Harcourt School Publishers & Holt, Rinehart and Winston

Continuity Across the Ages

Harcourt

HARCOURT SCHOOL PUBLISHERS & HOLT, RINEHART AND WINSTON

Our Programs

work hand in hand providing... **Continuity Across the Ages.**

K-12 Continuity

- ★ Patriotism
- ★ Democratic Values
- ★ Free Enterprise
- ★ Content
- ★ Skills

Grade K
Grade 1
Grade 2
Grade 3
Grade 4
Grade 5
Grade 6
Grade 6
Grade 7
Grade 8
Grade 9
Grade 10
Grade 11
Grade 12
Grade 12

These K–12 texts build solid foundations for student success in Social Studies by offering the following:

★ Depth of content develops thoughtful citizens, understanding past and present.

- Focusing attention on grade-level Texas Essential Knowledge and Skills throughout the elementary and secondary grade levels ensures understanding.
- Elementary Teacher's Editions also identify secondary level TEKS for which a base foundation of understanding is being built.
- At every level, depth of content and skills provide students with the tools they need to become active participants in their world.

★ Instructional support ensures students understand content.

- At every level, reading skills and strategies are taught, reinforced, and assessed to build cross-curricular reading skills.
- Primary sources provide opportunities for students to evaluate and analyze historical artifacts.
- Technology resources, including online multimedia biographies, allow students to explore in-depth Social Studies topics and enhance individual interests.
- Teaching materials provide exceptional resources at your fingertips to help Social Studies come alive to students.

★ Partnerships provide depth and breadth of expertise.

- CNN Turner Learning provides up-to-date information to keep content current and make sure the Social Studies content is relevant.
- MapQuest maps and skills illustrate events and help students gain skill proficiency.

3

HARCOURT SCHOOL PUBLISHERS & HOLT, RINEHART AND WINSTON

Our Editorial Team

Harcourt School Publishers and Holt, Rinehart and Winston together create programs that highlight content in patriotism, democratic values, and the free enterprise system, from kindergarten through high school. This collaborative effort evolved into a continuous series of books that build a strong Social Studies foundation in the elementary grades and prepare students for in-depth Social Studies content throughout secondary courses.

Don Lankiewicz
Vice President and Editor-in-Chief
Social Studies
Harcourt School Publishers

Sue Miller
Director
Social Studies
Holt, Rinehart and Winston

Our Authors

K-12 Continuity

Across the grades, the best in their fields meet to provide specialized expertise.

Dr. Tyrone Howard
Assistant Professor
UCLA Graduate School of Education & Information Studies
Los Angeles, California

Dr. Robert L Pennington
Professor
College of Business Administration
University of Central Florida
Orlando, Florida

Dr. Robert Bednarz
Professor
Department of Geography
Texas A&M University
College Station, Texas

Dr. Richard Diem
Professor of Education
University of Texas
San Antonio, Texas

Dr. Bruce E. Larson
Associate Professor of Teacher Education and Social Studies
Western Washington University
Bellingham, Washington

Dr. Robert J. Sager
Professor and Chair
Department of Earth Science
Pierce College
Lakewood, Washington

Dr. Michael J. Berson
Associate Professor
Social Science Education
University of South Florida
Tampa, Florida

Dr. Sherry L. Field
Associate Professor
The University of Texas at Austin
Austin, Texa

Dr. Thomas M. McGowan
Professor
Curriculum and Instruction
Arizona State University
Tempe, Arizona

Dr. Linda Kerrigan Salvucci
Associate Professor
Department of History
Trinity University
San Antonio, Texas

Dr. Paul Boyer
Professor and Director
Institute for Research in the Humanities
University of Wisconsin
Madison, Wisconsin

Dr. Robert P. Green, Jr.
Professor
School of Education
Clemson University
Clemson, South Carolina

Dr. Steven Kelman
Professor, John F. Kennedy School of Government
Harvard University
Cambridge, Massachusetts

Dr. Sterling Stuckey
Professor
Department of History
University of California
Riverside, California

Dr. Alison S. Brooks
Professor and Chair
Department of Anthropology
George Washington University
Washington, D.C.

Dr. David M. Helgren
Professor and Director
Center for Geographic Education
Chair, Department of Geography
San José State University
San José, California

Dr. Janice C. May
Professor
Department of Government
University of Texas at Austin
Austin, Texas

Larry Willoughby
Associate Professor
Department of History
Austin Community College
Austin, Texas

5

HARCOURT SCHOOL PUBLISHERS & HOLT, RINEHART AND WINSTON

Our Editorial Board Members & Consultants

Editorial Board Members

Dr. Laurel Carrington
Associate Professor
St. Olaf College
Northfield, Minnesota

Dr. Randolph B. Campbell
Regents Professor of History
University of North Texas
Denton, Texas

Mattie P. Collins
History Department Chair
Pine Bluff High School
Pine Bluff, Arkansas

Dr. Jesús F. de la Teja
Professor
Department of History
Southwest Texas State
  University
San Marco, Texas

Dr. Ronald Foore
Teacher
Booker T. Washington Magnet
  School
Tulsa, Oklahoma

Dr. Akira Iriye
Charles Warren Professor of
  American History
Harvard University
Cambridge, Massachusetts

Dr. Terry Jordan
Professor and the Walter
  Prescott Webb Chair in
  History and Ideas
Geography Department
University of Texas at Austin
Austin, Texas

Dr. Yasuhide Kawashima
Professor
Department of History
University of Texas, El Paso
El Paso, Texas

Rudy J. Martinez
Teacher
Thomas Edison High School
San Antonio, Texas

Barbara Mayo
Program Facilitator
Austin ISD
Austin, Texas

Elaine Parr
Teacher
Truitt Middle School
Cypress-Fairbanks ISD
Houston, Texas

Rick Rodriquez
Teacher
San Juan Middle School
Pharr-San Juan-Alamo ISD
San Juan, Texas

Lucinda Lucero Sachs
Teacher
Albuquerque School District
Albuquerque, New Mexico

Dr. Peter N. Stearns
Provost
George Mason University
Fairfax, Virginia

Velma Stredic
Teacher
Thomas Edison Middle School
Dallas ISD
Dallas, Texas

Dr. Nan E. Woodruff
Associate Professor
Department of History
Penn State University
University Park, Pennsylvania

Dr. Alfred Young
Professor
Department of History
Georgia Southern University
Statesboro, Georgia

Series Consultants/Specialists

Dr. Robert Bednarz
Professor
Department of Geography
Texas A&M University
College Station, Texas

Dr. Barbara Caffee
Social Studies Coordinator,
  K–12
Carrollton-Farmers Branch
  ISD
Carollton, Texas

Linda McMillan Fields
Social Studies Supervisor
Spring Branch ISD
Houston, Texas

Dr. Asa Hilliard III
Fuller E. Callaway Professor
  of Urban Education
Georgia State University
Atlanta, Georgia

Dr. Judith Irvin
Professor
Department of Education
Florida State University
Tallahassee, Florida

Dr. Thomas M. McGowan
Professor
Curriculum and Instruction
Arizona State University
Tempe, Arizona

Dr. John J. Patrick
Professor of Education
Indiana University
Bloomington, Indiana

Dr. Cinthia Suzel Salinas
Assistant Professor of
Education
University of Colorado
Boulder, Colorado

Dr. Phillip VanFossen
Associate Professor of Social
  Studies Education and
  Associate Director, Purdue
  Center for Economic
  Education
Purdue University
West Lafayette, Indiana

Dr. Hallie Kay Yopp
Professor
Department of Elementary,
Bilingual, and Reading
Education
California State University,
Fullerton
Fullerton, California

Our Partners

Harcourt School Publishers and Holt, Rinehart and Winston sought partners that could add a depth of understanding only their expertise could bring.

CNN—worldwide news coverage—helps bring Social Studies to life.
Unique videos for grades 4–6 make Social Studies relevant by taking students to explore landmarks and important sites featuring CNN news report footage. *CNN Presents* videos, for secondary grades, match current news and issues to historical, geographical, political, and economic topics.

ARGUS (Activities and Readings in the Geography of the United States)—the authority in US and World Geography—provides in-depth understanding of both physical and cultural landscapes. 
CD-ROMs, developed by the Association of American Geographers, provide in-depth information including case studies and a multitude of activities that integrate geography into Social Studies topics.

TIME FOR KIDS®—the leading current events classroom magazine—keeps content up-to-date.
Harcourt's exclusive Social Studies partnership with TIME FOR KIDS® provides online daily news stories for current events coverage… PLUS three nonfiction leveled books for each unit at the elementary grades… AND *Texas Extra*!

READING RAINBOW®—the Emmy Award-winning magazine format series—motivates learning and enhances classroom experience.
Students explore Social Studies through video field trips featuring segments from the READING RAINBOW television series promoting positive self-concept and literacy skills.

MAPQUEST—leader in map preparation—puts in-depth map information in the hands of each student.
MapQuest provides maps within the student textbooks. An additional CD-ROM provides a comprehensive program containing interactive and tutorial lessons that motivate your students to strengthen their map, graph, and computer skills.

HARCOURT SCHOOL PUBLISHERS & HOLT, RINEHART AND WINSTON

K-12 Continuity

Together, Harcourt School Publishers and Holt, Rinehart and Winston cover the content and skills all students need to become active, thoughtful citizens.

Major Understandings

History	K	1	2	3	4	5	6	7	8	9	10	11	12
understanding time patterns and relationships among events	•	•	•	•	•	•	•	•	•	•	•	•	•
sequence of events (indefinite time order)	•	•	•	•	•	•	•	•	•	•	•	•	•
chronology (definite time order)	•	•	•	•	•	•	•	•	•	•	•	•	•
cause and effect		•	•	•	•	•	•	•	•	•	•	•	•
historical points/frames of reference		•	•	•	•	•	•	•	•	•	•	•	•
identifying and using historical evidence	•	•	•	•	•	•	•	•	•		•	•	•
types of evidence	•	•	•	•	•	•	•	•	•		•	•	•
quality of evidence					•	•	•	•	•		•	•	•
understanding the importance of individuals and groups across time and place	•	•	•	•	•	•	•	•	•		•	•	•
leaders and achievers	•	•	•	•	•	•	•	•	•		•	•	•
ordinary people make a difference	•	•	•	•	•	•	•	•	•		•	•	•
founders and first persons	•	•	•	•	•	•	•	•	•		•	•	•
contributors to change	•	•	•	•	•	•	•	•	•		•	•	•
historical figures	•	•	•	•	•	•	•	•	•		•	•	•
reform movements		•	•	•	•	•	•	•	•	○	•	•	•
understanding the importance of issues, events, and ideas across time and place	•	•	•	•	•	•	•	•	•		•	•	•
innovations and inventions	•	•	•	•	•	•	•	•	•		•	•	•
impacts and turning points				•	•	•	•	•	•		•	•	•
revolutions and transformations		•	•	•	•	•	•	•	•		•	•	•
debates and controversies				•	•	•	•	•	•		•	•	•
economic, political, and social changes			•	•	•	•	•	•	•		•	•	•
understanding the times in which people lived	•	•	•	•	•	•	•	•	•		•	•	•
historical empathy	•	•	•	•	•	•	•	•	•		•	•	•
understanding origins, spread, and influence			•	•	•	•	•	•	•		•	•	•
growth and expansion			•	•	•	•	•	•	•		•	•	•
ideas and institutions			•	•	•	•	•	•	•		•	•	•
connecting and comparing past with present	•	•	•	•	•	•	•	•	•		•	•	•
celebrations, holidays, and customs	•	•	•	•	•	•	•	•	•		•	•	•
landmarks and monuments			•	•	•	•	•	•	•		•	•	•
comparing people, places, and environments	•	•	•	•	•	•	•	•	•		•	•	•

● ○ Bullets indicate levels at which understandings are introduced, taught, applied, reinforced, or extended.

	K	1	2	3	4	5	6	7	8	9	10	11	12
understanding the development of human systems		•	•	•	○	•	•	•	○	•	•	•	○
political		•	•	•	○	•	•	•	○	•	•	•	○
economic			•	•	○	•	•	•	○	•	•	•	○
social			•	•	○	•	•	•	○	•	•	•	○
culture			•	•	○	•	•	•	○	•	•	•	○
understanding impacts of turning points			○	•	○	•	○	•	○	•	○	•	○
political			○	•	○	•	○	•	○	•	○	•	○
economic			○	•	○	•	○	•	○	•	○	•	○
social		•	○	•	○	•	○	•	○	•	○	•	○
understanding development of civilizations		•	○	•	○	•	○	•	○	•	○	•	○
imperialism							○	•	○	•	○	•	○
importance of US		•	○	•	○	•	○	•	○	•	○	•	○

Geography

	K	1	2	3	4	5	6	7	8	9	10	11	12
understanding location	○	•	○	•	○	•	○	•	○	•	○	•	○
relative and absolute (exact) location	○	•	○	•	○	•	○	•	○	•	○	•	○
factors influencing location		•	○	•	○	•	○	•	○	•	○	•	○
understanding place	○	•	○	•	○	•	○	•	○	•	○	•	○
physical features (landforms, bodies of water, vegetation)	○	•	○	•	○	•	○	•	○	•	○	•	○
human or cultural features	○	•	○	•	○	•	○	•	○	•	○	•	○
understanding human-environment interactions	○	•	○	•	○	•	○	•	○	•	○	•	○
seasons and climate	○	•	○	•	○	•	○	•	○	•	○	•	○
land use and natural resources	○	•	○	•	○	•	○	•	○	•	○	•	○
conservation and pollution		•	○	•	○	•	○	•	○	•	○	•	○
population density				•	○	•	○	•	○	•	○	•	○
understanding movement	○	•	○	•	○	•	○	•	○	•	○	•	○
people (immigration, colonization, settlement patterns)		•	○	•	○	•	○	•	○	•	○	•	○
products (trade)		•	○	•	○	•	○	•	○	•	○	•	○
ideas (cultural borrowing and cultural diffusion)		•	○	•	○	•	○	•	○	•	○	•	○
understanding regions		•	○	•	○	•	○	•	○	•	○	•	○
physical regions		•	○	•	○	•	○	•	○	•	○	•	○
cultural regions		•	○	•	○	•	○	•	○	•	○	•	○
political regions		•	○	•	○	•	○	•	○	•	○	•	○
economic regions				•	○	•	○	•	○	•	○	•	○
functional regions						•	○			•			
time zones					○	•	○			•			

Economics

	K	1	2	3	4	5	6	7	8	9	10	11	12
understanding scarcity and economic choice	○	•	○	•	○	•	○	•	○	•	○	•	○
wants and basic needs	○	•	○	•	○	•				•			○
goods and services	○	•	○	•	○	•	○	•	○	•	○	•	○
production and consumption		•	○	•	○	•	○	•	○	•			○
trade-offs and opportunity cost			○	•	○	•	○						○
economic resources			•	○	•	○	•	○	•	○	•	○	•

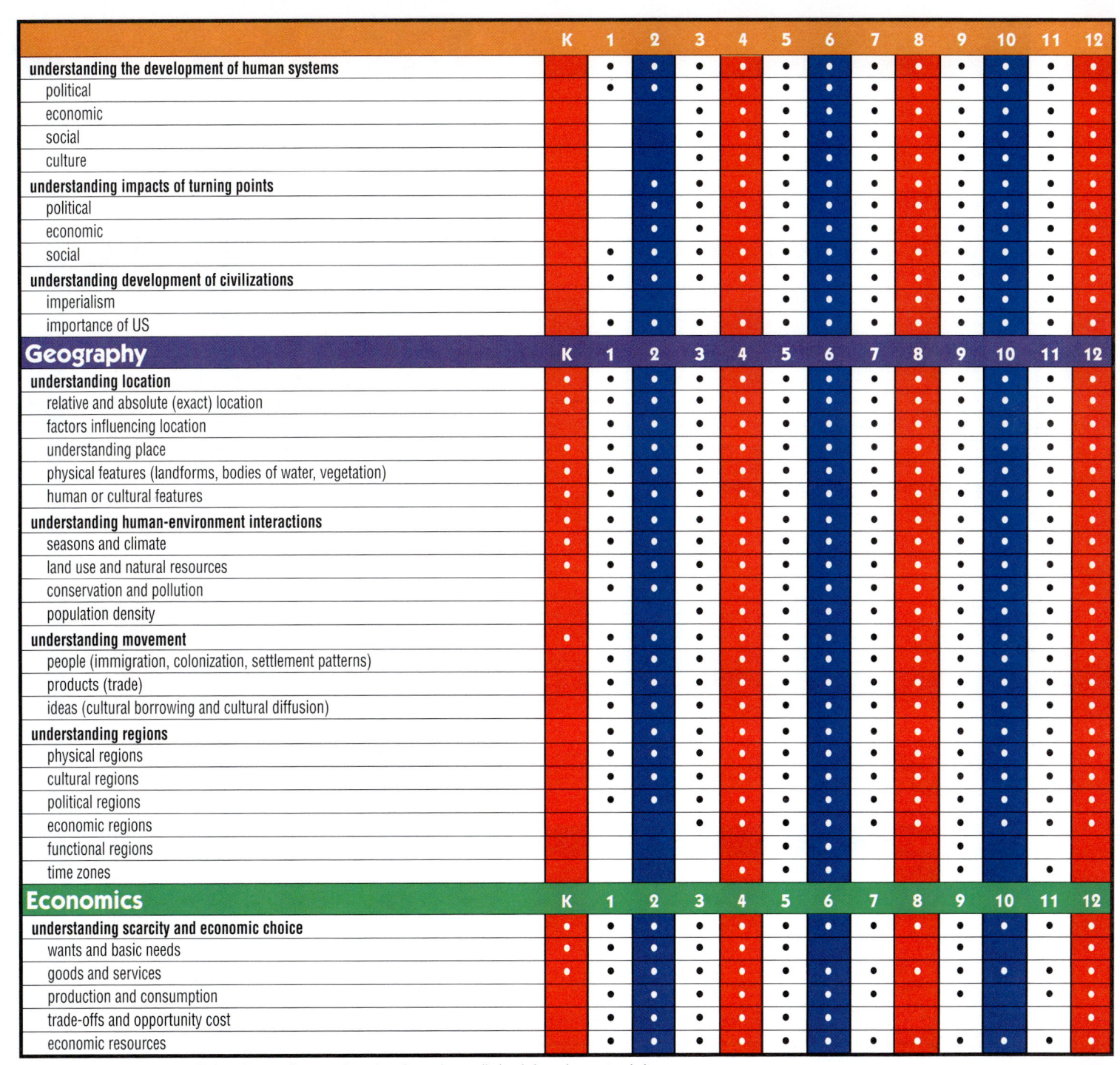

• ○ Bullets indicate levels at which understandings are introduced, taught, applied, reinforced, or extended.

HARCOURT SCHOOL PUBLISHERS & HOLT, RINEHART AND WINSTON

	K	1	2	3	4	5	6	7	8	9	10	11	12
spending, borrowing, saving, and investing		•	○	•	○	•	•		○				○
circular flow							•						○
understanding interdependence and income	•	•	○	•	○	•	•	•	○	•	○	•	○
transportation and communication links	•	•	○	•	○	•	•	•	○	•	○	•	○
mediums of exchange (barter and use of money)	•	•	○	•	○	•	•	•	○	•	○	•	○
trade	•	•	○	•	○	•	•	•	○	•	○	•	○
imports and exports (international trade)		•	○	•	○	•	•	•	○	•	○	•	○
understanding economic activities							•	•	○	•	○	•	○
primary, secondary, terciary, and quaternary industries							•		○				○
economic indicators						•	•	•	○		○	•	○
historical and geographic patterns						•	•	•	○	•	○	•	○
business organizations				•	○	•	•	•	○			•	○
consumer and personal economics				•	○	•	•						○
understanding markets and prices		•	○	•	○	•	•	•	○	•	○	•	○
supply and demand				•	○	•	•	•	○		○		○
profit motive and price				•	○	•	•	•	○		○		○
competition				•	○	•	•	•	○	•	○		○
market structure							•	•	○		○		○
understanding productivity and economic growth		•	○	•	○	•	•	•	○	•	○	•	○
value and importance of work		•	○	•	○	•	•	•	○	•	○	•	○
kinds of work (jobs)		•	○	•	○	•	•	•	○	•	○	•	○
division of labor and specialization		•	○	•	○	•	•	•	○	•	○	•	○
production process		•	○	•	○	•	•	•	○	•	○	•	○
factors of production							•	•	○	•	○	•	○
effects of technology		•	○	•	○	•	•	•	○	•	○	•	○
effects of government						•	•	•	○	•	○	•	○
understanding economic systems and institutions		•	○	•	○	•	•	•	○	•	○	•	○
public and private property			○	•	○	•	•				○	•	○
taxes		•	○	•	○	•	•	•	○	•	○	•	
free enterprise and entrepreneurship			○	•	○	•	•	•	○	•	○	•	○
command, traditional, and market systems							•		○		○		○
origins, spread, and influence						•	•	•	○	•	○	•	○
the Federal Reserve and financial institutions							•	•	○	•	○	•	○

Government

	K	1	2	3	4	5	6	7	8	9	10	11	12
understanding purposes of government		•	○	•	○	•	•	•	○	•	○	•	○
economic policy and free enterprise			○	•	○	•	•	•	○	•	○	•	○
promoting order and security		•	○	•	○	•	•	•	○	•	○	•	○
promoting well-being and common good		•	○	•	○	•	•	•	○	•	○	•	○
providing for distribution of benefits and burdens of society			○	•	○	•	•	•	○	•	○	•	○
providing means of peaceful conflict resolution			○	•	○	•	•	•	○		○	•	○
protecting rights and freedoms of individuals		•	○	•	○	•	•	•	○	•	○	•	○
changes over time			○	•	○	•	•	•	○	•	○	•	○

•○ Bullets indicate levels at which understandings are introduced, taught, applied, reinforced, or extended.

	K	1	2	3	4	5	6	7	8	9	10	11	12
understanding types of government (democracy, monarchy, dictatorship)		•	•	•	•	•	•	•	•	•	•	•	•
understanding democratic institutions		•	•	•	•	•	•	•	•	•	•	•	•
levels of government (local, state, national)			•	•	•	•	•	•	•		•	•	•
branches of government (executive, legislative, judicial)			•	•	•	•	•	•	•		•	•	•
government bodies (councils, boards, legislatures)		•	•	•	•	•	•	•	•	•	•	•	•
elected and appointed officials		•	•	•	•	•	•	•	•		•	•	•
government services and activities		•	•	•	•	•	•	•	•	•	•	•	•
government documents (Constitution, Bill of Rights, etc.)		•	•	•	•	•	•	•	•		•	•	•
political parties					•	•	•	•	•		•	•	•
understanding democratic processes		•			•	•	•	•	•		•	•	•
making, amending, and removing rules and laws				•	•	•	•	•	•		•	•	•
impact of Constitutional issues and Supreme Court decisions					•	•	•	•	•		•	•	•
enforcing laws		•	•	•	•	•	•	•	•		•	•	•
voting and elections		•	•	•	•	•	•	•	•		•	•	•
becoming a citizen					•	•	•	•	•		•	•	•
political debates and controversies						•	•	•	•		•	•	•
understanding geographic historical, and economic influences		•	•	•	•	•	•	•	•		•	•	•

Citizenship

	K	1	2	3	4	5	6	7	8	9	10	11	12
understanding national identity	•	•	•	•	•	•	•	•	•		•	•	•
flags, symbols, anthems, mottoes, and pledges	•	•	•	•	•	•	•	•	•		•	•	•
patriotic customs, celebrations, and traditions	•	•	•	•	•	•	•	•	•		•	•	•
understanding civic values	•	•	•	•	•	•	•	•	•		•	•	•
recognizing and respecting authority figures and leaders	•	•	•	•	•	•	•	•	•		•	•	•
accepting and respecting others	•	•	•	•	•	•	•	•	•		•	•	•
working for the common good		•	•	•	•	•	•	•	•		•	•	•
individuals as role models past and present	•	•	•	•	•	•	•	•	•		•	•	•
understanding democratic principles and institutions		•	•	•	•	•	•	•	•		•	•	•
citizens as the source of government's authority			•	•	•	•	•	•	•		•	•	•
due process and equal protection under the law			•	•	•	•	•	•	•		•	•	•
majority rule and minority rights			•	•	•	•	•	•	•		•	•	•
government by law			•	•	•	•	•	•	•		•	•	•
origins, spread, and influences			•	•	•	•	•	•	•		•	•	•
understanding rights and freedoms of citizens		•	•	•	•	•	•	•	•	•	•		•
voting rights, property rights, civil rights, human rights, economic rights		•	•	•	•	•	•	•	•	•	•		•
freedom of expression, worship, assembly, movement		•	•	•	•	•	•	•	•		•		•
comparisons among societies					•	•	•	•	•		•	•	•
understanding the responsibilities of citizens		•	•	•	•	•	•	•	•		•	•	•
voluntary responsibilities (voting, keeping informed)		•	•	•	•	•	•	•	•		•	•	•
responsibilities under the law (obeying laws, paying taxes)			•	•	•	•	•	•	•		•	•	•
understanding the impact of choices, points of view, and policies		•	•	•	•	•	•	•	•		•	•	•
comparisons among societies		•	•	•	•	•	•	•	•		•	•	•

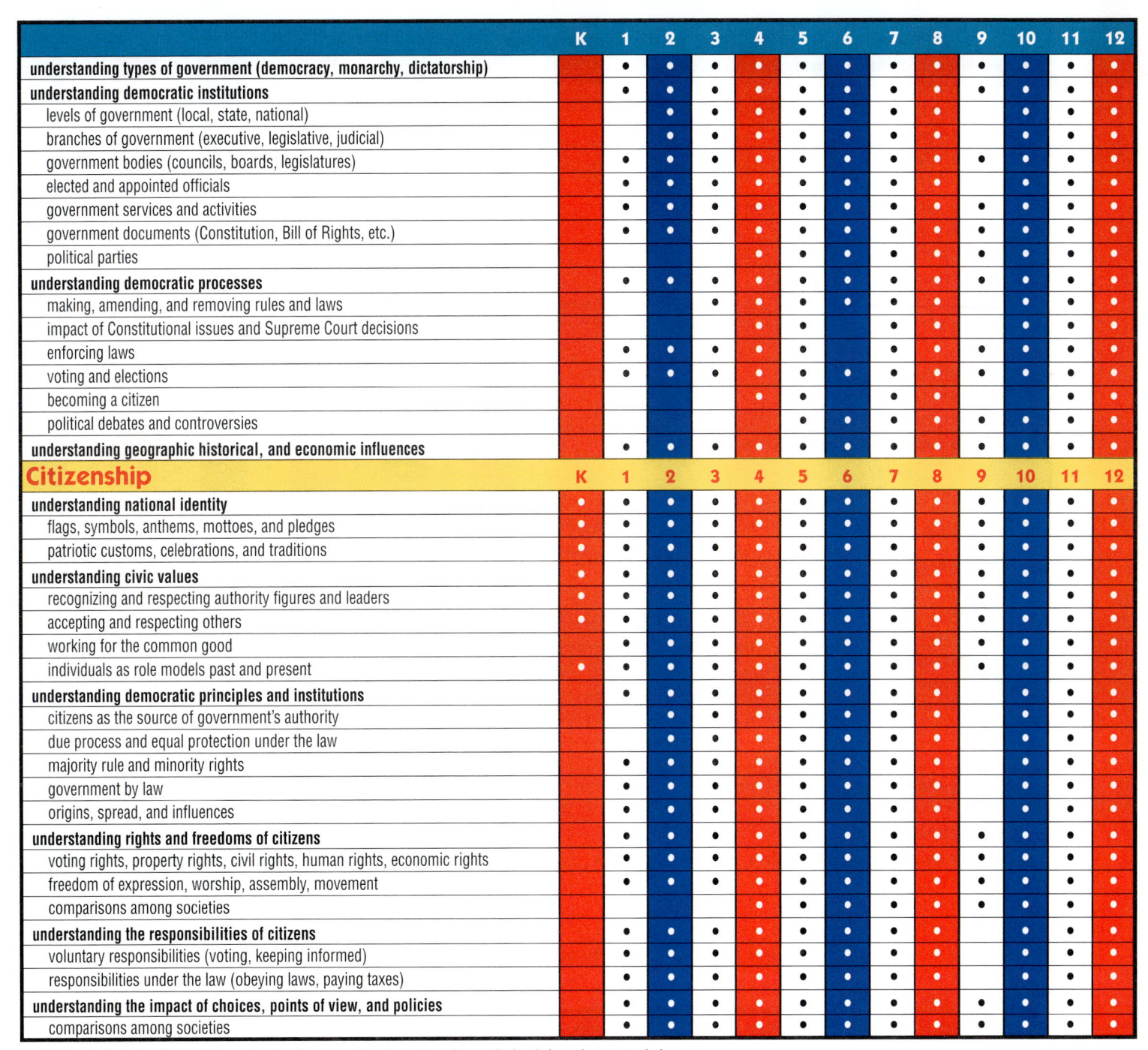

• ○ Bullets indicate levels at which understandings are introduced, taught, applied, reinforced, or extended.

HARCOURT SCHOOL PUBLISHERS & HOLT, RINEHART AND WINSTON

Culture	K	1	2	3	4	5	6	7	8	9	10	11	12
understanding ideas of shared humanity and unique identity	•	•	•	•	•	•	•	•	•	•	•	•	•
culture and cultural identity	•	•	•	•	•	•	•	•	•	•	•	•	•
customs, celebrations, and traditions (one's own and others)	•	•	•	•	•	•	•	•	•	•	•	•	•
cultural diversity and pluralism	•	•	•	•	•	•	•	•	•	•	•	•	•
multicultural societies	•	•	•	•	•	•	•	•	•	•	•	•	•
heroes	•	•	•	•	•	•	•	•	•	•	•	•	•
understanding social organizations and institutions	•	•	•	•	•	•	•	•	•	•	•	•	•
belonging to groups	•	•	•	•	•	•	•	•	•	•	•	•	•
family and community	•	•	•	•	•	•	•	•	•	•	•	•	•
social class structures				•	•	•	•	•	•	•	•	•	•
roles (gender, age, occupation)	•	•	•	•	•	•	•	•	•	•	•	•	•
religion and beliefs	•	•	•	•	•	•	•	•	•	•	•	•	•
education	•	•	•	•	•	•	•	•	•	•	•	•	•
governing and economic systems				•	•	•	•	•	•	•	•	•	•
changes over time	•	•	•	•	•	•	•	•	•	•	•	•	•
comparisons among groups or societies				•	•	•	•	•	•	•	•	•	•
understanding means of thought and expression	•	•	•	•	•	•	•	•	•	•	•	•	•
art, literature, music, dance, and architecture	•	•	•	•	•	•	•	•	•	•	•	•	•
language and communication	•	•	•	•	•	•	•	•	•	•	•	•	•
recreation	•	•	•	•	•	•	•	•	•	•	•	•	•
food preparation	•	•	•	•	•	•	•	•	•	•	•	•	•
understanding human relationships	•	•	•	•	•	•	•	•	•	•	•	•	•
between and among individuals		•	•	•	•	•	•	•	•	•	•	•	•
within a culture or society				•	•	•	•	•	•	•	•	•	•
between and among cultures or societies					•	•	•	•	•	•	•	•	•
philosophy and ethics			•	•	•	•	•	•	•	•	•	•	•
ideas and standards of behavior				•	•	•	•	•	•	•	•	•	•
resolving ethical issues						•	•	•	•	•	•	•	•
effects of belief on behavior			•	•	•	•	•	•	•	•	•	•	•

Science, Technology, and Society	K	1	2	3	4	5	6	7	8	9	10	11	12
understanding effects on daily life, past and present	•	•	•	•	•	•	•	•	•	•	•	•	•
transportation and communication	•	•	•	•	•	•	•	•	•	•	•	•	•
business and industry				•	•	•	•	•	•	•	•	•	•
understanding the relationship among science, technology, and society	•	•	•	•	•	•	•	•	•	•	•	•	•
contributions of individuals	•	•	•	•	•	•	•	•	•	•	•	•	•
political, economic, and social issues				•	•	•	•	•	•	•	•	•	•
influence of mathematics											•	•	•
understanding the relationship among science, technology, and the environment	•	•	•	•	•	•	•	•	•	•	•	•	•
human modification of the environment		•	•	•	•	•	•	•	•	•	•	•	•
use of natural resources	•	•	•	•	•	•	•	•	•	•	•	•	•

• ○ Bullets indicate levels at which understandings are introduced, taught, applied, reinforced, or extended.

Skills

Citizenship Skills

	K	1	2	3	4	5	6	7	8	9	10	11	12
working with others	•	•	•	•	•	•	•	•	•	•	•	•	•
solving problems as an individual and in groups	•	•	•	•	•	•	•	•	•	•	•	•	•
making choices and decisions as an individual and in groups	•	•	•	•	•	•	•	•	•	•	•	•	•
voting	•	•	•	•	•	•	•	•	•	•	•	•	•
economic choices			•	•	•	•	•	•	•	•	•	•	•
thoughtful decisions		•	•	•	•	•	•	•	•	•	•	•	•
resolving conflict	•	•	•	•	•	•	•	•	•	•	•	•	•
acting responsibly	•	•	•	•	•	•	•	•	•	•	•	•	•
identifying the consequences of a person's behavior	•	•	•	•	•	•	•	•	•	•	•	•	•
acting respectfully	•	•	•	•	•	•	•	•	•	•	•	•	•
of rules and laws	•	•	•	•	•	•	•	•	•	•	•	•	•
of democratic values	•	•	•	•	•	•	•	•	•	•	•	•	•
of differing points of view	•	•	•	•	•	•	•	•	•	•	•	•	•
identifying patriotic and cultural symbols	•	•	•	•	•	•	•	•	•	•	•	•	•
keeping informed	•	•	•	•	•	•	•	•	•	•	•	•	•
participating in a group or community	•	•	•	•	•	•	•	•	•	•	•	•	•
assuming leadership and being willing to follow		•	•	•	•	•	•	•	•	•	•	•	•

Map and Globe Skills

	K	1	2	3	4	5	6	7	8	9	10	11	12
understanding and using globes	•	•	•		•		•			•			
hemispheres			•	•	•	•				•			
poles		•	•	•	•	•			•				
parallels and meridians			•	•	•	•				•			
understanding the purpose and use of maps	•	•	•	•	•	•	•	•	•		•	•	•
map title	•	•	•	•	•	•	•	•	•		•	•	•
map key (legend)	•	•	•	•	•	•	•	•	•		•	•	•
compass rose (direction indicator)		•	•	•	•	•	•	•	•		•	•	•
map scale			•	•	•	•	•	•	•		•	•	•
grid system			•	•	•	•	•	•	•		•	•	•
comparing and contrasting maps and globes	•	•	•			•	•	•		•			
different scales					•	•	•			•			
projections and distortions						•	•			•			
understanding and using thematic maps	•	•	•	•	•	•	•	•	•		•	•	•
cultural maps			•	•	•	•	•	•	•		•	•	•
economic maps			•	•	•	•	•	•	•		•	•	•
historical maps			•	•	•	•	•	•	•	•	•	•	•
physical maps	•	•	•	•	•	•	•	•	•		•	•	•
political maps	•	•	•	•	•	•	•	•	•		•	•	•
population maps			•	•	•	•	•	•	•		•	•	•
time zone maps					•	•	•	•	•		•	•	•

• ○ Bullets indicate levels at which understandings are introduced, taught, applied, reinforced, or extended.

HARCOURT SCHOOL PUBLISHERS & HOLT, RINEHART AND WINSTON

	K	1	2	3	4	5	6	7	8	9	10	11	12
understanding and using map symbols	•	•	•	•	•	•	•	•	•	•	•	•	•
land and water	•	•	•	•	•	•	•	•	•	•	•	•	•
colors and patterns	•	•	•	•	•	•	•	•	•	•	•	•	•
object and picture symbols	•	•	•	•	•	•	•	•	•	•	•	•	•
lines and borders		•	•	•	•	•	•	•	•	•	•	•	•
routes and arrows	•	•	•	•	•	•	•	•	•	•	•	•	•
place symbols	•	•	•	•	•	•	•	•	•	•	•	•	•
relief and elevation				•	•	•	•	•	•	•	•	•	•
understanding directional terms and finding direction	•	•	•	•	•	•	•	•	•	•	•	•	•
cardinal directions		•	•	•	•	•	•	•	•	•	•	•	•
intermediate directions				•	•	•	•	•	•	•	•	•	•
understanding and measuring distance		•	•	•	•	•	•	•	•	•	•	•	•
miles and kilometers			•	•	•	•	•	•	•	•	•	•	•
insets		•	•	•	•	•	•	•	•	•	•	•	•
understanding and finding location		•	•	•	•	•	•	•	•	•	•	•	•
number and letter grids			•	•	•	•	•	•	•	•	•	•	•
lines of latitude and longitude					•	•	•	•	•	•	•	•	•
measurements in degrees, minutes, seconds						•	•	•	•	•	•	•	•

Chart and Graph Skills (Graphic Organizers)

	K	1	2	3	4	5	6	7	8	9	10	11	12
understanding and using time lines	•	•	•	•	•	•	•	•	•	•	•	•	•
calendars	•	•	•							•			•
horizontal time lines	•	•	•	•	•	•	•	•	•	•	•	•	•
vertical time lines					•	•	•	•	•		•		•
parallel time lines						•	•	•	•		•	•	
understanding and using tables and schedules	•	•	•	•	•	•	•	•	•	•	•	•	•
understanding and using graphs	•	•	•	•	•	•	•	•	•	•	•	•	•
picture graphs	•	•	•	•	•	•	•	•	•	•	•	•	•
single bar graphs		•	•	•	•	•	•	•	•	•	•	•	•
line graphs					•	•	•	•	•	•	•	•	•
double bar graphs					•	•	•	•	•	•	•	•	•
population pyramids						•	•		•		•		
circle (pie) graphs						•	•	•	•	•	•	•	•
comparing different graphs						•	•	•	•	•	•	•	•
climographs						•	•						
understanding and using diagrams and other graphic organizers	•	•	•	•	•	•	•	•	•	•	•	•	•
cutaway diagrams		•	•	•	•	•	•	•	•	•	•	•	•
flow charts			•	•	•	•	•	•	•	•	•	•	•
cartograms						•	•		•				

Reading and Critical Thinking Skills

	K	1	2	3	4	5	6	7	8	9	10	11	12
identifying cause-and-effect relationships	•	•	•	•	•	•	•	•	•	•	•	•	•
following sequence and chronology	•	•	•	•	•	•	•	•	•	•	•	•	•

• ○ Bullets indicate levels at which understandings are introduced, taught, applied, reinforced, or extended.

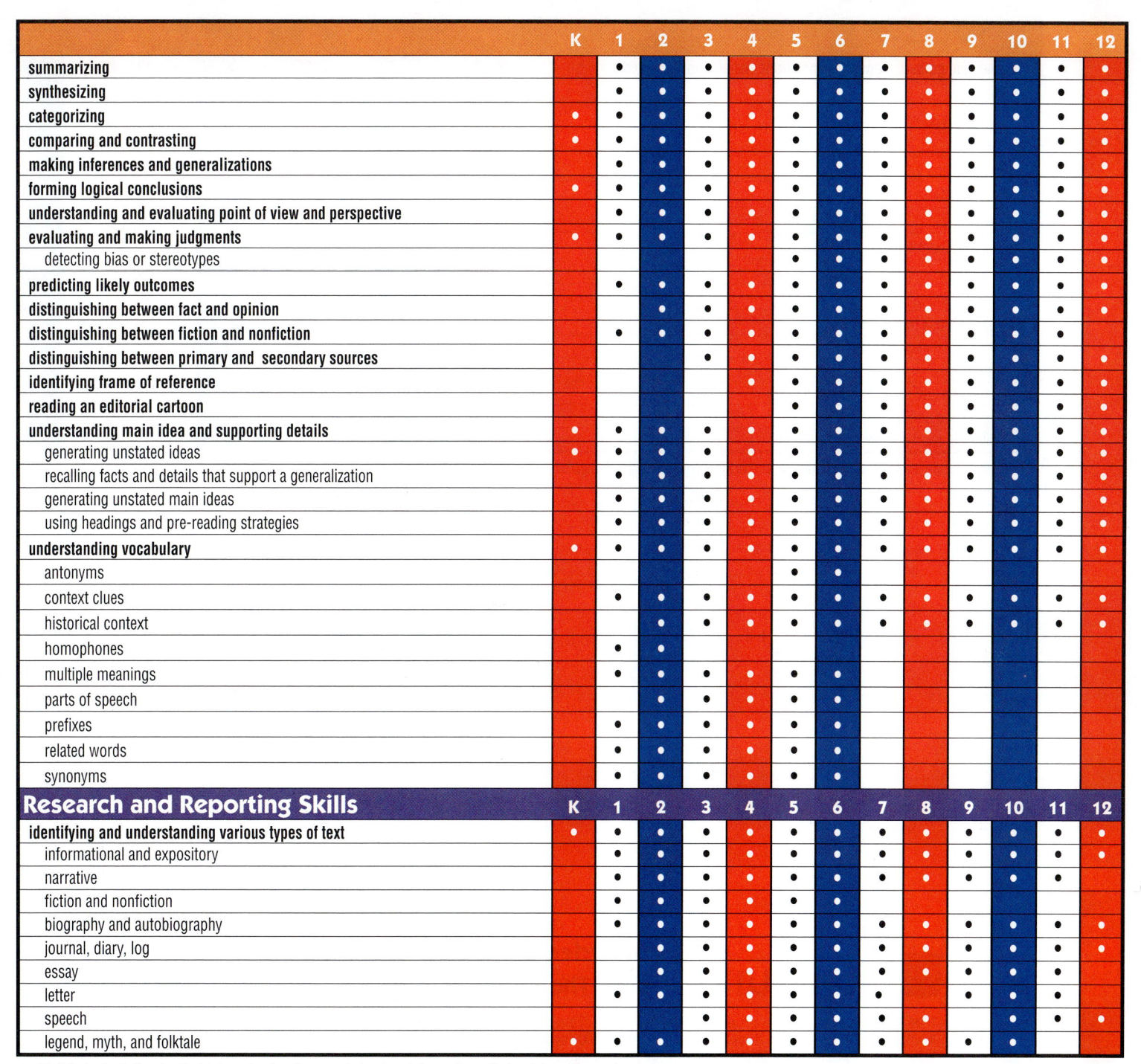

	K	1	2	3	4	5	6	7	8	9	10	11	12
summarizing		•	•	•	•	•	•	•	•	•	•	•	•
synthesizing		•	•	•	•	•	•	•	•	•	•	•	•
categorizing	•	•	•	•	•	•	•	•	•	•	•	•	•
comparing and contrasting	•	•	•	•	•	•	•	•	•	•	•	•	•
making inferences and generalizations		•	•	•	•	•	•	•	•	•	•	•	•
forming logical conclusions	•	•	•	•	•	•	•	•	•	•	•	•	•
understanding and evaluating point of view and perspective		•	•	•	•	•	•	•	•	•	•	•	•
evaluating and making judgments	•	•	•	•	•	•	•	•	•	•	•	•	•
detecting bias or stereotypes							•	•	•	•	•	•	•
predicting likely outcomes		•	•	•	•	•	•	•	•	•	•	•	•
distinguishing between fact and opinion			•	•	•	•	•	•	•	•	•	•	•
distinguishing between fiction and nonfiction		•	•	•	•	•	•	•	•	•	•	•	•
distinguishing between primary and secondary sources				•	•	•	•	•	•	•	•	•	•
identifying frame of reference					•	•	•	•	•	•	•	•	•
reading an editorial cartoon							•	•	•	•	•	•	•
understanding main idea and supporting details	•	•	•	•	•	•	•	•	•	•	•	•	•
generating unstated ideas	•	•	•	•	•	•	•	•	•	•	•	•	•
recalling facts and details that support a generalization		•	•	•	•	•	•	•	•	•	•	•	•
generating unstated main ideas			•	•	•	•	•	•	•	•	•	•	•
using headings and pre-reading strategies		•	•	•	•	•	•	•	•	•	•	•	•
understanding vocabulary	•	•	•	•	•	•	•	•	•	•	•	•	•
antonyms						•	•						
context clues		•	•	•	•	•	•	•	•	•	•	•	•
historical context			•	•	•	•	•	•	•	•	•	•	•
homophones		•	•										
multiple meanings		•	•	•	•	•	•						
parts of speech			•	•	•	•	•						
prefixes			•	•	•	•	•						
related words			•	•	•	•	•						
synonyms			•	•	•	•	•						

Research and Reporting Skills

	K	1	2	3	4	5	6	7	8	9	10	11	12
identifying and understanding various types of text	•	•	•	•	•	•	•	•	•	•	•	•	•
informational and expository		•	•	•	•	•	•	•	•	•	•	•	•
narrative		•	•	•	•	•	•	•	•	•	•	•	
fiction and nonfiction		•	•	•	•	•	•	•	•	•	•	•	•
biography and autobiography		•	•	•	•	•	•	•	•	•	•	•	•
journal, diary, log			•	•	•	•	•	•	•	•	•	•	•
essay			•	•	•	•	•	•	•	•	•	•	•
letter		•	•	•	•	•	•	•	•	•	•	•	•
speech				•	•	•	•	•	•	•	•	•	•
legend, myth, and folktale	•	•	•	•	•	•	•	•	•	•	•	•	•

• ○ Bullets indicate levels at which understandings are introduced, taught, applied, reinforced, or extended.

HARCOURT SCHOOL PUBLISHERS & HOLT, RINEHART AND WINSTON

	K	1	2	3	4	5	6	7	8	9	10	11	12
locating and gathering information in print and electronic sources	•	•	•	•	•	•	•	•	•	•	•	•	•
almanac				•	•	•	•	•	•	•	•	•	•
atlas and gazetteer		•	•	•	•	•	•	•	•	•	•	•	•
databases				•	•	•	•	•	•	•	•	•	•
dictionary and glossary		•	•	•	•	•	•	•	•	•	•	•	•
encyclopedia		•	•	•	•	•	•	•	•	•	•	•	•
Internet		•	•	•	•	•	•	•	•	•	•	•	•
library and community	•	•	•	•	•	•	•	•	•	•	•	•	•
newspapers		•	•	•	•	•	•	•	•	•	•	•	•
television and radio		•	•	•	•	•	•	•	•	•	•	•	•
expressing ideas in various ways	•	•	•	•	•	•	•	•	•	•	•	•	•
writing and dictating	•	•	•	•	•	•	•	•	•	•	•	•	•
speaking	•	•	•	•	•	•	•	•	•	•	•	•	•
dramatizing and role-playing simulations	•	•	•	•	•	•	•	•	•	•	•	•	•
constructing and creating	•	•	•	•	•	•	•	•	•	•	•	•	•
displaying, charting, drawing	•	•	•	•	•	•	•	•	•	•	•	•	•

• ○ Bullets indicate levels at which understandings are introduced, taught, applied, reinforced, or extended.

Harcourt

To order, call 1-800-225-5425.
Visit The Learning Site at www.harcourtschool.com

TIME FOR KIDS and the red border are registered trademarks of Time Inc. Used under license. Copyright © by Time Inc. All rights reserved. CNN NEWS-ROOM is a trademark of Cable News Network. Copyright © 2003 by Cable News Network, an AOL Time Warner Company. All rights reserved. Licensed by Turner Learning, an AOL Time Warner Company. Reading Rainbow is a registered trademark of GPN/WNED-TV. Any other service marks contained within this material are owned by their respective owners. HARCOURT and the Harcourt logo are trademarks of Harcourt, Inc. registered in the United States of America and/or other jurisdictions. Copyright © by Harcourt, Inc. All rights reserved. Printed in USA. 9997-41989-8

HOLT
Economics

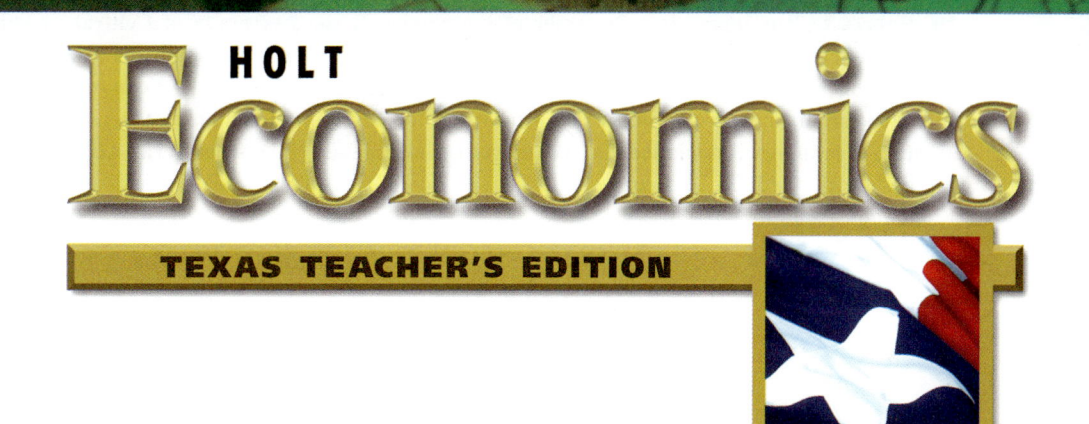

TEXAS TEACHER'S EDITION

Robert L. Pennington

HOLT, RINEHART AND WINSTON

A Harcourt Classroom Education Company

Austin • New York • Orlando • Atlanta • San Francisco • Boston • Dallas • Toronto • London

About the Author

Dr. Robert L. Pennington is a Professor of Economics at the University of Central Florida. He also is the director of the Florida Center for Economic Education. Additionally, Dr. Pennington is a member of the American Economic Association, the National Association of Economic Educators, the Association for Private Enterprise Education, the Southern Economics Association, and the Western Economics Association. Dr. Pennington received his Ph.D. from Texas A&M University. He has written, edited, and reviewed numerous books and articles dealing with economics and economic education.

Cover description: World currency; New York Stock Exchange; Texas flag

Cover credit: (World currency), Artbase Inc. Image #5304; (New York Stock Exchange), Artbase Inc. #NYC 0052; (Texas flag), ©Stockbyte

Copyright © 2003 by Holt, Rinehart and Winston

All rights reserved. No part of this publication may be reproduced or transmitted in any form or by any means, electronic or mechanical, including photocopy, recording, or any information storage and retrieval system, without permission in writing from the publisher.

Requests for permission to make copies of any part of the work should be mailed to the following address: Permissions Department, Holt, Rinehart and Winston, 10801 N. MoPac Expressway, Building 3, Austin, Texas 78759.

For acknowledgments, see page 542, which is an extension of the copyright page.

Copyright © 2000 CNN and CNNfyi.com are trademarks of Cable News Network LP, LLLP, a Time Warner Company. All rights reserved.
Copyright © 2000 Turner Learning logos are trademarks of Turner Learning, Inc., a Time Warner Company. All rights reserved.

Printed in the United States of America

ISBN 0-03-066656-2

1 2 3 4 5 6 7 8 9   032   06 05 04 03 02

CONTENT REVIEWERS

Donald G. Fell Economics
Florida Council on Economic Education

Warren Matthews, Economics
Houston Baptist University

Unit 1
John Tribble
Russell Sage College
Economics

Unit 2
John Clow
State University of New York, Oneonta
Microeconomics

Unit 3
Robert Reinke
University of South Dakota
Microeconomics and environmental economics

Unit 4
W. F. Mackara
East Tennessee State University
Economics

Unit 5
Gerald F. Draayer
Boise State University
Macroeconomics

Unit 6
Gail Tamaribuchi
University of Hawaii, Manoa
Economic education

EDUCATIONAL REVIEWERS

Don Bender
Shaler Area Senior High School
Pittsburg, Pennsylvania

Sharon Cruse
Central Hardin High School
Cecilia, Kentucky

Rachel Gragg
Clear Creek High School
League City, Texas

Richard Sipe
West Albany High School
Albany, Oregon

James G. Slenker
Liverpool High School
Liverpool, New York

Texas Reviewers

Martha Enriquez
Highland High School
San Antonio, Texas

Susan Storz
Plano East Senior High School
Plano, Texas

Beryl Bolton
Bellair High School
Bellair, Texas

Leslie Donovan
McCallum High School
Austin, Texas

Debbie Tettleton
Grand Prairie High School
Grand Prairie, Texas

Chris Newkirk
Bryan Adams High School
Dallas, Texas

Tom Gossett
MacArthur High School
San Antonio, Texas

Teresa Byers
Edison High School
San Antonio, Texas

Jane Nicholson
Boerne High School
Boerne, Texas

Woodie Meyer
Clark High School
San Antonio, Texas

David Echols
Adamson High School
Dallas, Texas

Roger Sullivan
Mission High School
Mission, Texas

Field Test Reviewers

Nicholas D. Confalone
Mansfield Senior High School
Mansfield, Ohio

Sharon Cruse
Central Hardin High School
Cecilia, Kentucky

George Dillow
Troy High School
Troy, Ohio

Alton Dale Gilmore
Tate High School
Gonzalez, Florida

Wayne Lechlitner
Venice High School
Venice, Florida

Christina B. Monroe
Chattanooga School of Arts and Science
Chattanooga, Tennessee

R. Kraig Rittenhouse
Warren Central High School
Vicksburg, Mississippi

Julia M. Sargent
George County High School
Lucedale, Mississippi

Richard Sipe
West Albany High School
Albany, Oregon

TEXAS EDITION

It's All About

The first step to success in the social studies classroom is capturing and sustaining the interest of your students. **HOLT ECONOMICS** is designed to be open and friendly to all students, so that they develop an enthusiasm for learning and an appreciation for the past.

HOLT ECONOMICS offers
- **Built-in Reading Support**
- **Complete TEKS coverage and daily preparation for TAKS ®**
- **Technology with Instructional Value**
- **The Best Teacher Management System in the Industry**

ECONOMICS IN ACTION engages your students' critical-thinking skills by showing them how to explore economic principles and discover how they are applied in everyday situations.

RELEVANCE

CNNfyi.com™ is a site designed to give students in grades 6–12 access to people, places, and environments around the globe while offering "real-world" articles, career and college resources, and online activities.

In-Text Features that Put Economics into Perspective

- Careers in Economics
- Case Studies
- Economics in Action
- Global Exchange
- Linking Economics and Geography
- Linking Economics and Government
- Linking Economics and History
- Linking Economics and Psychology
- Linking Economics and Science
- Linking Economics and Sociology

M1

Reading in the

TEXAS EDITION

Helping Students Make Sense of What They're Reading

An Essay by Dr. Judith Irvin, Ph.D. Reading Education

Who in middle and high schools helps students become more successful at reading and writing informational text? When I ask this question of a school faculty, the Language Arts/English teachers point to the social studies and science teachers because they are the ones with this type of textbook. The social studies and science teachers point to the Language Arts/English teachers because they are the ones that "do" words.

I advocate teachers taking an active role in helping students learn how to use text structure and context to understand what they read. Through consistent and systematic instruction that includes modeling of effective reading behavior, teachers can assist students in becoming better readers while at the same time helping them learn more content material.

The strategies in this book are designed to assist students with getting started, maintaining focus with reading, and organizing information for later retrieval. They engage students in learning material, provide the vehicle for them to organize and reorganize concepts, and extend their understanding through writing.

When teachers combine the teaching of reading and the teaching of content together into meaningful, systematic, and corrected instruction, students can apply what they have learned to understanding increasingly more difficult and complex texts as they progress through the school years.

At Holt, we don't assume that students know how or have any desire to make sense of what they're reading, and we develop our programs based on that assumption. We don't just ask students questions about content, we give them strategies to get to that content. Through design, research, and the help of experts like Dr. Judith Irvin, we make sure students' reading needs are covered with our programs.

Content Area

READING STRATEGIES FOR THE SOCIAL STUDIES CLASSROOM

Reinforce reading skills while teaching historical concepts. This resource contains a number of widely-tested and widely-accepted strategies to use with struggling and reluctant readers. Developed by Dr. Judith Irvin, Ph.D. Reading Education.

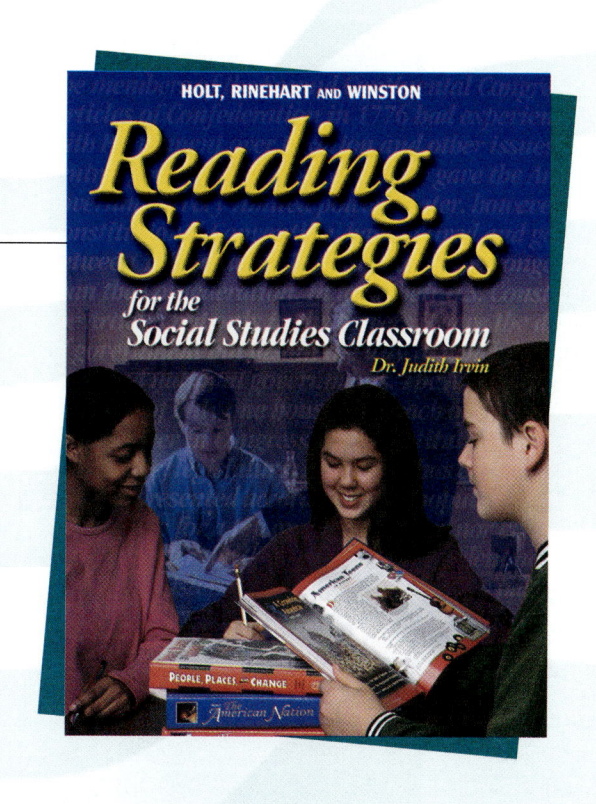

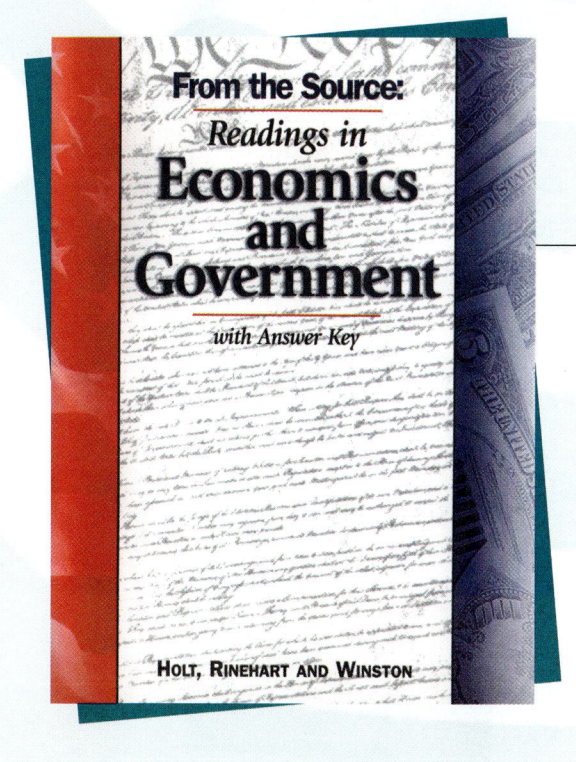

FROM THE SOURCE: READINGS IN ECONOMICS AND GOVERNMENT

These primary source readings, historical documents, legal statutes, and speeches—from notable figures such as Adam Smith, John Maynard Keynes, and David Ricardo—have brief introductions and critical-thinking questions that help students understand where these concepts originated.

Get Your Students

TEXAS EDITION

Your students love activities that get them involved with the content. That's why Holt offers active-learning resources that link directly to program content and provide a multitude of different lessons for large-group, small-group, and individual projects.

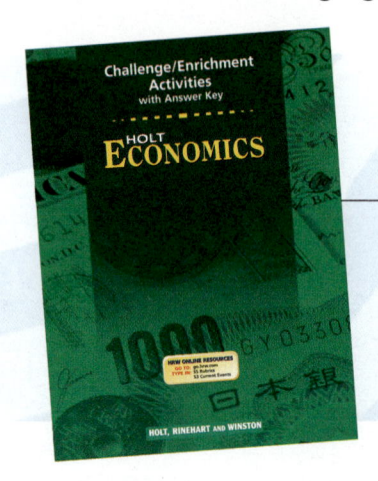

CHALLENGE/ENRICHMENT ACTIVITIES

These worksheets extend lessons through complementary activities and provide students with extra practice in critical thinking and researching economic issues.

SIMULATIONS AND STRATEGIES FOR TEACHING ECONOMICS

Engage your students with alternative lesson plans that pique their interest. Examples include contract negotiations and writing business and financial plans.

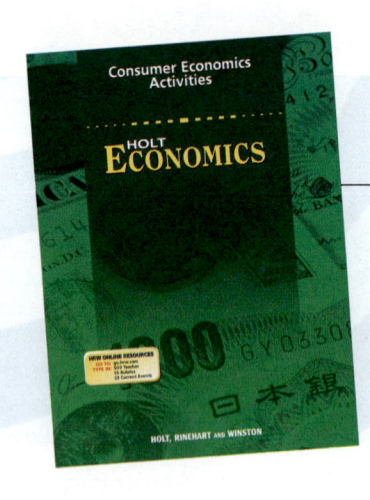

CONSUMER ECONOMICS ACTIVITIES

These additional activities help students with practical, everyday matters like calculating a mortgage payment based on the current interest rate. These activities provide experiences that tie the curriculum to real-world economic issues.

TEXAS CONNECTIONS TO ECONOMICS ★

This booklet contains all of the print program resources for each of the Texas-specific chapters. Worksheets, quizzes, and tests for Texas chapters are included in this resource.

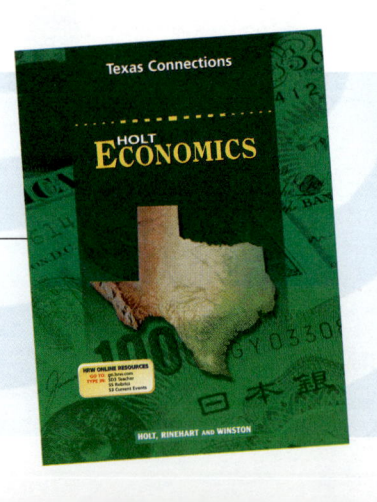

M4

Involved in Learning

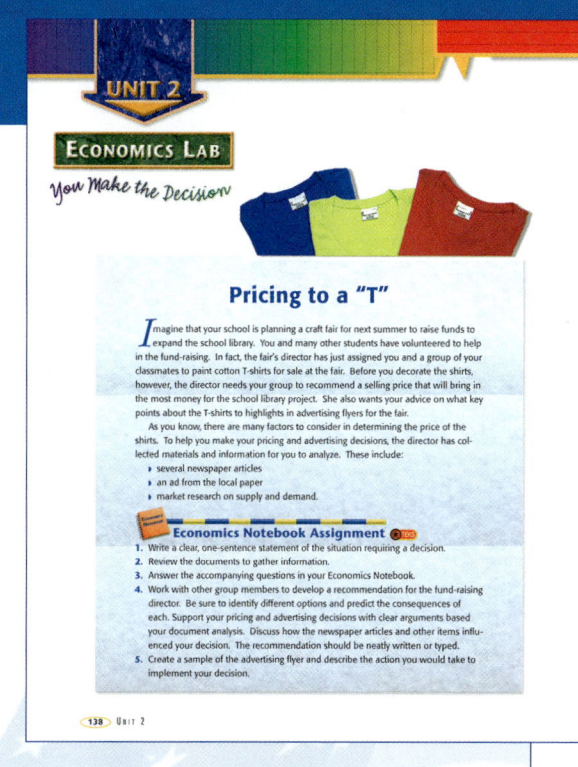

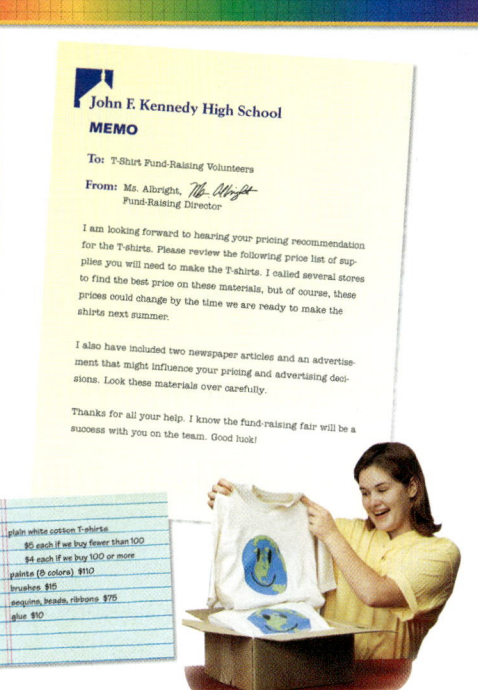

ECONOMIC LABS

These cooperative-learning projects challenge students to synthesize learning objectives and put them into practice. They also provide students with the opportunity to apply the information and ideas they have learned in the unit to a real-world situation.

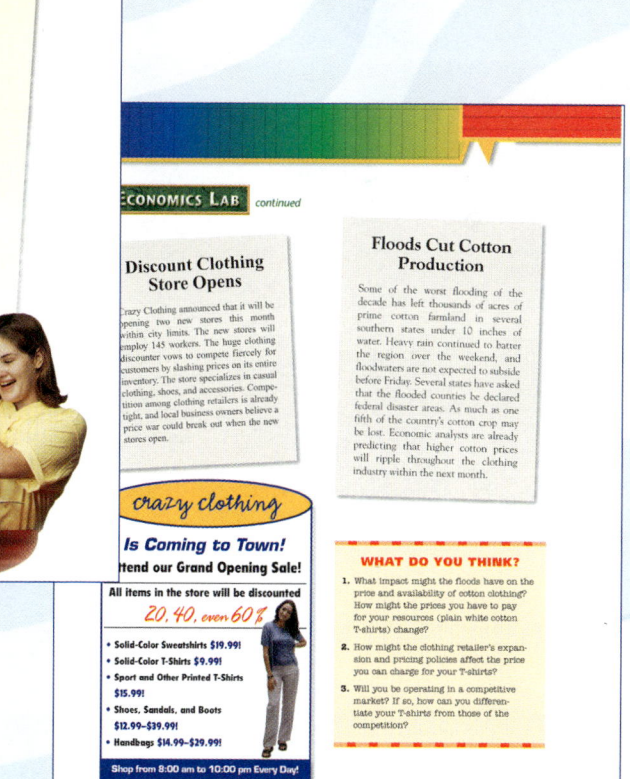

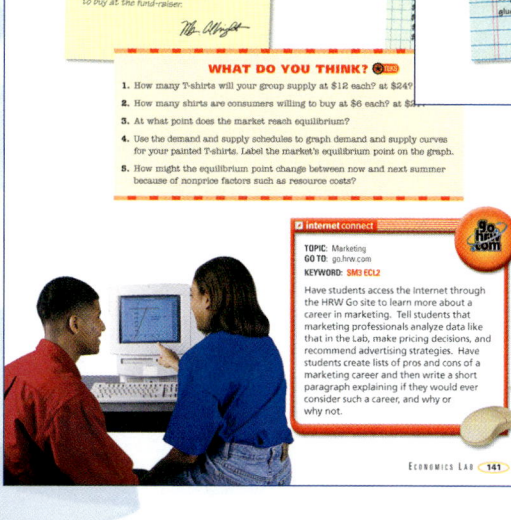

Joining Forces

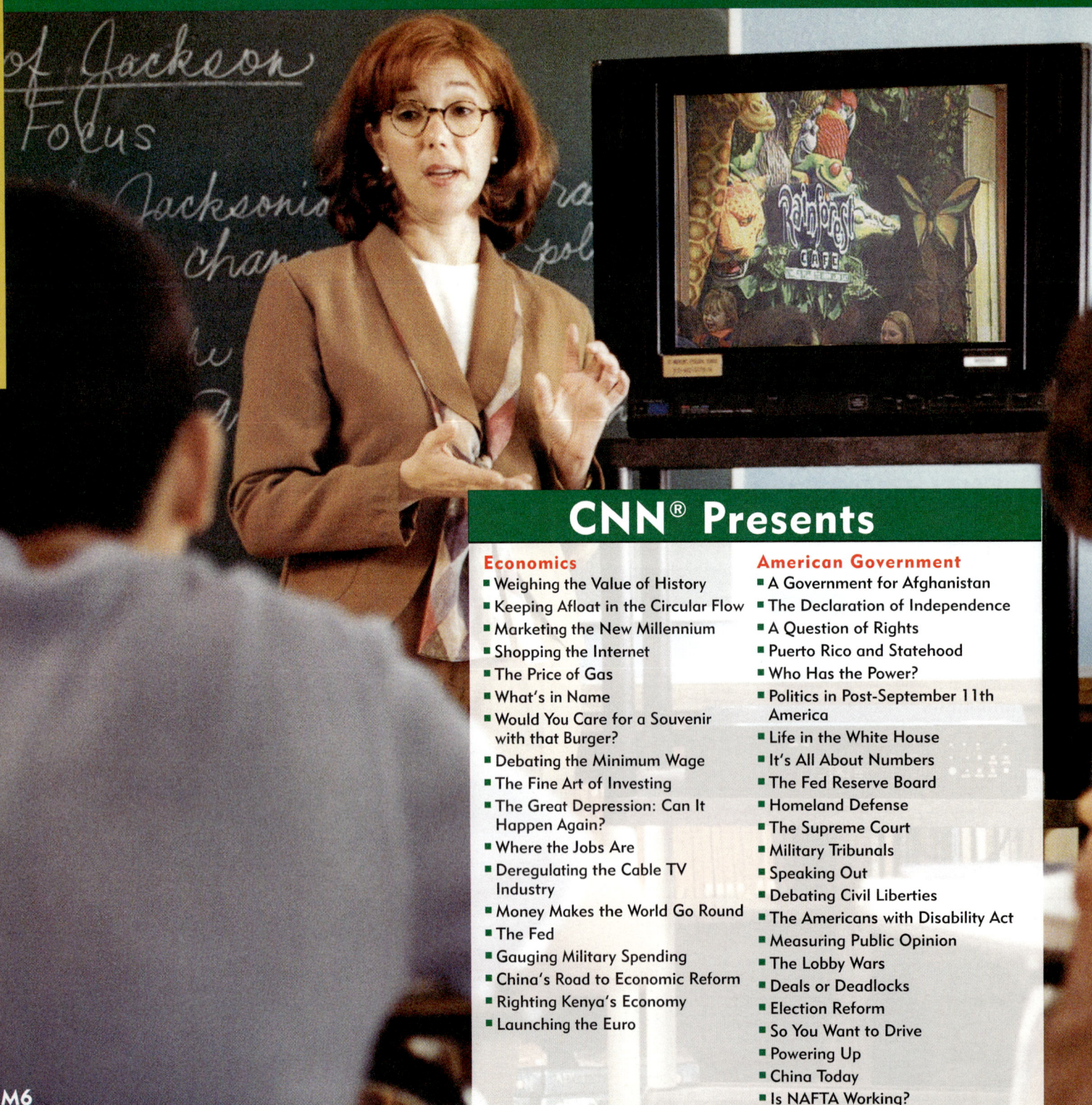

TEXAS EDITION

CNN® Presents

Economics
- Weighing the Value of History
- Keeping Afloat in the Circular Flow
- Marketing the New Millennium
- Shopping the Internet
- The Price of Gas
- What's in Name
- Would You Care for a Souvenir with that Burger?
- Debating the Minimum Wage
- The Fine Art of Investing
- The Great Depression: Can It Happen Again?
- Where the Jobs Are
- Deregulating the Cable TV Industry
- Money Makes the World Go Round
- The Fed
- Gauging Military Spending
- China's Road to Economic Reform
- Righting Kenya's Economy
- Launching the Euro

American Government
- A Government for Afghanistan
- The Declaration of Independence
- A Question of Rights
- Puerto Rico and Statehood
- Who Has the Power?
- Politics in Post-September 11th America
- Life in the White House
- It's All About Numbers
- The Fed Reserve Board
- Homeland Defense
- The Supreme Court
- Military Tribunals
- Speaking Out
- Debating Civil Liberties
- The Americans with Disability Act
- Measuring Public Opinion
- The Lobby Wars
- Deals or Deadlocks
- Election Reform
- So You Want to Drive
- Powering Up
- China Today
- Is NAFTA Working?

to Enrich your Classroom

CNNfyi.com

At **CNNfyi.com**, students will love exploring news stories written by experienced journalists as well as student bureau reporters complete with links to homework help and lesson plans.

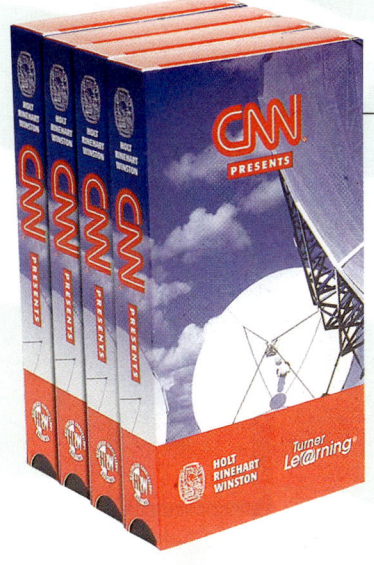

CNN PRESENTS VIDEO LIBRARY

The **CNN PRESENTS** video collection tackles the issue of making content relevant to students head on. Real-world news stories enable students to see the connections between classroom curriculum and today's issues and events around the nation and the world.

CNN PRESENTS...

- America: Yesterday and Today, Beginnings to 1914
- America: Yesterday and Today, 1850 to the Present
- America: Yesterday and Today, Modern Times
- American Government
- Economics
- Geography: Yesterday and Today
- Texas: Yesterday and Today
- September 11, 2001: Part One
- September 11, 2001: Part Two
- World Cultures: Yesterday and Today

Holt is proud to team up with **CNN/TURNER LEARNING** to provide you and your students with exceptional current and historical news videos and online resources that add depth and relevance to your daily instruction. This information collection takes your classroom to the far corners of the globe without students ever leaving their desks!

TEXAS EDITION

Your Multi-talented Classroom

HOLT RESEARCHER CD-ROM: ECONOMY AND GOVERNMENT

This fully searchable database tool includes biographies, state and nation profiles, Supreme Court cases, national and international organizations, and statistics. This outstanding research resource comes with an easy-to-use search engine, a link to **www.hrw.com**, a glossary, and a graphing tool.

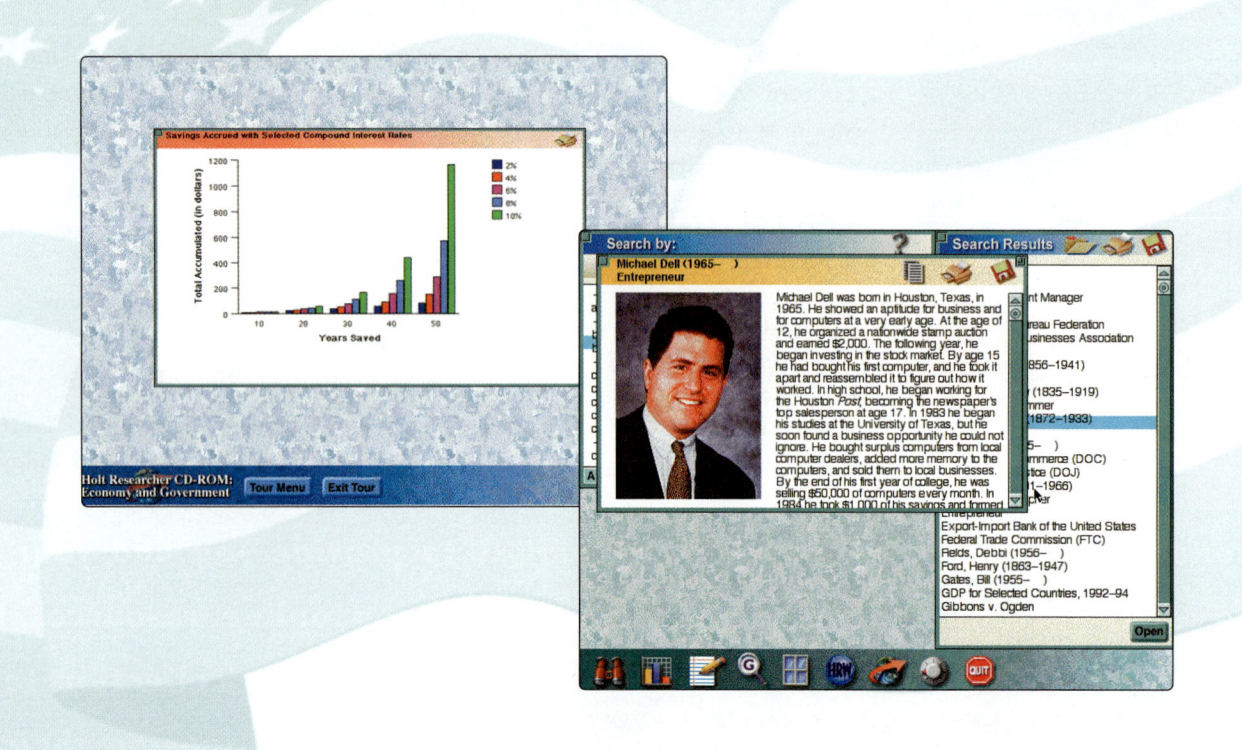

AWARD WINNER!

needs Multimedia Tools

HOLT ECONOMICS VIDEODISC
This exciting program presents in-depth case studies about topics such as the use of public lands or negotiating a multinational deal. Each case study enables you to present information and engage students in a whole new way.

AMERICAN CIVICS CITIZENSHIP SKILLS VIDEOCASSETTE AND VIDEODISC
Informative and enlightening, these eight segments include "The Roles of a Citizen," "The Critical Consumer," and "The Citizen and Local Media"; all designed to enhance how you teach citizenship skills.

Technology with

go.hrw.com FOR TEACHERS

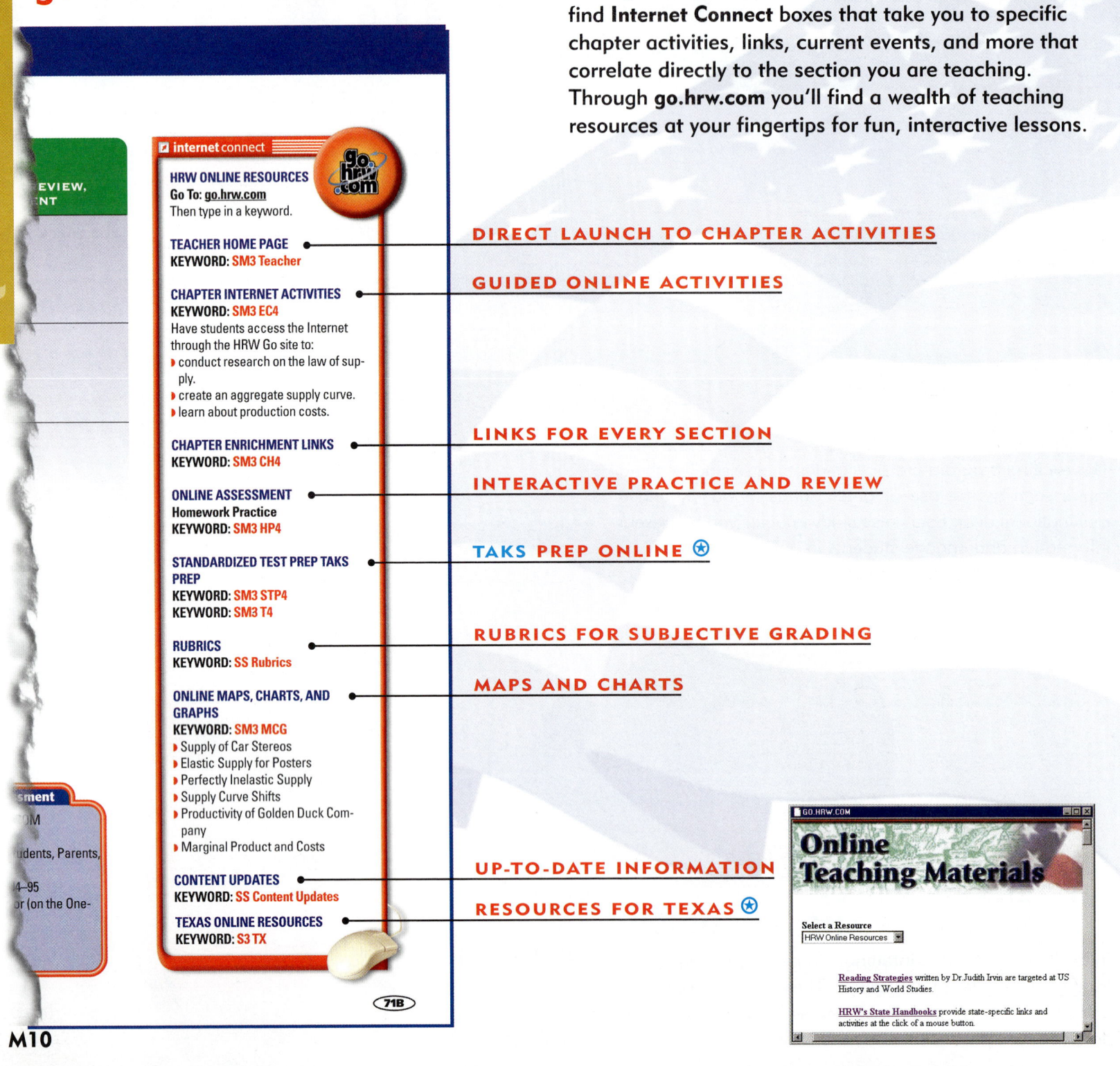

Throughout the *Annotated Teacher's Edition*, you'll find **Internet Connect** boxes that take you to specific chapter activities, links, current events, and more that correlate directly to the section you are teaching. Through **go.hrw.com** you'll find a wealth of teaching resources at your fingertips for fun, interactive lessons.

TEXAS EDITION

internet connect

HRW ONLINE RESOURCES
Go To: go.hrw.com
Then type in a keyword.

TEACHER HOME PAGE — DIRECT LAUNCH TO CHAPTER ACTIVITIES
KEYWORD: SM3 Teacher

CHAPTER INTERNET ACTIVITIES — GUIDED ONLINE ACTIVITIES
KEYWORD: SM3 EC4
Have students access the Internet through the HRW Go site to:
- conduct research on the law of supply.
- create an aggregate supply curve.
- learn about production costs.

CHAPTER ENRICHMENT LINKS — LINKS FOR EVERY SECTION
KEYWORD: SM3 CH4

ONLINE ASSESSMENT — INTERACTIVE PRACTICE AND REVIEW
Homework Practice
KEYWORD: SM3 HP4

STANDARDIZED TEST PREP TAKS PREP — TAKS PREP ONLINE ★
KEYWORD: SM3 STP4
KEYWORD: SM3 T4

RUBRICS — RUBRICS FOR SUBJECTIVE GRADING
KEYWORD: SS Rubrics

ONLINE MAPS, CHARTS, AND GRAPHS — MAPS AND CHARTS
KEYWORD: SM3 MCG
- Supply of Car Stereos
- Elastic Supply for Posters
- Perfectly Inelastic Supply
- Supply Curve Shifts
- Productivity of Golden Duck Company
- Marginal Product and Costs

CONTENT UPDATES — UP-TO-DATE INFORMATION
KEYWORD: SS Content Updates

TEXAS ONLINE RESOURCES — RESOURCES FOR TEXAS ★
KEYWORD: S3 TX

Online Teaching Materials

Select a Resource
HRW Online Resources

Reading Strategies written by Dr. Judith Irvin are targeted at US History and World Studies.

HRW's State Handbooks provide state-specific links and activities at the click of a mouse button.

Instructional Value

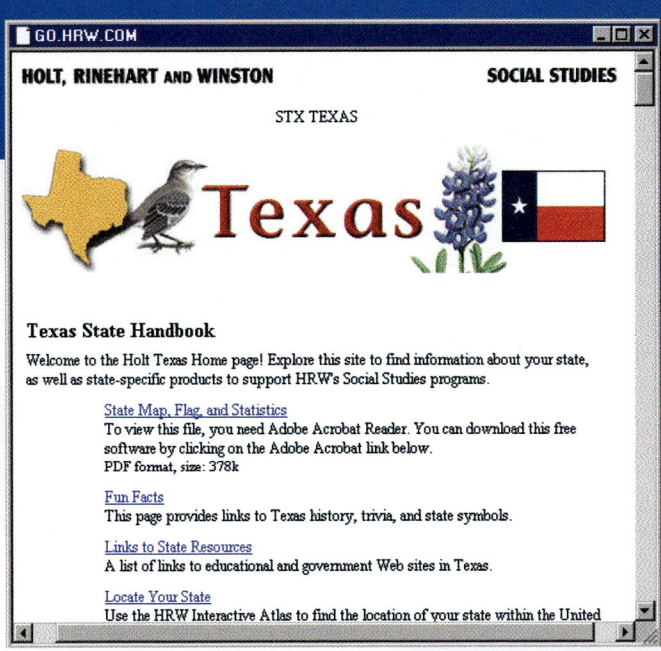

ONLINE TEACHING SUPPORT

Teacher materials on **go.hrw.com** offer you multiple resources for keeping content current. From **American History Maps and Charts** to **State Handbooks,** we've got it all.

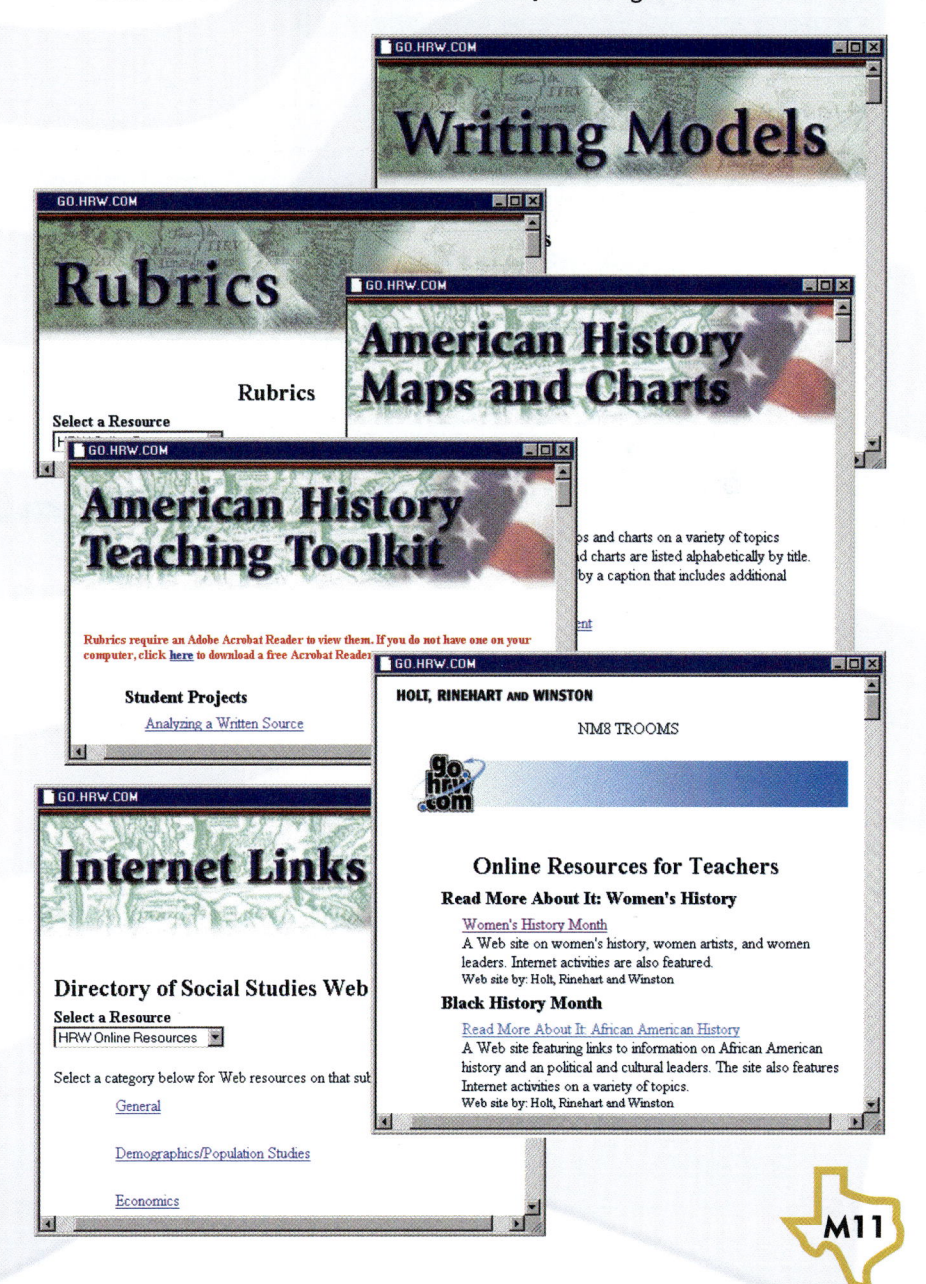

STATE HANDBOOKS

Visit **go.hrw.com**, type in the keyword **STX Texas**, and hit **go!** This site takes you to Texas fun facts, state map, flag, and statistics. There are also links to Texas state resources and products that are specifically made for Texas teachers and students.

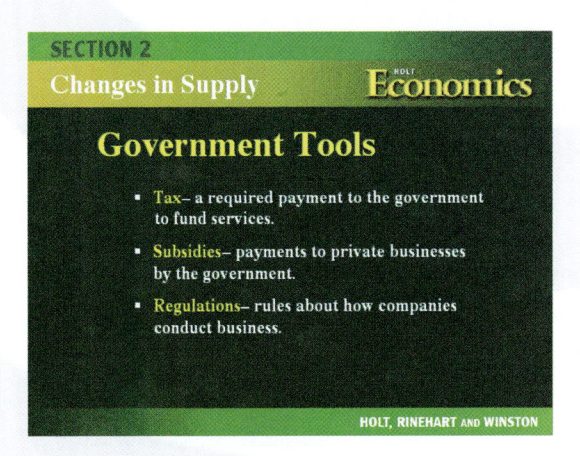

CLASSROOM PRESENTATION SUPPORT

Animated lecture notes help add visual support to your classroom presentations.

Technology that

TEXAS EDITION

Supreme Court Watch Online at go.hrw.com

The Holt American Government program includes an online resource that offers students up-to-date and comprehensive news about important Supreme Court events.

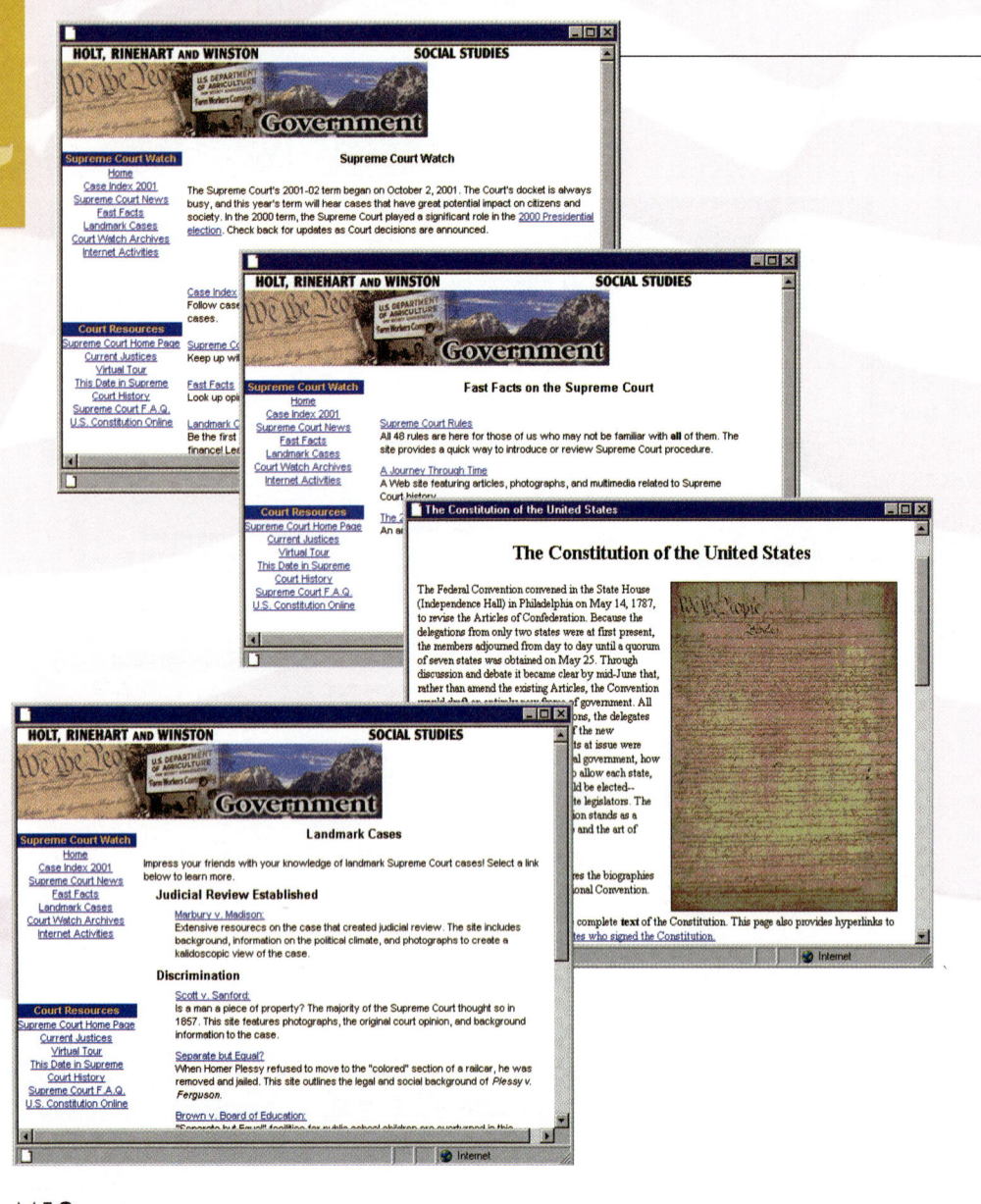

SUPREME COURT WATCH
- Case Index
- Supreme Court News
- Fast Facts
- Landmark Cases
- Court Watch Archives
- Internet Activities

Students may also visit pre-selected Court Resources including:
- Supreme Court Home Page
- Current Justices
- Virtual Tour
- This Date in Supreme Court History
- Supreme Court F.A.Q.

M12

Delivers Content

HOMEWORK PRACTICE AND TAKS PREP ONLINE ✪

This helpful tool allows students to practice and review content by chapter anywhere there is a computer. For even more **TAKS** practice, students can access **TAKS Prep Online** to complete interactive drills and review.

HRW ONLINE ATLAS

This helpful online tool contains over 300 well-rendered and clearly labeled country and state maps. The clean design and easy-to-use navigational tools make accessing information simple. These maps are continually updated so you can rest assured that you and your students have the latest and most accurate geographical content available. Maps are available in English and Spanish.

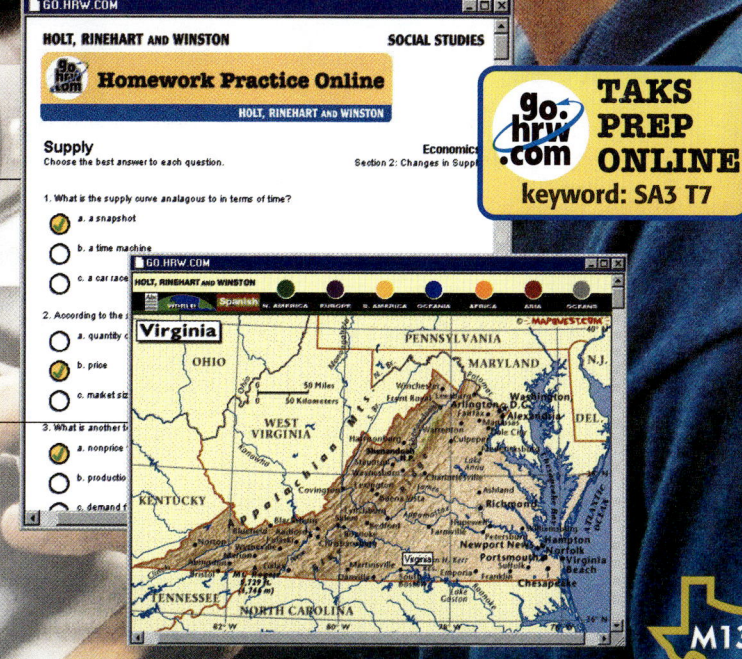

TAKS PREP ONLINE
keyword: SA3 T7

M13

Unique Teacher's
In-Text Chapter Planning

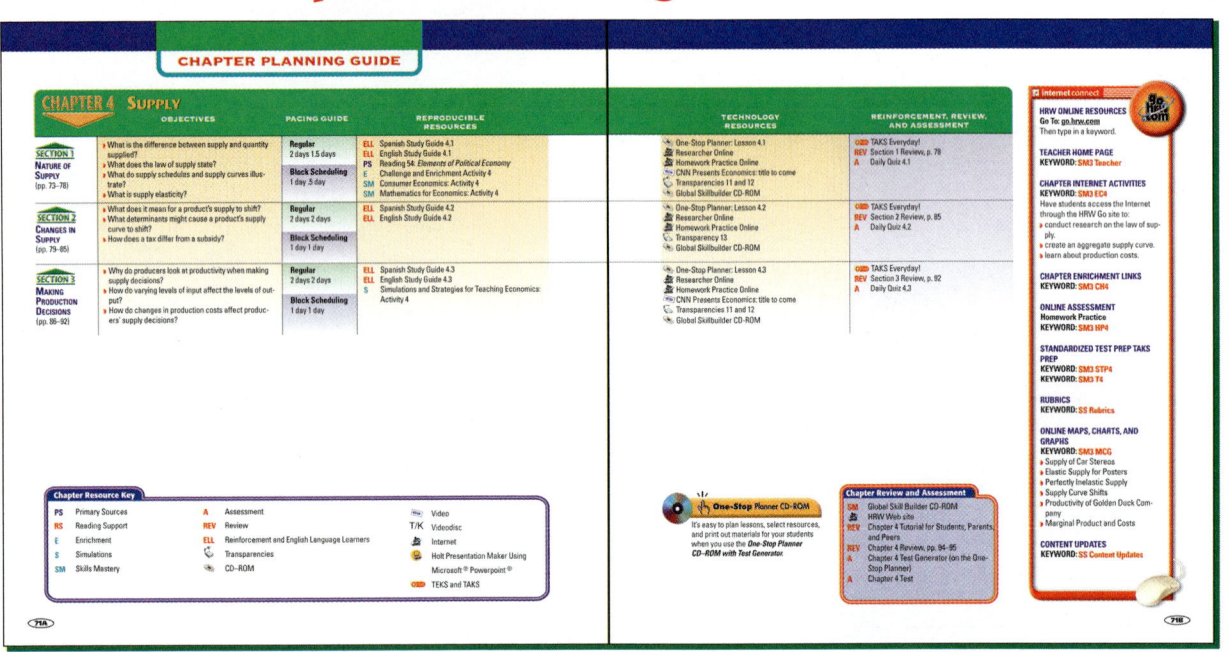

TEXAS EDITION

Holt Economics provides full **TEKS** coverage and comprehensive **TAKS** preparedness.

TEKS THROUGHOUT THE TEXT ★

Alignment to **TEKS** content requirements and Social Studies skills are noted in the **TEKS** correlation chart in your *Teacher's Edition* as well as throughout the text to help you plan and keep track of coverage.

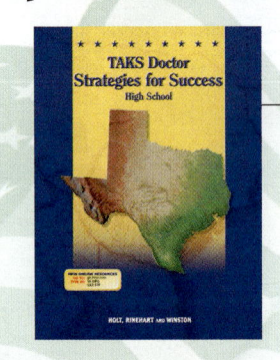

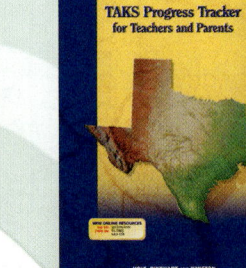

TAKS DOCTOR STRATEGIES FOR SUCCESS ★

Designed to help your students succeed—this resource provides creative teaching strategies to address various types of **TAKS** questions and objectives. Examples include mnemonic devices and other "how-to" strategies to help your students become familiar with the various types of standardized test questions.

TAKS PROGRESS TRACKER FOR TEACHERS AND PARENTS ★

Track your students' progress to ensure success! The ***Progress Tracker*** includes user-friendly forms to help you keep up with individual and classroom **TAKS** preparedness. Take the guessing out of the equation when it comes to **TAKS** preparedness and accountability.

M14

Management System

Everything you need is on one disc!

One-Stop Planner with Test Generator

ONE-STOP PLANNER CD-ROM WITH TEST GENERATOR

Holt brings you the most user-friendly management system in the industry with the **One-Stop Planner CD-ROM with Test Generator.** Plan and manage your lessons from this single disc containing all the teaching resources for **Holt Economics,** valuable planning and assessment tools, and more.

- **Editable lesson plans**
- **Classroom Presentations**
- **Easy-to-use test generator**
- **Previews of all teaching and video resources**
- **Easy printing feature**
- **Direct launch to go.hrw.com**
- **Online TAKS practice activities** ✪

M15

TEXAS EDITION

Energize

(Slide shown: Changes in Supply — Economics)

Government Tools
- **Tax** – a required payment to the government to fund services.
- **Subsidies** – payments to private businesses by the government.
- **Regulations** – rules about how companies conduct business.

HOLT, RINEHART AND WINSTON

Presentations That Benefit Learning

Animated lecture notes can be accessed with ease when you use Holt's **Presentation** tool found on the *One-Stop Planner CD-ROM*. This resource helps you spice up your presentations and gives you ideas to build on. You'll find Microsoft® PowerPoint® presentations that include lecture notes and animated graphic organizers for each chapter and section of your text.

Your Classroom Presentations

CHAPTER PLANNING GUIDE

Each chapter in the *Teacher's Edition* is preceded by this unique interleaf section. This two-page teacher's guide tells you what classroom resources are available. Working on Chapter 6 this week? No problem. Just check the listing of available print and technology resources for Chapter 6 to help plan your lessons.

This guide can also help you accommodate individual learning styles and block scheduling. Or if you are looking for alternative assessments, check the **Chapter Review** for a helpful array of portfolio projects, skills practice, and cooperative-learning activities.

Side Column Annotations that Spark Curiosity

- Careers in Economics
- Case Studies
- Economics in Action
- Global Exchange
- Linking Economics and Geography
- Linking Economics and Government
- Linking Economics and History
- Linking Economics and Psychology
- Linking Economics and Science
- Linking Economics and Sociology

M17

Assessment for

TEXAS EDITION

INTERACTIVE PRACTICE ACTIVITIES

SECTION 3 REVIEW

1. **Define and explain:** total product, marginal product, law of diminishing returns, fixed cost, depreciation, overhead, variable cost, total cost, marginal cost

2. **Identifying Concepts:** Copy the chart below. Use it to identify the three stages of production and to define what happens in each stage.

Stages of Production

3. **Finding the Main Idea**
   a. How do you determine what happens to productivity when a product's inputs change?
   b. What is the difference between fixed costs and variable costs?

4. **Writing and Critical Thinking**
   Summarizing: Imagine that the market for rubber ducks is extremely strong. As Manager of the Golden Duck Company, you are tempted to take advantage of the extra profit by producing 985 ducks. What factors would make you change your mind?
   Consider the following:
   • marginal costs
   • cost per duck

Homework Practice Online
keyword: xxx EC4

THIS SUPERIOR TEST GENERATOR REALLY WORKS!

REVIEW OF MAIN IDEAS

CHAPTER 4 Review

Writing a Summary

Using standard grammar, spelling, sentence structure, and punctuation, write a summary of the information in this chapter.

Identifying Ideas

1. law of supply
2. profit motive
3. cost of production
4. supply curve
5. determinant of supply
6. tax
7. law of diminishing returns
8. overhead
9. variable cost
10. marginal cost

Understanding Main Ideas

SECTION 1 (pp. 73–78)

1. Define the law of supply. Be sure to include how the profit motive relates to this law.
2. What causes movement along a supply curve—in other words, what prompts a change in the quantity supplied? How does this movement differ from a shift in supply?

SECTION 2 (pp. 79–85)

3. What determinants can cause a shift in supply? Give examples of at least three of these factors at work for a company that manufactures televisions.
4. In how many ways does new technology affect the supply curve? Give at least one example for each way you come up with.

SECTION 3 (pp. 86–92)

5. Explain what happens in the three stages of production described by the law of diminishing returns.
6. Explain the difference between the following types of costs: fixed, variable, total, marginal.

Reviewing Themes

1. **Productivity** What are the main ways for a producer to increase productivity of whatever the producer produces?
2. **Markets and Prices** If a product market is strong and the price is rising, how does that affect the supply of that product?
3. **Supply and Demand** Why would a larger supply of steel lead to an increase in the supply of automobiles on the market?

Thinking Critically

1. **Categorizing** Determine whether supply of the following products is elastic or inelastic: candy, diamonds, submarines, election campaign buttons. Explain your reasoning.
2. **Identifying Points of View** Why might a government grant subsidies to certain individuals or businesses?
3. **Competition and Market Structure** If a company has three different manufacturing plants and 10,000 employees, but wants to cut costs to increase productivity, where should the cuts come from and will those cuts be in variable, marginal, or fixed costs?

Writing About Economics

Review what you wrote in your Economics Notebook at the beginning of this chapter about the definition of *supply* and the things you believe you have supplied in the past month. Now that you have studied this chapter, would you change your definition and examples? Why or why not? Record your answer in your notebook.

94 CHAPTER 4

CRITICAL-THINKING REINFORCEMENT

OPPORTUNITIES FOR WRITING REINFORCEMENT

M18

Every Student

CONSISTENT TAKS TEST PREPARATION

TAKS EVERY DAY! ACTIVITIES AND PRACTICE

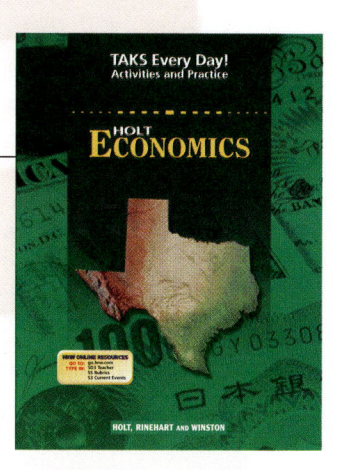

This resource will allow you and your students to devote time to **TAKS** preparation while maintaining your focus on content. Every section of the text has a **TAKS Every Day! Activity** that provides content-specific reinforcement plus grade-level practice in reading, math, and writing.

TAKS EVERY DAY! PRACTICE TESTS

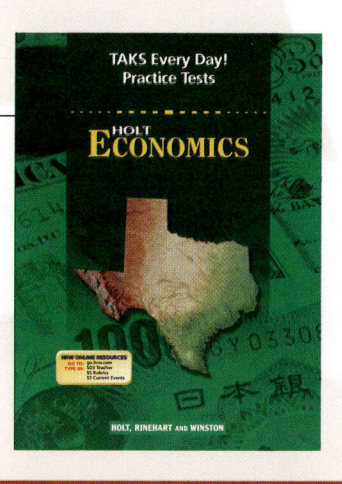

Don't let the **TAKS** test take your students by surprise. This resource exposes your students to a variety of question types—like multiple choice and short answer—commonly found in the **TAKS** test.

ACCESS ONLINE RUBRICS FOR GRADING PROJECTS AND PORTFOLIO ASSIGNMENTS

Additional Print and Technology Assessment Resources

- **Chapter Tests**
- **Daily Quizzes**
- **English Study Guides**
- **Spanish Study Guides**
- **Unit Tests and Unit Lab Activities**
- **Alternative Assessment Handbook**
- **Test Generator** (located on the *One-Stop Planner CD-ROM*)

Detailed Correlation of the
Texas Essential Knowledge and Skills (TEKS)
TO ECONOMICS

TEKS Objective	Main Coverage	
	Presentation	**Demonstration**
(1) Citizenship. The student understands the rights and responsibilities of consumers in the U.S. free-enterprise system.		
(A) Analyze the economic rights and responsibilities of individuals as consumers.	**Student Edition** Ch 2: 30–33 Ch 12: 282 CHB: 457–60 462–63, 469, 471–74, 472	Ch 1: 11C Ch 2: 30C, 42CR(mi)3 Ch 7: 162P Ch 9: 208C, 217C, 220CR(mi)6 Ch 12: 294P CHB: R4Q3, R8Q1, R15Q1, R15Q2, R21Q1, R24Q2
	Teacher's Edition Ch 1: 1C, 1D, 11 Ch 2: 30 Ch 7: 162 Ch 9: 217, 220	Ch 1: 1C, 1D
(B) Analyze the consequences of an economic decision made by an individual consumer.	**Student Edition** Ch 2: 30–33 Ch 12: 282 CHB: 458, 463, 473, 478	Ch 1: 2NA, 11C Ch 2: 30C, 42CR(mi)3 Ch 7: 145SR2, 162P Ch 9: 195P, 208C, 218SR2, 220CR(rt)1, 220CR(rt)3, 220CR(tc)1 CHB: R4Q3, R24Q2
	Teacher's Edition Ch 1: 11 Ch 7: 162 Ch 9: 208	Ch 8: 193G
(2) Citizenship. The student understands the rights and responsibilities of businesses in the U.S. free-enterprise system.		
(A) Analyze the economic rights and responsibilities of businesses.	**Student Edition** Ch 4: 93F Ch 7: 148 Ch 8: 177 CHB: 462, 466, 469	Ch 5: 107SR2 Ch 7: 148F1 Ch 8: 192CR(mi)3
	Teacher's Edition Ch 7: 148	Ch 7: 167G
(B) Analyze the consequences of an economic decision made by a business.	**Student Edition** Ch 3: 58 Ch 4: 85, 89, 91–93F Ch 8: 174F, 180, 188	Ch 1: 18SR3b Ch 4: 94CR(tc)3 Ch 6: 118F1 Ch 7: 150P Ch 10: 248CR(rt)3 Ch 12: 298CR(rt)3
	Teacher's Edition Ch 4: 80	Ch 3: 58 Ch 4: 71G, 71H Ch 5: 106 Ch 8: 167E, 167G, 189
(C) Analyze the ethics policy of a selected business.	**Student Edition** Ch 7: 165 Ch 12: 297F CHB: 461	Ch 7: 165F1, 165F2
	Teacher's Edition Ch 7: 143J	Ch 7: 143J

TEKS

TEKS Objective	Main Coverage	
	Presentation	**Demonstration**
(D) Identify and evaluate ordinances and regulations that apply to the establishment for various types of businesses.	**Student Edition** **Ch 7:** 146, 148 **Ch 12:** 284–286	**Ch 7:** 149SR1, 149SR3b, 166CR(rt)1 **Ch 12:** 285C, 286P, 290SR2, 290SR4, 298CR(mi)2, 299CR(ss)3
	Teacher's Edition **Ch 7:** 146, 148	**Ch 7:** 143D, 154 **Ch 12:** 277E

(3) Citizenship: The student understands the right to own, use, and dispose of private property.

(A) Analyze an example of the responsible purchase, use, or disposal of personal and business property.	**Student Edition** **Ch 2:** 29–33 **Ch 7:** 148 **CHB:** R19	**Ch 2:** 35SR3a **Ch 7:** 148F1, 148F2
	Teacher's Edition **Ch 2:** 21C, 21E **Ch 7:** 143D	**Ch 2:** 21C, 21E **Ch 7:** 143D
(B) Identify and evaluate examples of restrictions that the government places on the use of business and individual property.	**Student Edition** **Ch 2:** 30–33 **Ch 7:** 148	**Ch 2:** 30C, 41F1 **Ch 7:** 148F1, 148F2, 149SR3b, 166CR(rt)1
	Teacher's Edition 21E, 31	**Ch 2:** 21E, 33 **Ch 7:** 143D

(4) Economics. The student understands the basic principles of the U.S. free-enterprise system.

(A) Explain the basic principles of the U.S. free-enterprise system, including profit motive, voluntary exchange, private property rights, and competition.	**Student Edition** **Ch 2:** 29–33, 41 **Ch 4:** 74–75 **CHB:** 469	**Ch 2:** 29C, 30C, 32C, 35SR1, 42CR(id), 42CR(mi)4, 43CR(ss)4, 43CR(ss)2 **Ch 4:** 75P, 78SR1, 78SR3a, 83P, 84P, 94CR(id); 94CR(mi)1; 94CR(rt)2 **Ch 5:** 107SR4
	Teacher's Edition **Ch 2:** 21E, 21F	**Ch 4:** 71C, 71D
(B) Explain the benefits of the U.S. free-enterprise system, including individual freedom of consumers and producers, responsive prices, and investment opportunity.	**Student Edition** **Ch 2:** 29–33 **Ch 4:** 90 **Ch 5:** 97–100 **Ch 16:** 399 **CHB:** 458, 474, 475	**Ch 2:** 29C, 35SR3b, 42CR(rt)3 **Ch 5:** 98P, 100P, 102SR2, 114CR(rt)1 **Ch 7:** 158SR3a **Ch 9:** 203SR2, 203SR3b, 204P, 211F2, 218C **Ch 16:** 376NA **CHB:** R21Q1
	Teacher's Edition **Ch 5:** 97–100	**Ch 5:** 95C, 95D **Ch 9:** 193E

(5) Economics. The student understands the concepts of scarcity and opportunity costs.

(A) Explain why scarcity and choice are basic problems of economics.	**Student Edition** **Ch 1:** 8–9 **Ch 2:** 24–28, 39–40 **CHB:** 456, 458	**Ch 1:** 9C, 10SR3a, 10SR3c, 11C, 20CR(id), 20CR(mi)2, 20CR(rt)1, 20CR(tc)1 **Ch 2:** 28SR3b, 40C, 40SR3a, 42CR(mi)6, 43CRp **Ch 5:** 105SR1 **Ch 9:** 194NA **Ch 16:** 400CR(rt)4 **CHB:** R7Q1
	Teacher's Edition **Ch 1:** 8–9	**Ch 1:** 1E, 1G, 1H, 9

TEKS 1

TEKS Objective	Main Coverage	
	Presentation	**Demonstration**
(B) Interpret a production-possibilities curve and explain the concepts of opportunity costs and scarcity.	**Student Edition** **Ch 1:** 8–9, 11–14 **Ch 16:** 399 **Ch 17:** 416	**Ch 1:** 13G, 14G, 14SR1, 14SR2, 14SR3a, 14SR3b, 14SR3c, 14SR4, 20CR(mi)5, 20CR(tc)2, 20CR(rt)3, 21CR(ss)1, 21CR(ss)2 **Ch 5:** 105SR1 **Ch 17:** 413SR2, 416C, 424CR(mi)3, 424CR(tc)3 **U6Lab:** 452Q2
	Teacher's Edition **Ch 1:** 8–9S, 11–14S **Ch 17:** 416S	**Ch 1:** 1H, 13 **Ch 17:** 401E, 401F

(6) Economics. The student understands the circular-flow model of the economy.

(A) Interpret a circular-flow model of the economy and provide real-world examples to illustrate elements of the model.	**Student Edition** **Ch 2:** 34–35	**Ch 2:** 34C, 35SR2, 42CR(tc)2
	Teacher's Edition **Ch 2:** 21E, 21F	**Ch 2:** 21E, 21F, 34, 35
(B) Explain how government actions affect the circular-flow model.	**Student Edition** **Ch 2:** 34–35	**Ch 2:** 34C, 35SR2
	Teacher's Edition **Ch 2:** 21E, 21F, 34	**Ch 2:** 21E, 21F

(7) Economics. The student understands the interaction of supply, demand, and price.

(A) Identify the determinants that create changes in supply, demand, and price.	**Student Edition** **Pro:** T2–8, T11 **Ch 3:** 51–62 **Ch 4:** 79–85, 93 **Ch 8:** 170 **Ch 12:** 292–293 **Ch 16:** 394	**Pro:** T4C, T8SR3a **Ch 3:** 51P, 53P, 54C, 55C, 55SR1, 55SR 2, 55SR3a, 55SR4, 56P, 57P, 59P, 62SR1, 62SR2, 62SR3a, 62SR 3b, 62SR4, 64C, 65C, 67C, 68SR1, 68SR2, 68SR3b, 68SR4, 69F, 70CR(id), 70CR(w), 70CR(sum), 70CR(mi)1, 70CR(mi)2, 70CR(mi)4, 70CR(rt)1, 70CR(rt)3, 70CRtc1, 70CR(tc)2, 70CR(tc)3, 71CR(ss)1, 71CR(ss)4, 71CR(ic) **Ch 4:** 78C, 78SR1, 78SR3a, 78SR3b, 78SR4, 80C, 81P, 82P, 83P, 84P, 85P, 85SR1, 85SR2, 85SR3b, 85SR4, 94CR(id), 94CR(mi)3, 94CR(mi)4, 94CR(rt)2, 94CR(rt)3 **Ch 5:** 102SR4, 105P, 107P, 107SR1, 107SR2, 107SR4, 112SR1, 113F, 114CR(id), 114CR(mi)3, 114CR(tc)2, 114CR(tc)3 **Ch 6:** 122C, 122SR3d **U2Lab:** 141Q1–5 **Ch 8:** 192CR(mi)1 **Ch 9:** 213SR3b, 213SR4 **Ch 11:** 270CR(tc)1 **Ch 12:** 296SR3a, 298CR(mi)6; 298CR(tc)1 **Ch 16:** 400CR(rt)3
	Teacher's Edition **Ch 3:** 51–62 **Ch 4:** 76, 83, 84, 90 **Ch 11:** 270	**Pro:** TE **Ch 3:** 49C, 49D, 49E, 49F, 49H, 53 **Ch 4:** 74, 71E, 71F, 71 **Ch 5:** 95E **Ch 6:** 115F **Ch 9:** 193H
(B) Interpret a supply-and-demand graph using supply-and-demand schedules.	**Student Edition** **Ch 5:** 103–04	**Ch 3:** 54C, 55C, 67C, **Ch 4:** 74C, 78SR1, 94CR(id)4, **Ch 5:** 103C, 105P, 115CR(ss)1, 115CR(ss)2 **U2Lab:** 141Q1–5
	Teacher's Edition **Ch 5:** 103–04	**Ch 3:** 49D **Ch 4:** 71C, 71E , 74, **Ch 5:** 95E, 106

TEKS 2

TEKS Objective	Main Coverage	
	Presentation	**Demonstration**

(8) Economics. The student understands the role of financial institutions in saving, investing, and borrowing.

(A)	Explain the functions of financial institutions and how the role of financial institutions has changed over time.	**Student Edition** **Ch 13:** 308–17 **Ch 14:** 327–328 **CHB:** 464, 472	**Ch 13:** 314P, 314SR2, 314SR4, 322SR3b, 324CR(rt)2, 324(tc)3, 324CR(w), 325CRp
		Teacher's Edition **Ch 13:** 308–17	**Ch 13:** 299E, 299F
(B)	Analyze how financial institutions affect households and businesses.	**Student Edition** **Ch 13:** 315–20, 323F **CHB:** 472	**Ch13:** 310P, 322SR2, 323F2, 324CR(w), 324CR(mi)6, 324CR(tc)3, 324CR(tc)4
		Teacher's Edition **Ch 13:** 315–20, 323	**Ch 13:** 299G

(9) Economics. The student understands types of business ownership and types of market structures.

(A)	Explain the characteristics of sole proprietorships, partnerships, and corporations.	**Student Edition** **Ch 7:** 145–58	**Ch 7:** 149SR1, 152SR1, 152SR3a, 158SR1, 158SR3c, 158SR4, 164SR1,166CR(id), 166CR(w), 166CR(mi)4, 166CR(mi)5, 167CR(ss)2, 167CRp
		Teacher's Edition **Ch 7:** 145–58	**Ch 7:** 143C, 143E, 143F, 143G, 154
(B)	Analyze the advantages and disadvantages of sole proprietorships, partnerships, and corporations.	**Student Edition** **Ch 7:** 145–52, 156–58	**Ch 7:** 147P, 149SR2, 149SR3a, 149SR3b, 150P, 152SR2, 152SR3b, 152SR4, 157P, 158SR3a, 158SR3b, 166CR(mi)1, 166CR(mi)2, 166CR(mi)4, 166CR(rt)2, 166CR(rt)3, 166CR(tc)1 **U3Lab:** 223Q1–3
		Teacher's Edition **Ch 7:** 145–52, 156–58	**Ch 7:** 143C, 143D, 143E, 143F, 143H, 154
(C)	Describe characteristics and give examples of pure competition, monopolistic competition, oligopoly, and monopoly.	**Student Edition** **Ch 6:** 117–29 **Ch 12:** 286, 290 **Ch 16:** 382	**Ch 6:** 117P, 119C, 122SR1, 122SR2, 122SR3a, 122SR3b, 122SR3c, 122SR3d, 122SR4, 124C, 126P, 129SR1, 129S 2, 129SR3a, 129SR3b, 129SR4, 134SR4, 136CR(id), 136CR(mi)1, 136CR(mi)2, 136CR(mi)3, 136CR(mi)4, 136CR(rt)1, 136CR(rt)2, 136CR(tc)1, 136CR(tc)3
		Teacher's Edition **Ch 6:** 115C, 115D, 115E, 115F, 115G, 119	**Ch 6:** 115C, 115D, 115E, 115F, 115G, 121, 128

(10) Economics. The student understands traditional, command, and market economic systems.

(A)	Explain the characteristics and give examples of traditional, command, and market economic systems.	**Student Edition** **Ch 2:** 24–26 **Ch 16:** 377, 384, 393, 396, **Ch 17:** 414–15	**Ch 2:** 25C, 28SR1, 28SR2, 28SR3a, 42CR(id), 42CR(mi)2, 42CR(mi)3 **U1Lab:** 44NA, 46Q1–4, 47Q1–4 **Ch 16:** 377C, 380SR1, 380SR3b, 385SR3b, 387P, 388SR1, 388SR3, 389P, 393P, 398SR3a, 400CR(id), 400CR(mi)1, 400CR(rt)1, 400CR(rt)2, 400CR(tc)2, 400CR(w), 401CR(ss)3, 401CRp, 401CR(ic) **Ch 17:** 414P, 422SR2, 424CR(mi)4
		Teacher's Edition **Ch 17:** 414–15	**Ch 16:** 375C, 375D, 375E, 375F, 375G, 375I **Ch 17:** 401H

TEKS Objective	Main Coverage	
	Presentation	**Demonstration**
(B) Compare the U.S. system with other economic systems.	**Student Edition** Ch 2: 26 Ch 16: 382, 384 Ch 17: 414–15	**Ch 2:** 26C, 28SR2, 28SR3a, 35SR4, 42CR(mi)1 **U1Lab:** 44NA **Ch 16:** 380SR2, 385SR2, 388SR2b, 398SR3b, 400CR(mi)2, 400CR(tc)1, 400CR(tc)3, 400CR(tc)4
	Teacher's Edition Ch 17: 414–15	**Ch 16:** 375E, 375F, 375G, 375H

(11) Economics. The student understands the basic concepts of consumer economics.

(A) Analyze the factors involved in the process of acquiring consumer goods and services, including credit, interest, and insurance.	**Student Edition** Ch 1: 16 Ch 9: 214–15 **CHB:** 462, 463, 468, 471–73	**Ch 1:** 18SR1, 18SR2 **Ch 3:** 53P, 55SR4, 56P, 61F1 **Ch 9:** 214P, 215P, 218SR3a, 218SR3b, 218SR34, 220CR(w), 220CR(mi)6, 220CR(tc)1 **Ch 13:** 304C **Ch 16:** 392F1 **CHB:** R9463Q1, R9Q2
	Teacher's Edition Ch 1: 16 Ch 3: 53, 55, 56, 61 Ch 9: 214–15	**Ch 3:** 52 **Ch 9:** 193E, 193I **Ch 13:** 304
(B) Compare different means by which savings can be invested and the risks and rewards each poses to the consumer.	**Student Edition** Ch 9: 195–98, 201–03, 209–12 **CHB:** 478, 479	**Ch 7:** 158SR2 **Ch 9:** 199SR1, 199SR2, 199SR3a, 202P, 203SR1, 203SR2, 203SR3b, 204P, 210C, 213SR2, 213SR3b, 213SR3c, 220CR(w), 220CR(mi)1, 220CR(mi)3, 220CR(mi)4, 220CR(rt)2, 220CR(rt)3, 220CR(tc)1, 220CR(tc)3, 221CR(ss)2 **Ch 13:** 326NA
	Teacher's Edition Ch 9: 195–98, 201–03, 209–12	**Ch 7:** 143H **Ch 9:** 193C, 193D, 193E, 193H
(C) Analyze the economic impact of investing in stock and bond markets.	**Student Edition** Ch 9: 204–05, 210, 211 **CHB:** 476, 477, 478	**Ch 7:** 166CR(mi)3, 166CR(tc)2 **Ch 9:** 213SR2, 213SR4, 220CR(w), 220CR(mi)4, 220CR(rt)3, 221CR(ss)2 **CHB:** R24Q1, R24Q2, R24Q3, R24Q4, R24Q5
	Teacher's Edition Ch 9: 204–05, 210, 211	**Ch 7:** 143H **Ch 9:** 193G

(12) Geography. The student understands the geographic significance of the economic factors of production.

(A) Describe the effects of unequal distribution of economic factors of production.	**Student Edition** Ch 1: 19 Ch 18: 428	**Ch 11:** 263SR4 **Ch 17:** 406SR4, 407P, 424CR(rt)2 **Ch 18:** 430SR3a
	Teacher's Edition Ch 1: 19	**Ch 18:** 425C
(B) Analyze the locations of resources used in the production of an economic good and evaluate the significance of the locations.	**Student Edition** **Pro:** T1–3, T5–6, T9–10 Ch 1: 19 Ch 16: 393	**Pro:** T4SR4 **Ch 1:** 19F1, 19F2 **Ch 18:** 426N, 448CR(w)
	Teacher's Edition Ch 1: 19	**Ch 7:** 154

TEKS 4

TEKS Objective	Main Coverage	
	Presentation	**Demonstration**
(13) Geography. The student understands the reasons for international trade and its importance to the United States.		
(A) Explain the concepts of absolute and comparative advantages.	**Student Edition** **Ch 18:** 428	**Ch 18:** 428P, 430SR1, 448CR(id) 448CR(mi)2
	Teacher's Edition **Ch 18:** 425C, 426D	**Ch 18:** 425C, 425D
(B) Apply the concepts of comparative advantage to explain why and how countries trade.	**Student Edition** **Ch 18:** 428–430	**Ch 18:** 430SR2, 430SR3b, 430SR4, 448CR(rt)1, 448CR(w)
	Teacher's Edition **Ch 18:** 425C, 425D, 425H	**Ch 18:** 425C, 425D, 425H
(C) Analyze the impact of U.S. imports and exports on the United States and its trading partners.	**Student Edition** **Ch 10:** 239 **Ch 12:** 280F **Ch 16:** 382 **Ch 18:** 435, 437 **CHB:** 475	**Ch 10:** 238C, **Ch 12:** 283SR1, 298CR(id) **Ch 18:** 437C, 438C, 448CR(w)
	Teacher's Edition **Ch 18:** 425F, 425G, 425H	**Ch 18:** 425D, 425F
(14) Geography. The student understands the issues of free trade and the effects of trade barriers.		
(A) Compare the effects of free trade and trade barriers on economic activities.	**Student Edition** **Pro:** T12 **Ch 12:** 280F **Ch 16:** 382, 383, 397 **Ch 18:** 439–443	**Ch 12:** 283SR1,298CR(id) **Ch 16:** 400CR(rt)3 **Ch 18:** 440C, 441P, 443P, 446P, 446SR3a, 446SR3b, 448CR(mi)4, 448CR(tc)1, 448CR(tc)2, 448CR(w)
	Teacher's Edition **Pro:** TG **Ch 12:** 277D **Ch 18:** 425G, 440, 443	**Pro:** TG **Ch 4:** 71F **Ch 12:** 277D **Ch 18:** 425G
(B) Evaluate the benefits and costs of participation in international free-trade agreements.	**Student Edition** **Pro:** T11–12 **Ch 18:** 445, 447F	**Pro:** T12SR4, T14CR(rt)3 **Ch 18:** 446SR4, 447F1, 447F2 **U6Lab:** 453Q1–3
	Teacher's Edition **Pro:** TH **Ch 18:** 425G, 425H	**Pro:** TH **Ch 18:** 425G, 425H, 443, 444, 446, 447
(15) Government. The student understands the role that the government plays in the U.S. free-enterprise system.		
(A) Describe the role of government in the U.S. free-enterprise system.	**Student Edition** **Pro:** T7–9 **Ch 2:** 30, 33–34 **Ch 4:** 82 **Ch 5:** 108–10 **Ch 6:** 128–134 **Ch 8:** 174, 175, 183, 188 **Ch 10:** 238 **Ch 12:** 281, 284, 286, 287, 289–291, 291F, 293 **Ch 13:** 306, 308–14, 319, 322 **Ch 14:** 328, 330, 334, 335, 342–344 **Ch 15:** 349–52, 354–60, 362–64 **Ch 16:** 378, 384 **CHB:** 467, 468, 471	**Pro:** 8SR3b **Ch 2:** 33C, 35SR2, 42CR(tc)1 **Ch 5:** 108P, 110P, 112SR2, 114CR(id), 114CR(mi)4, 114CR(mi)5, 114CR(rt)2 **Ch 6:** 133P, 128P, 134SR1, 134SR3a, 134SR3b, 136CR(id) **Ch 7:** 148F2, 149SR3B, 166CR(id) **Ch 8:** 176SR4, 186P **Ch 9:** 212C **Ch 10:** 248CR(tc)2 **Ch 11:** 269F1, 270CR(rt)3 **Ch 12:** 284P, 287P, 289C, 290SR3a, 290SR4, 291P, 298CR(mi)4, 298CR(tc)2, 298CR(tc)1, 298CR(tc)4, 299CR(ss)4 **Ch 13:** 306P, 311P, 312P, 313F1, 314SR3b, 314SR4, 322SR3c, 324CR(rt)2, 324CR(mi)5, 324CR(mi)7, 324CR(rt)2 **Ch 14:** 336SR4, 346CR(rt)1, 346CR(rt)2 **Ch 15:** 354SR3, 364C, 366SR3a, 368CR(mi)1, 368CR(rt)2 **U5Lab:** 372Q1

TEKS 5

TEKS Objective	Main Coverage	
	Presentation	**Demonstration**
(15A) *continued*	**Teacher's Edition** **Pro:** T6 **Ch 4:** 81 **Ch 5:** 108–10 **Ch 13:** 306, 308–14, 319, 322 **Ch 15:** 349–52, 354, 355–60, 362–64	**Pro:** TF **Ch 4:** 71F **Ch 5:** 95G,95H, 109 **Ch 6:** 128 **Ch 8:** 167F **Ch 9:** 197 **Ch 12:** 277D, 277E, 277F, 288, 292 **Ch 13:** 299H, 312 **Ch 14:** 342 **Ch 15:** 347C, 347D, 347H **Ch 18:** 435
(B) Evaluate government rules and regulations in the U.S. free-enterprise system.	**Student Edition** **Pro:** T8 **Ch 2:** 33, 41 **Ch 5:** 109, 111–12, 113, **Ch 6:** 130–134 **Ch 8:** 174, 175 **Ch 12:** 286, 292, 293 **CHB:** 461, 467, 468, 471	**Ch 2:** 41F1, 42CR(rt)1 **Ch 5:** 112SR2, 112SR3a, 112SR3b, 112SR4, 113F, 114CR(id), 114CR(rt)2 **Ch 6:** 133P, 134SR3a, 134SR3b **Ch 7:** 148F1, 166CR(id),166CR(rt)1 **Ch 8:** 176SR4, 192CR(rt)3 **Ch 9:** 220CR(mi)6 **Ch 11:** 254F1, 268SR4 **Ch 12:** 285C; 290SR2; 290SR4; 293P; 296SR2; 296SR3a; 297F1, 297F2, 298CR(mi)6; 298CR(tc)1; 298CR(tc)4, 298CR(tc)5, 299CR(ss)Q4 **Ch 13:** 323F1, 323F2 **Ch 15:** 353F2
	Teacher's Edition **Pro:** T6 **Ch 5:** 109, 111–12, 113	**Pro:** TF **Ch 5:** 95G, 95H, 109 **Ch 7:** 166 **Ch 9:** 197 **Ch 12:** 277F, 277G
(16) Government. The student understands the goals of economic growth, stability, full employment, freedom, security, equity, and efficiency as they apply to U.S. economic policy.		
(A) Describe the goals of U.S. economic policy.	**Student Edition** **Ch 2:** 36, 38–39 **Ch 11:** 267–68 **Ch 12:** 284, 289, 290 **Ch 15:** 355–57, 364	**Ch 2:** 36C, 40SR2, 42CR(mi)5, 42CR(rt)1, 42CR(w), 43CR(ss)2, 43CR(ic) **Ch 11:** 268SR4, 270CR(w), 270CR(id), 270CR(rt)3 **Ch 12:** 288P; 290SR1; 290SR3b; 298CR(mi)Q5; 298CR(rt)1 **Ch 14:** 347CRp **Ch 15:** 356C, 364C, 366SR3a
	Teacher's Edition **Ch 11:** 267–68 **Ch 12:** 277E, 277F, 281 **Ch 15:** 355–57, 364	**Ch 11:** 249H **Ch 15:** 363
(B) Analyze how economic growth, stability, and full employment are measured.	**Student Edition** **Ch 2:** 38–39 **Ch 10:** 241–244 **Ch 11:** 251–52, 257–63	**Ch 2:** 40SR3b **Ch 10:** 229P, 232C, 233P, 235SR1, 235SR2, 235SR3a, 235SR3b, 235SR3c, 240SR1, 240SR3c, 242C, 246SR1, 248CR(mi)1, 248CR(mi)5, 248CR(rt)2, 248CR(tc)1 **Ch 11:** 251P, 256SR1, 256SR3a, 256SR3b, 257P, 263SR1, 263SR2, 268SR3a, 270CR(w), 270CR(id), 270CR(mi)1, 270CR(mi)5, 270CR(mi)6, 270CR(rt)1, **Ch 15:** 366SR4
	Teacher's Edition **Ch 11:** 251–52, 257–63	**Ch 10:** 227G **Ch 11:** 249C, 249D, 249E, 249F
(17) Government. The student understands the economic impact of fiscal policy decisions at the local, state, and national levels.		
(A) Identify types of taxes at the local, state, and national levels and the economic importance of each.	**Student Edition** **Ch 4:** 81, 82 **Ch 15:** 349–52, 359 **CHB:** 467, 469, 470	**Ch 4:** 85SR1, 94CR(id), 94CR(tc)2 **Ch 12:** 299CRp **Ch 15:** 354P, 354SR2, 354SR3a, 358P, 361SR2, 368CR(mi)1, 368CR(mi)3, 368CR(tc)1 **CHB:** R14Q2
	Teacher's Edition **Ch 4:** 82, 83 **Ch 15:** 349–52, 359	**Ch 15:** 347D

TEKS 6

TEKS Objective	Main Coverage	
	Presentation	**Demonstration**
(B) Analyze the categories of revenues and expenditures in the U.S. federal budget.	**Student Edition** **Ch 12:** 283 **Ch 15:** 351, 363	**Ch 12:** 283SR2, 283SR4 **Ch 15:** 351C, 354SR3b, 363C
	Teacher's Edition **Ch 15:** 351, 363	**Ch 4:** 71D **Ch12:** 277C **Ch 15:** 347G, 363
(C) Analyze the impact of fiscal policy decisions on the economy.	**Student Edition** **Ch 10:** 231, 231C, 238 **Ch 14:** 343–344 **Ch 15:** 358–59	**Ch 10:** 231C, 248CR(tc)2 **Ch 14:** 344SR3a **Ch 15:** 352M, 354SR4, 361P, 361SR3b, 368CR(mi)5, 368CR(rt)3, 368CR(rt)4, 368CR(tc)3 **U5Lab:** 371Q2, 373Q1–3
	Teacher's Edition **Ch 15:** 358–59	**Ch 15:** 347E, 347H

(18) Government. The student understands the role of the Federal Reserve System in establishing monetary policy.

(A) Explain the structure of the Federal Reserve System.	**Student Edition** **Ch 14:** 329–331, 332–336	**Ch 14:** 330M, 331SR2, 331SR3b, 331SR3c, 331SR4, 346CR(mi)1, 347CR(ic)
	Teacher's Edition **Ch 14:** 325C–D	**Ch 14:** 325C
(B) Analyze the three basic tools used to implement U.S. monetary policy.	**Student Edition** **Ch 14:** 339, 341–342	**Ch 12:** 297F2 **Ch 14:** 336SR2, 336SR3b, 336SR4, 337P, 339C, 344SR2, 344SR3b, 346CR(mi)3, 346CR(rt)3, 346CR(rt)5, 347CRp **U5Lab:** 373Q2
	Teacher's Edition **Ch 14:** 325G, 339	**Ch 14:** 325G

(19) History. The student understands economic ideas and decisions from the past that have influenced the present and those of today that will affect the future.

(A) Analyze the importance of various economic philosophers such as John Maynard Keynes, Karl Marx, and Adam Smith and their impact on the U.S. free-enterprise system.	**Student Edition** **Ch 2:** 25–27, 43 **Ch 15:** 356–357, 369 **Ch 16:** 382, 389, 390, 399F	**Ch 2:** 43F2 **Ch 15:** 361SR3a, 368CR(mi)2 **Ch 16:** 385SR4, 398SR2, 398SR4, 399F1, 400CR(id), 400CR(mi)4, 400CR(tc)4 **Ch 17:** 422SR4
	Teacher's Edition **Ch 15:** 356–357, 369 **Ch 16:** 390, 391	**Ch 2:** 27 **Ch 15:** 347E **Ch 16:** 375I, 375J
(B) Trace the history of the labor movement in the United States.	**Student Edition** **Ch 8:** 177–83 **CHB:** 467, 468	**Ch 8:** 176SR3b, 177P, 178P, 180C, 182C, 188P, 183SR2, 183SR3a, 183SR4, 192CR(mi)3, 192CR(mi)4, 192CR(rt)2, 193CR(ic) **CHB:** R14Q3
	Teacher's Edition **Ch 8:** 178, 179, 182, 188	**Ch 8:** 167E, 167F
(C) Analyze the impact of business cycles on U.S. history.	**Student Edition** **Ch 10:** 236–240	**Ch 9:** 211F1 **Ch 11:** 256SR4
	Teacher's Edition **Ch 9:** 227E, 227F	**Ch 10:** 227F

TEKS Objective	Main Coverage	
	Presentation	**Demonstration**
(D) Identify the contributions of entrepreneurs, past and present, such as Mary Kay Ash, Andrew Carnegie, and Bill Gates.	**Student Edition** Ch 6: 135 Ch 7: 146F, 161	Ch 6: 135F3, 136CR(id) Ch 7: 149SR4, 166CR(mi)5
	Teacher's Edition Ch 7: 146, 161	Ch 7: 143J, 160
(20) History. The student understands economic concepts embodied in historical documents including the U.S. Constitution.		
(A) Identify economic concepts in the U.S. Constitution, including property rights and taxation.	**Student Edition** CHB: 469	Ch 2: 41F2 CHB: R171
	Teacher's Edition Ch 2: 21E, 30, 31	Ch 2: 21E
(B) Analyze the impact of economic concepts in the U.S. constitution on contemporary issues and policies.	**Student Edition** Ch 12: 290 Ch 15: 364, 367 CHB: 470	Ch 15: 366SR3b, 367F1, 367F2
	Teacher's Edition Ch 15: 347D	Ch 15: 347D
(21) Culture. The student understands how societal values affect a nation's economy.		
(A) Analyze the societal values that determine how a country answers the basic economic questions.	**Student Edition** Ch 1: 9 Ch 2: 24–25, 40–41	Ch 1: 21CRp Ch 2: 40SR4, 43CRp Ch 16: 380SR4
	Teacher's Edition Ch 2: 21C, 21D, 21G, 21H	Ch 2: 21C, 21D, 21G, 21H
(B) Describe the societal values that influence traditional, command, and market economies.	**Student Edition** Ch 2: 24–27 Ch 16: 397, 399	Ch 2: 28SR3a, 28SR4, 43CRp Ch 16: 380SR4, 399F1, 399F2, 400CR(mi)3, 400CR(rt)4, 400CR(tc)2, 401CR(ss)4
	Teacher's Edition Ch 16: 396, 397	Ch 16: 375E, 375F, 375G
(22) Culture. The student understands the impact of the nation's culture on its level of economic development.		
(A) Describe the level of economic development of selected nations.	**Student Edition** Ch 16: 383, 385, 387–88, 390, 391, 396 Ch 17: 403–06, 407–09	Ch 16: 393P, 396P Ch 17: 404M, 406SR2, 424CR(tc)1
	Teacher's Edition Ch 16: 384, 387 Ch 17: 403–06, 407–09	Ch 8: 167D Ch 17: 401C, 401D, 401E, 401H

TEKS 8

TEKS Objective	Main Coverage	
	Presentation	**Demonstration**
(B) Analyze how societal values affect the economic development of nations.	**Student Edition** **Ch 17:** 412–13	**Ch 17:** 410F2, 411P, 413P, 413SR3a, 424CR(tc)2
	Teacher's Edition **Ch 2:** 21C, 21D, 24, 25, 38, 39 **Ch 16:** 396–97	**Ch 2:** 21C, 21D

(23) Social studies skills. The student applies critical-thinking skills to organize and use information acquired from a variety of sources, including electronic technology.

(A) Analyze information by sequencing, categorizing, identifying cause-and-effect relationships, comparing, contrasting, finding the main idea, summarizing, making generalizations and predictions, and drawing inferences and conclusions.	**Student Edition** **SHB:** S1–2, S9–11, S16–17	**Pro:** T4SR3b, T4SR4, T6P, T8SR3a, T8SR4, T12SR3a, T12SR3b, T12SR4, T13F1, T13F2, T14CR(tc)1, T14CR(tc)2, T14CR(tc)3 **Ch 1:** 7SR2, 7SR4, 10SR2, 10SR4, 14SR2, 14SR4, 18SR1, 18SR4, 21CR(ss)2, 21CR(ss)4 **Ch 2:** 40SR4, 43CR(ss)1–4, **Ch 3:** 55SR2, 55SR4, 62SR2, 62SR4, 68SR2, 68SR4, 70CR(tc)2, 70CR(tc)3, 71CR(ss)3, 71CR(ss)4 **Ch 4:** 73P, 75P, 77C, 77P, 78C, 78SR2, 78SR3a, 78SR3b; 78SR4; 79P, 80C, 81P, 82P; 83P, 84P, 85P, 85SR2; 85SR3a, 85SR3b; 85SR4, 87C, 89P; 91P 92SR2; 92SR3a, 92SR4, 94CR(mi)3; 94CR(mi)4, 94CR(mi)5; 94CR(mi)6, 94CR(rt)1; 94CR(rt)2, 94CR(rt)3, 94CR(tc)1, 94CR(tc)3, 95CR(ss)2, 95CR(ss)4 **Ch 5:** 102SR2, 102SR4, 107SR2, 107SR4, 112SR4, 113F, 114CR(mi)4, 114CR(rt)3, 114CR(tc)1, 114CR(tc)2, 114CR(tc)3, 114CR(w) **Ch 6:** 116NA, 122SR3b, 122SR4; 127P, 129SR2, 129SR3a, 129SR4, 136CR(mi)1, 136CR(mi)2, 136CR(tc)2, 136CR(tc)3, 137CR(ss)2 **U2Lab:** 141Q5 **Ch 7:** 149SR2, 149SR4, 152SR4, 158SR2, 158SR4, 162P, 164SR2, 164SR4, 166CR(rt)1, 166CR(tc)1, 167CR(ss)2, 167CR(ss)4 **Ch 8:** 170C; 172P; 176SR2, 176SR3a; 176SR4, 177P; 178P, 182C , 183SR2; 183SR3; 183SR4, 184P; 185P; 188P; 190P; 190SR2, 190SR3, 190SR4; 191F, 192CR(mi)1, 192CR(mi)2; 192CR(mi)4, 192CR(mi)5, 192CR(mi)6, 192CR(rt)3, 192CR(tc)1, 192CR(tc)2, 192CR(tc)3, 192CR(tc)4, 192CR(tc)5, 193CR(ss)2, 193CR(ic) **Ch 9:** 199SR2, 199SR4, 203SR2, 203SR4, 213SR4, 218SR2, 218SR4, 220CR(tc)1, 220CR(tc)2, 220CR(tc)3, 221CR(ss)4 **U3Lab:** 225Q2, 225Q4 **Ch 10:** 228NA, 229P, 231C, 232C, 233P, 234C, 235SR3a, 235SR3b, 235SR3c, 237F1, 238C, 238P, 240SR2, 240SR3a, 240SR3b, 240SR3c, 240SR4, 241P, 242C, 243P, 244P, 246SR2, 246SR3a, 246SR3b, 246SR4, 248CR(mi)1, 248CR(mi)2, 248CR(mi)3, 248CR(mi)4, 248CR(rt)1, 248CR(rt)2, 248CR(rt)3, 249CR(ic) **Ch 11:** 254F1, 254F2, 256SR2, 263SR2, 263SR3a, 263SR4, 268SR2, 268SR3b, 268SR4, 269F1, 269F2, 270CR(tc)1, 270CR(tc)2, 270(tc)3, 270CR(w), 271CR(ss)2 **U4Lab:** 275Q1–3 **Ch 12:** 279C, 280P, 283SR2, 283SR3a; 283SR3b, 283SR4, 284P, 285C; 286P, 287P; 288P, 290SR2; 290SR3a, 290SR3b, 290SR4; 292P; 293P, 294P, 296P, 296SR2; 296SR3a; 296SR4; 297F2, 298CR(mi)1; 298CR(mi)2, 298CR(mi)3; 298CR(mi)4, 298CR(mi)5, 298CR(mi)6, 298CR(rt)1, 298CR(rt)2, 298CR(rt)3, 298CR(tc)1, 298CR(tc)2, 298CR(tc)3, 298CR(tc)4, 298CR(tc)5, 299CR(ss)2, 299CR(ic) **Ch 13:** 307SR2, 307SR4, 313F1, 313F2, 314SR2, 314SR4, 322SR2, 322SR4, 323F2, 324CR(w), 325CR(ss)1 **Ch 14:** 326NA, 327P, 329C, 331SR3a, 331SR3b, 331SR3c, 331SR4, 333C, 335C, 336SR2, 336SR3a, 336SR3b, 336SR3c , 336SR4, 337P, 338P, 340F1, 343P, 344P, 344SR3a, 344SR3b, 344SR3c, 345F1, 345F2, 346CR(mi)2, 346CR(mi)3, 346CR(mi)4, 346CR(tc)1, 347CR(ss)4 **Ch 15:** 347CR(ss)4, 353F2, 354SR2, 354SR4, 361SR3b, 361SR4, 366SR2, 366SR4, 368CR(tc)1, 368CR(tc)3, 369CR(ss)3 **U5Lab:** 371Q1–2, 372Q1–3, 373Q1, 373Q3 **Ch 16:** 380SR2, 380SR3a, 380SR3b, 380SR4, 381P, 382P, 383P, 384P, 385SR2, 385SR3a, 385SR3b, 385SR4, 386P, 387P , 388P, 388SR1, 388SR2a, 388SR2b, 389P, 390P, 391P, 392F2, 393P, 395P, 396P, 398P, 398SR2, 398SRQ3b, 398SRQ4, 399F1, 399F2, 400CR(mi)1, 400CR(mi)2, 400CR(mi)3, 400CR(mi)4, 400CR(mi)5, 400CR(mi)6, 400CR(rt)1, 400CR(rt)2, 400CR(rt)3, 400CR(tc)1, 400CR(tc)2 , 400CR(tc)3, 400CR(tc)4, 400CR(w) , 401CR(ss)2, 401CR(ss)3, 401CR(ss)4, 401CR(ic) **Ch 17:** 406SR2, 406SR4, 407P, 408P, 412P, 413SR2, 413SR4, 420P, 422P, 422SR4, 424CR(mi)1, 424CR(rt)1, 424CR(tc)1–4 **Ch 18:** 430P, 430C, 430SR3b, 430SR4, 432P, 433P, 434F1, 436C, 437C , 438C , 438SR3a, 438SR4, 439P, 440C, 441P, 443P, 445C, 446P, 446SR4,

TEKS Objective	Main Coverage	
	Presentation	**Demonstration**
(23A) *continued*		448CR(rt)2, 448CR(w), 448CR(tc)3, 449CR(ic) **U6Lab:** 451Q1, 451Q3, 452Q1, 453Q1–3 **CHB:** R4Q1–3, R7Q1–3, R8Q1–3, R9Q1–3, R11Q1–3, R12Q1–3, R14Q1–3, R15Q1–2, R17Q1–3, R18Q1, R18Q3, R19Q1–2, R21Q1–3, R24Q1–2, R24Q4–5, R25Q1–3
	Teacher's Edition	**Pro:** TC, TE, TG, TH **Ch 1:** 9 **Ch 3:** 49D **Ch 4:** 71C; 71D; 71E; 71F, 71G, 71H **Ch 5:** 95G **Ch 6:** 115C, 115F, 115G, 115H **Ch 7:** 143J **Ch 8:** 167C; 167D, 167E, 167F, 167G, 167H **Ch 9:** 193C, 193H, 193J **Ch 10:** 227E **Ch 11:** 249C, 249F **Ch 12:** 277C, 277D, 277E; 277F, 277G **Ch 13:** 299D, 299E, 325C, 325F **Ch 14:** 330 **Ch 16:** 375C, 375D, 375E, 375F, 375G, 375H, 375I, 375J **Ch 18:** 425D, 425E, 425F, 425H
(B) Create economic models such as production-possibilities curves, circular-flow charts, and supply-and-demand graphs to analyze economic data.	**Student Edition** **SHB:** S19–20, S24–26	**Ch 1:** 21CRp **Ch 2:** 35SR2, 43CR(ic) **Ch 3:** 70CR(tc)2, 71CR(ss)2, 71CRp, 71CR(ic), **Ch 5:** 115CR(ss)1 **Ch 6:** 137CR(ic) **U2Lab:** 141Q4 **Ch 7:** 167CRp, 167CR(ic) **Ch 8:** 183SR2 **Ch 9:** 221CRp **U4Lab:** 272NA **Ch 12:** 283SR2, 290SR2, 296SR2, 299CRp **Ch 16:** 380SR2, 398SR2, 401CRp **Ch 17:** 422SR3b **U6Lab:** 452Q2
	Teacher's Edition	**Ch 3:** 49D, 49H **Ch 4:** 71C; 71F; 71H, 74 **Ch 5:** 95E, 106 **Ch 8:** 167E **Ch 12:** 277D; 277F **Ch 16:** 375I **Ch 18:** 425D, 444
(C) Create a product on a contemporary economic issue or topic using critical methods of inquiry.	**Student Edition** **SHB:** S21–22	**Ch 1:** 21CRp, 21CR(ic) **Ch 3:** 71CRp **U2Lab:** 141Q4 **Ch 7:** 167CRp, 167CR(ic) **Ch 8:** 193CRp, 193CR(ic) **Ch 9:** 221CRp, 221CR(ic) **Ch 10:** 249CRp, 249CR(ic) **Ch 11:** 271CRp **Ch 12:** 299CRp, 299CR(ic) **Ch 13:** 304, 325CRp **Ch 14:** 347CR(ic), 347CRp **Ch 15:** 369CR(ic), 369CRp **Ch 16:** 385SR2, 401CRp, 401CR(ic) **Ch 17:** 425CRp
	Teacher's Edition	**Pro:** TH **Ch 1:** 9, 13 **Ch 2:** 33 **Ch 4:** 71E, 71F, 74 **Ch 5:** 106, 109 **Ch 6:** 115C **Ch 7:** 154, 160 **Ch 8:** 167D; 167E; 167F **Ch 11:** 252, 261 **Ch 12:** 277C; 277D; 277E **Ch 13:** 312 **Ch 15:** 347H, 363 **Ch 16:** 375E, 375F, 375H, 375J
(D) Explain a point of view on an economic issue.	**Student Edition** **SHB:** S1, S3, S18–19, S21–22	**Pro:** T13F2 **Ch 4:** 85SR4; 88F1, 88F2; 92SR4; 94CR(tc)2; 94CR(tc)3 **Ch 5:** 99F2, 115CR(ic), 115CRp **Ch 6:** 134SR4, 135F1, 135F2, 136CR(tc)2, 136CR(tc)4, 137CR(ss)4, 137CR(ic) **Ch 8:** 181F1, 192CR(mi)3, 192CR(rt)2, 192CR(rt)6, 193CRp **Ch 9:** 211F2 **Ch 10:** 235SR4, 246SR4, 249CR(ss)4, 249CRp **Ch 11:** 270CR(w) **Ch 12:** 297F1; 298CR(rt)2; 298CR(tc)3; 298CR(w), 299CRp **Ch 13:** 325CR(ss)2, 325CR(ss)3 **Ch 14:** 344SR4, 346CR(rt)2, 346CR(rt)3, 346CR(rt)4, 346CR(tc)1, 346CR(tc)2, 347CRp **Ch 15:** 369CR(ic) **Ch 16:** 400CR(rt)4, 400CR(tc)4, 400CR(w) **Ch 18:** 449CR(ss)4
	Teacher's Edition	**Pro:** TD **Ch 2:** 33 **Ch 4:** 71C, 71G, 95H **Ch 5:** 109 **Ch 6:** 115F, 115G, 115H **Ch 8:** 167C; 167F; 167G; 167H **Ch 10:** 227F, 227G, 227H **Ch 12:** 277D; 277E; 277F; 277H **Ch 14:** 325C, 342 **Ch 16:** 375D, 375E, 375G, 375I **Ch 18:** 425G, 425H
(E) Analyze and evaluate the validity of information from primary and secondary sources for bias, propaganda, point of view, and frame of reference.	**Student Edition** **SHB:** S1, S3, S18, S20–21	**Pro:** T15CR(ss)3 **Ch 1:** 21CR(ss)3, 21CR(ss)4 **Ch 2:** 43CR(ss)1, 43CR(ss)3, 43CR(ss)4 **Ch 3:** 71CR(ss)3 **Ch 4:** 95CR(ss)Q3 **Ch 5:** 115CR(ss)3, 115CR(ss)4 **Ch 6:** 127P, 131P, 137CR(ss)1, 137CR(ss)2, 137CR(ss)3 **Ch 7:** 167CR(ss)3, 167CR(ss)4 **Ch 8:** 173C, 183SR4, 193CR(ss)3, 193CR(ss)4 **Ch 9:** 221CR(ss)1, 221CR(ss)2, 221CR(ss)3, 221CR(ss)4, 221CR(ic) **Ch 10:** 244P, 249CR(ss)3, 249CR(ss)4 **Ch 11:** 249CR(ss)3, 249CR(ss)4, 271CR(ss)3, 271CR(ss)4 **Ch 12:** 290SR4, 293P; 296SR4; 299CR(ss)3; 299CR(ss)4 **Ch 13:** 311P , 324CR(ss)3 **Ch 14:** 347CR(ss)3 **Ch 15:** 347CR(ss)3, 369CR(ss)1, 369CR(ss)3,

TEKS 10

TEKS Objective	Main Coverage	
	Presentation	**Demonstration**
(24A) *continued*		369CR(ss)4 **Ch 16:** 399F1–2, 401CR(ss)2, 401CR(ss)3, 401CR(ss)4 **Ch 17:** 425CR(ss)3, 425CR(ss)4 **Ch 18:** 432P, 449CR(ss)1, 449CR(ss)2, 449CR(ss)3, 449C(ss)4
	Teacher's Edition	**Ch 4:** 71F **Ch 8:** 167F **Ch 12:** 277D **Ch 16:** 375C, 375D
(F) Evaluate economic-activity patterns using charts, tables, graphs, and maps.	**Student Edition** SHB: S24–28	**Pro:** T11C, T15CR(ss)1, T15CR(ss)2 **Ch 1:** 21CR(ic), 21CR(ss)2 **Ch 3:** 54C, 55C, 57C, 64C, 65C, 67C, 70CR(tc)2, 71CR(ss)1, 71CR(ss)2 **Ch 4:** 73C, 74C; 78SR2; 78SR4; 85P; 85SR2, 87C; 90C, 92SR4; 94CR(mi)2, 95CR(ss)1; 95CR(ss)2 **Ch 5:** 103C, 105C, 106C, 109C, 110C, 115CR(ss)1, 115CR(ss)2 **Ch 6:** 119C, 122C, 122P, 124P, 137CR(ic) **Ch 7:** 145C, 151C, 153C, 156M, 167CR(ss)1 **Ch 8:** 169C; 170C; 173C, 176C; 179M, 180C, 182C; 193CR(ss)1; 193CR(ss)2 **Ch 9:** 196C, 209C, 221CRp **U3Lab:** 225Q1 **Ch 10:** 234C, 245C, 249CR(ss)1, 249CR(ss)2 **Ch 11:** 253C, 256C, 261C, 262C, 263C, 265C, 266C **U4Lab:** 273Q1–3, 274Q1–3, 275Q2 **Ch 12:** 279C; 281C; 283SR4, 289C; 299CR(ss)1; 299CR(ss)2 **Ch 13:** 316C, 325CR(ss)1, 325CR(ss)2 **Ch 14:** 341C, 347CR(ss)1, 347CR(ss)2 **Ch 15:** 351C, 363C **Ch 16:** 377C, 397C, 401CR(ss)1, 401CR(ss)2, 401CRp, 401CR(ic) **Ch 17:** 406C, 416C, 421C, 424CR(tc)3, 425CR(ss)1, 425CR(ss)2 **Ch 18:** 435M, 438C **U6Lab:** 451Q2–3
	Teacher's Edition	**Pro:** TD **Ch 4:** 71C, 71E, 71H, **Ch 5:** 95F, 106, 109 **Ch 7:** 143H, 160 **Ch 8:** 167C **Ch 11:** 249C, 249H, 261 **Ch 12:** 277C **Ch 13:** 299C **Ch 14:** 325H **Ch 15:** 363 **Ch 16:** 375D **Ch 17:** 401C, 401D **Ch 18:** 425D, 425F
(G) Use appropriate mathematical skills to interpret social studies information.	**Student Edition** SHB: S15, S24–26	**Pro:** T11C **Ch 1:** 21CR(ss)2 **Ch 2:** 43CR(ic) **Ch 3:** 70CR(tc)2, 71CR(ss)1, 71CR(ss)2, 71CR(ic) **Ch 4:** 73C, 74C, 87C, 90C, 95CR(ss)1; 95CR(ss)2 **Ch 5:** 103C, 105C, 115CR(ss)1 **Ch 6:** 137CR(ic) **Ch 7:** 145C, 151C, 153C, 156M, 167CR(ss)1 **Ch 8:** 169C; 170C; 173C; 176C; 180C; 193CR(ss)1; 193CR(ss)2 **Ch 9:** 205C, 208C, 221CR(ss)2, 221CRp **Ch 10:** 245C **Ch 11:** 266C, 270CR(mi)4, 271CRp, 271CR(ic) **U4Lab:** 273Q1, 274Q1–3 **Ch 12:** 279C; 281C; 289C; 299CR(ss)1; 299CR(ss)2, 299CRp **Ch 14:** 347CRp **Ch 15:** 369CRp **Ch 16:** 377C, 397C, 401CR(ss)1, 401CR(ss)2, **Ch 18:** 449CRp **U6Lab:** 452Q3
	Teacher's Edition	**Pro:** TD **Ch 4:** 71C, 71E; 71H **Ch 5:** 106, 109 **Ch 7:** 143H **Ch 8:** 167C **Ch 9:** 193E, 193H, 193I **Ch 10:** 227D **Ch 11:** 249F, 249H **Ch 12:** 277C **Ch 13:** 304 **Ch 15:** 363 **Ch 16:** 375C, 375D

(24) Social studies skills. The student communicates in written, oral, and visual forms.

(A) Use social studies terminology correctly.	**Student Edition** SHB: S19–20	**Pro:** T4SR1, T8SR1, T12SR1, T14CR(id) **Ch 1:** 7SR1, 10SR1, 14SR1, 18SR1, 20CR(id), 21CRp, 21CR(ic) **Ch 2:** 28SR1, 35SR1, 35C, 40SR1, 42CR(id), 43CRp **Ch 3:** 55SR1, 62SR1, 68SR1, 70CR(id), 71CRp **Ch 4:** 72NA, 77C; 78SR1; 80C; 85SR1; 85SR3a, 85SR3b, 85SR4, 92P, 92SR1; 92SR2; 94CR(mi)1; 94CR(mi)5; 94CR(tc)3 **Ch 5:** 102SR1, 107SR1, 112SR1, 114CR(id), 115CRp, 115CR(ic) **Ch 6:** 122SR1, 129SR1, 134SR1, 136CR1, 136CR(w) **Ch 7:** 149SR1, 152SR1, 158SR1, 164SR1, 166CR(id), 167CRp, 167CR(ic) **Ch 8:** 175P; 176SR1; 183SR1; 186P; 189P, 190SR1, 192CR(id), 193CR(ic) **Ch 9:** 199SR1, 203SR1, 213SR1, 218SR1 220CR(id), 221CRp **Ch 10:** 235SR1, 240SR1, 246SR1, 248CR(id), 249CRp, 249CR(ic) **Ch 11:** 256SR1, 263SR1, 268SR1, 270CR(id), 270CR(w) **Ch 12:** 283SR1; 290SR1; 296SR1; 298CR(id) **Ch 13:** 307SR1, 314SR1, 322SR1, 324CR(id), 324CR(w) **Ch 14:** 331SR1, 336SR1, 344SR1, 344SR4, 346CR(id), 346CR(w), 347CRp **Ch 15:** 354SR1, 361SR1, 366SR1, 366SR4, 368CR(id), 369CR(ic) **Ch 16:** 380SR1, 385SR1, 398SR1, 400CR(id) **Ch 17:** 402NA, 406SR1, 413SR1, 422SR1, 424CR(id) **Ch 18:** 430SR1, 438SR1, 446SR1, 448CR(id), 448CR(w), 449CRp, 449CR(ic) **CHB:** R252

TEKS 11

TEKS Objective	Main Coverage	
	Presentation	**Demonstration**
(24A) *continued*	**Teacher's Edition**	**Pro:** TC, TE, TG **Ch 1:** 7, 10, 13, 14, 18, 19 **Ch 2:** 33 **Ch 3:** 55, 62, 68, 69 **Ch 5:** 102, 106, 107, 109,112, 113 **Ch 6:** 122, 129, 134 **Ch 7:** 149, 152, 158, 164S, 165 **Ch 8:** 167C; 167E; 167G; 167H **Ch 9:** 193C, 199, 203, 207, 213, 218, 220 **Ch 10:** 227C, 227D, 227E, 227G **Ch 11:** 256, 263, 268, 269 **Ch 12:** 277C; 277E; 277G **Ch 13:** 307, 314S, 322, 323 **Ch 14:** 325C, 325E, 325G, 330, 342, 344 **Ch 15:** 354, 361, 363, 366, 367 **Ch 16:** 375C, 375E, 375G, 375I **Ch 17:** 401C, 406, 413, 422, 423 **Ch 18:** 430, 438, 446
(B) Use standard grammar, spelling, sentence structure, and punctuation.	**Student Edition** **SHB:** S15, S22–23	**Pro:** T14CRp(sum) **Ch 1:** 21CRp, 20CR(sum) **Ch 2:** 42CR(sum), 43CRp **Ch 3:** 70CR(sum), 71CRp **Ch 4:** 94CR(sum) **Ch 5:** 96NA, 114CR(sum), 115CRp, 115CR(ic) **Ch 6:** 136CR(sum) **Ch 7:** 166CR(sum), 167CRp, 167CR(ic) **Ch 8:** 192CR(sum), 193CR(ic) **Ch 9:** 220CR(sum), 221CRp **Ch 10:** 248CR(sum), 249CRp, 249CR(ic) **Ch 11:** 270CR(sum) **Ch 12:** 298CR(sum), 299CRp **Ch 13:** 300NA, 324CR(sum) **Ch 14:** 344SR4, 346CR(sum), 347CRp **Ch 15:** 348NA, 368CR(sum), 369CR(ic) **Ch 16:** 400CR(sum) **Ch 17:** 402NA, 424CR(sum), 425CR(ic), 425CRp **Ch 18:** 448CR(sum), 449CRp, 449CR(ic)
	Teacher's Edition	**Ch 1:** 13 **Ch 4:** 71F **Ch 5:** 106, 109 **Ch 8:** 167F; 167H **Ch 10:** 227D **Ch 14:** 330, 342 **Ch 15:** 363 **Ch 18:** 425D
(C) Transfer information from one medium to another, including written to visual and statistical to written or visual using computer software as appropriate.	**Student Edition** **SHB:** S23, S24–26	**Ch 3:** 71CR(ss)2 **Ch 5:** 115CR(ss)1, 115CRp **Ch 7:** 167CRp, 167CR(ic) **Ch 8:** 176SR2; 183SR2, 193CR(ic), 193CRp **Ch 9:** 221CRp **Ch 10:** 234SR2, 240SR2, 246SR2 **Ch 11:** 271CR(ic) **Ch 12:** 299CRp **Ch 13:** 325CR(ic) **Ch 14:** 331SR2, 336SR2, 344SR2, 347CR(ic) **Ch 16:** 401CR(ic), 401CRp **Ch 17:** 425CRp **Ch 18:** 446SR2, 449CRp
	Teacher's Edition	**Pro:** TC, TE, TG, TH **Ch 1:** 1J **Ch 4:** 71C; 71F; 71H **Ch 5:** 106, 109 **Ch 8:** 167D , 167E, 189 **Ch 9:** 193D **Ch 10:** 230 **Ch 12:** 277C; 277D; 277E; 277F; 277G; 277H **Ch 13:** 304 **Ch 15:** 350, 363 **Ch 16:** 375C, 375D, 375E, 375F, 375G, 375H, 375I, 375J **Ch 17:** 408 **Ch 18:** 425H, 444
(D) Create written, oral, and visual presentations of social studies information.	**Student Edition** **SHB:** S1–3, S19–21	**Pro:** T4SR2, T8SR2, T12SR2, T14CR(w) **Ch 1:** 7SR2, 10SR2, 14SR2, 18SR2, 21CR(ic) **Ch 2:** 28SR2, 40SR2, 42CR(w), 43CRp **Ch 3:** 55SR2, 62SR1, 68SR2, 70CR(w), 71CRp, 71CR(ic) **Ch 4:** 92SR2, 94CR(w), 95CRp, 95CR(ic) **Ch 5:** 96NA, 102SR2, 107SR2, 112SR2, 114CR(w), 115CR(ss)1, 115CR(ic), 115CRp **Ch 6:** 122SR2, 129SR2, 134SR2, 136CR(w), 137CRp **U2Lab:** 141Q4 **Ch 7:** 149SR2, 152SR2, 158SR2, 164SR2, 166CR(w), 167CR(ic), 167CRp **Ch 8:** 190SR2, 192CR(w), 193CR(ic), 193CRp **Ch 9:** 194N, 199SR2, 203SR4, 213SR2, 218SR2, 220CR(w), 221CR(ic), 221CRp **Ch 10:** 240SR2, 246SR2, 248CR(w), 248CR(w), 249CRp, 249CR(ic) **Ch 11:** 256SR2, 263SR2, 268SR2, 270CR(w) **Ch 12:** 298CR(w), 299CR(ic), 299CRp **Ch 13:** 300NA, 307SR2, 314SR2, 322SR2, 324CR(w), 325CRp, 325CR(ic) **Ch 14:** 326NA, 331SR2, 336SR2, 344SR2, 344SR4, 346CR(w), 347CR(ic) **Ch 15:** 348NA, 354SR2, 361SR2, 366SR2, 368CR(w), 369CRp, 369CR(ic) **Ch 16:** 380SR2, 385SR4, 400CR(w), 401CRp, 401CR(ic) **Ch 17:** 406SR2, 413SR2, 422SR2, 424CR(w), 425CRp, 425CR(ic) **Ch 18:** 430SR2, 438SR2, 446SR2, 448CR(w), 448CR(w), 449CRp, 449CR(ic)
	Teacher's Edition	**Pro:** TC, TE, TF, TG, T6, T10 **Ch 1:** 1D, 1F, 1H, 1J, 9, 13 **Ch 2:** 27, 33 **Ch 3:** 49D, 49F, 49G, 49H **Ch 4:** 71D; 71F; 71H **Ch 5:** 95D, 95H, 106, 109 **Ch 6:** 115H **Ch 7:** 143F, 143H **Ch 8:** 167D; 167E; 167F; 167G; 167H, 189 **Ch 9:** 193D, 193E, 193F, 193H, 193J **Ch 10:** 227C, 227D, 227E, 227G, 227H, 239 **Ch 11:** 249D, 249F, 249H **Ch 12:** 277C, 277D; 277E; 277F; 277G; 277H, 282, 288 **Ch 13:** 299D, 299E, 299F, 299G, 299H, 304, 312 **Ch 14:** 325C, 325D, 325E, 325F, 325G, 325H, 330, 342

TEKS 12

TEKS Objective	Main Coverage	
	Presentation	**Demonstration**
(24A) continued		**Ch 15:** 347D, 347F, 347G, 350, 363 **Ch 16:** 375C, 375D, 375E, 375F, 375G, 375H, 375I, 375J, 383, 394 **Ch 17:** 401D, 401E, 401F, 401G, 401H, 408, 420 **Ch 18:** 425D, 425F, 425G, 425H

(25) Social studies skills. The student uses problem-solving and decision-making skills, working independently and with others, in a variety of settings.

(A)	Use a problem-solving process to identify a problem, gather information, list and consider options, consider advantages and disadvantages, choose and implement a solution, and evaluate the effectiveness of the solution.	**Student Edition** **SHB:** S2, S3, S16–18, S20–21, S24–28	**U1Lab:** 44NA **Ch 8:** 190SR3b **U3Lab:** 222NA **Ch 10:** 248CR(tc)1, 248CR(tc)2, 248CR(tc)3 **Ch 11:** 271CRp **Ch 14:** 340F2 **Ch 16:** 388SR3, 398SR3a, 400CR(tc)1 **Ch 18:** 434F1, 434F2 **U6Lab:** 450NA
		Teacher's Edition	**Ch 4:** 71E **Ch 6:** 115E, 115G **Ch 8:** 167E; 167H **Ch 12:** 277D; 277F; 277H **Ch 16:** 375F, 375G, 375I
(B)	Use a decision-making process to identify a situation that requires a decision, gather information, identify options, predict consequences, and take action to implement a decision.	**Student Edition** **SHB:** S3, S16–18, S20–21, S24–28	**Ch 4:** 92SR4 **U2Lab:** 138NA **Ch 8:** 190SR4 **Ch 10:** 237F2 **U4Lab:** 272NA **U5Lab:** 370NA
		Teacher's Edition	**Ch 1:** 9 **Ch 4:** 71H **Ch 8:** 167H **Ch 12:** 277E **Ch 16:** 375H

(26) Science, technology, and society. The student understands the effect of science and technology on the economy.

(A)	Analyze the effect of technology on productivity.	**Student Edition** **Pro:** T2–3, T6–7 **Ch 4:** 83 **Ch 10:** 244 **Ch 16:** 393	**Pro:** T3M, T14CR(rt)2 **Ch 1:** 20CR(tc)3 **Ch 4:** 92SR3b, 94CR(mi)4 **Ch 9:** 219F2 **Ch 10:** 246SR2 **Ch 17:** 417P, 424CR(rt)3
		Teacher's Edition **Ch 4:** 80, 89	**Ch 1:** 9 **Ch 4:** 71F
(B)	Analyze the economic effects of the development of communication and transportation systems in the United States.	**Student Edition** **Ch 10:** 247	**Ch 6:** 128P **Ch 9:** 219F2 **Ch 10:** 247F1, 247F2
		Teacher's Edition **Ch 4:** 80	**Ch 6:** 128
(C)	Analyze the economic impact of obsolescence created by technological innovations.	**Student Edition** **Ch 11:** 253, 255	**Ch 11:** 255C
		Teacher's Edition **Ch 11:** 253, 255	**Ch 11:** 249D
(D)	Analyze how technological innovations change the way goods are manufactured, marketed, and distributed.	**Student Edition** **Ch 1:** 7 **Ch 4:** 83 **Ch 8:** 172 **Ch 18:** 442	**Ch 1:** 7SR4 **Ch 4:** 82P, 94CR(mi)4 **Ch 8:** 172P; 176SR2, 176SR4, 191F1 **Ch 18:** 448CR(mi)5

TEKS 13

TEKS Objective	Main Coverage	
	Presentation	**Demonstration**
(24A) *continued*	**Teacher's Edition** Ch 1: 7	Ch 1: 9
(27) Science, technology, and society. The student understands the economic effects of scientific discoveries and technological innovations on households, businesses, and government.		
(A) Give examples of types of economic information available as a result of technological innovations.	**Student Edition** Ch 9: 219	Ch 2: 43CR(ic) Ch 9: 219F1
	Teacher's Edition Ch 4: 80	Ch 9: 193G
(B) Explain how scientific discoveries and technological innovations create the need for rules and regulations to protect individuals and businesses.	**Student Edition** Ch 8: 191 Ch 12: 297	Ch 8: 176SR4, 183SR2 Ch 12: 298CR(tc)3
	Teacher's Edition Ch 8: 167G, 167H	Ch 8: 167G, 167H Ch 12: 277H

TEKS and TAKS Coverage by Section
FOR ECONOMICS

Chapter and Section	TEKS Covered	TAKS Prep
Skills Handbook		
Critical Thinking and the Study of Economics	23A, 23D, 23E, 24D, 25A, 25B	Exit Level Social Studies: 5
Reading Strategies	23A, 23E, 23F, 25B	Exit Level Social Studies: 5
Standardized Test-Taking Strategies	23G, 24A, 24B, 24D	Exit Level Social Studies: 5
Interactive Skill-Builder	23A, 23D, 23E, 23G, 24A, 24B, 24D	Exit Level Social Studies: 5
Prologue: The Texas Economy		
Section 1: The Texas Economy in the 1800s	12B, 23A, 23D, 23F, 23G, 24A, 24C, 24D, 26A	Exit Level Social Studies: 1, 2, 3, 5 TAKS Review Every Day! and TAKS Prep Online: Soc. Studies
Section 2: Boom and Bust in the Early 1900s	7A, 15A, 15B, 23A, 24A, 24C, 24D	Exit Level Social Studies: 1, 2, 3, 4, 5 TAKS Review Every Day! and TAKS Review Online: Soc. Studies
Section 3: Texas and the World	14A, 14B, 23A, 23C, 24A, 24C, 24D	Exit Level Social Studies: 1, 2, 3, 4, 5 TAKS Review Every Day! and TAKS Review Online: Soc. Studies
Chapter Review	14B, 23A, 23E, 23F, 24A, 24B, 24D, 26A	Exit Level Social Studies: 1, 2, 3, 4, 5
Chapter 1: What Is Economics?		
Section 1: An Economic Way of Thinking	1B, 23A, 24A, 24D, 26D	Exit Level Social Studies: 2, 3, 5 TAKS Review Every Day! and TAKS Review Online: Soc. Studies

Chapter and Section	TEKS Covered	TAKS Prep
Section 2: Scarcity and Choice	5A, 5B, 23A, 23B, 23C, 24A, 24D, 25B, 26D	Exit Level Social Studies: 3, 5 TAKS Review Every Day! and TAKS Review Online: Soc. Studies
Section 3: Opportunity Costs	1B, 5A, 5B, 23A, 23C, 24A, 24B, 24D	Exit Level Social Studies: 3, 5 TAKS Review Every Day! and TAKS Review Online: Soc. Studies
Section 4: Exchange	2B, 11A, 23A, 24A, 24C, 24D	Exit Level Social Studies: 2, 3, 5 TAKS Review Every Day! and TAKS Review Online: Soc. Studies
Chapter 1 Review	5A, 5B, 21A, 23A, 23B, 23C, 23E, 23F, 23G, 24A, 24B, 24D, 26A	Exit Level Social Studies: 2, 3, 5
Chapter 2: Economic Systems		
Section 1: Types of Economic Systems	5A, 10A, 10B, 19A, 21B, 23A, 24A, 24D	Exit Level Social Studies: 3, 5 TAKS Review Every Day! and TAKS Review Online: Soc. Studies
Section 2: Features of the U.S. Economy	1B, 3A, 3B, 4A, 4B, 6A, 6B, 10B, 15A, 23B, 23C, 23D, 24A, 24	Exit Level Social Studies: 3, 4, 5 TAKS Review Every Day! and TAKS Review Online: Soc. Studies
Section 3: The U.S. Economy at Work	5A, 16A, 16B, 21A, 23A, 24A, 24D	Exit Level Social Studies: 3, 4, 5 TAKS Review Every Day! and TAKS Review Online: Soc. Studies
Chapter 2 Review	1A, 3A, 3B, 4A, 4B, 5A, 6A, 10A, 10B, 15A, 15B, 16A, 16B, 21A, 21B, 23B, 23E, 23F, 23G, 24A, 24B, 24D, 27A	Exit Level Social Studies: 3, 4, 5
Unit 1 Economics Lab	23A, 23C, 23D, 24A, 24B, 24C, 24D, 23E, 25A	Exit Level Social Studies: 5

TEKS 15

Chapter and Section	TEKS Covered	TAKS Prep
Chapter 3: Demand		
Section 1: Nature of Demand	7A, 7B, 11A, 23A, 23B, 23F, 24A, 24D	Exit Level Social Studies: 3, 5 *TAKS Review Every Day!* and *TAKS Review Online:* Soc. Studies
Section 2: Changes in Demand	2B, 7A, 11A, 23A, 23F, 24A, 24D	Exit Level Social Studies: 3, 5 *TAKS Review Every Day!* and *TAKS Review Online:* Soc. Studies
Section 3: Elasticity of Demand	7A, 7B, 23A, 23B, 23F, 24A, 24D	Exit Level Social Studies: 3, 5 *TAKS Review Every Day!* and *TAKS Review Online:* ELA
Chapter 3 Review	7A, 23A, 23B, 23E, 23F, 23G, 24A, 24B, 24C, 24D	Exit Level Social Studies: 3, 5
Chapter 4: Supply		
Section 1: Nature of Supply	4A, 7A, 7B, 17B, 23A, 23B, 23C, 23D, 23F, 23G, 24A, 24C, 24D	Exit Level Social Studies: 3, 5 *TAKS Review Every Day!* and *TAKS Review Online:* Soc. Studies
Section 2: Changes in Supply	4A, 7A, 14A, 15A, 17A, 23A, 23B, 23C, 23D, 23E, 23F, 23G, 24A, 24C, 24D, 25A, 26A, 26B, 26D	Exit Level Social Studies: 3, 5 *TAKS Review Every Day!* and *TAKS Review Online:* Soc. Studies
Section 3: Making Production Decisions	2B, 23A, 23B, 23D, 23F, 23G, 24A, 24C, 24D, 25B	Exit Level Social Studies: 3, 5 *TAKS Review Every Day!* and *TAKS Review Online:* Soc. Studies
Chapter 4 Review	2B, 4A, 7A, 17A, 23A, 23D, 23E, 23F, 23G, 24A, 24B, 26A, 26D	Exit Level Social Studies: 3, 5
Chapter 5: Prices		
Section 1: The Price System	4B, 7A, 23A, 23D, 24A, 24D	Exit Level Social Studies: 3, 5 *TAKS Review Every Day!* and *TAKS Review Online:* Soc. Studies

Chapter and Section	TEKS Covered	TAKS Prep
Section 2: Determining Price	2A, 4A, 7A, 7B, 23A, 23B, 23C, 23F, 23G, 24A, 24B, 24C, 24D	Exit Level Social Studies: 3, 5 *TAKS Review Every Day!* and *TAKS Review Online:* Soc. Studies
Section 3: Managing Prices	7A, 15A, 15B, 23A, 23C, 23D, 23F, 23G, 24A, 24B, 24C, 24D	Exit Level Social Studies: 3, 4, 5 *TAKS Review Every Day!* and *TAKS Review Online:* Soc. Studies
Chapter 5 Review	4B, 7A, 7B, 15A, 15B, 23A, 23B, 23D, 23E, 23F, 23G, 24A, 24B, 24D	Exit Level Social Studies: 3, 4, 5
Chapter 6: Market Structures		
Section 1: Highly Competitive Markets	2B, 7A, 9C, 23A, 23C, 23F, 24A, 24	Exit Level Social Studies: 3, 5 *TAKS Review Every Day!* and *TAKS Review Online:* ELA
Section 2: Imperfectly Competitive Markets	7A, 9C, 15A, 23A, 23D, 23E, 24A, 24D, 25A, 26B	Exit Level Social Studies: 3, 4, 5 *TAKS Review Every Day!* and *TAKS Review Online:* Soc. Studies
Section 3: Market Regulation	9C, 15A, 15B, 23A, 23D, 23E, 24A, 24D, 25A	Exit Level Social Studies: 1, 3, 4, 5 *TAKS Review Every Day!* and *TAKS Review Online:* Math
Chapter 6 Review	9C, 15A, 19D, 23A, 23B, 23D, 23E, 23F, 23G, 24A, 24B, 24C, 24D	Exit Level Social Studies: 1, 3, 4, 5
Unit 2 Economics Lab	23A, 23C, 23D, 24A, 24B, 24C, 24D, 23E, 25B	Exit Level Social Studies: 5
Chapter 7: Business Organizations		
Section 1: Sole Proprietorships	2A, 2D, 3A, 3B, 9A, 9B, 15A, 15B, 19D, 23A, 23F, 23G, 24A, 24D	Exit Level Social Studies: 3, 4, 5 *TAKS Review Every Day!* and *TAKS Review Online:* Soc. Studies
Section 2: Partnerships	9A, 9B, 23A, 23F, 23G, 24A, 24D	Exit Level Social Studies: 3, 5 *TAKS Review Every Day!* and *TAKS Review Online:* Soc. Studies

TEKS 16

Chapter and Section	TEKS Covered	TAKS Prep	Chapter and Section	TEKS Covered	TAKS Prep
Section 3: Corporations	2D, 9A, 9B, 11B, 11C, 12B, 23A, 23C, 23F, 23G, 24A, 24D	Exit Level Social Studies: 3, 5 *TAKS Review Every Day!* and *TAKS Review Online: Soc. Studies*	**Section 4:** Borrowing and Credit	1A, 4B, 11A, 23A, 23G, 24A, 24D	Exit Level Social Studies: 3, 4, 5 *TAKS Review Every Day!* and *TAKS Review Online: Soc. Studies*
Section 4: Other Forms of Organization	1B, 9A, 19D, 23A, 23C, 23F, 24A, 24D, 26A	Exit Level Social Studies: 2, 3, 5 *TAKS Review Every Day!* and *TAKS Review Online: Soc. Studies*	**Chapter 9 Review**	1A, 1B, 11A, 11B, 11C, 15B, 23A, 23B, 23C, 23E, 23F, 23G, 24A, 24B, 24C, 24D	Exit Level Social Studies: 1, 3, 4, 5
Chapter 7 Review	2C, 2D, 3B, 9A, 9B, 11C, 15A, 15B, 19D, 23A, 23B, 23C, 23E, 23F, 23G, 24A, 24B, 24D	Exit Level Social Studies: 2, 3, 4, 5	**Unit 3 Economics Lab**	23A, 23C, 23D, 24A, 24B, 24C, 24D, 23E, 25A	Exit Level Social Studies: 5

Chapter 8: Labor and Unions

Chapter 10: Economic Performance

Chapter and Section	TEKS Covered	TAKS Prep	Chapter and Section	TEKS Covered	TAKS Prep
Section 1: The U.S. Labor Force	15B, 19B, 22A, 23A, 23C, 23D, 23E, 23F, 23G, 24A, 24B, 24C, 24D, 26D, 27B	Exit Level Social Studies: 3, 4, 5 *TAKS Review Every Day!* and *TAKS Review Online: Soc. Studies*	**Section 1:** Gross Domestic Product	16B, 17C, 23A, 23D, 23F, 23G, 24A, 24C, 24D	Exit Level Social Studies: 3, 5 *TAKS Review Every Day!* and *TAKS Review Online: Writing*
Section 2: The Growth of Labor Unions	2B, 15A, 19B, 23A, 23B, 23C, 23D, 23E, 23F, 23G, 24A, 24B, 24C, 24D, 25A, 27B	Exit Level Social Studies: 3, 4, 5 *TAKS Review Every Day!* and *TAKS Review Online: Soc. Studies*	**Section 2:** Business Cycles	13C, 16B, 23A, 23D, 24A, 24C, 24D, 25B	Exit Level Social Studies: 3, 5 *TAKS Review Every Day!* and *TAKS Review Online: Soc. Studies*
Section 3: Unions and Management	2A, 2B, 15A, 23A, 23D, 24A, 24B, 24C, 24D, 25A, 25B	Exit Level Social Studies: 3, 4, 5 *TAKS Review Every Day!* and *TAKS Review Online: Soc. Studies*	**Section 3:** Economic Growth	16B, 23A, 23D, 23E, 23F, 23G, 24A, 24C, 24D, 26A	Exit Level Social Studies: 3, 5 *TAKS Review Every Day!* and *TAKS Review Online: Soc. Studies*
Chapter 8 Review	7A, 15B, 19B, 23A, 23D, 23E, 23F, 23G, 24A, 24B, 24D	Exit Level Social Studies: 3, 4, 5	**Chapter 10 Review**	2B, 15A, 16B, 17C, 23A, 23C, 23D, 23E, 23F, 24A, 24B, 24D, 25A	Exit Level Social Studies: 3, 5

Chapter 9: Sources of Capital

Chapter 11: Economic Challenges

Chapter and Section	TEKS Covered	TAKS Prep	Chapter and Section	TEKS Covered	TAKS Prep
Section 1: Saving	1B, 11B, 15A, 15B, 223A, 23F, 24A, 24C, 24D	Exit Level Social Studies: 3, 5 *TAKS Review Every Day!* and *TAKS Review Online: Math*	**Section 1:** Unemployment	15B, 16B, 19C, 23A, 23C, 23F, 24A, 24D	Exit Level Social Studies: 1, 3, 4, 5 *TAKS Review Every Day!* and *TAKS Review Online: Soc. Studies*
Section 2: Investing	4B, 11B, 23A, 23G, 24A, 24D	Exit Level Social Studies: 3, 5 *TAKS Review Every Day!* and *TAKS Review Online: Soc. Studies*	**Section 2:** Inflation	12A, 16B, 23A, 23C, 23F, 24A, 24D	Exit Level Social Studies: 3, 5 *TAKS Review Every Day!* and *TAKS Review Online: ELA*
Section 3: Stocks, Bonds, and Futures	1B, 7A, 11B, 11C, 15A, 19C, 23A, 23F, 23G, 24A, 24D, 27A	Exit Level Social Studies: 1, 3, 4, 5 *TAKS Review Every Day!* and *TAKS Review Online: ELA*	**Section 3:** Poverty and Income Distribution	15B, 16B, 23A, 23F, 23G, 24A, 24D	Exit Level Social Studies: 3, 5 *TAKS Review Every Day!* and *TAKS Review Online: Math*

Chapter and Section	TEKS Covered	TAKS Prep
Section 3: Poverty and Income Distribution	15B, 16B, 23A, 23F, 23G, 24A, 24D	Exit Level Social Studies: 3, 5 *TAKS Review Every Day!* and *TAKS Review Online:* Math
Chapter 11 Review	7A, 15A, 16A, 16B, 23A, 23C, 23D, 23E, 23G, 24A, 24B, 24D, 25A	Exit Level Social Studies: 1, 3, 4, 5
Unit 4 Economics Lab	23A, 23C, 23D, 24A, 24B, 24C, 24D, 23E, 25B	Exit Level Social Studies: 3, 5

Chapter 12: Role of Government

Chapter and Section	TEKS Covered	TAKS Prep
Section 1: Growth of Government	13C, 14A, 15A, 17B, 23A, 23C, 23D, 23E, 23F, 23G, 24A, 24C, 24D, 25A	Exit Level Social Studies: 3, 5 *TAKS Review Every Day!* and *TAKS Review Online:* Soc. Studies
Section 2: Economic Goals	2D, 15A, 15B, 16A, 23A, 23B, 23C, 23D, 23E, 23F, 23G, 24A, 24C, 24D, 25A, 25B	Exit Level Social Studies: 3, 4, 5 *TAKS Review Every Day!* and *TAKS Review Online:* Math
Section 3: Government and the Public	1A, 7A, 15A, 15B, 23A, 23B, 23D, 23E, 24A, 24C, 24D, 25A, 25B, 27B	Exit Level Social Studies: 3, 4, 5 *TAKS Review Every Day!* and *TAKS Review Online:* Soc. Studies
Chapter 12 Review	2B, 2D, 7A, 13C, 14A, 15A, 15B, 16A, 18B, 23A, 23D, 23E, 23F, 23G, 24B, 24D, 27B	Exit Level Social Studies: 3, 4, 5

Chapter 13: Money and the Banking System

Chapter and Section	TEKS Covered	TAKS Prep
Section 1: Money	11A, 15A, 23A, 23C, 23F, 23G, 24A, 24C, 24D	Exit Level Social Studies: 3, 5 *TAKS Review Every Day!* and *TAKS Review Online:* Soc. Studies
Section 2: History of U.S. Banking	8A, 8B, 15A, 23A, 23C, 23E, 24A, 24D	Exit Level Social Studies: 1, 3, 4, 5 *TAKS Review Every Day!* and *TAKS Review Online:* Soc. Studies
Section 3: U.S. Banking Today	8A, 8B, 15A, 23A, 23F, 24A, 24D	Exit Level Social Studies: 1, 3, 4, 5 *TAKS Review Every Day!* and *TAKS Review Online:* Soc. Studies

Chapter and Section	TEKS Covered	TAKS Prep
Chapter 13 Review	8A, 8B, 15A, 15B, 23A, 23D, 23E, 23F, 24A, 24B, 24D	Exit Level Social Studies: 1, 3, 4, 5

Chapter 14: The Federal Reserve and Monetary Policy

Chapter and Section	TEKS Covered	TAKS Prep
Section 1: The Federal Reserve System	18A, 18B, 23A, 23D, 24A, 24B, 24C, 24D	Exit Level Social Studies: 1, 3, 4, 5 *TAKS Review Every Day!* and *TAKS Review Online:* Soc. Studies
Section 2: The Federal Reserve at Work	15A, 18A, 18B, 23A, 24A, 24C, 24D	Exit Level Social Studies: 3, 4, 5 *TAKS Review Every Day!* and *TAKS Review Online:* Soc. Studies
Section 3: Monetary Policy Strategies	15A, 17C, 18B, 23A, 23D, 23F, 24A, 24B, 24C, 24D, 25A	Exit Level Social Studies: 3, 4, 5 *TAKS Review Every Day!* and *TAKS Review Online:* ELA
Chapter 14 Review	15A, 16A, 18A, 18B, 23A, 23C, 23D, 23E, 23F, 23G, 24A, 24B, 24C, 24D	Exit Level Social Studies: 1, 3, 4, 5

Chapter 15: Fiscal Policy

Chapter and Section	TEKS Covered	TAKS Prep
Section 1: Defining Fiscal Policy	15A, 15B, 17A, 17B, 17C, 23A, 23F, 23G, 24A, 24C, 24D	Exit Level Social Studies: 3, 4, 5 *TAKS Review Every Day!* and *TAKS Review Online:* Soc. Studies
Section 2: Fiscal Policy Strategies	16A, 17A, 17C, 19A, 23A, 23B, 24A, 24D	Exit Level Social Studies: 3, 4, 5 *TAKS Review Every Day!* and *TAKS Review Online:* Math
Section 3: Fiscal Policy and the Federal Budget	15A, 16A, 16B, 17B, 17C, 23A, 23C, 23F, 23G, 24A, 24B, 24C, 24D	Exit Level Social Studies: 3, 4, 5 *TAKS Review Every Day!* and *TAKS Review Online:* Soc. Studies
Chapter 15 Review	15A, 17A, 17C, 19A, 20B, 23A, 23C, 23D, 23E, 23G, 24A, 24B, 24D	Exit Level Social Studies: 3, 4, 5
Unit 5 Economics Lab	23A, 23C, 23D, 24A, 24B, 24C, 24D, 23E, 25B	Exit Level Social Studies: 5

Chapter and Section	TEKS Covered	TAKS Prep
Chapter 16: Comparing Economic Systems		
Section 1: Development Models	10A, 10B, 21B, 23A, 23B, 23D, 23E, 23F, 23G, 24A, 24C, 24D	**Exit Level Social Studies:** 2, 3, 5 *TAKS Review Every Day!* and *TAKS Review Online:* **ELA**
Section 2: Capitalism	10, 10B, 19A, 21B, 23A, 23C, 23D, 24C, 24D, 25A	**Exit Level Social Studies:** 1, 2, 3, 4, 5 *TAKS Review Every Day!* and *TAKS Review Online:* **Soc. Studies**
Section 3: Socialism	10A, 10B, 21B, 23A, 23C, 23D, 24D, 25A, 25B	**Exit Level Social Studies:** 2, 3, 5 *TAKS Review Every Day!* and *TAKS Review Online:* **Soc. Studies**
Section 4: Communism	10A, 10B, 11A, 19A, 22A, 23A, 23B, 23C, 23D, 23F, 23G, 24A, 24C, 24D, 25A	**Exit Level Social Studies:** 1, 2, 3, 4, 5 *TAKS Review Every Day!* and *TAKS Review Online:* **Math**
Chapter 16 Review	5A, 7A 10A, 10B, 14A, 19A, 21B, 23A, 23B, 23C, 23D, 23E, 23F, 23G, 24B, 24C, 24D, 25A	**Exit Level Social Studies:** 1, 2, 3, 4, 5
Chapter 17: Developing Countries		
Section 1: Economic Development	5B, 12A, 22A, 23A, 23F, 24A, 24D	**Exit Level Social Studies:** 2, 3, 5 *TAKS Review Every Day!* and *TAKS Review Online:* **Soc. Studies**
Section 2: Challenges to Growth	5B, 12A, 22A, 22B, 23A, 24A, 24C, 24D	**Exit Level Social Studies:** 2, 3, 5 *TAKS Review Every Day!* and *TAKS Review Online:* **Soc. Studies**
Section 3: Paths to Economic Development	5B, 10A, 19A, 22A, 23A, 23B, 23F, 24A, 24D, 26A	**Exit Level Social Studies:** 2, 3, 5 *TAKS Review Every Day!* and *TAKS Review Online:* **Soc. Studies**

Chapter and Section	TEKS Covered	TAKS Prep
Chapter 17 Review	5B, 10A, 12A, 22A, 22B, 23A, 23E, 23F, 24A, 24B, 24C, 24D, 26A	**Exit Level Social Studies:** 2, 3, 5
Chapter 18: International Trade		
Section 1: Specialization and Interdependence	12A, 13A, 13B, 23A, 23B, 23F, 24A, 24B, 24D	**Exit Level Social Studies:** 2, 3, 5 *TAKS Review Every Day!* and *TAKS Review Online:* **Soc. Studies**
Section 2: Foreign Exchange and Currencies	13C, 13D, 23A, 23E, 23F, 24A, 24D, 25A	**Exit Level Social Studies:** 3, 5 *TAKS Review Every Day!* and *TAKS Review Online:* **Soc. Studies**
Section 3: Cooperation and Trade Barriers	14A, 14B, 23A, 23B, 23D, 24A, 24C, 24D	**Exit Level Social Studies:** 1, 2, 3, 4, 5 *TAKS Review Every Day!* and *TAKS Review Online:* **ELA**
Chapter 18 Review	12B, 13A, 13B, 13C, 13D, 14A, 14B, 23A, 23D, 23E, 23G, 24A, 24B, 24C, 24D, 26D	**Exit Level Social Studies:** 1, 2, 3, 4, 5
Unit 6 Economics Lab	23A, 23C, 23D, 24A, 24B, 24C, 24D, 23E, 25A	**Exit Level Social Studies:** 5
Consumer Handbook		
	1A, 1B, 4B, 5A, 11A, 11B, 11C, 17A, 19B, 20A, 23A, 24A	**Exit Level Social Studies:** 1, 5

TEKS 19

HOLT Economics

CONTENTS

How to Use Your Textbook xx
Themes in Economics xxiii
Skills Handbook S1
Economic Atlas A1

TEXAS EDITION

PROLOGUE: THE TEXAS ECONOMY · T1

| PROLOGUE | RESOURCE MANAGER | TA |

Lesson P.1 ....TC
Lesson P.2 ....TE
Lesson P.3 ....TG

Prologue

THE TEXAS ECONOMY · T1

1 The Texas Economy in the 1800s T1
2 Boom and Bust in the Early 1900s T5
3 Texas and the World T9

Economics in the News:
Economics and the Arts T13

UNIT 1: INTRODUCTION TO ECONOMICS · 1

| CHAPTER 1 | RESOURCE MANAGER | 1A |

Lesson 1.1 ....1C
Lesson 1.2 ....1E
Lesson 1.3 ....1G
Lesson 1.4 ....1I

Chapter 1

WHAT IS ECONOMICS? · 2

1 An Economic Way of Thinking 3

Careers in Economics:
Economist..5

Linking Economics and Geography:
Ecotourism..6

2 Scarcity and Choice..8

3 Opportunity Costs 11

Case Study:
Undamming the Deerfield 12

4 Exchange 15

Global Exchange:
Year-Round Produce....................................16

Economics in the News:
Economic Resources in
the Global Economy....................................19

| CHAPTER 2 | RESOURCE MANAGER | 21A |

Lesson 2.1 ....21C
Lesson 2.2 ....21E
Lesson 2.3 ....21G

iv TABLE OF CONTENTS

Chapter 2

ECONOMIC SYSTEMS — 22

1 Types of Economic Systems...........23
  Case Study:
  The Mbuti of Central Africa..............24
2 Features of the U.S. Economy........29
  Careers in Economics:
  Real Estate Agent...........................31
3 The U.S. Economy at Work 36
  Economics in Action:
  "Extra, Extra!"................................37
  Global Exchange:
  Immigration....................................39
  Economics in the News:
  Government Regulation of
  Private Property..............................41

Unit 1 Economics Lab........................44

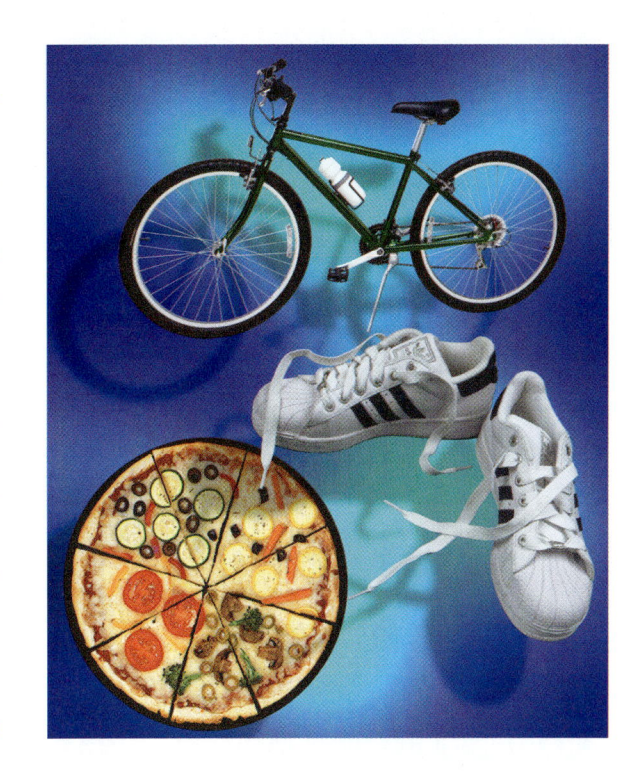

UNIT 2 — ELEMENTS OF MICROECONOMICS — 48

| CHAPTER 3 | RESOURCE MANAGER | 49A |

Lesson 3.1 ....49C
Lesson 3.2 ....49E
Lesson 3.3 ....49G

Chapter 3

DEMAND — 50

1 Nature of Demand.........................51
  Case Study:
  Generic Products............................53
2 Changes in Demand......................56
  Careers in Economics:
  Market Researcher.........................58
  Linking Economics and Psychology:
  Commercial Break..........................61
3 Elasticity of Demand 63
  Global Exchange:
  Movie Madness..............................66
  Economics in the News:
  Consumer Demand and the
  Food Distribution Industry 69

| CHAPTER 4 | RESOURCE MANAGER | 71A |

Lesson 4.1 ....71C
Lesson 4.2 ....71E
Lesson 4.3 ....71G

TABLE OF CONTENTS v

Chapter 4

SUPPLY 72

1 Nature of Supply 73
   Careers in Economics:
   Buyer 76
2 Changes in Supply 79
   Global Exchange:
   Acid Rain 81
   Case Study:
   Competition in Online Education 84
3 Making Production Decisions 86
   Economics in Action:
   Dialing for Dollars 88
   Economics in the News:
   Supply, Demand, and Computer Chips 93

CHAPTER 5	**RESOURCE MANAGER**	**95A**
Lesson 5.1		**95C**
Lesson 5.2		**95E**
Lesson 5.3		**95G**

Chapter 5

PRICES 96

1 The Price System 97
   Linking Economics and History:
   The Coming of the Computer Age 99
2 Determining Prices 103
   Careers in Economics:
   Sales Manager ....104  
   Case Study:
   Playstation 2 105
3 Managing Prices 108
   Global Exchange:
   International Bargain Hunters 111
   Economics in the News:
   California Power Crisis 113

CHAPTER 6	**RESOURCE MANAGER**	**115A**
Lesson 6.1		**115C**
Lesson 6.2		**115E**
Lesson 6.3		**115G**

Chapter 6

MARKET STRUCTURES 116

1 Highly Competitive Markets 117
   Economics in Action:
   Matchmaker, Matchmaker 118
   Careers in Economics:
   Advertising Account Manager 121
2 Imperfectly Competitive Markets 123
   Global Exchange:
   Driving Prices Up 125
3 Market Regulation 130
   Case Study:
   An Entertainment Monopoly? 132
   Economics in the News:
   Is Microsoft a Monopoly? 135

Unit 2 Economics Lab 138

UNIT 3 FREE ENTERPRISE AT WORK 142

| **Chapter 7** | **Resource Manager** | **143A** |

Lesson 7.1 ....143C
Lesson 7.2 ....143E
Lesson 7.3 ....143G
Lesson 7.4...143I

Chapter 7

BUSINESS ORGANIZATIONS 144

1 Sole Proprietorships 145

Careers in Economics:
Entrepreneur..146

Linking Economics and Government:
Government and the Responsibilities
of Business Ownership 148

2 Partnerships..150

3 Corporations 153

4 Other Forms of Organization......................159

Global Exchange:
Andrew Carnegie: Innovator of
Industrial Production 161

Case Study:
The Green Bay Packers 164

Economics in the News:
Business Ethics in a Global Economy 165

| **Chapter 8** | **Resource Manager** | **167A** |

Lesson 8.1 ....167C
Lesson 8.2 ....167E
Lesson 8.3 ....167G

Chapter 8

LABOR AND UNIONS 168

1 The U.S. Labor Force 169

Global Exchange:
Maquiladoras 174

Case Study:
Equal Pay for Equal Work 175

2 The Growth of Labor Unions 177

Economics in Action:
Union Summer 181

3 Unions and Management............................184

Careers in Economics:
Labor Relations Consultant........................187

Economics in the News:
Technology and Labor 191

TABLE OF CONTENTS vii

CHAPTER 9	RESOURCE MANAGER	193A
Lesson 9.1		193C
Lesson 9.2		193E
Lesson 9.3		193G
Lesson 9.4		193I

Chapter 9

SOURCES OF CAPITAL 194

1 Saving 195

Global Exchange:
Savings Around the World 198

2 Investing 200

3 Stocks, Bonds, and Futures 204

Careers in Economics:
Stockbroker 206

Linking Economics and History:
The Crashes of 1987 and 1929 211

4 Borrowing and Credit 214

Case Study:
Credit Card Incentives 216

Economics in the News:
Information Technology and
the Stock Market 219

Unit 3 Economics Lab 222

UNIT 4 — ELEMENTS OF MACROECONOMICS 226

LEADING ECONOMIC INDICATORS, 1995–1998

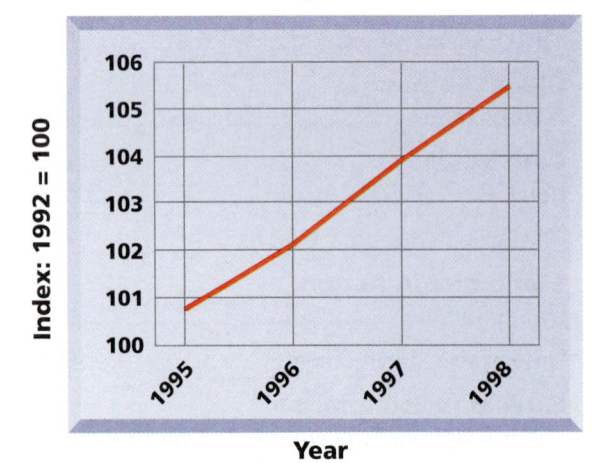

Source: U.S. Census Bureau, Statistical Abstract of the United States: 2000

CHAPTER 10	RESOURCE MANAGER	227A
Lesson 10.1		227C
Lesson 10.2		227E
Lesson 10.3		227G

Chapter 10

ECONOMIC PERFORMANCE 228

1 Gross Domestic Product 229

Global Exchange:
All Work and No Play 230

2 Business Cycles 236

Economics in Action:
How Does Your Garden Grow? 237

Careers in Economics:
Financial Analyst 239

3 Economic Growth 241

viii TABLE OF CONTENTS

Chapter 11	Resource Manager 249A
Lesson 11.1	249C
Lesson 11.2	249E
Lesson 11.3	249G

Chapter 11

ECONOMIC CHALLENGES 250

1 Unemployment 251

Linking Economics and Government:
Civilian Conservation Corps 254

Case Study:
Migrant Workers in California 255

2 Inflation 257

Careers in Economics:
Loan Officer 259

3 Poverty and Income Distribution 264

Global Exchange:
New Horizons 267

Economics in the News:
The Public Goods Gap 269

Unit 4 Economics Lab 272

Case Study:
Retraining 245

Economics in the News:
The Internet and the Global
Market Revolution 247

UNIT 5 — GOVERNMENT AND THE ECONOMY 276

Chapter 12	Resource Manager 277A
Lesson 12.1	277C
Lesson 12.2	277E
Lesson 12.3	277G

Chapter 12

ROLE OF GOVERNMENT 278

1 Growth of Government 279

Global Exchange:
Embargoes 280

Careers in Economics:
Civil Engineer 282

2 Economic Goals 284

3 Government and the Public 291

Case Study:
AmeriCorps 291

Economics in Action:
Young Lobbyist..295

Economics in the News:
E-Commerce and the Debate
over Personal Privacy...............................297

CHAPTER 13 RESOURCE MANAGER 299A
Lesson 13.1 ....299C
Lesson 13.2 ....299E
Lesson 13.3 ....299G

Chapter 13

MONEY AND THE BANKING SYSTEM 300

1 Money..301

Global Exchange:
Promoting Local Trade in
a Global Economy......................................303

Case Study:
Counterfeit Money.....................................306

2 History of U.S. Banking 308

Linking Economics and Science:
Shake, Rattle, and Roll 313

3 U.S. Banking Today...................................315

Careers in Economics:
Bank Teller..317

Economics in the News:
Financial Modernization and the
Repeal of the Banking Act of 1933 323

CHAPTER 14 RESOURCE MANAGER 325A
Lesson 14.1 ....325C
Lesson 14.2 ....325E
Lesson 14.3 ....325G

Chapter 14

THE FEDERAL RESERVE AND MONETARY POLICY 326

1 The Federal Reserve System 327

Careers in Economics:
Accountant..328

2 The Federal Reserve at Work 332

Global Exchange:
Sharing the Wealth 334

3 Monetary Policy Strategies 337

Case Study:
Alan Greenspan and Tight-Money Policy 338

Economics in Action:
Building Businesses in the Inner City 340

Economics in the News:
Has Alan Greenspan Lost
His Magic Touch? 345

CHAPTER 15 RESOURCE MANAGER 347A
Lesson 15.1 ....347C
Lesson 15.2 ....347E
Lesson 15.3 ....347G

Chapter 15

FISCAL POLICY 348

1 Defining Fiscal Policy................................349

Global Exchange:
Taxes..350

Linking Economics and Sociology:
Everything Old Is New Again....................353

2 Fiscal Policy Strategies..............................355

Careers in Economics:
Auditor..357

3 Fiscal Policy and the Federal Budget.........362

Case Study:
Balanced Budget Amendment....................366

Economics in the News:
The Commerce Clause and
Economic Legislation.................................367

Unit 5 Economics Lab.................................370

UNIT 6 — INTERNATIONAL ECONOMICS   374

CHAPTER 16 RESOURCE MANAGER 375A
- Lesson 16.1 .... 375C
- Lesson 16.2 .... 375E
- Lesson 16.3 .... 375G
- Lesson 16.4 .... 375I

Chapter 16

COMPARING ECONOMIC SYSTEMS   376

1. Development Models 377
   - **Careers in Economics:** Business Geographer 378
   - **Global Exchange:** Marketing Communism 379
2. Capitalism 381
   - **Case Study:** Capitalism, Singapore Style 385
3. Socialism 386
4. Communism 389

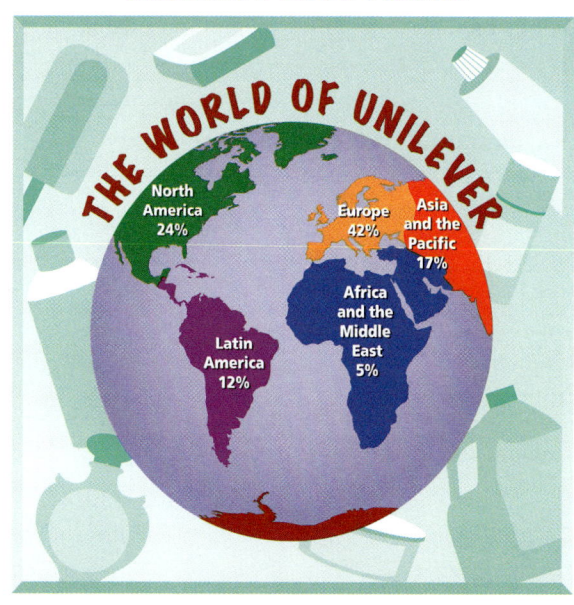

- **Economics in Action:** Brave New World 392
- **Economics in the News:** The Cold War and the American Economy 399

CHAPTER 17 RESOURCE MANAGER 401A
- Lesson 17.1 .... 401C
- Lesson 17.2 .... 401E
- Lesson 17.3 .... 401G

Chapter 17

DEVELOPING COUNTRIES   402

1. Economic Development 403
2. Challenges to Growth 407
   - **Careers in Economics:** Urban and Regional Planner 409
   - **Linking Economics and History:** How Many Worlds? 410
3. Paths to Economic Development 414
   - **Global Exchange:** Changing of the Guard 415
   - **Case Study:** Global Links 418
   - **Economics in the News:** Eastern Europe in the post-Communist Era 423

MULTINATIONAL CORPORATION: UNILEVER'S 2000 PROFITS

THE WORLD OF UNILEVER
- North America 24%
- Europe 42%
- Asia and the Pacific 17%
- Latin America 12%
- Africa and the Middle East 5%

TABLE OF CONTENTS   xi

CHAPTER 18 RESOURCE MANAGER 425A
Lesson 18.1 ....425C
Lesson 18.2 ....425E
Lesson 18.3 ....425G

Chapter 18

INTERNATIONAL TRADE 426

1 Specialization and Interdependence 427

Case Study:
The European Union 427

Careers in Economics:
Customs Inspector 429

2 Foreign Exchange and Currencies 431

Economics in Action:
An Education for the Global Economy 434

3 Cooperation and Trade Barriers 439

Global Exchange:
E-Commerce and the Global Economy 442

Economics in the News:
The NAFTA Debate 447

Unit 6 Economics Lab 450

REFERENCE SECTION R1

Consumer Handbook R2

World Economic Statistics R26

Glossary R38

Spanish Glossary R51

Index R67

Acknowledgments R90

FEATURES

CAREERS IN ECONOMICS

Economist...5	Business Geographer........................378
Real Estate Agent..................................31	Urban and Regional Planner.............409
Market Researcher................................58	Customs Inspector.............................429
Buyer...76	
Sales Manager.....................................104	
Advertising Account Manager............121	
Entrepreneur.......................................146	
Labor Relations Consultant................187	
Stockbroker..206	
Financial Analyst................................239	
Loan Officer..259	
Civil Engineer.....................................282	
Bank Teller...317	
Accountant...328	
Auditor...357	

CASE STUDY

Undamming the Deerfield....................12	Generic Products..................................53
The Mbuti of Central Africa..................24	Competition in Online Education........84
	Playstation 2......................................105
	An Entertainment Monopoly?............132
	The Green Bay Packers.......................164
	Equal Pay for Equal Work...................175
	Credit Card Incentives........................216
	Retraining..245
	Migrant Workers in California............255
	AmeriCorps...291
	Counterfeit Money..............................306
	Alan Greenspan and Tight-Money Policy........338
	Balanced Budget Amendment............366
	Capitalism, Singapore Style................385
	Global Links.......................................418
	The European Union...........................427

Economics in Action

"Extra, Extra!"	37
Dialing for Dollars	88
Matchmaker, Matchmaker	118
Union Summer	181
How Does Your Garden Grow?	237
Young Lobbyist	295
Building Businesses in the Inner City	340
Brave New World	392
An Education for the Global Economy	434

Economics in the News

Economics and the Arts	T13
Economic Resources in the Global Economy	19
Government Regulation of Private Property	41
Consumer Demand and the Food Distribution Industry	69
Supply, Demand, and Computer Chips	93
California Power Crisis	113
Is Microsoft a Monopoly?	135
Business Ethics in a Global Economy	165
Technology and Labor	191
Information Technology and the Stock Market	219
The Internet and the Global Market Revolution	247
The Public Goods Gap	269
The Economic Impact of September 11, 2001	297
Financial Modernization and the Repeal of the Banking Act of 1933	323
Has Alan Greenspan Lost His Magic Touch?	345
The Commerce Clause and Economic Legislation	367
The Cold War and the American Economy	399
Eastern Europe in the post-Communist Era	423
The NAFTA Debate	447

Global Exchange

Year-Round Produce	16
Immigration	39
Movie Madness	66
Acid Rain	81
International Bargain Hunters	111
Driving Prices Up	125
Andrew Carnegie: Innovator of Industrial Production	161
Maquiladoras	174
Savings Around the World	198
All Work and No Play	230
New Horizons	267
Embargoes	280
Promoting Local Trade in a Global Economy	303
Sharing the Wealth	334
Taxes	350
Marketing Communism	379
Changing of the Guard	415
E-Commerce and the Global Economy	442

xiv Table of Contents

Linking Economics and

GEOGRAPHY	Ecotourism	6
PSYCHOLOGY	Commercial Break	61
HISTORY	The Coming of the Computer Age	99
GOVERNMENT	Government and the Responsibilities of Business Ownership	148
HISTORY	The Crashes of 1987 and 1929	211
GOVERNMENT	Civilian Conservation Corps	254
SCIENCE	Shake, Rattle, and Roll	313
SOCIOLOGY	Everything Old Is New Again	353
HISTORY	How Many Worlds?	410

internet connect

President Lyndon B. Johnson	T15
Natural Resources	21
Unemployment Rates	43
Demand Schedules and Demand Curves	71
Law of Supply and Supply Curves	95
Nuclear Energy	115
Gas Prices in Your Community	141
Nonprofit Organizations	167
The Muckrakers	193
Careers in Financial Planning	225
Business Cycles and the Great Depression	249
The Consumer Price Index and Inflation	275
The Role of Government, Growth of Government	299
U.S. Currency	325
The Fed	347
Social Security	373
Comparing Economic Systems	401
The Peace Corps	425
IMF, Foreign Exchange, Cooperation	449

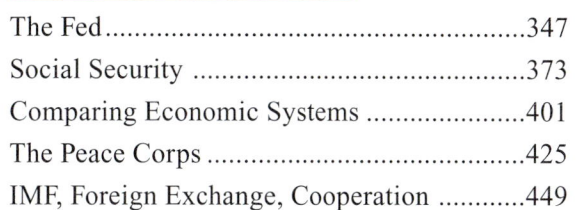

TABLE OF CONTENTS   XV

Tables, Charts, and Graphs

King Cotton in Texas	T4
Growth of High-Tech Jobs in Texas, 1980–2000	T11
Spindletop Oil Production, 1901–1921	T15
Scarcity	9
Kevin's Decision-Making Grid	11
The Production Possibilities Curve	13
Shifting Production Possibilities Curve	14
Types of Economic Systems	26
Circular Flow of Goods and Services	34
Demand Schedule	54
Demand for Car Stereos	55
Shifts in Demand	57
Elastic Demand for Pizza	64
Inelastic Demand for Soap	65
Movie Ticket Revenue and Demand Elasticity	67
Supply of Car Stereos	74
Elastic Supply for Posters	77
Perfectly Inelastic Supply	78
Supply Curve Shifts	80
Productivity of Golden Duck Company	87
Marginal Product and Costs	90
Demand and Supply Schedule for Tennis Shoes	103
Equilibrium Price for Tennis Shoes	103
Surplus and Shortage of Tennis Shoes	105
Equilibrium, Demand, and Supply Shifts	106
Price Ceiling and Shortage	109
Price Floor and Surplus	110
Competition and Market Structure	119
Shift in Demand and Equilibrium Price	122
Comparing Market Structures	124
U.S. Antitrust Legislation	133
Types of Business Organizations, 1997	145
Partnerships by Industry, 1997	151
Net Income of Businesses, 1997	153
Organization and Control in a Typical Corporation	154
New Business Incorporations and Business Failures, 1998	156
Conglomerate Combination	160
Labor Force, 1999	169
Equilibrium Wage	170
Education and Salary, 1998	173
Minimum Wage, 1950–2000	176
Changes in Union Membership	180
Major Labor Legislation	182
Compound Interest	196
National Savings Rates	197
Stock Splits	205
Understanding Stock Market Reports	208
Stock Market Performance	209

Absolute and Comparative Advantage

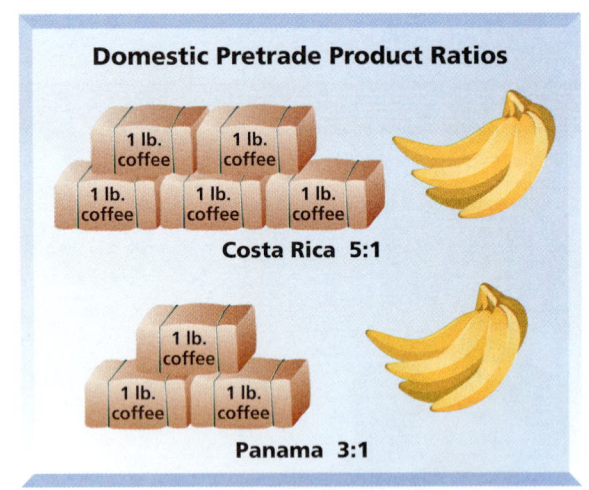

Domestic Pretrade Product Ratios

Costa Rica 5:1

Panama 3:1

Costa Rica–Panama

Trade Ratio 4:1

Treasury Bonds, Bills, and Notes 210
Security Regulations 212
Federal Regulation of Credit 217
Promoting Economic Growth
Through Saving and Credit 218
Gross Domestic Product, 2000 231
Nominal and Real GDP 232
National Income and
Product Accounts, 1999 234
Business Cycle 238
Real GDP Per Capita, 1970–1999 242
Labor Productivity, 1964–1999 245
Unemployment by Sex and Age, 1999 253
Fastest-Growing Occupations and Fastest-
Declining Industries, 1998–2008 255
Consumer Price Index, 1943–1999 261
Inflation Rate, 1943–1999 262
Real Value of the Dollar, 1982–1999 263
Poverty Rate, 1981–1999 265
Lorenz Curve, 1994 266

Gini Index, 1970–1998 266
Population Growth 279
Growth in Government Spending 281
How Federal, State, and
Local Dollars Are Spent 283

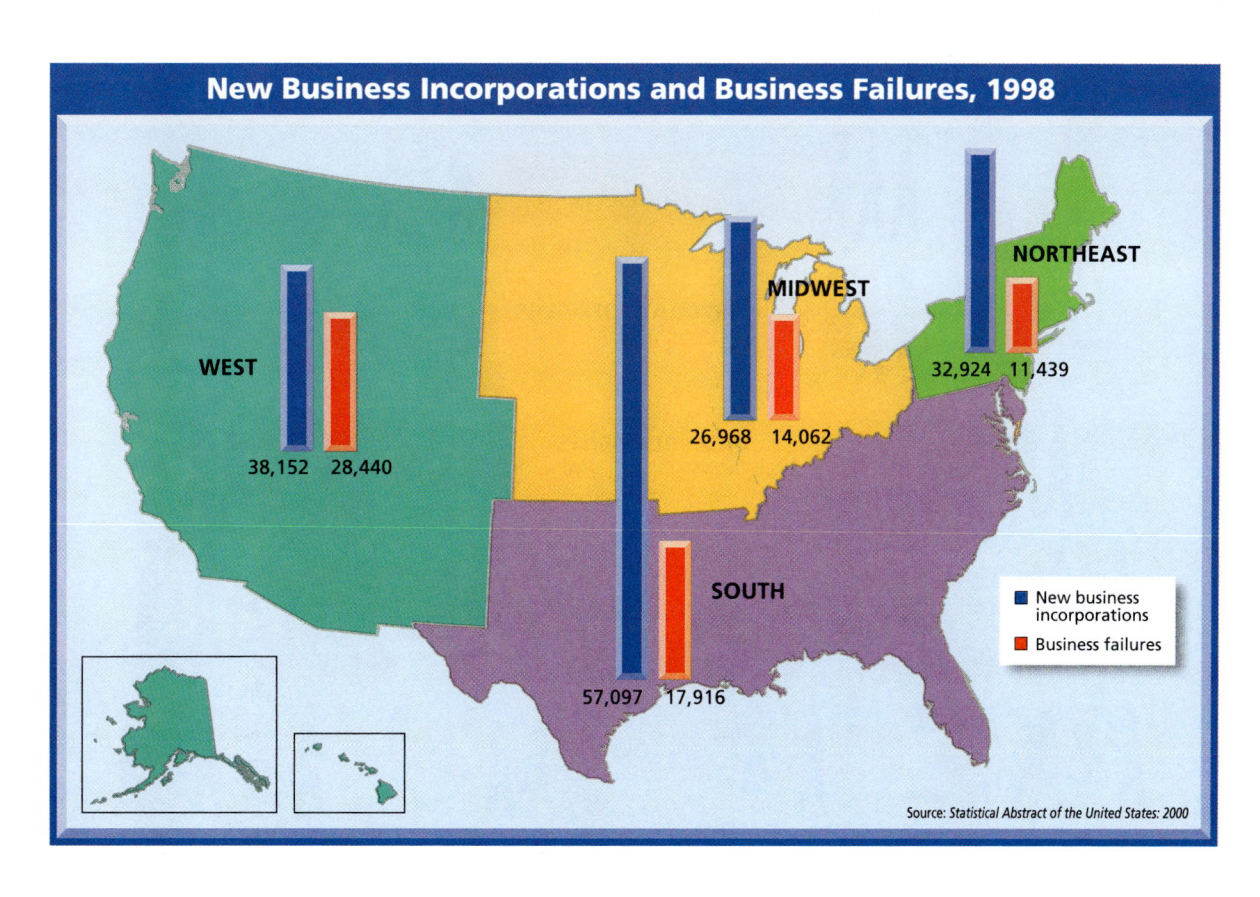

DECREASE IN DEMAND

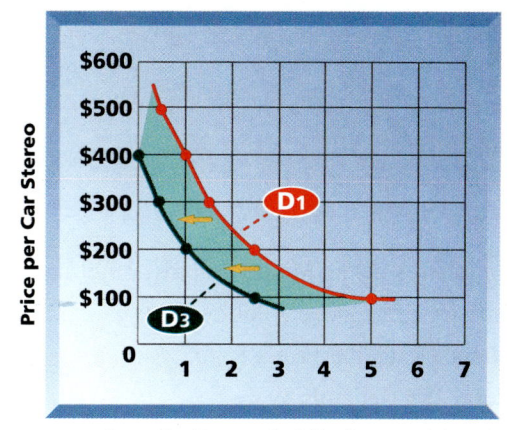

New Business Incorporations and Business Failures, 1998

WEST 38,152 28,440
MIDWEST 26,968 14,062
NORTHEAST 32,924 11,439
SOUTH 57,097 17,916

■ New business incorporations
■ Business failures

Source: *Statistical Abstract of the United States: 2000*

TABLE OF CONTENTS xvii

Federal Regulatory Agencies	285
Redistributing Income	289
Sources of Money's Value	304
Numbers of Financial Institutions, 1999	316
Bank Failures	321
Organization of the Fed	329
The Fed and Check-Clearing	333
Components of the Money Supply, 1999	335
Summary of Monetary Policy Tools	339
Discount Rate and Prime Rate	341
Federal Tax Receipts by Source, 1999	351
Fiscal Policy Models	356
Federal Expenditures, 2000	363
Federal Deficit, 1945–2000	364
Comparing Economic Systems	377

SOLE PROPRIETORSHIPS, 2000 BY SIZE OF RECEIPTS

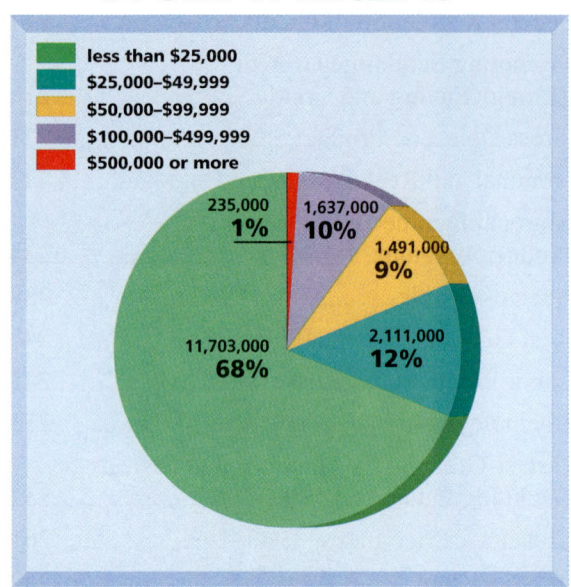

- less than $25,000
- $25,000–$49,999
- $50,000–$99,999
- $100,000–$499,999
- $500,000 or more

- 235,000 — 1%
- 1,637,000 — 10%
- 1,491,000 — 9%
- 2,111,000 — 12%
- 11,703,000 — 68%

ORGANIZATION AND CONTROL IN A TYPICAL CORPORATION

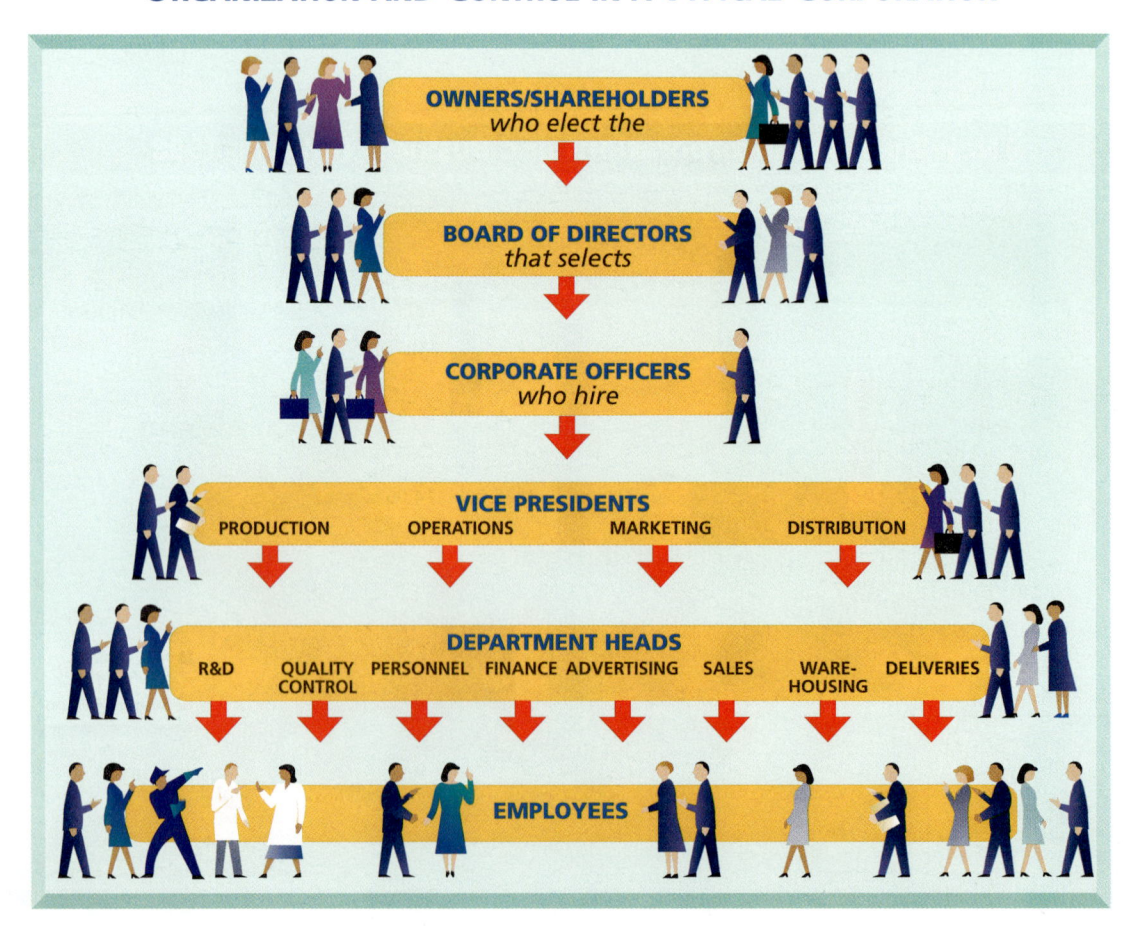

OWNERS/SHAREHOLDERS *who elect the*

↓

BOARD OF DIRECTORS *that selects*

↓

CORPORATE OFFICERS *who hire*

↓

VICE PRESIDENTS
PRODUCTION   OPERATIONS   MARKETING   DISTRIBUTION

↓

DEPARTMENT HEADS
R&D   QUALITY CONTROL   PERSONNEL   FINANCE   ADVERTISING   SALES   WAREHOUSING   DELIVERIES

↓

EMPLOYEES

xviii TABLE OF CONTENTS

Fall of the Soviet Union	394	Absolute and Comparative Advantage	430
Per Capita GDP: China, 1968–2000	397	U.S. International Trade (in billions of U.S. dollars),1997	435
Comparing Population Growth Rates, 1990–1995	406	Foreign Direct Investment in the United States, 1998	436
Production Possibilities Curve for Developing Nations	416	U.S. Balance of Trade (Goods and Services), 1960–1995	437
Multinational Corporation: Unilever's 1996 Sales	418	U.S. Imports and Exports, 1999–2000	438
Official Development Assistance from OECD Members	419	Average Tariff Rates in the United States, 1825–1995	440
External Debt of Developing Nations, 1995	421	North American Free Trade Agreement (highlights)	445

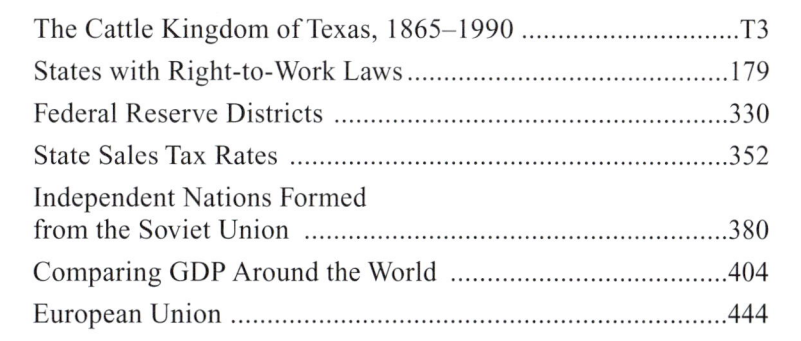

MAPS

The Cattle Kingdom of Texas, 1865–1990	T3
States with Right-to-Work Laws	179
Federal Reserve Districts	330
State Sales Tax Rates	352
Independent Nations Formed from the Soviet Union	380
Comparing GDP Around the World	404
European Union	444

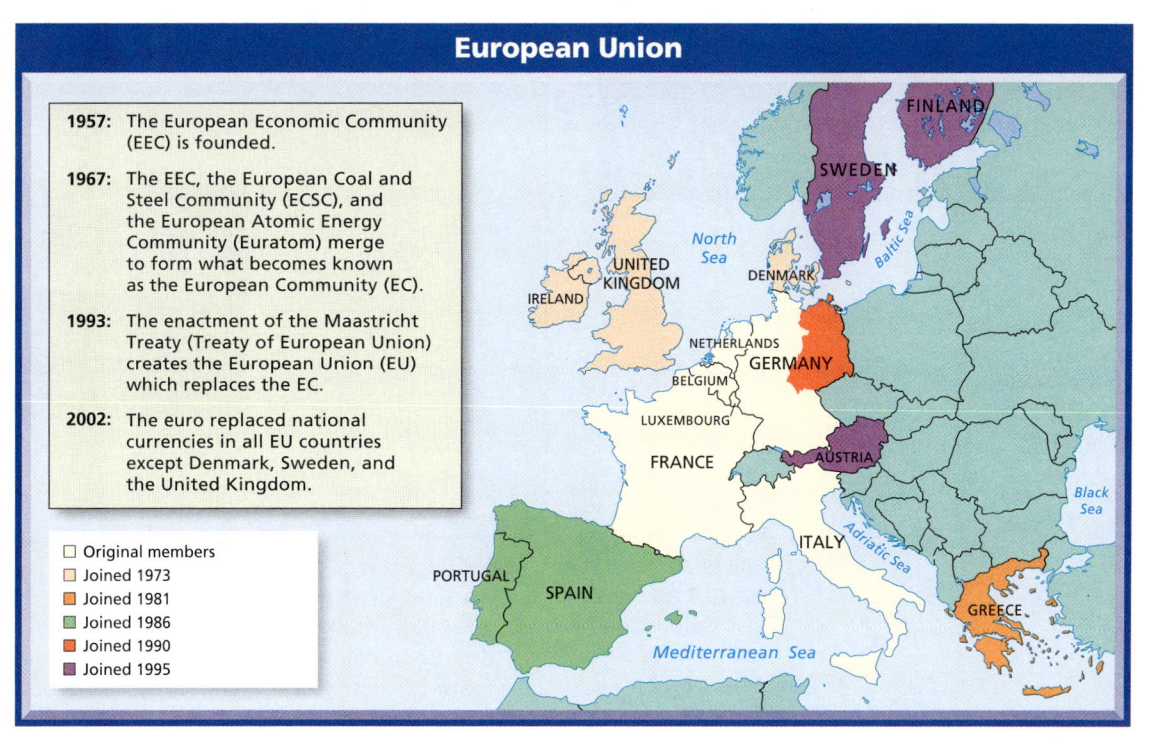

European Union

1957: The European Economic Community (EEC) is founded.

1967: The EEC, the European Coal and Steel Community (ECSC), and the European Atomic Energy Community (Euratom) merge to form what becomes known as the European Community (EC).

1993: The enactment of the Maastricht Treaty (Treaty of European Union) creates the European Union (EU) which replaces the EC.

2002: The euro replaced national currencies in all EU countries except Denmark, Sweden, and the United Kingdom.

- Original members
- Joined 1973
- Joined 1981
- Joined 1986
- Joined 1990
- Joined 1995

HOW TO USE YOUR TEXTBOOK

Use these built-in tools to read for understanding.

Why It Matters Today is an exciting way for you to make connections between what you are reading in your economics book and the world around you. In each chapter, you will be invited to explore a topic that is relevant to our lives today by using **CNNfyi.com** connections.

Read to Discover questions begin each section of *Holt Economics*. These questions serve as your guide as you read through the section. Keep them in mind as you explore the section's content.

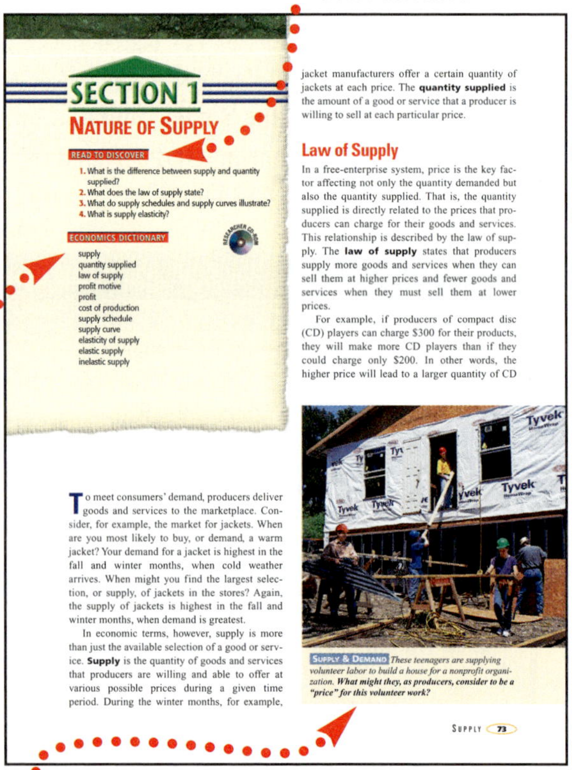

Economics Notebook activities invite you to explore how economic concepts relate to your own life, while at the same time honing your writing skills.

Economics Dictionary terms are introduced at the beginning of each section. The terms will be defined in context and are also defined on the *Holt Researcher CD–ROM*.

Interactive Captions accompany most of the book's rich images. Pictures are one of the most important primary sources social scientists can use to help analyze important issues. These features invite you to examine the images and make predictions about their content.

Use these review tools to pull together all the information you have learned.

Graphic Organizers will help you pull together important information from the section. You can complete the graphic organizer as a study tool to prepare for a test or writing assignment.

Homework Practice Online lets you log on to the go.hrw.com Web site to complete an interactive self-check of the material covered in the section.

Writing and Critical Thinking activities allow you to explore a section topic in greater depth and build your skills.

Building Social Studies Skills is a way for you to build your skills at analyzing information and gain practice in answering standardized-test questions.

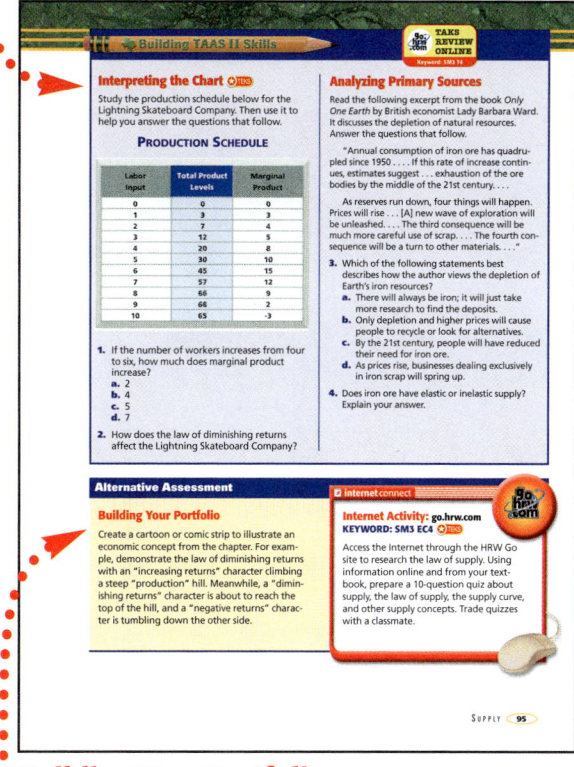

Thinking Critically questions ask you to use the information you have learned in the chapter to extend your knowledge. You will be asked to analyze information by using your critical thinking skills.

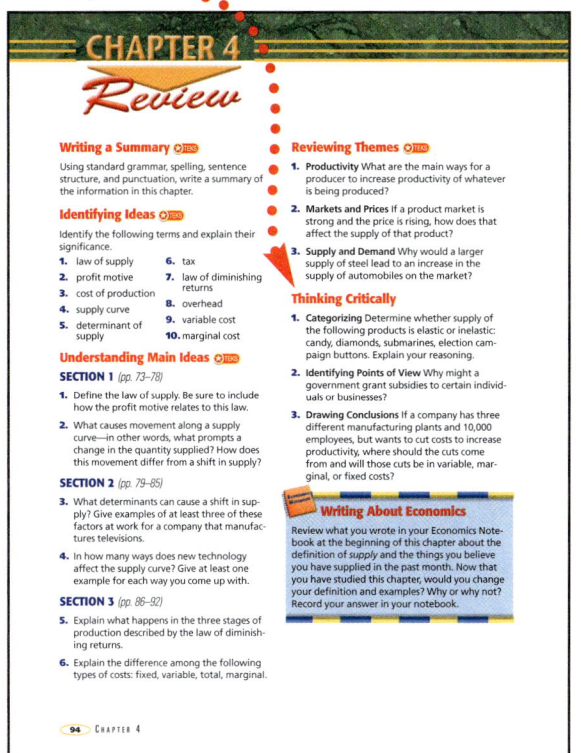

Building Your Portfolio is an exciting and creative way to demonstrate your understanding of economics.

Use these online tools to review and complete online activities.

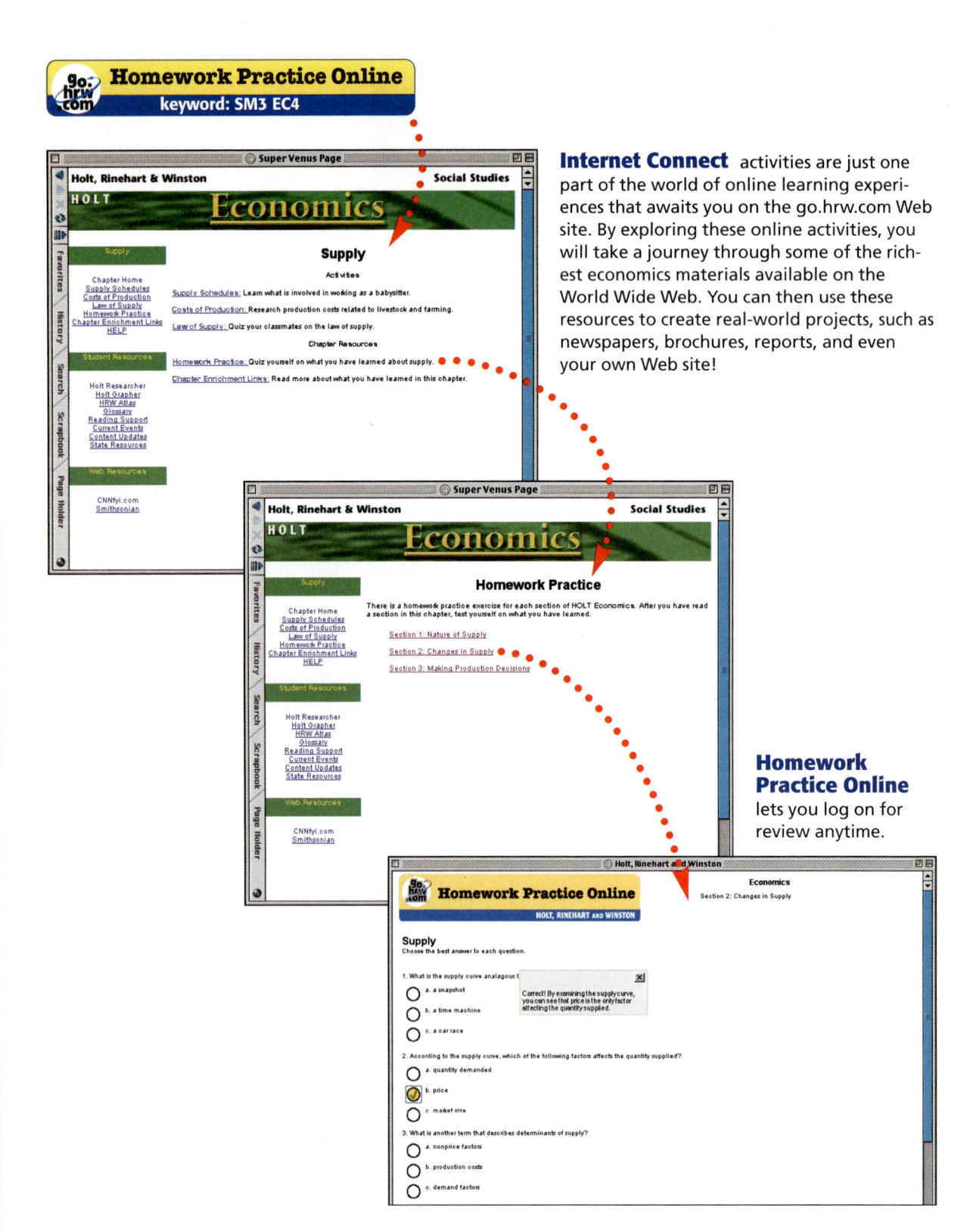

Internet Connect activities are just one part of the world of online learning experiences that awaits you on the go.hrw.com Web site. By exploring these online activities, you will take a journey through some of the richest economics materials available on the World Wide Web. You can then use these resources to create real-world projects, such as newspapers, brochures, reports, and even your own Web site!

Homework Practice Online lets you log on for review anytime.

HOW TO USE YOUR TEXTBOOK

THEMES IN ECONOMICS

Holt Economics examines the way in which economics affects the lives of individuals and how individuals, through their economic choices, shape their world. You will notice several recurrent themes in the study of economics.

SCARCITY & CHOICE	**ROLE OF GOVERNMENT**
OPPORTUNITY COST & TRADE-OFFS	**GROSS DOMESTIC PRODUCT**
PRODUCTIVITY	**AGGREGATE SUPPLY & AGGREGATE DEMAND**
ECONOMIC SYSTEMS	**UNEMPLOYMENT**
ECONOMIC INSTITUTIONS & INCENTIVES	**INFLATION & DEFLATION**
EXCHANGE, MONEY, & INTERDEPENDENCE	**MONETARY POLICY**
MARKETS & PRICES	**FISCAL POLICY**
SUPPLY & DEMAND	**INTERNATIONAL TRADE**
COMPETITION & MARKET STRUCTURE	**BALANCE OF PAYMENTS**
INCOME DISTRIBUTION	**INTERNATIONAL GROWTH & STABILITY**
MARKET FAILURES	

Skills Handbook

Critical Thinking and the Study of Economics ... S1

Reading Strategies ... S4

Standardized Test-Taking Strategies ... S12

Interactive Skill-Builder ... S16

CRITICAL THINKING AND THE STUDY OF ECONOMICS

Throughout *Holt Economics,* you are asked to think critically about the events and processes that shape your global, national, and local economy. Critical thinking is the reasoned judgment of information and ideas. People who think critically study information to determine its accuracy. They evaluate arguments and analyze conclusions before accepting their validity. Critical thinkers are able to recognize and define problems and develop strategies for resolving them.

The development of critical thinking skills is essential to effective economic habits. Such skills empower you to make informed economic choices. For example, critical thinking skills enable you to evaluate information you hear in news reports. In addition, critical thinking about economics enables you to be a skilled consumer and improves your ability to make wise decisions about budgeting, spending, and investing.

Helping you develop critical thinking skills is an important tool of *Holt Economics*. Using the following 14 critical thinking skills will help you better understand the concepts and forces involved in economics. Additional skills to help you understand economic concepts and processes can be found in the Interactive Skill-Builder, which begins on p. S16.

1. Identifying Points of View involves identifying the factors that color the outlook of a person or group. Someone's point of view includes beliefs and attitudes that are shaped by factors such as age, sex, religion, race, and economic status. This thinking skill helps us examine why people see things as they do, and reinforces the realization that people's views may change over time, or with a change in circumstances. A point of view that is highly personal or based on unreasoned judgment, is said to be *biased*.

2. Comparing and Contrasting involves examining events, situations, or points of view for their similarities and differences. *Comparing* focuses on both the similarities and the differences. *Contrasting* focuses only on the differences. For example, by comparing capitalism and democratic socialism you might note that although these economic systems have different levels of government control, they both are mixed economies. By contrasting, on the other hand, you might note that capitalism involves limited government control over the economy and democratic socialism involves moderate government control.

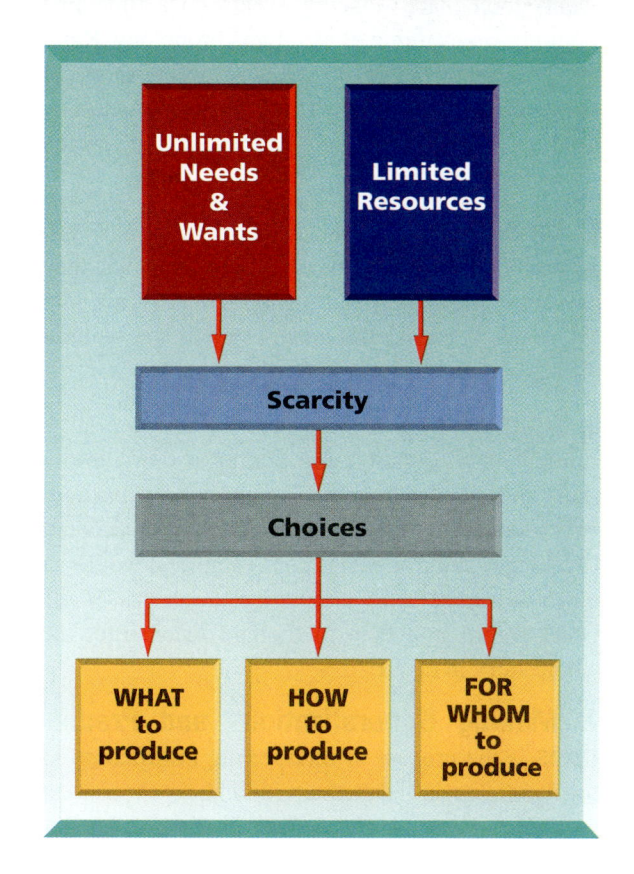

3. Analyzing Information is the process of breaking something down into its parts and examining the relationships among them. An *analysis* of something's parts enables you to better understand the whole. For example, to analyze the government's role in the economy, you might study taxation, the federal budget, and fiscal policy strategies.

4. Sequencing is the process of placing events in correct chronological order to better understand the relationships among these events. You can sequence events in two basic ways: according to *absolute* or *relative* chronology. Absolute chronology means that you pay close attention to the actual dates events took place. Placing events on a time line would be an example of absolute chronology. Relative chronology refers to the way events relate to one another. To put events in relative order, you need to know which one happened first, which came next, and so forth.

5. Categorizing is the process by which you group things together by the characteristics they have in common. By putting things or events into categories, it is easier to make comparisons and see differences among them.

6. Summarizing is the process of taking a large amount of information and boiling it down into a short and clear statement. Summarizing is particularly useful when you need to give a brief account of a longer story or event. For example, it would be much more useful to summarize the events of the Great Depression than to try and reconstruct the whole story in detail.

7. Making Generalizations and Predictions is the process of interpreting information to form more general statements and guess about what will happen next. A *generalization* is a broad statement that holds true for a variety of economic events or situations. Making generalizations can help you see the "big picture" of events, rather than just focusing on details. It is very important, however, that when making generalizations you try not to include situations that do not fit the statement. When this occurs, you run the risk of creating a stereotype, or overgeneralization. A *prediction* is an educated guess about an outcome. When you read economics, you should always be asking yourself questions like, "What will happen next? If this person does this, what will that mean for . . . ?", and so on. These types of questions help you draw on information you already know to see patterns in economics.

8. Drawing Inferences and Conclusions is forming possible explanations for an event, a situation, or a problem. When you make an *inference*, you take the information you know to be true and come up with an educated guess about what else you think is true about that situation. A *conclusion* is a prediction about the outcome of a situation based on what you already know. Often, you must be prepared to test your inferences and conclusions against new evidence or arguments.

9. Problem Solving is the process by which you pose workable solutions to difficult situations. The first step in the process is to identify a problem. Next you will need to gather information about the problem, such as its history and the various factors that contribute to the problem. Once you have gathered information, you should list and consider the options for solving the problem. For each of the possible solutions, weigh their advantages and disadvantages and, based on your evaluation, choose and implement a solution. Once the solution is in place, go back and evaluate the effectiveness of the solution you selected.

10. Decision Making is the process of reviewing a situation and then making decisions or recommendations for the best possible outcome. To complete the process, first identify a situation that requires a solution. Next, gather information that will help you reach a decision. You may need to do some background research to study the history of the situation, or carefully consider the points of view of the individuals involved. Once you have done your research, identify options that might resolve the situation. For each option, predict what the possible consequences might be if that option were followed. Once you have identified the best option, take action by making a recommendation and following through on any tasks that option requires.

11. Evaluating is assessing the significance or overall importance of something, such as the success of a tax cut or the impact of a trade deficit on economic growth. You should base your judgment on standards that others will understand and are likely to think important. An evaluation of a price increase for a particular product, for example, would assess the quantity of the product supplied by producers and the quantity demanded by consumers.

12. Supporting a Point of View involves identifying an issue, deciding what you think about the issue, and persuasively expressing your position on it. Your stand should be based on specific information. In taking a stand, even on a controversial issue such as labor unions, state your position clearly and give reasons to support it.

13. Studying Contemporary Issues and Problems involves identifying a current topic frequently discussed in the media, reading several sources of information on the topic, and evaluating that information. Finding space for all the waste a society creates, for example, is a contemporary problem you may be familiar with. You might feel the effects of it through recycling programs in your community or school. By studying this issue, you will be able to understand the cause of excess waste and evaluate solutions others have developed to ease the problem.

14. Applying a Model involves depicting something in its ideal state and evaluating how well a specific example matches the ideal. A model of an ideal capitalist economic system, for example, might be applied to the economy of Brazil. By evaluating how well each element of Brazil's economic system matches each element of a model capitalist system, you can determine whether or not Brazil has a capitalist economy or how close it matches an ideal system.

COMPARING ECONOMIC SYSTEMS

	Ownership of Natural Resources and Capital	
Allocation Choices	**Private**	**Government**
Private	**Market Capitalism** Examples: United States, Western Europe, Japan	**Market Socialism** Examples: Yugoslavia, China
Government	**Command Capitalism** Examples: many nations in Latin America, Africa, and the Middle East	**Command Socialism** Examples: Soviet Union, Cuba, North Korea

READING STRATEGIES

Becoming a Strategic Reader

by Dr. Judith Irvin

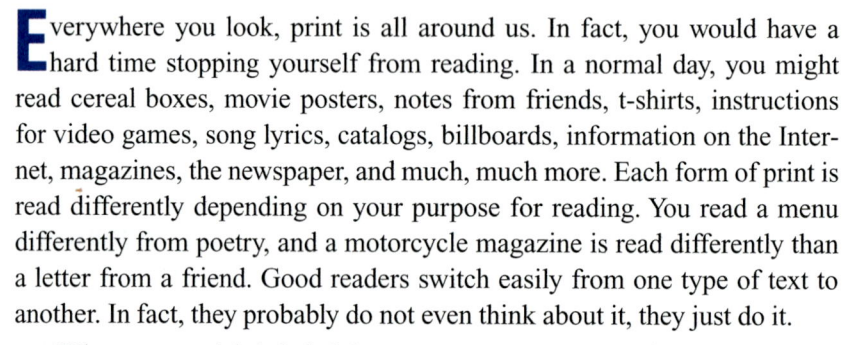

Everywhere you look, print is all around us. In fact, you would have a hard time stopping yourself from reading. In a normal day, you might read cereal boxes, movie posters, notes from friends, t-shirts, instructions for video games, song lyrics, catalogs, billboards, information on the Internet, magazines, the newspaper, and much, much more. Each form of print is read differently depending on your purpose for reading. You read a menu differently from poetry, and a motorcycle magazine is read differently than a letter from a friend. Good readers switch easily from one type of text to another. In fact, they probably do not even think about it, they just do it.

When you read, it is helpful to use a strategy to remember the most important ideas. You can use a strategy before you read to help connect information you already know to the new information you will encounter. Before you read, you can also predict what a text will be about by using a previewing strategy. During the reading you can use a strategy to help you focus on main ideas, and after reading you can use a strategy to help you organize what you learned so that you can remember it later. *Holt Economics* was designed to help you more easily understand the ideas you read. Important reading strategies employed in *Holt Economics* include:

A Tools to help you **preview and predict** what the text will be about

B Ways to help you **use and analyze visual information**

C Ideas to help you **organize the information** you have learned

SKILLS HANDBOOK

A. Previewing and Predicting

How can I figure out what the text is about before I even start reading a section?

Previewing and **predicting** are good methods to help you understand the text. If you take the time to preview and predict before you read, the text will make more sense to you during your reading.

1 Usually, your teacher will set the purpose for reading. After reading some new information, you may be asked to write a summary, take a test, or complete some other type of activity.

"After reading about supply, you will work with a partner to create a schedule and..."

Previewing and Predicting

step 1 Identify your purpose for reading. Ask yourself what you will do with this information once you have finished reading.

▼

step 2 Ask yourself what is the main idea of the text and what are the key vocabulary words you need to know.

▼

step 3 Use signal words to help identify the structure of the text.

▼

step 4 Connect the information to what you already know.

2 As you preview the text, use **graphic signals** such as headings, subheadings, and boldface type to help you determine what is important in the text. Each section of *Holt Economics* opens by giving you important clues to help you preview the material.

Looking at the section's **main heading** and sub-headings can give you an idea of what is to come.

Read to Discover questions give you clues as to the section's main ideas.

Economics Dictionary terms let you know the key vocabulary you will encounter in the section.

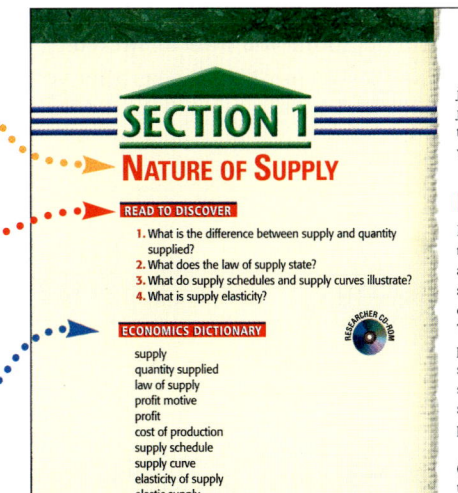

SECTION 1
NATURE OF SUPPLY

READ TO DISCOVER
1. What is the difference between supply and quantity supplied?
2. What does the law of supply state?
3. What do supply schedules and supply curves illustrate?
4. What is supply elasticity?

ECONOMICS DICTIONARY
supply
quantity supplied
law of supply
profit motive
profit
cost of production
supply schedule
supply curve
elasticity of supply
elastic supply

jacket manufacturers offer a certain quantity of jackets at each price. The **quantity supplied** is the amount of a good or service that a producer is willing to sell at each particular price.

Law of Supply

In a free-enterprise system, price is the key factor affecting not only the quantity demanded but also the quantity supplied. That is, the quantity supplied is directly related to the prices that producers can charge for their goods and services. This relationship is described by the law of supply. The **law of supply** states that producers supply more goods and services when they can sell them at higher prices and fewer goods and services when they must sell them at lower prices.

For example, if producers of compact disc (CD) players can charge $300 for their products, they will make more CD players than if they

SKILLS HANDBOOK S5

A. Previewing and Predicting (continued)

3 Other tools that can help you in previewing are **signal words**. These words prepare you to think in a certain way. For example, when you see words such as *similar to*, *same as*, or *different from*, you know that the text will probably compare and contrast two or more ideas. Signal words indicate how the ideas in the text relate to each other. Look at the list below for some of the most common signal words grouped by the type of text structures they include.

SIGNAL WORDS

Cause and Effect	Compare and Contrast	Description	Problem and Solution	Sequence or Chronological Order
because since consequently this led to…so if…then nevertheless accordingly because of as a result of in order to may be due to for this reason not only…but	different from same as similar to as opposed to instead of although however compared with as well as either…or but on the other hand unless	for instance for example such as to illustrate in addition most importantly another furthermore first, second …	the question is a solution one answer is	not long after next then initially before after finally preceding following on (date) over the years today when

4 Learning something new requires that you connect it in some way with something you already know. This means you have to think before you read and while you read. You may want to use a chart like this one to remind yourself of the information already familiar to you and to come up with questions you want answered in your reading. The chart will also help you organize your ideas after you have finished reading.

What I know	What I want to know	What I learned

S6 SKILLS HANDBOOK

B. Use and Analyze Visual Information

How can all the pictures, maps, graphs, and political cartoons with the text help me be a stronger reader?

Using visual information can help you understand and remember the information presented in *Holt Economics*. Good readers make a picture in their mind when they read. The pictures, charts, graphs, political cartoons, and diagrams that occur throughout *Holt Economics* are placed strategically to increase your understanding.

1 You might ask yourself questions like these:

Why did the writer include this image with the text?

What details about this image are mentioned in the text?

2 After you have read the text, see if you can answer your own questions.

Analyzing Visual Information

step 1 As you preview the text, ask yourself how the visual information relates to the text.

step 2 Generate questions based on the visual information.

step 3 After reading the text, go back and review the visual information again.

step 4 Connect the information to what you already know.

→ What are the people in this picture doing?

→ When was this picture likely taken?

→ What does this image tell me about economics?

B. Use and Analyze Visual Information (continued)

2 Maps, graphs, and charts help you organize information about a place. You might ask questions like these:

→ What is this a graph of?

→ What information was used to create the graph?

→ Why does the curve dip down on the right side of the graph?

PRODUCTIVITY OF GOLDEN DUCK COMPANY

Labor Input	Total Product	Marginal Product
0	0	0
1	10	10
2	50	40
3	110	60
4	175	65
5	245	70
6	320	75
7	400	80
8	485	85
9	575	90
10	675	100
11	875	200
12	985	110
13	1,000	15
14	975	-25
15	925	-50
16	825	-100

How do this graph and table support what I have read in the text?

What is the relationship between the graph and the table?

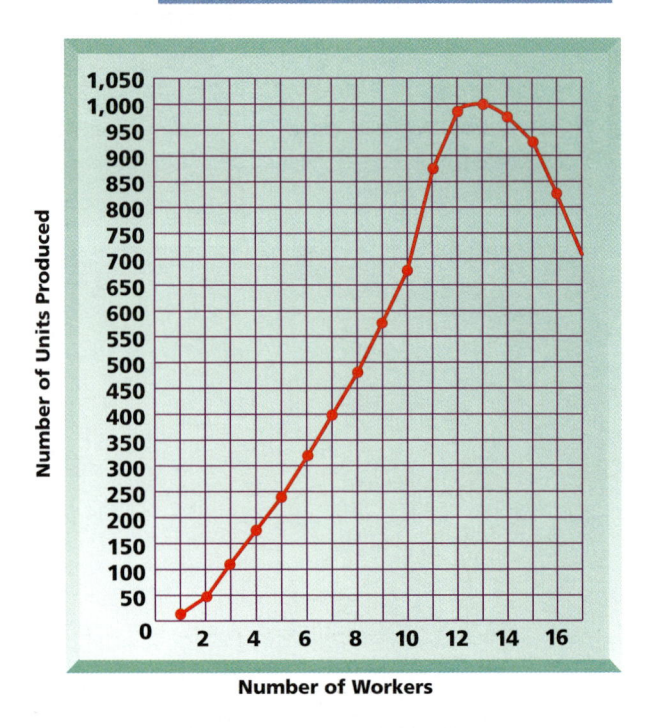

3 After reading the text, go back and review the visual information again.

4 Connect the information to what you already know.

SKILLS HANDBOOK

C. Organize Information

Once I learn new information, how do I keep it all straight so that I will remember it?

To help you remember what you have read, you need to find a way of **organizing information**. Two good ways of doing this are by using graphic organizers and concept maps. **Graphic organizers** help you understand important relationships—such as cause-and-effect, compare/contrast, sequence of events, and problem/solution—within the text. **Concept maps** provide a useful tool to help you focus on the text's main ideas and organize supporting details.

Identifying Relationships

Using graphic organizers will help you recall important ideas from the section and give you a study tool you can use to prepare for a quiz or test or to help with a writing assignment. Some of the most common types of graphic organizers are shown below.

▶ Cause and Effect

Economic events cause people to react in a certain way. Cause-and-effect patterns show the relationship between results and the ideas or events that made the results occur. You may want to represent cause-and-effect relationships as one cause leading to multiple effects,

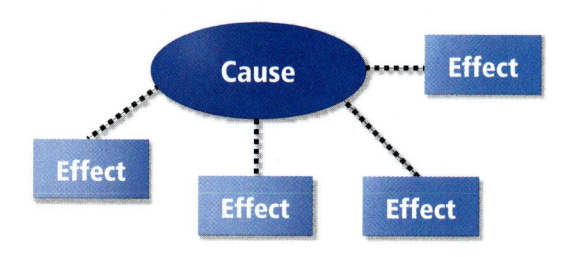

Cause → **Effect**, **Effect**, **Effect**, **Effect**

or as a chain of cause-and-effect relationships.

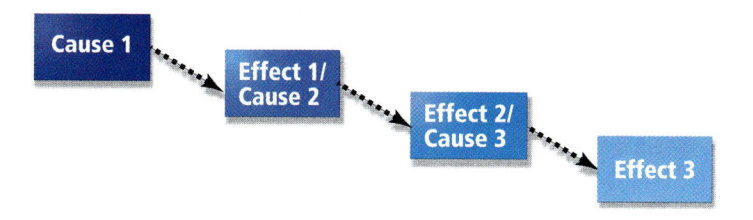

Cause 1 → **Effect 1/Cause 2** → **Effect 2/Cause 3** → **Effect 3**

Constructing Graphic Organizers

step 1 — Preview the text, looking for signal words and the main idea.

step 2 — Form a hypothesis as to which type of graphic organizer would work best to display the information presented.

step 3 — Work individually or with your classmates to create a visual representation of what you read.

C. Organize Information (continued)

◗ Comparing and Contrasting
Graphic Organizers are often useful when you are comparing or contrasting information. Compare-and-contrast diagrams point out similarities and differences between two concepts or ideas.

Characteristics | Shared Characteristics | Characteristics

◗ Sequencing
Keeping track of dates and the order in which events took place is essential to understanding end results. Sequence or chronological-order diagrams show events or ideas in the order in which they happened.

First Event → Next Event → Next Event → Last Event

◗ Problem and Solution
Problem-solution patterns identify at least one problem, offer one or more solutions to the problem, and explain or predict outcomes of the solutions.

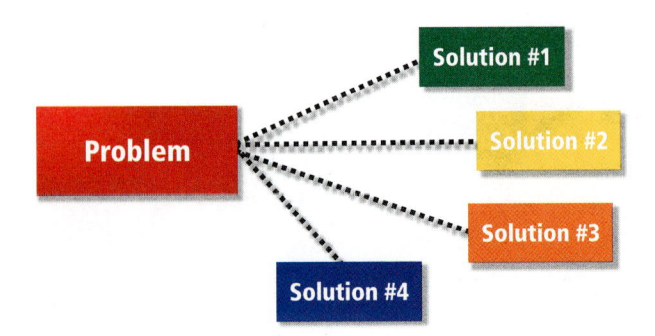

Problem → Solution #1, Solution #2, Solution #3, Solution #4

Skills Handbook

C. Organize Information *(continued)*

Identifying Main Ideas and Supporting Details

One special type of graphic organizer is the concept map. A concept map, sometimes called a semantic map, allows you to zero in on the most important points of the text. The map is made up of lines, boxes, circles, and/or arrows. It can be as simple or as complex as you need it to be to accurately represent the text.

Here are a few examples of concept maps you might use.

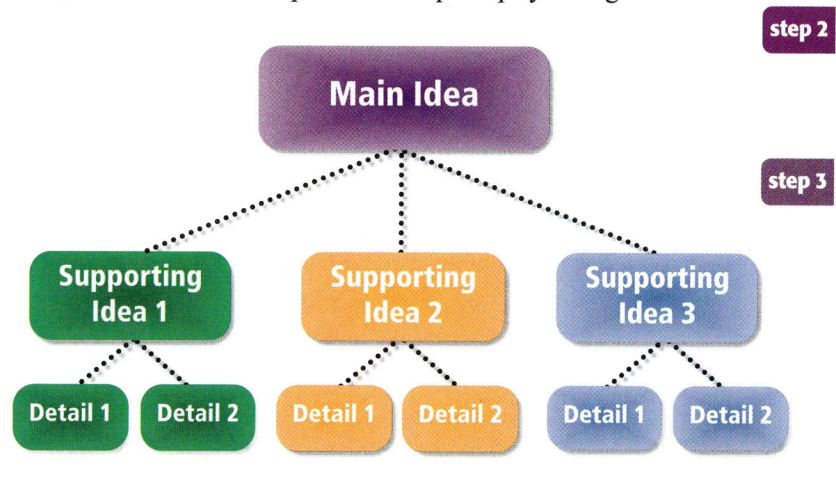

Constructing Concept Maps

step 1 Preview the text, looking at what type of structure might be appropriate to display on a concept map.

step 2 Taking note of the headings, bold-faced type, and text structure, sketch a concept map you think could best illustrate the text.

step 3 Using boxes, lines, arrows, circles, or any shapes you like, display the ideas of the text in the concept map.

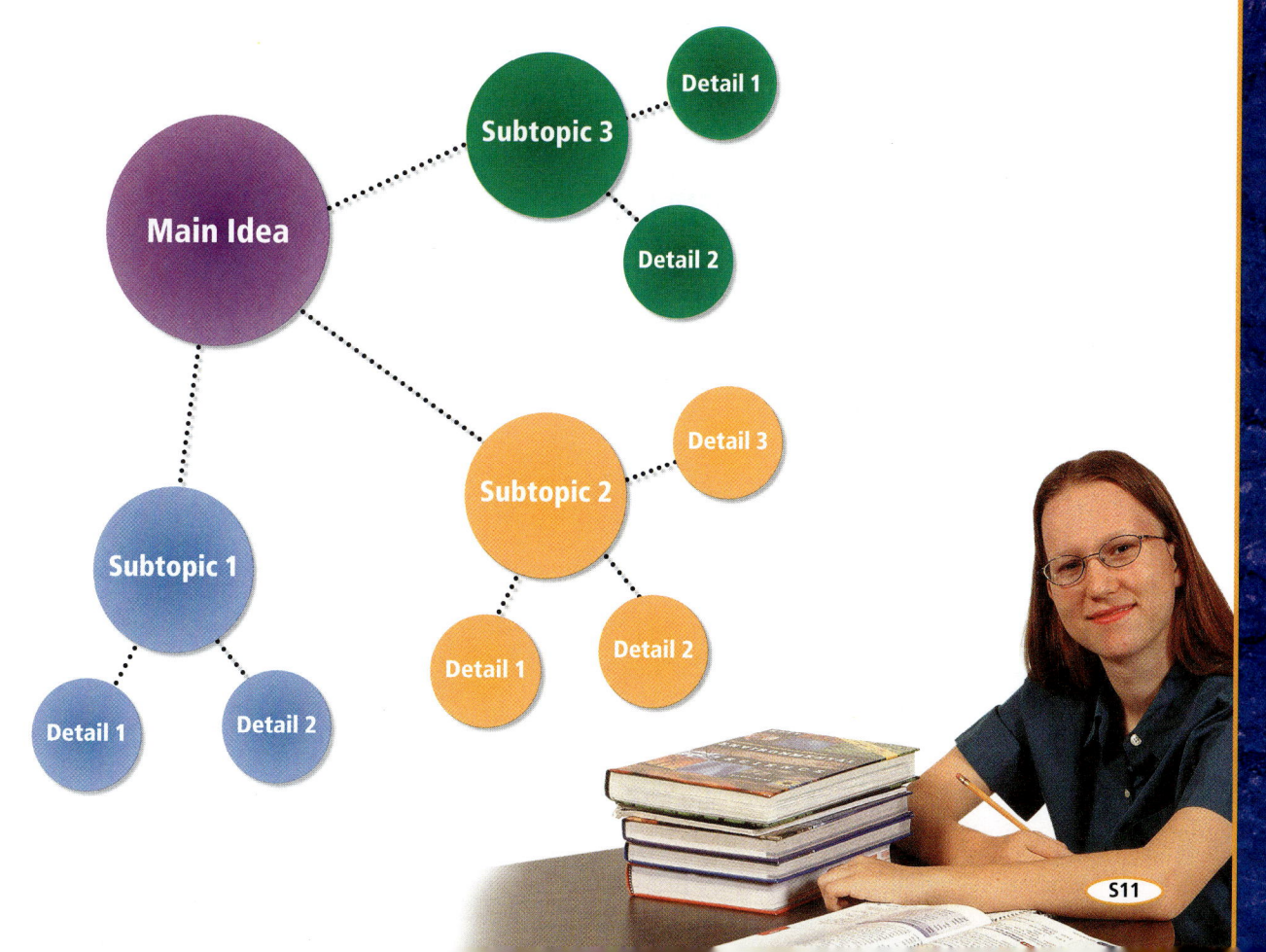

STANDARDIZED TEST-TAKING STRATEGIES

A number of times throughout your school career, you may be asked to take standardized tests. These tests are designed to demonstrate the content and skills you have learned. It is important to keep in mind that in most cases the best way to prepare for these tests is to pay close attention in class and take every opportunity to improve your general social studies, reading, writing, and mathematical skills.

Tips for Taking the Test

1. Be sure that you are well rested.
2. Be on time, and be sure that you have the necessary materials.
3. Listen to the teacher's instructions.
4. Read directions and questions carefully.
5. **DON'T STRESS!** Just remember what you have learned in class, and you should do well.

Practice the strategies at go.hrw.com

STANDARDIZED TEST PREP ONLINE
keyword: SM3 STP

Tackling Social Studies

The social studies portions of many standardized tests are designed to test your knowledge of the content and skills that you have been studying in one or more of your social studies classes. Specific objectives for the test vary, but some of the most common include the following:

1. Demonstrate an understanding of issues and events in history.
2. Demonstrate an understanding of geographic influences on historical issues and events.
3. Demonstrate an understanding of economic and social influences on historical issues and events.
4. Demonstrate an understanding of political influences on historical issues and events.
5. Use critical thinking skills to analyze social studies information.

Standardized tests usually contain multiple-choice and, sometimes, open-ended questions. The multiple-choice items will often be based on maps, tables, charts, graphs, pictures, cartoons, and/or reading passages and documents.

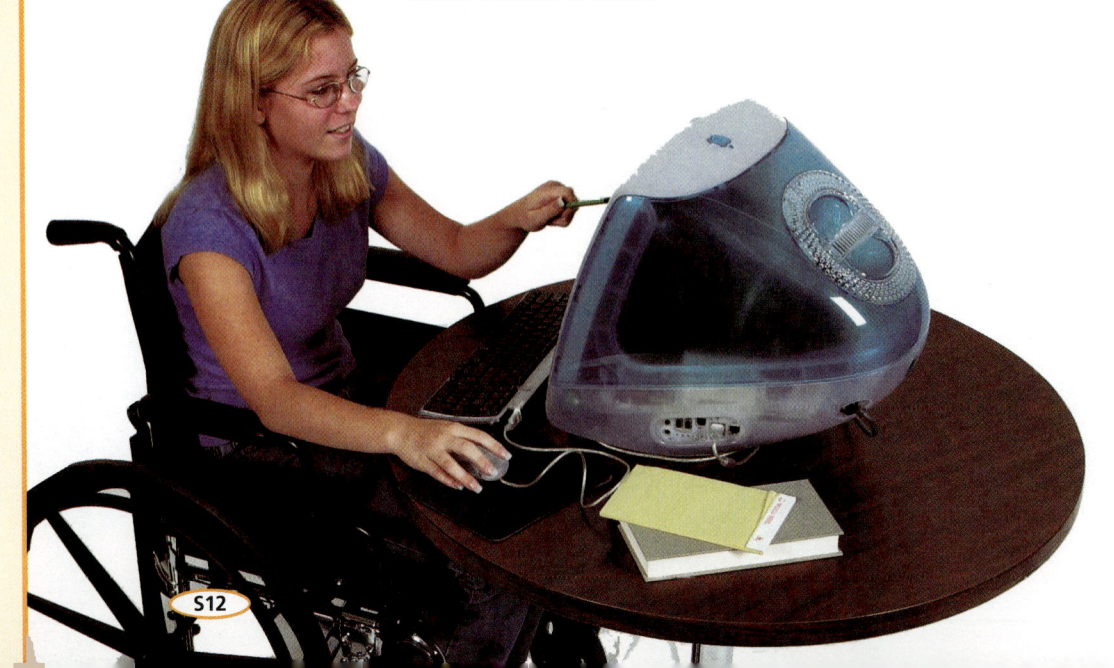

Tips for Answering Multiple-Choice Questions

1. If there is a written or visual piece accompanying the multiple-choice question, pay careful attention to the title, author, and date.
2. Then read through or glance over the content of the written or visual piece accompanying the question to familiarize yourself with it.
3. Next, read the multiple-choice question first for its general intent. Then reread it carefully, looking for words that give clues or can limit possible answers to the question. For example, words such as *most* or *best* tell you that there may be several correct answers to a question, but you should look for the most appropriate answer.
4. Read through the answer choices. Always read all of the possible answer choices even if the first one seems like the correct answer. There may be a better choice farther down in the list.
5. Reread the accompanying information (if any is included) carefully to determine the answer to the question. Again, note the title, author, and date of primary-source selections. The answer will rarely be stated exactly as it appears in the primary source, so you will need to use your critical thinking skills to read between the lines.
6. Think of what you already know about the time in history or person involved and use that to help limit the answer choices.
7. Finally, reread the question and selected answer to be sure that you made the best choice and that you marked it correctly on the answer sheet.

Strategies for Success

There are a variety of strategies you can prepare ahead of time to help you feel more confident about answering questions on social studies standardized tests. Here are a few suggestions:

1. Adopt an acronym—a word formed from the first letters of other words—that you will use for analyzing a document or visual piece that accompanies a question.

Helpful Acronyms

For a document, use SOAPS, which stands for

- **S** Subject
- **O** Overview
- **A** Audience
- **P** Purpose
- **S** Speaker/author

For a picture, cartoon, map, or other visual piece of information, use OPTIC, which stands for

- **O** Occasion (or time)
- **P** Parts (labels or details of the visual)
- **T** Title
- **I** Interrelations (how the different parts of the visual work together)
- **C** Conclusion (what the visual means)

2. Form visual images of maps and try to draw them from memory. Standardized tests will most likely include graphs and charts, showing important economic information about the United States and other countries. For example, you should be able to identify trends in key economic indicators, such as inflation and unemployment. You should also be able to analyze the distribution of natural resources in various regions and explain the importance of this distribution of productivity and the balance of trade.
3. When you have finished studying an economic concept or structure, try to think of who or what might be important enough for a standardized test. You may want to keep your ideas in a notebook to refer to when it is almost time for the test.
4. Standardized tests will likely test your understanding of the political, economic, and social processes that shape a country's history, culture, and geography. Questions may also ask you to understand the impact of economic factors on major events. For example, some may ask about the effects of the business

cycle on the U.S. free-enterprise system. In addition, questions may test your understanding of economic concepts, such as supply and demand, on people's lives.

5. For the skills area of the tests, practice putting major events and personalities in order in your mind. Sequencing people and events by dates can become a game you play with a friend who also has to take the test. Always ask yourself "why" this event is important.

6. Follow the tips under "Ready for Reading" below when you encounter a reading passage in social studies, but remember that what you have learned about economics can help you in answering reading-comprehension questions.

Ready for Reading

The main goal of the reading sections of most standardized tests is to determine your understanding of different aspects of a piece of writing. Basically, if you can grasp the main idea and the writer's purpose and then pay attention to the details and vocabulary so that you are able to draw inferences and conclusions, you will do well on the test.

Tips for Answering Multiple-Choice Questions

1. Read the passage as if you were not taking a test.

2. Look at the big picture. Ask yourself questions like, "What is the title?", "What do the illustrations or pictures tell me?", and "What is the writer's purpose?"

3. Read the questions. This will help you know what information to look for.

4. Reread the passage, underlining information related to the questions.

5. Go back to the questions and try to answer each one in your mind before looking at the answers.

6. Read all the answer choices and eliminate the ones that are obviously incorrect.

Types of Multiple-Choice Questions

1. **Main Idea** This is the most important point of the passage. After reading the passage, locate and underline the main idea.

2. **Significant Details** You will often be asked to recall details from the passage. Read the question and underline the details as you read, but remember that the correct answers do not always match the wording of the passage precisely.

3. **Vocabulary** You will often need to define a word within the context of the passage. Read the answer choices and plug them into the sentence to see what fits best.

4. **Conclusion and Inference** There are often important ideas in the passage that the writer does not state directly. Sometimes you must consider multiple parts of the passage to answer the question. If answers refer to only one or two sentences or details in the passage, they are probably incorrect.

Tips for Answering Short-Answer Questions

1. Read the passage in its entirety, paying close attention to the main events and characters. Jot down information you think is important.

2. If you cannot answer a question, skip it and come back later.

3. Words such as *compare, contrast, interpret, discuss,* and *summarize* appear often in short-answer questions. Be sure you have a complete understanding of each of these words.

4. To help support your answer, return to the passage and skim the parts you underlined.

5. Organize your thoughts on a separate sheet of paper. Write a general statement with which to begin. This will be your topic statement.

6. When writing your answer, be precise but brief. Be sure to refer to details in the passage in your answer.

Targeting Writing

On many standardized tests you will occasionally be asked to write an essay. In order to write a concise essay, you must learn to organize your thoughts before you begin writing the actual composition. This keeps you from straying too far from the essay's topic.

Tips for Answering Composition Questions

1. Read the question carefully.
2. Decide what kind of essay you are being asked to write. Essays usually fall into one of the following types: persuasive, classificatory, compare/contrast, or "how to." To determine the type of essay, ask yourself questions like, "Am I trying to persuade my audience?", "Am I comparing or contrasting ideas?", or "Am I trying to show the reader how to do something?"
3. Pay attention to keywords, such as *compare, contrast, describe, advantages, disadvantages, classify,* or *speculate.* They will give you clues as to the structure that your essay should follow.
4. Organize your thoughts on a separate sheet of paper. You will want to come up with a general topic sentence that expresses your main idea. Make sure this sentence addresses the question. You should then create an outline or some type of graphic organizers to help you organize the points that support your topic sentence.
5. Write your composition using complete sentences. Also, be sure to use correct grammar, spelling, punctuation, and sentence structure.
6. Be sure to proofread your essay once you have finished writing.

Gearing Up for Math

On most standardized tests you will be asked to solve a variety of mathematical problems that draw on the skills and information you have learned in class. If math problems sometimes give you difficulty, have a look at the tips below to help you work through the problems.

Tips for Solving Math Problems

1. Decide what is the goal of the question. Read or study the problem carefully and determine what information must be found.
2. Locate the factual information. Decide what information represents key facts—the ones you must have to solve the problem. You may also find facts you do not need to reach your solution. In some cases, you may determine that more information is needed to solve the problem. If so, ask yourself, "What assumptions can I make about this problem?" or "Do I need a formula to help solve this problem?"
3. Decide what strategies you might use to solve the problem, how you might use them, and what form your solution will be in. For example, will you need to create a graph or chart? Will you need to solve an equation? Will your answer be in words or numbers? By knowing what type of solution you should reach, you may be able to eliminate some of the choices.
4. Apply your strategy to solve the problem and compare your answer to the choices.
5. If the answer is still not clear, read the problem again. If you had to make calculations to reach your answer, use estimation to see if your answer makes sense.

INTERACTIVE SKILL-BUILDER

Economics is a part of almost every aspect of our daily lives. To grasp this relationship, you will need to understand the forces that shape economics. The skills covered in this handbook will enable you to analyze economic concepts and processes. The handbook will also introduce you to key sources of economic information that can be presented in a variety of forms. Your understanding and appreciation of economics will grow as your study skills improve. Your study of economics also will provide you with opportunities to sharpen your research, writing, and test-taking abilities.

1 FINDING THE MAIN IDEA

In the study of economics, significant events and concepts sometimes get lost among surrounding issues. The ability to identify central elements is a key to understanding any complex issue. This book is designed to help you focus on the most important concepts in economics. The focus questions at the beginning of each section are intended to guide your reading and the chapter summary reinforces the main ideas presented. But not everything you read is structured this way. Applying these general guidelines will help you identify the main ideas in what you read.

How to Identify the Main Idea

Read any introductory material. Read the title and the introduction, if there is one, which may point out the material's main ideas.

Have questions in mind. Formulate questions about the subject that you think might be answered by the material. Having such questions in mind will focus your reading.

Note the outline of ideas. Pay attention to any headings or subheadings, which may provide a basic outline of the major ideas.

Distinguish supporting details. As you read, distinguish sentences providing additional details from the general statements they support. A trail of facts, for instance, may lead to a conclusion that expresses a main idea.

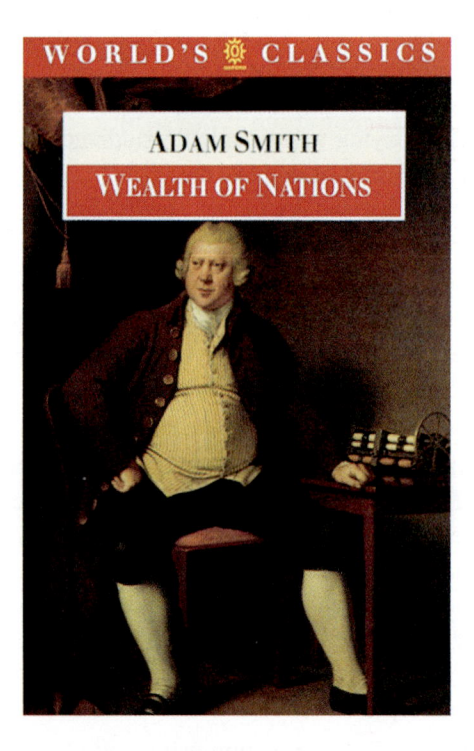

Applying Your Skill

Read the paragraph below, from the Chapter 6 subsection "Era of Big Business," to identify its main idea.

"At first the U.S. government did not interfere with the trusts [huge monopolies]. Most economists and policy-makers at the time believed firmly in a laissez-faire economic philosophy. This philosophy states that economic systems prosper when the government does not interfere with the market in any way. (Laissez-faire is a French term meaning 'let people do [as they will].') Thus, the federal

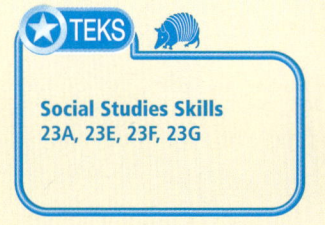

★ TEKS

Social Studies Skills
23A, 23E, 23F, 23G

SKILLS HANDBOOK

government initially favored leaving the market and the trusts alone."

As the lead sentence indicates, the paragraph focuses on the nature of government involvement in the U.S. economy at a specific point in time. Details about economic philosophy are included to provide background and a more complete understanding of the government's actions. The main idea is clearly stated in the final sentence.

Practicing Your Skill TEKS

Now read the third paragraph of the subsection on page 130 and answer the following questions.
1. What is the paragraph's main idea? How does the writer support that idea?
2. What is the relationship between the main ideas in this paragraph and the one excerpted above? Combine them into one statement that summarizes both paragraphs.

2 IDENTIFYING CAUSE AND EFFECT

Identifying and understanding cause-and-effect relationships is fundamental to interpreting economic concepts. A *cause* is any action that leads to an event; the outcome of that action is an *effect*. To investigate both why an economic event took place and what happened as a result of that event, economists ask questions such as What is the immediate activity that triggered the event? and What is the background leading up to the event? Your task is simpler than the economist's: to trace what he or she has already determined or theorized about the web of actions and outcomes.

How to Identify Cause and Effect

Look for clues. Certain words and phrases are immediate clues to the existence of a cause-and-effect relationship.

Cause & Effect Clues

as a result of	aftermath of
because	as a consequence of
brought about	depended on
inspired	gave rise to
led to	originated from
produced	outcome
provoked	outgrowth
the reason for	proceeded from
spurred	resulted in

Identify the relationship. Read carefully to identify how events are related. Writers do not always directly state the link between cause and effect. Sometimes a reader has to *infer*, or determine, the cause or the effect from the information.

Check for complex connections. Beyond the immediate, or superficial, cause and effect, check for other, more complex connections. Note, for example, whether (1) there were additional causes of a given effect; (2) a cause had multiple effects; and (3) these effects in turn caused any additional effects.

Applying Your Skill

The diagram below presents an important cause-and-effect relationship in the concept of demand. The diagram describes the effects of price ceilings on rents. Note how an effect may in turn become a cause.

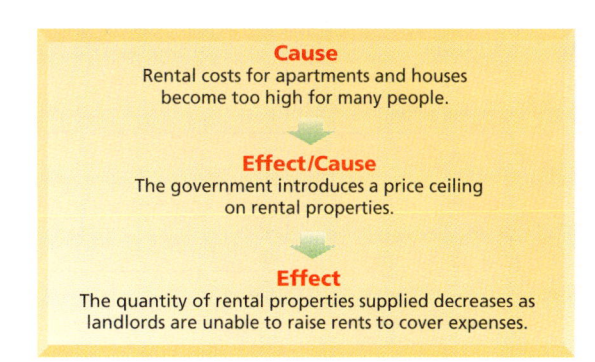

Cause
Rental costs for apartments and houses become too high for many people.

↓

Effect/Cause
The government introduces a price ceiling on rental properties.

↓

Effect
The quantity of rental properties supplied decreases as landlords are unable to raise rents to cover expenses.

Practicing Your Skill TEKS

Think about your own economic activities, such as holding a part-time job or buying a concert ticket. Show how cause and effect have played a role in your choices. Draw a chart showing the relationships between the actions and the outcomes. Then write a paragraph that explains the connections.

Practicing Your Skill Answers

Students should read the paragraph that starts, "By the 1800s, however, many people...," on page 130.

1. The paragraph's main idea is that the federal government passed several laws in the 1880s intended to control unfair business practices in the United States. The writer supports this idea by stating that the reason the government changed its economic philosophy toward trusts was because people had grown concerned over the power of the trusts. ★23A

2. The U.S. federal government, which favored a laissez-faire economic policy, initially left trusts alone. However, during the 1880s, the American public grew increasingly concerned over the amount of control the trusts had over the economy. In response to this concern, the government passed a number of important laws intended to control unfair business practices in the United States. ★23A

Practicing Your Skill Answers

To assess this skill activity, see Rubric 6: Cause and Effect and Rubric 7: Charts in the *Alternative Assessment Handbook*. ★23A

SKILLS HANDBOOK S17

3 DISTINGUISHING FACT FROM OPINION

The ability to distinguish facts from opinions is essential in judging the soundness of an argument or the reliability of an economic analysis. A fact can be proved or observed; an opinion, on the other hand, is a personal belief or conclusion. One often hears facts and opinions mixed in everyday conversation—as well as in advertising, political debate, and government policy statements. Thus, in an argument, opinions do not carry as much weight as facts, although some opinions can be supported by facts.

How to Distinguish Fact from Opinion

Identify the facts. Begin by asking yourself whether the statement at hand can be proven. Determine whether the idea can be checked for accuracy in a source such as an almanac or encyclopedia. If so, it is probably factual. If not, it probably contains an opinion.

Identify the opinions. Look for clues that signal a statement of opinion—for example: phrases such as *I think* or *I believe*. Comparative words like *greatest* or *more important* and value-laden words like *extremely* or *ridiculous* imply a judgment, and thus an opinion.

Reprinted with permission, "Star Tribune", Minneapolis

STEVE SACK
Courtesy Minneapolis Star-Tribune

Applying Your Skill

Economic policy reflects the opinions of decision makers. For example, read the following excerpt from President Franklin D. Roosevelt's first inaugural address.

"Values have shrunken to fantastic levels; taxes have risen; our ability to pay has fallen; government of all kinds is faced by serious curtailment [shortening] of income; the means of exchange are frozen in the currents of trade; the withered leaves of industrial enterprise lie on every side; farmers find no markets for their produce; the savings of many years in thousands of families are gone. . . .

"Our greatest primary task is to put people to work. This is no unsolvable problem if we face it wisely and courageously. It can be accomplished in part by direct recruiting by the government itself, treating the task as we would treat the emergency of war, but at the same time, through this employment, accomplishing greatly needed projects to stimulate and reorganize the use of our natural resources. . . ."

While the first paragraph in this excerpt presents facts that can be proven or disproven, the second paragraph presents Roosevelt's opinion of how the government should respond to the Great Depression.

Practicing Your Skill

The excerpt that follows is from Andrew Carnegie's essay "The Gospel of Wealth." Read the excerpt and answer the questions on the next page.

"This, then, is held to be the duty of the man of wealth: To set an example of modest . . . living, shunning display or extravagance; to provide moderately [reasonably] for the legitimate [proper] wants of those dependent upon him; and, after doing so, to consider all surplus revenues which come to him simply as trust funds, which he is called upon to administer . . . as a matter of

---

Practicing Your Skill
Answers

1. statement of opinion ⭐23E
2. He uses the words *duty, trust funds, trustee, agent,* and *ability to administer.* ⭐23E
3. Carnegie has a high opinion of the wealthy, which is evident through his use of the following phrase to describe how the wealthy can help the poor: "bringing to their service his superior wisdom, experience, and ability to administer, doing for them better than they would or could do for themselves." ⭐23E

SKILLS HANDBOOK

duty in the manner which, in his judgment, is best calculated to produce the most beneficial results for the community—the man of wealth thus becoming the mere trustee and agent for his poorer brethren, bringing to their service his superior wisdom, experience, and ability to administer, doing for them better than they would or could do for themselves. . . ."

1. Is this excerpt a statement of fact or a statement of opinion?
2. What words does Carnegie use to describe why the wealthy should support those with more limited finances?
3. Which words provide clues to Carnegie's view of the wealthy?

4 BUILDING VOCABULARY

The study of economics may challenge your reading comprehension. You will probably encounter many new and unfamiliar words. But with regular effort you can master them and turn reading economics into an opportunity to enlarge your vocabulary. Following the steps outlined below will assist you in this endeavor.

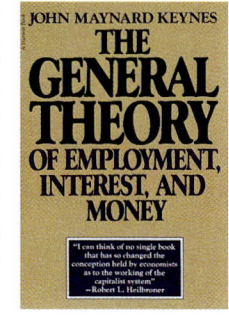

How to Build Vocabulary

Identify unusual words. As you read, be aware of words that you cannot pronounce or define. Keep a list of these words. Words that are somewhat familiar are the easiest to learn.

Study context clues. Study the sentence and paragraph carefully where you find each new term. This *context*, or setting, may give you clues to the word's meaning. The word may be defined by either an example or another, more familiar word that means the same thing.

Use the dictionary. Use a dictionary to help you pronounce and define the words on your list. Review new vocabulary. Look for ways to use the new words—in homework assignments, conversation, or classroom discussions. The best way to master a new word is to use it.

Practicing Your Skill

1. What is context? How can it provide clues to a word's meaning?
2. As you read a chapter, list any unusual words that you find. Write down what you think each word means, and then check your definitions against those that you find in a dictionary.

5 CONDUCTING RESEARCH

To complete research papers or special projects, you may need to use resources beyond this textbook. For example, you may want to research specific subjects or business organizations not discussed here, or to learn additional information about a certain topic. Doing such research typically involves using the resources available in a library.

```
The general theory of employment, interest, and money
    by John Maynard Keynes.
    San Diego : Harcourt, Brace, Jovanovich, 1964 [1991 printing]
    xii, 403 p. : ill. ; 21 cm.
    Originally published: 1953.
    "A Harvest/HBJ book."
    Includes bibliographical references and index.
Subjects:
    Economics.
    Money.
    Monetary policy.
    Interest.
Search for other works by:
    Keynes, John Maynard, 1883-1946.
```

Language	Call Number	LCCN	Dewey Decimal	ISBN/ISSN
English (eng)	HB99.7 .K378 1964	91006533 //r91	330.15/6	0156347113 : $8.95

Practicing Your Skill Answers

1. Context refers to setting, that is, the words or sentences that surround a word or phrase. The context can provide clues to the meaning of an unknown word because the surrounding sentences may provide a definition of the word or examples that clarify the word's meaning.

2. Encourage students to use the glossary in the back of the textbook or the Electronic Glossary on the *Holt Researcher CD-ROM* to look up the meaning of any economics terms that they do not understand.

Practicing Your Skill Answers ⭐23E

1. the Dewey decimal system and the Library of Congress system

2. specialized CD-ROMs, encyclopedias, economic dictionaries, almanacs (e.g., *The World Almanac, Book of Facts*), yearbooks, periodical indexes

3. periodical indexes, such as the *Readers' Guide to Periodical Literature* and the *New York Times Index*

How to Find Information

To find a particular book, you need to know how libraries organize their materials. Books of fiction are alphabetized according to the last name of the author. To classify nonfiction books, libraries use the Dewey decimal system and the Library of Congress system. Both systems assign each book a *call number* that tells you where it is shelved.

To find a particular book's call number, look in the library's *card catalog*. The catalog lists books by author, by title, and by subject. If you know the author or title of the book, finding it is simple. If you do not know this information, or if you just want to find any book about a general subject, look under an applicable subject heading. Many libraries have computerized card catalogs. These catalogs generally contain the same information as a traditional card catalog, but take up less space and are easier to update and to access.

Librarians can assist you in using the card catalog and direct you to a book's location. They also can suggest additional resources. Many libraries now rely on computerized resources and have access to the Internet. Specialized CD–ROMs such as the *Holt Researcher CD–ROM: Economics and Government* also provide access to statistics and other government information.

How to Use Resources

In a library's reference section, you will find encyclopedias, specialized dictionaries, atlases, almanacs, and indexes to material in magazines and newspapers. *Encyclopedias* often will be your best resource. Encyclopedias include economic, political, and geographic data on individual nations, states, and cities, as well as biographical sketches of important historical figures. Entries often include cross-references to related articles.

Specialized dictionaries exist for almost every field. For example, an economics dictionary will focus on defining economic concepts.

To find up-to-date facts about a subject, you can use almanacs, yearbooks, and periodical indexes. References like *The World Almanac and Book of Facts* include economic information and a variety of statistics about population, the environment, sports, and so on. Encyclopedia yearbooks keep up with recent, significant developments not fully covered in encyclopedia articles.

Periodical indexes, particularly *Readers' Guide to Periodical Literature*, can help you locate informative, current articles published in magazines. The *New York Times Index* catalogs the news stories published in the *Times*—the U.S. daily newspaper with perhaps the most in-depth coverage of national and world events.

Practicing Your Skill ⭐TEKS

1. In what two ways are nonfiction books classified?

2. What kinds of references contain information about economics?

3. Where would you look to find the most recent coverage of a political or social issue?

6 ANALYZING PRIMARY SOURCES

There are many sources of firsthand economic information, including editorials, policy statements, and legal documents. All of these are primary sources. Newspaper reports and editorial cartoons also are considered to be primary sources, although they are generally written after the fact. Because they permit a close-up look at a given topic—and often a chance to get inside people's minds—primary sources are valuable analytical tools.

Secondary sources are descriptions or interpretations of events that are written after the events have occurred and by persons who did not participate in the events describe. Books such as *Holt Economics*, biographies, encyclopedias, and other reference works are secondary sources.

How to Analyze Primary Sources ⭐TEKS

1. Study the material carefully. Consider the nature of the material. Is it verbal or visual? Is it

SKILLS HANDBOOK

based on firsthand information or on the accounts of others? What is the author's frame of reference? Note the major ideas and details.

2. Consider the audience.
Ask yourself: For whom was this message originally meant? Whether a message was intended, for instance, for the general public or for a specific, private audience may have shaped its style or content.

3. Check for bias.
Watch for words or phrases that present a one-sided view of a person or situation. Determine if the information represents fact or opinion, or is a piece of propaganda.

4. When possible, compare sources.
Study more than one source on a topic. Comparing sources gives you a more complete, balanced account of the topic.

Practicing Your Skill

1. What distinguishes secondary sources from primary sources?
2. What advantage do secondary sources have over primary sources?
3. Of the following, identify which are primary and which are secondary sources: a newspaper, a biography, an editorial cartoon, a deed to property, a snapshot of a family vacation, a magazine article about the economics of Thailand. How might some of these sources prove to be both primary and secondary sources?

7 WRITING ABOUT ECONOMICS

Holt Economics presents several writing opportunities in the Section Reviews, Chapter Reviews, and Unit Labs. Following these guidelines will improve your writing about economics as well as other subjects.

How to Write with a Purpose

Always keep your purpose for writing in mind. That purpose might be to analyze, evaluate, synthesize, inform, persuade, hypothesize, or take a stand. As you begin, your purpose will determine the most appropriate approach to take and when you are done, it will help you evaluate your success.

Each purpose for writing requires its own form, tone, and content. The point of view you are adopting will shape what you write, as will your intended audience: whoever will be reading what you write.

Some writing assignments in *Holt Economics* ask you to create a specific type of writing, such as a newspaper editorial or an advertisement.

- A newspaper *editorial* is a public statement of an opinion or a viewpoint. It takes a stand on an issue and gives reasons for that stand.
- An *advertisement* is an announcement to promote a product or an event. Effective ads are direct and to the point, and use memorable language, such as jingles and slogans, to highlight important features.

How to Write a Paper or an Essay

Each writing opportunity will have specific directions about what and how to write. Regardless of the particular topic you choose, you should follow certain basic steps.

There are five major stages to writing a paper or essay: prewriting, creating an outline, writing a first draft, evaluating and revising your draft to

---

Practicing Your Skill Answers

1. Primary sources are firsthand accounts or sources of information. Secondary sources are descriptions or interpretations of events that are written after the events have occurred and by persons who did not participate in the events they are describing.

2. secondary sources, because they are written after the fact, and thus often can provide a more unbiased and complete description or interpretation of an event than a primary source does

3. primary—newspaper, editorial cartoon, deed to property, snapshot of family vacation; secondary—magazine article about the economics of Thailand; newspapers and magazines may contain both primary and secondary source material. Newspapers may have articles interpreting historical events, and magazine articles may include excerpts from primary source documents

SKILLS HANDBOOK S21

eliminate any awkward passages, and proofreading and producing a final draft of your paper for presentation. Each of these stages can be further divided into more specific steps and tasks. The guidelines outlined below can help you improve your writing abilities.

Prewriting

Choose a topic. Select a topic for your paper. Take care to narrow your subject so that you will be able to develop and support a clear argument.

Identify your purpose for writing the essay or paper. Read the directions carefully to identify the purpose for your writing. Keep that purpose in mind as you plan and write your paper.

Determine your audience. When writing for a specific audience, choose the tone and style that will best communicate your message.

Collect information. Write down your ideas and the information you already know about your topic, and do additional research if necessary. Your writing will be more effective if you have many details at hand.

```
              Communism in the Soviet Union
  I. Political philosophies of Marx
 II. Rise of communism
     A. War communism
        1. Private property abolished
        2. Land redistributed
        3. Factories brought under government control
     B. New Economic Policy
        1. Some private incentives restored
        2. Larger enterprises controlled by government
     C. Stalin's rule
        1. Introduced Five-Year Plans
        2. Emphasized heavy industries
        3. Began system of collectivization
     D. Central planning
     E. Production
        1. Shift toward more consumer goods after Stalin's death
        2. Low agricultural output necessitated food imports
     F. Soviet problems
III. Beginnings of reform
     A. Collapse of the Soviet Union
        1. Dissatisfaction with standard of living
        2. Perestroika introduced by Gorbachev
        3. Price hikes failed to correct shortages
        4. Republics of Soviet Union declare independence
     B. Russian reform
        1. Yeltsin begins transition to market capitalism
        2. Prices and production largely free of government control
        3. Many state-owned firms privatized
```

How to Create an Outline

Think and plan before you begin writing your first draft. Organize themes, main ideas, and supporting details into an outline.

Order your material. Decide what information you want to emphasize or focus on. Order or classify your material with that in mind. Determine what information belongs in an introduction, what should make up the body of your paper, and what to leave for the conclusion.

Identify main ideas. Identify the main ideas to be highlighted in each section. Make these your outline's main headings.

List supporting details. Determine the important details or facts that support each main idea. Rank and list them as subheadings, using additional levels of subheadings as necessary. Never break a category into subheadings unless there at least two: no As without Bs, no 1s without 2s.

Put your outline to use. Structure your essay or report according to your outline. Each main heading, for instance, might form the basis for a topic sentence to begin a paragraph. Subheadings would then make up the content of the paragraph. In a more lengthy paper, each subheading might be the main idea of a paragraph.

Writing the Draft

In your first draft, remember to use your outline as a guide. Each paragraph should express a single main idea or set of related ideas, with details for support. Be careful to show the relationships between ideas and to use proper *transitions*—sentences that build connections between paragraphs.

Evaluating and Revising the Draft

Review and edit. Revise and reorganize your draft as needed to make your points. Improve sentences by adding appropriate adjectives and adverbs. Omit words, sentences, or paragraphs that are unnecessary or unrelated to a main idea. Check your work to make sure you have covered all details.

Evaluate your writing style. Make your writing clearer by varying the sentence length and rephrasing awkward sentences. Replace inexact wording with more precise word choices.

Proofreading

Proofread your paper carefully. Check for proper spelling, punctuation, and grammar.

Write your final version. Prepare a neat and clean final version. Appearance is important; it may not affect the quality of your writing itself, but it can affect the way your writing is perceived and understood.

Practicing Your Skill

1. What factor—more than any other—should affect how and what you write? Why?
2. Why is it important to consider the audience for your writing?
3. What is involved in the editing of a first draft?

8 LEARNING FROM VISUALS

Visuals are graphic images that can provide information about culture and society. These clues are available in a broad range of formats, including photographs, paintings, television, web sites, and political cartoons. Visual images record a large amount of diverse data. To extract this data, you must carefully examine the details in the image.

How to Study Visuals

Identify the subject. Look at the content of the picture. What is the main focus? For example, is it a group of people, a building, or a particular event? Who is the intended audience? What do you think the creator of the image is trying to convey? Read the title, captions or listen to the dialogue to pick up clues to its subject matter.

Examine the details. Gather subtle information from the image. Are there clues about time or place? Look at details such as clothing style, architecture, and the arrangement of the image's components to further evaluate its effect and meaning.

Identify the tone. Most people think that visuals present only facts. A visual image, however, also exposes feelings about a subject. What do the images reveal about peoples' feelings? How do you feel when you look at the picture? Does it make you laugh, or feel sad or angry? Try to identify what specific elements in the image evoke this feeling.

Put the data to use. Combine the information you gathered from the visual images and written or spoken words to analyze a particular subject.

Practicing Your Skill

1. What is the subject of the cartoon on this page?
2. What symbols and images does the cartoonist use to convey his message?
3. What is the cartoonist's opinion about Greenspan's economic policy? Do you agree? Explain your answer.

(Continued from page S23)

of restraining inflation. A couple in bed represent the American public. Having been asleep, they are unaware of what is really going on and are surprised that inflation is a problem. They are growing fearful of it all the same because of the Fed's warnings. ⭐23E

3. that it is an over-reaction; answers will vary. ⭐23E

Practicing Your Skill
Answers ⭐23F, 23G

1. public opinion of current (1992) economic conditions in the United States

2. The data is presented in the form of percentages so that readers can know immediately how many people out of the total sample thought a certain way. If the poll gives numbers instead of percentages, it is not clear if the numbers represent a large or small part of those polled unless the total sample size is provided as well.

3. that the majority of those polled rated U.S. economic conditions in 1992 as either poor or fair

9. UNDERSTANDING MEASUREMENT CONCEPTS AND METHODS

Measurements can give us information about the magnitude, amount, or size of a particular item. Measurements usually are presented in the form of numbers. Finding the information you need from these numbers however, may be difficult unless you know what to look for. Understanding measurement methods and learning to read the results of measurements is key to learning about economics and many other subjects.

Many measurements in *Holt Economics* are statistics. These are facts presented in the form of numbers and are typically arranged to show applicable information about a subject. Statistics often are presented in the form of percentages or ratios.

READING PUBLIC OPINION POLLS

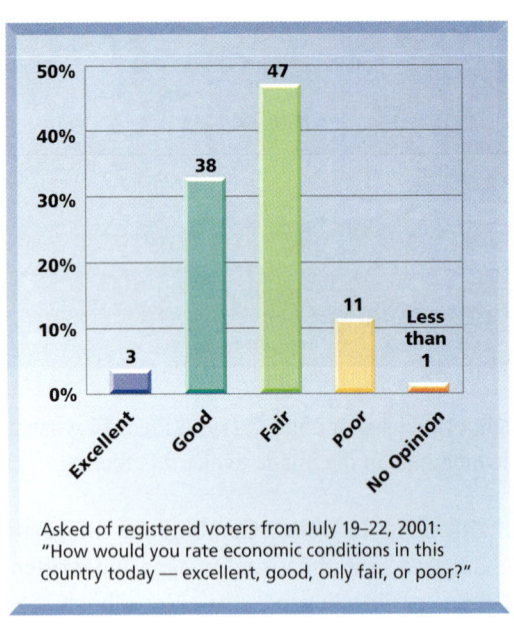

Rating	Percentage
Excellent	3
Good	38
Fair	47
Poor	11
No Opinion	Less than 1

Asked of registered voters from July 19–22, 2001: "How would you rate economic conditions in this country today — excellent, good, only fair, or poor?"

Source: *The Gallup Poll: 2001*

Measurements can provide a wide variety of information. For example, you might read measurements that tell you how many people in your state agree with raising the speed limits or what the rate of inflation was over the past year.

How to Read Measurements ⭕TEKS

Look for clues. Use the information presented with measurements to help you understand their significance. If the measurements appear in a chart or graph, read the title or labels to find clues. If the numbers appear in the text, read the paragraph surrounding them to gain more information.

Identify form. What form is the measurement in? Is it expressed as a percentage? a ratio?

Evaluate the method and purpose of measurement. How was the data collected—through a poll, government census, or price analysis? Why was this information collected and who will use it?

Put the data to use. Use the information in the measurement to build a mental picture of the data or group described. Draw conclusions from the information presented.

Practicing the Skill

1. What is the subject of this data?
2. Why do you think the data is presented in the form of percentages?
3. What conclusions can be drawn from the data?

10. UNDERSTANDING CHARTS AND GRAPHS

Charts and graphs are means of organizing and presenting information visually. They categorize and display data in a variety of ways, depending on their subject. Several types of charts and graphs are used in this textbook.

Charts

Charts commonly used in economics include tables, flowcharts, and organizational charts. A *table* lists and categorizes information. A *flowchart* shows a sequence of events or the steps in a

SKILLS HANDBOOK

CIRCULAR FLOW MODEL OF GOODS AND SERVICES

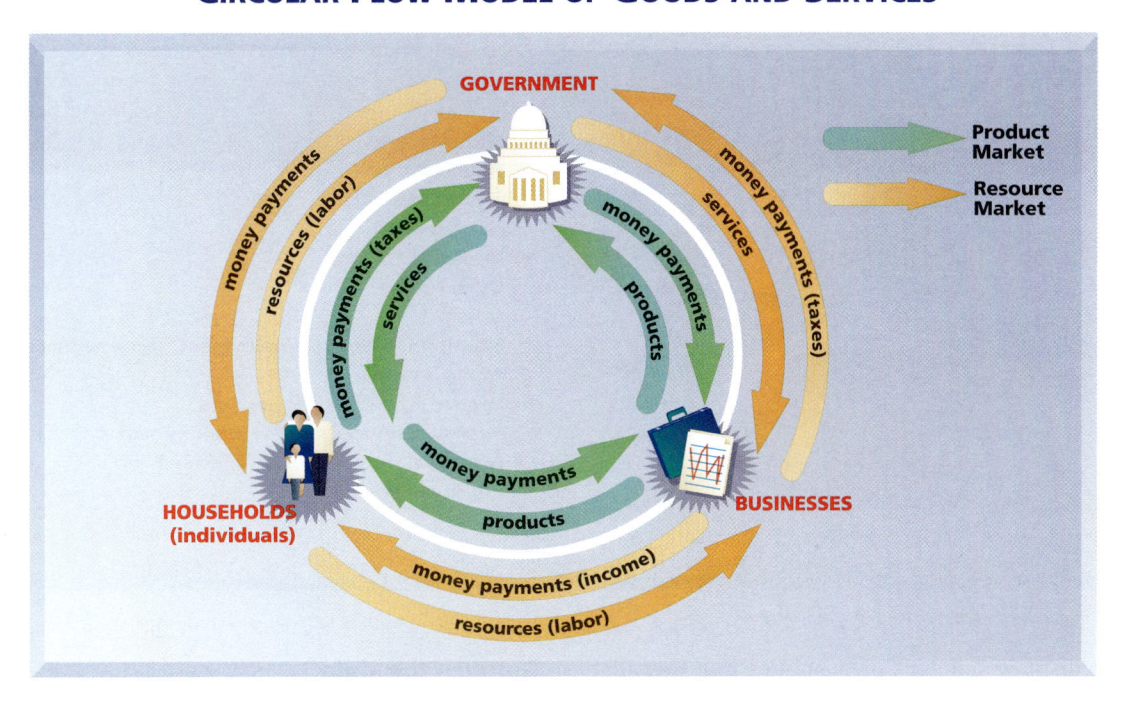

process. Cause-and-effect relationships are often shown by flowcharts. For example, see the Circular Flow Model of Goods and Services chart. An *organizational chart* displays the structure of an organization, indicating the ranking or function of its internal parts and the relationships among them.

How to Read a Chart

Read the title. Read the title to identify the focus or purpose of the chart.

Study the chart's elements. Read the chart's headings, subheadings, and labels to identify the categories used and the specific data given for each category.

Analyze the details. When reading quantities, note increases or decreases in amounts. When reading dates, note intervals of time. When viewing an organizational or flowchart, follow directional arrows or lines.

Put the data to use. Form generalizations or draw conclusions based on the data.

Graphs

There are several types of graphs, each of which is well suited for a particular purpose. A *line graph* plots information by dots connected by a line. This line also can be called a *curve*. A line graph such as the one below shows changes or trends. A *bar*

PRODUCTION CURVE

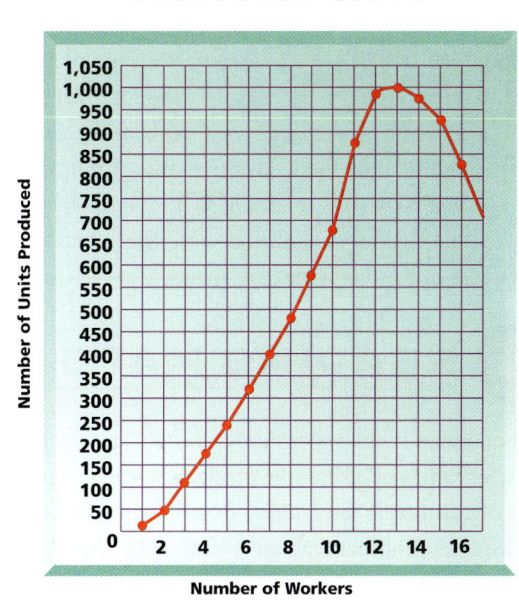

SKILLS HANDBOOK S25

FEDERAL EXPENDITURES, 2000

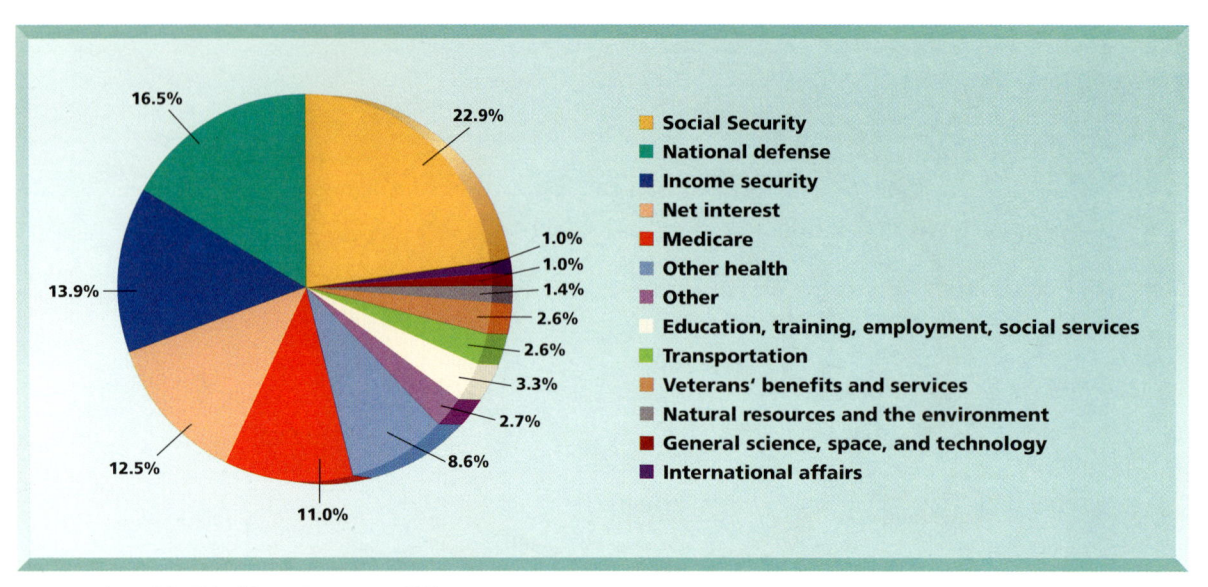

22.9%	Social Security
16.5%	National defense
13.9%	Income security
12.5%	Net interest
11.0%	Medicare
8.6%	Other health
2.7%	Other
3.3%	Education, training, employment, social services
2.6%	Transportation
2.6%	Veterans' benefits and services
1.4%	Natural resources and the environment
1.0%	General science, space, and technology
1.0%	International affairs

Source: *Budget of the United States Government: 2000*

graph displays amounts or quantities in a way that makes comparisons easy. A *pie graph*, or *circle graph*, such as the one above, displays proportions by showing sections of a whole as if they were slices of a pie.

How to Read a Graph

Read the title. Read the title to identify the subject and purpose of the graph. Note the kind of graph it is, remembering what each kind is designed to emphasize.

Study the labels. To identify the type of information presented in the graph, read the label for each axis. The *horizontal axis* runs from left to right, generally at the bottom of the graph, while the *vertical axis* runs up and down, generally along the left-hand side. In addition, note the intervals of any dates or amounts that are listed.

Analyze the data. Note increases or decreases in quantities. Look for trends, relationships, and changes in the data.

Put the data to use. Use the results of your analysis to form generalizations and draw conclusions.

Applying Your Skill

Study the pie graph above. You can see how the federal government plans expenditures.

Practicing Your Skill ★TEKS

Use the line graph "Production Curve" on page S25 to answer the following questions:

1. Describe the type of data illustrated and the intervals used for (a) the horizontal axis and (b) the vertical axis.
2. What generalizations or conclusions can you draw from the information in this graph?

11 READING MAPS

Economics and geography often are related. Economics describes the production and consumption of resources. Geography describes how physical environments affect human events and how people influence the environment around them. Geographers have developed six essential elements—the world in spatial terms, places and regions, physical systems, human systems, environment and society, and the uses of geography—to organize this information into a format that is useful for everyone.

**Practicing Your Skill
Answers** ★23F

1. The graph illustrates worker productivity (the number of units that different numbers of workers can produce). The graph also illustrates the law of diminishing returns, covered in Chapter 4. The horizontal axis provides data in intervals of two; the vertical axis provides data in intervals of 50.

2. Increasing the number of workers increases the number of units produced, up to a certain point. Past this point, increasing the number of workers results in decreased production.

Geographic information for all six elements can be presented in text or represented visually in maps. Maps convey a wealth of varied information through colors, lines, symbols, and labels. To read and interpret maps, you must understand their language and symbols.

Types of Maps

A map is an illustration drawn to scale of all or part of the earth's surface. Types of maps include physical maps, political maps, and special-purpose maps. *Physical maps* illustrate the natural landscape of an area. *Physical maps* often use shading to show relief—the rises and falls in the surface of the land—and colors to show elevation, or height above sea level.

Political maps illustrate political units such as states and nations, by employing color variations, lines to mark boundaries, dots for major cities, and stars or stars within circles for capitals. Political maps show information such as territorial changes or military alliances. See the map on page S28.

Special-purpose maps present specific information such as the routes of explorers, the outcome of an election, regional economic activity, or population density. The map shown below is a special-purpose map.

Many maps combine various features of the types listed above. For example, a map may combine information from a political and a special-purpose map by showing national boundaries as well as trade routes.

Map Features

Most maps have a number of features in common. Familiarity with these basic elements makes reading any map easier.

Titles, legends, and labels
A map's *title* tells you what the map is about, what area is shown, and usually, what time period is being represented. The *legend*, or key, explains symbols, colors, or shadings used on the map. *Labels* designate political and geographic place-names as well as physical features like mountain ranges, oceans, and rivers.

The global grid
The *absolute location* of any place on the earth is given in terms of *latitude* (degrees north or south of the equator) and *longitude* (degrees east or west of the prime meridian). The symbol for a degree is °. Degrees are divided into 60 equal parts called minutes, which are represented by the symbol '. The global grid is created by the intersecting lines of latitude (parallels) and lines of longitude (meridians). Lines of latitude and

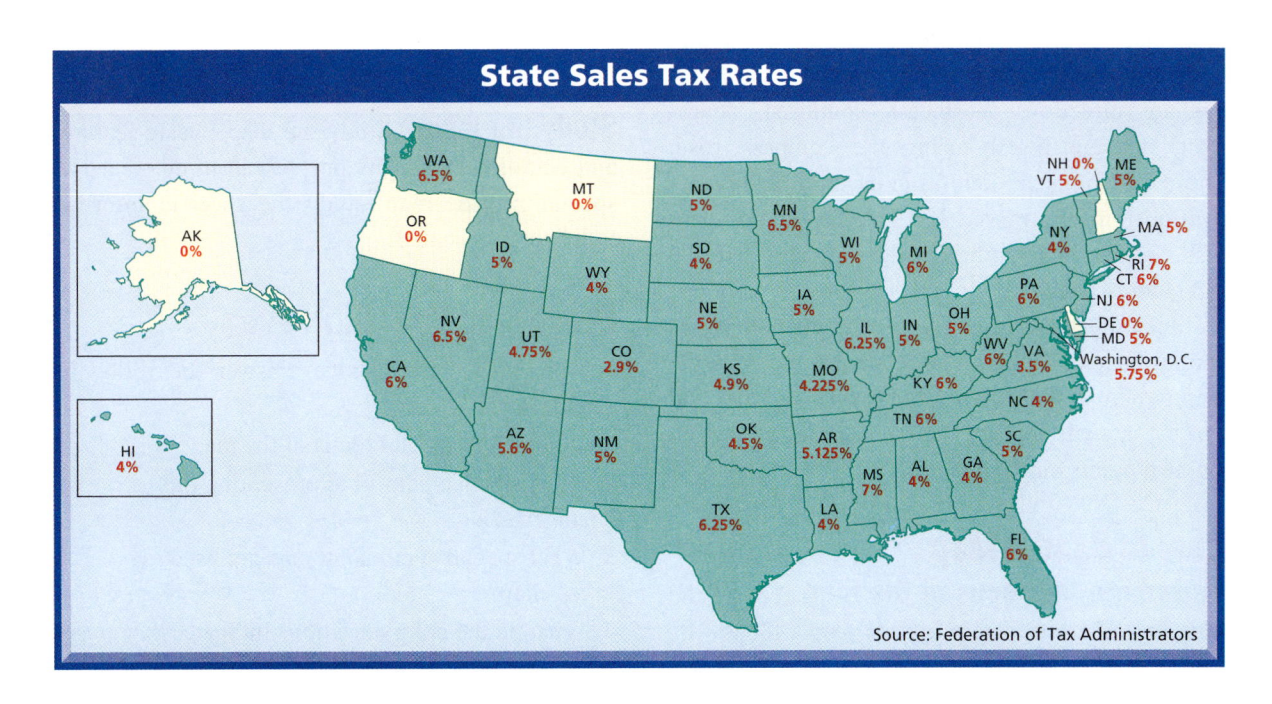

State Sales Tax Rates

State	Rate	State	Rate	State	Rate
AK	0%	KY	6%	NY	4%
AL	4%	LA	4%	OH	5%
AR	5.125%	MA	5%	OK	4.5%
AZ	5.6%	MD	5%	OR	0%
CA	6%	ME	5%	PA	6%
CO	2.9%	MI	6%	RI	7%
CT	6%	MN	6.5%	SC	5%
DE	0%	MO	4.225%	SD	4%
FL	6%	MS	7%	TN	6%
GA	4%	MT	0%	TX	6.25%
HI	4%	NC	4%	UT	4.75%
IA	5%	ND	5%	VA	3.5%
ID	5%	NE	5%	VT	5%
IL	6.25%	NH	0%	WA	6.5%
IN	5%	NJ	6%	WI	5%
KS	4.9%	NM	5%	WV	6%
		NV	6.5%	WY	4%
				Washington, D.C.	5.75%

Source: Federation of Tax Administrators

Independent Nations Formed from the Soviet Union

Practicing Your Skill
Answers ★23F

1. The 15 independent nations formed from the Soviet Union after it dissolved in 1991.

2. A map can show the size and geographic location of the former Soviet Union as well as the size and location of each of the 15 countries formed from it.

3. none are used

4. A neutral color is used to indicate nonsubject matter, a blue to indicate water, and other colors to indicate each of the 15 subject countries.

---

longitude may sometimes be indicated by tick marks near the edge of the map or by lines across an entire map. Many maps also have locator maps, which show the subject area's location in relation to a larger area, such as a continent or the world.

Directions and distances Most maps in this textbook have a *compass rose*, or *directional indicator*. The compass rose indicates the four cardinal or primary points—using N for north, S for south, E for east, and W for west. You can also find intermediate directions—northeast, southeast, southwest, and northwest—using the compass rose. These directions are helpful in describing the relative location of a place. (If a map has no compass rose, assume that north is at the top, east is to the right, and so on.)

Many maps include a *scale*, showing both miles and kilometers, to help you relate distances on the map to actual distances on the earth's surface. You can use a scale to find the true distance between any two points on the map.

How to Read a Map

Determine the focus of the map. Read the title and labels to determine the map's focus—its subject and the geographic area it covers.

Study the map legend. Read the legend and become familiar with any special symbols, lines, colors, and shadings used in the map.

Check directions and distances. Use the directional indicator and scale as needed to determine direction, location, and distance.

Check the grid lines. Refer to lines of latitude and longitude, or to a locator map, to fix the location in relation larger area.

Study the map. Study the map's basic features and details, keeping its purpose in mind. If it is a special-purpose map, study the specific information being presented.

Practicing Your Skill TEKS

For the map shown above, answer the following questions.

1. What is the special focus of the map?
2. How is a map helpful in presenting this information?
3. What special symbols, if any, are used in the map?
4. What do the color variations indicate?

SKILLS HANDBOOK

ECONOMIC ATLAS

United States: Political A2

United States Population Density A4

Per Capita Personal Income in Current Dollars A4

United States Unemployment Rate A5

National Resources of the United States A5

The World: Political A6

**United States Balance of Trade
with Selected Nations, 1999** A8

World Population Density A8

World Labor in Agriculture A9

World Urban Population A9

United States: Political

Economic Atlas — A2

ECONOMIC ATLAS — A3

United States Population Density

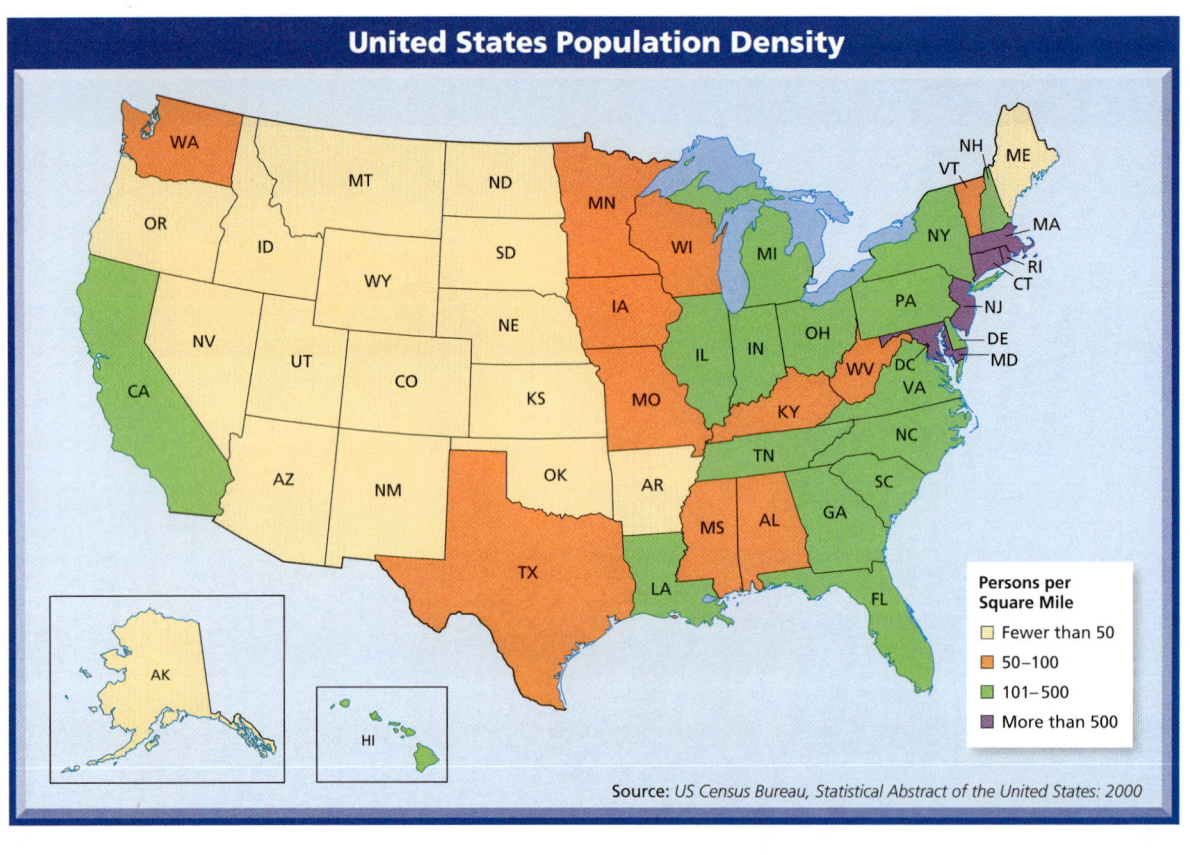

Persons per Square Mile
- Fewer than 50
- 50–100
- 101–500
- More than 500

Source: *US Census Bureau, Statistical Abstract of the United States: 2000*

Per Capita Personal Income in Current Dollars

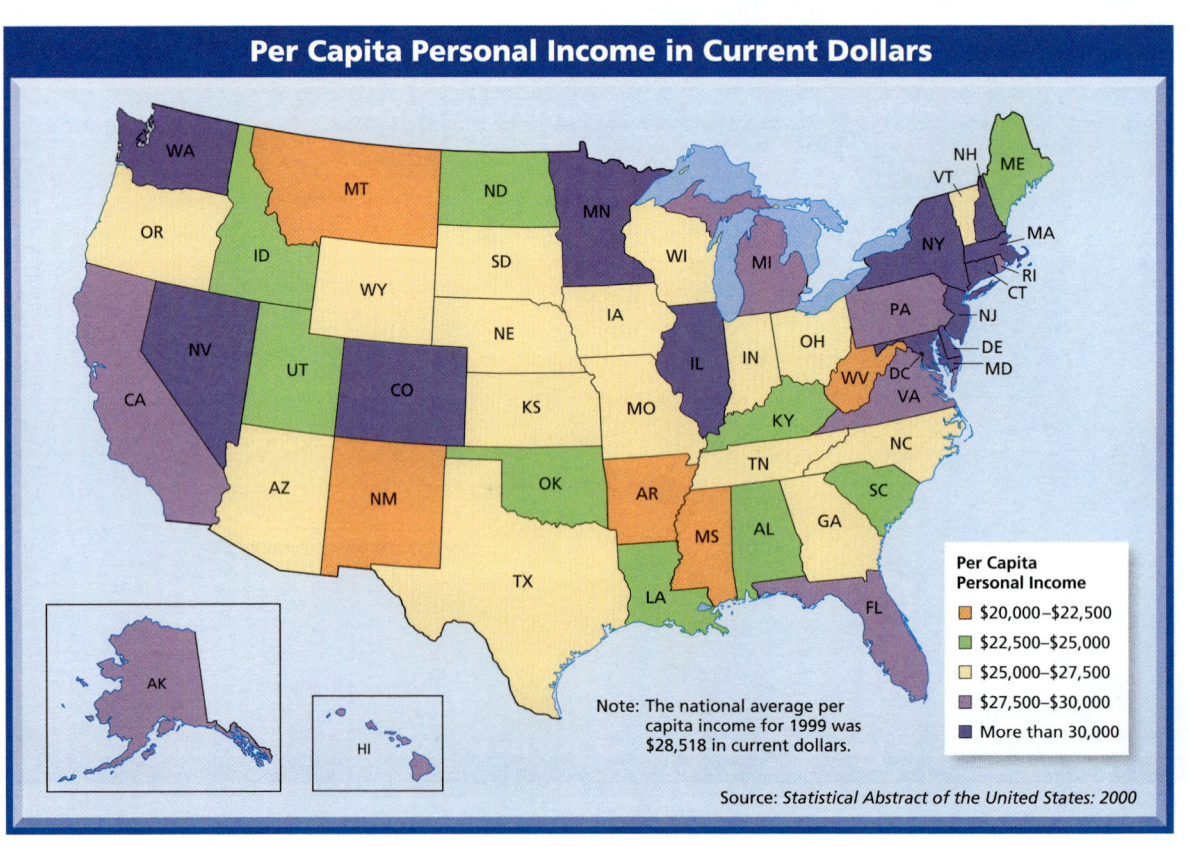

Per Capita Personal Income
- $20,000–$22,500
- $22,500–$25,000
- $25,000–$27,500
- $27,500–$30,000
- More than 30,000

Note: The national average per capita income for 1999 was $28,518 in current dollars.

Source: *Statistical Abstract of the United States: 2000*

ECONOMIC ATLAS

United States Unemployment Rate

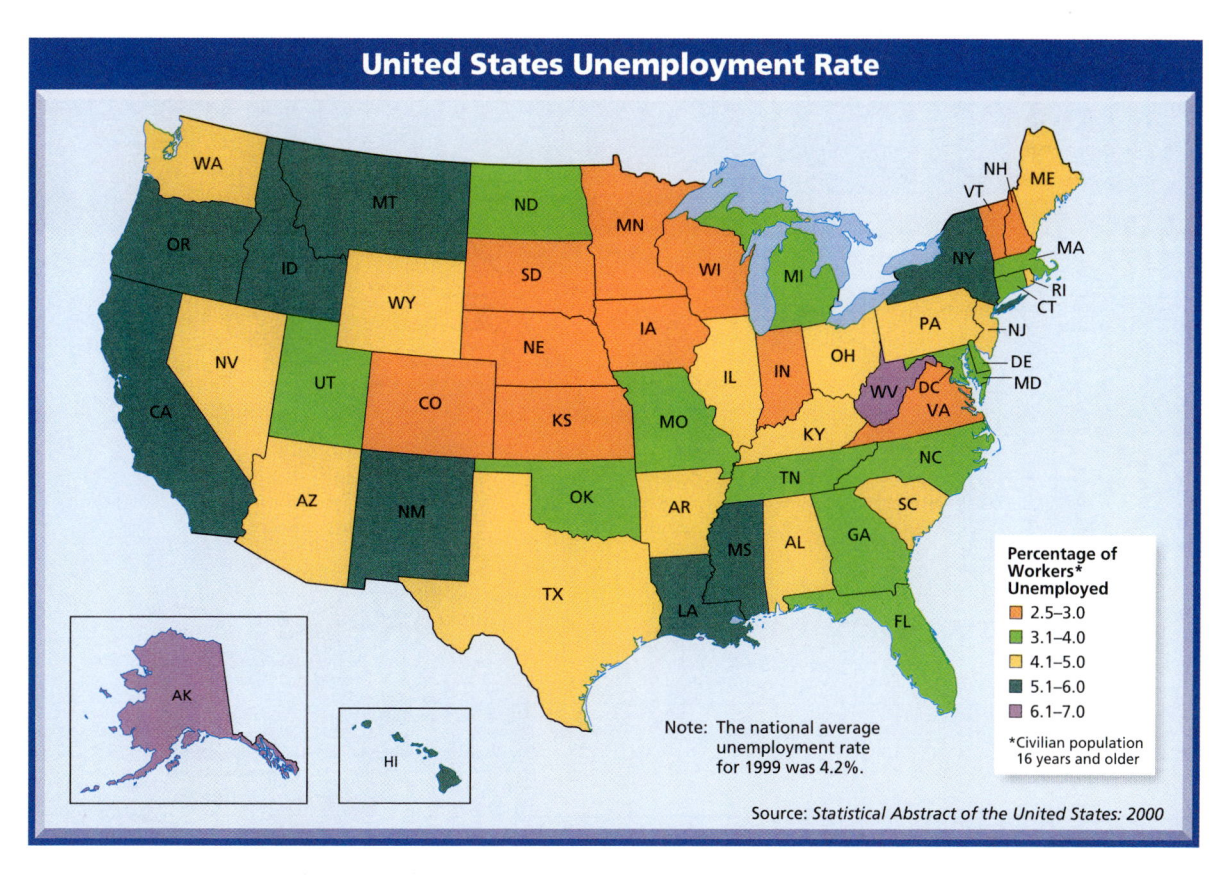

Percentage of Workers* Unemployed
- 2.5–3.0
- 3.1–4.0
- 4.1–5.0
- 5.1–6.0
- 6.1–7.0

*Civilian population 16 years and older

Note: The national average unemployment rate for 1999 was 4.2%.

Source: *Statistical Abstract of the United States: 2000*

Natural Resources of the United States

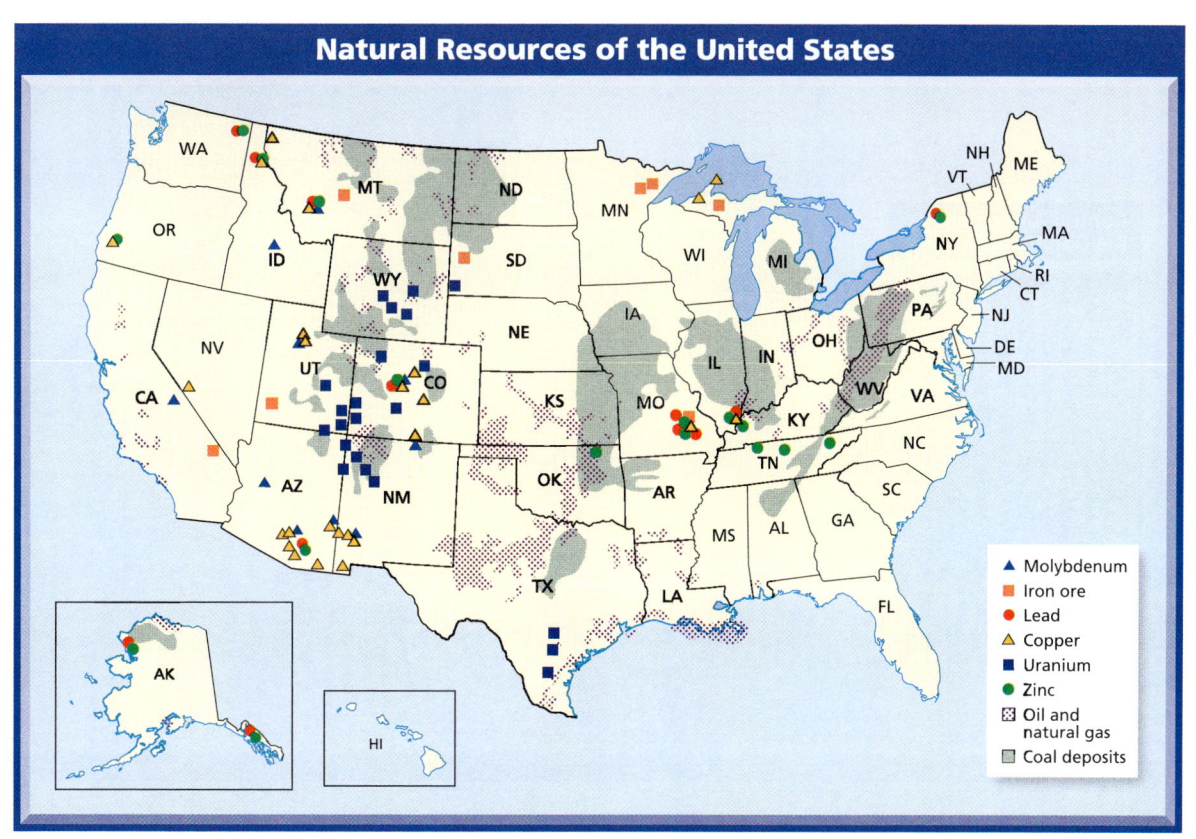

- ▲ Molybdenum
- ■ Iron ore
- ● Lead
- △ Copper
- ■ Uranium
- ● Zinc
- ▦ Oil and natural gas
- ▓ Coal deposits

ECONOMIC ATLAS A5

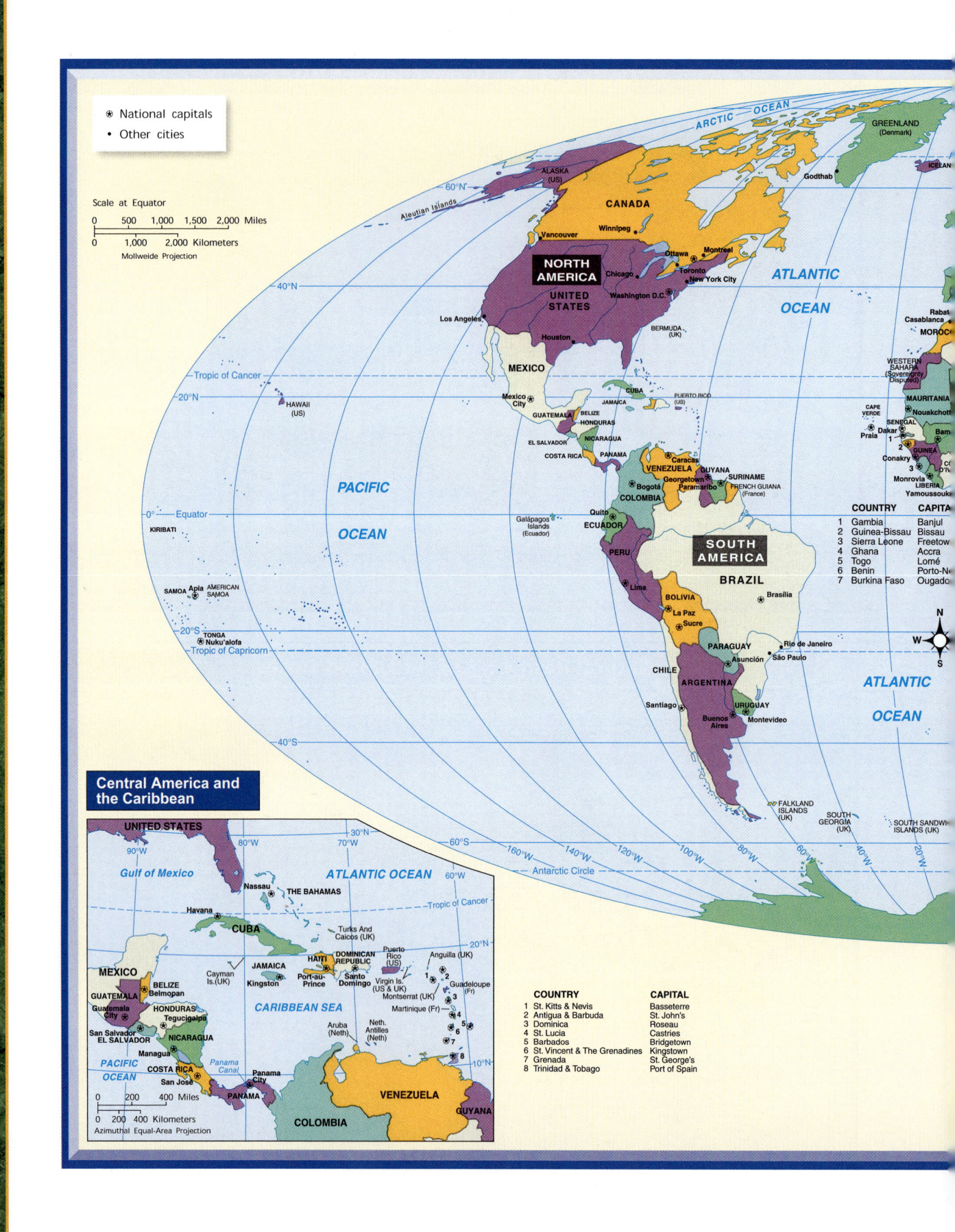

Economic Atlas

- ⊛ National capitals
- • Other cities

Scale at Equator
0 500 1,000 1,500 2,000 Miles
0 1,000 2,000 Kilometers
Mollweide Projection

COUNTRY	CAPITAL
1 Gambia	Banjul
2 Guinea-Bissau	Bissau
3 Sierra Leone	Freetown
4 Ghana	Accra
5 Togo	Lomé
6 Benin	Porto-Novo
7 Burkina Faso	Ouagadougou

Central America and the Caribbean

COUNTRY	CAPITAL
1 St. Kitts & Nevis	Basseterre
2 Antigua & Barbuda	St. John's
3 Dominica	Roseau
4 St. Lucia	Castries
5 Barbados	Bridgetown
6 St. Vincent & The Grenadines	Kingstown
7 Grenada	St. George's
8 Trinidad & Tobago	Port of Spain

0 200 400 Miles
0 200 400 Kilometers
Azimuthal Equal-Area Projection

A6 Economic Atlas

COUNTRY	CAPITAL
1 Czech Republic	Prague
2 Slovakia	Bratislava
3 Slovenia	Ljubljana
4 Croatia	Zagreb
5 Bosnia and Herzegovina	Sarajevo
6 Macedonia	Skopje
7 Yugoslavia (Serbia and Montenegro)	Belgrade
8 Lithuania	Vilnius
9 Latvia	Riga
10 Estonia	Tallinn

ECONOMIC ATLAS A7

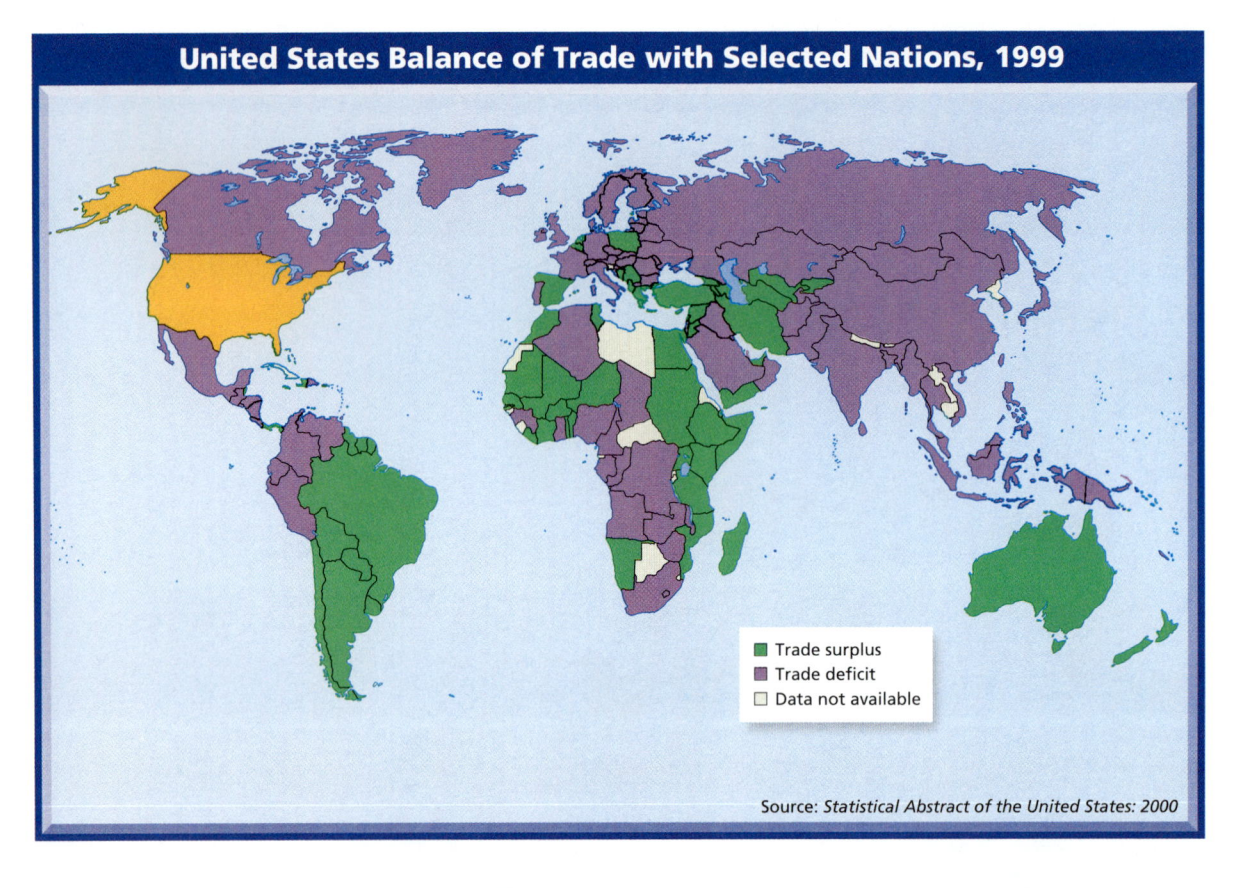

United States Balance of Trade with Selected Nations, 1999

- Trade surplus
- Trade deficit
- Data not available

Source: *Statistical Abstract of the United States: 2000*

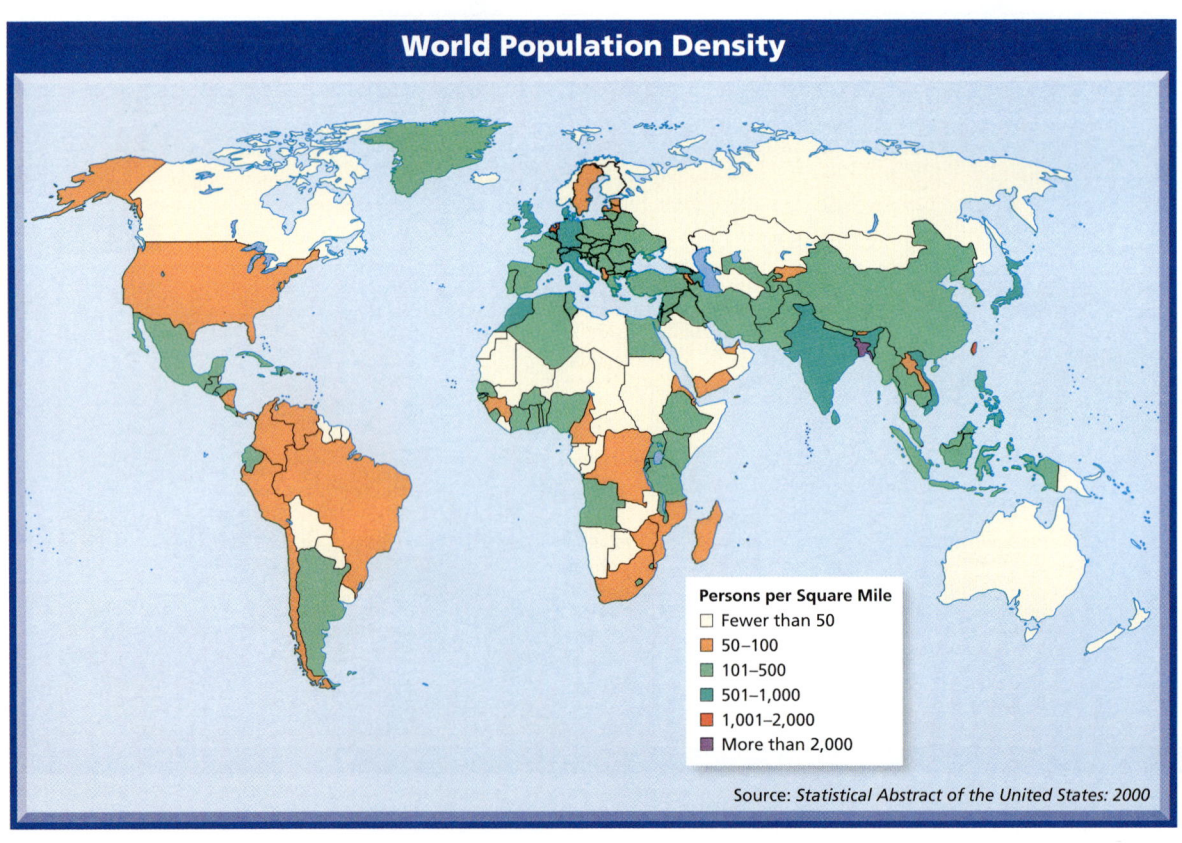

World Population Density

Persons per Square Mile
- Fewer than 50
- 50–100
- 101–500
- 501–1,000
- 1,001–2,000
- More than 2,000

Source: *Statistical Abstract of the United States: 2000*

Economic Atlas

World Labor in Agriculture

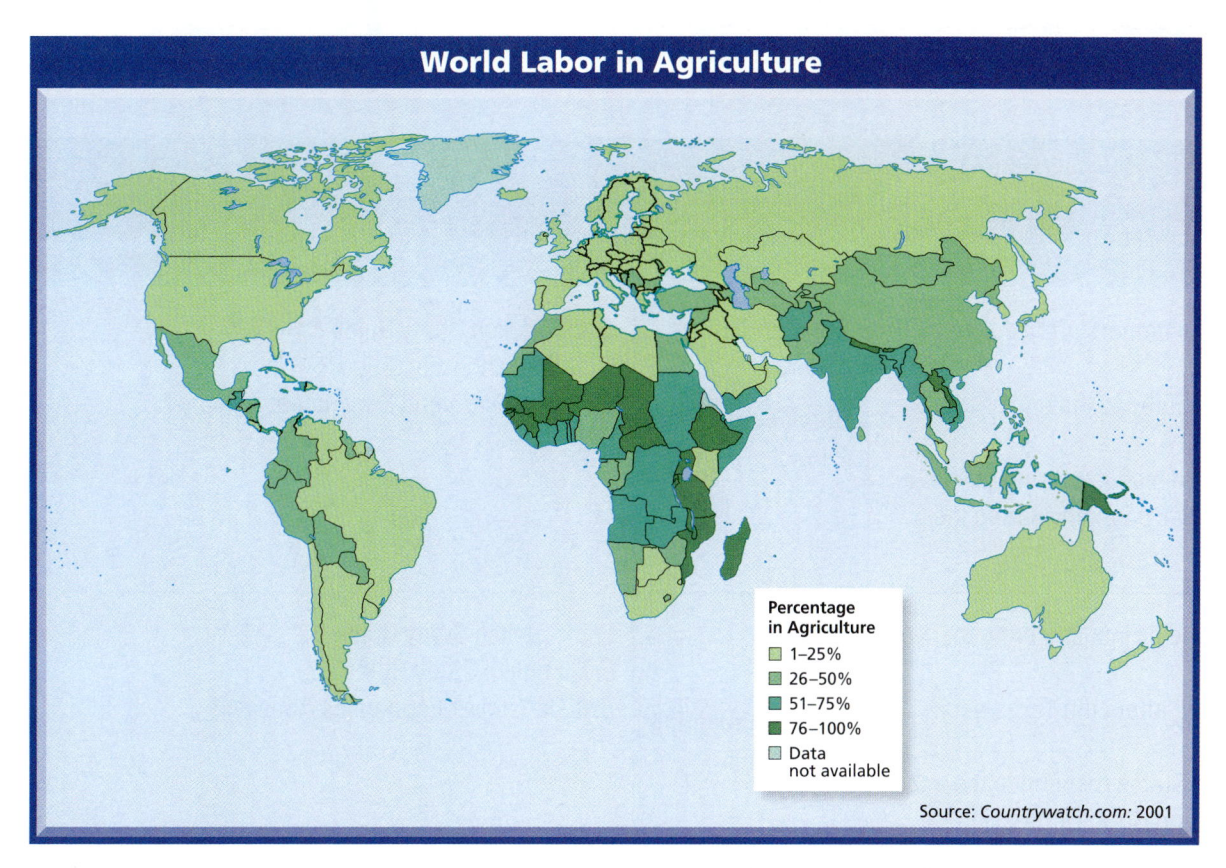

Percentage in Agriculture
- 1–25%
- 26–50%
- 51–75%
- 76–100%
- Data not available

Source: *Countrywatch.com:* 2001

World Urban Population

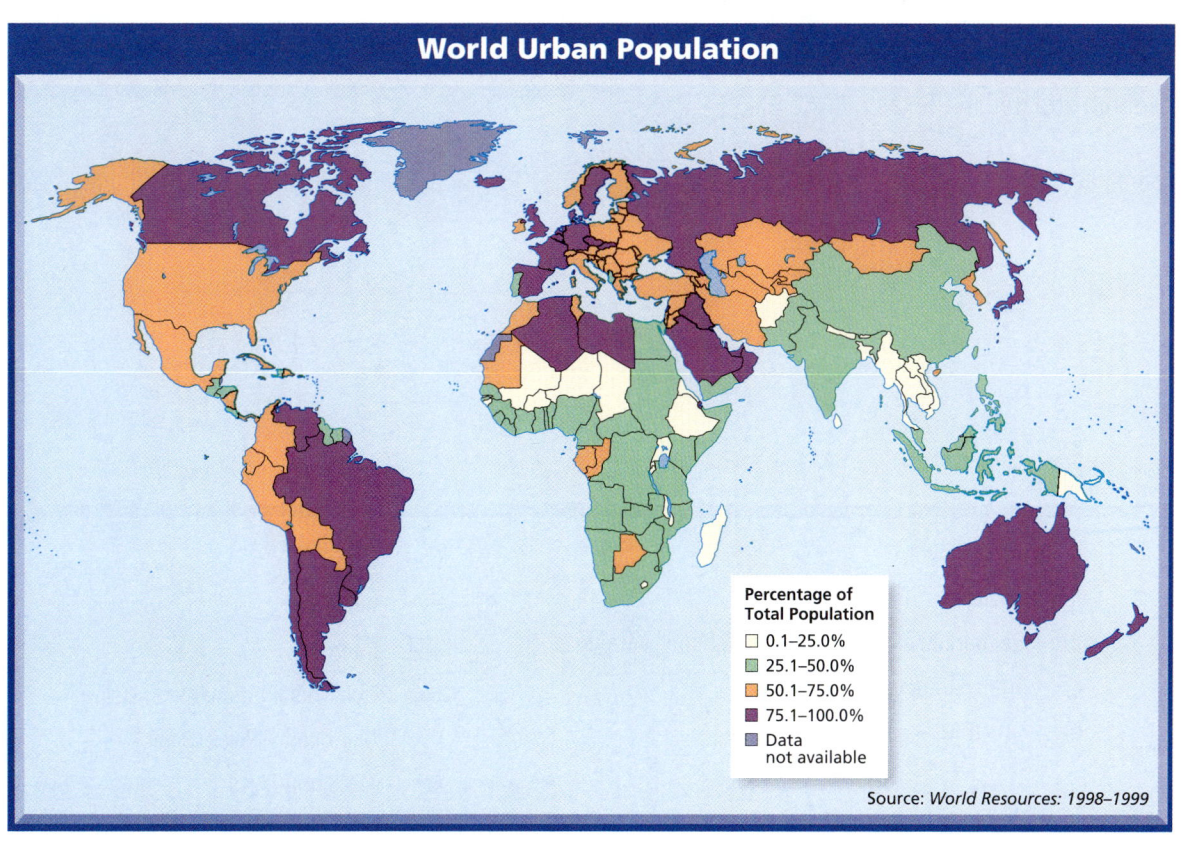

Percentage of Total Population
- 0.1–25.0%
- 25.1–50.0%
- 50.1–75.0%
- 75.1–100.0%
- Data not available

Source: *World Resources: 1998–1999*

ECONOMIC ATLAS

CHAPTER RESOURCE MANAGER

PROLOGUE: The Texas Economy

	OBJECTIVES	PACING GUIDE	REPRODUCIBLE RESOURCES
SECTION 1 **THE TEXAS ECONOMY IN THE 1800S** (pp. T1–T4)	▸ Why did many Texas farmers grow cotton in the 1800s? ▸ What factors contributed to the end of the cattle drives? ▸ Why did industry and manufacturing remain a small part of the Texas economy during the 1800s?	**Regular** 1.5 days **Block Scheduling** 1 day	**ELL** Spanish Study Guide P.1 **ELL** English Study Guide P.1 **E** Challenge and Enrichment Activity P
SECTION 2 **BOOM AND BUST IN THE EARLY 1900S** (pp. T5–T8)	▸ What benefits did the oil industry bring to Texas? ▸ How did World War I affect the Texas economy? ▸ How did the United States respond to the economic crisis called the Great Depression?	**Regular** 1.5 days **Block Scheduling** 1 day	**ELL** Spanish Study Guide P.2 **ELL** English Study Guide P.2 **SM** Consumer Economics Activity P
SECTION 3 **TEXAS AND THE WORLD** (pp. T9–T12)	▸ What industries developed in Texas after World War II? ▸ How has medical research affected the Texas economy? ▸ How has Texas become tied to the global economy?	**Regular** 1.5 days **Block Scheduling** 1 day	**ELL** Spanish Study Guide P.3 **ELL** English Study Guide P.3

Chapter Resource Key

- **PS** Primary Sources
- **RS** Reading Support
- **E** Enrichment
- **S** Simulations
- **SM** Skills Mastery
- **A** Assessment
- **REV** Review
- **ELL** Reinforcement and English Language Learners
- Transparencies
- CD-ROM
- Video
- Videodisc
- Internet
- Holt Presentation Maker Using Microsoft® PowerPoint®
- TEKS and TAKS

TECHNOLOGY RESOURCES	REINFORCEMENT, REVIEW, AND ASSESSMENT
• One-Stop Planner: Lesson P.1 • Researcher Online • Homework Practice Online • Global Skillbuilder CD-ROM	**REV** Section 1 Review, p. T4 **A** Daily Quiz P.1 ★ TAKS Every Day!
• One-Stop Planner: Lesson P.2 • Researcher Online • Homework Practice Online • Global Skillbuilder CD-ROM	**REV** Section 2 Review, p. T8 **A** Daily Quiz P.2 ★ TAKS Every Day!
• One-Stop Planner: Lesson P.3 • Researcher Online • Homework Practice Online • Global Skillbuilder CD-ROM	**REV** Section 3 Review, p. T12 **A** Daily Quiz P.3 ★ TAKS Every Day!

Chapter Review and Assessment
SM Global Skillbuilder CD-ROM
  HRW Go site
REV Reteaching Activity P
REV Prologue Review, pp. T15–T16
A Prologue Test Generator (on the One-Stop Planner)
A Prologue Test
A Alternative Assessment Handbook

One-Stop Planner CD-ROM
It's easy to plan lessons, select resources, and print out materials for your students when you use the **Texas One-Stop Planner CD-ROM with Test Generator**.

Print Resources also available in *Texas Connections to Economics*.

---

internet connect

HRW ONLINE RESOURCES
Go To: go.hrw.com
Then type in a keyword.

TEACHER HOME PAGE
KEYWORD: **SM3 Teacher**

CHAPTER INTERNET ACTIVITIES
KEYWORD: **SM3 ECP**
Choose an activity to:
▸ interview President Lyndon B. Johnson.
▸ learn about the impact of Spindletop on the Texas oil industry.
▸ create thematic maps of Texas.

CHAPTER ENRICHMENT LINKS
KEYWORD: **SM3 CHP**

HOLT RESEARCHER ONLINE
KEYWORD: **Holt Researcher**

ONLINE ASSESSMENT
Homework Practice
KEYWORD: **SM3 HPP**
TAKS Review
KEYWORD: **SM3 TP**
Rubrics
KEYWORD: **SS Rubrics**

CONTENT UPDATES
KEYWORD: **SS Content Updates**

HOLT PRESENTATION MAKER
KEYWORD: **SM3 PPTP**

ONLINE READING SUPPORT
KEYWORD: **SS Strategies**

CURRENT EVENTS
KEYWORD: **S3 Current Events**

TEXAS ONLINE RESOURCES
KEYWORD: **S3 TX**

LESSON P.1 — THE TEXAS ECONOMY IN THE 1800s

TEXTBOOK PAGES T1–T4

HOLT PRESENTATION MAKER Access Illustrated LECTURE NOTES using Microsoft® PowerPoint® on the One-Stop Planner CD-ROM

OBJECTIVES

- Explain why many Texas farmers grew cotton in the 1800s.
- Identify the factors that contributed to the end of the cattle drives.
- Examine why industry and manufacturing remained a small part of the Texas economy during the 1800s.

MOTIVATE

Have students each write a series of sentences describing what they think life was like for farmers and ranchers on the Texas frontier in the 1800s. Call on student volunteers to share their sentences with the class. *(Sentences will vary but may include that life was difficult, and people worked hard. Students' ideas may also reflect a romanticized vision of frontier and cowboy life.)* Tell students that in this section they will learn about farming, ranching, and manufacturing in 1800s Texas and the effect it had on the lives of Texans and on the Texas economy.

TEACH

Building a Vocabulary

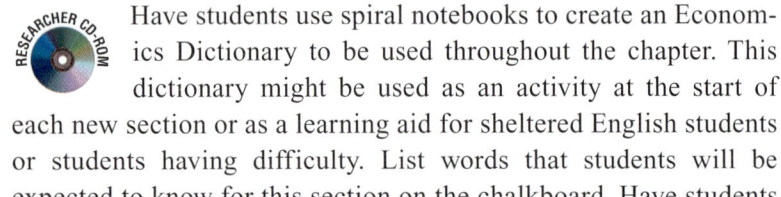

Have students use spiral notebooks to create an Economics Dictionary to be used throughout the chapter. This dictionary might be used as an activity at the start of each new section or as a learning aid for sheltered English students or students having difficulty. List words that students will be expected to know for this section on the chalkboard. Have students use the information provided in the textbook or on the *Researcher CD-ROM* to list, define, and give an example of each term. ★24A

Understanding Main Concepts

Have students describe the general state of agriculture in Texas in the early 1800s. *(Seventy percent of Texans were farmers who raised cows and hogs and planted crops, such as corn and wheat, for food and goods they needed for their daily lives).* Ask them how farmers made extra money during these times *(by selling surplus: butter, chickens, and eggs, and eventually raising and exporting sheep).* Have students define the term *cash crop (a crop grown and sold for profit)*. Ask for student volunteers to provide examples of Texas cash crops *(cotton and sugarcane)*. Review with the class factors necessary to make raising these crops profitable for farmers *(slavery, proximity to textile mills and processing plants, and railroads)*. ★23A

Identifying Cause and Effect, Organizing Ideas

Organize the class into small groups. Have each group begin this exercise by listing each of the factors that contributed to the end of the cattle drives *(Texas fever, legislation, barbed wire, windmills, refrigerated railroad cars, sheep ranching, and harsh winters)*. Then have them expand each item on the list to a one- to two-sentence explanation of the circumstance and its effect on the industry. *(For example: The fear of Texas fever spreading led to legislation restricting drives through some states.)* Finally, have each group use their sentences as the basis for a flowchart that visually depicts the series of causes that resulted in the decline in Texas ranching. ★23A

Comparing and Contrasting

Now have students write a brief essay comparing and contrasting the agriculture, cattle, and manufacturing industries in Texas during the 1800s. Have students describe the effect that each of the industries had on the state's economy at that time, including the benefits that it brought. ★23A, 24D

CLOSE

Review with the class the significance of farming, ranching, and manufacturing in 1800s Texas. Then have students predict how these industries fared as the state moved into the 1900s.

OPTIONS

Students Having Difficulty

Pair students having difficulty with students who have mastered the lesson material. Have pairs discuss the following questions and then write sentences or brief paragraphs to answer them:

- Why were farming and ranching so prevalent in Texas in the 1800s? *(ample land, promotion by the railroad companies, opportunity for profit)*
- What factors brought changes to farming? *(new technologies such as barbed wire, the steel plow, and windmills)*
- What factors brought changes to ranching? *(legislation, disease, barbed wire, and improved farming and transportation technology)*
- Why was industrial activity so minimal in the 1800s? *(People made most of what they needed at home, had little extra money to spend, or got what they needed imported from other places.)*

Interpersonal Learners, Linguistic Learners

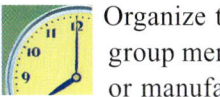

Organize these students into groups of three. Assign each group member one of the following roles: farmer, rancher, or manufacturer. Ask each group to imagine that they are operating their business in 1800s Texas as the open range was closing. Invite each group to write and enact a skit that depicts the changing economic circumstances of the time from the point of view of each member in relation to his or her assigned industry. Encourage students to suggest solutions that may have helped stabilize the situation of each group member's industry. ★23D

Gifted Learners, Linguistic Learners, Logical-Mathematical Learners

Have these students conduct research on the cattle industry in recent years. Tell them to locate figures for Texas as well as for the entire nation. Have students use the *Researcher Online,* the library, in-class resources, and the Internet to find information. Have students compile figures that would help them address the following questions: How has Texas cattle production changed in the past century? How has U.S. cattle production changed in the past century? What relationship, if any, can be seen between the two? Have students display their results in a chart or graph that illustrates the statistics they found. Have them also include a brief paragraph that explains the national and Texan trends in cattle production. ★23F, 23G, 24C

REVIEW

Have students complete the Section 1 Review on page T4. Use the answers in the Annotated Teacher's Edition to assess student mastery of this section.

ASSESS

To assess student mastery of this section, have students complete Daily Quiz P.1 in *Texas Connections to Economics*. For additional assessment options, see *Alternative Assessment Handbook* on the *One-Stop Planner CD-ROM*.

ADDITIONAL RESOURCES

Kelton, Elmer, Kathleen Jo Ryan, Genevieve Morgan, and Tommy Lee Jones. *Texas Cattle Barons: Their Families, Land, & Legacy.* 1999. Ten Speed Press.

Lowe, Richard G., and Randolph B. Campbell. *Planters and Plain Folk: Agriculture in Antebellum Texas.* 1987. Southern Methodist University Press.

Maxwell, Robert S., and Robert D. Baker. *Sawdust Empire: The Texas Lumber Industry, 1830-1940.* 1983. Texas A&M University Press.

LESSON P.2 BOOM AND BUST IN THE EARLY 1900s

TEXTBOOK PAGES T5–T8

HOLT PRESENTATION MAKER Access Illustrated LECTURE NOTES using Microsoft® PowerPoint® on the One-Stop Planner CD-ROM

OBJECTIVES

- Identify the benefits the oil industry brought to Texas.
- Describe how World War I affected the Texas economy.
- Analyze how the United States responded to the economic crisis called the Great Depression.

MOTIVATE

Invite students to suggest how many of the items they rely upon each day are related to the oil industry. Encourage them to consider items directly related, such as gas, as well as those that are indirectly related, such as items that were shipped to a store so that they could purchase them. Write the term *petrochemicals* on the chalkboard. Explain to students that many products, such as rubber, are made from a petroleum base. Tell students that they will learn about how the market for oil expanded in the 1900s, which led to expansion of the oil industry in Texas.

TEACH

Building a Vocabulary

List the important terms for this section on the chalkboard and tell students to add them to their Economics Dictionary. Tell students to use the information provided in the text or on the *Researcher CD-ROM* to list, define, and give an example of each term. ★24A

Identify Cause and Effect, Evaluate Ideas

Have students define the term *petroleum*. (*Petroleum is another word for oil.*) Then review with the class the series of events that led to the boom in the Texas oil industry. Call on volunteers to list each event in a cause and effect chart on the chalkboard. (*Kerosene was invented, increasing the demand for oil. Major oil field was discovered in Corsicana, causing the Texas oil industry to take off. Spindletop oil strike occurs, raising the Texas oil production to 20 percent of the national total. Texas oil companies expand, boosting the economy and creating new jobs. Automobile popularity rises, increasing the market for petrochemical products and the demand for oil and gas. New pipelines are laid, increasing the speed and reducing the cost of transporting oil to the rest of the nation. Research and exploration lead to more Texas oil strikes.*) Then have students write a concluding paragraph summarizing the benefits that oil brought to Texas at this time. (*Thousands of jobs were created, millions were collected in tax revenues, and some oil profits were applied to state hospitals, universities, and charities.*) ★23A, 24C

Analyze Ideas

Discuss with the class the condition of the Texas economy just prior to World War I. (*Industrial jobs had increased, but farmers, who made up the majority of Texans at the time, were struggling. Many had lost their land and were tenant farming.*) Tell students that World War I increased the demand for food and clothing for use in the armed services. Texas met this demand by increasing agricultural and textile production. Ask students what other industries benefited from World War I (*oil and lumber*). Call on student volunteers to explain why (*for fuel and petrochemical products such as rubber*). Then ask students to write a paragraph explaining what happened to the Texas economy when the war ended. (*The boom ended as the country returned to a peacetime economy. Soldiers flooded the job market, displacing African Americans and women. The demand and price for farm products fell, causing a return of hard times to farmers.*) ★7A, 24D

Compare and Contrast

Have students write and give an oral report that compares and contrasts the national effects of the Great Depression with the circumstances as they occurred in Texas at that time. Provide students with a brief review of the material before they begin. (*Texans farmed and supplied their own food for a time. Eventually oil and farm overproduction caused the Texas economy to crash as badly as the national economy. The Texas government enacted measures to stem the tide of the depression, as the Roosevelt administration did.*) ★24D

CLOSE

Discuss with students whether they think that the government could have intervened in industrial matters prior to the war or the Great

Depression to help grow and stabilize the Texas economy. Have them consider whether the government has the right to do so and whether they think that such methods are even effective in avoiding the effects of a market downturn. ★15A, 15B

OPTIONS

Musical-Rhythmic Learners

Organize these students into groups and have them write a song in tribute to the benefits that the oil industry brought to Texas in the early 1900s. Suggest that students begin by listing and then elaborating on these benefits. They can then use their completed lists as an outline when writing their group's song. Encourage students to be creative and select any genre of music that they feel is appropriate to their purpose. Have each group perform their song for the class.

English Language Learners

Pair sheltered English students with students fluent in English. Tell each pair to create a storyboard that shows how World War I affected the Texas economy. Storyboards should depict Texas production during the war as well as the changes that took place after the war. *(For example, food and textiles can be shown being shipped during the war and sitting in warehouses after the war.)* Encourage students to include descriptive captions. Have them include their storyboards in their portfolios.

Gifted Learners, Linguistic Learners

Have students select a Texas oil company that began in the 1900s and obtain information on its origins. Have students use the *Researcher Online,* the library, in-class resources, and the Internet to find information. Tells students to use the information they find to create a horizontal time line with entries above and below. The entries on top should trace the history of their selected oil company and the entries below should depict state, national, and international events that affected the oil industry at that time *(for example the Texas oil boom, the Great Depression, and World War I)*. Students may wish to place their annotated time lines in their portfolios. ★24D

REVIEW

Have students complete the Section 2 Review on page T8. Use the answers in the Annotated Teacher's Edition to assess student mastery of this section.

ASSESS

To assess student mastery of this section, have students complete Daily Quiz P.2 in *Texas Connections to Economics*. For additional assessment options, see *Alternative Assessment Handbook* on the *One-Stop Planner CD-ROM*.

ADDITIONAL RESOURCES

Buenger, Walter L. *The Path to a Modern South: Northeast Texas between Reconstruction and the Great Depression.* 2001. University of Texas Press.

Galbraith, John Kenneth. *The Great Crash 1929.* 1997. Mariner Books.

Spellman, Paul N. *Spindletop Boom Days (Clayton Wheat Williams Texas Life Series, No. 9).* 2001. Texas A&M University Press.

LESSON P.3 TEXAS AND THE WORLD

TEXTBOOK PAGES T9–T12

HOLT PRESENTATION MAKER Access Illustrated LECTURE NOTES using Microsoft® PowerPoint® on the One-Stop Planner CD-ROM

OBJECTIVES

- Describe the industries that developed in Texas after World War II.
- Explain how medical research has affected the Texas economy.
- Identify how Texas has become tied to the global economy.

MOTIVATE

Option 1: Ask students to identify major industries that fuel the economy in your region. *(Answers will vary depending upon your region.)* Ask them to explain why they selected these industries. *(These industries provide the most jobs, goods, or services in the community.)* Ask students: How do you think these industries became so important to our local community? Tell the class that in this section they will learn about the need for diversification and desire for globalization of the Texas economy.

Option 2: Find several stories in a local newspaper that highlight the presence of the aerospace, medical research, and high-tech industries in Texas. Share these stories with the class. Discuss with students the kinds of changes these stories exemplify in Texas industry over the years *(a shift from agriculture and oil toward aerospace, medical research, and high-tech).* Tell the class that in this section they will learn about how and why Texas broadened its economy to accommodate these new industries.

TEACH

Building a Vocabulary

List the important terms for this section on the chalkboard and tell students to add them to their Economics Dictionary. Tell students to use the information provided in the text or on the *Researcher CD-ROM* to list, define, and give an example of each term. ★24A

Understanding Main Concepts

Review with the class the various industries that developed in Texas after World War II *(aircraft and ship building, chemical production, steel manufacturing, weapons production, and the aerospace and electronics industries).* Have students work with a partner to describe how each of these industries relates to the nation's defense during the hot and cold war periods. Reconvene as a class and call on volunteers to share their descriptions with the class. *(Students' descriptions will vary but in general should note that each of these industries directly supports the national defense of the time.)* ★23A

Identifying Cause and Effect, Analyzing Ideas

Remind students that while Texas's dependence on the oil industry benefited the state in the 1970s, it resulted in serious financial setbacks in the 1980s through the mid-1990s. Have students create a chart that tracks the causes and effects that led to greater diversification in the industries supporting the Texas economy today. Assist students by reviewing the events as a class before they begin. *(International oil prices rose in the 1970s, increasing demand for less expensive Texas-supplied oil. Prices dropped in the 1980s, leading to job loss and problems in the banking and real estate industries. Finally, changing demands for goods resulted in diversification of the Texas economy through expansion of the high-tech, health care, and tourism industries.)* ★23A

Organizing Ideas, Creating Charts and Graphs

Write the term *globalization* on the chalkboard. Ask for student volunteers to help define this term. *(Globalization is a term for the process in which a nation increases its economy's interdependence with the rest of the world.)* Remind students that the process of globalization in Texas occurred gradually over time. Organize the class into groups of three or four. Have each group make a flowchart that illustrates the series of events that led Texas to become tied to the global economy. *(Texas established an Office of International Business, many nations moved their consulates to Texas, in 1994 NAFTA brought more goods and jobs in from Mexico; Texas maintains Free Trade Zones)*

Ask for volunteers to share their flowcharts. Refer students who need additional instruction on the skills used in this activity to the *Global Skillbuilder CD-ROM*, Lesson 12: Creating Graphic Organizers. ★14A, 24C

CLOSE

Discuss with students the changes that have taken place in the Texas economy due to the broadening focus of industry and globalization since World War II. Ask for student volunteers to share with the class any insights they have about the future of industry in Texas. Poll the class to find out what industry each student is interested in working in when he or she is an adult.

OPTIONS

Interpersonal Learners

Discuss with students the effects that both diversification and globalization have had on the Texas economy. Ask them to consider local businesses that they think have benefited from these shifts in Texas industry. Have students contact people who work in these industries and conduct interviews with them to identify how diversification and globalization have impacted the economy both locally and statewide. Ask students to evaluate the effectiveness of these factors. Did it make sense for Texas to move beyond oil and agriculture and into the worldwide marketplace in the mid- to late-1900s? ★14B

Students Having Difficulty

Pair students having difficulties with students who have mastered the lesson material. Have each pair classify the following aspects of the post-World War II Texas economy according to these three categories: defense, high-tech, and medical research. Tell students that many of the items will belong in more than one category. ★23A
- aerospace
- electronics
- artificial heart
- weapons production
- semiconductors
- arterial bypass

Gifted Learners, Linguistic Learners

Ask students to conduct research on a Texas company currently involved in either the defense, high-tech, or medical industries. Have students use the *Researcher Online,* the library, in-class resources, and the Internet to find information. Ask students to discover when the company originated, what its primary product or service is, who its key customers are, and what its financial outlook is in light of the world marketplace. Have students summarize their findings in an oral report that can be presented to the class. Encourage students to use charts or graphs to help further clarify the significance of their findings. ★23A, 23C, 24C, 24D

REVIEW

Have students complete the Section 3 Review on page T12. Use the answers in the Annotated Teacher's Edition to assess student mastery of this section.

ASSESS

To assess student mastery of this section, have students complete Daily Quiz P.3 in *Texas Connections to Economics.* For additional assessment options, see *Alternative Assessment Handbook* on the *One-Stop Planner CD-ROM.*

ADDITIONAL RESOURCES

Burrows, William E., and Walter Cronkite. *The Infinite Journey: Eyewitness Accounts of NASA and the Age of Space.* Discovery Channel Inc. 2000.

Folsom, Ralph H. *NAFTA in a Nutshell.* West Group. 1999.

Kinsey-Goman, Carol. *The Human Side of High-Tech: Lessons from the Technology Frontier.* John Wiley & Sons. 2000.

PROLOGUE

TOPICS INCLUDE

- agriculture
- the cattle industry
- manufacturing
- oil
- petrochemicals
- war and economic growth
- the Great Depression
- the aerospace industry
- economic diversification
- global trade

ECONOMICS NOTEBOOK

The Economics Notebook is a journal activity that encourages students to consider basic concepts of economics that relate to their lives. A follow-up notebook activity appears on page T15.

WHY IT MATTERS TODAY

To find additional information dealing with economic activities today in Texas, visit CNNfyi.com or have students complete the ECONOMICS IN THE NEWS activity on page T13.

CNNfyi.com

PROLOGUE

THE TEXAS ECONOMY

Texans have engaged in numerous economic activities since 1845, the year Texas became a state. For much of the state's history, Texans have enjoyed the benefits of the natural resources of the land, from its fertile soil to its grasslands to the deposits of oil deep beneath Earth's surface. In recent years Texans have sought to diversify the state's economy, and today visitors can find both farmers and computer programmers living and working in Texas.

ECONOMICS NOTEBOOK

In your Economics Notebook write a paragraph describing the resources and events that have created the most economic activity in Texas.

WHY IT MATTERS TODAY

Today Texans are engaged in many economic activities. Use CNNfyi.com or other **current events** sources to find information about one or more of these activities. Record your findings in your Economics Notebook.

CNNfyi.com

SECTION 1

THE TEXAS ECONOMY IN THE 1800s

READ TO DISCOVER

1. Why did many Texas farmers grow cotton in the 1800s?
2. What factors contributed to the end of the cattle drives?
3. Why did industry and manufacturing remain a small part of the Texas economy during the 1800s?

ECONOMICS DICTIONARY

cash crops
commercial farming

How many of the foods you eat today are grown right here in Texas? As it was in the past, agriculture remains an important part of the Texas economy.

Texas Agriculture

In the 1800s Texas was a rural state—95 percent of Texans lived in rural areas in 1850—and the Texas economy was based on farming and ranching. In 1860 some 70 percent of Texans were farmers. These farmers grew a variety of crops, including corn, sweet potatoes, and wheat, and raised cows for milk products and hogs for meat. For extra money, some farm families sold butter, chickens, and eggs. As wool became an important Texas export, sheep also provided an extra source of income for Texas farmers.

In addition to growing food crops, Texan farmers produced **cash crops,** such as cotton and sugarcane, to sell for a profit. In response to the growing demand from northern textile mills, cotton production in Texas increased from 60,000 bales in 1849 to 400,000 bales 10 years later. Because cotton was a labor-intensive crop and because many Texans immigrated from southern slave states, some Texans relied upon slave labor to plant, pick, and process it for sale. In 1860 some 2,000 planters lived in Texas. These planters—large-scale farmers who held at least 20 slaves—lived in relative comfort and exercised economic and political influence far beyond their small numbers.

In the years after the Civil War, the expansion of the state's railroad system brought new settlers to Texas. Railroad companies promoted settlement by distributing brochures throughout the United States that advertised the rich farmland available in Texas. Thousands of settlers in search of opportunity journeyed to the state, where the railroads sold parcels of land to the prospective farmers. Partly as a result of this migration, the number of farms in Texas rose from about 61,000 in 1870 to 350,000 by 1900.

The lure of inexpensive land drew many farmers to West Texas, where they had to practice dry-farming techniques, such as terracing, to keep moisture in the soil. Texas farmers also used threshers and other mechanical farm tools to increase production. Such developments made **commercial farming**—the large-scale production of agricultural goods to sell for profit—an important sector of the Texas economy. Most farmers raised cotton, which promised high profits and which grew well in many parts of the state. Texas farmers produced some $57 million in cotton in 1880 alone. Farmers relied upon railroads to ship cotton to textile mills, most of which were located outside the state.

The integration of Texas agriculture into national and international markets brought opportunities but also challenges to Texas farmers, who were now vulnerable to supply and price changes in world markets. Unfortunately, the increased production of cotton and other crops

---

SECTION 1

THE TEXAS ECONOMY IN THE 1800s

Lesson Plans
For teaching strategies, see Lesson P.1 located at the beginning of this chapter, or the One-Stop Planner strategy P.1.

Economics Dictionary
To reinforce the section's vocabulary terms, refer students to the Electronic Glossary on the *Researcher CD-ROM*.

Section Assessment
To assess students' mastery of this section, have them complete Daily Quiz P.1 in *Texas Connections to Economics*.

TEKS

Content
12B, 26A
Social Studies Skills
23A, 23D, 23F, 23G, 24A, 24C, 24D

Cultural Perspectives

Following the Civil War, people came from many places to live in Texas. They emigrated from Europe, from countries such as Germany and Czechoslovakia. Many of these people came from farming families, making it easier to adjust to their new life in the United States. These immigrants brought with them a rich cultural heritage. The Czech immigrants who settled in Texas were eager to preserve their Catholic religious heritage. Over time, they built beautiful churches with high vaulted ceilings and stained-glass windows. Czech settlers decorated the interior of these churches with elaborate paintings of angels, flowers, and symbols. One Czech church features 66 types of flowers, vines, and shrubs on its ceiling. Today services and festivals held at the painted churches of Fayette County draw thousands of visitors. Such craftsmanship came out of these immigrants' pride in who they were when they arrived in Texas.

Caption Answer

The cattle drives allowed ranchers to send their cattle to the cattle towns in Missouri and Kansas, where they could be shipped to eastern markets for a higher profit.

---

was not matched by growing demand, and prices for agricultural goods fell throughout the late 1800s. Between 1874 and 1897 wheat prices fell from 94 to 63 cents per bushel. During this same period, cotton prices dropped from 11 to 6 cents per pound. Farmers also had to contend with rising costs for land and farm machinery and with destructive pests such as the boll weevil. Many migrants from the United States and Mexico could no longer afford farms and found work as agricultural laborers. Others worked as tenant farmers or sharecroppers, paying rent for farmland by giving up a percentage of their crops. In response to these many problems, farm organizations and agricultural scientists encouraged farmers to grow a variety of crops. However, most Texas farmers continued to produce cotton, which promised higher profits than other crops.

The Cattle Industry

After cotton, cattle was the state's second-most-valuable export during the 1800s. As one visitor to the state noted, Texas "is especially suited to livestock raising, because it has an abundance of good water and grazing." Cattle provided food, hides, and tallow, which was used to make soap and candles.

Early Developments Until the 1860s Texas cattle were usually sold at local auctions. The growth of the Texas cattle industry was limited because the region still had a fairly small population. Some ranchers sought new markets, driving herds to port towns in Texas, from which the cattle were shipped to locations such as New Orleans and Havana, Cuba. After gold was discovered in California, Texans drove a limited number of cattle west to feed the growing population of miners in the region. Yet transporting cattle great distances was a difficult and dangerous process.

When the Civil War broke out, the demand for Texas beef increased rapidly, in part because the Confederate army needed meat to feed its troops. By 1863, however, Union forces had blocked trade from Confederate states, including Texas. As a result, the number of cattle in Texas grew rapidly. By the end of the Civil War, some 5 million cattle roamed the state, many of them mavericks, or unclaimed cattle.

The Cattle Drives Recognizing the economic opportunity that the immense herds offered, Texans sought new markets for their cattle. The northeastern United States, with its large population and smaller agricultural economy, was one potential market for Texas beef that promised great profits. Cattle that sold in Texas for $3 to $6 a head could be sold in New York for as much as $80.

Texas ranchers could not drive cattle to eastern markets because of the distance involved and the many populated farm areas that the herds would have to cross. They could, however, drive the cattle to midwestern states such as Missouri or Kansas, from which the cattle could be sent by rail to meat-processing plants in St. Louis and Chicago. During the fall and winter, cattle grazed on the open range, or unfenced lands, of Texas. In the spring cowboys rounded up the cattle and drove the herds north. Texas longhorns—hearty animals that performed well on the long drives—also carried ticks that spread a deadly cattle disease called Texas fever. Farm cattle in Missouri and Kansas died in large numbers, prompting those states to enact legislation restricting longhorn drives.

MARKETS & PRICES *Roping steers was just one of the many difficult challenges cowboys faced on cattle drives.* **How did cattle drives open up new markets for Texas ranchers?**

The Cattle Kingdom of Texas, 1865–1890

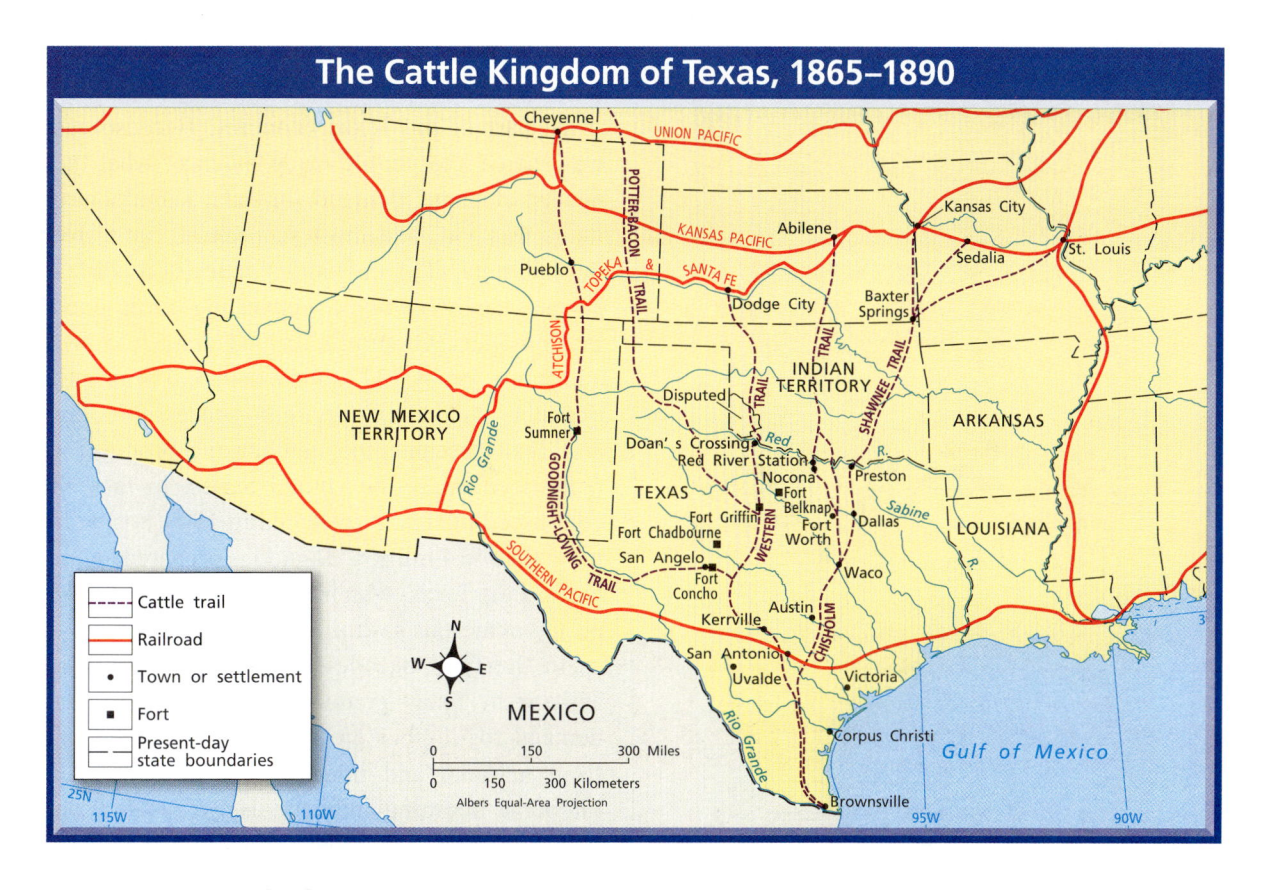

FIGURE P.1 The use of cattle trails and railroads allowed Texas ranchers to sell their livestock in national markets. **How did technological advances affect productivity in the cattle industry?**

In response to these restrictions, some Texas ranchers drove their herds farther west to small towns such as Abilene, Kansas, which had new railheads. By 1871 some 600,000 or 700,000 cattle arrived in Abilene, where weary cowboys spent their hard-earned money on hot baths, clean clothes, and good food. Other cattle ranchers, such as Charles Goodnight, drove their cattle west to New Mexico and Colorado to provide beef to American Indian reservations, military posts, and mining camps.

The success of the trail drives led to the development of huge ranches throughout the state. The XIT Ranch in the Texas Panhandle eventually covered some 3 million acres of land and was home to some 150,000 head of cattle. The cowboys who worked on these ranches and drove the herds north provided an image of Texas that remains popular today. In reality, however, the age of the cattle drives was soon over. Technological advances hastened the demise of the drives. Barbed wire closed the open range, and windmills made it possible for farmers to grow crops on the Plains, thereby increasing competition for land in Texas. Railroads with refrigerated cars also eventually came to Texas, eliminating the need for long cattle drives. Cattle ranchers also competed with sheep ranchers, who benefited from expanding wool markets. In addition, several harsh winters in the 1880s killed thousands of cattle, weakening the Texas ranching industry. Despite the end of the cattle drives, ranching remained an important part of the Texas economy at the close of the 1800s.

Manufacturing in Texas

Although farming and ranching dominated the Texas economy in the 1800s, some Texans worked as blacksmiths, carpenters, and saddle and wagon

---

Caption Answer
Barbed wire and railroads increased efficiency and opened new markets.

Across the Curriculum

MATH Some Texans made large profits from cattle drives. Texan M. A. Withers bought 600 longhorns for $5,400. In 1868 he spent $4 per head to drive the cattle to Abilene, Kansas, where he sold the herd for $16,800.
Critical Thinking: What was Withers' profit?
Answer: $9,000 (600 x 4 = 2,400; 5,400 + 2,400 = 7,800; 16,800 – 7,800 = $9,000) ■
23G

Across the Curriculum

SCIENCE The cattle disease *Texas fever* struck rapidly and was often fatal. The disease seemed to appear after Texas longhorns passed through an area, but no one knew the cause. In the 1890s, scientists learned that a microscopic organism spread by cattle ticks caused Texas fever. In Texas, where the disease was widespread, most cattle were infected at an early age, greatly increasing their chance of survival. Even after recovery, however, cattle could still spread the disease through ticks.
Critical Thinking: What do you think were some effects of the discovery of how Texas fever was spread?
Answer: Students might mention that ranchers tried to control ticks to stop the spread of the disease or that some other state leaders tried to keep Texas cattle out of their states. ■

THE TEXAS ECONOMY

Caption Answer
The price fell. The increase in supply from overproduction did not match the demand in the marketplace. ★7A

SECTION 1 REVIEW ANSWERS

1. cash crops (T1), commercial farming (T1) **24A**

2. agriculture—cotton; expanded greatly in the late 1800s; dependence on one crop, pests, ranching—cattle and sheep; expanded after the Civil War and opening of cattle trails; long distance to market, bad weather, manufacturing—processing farm products, lumber; gradually increased in the late 1800s; state remained mainly agricultural and imported most of its manufactured goods **24D**

3a. Cotton production initially offered large profits, but overproduction in the late 1800s led to declining profits and economic difficulties for many Texas farmers.

3b. to journey to rail heads, where the cattle could be shipped to slaughterhouses in the east **23A**

4. Students' responses will vary but should demonstrate accurate knowledge of the environmental hardships faced by Texas ranchers in the late 1800s as well as the significance of a ranch's distant location from the market. **12B, 23A**

T4

King Cotton in Texas

[Graph showing Cotton Production and Prices, 1872–1900]
- Cotton Produced in Texas (in 100,00 Bales)
- Prices (cents per pound)

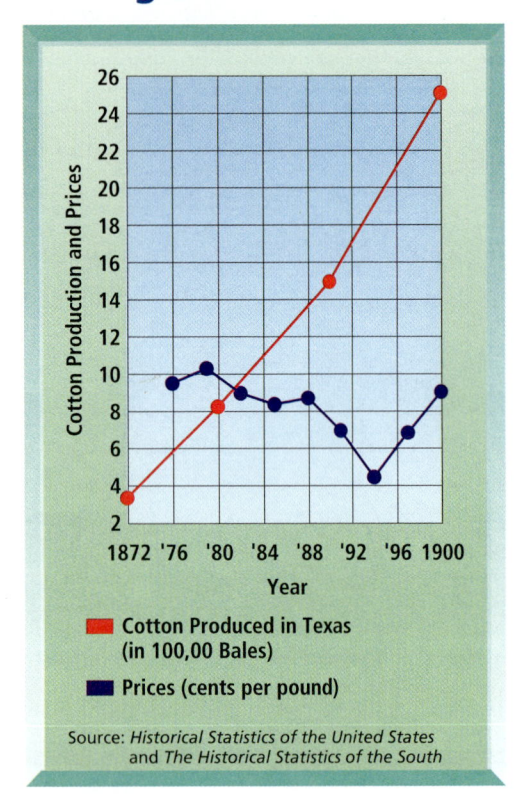

Source: *Historical Statistics of the United States* and *The Historical Statistics of the South*

FIGURE P.2 Cotton production expanded rapidly during the late 1800s. **In general, what happened to the price of cotton as production increased? Why did this occur?** ★TEKS

makers. Texas also had a number of doctors, lawyers, and merchants. Yet industry remained a small part of the Texas economy. Because cash was scarce and people made much of what they needed at home, demand for most manufactured items was low, and most such items came from out of state. The industries that succeeded in Texas usually involved converting farm goods into products. Gristmills ground grain into meal and flour, and by 1870, more than 530 flour mills operated in Texas. Cotton gins processed cotton, and Texas became the number-one producer of cottonseed oil in the United States. In fact, the cottonseed oil Texas produced in 1900 was worth more than $14 million. Tanneries prepared animal hides. East Texas, which was rich in lumber, supported numerous sawmills.

In the final decades of the 1800s industrial activity in Texas gradually increased. Growing demand for lumber on the part of railroads and from national and international markets made lumber a booming industry. Between 1870 and 1900 the state's lumber production increased eightfold. Stockyards and meatpacking plants developed near railroad junctions. Despite such growth, less than 2 percent of the Texas population held manufacturing jobs in 1900.

SECTION 1 REVIEW

★TEKS Q: 1, 2, 4

1. Identify and Explain:
cash crops
commercial farming

2. Analyzing Information: Copy the chart below. Use the chart to describe the Texas economy in the 1800s.

	Agriculture	Ranching	Industry
Markets			
Growth			
Problems			

Homework Practice Online
keyword: SM3 HPTX

3. Finding the Main Idea
a. What opportunities and problems did cotton cultivation create in Texas?
b. Why did ranchers drive cattle herds north from Texas?

4. Writing and Critical Thinking
Summarizing: Imagine that you are a Texas rancher in the late 1800s. Discuss some of the challenges facing your industry and how you have overcome them.
Consider the following:
• environmental hardships
• the significance of your ranch's location in relation to the market

T4 PROLOGUE

SECTION 2

BOOM AND BUST IN THE EARLY 1900s

READ TO DISCOVER
1. What benefits did the oil industry bring to Texas?
2. How did World War I affect the Texas economy?
3. How did the United States respond to the economic crisis called the Great Depression?

ECONOMICS DICTIONARY
Spindletop strike
petroleum
vertical integration
horizontal integration
petrochemicals
demobilization
Great Depression
proration
New Deal

Throughout its history the Texas economy has undergone cycles of boom and bust. In good times and bad, however, Texas entrepreneurs have looked for innovative ways to use the state's natural resources.

The Texas Oil Industry

On January 10, 1901, a giant plume of oil that could be seen more than 10 miles away shot out of an oil well on Spindletop Hill near Beaumont. The **Spindletop strike,** which made newspaper headlines around the world, signaled a major shift in the Texas economy. In the 1900s the land of farmers and cowboys would also become a land of oil barons and oil-field workers as the petroleum industry became an important part of the Texas economy.

The Market The demand for oil had risen dramatically after scientists developed kerosene, a new form of fuel used for lighting derived from **petroleum,** or oil. Texans had drilled for oil as early as 1866, but initial efforts to discover oil were not very successful. In 1889 Texas produced only 48 barrels of oil, compared to the 35 million barrels produced in the rest of the United States.

The Texas oil industry took off in 1894, when a major oil field was discovered in Corsicana. In 1900 the Corsicana field yielded about 839,000 barrels of oil. Businesses constructed refineries to process crude oil and convert it into usable products such as kerosene or lubricants. Yet production at the Corsicana field was dwarfed by the astounding output of the Spindletop oil field. Spindletop produced more than 17 million barrels of oil in 1902, some 20 percent of the oil produced in the United States.

New Business Strategies The discovery of oil at Spindletop led to a boom in the Texas economy and created many new jobs. About 500 oil

MARKETS & PRICES *The Spindletop strike led to an oil boom in Texas.* **How did the strike affect the Texas economy?**

SECTION 2

BOOM AND BUST IN THE EARLY 1900s

Lesson Plans
For teaching strategies, see Lesson P.2 located at the beginning of this chapter, or the One-Stop Planner strategy P.2.

Economics Dictionary
To reinforce the section's vocabulary terms, refer students to the Electronic Glossary on the *Researcher CD-ROM*.

Section Assessment
To assess students' mastery of this section, have them complete Daily Quiz P.2 in *Texas Connections to Economics*.

Caption Answer
The boom brought many new jobs to the state and boosted other industries, such as refining and petrochemicals.

TEKS
Content
7A, 15A, 15B
Social Studies Skills
23A, 24A, 24C, 24D

Themes in Economics

THE ROLE OF GOVERNMENT

Early Texas roads may have been little more than bumpy trails, but today's Texas highways are considered to be some of the best in the nation. More than 70,000 miles of highways criss-cross Texas. A state gasoline tax, vehicle registration fees, and federal assistance help finance and maintain the state's highway system. ★23A

Caption Answer

Answers could include oil-field workers, refinery workers, store owners, wagon drivers, oil equipment suppliers ★23A

---

internet connect

TOPIC: Spindletop
GO TO: go.hrw.com
KEYWORD: SM3 ECP

Have students access the Internet through the HRW Go site to conduct research on Spindletop. Have students imagine themselves transported via time machine to 1901, Beaumont, Texas. Students should collect all the information they can and then "return" to the present where they present their findings to the class. Students should consider the impact of Spindletop on Texas and the U.S. oil industry. ★24D

---

companies operated in nearby Beaumont, which swelled in population to some 40,000 residents. Spindletop produced so much oil, however, that prices quickly dropped, reaching an all-time low of three cents a barrel in 1902. The slumping prices drove many small oil companies out of business. In order to survive, oil companies relied upon business strategies to increase efficiency and cut costs. Some companies practiced **vertical integration**—owning the businesses involved in each step of a manufacturing process. For example, the Texas Company drilled for oil, owned refineries, and operated barges and railroad tanker cars that transported oil. Most large oil companies also practiced **horizontal integration**—owning many businesses in a particular field. Large oil corporations ran many refineries—factories where crude oil is converted into usable products. These refineries shared supplies and resources to make business more efficient. Some of the companies that practiced vertical and horizontal integration became quite wealthy and powerful.

Boom Times The growing popularity of automobiles expanded the market for petroleum products and increased oil company profits. Automobiles used gasoline, an oil by-product that had long been regarded as waste. As more Americans purchased cars, demand for gasoline increased, and the Texas oil industry's production of gasoline helped keep Americans on the nation's roads and highways. The oil industry also benefited from the sale of natural gas, another product of the Texas oil fields. New technology allowed for the development of pipelines that could safely transport natural gas to distant markets.

Continued demand for oil and natural gas prompted research and exploration, which led to the discovery of additional fields throughout the state. The first successful oil strike in the Panhandle took place in 1921. Six years later, Panhandle oil fields produced some 39 million barrels of oil in a single year. Major West Texas oil fields included the Yates, Hobbs, and Big Lake oil fields. In 1930 a wildcatter, or someone who drills for oil independently, named C. M. Joiner confounded experts when he discovered a major oil field in East Texas, where geologists had claimed there was very little oil. The East Texas field soon became one of the largest in the world.

The booming oil industry affected Texas in many ways. The industry created thousands of jobs for Texans. Boomtowns, raw and rough towns filled with people eager to become rich, sprang up near new oil fields. The state government taxed oil-field production—in 1919 tax

ECONOMIC INSTITUTIONS & INCENTIVES *People flocked to boomtowns seeking jobs in the oil business.* **What types of jobs do you think the oil boom generated?**

revenues from oil reached $1 million. Some oil producers also used their huge profits to contribute millions to hospitals, universities, and charities in the state.

Industry and Agriculture

The oil boom of the early 1900s also furthered the growth of industry in Texas, as many Texans found work in the industries related to the oil business. **Petrochemicals,** products made from oil and gas, became an important part of the Texas economy. Petrochemicals include synthetic rubber, plastics, and carbon black, which is used to make ink, tires, and other products.

The growth of the oil industry, railroads, and the textile industry increased the number of industrial jobs in Texas. By 1920 some 16 percent of the Texas workforce was employed in industry. At the same time, the number of Texans involved in agriculture declined by about 24 percent. Life on Texas farms had never been easy, requiring a lot of hard work and offering few luxuries. Technologies such as gasoline-powered tractors and electric irrigation pumps increased production, which led to surpluses and declining prices for farm goods. As a result, many Texas farm families had difficulty paying their debts, and thus the number of tenant farmers and sharecroppers rose. As one newspaper noted, "There is something rotten in Texas when more than half of our farm families are landless tenants." The struggles of farm life led many rural families to move to urban areas in search of new opportunities.

Hard Times

The economic demands of World War I provided some relief for farmers and other Texans. To feed and clothe U.S. soldiers, Texans stepped up agricultural production, borrowing money to purchase land and equipment. Oil and lumber production also increased, and the Texas economy reached almost full employment during the war. In addition, federal spending in Texas increased as the state became home to several military installations. Yet at war's end, the process of **demobilization,** or moving from a wartime to a peacetime economy, ended the boom. Soldiers returning home needed jobs, often displacing women and African Americans who had found industrial work during the war. Reduced demand led to declining prices for agricultural goods—cotton fell from 42 cents a pound in 1920 to less than 10 cents a pound a year later—and Texas farmers again endured hard times.

The Great Depression Times went from bad to worse in 1929, the first year of a global economic downturn called the **Great Depression.** The depression was less severe in Texas than it was in many other states. The oil industry initially continued to provide jobs. However, as

SUPPLY & DEMAND *Texas farmers faced the environmental challenge of terrible dust storms during the 1930s.* **What other problems did farmers face?**

Cultural Perspectives

Many inventions were created to facilitate the production and use of oil. Elijah McCoy, the son of runaway slaves, contributed a lubricating cup that fed oil to parts of a machine while it was running. McCoy who was schooled as an engineer in Scotland, could not find a job in his chosen profession. Although many companies were looking for engineers, none would hire an African American. He eventually took a job shoveling coal and lubricating machines. He noticed that the companies lost production time because the machines had to be stopped, lubricated by hand, then restarted. McCoy worked for two years, spending his own money and using scrap metal, to create his automatic lubricator. After patenting his invention, McCoy soon improved upon his creation and developed other lubricating devices. Others tried to sell their own versions of the automatic lubricator, but buyers knew that McCoy's was the most dependable. Before buying they would ask, "Is this the *real* McCoy?" ■

Caption Answer
Overproduction of cash crops, such as cotton, led to falling prices.

THE TEXAS ECONOMY T7

SECTION 2 REVIEW ANSWERS

1. petroleum (T5), Spindletop strike (T5), vertical integration (T6), horizontal integration (T6), petrochemicals (T7), demobilization (T7), Great Depression (T7), proration (T8), New Deal (T8) **24A**

2. jobs—brought many new jobs to the state, industries—many related industries, such as refineries, developed, taxes—state able to gain much revenue from taxes on oil **24D**

3a. As farmers and oil companies produced more, prices fell. **7A, 23A**

3b. created jobs to help unemployed Americans survive and to foster economic growth **15A**

4. Students' explanations will vary but should reflect an understanding of the benefits of and reasons for the use of vertical and horizontal integration. **23A**

---

time passed the depression deepened. Businesses laid off workers to reduce expenses. Unemployed workers could not afford to buy many goods, and falling demand led to business failures and more layoffs. By 1932 some 300,000 Texans were unemployed.

Economic conditions worsened as overproduction led to a crisis in the oil industry and in agriculture. The discovery of the East Texas oil field in 1930 created a surplus, and oil prices fell from more than $1 per barrel to a dangerously low 8 cents per barrel. In an effort to limit production, Governor Ross Sterling declared martial law in four East Texas counties in 1931. Sterling sent in the National Guard to enforce **proration,** a system under which each well could produce only a specified amount of oil each day.

Like oil companies, Texas farmers continued to overproduce, which drove cotton prices down to less than six cents a pound in 1932. Some farmers burned their crops. One newspaper noted, "There is no waste in burning something that . . . is hardly worth hauling to town."

The New Deal The Great Depression lasted throughout the decade of the 1930s. The economic crisis was so severe that the federal government, under the direction of President Franklin Roosevelt, created numerous programs to assist citizens and promote economic recovery. Roosevelt's program, called the **New Deal,** created jobs by funding public works—government-sponsored building projects for public use. Some 100,000 Texans found work in the Civilian Conservation Corps (CCC), which built and repaired bridges, dams, and roads. The Works Progress Administration (WPA) constructed dams along the Colorado River, and the National Youth Administration (NYA) created jobs for young people. The Texas chapter of the NYA was headed by a young Texan named Lyndon B. Johnson. Texas NYA workers constructed the first highway rest stops in the nation, an innovation that quickly spread to other states. With money in their pockets, Texans could buy goods and, it was hoped, spur economic recovery.

The New Deal did not end the Great Depression, however. The economy remained weak until the early 1940s, when another global event changed the lives of Texans and other Americans. In 1941 the Japanese bombed Pearl Harbor, drawing the United States into a long and bloody war.

SECTION 2 REVIEW

★ TEKS 1, 2, 3a, 3b, 4

1. Identify and Explain:
- Spindletop strike
- petroleum
- vertical integration
- horizontal integration
- petrochemicals
- demobilization
- Great Depression
- proration
- New Deal

2. Identifying Cause and Effect: Copy the web diagram below. Use the diagram to show how the oil industry affected the Texas economy.

(Web diagram: Oil Industry connected to Jobs, Industries, Taxes)

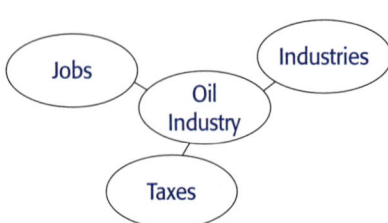

3. Finding the Main Idea
- **a.** How did overproduction hurt farmers and the Texas oil industry?
- **b.** How did the federal government respond to the crisis of the Great Depression?

4. Writing and Critical Thinking
Evaluating: Imagine that you are an oil industry executive. Explain to a newspaper reporter the benefits of horizontal and vertical integration.
Consider the following:
- efforts to control costs
- the benefits of increased efficiency

Homework Practice Online
keyword: SM3 HPTX

SECTION 3

TEXAS AND THE WORLD

READ TO DISCOVER
1. What industries developed in Texas after World War II?
2. How has medical research affected the Texas economy?
3. How has Texas become tied to the global economy?

ECONOMICS DICTIONARY
aerospace
Manned Spacecraft Center
Michael DeBakey
globalization
North American Free Trade Agreement
maquiladoras

Since World War II, Texas has become increasingly linked to the national and global economies. Many people have come to Texas seeking jobs and economic opportunities.

War and Economic Growth

World War II did what the New Deal had not—it ended the Great Depression. Even before the Japanese attack on Pearl Harbor, Americans had been providing weapons and supplies to the allies. This, along with the rapid U.S. mobilization after the attack, transformed the American economy. Approximately 500,000 Texans moved from rural areas to cities to look for work in booming industries, including aircraft and ship construction, chemical production, and steel manufacturing. In addition, some 750,000 Texas men and women found employment in the nation's armed forces. The Texas economy also grew as a result of federal spending in the state, which served as a wartime training center for 1.2 million soldiers and 200,000 pilots.

Military spending remained important to the Texas economy after World War II ended in 1945. The Cold War, the name given to the tensions that existed between the United States and the Soviet Union after 1945, led the United States government to continue defense spending. Increases in military spending promoted economic growth in Texas, which by 1955 led the United States in the production of helium, oil, petrochemicals, and sulfur. The Texas aircraft industry, which had boomed during World War II, continued to thrive because of increased civilian travel and military demands. Texas became a center for weapons production. By 1965 the Texas firm of General Dynamics had become the leading weapons exporter in the United States.

The military's need for rockets also helped launch the state's **aerospace** industry, which manufactured airplanes as well as missiles. The electronics industry also gained a strong presence in the state as firms like Texas Instruments assisted in the development of missiles. In addition, other Texas industries produced goods and services for the personnel stationed at the many military installations in the state.

ROLE OF GOVERNMENT *During World War II and the Cold War, Texas was home to a growing aircraft industry.* **How did defense spending help the Texas economy?**

THE TEXAS ECONOMY T9

Caption Answer
The location of the Manned Spacecraft Center in Houston brought many new jobs to the area and helped attract high-tech industries to the state.

internet connect
TOPIC: Economic Map of Texas
GO TO: go.hrw.com
KEYWORD: SM3 ECP

Have students access the Internet through the HRW Go site to research various parts of the Texas economy. Individually or in groups, have students create thematic maps of the state showing the location of various industries and institutions important to the economy. For instance, they may wish to include the Johnson Space Center, the Texas Medical Center, Spindletop, high-tech industries, tourist locations, universities, and other economic engines mentioned on the Web or in the chapter. ★24D

Caption Answer
New jobs have brought increased prosperity to the state, but downturns in the technology industries have also caused economic hardships for some Texans.

PRODUCTIVITY *The Manned Spacecraft Center in Houston served as Mission Control for landings on the Moon.* **How did space technology affect the economy?**

While rapid industrial growth drew many Texans to urban areas, the rural population continued to decline. Texas cities took on a new look, with towering skyscrapers, four-lane expressways filled with automobiles and passenger planes cruising in the skies overhead. Reflecting on economic and urban growth in Texas, one journalist noted that "quiet towns are being transformed, almost violently, into large cities with towering skylines."

High-Tech Texas

As the home of a vibrant aerospace industry, Texas was a logical choice to become a center of the nation's space program in the late 1950s and 1960s. In 1961 Houston became the home of the **Manned Spacecraft Center,** which served as the Mission Control Center for all human U.S. space flights. Renamed the Lyndon B. Johnson Space Center in 1973, the facility brought many jobs to Texas. Engineers and technicians at the center researched, developed, and built the first space shuttle, which was launched in 1981. With thousands of employees, the center was also a primary source for space-station and space-medicine research.

In addition to becoming a center for defense and space research, Texas rapidly became a leader in electronics. Drawn by low labor costs, good climate, and proximity to markets, many electronics firms moved to Texas. These companies manufactured a variety of electronic devices, including transistors, television sets, and computers. New technological developments in communications, radar, and other systems led to even greater growth, and by 1963 nearly 300 businesses in the state produced electronic devices. Several Texas firms became world leaders in electronics, adding billions of dollars to the state's economy. These companies also provided national and international markets with new technology developed and manufactured in Texas.

As computer technology became more important to business operations, Texas companies designed and manufactured semiconductors and microchips to meet the national and international demand. Austin became a high-tech research center as several companies built facilities there during the 1960s and 1970s.

Scientific research in medicine also spurred economic growth. In the 1960s Texas doctors and scientists studied new treatments for cancer, evaluated new drugs, and developed other medical innovations. Texas doctors such as **Michael DeBakey,** who performed the first arterial bypass to repair a damaged heart, helped revolutionize

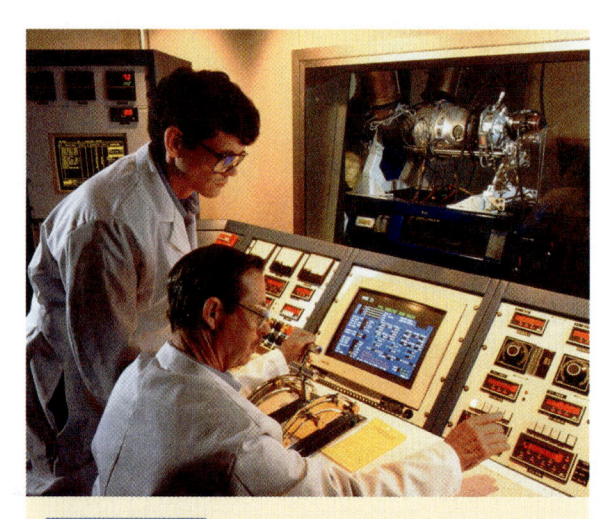

PRODUCTIVITY *In recent years Texas has become one of the world's leading high-tech centers.* **How has an increase in high-tech jobs presented Texans with new opportunities and challenges?**

T10 PROLOGUE

improved. Successful industrial development led to an improved quality of life for many Texans, which in turn attracted more people to the state.

Economic Diversification

Over the course of the 1900s the Texas economy had become increasingly tied to the global economy. This became apparent during the 1970s, when Texans benefited from rising international oil prices. The entire state economy continued to grow until oil prices dropped in the early 1980s. Oil production in the state declined, causing some one third of workers in the Texas oil industry to lose their jobs between 1982 and 1994. As oil prices fell, the real estate and banking industries experienced financial problems. Texas banks, which had greatly profited from a strong real estate market, were hit hard when real estate prices collapsed in the 1980s. In addition, banks suffered when oil companies and other industries that were not doing well defaulted on loans. Between 1985 and 1992, about 470 banks went out of business. First the Texas economy and then the national economy went into recession.

Changing demand for goods in national and international markets prompted Texans to diversify the state's industrial base, helping Texas to recover from the downturn of the late 1980s. Changes in the economy were reflected in shifting sources of state revenue. In 1993 state government received only 7 percent of its income from oil activities, down from 25 percent just a decade earlier. Many Texans found work in high-tech industries or in service-related industries, such as health care and tourism. In the late 1990s two Texas companies—Compaq of Houston and Dell Computer Corporation of Round Rock—led the world in computer production. Some 25 percent of Texans who worked in manufacturing produced computers or other electronic devices. The value of Texas high-tech exports totaled some $36.5 billion in 1997.

Although industry dominated the Texas economy in the 1990s, agribusiness—the farming and processing of agricultural goods—remained important, contributing about $40 billion a year

or medical research, Texas has drawn patients from around the world for treatment. Medical technologies developed in Texas, such as the artificial heart, are used throughout the world to treat patients. As a result of these scientific and medical advances, many high-tech technology firms moved their operations to Texas. In 1998 Dr. Ferid Murad of the University of Texas received the Nobel Prize in medicine for his research on the relationship between chemicals and the heart. Texas remained a high-tech center into the twenty-first century.

The booming Texas high-tech and medical-technology industries affected not only the markets in which they operated but also the cities in which they were based. As the populations of the cities grew dramatically, world-class buildings and new sports arenas were built, and museums and other attractions were established or

Themes in Economics

INTERNATIONAL TRADE The growing domestic demand for fossil fuels made the United States increasingly dependent upon foreign oil. In 1960 the United States imported 19 percent of its oil; by 1974 that number had risen to 39 percent. Americans were particularly dependent upon Middle Eastern oil resources. In the mid-1970s, as much as half of all imported oil came from the that region. As political circumstances in the Middle East began to affect the price of oil in the United States, the United States looked to Texas for less expensive oil.

Themes in Economics

THE ROLE OF GOVERNMENT Many labor leaders in the United States feared that the North American Free Trade Agreement (NAFTA) would lead to the loss of jobs for Americans. Because labor unions represented a powerful force within the Democratic Party, many Democrats in Congress refused to support NAFTA. President Clinton decided to ally with Republicans to secure its passage. NAFTA passed in the House by a 234-to-200 vote and in the Senate by a 61-to-38 vote.

Caption Answer
about 40,000 ★ 23F, 23G

SECTION 3 REVIEW ANSWERS

1. aerospace (T9), Manned Spacecraft Center (T10), Michael DeBakey (T10), globalization (T12), North American Trade Agreement (T12), maquiladora (T12) **24A**

2. Student responses will vary, but their tree maps should include examples from the space program, medical research, high-tech industries, and NAFTA. **24D**

3a. The state had developed defense and aircraft industries, which provided the basis for space facilities. **23A**

3b. Advanced research brought experts and research money into the state. **23A**

4. Students' responses will vary but should include a discussion of the effect of NAFTA and the impact of economic downturns. Some responses might include: opportunities—increased jobs, new international markets; challenges—increased pollution, growth outpacing infrastructure **14B, 23A**

---

to the state's economy by the end of the 1990s. Texas led the nation in production of cotton and hay, and it exported large amounts of grapefruit, oranges, and peanuts.

Global Trade

In 1998, state officials announced that if Texas were still an independent nation, it would be the 11th largest economy in the world. The state's booming economy reflected its increasing interdependence with the rest of the world, a process called **globalization.** Dozens of nations ranging from Albania to Venezuela maintain consulates, or diplomatic offices, in Texas. These consulates work to improve trade between Texas and other nations. In addition, Texas maintains several Foreign Trade Zones, areas in which export regulations are reduced in an effort to promote trade. In 2000 Texas had 26 such zones.

The Texas economy received a large boost in 1994 when the **North American Free Trade Agreement** (NAFTA), which eliminated many trade barriers between Canada, Mexico, and the United States, went into effect. Many of the trade goods flowing to and from Mexico pass through Texas, bringing more jobs to the state. In 1999 about $41 billion worth of goods—almost half the state's exports—went to Mexico.

Globalization brought many benefits to Texas, but it also brought challenges. Increased trade along the Texas-Mexico border led to rapid population growth in the region. Many cities along the border could not build an infrastructure—public works such as roads and water systems—quickly enough to keep pace with population gains. In addition, hundreds of *maquiladoras,* or factories, appeared along the Mexican border, contributing to the air and water pollution in the region. These new factories, however, brought jobs and economic development to the region. Finally, international economic downturns still affected the Texas economy. For example, when Mexico experienced a financial crisis in 1995, computer exports from Texas to that country fell dramatically.

Despite these challenges, Texans recognized that globalization was essential to economic growth in Texas, and the state government worked to advance the process. Texas also maintains an Office of International businesses and conducts overseas trade shows. As a result of these and other efforts, Texas is a major exporter of goods from the United States to global markets.

SECTION 3 REVIEW

★ TEKS 1, 2, 4

1. **Identify and Explain:**
   aerospace
   Manned Spacecraft Center
   Michael DeBakey
   globalization
   North American Free Trade Agreement
   maquiladoras

2. **Categorizing** Copy the graphic organizer below. Use the organizer to show the diversification of the Texas economy in the late 1900s.

   (Medical Research, High-Tech Industries, Space Program, NAFTA)

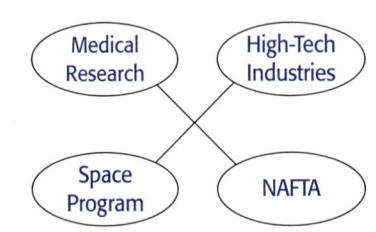

3. **Finding the Main Idea**
   a. Why did Texas become the center for the nation's space program?
   b. How has medical research affected the Texas economy?

4. **Writing and Critical Thinking**
   Evaluating: What opportunities and challenges do international markets create for Texas?
   Consider the following:
   • the effect of NAFTA
   • the effects of international economic downturns

Homework Practice Online
keyword: SM3 HPTX

Economics IN THE NEWS

Economics and the Arts

A study released in January 2001 revealed the importance of the arts to the Texas economy. The study, entitled "The Arts, Culture, and the Texas Economy," reported that in the year 2000 the combined effect of artistic endeavors created about 1.9 million jobs in Texas. These endeavors included art exhibits, opera, history, and photography and non-artistic work that supports the arts. These jobs generated some $61.7 billion in personal income for Texans. The report concluded that about 20 percent of tourist spending in the state was related to the arts.

The regions in Texas that benefited most from the economic effects of the arts were the most-populated urban areas. Some 78 percent of the total amount of money people spent on the arts in Texas took place in metropolitan areas: Dallas, Houston, Fort Worth–Arlington, San Antonio, and Austin–San Marcos. The study argued, however, that Texans in rural areas benefit from the arts too, as artistic projects and the people who operate them make use of agricultural goods produced in rural areas.

Ray Perryman, one of the report's authors, concluded that "if you limit the exposure of people to the arts, you limit the long-term ability of the economy to expand." George Pond of the Texas Cultural Trust Council declared that financial support and planning for the arts are "as important as putting in a water pipeline. I could argue they're more important." Perryman, Pond, and other supporters of the arts in Texas hoped that the report would spur Texas to spend more on the arts, both for their "celebration of life" and their economic benefits. Pond noted that in 2000 the Texas state government spent only 17 cents per person on cultural arts, whereas the national average for arts spending by states that year was $1.44.

What Do You Think? ★TEKS

1. How do the cultural arts affect the Texas economy?
2. In your opinion, what role should the government play in spending for the arts? Explain your answer.

WHY IT MATTERS TODAY

The arts are only one aspect of the diverse Texas economy. Use CNNfyi.com or other **current events** sources to find additional information on issues affecting the Texas economy. Record your findings in your Economics Notebook.

CNNfyi.com

Many Texans enjoy visiting art exhibits, like this outdoor show in Austin.

Economics in the News Answers

1. In 2000 the arts accounted for about 1.9 million jobs, generating some $6.7 billion in personal revenue. 23A

2. Student responses will vary, but students should provide reasons to support their opinions. They may also rely on recent news stories and information. 23A, 23D

PROLOGUE Review Answers

Writing a Summary

Summaries should focus on the main points of each section. These may be found in the Read to Discover questions at the start of each section. Summaries should also use standard grammar, spelling, sentence structure, and punctuation. 24B, 24D

Identifying People and Ideas

cash crop (T1), commercial farming (T1), Spindletop strike (T5), vertical integration (T6), petrochemicals (T7), proration (T8), New Deal (T8), aerospace (T9), Michael Debakey (T10), North American Free Trade Agreement (T12) 24A

Understanding Main Ideas

1. The booming market declined by the end of the century.

2. Texas had the cattle needed to meet the growing demand for beef in the United States.

PROLOGUE Review

(Continued from page T13)

3. Hardships include bad weather and difficulty getting cattle to market.

4. created new petrochemical industries

5. It put some 300,000 Texans out of work, requiring federal intervention to help the state recover.

6. CCC, WPA, NYA,

7. space program, electronics, medical research

8. Diversity allowed the economy to weather downturns in some industries.

9. benefits—increased jobs, new markets; costs—increased pollution, growth outpacing infrastructure

Reviewing Themes

1. Its proximity to Mexico created economic opportunities.

2. Students should note the affect of railroads and barbed wire on the industry. **26A**

3. It has given Texas more markets but made it vulnerable to economic downturns in other countries. **14B**

Thinking Critically

1. Students should note that it has become diverse, including manufacturing and high-tech research. **23A**

2. When cotton and oil were overproduced, prices dropped, reducing income in Texas. **23A**

3. marks a turning point because it was followed by an oil boom that influenced the economy throughout the 1900s **23A**

Writing A Summary ⭐TEKS

Using standard grammar, spelling, sentence structure, and punctuation, write a summary of the information in this chapter.

Identifying People and Ideas ⭐TEKS

1. cash crop
2. commercial farming
3. Spindletop strike
4. vertical integration
5. petrochemicals
6. proration
7. New Deal
8. aerospace
9. Michael DeBakey
10. North American Free Trade Agreement

Understanding Main Ideas

SECTION 1 *(pp. T1–T4)*

1. How did the cotton market change over the course of the 1800s?
2. Why did the cattle industry boom after the Civil War?
3. What hardships did Texas ranchers face in the 1800s?

SECTION 2 *(pp. T5–T8)*

4. How did the oil boom contribute to industrial growth in Texas?
5. How did the Great Depression affect the Texas economy?
6. What New Deal Programs tried to help fight the effects of the depression?

SECTION 3 *(pp. T9–T12)*

7. What industries developed in Texas after World War II?
8. How did a diversified economy benefit Texans?
9. What have been some benefits and costs for Texas with U.S. participation in NAFTA?

Reviewing Themes ⭐TEKS

1. **Markets & Prices** How did the geographic location of Texas affect its economy in the 1900s?
2. **Productivity** How did technology influence the Texas cattle industry?
3. **International Trade** How has global trade affected the Texas economy?

Thinking Critically

1. **Summarizing** How did the Texas economy change during the 1900s?
2. **Analyzing Information** How did overproduction of some goods weaken the Texas economy?
3. **Evaluating** What is the importance of the Spindletop strike to the economic history of Texas?

Writing about Economics ⭐TEKS

Look back at the economic activities you described in your Economics Notebook at the start of the chapter. Do you still agree with your choices? In your Notebook, revise your answer or explain why you still think your choices are correct.

Building Social Studies Skills

Interpreting the Chart

Spindletop Oil Production 1901–21

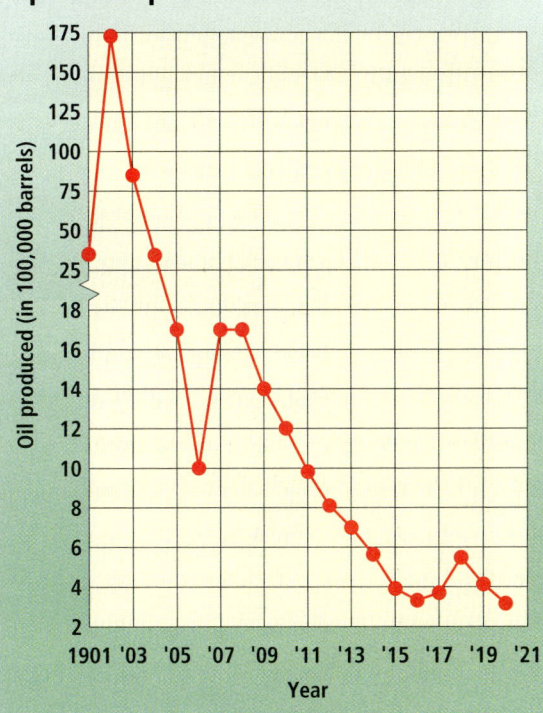

Oil produced (in 100,000 barrels) vs Year (1901–'21)

Source: Carl Coke Rister, *Oil! Titan of the Southwest*

1. By how much did Spindletop oil production change between 1902 and 1910?
   a. dropped 16.2 million barrels
   b. rose 16.2 million barrels
   c. dropped 18.6 million barrels
   d. rose 18.6 million barrels

2. Based on your knowledge of the chapter, what do you think caused the change?

Analyzing Primary Sources

Read the following excerpt from an oral history of oil drilling as remembered by Electra resident E. M. Friend.

"Doc got hold of a little old spudding [digging] machine and got to drilling those shallow wells. . . . His old machine didn't amount to much. He kept it fixed up with bailing wire and anything he could get hold of. . . . And so his brother had a little money and his father had a little money. They kind of throwed in together and bought them a rotary drill. And they got some contracts and I imagine they were just about the luckiest drillers in the country. And they had the one rig, then they built it up to three or four. And when things got quiet in Electra, the East Texas oil field opened up and they went down there. And their luck still held good, by George."

3. What led to Doc's success as an oil producer?
   a. using bailing wire on his old drilling machine
   b. buying new technology
   c. drilling in many different regions at once
   d. only drilling in Electra

4. Is this oral history a primary source of the events in Electra or a secondary one? Explain your answer.

Alternative Assessment

Building Your Portfolio

Create an illustrated tree map that shows how the Texas economy has been integrated into the national and world economy since the 1800s. You should conduct research to find some specific examples of companies that fit into the various categories on the map. Include these examples on your map and present your work to the class.

internet connect

Internet Activity: go.hrw.com
KEYWORD: SM3 ECTX

Access the Internet through the HRW Go site to conduct research on President Lyndon B. Johnson. Work in pairs to write the script for an interview between a reporter and President Johnson. Include questions about Johnson's childhood, his wife, life in Texas, efforts as president, and any other topics of interest. Take turns presenting your interviews to the class.

TAKS REVIEW ONLINE
Keyword: SM3 TP

Writing about Economics
Students may or may not revise their choices, but should provide some explanation in either case. 24D

Building Social Studies Skills
1. a 25F
2. Students should note that the rush to Spindletop probably led to overproduction. 23F
3. b 23E
4. primary because Friend was present at the events being discussed

THE TEXAS ECONOMY T15

UNIT 1

Lesson Options

Suggestions for customizing the material in Unit 1 to fit the specific schedule and curriculum of your classroom are located at the beginning of each chapter.

Main Ideas

Ask each student to read the Main Ideas and to briefly answer each question in writing. Later, when you have finished Unit 1, ask students to return to their original answers and to revise them using what they learned in the unit.

Economics Lab

The Unit 1 Economics Lab appears on pages 44–47. This lab project is a real-world assignment in which students will work in groups to choose the best economic system for a new international settlement planned for the Moon. During the course of the project, students will consider the pros and cons of the world's three major economic systems: capitalism, democratic socialism, and authoritarian socialism (or communism). Support materials for the lab appear in *Unit Tests and Unit Lab Activities with Answer Key.* ★21A

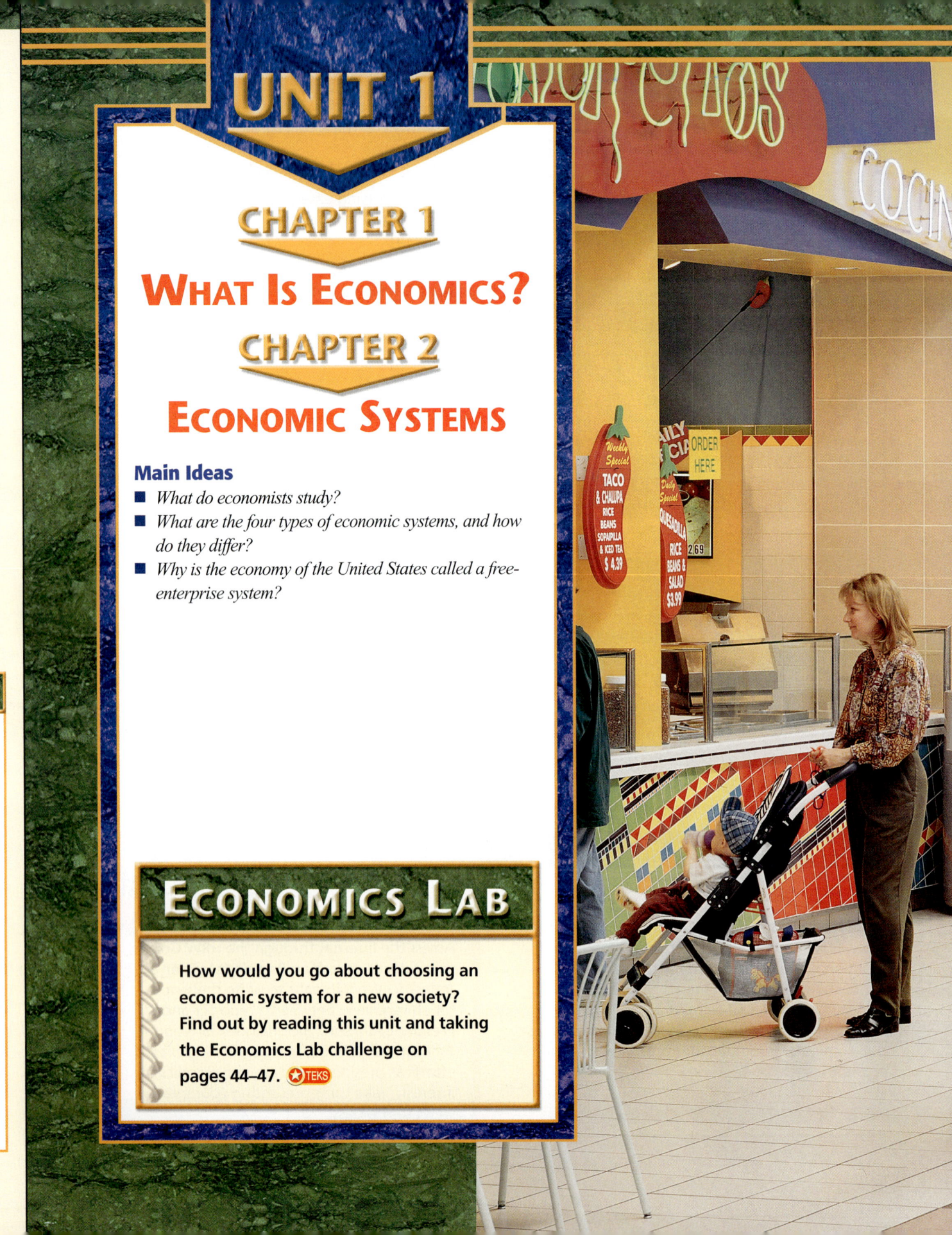

UNIT 1

CHAPTER 1
WHAT IS ECONOMICS?

CHAPTER 2
ECONOMIC SYSTEMS

Main Ideas

- *What do economists study?*
- *What are the four types of economic systems, and how do they differ?*
- *Why is the economy of the United States called a free-enterprise system?*

Economics Lab

How would you go about choosing an economic system for a new society? Find out by reading this unit and taking the Economics Lab challenge on pages 44–47. ★TEKS

Introduction to Economics

Unit 1 Overview

Unit 1 introduces students to the study of economics and to fundamental concepts such as scarcity and choice, trade-offs and opportunity cost, productivity, money and exchange, interdependence, and markets. Students will examine how individuals and different societies address the three basic economic questions: what to produce, how to produce, and for whom to produce. They will also study the factors of production, the circular-flow model, the main economic systems in the world, the main features of a free-enterprise system, and the main features and goals of the U.S. economy.

Teaching with Photographs

This photograph shows a food court at a popular shopping mall. Eating at a mall involves making several economic choices. People must decide where to eat, how much to spend, and what to order. As a motivating activity for this unit, ask students to point out the types of economic choices illustrated in the photograph.

CHAPTER RESOURCE MANAGER

CHAPTER 1: WHAT IS ECONOMICS?

Section	Objectives	Pacing Guide	Reproducible Resources
SECTION 1 **An Economic Way of Thinking** (pp. 3–7)	• What is economics? • What are the factors of production? • What is the goal of entrepreneurship?	Regular: 1 day; Block Scheduling: 0.5 day	ELL Spanish Study Guide 1.1; ELL English Study Guide 1.1; SM Consumer Economics: Activity 1
SECTION 2 **Scarcity and Choice** (pp. 8–10)	• Why is scarcity a basic problem of economics? • What issues must producers address to distribute resources? • Why do producers study productivity?	Regular: 1.5 days; Block Scheduling: 0.5 day	ELL Spanish Study Guide 1.2; ELL English Study Guide 1.2; PS Reading 60: Principles of Economics, Alfred Marshall
SECTION 3 **Opportunity Costs** (pp. 11–14)	• Why is sacrifice an important element of economic choice? • What assumptions are involved in creating a production possibilities curve? • Why might future production possibilities differ from current production possibilities?	Regular: 1.5 days; Block Scheduling: 1 day	ELL Spanish Study Guide 1.3; ELL English Study Guide 1.3; SM Mathematics for Economics: Activity 1
SECTION 4 **Exchange** (pp. 15–18)	• What are the difficulties associated with barter? • Why is true self-sufficiency rare? • What are the economic benefits of interdependence?	Regular: 1.5 days; Block Scheduling: 1 day	ELL Spanish Study Guide 1.4; ELL English Study Guide 1.4; E Challenge and Enrichment: Activity 1; E Simulations and Strategies for Teaching Economics: Activity 1

Chapter Resource Key

- **PS** Primary Sources
- **RS** Reading Support
- **E** Enrichment
- **S** Simulations
- **SM** Skills Mastery
- **A** Assessment
- **REV** Review
- **ELL** Reinforcement and English Language Learners
- Transparencies
- CD-ROM
- Video
- Videodisc
- Internet
- Holt Presentation Maker Using Microsoft® PowerPoint®
- TEKS and TAKS

TECHNOLOGY RESOURCES	REINFORCEMENT, REVIEW, AND ASSESSMENT
One-Stop Planner: Lesson 1.1 Researcher Online Homework Practice Online CNN Presents Economics: Weighing the Value of History Global Skillbuilder CD-ROM	REV Section 1 Review, p. 7 A Daily Quiz 1.1 ★ TAKS Every Day!
One-Stop Planner: Lesson 1.2 Researcher Online Homework Practice Online Transparency 1 Global Skillbuilder CD-ROM	REV Section 2 Review, p. 10 A Daily Quiz 1.2 ★ TAKS Every Day!
One-Stop Planner: Lesson 1.3 Researcher Online Homework Practice Online Holt Economics Videodisc: Land Use: Development in Dana Point Transparencies 2 and 3 Global Skillbuilder CD-ROM	REV Section 3 Review, p. 14 A Daily Quiz 1.3 ★ TAKS Every Day!
One-Stop Planner: Lesson 1.4 Researcher Online Homework Practice Online Global Skillbuilder CD-ROM	REV Section 4 Review, p. 18 A Daily Quiz 1.4 ★ TAKS Every Day!

Chapter Review and Assessment

SM Global Skillbuilder CD-ROM
HRW Go site
REV Reteaching Activity 1
REV Chapter 1 Review, pp. 20–21
A Chapter 1 Test Generator (on the One-Stop Planner)
A Chapter 1 Test
A Alternative Assessment Handbook

One-Stop Planner CD-ROM

It's easy to plan lessons, select resources, and print out materials for your students when you use the *Texas One-Stop Planner CD-ROM with Test Generator*.

---

internet connect

HRW ONLINE RESOURCES
Go To: go.hrw.com
Then type in a keyword.

TEACHER HOME PAGE
KEYWORD: SM3 Teacher

CHAPTER INTERNET ACTIVITIES
KEYWORD: SM3 EC1
Choose an activity to:
▶ research natural resources.
▶ understand assembly lines.
▶ learn about the economy of Nauru.

CHAPTER ENRICHMENT LINKS
KEYWORD: SM3 CH1

HOLT RESEARCHER ONLINE
KEYWORD: Holt Researcher

ONLINE ASSESSMENT
Homework Practice
KEYWORD: SM3 HP1
TAKS Review
KEYWORD: SM3 T1
Rubrics
KEYWORD: SS Rubrics

CONTENT UPDATES
KEYWORD: SS Content Updates

HOLT PRESENTATION MAKER
KEYWORD: SM3 PPT1

ONLINE READING SUPPORT
KEYWORD: SS Strategies

CURRENT EVENTS
KEYWORD: S3 Current Events

TEXAS ONLINE RESOURCES
KEYWORD: S3 TX

1B

LESSON 1.1 AN ECONOMIC WAY OF THINKING

TEXTBOOK PAGES 3–7

HOLT PRESENTATION MAKER
Access Illustrated LECTURE NOTES using Microsoft® PowerPoint® on the One-Stop Planner CD-ROM

OBJECTIVES

- Define economics.
- Identify the factors of production.
- Determine the goal of entrepreneurship.

MOTIVATE

Ask students to name some of the goods and services they have bought over the past few days. Make a list of these products on the chalkboard. Then ask students to list some of the choices they made when deciding to buy these products. List these choices on the chalkboard as well. Next, ask students which of the choices listed might be considered economic choices. Guide students in their responses to help them understand the meaning of the term *economics*. As a class, come up with a working definition of the word. Write this definition on the chalkboard and tell students to keep this definition in mind as they read Section 1 of the chapter.

TEACH

Building a Vocabulary

Have students use spiral notebooks to create an Economics Dictionary to be used throughout the chapter. This dictionary might be used as an activity at the start of each new section or as a learning aid for sheltered English students or students having difficulty. List words that students will be expected to know for this section on the chalkboard. Have students use the information provided in the text or on the *Researcher CD-ROM* to list, define, and give an example of each term.

Understanding Main Concepts

Review with students the definition of economics on the chalkboard. Ask: Why is an understanding of economics important? *(An understanding of economics helps people take advantage of the opportunities available to them and make wise choices about how to spend and invest their money and time.)* Next, ask students to describe the two main groups of economic decision makers *(consumers and producers)*. Have students describe ways in which they serve as consumers and producers. Make certain that students understand the difference between these two economic terms.

Organizing Ideas

Have students name some of the decisions that consumers and producers must make. Then tell students that this network of decisions forms the basis of an economic system. With input from students, create a flowchart on the chalkboard that organizes the economic flow from producers to consumers. The flowchart should include producers, the factors of production they use, the goods and services they create with these resources, and the consumers who buy these products (a sample flowchart appears below). Leave room in the flowchart for students to list specific examples of each item. Tell students to copy the flowchart in their notes. Refer students who need additional instruction on the skills used in this activity to the *Global Skill Builder* Lesson 12: Creating Graphic Organizers.

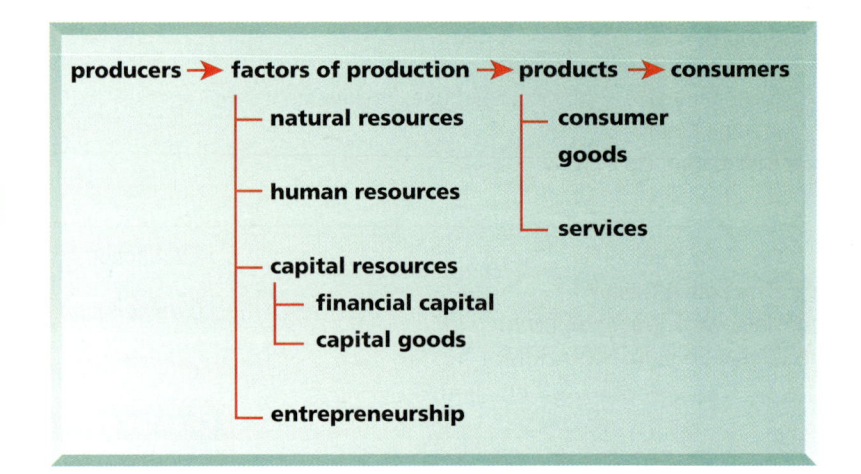

```
producers → factors of production → products → consumers
              ├─ natural resources       ├─ consumer
              │                          │   goods
              ├─ human resources         │
              │                          └─ services
              ├─ capital resources
              │    ├─ financial capital
              │    └─ capital goods
              └─ entrepreneurship
```

Solving Problems

Organize students into groups and tell them that they are going to focus on just one of the factors of production—entrepreneurship. Tell students that each group will play the role of entrepreneurs who have decided to produce an entertainment guide for their high school. The guide will provide highlights of upcoming events as well as listings of local restaurants, coffee shops, clubs, movie theaters, recreation facilities, and other places of interest to high school students. Direct each group to brainstorm and answer the following question: What natural resources, human resources, and capital resources will we need to produce and sell our entertainment guide? Give students 10 to 15 minutes to complete the activity. Then have selected groups share their answers with the class. Ask students why they think people choose to become entrepreneurs. Use students' responses to lead into a discussion about the importance of entrepreneurship in an economic system.

CLOSE

Review with students the importance of choices and decisions in economics. Then call on volunteers to answer the question: How does economics affect you? Use students' responses to review the importance of economic choices and decisions in people's everyday lives.

OPTIONS

Sheltered English Students

Pair sheltered English students with students fluent in English. Have each pair create a poster illustrating the information in the flowchart that the class created earlier. Student pairs should also write a caption explaining the economic flow shown in their poster.

Students Having Difficulty

Pair students having difficulty with students who have mastered the material. Write the following sets of terms on the chalkboard:
- producers and consumers
- needs and wants
- goods and services
- capital goods and consumer goods

Have student pairs compare and contrast the two terms in each set. Then, for each set, have students list examples of each term.

Linguistic Learners

Have students use the *Researcher Online,* the library, in-class resources, and the Internet to learn about a successful entrepreneur, preferably someone who is close to their own age. Students should learn about the entrepreneur's life, the new idea or product he or she came up with, and the problems he or she faced along the way. Students also should examine the risks and advantages of being an entrepreneur. If possible, have students interview the entrepreneur they are researching. In a follow-up activity, have students share what they have learned in a presentation to the class. Encourage students to use visual aids to enhance their presentations. The *Researcher Online* includes a description of what a career as an entrepreneur involves as well as biographies of some well-known entrepreneurs. ★24D

After discussing how the introduction of technology can make the production of products more efficient, organize students into groups. Have each group research an example of recent technology that has been introduced and made production more proficient. Each group should then create a presentation explaining its research. Have each group present its material to the class. ★24D

REVIEW

Have students complete the Section 1 Review on page 7. Use the answers in the Annotated Teacher's Edition to assess student mastery of this section.

ASSESS

To assess student mastery of this section, have students complete Daily Quiz 1.1 in *Daily Quizzes with Answer Key.* For additional assessment options, see *Alternative Assessment Handbook* on the *One-Stop Planner CD-ROM.*

ADDITIONAL RESOURCES

Phillipson, Ian. *How to be an Entrepreneur: A Guide for the Under 25s.* 1995. Kogan Page.

Walstad, William, and John C. Soper, eds. *Effective Economic Education in the Schools.* 1991. Joint Council on Economic Education, National Education Association.

How to Become a Teenage Entrepreneur. Life Skills Unlimited. (video)

LESSON 1.2 SCARCITY AND CHOICE

TEXTBOOK PAGES 8–10

> **HOLT PRESENTATION MAKER**
> Access Illustrated LECTURE NOTES using Microsoft® PowerPoint® on the One-Stop Planner CD-ROM

OBJECTIVES

- Determine why scarcity is a basic problem of economics. ★5A
- Identify the issues that producers must address to distribute resources.
- Explain why producers study productivity.

MOTIVATE

Write the term *scarcity* on the chalkboard. Ask students to suggest a number of natural resources that are considered scarce in the community or state in which you live. Write these resources on the chalkboard. *(Section 1 of this chapter lists examples of natural resources, such as water, timber, oil, and minerals.)* Have students discuss why each resource that the class listed is considered scarce. Have students suggest a definition for the term *scarcity*. Write the definition on the chalkboard and have students write it in their notes. Then discuss with the class what kinds of choices local governments, communities, or families must make in dealing with scarce resources. For example, if you live in a dry region, encourage students to discuss how people deal with water scarcity in local agriculture or in the types of yards they design. If you live in a region with little timber, ask students to suggest what other materials are used in the area to make homes and buildings. Tell students to think about this discussion and the choices their community makes concerning scarce resources as they read Section 2 of the chapter.

Ask students to name several large, successful national or multinational corporations *(such as IBM, Levi Strauss & Co., or Toyota)*. Once you have compiled a list on the chalkboard, ask students to suggest what choices these companies made that helped them grow and become successful. Choose one or more of the corporations on the list and ask students the following questions: Why do you think this company decided to produce the goods and services that it produces? Who is the company's intended market? What natural, human, and capital resources does the company need and use? Are any of these resources extremely scarce or expensive? What methods do you think the company might use to save money while producing quality goods as quickly as possible? Why do you think this company is successful? Have the class discuss each question. Then tell students to think about this discussion as they read Section 2 of the chapter.

TEACH

Building a Vocabulary

List the important terms for this section on the chalkboard and tell students to add them to their Economics Dictionary. Tell students to use the information provided in the text or on the *Researcher CD-ROM* to list, define, and give an example of each vocabulary term.

Understanding Main Concepts

Remind students of the definition of the term *scarcity*. *(Scarcity is a condition caused by the combination of limited economic resources and unlimited human wants.)* Ask students how people respond to scarcity. *(People must decide how to allocate, or distribute, resources in order to satisfy the greatest number of needs and wants.)* Next, ask students to list the three basic economic questions that individuals, businesses, and societies must address when deciding how best to allocate scarce resources *(what to produce, how to produce, and for whom to produce)*. Write these three questions on the chalkboard, and have the class discuss what each question entails.

Ask students to suggest the name of a company with which they are familiar. As a class, have students explain how this company answers the three economic questions. Have students repeat the activity with other companies until you are sure that the class understands the concepts being discussed. ★5A

Solving Problems

Next, tell students that they are going to apply these concepts to a hypothetical business of their own. Organize students into groups of three or four. Tell each group to choose a type of business and imagine that they are planning to start a business of this type. Instruct each group to decide what to produce and how and for whom to produce it. In addition, each group should create a list of some of the main factors of production that they will need to run their business. *(For example, for a farm, these might include: labor, farm machinery, and fertilizer; for an automobile factory: labor, assembly lines, machinery, steel, rubber, and plastic; for a law firm: lawyers and legal secretaries, computers, telephones, photocopiers, paper, and reference books.)* Give students about 15 minutes to complete this activity. Ask for volunteers from different groups to share their results with the class.

Mastering Concepts, Writing About Economics

Explain to students that once producers decide what, how, and for whom to produce, they must then carry out these decisions. In doing so, producers try to use their resources as wisely as possible to deal with the problem of scarcity. Ask students to recall from the chapter how producers determine if they are using their resources wisely *(by studying productivity).* Discuss with the class what is meant by productivity. *(Productivity is the level of output that results from a given level of input.)* Call on volunteers to list the three methods for boosting productivity that are discussed in the text *(division of labor and specialization, shortcuts, and mechanization).* Ask students to provide some examples of each method. Then have students use standard grammar, spelling, sentence structure, and punctuation to write a few paragraphs that explain the benefits and problems with each of these methods of boosting productivity. ⭐24A

CLOSE

Ask volunteers to share their paragraphs with the class. Have students discuss whether some methods of increasing productivity are more useful for certain types of businesses than others. Then have students discuss why the efficient use of resources is important in determining the success of a business.

OPTIONS

Students Having Difficulty

Pair students having difficulty with students who have mastered the material. Instruct each pair to write one or two sentences that use the idea of scarcity. Have them do the same thing for the terms *allocate, productivity, efficiency, division of labor, specialization,* and *mechanization.* You might have students use these terms in sentences that create a short story about the efforts of entrepreneurs to start businesses. Suggest that students use their textbooks, the Electronic Glossary on the *Researcher CD-ROM,* dictionaries, and encyclopedias to clarify the meaning of each term.

Linguistic Learners

Instruct each student to write a brief essay describing how chores and other important tasks are accomplished in their households. Tell students to consider how the concepts of productivity, division of labor, and specialization apply to the way their families organize and complete chores and other tasks. Students should consider the methods that members of their households currently use to increase efficiency and productivity, such as employing shortcuts and using machines (for example, washing machines, dishwashers, and breadmakers). Finally, tell students to suggest ways in which chores and other tasks in their households might be accomplished more efficiently. Ask several volunteers to share their essays with the class. ⭐24D

Gifted Learners

Have students use the *Researcher Online,* the library, in-class resources, or the Internet to explore how a specific small business, company, or corporation has tried to increase its productivity and efficiency. You might organize students into groups or have them work individually to complete this exercise. Instruct students to prepare brief reports explaining and illustrating how the business they examined has boosted productivity through the use of division of labor and specialization, shortcuts, and mechanization. In addition, encourage students to examine other methods that the business they examined is using to increase productivity and how productivity methods in that industry have changed over time. Suggest that students include illustrations, graphs, charts, or tables to enrich their reports. ⭐24D

REVIEW

Have students complete the Section 2 Review on page 10. Use the answers in the Annotated Teacher's Edition to assess student mastery of this section.

ASSESS

To assess student mastery of this section, have students complete Daily Quiz 1.2 in *Daily Quizzes with Answer Key.* For additional assessment options, see *Alternative Assessment Handbook* on the *One-Stop Planner CD-ROM.*

ADDITIONAL RESOURCES

Billings, Henry. *Introduction to Economics.* 1990. EMC.
Saunders, Phillip, and National Council on Economic Education. *A Framework for Teaching the Basic Concepts.* 1993. Economics America, National Council on Economic Education.
Watts, Michael. *Focus: High School Economics.* 1996. National Council on Economic Education.

LESSON 1.3 OPPORTUNITY COSTS

TEXTBOOK PAGES 11–14

HOLT PRESENTATION MAKER
Access Illustrated LECTURE NOTES using Microsoft® PowerPoint® on the One-Stop Planner CD-ROM

OBJECTIVES

- Understand why sacrifice is an important element of economic choice.
- Identify the assumptions involved in creating a production possibilities curve.
- Determine why future production possibilities might differ from current production possibilities.

MOTIVATE

Tell students to imagine the following scenario: You belong to your school's Young Entrepreneurs Organization. This coming Saturday evening, the club is holding a fund-raiser to earn money for an upcoming trip. As a member, you should attend. A few days before the fund-raiser, however, some of your friends tell you that they have tickets to a sold-out Saturday night concert for your favorite band. They want you to join them, and have an extra ticket they will sell you for $20. While wondering what to do, the person you have been dying to go out with walks up and asks if you would like to see a movie together Saturday evening. Your head starts to swim. What do you do? You want to do all three activities, but you know you can do only one. Which do you choose?

Tell students that one way to choose from among alternatives is to use a decision-making grid. On the chalkboard, draw the following grid. Have students suggest the benefits and trade-offs of each choice, and then have the class rank the choices based on which ones provide the most benefits with the least number of trade-offs. Tell students to keep this activity in mind as they read Section 3.

Alternatives	Benefits	Trade-offs
Go to fund-raiser		
Go to concert		
Go on date		

Next, ask student to suggest different environmental problems that exist in the United States today *(some examples include water pollution, air pollution, clear-cut forests, and toxic waste dumps)*. Have students discuss possible causes of these problems and speculate on what benefits people might have hoped to gain through actions and decisions that ultimately hurt the environment. Then ask students to suggest whether they think the benefits or gains have been worth the environmental costs. Tell students to consider the benefits and trade-offs of the choices they make as they read Section 3.

TEACH

Building a Vocabulary

List the important terms for this section on the chalkboard and tell students to add them to their Economics Dictionary. Tell students to use the information provided in the text or on the *Researcher CD-ROM* to list, define, and give an example of each vocabulary term.

Understanding Main Concepts

Ask students why scarcity requires producers and consumers to make sacrifices *(because there are a limited number of resources, and if a resource is used to produce one good, that same resource cannot be used to produce something else—one good is sacrificed for another)*. Next, discuss with students the meanings of the terms *trade-off* and *opportunity cost* and the difference between the two *(when one good is sacrificed for another, that sacrifice is called a trade-off; an opportunity cost is the cost of this sacrifice—the value of the next best alternative given up to obtain that good)*. ⭐5A

Learning from Visuals

Tell students that trade-offs and opportunity costs can be illustrated using a type of graph called a production possibilities curve. Have students examine the graph in Figure 1.3 (Transparency 2). Ask students to explain what the graph depicts. Make certain that students understand that the opportunity cost of making one type of car is the number of cars of another type that cannot be made. Point out that a production possibilities curve is a model, or a simplified version of reality based on specific assumptions. Ask volunteers to recall from their reading what two assumptions production possibilities curves include *(first, that the amount of available resources and technology will not change during the period being studied; and second, that all the natural, human, and capital resources are being used as efficiently as possible)*. Discuss why economists and businesspeople find models helpful in making business decisions *(models are useful tools that help people understand how the real world works).* ⭐5A

Applying Ideas, Creating Charts and Graphs

Explain to students that production possibilities curves are models of current conditions. Ask students why these conditions might change *(because technology and the amount of available resources do not remain constant in the real world, and producers do not always use factors of production as efficiently as possible).* Have students examine the production possibilities curve in Figure 1.4 (Transparency 3). Discuss with them briefly why and how the curve's "shift to the right" occurred. Then, organize students into groups of two and give each pair a posterboard. Tell the groups to choose an industry or business and create a production possibilities curve for two products. Have each group develop a scenario that would shift the production possibilities curve to the right and then create a second graph that shows how the curve has shifted. Next, each group should write a paragraph explaining what changing factors caused the shift *(e.g., if a group uses the example of a clothing company, they might argue that the company decided to double their production of jeans because they suddenly were offered blue denim for half price).* Refer students who need additional instruction on the skills used in this activity to the *Global Skillbuilder* Lesson 11: Presenting Data Graphically. ⭐5B, 24D

Applying, Analyzing, and Debating Ideas

Tell students that they are now going to apply the information they have learned. Organize students into groups of four. Instruct each group to imagine that they are the managers of a large company that is deciding whether to move its main factory from the United States to Mexico. Have each group debate the benefits versus the trade-offs and opportunity costs of moving the factory to Mexico. Assign two students in each group to support moving the factory to Mexico, and two students to support keeping the factory in the United States. After 15 to 20 minutes, have students regroup as a class and ask for volunteers to discuss which trade-offs or benefits were most convincing in their debates. You might also want to have each student write a brief paragraph summarizing the debate.

CLOSE

Review with students the importance of trade-offs and opportunity costs in making economic decisions and how companies use production possibilities curves to help make these decisions. ⭐5A

OPTIONS

Gifted Learners

Have interested students explore the benefits, trade-offs, and opportunity cost of an economic action that involved the environment, such as damming a river, using pesticides in farming, or strip-mining a mountain. Encourage students to use the Internet and recent newspapers and magazines to research this project, perhaps focusing on a debate that is featured in editorials. Have students create a presentation that analyzes the problem and shows the benefits, trade-offs, and opportunity cost of the action taken. Students also should state whether they think the trade-offs involved were worth the benefits. ⭐5A

Linguistic Learners

Organize students into groups of two. Have each pair work together to write a three-paragraph newspaper article, with headline, that explains the benefits, trade-offs, and opportunity cost of a real or hypothetical business decision. Student pairs can use newspapers and magazines, the library, and the Internet to research current business decisions, or they can make up a business decision on which to base their article. Once students have finished writing their articles, have them exchange and read one other student's article. Finally, have pairs discuss their articles. ⭐24D

REVIEW

Have students complete the Section 3 Review on page 14. Use the answers in the Annotated Teacher's Edition to assess student mastery of this section.

ASSESS

To assess student mastery of this section, have students complete Daily Quiz 1.3 in *Daily Quizzes with Answer Key.* For additional assessment options, see *Alternative Assessment Handbook* on the *One-Stop Planner CD-ROM.*

ADDITIONAL RESOURCES

Anderson, Curt L. *Economics and the Environment.* 1996. Economics America, National Council on Economic Education.

Joint Council on Economic Education. *Choices and Changes: Teacher Resource Material.* 1992. Joint Council on Economic Education.

LESSON 1.4 EXCHANGE

TEXTBOOK PAGES 15–18

HOLT PRESENTATION MAKER: Access Illustrated LECTURE NOTES using Microsoft® PowerPoint® on the One-Stop Planner CD-ROM

OBJECTIVES

- Identify and describe the difficulties associated with barter.
- Explain why true self-sufficiency is rare.
- Identify the economic benefits of interdependence.

MOTIVATE

Have students use the *Researcher Online,* the Internet, or the most recent *World Almanac* or *Statistical Abstract of the United States* to see which countries have the largest trade deficits (if time is limited, you might gather this data for students). Ask them to suggest why these deficits might occur. Then ask them why one country might need to trade with another country for different goods and services that it does not provide for itself. Tell students to think about these issues as they read Section 4.

TEACH

Building a Vocabulary

List the important terms for this section on the chalkboard and tell students to add them to their Economics Dictionary. Tell students to use the information provided in the text or on the *Researcher CD-ROM* to list, define, and give an example of each vocabulary term.

Role-Playing, Drawing Conclusions

Ask a student to define the concept of barter *(direct trade in which one set of goods is exchanged for another).* Write this definition on the chalkboard. Then organize the class into groups representing five sets of countries:

- countries rich in oil, in need of timber
- countries rich in timber, in need of minerals
- countries rich in food, in need of microchips
- countries rich in minerals, in need of food
- countries rich in microchips, in need of oil

Give each group one index card that identifies the resource it has, and a second card that identifies the resource it needs (groups should memorize the resources they have and need). Explain that the purpose of the activity is for groups to barter with other groups to obtain the resources they need. Tell groups that they can trade only a "resource rich" card for a "resource needed" card (when trading, groups should exchange actual cards); they cannot trade a "resource needed" card for another "resource needed" card. Emphasize to students that offers of money or credit are not allowed. Have all groups begin their bartering efforts at the same time. Give students about 10 minutes to complete the exercise. At the end of this time, ask how many groups were successful in getting the resource they needed. Ask those groups who were unsuccessful what problems they faced. Then have students discuss why bartering can be a difficult and complicated process.

Organizing Ideas

Ask students to name the two other types of exchange that developed because of the difficulties connected with barter *(money and credit).* Organize students into groups of three or four. Tell each group to create a table that lists at least two to three benefits and drawbacks for each of the three types of exchange: barter, money, and credit. Give students about 10 minutes to complete this activity. Then reconvene the class and ask volunteers to call out some of the items that they wrote down. Discuss the items as a class. At the same time, create a table on the chalkboard that lists the correct benefits and drawbacks of each exchange.

Analyzing Ideas, Mastering Concepts

Ask students why individuals and countries participate in exchanges *(to obtain goods they cannot make themselves).* Write the term *self-sufficiency* on the chalkboard. Ask students to define the term. Then ask students for examples of past or current nations or civilizations that were or are self-sufficient *(most American Indian societies were self-sufficient to some extent, as were most African peoples before colonization and European American pioneers in the American West).* Discuss with the class why self-sufficiency is so difficult and rare, and why most people are dependent on others for many of their needs and wants. *(Self-sufficiency is rare because few people have the skills and resources to make all the things that they want and need.)*

Ask students how nations deal with their lack of self-sufficiency. *(Nations deal with their lack of self-sufficiency by obtaining products they cannot produce themselves through trade or by colonizing or conquering other societies or nations.)* Write the term *interdependence* on the chalkboard. Discuss with students why nations are economically interdependent. Then have students discuss and analyze the benefits and challenges of interdependence.

Demonstrating Understanding, Drawing Conclusions

Tell students that examples of economic interdependence occur every day. Organize students into groups of three or four. Give each group a newspaper section that covers either local, national, or international news. Tell each group to make a list of each example of economic interdependence that they find in the newspaper section. For each item on the list, have groups list the benefits and drawbacks, if any, for the individuals, groups, or nations involved. When students are through, have volunteers from each group share with the class some of the situations of economic interdependence they found in their newspaper sections. Discuss the benefits and drawbacks of economic interdependence. Then ask students how they and their families are economically interdependent with producers outside of their homes.

CLOSE

Ask students which exchange method they think is preferable when trading in interdependent relationships: barter, money, or credit. Next, ask students whether they think individuals and countries should try to work for greater self-sufficiency or greater interdependence. Finally, have students discuss the following question: Are there any industries in which it might be desirable and realistic for the United States to be more self-sufficient, and if so, why?

OPTIONS

Sheltered English Students, Visual-Spatial Learners

Organize students into groups of two to four. Each group should include a mixture of sheltered English students and students fluent in English. Have students use the *Researcher Online,* the library, in-class resources, and the Internet to find data from which to make a graph, table, or map that illustrates a variety of interdependent economic relationships within the United States or between various countries. ★24C, 24D

Students Having Difficulty

Pair students having difficulty with students who have mastered the material. Have one student in each pair play the role of an economist, while the other student plays the role of a reporter. Tell each pair to create an interview in which the reporter asks the economist how different methods of exchange work and the benefits and drawbacks of each method. The reporter should also ask why economic self-sufficiency is rare, and what the economic benefits of interdependence are. Students may wish to prepare their questions and answers on paper before conducting their "interviews." If necessary, have students refer to their textbooks or to the *Researcher CD-ROM* to clarify the meanings of exchange systems, self-sufficiency, and interdependence. Following the activity, have each student write a brief summary of the interview in which he or she participated.

Gifted Learners

Encourage interested students to explore how economic interdependence operates within a specific industry or company. Have students present their findings in a report that includes graphs, charts, maps, tables, or illustrations. Once students have presented their findings, lead them in a conversation on whether economic interdependence is reliant on the type of industry being discussed or if it exists among all industries. Call on volunteers to present their point of view before the class. Finally, have students identify factors that seemed to lead to economic interdependence. ★24D

REVIEW

Have students complete the Section 4 Review on page 18. Use the answers in the Annotated Teacher's Edition to assess student mastery of this section.

ASSESS

To assess student mastery of this section, have students complete Daily Quiz 1.4 in *Daily Quizzes with Answer Key.* For additional assessment options, see *Alternative Assessment Handbook* on the *One-Stop Planner CD-ROM.*

RETEACH

For students having difficulty with the lessons, have them complete Reteaching Activity 1. This activity is located in *Reteaching Activities with Answer Key.*

ADDITIONAL RESOURCES

MacMillan, Bill, and Gordon Fell. *Atlas of Economic Issues.* 1992. Facts on File.

CHAPTER 1

TOPICS INCLUDE

- economic choices and decisions
- factors of production
- scarcity
- what to produce, how to produce, and for whom to produce
- productivity
- division of labor and specialization
- trade-offs and opportunity costs
- production possibilities curves
- forms of exchange
- economic interdependence and self-sufficiency

ECONOMICS NOTEBOOK

The Economics Notebook is a journal activity that encourages students to consider basic concepts of economics that relate to their lives. A follow-up notebook activity appears on page 20. *1B*

WHY IT MATTERS TODAY

To find additional lesson plans dealing with economic decisions, visit CNNfyi.com or have students complete the ECONOMICS IN THE NEWS activity on page 19.

CNNfyi.com

CHAPTER 1

WHAT IS ECONOMICS?

Economics touches every aspect of your life—every time you make a choice. You might think of economics as the study of choices—the food you eat, the clothes you wear, the movies you see, and the music you buy. By studying your choices as well as the choices of others, you will see how economics shapes the world around you and, in turn, how you can shape your world.

ECONOMICS NOTEBOOK

In your Economics Notebook, list your daily activities. How does choice influence your activities? Which activities would you describe as "economic"?

WHY IT MATTERS TODAY

Many businesses depend on factors of production located in different places. Use CNNfyi.com or other **current events** sources to find other examples of businesses using economic factors of production located in different places. Record your findings in your Economics Notebook.

CNNfyi.com

SECTION 1

AN ECONOMIC WAY OF THINKING

READ TO DISCOVER

1. What is economics?
2. What are the factors of production?
3. What is the goal of entrepreneurship?

ECONOMICS DICTIONARY

economics
economist
microeconomics
macroeconomics
consumers
producers
goods
services
resources
factors of production
natural resources
human resources
capital resources
capital goods
consumer goods
technology
entrepreneurship
entrepreneur

How do you decide what food to eat, what clothes to wear, and what movies to see? The study of the choices that people make to satisfy their needs and wants is called **economics**. A person who studies these economic choices is called an **economist**.

Economists generally classify economic actions into two categories: microeconomics and macroeconomics. **Microeconomics** is the study of the choices made by economic actors such as households, companies, and individual markets. Although the term *micro* means "small," microeconomics can focus on large participants in the economy. For example, the production at one company—even one as large as Exxon Mobil Corporation, whose total output exceeds that of some nations—is considered a microeconomic topic because only a single economic actor is involved.

Macroeconomics, on the other hand, examines the behavior of entire economies. For example, unemployment in the United States is a macroeconomic topic.

What can you learn from economics? By examining the economic choices you make, you can take advantage of the opportunities available to you—from choosing where to eat lunch to deciding whether to go to college, from buying a pair of jeans to choosing a career.

The first step in examining the economic choices you make is to develop an economic way of thinking. As you will see, you already understand many economic concepts, even if you think of economics as an unfamiliar subject. Whether you realize it or not, you take economic action every day. Now you must expand your understanding and think economically.

Economic Decisions

How does an economist view the world? Economists pay attention to economic decisions, observing not only who makes them but also how those decisions are made.

Who Makes Decisions? You do! You may choose to buy concert tickets or to start a tutoring business. The people around you also make decisions, as do people around the world.

In economic terms, there are two large groups of economic decision makers. The people who decide to buy things are called **consumers**. The people who make the things that satisfy consumers' needs and wants are called **producers**. Consumers choose what to buy, and producers choose what to provide and how to provide it. This network of decisions is the basis of all economic systems. Every society around the world

---

SECTION 1

AN ECONOMIC WAY OF THINKING

Lesson Plans
For teaching strategies, see Lesson 1.1 located at the beginning of this chapter or the One-Stop Planner Strategy 1.1.

Economics Dictionary
To reinforce the section's vocabulary terms, refer students to the Electronic Glossary on the *Researcher CD-ROM*.

Section Assessment
To assess students' mastery of this section, have them complete Daily Quiz 1.1 in *Daily Quizzes with Answer Key*.

TEKS

Content
1B, 26D
Social Studies Skills
23A, 24A, 24D

Caption Answer
Answers will vary but should reflect an understanding of the economic meanings of goods and services.

Themes in Economics

SCARCITY & CHOICE The air you breathe is a free natural resource, but how healthful is it? As smog increases in some cities, unpolluted air is becoming a scarce resource and a hot commodity. "Oxygen bars", where patrons pay to inhale pure oxygen, have popped up everywhere, from Tokyo and Beijing to Toronto and New York. At an oxygen bar in Los Angeles, patrons can receive a 20-minute blast of pure oxygen for about $16.

Proponents claim that inhaling pure oxygen strengthens the immune system, purifies the body, and boosts alertness. Some doctors, however, point out that breathing pure oxygen can be harmful, particularly for people with lung problems. In addition, officials note that handling pure oxygen poses a fire hazard. ■

Caption Answer
human resources

SCARCITY & CHOICE *You make decisions every day based on your needs and wants.* **What goods and services do you need and want during an average day?**

has an economic system, whether that society consists of a neighborhood or a nation.

How Do You Make Decisions?

You make economic choices based on your needs and wants, which reflect your desires for certain goods and services. Economists generally classify as needs those goods and services that are necessary for survival, such as food, clothing, and shelter. Wants are those goods and services that people consume beyond what is necessary for survival, such as magazines, television sets, and car washes.

As you can see, the economic decisions you make also focus on goods and services. In economic terms, **goods** are physical objects that can be purchased. A pizza, a bicycle, and a pair of tennis shoes are examples of goods. **Services** are actions or activities that are performed for a fee. Lawyers, plumbers, teachers, and taxicab drivers perform services. The term *product* often refers to both goods and services.

Economic Resources

Economists also are interested in the environment in which people make decisions. What do you see when you look around you? People, cars, trees, buildings? An economist sees these same things as economic resources. A **resource** is anything that people use to make or obtain what they need or want.

Resources that can be used to produce goods and services are called **factors of production**. Economists usually divide these factors of production into four categories:

- natural resources,
- human resources,
- capital resources, and
- entrepreneurship.

Natural Resources Items provided by nature that can be used to produce goods and to provide services are called **natural resources**. Natural resources can be found on or in Earth, or in Earth's atmosphere. Examples of natural resources on or in Earth are farmland in California, trout-filled rivers in Montana, oil fields in Oklahoma, and coal mines in West Virginia. Atmospheric resources include sunlight, wind, and rain.

A natural resource is considered a factor of production only when it is scarce and some payment is necessary for its use. For example, the air you breathe on the beach is not a factor of production because it is not scarce and you do not

SCARCITY & CHOICE *Economic resources that are used to produce goods and services are called factors of production.* **Of which factor of production is this attorney an example?**

CHAPTER 1

CAREERS IN ECONOMICS

Economist

How many potential car buyers live in Savannah, Georgia? How much are people willing to pay for a pair of in-line skates? What goods and services does the United States export to other countries? How does the income of an orchard owner in Oregon compare to the income of an orchard owner in Virginia? Economists answer these questions—and many others—on a daily basis.

Economists collect information on many aspects of the economy. They can determine how a society such as that of the United States uses its land, labor, raw materials, and machinery. Economists also try to identify why producers choose to provide certain goods and services, as well as the costs and benefits of consuming those products.

How can you become an economist? Generally you will need a college degree in economics. Additionally, courses in mathematics, government, international relations, and other social sciences can help you understand how economic developments affect individuals and societies. Computer skills also are critical because economists rely on computers to help collect, sort, and interpret data. Some economists also earn a master's degree or doctorate.

As an economist, you might be employed by a private company such as a research firm, management-consulting firm, bank, or insurance company. Economists also work for federal, state, and local governments. For example, economists at the Federal Trade Commission (FTC) analyze industries to help enforce fair business practices. Economists in the Department of Commerce study production, distribution, and consumption of goods and services.

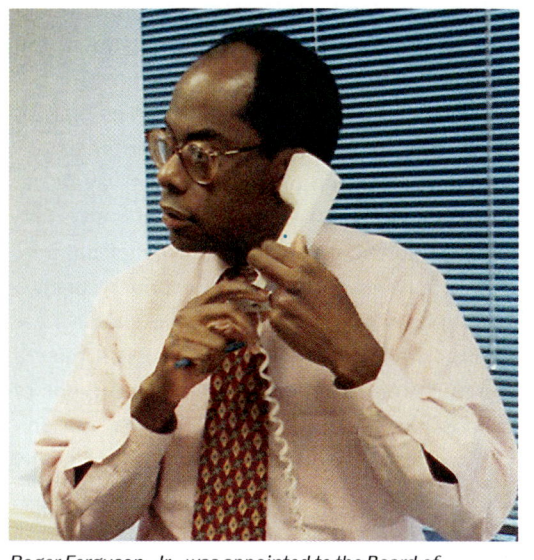

Roger Ferguson, Jr., was appointed to the Board of Governors of the Federal Reserve System by President Bill Clinton in 1997.

---

have to pay to breathe it. If you go scuba diving, however, you have to pay for the bottled air in the scuba tanks.

Human Resources Any human effort exerted during production is considered a **human resource**. The effort can be either physical or intellectual. Assembly-line workers, ministers, and store clerks all are human resources.

Capital Resources The manufactured materials used to create products are called **capital resources**. Capital resources include capital goods and the money used to purchase them. **Capital goods** are the buildings, structures, machinery, and tools used in the production process. Department stores, factories, dams, computers, and hammers are examples of capital goods.

Careers in Economics
To help students learn about other careers in economics, refer them to the Careers section on the *Researcher Online*.

Profiles in Economics
The Biographies section on the *Researcher Online* contains biographical profiles on the following economists: Milton Friedman, John Kenneth Galbraith, John Maynard Keynes, W. Arthur Lewis, Alfred C. Marshall, Karl Marx, Alice Rivlin, Adam Smith, Laura D'Andrea Tyson, and Barbara Ward.

Global Connections
Many regions of the world are associated with certain natural resources. Oklahoma and Texas are known for their oil, as are Kuwait and Saudi Arabia. South Africa is known for its diamond mines, and Colombia is known for its coffee beans. The primary natural resources of some regions are not as well known, however. For example, about a third of the world's cork trees grow in Portugal. It is not surprising then that Portugal leads the world in cork production, and a Portuguese company, Corticeira Amorim, is the world's leading producer of wine corks.

WHAT IS ECONOMICS?

What Do You Think?
Answers

1. Answers will vary, but students should exhibit an understanding of the difficulties involved in balancing economic and environmental demands at special tourist destinations. Students should support their opinions with examples from the text.

2. Answers will vary but might include the following: Ecotourism might help preserve a region's natural areas and thus ensure continued revenue from tourism for a longer period of time. Other industries in the region might adopt ecotourist methods, resulting perhaps in higher prices but decreased environmental problems. Regulations controlling ecotourism might increase to the point where many tourist attractions cannot turn a profit, which could increase unemployment and hurt the economy. Regulations controlling ecotourism might lead to better and more standardized methods of operation, lowering costs and increasing profits at ecotourist attractions.

Caption Answer

through ecotourism

LINKING ECONOMICS and GEOGRAPHY

Ecotourism

You may have read news stories describing the harmful effects of tourism on the environment. Hotel construction can disturb the habitats of native animals and plants. Speedboats can frighten and sometimes injure—or even kill— aquatic animals. Litter can disrupt habitats and the food chain.

At the same time, however, tourism provides income for many regions. How can this economic need be balanced with the need to preserve the environment and respect local traditions? Some countries hope to find the answer in ecotourism.

In its ideal form, ecotourism is travel to natural areas in a way that conserves the environment and sustains the well-being of the local people. The country of Costa Rica, for example, relies on ecotourism in its efforts to preserve its rain forests.

The construction of an aerial tramway in the canopy (treetop level) of the rain forest is an example of the potential for a mutually beneficial relationship between nature and the economy. Using a converted ski lift along a one-mile course near Braulio Carrillo National Park, biologists offer a 90-minute tour that allows visitors to see one of the most diverse populations of plants and animals on Earth. Although the tram attracts nearly 100 people a day, its operators have tried to minimize its impact on the environment. Each car carries only five people and is spaced at a considerable distance from other cars on the cable.

Construction materials for the tramway were brought in by helicopter, eliminating the need to build a road beneath. Whenever possible, trees were pulled out of the way of the cable with ropes to avoid cutting them down. Development of the tramway has preserved an ecological sanctuary and provides the region with a steady source of income.

Despite the fact that ecotourism is a fast-growing segment of the travel industry, many environmentalists argue that the word itself has no meaning. In the United States alone, more than 200 outfitters offer excursions termed "ecotours." A *U.S. News & World Report* investigation, however, determined that many ecotours do not give environmental concerns a high priority. In the Galápagos Islands, for example, all the tour boats dump sewage directly into the ocean.

In addition to environmental concerns, some people argue that ecotourism has fallen short of its economic goals. Tour profits often do not find their way into local businesses and salaries. Most profits go to the tour companies, which are usually based in other countries.

Despite these shortcomings, supporters argue that ecotourism has worked in many areas. Governments now are trying to improve ecotourism programs through a combination of educational efforts and regulation.

What Do You Think?

1. Is it possible to meet both economic and environmental demands at these special tourist destinations? Explain your answer.
2. What are the possible long-term effects of ecotourism on a region's economy?

How does Costa Rica reconcile the often conflicting demands of tourism and environmental protection?

Capital goods are the manufactured resources that are used in making finished products. These finished products—the goods and services that people buy—are called **consumer goods**.

Some products can be either capital goods or consumer goods, depending on how they are used. A bicycle purchased for personal use is a consumer good. The same bicycle would be classified as a capital good, however, if it is purchased by a New York City messenger service for use in making deliveries.

Technology is the use of technical knowledge and methods to create new products or make existing products more efficiently. For example, advances in computer technology have dramatically changed how work is done. In some highly automated plants, computers direct production by issuing electronic instructions to robots on assembly lines.

Entrepreneurship

The combination of organizational abilities and risk taking involved in starting a new business or introducing a new product is called **entrepreneurship**. The goal of entrepreneurship is to develop a new mix of the other factors of production, creating something of value. An **entrepreneur** is a person who attempts to start a new business or introduce a new product—risking economic failure in return for the possibility of financial gain.

Many entrepreneurs begin their businesses by finding answers to their own questions. Texan Michael Dell grew up tinkering with computers and noticed that salespeople frequently were not able to answer his questions. Convinced that computer stores provided inadequate services, he went into business for himself. One year after starting college, Dell had earned more than $700,000.

In 1985 Dell also developed a clone, or copy, of the IBM personal computer (PC). His company—known as Dell Computer Corporation—created an innovative distribution method by selling its merchandise directly by telephone or mail order. Without the markup that retail stores charged, Dell computers sold at less than half the price of IBM computers. The company started selling PCs through its Web site in 1996. Dell Corporation is now the world's top direct seller of computers, with net revenues of about $25 billion in 2000.

SECTION 1 REVIEW

Q: 1, 2, 4

1. Identify and Explain:
- economics
- economist
- microeconomics
- macroeconomics
- consumers
- producers
- goods
- services
- resources
- factors of production
- natural resources
- human resources
- capital resources
- capital goods
- consumer goods
- technology
- entrepreneurship
- entrepreneur

2. Categorizing: Copy the chart below. Use it to provide examples of various natural resources, human resources, and capital resources.

Natural Resources	Human Resources	Capital Resources

3. Finding the Main Idea

a. Provide examples of your daily economic decisions. What are the key influences on these decisions?

b. You use the factors of production every day. For example, you use a human resource—your own effort—to finish your homework. What other factors of production do you use in your daily activities?

4. Writing and Critical Thinking

Drawing Conclusions: Why might entrepreneurs be particularly good at putting technology to innovative use?

Consider the following:
- characteristics of successful entrepreneurs
- Dell Computer Corporation's methods of distribution

Homework Practice Online
keyword: SM3 HP1

SECTION 1 REVIEW ANSWERS

1. economics (3), economist (3), microeconomics (3), macroeconomics (3), consumers (3), producers (3), goods (4), services (4), resources (4), factors of production (4), natural resources (4), human resources (5), capital resources (5), capital goods (5), consumer goods (7), technology (7), entrepreneurship (7), entrepreneur (7) **24A**

2. Answers will vary but might include natural resources—timberland, diamond mines; human resources—bankers, teachers; and capital resources—printing presses, bulldozers. **23A, 24D**

3a. Answers will vary but might include where to eat lunch, how much time to spend on homework, or what clothes to buy. Students should mention needs and wants for goods and services.

3b. Answers should show an understanding of the factors of production. Students might mention that they use capital goods such as pens, paper, and computers to complete homework, write papers, and create projects.

4. Answers will vary but students might mention that entrepreneurs have organizational, problem-solving, and risk-taking abilities coupled with the desire for financial gain. For example, Michael Dell took advantage of the Internet to cut costs and distribute computers more efficiently than his competitors. **23A, 26D**

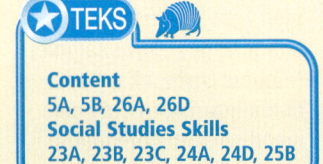

SECTION 2

SCARCITY AND CHOICE

READ TO DISCOVER
1. Why is scarcity a basic problem of economics?
2. What issues must producers address to distribute resources?
3. Why do producers study productivity?

ECONOMICS DICTIONARY
scarcity
allocate
productivity
efficiency
division of labor
specialization

You have learned that economists study the decisions that people make about using a variety of resources. Why do people need to make these decisions?

Consider an economic decision you may have faced many times: how to spend a limited amount of money from an allowance, a birthday gift, or your paycheck. You can use the money to buy several compact discs (CDs), movie tickets for your friends, or a new outfit for school. But you cannot buy all these things. Because your resources (money) are limited, you are forced to make an economic decision—to choose how you will spend the money. Such limitations on resources—and how people respond to them—are a part of every aspect of economics.

Scarcity

All resources are limited. People's wants, however, are unlimited. This combination of limited economic resources and unlimited wants results in a condition known as **scarcity**. Scarcity is the most basic problem of economics, because it forces people to make decisions about how to use resources effectively (see Figure 1.1).

Many factors contribute to scarcity. Low amounts of rainfall, for example, may lead to poor harvests and therefore to a scarcity of fruits and vegetables at grocery stores. During World War II silk and nylon were used to make parachutes—creating a scarcity of women's stockings, which had been produced from those materials during peacetime.

Identifying Economic Questions

How do you—and other people—respond to scarcity? Limited amounts of products require people to make decisions. People decide how to **allocate**, or distribute, resources in order to satisfy the greatest number of needs and wants. To allocate resources effectively, an economic

SCARCITY & CHOICE *Scarcity is the most basic problem of economics.* **How does recycling allow for a more effective use of scarce resources?**

CHAPTER 1

system or a society must address three basic economic questions:

- what to produce,
- how to produce, and
- for whom to produce.

The answers to these questions help a society determine the best distribution of resources to meet its needs and wants.

What to Produce A society's needs and wants can never be met completely. Therefore, the society's economic system must determine the urgency of those needs and wants. Suppose that a large number of people decide to move to a particular city and that many of them have school-age children. Should the city build a new school to accommodate these students, or should more money be spent on school buses and drivers so that more students can attend existing schools? What if a new school *and* additional buses are necessary? The city must decide what resources will be allocated for construction and what resources will be allocated for transportation.

How to Produce A society can allocate resources in many different ways. During construction of the new school, for example, the builder must decide how the roof will be built. Suppose that a worker can attach shingles using either a hammer and nails or a nail gun. Either method will result in a stable, well-made roof. A worker using a nail gun will work faster—and tire more slowly—than a worker using a hammer. How does the builder choose a method of production? If unemployment is high, the builder may decide that hiring additional workers is less expensive than investing in equipment. If workers demand high wages, the builder may decide to hire fewer workers and provide them with equipment that increases their speed.

For Whom to Produce A society must determine how to distribute the goods and services that it produces. For example, who will attend the new school? Will any students at existing schools be transferred to the new school? How will city residents pay for construction? To allocate resources effectively, a society must consider who will consume goods and services.

Productivity

After choosing what, how, and for whom to produce, a society must carry out these decisions. In doing so, the society tries to make sure that its resources are used as effectively as possible. Remember, the problem of scarcity forces people to find ways to use resources wisely.

Economists determine if resources are being used wisely by studying productivity. **Productivity** is the level of output that results from a given level of input. For example, suppose that the

SCARCITY

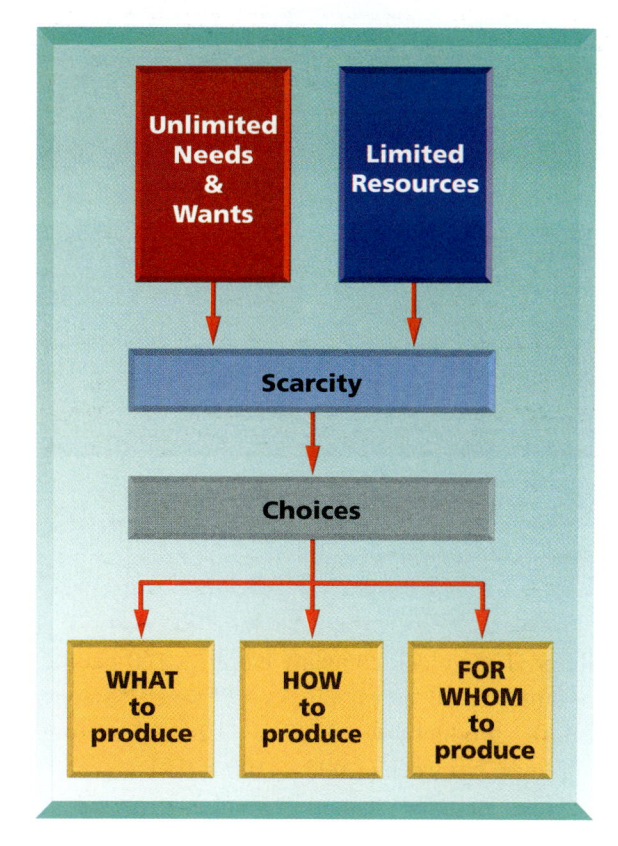

FIGURE 1.1 The combination of unlimited needs and wants and limited resources results in a condition called scarcity. **What three economic decisions does scarcity force a society to make?**

Transparency
An overhead transparency of Figure 1.1 is available in *Transparency Resources.* See Transparency 1: Scarcity.

Caption Answer
how to produce, what to produce, and for whom to produce ★5A

internet connect

TOPIC: Specialization and Division of Labor
GO TO: go.hrw.com
KEYWORD: SM3 EC1

Have students access the Internet through the HRW Go site to conduct research on Henry Ford and the automobile assembly line. Have students design their own assembly lines to build products of their choice. They can be products that the students invent or ones that already exist. Have students draw each task required in production on a flow chart, illustrating the principles of specialization and division of labor used to increase productivity. ★23B, 23C, 24D, 25B, 26A, 26D

WHAT IS ECONOMICS?

Caption Answer
It enables each employee to work faster and produce more, which increases efficiency and productivity.

SECTION 2
REVIEW ANSWERS

1. scarcity (8), allocate (8), productivity (9), efficiency (10), division of labor (10), specialization (10) 5A, 5B, 24A

2. Students should identify the following questions: what to produce, how to produce, and for whom to produce. 23A, 24D

3a. because all resources are limited 5A

3b. because it involves making the most effective use of scarce resources

3c. Scarcity forces people to make decisions about how to use resources effectively. These choices affect all aspects of an economy. 5A

4. Answers will vary but might include the following: Students choose what to produce based on instructions and homework assignments. Students choose how to produce based on the tools available to them (pencils, pens, graph paper, posterboard, computers) and the type of product they are producing (homework, writing assignments, charts, presentations). Students choose for whom to produce based on who will be grading or assessing the final product (teachers, fellow students). 23A

PRODUCTIVITY *Workers on an assembly line demonstrate the concept of specialization.* **How does specialization benefit a producer?**

Sleepy Time clock company employs 100 people to build 1,000 alarm clocks per week. Sleepy Time's productivity thus is 10 clocks per employee per week (1,000 ÷ 100 = 10).

Now imagine that the company president decides that productivity is too low and asks staff members to suggest improvements. The finance manager for Sleepy Time points out that each worker builds an entire clock from start to finish. She suggests that the company find ways to improve **efficiency**, which is the use of the smallest amount of resources to produce the greatest amount of output.

One option might be for the factory to introduce a **division of labor**, assigning a small number of tasks to each worker. For example, one worker might attach the clock face, and another might install the power switch. Because these steps are performed repeatedly, workers gain expertise in their assigned tasks. This focus on one activity is known as **specialization**. The process of specialization allows each employee to work faster and to produce a greater number of alarm clocks. Introducing division of labor would enable the Sleepy Time company to increase production to 5,000 alarm clocks per week.

On the other hand, the Sleepy Time company might decide to increase efficiency by finding shortcuts that allow workers to construct clocks more quickly. Now only 25 employees would be needed to produce 1,000 clocks per week. Although the company produces the same number of clocks, productivity increases because input—the number of workers—is reduced.

A third option might involve mechanization. Some of the workers might be replaced by machines that work faster and longer—and therefore at a lower cost per unit—than employees.

SECTION 2 REVIEW

★TEKS Q: 1, 2, 3a, 3c, 4

1. Identify and Explain:
scarcity
allocate
productivity
efficiency
division of labor
specialization

2. Summarizing: Copy the diagram below. Use it to identify the three questions that all economic systems address.

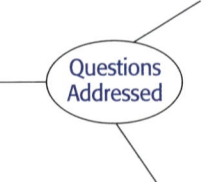

Questions Addressed

3. Finding the Main Idea
   a. Why do societies need to make choices about distributing resources?
   b. Why is productivity important to a society?
   c. Why are scarcity and choice basic problems of economics?

4. Writing and Critical Thinking
   Analyzing Information: How do you decide to allocate your limited time and effort in your studies?
   Consider the following:
   • how you answer the three main production questions when studying
   • which classes require additional study time
   • how much time you have available for studying

Homework Practice Online
keyword: SM3 HP1

CHAPTER 1

SECTION 3

OPPORTUNITY COSTS

READ TO DISCOVER

1. Why is sacrifice an important element of economic choice?
2. What assumptions are involved in creating a production-possibilities curve?
3. Why might future production possibilities differ from current production possibilities?

ECONOMICS DICTIONARY

trade-off
opportunity cost
production possibilities curve

As you have learned, scarcity requires producers and consumers to make choices. Similarly, a society must answer the three economic questions of what to produce, how to produce, and for whom to produce. What are the results of these economic decisions?

Trade-Offs and Opportunity Costs

Choosing among alternative uses for available resources forces individuals to make decisions. If a resource is used to produce or consume one good, that same resource cannot be used to produce or consume something else. One good is sacrificed for another. In economic terms this sacrifice is called a **trade-off**. The cost of this trade-off—the value of the next best alternative that is given up to obtain the preferred item—is called the **opportunity cost**.

People face trade-offs and opportunity costs every day. Consider the following example. Michelle Tanabe has two events she would like to attend in the same week—a concert and an ice hockey game. Tickets for the concert and the hockey game cost the same amount. Unfortunately, Michelle has only enough money to purchase one ticket. She must make a trade-off because she cannot afford to buy both tickets. If she spends money on a ticket to the concert, the alternative choice—the ticket to the hockey game—is the opportunity cost of buying the concert ticket.

The above example is a simple, two-item choice. Most choices, however, involve many more trade-offs (see Figure 1.2). When resources are used to build a factory, the trade-off is not between the factory and one other use of the resources. All of the workers, equipment, and financial input used to construct the factory could be used to build many combinations of homes, offices, and shopping centers. These factors of production might also be used in fields

KEVIN'S DECISION-MAKING GRID

ALTERNATIVES	CRITERIA			
	Cost Within Budget?	Acceptable to Parents?	Lasting Benefit?	Entertaining?
Go to Choir Practice	yes	yes	yes	yes
Go out to Dinner	no	no	no	yes
Watch Television	yes	possibly	no	yes
Do Homework	yes	yes	yes	no
Go to Football Game	yes	no	no	yes

FIGURE 1.2 Kevin has $10 left from his allowance. **Based on his decision-making grid, what is his best choice for a Friday-night activity? What are the trade-offs? What is the opportunity cost?** TEKS

WHAT IS ECONOMICS? 11

Holt Economics Videodisc

The videodisc segment Land Use: Development in Dana Point complements the Chapter 1 Case Study, Undamming the Deerfield. Barcodes for the Spanish version of the video segment are available in *Holt Economics Videodisc Teacher's Guide.*

PLAY SEGMENT 1

PAUSE

RESUME PLAY

PLAY OPTION A

PLAY OPTION B

PLAY EPILOGUE

Caption Answer
The river generates less hydroelectric power for New England Power.

---

other than construction. For example, investors might decide to deposit their money in savings accounts, or the land might be used as a park.

Although many trade-offs may be possible within a set of choices, only one of these—the next best choice—is considered the opportunity cost. For example, suppose that you are deciding how to spend your Saturday afternoon. You can choose between a trip to the beach, a visit to a carnival, and a hike in a nearby park. After some thought, you decide that you are not interested in going on a hike, and that although the carnival would be fun, you would prefer to go to the beach. Both the carnival and the hike are considered trade-offs. However, only your *second-best* choice—the carnival—is considered an opportunity cost of going to the beach.

CASE STUDY

Undamming the Deerfield

OPPORTUNITY COST & TRADE-OFFS Across the country the effects of dam construction on rivers are being reconsidered. Rivers have long provided power to turn machinery in mills and to run electric generators. In fact, the federal government has licensed hundreds of dams in order to advance the nation's industrial development. Although both industry and consumers have benefited from this development, the rivers and the communities along them have often been harmed in some unexpected economic ways.

For example, the Deerfield River, which runs through Vermont and Massachusetts, has a series of 10 dams that were built along its course in the early 1900s. At the time, government officials and many residents believed that the benefits of building the dams to generate hydroelectric power outweighed the interruption of the river's natural flow. In recent years, however, this trade-off has been reevaluated. Why?

The dams affected the environment of the river's fish species including salmon, which could no longer return upstream to spawn. As a result, the area's fishing industry suffered. Likewise, the dams limited the river's potential as a site for water sports. Finally, the local ecosystem was jeopardized by the presence of the dams. Wildlife and water quality declined.

As a result, in 1995 New England Power, owner of nine of the dams, agreed to adapt its water usage to meet these economic and environmental concerns. As more water is released from the dams, dry stretches of river are once again able to support life. The construction of fish runs allows salmon to travel along the river as they had not in decades. Additionally, periodic water releases from one of the dams created one of the country's most exciting whitewater kayak runs.

This reevaluation of water use along the Deerfield River shows how trade-offs and opportunity costs can change over time. By periodically reviewing these types of decisions, producers and consumers can make the best trade-offs and limit the effects of opportunity costs.

Production Possibilities

Trade-offs and opportunity costs can be illustrated using a production possibilities curve. A **production possibilities curve** shows all of the possible combinations of two goods or services that can be produced within a stated time period, given two important assumptions. First, it is assumed that the amount of available resources

OPPORTUNITY COST & TRADE-OFFS *Reevaluation of public use of New England's Deerfield River has created new opportunities to kayak its whitewater rapids.* **What are the trade-offs of recreational use of the river?**

and technology will not change during the period being studied. Second, it is assumed that all of the natural, human, and capital resources are being used in the most efficient manner possible.

The above assumptions are important because they determine which production combinations will fall on the curve and which will not. All of the combinations on the curve meet these assumptions. Combinations that lie inside (below) the curve, on the other hand, represent an inefficient use of existing resources. Combinations that lie outside (above) the curve represent production impossibilities, given existing technology. Each production combination is measured in terms of opportunity costs. That is, more of one good can be produced only by making less of the other good.

Keep in mind that a production possibilities curve is a model, or a simplified version of reality based on specific assumptions. Models are useful tools that help people understand how the real world works. Because the production possibilities curve is based on assumptions relating to current conditions, it is a helpful model.

Current Production Possibilities Figure 1.3 shows the possible production options that would be available to the U.S. automotive industry if it concentrated its current resources on the production of only two types of cars: economy and luxury. Like all production possibilities curves, this curve is based on the assumptions that the amount of resources—raw materials, labor, and capital goods—will not change and that those resources will be used efficiently.

The curve that connects points A through E shows the production combinations that meet the stated assumptions. At point A, all resources are devoted to the production of luxury cars. Point E represents the other extreme—all resources are devoted to the production of economy cars. In these two extreme cases (points A and E), the opportunity cost of producing one class of cars is the entire production capacity of the other class of cars.

Consumers are interested in purchasing a variety of cars, however, so automobile companies probably would not choose to limit production to either luxury or economy cars. Instead, automobile companies would most likely produce some combination of the two classes of cars. These combinations are represented by points B, C, and D on the curve. The opportunity cost of producing a certain number of one class of cars would be the number of cars of the other class that could not be produced. For example, the production of 5 million economy cars would limit the production of luxury cars to 2.5 million.

Two additional points, F and G, are included in the graph. Point F, which lies outside the curve, is a production impossibility given the current levels of technology and other resources. No matter how the automotive industry mixes the existing factors of production, it cannot produce

THE PRODUCTION POSSIBILITIES CURVE

Production of Economy Cars (in millions) (y-axis, 0–9)
Production of Luxury Cars (in millions) (x-axis, 0–6)

Points: E (0, 7), D (1, 6), C (3, 4.5), B (4, 3), A (5, 0.5), F (5, 5), G (2, 3)

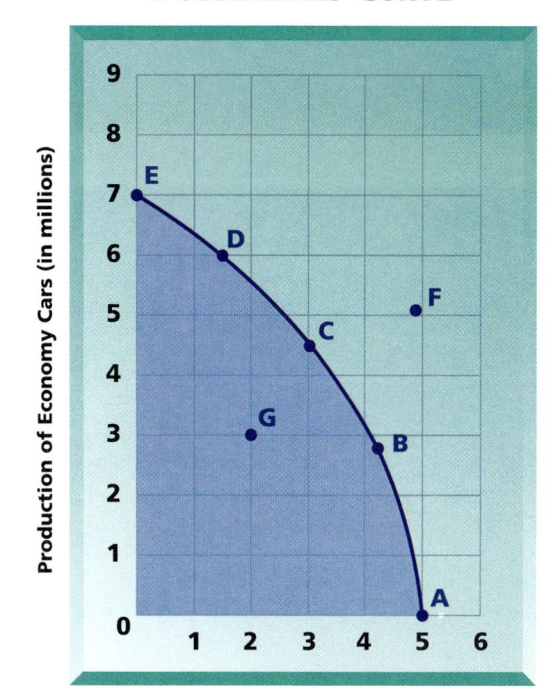

FIGURE 1.3 The production possibilities curve is a helpful model for understanding efficient use of resources. **What two assumptions must be considered when studying a production possibilities curve? According to the graph, is it more efficient to produce luxury cars or economy cars?**

Transparency

An overhead transparency of Figure 1.4 is available in *Transparency Resources*. See Transparency 3: Shifting Production Possibilities Curve.

Caption Answer

a decrease in available resources ⭐5B

SECTION 3
REVIEW ANSWERS

1. trade-off (11), opportunity cost (11), production possibilities curve (12) **5B, 24A**

2. Answers will vary but should reflect an understanding of opportunity cost. Some students may have more than one optimal choice. **1B, 5B, 23A, 24D**

3a. that the amount of available resources and technology will not change during the period being studied and that all the natural, human, and capital resources are being used in the most efficient manner possible **5B**

3b. an inefficient use of existing resources **5B**

3c. by causing the curve to shift to the right **5B**

4. Answers will vary but should reflect an understanding of trade-offs and opportunity costs. **5B, 23A**

SHIFTING PRODUCTION POSSIBILITIES CURVE

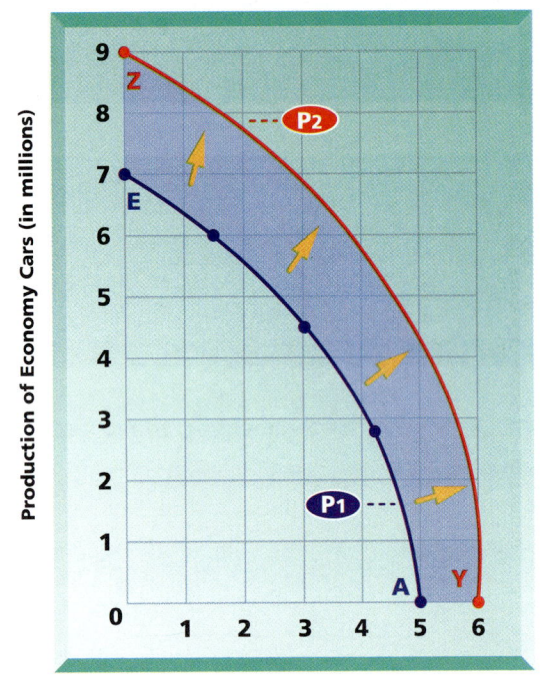

FIGURE 1.4 A shift of the production possibilities curve to the right indicates that improvements in technology have occurred or that new resources are available. **What conditions would cause the curve to shift to the left?** ⭐TEKS

at this high a level. Point G, which lies inside the curve, represents an inefficient use of resources. If the existing factors of production were used more efficiently, the industry should be able to produce at a level represented by one of the points on the production possibilities curve, instead of at the level of point G.

Future Production Possibilities In the real world, technology and the factors of production do not remain constant. When improvements in technology occur or new resources become available, the entire production possibilities curve changes. A new curve is formed to the right of the old curve. Economists say that the curve has "shifted to the right."

The production possibilities curve in Figure 1.4 shows a shift to the right. The new curve, which connects points Y and Z, represents the expanded production that results from advances in technology or the introduction of new resources. The new curve, like the old one, makes the standard assumptions of fixed resources and efficiency. If the assumptions change—if new technology or resources become available—the curve again shifts to the right. The curve may also shift to the left if resources become unavailable.

SECTION 3 REVIEW

⭐TEKS Q: 1, 2, 3a, 3b, 3c, 4

1. Identify and Explain:
 trade-off
 opportunity cost
 production possibilities curve.

2. Categorizing: Assume that you have $50 and need to decide how best to spend the money. Fill in the grid. Which choice satisfies the greatest number of criteria? What is the opportunity cost of this choice?

	Within Range?	Acceptable To Parents?	Lasting Use?
Jeans			
Pizza			
Rock Tickets			

Homework Practice Online
keyword: SM3 HP1

3. Finding the Main Idea

a. What assumptions determine the production possibilities curve?

b. What condition is represented by a point lying inside, or below, the production possibilities curve?

c. How can an increase in available resources affect the production possibilities curve?

4. Writing and Critical Thinking

Summarizing: From your own experience, describe a recent economic choice you have made.
Consider the following:
• the trade-offs involved in making the choice
• the opportunity cost involved in making the choice

14 CHAPTER 1

SECTION 4

EXCHANGE

READ TO DISCOVER

1. What are the difficulties associated with barter?
2. Why is true self-sufficiency rare?
3. What are the economic benefits of interdependence?

ECONOMICS DICTIONARY

exchange
barter
money
credit
value
utility
self-sufficiency
interdependence

How do producers find out if they indeed have determined the most efficient and productive method of using resources? If consumers purchase more calculators from Texas Instruments than from Radio Shack, Texas Instruments knows that it made the correct economic decisions. Producers gain this information through a process called **exchange**, in which producers and consumers agree to provide one type of item in return for another.

Forms of Exchange

The principle of exchange has existed throughout history. Exchange can take one of three forms: barter, money, or credit.

Barter In many societies—today and in the past—people exchanged one set of goods for another. This direct trade is known as **barter**. Barter relies on bargaining and often results in complicated transactions. Suppose that two students agree to trade lunches. One student may offer a turkey sandwich in exchange for a carton of chocolate milk. The student who has the milk, however, may only be willing to trade for an apple. For the exchange to be completed, therefore, the student with the turkey sandwich must find a *third* person who has an apple—and hope that this person is willing to participate in the lunchtime trade.

Money The difficulties of barter commonly lead to the development of a standardized means of exchange. This means of exchange is called money. **Money** is any item that is readily accepted by people in return for goods and services. When you think of money, you probably

EXCHANGE, MONEY, & INTERDEPENDENCE *Traders from throughout the former Soviet Union flock to the border town of Pogranichnyy, Russia, to barter goods with Chinese businesspeople.* **What are some of the difficulties associated with barter?**

WHAT IS ECONOMICS? 15

Themes in Economics

EXCHANGE, MONEY, & INTERDEPENDENCE In the early 1990s, credit card companies began targeting lower-income families and college students. As a result, many people racked up more debt than they could handle. In 1999 about 1.4 million people in the United States filed for personal bankruptcy, an increase of more than 62 percent from 1995. Experts cite consumers' rash use of credit cards as one cause.

Credit counseling services suggest that people avoid the credit trap by

- obtaining credit cards with low interest rates and no annual fee.
- not using credit cards for cash advances, which have higher interest rates.
- paying off as much debt each month as possible.
- paying off the card with the highest interest rate first.
- checking their credit reports for inaccuracies. ■

Global Exchange

Year-Round Produce

Have you ever wondered why you can buy fresh tomatoes or peaches all year long, even though these fruits generally grow only in the summer? Perhaps you have noticed kiwi fruit from New Zealand or grapes from Chile available at your local supermarket in the winter. Although you probably have grown accustomed to fresh produce year-round, this luxury has not always been available to consumers.

What makes it possible for you to enjoy fresh produce anytime you want? Relatively recent technological developments permit fresh produce to be transported from countries around the world to your local store.

For example, in 1995 British Airways World Cargo announced the opening of a new warehouse devoted to perishable cargo, such as fresh flowers and produce. Trained specialists oversee shipping and storage and rely on equipment such as blast chillers and ethylene scrubbers to ensure that the warehouse remains a safe environment for fresh produce.

These and other developments in rapid shipping and advanced refrigeration equipment mean that distant countries can supply their produce to U.S. markets. Chile, for example, grows most of its produce between October and April, because its location south of the equator makes these the warmest months of the year. "Reversed" seasons in Southern Hemisphere countries such as Chile and New Zealand complement the growing season in the Northern Hemisphere and extend the season for fresh products and produce.

---

imagine bills and coins such as dollars, pesos, lire, shekels, and yen. In various societies many other items have been used as money, however, including precious metals, salt, beads, and cocoa beans.

Money has three functions. It serves as

- a standardized item that is generally traded for goods or services,
- a measure of value that allows both producers and consumers to determine and express worth, and
- a store of value that can be saved and used to purchase items at a later date.

Credit A third form of exchange, called **credit**, allows consumers to use items before completing payment for the merchandise. Credit allows consumers to pay for an item over a specified period of time. For example, you may decide to buy a portable stereo priced at $200. You do not have $200 at the moment, however, so you arrange to pay for the stereo over a period of six months. The use of credit allows you to take your stereo home today—even though you have not made all of your payments.

Consumers who fail to make the necessary credit payments, however, may be required to return the merchandise for which they are paying. They also risk losing future opportunities to receive credit.

Many societies combine different forms of exchange within their economies. For example, both money and credit are important to the U.S. economy as a whole, while individuals within the U.S. economy sometimes may rely on barter. A plumber, for example, may agree to fix his neighbor's clogged drain in exchange for help with building a covered patio. You will learn more about credit and other common forms of exchange in later chapters.

Value

How do consumers and producers determine the worth of items in an exchange? In order to avoid the problems of barter, goods and services are assigned a **value** that can be expressed as an amount of money, or price. Suppose, for example, that Craig Patterson collects stamps. The value of his collection is determined by how much another collector would be willing to pay for the stamps.

Which do you think are more likely to carry higher values—needs or wants? Many needs, such as water, have low monetary values. Water is necessary to life, but it is not expensive. A want such as a diamond necklace, on the other hand, is very expensive even though it is not a necessity.

Why do many wants carry higher values than many needs? In the example described above, consider the availability of each item. Diamonds are extremely rare, while water is plentiful in most regions of the world. Scarcity, therefore, can create value.

Value is also determined by the degree to which a product has **utility**, or usefulness to a person. Utility can be more difficult to determine than scarcity, because one person may find a product useful while another finds the product to be of no use at all. Do diamonds and water have utility? Yes, both are useful. Water is necessary to life, and diamonds are both a popular gemstone and an important tool in some industries.

Water, therefore, has utility but is not scarce, while diamonds have both utility and scarcity. This combination of utility and scarcity forms the basis for determining value.

The determination of value allows producers and consumers to decide the relative worth of goods and services in an exchange. Consider again the case of Craig Patterson. Some of the stamps in his collection are very rare, while others are not. Additionally, other stamp collectors are likely to feel that his collection has a high utility, while noncollectors may disagree. The value of Craig's collection, therefore, depends on the scarcity and the utility of the stamps.

Interdependence

Why would you participate in an exchange? For an exchange to be successful, each participant must be able to provide goods and services that the other wants but does not possess. If both people are satisfied with the goods and services they already have, an exchange will not take place. The principle of exchange depends on unmet needs and wants.

Are you able to produce all of the goods and services you need? People—or societies—demonstrate **self-sufficiency** when they can fulfill all of their needs without outside assistance. True self-sufficiency is rare, however, because resources are limited. To produce everything you need would require a tremendous supply of tools, equipment, and raw materials. In addition, self-sufficiency demands extensive skills and knowledge in a variety of fields.

Instead of being self-sufficient, people tend to specialize in certain areas of production and rely

EXCHANGE, MONEY, & INTERDEPENDENCE *Amish settlements, located primarily in Ohio and Pennsylvania, attempt to be completely self-sufficient by fulfilling all their residents' needs without outside assistance.* ***Why do most societies fulfill wants and needs through interdependence and exchange?***

Global Connections

Scarcity can sometimes increase the value of a product to shocking levels. In Japan, Nike's Air Max® tennis shoes were hot items with teens during the late 1990s. The most desired models were also the hardest to find. At one point, used pairs of the Yellow Max, a discontinued model, sold for about $900. ■

Caption Answer

because self-sufficiency requires a tremendous supply of tools, equipment, and raw materials as well as people with extensive skills and knowledge in a variety of fields

WHAT IS ECONOMICS? 17

SECTION 4 REVIEW ANSWERS

1. exchange (15), barter (15), money (15), credit (16), value (17), utility (17), self-sufficiency (17), interdependence (18) **11A, 24A**

2. Students should mention barter, which often requires complex transactions between multiple parties; money, which provides a standardized means of exchange; credit, which allows consumers to use items before completing payment. **11A, 24D**

3a. Answers will vary but may include: benefits—people and nations can specialize in what they produce and can rely on others for additional products; risks—it presents a challenge if a product becomes unavailable.

3b. Answers will vary but students might mention the inefficiency of producing a good that is unsuited to a particular climate. **2B**

4. Answers will vary, but in most schools, teachers and other school officials specialize in particular fields or duties (e.g., geography, English, or counseling) and rely on others to provide specialized instruction or work in other areas. **23A**

---

on others for additional goods and services. For example, a landowner in the Rio Grande valley of Texas is more likely to cultivate grapefruit than to fish for Atlantic cod, because the region's soil and climate are well suited to citrus crops—and because Texas is a long way from the North Atlantic. The landowner in Texas must rely on fishing companies in the New England states to provide cod, just as fishing-boat captains who want grapefruit must rely on citrus farmers in Texas and other states with appropriate soil and climate conditions.

This reliance among economic actors is known as interdependence. **Interdependence** means that events or developments in one region of the world or sector of the economy influence events or developments in other regions or sectors. Increased home construction may encourage a paint company to expand production and hire additional workers. Bad weather in Oregon and Washington may lead to a poor apple crop, which in turn can increase the price of apple juice and frozen apple turnovers.

Interdependence encourages individuals, industries, and regions to meet particular needs and wants. If you know that you can purchase clothing at a nearby store, you do not need your own loom. Sometimes, however, interdependence can present challenges if the good or service becomes unavailable. For example, in 1990 Iraq invaded Kuwait, a small, oil-rich country. Many people feared that a stoppage of oil production and shipments would weaken the economies of the countries that received their oil supplies from Kuwait. Although interdependence offers many benefits, it also can pose the threat of economic vulnerability.

EXCHANGE, MONEY, & INTERDEPENDENCE *Societies can specialize in the production of certain goods and services when they practice interdependence.*

SECTION 4 REVIEW

★TEKS Q: 1, 2, 3b, 4

1. Identify and Explain:
- exchange
- barter
- money
- credit
- value
- utility
- self-sufficiency
- interdependence

2. Summarizing: Copy the diagram below. Use it to identify three forms of exchange along with the characteristics of each form of exchange.

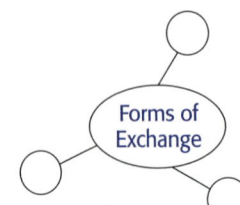

Forms of Exchange

3. Finding the Main Idea
a. Describe the benefits and risks of interdependence.
b. Why might interdependence lead to increased economic efficiency?

4. Writing and Critical Thinking
Drawing Inferences: How do forms of interaction within your school demonstrate interdependence?
Consider the following:
- Do some math teachers also teach English classes?
- Do teachers also act as administrators?

Homework Practice Online
keyword: SM3 HP1

18 CHAPTER 1

Economics IN THE NEWS

Economic Resources in the Global Economy

Economic resources—be they natural, capital, human, or entrepreneurial—often come from different locations, especially in an increasingly interdependent and global economy. For instance, one of the most important factors entrepreneurs must consider when producing their goods and services is labor. However, finding workers at the right price and with the right skills can often be difficult. One strategy American businesses use is to locate where labor costs are low, such as in rural areas where good jobs are in short supply. Many American companies also look to other countries to supply their labor needs.

One example is Mexico's *maquiladora*—twin plant or production-sharing—program. Since the 1960s, Mexico has allowed foreign businesses to set up factories called *maquiladoras*. (The term *maquiladora* comes from the Spanish word *maquilar*, which means "to submit something to the action of a machine.") By locating factories in Mexico, U.S. companies are able to use less-expensive Mexican labor. More than 3,000 businesses participate in the program, including most of America's largest manufacturing companies. In fact, 98 percent of the companies are U.S.-based. The *maquiladora* program employs more than 1 million Mexican workers, producing everything from automobile parts to candy.

In recent years, America's computer and Internet-related companies have also begun to use foreign labor. For instance, with rapid economic growth has come an increased demand for skilled customer-service representatives to answer questions over the telephone. Companies such as Microsoft and Sun Microsystems have set up call centers in foreign countries to take advantage of lower labor costs. Two of the most popular countries are India and Ireland, because both countries have well-educated English-speaking populations.

With improved global communication and increasing reliance on the Internet, companies can employ staff in other countries to serve customers here in the United States.

Many American workers object to the movement of jobs out of the country, arguing that it leaves fewer jobs to go around for American workers. They also argue that all workers, be they American or foreign, deserve adequate wages. Finally, they object to the fact that many foreign countries have less strict health, safety, and environmental regulations than the United States.

What Do You Think? TEKS

1. Which of the factors of production are American businesses increasingly getting from foreign countries?
2. Why might American companies move labor-intensive operations to Mexico?
3. How do lower wages increase the productivity and efficiency of a business?

WHY IT MATTERS TODAY

Many businesses depend on factors of production located in different places. Use **CNNfyi.com** or other **current events** sources to find other examples of businesses using economic factors of production located in different places. Record your findings in your Notebook.

CNNfyi.com

Economics in the News Answers

1. labor; labor costs are less expensive in many foreign countries 12B
2. Labor costs less in Mexico, but Mexico is still close to the U.S. market.
3. by reducing production costs

CHAPTER 1
Review Answers

Writing a Summary

Summaries should focus on the main points of each section. These may be found in the Read to Discover questions at the start of each section. Summaries should also use standard grammar, spelling, sentence structure, and punctuation. 24B, 24D

Identifying Ideas

economics (3), factors of production (4), natural resources (4), human resources (5), capital resources (5), entrepreneurship (7), scarcity (8), trade-off (11), opportunity cost (11), production possibilities curve (12), exchange (15), credit (16) 24A

Understanding Main Ideas

1. microeconomics—study of specific economic actors; macroeconomics—study of entire economies
2. It forces people to decide how to use resources effectively. 5A
3. what, how, and for whom to produce

CHAPTER 1 Review

(Continued from page 19)

4. Workers do a few tasks repeatedly and therefore become experts at those tasks and do them faster.

5. The resources and technology will not change during the period being studied; all resources are being used as efficiently as possible. **5B**

6. Countries do not have to produce all of the goods they consume and can specialize in the production of certain goods while trading for others.

Reviewing Themes

1. Human needs and wants are always greater than the resources available to satisfy those needs. **5A**

2. by money; scarcity, limited resources

3. The curve shows all possible combinations of goods or services that can be produced within a stated time period. **5B**

Thinking Critically

1. Students will likely view shoes as consumer goods, projectors as consumer or capital goods, and forklifts as capital goods.

2. Resources are unlimited, yet class members may have unlimited needs and wants. **5B**

3. Entrepreneurs use other resources to start new businesses or to produce new products. Technology creates new resources and improves existing ones. **26A**

Writing a Summary

Using standard grammar, spelling, sentence structure, and punctuation, write a summary of the information in this chapter.

Identifying Ideas

1. economics
2. factors of production
3. natural resources
4. human resources
5. capital resources
6. entrepreneurship
7. scarcity
8. trade-off
9. opportunity cost
10. production possibilities curve
11. exchange
12. credit

Understanding Main Ideas

SECTION 1 *(pp. 3–7)*

1. What is the difference between microeconomics and macroeconomics?

SECTION 2 *(pp. 8–10)*

2. Why is scarcity important in economics?
3. What three production issues must an economic system address?
4. How can division of labor and specialization increase productivity?

SECTION 3 *(pp. 11–14)*

5. Identify the assumptions on which the production possibilities curve is based.

SECTION 4 *(pp. 15–18)*

6. Describe the benefits of interdependence.

Reviewing Themes

1. **Scarcity & Choice** Why is scarcity considered the most basic problem of economics?
2. **Exchange, Money, & Interdependence** How is value represented in an economic system with a standardized means of exchange? What conditions lead to economic interdependence?
3. **Opportunity Cost & Trade-Offs** How can a production possibilities curve be used to illustrate trade-offs and opportunity costs?

Thinking Critically

1. **Categorizing** Determine whether the following products are capital goods or consumer goods: tennis shoes, motion picture projectors, forklifts. Explain your answers.
2. **Making Generalizations** Consider the resources that are available in your classroom, such as reference books, chalk, and display areas. How do these resources reflect the principle of scarcity?
3. **Analyzing Information** Explain how entrepreneurship and technology relate to natural, human, and capital resources.

Writing about Economics

Review what you wrote about your economic activities in your Economics Notebook at the beginning of this chapter. Now that you have studied this chapter, would you change your evaluation? Why or why not? Revise what you wrote earlier, if necessary, and put your ideas in terms of scarcity, trade-offs, and opportunity costs.

Building Social Studies Skills

Interpreting the Graph

Study the graph below. Then use it to help you answer the questions that follow.

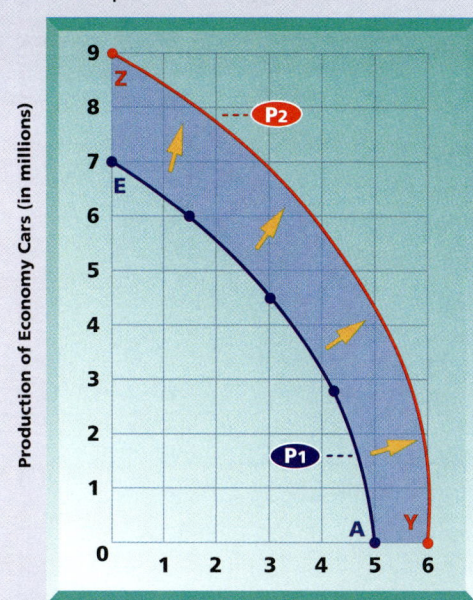

Production of Economy Cars (in millions) vs **Production of Luxury Cars (in millions)**

1. What does the curve's shift to the right mean?
   a. Improvements in technology have occurred, or new resources are available.
   b. Available resources have decreased, or there are diminishing returns to technology.
   c. Efficiency has decreased.
   d. None of the above.
2. Do you think production possibilities curves might "shift to the right" more often than they "shift to the left"? Explain your answer.

Analyzing Primary Sources

Read the following excerpt by English economist Alfred Marshall (1842–1924). Then answer the questions.

"The steadiest motive to ordinary business work is the desire for the pay.... It is this definite and exact money measurement of the steadiest motives ... which has enabled economics far to outrun every other branch of the study of man.

"But of course economics.... deals with the ever changing and subtle forces of human nature....

"*Economic laws* ... relate to branches of conduct in which the strength of the motives chiefly concerned can be measured by a money price....

"For there is a continuous gradation [progression] from social laws ... that can be measured by price, to social laws in which such motives have little place; and which are therefore generally as much less precise and exact than economic laws."

3. What is Marshall's point of view?
   a. Economic motives are difficult to measure, which makes economics an imprecise science.
   b. Economic motives are steady and measurable, which makes economics more exact than other social sciences.
   c. Social tendencies, are not measurable.
   d. None of the above.
4. What evidence might contradict Marshall's claims that the steadiest motive to work is the desire for pay?

Alternative Assessment

Building Your Portfolio

With your group, develop an idea for a new study aid. Respond to the three production questions of what to produce, how to produce, and for whom to produce. Assign each member of the group a task, and create an advertisement that describes what the product is, how it is made, and the audience it targets. Draw three production possibilities curves for your product: one showing current production, one assuming increased technology, and one forecasting increased resources.

Internet Activity: go.hrw.com
KEYWORD: SM3 EC1

Access the Internet through the HRW Go site to conduct research on natural resources in the United States. You may also refer to your textbook. Then create a U.S. map that shows the location of natural resources such as minerals, energy sources, farmland, and marine life. Write a caption evaluating the importance of the resources' locations.

Writing about Economics
Answers will vary, but students should organize their activities in terms of choice and relate each of the three factors to their activities in some way.

Building Social Studies Skills

1. a 5B
2. Answers will vary, but students should base their opinions on whether they believe that new technology and new resources are causing an increase in production potential. 23A, 23F, 23G,
3. b 23E
4. Answers will vary. Students might suggest that job satisfaction or political goals can override the desire for pay in some cases. Students should support their arguments with specific examples.
23A, 23E

CHAPTER RESOURCE MANAGER

CHAPTER 2 ECONOMIC SYSTEMS

	OBJECTIVES	PACING GUIDE	REPRODUCIBLE RESOURCES
SECTION 1 **TYPES OF ECONOMIC SYSTEMS** (pp. 23–28)	▶ How are the three basic economic questions answered in traditional, command, and market economies? ▶ What are the roles of self-interest and incentives in a market economy? ▶ What types of mixed economies exist today?	**Regular** 2 days **Block Scheduling** 1 day	**ELL** Spanish Study Guide 2.1 **ELL** English Study Guide 2.1 **PS** Reading 50: The Wealth of Nations **PS** Reading 58: Das Kapital
SECTION 2 **FEATURES OF THE U.S. ECONOMY** (pp. 29–35)	▶ What are the basic principles of free enterprise in the United States? ▶ What are the two markets of the circular flow model? ▶ How does the circular flow model reflect exchange?	**Regular** 2 days **Block Scheduling** 1 day	**ELL** Spanish Study Guide 2.2 **ELL** English Study Guide 2.2
SECTION 3 **THE U.S. ECONOMY AT WORK** (pp. 36–40)	▶ How do nations decide how to use scarce resources? ▶ What are the major goals of U.S. economic policy? ▶ Why do economic goals sometimes conflict?	**Regular** 1.5 days **Block Scheduling** 0.5 day	**ELL** Spanish Study Guide 2.3 **ELL** English Study Guide 2.3 **E** Challenge and Enrichment: Activity 2

Chapter Resource Key

PS	Primary Sources	**A**	Assessment		Video
RS	Reading Support	**REV**	Review		Videodisc
E	Enrichment	**ELL**	Reinforcement and English Language Learners		Internet
S	Simulations		Transparencies		Holt Presentation Maker Using Microsoft® PowerPoint®
SM	Skills Mastery		CD-ROM		TEKS and TAKS

TECHNOLOGY RESOURCES	REINFORCEMENT, REVIEW, AND ASSESSMENT
◦ One-Stop Planner: Lesson 2.1 ◦ Researcher Online ◦ Homework Practice Online ◦ CNN Presents Economics: Keeping Afloat in the Circular Flow ◦ Transparency 4: Types of Economic Systems ◦ Global Skillbuilder CD-ROM	**REV** Section 1 Review, p. 28 **A** Daily Quiz 2.1 ★ TAKS Every Day!
◦ One-Stop Planner: Lesson 2.2 ◦ Researcher Online ◦ Homework Practice Online ◦ Transparency 5: Circular Flow of Goods and Services ◦ Global Skillbuilder CD-ROM	**REV** Section 2 Review, p. 35 **A** Daily Quiz 2.2 ★ TAKS Every Day!
◦ One-Stop Planner: Lesson 2.3 ◦ Researcher Online ◦ Homework Practice Online	**REV** Section 3 Review, p. 40 **A** Daily Quiz 2.3 ★ TAKS Every Day!

Chapter Review and Assessment
SM Global Skillbuilder CD-ROM
 HRW Go site
REV Reteaching Activity 2
REV Chapter 2 Review, pp. 41–43
A Chapter 2 Test Generator (on the One-Stop Planner)
A Chapter 2 Test
A Alternative Assessment Handbook

One-Stop Planner CD-ROM
It's easy to plan lessons, select resources, and print out materials for your students when you use the *Texas One-Stop Planner CD-ROM with Test Generator.*

---

internet connect

HRW ONLINE RESOURCES
Go To: **go.hrw.com**
Then type in a keyword.

TEACHER HOME PAGE
KEYWORD: **SM3 Teacher**

CHAPTER INTERNET ACTIVITIES
KEYWORD: **SM3 EC2**
Choose an activity to:
▶ answer questions about Adam Smith's life and philosophy.
▶ research the role of the U.S. government in the free-enterprise system.
▶ research unemployment in the United States and abroad.

CHAPTER ENRICHMENT LINKS
KEYWORD: **SM3 CH2**

HOLT RESEARCHER ONLINE
KEYWORD: **Holt Researcher**

ONLINE ASSESSMENT
Homework Practice
KEYWORD: **SM3 HP2**
TAKS Review
KEYWORD: **SM3 T2**
Rubrics
KEYWORD: **SS Rubrics**

CONTENT UPDATES
KEYWORD: **SS Content Updates**

HOLT PRESENTATION MAKER
KEYWORD: **SM3 PPT3**

ONLINE READING SUPPORT
KEYWORD: **SS Strategies**

CURRENT EVENTS
KEYWORD: **S3 Current Events**

TEXAS ONLINE RESOURCES
KEYWORD: **S3 TX**

LESSON 2.1 TYPES OF ECONOMIC SYSTEMS

TEXTBOOK PAGES 23–28

HOLT PRESENTATION MAKER
Access Illustrated LECTURE NOTES using Microsoft® PowerPoint® on the One-Stop Planner CD-ROM

OBJECTIVES

- Explain how the three basic economic questions are answered in traditional, command, and market economies. ★10A
- Describe the roles of self-interest and incentives in a market economy.
- Describe the types of mixed economies that exist today.

MOTIVATE

Remind students that in Chapter 1 they examined the ways individuals make economic decisions. Tell students that they are now going to focus on the ways nations and governments make economic decisions. Write the following questions on the chalkboard:

- Which factors influence economic decisions made in your school?
- Who makes these decisions?
- What are these decisions based on?

Have students discuss each question in turn. As students answer the questions, write their answers on the chalkboard. Then have students answer the three questions for the United States instead of their school. Once again, write students' answers on the chalkboard. Tell students to write down these questions and answers, and then to write down how these answers might differ for different economic systems and countries, as they read through Section 1 of the chapter. ★10B

TEACH

Building a Vocabulary

Have students use spiral notebooks to create an Economics Dictionary to be used throughout the chapter. This dictionary might be used as an activity at the start of each new section or as a learning aid for sheltered English students or students having difficulty. List words that students will be expected to know for this section on the chalkboard. Have students use the information provided in the text or on the *Researcher CD-ROM* to list, define, and give an example of each term.

Comparing and Contrasting Concepts

Have students examine Figure 2.1: Types of Economic Systems (Transparency 4). Review each economic system as a class. Then call on students to describe how each of the societies and countries listed is representative of its economic system. Next, have students compare and contrast the three types of economic systems and discuss the advantages and disadvantages of each. ★10A

Applying a Model, Making Decisions

After reviewing the general characteristics of traditional, command, and market economies, organize students into groups of three or four. Assign each group to be representatives of either a traditional, command, or market economy. Have each group decide how their school will be run based on the economic system they represent. Each group should create a table illustrating how the school will answer the three basic economic questions of what to produce, how to produce, and for whom to produce. Students should also consider the societal values that influence traditional, command, and market economies. When students finish, have groups discuss their results and decide on a master economic plan. Have volunteers present the economic plans to the rest of the class. ★21B

Evaluating and Applying Ideas

Ask students which economic system they prefer: traditional, command, or market? Explain that most people in the United States prefer a market economy because it is the economic system closest to that of the U.S. economy. Ask students how the market regulates economic activity *(self-interest)*. Then ask how people decide what economic choices are in their self-interest *(through incentives)*. Discuss with students the roles of self-interest and incentives in a market economy.

Review with students how the newspaper carrier example in the textbook (on pages 26 and 27) illustrates the roles of self-interest and incentives in a market economy. Then organize students into groups of three or four. Have each group select a job. (Students might choose one of the jobs described in the Careers section on the *Researcher Online.*) Next, have students create a diagram showing how the job they selected benefits society and listing the incentives the job provides. Ask several volunteers to share their diagrams. Refer students who need additional instruction on the skills used in this lesson to the *Global Skillbuilder* Lesson 12: Creating Graphic Organizers.

Classifying Ideas

Ask students how most of the economies that exist today are classified. *(They are classified as mixed economies.)* Call on a student to define mixed economies for the class. *(A mixed economy combines elements of the pure economic models to answer the three basic economic questions.)* Write the definition on the chalkboard. Then ask students to list the three main categories of mixed economies *(authoritarian socialism, capitalism, and democratic socialism).* Discuss with students the characteristics of each system. Have students describe the role of government and individuals in each system. To help students organize their ideas, have them create a table similar to the one below. ⭐23A

Mixed Economy	Economic Model Closest to	What to Produce	How to Produce	For Whom to Produce	Current Examples
Authoritarian Socialism (Communism)					
Capitalism					
Democratic Socialism					

CLOSE

Review with students the questions they discussed at the beginning of class. Ask students which economic system they now think best describes how their school is run and why. Use students' responses to review the characteristics of the economic systems covered in Section 1 of Chapter 2.

OPTIONS

Gifted Learners

Have students research the author Ayn Rand's philosophy of objectivism and determine which economic system it most resembles. Next, have students write an essay comparing and contrasting the philosophies of Ayn Rand and Adam Smith, or create and perform a dialogue between Ayn Rand and Adam Smith on the topic of the role of self-interest.

Linguistic Learners

Tell students to imagine that Adam Smith is running for president of the United States and that they are his speech writers. Have students write a speech justifying Smith's *laissez-faire* approach to economics. Then have students use the *Researcher Online,* the library, and in-class resources to research Smith's theories and apply them to current economic trends. Students should work to make their speeches persuasive and contemporary, and address the importance and impact of Adam Smith on the U.S. free-enterprise system. Have selected students present their speeches to the class. ⭐19A

Sheltered English Students

Pair sheltered English students with speakers fluent in English. Have each pair create a poster illustrating the three types of economic systems—traditional, command, and market. Posters should show how the three basic economic questions are answered in each system.

REVIEW

Have students complete the Section 1 Review on page 28. Use the answers in the Annotated Teacher's Edition to assess student mastery of this section.

ASSESS

To assess student mastery of this section, have students complete Daily Quiz 2.1 in *Daily Quizzes with Answer Key.* For additional assessment options, see *Alternative Assessment Handbook* on the *One-Stop Planner CD-ROM.*

ADDITIONAL RESOURCES

Coats, A.W. *On the History of Economic Thought.* 1992. Routledge.

Holton, Robert J. *Economy and Society.* 1992. Routledge.

Rothschild, Emma. *Economic Sentiments: Adam Smith, Condorcet, and the Enlightenment.* 2001. Harvard University Press.

Smith, Adam. *The Wealth of Nations.* 1991. Prometheus Books.

LESSON 2.2 FEATURES OF THE U.S. ECONOMY

TEXTBOOK PAGES 29–35

> **HOLT PRESENTATION MAKER**
> Access Illustrated LECTURE NOTES using Microsoft® PowerPoint® on the One-Stop Planner CD-ROM

OBJECTIVES

- Explain the basic principles of free enterprise in the United States. ★4A
- Name the two markets of the circular flow model.
- Explain how the circular flow model reflects exchange.

MOTIVATE

Write the term *free enterprise* on the chalkboard. Have students analyze the term by dissecting it one word at a time. Ask students to define the word *free*, then the word *enterprise*. You might have students use word association to define each term. As students provide responses for each word, write them on the chalkboard. Then ask students to combine the definitions in order to form a working definition of *free enterprise*.

Tell students that the capitalist economy of the United States is called a free-enterprise system because individuals in the United States have a great number of economic freedoms. Ask students to suggest what they think some of these economic freedoms are. Write students' suggestions on the chalkboard.

TEACH

Building a Vocabulary

List the important terms for this section on the chalkboard and tell students to add them to their Economics Dictionary. Tell students to use the information provided in the textbook or on the *Researcher CD-ROM* to list, define, and give an example of each term.

Understanding Main Concepts, Comparing and Contrasting

Have students review their original definition of *free enterprise* and revise it as necessary. Next, have students list the five features of a free-enterprise system *(the right to own private property and enter into contracts, make individual choices, engage in economic competition, make decisions based on self-interest, and participate in the economy with limited government involvement and regulation)*. As students name the features, write them on the chalkboard next to the list of economic freedoms that students made at the start of class. Have students review their list of economic freedoms. Ask them how their list fits with the five main features of a free-enterprise system. Make certain that students understand each of the five concepts. Then ask them what separates the U.S. economy from the pure market model *(limited government intervention and regulation)*.

Next, ask students to consider a fast-food restaurant. Ask them to give examples of how a fast-food restaurant demonstrates each of the five features or benefits of a free-enterprise economy. Finally, share with students the information from the sidebar on p. 31. Have them research and evaluate government restrictions on the use of individual property. ★3A, 3B, 4B

Demonstrating Understanding, Role-Playing

Organize students into five groups, one for each basic principle of free enterprise in the United States. Have each group create and perform a skit that showcases the group's principle of free enterprise. Each member of the group should participate in the skit. After each skit, have students in the audience provide feedback.

Using Economic Models

Ask students to name and define the roles of the three main economic actors in a free-enterprise economy *(producers, consumers, and the government)*. Explain to students that in a free-enterprise system, resources, products, and money payments are exchanged among these different actors in the economy. Have students examine the circular flow model on page 34 of their textbook (Transparency 5). Tell students that this model represents a simplified view of how the U.S. economy functions. Ask students what is represented by the green arrows *(the product market, which represents all of the exchanges of goods and services in the economy)*. Then ask what is represented by the gold arrows *(the resource market, which represents the exchange of resources among households and business firms and the government)*.

Explain to students that exchanges in the product and resource markets involve two different types of flows—the flow of resources and products and the flow of money payments. Call on students to describe how the circular flow model illustrates each of these flows. Then have students provide some real-life

21E

examples of exchanges. Refer students who need additional instruction on the skills used in this lesson to the *Global Skillbuilder* Lesson 13: Interpreting Diagrams.

Classifying and Organizing Information

On the chalkboard make a table similar to the one below, except do not fill in the bulleted items. Have students classify each exchange in the circular flow model and indicate where the exchange should go in the table. Complete the table as a class. Then call on students to describe specific exchanges that they or someone they know has made recently. Have students classify each exchange according to its place in the circular flow model and record their answer in the appropriate place in the table.

Flow	Product Market	Resource Market
Resources and Products	• Businesses supply goods and services to households and government in exchange for payment • Government supplies services to households in exchange for taxes.	• Households supply resources (labor) to businesses and government in exchange for income. • Government supplies services to businesses in exchange for taxes.
Money Payments	• Households and government make payments to businesses in exchange for goods and services. • Households make payments (taxes) to government in exchange for services.	• Businesses and government make payments (income) to households in exchange for resources. • Businesses make payments (taxes) to government in exchange for services.

CLOSE

Review the five features of free enterprise in the United States. Then ask students to describe the flow and exchange of resources, products, and money payments in the U.S. economy, using the circular flow model as a visual aid.

OPTIONS

Sheltered English Students

Pair sheltered English students with fluent speakers. Have each pair use newspapers and magazines to create a collage illustrating the five basic principles of the free-enterprise system in the United States. Each pair should write a caption that explains how the collage represents the features of a free-enterprise system.

Body-Kinesthetic Learners, Students Having Difficulty

To help students better understand the exchanges shown in the circular flow model, have the class create a representation of the model by using their own bodies in motion. Provide students with placards or signs they can carry to identify their role within the circular flow model. As students move through the model, have them explain the market, flow, and exchange that they represent.

Gifted Learners

Explain to students that at times in the history of the United States, government regulation of the economy has come into conflict with individual freedom. Have students use the Supreme Court Docket on the *Researcher Online*, the library, in-class resources, and the Internet to research such a conflict. Tell students to write a report describing and analyzing the conflict, explaining how it was resolved, and giving their opinion of the resolution.

REVIEW

Have students complete the Section 2 Review on page 35. Use the answers in the Annotated Teacher's Edition to assess student mastery of this section.

ASSESS

To assess student mastery of this section, have students complete Daily Quiz 2.2 in *Daily Quizzes with Answer Key*. For additional assessment options, see *Alternative Assessment Handbook* on the *One-Stop Planner CD-ROM*.

ADDITIONAL RESOURCES

Friedman, Milton. *Capitalism and Freedom*. 1993. Blackstone Audio Books. (audio cassette)

Schwartz, Louis, and John J. Flynn. *Supplement to Free Enterprise and Economic Organization*. 1998. Foundation Press, Inc.

Stein, Herbert, and Murray Foss. *The New Illustrated Guide to the American Economy*. 1995. AEI Press.

Thurow, Lester, and Robert Heilbroner. *Economics Explained*. 1994. Touchstone Books.

Wentworth, Donald, et al. *United States History: Focus on Economics*. 1996. Economics America, National Council on Economic Education.

LESSON 2.3 THE U.S. ECONOMY AT WORK

TEXTBOOK PAGES 36–40

HOLT PRESENTATION MAKER
Access Illustrated LECTURE NOTES using Microsoft® PowerPoint® on the One-Stop Planner CD-ROM

OBJECTIVES

▸ Describe how nations decide how to use scarce resources.
▸ List and define the major goals of U.S. economic policy. ★16A
▸ Explain why economic goals sometimes conflict.

MOTIVATE

Write the following statement on the chalkboard: Should the U.S. government provide health-care coverage to all U.S. citizens? Encourage students to discuss the question. Guide students in examining the arguments supporting and opposing government-sponsored health care. Ask students to suggest some of the benefits and trade-offs of the U.S. government providing health coverage to all citizens.

After a brief period of discussion, explain to students that this issue, like many others in the United States, involves conflicting goals. Ask students what they think the goals of the U.S. economy should be. List students' suggestions on the chalkboard. Tell students to keep this list in mind as they read through Section 3 of the chapter.

TEACH

Building a Vocabulary

List the important terms for this section on the chalkboard and tell students to add them to their Economics Dictionary. Tell students to use the information provided in the textbook or on the *Researcher CD-ROM* to list, define, and give an example of each term.

Understanding Main Concepts

Ask students how nations decide how to use scarce resources *(by setting goals)*. Then ask students to name and define the six major goals of U.S. economic policy *(economic freedom, efficiency, equity, security, stability, and growth)*. As students list each economic goal, ask them to provide examples of that goal. Then ask students if they can think of any current events in the news that illustrate one or more of the six economic goals. Encourage students to discuss each example. ★16A

Acquiring Information

Provide (or have students bring) several recent newspapers and magazines to class. Organize students into six groups, one for each of the six major goals of U.S. economic policy. Tell students that businesses and policymakers daily deal with issues involving the six U.S. economic goals. Instruct each student to find a newspaper or magazine article that illustrates or represents his or her group's assigned goal. When students are through, have them regroup and select the article that best illustrates their group's economic goal. Then have a representative from each group summarize the selected article for the rest of the class and explain how it relates to the group's assigned goal. ★16A

Analyzing Ideas

Review with students the list of economic goals they made at the beginning of class. Point out any differences between this list and the six economic goals listed in the textbook. Tell students that people in the United States have a variety of opinions as to what the economic goals of the United States should be and which goals should take priority. Even when policymakers agree on economic goals, they cannot pursue every goal at the same time. Explain that it is inevitable that economic goals will conflict in a diverse society where different groups of people experience various needs and wants at the same time.

Review with students the question they discussed at the start of class: Should the U.S. government provide health coverage to all U.S. citizens? Ask which of the six main economic policy goals are involved in this issue. Then ask how these goals conflict and what trade-offs are involved. After a brief period of discussion, have students analyze and discuss other current news events that involve conflicting economic goals and trade-offs. ★16B

Role-Playing, Recognizing Point of View

Organize students into groups of two or three and assign each group a different role, such as that of a college student, an environmental activist, a CEO of a large corporation, a single mother on welfare, an elderly couple depending on government-subsidized health care, a business entrepreneur, etc. Tell the groups to consider goals of U.S. economic policy from the perspective of their assigned roles. Have the members of each group map out what they think the short-term and long-term goals of the U.S. economy should be and why. Then have the groups hold an economic summit and present their goals. Call on representatives to present their group's goals to the class. After each presentation, give other groups time to respond and ask questions. Throughout the summit, help students understand how different groups have differing needs and wants, and thus have differing ideas about what the economic goals of the United States should be. ⭐16A

CLOSE

Ask students which of the six main economic goals they think are the most important and why. Then ask the class what they think the short-term and long-term goals for U.S. economic policy should be. As students try to come to a consensus, point out how hard it can be for policymakers to choose what actions to take when different groups support conflicting goals.

OPTIONS

Students Having Difficulty

Organize students into groups of two or three, pairing students having difficulty with students who have mastered the material. Tell each group to imagine that they are economic advisers preparing to address a group of newly elected U.S. legislators. As economic advisers, it is their job to explain to all new legislators the importance of each of the six economic policy goals of the United States, and how and why these goals can conflict. Tell each group to create materials, such as charts and posters, for their presentation. Each group member should participate in preparing materials. ⭐16A

Gifted Learners

Refer students to the Global Exchange feature about immigration on page 39. Have students use the *Researcher CD-ROM,* the library, in-class resources, and the Internet to research questions about immigration and economics. Where are immigrants to the United States coming from? What sort of economic systems are in place in these countries? Tell students to compare and contrast the economic systems and national economic goals of these countries with those of the United States. Have students present their findings in a briefing paper that includes original charts and graphs. Students may want to include their papers in their portfolios.

Linguistic Learners

Have students write two to four paragraphs in response to the following question: How do the economic goals of the United States help policymakers reach decisions regarding the U.S. economy? Tell students that they should address each of the six economic policy goals of the United States in their papers. In addition, encourage students to provide actual examples of ways in which prioritizing goals has helped policymakers reach decisions.

Visual-Spatial Learners

Have students choose a period of time in U.S. history and compare and contrast the economic goals and priorities of that period with those of today. Have students use newspaper and magazine clippings to create a collage that illustrates and compares the important economic goals of the two periods. Students may want to include their collages in their portfolios.

REVIEW

Have students complete the Section 3 Review on page 40. Use the answers in the Annotated Teacher's Edition to assess student mastery of this section.

ASSESS

To assess student mastery of this section, have students complete Daily Quiz 2.3 in *Daily Quizzes with Answer Key.* For additional assessment options, see *Alternative Assessment Handbook* on the *One-Stop Planner CD-ROM.*

RETEACH

For students having difficulty with the lessons, have them complete Reteaching Activity 2. This activity is located in *Reteaching Activities with Answer Key.*

ADDITIONAL RESOURCES

Finkelstein, Joseph. *The American Economy: From the Great Crash to the Third Industrial Revolution.* 1992. Harlan Davidson.

Rivlan, Alice M. *Reviving the American Dream: The Economy, the States, and the Federal Government.* 1992. Brookings Institution.

CHAPTER 2

TOPICS INCLUDE

- traditional, command, and market economies
- role of self-interest and incentives in market economies
- authoritarian socialism
- capitalism
- democratic socialism
- U.S. free-enterprise system
- circular flow model
- exchanges in the product and resource markets
- goals of the U.S. economy
- conflicts and trade-offs with economic goals

ECONOMICS NOTEBOOK

The Economics Notebook is a journal activity that encourages students to consider basic concepts of economics that relate to their lives. A follow-up notebook activity appears on page 41.

WHY IT MATTERS TODAY

To find additional lesson plans dealing with economic systems, visit CNNfyi.com or have students complete the ECONOMICS IN THE NEWS activity on page 42.

CNNfyi.com

CHAPTER 2

ECONOMIC SYSTEMS

As you have learned, there are three basic economic questions: what to produce, how to produce, and for whom to produce. Like individuals, societies also must answer these basic production questions, and they do so in different ways. For example, in some societies the government makes the production decisions, while in others these decisions are made by business owners. In all societies, however, production decisions are designed to meet people's needs and wants. The decisions form an interlocking network of production and consumption, and are the basis of all economic systems.

In this chapter you will learn how different societies make production decisions. You also will learn about the U.S. economy—what it is supposed to do and how it affects you.

ECONOMICS NOTEBOOK

In your Economics Notebook, list your personal economic goals. For example, you may want to buy a new jacket or take a trip. Which of your economic goals are short-term, and which are long-term? Explain your answers.

WHY IT MATTERS TODAY

When resources are scarce, a society must decide what it can and cannot produce with them. Visit CNNfyi.com or other **current events** sources to find out more about how U.S. society makes decisions about the use of its resources.

CNNfyi.com

SECTION 1

TYPES OF ECONOMIC SYSTEMS

READ TO DISCOVER

1. How are the three basic economic questions answered in traditional, command, and market economies?
2. What are the roles of self-interest and incentives in a market economy?
3. What types of mixed economies exist today?

ECONOMICS DICTIONARY

traditional economy
command economy
market economy
market
self-interest
incentive
mixed economy
authoritarian socialism
communism
capitalism
democratic socialism

You know that scarcity affects all aspects of economics and that it requires economic actors—individuals, businesses, and governments—to make choices. You, for example, have a limited amount of money and time—a basic economic problem. This scarcity forces you to make choices among ways to spend your money and your time—another common economic problem. In other words, scarcity results from the combination of limited resources and unlimited wants.

Nations also must make choices in order to use their natural, human, capital, and entrepreneurial resources efficiently. A nation—or, more directly, its leaders—must address the three basic economic questions: what to produce, how to produce, and for whom to produce.

A nation's responses to these questions are determined by its economic system. An economic system reflects the process a nation—or any society—follows to produce goods and services. There are four types of economic systems: traditional, command, market, and mixed.

In truth, all economies are mixed. Pure traditional, pure command, and pure market systems are models that do not exist in the world today. A few mixed economies are closest to the pure traditional model and are classified as traditional economies. Mixed economies that are closest to the pure command model are classified as command economies. Similarly, mixed economies that are closest to the pure market model are classified as market economies. See Figure 2.1 on page 26 for a summary of types of economic systems.

ECONOMIC SYSTEMS *In a traditional economy, children—such as this Navajo girl—often carry on the economic roles played by their parents.*

SECTION 1

TYPES OF ECONOMIC SYSTEMS

Lesson Plans
For teaching strategies, see Lesson 2.1 located at the beginning of this chapter or the One-Stop Planner Strategy 2.1.

Economics Dictionary
To reinforce the section's vocabulary terms, refer students to the Electronic Glossary on the *Researcher CD-ROM*.

Section Assessment
To assess students' mastery of this section, have them complete Daily Quiz 2.1 in *Daily Quizzes with Answer Key*.

TEKS
Content
5A, 10A, 10B, 19A, 21B
Social Studies Skills
23A, 24A, 24D

Global Connections

Today's rapidly changing world threatens the existence of some traditional economies. The Kaiowá tribe, located near the Paraguay-Brazil border, have led a simple life of fishing and farming for centuries.

In the 1940s, however, the Brazilian government began redistributing Kaiowá land to commercial farmers. Over time, the Kaiowá have lost a large percentage of their tribal lands to agribusiness and to other, more dominant tribes. In 1945 Kaiowá tribal lands measured some 25,000 square miles; by 1996 they had dwindled to about 172 square miles, less than an acre per person.

With the loss of their land, the Kaiowá are seeing their way of life slip away. Kaiowá men have been forced to find work on commercial farms or in distilleries to survive. The Brazilian Government Indian Protection Agency has attempted to intervene on behalf of the Kaiowá, but with limited success. ■

Caption Answer

The Mbuti produce goods for themselves and for trade with neighboring tribes.

Traditional Economies

As you might guess, a **traditional economy** is based on a society's values—its customs and traditions. In other words, the answers to the three economic questions are found in the past. Contemporary economic activities are based on the collection of rituals, habits, laws, and religious beliefs developed by the group's ancestors.

In a traditional economy, children often carry on the economic roles played by their parents. This means that tradition determines in large part what is produced. For example, if you lived in a society with a traditional economy and one of your parents earned a living by catching fish in the nearby river, you would earn your living in the same way. Tradition decides what you produce—fish. Note also that traditional economic roles generally are passed down from father to son and from mother to daughter, because in traditional economies men and women often perform distinct tasks.

Custom determines how items will be produced in a traditional economy. For example, hundreds of years ago some American Indian tribes planted corn when oak leaves grew to the size of a squirrel's ear. This timing was based on traditional agricultural practices rather than individual decisions.

For whom are goods produced in a traditional economy? Economic activities tend to be centered around traditional family and social units such as a tribe. The goods and services that are produced are distributed among the group's members. By sharing products, members of a traditional economy work to maintain the entire group rather than just themselves. For example, members of Inuit tribes in Canada share equally in the results of a hunt. When a seal or other large animal is killed, the meat is divided among the members of the hunting party. Hunters then share their meat with family members in an effort to help the entire community survive the harsh winter.

Traditional economic systems still exist in parts of North America, Latin America, Asia, and Africa. For example, the Dinka of central Africa herd cattle and grow crops on the southern plains of the Sudan as their ancestors have done for centuries. Other traditional economies include the San of the Kalahari Desert and the Aborigines of Australia. The Mbuti of central Africa are also organized into a traditional economic system.

CASE STUDY

The Mbuti of Central Africa

ECONOMIC SYSTEMS The Mbuti are inhabitants of the Ituri Forest in Democratic Republic of the Congo in central Africa. The 35,000 Mbuti live, work, and travel in bands, or small groups, of 30 people or less, and members of a band view themselves as a family. Because the Mbuti have a traditional economy, they rely on long-standing customs to answer the three basic economic issues of what, how, and for whom to produce.

The main duty of all band members is to provide food, and the Ituri Forest offers an abundance of natural resources. The Mbuti are hunter-gatherers. They collect roots, mushrooms, fruits, berries, and nuts. In addition, they hunt for wild game using nets, spears, bows, and arrows, which sometimes are dipped in poison. The men hunt, and the women and children gather and prepare the food. Tradition dictates which

ECONOMIC SYSTEMS *In the Mbuti tribe's economy, tradition determines which tasks will be done by men, women, and children.* **For whom do the Mbuti produce?**

jobs will be done by men and which will be done by women, as well as what duties children will perform.

Although members of traditional economies generally resist change, the Mbuti have adopted new tools in recent years. Neighboring tribes produce metal machetes and knives. The Mbuti trade for these items because they do not have the necessary resources and skills to produce metal tools.

Command Economies

While a traditional economy relies on past customs, a pure **command economy** relies on government officials to answer the three basic economic questions. The officials—sometimes called central planners—have the power to decide what products will be made and how these products will be produced. These planners also decide who will receive the products once they are completed. Command economies may also be called planned economies.

Because central planners make decisions about what, how, and for whom to produce, individuals in a command economy have little or no say in economic choices. The government maintains complete control over the factors of production.

Although pure command economies no longer exist, they were quite common in the past. For example, during the Old Kingdom period of Egyptian history (2700–2200 B.C.), the pharaoh, or monarch, ruled both the economy and the government of Egypt. The monarch owned the land, controlled all trade, collected taxes, and supervised the building of the kingdom's pyramids, dams, canals, and granaries.

During the Zhou Dynasty (1122–221 B.C.) in China, emperors were able to control resources by distributing land to supporters called vassals. The vassals pledged their military and political loyalty to the emperor in return for the land grants.

A similar system existed in Western Europe during the Middle Ages. Monarchs and other feudal lords granted resources such as land—called fiefs—to vassals in exchange for loyalty, military support, and payment. These vassals granted peasants the right to work the lands in exchange for money, crops, or livestock. The lord had absolute control over the use of human, natural, and capital resources on the manor and therefore made all decisions about what, how, and for whom to produce.

ECONOMIC SYSTEMS *Egyptians, such as those shown posting taxes on the Old Kingdom tomb above, lived in a command economy.* **Who controls production in a command economy?**

Market Economies

In a pure **market economy**, individuals answer the three basic economic questions. The government has no say in what, how, and for whom goods are produced, and the factors of production are owned by individuals. People can buy, sell, and produce anything they want.

This free exchange of goods and services is referred to as the **market**. The market provides the only form of control over what goods and services are bought and sold. The United States, Germany, and Japan have economies based on the concept of market economics.

Self-Interest How does the market regulate economic activity? One of the first people to explain this process of market regulation was Adam Smith (1723–1790), a Scottish economist and philosopher. In 1776 Smith published his ideas in the book *An Inquiry into the Nature and Causes of the Wealth of Nations*.

Caption Answer
government officials sometimes called central planners ★10A

Across the Curriculum

HISTORY & GOVERNMENT The Zhou came to power in China after conquering the Shang Dynasty in 1122 B.C. Shang rulers believed that their right to rule was passed down through their ancestors. Similarly, later Western rulers defended their legitimacy to rule through their lineage and the divine right of kings.

Zhou rulers, however, believed that their right to rule came from the gods. The gods chose the family most morally worthy to rule China and conferred on them the Mandate of Heaven. When a family was no longer morally worthy to rule, the gods chose another family. When they conquered the Shang, the Zhou rulers claimed that the Mandate of Heaven was now theirs and that they were the new Sons of Heaven. In this way, the emperor and his kinsmen justified their feudal authority over the people. ■

Profiles in Economics

For a biography of Adam Smith and other noted people in economics, refer students to the Biographies section on the *Researcher Online*.

Enhancing the Lesson

For more information on Adam Smith's theory of the role of self-interest in a market economy, see Reading 50: *The Wealth of Nations* in *From the Source: Readings in Economics and Government with Answer Key*.

Transparency

An overhead transparency of Figure 2.1 is available in *Transparency Resources*. See Transparency 4: Types of Economic Systems.

Caption Answer

United States—market economy in which individuals determine the answers to the three basic economic questions; Australian Aborigines—traditional economy in which tradition, custom, and economic roles determine the answers to the three basic economic questions ★10B

He contended that when the government is not involved in the economy, the market is driven purely by **self-interest**—the impulse that encourages people to fulfill their needs and wants.

Although some people believe that self-interest leads individuals to ignore the needs of others, Smith argued that self-interest benefits all of society by helping the economy grow. According to Smith, in a market exchange each person attempts to gain the greatest possible advantage from the transaction. While individuals work to meet their own needs and wants, however, self-interest acts as an "invisible hand" that also leads them to do what is best for society—even if they are unaware of how their actions may benefit others.

How can self-interest benefit others? Suppose that you have a job as a newspaper carrier. Why did you accept this job?

Adam Smith

(a) You believe that everyone deserves a newspaper.
(b) It is a good newspaper, and more people should read it.
(c) You are paid to deliver the newspaper.

Probably your answer is *c*. You deliver newspapers because you are paid to do so. At the same time, however, newspaper delivery makes it easier for people to learn about world and community events. Thus, your self-interest benefits other members of society.

Smith believed that government involvement in the economy conflicts with self-interest and limits the ability of the "invisible hand" to regulate the market. Suppose that the government set a limit on how many newspapers you could be paid to deliver each day. Would you try to sell newspaper subscriptions to people who moved into houses along your route? Probably not, because once you reach the maximum number of deliveries, additional subscriptions would offer you no personal benefit and would not be in your self-interest. The government policy, therefore, effectively would have limited newspaper circulation, reducing the benefits to you and to society as a whole.

TYPES OF ECONOMIC SYSTEMS

Economic Systems	WHAT to Produce	HOW to Produce	FOR WHOM to Produce	Examples
TRADITIONAL	• determined by tradition • economic roles often passed from generation to generation	• determined by custom	• usually centered around traditional family and social units such as a tribe	• Aborigines of Australia • Mbuti of central Africa • Inuit of Canada
COMMAND	• determined by government officials	• determined by government officials	• determined by government officials	• Old Kingdom Egypt • Middle Ages in Europe • Zhou Dynasty in China
MARKET	• determined by individuals	• determined by individuals	• determined by individuals	• United States • Canada • Australia

FIGURE 2.1 Economic systems are defined by the way they answer the three basic economic questions. **How does the U.S. economic system differ from that of Australian Aborigines?**

Incentives In a market economy, how do you decide what economic choices are in your self-interest? You—and other individuals in the economy—respond to incentives. An **incentive** is something that encourages you to behave in a particular way.

For example, the newspaper may offer you a bonus for every 50 new subscribers you sign up. This financial reward acts as an incentive, encouraging you to sell as many subscriptions as there are customers who want to buy them.

Incentives also can take the form of penalties. The newspaper may, for example, have a policy that financially penalizes its carriers if they do not sell at least 10 subscriptions per month: $2 is deducted from a carrier's monthly paycheck for each of the 10 subscriptions the carrier fails to sell. This penalty, like the bonus, acts as an incentive and encourages carriers to sell subscriptions. Negative incentives, however, can have additional consequences. As a carrier, you might become angry at the newspaper for docking your wages and decide to quit.

Mixed Economies

A **mixed economy** combines elements of traditional, market, and command economic models to answer the three basic economic questions. Because each nation's economy is a different blend of these three economic models, economists classify them according to the degree of government control. The three main categories of mixed economies are

- authoritarian socialism,
- capitalism, and
- democratic socialism.

Authoritarian Socialism Mixed economies that are closest to the pure command model are said to practice **authoritarian socialism**, which is also known as **communism**. In these economies the government owns or controls nearly all the factors of production.

How does a nation practicing authoritarian socialism answer the basic questions of what,

ECONOMIC SYSTEMS *Top to bottom: a Cuban worker cutting sugarcane in an authoritarian socialist economy; U.S. soldiers training in a capitalist economy; a government-owned airplane being built during France's democratic socialist era.*

---

internet connect

TOPIC: Adam Smith
GO TO: go.hrw.com
KEYWORD: SM3 EC2

Have students access the Internet through the HRW Go site to conduct research on Adam Smith. With a partner, each student should write a series of questions that he or she would like to ask Adam Smith about his life and his thoughts on modern economics. They should include at least one question on how Smith has influenced the U.S. free-enterprise system. Then, have students answer these questions as they believe that he would. Students should be prepared to present the interview, with one playing the role of the reporter and the other the role of Adam Smith. ★19A, 24D

Enhancing the Lesson

For a critique of capitalism, see Reading 58: Das Kapital, in *From the Source: Readings in Economics and Government with Answer Key.*

SECTION 1 REVIEW ANSWERS

1. traditional economy (24), command economy (25), market economy (25), market (25), self-interest (26), incentive (27), mixed economy (27), authoritarian socialism (27), communism (27), capitalism (28), democratic socialism (28) **10A, 24A**

2. three main branches: traditional, command, and market; smaller branches: should list how each economic system determines what is produced, how and for whom, and should give several real-world examples. Refer to the chart on p. 26. **10A, 24D**

3a. traditional—custom and tradition determine what, how, and for whom products are made; command—government decides what, how, and for whom products are made; market—individuals answer these questions. Answers will vary. Students should demonstrate an understanding of the values of societies under each system. **10A, 21B**

3b. scarcity and choice; because not all needs can be fulfilled, people are forced to choose between conflicting goals **5A**

4. authoritarian socialism (communism)—government owns or controls nearly all factors of production; capitalism—individuals own factors of production and address the economic questions; democratic socialism—government owns several key industries and individuals own the rest **21B**

---

how, and for whom to produce? For example, government officials in Cuba develop long-term plans outlining how the nation's resources will be used. This long-range planning serves to limit the decision-making power of individuals.

Capitalism While economies closest to the command model are said to practice authoritarian socialism, those closest to the market model are said to practice capitalism. In an economy based on **capitalism**, individuals own the factors of production and answer the basic economic questions. The economies of the United States, Canada, Mexico, Japan, and Taiwan are classified as capitalist.

For example, you can decide what to produce when you select a career. Your decision to be an electrician, an engineer, a reporter, or a fashion designer determines what is produced. This choice is not based on the jobs held by your parents and grandparents, or on the national goals of a central planner, but on your interests and skills as an individual.

Although the government of a capitalist nation may enact some regulations, its involvement in the economy is relatively limited. What is the government's role in a capitalist economy? Taxation and spending policies enable the government to provide a variety of services, including education, social welfare programs, and national defense. The government also may regulate health and safety standards in the workplace. In spite of this government activity, however, private ownership and free choice—rather than central planning—remain the basis of capitalism.

Democratic Socialism The third type of mixed economy falls between authoritarian socialism and capitalism. In this type of mixed economy, called **democratic socialism**, the government owns some of the factors of production. In most cases, government ownership is limited to key industries such as electrical utilities and telephone networks, which are of national concern. Individuals are able to influence economic planning through the election of government officials.

The economies of many European nations, including Sweden, Poland, and France, have included elements of democratic socialism. In addition, the economies of many of the world's less industrialized countries, such as Tanzania, Angola, and Mozambique, have been classified as democratic socialist.

SECTION 1 REVIEW

★TEKS Q: 1, 2, 3a, 3b, 4

1. Identify and Explain:
   traditional economy
   command economy
   market economy
   market
   self-interest
   incentive
   mixed economy
   authoritarian socialism
   communism
   capitalism
   democratic socialism

2. Categorizing: Copy the diagram below. Use it to compare traditional, command, and market economic systems. Give examples of each economy.

Types of Economic Systems

	Traditional	Command	Market
What			
How			
For Whom			
Example			

Homework Practice Online
keyword: SM3 HP2

3. Finding the Main Idea

a. What are the differences among traditional, command, and market economic systems? Describe the societal values influencing each system.

b. What are two basic economic problems that individuals and nations face? Why?

4. Writing and Critical Thinking

Comparing: Examine the three main categories of mixed economies: authoritarian socialism, capitalism, and democratic socialism. How are they similar and how are they different?

Consider the following:
• social values
• ownership of factors of production

CHAPTER 2

SECTION 2
FEATURES OF THE U.S. ECONOMY

READ TO DISCOVER

1. What are the basic principles of free enterprise in the United States?
2. What are the two markets of the circular flow model?
3. How does the circular flow model reflect exchange?

ECONOMICS DICTIONARY

free enterprise
private property
contracts
competition
voluntary exchange
product market
resource market
income

You have learned that nations have different economic systems. Why does a nation develop a particular economic system? The answer is that nations, like individuals, make choices that will satisfy needs and wants. Therefore, a nation will develop the economic system that it believes is most likely to meet the needs of its citizens.

The United States has a capitalist economy and leans toward the market model, which is driven by individuals. Individuals in the United States are free to exchange their goods and services, seek jobs of their own choosing, use their resources as they wish, and own and operate businesses.

In fact, individuals in the United States have a great number of economic freedoms. Because of these freedoms, the capitalist economy of the United States is sometimes called a free-enterprise system. Enterprise is another word for business. Thus, **free enterprise** is a system under which business can be conducted freely with little government intervention. The U.S. free-enterprise system also includes such benefits for individuals as investment opportunities and prices that respond to competition.

Free Enterprise in the United States

The free-enterprise system of the United States is based on five main features. In the United States, individuals have the right to

- own private property and enter into contracts,
- make individual choices,
- engage in economic competition,
- make decisions based on self-interest, and
- participate in the economy with limited government involvement and regulation.

The final feature—limited government intervention and regulation—is what separates the U.S. economy from the pure market model.

Private Property and Contracts Goods that are owned by individuals and by businesses, rather than by the government, are considered **private property**. Your own private property might include clothes, compact discs (CDs), and

ECONOMIC SYSTEMS *The U.S. economy is based on the market model, which is driven by individuals. Which of the five main features of a free-enterprise system separate the U.S. economy from the pure market model?* ⭐TEKS

ECONOMIC SYSTEMS **29**

Caption Answer

the right to make individual choices, engage in economic competition, make decisions based on self-interest, and participate in the economy with limited government involvement and regulation ⭐4A

Global Connections

Although the right to own private property has been central to the U.S. economy throughout history, the idea is not necessarily an easy one to introduce into a culture unused to it. For example, after the Soviet Union collapsed in the early 1990s, Russia began efforts to privatize its economy. Public reaction to government reforms was mixed, however. Those who favored the reforms tended to be young, well-educated urbanites. Those living in villages and small towns—roughly two thirds of the population—as well as older citizens, were more apprehensive, however. Farmers, in particular, feared privatization of the collective farms in which they worked and lived, because it required large capital investments most could not afford. ■

Caption Answer

They can lease all or part of their house, sell it, expand it, or use it for a business. Zoning regulations may limit owners' ability to use their house for a business. ⭐1B, 3B

BABY BLUES

BABY BLUES reprinted with special permission of King Features Syndicate, Inc.

ECONOMIC SYSTEMS *In the United States, individuals have the right to own private property.* **What are the other four features of free enterprise in the United States?** ⭐TEKS

books. A business's private property might include a factory, office building, machinery, and other equipment, as well as the land on which the factory and office buildings are located.

Individuals and business owners can use their property or dispose of it as they wish. They can buy as much private property as they can afford. They also can sell as much as they wish, so long as a buyer is willing and able to purchase the property.

Individuals also have the right to enter into agreements with one another to buy and sell goods and services. These agreements are called **contracts**. If Peter Donnelly agrees to sell a CD to his friend Adam Barker for $10, they have a contract. Peter agrees to supply the CD, and Adam agrees to supply $10 in exchange.

A contract can be either oral or written, but regardless of its form, it is legally binding. In other words, a contract represents an economic decision that is made by an individual consumer and has legal consequences. If any person fails to fulfill the terms of the contract, the issue may be taken to court in order to ensure that the agreement is carried out or that a satisfactory compromise is reached.

Individual Choice Property owners, laborers, producers, and consumers in the United States enjoy freedom of choice. This freedom of choice is closely linked to the right to own private property and to enter into contracts. Property owners are free to use or dispose of their private property as they choose within the laws set forth by the local government involving zoning and other land-use ordinances. Laborers are free to pursue job opportunities. Producers are free to make whatever goods and services they wish. Consumers are free to buy those goods and services that best meet their needs and wants.

Suppose Toussaint Waller owns several acres of undeveloped land. He is free to choose how to use the land. He may live on the land himself, or he may sell it to a developer for construction of homes and businesses. Perhaps Toussaint will

ECONOMIC SYSTEMS *What economic choices might this couple make about the use of their house? How might government restrictions limit their choices?* ⭐TEKS

30 CHAPTER 2

give the land to the city for use as a park, or perhaps he will leave the land undeveloped, thus providing a space for plants and wildlife.

Suppose that Toussaint sells the land to the BuildQuik development company, which constructs a small shopping center and parking lot on the property. These two initial individual choices—Toussaint's decision to sell the land and BuildQuik's decision to use the land for a shopping center—will set off a series of other economic choices and opportunities. Construction workers may choose whether to pursue a job with BuildQuik. The new stores will provide others with a choice of sales and management positions. BuildQuik also may decide to hire security guards to patrol the parking lot, and

CAREERS IN ECONOMICS

Real Estate Agent

Think about your dream home. How might you look for it? You might visit every home in the city or town of your choice. Perhaps you might call people on the phone and ask if their homes are for sale. Neither of these is a practical approach—you would simply waste time and money. Instead, you would probably rely on an efficient method with proven results—hiring a real estate agent.

A real estate agent lists new properties for sale and shows them to potential buyers. Real estate agents have to be part salesperson and part private detective. Your real estate agent will need to find out what type of neighborhood you want to live in, what kind of house you would like, and how much you can afford to pay, to match your needs to the seller's product.

Once a match is made, agents help both parties negotiate a price and help buyers find financing. In addition, agents make sure that all conditions of the purchase, such as inspections, are carried out before the sale is final. Because these responsibilities involve working with people, real estate agents need excellent interpersonal and communication skills.

Most real estate agents are associated with brokers or agencies but are responsible for building their own client base. Although no standard formal training is required to sell real estate, agents must obtain a state broker's license. In addition, most agents take courses sponsored by the National Board of Realtors. College-level courses in economics, marketing, and finance also are helpful because agents often are required to put together—and explain—complicated mortgage packages for home buyers.

Why do people become real estate agents? Flexibility, potential for profits, and opportunities to work with the public make real estate agent a popular occupation.

Real estate agents match the needs and wants of home buyers with those of home sellers.

Themes in Economics

OPPORTUNITY COST & TRADE-OFFS The Fifth Amendment to the U.S. Constitution states that "private property [shall not] be taken for public use, without just compensation." This clause, known as the takings clause, is at the center of a controversy over whether the government should compensate property owners when regulations reduce land values.

On one side of the issue are business interests, who think that many regulations overly restrict property use. These groups support laws, known as takings bills, that require the government to compensate property owners whenever a regulation decreases a property's value by more than a certain percentage.

On the other side of the issue are environmental and advocacy groups who oppose takings bills. These groups claim that these bills are costly to implement, can hinder or prevent environmental legislation from being passed, and can hurt existing environmental protections. These groups consider the courts the proper arena for deciding issues involving regulations and losses to property values. ■

Careers in Economics

To help students learn about other careers in economics, refer them to the Careers section on the *Researcher CD-ROM*.

Global Connections

In India, prior to 1991 the government controlled almost all aspects of the nation's markets—from production levels and wages to suppliers and prices. Product choices were limited, and what was available was often poorly made, overpriced, and hard to get. In general, service was terrible, and companies had little incentive to improve. Indians looking to buy a car, for example, had only a few domestic models from which to choose. Foreign cars were unavailable. As a result, almost every Indian drove a Hindustan Ambassador, an underpowered car available only in cream, which took months to get.

In 1991, however, the Indian government opened up many of the nation's markets to competition. Faced with new rivals for market share, many companies had to lower prices and improve quality and service to compete. As a result, Indian consumers have begun to demand—and expect—a higher level of quality and service. ■

Caption Answer

It encourages producers to improve existing products and develop new ones, and to sell products at a reasonable price that consumers are willing to pay.
★ 4A

---

maintenance workers to repair plumbing and electrical problems in the shops. Laborers in many careers therefore are free to pursue these job opportunities.

Producers, like property owners and laborers, are able to make choices. The new shopping center provides space for a number of businesses. Why might a business owner decide to rent space in a new shopping center? Perhaps the business owner believes that many people in the area around the shopping center would be interested in a particular good or service. For example, the owner of the Good Food supermarket chain may feel that the shopping center is a prime location for a grocery store because of the number of consumers living in the area. Therefore, the Good Food supermarket, a business, can purchase, use, and dispose of property just like an individual.

Consumers also make choices. The shops constructed by BuildQuik at the new Waller Shopping Center provide goods and services. Consumers can decide to buy those goods and services that best meet their needs and wants. For example, the shopping center may include the Good Food supermarket, a pharmacy, a dry cleaner, and a children's furniture boutique. Rick Salazar, who has two children, might choose to buy furniture at the boutique if he likes the merchandise and thinks the prices are affordable.

ECONOMIC SYSTEMS *Competition is the economic rivalry that exists among businesses selling the same or similar products.* **Why is competition important in a free-enterprise system?** ★ TEKS

Competition Free enterprise gives businesspeople the right to choose what, how, and for whom to produce. Sometimes two or more businesspeople make the same production choices. These choices lead the businesspeople and their companies into competition. **Competition** is the economic rivalry that exists among businesses selling the same or similar products. Competition is important because it encourages producers to improve existing products and develop new ones in order to attract customers.

For example, suppose that Gillian Petrakis wants to buy a portable compact disc player. The Genco Electronics Company wants consumers like Gillian to buy one of their CD players instead of one produced by the Sanford Corporation or any of the many other electronics firms. Therefore, Genco will try to produce portable CD players that have better sound and need fewer batteries than CD players produced by their competitors. Similarly, the A-1 Appliance Store will try to sell CD players at a lower price than the Acme Appliance Store so that Gillian will choose to buy her CD player at A-1 Appliance. This high level of competition thus allows Gillian to find a portable CD player with the features she wants—at a price she is willing to pay.

Self-Interested Decisions As Adam Smith indicated, self-interest is the force that directs the actions of individuals and firms in a market system. In the United States, free enterprise allows producers and consumers to make choices for their own benefit. When producers and consumers unconditionally purchase and sell products, and they believe that the opportunity costs of such a trade are acceptable to both parties, the transaction is called a **voluntary exchange.** Both parties expect to benefit in such an exchange.

Consider Toussaint Waller's decision to sell his land. He decided to sell the land to the BuildQuik development company because he felt that he would benefit from the voluntary exchange. Although the sale of the land also resulted in increased benefits to many other people in the form of more employment and more goods and services, Toussaint's decision was made on the basis of self-interest.

ECONOMIC INSTITUTIONS & INCENTIVES *The federal government provides national parks for public use.* **What reasons might the government have for preserving wilderness areas?** ★TEKS

Limited Government Involvement Because the United States has a market economy, most production decisions are made by individuals or businesses—not by the government. The government does play an important role, however, by regulating the economy. For example, the government establishes health and safety laws, monitors banking practices, and prohibits discrimination in the workplace.

The government also provides public services. Funds are raised through taxation and spent on goods and services for members of society. For example, federal taxes are used to pay for national defense. Similarly, public education relies on funds from state and local taxes. The government also redistributes wealth by using funds from citizens' taxes to help needy individuals and struggling businesses. Finally, the government attempts to keep the economy stable by holding down prices and unemployment and by encouraging economic growth.

Economic Actors in Free Enterprise

Free enterprise is driven by the decisions of producers and consumers, with a limited amount of government involvement. How do these three economic actors—producers, consumers, and the government—interact in the U.S. economy?

Producers As noted in Chapter 1, producers provide goods and services in the market. Through a combination of human resources, natural resources, and capital resources, producers work to satisfy the needs and wants of consumers. In doing so, producers rely on entrepreneurship to develop new products and production methods.

In a free-enterprise system, a successful producer also can benefit other economic actors. Suppose that Ross Anderson owns a company that produces digital pagers. If his business is successful—in other words, if the company makes more money than it spends—he may be able to expand his operations and hire more workers. Ross may choose to spend money on product development, creating new models of pagers with more features, thus providing consumers with new products.

Consumers Consumers influence production by purchasing goods and services. If Hannah Carroll feels that Ross's company provides quality digital pagers, she may choose to buy one. On the other hand, free-enterprise ensures a variety of goods, and Hannah may prefer the features or price of a pager produced by a different company. Consumers such as Hannah communicate with producers by making these decisions. The level of product sales tells Ross if his company has accurately answered the basic economic questions of what, how, and for whom to produce.

Government As you know, government plays a limited but important role in the free-enterprise system of the United States. Although producers and consumers provide answers to the three basic economic questions of what, how, and for whom to produce, the government oversees and regulates the effects of these decisions on the economy as a whole. For example, Ross's company must produce its pagers in a factory that meets federal safety standards.

Caption Answer
to ensure that future generations will be able to see and appreciate the natural beauty of these areas and to protect the natural resources found there and the habitats of the creatures that live there ★15A

internet connect
TOPIC: Government Involvement in the U.S. Economy
GO TO: go.hrw.com
KEYWORD: SM3 EC2

Have students access the Internet through the HRW Go site to conduct research on the role of the U.S. government in the free-enterprise system. Have students create a list of the pros and cons of U.S. government participation in the economy.
★3B, 23C, 23D, 24A, 24D

ECONOMIC SYSTEMS **33**

Transparency
An overhead transparency of Figure 2.2 is available in *Transparency Resources*. See Transparency 5: Circular Flow of Goods and Services.

Caption Answer
The government's role is to raise money through taxes so that it can provide services and money to households and businesses. ★6A, 6B

Themes in Economics

THE ROLE OF GOVERNMENT

Adam Smith believed that government involvement in the economy conflicts with self-interest. Nevertheless, he did support a limited role for government. In his book, *A Theory of Moral Sentiments*, published in 1759, Smith wrote that government intervention was needed to alleviate what he saw as the social costs of capitalism—alienation and a loss of values. He believed that government's role was to improve the public good, ensure justice, protect property, limit monopolies, provide defense, and fund education and the building of roads, bridges, and canals. Much of the current dialogue regarding government's proper role in our society and economy reflects Smith's ideas. ■

CIRCULAR FLOW OF GOODS AND SERVICES

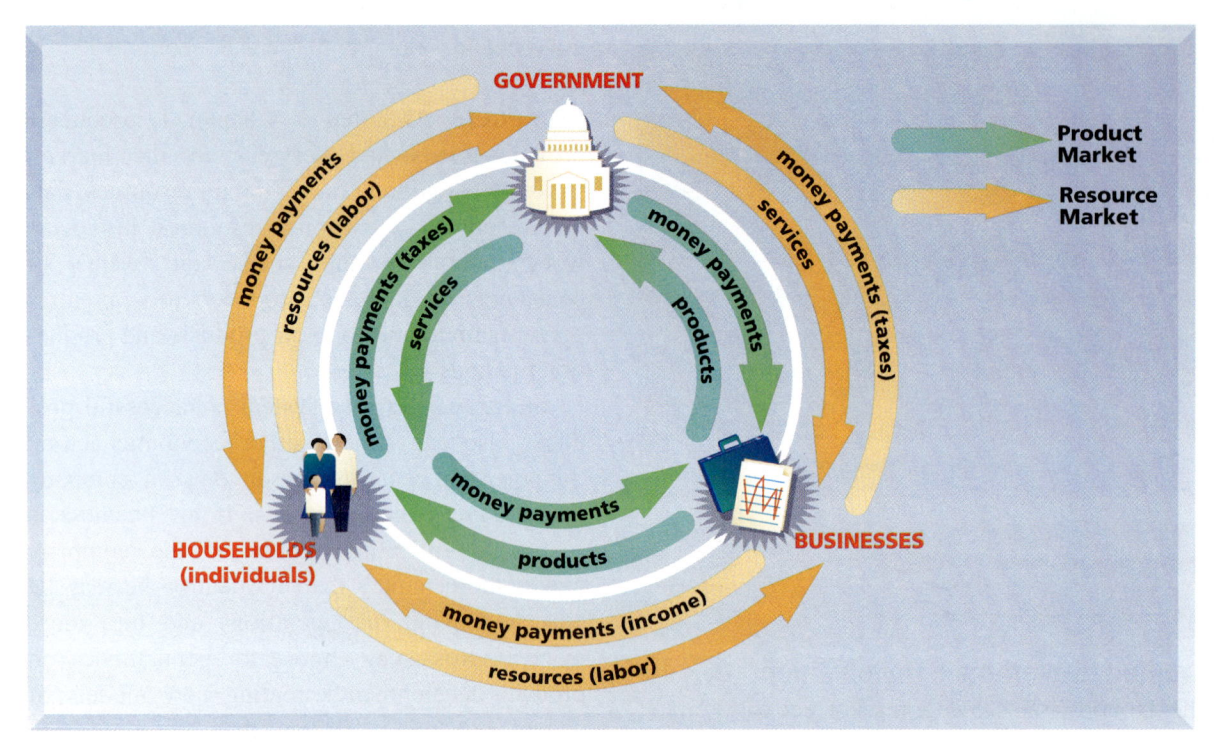

FIGURE 2.2 This circular flow model illustrates the exchange of resources, products, and money payments in the U.S. economy. **What is the government's role according to the circular flow model?** ★TEKS

Government, producers, and consumers play different—but connected—roles in a market system. To answer the economic questions of what, how, and for whom to produce, these economic actors also rely on a system of exchange.

Circular Flow Model

In a free-enterprise system, resources, products, and money payments are exchanged among the different actors in the economy. This exchange can be traced in a circular flow model. The model, shown in Figure 2.2, is a simplified view of how the U.S. economy functions.

Markets The circular flow model has two parts. The green arrows are the **product market**, which represents all of the exchanges of goods and services in the economy. Businesses develop products for sale to both households and the government. Households and the government then pay the businesses for the products.

The gold arrows are the resource market. The **resource market** represents the exchange of resources between households—individuals like you who own the factors of production (natural, human, and capital resources)—and business firms and the government, who are the users of the resources.

The money paid to households by business firms and the government in exchange for the households' resources is called **income**. Households receive income such as rents (in exchange for natural resources), wages (in exchange for labor), and interest (in exchange for capital).

Flows Exchanges in the product and resource markets involve two different types of flows—the flow of resources and products and the flow of

34 CHAPTER 2

payments. Households supply the resources to businesses and the government in the resource market. Businesses then make products, which are sold to households and the government in the product market. For example, if you work in a restaurant, you (as a member of a household) provide a human resource (your labor) to the business. The business in turn provides food and service to customers, who, like you, are members of households.

Likewise, the government produces goods and services for the benefit of businesses and households. The government produces goods and services by using the resources that it purchases from households in the resource market.

In the resource market, businesses and the government make payments to households in exchange for the households' resources. Once households receive this payment, they continue circulating the money by purchasing goods and services in the product market. By doing this, households return money to businesses. Consider your job at the restaurant. The restaurant pays you for your work. In turn, customers such as yourself pay the restaurant for the food provided.

ECONOMIC SYSTEMS *In a free-enterprise system, resources, products, and money payments can be exchanged among different parts of the economy.* **Is the sale of cookies at a bake sale part of the product market or the resource market?**

Businesses use the payments from households and the government to purchase additional resources from households. The money flow continues as businesses and households make payments to the government. These payments take the form of taxes. The government uses the payments to provide goods and services to businesses and households.

SECTION 2 REVIEW

TEKS Q: 1, 2, 3a, 3b, 4

1. Identify and Explain:
- free enterprise
- private property
- contracts
- competition
- voluntary exchange
- product market
- resource market
- income

2. Summarizing: Copy the diagram below. Use it to give two examples of the flow of goods and services between government, businesses, and households.

Flow of Goods and Services
(Government, Households, Businesses triangle diagram)

3. Finding the Main Idea
  a. Give examples of responsible purchase, use, and disposal of property by an individual and by a business.
  b. What are the benefits to producers and consumers of the U.S. free-enterprise system?

4. Writing and Critical Thinking
  Comparing: Describe how the U.S. economy is similar to, and yet different from, a pure market economy.
  Consider the following:
  - government intervention
  - individual choice
  - ownership of factors of production

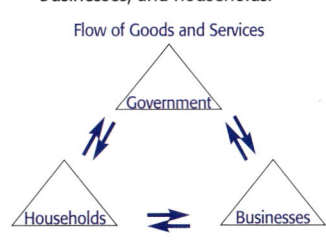

Homework Practice Online
keyword: SM3 HP2

ECONOMIC SYSTEMS 35

SECTION 3

THE U.S. ECONOMY AT WORK

READ TO DISCOVER
1. How do nations decide how to use scarce resources?
2. What are the major goals of U.S. economic policy?
3. Why do economic goals sometimes conflict?

ECONOMICS DICTIONARY
full employment
price stability
standard of living

What are your goals? You may hope to go to college or find a high-paying job. To reach your goals, you will need to take particular actions. For example, if you want to be an electrician, you will need to acquire skills and knowledge.

Nations—or economic systems—also set goals. As you have learned, economic systems are made up of economic actors. Households, businesses, and government officials together determine the general objectives—or goals—of their economic system. The government works toward the nation's economic objectives as the elected representatives of these actors. By setting goals, a nation's policymakers can choose how to use scarce resources.

U.S. Economic Goals

The United States has six major goals for its economic policy, many of which are also held by other nations around the world. These goals are economic

- freedom,
- efficiency,
- equity,
- security,
- stability, and
- growth.

Economic Freedom Maintaining freedom of choice in the marketplace is at the heart of economic freedom. In a free-enterprise system, consumers are free to decide how to spend their incomes on goods and services. Workers are free to choose an occupation, change jobs, or join a union. Savers and investors are free to decide when, where, and how to save or invest their money. Businesspeople are free to open new

---

THE WIZARD OF ID   by Brant parker and Johnny hart

ECONOMIC INSTITUTIONS & INCENTIVES Security is one of the goals of the U.S. economy. *What are the other five goals? Which goals are implied in this cartoon?*

Teacher Sidebar

SECTION 3

THE U.S. ECONOMY AT WORK

Lesson Plans
For teaching strategies, see Lesson 2.3 located at the beginning of this chapter.

Economics Dictionary
To reinforce the section's vocabulary terms, refer students to the Electronic Glossary on the *Researcher CD-ROM*.

Section Assessment
To assess students' mastery of this section, have them complete Daily Quiz 2.3 in *Daily Quizzes with Answer Key*

Caption Answer
freedom, efficiency, equity, stability, and growth; freedom and security ⭐16A

TEKS

Section 3
Content
5A, 16A, 16B, 21A
Social Studies Skills
23A, 24A, 24D
Chapter Review
Content
1B, 3A, 3B, 4A, 4B, 5A, 6A, 10A, 10B, 15A, 15B, 16A, 16B, 21A, 21B, 27A
Social Studies Skills
23B, 23E, 23F, 23G, 24A, 24B, 24D

36 CHAPTER 2

Economics in Action

"Extra, Extra"

What would teens write about if they had the opportunity to publish their own work? The latest fashion trends? Celebrity profiles? Fad diets? The answer may surprise you. Although these topics are standard fare in many publications targeted at teen audiences, young writers are actually concerned about a wide variety of issues. Teenagers' writing can be found in newspapers and magazines focusing on the environment, sports, fiction, and even economics.

In fact, some publications contain only stories by teen authors. For example, *Teen Ink*, run by John and Stephanie Meyers, is a newspaper written entirely by teenagers. The Meyers determined that "teens didn't need another publication with adults trying to figure out what they wanted to hear." So, they decided to create a newspaper that would provide teenagers with the opportunity to write articles that expressed their own thoughts and opinions.

Writing poetry, essays, and reviews offers students a way to present their ideas creatively and develop confidence in their writing skills. The Meyers believe that these rewards are improving teens' sense of self-worth and see *Teen Ink* as an investment in the future. David Anable, former chair of the Boston University journalism school and a member of the newspaper's board, believes that teen papers give student journalists a chance "to learn the craft and write with enthusiasm, not reluctance."

Contributors to the paper write about a number of controversial topics, submit articles on sports, music, and travel, and provide reviews of colleges. A recent issue of the newspaper contained articles on topics ranging from environmental issues and animal rights, to an opinion piece calling for teenagers to have a greater voice in the American political system even though most are too young to vote.

Newspapers written by teenagers have also reported important international events. For instance, teen journalists for *Vox*, an Atlanta-based newspaper written for and by high school students, covered the Summer Olympic Games in Atlanta.

Some of the teen journalists' stories were also picked up by nationally syndicated publications, including *CNN.com* and *USA Today*. One student, for example, sold a story to *CNN.com* about how nearly 1,500 volunteers for the Atlanta games provided translating services for athletes who did not speak English. A second student sold a story on the closing-ceremony performance by members of Atlanta's *Symphony Youth*. Although the reporters were paid a modest fee for their work, one of the teen journalists pointed out that the real reward was the experience of being one of the first teenagers to report on such a prestigious event.

What Do You Think?

1. In your opinion, what are the potential benefits to readers of teen writing and publishing?
2. If you were hired to write for a teen publication, what issues would you want to cover?

Publications such as Teen Ink *provide teen writers with a forum for their work.*

What Do You Think? Answers

1. Writing articles for actual publication gives teens hands-on experience that will help them later in their careers, teaches them to deal with work schedules and responsibility, encourages them to stay informed about current events, provides a sense of pride and accomplishment, and gives other teens access to articles that discuss issues relevant to them.

2. Answers will vary but might include topics such as dating and relationships, college and career planning, music and art, theater and movies, sports, politics, business and economics, science and technology, ethics, and racism and discrimination.

Caption Answer

(top)
It increases economic stability, efficiency, and growth.

Themes in Economics

ECONOMIC FREEDOM & EQUITY

Economist Milton Friedman argues in his book, *Free to Choose: A Personal Statement* (1980), which he co-authored with his wife Rose, that economic freedom promotes economic equity. He writes:

"Everywhere in the world there are gross inequities of income and wealth.... In the past century a myth has grown up that free market capitalism... increases such inequalities, that it is a system under which the rich exploit the poor.

"Nothing could be further from the truth. Wherever the free market has been permitted to operate, wherever anything approaching equality of opportunity has existed, the ordinary man has been able to attain levels of living never dreamed of before....

"A society that puts equality—in the sense of equality of outcome—ahead of freedom will end up with neither equality nor freedom.... On the other hand, a society that puts freedom first will, as a happy by-product, end up with both greater freedom and greater equality.... [Freedom] preserves the opportunity for today's disadvantaged to become tomorrow's privileged." ■

ECONOMIC INSTITUTIONS & INCENTIVES *A key concern of economic stability is full employment.* **How does low unemployment benefit the U.S. economy?**

businesses, change from one business to another, and expand or close existing enterprises.

Economic Efficiency The goal of economic efficiency has to do with efforts to make the best use of scarce resources. Of course, scarcity is a basic problem of economics. Economic efficiency can be measured by how many goods and services a nation's workers produce. The more products each worker produces, the more efficient the economy will be.

Economic Equity Economic equity, which is sometimes called economic justice, is hard to identify because it deals with questions of fairness and of right and wrong. Policymakers often face problems when trying to arrive at a fair decision. By studying the costs and benefits of a proposed course of action, policymakers try to judge whether a particular choice is fair. For example, policymakers in the United States attempt to ensure that members of society share in the costs and benefits of the free-enterprise system as equally as possible.

Economic Security The goal of economic security refers to a nation's efforts to protect its members from poverty, business and bank failures, medical emergencies, and other situations that would harm the economic well-being of individual citizens and the nation as a whole. Economic security can result from individual and government actions. For example, you—and other consumers—can guard against the unexpected by purchasing different kinds of insurance or by saving some of your money. On the government level, federal, state, and local governments can promote economic security through such actions as providing unemployment compensation, insuring bank deposits, and giving economic assistance to troubled businesses.

Economic Stability The goal of economic stability involves two concerns—achieving full employment and achieving stable prices. **Full employment** is the lowest possible level of unemployment in the economy. Although there will always be some amount of unemployment as workers move and change jobs and as new businesses open and others close, economic stability focuses on keeping the level of unemployment as low as possible. The U.S. government releases employment statistics periodically.

The other element of economic stability is price stability. **Price stability** is achieved when the overall price level of the goods and services available in the economy is relatively constant. Price stability refers to the prices of all products taken together—not to changes in the price of an individual product.

ECONOMIC INSTITUTIONS & INCENTIVES *A nation's standard of living is measured by per capita consumption during a specific period of time.* **How is standard of living related to economic growth?**

Economic Growth Economic growth has to do with efforts to increase the amount of goods and services produced by each worker in the economy. The difference between simply increasing the economy's production and increasing the production from each worker is important. If the total number of workers increases more quickly than total production, on average each worker produces less. Lower production from each worker means that fewer goods and services are available for each person to consume.

A decrease in the number of available goods and services results in a decline in a nation's standard of living. **Standard of living** refers to people's economic well-being. Economists measure a nation's standard of living by how much the average person in that country is able to consume in a given period of time—usually one year. The standard of living improves when production from each worker increases faster than the total population, thus providing more goods and services for each person.

Economic Goals and Trade-Offs

Are you able to pursue all of your personal goals at the same time? Probably not. Sometimes you may have to decide that one goal is more important than another. For example, you may want to go to college and buy a car. If you cannot afford to do both at the same time, you may have to choose one goal over another. Although you can work toward more than one goal over a period of time, you may have to make trade-offs at one particular point in time. Making one monetary choice over another is a basic problem of economics.

The goals of an economic system also can be affected by trade-offs. At various times, people's needs and wants may conflict. As a result, although different nations may share a number of economic goals, those nations will prioritize those goals differently.

Priorities Must Be Assigned Scarcity forces individuals, businesses, and governments to make choices among various needs and wants. Nations also must decide which goals are most

Global Exchange

Immigration

Nearly 660,000 people legally immigrated to the United States in 1998 alone. Why do people want to move to this country? And how do they obtain legal status to live and work here?

Many immigrants come to the United States seeking employment. Relatively high wages and a high standard of living attract people from countries around the world. Additionally, television and movies often present an idealized image of life in the United States.

To obtain permission to live in the United States, an immigrant must apply for and meet the requirements of a visa. Most visas are sought by—and granted to—people who already have relatives living in the United States. Those without relatives may be considered for legal admission—known as "permanent resident status" and represented by a green card—based on their occupational skill level.

Highly skilled workers, such as doctors, teachers, and computer programmers, can obtain green cards relatively easily. The government allowed 140,000 highly skilled workers to immigrate in 1998 because these workers are needed in the U.S. economy.

A backlog of less-skilled workers seeking green cards exists, however, because their work is not in as high demand. Only 50,000 less-skilled workers were admitted into the United States in 2001. To admit these workers fairly, the U.S. Department of State conducts a visa lottery, randomly selecting and awarding green card visa numbers to eligible persons.

Profiles in Economics

For a biography of Milton Friedman and other noted people in economics, refer students to the Biographies section on the *Researcher CD-ROM*.

Themes in Economics

OPPORTUNITY COST & TRADE-OFFS The debate over health-care reform in the United States illustrates how different economic goals can come into conflict. Opponents of health-care reform state that increasing health-care coverage will limit economic freedom by restricting consumers' choices and requiring people to pay higher taxes to provide coverage for others.

Supporters of health-care reform state that expanded coverage will increase economic equity by ensuring that all U.S. citizens have access to a minimum level of health care. The groups on this side of the debate cite that many people in the United States, particularly disadvantaged people without health insurance, currently cannot afford adequate medical care. ■

Caption Answer

(page 38, bottom)
A nation's standard of living improves when the amount of goods and services each worker produces increases—in other words, when the economy grows.

ECONOMIC SYSTEMS 39

Caption Answer
Answers will vary but should reflect an understanding that the resources cannot be used in other ways to promote different economic goals. ★5A

SECTION 3
REVIEW ANSWERS

1. full employment (38), price stability (38), standard of living (39) 24A

2. goals–freedom, efficiency, equity, security, stability, and growth 16A, 24D

3a. Scarcity forces individuals, businesses, and governments to prioritize and make choices; not all needs and desires can be met. Choice is a basic economic problem because not all available choices can be selected. 5A

3b. economic growth–measured by changes in the standard of living; economic stability–by employment rate and price fluctuation; economic security–by a nation's poverty level, by the number of failed businesses and banks, and by the number of emergencies that might harm the national economy 16B

4. Different socioeconomic groups will have conflicting goals. Also, even if different groups have the same economic goal, they may differ on the various ways to achieve this goal. 21A, 23A

ECONOMIC INSTITUTIONS & INCENTIVES *Conflicts among goals force nations to prioritize their needs and wants.* **What are the trade-offs when resources are used to clean up pollution?** ★TEKS

important and assign resources to them first. In World War II, for example, national defense and security became high priorities. The factors of production were shifted from business and industry to the war effort.

Priorities Can Change Policymakers at all levels must decide which goals are most important according to the particular needs and wants of the time. For example, during the 1970s dramatic price increases encouraged many people in the United States to focus on economic stability. During the 1980s, however, concerns about unemployment and low productivity encouraged U.S. policymakers to focus on economic security and economic growth.

Priorities Can Conflict Even at a single point in history, conflicts among goals arise because different groups in the nation have different needs. Low-income workers or the elderly, for example, generally are more concerned with economic security and equity than with other economic goals. Many businesspeople, on the other hand, want to emphasize economic growth and efficiency.

Solutions Can Conflict Even if groups in a society agree on priorities, they may have conflicting ideas about the best means to achieve the selected goals. These differences are not always easy to resolve. For example, two groups of policymakers may agree that the most important goal is economic growth, but may propose strikingly different methods of achieving that growth. Suppose that one group believes that the government should raise taxes and use the money to help new businesses grow. The other group, however, wants to lower taxes to let businesses and individuals make and buy more goods to stimulate growth.

SECTION 3 REVIEW

★TEKS Q: 1, 2, 3a, 3b, 4

1. Identify and Explain:
   full employment
   price stability
   standard of living

2. Identifying Concepts: Copy the diagram below. Use it to describe the six major goals for U.S. economic policy.

(diagram: U.S. Economic Policy Goals)

Homework Practice Online
keyword: SM3 HP2

3. Finding the Main Idea
   a. Why are scarcity and choice basic problems of economics?
   b. How are economic growth, stability, and security measured?

4. Writing and Critical Thinking
   Analyzing Information: Discuss how economic priorities and solutions can conflict.
   Consider the following:
   • scarcity and choice
   • societal values
   • stability versus growth

CHAPTER 2

Economics IN THE NEWS

Government Regulation of Private Property

As you know, one of the main features of the free-enterprise system is the right to own private property. In fact, the U.S. Constitution specifically protects individuals' rights to own property and to use it as they see fit. However, government does have the power to regulate some uses of property—such as those affecting health and safety—to benefit the economy and society as a whole. Moreover, such government regulations often have to reconcile conflicting social and economic priorities.

One of the ways that governments regulate property is through land-use regulations such as zoning laws, which restrict certain types of property usage (such as manufacturing) to certain areas, or prohibit them outright. However, since zoning laws infringe on property rights, they can often be highly controversial.

One such controversy involves the central Texas town of Georgetown. During the 1990s, the town experienced rapid economic growth, mainly due to the region's booming high-tech economy. At first, Georgetown's city government encouraged economic growth by avoiding zoning restrictions that might discourage businesses from locating in the city.

As the town's economy grew, however, so did its population. By the end of the 1990s, population growth was beginning to harm the town's quality of life. Traffic congestion was on the rise, and excessive commercial development can threaten a town's water supply.

In 2001, Georgetown's city council responded to changing circumstances by passing new, stricter zoning laws regulating commercial development. Among other things, the laws raised the percentage of each piece of property that had to be left free from development and required that developers preserve trees and other vegetation and help pay for road improvements and traffic studies.

Georgetown's Chamber of Commerce, developers, and other activists protested the changes, especially since the city council passed the new zoning regulations with little notice. They argued that by raising the costs of development and restricting the ways that a property could be used, the regulations slowed the town's economic growth. The city council countered that the changes were needed to preserve the town's quality of life, and if they had not acted so quickly, developers would have had a chance to start more projects before the new regulations were in place.

City council meetings involving land use frequently draw large numbers of residents. Controversy is common, and council members are called on to make hard decisions that are sometimes challenged in the courts.

What Do You Think? ★TEKS

1. What effect does zoning have on property rights?
2. Identify economic concepts in the U.S. Constitution regarding property rights.

▶ WHY IT MATTERS TODAY

Even though private property owners are generally allowed to use their land as they see fit, the government does have the power to regulate some uses of property. At the end of this chapter, visit CNNfyi.com or other **current events** sources to learn more about government regulation of private property.

CNNfyi.com

Economics in the News Answers

1. It restricts property rights by prohibiting property from being used for certain purposes. 3B, 15B
2. The Constitution provides for individuals to own property and use it as they see fit. 20A

CHAPTER 2 Review Answers

Writing a Summary

Summaries should focus on the main points of each section. These may be found in the Read to Discover sections at the start of each section. Summaries should also use standard grammar, spelling, sentence structure, and punctuation. 24B, 24D

Identifying Ideas

traditional economy (24), command economy (25), market economy (25), market (25), self-interest (26), incentive (27), mixed economy (27), authoritarian socialism (27), communism (27), capitalism (28), democratic socialism (28), free enterprise (29), private property (29), contracts (30), competition (32), voluntary exchange (32), product market (34), resource market (34), income (34), full employment (38), price stability (38), standard of living (39) 4A, 10A, 24A

Understanding Main Ideas

1. traditional—custom and tradition determine what,

41

CHAPTER 2 Review

(Continued from page 41)

how, and for whom products are made; command–the government answers these questions. In the U.S. economy, what, how, and for whom products are made are determined by individuals with limited government intervention. **10B**

2. capitalist economy as individuals determine what, how, and for whom to produce **10A**

3. See Figure 2.1 on p. 26. **10A**

4. If an individual fails to fulfill the terms of a contract, the issue may be taken to court to make certain that the agreement is carried out or that a satisfactory compromise is reached. **1B**

5. Individuals and business owners can buy, use, or dispose of their private property as they wish. Voluntary exchange occurs when producers and consumers purchase and sell products based on their deciding that the opportunity costs of the trades are acceptable. **4A**

6. freedom, efficiency, equity, security, stability, and growth **16A**

7. scarcity *M* because there are a limited number of resources available; choice *M* because some choices must be eliminated in the decision process **5A**

Reviewing Themes

1. prevent producers from misrepresenting the value or merit of their goods and services; answers will vary **4A, 15B, 16A**

2. Answers will vary but should exhibit an under-

Writing a Summary

Using standard grammar, spelling, sentence structure, and punctuation, write a summary of the information in this chapter.

Identifying Ideas

1. traditional economy
2. command economy
3. market economy
4. market
5. self-interest
6. incentive
7. mixed economy
8. authoritarian socialism
9. communism
10. capitalism
11. democratic socialism
12. free enterprise
13. contracts
14. competition
15. product market
16. resource market
17. income
18. full employment
19. price stability
20. standard of living

Understanding Main Ideas

SECTION 1 *(pp. 23–28)*

1. How does the U.S. economic system compare to traditional and command economic systems?

2. In which category of mixed economic systems does the U.S. fit? Explain your answer.

3. Give an example of a traditional economic systems.

SECTION 2 *(pp. 29–35)*

4. What are the consequences to an individual consumer who enters into a contract?

5. What are the economic principles of private property and voluntary exchange?

SECTION 3 *(pp. 36–40)*

6. What are the goals of U.S. economic policy?

7. Why are scarcity and choice basic economic problems?

Reviewing Themes

1. Economic Systems How do laws against false advertising promote economic equity? Which of these goals of the U.S. economy might these laws promote? Explain your answer.

2. Competition and Market Structure What types of economic competition do you experience during the course of one week? In what ways do you perform as an economic actor?

3. Economic Systems What are the benefits of the U.S. free-enterprise system to producers and to consumers?

Thinking Critically

1. Making Generalizations A city imposes restrictions on water use during a drought. Which economic goals are city leaders emphasizing? Explain your answer.

2. Summarizing Give two real-world examples illustrating elements of the circular flow model.

Writing about Economics

Review what you wrote in your Economics Notebook at the beginning of this chapter about your personal economic goals. How do your short-term and long-term goals fit in with the economic goals of the United States? Record your answer in your Notebook.

Building Social Studies Skills

Interpreting the Visual Record 🟠TEKS

Study the cartoon below. Then use it to help you answer the questions that follow.

[THE WIZARD OF ID cartoon by Brant Parker and Johnny Hart]

Panel 1: "I HAVE GOOD NEWS AND BAD NEWS"
Panel 2: "...THE BAD NEWS IS, THERE IS NO MONEY LEFT FOR SOCIAL SECURITY...."
Panel 3: "...THE GOOD NEWS IS, YOU CAN WORK UNTIL YOU ARE NINETY"

1. In this cartoon, the king is speaking to what audience?
   a. other members of the royalty
   b. his relatives
   c. the peasants
   d. visitors from another country

2. If freedom and security are the economic goals addressed in this cartoon, what are the other four goals of the U.S. economy?

Analyzing Primary Sources 🟠TEKS

Janet Prindle and Farha-Joyce Haboucha are financial planners who manage more than $300 million in socially responsive investments. Their opinion article discusses the relevance of Adam Smith's economic theory today.

"The father of capitalism, Adam Smith (1723-1790), was perhaps history's most misunderstood philosopher. He was a progressive, even radical, thinker a far cry from his image in economic and political debates today....

"If Adam Smith were alive, he would be a socially responsive investor. He clearly thought the financial success of an enterprise depended in large measure on the degree to which it contributed to the social good.... The way to improve society is to grow the economy. Increasing production increases wealth, which increases wages and purchasing power. The question for policy makers is how to facilitate this chain of cause and effect.

"And it is this question that leads Smith to develop his famous theory of the 'invisible hand.' We do not gain our supper through the benevolence [kindness] of the butcher. The butcher labors to promote his own interest, which includes a need to be seen as benevolent [kind]. This need and the pressures of a competitive environment produce the positive social effects: the growth of production, wealth, wages, and purchasing power."

3. What does a competitive environment produce?
   a. growth of purchasing power
   b. growth of wages and wealth
   c. growth of production
   d. all of the above

4. How do the authors interpret Smith's theory of the "invisible hand"?

Alternative Assessment

Building Your Portfolio 🟠TEKS

For each of the three types of mixed economies, select a country not mentioned in this chapter and research its economy. How do people in that country decide what, how, and for whom to produce? Prepare a brief written report for each country that is researched.

internet connect

Internet Activity: go.hrw.com
KEYWORD: SM3 EC2 🟠TEKS

Access the Internet through the HRW Go site to conduct research on unemployment in the United States and/or several foreign countries. Use the HOLT Grapher to create a chart or graph of the unemployment rate in the United States over time, or of the unemployment rate of the U.S. compared with that of other countries.

---

standing of economic competition and participants.

3. producers–make a profit, expand operations, and improve or develop a particular product; consumers–purchase a specific product, thereby influencing the producer 4B

Thinking Critically

1. economic efficiency by using scarce resources efficiently; economic equity by ensuring that all have access to water; economic security by preventing water depletion 15A

2. Answers will vary. Examples could include citizens paying taxes and receiving police, fire, and sanitation services; or businesses selling equipment to the government. 6A

Writing about Economics

Students should discuss their personal economic goals in terms of the economic goals of the United States presented in this chapter. 16A

Building Social Studies Skills

1. c 23E
2. efficiency, equity, stability, and growth 16A
3. d 23E
4. Competition and self-interest motivate producers to act benevolently and offer quality products at fair prices. 4A, 23E

ECONOMIC SYSTEMS

UNIT 1

LAB OBJECTIVES

During the lab, students will
- research democratic socialism, authoritarian socialism (communism), and capitalism.
- outline the main aspects of each economic system.
- examine and discuss the benefits and limitations of each economic system.
- prepare a written speech recommending the best economic system for a new moon settlement.

Using the Lab

Before beginning the lab, organize students into groups and distribute copies of the Unit 1 Lab Activity found in *Unit Tests and Unit Lab Activities with Answer Key*. Have students read the assignment on this page and then discuss the assignment as a class. Point out the documents on pages 45–47 that students will use during the lab.

The What Do You Think? questions on pages 46 and 47 will help guide students during the project. In addition, the lab activity sheet includes a step-by-step checklist for students to monitor their progress.

★ 10A, 10B, 25A

UNIT 1

ECONOMICS LAB

You Solve the Problem

Economist for a Day

*I*magine that a new international settlement has been planned for the moon. You and your classmates have been chosen by the Earth Federation to be part of the Federation's Moon Settlement Economics Committee. As members of this committee, your group is responsible for designing the economic system to be used in the settlement.

Because this is an international endeavor, you need to consider the pros and cons of all three modern economic systems on Earth: capitalism, democratic socialism, and authoritarian socialism (or communism). The Federation has supplied you with some basic information to begin your comparison. It also has included the following three documents for you to review:
- a letter from a citizen in the country Richtany,
- a newspaper editorial from the country of Ziber,
- and a speech about the benefits of capitalism in Carnegia.

Economics Notebook Assignment ★TEKS

1. Write a clear, one-sentence statement of the problem to solve.
2. Review the documents on the following pages to gather information.
3. Write your notes and answers to the questions that accompany the documents in your Economics Notebook.
4. Meet with your group and create an outline that summarizes the most important points about each system. Discuss your findings and formulate an argument for the economic system your group thinks will work best on the moon. In your discussion, be sure to consider the different options and the advantages and disadvantages of each.
5. Write a speech to present your group's solution for implementation. Make sure to support your recommendation with facts from the documents provided by the Federation. Provide some information evaluating how effective you think your solution will be.

EARTH FEDERATION

To: Moon Settlement Economics Committee
From: Earth Federation Executive Council

The General Assembly is looking forward to hearing your recommendation and plans for an economic system on the moon. Please use the attached information about the world's current economic systems to aid your research. We also have included a letter, a newspaper editorial, and a speech, each of which argues for one of the three systems.

Once you have made your determination, be sure to address these issues in your speech:
- How will the settlement answer the three basic economic questions?
- Who will own the factors of production?
- What will be the trade-offs in your system?

We realize that your task is a difficult one. However, it is vitally important to the success of the planned moon settlement, as well as to all space colonization efforts in the future, that you make a well-researched recommendation to the Earth Federation. Thank you for your time and effort.

EARTH FEDERATION

	Capitalism	**Democratic Socialism**	**Authoritarian Socialism/Communism**
Type of Political System	Nations are mainly democratic.	Some nations tend to be democracies, while other nations lean toward totalitarianism.	Most nations have a one-party totalitarian government.
Central Planning in the Economy	Governments influence economic activity through tax credits, subsidies, low-interest loans, other financial incentives, and regulations.	Governments directly control production in large, state-owned facilities and are involved in planning the use of resources.	Almost all economic decisions are made by a single political party. Specific economic plans are devised by agencies in charge of planning for a particular industry.
Economic Freedom of Workers	Workers choose jobs that fit their qualifications. Some join unions for collective bargaining power.	Workers choose jobs that fit their qualifications. Many join unions that bargain with private firms and governments.	The government controls employment and holds the power to reject job transfers. Unions are strictly controlled, and strikes are prohibited.
Examples	Carnegia	Richtany	Ziber

Economics Lab 45

What Do You Think?
Answers
1. government and individuals 10A
2. Individuals give up some freedoms to the government in exchange for industry regulation, social programs, and protection against unemployment, market failures, and discrimination. 10A
3. Individuals would need to budget more money for taxes, but less for medical and other services. Choices are somewhat limited to promote economic equity, security, and stability. 10A
4. monetary compensation 10A

What Do You Think?
Answers
1. the government 10A
2. Individuals exchange freedoms for government protection and regulation. 10A
3. Individuals would need to budget more money for taxes, but little for housing or medical and other services. Choices would be limited, and the government would set economic goals. 10A
4. special government perks 10A

46

ECONOMICS LAB continued

From the Desk of Judit Steger

Dear Earth Federation Members,

As plans for the new moon settlement get under way, I am troubled by the widespread interest in establishing an economic system with little or no government intervention. In their unquenchable thirst for profits, some manufacturers have forgotten the ruin that an unregulated economy can bring on people who are prevented from working by age, illness, or disability. Without governmental protections for unemployment and market failures, even those who are able to work will be left vulnerable to economic depressions.

The citizens of Richtany believe that our system of democratic socialism will work best on the moon. Although most factors of production should be left in private hands, the moon settlement should own some of its major industries and use taxes to fund social programs that protect all of its citizens. We have both a moral and an economic obligation to provide social programs such as health care, education, and retirement pensions to the citizens of this new international settlement. I hope that when making your decision you will not ignore the value of moderate government control of the economy.

Sincerely,
Judit Steger

WHAT DO YOU THINK? ▶
1. Who owns the factors of production in this system (right)?
2. What are the trade-offs in this system?
3. How would this system affect an individual's budget, economic choices, and economic goals?
4. What are the incentives to produce in this system?

46 UNIT 1

◀ WHAT DO YOU THINK?
1. Who owns the factors of production in this system (left)?
2. What are the trade-offs in this system?
3. How would this system affect an individual's budget, economic choices, and economic goals?
4. What are the incentives to produce in this system?

The Promise of Communism

The people of Ziber believe that authoritarian socialism, or communism, is a strong and fair economic system. We hope that the new moon settlement will model its economic system on that of this country and the economic theories of Karl Marx. Economic factors determine social and political change throughout the world. In many countries, the proletariat, or working class, is oppressed and exploited by those who own the factors of production. By owning the factors of production in Ziber, workers have created a classless society.

We believe that the government should own nearly all the industries in the settlement and should closely regulate any small private businesses. The government can then use these revenues to finance social programs such as low-cost public housing, free health care, and education and retirement pensions.

Three Cheers for Capitalism

Way back in 1993, Malcolm S. Forbes, Jr., encouraged all of us to give "Three Cheers" for the benefits of a capitalist economy. He said, "Capitalism works better than any of us can conceive. It is also the only moral system of exchange. It encourages individuals to freely devote their energies and impulses to peaceful pursuits, to the satisfaction of others' wants and needs, and to constructive action for the welfare of all.

"Capitalism is not a top-down system; it cannot be mandated [decreed] or centrally planned. It operates from the bottom up, through individuals—individuals who take risks, who often 'don't know any better,' who venture into areas where, according to conventional [customary] wisdom, they have no business going, who see vast potential where others see nothing. . . .

"There is another important thing to remember about capitalism: failure is not a stigma [sign of disgrace] or a permanent obstacle. It is a spur to learn and try again. Edison invented the lightbulb on, roughly, his ten-thousandth attempt. If we had depended on central planners to direct his experiments, we would all be sitting around in the dark today. . . .

"[Capitalism] stands not for accumulated wealth or greed but for human innovation, imagination, and risk-taking. It cannot be measured in mathematical models or quantified in statistical terms, which is why central planners and politicians always underestimate it."

Forbes's comments still are true today. That is why the people of Carnegia strongly urge the Earth Federation to use capitalism as the economic system for the moon settlement. Thank you.

◀ WHAT DO YOU THINK?

1. Who owns the factors of production in this system?
2. What are the trade-offs in this system?
3. How would this system affect an individual's budget, economic choices, and economic goals?
4. What are the incentives to produce in this system?

internet connect

Internet Activity: go.hrw.com
KEYWORD: SM3 ECL1

Access the Internet through the HRW Go site to find information on the economic history of Russia (formerly the Soviet Union). Create an annotated time line that details the changes the country has undergone over the years as it has changed its economic structure. Be sure to indicate any challenges changing from one economic structure to another has caused for the country.

What Do You Think?
Answers

1. individuals 10A
2. Individuals give up some economic stability, equity, and security in exchange for greater economic freedom and growth. 10A
3. Individuals' budgets, choices, and economic goals are based on satisfying needs and wants and are determined by the market. 10A
4. monetary compensation 10A

UNIT 2

Lesson Options
Suggestions for customizing the material in Unit 2 to fit the specific schedule and curriculum of your classroom are available at the beginning of each chapter.

Main Ideas
Ask each student to read the Main Ideas and briefly answer each question in writing. Later, when you have finished Unit 2, ask students to return to their original answers and revise them using what they learned in the unit.

Economics Lab
The Unit 2 Economics Lab appears on pages 138–41. This lab project is a real-world assignment in which students will work in groups to make pricing and advertising recommendations for hand-painted T-shirts to be sold at a school fund-raiser. Support materials for the lab appear in *Unit Tests and Unit Lab Activities with Answer Key.* ⭐7A

UNIT 2

CHAPTER 3
DEMAND

CHAPTER 4
SUPPLY

CHAPTER 5
PRICES

CHAPTER 6
MARKET STRUCTURES

Main Ideas
- *What factors can cause a product's demand to fluctuate?*
- *What factors determine a product's supply?*
- *How can the structure of a market influence consumers' purchases?*

Economics Lab
How much money can you raise by decorating T-shirts? Find out by reading this unit and taking the Economics Lab challenge on pages 138–41. ⭐TEKS

Elements of Microeconomics

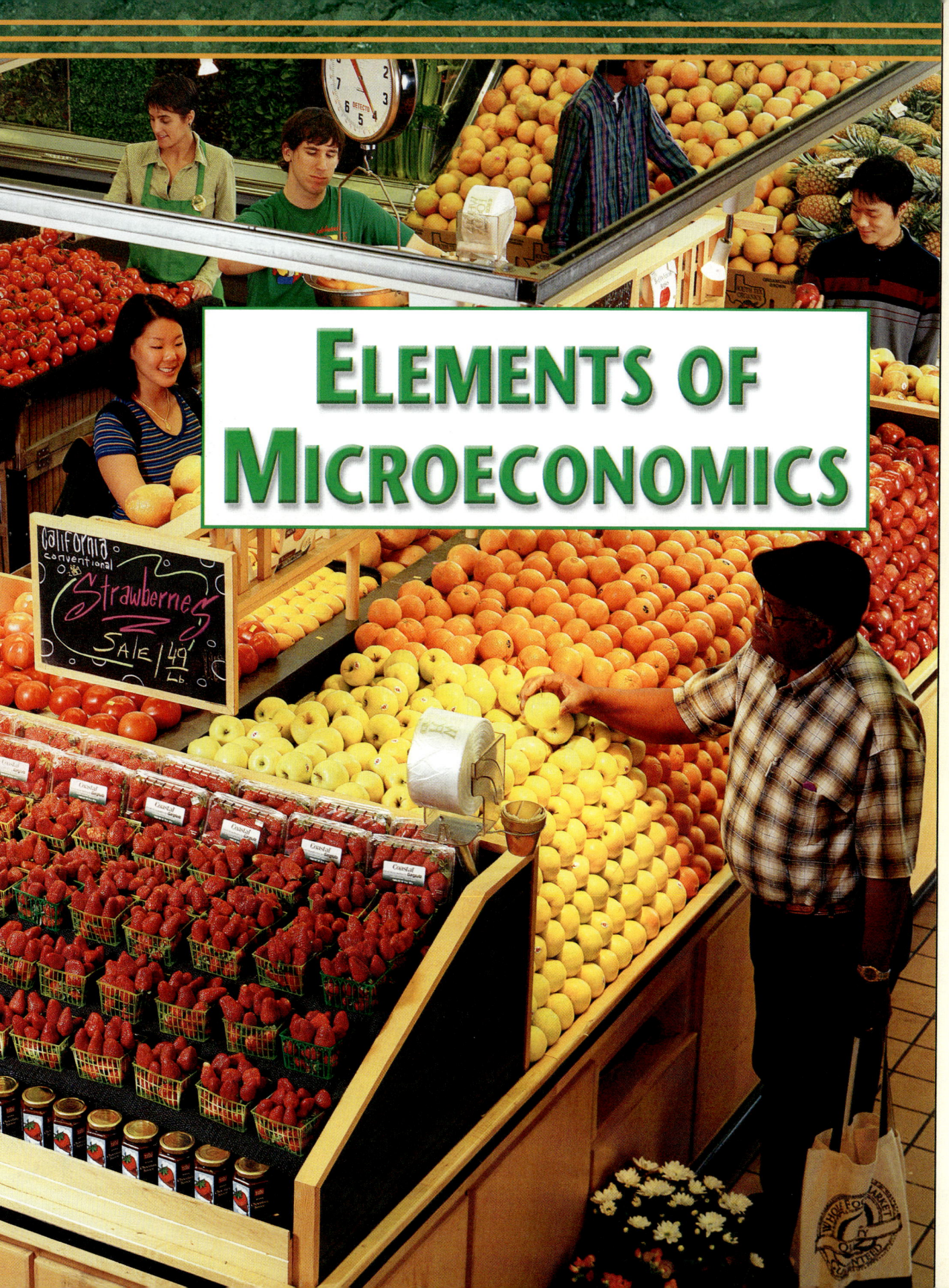

Unit 2 Overview

Unit 2 covers the basic microeconomic concepts of demand, supply, price, and market structures. Students will study the laws of demand and supply, demand and supply schedules and curves, elasticity of demand and supply, how businesses and markets set prices, price regulation, competitive and noncompetitive market structures, and market regulation.

Teaching with Photographs

This photograph shows the variety of fruits and vegetables available for sale at a grocery store. Although produce imported from around the world is available year-round in American grocery stores, many fruits and vegetables remain somewhat seasonable. For example, in the United States, strawberries are more expensive and scarce during the winter than during the summer.

As a motivating activity for the unit, ask students what produce in their local grocery stores is seasonable and why it is more expensive in the off-season.

CHAPTER RESOURCE MANAGER

CHAPTER 3 DEMAND

	OBJECTIVES	PACING GUIDE	REPRODUCIBLE RESOURCES
SECTION 1 **NATURE OF DEMAND** (pp. 51–55)	▸ How does demand differ from the quantity demanded? ▸ What does the law of demand state? ▸ What do demand schedules and demand curves illustrate?	**Regular** 1.5 days **Block Scheduling** 1 day	**ELL** Spanish Study Guide 3.1 **ELL** English Study Guide 3.1
SECTION 2 **CHANGES IN DEMAND** (pp. 56–62)	▸ What does it mean for a product's demand to shift? ▸ What factors can shift demand for a product? ▸ How do substitute goods differ from complementary goods?	**Regular** 1.5 days **Block Scheduling** 1 day	**ELL** Spanish Study Guide 3.2 **ELL** English Study Guide 3.2 **PS** Reading 67: The Affluent Society **E** Challenge and Enrichment Activity 3 **SM** Consumer Economics Activity 3
SECTION 3 **ELASTICITY OF DEMAND** (pp. 63–68)	▸ What is demand elasticity? ▸ What is the difference between elastic and inelastic demand? ▸ How is demand elasticity measured?	**Regular** 1.5 days **Block Scheduling** 1 day	**ELL** Spanish Study Guide 3.3 **ELL** English Study Guide 3.3 **SM** Mathematics for Economics: Activity 3

Chapter Resource Key

- **PS** Primary Sources
- **RS** Reading Support
- **E** Enrichment
- **S** Simulations
- **SM** Skills Mastery
- **A** Assessment
- **REV** Review
- **ELL** Reinforcement and English Language Learners
- Transparencies
- CD-ROM
- Video
- Videodisc
- Internet
- Holt Presentation Maker Using Microsoft® PowerPoint®
- TEKS and TAKS

TECHNOLOGY RESOURCES	REINFORCEMENT, REVIEW, AND ASSESSMENT
• One-Stop Planner: Lesson 3.1 • Researcher Online • Homework Practice Online • CNN Presents Economics: Marketing the New Millennium • Transparency 6 • Global Skillbuilder CD-ROM	**REV** Section 1 Review, p. 55 **A** Daily Quiz 3.1 ★ TAKS Every Day!
• One-Stop Planner: Lesson 3.2 • Researcher Online • Homework Practice Online • Transparency 7 • Global Skillbuilder CD-ROM	**REV** Section 2 Review, p. 62 **A** Daily Quiz 3.2 ★ TAKS Every Day!
• One-Stop Planner: Lesson 3.3 • Researcher Online • Homework Practice Online • Transparencies 8, 9, and 10 • Global Skillbuilder CD-ROM	**REV** Section 3 Review, p. 68 **A** Daily Quiz 3.3 ★ TAKS Every Day!

Chapter Review and Assessment

SM Global Skillbuilder CD-ROM
 HRW Go site
REV Reteaching Activity 3
REV Chapter 3 Review, pp. 70–71
A Chapter 3 Test Generator (on the One-Stop Planner)
A Chapter 3 Test
A Alternative Assessment Handbook

One-Stop Planner CD-ROM

It's easy to plan lessons, select resources, and print out materials for your students when you use the **Texas One-Stop Planner CD-ROM with Test Generator.**

---

internet connect

HRW ONLINE RESOURCES
Go To: go.hrw.com
Then type in a keyword.

TEACHER HOME PAGE
KEYWORD: SM3 Teacher

CHAPTER INTERNET ACTIVITIES
KEYWORD: SM3 EC3
Choose an activity to:
▶ create demand schedules and demand curves.
▶ research salaries paid for different professions.
▶ create a marketing plan.

CHAPTER ENRICHMENT LINKS
KEYWORD: SM3 CH3

HOLT RESEARCHER ONLINE
KEYWORD: Holt Researcher

ONLINE ASSESSMENT
Homework Practice
KEYWORD: SM3 HP3
TAKS Review
KEYWORD: SM3 T3
Rubrics
KEYWORD: SS Rubrics

CONTENT UPDATES
KEYWORD: SS Content Updates

HOLT PRESENTATION MAKER
KEYWORD: SM3 PPT3

ONLINE READING SUPPORT
KEYWORD: SS Strategies

CURRENT EVENTS
KEYWORD: S3 Current Events

TEXAS ONLINE RESOURCES
KEYWORD: S3 TX

LESSON 3.1 NATURE OF DEMAND

TEXTBOOK PAGES 51–55

HOLT PRESENTATION MAKER: Access Illustrated LECTURE NOTES using Microsoft® PowerPoint® on the One-Stop Planner CD-ROM

OBJECTIVES

- Describe how demand differs from the quantity demanded.
- Explain what the law of demand states.
- Explain what demand schedules and demand curves illustrate.

MOTIVATE

Tell students to imagine that they each have $30 and would like to purchase some compact discs (CDs). Tell them that they do not necessarily want to spend all their money, however. Ask them how many CDs they would purchase if the price were $5 per CD. Keep raising the price by $5 until you reach a price of $30 per CD. Tally the total number of CDs students would purchase at each price and record the answers in the form of a demand schedule. Tell students to keep this activity in mind as they read Section 1.

TEACH

Building a Vocabulary

Have students use spiral notebooks to create an Economics Dictionary to be used throughout the chapter. This dictionary might be used as an activity at the start of each new section or as a learning aid for sheltered English students or students having difficulty. List words that students will be expected to know on the chalkboard. Have students use the information provided in the text or on the *Researcher CD-ROM* to list, define, and give an example of each term.

Understanding Main Concepts

Have students name some of the products that they would like to buy in the near future. Ask if they can add to the demand for these products now—in other words, are they able to buy these products now? Explain that a consumer must be both willing and able to buy a product to add to the demand for that product.

Write the terms *demand* and *quantity demanded* on the chalkboard. Tell students that economists and businesses differentiate between these two economic terms. Have students define each term *(demand—the amount of a good or service a consumer is willing and able to buy at various possible prices during a given time period; quantity demanded—the amount of a good or service that a consumer is willing and able to buy at each particular price).*

Using Charts and Graphs

To help students better understand the distinction between demand and quantity demanded, direct their attention back to the demand schedule that they created at the start of class. Call on students to identify the total classroom demand for CDs and the quantity of CDs demanded at different prices. Continue to examine the chart as necessary to make certain that students understand the distinction between demand and quantity demanded.

Understanding Main Concepts

Ask students to name the law that describes the interplay between price and quantity demanded *(the law of demand)*. Have a student define the law of demand *(an increase in a good's price causes a decrease in the quantity demanded, and vice versa)*. Write the definition on the chalkboard. As you discuss the law of demand with students, show how the demand schedule they created for the classroom demand for CDs illustrates the law.

Next, ask students to name and define the three economic determinants that help explain the law of demand *(income effect, substitution effect, and diminishing marginal utility)*. Have students apply these three concepts to the classroom demand for CDs. For example, to illustrate the substitution effect, students might mention that they would buy cassettes instead of CDs if the latter cost more than $15. Then have students give examples of each of the three concepts at work. ⭐7A

Predicting Outcome, Applying Ideas

Provide several local in-store circulars, sales fliers, and newspaper advertisements. Organize students into groups of three or four. Tell each group to find an example of a business that recently raised or lowered its prices for a good or service. Instruct groups to predict how the price change will affect consumer demand for the good or service. Tell students to consider the law of demand, the income effect, the substitution effect, and diminishing marginal utility when making their predictions. Give each group 10 to 15 minutes to complete the exercise. Ask for volunteers from different groups to share their predictions with the class. ⭐23A

Using Economic Models

Review with the class the benefits of using economic models. Explain that demand schedules and demand curves are models that help economists and businesses better understand and predict consumer demand. Ask students to identify the type of economic model that they have been using throughout the lesson so far *(a demand schedule)*. Ask students why businesses might use a demand schedule *(to more easily see the interaction between price and quantity demanded so as to select the best price to charge for a good or service)*.

Have students examine Figure 3.2: Demand for Car Stereos (Transparency 6). Ask them what a demand curve shows and why it is useful *(it plots all of the information listed in a demand schedule; it shows at a glance the rate of change in quantity demanded at each price)*. As a class, have students interpret the information in the demand curve. Refer students who need more instruction on the skills used in this lesson to the *Global Skillbuilder* Lesson 10: Reading Graphs. ⭐7B

Creating Charts and Graphs

Organize students into groups of two or three. Give each group some poster board and some felt-tip markers. Tell each group to develop a demand schedule and a demand curve that shows the demand for a product or service. Each group should write captions that explain the information shown in their demand schedules and demand curves. Students can also use the Graphing Tool on the *Researcher Online* to create their graphs. Refer students who need additional instruction on the skills used in this lesson to the *Global Skillbuilder* Lesson 11: Presenting Data Graphically. ⭐23B

CLOSE

Summarize the information covered in the lesson. Then lead students in a discussion about how businesses use their knowledge of the law of demand, the income effect, the substitution effect, and diminishing marginal utility when advertising products.

OPTIONS

Sheltered English Students, Visual-Spatial Learners

Organize students into groups of two or three. Group sheltered English students with students fluent in English. Have each pair create a comic strip that incorporates the main concepts covered in Section 1. Students' comic strips might be stories that address several concepts at once, or they might illustrate each concept separately. Students should include dialogue or captions with their comic strips. ⭐24D

Body-Kinesthetic Learners, Interpersonal Learners

Organize students into groups of two or three. Assign each group one of the economic concepts from the chapter. Tell each group to prepare a short skit illustrating their assigned economic concept in action. Give students 15 to 20 minutes to prepare their skits. ⭐24D

Linguistic Learners

Invite a local businessperson who uses demand schedules and demand curves to speak to your class. Ask the speaker to describe how the law of demand affects his or her business, how he or she uses demand schedules and demand curves at work, and how his or her business tries to increase demand for its product. If possible, have the speaker show the class actual demand schedules and demand curves to interpret. Encourage students to prepare several questions beforehand to ask the speaker. ⭐7A, 7B

REVIEW

Have students complete the Section 1 Review on page 55. Use the answers in the Annotated Teacher's Edition to assess student mastery of this section.

ASSESS

To assess student mastery of this section, have students complete Daily Quiz 3.1 in *Daily Quizzes with Answer Key*. For additional assessment options, see *Alternative Assessment Handbook* on the *One-Stop Planner CD-ROM*.

ADDITIONAL RESOURCES

Creedy, John. *Demand and Exchange in Economic Analysis.* 1992. Edgar Elgar.

Flickman, Lawrence. *Consumer Society in American History: A Reader.* 1999. Cornell University Press.

Hildenbrand, Werner. *Market Demand: Theory and Empirical Evidence.* 1994. Princeton University Press.

Mander, Eric. *The Laws of Choice: Predicting Consumer Behavior.* 1997. Free Press.

LESSON 3.2 CHANGES IN DEMAND

TEXTBOOK PAGES 56–62

HOLT PRESENTATION MAKER
Access Illustrated LECTURE NOTES using Microsoft® PowerPoint® on the One-Stop Planner CD-ROM

OBJECTIVES

- Explain what it means for a product's demand to shift.
- Identify and describe the factors that can shift demand for a product. ⭐7A
- Explain how substitute goods differ from complementary goods.

MOTIVATE

Ask students to suggest how their spending might change if they suddenly had a job that paid $40,000 a year. Ask them if their demand for luxury items might increase. Next, discuss how their demand for certain goods might change if their salary was suddenly cut to $20,000 a year, or if they suddenly became unemployed. Emphasize that people's demand for goods and services can change due to factors other than price. Ask students to suggest what some of these factors might be. For example, encourage them to imagine what might happen to the demand for a product if it suddenly became unpopular. Tell students to keep the factors they listed in mind as they read through Section 2 of the chapter.

TEACH

Building a Vocabulary

List the important terms for this section on the chalkboard and tell students to add them to their Economics Dictionary. Tell students to use the information provided in the text or on the *Researcher CD-ROM* to list, define, and give an example of each term.

Applying a Model

Ask students to recall the definition of a demand curve. *(It shows the quantity of a good or service demanded at each price during a specific period of time.)* Remind students that demand curves are accurate only for a specific period of time, and that price is the only factor affecting the quantity demanded. Have students examine Figure 3.3: Shifts in Demand (Transparency 7). Ask them what happens if the price of car stereos increases. *(The intersection of the new price and the quantity demanded moves to a different point along the demand curve.)* Next, ask what would happen if the popularity of this model of car stereo increased due to a successful advertising campaign. *(The entire demand curve will shift to the right. In other words, the quantity of car stereos demanded at each and every price will increase.)* Refer students who need additional instruction on the skills used in this lesson to the *Global Skill Builder* Lesson 10: Reading Graphs. ⭐7A

Analyzing Ideas, Role-Playing

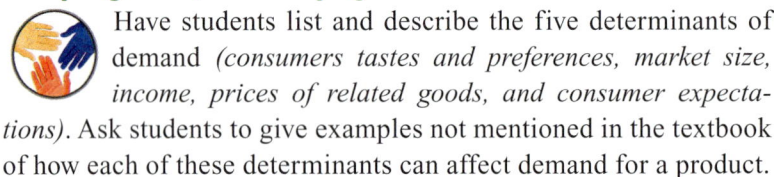

Have students list and describe the five determinants of demand *(consumers tastes and preferences, market size, income, prices of related goods, and consumer expectations)*. Ask students to give examples not mentioned in the textbook of how each of these determinants can affect demand for a product.

Organize students into groups of four or five. Tell each group to imagine that they are the managers of a local store that specializes in specific products, such as audio CDs, adventure trips, computer games, skateboards and skateboarding equipment, etc. They are preparing to order inventory for the coming year and are trying to predict how demand for their products may change during that time period. Each group should address how each of the five determinants of demand might affect demand for their products in the coming year. Encourage groups to consider what might happen if several factors changed during the year, as well as what might happen if only one factor changed but others remained the same. When students are through, have them share their predictions with the class. Encourage the class to discuss each group's predictions. ⭐7A

Classifying Information

Tell students that they are now going to focus on just one of the determinants of demand: the prices of related goods. Write the terms *substitute goods* and *complementary goods* on the chalkboard or on an overhead transparency. Have students distinguish between the two terms and describe how changes in the prices of related products can shift the demand for substitute and complementary goods. Then organize students into groups of two to four (You may wish to pair students who appear to be mastering the concepts of substitute and complementary goods with students who are having difficulty.) Draw a chart similar to the one on page 49F. Fill in the first row as shown, as an example, or

49E

Product	Substitute Good	Complementary Good
butter	margarine	bread

ask the class to provide a few examples. Then tell each group to create a similar chart and provide at least five more examples. ⭐7A

CLOSE

Have students discuss ways that businesses can influence shifts in demand. Use one business or industry as an example, such as an auto manufacturer. Call on volunteers to suggest what a manager might do, besides changing price, to boost demand or to deal with factors that are decreasing demand. ⭐7A

OPTIONS

Interpersonal Learners

Organize students into groups of three to five. Tell each group to imagine that they are the officers of a school club. To raise money for the club, they are selling tickets to a dance. Each group's task is to think of ways to increase ticket sales without lowering ticket prices. Tell students to consider each of the five determinants of demand when thinking of suggestions. Have students summarize their ideas and present them to the rest of their club (the class). ⭐7A

Body-Kinesthetic Learners

Have students visit local stores and research the prices of various products and their substitute and complementary goods. Students might work individually or in groups to complete this assignment. Students should record the prices for at least 10 products and their substitute goods and at least 10 products and their complementary goods. In addition, have students record whether any of the products are on sale and how that affected the price of related goods (e.g., are related goods also on sale). Have volunteers report their findings to the class. Then ask: If a product was on sale, was its complementary good also on sale? If not, ask students if they think demand for both products would increase anyway, even though only one product was on sale. ⭐7A

Gifted Learners

Have students read the feature Linking Economics and Psychology: Commercial Break on page 61 of the textbook. Tell students to use the library, in-class resources, and the Internet to research how a particular business or manufacturer used a focus group to plan a successful advertising campaign. Have students present their findings in a brief oral report. ⭐24D

Intrapersonal Learners, Linguistic Learners

Have students write a short paper on brand-name and generic, or store-brand, products. Students should address how their own buying habits are influenced by brand names and by the availability of lower-priced substitute products. For example, do students always drink the same brand of soft drink or buy certain brands of clothing? Students may want to add their papers on brand-name and generic products to their portfolios. ⭐7A, 24D

REVIEW

Have students complete the Section 2 Review on page 62. Use the answers in the Annotated Teacher's Edition to assess student mastery of this section.

ASSESS

To assess student mastery of this section, have students complete Daily Quiz 3.2 in *Daily Quizzes with Answer Key*. For additional assessment options, see *Alternative Assessment Handbook* on the *One-Stop Planner CD-ROM*.

ADDITIONAL RESOURCES

Edmunds, Holly. *The Focus Group Research Handbook.* 1999. American Marketing Association.

Hanna, Nessim, and Richard Wozniak. *Consumer Behavior.* 2000. Prentice Hall.

Ott, Rick. *Creating Demand.* 1999. Symmetric Systems, Inc.

Thurow, Lester, and Robert Heilbroner. *Economics Explained.* 1998. Touchstone Books.

Witt, Ulrich. *Escaping Satiation.* 2001. Springer Verlag.

LESSON 3.3 ELASTICITY OF DEMAND

TEXTBOOK PAGES 63–68

HOLT PRESENTATION MAKER
Access Illustrated LECTURE NOTES using Microsoft® PowerPoint® on the One-Stop Planner CD-ROM

OBJECTIVES

- Define demand elasticity.
- Describe the difference between elastic and inelastic demand.
- Explain how demand elasticity is measured.

MOTIVATE

On the chalkboard or on an overhead transparency, draw three demand curves—one that is almost vertical, one that is almost horizontal, and one that is almost horizontal to a certain price and then almost vertical. Have students describe what each graph illustrates *(almost horizontal—a small change in price results in a large change in quantity demanded; almost vertical—a change in price has little impact on quantity demanded; mixture—a change in price results in a large change in quantity demanded until the price reaches a certain point, and then a price change has little effect on quantity demanded).* Have students speculate about what type of products these graphs might represent. Tell students to keep this activity in mind as they read through Section 3 of the chapter.

TEACH

Building a Vocabulary

List the important terms for this section on the chalkboard and tell students to add them to their Economics Dictionary. Tell students to use the information provided in the text or on the *Researcher CD-ROM* to list, define, and give an example of each term.

Understanding Main Concepts

Have students define the term *elasticity of demand (the degree to which changes in a good's price affect the quantity demanded by consumers).* Discuss with students why businesspeople are interested in their products' elasticity of demand *(to help determine the degree to which changing prices affect quantity demanded so that they can determine if a price change will be profitable).*

Next, ask students to name the two types of demand elasticity *(elastic demand and inelastic demand).* List the three characteristics that determine whether a product has elastic or inelastic demand— whether the product is a necessity, the number of readily available substitutes for the product, and whether the product's cost represents a small or large portion of consumers' incomes—on the chalkboard. Have students use this list to describe the characteristics of products with elastic demand and of those with inelastic demand.

Applying Economic Models

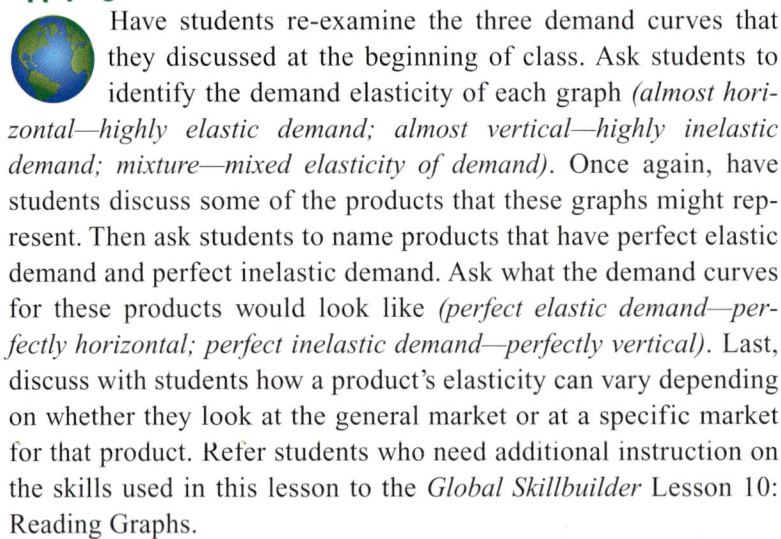

Have students re-examine the three demand curves that they discussed at the beginning of class. Ask students to identify the demand elasticity of each graph *(almost horizontal—highly elastic demand; almost vertical—highly inelastic demand; mixture—mixed elasticity of demand).* Once again, have students discuss some of the products that these graphs might represent. Then ask students to name products that have perfect elastic demand and perfect inelastic demand. Ask what the demand curves for these products would look like *(perfect elastic demand—perfectly horizontal; perfect inelastic demand—perfectly vertical).* Last, discuss with students how a product's elasticity can vary depending on whether they look at the general market or at a specific market for that product. Refer students who need additional instruction on the skills used in this lesson to the *Global Skillbuilder* Lesson 10: Reading Graphs.

Classifying Information

Organize the class into groups of three to five. Tell each group to draw a chart with two columns, one with the heading *elastic demand,* and the other with the heading *inelastic demand.* Under each heading students should list the three characteristics that define that type of demand. Then they should list at least five examples of products with that type of demand. After 10 to 15 minutes, call on students to share some of their examples with the class. ★24D

Learning from Visuals

Ask students to name one simple method that business people use to measure demand elasticity *(total-revenue test).* Then ask why businesspeople use this test *(to determine the price to charge for a product to maximize total revenue).* Have students use Figure 3.6: Movie Ticket Revenue and Demand Elasticity (Transparency 10) to describe how the total-revenue test measures demand elasticity. Ask students what a drop in a business's total revenue following a price increase indicates *(elastic demand for the business's product)*. Then ask what a rise in a business's total revenue following a price increase indicates *(inelastic demand for the business's product)*.

Creating Charts and Graphs

Organize students into groups of three or four. Tell students to imagine that they are business managers trying to sell a product. Each group should decide on a product to sell and then create a hypothetical, yet realistic, demand schedule and demand curve for that product. The table and graph should resemble those in Figure 3.6. Students may want to use the Graphing Tool on the *Researcher Online* to create their graphs. Next, each group should identify at which prices demand for their product is elastic, at which prices it is inelastic, and at what price total revenue is maximized. (It is not necessary that students choose a product with mixed elasticity of demand across prices.) Refer students who need additional instruction on the skills used in this lesson to the *Global Skillbuilder* Lesson 11: Presenting Data Graphically. ⭐23B

CLOSE

Lead students in a discussion about how businesses or manufacturers might be able to change demand elasticity for their product to increase revenue. For example, a manufacturer who produces a product with elastic demand might use an ad campaign to convince consumers that the product is a necessity, that it has few readily available substitutes, and that its cost is not that high given its worth to consumers.

OPTIONS

Students Having Difficulty, Sheltered English Students

Pair students having difficulty with students who have mastered the material. Give each pair a posterboard. Tell each pair to draw a line down the center of their posterboard and to write the definition of elastic demand at the top of one side and the definition of inelastic demand at the top of the other. Then have the pairs cut out pictures from newspapers and magazines to create two collages of products, one for each type of demand elasticity. Have students indicate why each of the different images they selected exhibits elastic or inelastic demand. ⭐24D

Gifted Learners

Organize students into groups of four or five. Tell groups to imagine that they are market researchers working for a large corporation. Their company has come up with a new product that they want to test market. Each group's task is to create a market survey to determine the quantity of the product that people in their community would demand at different prices. Each group should think of a new and innovative product, decide on a variety of prices to charge, survey at least 50 people in their community about how much of the product they would buy at different prices, compile the results into a demand schedule and a demand curve, indicate whether the product has elastic or inelastic demand (or a mixture), and determine the price to charge to maximize revenue. Students may want to use the Graphing Tool on the *Researcher Online* to create their graphs. Have each group present their results to the class. ⭐7A, 23B

REVIEW

Have students complete the Section 3 Review on page 68. Use the answers in the Annotated Teacher's Edition to assess student mastery of this section.

ASSESS

To assess student mastery of this section, have students complete Daily Quiz 3.3 in *Daily Quizzes with Answer Key*. For additional assessment options, see *Alternative Assessment Handbook* on the *One-Stop Planner CD-ROM*.

RETEACH

For students having difficulty with the lessons, have them complete Reteaching Activity 3. This activity is located in *Reteaching Activities with Answer Key*.

ADDITIONAL RESOURCES

Dutka, Alan. *AMA Handbook for Customer Satisfaction: A Complete Guide to Research, Planning, and Implementation.* 1995. NTE Publishing Group.

Ziccardi, Donald, and David Moin. *Masterminding the Store: Advertising, Sales Promotion, and the New Market Reality.* 1997. John Wiley and Sons.

CHAPTER 3

TOPICS INCLUDE

- consumer demand
- law of demand
- income effect
- substitution effect
- diminishing marginal utility
- movement along the demand curve
- determinants of demand
- shifts in the demand curve
- substitute goods
- complementary goods
- elasticity of demand
- maximizing total revenue

ECONOMICS NOTEBOOK

The Economics Notebook is a journal activity that encourages students to consider basic concepts of economics that relate to their lives. A follow-up notebook activity appears on page 70.

WHY IT MATTERS TODAY

To find additional lesson plans dealing with demand, visit CNNfyi.com or have students complete the ECONOMICS IN THE NEWS activity on page 69.

CNNfyi.com

CHAPTER 3

DEMAND

As a consumer, your role in market demand is governed by some fundamental economic concepts. In this chapter you will explore these concepts, including the law of demand, shifts in demand, and elasticity of demand. You also will learn to use demand schedules and demand curves—key tools of every economist and every economics student.

ECONOMICS NOTEBOOK

In your Economics Notebook, write what you think the term *demand* means. List five things that you think you have demanded, in economic terms, in the past month.

WHY IT MATTERS TODAY

Consumer demand shapes production decisions in many industries. Use CNNfyi.com or other **current events** sources to find additional examples of the impact of consumer demand. Record your findings in your Notebook.

CNNfyi.com

50

SECTION 1

NATURE OF DEMAND

READ TO DISCOVER

1. How does demand differ from the quantity demanded?
2. What does the law of demand state?
3. What do demand schedules and demand curves illustrate?

ECONOMICS DICTIONARY

demand
quantity demanded
law of demand
purchasing power
income effect
substitution effect
diminishing marginal utility
demand schedule
demand curve

You have wanted, or demanded, many things in your life. Everyone has. In economic terms, however, the concept of demand means more than simply wanting something.

Consider Linda Armstrong's situation. Suppose that she has been saving to buy a new car ever since she graduated and started her job a year ago. Linda wants a sports car that has a good safety record and a reputation for needing few repairs. After shopping around, Linda realizes that the cost of a new sports car is beyond her budget. At this point, she cannot afford the car she wants. Instead, she will have to look for a used sports car, buy a less expensive car, or wait until she can afford her first choice in cars.

At this particular time, Linda cannot add to the demand for new sports cars. This does not mean that she might not be part of that demand at some time in the future—if and when she can afford such a car.

As you can see from Linda's example, **demand** in economic terms is the amount of a good or service that a consumer is willing and able to buy at various possible prices during a given time period. **Quantity demanded** is a slightly different concept that describes the amount of a good or service that a consumer is willing and able to buy at each particular price during a given time period.

This definition of demand contains two important conditions. First, the consumer must be willing *and* able to buy the good or service. In other words, the person must not only want the product but also have the means to pay for it. Linda did not meet this condition because she could not afford the car she wanted. Second, demand for the product must be examined for a *specific time period*—a day, a week, a month, a year, or some other definite period. The time period under study must be specific because various factors that change over time can affect the demand for a product.

SUPPLY & DEMAND *Demand is more than just the desire to purchase a product.* **What conditions must a consumer meet in order to add to the demand for sports cars?**

DEMAND 51

Themes in Economics

SUPPLY & DEMAND In an attempt to increase consumer demand, businesses often use price-cutting strategies such as coupons, sales, specials, and rebates. These strategies are particularly popular with companies selling products in a highly competitive market and for which there are many available substitutes, as in the fast-food industry or the automotive industry. ■

---

internet connect

TOPIC: Purchasing Power
GO TO: go.hrw.com
KEYWORD: SM3 EC3

Have students access the Internet through the HRW Go site to conduct research on salaries paid for different professions. Then have each student choose a profession he or she is interested in and create a budget based on the first year's salary for that profession. Each student should estimate the purchasing power he or she will have. Remind students to include taxes, rent, insurance costs, transportation costs, and so on as they prepare their budgets. ★11A

Law of Demand

Linda's situation illustrates a basic economic principle: In a free-enterprise system, price is the main variable affecting demand. Specifically, there is an inverse, or opposite, relationship between price and the quantity demanded. This relationship is described by the **law of demand**, which states that an increase in a good's price causes a decrease in the quantity demanded and that a decrease in price causes an increase in the quantity demanded.

Suppose that you want to buy a compact disc (CD) player. You expect to buy a CD player for about $200, and you have saved that amount. One Saturday you go to the Avalon Electronics Store. When you arrive at the store, you discover that the price of CD players has increased from $200 to $300. You are not able to pay $300 for a CD player because you have not saved that much money. Even if you were able to pay the higher price, you might not be willing to do so. Similarly, some other consumers also will be unwilling or unable to buy CD players at the higher price. In other words, the price increase will lead to a decrease in the quantity demanded. In contrast, if the price for CD players falls to $100, the quantity demanded will increase as consumers are willing and able to buy more CD players.

Three economic concepts help explain the law of demand: the income effect, the substitution effect, and diminishing marginal utility. Together these concepts account for the inverse effect that changes in price have on the quantity demanded.

Income Effect
The amount of money, or income, that people have available to spend on goods and services is called their **purchasing power**. As a consumer's purchasing power increases, his or her demand for goods and services also tends to increase. On the other hand, a decrease in a consumer's purchasing power tends to decrease his or her demand. Any increase or decrease in consumers' purchasing power caused by a change in price is called the **income effect**.

For example, if a store lowers the price of its CDs from $15 to $10, a consumer can buy more CDs with the same amount of income. A person spending $30 can buy three CDs at the new price of $10, but could have purchased only two CDs at the previous price of $15. The lower price thus increases the consumer's purchasing power and increases the quantity of CDs demanded from two to three.

The income effect also exists when the price of a product rises and an individual can buy less of the product with the same amount of income. If the price of CDs jumps to $18, a consumer with $30 to spend does not have enough money to buy more than one CD. The consumer's purchasing power has decreased, resulting in a decrease in the quantity of CDs demanded from two to one.

In general, the income effect has a strong and predictable influence on the quantity demanded. Keep in mind, however, that the income effect does not always come into play. Although the price of CDs falls from $15 to $10, some people still may want only the two CDs they originally intended to buy at the higher price. Even though consumers' increased purchasing power has made them *able* to buy three CDs at the new price, they might not be *willing* to do so.

Likewise, people who really want these two CDs may be willing and able to buy them even if the price rises to $18. Although consumers' purchasing power has decreased, the quantity demanded would remain at two CDs instead of falling to one or none.

Substitution Effect
The **substitution effect** describes the tendency of consumers to substitute a similar, lower-priced product for another product that is relatively more expensive. This effect helps explain the relationship between price and the quantity demanded. For example, when the price of steak increases, many consumers reduce the quantity of beef demanded and buy more chicken, a lower-priced substitute. The substitution effect helps explain why higher beef prices cause a decrease in the quantity of beef demanded and an increase in the demand for chicken.

Like the income effect, the substitution effect sometimes does not apply. If an essential good or service has no readily available substitute, a rise

SUPPLY & DEMAND *Generic products and store brands allow consumers to substitute similar, lower-priced goods for more expensive products.* **When does the substitution effect not apply to demand?**

Generic products had their highest U.S. sales to date in 1982, during a period of poor economic performance. Consumer purchasing power at that time had fallen, and many people chose to substitute lower-priced generic products for higher-priced brand names.

When the U.S. economy improved in the mid- and late 1980s, the demand for generic products decreased. Consumers' purchasing power had been restored to the point where many consumers who preferred brand-name products could afford to switch back to buying them.

Generic products still can be found on store shelves, however. In the 1990s many stores substituted "store" brands for their generic products. Instead of traditional generic packaging, these store brands feature more sophisticated packages and labels. The cost of redesigning and repackaging raises the price of generic and store-brand products somewhat, but they continue to cost less than brand-name products because of lower advertising costs.

in price may not lower the quantity demanded. Milk, for example, does not have a lower-priced, readily available substitute. Thus, a rise in the price of milk likely will not cause consumers to switch to a substitute. Most people will consume about the same amount of milk in spite of the higher price.

CASE STUDY

Generic Products

SUPPLY & DEMAND Consumer demand for generic products is an example of the substitution effect at work. Generic products are nonbrand-name products. You may have purchased or seen such products on store shelves. When generic products were first introduced, they typically featured plain, white, or yellow packaging with black lettering.

Long popular in Europe, generic products were first introduced to the U.S. market in 1977. They sell for up to 40 percent less than brand names even though the quality is roughly the same. How can generic products sell for so much less? They do not have costly packaging and are not the focus of expensive advertising campaigns like brand-name products.

Diminishing Marginal Utility The third concept involved in explaining the law of demand is based on utility. As noted in Chapter 1, utility describes the usefulness of a product, or the amount of satisfaction that an individual receives from consuming a product. A product's overall utility typically increases as more of the product is consumed. However, as more units of a product are consumed, the satisfaction received from consuming each additional unit declines. Economists call this **diminishing marginal utility** because the marginal, or additional, utility of each unit consumed diminishes, or lessens, with each additional unit.

Suppose that you and your friends play basketball on a Saturday morning. After the game, you all have lunch at the restaurant with the best tacos in town. The first taco is well worth the $1 it costs. In fact, you are so hungry you would have paid $1.50 for it. The second taco also is worth at least $1 to you.

As you consider eating a third taco, however, you realize that you are starting to get full. You are still a little hungry but not as hungry as you

DEMAND 53

Themes in Economics

SUPPLY & DEMAND Total utility measures the total amount of satisfaction an individual receives from consuming one or more units of a product. Marginal utility is the additional amount of satisfaction an individual receives from consuming just one more unit of a product. In keeping with the law of diminishing marginal utility, a product's marginal utility decreases with each additional purchase made. ∎

Caption Answer
3,750 ⭐ 7B, 23F

---

were before eating the first and second tacos. The third taco is not worth $1 to you. The restaurant is running a special, however. If you order two tacos, a third one is half price. At the lower price of 50 cents, the third taco is worth the cost to you. You eat the third taco and are full.

Although the total utility of eating the tacos has increased, the marginal utility has decreased with each taco consumed. What about a fourth taco? You cannot eat anything more, so you certainly would not be willing to pay $1—or even 50 cents—for a fourth taco. Even if this taco were free, you might not order it.

Diminishing marginal utility helps explain why the demand for a product is not limitless. At some point, consumers cannot use any more of a product. There is a limit to a product's utility to consumers and thus a limit to consumers' demand.

Demand Schedules

One useful way to show the relationship between the price of a good or service and the quantity that consumers demand is a **demand schedule**. This schedule lists the quantity of goods that consumers are willing and able to buy at a series of possible prices.

A demand schedule allows you to see the interaction of price and demand in a simple table format. Suppose that Ellen Lisiewicz, a jewelry store owner, wants to know how many Right On Time watches she can sell at various prices during a one-month period. Ellen may develop a demand schedule that indicates the quantity of watches demanded at several prices so that she can determine—and charge her customers—the most profitable price for the watch.

An example of a demand schedule appears in Figure 3.1. The schedule lists the quantity of watches demanded during the month at several possible prices. You can see that as prices increase from $100 to $600, the quantity demanded decreases. When the price is $100, the quantity of watches demanded is 5,000. When the price is $600 or higher, consumers do not buy any watches.

Demand Curves

Demand curves are another way to show the relationship between the price of a product and the quantity demanded. A **demand curve** plots this information on a graph.

In Figure 3.2, for example, demand curve D_1 plots all of the possible combinations of prices and quantities demanded during a one-month period for car stereos listed in the demand schedule on the left. The quantities that consumers might purchase appear along the horizontal axis at the bottom of the graph, increasing from left to right. The possible prices of the stereos appear along the vertical axis at the left side of the graph, increasing from bottom to top.

Each point plotted on the graph represents a specific combination of price and quantity demanded. The curve slopes downward, reflecting the greater quantity that consumers will buy at lower prices.

Why might a business owner plot a demand curve rather than simply referring to a demand

DEMAND SCHEDULE

Price per Watch	Quantity Demanded
$600	0
$500	1,500
$400	2,750
$300	3,750
$200	4,500
$100	5,000

FIGURE 3.1 A demand schedule shows the interaction between price and demand during a specific period. **During a one-month period, how many watches are demanded at $300?** ⭐ TEKS

DEMAND FOR CAR STEREOS

DEMAND SCHEDULE

Price per Car Stereo	Quantity Demanded
$500	500
$400	1,000
$300	1,500
$200	2,500
$100	5,000

DEMAND CURVE

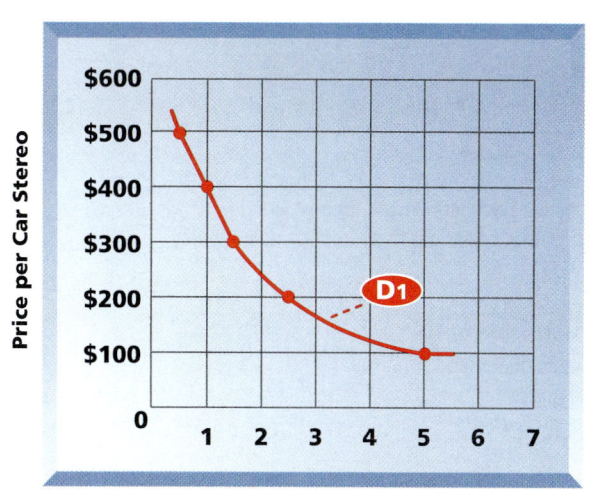

FIGURE 3.2 A demand curve plots all of the information listed in a demand schedule. **If the price increases from $300 to $400, how will the demand for car stereos change in a given month?**

---

schedule? A demand curve can show at a glance the rate of change at each price. In some cases the demand curve will appear to be straight, as each change in price results in the same change in the quantity of the product demanded. Other demand curves, such as the one shown above in Figure 3.2, may reflect greater changes in the quantity of a product demanded at some prices than at others and therefore will have a more "curved" appearance.

SECTION 1 REVIEW

Q: 1, 2, 3a, 4

1. **Identify and Explain:**
   demand
   quantity demanded
   law of demand
   purchasing power
   income effect
   substitution effect
   diminishing marginal utility
   demand schedule
   demand curve

2. **Summarizing:** Copy the graphic organizer. Use it to summarize the economic concepts that help explain the law of demand.

   Law of Demand
   Price changes have an inverse effect on quantity demanded.

3. **Finding the Main Idea**
   a. Explain the difference between demand and quantity demanded.
   b. What is the difference between a demand schedule and a demand curve?

4. **Writing and Critical Thinking**
   Identifying Cause and Effect: Give one personal example of each of the following concepts: income effect, substitution effect, and diminishing marginal utility.
   Consider the following:
   • the inverse relationship between price and quantity demanded
   • other factors affecting demand

Homework Practice Online
keyword: SM3 HP3

DEMAND 55

SECTION 2

CHANGES IN DEMAND

READ TO DISCOVER
1. What does it mean for a product's demand to shift?
2. What factors can shift demand for a product?
3. How do substitute goods differ from complementary goods?

ECONOMICS DICTIONARY
determinants of demand
substitute goods
complementary goods

As noted in the previous section, a demand curve like the one in Figure 3.2 on page 55 illustrates a product's market during a specific period of time. In effect, the demand curve in Figure 3.2 is a snapshot of the car stereo market. And because the picture is taken at a single point in time, the only factor affecting the demand for car stereos is the one shown in the picture (graph): price. In other words, at the time this picture of the car stereo market was taken, nothing but a change in price could have caused a change in the quantity demanded.

By examining the demand curve, you can see that price is the only factor affecting the quantity demanded. Look again at the D_1 curve in Figure 3.2. What would have to happen for the number of car stereos demanded to increase from 2,500 to 5,000? The graph shows that only a drop in the price from $200 to $100 will cause this change in the quantity demanded. Such a decrease in price will cause the intersection of price and demand to move to a new point along the demand curve.

Demand Shifts

Markets do not stand still, however, so new snapshots of demand for a product must be taken periodically. Indeed, the passage of time allows factors other than price to influence demand significantly. In economic terms, these factors can shift the entire demand curve of a product to the right or left, instead of simply causing movement along the old demand curve.

Figure 3.3 shows the old D_1 demand curve for car stereos from Figure 3.2, as well as two new demand curves. If, after the passage of time, a factor other than price causes an increase in demand for car stereos, the entire curve shifts to the right (D_2). Conversely, if this factor causes a decrease in demand, the entire curve shifts to the left (D_3). A shift in either the D_2 or D_3 curve means that a different quantity of car stereos is demanded at *each* and *every* price. This group of factors is called the **determinants of demand**.

SUPPLY & DEMAND *Concert ticket sales reflect a music group's popularity. How can consumer tastes and preferences influence demand?*

SHIFTS IN DEMAND

INCREASE IN DEMAND

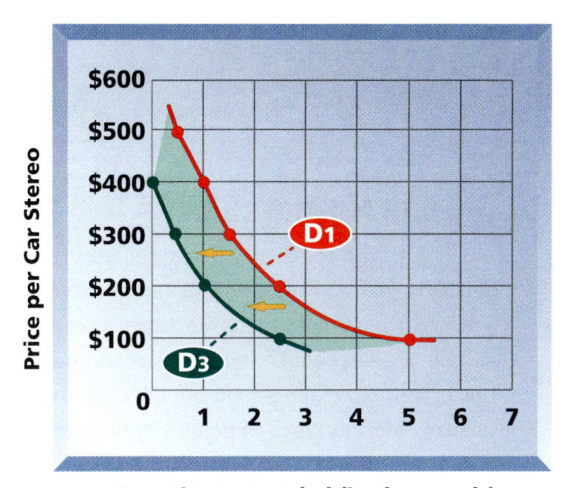

DECREASE IN DEMAND

FIGURE 3.3 Many nonprice factors can shift the entire demand curve. **How do demand curves D_2 and D_3 reflect shifts in demand?** ★TEKS

What can cause these shifts in demand? The determinants of demand include

- consumer tastes and preferences
- market size
- income
- prices of related goods
- consumer expectations.

Change in any one of these determinants can cause a change in the overall demand for a good or a service.

Consumer Tastes and Preferences

Changes in consumer tastes and preferences can have a major effect on demand for products. For example, think about the bands and singers you like. Are they the same ones your parents listen to? Are they even the same ones you liked just two or three years ago? Chances are they are not the same. The popularity of recording artists rises and falls frequently.

What happens to the demand curve when consumer preference for a recording artist grows? For example, if the popularity of a new group called the Mock Turtles rises, the demand for the group's music also increases. The demand curve shifts to the right as consumers become willing to buy more Mock Turtles CDs at each and every price.

What happens when the Mock Turtles' next release receives terrible reviews from music critics? Some consumers no longer like the group, decreasing the quantity of Mock Turtles CDs demanded. As the group's popularity falls, the demand curve shifts to the left. Consumers will now buy fewer of the group's CDs at each and every price.

Market Size

Changes in the size of a market tend to affect demand. As a market expands, it has more consumers than before. A larger number of consumers in turn means a greater potential demand. Likewise, if a market contracts, it loses consumers, creating a smaller potential demand.

Markets expand and contract for several reasons. Decisions by private businesses are one

---

Transparency

An overhead transparency of Figure 3.3 is available in *Transparency Resources*. See Transparency 7: Shifts in Demand.

Caption Answer

In each, a different quantity of car stereos is demanded at each and every price—D_2 shows an increase in demand; D_3 shows a decrease in demand.
★7A, 23F

Cultural Perspectives

Health trends can increase consumer demand for certain foods or products. In the early 1990s many medical journals and health magazines began touting bananas as the "perfect portable snack." Bananas are extremely low in fat, low in calories, high in fiber, and a rich source of potassium and vitamins B_6 and C. As a result of this promotion, consumer demand for bananas rose dramatically. From 1990 to 1998, per capita banana consumption increased 26 percent.

DEMAND 57

Careers in Economics

To help students learn about other careers in economics, refer them to the Careers section on the *Researcher Online*.

Across the Curriculum

TECHNOLOGY Virtual reality may be changing the way market researchers conduct their work. Computer-simulated shopping programs enable researchers to examine consumers' reactions to products in an environment that resembles an actual shopping experience. As an added incentive, computer-simulated programs are often less expensive and more reliable than other commonly used market research tools, such as questionnaires, focus groups, and test markets. ■

---

internet connect

TOPIC: Demand Shifts, Advertising
GO TO: go.hrw.com
KEYWORD: SM3 EC3

Have students access the Internet through the HRW Go site to conduct research on De Beers, the company that has promoted the diamond as a symbol of love. The De Beers advertising campaigns helped to greatly increase the demand for diamond jewelry. Have students outline a marketing plan to increase demand for a product that is currently out of favor in the marketplace. ★2B

CAREERS IN ECONOMICS

Market Researcher

Imagine that one Saturday you and your friends decide to go to the mall. As you enter the building, a woman at a demonstration table asks you to sample a new product and to answer some questions. You agree and spend the next few minutes tasting different types of peanut butter and comparing package labels.

Why is this woman asking questions about peanut butter? She is a market researcher. In order to know what products to make and how to present these products, companies need to find out what consumers like and dislike. Do consumers want organic peanut butter? Does a yellow label catch their eye more than a white one? Market researchers help companies answer these types of questions.

Sometimes market researchers conduct surveys, as in the "taste test" example above. Market researchers also rely on information collected by governments and businesses. For example, a toy company may use U.S. census data to pinpoint communities with large numbers of children in the population.

Market researchers need specific skills to do their job well. Because they deal with the public, researchers must have good communications skills. They also must be able to analyze statistics and other data they collect. Most market research companies use computers to collect, organize, and analyze the massive amounts of data they handle, so good computer skills are necessary as well.

Market researchers provide companies with valuable insight into consumer habits and demand. Without this type of information, a company might develop the world's most delicious peanut butter—but not sell a jar of it because it is hidden behind an unattractive label.

Market researchers analyze consumer tastes and preferences.

---

cause of changes in market size. For example, suppose that Recreational Equipment Inc. (REI) launches a national advertising campaign for its boots and other hiking gear. People across the United States see the advertisements and learn about REI's products. More people take up hiking, thereby expanding the market and increasing demand for hiking products made by producers throughout the market. Because the quantity of hiking products demanded changes at each and every price, the entire demand curve shifts to the right. In contrast, decreased demand would cause the market to shrink and the demand curve to shift to the left.

Governments also make policy decisions that affect the size of markets. For example, North

CHAPTER 3

Vietnam's victory in the Vietnam War led the United States to break off trade and diplomatic relations with Vietnam. In 1995, however, relations were restored. Suddenly, many U.S. companies found a whole new group of consumers for their goods in Vietnam. The demand curve for their products shifted to the right.

A third force affecting market size is new technology. Technology can create new products and markets, sometimes at the expense of older ones. The invention of small video cameras, or camcorders, for example, created a new market. The popularity of camcorders also caused the market for 16-millimeter movie cameras—and projectors to contract until it virtually disappeared. Over time, the demand curve for camcorders shifted to the right, while the demand curve for 16-millimeter movie cameras shifted farther and farther to the left.

SUPPLY & DEMAND *Advertising can affect the size of markets, thereby increasing or decreasing demand.* ***At what market is this targeted?***

Income

Generally, when income increases, people have more money to spend. This increased spending results in a greater demand for goods and services, and thus in a shift to the right in the demand curve for the products people buy. Because of their higher incomes, consumers are willing and able to buy more products at every price. Similarly, a decrease in income leads to a decrease in demand because consumers are less willing and able to spend money and contribute to the demand for products.

Although the demand for most goods increases as income rises, a few exceptions exist. Suppose that a family eats beef for dinner once a week. As the household's income increases, the family switches from ground beef to the higher-priced—but now affordable—steak. This increase

SUPPLY & DEMAND *A decrease in income decreases demand because consumers have less money to spend, regardless of price.* ***How is a change in income different from the income effect?***

Caption Answer
teenagers

Across the Curriculum

PSYCHOLOGY Noted psychologist Abraham Maslow developed the theory of the hierarchy of needs. This theory ranks human needs and desires in a hierarchy in order of importance. At the bottom of the hierarchy are physiological needs, such as food and water, and safety needs, such as security and stability. Maslow believed that people satisfy these lower-level, or basic, needs before trying to satisfy higher-level needs, such as love, acceptance, and self-actualization.

Maslow's theory may provide relevant insight into the way consumers' demands change as their incomes increase. For example, when incomes are low, consumers tend to spend proportionately more of their incomes on necessities such as food, housing, and electricity. As incomes increase, consumers spend proportionately more on luxuries such as movies, concerts, and restaurant dining. ■

Caption Answer
change in income—shift in the demand curve at every price; income effect—changes in consumers' purchasing power because of a change in a product's price

Caption Answer
It will probably increase the demand for frozen yogurt.

Themes in Economics

SUPPLY & DEMAND Economists measure the degree of substitutability between products by calculating the cross-price elasticity of demand. For example, if a soft drink company lowers the price of Cola A, how will the price cut affect sales of Cola B, which the company also produces? To determine the answer, economists divide the percentage of the change in the quantity demanded of Cola B by the percentage of Cola A's price change.

If the result is a positive value, then the two goods are substitute goods, such as butter and margarine. If the result is a negative value, then the two goods are complementary goods, such as paint and paintbrushes. If the result is zero, then the two goods are independent goods—that is, changing the price of one good has no effect on the quantity demanded of the second good. Desks and skateboards are independent goods. ■

SUPPLY & DEMAND *Goods that can be used to replace the purchase of similar goods when prices rise are called substitute goods.* **How might an increase in the price of ice cream affect the demand for frozen yogurt?**

in the demand for steak causes the demand for ground beef to decrease. In this situation the income effect is working in reverse. The higher-priced steak is being purchased rather than the lower-priced hamburger.

It is important to note that a change in people's income is similar to, as well as different from, the income effect. As noted in Section 1, the income effect deals with changes in consumers' purchasing power caused by a change in a product's price. For example, if Paul Sakamoto earns $18,000 a year and the price of various goods falls, his purchasing power increases as the $18,000 buys more of the same goods than it bought at higher prices. This results in a change in the quantity demanded, or movement along the demand curve.

In contrast, a change in a person's income brings a different amount of money into that person's household. For example, suppose that Paul receives a raise from $18,000 a year to $19,000. Paul has more money to spend, and his demand probably will increase. This results in completely new demand curves for the goods Paul buys. In this case, the actual change in income, rather than a change in price, causes the shift in demand as more product is bought at the same price.

Prices of Related Goods

The demand for a good is often connected to the demand for related goods. This means that changes in a product's price can affect demand for the product's related goods. There are two types of related goods: substitute goods and complementary goods.

Substitute Goods
Goods that can be used to replace the purchase of similar goods when prices rise are called **substitute goods**. As noted in Section 1, consumers' tendency to switch to lower-priced substitutes is called the substitution effect.

How do price changes for one good affect demand for its substitutes? Consider two similar products—butter and margarine. Price changes for butter can affect the demand for margarine. When the price of butter increases, many people consume less butter and use margarine instead. Thus, the demand for margarine—a substitute good—increases. Likewise, when the price of butter decreases, many people who use margarine switch to butter, and the overall demand for margarine decreases.

By definition then, an increase in a product's price leads to increased demand for the product's substitute goods. Meanwhile, a decrease in the product's price leads to a decrease in the demand for the product's substitute goods.

Complementary Goods
Goods that are commonly used with other goods are known as **complementary goods**. Paintbrushes and paint, for example, are complementary goods. As the price of a gallon of paint increases, the quantity of paint demanded *and* the quantity of paintbrushes demanded decreases. Along the same lines, if paint goes on sale, the quantity of both paint and paintbrushes demanded rises, even though the price of the paintbrushes has not changed.

Thus, an increase in a product's price causes decreased demand for that product's complementary goods. Similarly, a decrease in the product's

LINKING ECONOMICS and PSYCHOLOGY

Commercial Break

Could you become a better athlete simply by driving a different type of car? Of course not—and car manufacturers know this too. One car commercial shows golf star Tiger Woods failing miserably at teaching a group of people how to play golf. As Woods then drives off in a new car, the commercial suggests that while a person may never play golf like Tiger, by buying the advertised car they can still drive like him. Although the commercial pokes fun at the idea that the correct purchase can change your life, many other commercials encourage this attitude. Why?

Advertisers know that tapping into fantasies and emotions is a powerful way to reach consumers and increase demand for products. In fact, advertisers spend a great deal of money studying the psychological makeup of consumers—their attitudes, emotions, and behaviors. They use these findings to try to influence consumers' buying decisions and raise demand.

Some advertisements, for example, play to consumers' anxieties and fears. Consider the back-to-school advertisement for athletic shoes that likens school to a reality show where wearing the wrong shoes can get you voted out the first day. The advertisement directly plays to many teenagers' fears of not fitting in at school.

Other advertisements try to appeal to consumers' fantasies of who they want to be. For instance, a commercial in the 1990s suggested that if consumers bought their sports drink they could "be like Mike." This ad was intended to appeal to the many young fans of Michael Jordan. Of course, a sports drink can hardly improve someone's dunk shots—much less make that person taller.

Advertisers have several methods of determining the best way to appeal to consumers' emotions. One method is through focus groups. People in a focus group participate in activities designed to reveal opinions about and emotional responses to a product. Members of focus groups draw pictures to illustrate their reactions to a product, role-play scenarios that represent their need for or feelings about a product, and tell stories about how they might use a product. Based on the focus group results, advertisers develop campaigns to reinforce consumers' positive feelings about the product and relieve any anxieties they may have.

What does the link between psychology and advertising mean to you? As an alert consumer, you should always view advertising with a critical eye. Be aware of how ads try to tap into your fantasies and fears. Ask yourself if the product is what you need and can afford—not just if it will make you feel like a sports star.

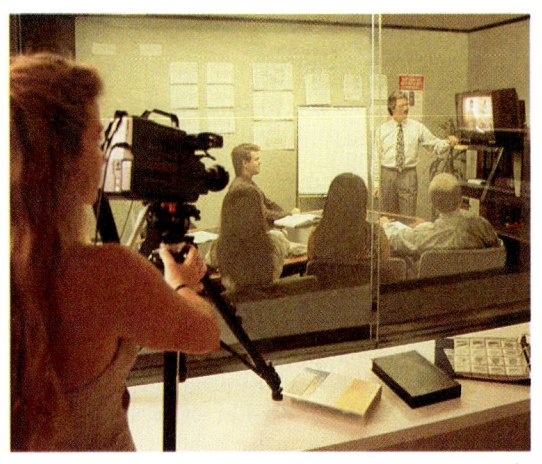

Advertising focus groups are designed to reveal consumers' opinions about and emotional responses to a product.

What Do You Think? ⭐TEKS

1. What are some of the positive and negative aspects of using psychological research in developing advertising campaigns?
2. In what ways can an understanding of psychology help consumers evaluate an advertisement?

Enhancing the Lesson
For more information about the relationship between consumer demand and advertising, see Reading 67: *The Affluent Society* in *From the Source: Readings in Economics and Government with Answer Key*.

What Do You Think? Answers

1. positive aspects—advertising campaigns are more successful, and producers sell more as a result; consumers feel better about the products they buy; advertisements are more exciting and interesting; advertisements are better able to inform consumers about the products they want; negative aspects—consumers may decide to buy a product based on emotional responses to advertising, not because they actually need the product or because it is a good buy; advertisements may not provide as much actual product information. ⭐11A

2. If consumers understand the methods advertisers are using to try to influence their buying behavior, they will be better able to ignore the psychology of advertising and focus on making the best economic decision.

price results in an increased demand for that product's complementary goods. Note that the effect of a price change on a product's complementary goods is the opposite of the effect of such a change on that product's substitute goods.

Consumer Expectations

Have you ever bought something in anticipation of having more money from a new job or from a raise in your allowance? If so, you probably shifted demand by way of expectations of your future income. Consumer expectations can dramatically influence shifts in the demand curve.

Suppose that you work at a restaurant on the weekends. The owner announces that all employees will receive a raise of 50 cents per hour. You have been hoping to buy a particular book, and you know that soon you will be able to afford the purchase. After some thought, you decide to buy the book today—even though you will not receive your raise for two weeks. By taking this approach, you have increased the demand for the book even though your income has not yet increased.

If, on the other hand, you anticipate a lower income because of a series of layoffs at the restaurant, you probably will choose to delay many of your purchases. Generally, when consumers are pessimistic about their future incomes, the overall level of demand for goods and services in the economy decreases.

SUPPLY & DEMAND *Paint brushes and paint are complementary goods.* **What other complementary goods come to mind?**

SECTION 2 REVIEW

Q: 1, 2, 3a, 3b, 4

1. **Identify and Explain:**
   determinants of demand
   substitute goods
   complementary goods

2. **Identifying Cause and Effect:** Copy the graphic organizer. Use it to explain how a change in the price of a product affects demand for its substitute goods and its complementary goods.

   Effects of Price Change on Demand for Substitute Goods and Complementary Goods

   Homework Practice Online
   keyword: SM3 HP3

3. **Finding the Main Idea**
   a. How is a shift in demand different from a change in the quantity demanded?
   a. Name the five main determinants that can cause shifts in demand. Give at least two examples of how each of these determinants have affected your demand for a product.

4. **Writing and Critical Thinking**
   Making Predictions: Suppose that consumers' expectations about the overall economy are high. As a result, people make large purchases in anticipation of better wages. Unfortunately, over the next few months the economy does not perform as well as they had hoped.
   Consider the following:
   • what will happen to the general level of demand
   • how this experience will affect consumer expectations in the future

---

Caption Answer
Answers will vary. Some examples include computers and printers, hamburger patties and hamburger buns, and bicycles and bicycle helmets.

SECTION 2 REVIEW ANSWERS

1. determinants of demand (56), substitute goods (60), complementary goods (62) **7A, 24A**

2. Increasing a product's price causes an increase in demand for the product's substitute goods and a decrease in demand for the product's complementary goods; decreasing a product's price has the opposite effect. **7A, 23A, 24D**

3a. A shift in demand refers to a change in the demand of a product at each and every price; a change in the quantity demanded refers to a change in the demand of a product at a specific price. **7A**

3b. consumer tastes and preferences, market size, income, prices of related goods, and consumer expectations; Examples will vary but should reflect an understanding of each concept. **7A**

4. Demand decreases. Future consumer expectations will probably not be so high or optimistic. **7A, 23A**

SECTION 3
ELASTICITY OF DEMAND

READ TO DISCOVER
1. What is demand elasticity?
2. What is the difference between elastic and inelastic demand?
3. How is demand elasticity measured?

ECONOMICS DICTIONARY
elasticity of demand
elastic demand
inelastic demand
total revenue

As you have learned, the law of demand describes the inverse relationship between price and the quantity demanded. For example, if a movie theater increases the price of its matinees from $4 to $5, fewer people are likely to attend these showings. The quantity of movie tickets demanded decreases because of the ticket-price increase. But how much does the quantity demanded decrease when a product's price increases? How many fewer people will go to the matinees at the higher price?

Manufacturers, sellers, and other businesspeople need to know this type of information in order to make good business decisions. Will lowering their products' prices by 10 or 20 percent increase the quantity demanded and the theaters' income? Can they afford to lower their prices at all? If they increase prices, will their income still be high enough to stay in business?

Businesspeople can answer questions such as those described above by determining the elasticity of demand for their products. **Elasticity of demand** is the degree to which changes in a good's price affect the quantity demanded by consumers. The demand for a product can be elastic or inelastic.

Elastic Demand

Elastic demand exists when a small change in a good's price causes a major, opposite change in the quantity demanded. Thus, demand is elastic when a small decrease in a good's price causes a significant increase in the quantity demanded. Demand is also elastic when a small increase in a good's price results in a significant decrease in the quantity demanded.

Certain kinds of goods tend to have elastic demand. A good's elasticity can change if

- the product is not a necessity
- there are readily available substitutes or
- the product's cost represents a large portion of consumers' income.

SUPPLY & DEMAND *Portable tape players often are expensive and are not a necessity.* **Is the demand for portable tape players elastic or inelastic?**

DEMAND 63

Sidebar

Transparency

An overhead transparency of Figure 3.4 is available in *Transparency Resources*. See Transparency 8: Elastic Demand for Pizza.

Caption Answer

The curve is almost horizontal, showing that a small increase in the price of pizza causes a large decrease in the quantity demanded. ★7A, 23F

Themes in Economics

THE ROLE OF GOVERNMENT

Electricity is a good that is both essential and has few available substitutes. As a result, it has a highly inelastic demand. Because electricity can be efficiently produced only in large quantities, natural monopolies occur. To prevent monopolistic producers from charging consumers exorbitantly high prices, the U.S. government regulates the prices these utility companies can charge. ■

Caption Answer

Answers will vary. Some examples include salt, flour, and gasoline.

ELASTIC DEMAND FOR PIZZA

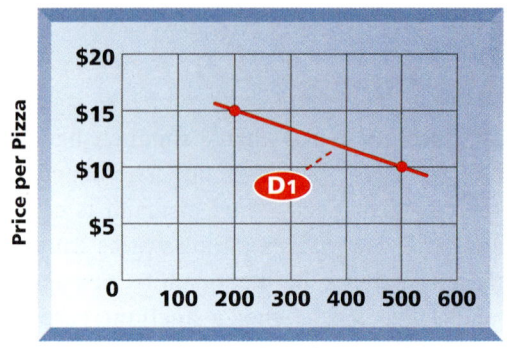

FIGURE 3.4 A product has elastic demand when small changes in price result in major changes in demand. **How does the slope of the demand curve above indicate elastic demand for pizza?** ★TEKS

You can apply these three factors to determine if a product has elastic demand. Consider pizza, for example. Though some people are very fond of pizza, it is not a necessity. In addition, pizza has readily available substitutes. In fact, pizza has many substitutes, such as sandwiches and tacos. Competing restaurants often are located next to each other, so substitutes generally are only a few steps away.

Consider the third factor—the cost of a product compared to consumers' income. Here, the effect is not so clear-cut. If the price of the pizza represents a relatively large portion of your weekly income as a student, a rise in the price of pizza can have a large impact on your weekly budget. So if the price of a small pizza rose from $4.50 to $5.50, you probably would eat less pizza and switch to a less expensive meal.

The price of pizza represents a much smaller portion of the incomes earned by people with full-time jobs, however. A rise in the price of pizza might not affect their quantity demanded as much as it affects yours. Overall, however, the fact that pizza is not a necessity and that so many substitutes are readily available results in an elastic demand.

You can see the elastic demand for pizza in Figure 3.4. The curve indicating elasticity (D$_1$) is almost horizontal, showing that a small increase in the price of pizza causes a large decrease in the quantity demanded as consumers switch to lower-priced substitutes. Likewise, a relatively small decrease in price causes a large increase in quantity demanded as sandwich-purchasers switch to pizza.

Inelastic Demand

Inelastic demand exists when a change in a good's price has little impact on the quantity demanded. Certain kinds of goods tend to have inelastic demand. A good usually has inelastic demand if

- the product is a necessity
- there are few or no readily available substitutes for the product or
- the product's cost represents a small portion of consumers' income.

Salt is an example of a good with inelastic demand. It is a necessity, it has few substitutes, and at a price of about 40 cents a box, salt represents a small portion of people's incomes. Even if the price of salt doubled, most people would

SUPPLY & DEMAND *Soap is a good that has inelastic demand.* **What kinds of goods tend to have inelastic demand?**

CHAPTER 3

Elasticity in Specific and General Markets

In determining a product's elasticity, remember that consumers' responses to price changes can vary, depending on whether you are looking at a specific or general market for that product. Think again of the photograph metaphor—that is, think of looking at a product's demand as taking a snapshot at a particular point in time. When you take this picture, you can take a close-up shot or you can step back and take a wide-angle shot. The close-up shot reveals the specific market, capturing only a small part of the product's overall "scene." In contrast, the wide-angle shot shows the larger, general market for the product. This picture includes all the background of the product's market.

But how does the scope of the picture—whether it is a close-up shot or a wide-angle shot—affect how you will view the elasticity of demand for a product? Consider the market for a basic necessity: flour. If you take a wide-angle picture of this market, demand is inelastic. If the consume the same amount because they must use salt, there is no alternative, and the higher price of 80 cents still represents only a tiny portion of their income.

Consider another example—soap. Is demand for this product elastic or inelastic? Determine how the three factors affect this product. It is essential—soap is necessary for washing.

This product does not have readily available substitutes. There are not many alternatives to soap. Other cleaning substances generally are too harsh for use on skin, making these substances poor substitutes.

Look at what portion of people's incomes the cost of soap represents. Soap is inexpensive and represents a small portion of people's incomes. Even if the price of soap doubled, it still would be very affordable.

The graph in Figure 3.5 illustrates the inelastic demand curve for soap. The demand curve D_1 on the graph is almost vertical, showing that even after a large increase in the price of soap there is a relatively small change in the quantity of soap demanded by consumers.

SUPPLY & DEMAND *Flour is a necessary good with inelastic demand in a general market.* **Under what circumstances might the demand for flour be elastic?**

INELASTIC DEMAND FOR SOAP

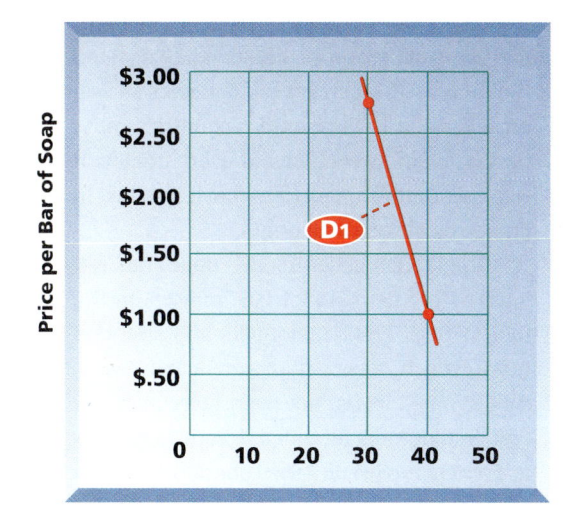

FIGURE 3.5 The quantity of soap demanded during a one-month period indicates demand elasticity. **What is the relationship between price and demand for products with inelastic demand?**

Caption Answer
when the demand for flour is examined in a specific, local market

Themes in Economics

SUPPLY & DEMAND Time is another factor that affects a product's demand elasticity. When a product's price changes, it takes consumers and the market time to respond to the change. Therefore, in general, the more time that passes following a price change, the more elastic a product's demand becomes.

For example, an increase in the admission price of amusement parks will result in some drop in quantity demanded right away. However, some people will have already made plans to attend the park and will not have time to change these plans. They will go to the park despite the rise in the price of admission. As time passes, though, more people will have time to choose other, cheaper vacation destinations.

Transparency

An overhead transparency of Figure 3.5 is available in *Transparency Resources*. See Transparency 9: Inelastic Demand for Soap.

Caption Answer

A change in the product's price has little impact on the quantity demanded.

7A, 23F

DEMAND 65

Across the Curriculum

MATHEMATICS To calculate a product's elasticity of demand in response to a price change, economists divide the percentage that the product's quantity demanded changed by the percentage that the product's price changed. For example, if a 10 percent price increase for movie tickets results in a 45 percent drop in quantity demanded, then the movie tickets' elasticity of demand, represented by the symbol E_d, is 4.5. If $E_d > 1$, as it is in this case, then demand is elastic. On the other hand, if a 10 percent price increase in movie tickets results in a 2 percent drop in prices, then the movie tickets' elasticity of demand is $E_d = 0.2$. If $E_d < 1$, as it is in this case, then demand is inelastic. ■

Enhancing the Lesson

For more information on the European Union, see the International Organizations section on the *Researcher Online*.

Global Exchange

Movie Madness

What movies are hot at the box office in other countries? Probably the same movies you are going to see. The demand for movies made in the United States is high around the world.

In fact, many movies—no matter how successful they may be in the United States—earn a large percentage of their profits in other countries. For instance, while the movie *Titanic* made over $601 million in the United States, it made over $1.2 billion abroad! American movies have become so popular overseas that U.S. film studios are beginning to add more foreign locations and film stars to their movies to help attract even larger foreign audiences.

Despite the enormous popularity of U.S. movies overseas, a film's success is not always welcomed by foreign trade officials. In a recent international trade agreement, members of the European Union (EU) decided that at least 51 percent of all movies shown on television in EU member countries must be European. French law is even stricter. It requires that 60 percent of movies shown in France be of European origin.

The French government's policy has not lowered the demand for U.S. movies. In the mid-1980s, French filmgoers still attended more French movies than American movies. By the mid-1990s, however, twice as many French filmgoers attended American movies as French movies. In 1999 about 56 percent of the total box-office receipts in France went to American films, while only 31 percent went to French films. Governments do not seem to have very much luck in regulating consumer demand.

---

price of flour rises, the quantity demanded does not decrease proportionately. People still will consume about the same amount of flour because it is a basic staple that has no substitutes and it does not require a large portion of people's income.

If, however, you take a close-up shot of a specific, local market for flour, demand is elastic. Suppose that one of four grocery stores in town raises the price of flour by 75 cents per sack. The quantity of flour demanded at that store likely will fall off—not because people switch to lower-priced substitutes or consume less flour, but because they will buy the lower-priced flour at the other three grocery stores in town.

For these grocery store owners, demand for flour on the local level is elastic because of competition, even though the overall, general market for flour is inelastic. Looking only at the general, inelastic market for flour instead of at the specific, elastic market would lead these business owners to make incorrect pricing decisions based on incomplete and inaccurate information.

Measuring Elasticity

As noted at the beginning of this section, movie theater owners and other businesspeople try to determine demand elasticity so that they can set prices for their products. Businesspeople also can measure demand elasticity for their goods and services.

One of the simplest ways to measure demand elasticity is through the total-revenue test. **Total revenue**—sometimes called total receipts—refers to the total income that a business receives from selling its products. By monitoring any changes in a business's (or market's) total revenue before and after changes in the price of a product, you can determine the elasticity of demand for that product.

Keep in mind that the degree of elasticity of a product can vary for different price ranges. In fact, demand for a product can be elastic over one range of prices and inelastic over another. The total-revenue test indicates these changes in demand elasticity.

MOVIE TICKET REVENUE AND DEMAND ELASTICITY

DEMAND ELASTICITY AND TOTAL REVENUE

Price per Ticket	Quantity Demanded	Total Revenue
$5.00	10,000	$50,000
$4.50	22,500	$101,250
$4.00	30,000	$120,000
$3.50	31,250	$109,375
$3.00	32,500	$97,500
$2.50	33,750	$84,375

EFFECT OF DEMAND ELASTICITY AND TOTAL REVENUE

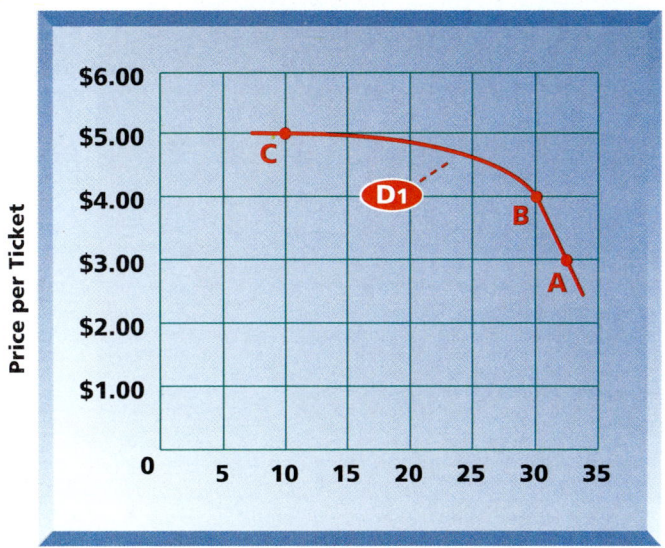

FIGURE 3.6 Demand for some products may be elastic in some price ranges and inelastic in other ranges. **During a one-month period, what price range shows inelastic demand for movie tickets?**

Total Revenue and Elastic Demand A drop in a business's total revenue from a price increase indicates elastic demand for the product. If, for example, movie theater owners raise the price of a matinee ticket from $4 to $5, many people likely will rent movies on videotape instead of going to movie theaters. Thus, even though the price per ticket is higher, the theater owners' total revenue decreases because so many more people will stay away from the theaters at the higher $5 price.

You can see this decrease in total revenue in the table in Figure 3.6. The table shows that when the price is $4 per ticket, the number of tickets sold during a one-month period is 30,000. The total revenue earned by the movie theaters in this town for this period of time is $120,000 ($4 × 30,000). When the price is raised to $5 per ticket, however, the number of tickets sold decreases to 10,000. Total revenue in turn decreases to $50,000 ($5 × 10,000). The drop in total revenue indicates that the demand for movie tickets in this price range is elastic.

You can confirm this elasticity of demand by looking at the demand curve in Figure 3.6. The portion of the graph from point B to point C ($4 to $5) is not very steep. It shows that this change in price results in a drop in total revenue. In contrast, if the price was $5, then lowering the price to $4 would raise total revenue from $50,000 to $120,000. If lowering the price of a product raises total revenue, then demand is elastic.

Total Revenue and Inelastic Demand In contrast, a rise in a business's total revenue because of a price increase indicates inelastic demand for the business's good or service. Look again at the table in Figure 3.6. If the price of a movie ticket is only $2.50, some 33,750 people go to matinees. Total revenue is $84,375 ($2.50 × 33,750). If the price is raised to $3.50, the number of people attending the matinees

DEMAND 67

Transparency
An overhead transparency of Figure 3.6 is available in *Transparency Resources*. See Transparency 10: Movie Ticket Revenue and Demand Elasticity.

Caption Answer
$3.00 to $4.00 (point A to B) 7A, 7B, 23F

Themes in Economics

COMPETITION & MARKET STRUCTURE Demand for mobile phones has soared in recent years. In 2000, worldwide purchases of mobile phones, which totaled more than 400 million units, outstripped the total sales of personal computers, pagers, laptops, televisions, and cars combined. Despite the continued growth in mobile phone sales, there is concern that demand may be slackening. In addition, many mobile phones cannot provide consumers with speedy and convenient access to the Internet. However, some analysts predict that new technology that speeds up data transfer on wireless phones will soon be available. Such an improvement in technology could spark new demand for the next generation of mobile phones. ■

Caption Answer

with the total-revenue test

SECTION 3
REVIEW ANSWERS

1. elasticity of demand (63), elastic demand (63), inelastic demand (64), total revenue (66) **7A, 24A**

2. elastic demand—not necessities, have readily available substitutes, cost a large portion of consumers' incomes; inelastic demand—necessities, no readily available substitutes, cost a small portion of consumers' incomes **7A, 23A, 24D**

3a. It helps producers set the best prices for their products.

3b. Demand for a product may be inelastic in general, but elastic in a specific market. Also, the degree of a product's demand elasticity can vary across price ranges. Examples will vary. **7A**

3c. A drop in total revenue after a price increase indicates elastic demand; an increase indicates inelastic demand.

4. The term *elasticity* describes the ability to adapt to and recover from change; it is a good term to describe elastic and inelastic demand because these concepts refer to how consumer demand adapts to price changes. **7A, 23A**

---

thus causes an increase in total revenue to $109,375 ($3.50 × 31,250). The rise in total revenue indicates that the demand for movie tickets in this price range is inelastic. Changes in total revenue and changes in price move the same direction on an inelastic demand curve.

The curve in Figure 3.6 illustrates this inelastic demand. From point A to point B ($3 to $4), the curve is very steep. It shows that a change in price in this part of the graph results in an increase in total revenue.

Maximizing Total Revenue Look again at the table in Figure 3.6. At what point is total revenue maximized for the movie theater owners? In other words, at this point in time and for this particular market, what is the price that theaters should charge to achieve the highest revenue? You can see that at $4 per ticket, 30,000 people flock to the matinees, for a total revenue of $120,000 ($4 × 30,000). If movie theaters charge either more or less than $4, total revenue drops. At the price of $4, therefore, the movie theaters' total revenue is highest. Measuring the varying elasticity of demand for their product directs the owners toward the pricing decision that will earn the most revenue.

SUPPLY & DEMAND *Businesspeople—such as movie theater owners—need to measure demand elasticity in order to set prices.* **How can demand elasticity be measured?**

remains high—31,250. Even after the price increase, many consumers consider matinees to be worthwhile, lower-priced entertainment than other recreational activities. The price change

---

SECTION 3 REVIEW

1. Identify and Explain:
elasticity of demand
elastic demand
inelastic demand
total revenue

2. Summarizing: Copy the chart below. Use it to describe and give examples of the type of products that tend to have elastic demand and the type that tend to have inelastic demand.

Elastic Demand	Inelastic Demand

Homework Practice Online
keyword: SM3 HP3

★TEKS Q: 1, 2, 3b, 4

3. Finding the Main Idea

a. Why is determining demand elasticity important in economics?

b. How can a product have both elastic and inelastic demand? Think of an example that is not used in the book to illustrate this situation.

c. How does the total-revenue test indicate demand elasticity?

4. Writing and Critical Thinking

Drawing Conclusions: Look up the word *elasticity* in a dictionary. Explain why this term is appropriate in describing the two different types of demand.

Consider the following:
- products that have elastic demand
- products that have inelastic demand

68 CHAPTER 3

Economics IN THE NEWS

Consumer Demand and the Food Distribution Industry

Until recently, boxes of Wheaties™ cereal contained both curly and flat flakes. However, market researchers found that consumers preferred curly to flat flakes. As a result, General Mills, the manufacturer of Wheaties™, began buying only the strain of wheat that produced curly flakes. This purchasing decision forced farmers and grain handlers to handle wheat that produces curly flakes separately.

This is just one example of how consumer demand shapes the food industry. In recent years, social changes, technological advances, and new business management practices have produced fundamental changes in the food industry.

Economists have found that several factors have changed consumer tastes and helped make the food industry more responsive to changes in consumer demand. One factor is the rise of women in the workforce. The typical household now has more income to spend on food but less time to prepare it. Thus, there has been increased demand for ready-made foods. At the same time, consumers have developed tastes for a wider variety of foods, making it more important for food stores to keep track of changes in consumer demand.

A second factor involves technological changes that have made it easier for grocery stores to monitor changes in consumer demand. One such example is the bar code, which began replacing paper price tags in the 1970s. By scanning bar codes, grocers can collect and computerize information about products, allowing them to more efficiently keep track of, among other things, how much of a particular item is being sold.

A third factor, changes in business practices, has also enabled retailers to respond to consumer demand quickly and efficiently. Wal-Mart pioneered many of the new practices in the 1980s. It was the first company to purchase and restock items daily and to share information and cooperate more closely with its suppliers. Such cooperation was aided by advances in information technology, which allow stores and distributors to share information, such as that scanned from bar codes.

Another change in business practices has been the consolidation of grocery stores into ever-larger chains. Large grocery store chains are more efficient. By purchasing and transporting goods in larger quantities, they can cut costs. For instance, their greater purchasing power allows them to buy larger quantities of an item at a lower unit cost. All of these changes have made the food industry, the nation's largest retail industry, more efficient and responsive to changing consumer demands.

Closely tracking consumer demand and coordinating shipments from warehouses to arrive on store shelves in time is important across a number of industries, from food to durable goods.

What Do You Think? TEKS

1. In which direction does increased efficiency in the food industry move the demand curve?
2. Which of the determinants of demand is discussed in the feature?

> **WHY IT MATTERS TODAY**
> Changing business practices have an effect on the items that you purchase. Use CNNfyi.com or other **current events** sources to find additional examples of changing business practices. Record your findings in your Notebook.
>
> CNNfyi.com

Economics in the News Answers

1. to the right **7A**
2. consumer tastes and preferences **7A**

CHAPTER 3
Review Answers

Writing a Summary

Summaries should focus on the main points of each section. These may be found in the Read to Discover questions at the start of each section. Summaries should also use standard grammar, spelling, sentence structure, and punctuation. **7A, 24B, 24D**

Identifying Ideas

demand (51), law of demand (52), purchasing power (52), income effect (52), substitution effect (52), diminishing marginal utility (53), demand schedule (54), demand curve (54), determinants of demand (56), substitute goods (60), complementary goods (62), elasticity of demand (63) **7A, 24A**

Understanding Main Ideas

1. An increase in a product's price causes a decrease in quantity demanded, and vice versa. Consumer purchasing power, the availability of cheaper substitutes, and the tendency of a product's utility to diminish with additional purchases all contribute to the inverse effect of price changes on quantity demanded. **7A**

CHAPTER 3 Review

(Continued from page 69)

2. price; a shift in demand is a change in demand at every price and is the result of factors other than price **7A**

3. Complementary goods are commonly used with other goods. Substitute goods can replace similar goods when prices rise. Ice cream—ice cream cones/frozen yogurt, baseball tickets—hot dogs/hockey tickets, pencils—paper/pens

4. It helps them set the best prices for their products to maximize total revenues; by using the total-revenue test. **7A**

Reviewing Themes

1. There is an inverse relationship between a product's price and the quantity of demand for the product. **7A**

2. The total-revenue test is used to measure a product's elasticity of demand. A drop in total revenue following a price increase indicates elastic demand, while a rise in revenue following a price increase indicates inelastic demand.

3. The determinants of demand are consumer tastes and preferences, market size, income, prices of related goods (substitute goods and complementary goods), and consumer expectations. **7A**

Thinking Critically

1. apples—elastic (not a necessity, readily available substitutes, cost not a large portion of income); heart medicine—inelastic (a necessity, no substitutes, cost not a large portion of income); gasoline—inelastic (often a necessity, few

Writing a Summary ★TEKS

Using standard grammar, spelling, sentence structure, and punctuation, write a summary of the information in this chapter.

Identifying Ideas ★TEKS

1. demand
2. law of demand
3. purchasing power
4. income effect
5. substitution effect
6. diminishing marginal utility
7. demand schedule
8. demand curve
9. determinants of demand
10. substitute goods
11. complementary goods
12. elasticity of demand

Understanding Main Ideas ★TEKS

SECTION 1 *(pp. 51–55)*

1. State the law of demand in your own words. Be sure to include how the income effect, the substitution effect, and diminishing marginal utility relate to the law of demand.

2. What causes movement along a demand curve—in other words, a change in the quantity demanded? How does this movement differ from a shift in demand?

SECTION 2 *(pp. 56–62)*

3. What is the difference between a complementary good and a substitute good? Give an example of each kind of good for each of these products: ice cream, baseball game tickets, pencils.

SECTION 3 *(pp. 63–68)*

4. Why is determining demand elasticity important to business owners? How can business owners measure demand elasticity?

Reviewing Themes ★TEKS

1. **Supply and Demand** What does the law of demand state about the relationship between price and quantity demanded?

2. **Supply and Demand** How is elasticity of demand measured?

3. **Supply and Demand** What are the factors that can cause shifts in demand?

Thinking Critically ★TEKS

1. **Drawing Conclusions** Determine whether demand for each of the following products is elastic or inelastic: Granny Smith apples, heart medicine, gasoline. Explain your reasoning.

2. **Making Generalizations** Describe what happens to the demand curve for turkey in the United States in November. What happens to the curve after the holidays? Why do these changes occur? Plot a demand curve that assumes that turkey normally costs $1 a pound but increases to $2.25 a pound at Thanksgiving, while demand soars from 30 million to 90 million pounds in that time.

3. **Identifying Cause and Effect** Suppose that some children are planning to run a lemonade stand in your neighborhood this weekend. Given your newfound knowledge of demand, what advice would you give them in setting prices?

Writing about Economics

Review what you wrote about the term *demand* in your Economics Notebook at the beginning of this chapter. Would you revise your definition of demand now? Do you think your understanding of the law of demand will have an effect on your economic behavior in the future? Write a one-paragraph response in your Notebook.

Building Social Studies Skills

Interpreting the Chart ⭐TEKS

Study the chart below. Then use it to answer the questions that follow.

DEMAND SCHEDULE

Price per Hair Dryer	Quantity Demanded
$40	0
$30	10,000
$20	30,000
$10	40,000

1. What relationship does this chart show between hair dryers' prices and their demand.
   a. As demand increases, prices increase.
   b. As demand decreases, prices decrease.
   c. As price decreases, demand increases.
   d. There is not a clear relationship between price and demand.

2. Why do you think that there is demand elasticity for hair dryers. Use the demand schedule to create a graph of the demand curve for hair dryers.

Analyzing Primary Sources ⭐TEKS

Read the excerpt below from *Community College Times*. Then answer the questions that follow.

"California's summer budget battles are becoming commonplace, but they are placing community colleges and their students in uncommon positions.

"In a compromise hammered out behind closed doors last week [June 1993], legislators agreed to a budget that assumes a 50 percent increase in community colleges' fees—from the current $10 per unit to $15 per unit. The total price tag for a semester would not exceed $150. . . .

"Exactly what effect the new fees will have on community college student enrollment is unknown, but last year's big fee hike—coupled with other budgetary changes. . . was blamed for a 112,000 drop in attendance [last year]."

3. What is the author's point of view regarding student enrollment?
   a. Enrollment is increasing as a result of the economy.
   b. Enrollment is decreasing as a result of increased fees and tuition.
   c. Enrollment is remaining nearly the same.
   d. Decreases in students' fees are increasing enrollment.

4. The article states that the effect of the new fees on community college enrollment is "unknown." What effect do you predict they will have? Explain your answer.

Alternative Assessment

Building Your Portfolio ⭐TEKS

With your group, create a movie poster that "advertises" or illustrates one basic economic concept from the chapter. For example, you might create a poster of the movie *Cereal and Milk: A Love Story of Two Complementary Goods*. The poster should explain in words and images the economic concept your group has chosen. Assign members of the group to design the poster's layout, draw or find images, and write copy.

internet connect

Internet Activity: go.hrw.com
KEYWORD: SM3 EC3 ⭐TEKS

Access the Internet through the HRW Go site and navigate to the Department of Energy Web site. One table shows U.S. consumption of gasoline in barrels and the other shows price per gallon of gasoline for the past 50 years. Create demand schedules and demand curves to represent data for several years.

---

readily available substitutes, cost not a large portion of income) **7A, 23A**

2. It shifts to the right and then shifts back after the holidays. Turkey is commonly served during the holidays, so demand increases at each price. Graph should show price on the vertical axis, quantity on the horizontal axis, and a line moving left to right and upward to indicate increased demand despite increased price. **7A, 23A, 23B, 23F, 23G**

3. Answers should reflect an understanding of the income effect, the substitution effect, diminishing marginal utility, and elasticity of demand. **7A, 23A**

Writing about Economics

Students should discuss their initial definitions of demand as well as the ways, if any, that their understandings have changed. Students should also try to anticipate how their understanding of the law of demand might affect their consumption of goods in the future. **24D**

Building Social Studies Skills

1. c **7A, 23F, 23G**

2. Hair dryers are not a necessity. Demand curves should slope downward. **7A, 23B, 23F, 23G, 24C**

3. b **23E**

4. Students should predict that demand will probably decrease. Students should discuss the relationship between price and demand. **7A, 23A**

DEMAND 71

CHAPTER RESOURCE MANAGER

CHAPTER 4 SUPPLY

	OBJECTIVES	PACING GUIDE	REPRODUCIBLE RESOURCES
SECTION 1 **NATURE OF SUPPLY** (pp. 73–78)	▸ What is the difference between supply and quantity supplied? ▸ What does the law of supply state? ▸ What do supply schedules and supply curves illustrate? ▸ What is supply elasticity?	**Regular** 1.5 days **Block Scheduling** .5 day	**ELL** Spanish Study Guide 4.1 **ELL** English Study Guide 4.1 **PS** Reading 54: Elements of Political Economy **E** Challenge and Enrichment: Activity 4 **SM** Consumer Economics: Activity 4 **SM** Mathematics for Economics: Activity 4
SECTION 2 **CHANGES IN SUPPLY** (pp. 79–85)	▸ What does it mean for a product's supply to shift? ▸ What determinants might cause a product's supply curve to shift? ▸ How does a tax differ from a subsidy?	**Regular** 2 days **Block Scheduling** 1 day	**ELL** Spanish Study Guide 4.2 **ELL** English Study Guide 4.2
SECTION 3 **MAKING PRODUCTION DECISIONS** (pp. 86–92)	▸ Why do producers look at productivity when making supply decisions? ▸ How do varying levels of input affect the levels of output? ▸ How do changes in production costs affect producers' supply decisions?	**Regular** 2 days **Block Scheduling** 1 day	**ELL** Spanish Study Guide 4.3 **ELL** English Study Guide 4.3 **S** Simulations and Strategies for Teaching Economics: Activity 4

Chapter Resource Key

PS	Primary Sources	**A**	Assessment		Video
RS	Reading Support	**REV**	Review		Videodisc
E	Enrichment	**ELL**	Reinforcement and English Language Learners		Internet
S	Simulations		Transparencies		Holt Presentation Maker Using Microsoft® PowerPoint®
SM	Skills Mastery		CD-ROM		TEKS and TAKS

TECHNOLOGY RESOURCES	REINFORCEMENT, REVIEW, AND ASSESSMENT
• One-Stop Planner: Lesson 4.1 • Researcher Online • Homework Practice Online • CNN Presents Economics: Shopping the Internet • Transparencies 11 and 12 • Global Skillbuilder CD-ROM	**REV** Section 1 Review, p. 78 **A** Daily Quiz 4.1 ★ TAKS Every Day!
• One-Stop Planner: Lesson 4.2 • Researcher Online • Homework Practice Online • Transparency 13 • Global Skillbuilder CD-ROM	**REV** Section 2 Review, p. 85 **A** Daily Quiz 4.2 ★ TAKS Every Day!
• One-Stop Planner: Lesson 4.3 • Researcher Online • Homework Practice Online • Transparencies 14 and 15 • Global Skillbuilder CD-ROM	**REV** Section 3 Review, p. 92 **A** Daily Quiz 4.3 ★ TAKS Every Day!

Chapter Review and Assessment

SM Global Skillbuilder CD-ROM
HRW Go site
REV Reteaching Activity 4
REV Chapter 4 Review, pp. 94–95
A Chapter 4 Test Generator (on the One-Stop Planner)
A Chapter 4 Test
A Alternative Assessment Handbook

internet connect

HRW ONLINE RESOURCES
Go To: go.hrw.com
Then type in a keyword.

TEACHER HOME PAGE
KEYWORD: SM3 Teacher

CHAPTER INTERNET ACTIVITIES
KEYWORD: SM3 EC4
Choose an activity to:
• conduct research on the law of supply.
• create an aggregate supply curve.
• learn about production costs.

CHAPTER ENRICHMENT LINKS
KEYWORD: SM3 CH4

HOLT RESEARCHER ONLINE
KEYWORD: Holt Researcher

ONLINE ASSESSMENT
Homework Practice
KEYWORD: SM3 HP4
TAKS Review
KEYWORD: SM3 T4
Rubrics
KEYWORD: SS Rubrics

CONTENT UPDATES
KEYWORD: SS Content Updates

HOLT PRESENTATION MAKER
KEYWORD: SM3 PPT4

ONLINE READING SUPPORT
KEYWORD: SS Strategies

CURRENT EVENTS
KEYWORD: S3 Current Events

TEXAS ONLINE RESOURCES
KEYWORD: S3 TX

One-Stop Planner CD-ROM

It's easy to plan lessons, select resources, and print out materials for your students when you use the **Texas One-Stop Planner CD-ROM with Test Generator**.

LESSON 4.1 NATURE OF SUPPLY

TEXTBOOK PAGES 73-78

HOLT PRESENTATION MAKER
Access Illustrated LECTURE NOTES using Microsoft® PowerPoint® on the One-Stop Planner CD-ROM

OBJECTIVES

- Explain the difference between supply and quantity supplied.
- Explain what the law of supply states.
- Explain what supply schedules and supply curves illustrate.
- Describe supply elasticity.

MOTIVATE

Present the following scenario: To help defray the growing costs associated with the Senior Prom, this year's senior class has decided to raise money by holding a bake sale. The officers of the senior class have decided to sell cupcakes for $1 apiece, small cakes for $10, medium cakes for $18, large cakes for $24, and specialty cakes for $30. The officers are trying to decide how many of each size cake to make for the sale and are hoping that the economics classes might be able to give them some advice. Ask students what advice they would give the senior class officers. Encourage class discussion. Then tell students to keep this scenario in mind as they read through Section 1. ★23A, 23D

TEACH

Building a Vocabulary

Have students use spiral notebooks to create an Economics Dictionary to be used throughout the chapter. This dictionary might be used as an activity at the start of each new section or as a learning aid for sheltered English students or students having difficulty. List words that students will be expected to know for this section on the chalkboard. Have students use the information provided in the textbook or on the *Researcher CD-ROM* to list, define, and give an example of each term. ★24A

Understanding Main Concepts

Have students define the terms *supply* and *quantity supplied* (*supply*—the quantity of goods and services that producers are willing to sell at various possible prices during a given time period; *quantity supplied*—the quantity of a good or service that producers are willing to sell at each particular price during a given time period.) Then ask them to name the law that describes the interplay between price and quantity supplied (*the law of supply*). Have a student define the law of supply. (*Producers supply more goods and services when they can sell them at higher prices and fewer goods and services when they must sell them at lower prices.*) Ask why producers vary their supply of goods and services according to the law of supply. (*They are in pursuit of profits.*) Make certain that students understand the definition of profit (*total revenue minus the costs of production*). ★4A, 24A

Applying Ideas, Using Models

Remind students of the scenario they discussed at the start of class. Have them reconsider the scenario in light of the law of supply. Ask again how many cakes they would recommend supplying at each price based on the information available. Construct a supply schedule similar to the one below based on the class's responses.

Price per Cake	Quantity of Cake Supplied
$30	
$24	
$18	
$10	
$1	

Remind students that a supply schedule is a tool that shows the relationship between the price of a good or service and the quantity that producers will supply. Ask students to name another model that economists use to show the relationship between price and supply (*a supply curve*). Ask what a supply curve illustrates (*the information in a supply schedule*). Have students plot a supply curve based on the information in the class's supply schedule. Students may want to use the Graphing Tool on the *Researcher Online* to create their graphs. Refer students who need additional instruction on the skills used in this lesson to the *Global Skillbuilder* Lesson 11: Presenting Data Graphically. ★7B, 23B, 23F, 24C

Classifying Ideas

Tell students that they can determine if they made wise supply decisions by examining the elasticity of supply. Ask a student to define elasticity of supply *(the degree to which price changes affect the quantity supplied)*. Tell students that a product's supply, like its demand, can be either elastic or inelastic. Have students define the characteristics of elastic and inelastic supply *(elastic supply—product can be made quickly, cheaply, and using a few, readily available resources; inelastic supply—making the product requires a great deal of time, money, and resources that are not readily available)*. Have students provide some examples not mentioned in the textbook of products with elastic and inelastic supply. Then ask students if the senior bake sale cakes have elastic or inelastic supply, and why *(elastic supply because they satisfy the three characteristics)*.

Ask students if their supply decisions created a supply curve with elastic supply. Then discuss what supply curves would look like for products with perfectly elastic and perfectly inelastic supply *(perfectly elastic—horizontal line; perfectly inelastic—vertical line)*. Have students suggest situations where supply would be perfectly elastic and perfectly inelastic. ★23A

Comparing and Contrasting

Provide students with (or have them bring) a number of magazines, newspapers, and advertising inserts. Divide the class in half. Tell half of the students to find examples of products that they think have elastic supply, and the other half to find examples of products that they think have inelastic supply. When students are through, have volunteers share what they found with the class. ★23A

CLOSE

Call on students to summarize the material covered in the lesson. Then ask students if they as producers would rather face an elastic supply curve or an inelastic supply curve. Tell students to remember to consider the profit motive when discussing the question. ★4A, 23A

OPTIONS

Gifted Learners

Have students prepare reports on the federal government's treatment of profits since the 1930s. Have students use the *Researcher Online*, the library, in-class resources, and the Internet to find information. ★4A, 17B

Body-Kinesthetic Learners

Organize students into groups of two or three. You might want to pair students having difficulty with students who have mastered the material. Assign each group one of the economic concepts from the chapter. Tell each group to prepare a short skit illustrating their assigned economic concept in action. Give students 15 to 20 minutes to prepare their skits. Then have volunteers perform their skits. Open the performance up for discussion to make the performers answer questions about their concept. ★24A, 24D

Linguistic Learners

Have each student examine the financial sections of newspapers and magazines to find an instance demonstrating the law of supply. Tell students to write two or three paragraphs summarizing their example and explaining how it relates to the law of supply. Students may want to include their papers in their portfolios. ★23A

Visual-Spatial Learners

Have students create a comic strip or cartoon that visually depicts the concepts of elastic and inelastic supply. Tell students to look at the comic strip in Section 1 of the chapter for ideas. Have several volunteers share their cartoons with the class. Encourage the class to discuss how each cartoon depicts elastic and inelastic supply. Students may want to include their cartoons in their portfolios. ★24D

REVIEW

Have students complete the Section 1 Review on page 78. Use the answers in the Annotated Teacher's Edition to assess student mastery of this section.

ASSESS

To assess student mastery of this section, have students complete Daily Quiz 4.1 in *Daily Quizzes with Answer Key*. For additional assessment options, see *Alternative Assessment Handbook* on the *One-Stop Planner CD-ROM*.

ADDITIONAL RESOURCES

Fanning, Connell, et al. *The General Theory of Profit Equilibrium: Keynes and the Entrepreneur Economy.* 1998. St. Martin's Press.

LESSON 4.2 CHANGES IN SUPPLY

TEXTBOOK PAGES 79–85

HOLT PRESENTATION MAKER
Access Illustrated LECTURE NOTES using Microsoft® PowerPoint® on the One-Stop Planner CD-ROM

OBJECTIVES

- Explain what it means for a product's supply to shift.
- Identify determinants that might cause a product's supply curve to shift. ★7A
- Describe the difference between a tax and a subsidy.

MOTIVATE

Remind students of the definition of profit *(total revenues minus costs of production)*. Have students review what some of the costs of production are *(wages and salaries, rent, interest on loans, utilities, raw materials, and any other goods and services used to manufacture a product)*. Then tell students to imagine that they own a coffee plantation. A recent strike by coffee bean pickers has increased their costs of production, cutting into their profits. Ask students how this situation will affect the amount of coffee that they supply at each price. *(It will result in a decrease.)* Have students consider and debate options for correcting the situation.

After a brief period of discussion, explain to students that supply, like demand, is affected by factors other than price. Ask students to suggest what some of these factors might be. Tell students to keep the factors in mind as they read through Section 2. ★7A, 23C, 25A

TEACH

Building a Vocabulary

List the important terms for this section on the chalkboard and tell students to add them to their Economics Dictionary. Tell students to use the information provided in the text or on the *Researcher CD-ROM* to list, define, and give an example of each term. ★24A

Applying an Economic Model

Ask students to recall the definition of a supply curve. *(A supply curve shows the quantity of a good or service supplied at each price during a specific period of time.)* Remind students that a supply curve depicts supply for a specific period of time, and that price is the only factor affecting the quantity supplied. Have students examine Figure 4.4: Supply Curve Shifts (Transparency 13). Ask students what happens if the price of car stereos increases from $200 to $400. *(The intersection of the new price and the quantity supplied moves to a different point along the supply curve.)*

Next, ask students what it means for a product's supply to shift. *(A product's supply shifts when producers supply a different quantity of the product at each and every price.)* Then ask what would happen if a technological advance made it cheaper to produce this model of stereo. *(The producer would increase the quantity of car stereos supplied at each and every price, thereby shifting the entire supply curve to the right.)* Call on students to describe why this shift in supply occurs. *(If stereos are cheaper to make, then there is more potential for profit, so producers supply more product.)* Refer students who need additional instruction on the skills used in this lesson to the *Global Skillbuilder* Lesson 10: Reading Graphs. ★7B, 23A, 23F, 23G

Analyzing Ideas

Have students list and describe the six determinants of supply *(prices of resources, government tools, technology, competition, prices of related goods, and producer expectations)*. Then ask students to give examples not mentioned in the text of how each of these determinants can affect supply. Next, ask students how the supply curve of coffee would shift in each of the following situations:

- this year's coffee bean harvest is the largest to date *(right)*
- coffee bean pickers go on strike *(left)*
- Congress approves a tax cut for small businesses *(right)*
- agricultural subsidies for coffee bean plantations are decreased *(left)*
- Congress passes a law regulating how brewed coffee must be stored until it is served *(right)*
- a new invention makes it easier and faster to harvest coffee beans *(right)*
- coffee shops increase in popularity, and their numbers increase rapidly *(right)*
- the price of herbal teas increases because of their popularity with college students *(left)*
- producers expect the popularity of coffee shops to continue to increase *(right)* ★7A, 23A, 23E

71E

Identifying Cause and Effect

Organize students into six groups and assign each group one of the determinants of supply. Tell students to imagine that they are opening a pizzeria. Each group's task is to analyze its assigned determinant of supply in relation to the start-up of the pizzeria and then prepare a supply briefing to present to the class. Questions students might consider include: What types of resources are necessary to run a pizzeria? What factors could cause a change in the price and/or availability of needed resources? What kinds of technology are involved in running a pizzeria? In what ways might changing technology affect supply in this business? How does competition affect the pizzeria market? What kinds of related goods are involved in the pizzeria business? How might a change in the price of related goods affect this business? On what should expectations of future sales and demand be based? ★7A, 23A, 23C, 24D, 26A

Comparing and Contrasting

Tell students that they are now going to focus on just one of the determinants of supply: government tools. Write the terms *tax*, *subsidy*, and *regulation* on the chalkboard. Have students distinguish among the three terms and describe how each can shift supply. Then have students discuss the benefits and disadvantages of each for producers, consumers, and government. ★7A, 15A, 23A, 24A

CLOSE

Review with students what it means for a product's supply to shift, and the determinants that can cause this shift. Then have students suggest how various historical and recent technological advances have affected supply in various markets. ★23A, 26D

OPTIONS

Students Having Difficulty

Pair students having difficulty with students who have mastered the material. Tell each pair of students to make an outline of the main concepts covered in Section 2 of the chapter.

Gifted Learners

As a class, discuss what is meant by supply shocks. Then have students research the OPEC oil embargo of the 1970s and write a report on the impact of this event on the supply of various products in the United States. Have students use the *Researcher Online*, the library, in-class resources, and the Internet to find information. Students might want to enhance their reports with charts, graphs, and illustrations. When students are through, discuss the event as a class, and ask students if they can name any other supply shocks in the history of the United States. ★14A, 23B, 23C, 23E, 24B, 24C, 24D

Linguistic Learners

Have students use the *Researcher Online*, the library, in-class resources, and the Internet to research a specific company or business to determine which employees are responsible for analyzing the determinants of supply for that business's product. Tell students to imagine that they are going to interview one of these individuals and to prepare at least 10 interview questions to ask. Have students actually conduct the interviews, if possible. Have those students who conducted actual interviews share their findings and experiences with the class. ★23C, 23E, 24D

REVIEW

Have students complete the Section 2 Review on page 85. Use the answers in the Annotated Teacher's Edition to assess student mastery of this section.

ASSESS

To assess student mastery of this section, have students complete Daily Quiz 4.2 in *Daily Quizzes with Answer Key*. For additional assessment options, see *Alternative Assessment Handbook* on the *One-Stop Planner CD-ROM*.

ADDITIONAL RESOURCES

Buckley, Andrew. *Buying Electricity and Gas in the Competitive Marketplace*. 1998. Grover Publishing Ltd.

Colin, Wren. *Industrial Subsidies: The U.K. Experience*. 1996. St. Martin's Press.

Finegan, Brian. *The Federal Subsidy Beast: The Rise of a Supreme Power in a Once Great Democracy*. 2000. Alary Press.

LESSON 4.3 MAKING PRODUCTION DECISIONS

TEXTBOOK PAGES 86–92

HOLT PRESENTATION MAKER Access Illustrated LECTURE NOTES using Microsoft® PowerPoint® on the One-Stop Planner CD-ROM

OBJECTIVES

- Explain why producers look at productivity when making supply decisions.
- Describe how varying the levels of input affects the levels of output.
- Explain how changes in production costs affect producers' supply decisions.

MOTIVATE

Place a medium-sized table in the front of the class. On this table, place three pairs of scissors, two tape dispensers or staplers, and several packages of construction paper. Have two students sit at the table. Tell them that they are employees with the Fabulous Paper Chain Company and that this table is their "factory." The students' task is to create as many 3-ring paper chains as possible in five minutes. At the end of five minutes, stop them and count the number of paper chains that they have produced. Record this number on the board.

Next, have two more students join the company as new workers. Once again, give the students five minutes to create as many 3-ring paper chains as possible. After five minutes, record how many additional paper chains have been made. Continue to repeat the exercise, adding several more students to the group of workers each time until the entire class is working. Then have students analyze the effect of adding workers on the number of paper chains produced. Help students see that at some point, the addition of new workers did not result in increased marginal product or total product. Tell students to keep this activity in mind as they read through Section 3. ★2B, 23A, 23D

TEACH

Building a Vocabulary

List the important terms for this section on the chalkboard and tell students to add them to their Economics Dictionary. Tell students to use the information provided in the text or on the *Researcher CD-ROM* to list, define, and give an example of each term. ★24A

Understanding Main Concepts

Review with students the definition of productivity *(the amount of goods and services produced per unit of input)*. Then ask them why producers examine productivity when making supply decisions *(to maximize efficiency and profits)*. Next, ask what producers examine when trying to increase productivity *(how varying the level of input affects total product and marginal product)*. Have students examine Figure 4.5: Productivity of the Golden Duck Company (Transparency 14) and define total product and marginal product *(total product—all the product a company makes with a given amount of input during a given period of time; marginal product—the change in output generated by adding one more unit of input)*. Make certain that students understand how to calculate marginal product *(total product at one level of input minus total product at the previous level of input)*. Then ask them to name the basic economic principle that describes the effect that varying the level of an input has on total and marginal product *(the law of diminishing returns)*. Have students describe what this law states *(as more of one input is added to a fixed supply of other resources, productivity increases up to a point, after which the marginal product diminishes and eventually results in negative marginal product and decreased total product)*. Ask students to list and define the three stages of production that the law of diminishing returns predicts *(increasing marginal returns, diminishing marginal returns, and negative marginal returns)* and identify each stage in Figure 4.5. Refer students who need additional instruction on the skills used in this lesson to the *Global Skillbuilder* Lesson 10: Reading Graphs. ★2B, 23A

Mastering Concepts, Creating Charts and Graphs

Have students re-examine the number of paper chains that they produced with varying levels of student workers. Then ask them to identify the stages of increasing marginal returns, diminishing marginal returns, and negative marginal returns. Next, organize students into groups of two or three. Tell the groups to create a production schedule and a production curve for the paper-chain activity using Figure 4.5 as a guide. Each group should indicate on their graph the three stages of the law of diminishing returns. Students may want to use the

Graphing Tool on the *Researcher Online* to create their graphs. Refer students who need additional instruction on the skills used in this lesson to the *Global Skillbuilder* Lesson 11: Presenting Data Graphically. ★23B, 23F, 24C, 24D

Classifying Information

Tell students that, in addition to productivity, producers also look at their costs of production when making supply decisions. Briefly review with students what they learned about producers' costs of production in Sections 1 and 2. Then ask why producers are interested in analyzing their costs of production *(because these costs directly affect profit, and by analyzing them, producers can determine appropriate production goals and potential profits)*. Next, ask students to name and define the four categories of production costs that producers analyze *(fixed costs or overhead, variable costs, total costs, and marginal costs)*.

Have students examine Figure 4.6: Marginal Product and Costs (Transparency 15) and describe what it shows. Use the chart to guide students in a discussion about how changes in production costs affect producers' supply decisions. To make certain that students understand how marginal costs are calculated, have them determine the marginal costs for several different increases in the level of production at the Golden Duck Company. Then ask students: Based on Figure 4.6, how many workers should the Golden Duck Company employ, and why? *(They should employ 11 workers because that is when marginal product is maximized and marginal costs are lowest.)* ★2B, 23A, 23F, 23G, 25B

CLOSE

Review with students all the economic concepts that producers examine when making supply decisions—the laws of demand and supply, elasticity of demand and supply, shifts in the demand and supply curves, productivity, and the costs of production. Encourage students to examine how producers synthesize this information to make production decisions, set prices, and maximize profits.

OPTIONS

Sheltered English Students

Pair sheltered English students with students fluent in English. Tell each pair to create a poster that visually represents or depicts the law of diminishing returns. Each pair should write a descriptive caption as well. Students may want to include their posters in their portfolios. ★23A, 24C, 24D

Students Having Difficulty

Pair students having difficulty with those who have mastered the material. Write the following sets of terms on the chalkboard. Then tell student pairs to compare and contrast the terms in each set.
- total product and marginal product
- fixed costs and variable costs
- total costs and marginal costs ★23A, 24A

Musical-Rhythmic Learners

Encourage students (or groups of students) with musical-rhythmic gifts to create a rap or other type of song that describes what happens in each stage of the law of diminishing returns. Have students perform their songs for the class. Students may want to include their songs in their portfolios. ★24D

REVIEW

Have students complete the Section 3 Review on page 92. Use the answers in the Annotated Teacher's Edition to assess student mastery of this section.

ASSESS

To assess student mastery of this section, have students complete Daily Quiz 4.3 in *Daily Quizzes with Answer Key*. For additional assessment options, see *Alternative Assessment Handbook* on the *One-Stop Planner CD-ROM*.

RETEACH

For students having difficulty with the lessons, have them complete Reteaching Activity 4. This activity is located in *Reteaching Activities with Answer Key*.

ADDITIONAL RESOURCES

Fuller, Jim and Jeanne Farrington. *From Training to Performance Improvement: Navigating the Transition*. 1999. Jossey-Bass Inc.

Hickman, Craig R. *The Productivity Game: An Interactive Business Game Where You Make or Break the Company*. 1995. Prentice Hall Trade.

Otabil, Mensa. *Four Laws of Productivity*. 1997. Pneuma.

CHAPTER 4

TOPICS INCLUDE

- supply
- quantity supplied
- law of supply
- profit motive
- profit
- revenue
- cost of production
- supply schedule
- supply curve
- elasticity of supply
- supply shifts
- tax
- subsidy
- regulation
- productivity
- total and marginal product
- total and marginal cost
- law of diminishing returns
- fixed and variable cost
- depreciation
- overhead

ECONOMICS NOTEBOOK

The Economics Notebook is a journal activity that encourages students to consider basic concepts of economics that relate to their lives. A follow-up notebook activity appears on page 94.

WHY IT MATTERS TODAY

To find additional lesson plans dealing with the way supply affects the economy, visit CNNfyi.com or have students complete the ECONOMICS IN THE NEWS activity on page 93.

CNNfyi.com

CHAPTER 4

SUPPLY

Like most people, you probably think of yourself only as part of demand—as a consumer of goods and services. But you also are a producer, or supplier of goods and services. For example, you may have supplied your labor delivering newspapers or working on community projects.

Like your role in market demand, your role in market supply is governed by some fundamental economic principles. This chapter explores these principles, including the law of supply, elasticity of supply, and shifts in supply. You also will learn to use supply schedules and supply curves, another set of basic economic tools. Additionally, you will learn how production decisions affect supply.

ECONOMICS NOTEBOOK

In your Economics Notebook, write what you think the term *supply* means. List five things you think you have supplied, in economic terms, in the past month.

WHY IT MATTERS TODAY

Whether growing your own food or supplying electricity to an entire city, the supply of goods and services is essential to any economy. At the end of this chapter visit CNNfyi.com to learn more about how the law of supply affects your life.

CNNfyi.com

SECTION 1
NATURE OF SUPPLY

READ TO DISCOVER
1. What is the difference between supply and quantity supplied?
2. What does the law of supply state?
3. What do supply schedules and supply curves illustrate?
4. What is supply elasticity?

ECONOMICS DICTIONARY
supply
quantity supplied
law of supply
profit motive
profit
cost of production
supply schedule
supply curve
elasticity of supply
elastic supply
inelastic supply

To meet consumers' demand, producers deliver goods and services to the marketplace. Consider, for example, the market for jackets. When are you most likely to buy, or demand, a warm jacket? Your demand for a jacket is highest in the fall and winter months, when cold weather arrives. When might you find the largest selection, or supply, of jackets in the stores? Again, the supply of jackets is highest in the fall and winter months, when demand is greatest.

In economic terms, however, supply is more than just the available selection of a good or service. **Supply** is the quantity of goods and services that producers are willing and able to offer at various possible prices during a given time period. During the winter months, for example, jacket manufacturers offer a certain quantity of jackets at each price. The **quantity supplied** is the amount of a good or service that a producer is willing to sell at each particular price.

Law of Supply

In a free-enterprise system, price is the key factor affecting not only the quantity demanded but also the quantity supplied. That is, the quantity supplied is directly related to the prices that producers can charge for their goods and services. This relationship is described by the law of supply. The **law of supply** states that producers supply more goods and services when they can sell them at higher prices and fewer goods and services when they must sell them at lower prices.

For example, if producers of compact disc (CD) players can charge $300 for their products, they will make more CD players than if they could charge only $200. In other words, the higher price will lead to a larger quantity of CD

SUPPLY & DEMAND *These people are supplying volunteer labor to build a house for a nonprofit organization. What might they, as producers, consider to be a "price" for this volunteer work?*

SUPPLY 73

Transparency
An overhead transparency of Figure 4.1 is available in *Transparency Resources*. See Transparency 11: Supply of Car Stereos.

Caption Answer
It will increase by 1,000 units. ★7B, 23F, 23G

---

internet connect

TOPIC: Supply Schedule, Elasticity of Supply
GO TO: go.hrw.com
KEYWORD: SM3 EC4

Have students access the Internet through the HRW Go site to learn what is involved in working as a baby-sitter. In many communities baby-sitters are in short supply and are able to charge high hourly rates. Have students consider the pros and cons of baby-sitting, then develop individual supply schedules: how many hours of baby-sitting would each supply at what price? Have students compare results and create an aggregate supply curve for the class. How elastic is the supply? ★7A, 7B, 23B, 23C

---

players supplied. At the lower price, producers will supply a smaller quantity.

What causes producers to vary their supply of goods and services in this way? Their actions are based on the **profit motive**. This desire to make money helps explain the law of supply.

Profit Motive The amount of money remaining after producers have paid all of their costs is called **profit**. A business makes a profit when revenues are greater than **costs of production**. These costs include wages and salaries, rent, interest on loans, bills for electricity, raw materials, and any other goods and services used to manufacture a product.

To make a profit, producers must provide the goods and services that consumers want—at prices that consumers are willing and able to pay. For example, suppose that the Twin Wheels Bicycle Company is designing a new children's bike, aimed at 6- and 7-year-olds. The company is considering adding a tiny onboard computer system to the bike, much like those used in automobiles. The system will give young riders information such as their speed, direction, and tire pressure.

The system is so costly that the company would have to charge $1,000 for each bike. At this point the company owners tell the designers that the onboard computer system is not worth making. The owners know that the vast majority of consumers are not willing and able to pay $1,000 for a children's bike. If the company supplies this bike in the marketplace, it will not make a profit.

Profit and Markets The profit motive has a far-reaching effect in free-enterprise markets. It not only governs how individual companies like Twin Wheels make decisions, it also helps direct the use of resources in the entire market.

For example, imagine that Twin Wheels introduces a line of children's bikes that sell for $150. The new model is extremely popular, and the company sells thousands of bikes and makes

---

SUPPLY OF CAR STEREOS

SUPPLY SCHEDULE

Price per Car Stereo	Car Stereos Supplied
$500	4,000
$400	3,750
$300	3,500
$200	2,500
$100	0

SUPPLY CURVE

FIGURE 4.1 A supply curve plots information from a supply schedule. **If the price of a car stereo changes from $200 to $300, how will the quantity supplied change during a given month?** ★TEKS

SUPPLY & DEMAND *The profit motive plays a key role in the law of supply.* **How does the profit motive help direct producers' use of resources?**

good profits. The company increases its production of the bike in pursuit of more profits.

Twin Wheels is not the only company to take notice of the market's high demand, however. On a broader scale, the company's sales and profits encourage other bicycle manufacturers to make more children's bikes. New bicycle manufacturers also may enter the market. All of these companies are pursuing profits.

What happens if Twin Wheels finds demand low for its new line of children's bikes? Even after lowering the price of the bikes, it barely makes back its investment. The company decides to decrease production of the bikes.

Likewise, the company's low sales and profits signal other suppliers that consumer demand in this market is low. Other bicycle manufacturers decrease their production of children's bikes and use their resources to make products that earn higher profits. The low demand also discourages new manufacturers from entering the market because they cannot expect to make good profits. In this way, profits help direct the use of resources.

Supply Schedules

One useful tool that shows the relationship between the price of a good or service and the quantity that producers will supply is a **supply schedule**. This schedule lists each quantity of a product that producers are willing to supply at various market prices.

An example of a supply schedule appears in Figure 4.1. The schedule lists the number of car stereos that the Audio Blast Company is willing to supply at several possible prices. You can see that as prices increase from $100 to $500, the quantity supplied increases. When the price is $100, the quantity of stereos supplied is zero. When the price is $500, Audio Blast supplies 4,000 stereos.

Supply Curves

Supply curves are another way to show the relationship between the price of a good or service and the quantity supplied. A **supply curve** plots on a graph the information from a supply schedule.

The supply curve S_1 in Figure 4.1, for example, shows all of the possible combinations of prices and quantities for Audio Blast's stereos, as listed in the supply schedule. The quantities of stereos that Audio Blast will supply appear along the horizontal axis, increasing from left to right. The possible prices of those stereos appear along the vertical axis, increasing from bottom to top.

Each point plotted on the graph represents a specific combination of price and quantity supplied. The curve slopes upward, reflecting the

---

Caption Answer
The profit motive encourages producers to use resources wisely, thus keeping production costs low and increasing profits. 4A, 23A

Cultural Perspectives

Fuzzy dice, pet rocks, and nose rings are all examples of fads, or consumer trends. Fads often develop around items with high elastic supply that can be made quickly and inexpensively. Thus, producers can easily adjust supply to meet rapidly changing consumer demand.

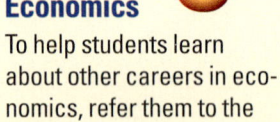

Careers in Economics

To help students learn about other careers in economics, refer them to the Careers section on the *Researcher Online*.

---

greater quantity that producers will supply at higher prices. Note that this is the opposite of what happens to demand curves, such as the one in Figure 3.2 on page 55.

Elasticity of Supply

The law of supply, supply schedules, and supply curves all point out the relationship between price and quantity supplied. They show that high prices for products lead to a large quantity of those products supplied, and low prices lead to a small quantity supplied. But how much of a change in price causes how much of a change in quantity supplied? As with demand, the answer lies in how elastic the supply of a product is.

Elasticity of supply is the degree to which price changes affect the quantity supplied. A

CAREERS IN ECONOMICS

Buyer

Do you like to shop? Imagine being paid to buy the latest fashions, the hottest music, or the fastest computers. As a buyer, you would be required to make these kinds of purchases every day—but not for your own consumption.

Buyers are hired by stores to purchase merchandise from manufacturers. The stores then resell this merchandise to customers. All sizes of retail businesses—from small shops to large department store chains—employ buyers to determine what to buy, how much to buy, and from whom to buy consumer goods.

In effect, buyers must predict the future. Their job is to estimate what demand for particular products will be, and to choose the mix of prices, sizes, types, and colors. For example, when a buyer orders hot-pink sweaters for the fall line of clothes, he or she is estimating that the fashion tastes of shoppers and cooler weather will increase demand for this particular item.

Buyers have to replenish supplies quickly and economically as merchandise is sold. In addition, buyers price merchandise, create product displays, and manage sales personnel. They also must be good with numbers and able to use computers to track merchandise and inventory.

Buyers need to be skillful communicators. Those who are able to express their ideas to vendors, salespeople, managers, and customers generally obtain the best deals.

Most employers require a college education for this position. Courses in business management, merchandising, marketing, and math are helpful. A career as a professional buyer demands a lot of time and energy. Many buyers, however, find their role as the critical link between the consumer and producer to be exciting and rewarding.

Buyers use their knowledge of the market to predict demand and provide an adequate supply of goods and services.

76 CHAPTER 4

SUPPLY & DEMAND *Prices for sports team memorabilia may increase during a successful season.* **How does this increase reflect the law of supply?** ⭐TEKS

product's supply, like demand, can be either elastic or inelastic.

Elastic Supply What goods tend to have elastic supply? **Elastic supply** exists when a small change in price causes a major change in the quantity supplied. Products with elastic supply usually can be made

▸ quickly,
▸ inexpensively, and
▸ using a few, readily available resources.

Suppliers can change the production rates of such goods easily in order to meet changing consumer demand.

Sports teams' souvenirs, such as T-shirts, posters, and hats, are examples of products with elastic supply. Consider what happens when a football team wins the Super Bowl. Demand for the team's souvenirs soars. They become more valuable to consumers, and prices rise.

What happens to the supply of these goods? Because these souvenirs can be produced quickly and inexpensively, the supply expands rapidly. In fact, within a few days of the team's victory, stores are literally flooded with the souvenirs.

The relatively small change in price results in an enormous change in supply.

You can see the elastic supply for posters of Super Bowl champions in Figure 4.2. The supply curve S₁ is more horizontal than vertical, showing that a small change in the price of posters causes a large change in the quantity of posters supplied. For example, at the price of $4.50, producers supply 100,000 posters. If the price increases to $9, producers supply 700,000 posters. A 100 percent increase in price leads to a 600 percent increase in the quantity supplied.

Inelastic Supply Some goods tend to have an inelastic supply. **Inelastic supply** exists when a change in a good's price has little impact on the quantity supplied. A product usually has an inelastic supply if production requires a great deal of

▸ time,
▸ money, and
▸ resources that are not readily available.

Suppliers cannot easily change the production rates of such goods in order to meet changing consumer demand.

ELASTIC SUPPLY FOR POSTERS

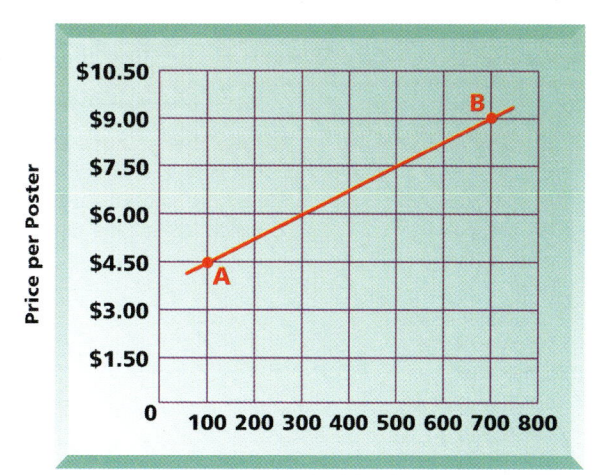

Quantity Supplied (in thousands)

FIGURE 4.2 A relatively horizontal line indicates elastic supply for posters during this one-week period. **What conditions are necessary for supply to be elastic?**

SUPPLY **77**

Caption Answer
A great deal of time, money, and resources that are not readily available are required to produce it. ⭐ **7A, 23A**

SECTION 1
REVIEW ANSWERS

1. supply (73), quantity supplied (73), law of supply (73), profit motive (74), profit (74), cost of production (74), supply schedule (75), supply curve (75), elasticity of supply (76), elastic supply (77), inelastic supply (77) **4A, 7A, 24A**

2. Winning the World Series leads to increased demand for a team's souvenirs, this causes the price to rise, rising prices lead to an increase in production, which leads to an increase in supply. **23A, 23F**

3a. In order to maximize profits, producers supply more products at higher prices and fewer products at lower prices. **4A, 7A, 23A**

3b. elastic—products can be made quickly, cheaply, and with a few, readily available resources; inelastic—products require a great deal of time, money, and hard-to-find resources. **7A, 23A**

4. Figure 4.1 represents a supply curve and Figure 3.2 represents a demand curve. In a supply curve, as the price increases, supply also increases in order to take advantage of increasing profits. In a demand curve, higher prices lead to decreased demand. As demand drops, prices fall. **7A, 23A, 23F**

PERFECTLY INELASTIC SUPPLY

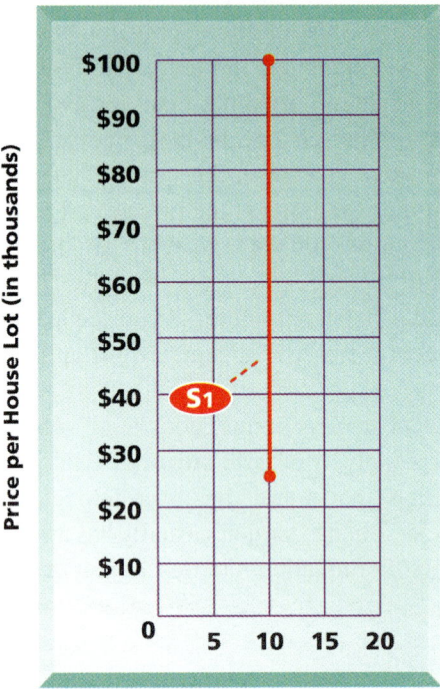

[Graph: Price per House Lot (in thousands) vs. Quantity Supplied, showing a vertical line at quantity = 10, with S1 marked at $40]

FIGURE 4.3 If a producer cannot increase supply regardless of price, supply is perfectly inelastic as it is for these house lots during a one-year period. **What characteristics indicate that a product has inelastic supply?** ⭐TEKS

Gold is one example of a product with a traditionally inelastic supply. If the price of gold rises, the quantity of gold supplied does not change much. Gold is a rare metal that is expensive to mine and requires time to refine, or purify. For these reasons, gold has an inelastic supply. Other rare, labor-intensive, and expensive items such as fine art and space shuttles have inelastic supply as well.

A perfectly inelastic supply exists when producers, regardless of price, cannot increase the quantity supplied. You can see a perfectly inelastic supply curve in Figure 4.3. Suppose that a building contractor wants to develop beachfront property and build Sandy Shores Homes. The contractor divides a piece of shoreline property into 10 lots. The lots are sized as small as local laws will allow. No matter what price the developer sets for each of the lots, the supply of shoreline properties at Sandy Shores is fixed. If demand is high, the developer might price the lots at $100,000 each. If demand is low, the developer might only be able to charge $25,000. At either price, however, the quantity supplied is 10 lots. Because price changes do not cause any change to the quantity of lots supplied, the supply of lots is perfectly inelastic.

SECTION 1 REVIEW

1. Identify and Explain:
- supply
- quantity supplied
- law of supply
- profit motive
- profit
- cost of production
- supply schedule
- supply curve
- elasticity of supply
- elastic supply
- inelastic supply

2. Identifying Cause and Effect: Copy the cause-and-effect chart below. Use it to describe how winning the World Series can rapidly increase the supply of a baseball team's souvenirs.

Cause: Yankees win the World Series
↓
Effect/Cause
↓
Effect/Cause

Homework Practice Online
keyword: SM3 HP4

⭐TEKS Q: 1, 2, 3a, 3b, 4

3. Finding the Main Idea
a. What is the law of supply and how does the profit motive help explain it?
b. What are the characteristics of products with elastic supply and those with inelastic supply?

4. Writing and Critical Thinking

Drawing Inferences: Look back at Figure 4.1 on page 74 and at Figure 3.2 on page 55. What makes these curves go in opposite directions?
Consider the following:
- the law of supply
- the law of demand
- the effect of price on the supply of and demand for a particular good or service.

SECTION 2
CHANGES IN SUPPLY

READ TO DISCOVER
1. What does it mean for a product's supply to shift?
2. What determinants might cause a product's supply curve to shift?
3. How does a tax differ from a subsidy?

ECONOMICS DICTIONARY
determinants of supply
tax
subsidy
regulation

Like demand curves, supply curves illustrate a product's market at a specific period of time. The supply curve in Figure 4.1 on page 74, for example, is a snapshot of Audio Blast's stereo supply. Again, because the picture is taken at a set point in time, the only factor affecting the quantity of stereos supplied is the one factor shown in the picture (graph): price. Nothing but a price change is affecting the quantity of stereos supplied by Audio Blast at the time this picture was taken.

By examining the supply curve, you can see that price is the only factor affecting the quantity supplied. Look again at the S_1 curve in Figure 4.1. What would have to happen for the number of car stereos supplied to increase from 2,500 to 4,000? The graph shows that only an increase in price from $200 to $500 will cause this change in the quantity supplied. Such an increase in price will result in the intersection of price and quantity supplied moving from point to point along the supply curve.

Supply Shifts

You already know, however, that markets do not stand still. New snapshots of a product's supply must be taken periodically because supply, like demand, is affected by factors other than price. In economic terms, these **determinants of supply**—or nonprice factors—can shift the entire supply curve of a product, instead of simply changing the quantity supplied along the original supply curve.

Figure 4.4 on page 80 shows movement of the entire S_1 supply curve from Figure 4.1. If the determinants of supply cause an increase in the supply of car stereos, the entire curve shifts to the right (S_2). Similarly, if the supply determinants cause a decrease in supply, the entire curve shifts to the left (S_3). A shift to either the S_2 or S_3

BLONDIE

BLONDIE reprinted with special permission of King Features Syndicate, Inc.

SUPPLY & DEMAND *Businesses earn profits when revenues exceed the costs of production.* **How can a change in the price of resources affect the supply curve?**

Global Connections

U.S. companies have often located plants and offices in other countries that have an abundance of labor willing to work for low wages. By paying less for labor, these companies are able to reduce production costs and thereby increase profits. IBM, Texas Instruments, and Motorola established programming offices in Bangalore, India, to take advantage of the glut of skilled programmers there who would work for lower wages than U.S. programmers.

Improved technology, such as advances in telecommunications, has helped create this growing global labor force. In another example, satellite connections enable remote data entry workers in Jamaica to handle calls, make airline reservations, and process plane tickets for consumers in the United States. ■

Transparency

An overhead transparency of Figure 4.4 is available in *Transparency Resources*. See Transparency 13: Supply Curve Shifts.

Caption Answer

prices of resources, government tools, technology, competition, prices of related goods, and producer expectations ★7A, 23A, 24A

---

curve means that a different quantity of car stereos is supplied at *each and every* price.

What causes these shifts in supply? The determinants of supply include

- prices of resources,
- government tools,
- technology,
- competition,
- prices of related goods, and
- producer expectations.

A change in one of these determinants can cause a change in the overall supply of a product.

Prices of Resources

One of the most common determinants that can shift the supply curve is a change in the price of resources, or factors of production. A resource is anything that is used in the production of a good or service. Resources include raw materials, electricity, and workers' wages. These resources contribute to a business's costs of production. Thus, any price change for a resource increases or decreases a business's production costs.

When the price of a resource falls, production costs fall accordingly. In turn, lower production costs mean that a business can supply more of the product for the same cost as before. Lower costs also generally go hand-in-hand with higher profits, which encourage the business to expand supply even more. For these reasons, a decrease in the price of a resource often causes producers to supply more product to the market at each and every price.

Suppose that the Fruit Bonanza Company makes fruit juices. The base ingredient of all of their juices is apple juice. An unexpectedly large crop of apples this year has been produced, reducing the price of apples by 10 cents a pound.

Given the large amount of apples that Fruit Bonanza buys, this price change significantly reduces the company's production costs. Lower costs allow the company to make more profit on the sale of each bottle of juice at each and every price. The higher profits encourage the owners of Fruit Bonanza to increase production even further. Thus, the supply curve shifts to the right as the company offers more bottles of juice at each and every price.

SUPPLY CURVE SHIFTS

INCREASE IN SUPPLY

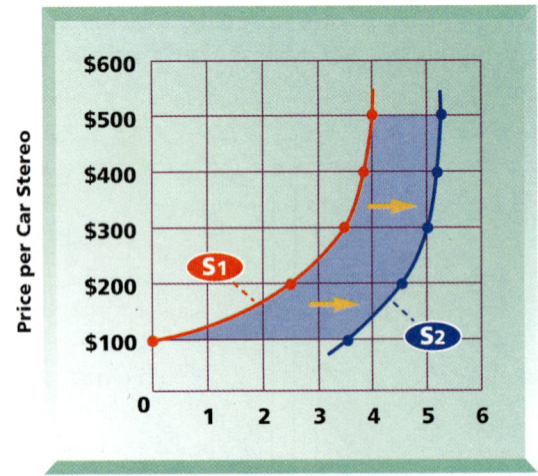

DECREASE IN SUPPLY

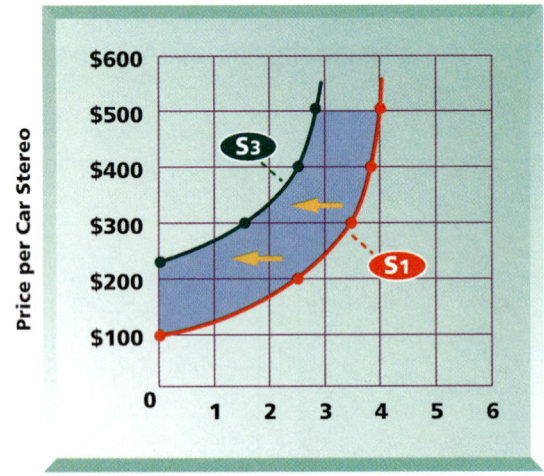

FIGURE 4.4 A shift in the supply curve results in new quantities of car stereos supplied at all possible prices. **What determinants cause a shift in the supply curve?** ★TEKS

SUPPLY & DEMAND *An unexpectedly large crop of apples lowers the cost of products made with apples. What would happen to the supply curve for applesauce in this instance?* ⭐TEKS

The opposite happens if the cost of a resource increases. If the price of apples rises by 10 cents a pound, for example, Fruit Bonanza's production costs also rise. Higher production costs mean that the company cannot supply as much of the product for the same cost as before. Higher costs also mean lower profits. The prospect of lower profits causes Fruit Bonanza to produce even less juice. Thus, the supply curve shifts to the left as the company offers less juice to the market at each and every price.

Government Tools

Various government tools can cause the supply curve for goods and services to shift either to the right or the left. The three main tools are taxes, subsidies, and regulation.

Taxes Like individual citizens, producers must pay taxes. A **tax** is a required payment of money to the government to help fund government services. Businesses may have to pay taxes on the materials they use, the property they own, and the profits they make. Taxes add to a business's

Global Exchange

Acid Rain

Every government creates regulations that are designed to protect its citizens. Although such government regulations are applied within national borders, sometimes the problems they address do not recognize borders. Along the U.S.-Canada border, for example, the problem of acid rain introduced a sour note in the two countries' relations.

Acid rain is caused by sulfur dioxide and nitrogen oxides. Factories, cars, and refineries release these gases into the air, where they mix with water vapor. This falls to the earth as acid rain.

Why is acid rain a concern? Acid rain changes the soil's mineral content, altering the growth of plants. Some plants die; others grow but are not healthy. Acid rain also contaminates lakes and streams, killing fish and other aquatic animals.

For many years the problem of acid rain strained relations between the United States and Canada as airborne pollutants drifted across the border between the two countries. Canada has national air quality standards and strict emission limits for its cars and factories. It is relatively recently that U.S. policies, which are enforced at the state level, have begun to change.

During the 1990s a number of U.S. companies began participating in a new, market-based program. Each company received a pollution "allowance." When a company emitted more pollution than it was "allowed," it had to buy allowances from lower-polluting companies. This program helped lower pollution rates as companies bought newer equipment in the hope of selling their unused allowances.

Caption Answer
It would shift to the right. ⭐7A, 23A

Cultural Perspectives

Why does job growth boom one year in McAllen, Texas, and Boise City, Idaho, while it slows in New York City and San Francisco. Why does business grow faster in some areas than others? Taxes are one major factor. Cities like McAllen and Boise City have lower taxes than New York City and San Francisco. Lower taxes mean lower production costs for businesses. Cities often try to lure new business by offering them tax breaks.

Offering tax incentives to encourage business growth can backfire, however. Businesses, particularly high-tech companies, need a large supply of educated workers. Because education is largely funded through tax revenue, cutting taxes can hurt the quality of local education. For example, Columbus, Georgia's largest employer, Synovus Financial Corp., threatened to relocate to another state because it could not find enough skilled programmers in the area to hire. As a result, the state of Georgia put together a $23 million incentive plan that included educational spending and tax breaks to encourage the company to stay in Georgia. ◼

SUPPLY 81

Caption Answer

Improved technology usually reduces production costs and increases profits. As a result, suppliers will likely increase supply at each and every price, shifting the supply curve to the right. ★7A, 23A, 26D

Across the Curriculum

HISTORY Sugar subsidies played a crucial role in the U.S. annexation of Hawaii in 1898. In 1876 the United States and Hawaii had formalized a treaty allowing Hawaiian sugar producers to export sugar to the United States without paying a tariff. Because the United States placed a tariff on other imported sugar, the treaty gave Hawaiian sugar producers a competitive advantage and put them on level ground with U.S. domestic sugar producers.

The McKinley Tariff Act of 1890, however, eliminated tariffs on all imported sugar. In addition, to give domestic sugar planters a competitive advantage, the act granted U.S. sugar planters a subsidy of two cents per pound of sugar. The law hurt Hawaiian planters and devastated the Hawaiian sugar market.

This event is one of the pivotal factors that led a large number of Hawaiian planters, many of whom were from the United States, to push for the U.S. annexation of Hawaii. Many native Hawaiians and U.S. sugar producers fought Hawaii's annexation, but without success. ■

PRODUCTIVITY *The Ford assembly line revolutionized automobile production.* ***How can technology cause the supply curve to shift?*** ★TEKS

production costs, just like the cost of rent or raw materials does.

How do taxes affect supply? Higher taxes mean that businesses are faced with higher costs and the prospect of making less profit and will supply less of their product to the market. Thus, the supply curve shifts to the left.

Subsidies Payments to private businesses by the government are called **subsidies**. For example, to ensure consumers an affordable supply of flour, cereal, and other essential wheat products, the government might grant a subsidy to wheat farmers. By lowering the costs of planting wheat—compared to the costs of planting a nonsubsidized crop—the subsidy encourages Gary Bryant, a wheat farmer, to plant more wheat. The lower costs of planting wheat also promise Gary greater profits on the sale of his wheat. The supply curve for wheat shifts to the right.

Subsidies and taxes thus have opposite effects on supply. As you can see from the above example, subsidies can reduce a business's production costs. These lower costs mean higher profits, which encourage producers to supply more of their product at each and every price.

Keep in mind, however, that subsidies have a cost. Taxpayers fund subsidies given to farmers and other private businesses.

Regulation To protect the public, the government passes many kinds of **regulations**, or rules, about how companies conduct business. Regulations are designed to prevent pollution, discrimination, and other problems that affect citizens. Loose government regulations tend to increase supply. Strict regulations, on the other hand, tend to decrease supply.

For example, strict pollution controls force companies to spend more money on finding safe ways to dispose of waste and toxic materials. Complying with the regulations thus increases the companies' production costs. As you have learned, higher production costs prevent producers from supplying as many goods and services, and the supply curve for their products shifts to the left.

Technology

New technology, such as a new tool or chemical process, can have a powerful impact on supply by

CHAPTER 4

changing the way in which products are made. Usually, new technology makes production more efficient and less expensive. This causes the costs of production to decrease. In turn, producers are able to supply more goods and services at each and every price because their costs are lower and their profits are higher.

Consider the case of automobiles. The first cars were produced individually by several workers. Because each car was made up of thousands of parts, production was time-consuming and expensive. In the early 1900s, however, technology revolutionized automobile production. Around 1913 Henry Ford used a new production technique—the assembly line—to make cars in his Detroit-area factory. Car frames moved along a conveyor belt past workers who performed their specified tasks in the assembly process. New machines produced the individual automobile parts, which were carried to workers on the assembly line.

This new technology had dramatic results. Assembly time was reduced significantly for Ford's Model T automobile. For the same amount of time and money as before, Ford's company could now produce many more Model T automobiles. Therefore, the supply curve for automobiles shifted to the right as it became profitable for producers to offer more cars at each and every price.

Keep in mind that technology also has a cost. A company may have to pay researchers or other companies for the desired technology. It is not uncommon for new technology to *add* to the costs of production at first. Henry Ford had to pay a great deal of money to install the new machines and the assembly line in his factory. However, Ford calculated that the increased efficiency and increased profitability of the new technology would outweigh the initial cost of installation.

Competition

Competition tends to increase supply, while a lack of competition tends to decrease supply. Why is this so?

Consider the market for home video games. When the first company offered these games, the selection was extremely limited. Demand for these games rose quickly, however, generating high sales and good profits for the company. These profits encouraged dozens of new video firms to enter the market. The supply and selection of games soon skyrocketed.

As this example shows, a larger number of suppliers in a market tends to increase supply. Each producer competes for a share of the market demand by supplying more of the product. This shifts the supply curve to the right as producers offer more goods at each and every price for the product.

Remember that suppliers can leave as well as enter a market. If the demand for video games were to fall, there would be more games (more supply) on the market than consumers wanted to purchase. Supply would be higher than demand. Some companies would not sell all of their games and might not make enough profit. These companies might then leave the market. Supply would shrink as fewer producers competed to deliver games to the market.

SUPPLY & DEMAND *Strong competition tends to increase supply, while weak competition tends to decrease supply.* **How might the entry of new carriers into the airline industry affect airfares?**

Across the Curriculum

TECHNOLOGY In the late 1790s the United States was on the brink of war with France and needed a large supply of muskets. Manufacturing techniques at that time were slow and inefficient, however. Artisans created most items. Each item was slightly different, and if a part broke, a new one had to be custom-made. A government arsenal in Massachusetts, for example, produced only 245 muskets in two years.

Inventor Eli Whitney approached the government with an idea for improving weapons production by producing interchangeable parts. Each part for a certain model of gun would be identical and could be used in any gun of that model. If a part broke, it could be easily replaced. The government liked Whitney's idea and gave him $5,000 to start his business. Although it took Whitney more than two years to build the necessary equipment, his shop produced 500 muskets during its first few months of production. Other industries quickly adopted the idea of interchangeable parts, laying the groundwork for later mass production techniques. ■

Caption Answer
Airfares might decrease in price. 4A, 7A, 23A

SUPPLY 83

Global Connections

Health scares linked to a particular product can result in increased supplies of related goods. In the late 1980s and early 1990s, an epidemic of Bovine Spongiform Encephalopathy, or mad cow disease, developed among cattle in Great Britain. In March 1996, British scientists reported that human beings could get a rare and fatal brain disorder by eating beef from cattle with mad cow disease. Sales of beef—long a staple of the British diet—fell by 30 percent that month. Hungry Britons with a craving for meat turned to lamb, pork, and chicken as substitutes. At the same time, British grocers and butchers cut beef supplies and started supplying more exotic meats such as ostrich from the United States, kangaroo from Australia, and crocodile from Zimbabwe. Tesco, the first British supermarket chain to supply ostrich meat, even provided preparation tips to help uncertain shoppers. ■

Caption Answer

Producers in a competitive market compete for shares of that market's demand by supplying more product at each price. ★4A, 7A, 23A

CASE STUDY

Competition in Online Education

Online education is one of many business opportunities on the Internet. One estimate expects the market to reach $25.3 billion by 2003. In 1999 Powered Inc., based in Austin, Texas, decided to enter the field. The company planned to specialize in creating Web-based educational classes.

At first, the small company was one of only a few companies pursuing the online education market. It quickly signed deals with several high-profile companies, such as bookstore chain Barnes & Noble, for whom it created Barnes & Noble University. The site offers free educational courses in the hope that customers will purchase the courses' reading materials from the bookstore.

Powered's success soon led to its being joined in the field by several larger, well-established companies with previous experience providing educational training for corporations. This means an increased supply of online education offerings. The supply curve for online education has shifted to the right. Many traditional universities also offer their courses over the Internet, further increasing supply and competition for smaller companies such as Powered.

Powered's client list continues to grow. However, the company still faces strong competition in the years ahead.

COMPETITION & MARKET STRUCTURE *The popularity of the Internet has encouraged more Internet service providers to enter the market.* **How can competition contribute to an increase in quantity supplied?** ★TEKS

Prices of Related Goods

The supply for one good often is connected to the supply for its related goods. This means that changes in a product's price can affect the supply for the product's related goods.

For example, think again of Gary Bryant, the wheat farmer. In addition to wheat, Gary has several other choices of crops—corn, soybeans, and hay, for example. These goods are related as far as Gary is concerned because they share a common feature: they are potential crops that he may choose to plant.

Gary had planned to plant wheat, until the price of wheat dropped suddenly. The price of corn is now higher relative to the price of wheat. Because Gary can earn more profit on corn, he decides to plant corn instead of wheat. Thus, the drop in wheat prices results in an increase in the supply of its related good—corn—even though the price of corn did not change. The supply curve for corn shifts to the right.

Likewise, if the price of wheat were to rise relative to corn, more farmers would choose to plant wheat instead of corn in order to earn more profit. The rise in the price of wheat would result in a decrease in the supply of corn. The corn supply curve would shift to the left.

Producer Expectations

Just as consumers sometimes make current buying decisions based on their expectations of future income, suppliers make current production decisions based on their expected future income. Producers' income, of course, depends on the prices they can charge for their products. The expectations they have of future changes in the price of their products can affect how much of their product they supply to the market now.

For example, suppose that Sports Madness, a sports equipment manufacturer, expects the price of its basketballs to increase in the next few months. The company believes that the start of the school year—and later, the basketball season—will increase demand and prices. It decides to increase production of its basketballs now in order to meet the expected increase in demand. Thus, the supply curve for basketballs shifts to the right.

The effect of expectations on supply are difficult to predict, however. In the same situation, another sports manufacturer might decide to withhold a large portion of its basketballs by storing them in a warehouse. The company plans to deliver these basketballs to the market in a couple of months when prices will be higher. This decision leads to a decrease in the current supply of basketballs and shifts the supply curve in the opposite direction—to the left.

Manufacturers face similar options when they expect the price of their products to fall in the future. For example, if the above companies expect the price of basketballs to fall when the season ends, they may increase their production now in order to sell as many basketballs as possible before the price falls. Their expectations of future prices cause the supply curve to shift to the right. On the other hand, they may decrease their immediate production, anticipating that demand and prices will be lower. This decrease would shift the supply curve to the left.

SUPPLY & DEMAND *Suppliers make production decisions based on their expected future income.* **What happens to the supply curve for Valentine candy on February 15th?** TEKS

SECTION 2 REVIEW

TEKS Q: 1, 2, 3a, 3b, 4

1. **Identify and Explain:**
   determinants of supply
   tax
   subsidy
   regulation

2. **Analyzing Information:** Copy the web organizer below. Use it to identify the six main determinants of supply.

   (web organizer with center "Determinants of Supply" and six connected circles)

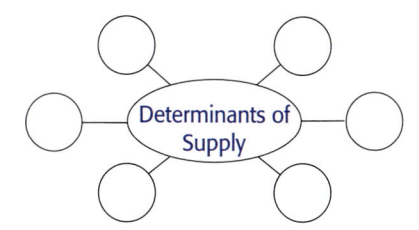

3. **Finding the Main Idea**
   a. How is a shift in the supply curve different from a change in the quantity supplied?
   b. How can taxes and subsidies affect supply?

4. **Writing and Critical Thinking**
   Summarizing: Think about the determinants of supply. In what ways are all of them related?
   Consider the following:
   - the determinants of supply
   - the supply curve

Homework Practice Online
keyword: SM3 HP4

SUPPLY 85

Caption Answer
It shifts to the left. 7A, 23A, 23F

SECTION 2 REVIEW ANSWERS

1. determinants of supply (79), tax (81), subsidy (82), regulation (82) 7A, 17A, 24A

2. prices of resources, government tools, technology, competition, prices of related goods, and producer expectations 7A, 23A, 23F

3a. A change in quantity supplied is indicated by movement along the supply curve; a shift in supply is indicated by the movement of the entire supply curve to the right or left. 23A, 24A

3b. Higher taxes increase production costs, which decreases profits, which leads businesses to decrease supply. Subsidies reduce production costs, which increases profits, which leads businesses to increase supply. 7A, 23A, 24A

4. Each determinant of supply affects producer decisions regarding production and the amount of a good or service to supply. Each determinant can shift the supply curve to either the right or the left. 7A, 23A, 23D, 24A

SECTION 3

MAKING PRODUCTION DECISIONS

Lesson Plans
For teaching strategies, see Lesson 4.3 located at the beginning of this chapter or the One-Stop Planner Strategy 4.3.

Economics Dictionary
To reinforce the section's vocabulary terms, refer students to the Electronic Glossary on the *Researcher CD-ROM*.

Section Assessment
To assess students' mastery of this section, have them complete Daily Quiz 4.3 in *Daily Quizzes with Answer Key*.

TEKS

Section 3
Content
2B, 26A
Social Studies Skills
23A, 23B, 23D, 23F, 23G, 24A, 24C, 24D, 25B
Chapter Review
Content
2B, 4A, 7A, 17A, 26A, 26D
Social Studies Skills
23A, 23D, 23E, 23F, 23G, 24A, 24B

86

SECTION 3

MAKING PRODUCTION DECISIONS

READ TO DISCOVER
1. Why do producers look at productivity when making supply decisions?
2. How do varying levels of input affect the levels of output?
3. How do changes in production costs affect producers' supply decisions?

ECONOMICS DICTIONARY
total product
marginal product
law of diminishing returns
fixed cost
depreciation
overhead
variable cost
total cost
marginal cost

You make production decisions every day. For example, you decide how to complete (produce) your homework assignments. You decide how to make your lunch. You decide how to make decorations for a school dance. Although you probably are unaware of it, when you make these types of daily choices, you go through a decision-making process much like the one that manufacturers use every day.

How do you and other suppliers make production decisions? You already know part of the answer. As noted in this chapter and in Chapter 3, the amount of goods produced is influenced by the laws of demand and supply, elasticity of demand and supply, and shifts in the demand and supply curves.

86 CHAPTER 4

There are two pieces of the puzzle left to examine, however. Production levels also are influenced by productivity and the costs of production. Manufacturers must consider these two factors before deciding how much to produce for the market.

Productivity

As noted in Chapter 1, productivity is the amount of goods and services produced per unit of input. In other words, productivity tells business owners how efficiently their resources are being used in production.

Think about your own productivity regarding homework. Imagine that you have a test tomorrow in one of your classes. You estimate that it will take you about three hours to study for it. That is, for every three hours of input (study time) you produce one unit of output (a good grade on a test). Can you be more productive? Perhaps by studying with a friend—discussing the material and quizzing each other—you can increase the effectiveness of your study time. This type of studying allows you to produce a good grade on the test with only two hours of input instead of three.

Of course, productivity in businesses is much more complex—and involves more inputs—than the above example. But like you, business owners must examine their productivity in order to maximize efficiency and profits. And like you, they consider varying the amount of their inputs in order to increase productivity. To do this, business owners look at their total product, marginal product, and how the two figures change as inputs change.

Total Product To understand how output is affected by changes in input, a company first must calculate its output. All of the product a company makes in a given period of time—with a given amount of input—is called its **total product**, or total output. The table in Figure 4.5 contains a production schedule for the Golden Duck Company. The second column of the table lists the possible total product levels for the company. Golden can make anywhere between zero and 1,000 rubber ducks a day as it uses zero to 13 units of labor.

Marginal Product To maximize productivity, business owners also need to know their marginal product. **Marginal product** is the change in output generated by adding one more unit of input. How do businesses calculate marginal product?

Return to the production schedule in Figure 4.5. The third column lists the marginal product for each level of production. That is, it shows how many additional units (ducks) are produced at each level of input. For example, if labor input increases from zero to 1, the marginal product is 10 because 10 ducks are produced. If the level of input rises again to 2, the marginal product is 40 because 40 more ducks are produced than before the increase (50 − 10 = 40).

Law of Diminishing Returns

Once total and marginal product have been calculated, a company is ready to vary one of its inputs to see the effect on output. This effect is governed by a basic economic principle: the **law of diminishing returns**. This law describes the effect that varying the level of an input has on total and marginal product. It states that as more of one input is added to a fixed supply of other resources, productivity increases up to a point. At some point, however, the marginal product will diminish. Eventually, it will result in negative marginal product.

Keep in mind that this principle applies to situations in which only *one* input is varied. Of course, a company like Golden would want to vary several of its inputs to find the most efficient combination. It might increase the number of its workers *and* add more machines to its

Across the Curriculum

SCIENCE Farmers apply the law of diminishing returns in determining how much fertilizer to use to produce maximum crop yields. As a farmer applies more fertilizer to crops, total and marginal output increase up to a certain point. Beyond that point, adding more fertilizer results in diminished increases in crop production. To maximize profits, farmers must balance the costs of buying extra fertilizer with the returns they get in increased crop value. ■

Transparency

An overhead transparency of Figure 4.5 is available in *Transparency Resources*. See Transparency 14: Productivity of Golden Duck Company.

Caption Answer

As the level of labor input is increased, productivity increases up to a point (through the addition of the eleventh worker). After that, adding additional labor decreases productivity and eventually results in negative marginal product and decreased total product. 23A, 23F, 23G

PRODUCTIVITY OF GOLDEN DUCK COMPANY

PRODUCTION SCHEDULE

Labor Input	Total Product	Marginal Product
0	0	0
1	10	10
2	50	40
3	110	60
4	175	65
5	245	70
6	320	75
7	400	80
8	485	85
9	575	90
10	675	100
11	875	200
12	985	110
13	1,000	15
14	975	-25
15	925	-50
16	825	-100

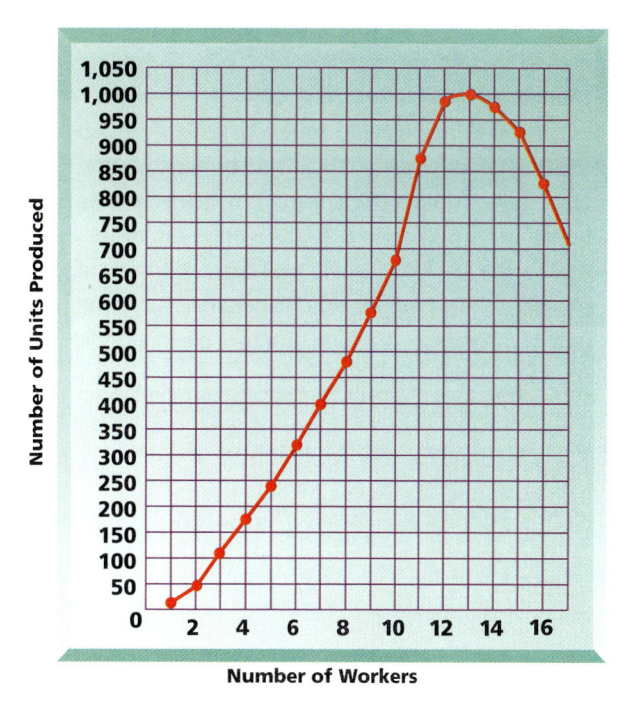

FIGURE 4.5 Production schedules and production curves illustrate productivity during a specific period of time. **How does this production curve reflect the law of diminishing returns at the Golden Duck factory?** TEKS

What Do You Think?
Answers

1. Answers will vary but might include businesses that do not require much initial capital or labor, such as pet-sitting, child care, tutoring, yard care, computerized services, and services that can be marketed over the Internet. ⭐23A

2. Answers will vary but should reflect an understanding of the laws of supply and demand. ⭐23D

ECONOMICS IN ACTION

Dialing for Dollars

You may think of business leaders as men and women who have been part of the corporate world for many years. There are, however, some young people out there who already own and run their own businesses.

Bill Cunningham has been in business for himself since he was 17. While he was still in high school, Bill gained valuable experience working for a telemarketing company at night. Then with a telephone and about $700 in savings, he started his own business. He established Dial USA, a telemarketing firm based in Dallas.

Bill felt that telemarketing was an ideal business for a young entrepreneur. He said, "If I were to go to someone's office and try to sell him a copy machine in person at 17, it would be difficult. However, if I were able to communicate clearly and maturely over the telephone, I had a fighting chance."

Bill was responsible for every aspect of Dial USA's business. He had to find customers, pay the bills, and establish prices and policies. In the beginning, he also was Dial USA's only employee.

As the company grew, however, Bill needed people to help him. He was responsible for hiring new employees, training them, paying their salaries, and making sure that the company ran smoothly and earned a profit. Although Bill was happy to earn a profit, it was not the primary reason that he went into business. Bill said, "You don't go into business to make money. You go in because you are a creator. Money's a by-product, a way of keeping score." After only three years, Dial USA's "score" was an impressive $1.2 million in revenues, and Bill's client list continued to grow.

Why would a company hire a telemarketer like Dial USA? Telemarketers fill an important need by selling products, which allows a company's staff to concentrate on developing goods and services.

Making an organization known to the public is one of Dial USA's most important tasks. For example, Dial USA was hired by the Center for Success in Learning, an organization that develops techniques and programs for learning-challenged children. The center needed to raise funds, so Bill's company advertised a benefit rodeo. In a matter of weeks, Dial USA helped the Center for Success in Learning earn $35,000, which allowed the organization to stay in business.

Telemarketers usually are paid commissions, which means that instead of earning a fixed wage for every hour of work, their pay is based on the number of products sold. The more tickets Bill sold for the benefit rodeo, for example, the more money he made for himself as well as for the center. Bill said, "I believed that we could make a difference and make a profit at it."

Running a business takes hard work and determination. To any budding entrepreneurs, Bill suggests, "Examine all your options. But when you make up your mind, have laser-guided focus to work hard on your goals."

Bill Cunningham started his telemarketing company—Dial USA—at the age of 17.

What Do You Think? ⭐TEKS

1. What kinds of businesses offer a young entrepreneur the best chances for success? Explain your answer.

2. If you were starting your own business, what would you choose to do? Why?

factory. Varying several inputs at once, however, makes it difficult to determine clear cause-and-effect results. If production does increase at the Golden plant, was it a result of hiring more workers, adding new machines, or both? By looking at only one input at a time, the effect on total output is clearer.

The three stages of production that can be predicted by the law of diminishing returns are called increasing marginal returns, diminishing marginal returns, and negative marginal returns. The effect on output of varying levels of input can be seen by looking closely at these three stages.

Increasing Marginal Returns Look again at the production schedule in Figure 4.5 on page 87. The first column shows one input in making rubber ducks: labor. As this input varies, so do the output levels of the company. Clearly, if there are no workers, no product is made. With one worker, the company makes 10 ducks a day. As the number of workers increases to 13, total product levels continue to increase. Extra workers allow each person to specialize, or concentrate, on a particular part of the process. This increases production.

Notice how the marginal product in column three also continues to increase with the addition of the first 11 workers. As each of these first 11 workers are added, output rises at a faster rate. The first worker boosts production by 10 units, the second by 40, the third by 60, and so on until the eleventh worker, who raises output by 200 units.

You can also see this rise in production in the production curve in Figure 4.5. The vertical axis of the graph shows Golden's total product, or output. The one varying input (labor) appears on the horizontal axis. As the number of workers increases from zero to 11, the total output rises at a steep rate.

Diminishing Marginal Returns As the law of diminishing returns predicts, however, at some point output begins to increase at a diminished, or lower, rate. The twelfth worker only adds 110 units, whereas the eleventh worker added 200 units. Perhaps there is not enough machinery in the factory to keep the twelfth worker fully employed. Thus, even though total product continues to increase with the twelfth worker, marginal product begins to decrease. That is, total output increases at a slower rate than it did with workers 1 through 11.

The production curve in Figure 4.5 reflects this drop in the rate of increased production. As the number of workers increases from 11 to 12, the rise in total output begins to level off. Production with these workers is not rising as fast as in the first part of the graph.

Negative Marginal Returns The fourteenth, fifteenth, and sixteenth workers make the situation even worse. At this point, workers are getting in each other's way, creating bottlenecks on the assembly line and actually lowering the level of output. In addition, the overcrowding results in frustrated workers and low morale, which further erodes productivity. The fourteenth worker, for example, lowers total production by 25 units.

You can see this drop in total product in the production curve. The graph curves downward after the addition of the fourteenth, fifteenth, and

PRODUCTIVITY *How many people does it take to change a lightbulb?* **Why do producers pay attention to marginal returns?**

Caption Answer
to determine the level of input needed to maximize profits ★23A

Across the Curriculum

TECHNOLOGY New technology often can help an industry improve output. However, the law of diminishing returns can still come into play. In the fishing industry, technology such as electronic fish-finding equipment, global-positioning systems, computers, and satellite linkups have greatly improved navigation, weather tracking, and fish hauls. Smaller fishing boats in particular rely on sophisticated high-tech equipment to compete with larger boats and crews.

Fishing operations using state-of-the-art equipment have gotten so good at finding fish, however, that many fish populations are dwindling. Along the New England coast, the fish population has become severely depleted. New England fishing operations are now seeing negative returns on their investments in high-tech equipment. Fish hauls, which increased steadily during the late 1970s, have declined since 1980. The U.S. government has responded by limiting fishing along the New England coast to help fish populations increase. ■

SUPPLY 89

Themes in Economics

MARKETS & PRICES Environmental trends can affect supply in an industry by affecting the price of its resources. For example, during the late 1990s increased pressures on the paper industry to limit logging in national forests caused the price of wood pulp to escalate. At the same time, increased recycling caused the price of wastepaper to drop. Raw materials can account for as much as 40 percent of a paper mill's production costs. As a result, paper mills that specialized in using wastepaper to produce recycled paper products saw increased profits while many other paper mills saw profits drop. As more cities and states require recycling, the supply of recycled paper products likely will continue to increase at each and every price. ■

Transparency
An overhead transparency of Figure 4.6 is available in *Transparency Resources*. See Transparency 15: Marginal Product and Costs.

Caption Answer
at the point of 11 workers producing 875 total units at a total cost of $5,765 ★23F, 23G

---

sixteenth workers. This reflects the negative marginal returns to labor.

Production schedules and curves like the ones in Figure 4.5 help businesspeople apply the law of diminishing returns to their production decisions. By discovering the point at which their inputs are most efficiently used, they can set production levels that will maximize profits.

Costs of Production

Manufacturers must also look at their costs of production when deciding how much to supply to the market. As noted in Section 1, a business's costs of production include any goods and services used to make a product. Manufacturers are particularly interested in their costs of production because these costs directly affect the amount of profit their business makes.

For example, imagine that you start your own lawnmowing service. Two of your customers want to have their lawns mowed by 10 A.M. Saturday. They are willing to pay you the same amount of money—$15. One lawn takes one hour to mow, and the other takes two.

You know you only have time to complete one of the assignments by the deadline. How do you choose? For a cost of two hours' work, you have the potential to earn $15. You can earn the same amount of money by working for one hour on a different lawn. But your cost in earning that money is lower—one hour of work instead of two. In search of the highest profit with the lowest cost, you decide that on Saturday morning you will mow the lawn that takes one hour to complete.

Manufacturers and other suppliers deal with complicated production costs and must consider many factors. To make analyzing costs easier, most producers divide them into several categories: fixed, variable, total, and marginal. Analyzing these various production costs helps

MARGINAL PRODUCT AND COSTS

Labor Input	Total Product	Marginal Product	Fixed Costs	Variable Costs	Total Costs	Marginal Costs
0	0	0	$3,400	$0	$3,400	–
1	10	10	3,400	215	3,615	$21.50
2	50	40	3,400	430	3,830	5.38
3	110	60	3,400	645	4,045	3.58
4	175	65	3,400	860	4,260	3.31
5	245	70	3,400	1,075	4,475	3.07
6	320	75	3,400	1,290	4,690	2.87
7	400	80	3,400	1,505	4,905	2.69
8	485	85	3,400	1,720	5,120	2.53
9	575	90	3,400	1,935	5,335	2.39
10	675	100	3,400	2,150	5,550	2.15
11	875	200	3,400	2,365	5,765	1.08
12	985	110	3,400	2,580	5,980	1.95
13	1,000	15	3,400	2,795	6,195	14.33
14	975	-25	3,400	3,010	6,410	–
15	925	-50	3,400	3,225	6,625	–
16	825	-100	3,400	3,440	6,840	–

FIGURE 4.6 Marginal costs indicate the cost of producing one more unit of output. **At what point are marginal costs lowest for the Golden Duck Company?** ★TEKS

producers determine production goals and potential profits.

Fixed Costs Some production costs do not change no matter how many goods are made. For example, whether the Golden Duck factory produces 10 ducks a day or 1,000—or even if it produces none—the rent that the factory pays stays the same. Production costs that do not change as the level of output changes are called **fixed costs**. Fixed costs include rent, interest on loans, property insurance premiums, local and state property taxes, and salaries.

Fixed costs also include routine wear and tear on machines and other capital goods. In the Golden Duck factory, for example, the machine that molds the toys was purchased five years ago. Each year, a portion of the value of that machine has been considered a fixed cost. Why?

Each year, the molding machine is older and less efficient. The older it becomes, the less value it has. This aging of the machine—and other capital goods—is thus seen as a cost.

Businesses do not determine the amount of **depreciation**, or lessening in value, on each and every capital good they own because these calculations would take too much time. Instead, tax laws and standard accounting practices allow them to divide the cost of a capital good over the life of the good.

You can see the total weekly fixed costs for the Golden Duck Company in Figure 4.6. The first three columns are the production schedule from Figure 4.5. Column 4 shows the fixed costs for each level of production. Notice that the fixed costs listed in this column do not change even though the production level changes. Whether the company produces zero ducks or 1,000 ducks a day, the company's total fixed costs, also called **overhead**, remain $3,400.

Variable Costs Unlike fixed costs, **variable costs** change as the level of output changes. Variable costs include raw materials and wages. In the case of the rubber duck factory, for example, as production rises from 10 to 1,000 ducks a day, the number of workers also rises. The wages

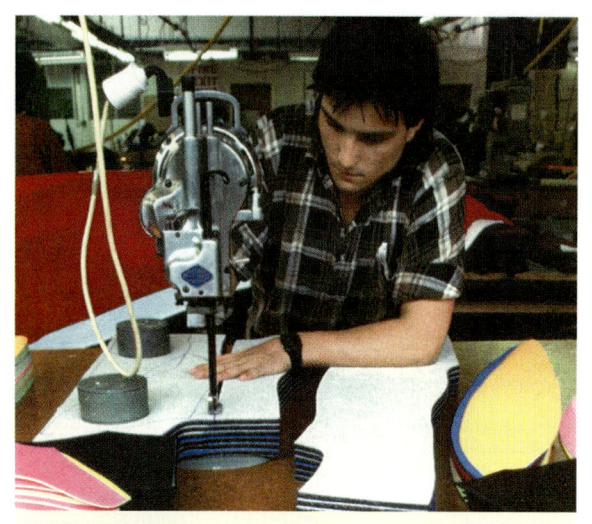

PRODUCTIVITY *Production costs are important to manufacturers because these costs directly affect their business's level of profits.* **What production costs can you identify in this photograph?**

of these workers are an added, or variable, cost. So are the added materials used to make the additional 990 ducks.

You can see Golden's variable costs in Figure 4.6. Column 5 shows the total variable costs of making ducks at each production level. As you would expect, the variable costs listed in column 5 change as production levels change. When no ducks are made, for example, variable costs are $0. At a production level of 1,000 ducks a day, variable costs are $2,795.

Total Costs The sum of the fixed and variable production costs is a company's **total costs**. At zero output a firm's total costs are equal to its fixed costs. If a company is not producing anything, it does not have any variable costs—no workers to be paid and no raw materials to be bought. Thus, its fixed costs are its total costs.

As soon as production begins, however, so do a company's variable costs. This in turn raises the company's total costs. Look again at Figure 4.6 on page 90. At a production level of 1,000 ducks a day, what are Golden's total costs per week? Adding the company's fixed costs ($3,400) and variable costs ($2,795) at this production level reveals weekly total costs of $6,195.

SUPPLY **91**

Caption Answer
Divide the variable, or additional, cost of increasing production by the number of additional units that are to be made. ⭐24A

SECTION 3
REVIEW ANSWERS

1. total product (86), marginal product (87), law of diminishing returns (87), fixed cost (91), depreciation (91), overhead (91), variable cost (91), total cost (91), marginal cost (92) 24A

2. increasing returns—additional inputs result in additional total and marginal product; diminishing returns—total product increases but marginal product decreases; negative returns—total product decreases 23A, 24A, 24D

3a. by examining how total and marginal product changes as inputs change 23A

3b. increases productivity. 26A

4. Marginal costs are higher per duck when the company employs 12 people as opposed to 11 people. However, the extra profit earned on the sale of those extra ducks might be worth it as long as their cost is not more than the marginal cost. 23A, 23F, 25B

PRODUCTIVITY *To make wise production decisions, a tennis ball company must determine the additional costs of producing one more unit of output.* **How is marginal cost calculated?**

Marginal Costs To make production decisions, businesspeople need to know not only their company's total costs but also the marginal costs for the company. **Marginal costs** are the additional costs of producing one more unit of output. How do businesses determine marginal costs?

As you know, fixed costs do not change as production levels change. Therefore, to determine marginal costs as production levels change, a business must look at its variable costs alone. If Golden wants to increase production from 875 to 1,000 ducks a day, its variable costs increase by $430, from $2,365 to $2,795. The marginal cost of making each new duck is the additional cost ($430) divided by the number of additional ducks (125): $430 ÷ 125 = $3.44.

This figure means that each additional duck (numbers 876 to 1,000) costs $3.44 to make. If Golden wants to increase production from 875 to 999 ducks instead of to 1,000, it can calculate how much this will cost: 124 additional ducks at a marginal cost of $3.44 equals $426.56.

This allows businesspeople to calculate the exact cost of any change in production levels. Many businesspeople do indeed make marginal production decisions—decisions to produce a few more or a few less units of output. Marginal costs allow the business to determine the profitability of increasing or decreasing production by a few units.

SECTION 3 REVIEW

⭐TEKS Q: 1, 2, 3b, 4

1. **Define and Explain:**
   total product
   marginal product
   law of diminishing returns
   fixed cost
   depreciation
   overhead
   variable cost
   total cost
   marginal cost

2. **Summarizing:** Copy the chart below. Use it to identify the three stages of production and to define what happens in each stage.

   Stages of Production

3. **Finding the Main Idea**
   a. How do you determine what happens to productivity when a product's inputs change?
   b. How does technology affect productivity?

4. **Writing and Critical Thinking**
   Summarizing: Imagine that the market for rubber ducks is extremely strong. As manager of the Golden Duck Company, you are tempted to take advantage of the extra profit by producing 985 ducks. What factors would make you change your mind?
   Consider the following:
   • marginal costs
   • cost per duck

Homework Practice Online
keyword: SM3 HP4

Economics IN THE NEWS

Supply, Demand, and Computer Chips

Computer chip manufacturers benefited greatly from the high-tech boom of the 1990s. Computer chips are used to control electronic devices, from digital watches and automobiles to personal computers. The microprocessor, the most sophisticated type of computer chip, allows computers to execute millions of instructions a second from computer programs.

Computer chip producers have benefited greatly from the explosion of personal computer sales in the 1990s. Chip manufacturers such as Intel and Advanced Micro Devices (AMD) expanded rapidly in an effort to keep up with demand. By 2000, chip sales for personal computers alone had risen to $50 billion for the year.

However, in 2001, the U.S. economy began to slow down rapidly. The downturn hurt the sales of personal computers, which in turn caused the sales of computer chips to fall. Analysts predicted that sales of computer chips would drop by about 25 percent, only reaching $38 billion by year's end.

In a short period of time, chip manufacturers had gone from barely keeping up with demand to an oversupply of chips. As a result, a price war began between chip manufacturers seeking to sell their excess chips. Chip prices plummeted. Intel, for instance, slashed prices on its most advanced chips by 50 percent. The price of other types of computer chips fell even further. For instance, in July 2000 personal computer manufacturers such as Dell paid $12.64 for 128 megabytes of computer memory chips. A year later they were paying $2.39.

Falling prices will force chip manufacturers to cut costs. As a result, AMD may have to postpone plans to build a new manufacturing plant to produce its next generation of more-advanced computer chips and Intel may have to drop plans to expand its workforce.

The price of and demand for computer parts such as microprocessors, or chips, fluctuate when computer makers experience shifts in demand for their own products.

At the same time, other sectors of the computer industry may benefit from decreasing chip prices. For companies that specialize in manufacturing and selling personal computers, such as Dell, lower chip prices mean reductions in their costs of production. Dell can then lower its price to consumers. In fact, such reductions, along with future technological advances, such as new operating systems, may stimulate personal computer sales to the point where chip manufacturers may once again see record sales.

What Do You Think? TEKS

1. According to the law of supply, how will computer chip manufacturers react to falling prices for computer chips?
2. What impact does falling computer chip prices have on the costs of production of personal computer manufacturers?

WHY IT MATTERS TODAY

Businesses are affected by changes in the supply of resources. The changes businesses deal with affect the overall prices of goods you purchase. Use CNNfyi.com or other **current events** sources to find additional information on changes in factors relating to supply.

CNNfyi.com

Economics in the News Answers

1. They will reduce supply by producing fewer chips. 7A
2. It lowers their costs of production. 7A, 23A

CHAPTER 4
Review Answers

Writing a Summary

Summaries should focus on the main points of each section. These may be found in the Read to Discover questions at the start of each section. Summaries should also use standard grammar, spelling, sentence structure, and punctuation. 24B, 24D

Identifying Ideas

law of supply (73), profit motive (74), cost of production (74), supply curve (75), determinants of supply (79), tax (81), law of diminishing returns (87), overhead (91), variable cost (91), marginal cost (92) 4A, 7A, 17A

Understanding Main Ideas

1. Producers supply more products at higher prices and fewer products at lower prices. Producers make supply decisions based on maximizing profit. 4A, 24A
2. change in price; shift is caused by changes in supply at each and every price 23F

93

CHAPTER 4 Review

3. prices of resources (e.g., labor costs), government tools (e.g., production standards), technology (e.g., HDTV), competition (e.g., other TV makers), prices of related goods (e.g., movie tickets), and producer expectations (e.g., increased sales during holidays) **7A, 23A**

4. The technology itself usually makes production more efficient, thereby lowering the cost of production, which moves the supply curve to the right; the development of new technology, however, has a cost, and this cost increases the cost of production, which moves the supply curve to the left. **7A, 23A, 26A, 26D**

5. increasing returns—increasing input increases total and marginal product; diminishing returns—increasing input increases total product but decreases marginal product; negative returns—increasing input decreases total product **23A, 24A**

6. fixed costs—do not change with output level; variable costs—change with output level; total costs—sum of fixed and variable costs; marginal costs—cost of making one more unit of output **23A**

Reviewing Themes

1. Producers can increase inputs in order to increase output (productivity). This is usually done by hiring more workers or installing more efficient machinery and methods. **23A**

2. When markets are strong and prices are high, more producers try to take advantage of consumer demand in order to make a profit.

(Continued on page 95)

94

Writing a Summary

Using standard grammar, spelling, sentence structure, and punctuation, write a summary of the information in this chapter.

Identifying Ideas

Identify the following terms and explain their significance.

1. law of supply
2. profit motive
3. cost of production
4. supply curve
5. determinant of supply
6. tax
7. law of diminishing returns
8. overhead
9. variable cost
10. marginal cost

Understanding Main Ideas

SECTION 1 *(pp. 73–78)*

1. Define the law of supply. Be sure to include how the profit motive relates to this law.

2. What causes movement along a supply curve—in other words, what prompts a change in the quantity supplied? How does this movement differ from a shift in supply?

SECTION 2 *(pp. 79–85)*

3. What determinants can cause a shift in supply? Give examples of at least three of these factors at work for a company that manufactures televisions.

4. In how many ways does new technology affect the supply curve? Give at least one example for each way you come up with.

SECTION 3 *(pp. 86–92)*

5. Explain what happens in the three stages of production described by the law of diminishing returns.

6. Explain the difference among the following types of costs: fixed, variable, total, marginal.

Reviewing Themes

1. **Productivity** What are the main ways for a producer to increase productivity of whatever is being produced?

2. **Markets and Prices** If a product market is strong and the price is rising, how does that affect the supply of that product?

3. **Supply and Demand** Why would a larger supply of steel lead to an increase in the supply of automobiles on the market?

Thinking Critically

1. **Categorizing** Determine whether the supply of candy and diamonds is elastic or inelastic. Explain your reasoning.

2. **Identifying Points of View** Why might a government grant subsidies to certain individuals or businesses?

3. **Drawing Conclusions** If a company has three different manufacturing plants and 10,000 employees, but wants to cut costs to increase productivity, where should the cuts come from and will those cuts be in variable, marginal, or fixed costs?

Writing about Economics

Review what you wrote in your Economics Notebook at the beginning of this chapter about the definition of *supply* and the things you believe you have supplied in the past month. Now that you have studied this chapter, would you change your definition and examples? Why or why not? Record your answer in your notebook.

CHAPTER 4

Building Social Studies Skills

Interpreting the Chart

Study the production schedule below for the Lightning Skateboard Company. Then use it to help you answer the questions that follow.

PRODUCTION SCHEDULE

Labor Input	Total Product Levels	Marginal Product
0	0	0
1	3	3
2	7	4
3	12	5
4	20	8
5	30	10
6	45	15
7	57	12
8	66	9
9	68	2
10	65	-3

1. If the number of workers increases from four to six, how much does marginal product increase?
   a. 2
   b. 4
   c. 5
   d. 7
2. How does the law of diminishing returns affect the Lightning Skateboard Company?

Analyzing Primary Sources

Read the following excerpt from the book *Only One Earth* by British economist Lady Barbara Ward. It discusses the depletion of natural resources. Answer the questions that follow.

"Annual consumption of iron ore has quadrupled since 1950 . . . . If this rate of increase continues, estimates suggest . . . exhaustion of the ore bodies by the middle of the 21st century. . . .

As reserves run down, four things will happen. Prices will rise . . . [A] new wave of exploration will be unleashed. . . . The third consequence will be much more careful use of scrap. . . . The fourth consequence will be a turn to other materials. . . ."

3. Which of the following statements best describes how the author views the depletion of Earth's iron resources?
   a. There will always be iron; it will just take more research to find the deposits.
   b. Only depletion and higher prices will cause people to recycle or look for alternatives.
   c. By the 21st century, people will have reduced their need for iron ore.
   d. As prices rise, businesses dealing exclusively in iron scrap will spring up.
4. Does iron ore have elastic or inelastic supply? Explain your answer.

Alternative Assessment

Building Your Portfolio

Create a cartoon or comic strip to illustrate an economic concept from the chapter. For example, demonstrate the law of diminishing returns with an "increasing returns" character climbing a steep "production" hill. Meanwhile, a "diminishing returns" character is about to reach the top of the hill, and a "negative returns" character is tumbling down the other side.

internet connect

Internet Activity: go.hrw.com
KEYWORD: SM3 EC4

Access the Internet through the HRW Go site to research the law of supply. Using information online and from your textbook, prepare a 10-question quiz about supply, the law of supply, the supply curve, and other supply concepts. Trade quizzes with a classmate.

(Continued from page 94)

Therefore, supply increases as similar products arrive on the market. **4A, 7A, 23A**

3. More steel will make steel cheaper so more cars can be made more cheaply. **7A, 23A**

Thinking Critically

1. candy—made quickly and cheaply, resources readily available (elastic); diamonds—hard to find, time-consuming, and costly to refine (inelastic) **23A**

2. to ensure an adequate supply of essential products; to increase economic activity in a city or region. **17A, 23D**

3. The employer can lay off employees to decrease marginal costs, and this would also decrease variable costs of employee salaries. The company could also get rid of one building, which would be a fixed cost. **2B, 23A, 23D, 24A**

Writing about Economics

Students should explain their reasons for being loyal to the products they listed. They should also identify factors such as celebrity endorsements and brand recognition. **24B**

Building Social Studies Skills

1. d **23F, 23G**

2. Increasing labor input to six workers increases production output. After that, marginal product decreases. **23A, 23F, 23G**

3. b **23E**

4. inelastic—is costly to mine and is not readily available **23A, 23E**

SUPPLY 95

CHAPTER RESOURCE MANAGER

CHAPTER 5 PRICES

	OBJECTIVES	PACING GUIDE	REPRODUCIBLE RESOURCES
SECTION 1 **THE PRICE SYSTEM** (pp. 97–102)	▶ What is the role of the price system? ▶ What are the benefits of the price system? ▶ What are the limitations of the price system?	**Regular** 1.5 days **Block Scheduling** 0.5 day	**ELL** Spanish Study Guide 5.1 **ELL** English Study Guide 5.1 **PS** Reading 64: Price Making in a Democracy
SECTION 2 **DETERMINING PRICES** (pp. 103–07)	▶ What is market equilibrium? ▶ How does the price system handle product surpluses and shortages? ▶ How do shifts in demand and supply affect market equilibrium?	**Regular** 2 days **Block Scheduling** 1 day	**ELL** Spanish Study Guide 5.2 **ELL** English Study Guide 5.2 **E** Challenge and Enrichment: Activity 5 **SM** Mathematics for Economics: Activity 5 **E** Simulations and Strategies for Teaching Economics: Activity 5
SECTION 3 **MANAGING PRICES** (pp. 108–12)	▶ Why do governments sometimes set prices? ▶ What do governments try to accomplish through price floors, price ceilings, and rationing? ▶ What happens when governments manage prices?	**Regular** 2 days **Block Scheduling** 1 day	**ELL** Spanish Study Guide 5.3 **ELL** English Study Guide 5.3 **SM** Consumer Economics: Activity 5

Chapter Resource Key

- **PS** Primary Sources
- **RS** Reading Support
- **E** Enrichment
- **S** Simulations
- **SM** Skills Mastery
- **A** Assessment
- **REV** Review
- **ELL** Reinforcement and English Language Learners
- Transparencies
- CD-ROM
- Video
- Videodisc
- Internet
- Holt Presentation Maker Using Microsoft® PowerPoint®
- TEKS and TAKS

95A

TECHNOLOGY RESOURCES	REINFORCEMENT, REVIEW, AND ASSESSMENT
• One-Stop Planner: Lesson 5.1 • Researcher Online • Homework Practice Online • CNN Presents Economics: The Price of Gas • Global Skillbuilder CD-ROM	**REV** Section 1 Review, p. 102 **A** Daily Quiz 5.1 ★ TAKS Every Day!
• One-Stop Planner: Lesson 5.2 • Researcher Online • Homework Practice Online • Transparencies 16, 17, and 18 • Global Skillbuilder CD-ROM	**REV** Section 2 Review, p. 107 **A** Daily Quiz 5.2 ★ TAKS Every Day!
• One-Stop Planner: Lesson 5.3 • Researcher Online • Homework Practice Online • Transparencies 19 and 20 • Global Skillbuilder CD-ROM	**REV** Section 3 Review, p. 112 **A** Daily Quiz 5.3 ★ TAKS Every Day!

Chapter Review and Assessment

- **SM** Global Skillbuilder CD-ROM
- HRW Go site
- **REV** Reteaching Activity 5
- **REV** Chapter 5 Review, pp. 114–15
- **A** Chapter 5 Test Generator (on the One-Stop Planner)
- **A** Chapter 5 Test
- **A** Alternative Assessment Handbook

One-Stop Planner CD-ROM

It's easy to plan lessons, select resources, and print out materials for your students when you use the *Texas One-Stop Planner CD-ROM with Test Generator*.

---

internet connect

HRW ONLINE RESOURCES
Go To: go.hrw.com
Then type in a keyword.

TEACHER HOME PAGE
KEYWORD: SM3 Teacher

CHAPTER INTERNET ACTIVITIES
KEYWORD: SM3 EC5
Choose an activity to:
▸ understand the benefits and limitations of nuclear energy.
▸ research gasoline prices in the United States.
▸ learn about the minimum wage.

CHAPTER ENRICHMENT LINKS
KEYWORD: SM3 CH5

HOLT RESEARCHER ONLINE
KEYWORD: Holt Researcher

ONLINE ASSESSMENT
Homework Practice
KEYWORD: SM3 HP5
TAKS Review
KEYWORD: SM3 T5
Rubrics
KEYWORD: SS Rubrics

CONTENT UPDATES
KEYWORD: SS Content Updates

HOLT PRESENTATION MAKER
KEYWORD: SM3 PPT5

ONLINE READING SUPPORT
KEYWORD: SS Strategies

CURRENT EVENTS
KEYWORD: S3 Current Events

TEXAS ONLINE RESOURCES
KEYWORD: S3 TX

95B

LESSON 5.1 THE PRICE SYSTEM

TEXTBOOK PAGES 97–102

HOLT PRESENTATION MAKER
Access Illustrated LECTURE NOTES using Microsoft® PowerPoint® on the One-Stop Planner CD-ROM

OBJECTIVES

- Explain the role of the price system.
- Describe the benefits of the price system. ★4B
- Identify the limitations of the price system.

MOTIVATE

Show the class some advertisements from a local newspaper in which you have blacked out all of the prices. Ask the students how they would choose between the products advertised if all the items cost the same price. Call on students to suggest what difficulties they might encounter if prices did not exist at all. *(Students might suggest that producers and consumers would have a difficult time exchanging goods and services. Producers could not judge the value of resources required to produce goods or services, or the level of consumer demand for a product. Consumers could not judge the value of one good compared with another.)* Tell students to consider the benefits and limitations of prices as they read through Section 1 of the chapter.

TEACH

Building a Vocabulary

Have each student use a spiral notebook to create an Economics Dictionary to be used throughout the chapter. This dictionary might be used as an activity at the start of each new section or as a learning aid for English Language Learners or students having difficulty. List words that students will be expected to know for this section on the chalkboard. Have students use the information provided in the text or on the *Researcher CD-ROM* to list, define, and give an example of each term.

Understanding Main Concepts

Ask students to list the main goals of producers. As students mention different goals, create a list on the chalkboard. Do the same thing for the goals of consumers. Then have students compare the two lists and discuss how producers' and consumers' goals can conflict. Ask students how producers and consumers resolve their conflicting goals *(through the price system).*

Call on students to explain the role of the price system. Ask students what role the price system plays in motivating producers and consumers to balance the forces of supply and demand. *(The price system helps producers and consumers communicate how much products cost to make, what they are worth to both producers and consumers, and the level of demand for them. Through prices, producers and consumers negotiate and compromise by either accepting or rejecting the prices of goods and services.)*

Analyzing and Applying Ideas

Tell the class that the price system not only plays an important role in free-enterprise markets but offers many benefits as well. On the chalkboard, write *Benefits of the Price System.* Under this heading, list the five benefits of the price system: *information, incentives, choice, efficiency,* and *flexibility.* Briefly discuss each benefit with the class.

Next, tell the class that the price system has limitations as well as benefits. On the chalkboard, write *Limitations of the Price System.* Under this heading, list the three limitations of the price system: *externalities, public goods,* and *instability.* Once again, briefly discuss each limitation with the class.

Organize the class into groups of three to five students. Tell each group to think of one or two examples not mentioned in the text that illustrate each of the five benefits and three limitations of the price system. When the groups are done, call on volunteers from each group to share some of their examples with the class. ★4B

Role-Playing

Have two volunteers stand up in front of the class. Tell student A to imagine that he or she is a producer who has five pizzas to sell. Each pizza cost $5 to make, and the producer would like to sell all five while making as much profit as possible. Tell Student B to imagine that he or she is a consumer who wants to buy some pizza to serve at a party. The consumer has $100 to spend and wants to buy as much pizza as possible for as little money as possible. Have the two students act out their roles until they agree on a price and an exchange is made. When they are done, have the class provide feedback and point out ways in which the price system helped the two students communicate and come to an agreement.

Then organize the class into groups of two or three. Have each group create a similar type of scenario that illustrates the role of the price system in helping producers and consumers communicate. Have volunteers act out their scenarios for the class.

CLOSE

Review with the class the role of the price system and its benefits and limitations. Then have students discuss whether the benefits of the price system outweigh the limitations. ★4B

OPTIONS

Students Having Difficulty, English Language Learners

Pair students having difficulty or students acquiring English with fluent students who have mastered the material. Tell each pair to create a chart that illustrates the role, benefits, and limitations of the price system. Have each pair write a caption describing the importance of the price system, and what its chart illustrates. Refer students who need additional instruction on the skills used in this lesson to the *Global Skillbuilder* Lesson 12: Creating Graphic Organizers. ★4B, 24D

Gifted Learners

Tell students to research how the price of one product varies throughout the nation. Students should examine the reasons for price variations, whether regional supply and demand for the product varies, and who the major suppliers of the product are. Have students prepare a presentation summarizing their findings to give to the class. Students may want to include summaries of their presentations in their portfolios. ★24D

Interpersonal Learners, Linguistic Learners

Organize students into groups of three to five. Provide students with several local and national newspapers and news magazines. Tell each group to use newspapers and magazines to find examples of how companies and the government have dealt with negative and positive externalities. In addition, encourage students to find articles that mention government attempts to increase, decrease, or otherwise change the way the United States pays for public goods. Each group should select one article to share with the class. Have a volunteer from each group summarize the selected articles for the class.

Visual-Spatial Learners

Tell students to create a print advertisement "selling" or "promoting" the price system. The ad should explain the role and importance of the price system and how it benefits both producers and consumers. Tell students to include both text and illustrations in their ads. You might want to suggest that students create their ads around a catchy slogan or a striking image. ★4B, 24D

REVIEW

Have students complete the Section 1 Review on page 102. Use the answers in the Annotated Teacher's Edition to assess student mastery of this section.

ASSESS

To assess student mastery of this section, have students complete Daily Quiz 5.1 in *Daily Quizzes with Answer Key*. For additional assessment options, see *Alternative Assessment Handbook* on the *One-Stop Planner CD-ROM*.

ADDITIONAL RESOURCES

Fischer, David Hackett. *The Great Wave: Price Revolutions and the Rhythm of History.* 2000. Oxford University Press.

Heilbroner, Robert L. *The Making of Economic Society.* 2001. Prentice Hall.

Stein, Herbert and Murray Foss. *The New Illustrated Guide to the American Economy.* 1995. AEI Press.

Focus: High School Economics, National Council on Economic Education. (instructional activities)

LESSON 5.2 DETERMINING PRICES

TEXTBOOK PAGES 103–07

HOLT PRESENTATION MAKER Access Illustrated LECTURE NOTES using Microsoft® PowerPoint® on the One-Stop Planner CD-ROM

OBJECTIVES

- Explain what market equilibrium is.
- Identify how the price system handles product surpluses and shortages.
- Describe how shifts in demand and supply affect market equilibrium.

MOTIVATE

Tell students to consider how price can affect the supply of and demand for a product. Then ask students to describe what they think would happen if one music store in town decided to lower the price of all its compact discs (CDs) to 50 cents. *(Students might suggest that consumers would rush to the store to buy CDs and that the store would probably run out of stock rather quickly. In addition, the store would probably lose money because the price would be too low for it to make a profit.)* Then ask students to describe what they think would happen if one music store decided to charge twice as much for its CDs as other stores. *(Students might suggest that few consumers would choose to shop at the store, resulting in surplus stock and possibly causing the store to go out of business.)* Explain to students that prices that are too low or too high can result in imbalances between supply and demand. Tell students to think about how the price system can correct these imbalances as they read the section. ★7A

TEACH

Building a Vocabulary

List the important terms for this section on the chalkboard and tell students to add them to their Economics Dictionaries. Tell students to use the information provided in the text or on the *Researcher CD-ROM* to list, define, and give an example of each vocabulary term.

Understanding Main Concepts

Have students look at Figure 5.1: Demand, Supply, and Equilibrium Price for Tennis Shoes (Transparency 16). Briefly review with students what supply-and-demand schedules and curves show and why producers use them. Then tell the class that producers plot a product's demand and supply curves on the same graph to determine the price at which supply and demand are in market equilibrium. Ask a student to point out where market equilibrium occurs in Figure 5.1 *(at the point E)*. Then ask a student to define the term *market equilibrium* and write the definition on the chalkboard. *(Market equilibrium occurs when the quantity supplied and the quantity demanded for a product are equal at the same price.)* Refer students who need additional instruction on the skills used in this activity to the *Global Skillbuilder* Lesson 10: Reading Graphs. ★7B

Understanding, Using, and Creating Charts and Graphs

On the chalkboard, draw a demand and supply schedule similar to the one below. Organize students into groups of two to three. Tell them to use the demand and supply schedule to plot demand and supply curves on one graph, as in Figure 5.1. Tell students to label the demand curve and the supply curve, indicating the equilibrium point. Students may want to use the Graphing Tool on the *Researcher Online* to create their graphs. Refer students who need additional instruction on the skills used in this activity to the *Global Skillbuilder* Lesson 11: Presenting Data Graphically. ★7B, 23B

Demand and Supply Schedule for Football Tickets

Price per Ticket	Quantity Demanded	Quantity Supplied
$15	150,000	0
$30	120,000	30,000
$45	90,000	60,000
$60	60,000	90,000
$75	30,000	120,000
$90	0	150,000

Identifying Cause and Effect, Learning from Visuals

Explain to students that the price system steers supply and demand toward market equilibrium but that this process is not instantaneous. A certain amount of trial and error is involved as producers change prices and quantity supplied to eliminate surpluses and shortages. Call on volunteers to define a surplus and a shortage. *(A surplus exists when the quantity supplied exceeds the quantity demanded. A shortage exists when the quantity demanded exceeds the quantity supplied.)* Write the definitions on the chalkboard.

Have students examine Figure 5.2: Surplus and Shortage of Tennis Shoes (Transparency 17). Call on a student to explain why setting the price for tennis shoes at $90 results in a surplus. Have the student describe how the graph illustrates this surplus. Then ask another student to describe the process by which the price system resolves this surplus. Next, have students do the same thing for the shortage that occurs when the price for tennis shoes is $30.

Remind students of the questions they discussed at the start of the lesson. Ask them if their predictions about what happens when producers set prices for CDs too low or too high were correct. If they weren't, have students explain again what would happen in each case. ⭐23F

Organizing Ideas, Demonstrating Understanding

Organize students into groups of two or three. Tell each group to create two flowcharts: one that shows the process by which surpluses occur and the price system resolves them, another that shows the process by which shortages occur and the price system resolves them. When students are done, have volunteers share their flowcharts with the class. Provide feedback as necessary. You may want to draw two "correct" flowcharts on the chalkboard and have students copy them in their notes. Refer students who need additional instruction on the skills used in this activity to the *Global Skillbuilder* Lesson 12: Creating Graphic Organizers.

Identifying Cause and Effect, Learning from Visuals

Remind students that a variety of factors can shift a product's entire demand or supply curve to the right or left. Quickly review these factors. Then ask students to describe what happens to the equilibrium point when a product's demand or supply curve shifts. *(The equilibrium point shifts to the new intersection of the demand and supply curves.)* Have students examine Figure 5.3: Equilibrium, Demand, and Supply Shifts (Transparency 18). Call on students to explain how the shift in the demand curve in the graph on the left shifts the equilibrium point. Next, have students explain how the shift in the supply curve in the graph on the right shifts the equilibrium point. ⭐7A, 23F

CLOSE

Review with the class the main concepts discussed during the lesson. Then ask students to mention any recent shortages of surpluses that they know of. Instruct students to discuss why these imbalances occurred and to predict what they think the market and producers will do to try and correct these imbalances.

OPTIONS

Students Having Difficulty

Pair students having difficulty with students who have mastered the material. Tell each pair to make an outline of the main concepts covered in the section.

Linguistic Learners

Have students research the causes and effects of a recent surplus or shortage. Students may want to focus on food products, toys, computers, or any other good or service with a supply or demand that can shift rapidly. Have students use the *Researcher Online,* the library, in-class resources, and the Internet to find information. Have students summarize their findings in a report that includes charts and graphs illustrating the supply and demand imbalance and any changes in this imbalance. Students may want to use the Graphing Tool on the *Researcher Online* to create their graphs. Students may want to include their reports in their portfolios.

REVIEW

Have students complete the Section 2 Review on page 107. Use the answers in the Annotated Teacher's Edition to assess student mastery of this section.

ASSESS

To assess student mastery of this section, have students complete Daily Quiz 5.2 in *Daily Quizzes with Answer Key.* For additional assessment options, see *Alternative Assessment Handbook* on the *One-Stop Planner CD-ROM.*

ADDITIONAL RESOURCES

Baumol, William, and Alan Blinder. *Microeconomics: Principles and Policy.* 2000. Harcourt College.

Jacobs, Eva ed., *Handbook of Labor Statistics: Employment, Earnings, Prices, Productivity, and other Labor Data.* 2000. Bernan Associates.

Thurow, Lester, and Robert Heilbroner. *Economics Explained.* 1998. Touchstone Books.

Economics at Work. National Council on Economic Education. (one-semester multimedia curriculum)

LESSON 5.3 MANAGING PRICES

TEXTBOOK PAGES 108–112

HOLT PRESENTATION MAKER
Access Illustrated LECTURE NOTES using Microsoft® PowerPoint® on the One-Stop Planner CD-ROM

OBJECTIVES

- Describe why governments sometimes set prices. ★15A
- Analyze what governments try to accomplish through price floors, price ceilings, and rationing. ★15A
- Explain what happens when governments manage prices.

MOTIVATE

Have students discuss each of the following scenarios:
- It is 1942 and World War II has erupted. In the United States, many products, such as meat and gasoline, are in short supply. What steps might the U.S. government take to allocate scarce goods?
- The high-tech industry is booming in your city. Hundreds of people earning high wages are moving into the city each month. Rapidly rising apartment prices are the result. Many poorer residents can no longer afford to live in the city and are having to move to less desirable areas. What should the local government do, if anything?
- Increasing numbers of people are moving to a new settlement on Mars in hopes of economic gain. Unfortunately, jobs are scarce, and competition is stiff. Wages have dropped to all-time lows as people, desperate for work, accept any pay offered. Many people live in slums and can barely afford to buy food and clothing. What should the government on Mars do, if anything?

Tell students to keep these scenarios in mind as they read the section.

TEACH

Building a Vocabulary

List the important terms for this section on the chalkboard and tell students to add them to their Economics Dictionaries. Tell students to use the information provided in the text or on the *Researcher CD-ROM* to list, define, and give an example of each vocabulary term.

Understanding Main Concepts

Write the terms *price ceilings, price floors,* and *rationing* on the chalkboard. Ask students to define each term and to explain why governments use each of these forms of intervention *(price ceilings —government regulations that establish maximum prices for a particular product to ensure that consumers can purchase basic necessities; price floors—government regulations that establish minimum prices for a particular product to ensure that producers and workers earn a basic level of income and that producers earn enough profit to make it worthwhile to produce needed goods and services; rationing—a system in which a government or other institution determines how a product will be distributed because it is extremely scarce).*

Next, ask students to explain why most economists advise against the use of price ceilings and price floors except in rare situations. *(Interfering in the normal interaction between supply and demand can cause unintended imbalances and can prevent markets from reaching equilibrium.)* Then ask students to explain the negative consequences of using price ceilings, price floors, and rationing programs. *(Price ceilings tend to result in shortages; price floors tend to result in surpluses; rationing can distribute goods unfairly, is costly to put into effect, and tends to foster black markets.)* ★15A, 15B

Identifying Cause and Effect, Evaluating Solutions

Have students review the three scenarios they discussed at the start of class. For each scenario, ask students which method of intervention is the most appropriate—price ceilings, price floors, or rationing—and what the positive and negative consequences might be of using that method. Then have the class vote on whether the government should intervene in each case.

Next, ask students to describe some other situations in which governments might need to use price ceilings, price floors, or rationing, and to explain the positive and negative consequences of each. ★15A, 15B, 23A

Solving Problems

Organize students into groups of four or five and assign each group one of the situations that students mentioned in the previous activity. Tell students to imagine that they are government or institution leaders. Their task is to decide whether the situation requires intervention and, if so, whether they should use price ceilings, price floors, or a rationing program. Tell each group to write a brief statement explaining the situation they face, the solution they chose, and why they chose this solution. Then call on volunteers to share their group's scenario and solution or have students hand in their statements for evaluation. ⭐15A

Debating Ideas, Taking a Stand

Have the class choose one of the scenarios discussed during the lesson. Then organize the class into two groups. Tell one group to discuss arguments supporting intervention and the other group to discuss arguments opposing intervention. Give each group 15 to 20 minutes to prepare their arguments. Then have each group select three representatives to present the group's arguments in a debate. Following the debate, have the students in the audience provide feedback. ⭐15A, 15B, 24D

CLOSE

Review the main concepts discussed during the lesson. Then ask students what the consequences might be if the U.S. government never used price ceilings, price floors, or rationing programs.

OPTIONS

Students Having Difficulty

Pair students having difficulty with students who have mastered the material. Tell each pair to discuss and answer the following questions:
- Why do governments sometimes set prices?
- What do governments try to accomplish by using price floors, price ceilings, and rationing programs?
- What are some of the advantages and disadvantages of government intervention in the price system? ⭐15A, 15B

Gifted Learners

Have students research the use of price ceilings, price floors, or rationing programs either at a certain point in history or throughout a period in history. Students can present the information they find in either a written report or in charts and graphs. For example, a student researching the history of the minimum wage in the United States might create a chart that shows the date on which the minimum wage was first instituted and why, the dates it was increased, and the public reaction to these increases. Have students use the library, in-class resources, and the Internet to find information on their topics. Students may want to include their presentations in their portfolios. ⭐15A, 24D

Intrapersonal Learners, Linguistic Learners

Have each student write an essay in response to the following question: Should the government interfere in the price system through the use of price ceilings, price floors, and rationing programs? Students may want to include their essays in their portfolios. ⭐15B, 23D, 24A

Interpersonal Learners

Invite a state or local politician knowledgeable about the use of price-intervention policies to speak to the class about issues such as rent control and minimum wage. Have students prepare questions for the speaker in advance. Following the presentation, have each student write a summary of the discussion. ⭐24D

Visual-Spatial Learners

Show students the film "The Power of the Market," the first of the "Free to Choose" series, available from the Americanism Educational League, P.O. Box 5986, Buena Park, CA 90622. Then have each student write an essay on why he or she is for or against the price system.

REVIEW

Have students complete the Section 3 Review on page 112. Use the answers in the Annotated Teacher's Edition to assess student mastery of this section.

ASSESS

To assess student mastery of this section, have students complete Daily Quiz 5.3 in *Daily Quizzes with Answer Key*. For additional assessment options, see *Alternative Assessment Handbook* on the *One-Stop Planner CD-ROM*.

RETEACH

Instruct students having difficulty with the lessons to complete Reteaching Activity 5. This activity is located in *Reteaching Activities with Answer Key*.

ADDITIONAL RESOURCES

Dowd, Douglas. *Against the Conventional Wisdom: A Primer for Current Economics Controversies and Proposals.* 1997. Westview Press.

Levin-Waldman, Oren. *The Case of the Minimum Wage.* 2001. State University of New York Press.

CHAPTER 5

TOPICS INCLUDE

- benefits and limitations of the price system
- market failures
- negative and positive externalities
- market equilibrium
- surpluses and shortages
- shifts in market equilibrium
- benefits and liabilities of managing prices
- rationing and black markets

ECONOMICS NOTEBOOK

The Economics Notebook is a journal activity that encourages students to consider basic concepts of economics that relate to their lives. A follow-up notebook activity appears on page 114.

WHY IT MATTERS TODAY

To find additional lesson plans dealing with prices, visit CNNfyi.com or have students complete the ECONOMICS IN THE NEWS activity on page 113.

CNNfyi.com

CHAPTER 5

PRICES

Self-interest leads producers and consumers to have different goals in the marketplace. How can consumers and producers compromise? How can consumers and producers determine a level of production that satisfies consumers' desire for affordable goods and the producers' desire to make a profit? Consumers and producers communicate through the price system. In this chapter you will learn how the price system works in a free-enterprise system as well as how the market responds to surpluses and shortages.

ECONOMICS NOTEBOOK

In your Economics Notebook, list three items that you have purchased recently and indicate how much you paid for them. Explain what you think these prices told you about the products.

WHY IT MATTERS TODAY

Government regulation of prices continues to be a controversial topic. Use CNNfyi.com or other current events sources to find additional instances of controversies generated by the issue.

CNNfyi.com

96

SECTION 1
THE PRICE SYSTEM

READ TO DISCOVER
1. What is the role of the price system?
2. What are the benefits of the price system?
3. What are the limitations of the price system?

ECONOMICS DICTIONARY
market failure
externality
public good

How does the price system allow producers and consumers to communicate with each other? As you know, producers and consumers have different goals. To meet their goals, the two groups must work together. The price system guides producers and consumers to balance the forces of supply and demand by reaching compromises on production levels. That is, a free-enterprise economy primarily relies on the price system to answer the basic economic questions of what, how, and for whom to produce.

In this section you will learn not only how the price system works but also how well it works. The price system has both benefits and limitations in coordinating production decisions among producers and consumers.

The Language of Prices

Every time you buy a good or service, you are speaking the "language" of prices. It may sound strange to say that prices are a language, but prices do indeed serve as the main form of communication between producers and consumers in a free-enterprise market.

Prices are the way in which producers tell consumers how much it costs to produce and distribute a good or service. In essence, the price of a pizza translates to you, the consumer, as "If you want this amount of pizza, you have to pay this price." If you buy the pizza, your response to producers is "Yes, I want this amount of pizza at this price." If you do not buy the pizza, your response is "No, I do not want this amount of pizza at this price."

If consumers buy a product at the established price, producers may be satisfied and maintain current production levels and prices. On the other hand, producers may decide to try to increase their profits. The owner of Palatial Pizza, for example, communicates this decision to consumers by increasing the price of a pizza. Consumers then have the chance to respond to Palatial Pizza's decision by accepting or rejecting the new price. If the price increase is acceptable, consumers will continue to buy about the same amount of pizza from Palatial, and revenue will increase. If the price increase is not acceptable, consumers will buy fewer pizzas from Palatial Pizza, causing revenue to fall.

In contrast, if consumers do not buy a product at the established price, producers must determine whether they can charge a lower price for the product and still make a profit. If they can, producers communicate this to consumers by reducing prices.

Benefits of the Price System

Using the price system as a form of communication between producers and consumers has several benefits. It provides

- information,
- incentives,
- choice,
- efficiency, and
- flexibility.

Information Producers and consumers can gather information through the price system. For example, the prices of resources tell producers

PRICES 97

Caption Answer

information, choice, efficiency, and flexibility ⭐4B

Global Connections

In Hungary, restaurants often do not list prices on the foreign-language versions of their menus. As a result, tourists dining out in Hungary can end up paying much higher prices than Hungarian diners, whose menus include prices. One Budapest restaurant charged a tourist 11,000 forints ($65) for two bowls of goulash. On the Hungarian menu, the price of one bowl of goulash was only 550 forints ($3). Another tourist was shocked when his bill for a dinner for four came to more than $6,000. ■

Themes in Economics

MARKETS & PRICES Payless ShoeSource shows the benefit of offering strong price incentives. To attract customers, Payless provides low-priced knockoffs of higher-priced shoes. The shoe chain is able to keep prices low because it minimizes costs. Shelves are tightly packed in order to display a large number of shoes in a small space. Customers help themselves, eliminating the need for salespeople. The strategy has paid off. In 2000 Payless was the number-one shoe retailer in the United States. ■

CALVIN & HOBBES Copyright 1989 Watterson. Reprinted with permission of Universal Press Syndicate. All rights reserved.

MARKETS & PRICES *Using the price system as a form of communication between producers and consumers provides several benefits, including incentives.* **What are the other benefits of the price system?** ⭐TEKS

how much they must pay to make their products. The market would be quite different if producers did not know this information. Businesses would make random decisions about what to produce because they would have no idea whether one product would be more profitable than another. A producer would have no way of knowing whether it would be more profitable to produce skateboards or microprocessors.

Like producers, consumers gather information through the price system. Consumers need to know the prices of goods and services to make informed buying decisions. Without prices, how could you shop effectively? You would have no way of knowing how the cost of a sweater compares with that of a jacket. Prices inform consumers of the relative worth of the goods and services they purchase.

Incentives The price system also provides producers and consumers with incentives to participate in the market. As noted in Chapter 2, an incentive is something that encourages you to behave in a particular way. High prices, when combined with low costs, generally encourage producers to supply more goods and services. This reflects the law of supply—that high prices encourage increases in the quantity supplied, while low prices encourage reductions in the quantity supplied. Low prices, meanwhile, give consumers an incentive to buy more goods and services. This, in turn, reflects the law of demand, which states that high prices generally encourage reductions in the quantity demanded, while low prices tend to encourage increases in the quantity demanded. If there were no price incentives, producers and consumers would have a much more difficult time exchanging goods and services.

Choice By encouraging participation in markets, the price system also increases the choices available in those markets. The higher the incentive to supply products to the marketplace, the greater the choice of products supplied.

For example, consider the athletic-clothing market. Demand for this type of clothing is high, which drives prices and profits higher in relation to many "basic" clothes like jeans and T-shirts. These higher prices and profits encourage competition among the various clothing manufacturers in this market.

In competing with one another, the manufacturers create hundreds of different products, trying to match consumer preferences and generate the most profit. As a result, consumers can select from a wide range of styles and prices for athletic clothing and can choose to buy a $300 designer nylon jogging suit or a pair of $20 cotton sweatpants.

Efficiency Efficiency is a key benefit of the price system. The system brings about efficiency in two main ways. First, it provides for the wise

98 CHAPTER 5

LINKING ECONOMICS and HISTORY

The Coming of the Computer Age

How would you describe a typical computer? You may think of monitors, hard drives, disk drives, and CD-ROM drives. Despite having all of these features, computers usually are small enough to sit on top of a desk. The computer has not always been so compact, however.

The first modern computer, called the Electronic Numerical Integrator and Computer (ENIAC), measured 50 by 30 feet. Development costs for the ENIAC, which was completed in 1945, totaled $400,000.

Over the next decade, computers were transformed from basic mathematical instruments into data-processing machines. The first successful business computer—the 1401®, created by International Business Machines (IBM)—rented for $2,500 per month in 1960 (equivalent to a purchase price of $150,000 at that time).

How did these large and costly computers, known as mainframes, develop into the desktop models we know today? During the 1950s and 1960s a "revolution in miniature" swept the electronics industry. Large vacuum tubes were replaced by smaller transistors. Transistors then evolved into integrated circuits, or microchips, which measured only two tenths of an inch by one tenth of an inch. These tiny chips cost about $1,000 when they were first introduced in 1971, but within two years competition from other producers had driven the price down to $100.

Electronic innovations also enabled components to be produced more efficiently, lowering the price of the entire computer. By 1970 a "minicomputer" cost about $20,000.

The Altair 8800®—introduced in January 1975—is considered to be the first personal computer because it cost about $400 unassembled. The Altair consisted of only a single box with a panel of switches and neon bulbs. It had neither a display screen nor a keyboard and contained very little memory.

By 1977 the "microcomputer" was transformed from a hobbyist's machine into a consumer product. One of the many firms to join the market in the late 1970s was Apple Computer, selling a "home/personal computer" for $1,298 (excluding a monitor) in 1977.

Not to be outdone, in 1981 IBM launched a personal computer (PC) that sold for $2,880. Most software available at the time was easily converted to run on the PC, encouraging other companies to make clones, or copies, of the IBM computer.

Competition and technological developments have led to a decrease in the price of PCs, thereby making computers affordable for the majority of Americans. It was estimated that about 75 percent of American households owned PCs in 2000.

What Do You Think?

1. How do you think computers will change during the next 10 years?
2. Do you think that personal computers will become more or less affordable in the future? Explain your answer.

The first modern computer—the ENIAC—was extremely large and costly compared to today's machines.

What Do You Think? Answers

1. Answers will vary but should include specific examples or reasons to support the opinion given. Students may say that PCs will probably become even smaller and more portable while at the same time becoming more powerful. PCs will probably contain more memory, be easier to use, and be able to run more complex and varied software.

2. Answers will vary but should include specific examples or reasons to support the opinion given. Students may answer that, based on past pricing trends in the computer industry, PCs most likely will be more affordable in the future. As a result of strong competition, rapid technological developments, the growing popularity of the Internet, and unforeseen applications, demand for PCs probably will remain constant, and thus future prices will probably remain low. 23D

Caption Answer

by telling producers what consumers want to buy so that producers can use resources to make what consumers want; by quickly signaling the value of a good or service in relation to others so that producers and consumers can easily compare prices of resources and products ⭐4B

Global Connections

Supply and demand for a product is not always the same in every market. For example, in the mid-1990s Levi Strauss & Co.'s 501® blue jeans sold for about $30 in the United States but for $80 or more overseas. The reason is that Levi's® blue jeans were a status symbol among Asian and European youth. Thus, overseas consumers were willing to pay more for Levi's blue jeans than were U.S. shoppers. The flexibility of the price system enables producers to match prices to varying consumer demand in different markets. ■

Caption Answer

negative externality

MARKETS & PRICES *Prices immediately signal the value of a good in relation to another good.* **How does the price system encourage efficiency?** ⭐TEKS

use of resources. Prices tell producers which products consumers want to buy. High prices encourage producers to use resources to provide goods and services that consumers want. Low prices lead producers to stop using resources to provide goods and services that consumers do not want.

Without prices to indicate consumer demand, producers could unknowingly waste raw materials, their workers' labor, and other resources by making products that would sit unpurchased on store shelves. The pricing system tells producers how best to use their resources—natural, human, capital, and entrepreneurial—to meet consumer demand.

The price system also encourages efficiency by quickly delivering information to producers and consumers. Prices immediately signal the value of a good or service in relation to other goods or services. Producers can easily compare the prices of resources, and consumers can do the same for goods and services. As a result, both groups can make decisions efficiently.

Think about how long it would take you to buy a pair of jeans at the mall if you could not compare prices. You might find four pairs you like equally, but be unable to determine which ones cost a lot of money and which ones are relatively inexpensive. The decision about which pair to buy would take you much longer—so long, in fact, that you might become frustrated and decide not to buy any jeans at all. By eliminating some choices, the price system allows consumers to make decisions efficiently.

Flexibility One of the price system's greatest strengths is its ability to deal with change. The supply and demand of goods changes almost constantly. A hit movie or music video can increase consumer demand for a particular hair or clothing style overnight. Sudden events such as floods, freezes, and work stoppages can reduce the supply of crops or manufactured goods. The price system can accommodate these changes quickly.

If, for example, a freeze destroys a large portion of the orange crop, the price of oranges increases. The higher prices determine how the low orange supply will be distributed: only those

MARKETS & PRICES *Limitations of the price system are known as market failures.* **What type of market failure is caused by a logging company that fails to plant new trees?**

100 CHAPTER 5

people who are willing and able to pay the higher price can satisfy their demand for oranges.

If prices did not rise, the quantity of oranges demanded would be much higher than the quantity supplied. Consumers would have to compete for oranges—possibly by standing in long lines—only to have the supply run out before each person was able to make a purchase. In this case, many consumers who are willing and able to buy the lower-priced fruit would be unable to satisfy their demand.

Limitations of the Price System

On the whole, the price system is an effective way to coordinate the decisions of consumers and producers in a free-enterprise economy. The system does have limitations, however. These limitations are sometimes referred to as **market failures** because the market—or the price system—fails to account for some costs and therefore cannot distribute them appropriately.

Externalities
One limitation of the price system is that it may not take into account all of the costs and benefits of production. The production of goods sometimes results in side effects for people not directly connected with the production or consumption of the goods. These side effects are called **externalities** and can be either negative or positive.

A negative externality exists when someone who does not make or consume a certain product nonetheless bears part of the cost of its production. Pollution is an example of a negative externality. Suppose that the air and water pollution emitted by the Paragon Paper factory affects a wide geographic area. If Paragon Paper is not held responsible for the costs of any negative health and environmental problems caused by this pollution, the price of the factory's goods is not an accurate measure of their entire cost. Instead, part of the cost—the externality cost of pollution—is "paid" by the people living near the Paragon Paper factory, rather than by the company and the consumers who buy Paragon's goods. In such situations the price system fails to assign the entire cost of production to the producers and consumers of the products.

A positive externality exists when someone who does not sell or buy a certain product nonetheless benefits from its production. For example, imagine that many workers eat lunch at The Hard Hat, a restaurant near the Paragon Paper factory. The Hard Hat's location allows it to benefit from the factory's production, even though it does not consume the factory's goods. The restaurant pays no part of the production cost, but it benefits from that production. Instead, the Paragon Paper factory and consumers who buy the factory's goods bear the entire cost. In such situations the price system fails to assign the entire cost of production to all those who benefit from that production.

Public Goods
The price system also fails to assign the cost of public goods to all consumers. A **public good** is any good or service that is

MARKETS & PRICES *The benefits of this home security system extend to nearby neighbors even though they did not pay for it.* **What positive externalities are you aware of in your community?**

Across the Curriculum

HISTORY & GOVERNMENT The U.S. government penalizes firms that pass the costs of pollution on to others. The Environmental Protection Agency (EPA), established in 1970 under President Richard Nixon, oversees this task. The EPA's goal is to protect the environment and to work with state and local governments to control and reduce air, water, solid waste, pesticide, radiation, and toxic-substance pollution. Through industry regulation, the EPA and other government agencies work to prevent and alleviate negative externalities.

Caption Answer
Answers will vary but should reflect an understanding of positive externalities.

Cultural Perspectives
An example of a positive externality is the growth of automobile factories in the southern United States. During the 1990s, foreign car manufacturers such as Mercedes-Benz and Toyota built several plants in the South to take advantage of the region's cheap labor and low taxes, among other things. Local industries have benefited, particularly those that provide parts and other resources to these factories.

Caption Answer
If people are not forced to pay for public goods, the market fails to distribute their costs appropriately.

SECTION 1 REVIEW ANSWERS

1. market failure (101), externality (101), public good (101) **24A**

2. information—price labels help shoppers make informed buying decisions; incentives—sales, specials, and discounts help increase demand; choice—multiple brands are available for products in high demand; efficiency—consumers can easily compare product value; flexibility—prices change frequently as supply and demand change **4B, 23A, 24D**

3a. by balancing the forces of supply and demand

3b. Examples will vary but might include the following: negative externality—destruction of animal habitat; positive externality—increased business because of a local tourist attraction; public good—roadways.

4. Answers will vary but students might suggest that they would buy brands they trust or base their buying decisions on past prices. **7A, 23A**

MARKETS & PRICES *Law enforcement is one example of a public good.* **How can public goods be market failures?**

consumed by all members of a group. Public goods include national defense, the judicial system, and law enforcement. If the government did not require people to pay for these goods and services through taxes, some of those who benefit from them would be unwilling to pay.

For example, if paying for local police protection were voluntary, some citizens would choose not to pay. Yet as soon as the municipal government supplied this service to the paying citizens, everyone in the community would benefit from, or consume, the service. Suppose that crimes occurred throughout the community, and the police arrested those responsible. All residents—even those who had not contributed to the budget for police protection—would benefit. In these situations the price system does not fairly distribute the cost of public goods.

Instability Although the price system's ability to adapt to change is generally considered a benefit, this flexibility can make the system somewhat unstable. As the system reacts to severe weather, natural disasters, worker protests, and other events, prices can swing quickly between extremes. A drastic drop in prices might cause some companies to go out of business. A tremendous price increase may make a certain necessity so expensive that most people cannot afford it. Even less-dramatic price swings can prevent the market from functioning smoothly, because producers and consumers cannot rely on stable prices when making business or purchasing decisions.

SECTION 1 REVIEW

TEKS Q: 1, 2, 4

1. Identify and Explain:
- market failure
- externality
- public good

2. Categorizing: Copy the graphic organizer below. Use it to identify and explain the five main benefits of the price system evident in a grocery store.

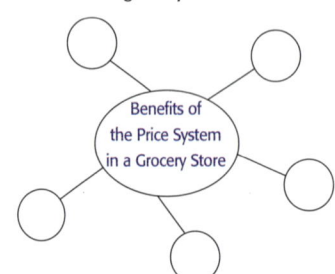

Benefits of the Price System in a Grocery Store

3. Finding the Main Idea
  a. How do prices coordinate the decisions of producers and consumers?
  b. Give one example not mentioned in the text of each of the following: negative externality, positive externality, public good.

4. Writing and Critical Thinking
  Drawing Inferences: Suppose that you go to the grocery store and that none of the products have prices listed. How would you decide what and how much to buy?
  Consider the following:
  - how you have made your buying decisions in the past
  - factors that might influence this decision

Homework Practice Online
keyword: SM3 HP5

102 CHAPTER 5

SECTION 2
DETERMINING PRICES

READ TO DISCOVER
- market equilibrium
- surplus
- shortage

ECONOMICS DICTIONARY
1. What is market equilibrium?
2. How does the price system handle product surpluses and shortages?
3. How do shifts in demand and supply affect market equilibrium?

If the price system is a type of unspoken language, how can you see—as well as feel—its influence on the decisions made by producers and consumers? You can see the price system at work most clearly in how it determines the amounts and prices of goods and services available in the marketplace.

Equilibrium

The price system helps producers and consumers reach **market equilibrium**, a situation that occurs when the quantity supplied and the quantity demanded for a product are equal at the same price. At this equilibrium point, the needs of both producers and consumers are satisfied, and the forces of supply and demand are in balance. When a market reaches its equilibrium point, producers and consumers have communicated effectively.

You can see the equilibrium point for a product by plotting its demand and supply curves on the same graph. Examine Figure 5.1. The table on the left shows the demand and supply schedules for tennis shoes. The graph on the right plots this information in a demand curve (D_1) and a

DEMAND AND SUPPLY SCHEDULE FOR TENNIS SHOES

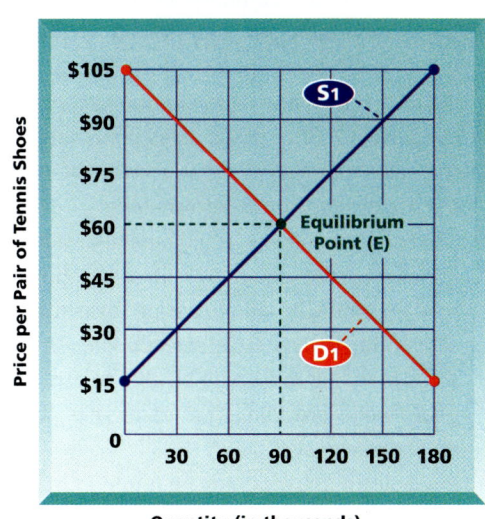

Price per Pair of Tennis Shoes	Quantity Demanded	Quantity Supplied
$15	180,000	0
$30	150,000	30,000
$45	120,000	60,000
$60	90,000	90,000
$75	60,000	120,000
$90	30,000	150,000
$105	0	180,000

FIGURE 5.1 Market equilibrium occurs when the quantity supplied and the quantity demanded for a product are equal at the same price. **Use the schedule to read the graph and identify the quantity demanded and quantity supplied at a price of $75.**

Themes in Economics

MARKETS & PRICES

Many businesses use an approach called yield, or revenue, management to set prices. With this approach, businesses raise or lower prices for the same product based on season, time of day, or type of customer. This pricing system is popular in service industries such as airlines, restaurants, and theaters. A restaurant may charge higher prices during peak hours, such as lunchtime, and lower prices for the same dishes during non-peak hours. Airlines charge higher fares during peak periods, such as holidays, and theaters may charge more for a seat on a Friday night than on a Tuesday night. Ask students how yield management can help producers avoid surpluses and shortages. ∎

Careers in Economics

To help students learn about other careers in economics, refer them to the Careers section of the *Researcher Online*.

---

supply curve (S_1). The vertical axis lists the possible prices for a pair of tennis shoes. The horizontal axis lists the quantities that could be demanded and supplied.

The point at which these two curves intersect (point E) is the market equilibrium for tennis shoes. Equilibrium exists at a price of $60 and a quantity of 90,000 pairs of shoes.

How does the price system actually steer producers and consumers toward the equilibrium point? The process does not take place instantly. In fact, a certain amount of trial and error may be necessary, as producers change prices and quantities of the goods and services supplied. This adjustment process works to eliminate surpluses and shortages—situations in which the forces of

CAREERS IN ECONOMICS

Sales Manager

Suppose that your family is planning to go on vacation, and you need to earn spending money. You apply for a retail sales position at a department store in the mall. To prepare for your interview, you research the store and the role of the person who may be your supervisor.

What is a sales manager's job? A sales manager identifies applicants who seem likely to be effective salespeople and then teaches them about store and company policies. Additionally, the sales manager determines demand and establishes sales goals. How hot are in-line skates? How many pairs should salespeople sell every week? Once these sales goals are defined, the sales manager must supervise the salespeople and evaluate their performance.

Sales managers need specific skills. They generally have experience in sales. However, a manager must be able to assign tasks rather than attempting to outsell the salespeople. An effective sales manager must also be able to explain sales goals while providing the leadership needed to meet these goals.

Sales managers may be found in many businesses. For example, the sales manager for Sony or Panasonic may supervise sales of television sets and stereos to department stores. The sales manager for a department store, such as Sears or J.C. Penney, oversees the retail sales clerks who sell the televisions and stereos to consumers.

Stores and companies need sales managers to analyze market demand, establish realistic objectives, and hire and train people to meet sales goals. Without these managers, a company might ignore potential consumers because of a lack of attention to the market and popular demand.

Sales managers are responsible for determining demand, teaching sales staff, and establishing sales goals.

supply and demand are not in balance and the market has not reached equilibrium.

Surpluses A **surplus** exists when the quantity supplied exceeds the quantity demanded at the price offered. You can see an example of a surplus in Figure 5.2. Points A and B demonstrate what happens if producers decide to charge $90 for the shoes. At this price producers are willing to supply 150,000 pairs of tennis shoes (point B). The quantity demanded at this price, however, is lower than 150,000 pairs. At a price of $90, consumers are willing and able to buy only 30,000 pairs of shoes (point A). The result is a surplus of 120,000 pairs (150,000 – 30,000 = 120,000).

The surplus tells producers that they are charging too much for their shoes. After re-examining costs, producers decide they can lower their price and still make a profit. The lower price increases the quantity demanded and decreases the quantity supplied, eliminating the surplus and steering the market toward equilibrium (point E).

SURPLUS AND SHORTAGE OF TENNIS SHOES

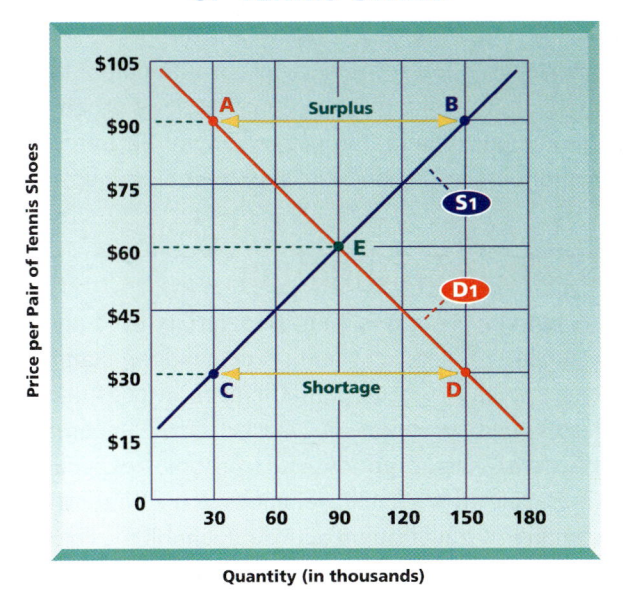

FIGURE 5.2 The process of price determination may involve a period of trial and error. **What are the consequences of charging $90 per pair? $45 per pair?**

MARKETS & PRICES *The price system steers producers and consumers toward market equilibrium.* **How might a bookstore react to a surplus of books?**

Shortages A **shortage** exists when the quantity demanded exceeds the quantity supplied at the price offered. An example of a shortage appears in Figure 5.2. Points C and D show what happens if producers decide to charge only $30 for their shoes. At this price they are willing to produce 30,000 pairs of tennis shoes (point C). The quantity demanded at this price, however, is greater than 30,000 pairs. At a price of $30, consumers are willing and able to buy as many as 150,000 pairs of shoes (point D). The result is a shortage of 120,000 pairs (150,000 – 30,000 = 120,000).

How do producers react to this situation? The shortage tells them that they are charging too little for the shoes. They decide to raise the price. The higher price decreases the quantity demanded and increases the quantity supplied, eliminating the shortage and steering the market toward equilibrium (point E).

CASE STUDY

Sony® PlayStation 2®

MARKETS & PRICES Every year as the holidays approach, manufacturers hope that they have the year's hot new gift. In years past, demand for the

EQUILIBRIUM, DEMAND, AND SUPPLY SHIFTS

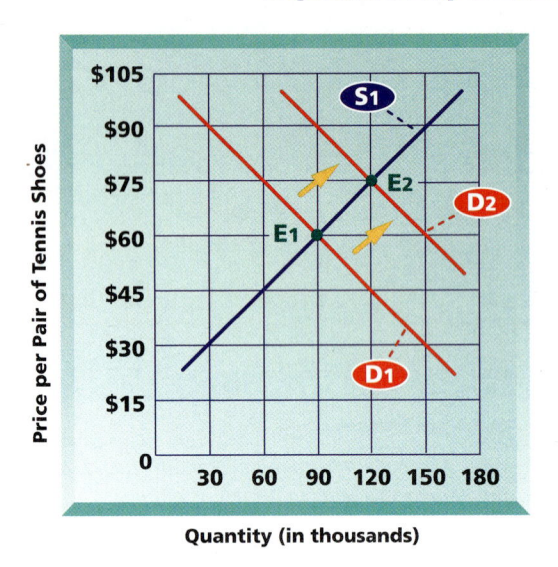

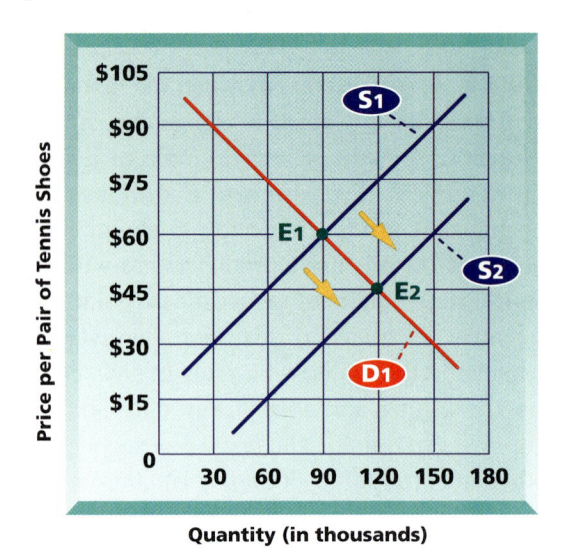

FIGURE 5.3 Many factors can shift a product's demand or supply curve. **What happens to the equilibrium point when either the demand or supply curve shifts?**

---

most popular toys, such as the Tickle Me Elmo™ doll or Mighty Morphin Power Rangers®, has outstripped supply, forcing gift shoppers to endure long lines at the toy store.

In 2000 the main contender for the year's hottest holiday gift was Sony's new PlayStation 2 video game system. With state-of-the-art graphics and a built-in DVD and CD player, the game was a "must have" gift for kids of all ages.

However, because of a shortage of computer parts, the game system was in short supply. On its official release date in October 2000, thousands of eager consumers lined up to buy the game system. High demand meant many stores had to turn away customers. Online toy store Toysrus.com sold out its supply in an astounding 30 seconds!

With an estimated 500,000 games sold in the first two days, PlayStation 2 was the most popular electronic consumer item ever in terms of initial sales. By comparison, it took nine months to sell 315,000 DVD players when they were first introduced in 1996.

With stores sold out, many disappointed buyers turned to Internet auction sites such as eBay, where the game systems, which originally cost $300, were going for as much as $1,300. Meanwhile, retailers predicted they would not catch up with demand until March 2001.

Shortages—and surpluses—occur throughout the marketplace. The price system steers all producers and consumers toward market equilibrium by responding to demand and supply imbalances.

Shifts in Equilibrium

As noted in Chapters 3 and 4, a variety of factors can shift a product's entire demand or supply curve to the right or left. Changes in consumer tastes and preferences, market size, income, prices of related goods, and consumer expectations can all shift the demand curve. Similarly, changes in government actions, technology, competition, producer expectations, and the prices of resources and related goods can all shift the supply curve. When either the demand or the supply curve shifts, the equilibrium point also shifts to the new intersection of the curves.

You can see an equilibrium shift in Figure 5.3. The graph on the left shows the results of a shift in demand for tennis shoes. Suppose that the tennis championship at Wimbledon is won by a new teenage athlete. As a result of publicity for the sport, consumer preference for tennis shoes increases. Consumers now are willing to buy more tennis shoes at every possible price, so the demand curve shifts to the right from D_1 to D_2.

What happens to the equilibrium point? It moves from point E_1 on the old demand curve to point E_2 on the new demand curve. The new equilibrium price is $75, and the new equilibrium quantity is 120,000 pairs of shoes.

The graph on the right, however, shows the results of a shift in supply for tennis shoes. Suppose that many firms install new machinery in their factories. The new technology speeds up production and allows the companies to supply more shoes to the market at each and every price. As a result, the supply curve shifts from S_1 to S_2.

What happens to the equilibrium point? It moves from point E_1 on the old supply curve to point E_2 on the new supply curve. The new equilibrium price is $45, and the new equilibrium quantity is 120,000 pairs of shoes. The quantity of tennis shoes demanded and the quantity supplied are once again equal at the same price.

MARKETS & PRICES *During a recent holiday season, enormous demand for the Tickle Me Elmo™ doll caused widespread shortages.* **What were the likely results of this shortage?**

SECTION 2 REVIEW

1. Identify and Explain:
   market equilibrium
   surplus

2. Identifying Cause and Effect:
   Copy the graphic organizer below. Use it to explain how the price system responds to surpluses and shortages.

   Market Equilibrium
   Surplus   Shortage

3. Finding the Main Idea
   a. When is a market in equilibrium?
   b. How do shifts in the supply and demand curves affect market equilibrium?

4. Writing and Critical Thinking
   Making Predictions: Predict what would happen to both consumers and producers if a company did not change its product's price when faced with a surplus? When faced with a shortage?
   Consider the following:
   • the response of the price system to surpluses
   • the response of the price system to shortages

Homework Practice Online
keyword: SM3 HP5

Caption Answer
increased prices followed by decreasing quantity demanded and increasing quantity supplied 7A

SECTION 2 REVIEW ANSWERS

1. market equilibrium (103), surplus (105), shortage (105) 7A, 24A

2. surplus—drop in prices, increasing quantity demanded, decreasing quantity supplied, eliminating the surplus, moving the market toward equilibrium; shortage—rise in prices, decreasing quantity demanded, increasing quantity supplied, eliminating the shortage, moving the market toward equilibrium 2A, 7A, 23A, 24D

3a. when quantity supplied and quantity demanded for a product are equal at the same price

3b. They shift the equilibrium point to the new intersection of the curves.

4. With a surplus, not enough consumers would be willing and able to buy the product, and producers would lose profits on unsold items. With a shortage, consumers would have to wait for or fight over limited supplies, and producers would sell out and lose potential profits. 4A, 23A

SECTION 3

MANAGING PRICES

READ TO DISCOVER
1. Why do governments sometimes set prices?
2. What do governments try to accomplish through price floors, price ceilings, and rationing?
3. What happens when governments manage prices?

ECONOMICS DICTIONARY
price ceiling
price floor
minimum wage
rationing
black market

As noted in Section 1, the price system has a number of limitations. The price system does not accurately assign the costs of, or determine who should pay for, the costs of externalities like pollution. Nor does it accurately distribute the costs and benefits of public goods like national defense. In addition, the system's occasional instability can complicate the attempts of producers and consumers to predict prices and plan for the future.

To address these limitations, governments sometimes become involved in the marketplace. Just as governments assign the costs of public goods, governments also can choose to assign the costs of externalities—for example, by making companies reduce the amount of pollution they emit and pay for any damage caused by that pollution. To keep the market functioning smoothly and to avoid instability caused by dramatic price swings, governments at times may choose to set prices and ration goods.

Setting Prices

Governments sometimes set prices to protect producers and consumers from dramatic price swings. They accomplish this through price ceilings and price floors.

Price Ceilings A **price ceiling** is a government regulation that establishes a maximum price for a particular good. Producers cannot charge prices above this set level.

Consider rent controls, for example. Suppose that the city of New Populous is experiencing a population boom. So many people want to live in the city that prices for apartments and other rental properties have skyrocketed. As a result, many people who work in New Populous cannot afford to rent apartments or houses in town near their jobs. Such a situation results from the forces of supply and demand. The high demand for the limited supply of New Populous rental properties drives up rents as consumers compete with one another by paying higher prices (rent).

Like many other communities, however, New Populous feels that affordable housing is an important priority. Therefore, to ensure that its citizens can afford to live in the city, the New Populous city council decides to intervene in the

MARKETS & PRICES *Rent control is one example of a price ceiling.* **Why do governments sometimes set prices?**

PRICE CEILING AND SHORTAGE

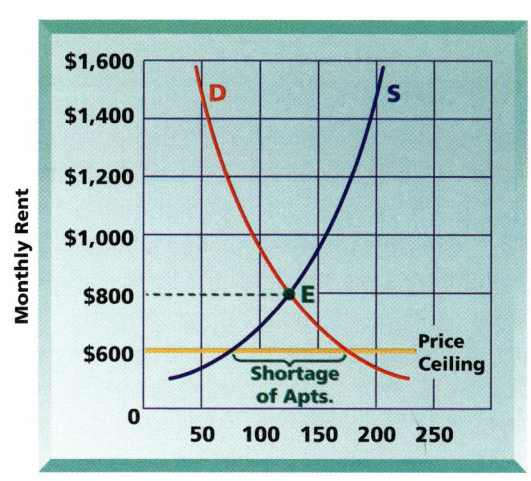

FIGURE 5.4 Price ceilings are governmental regulations that set the maximum legal price for a particular product. **How does this graph illustrate the consequences of setting price ceilings?** ⭐TEKS

market by setting a price ceiling on rents for apartments within city limits.

Price Floors Price floors are more common than price ceilings. A **price floor** is a government regulation that establishes a minimum level for prices.

In certain situations the government sets price floors for agricultural products. Suppose that good weather results in an unusually large corn crop. The huge supply drives the price of corn so low that farmers cannot make enough money to pay their bills, let alone make a profit. Many farmers face losing their land. To prevent this from happening, the government sets a base price for corn that will guarantee farmers a minimum level of income.

The **minimum wage** is another example of a price floor. Established by federal law, this wage is the lowest amount an employer legally can pay a worker for a job. In some types of work the number of workers exceeds the number of available jobs. As workers compete for jobs, they are willing to accept increasingly lower wages. Wages may fall so low that many people cannot earn enough money on which to live. To help prevent this from happening, the government sets a minimum wage, ensuring workers a certain level of income.

Consequences of Setting Prices

Most economists advise against the use of price ceilings and price floors. Interfering in the normal interaction between supply and demand can cause unintended imbalances and can prevent markets from reaching equilibrium. Price ceilings tend to result in shortages, and price floors tend to result in surpluses. Think again about some of the examples already discussed.

The government of New Populous hopes that rent controls—a price ceiling—will result in affordable housing. The government sets the price of a two-bedroom apartment at $600 per month, while the equilibrium price is $800. (See Figure 5.4.) Unfortunately, by keeping rents artificially low, rent controls tend to shrink the supply of rental properties. Notice that a price ceiling of $600 creates a shortage of 100,000 (175,000 − 75,000 = 100,000) apartments. How does this happen?

MARKETS & PRICES *Minimum-wage jobs ensure workers a certain level of income.* **What form of government price setting does this exemplify?**

PRICES 109

Transparency

An overhead transparency of Figure 5.5 is available in *Transparency Resources*. See Transparency 20: Price Floor and Surplus.

Caption Answer
$2.00 and $2.50 ⭐23F

Across the Curriculum

HISTORY During World War II each family in the United States received a ration coupon book. Each person was allotted 64 "red" points and 48 "blue" points each month. Red points were used to purchase foods such as meat and butter. Blue points were used to buy canned goods and other processed foods. Grocery stores displayed the number of points an item required along with its sales price. ■

Caption Answer
Answers will vary but should reflect an understanding of rationing. ⭐15A

PRICE FLOOR AND SURPLUS

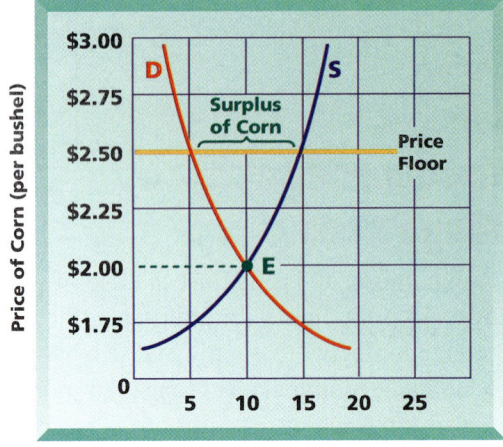

FIGURE 5.5 Price floors set the minimum legal price for a particular product. **Give the equilibrium price for corn and identify the price floor.** ⭐TEKS

Remember that the law of supply explains that higher prices encourage increases in the quantity supplied, and lower prices encourage reductions in the quantity supplied. By lowering prices, and therefore the potential profits that landlords can make on their properties, rent control programs discourage landlords from building new rental units. Likewise, landlords are less willing to invest money in repairing existing rent-controlled properties because they cannot increase rents to cover these expenses.

Thus, instead of increasing the quantity of affordable housing supplied, over time rent controls actually tend to decrease the quantity supplied. Because landlords cannot change prices according to their costs and in response to demand, the market does not reach equilibrium.

Now think again about the government's corn-pricing policy. As shown in Figure 5.5, a price floor of $2.50 per bushel encourages farmers to maintain a high level of corn production. Even when the market is flooded with surplus corn, farmers know that the price floor guarantees them a minimum income. By sending incorrect signals to farmers, the artificially high prices prevent the market from reaching equilibrium.

Rationing

Sometimes the supply of a good is so low that a government rations the good. **Rationing** is a system in which a government or other institution decides how to distribute a product. Under a rationing system, a product is distributed on the basis of policy decisions rather than on the basis of prices determined by supply and demand.

Rationing seldom occurs in a free-enterprise system. In the United States, rationing has occurred mainly during wars and other crises. During World War II, for example, the U.S. government rationed many goods, such as tires, gasoline, meat, butter, and coffee. To coordinate its rationing efforts, the government distributed books of coupons that allowed citizens to buy specific amounts of rationed goods.

A national crisis is not the only time rationing might occur. Consider college sports tickets. Often the number of people who want to see a college team's games is greater than the number of tickets available. Under the price system, this shortage would be eliminated as the excess quantity demanded drove up prices. Fewer fans would be willing to pay the higher prices, and the quantity demanded would decrease.

Most colleges, however, believe that students and alumni should have priority over the general public when buying tickets for home games. To make sure that affordable tickets are available to

MARKETS & PRICES *During the 1970s, oil shortages in the United States forced gasoline rationing.* **What current examples of rationing can you identify?** ⭐TEKS

110 CHAPTER 5

these groups, colleges usually ration by setting aside tickets for alumni and for students.

Consequences of Rationing

Many people feel that rationing is an unwise economic policy. Critics charge that the system

- is unfair,
- is expensive, and
- creates black markets.

Unfairness One criticism of rationing is that it distributes goods and services unfairly. In the case of college sports tickets, for example, many people in the general public believe they have as much right to attend a team's games as do alumni and students. By rationing tickets, the college is giving both students and alumni special treatment over the general public.

Critics of rationing point out that the price system does not favor any one person or group over another. Prices are neutral because all consumers are treated equally. If the college tickets were distributed under the forces of supply and demand instead of under rationing, students, alumni, and the general public all would have an equal chance to buy tickets.

Cost Another criticism of rationing is that it is costly to put into effect. Colleges devote employees' work hours to carrying out and tracking the ticket rationing. Likewise, a government must not only determine who is to receive rationed goods and in what amounts but also must print and distribute ration coupons. In addition, a method of enforcing the rationing program must be developed to ensure that people do not receive more rationed goods than they should. These tasks can use significant amounts of human resources and financial capital.

Unlike rationing, the price system has no such administrative costs. When prices are determined by the normal interaction of supply and demand, governments and other institutions do not have to spend time and resources managing the distribution of goods and services.

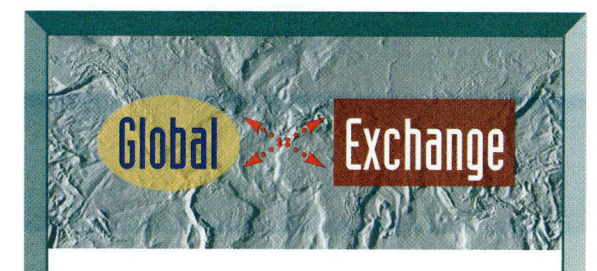

Global Exchange

International Bargain Hunters

Many Japanese vacationers in the United States spend much of their time—and a third of their travel budget—shopping. Prices in the United States are often dramatically lower than in Japan, allowing Japanese travelers to buy items that would be less affordable at home.

Many items that tourists buy—including electronic equipment, designer clothing, and jewelry—are purchased as gifts for family members. Some tourists, however, pay for their trip by selling the items that they have purchased overseas.

How high are prices in Japan? A pound of rice in Japan, for example, is about seven times more expensive than in other parts of the world. In 2001 a case of Coca-Cola cost about $23.

Even though a slump in the Japanese economy since the mid-1990s has lowered retail prices, many of these prices would still seem high to U.S. consumers. For example, it is not unusual to pay $100 or more for a ticket to a music concert, and a pair of Nike athletic shoes can cost as much as $300.

Some retailers have tried to lower prices in Japan. For example, Kou's—a discount warehouse—provides bulk products in the style of Sam's Club or Costco in the United States. Japanese entrepreneurs have also begun to set up online shopping services that offer discount prices. In fact, one site specializes in selling foreign goods.

Prices still remain high for many consumer goods in Japan. Thus, for many Japanese, overseas shopping may continue to yield bargains.

Global Connections

Following the Soviet Union's collapse, Cuba lost about $8 billion a year in aid and subsidies that the Soviet Union had provided. At the same time, harvests of Cuba's main cash crop, sugarcane, were poor. As a result, Cuba's economy declined, reaching its lowest point in 1994. These factors, combined with U.S. trade sanctions and Cuba's limited agricultural diversity, created severe shortages.

To help make limited goods available to everyone, the Cuban government instituted rationing. Rationed goods were available weekly, monthly, or, as was most often the case, whenever they happened to arrive. Some items, such as chicken and soap, were almost impossible to get.

Researchers estimated that the daily average caloric intake per person in Cuba dropped from 2,835 calories in 1989 to a low of about 1,863 calories in 1994.

Today, thanks to urban agricultural production, caloric intake has climbed by 40 percent. Still, food costs are high for consumers, partly because the Cuban government relies on a system of price floors and price ceilings.

Caption Answer
unfair distribution of products, high administrative costs

SECTION 3 REVIEW ANSWERS

1. price ceiling (108), price floor (109), minimum wage (109), rationing (110), black market (112) **7A, 24A**

2. may lead to unfair distribution, high administration costs, and black markets **15A, 15B, 24D**

3a. to ensure that consumers can purchase this basic necessity at a reasonable price; to ensure producers of both a basic level of income and enough profit to make it worthwhile to produce this needed good **15B**

3b. Price ceilings tend to result in shortages, price floors in surpluses. **15B**

4. Answers will vary but should reflect an understanding of the trade-offs of managing prices. **15B, 23A**

MARKETS & PRICES *Ticket scalpers represent the black market that can be created by rationing.* **What are other possible consequences of rationing?**

Black Markets The third problem with rationing is that it tends to encourage **black markets**, in which goods are exchanged illegally at prices that are higher than officially established prices. Rationing encourages black markets because it succeeds in distributing goods among consumers but does not completely satisfy consumer demand.

After the college rations its tickets, for example, the quantity demanded remains high. Instead of allowing all consumers to compete for the tickets—which would drive up ticket prices and reduce the quantity demanded—the rationing program keeps prices artificially low. The high quantity demanded means that many people—including students and alumni—remain willing and able to buy tickets. Black markets have developed to meet this remaining demand.

At a sold-out football game, for example, the black market takes the form of people outside the gates offering to sell tickets—at prices higher than those set by the college. These black marketers, who buy rationed tickets from students and alumni who decide not to use them, sell them to the general public for a profit.

What is wrong with black markets? First, black markets are unfair. For example, if you buy a ticket from a black marketer, you may pay a great deal more than someone who bought a rationed ticket. Is it fair for you to pay so much more for the same good?

Black markets also pose other problems for consumers. For example, if the ticket you bought turns out to be fake, you probably cannot get your money back. Additionally, many governments outlaw black-market activity because it defeats the very purpose of a rationing program—determining which consumers receive how much of a good.

SECTION 3 REVIEW

★TEKS Q: 1, 2, 3a, 3b, 4

1. Identify and Explain:
- price ceiling
- price floor
- minimum wage
- rationing
- black market

2. Identifying Cause and Effect: Copy the graphic organizer below. Use it to show three consequences of government rationing programs.

Consequences of Government Rationing Programs

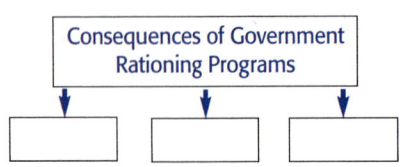

3. Finding the Main Idea

a. Why might the government place a $1 price ceiling on a gallon of milk? Why might it place a $5 price floor on a bushel of wheat?

b. What are the probable results of both the price ceiling and the price floor in question 3a?

4. Writing and Critical Thinking

Supporting a Point of View: Should the government try to manage prices in some situations? Why or why not? Give at least one example not used in the book to support your answer.

Consider the following:
- the consequences of setting price floors and ceilings
- the types of situations that might cause the government to manage prices

Homework Practice Online
keyword: SM3 HP5

112 CHAPTER 5

Economics IN THE NEWS

California's Power Crisis

Until 1996 the state of California, like most states, regulated its electricity rates. The state's electrical power was generated and distributed by two companies, while a state commission set the rates power companies could charge. However, Californians still paid higher-than-average rates for their electricity. Many economists blamed the problem on a lack of competition.

In 1996 California became one of the first states to deregulate its power industry. The deregulation law required the two power companies that then controlled the market to sell their power plants and concentrate on the distribution of power to consumers. At the same time the new law allowed power companies from outside the state to sell power to the two distributors. State officials hoped that greater competition from deregulation would result in lower electricity rates for consumers.

However, things did not work out the way supporters of deregulation had hoped. Deregulation went into full effect in April 1998. By 2000 electricity prices had begun to skyrocket. For example, one San Diego business owner's electricity bill went from about $500 to $1,300 a month in just five months. Soon electricity customers were up in arms. In San Diego, consumer groups paid for television advertisements urging consumers to refuse to pay the higher bills.

What went wrong? While opinions vary, economists agree that a major part of the problem was related to an increase in demand without a corresponding increase in supply. With its booming economy and population growth, the state's energy needs had grown by 30 percent while production had grown by only 10 percent. The state's power producers were also accused of fueling the shortage by intentionally reducing supply to increase prices.

Rolling blackouts in California forced many businesses to close for lack of power.

Meanwhile, the shortage continued. Soon the state was forced to ration electricity. State officials resorted to rolling blackouts, or turning off power to customers on a periodic basis. Customers whose electricity use involved life-and-death situations—such as hospitals—were exempt, but homes, schools and businesses were forced to deal with no power.

In June 2001 the federal government responded to the crisis by regulating electricity prices. At the same time Californians increased efforts to conserve electricity. Both efforts provided some short-term relief. During the summer of 2001, state officials were able to avoid rolling blackouts.

What Do You Think?

1. Which types of price management did the government use during the crisis?
2. What effect might price ceilings have on the market for electricity?

WHY IT MATTERS TODAY

Regulation of public utilities can affect the amount of money that consumers have to spend. Use CNNfyi.com or other **current events** sources to find other examples of government control of prices and the effects of price regulation.

Economics in the News Answers

1. price setting and rationing 15B
2. They prevent the market from reaching equilibrium. By lowering prices they may increase demand without providing an incentive for increasing supply. 7A, 15B, 23A

CHAPTER 5 Review Answers

Writing a Summary

Summaries should focus on the main point of each section. These may be found in the Read to Discover questions at the start of each section. Summaries should also use standard grammar, spelling, sentence structure, and punctuation. 24B, 24D

Identifying Ideas

market failure (101), externality (101), public good (101), market equilibrium (103), surplus (105), shortage (105), price ceiling (108), price floor (109), minimum wage (109), rationing (110) 7A, 15A, 24A

Understanding Main Ideas

1. It does not account for all of the costs and benefits of production, and the system can be unstable.
2. Prices are the way producers tell consumers how much it costs to make and distribute a product, and consumers tell producers how

(Continued on page 114)

CHAPTER 5 Review

Writing a Summary

Using standard grammar, spelling, sentence structure, and punctuation, write a summary of the information in this chapter.

Identifying Ideas

1. market failure
2. externality
3. public good
4. market equilibrium
5. surplus
6. shortage
7. price ceiling
8. price floor
9. minimum wage
10. rationing

Understanding Main Ideas

SECTION 1 (pp. 97–102)

1. Describe the limitations of the price system.

SECTION 2 (pp. 103–07)

2. Explain the role of the price system. Be sure to include how the price system encourages market equilibrium.
3. How can a shift in demand influence a market's equilibrium point?

SECTION 3 (pp. 108–12)

4. Why might a government establish a price floor on one good or service and a price ceiling on another?
5. Why might a government begin rationing items in the market?

Reviewing Themes

1. **Markets & Prices** How does the price system encourge efficiency?
2. **Markets & Prices** Why do governments sometimes set prices?
3. **Supply & Demand** How can public goods be considered market failures?

Thinking Critically

1. **Categorizing** Explain why you believe that each of the following is or is not a public good: fire protection, newspaper publication, road maintenance.
2. **Finding the Main Idea** How can an advertising campaign cause a shift in a market's equilibrium?
3. **Supporting a Point of View** You are in charge of selling tickets to your school play. Do you establish a rationing system to ensure that each performer's family is able to attend opening night? Why or why not?

Writing about Economics

Review what you wrote in your Economics Notebook at the beginning of this chapter about prices for items you have purchased recently and what those prices told you about the products. Now that you have studied this chapter, would you change your description of what you learned from the prices? Why or why not? Record your answers in your notebook.

(Continued from page 113)

much they are willing and able to pay for a product. The point, or price, at which consumer demand equals supply is the market's equilibrium point.

3. It can shift the market's equilibrium point. **7A**

4. Price ceilings help ensure reasonable prices for consumers. Price floors help ensure producers of both a basic level of income and enough profit to make it worthwhile to produce needed goods and services. **15A, 23A**

5. to ensure fair access to products at reasonable prices when supplies are low **15A**

Reviewing Themes

1. by telling producers what consumers want to buy so that producers can use resources to make what consumers want; by quickly signalling the value of a good and service in relation to others so that producers and consumers can easily compare prices of resources and products **4B**

2. to protect producers and consumers from dramatic price swings **15A**

3. If people are not forced to pay for public goods, the market fails to distribute their costs appropriately. **23A**

Thinking Critically

1. fire protection—public good because benefits all; newspaper—not a public good because benefits only those who pay for it; road maintenance—public good because benefits all **23A**

Building Social Studies Skills

Interpreting the Chart

Read the chart and answer the questions.

Price per Motor Scooter	Quantity Demanded	Quantity Supplied Before New Assembly Line (S$_1$)	Quantity Supplied After New Assembly Line (S$_2$)
$250	600,000	0	200,000
$500	500,000	100,000	300,000
$750	400,000	200,000	400,000
$1,000	300,000	300,000	500,000
$1,250	200,000	400,000	600,000
$1,500	100,000	500,000	700,000
$1,750	0	600,000	800,000

1. How might the application of new technology affect the production process?
   a. Negative externalities will negate the effects of new technology.
   b. New technology will lead to decreased efficiency.
   c. New technology will lead to greater efficiency.
   d. None of the above.

2. What would happen to the supply curve if the new assembly line broke down?

Analyzing Primary Sources

Read the following excerpt from a *New York Times* article regarding the service Napster. Then answer the questions.

"One of the advantages of MP3 [a type of file] sharing is that you can get songs that aren't out on CD yet.... It's a great way to see if the whole CD is worth its inflated price." [Craig Newell, 17-year-old music consumer]

"File sharing is misnamed. When I share something with you, I only have a portion of it left for me." [Hilary Rosen, president of the Recording Industry Association of America]

"The problem is that record companies now charge so much ... that people feel justified in stealing" [Esther Dyson, author and venture capitalist]

3. How might each person's frame of reference be characterized in this discussion?
   a. The participants are disinterested.
   b. Each person's frame of reference has been largely determined by his or her status as a producer or a consumer.
   c. Frame of reference is irrelevant.
   d. Each person shares a consumer's frame of reference.

4. How might the participants' views reflect their economic or professional interests?

Alternative Assessment

Building Your Portfolio

Conduct a panel discussion about introducing a price floor for soybeans. Choose one member of the group to act as mediator and organize the rest of the group into two teams. One team should argue in favor of the price floor, while the other group should argue against it. Ask the rest of the class to summarize each team's key arguments in their notes and hold a vote to determine which team presented its argument most effectively.

internet connect

Internet Activity: go.hrw.com
KEYWORD: SM3 EC5

Access the Internet through the HRW Go site to research the costs and benefits of nuclear energy. Then write a letter to your local newspaper by first writing a letter in favor of building a nuclear power plant in your town. Write a second letter arguing against building a nuclear power plant. Discuss the concepts of externalities, public goods, and real costs in your letters.

---

2. It can increase consumer demand, thus moving the demand curve to the right and shifting the market's equilibrium point. 7A, 23A

3. Answers should reflect an understanding of rationing and its trade-offs. 7A, 23A

Writing about Economics

Students may or may not change their descriptions of what they learned from the prices they paid; however, they should be able to support their responses using concepts such as the price system, surpluses, shortages, and so on. 23A, 24D

Building Social Studies Skills

1. c 7B, 23B, 23F, 23G, 24D
2. The curve would shift upward and to the left. 7B, 23F
3. b 23E
4. Answers will vary, but students might mention that Craig Newell, a consumer, benefited from Napster by evaluating individual songs from CDs, or that Hilary Rosen, representing the recording industry, has an interest in promoting that industry's viewpoint. 23E

CHAPTER RESOURCE MANAGER

CHAPTER 6 — MARKET STRUCTURES

	OBJECTIVES	PACING GUIDE	REPRODUCIBLE RESOURCES
SECTION 1 **HIGHLY COMPETITIVE MARKETS** (pp. 117–22)	▸ What is perfect (pure) competition? ▸ What is monopolistic competition? ▸ How do sellers differentiate their products under monopolistic competition?	**Regular** 1.5 days **Block Scheduling** 1 day	**ELL** Spanish Study Guide 6.1 **ELL** English Study Guide 6.1 **PS** Reading 39: Interstate Commerce Act of 1887 **E** Challenge and Enrichment: Activity 6 **SM** Mathematics for Economics: Activity 6
SECTION 2 **IMPERFECTLY COMPETITIVE MARKETS** (pp. 123–29)	▸ How is an oligopoly structured? ▸ What is a monopoly? ▸ What types of monopolies exist? ▸ What factors affect prices in oligopolies and monopolies?	**Regular** 1.5 days **Block Scheduling** 1 day	**ELL** Spanish Study Guide 6.2 **ELL** English Study Guide 6.2 **SM** Consumer Economics: Activity 6
SECTION 3 **MARKET REGULATION** (pp. 130–34)	▸ What was the relationship between the U.S. government and business before the 1880s? ▸ What was the purpose of early antitrust legislation? ▸ How has the government enforced antitrust legislation?	**Regular** 1.5 days **Block Scheduling** 1 day	**ELL** Spanish Study Guide 6.3 **ELL** English Study Guide 6.3 **PS** Reading 40: Sherman Antitrust Act of 1890 **PS** Reading 42: Federal Trade Commission Act of 1914 **S** Simulations and Strategies for Teaching Economics: Activity 6

Chapter Resource Key

- **PS** Primary Sources
- **RS** Reading Support
- **E** Enrichment
- **S** Simulations
- **SM** Skills Mastery
- **A** Assessment
- **REV** Review
- **ELL** Reinforcement and English Language Learners
- Transparencies
- CD-ROM
- Video
- Videodisc
- Internet
- Holt Presentation Maker Using Microsoft® PowerPoint®
- TEKS and TAKS

TECHNOLOGY RESOURCES

- One-Stop Planner: Lesson 6.1
- Researcher Online
- Homework Practice Online
- CNN Presents Economics: What's in a Name
- Transparencies 21 and 22
- Global Skillbuilder CD-ROM

- One-Stop Planner: Lesson 6.2
- Researcher Online
- Homework Practice Online
- Transparency 23
- Global Skillbuilder CD-ROM

- One-Stop Planner: Lesson 6.3
- Researcher Online
- Homework Practice Online
- Holt Economics Videodisc: Preserving Competition: Skiing In New England
- Transparency 24
- Global Skillbuilder CD-ROM

REINFORCEMENT, REVIEW, AND ASSESSMENT

REV Section 1 Review, p. 122
A Daily Quiz 6.1
★ TAKS Every Day!

REV Section 2 Review, p. 129
A Daily Quiz 6.2
★ TAKS Every Day!

REV Section 3 Review, p. 134
A Daily Quiz 6.3
★ TAKS Every Day!

Chapter Review and Assessment
- **SM** Global Skillbuilder CD-ROM
- HRW Go site
- **REV** Reteaching Activity 6
- **REV** Chapter 6 Review, pp. 136–37
- **A** Chapter 6 Test Generator (on the One-Stop Planner)
- **A** Chapter 6 Test
- **A** Alternative Assessment Handbook

---

internet connect

HRW ONLINE RESOURCES
Go To: go.hrw.com
Then type in a keyword.

TEACHER HOME PAGE
KEYWORD: SM3 Teacher

CHAPTER INTERNET ACTIVITIES
KEYWORD: SM3 EC6
- research gas prices.
- create ads for two stores.
- create a table depicting the four types of monopolies.

CHAPTER ENRICHMENT LINKS
KEYWORD: SM3 CH6

HOLT RESEARCHER ONLINE
KEYWORD: Holt Researcher

ONLINE ASSESSMENT
Homework Practice
KEYWORD: SM3 HP6
TAKS Review
KEYWORD: SM3 T6
Rubrics
KEYWORD: SS Rubrics

CONTENT UPDATES
KEYWORD: SS Content Updates

HOLT PRESENTATION MAKER
KEYWORD: SM3 PPT6

ONLINE READING SUPPORT
KEYWORD: SS Strategies

CURRENT EVENTS
KEYWORD: S3 Current Events

TEXAS ONLINE RESOURCES
KEYWORD: S3 TX

One-Stop Planner CD-ROM

It's easy to plan lessons, select resources, and print out materials for your students when you use the *Texas One-Stop Planner CD-ROM with Test Generator.*

LESSON 6.1 HIGHLY COMPETITIVE MARKETS

TEXTBOOK PAGES 117–22

HOLT PRESENTATION MAKER — Access Illustrated LECTURE NOTES using Microsoft® PowerPoint® on the One-Stop Planner CD-ROM

OBJECTIVES

- Define perfect competition.
- Define monopolistic competition.
- Explain how sellers differentiate their products under monopolistic competition.

MOTIVATE

Tell students that Coca-Cola® and McDonald's® are some of the world's most profitable and recognizable brand names. Ask students to name some other well-known brand names. Have students speculate why these brands are so well known and trusted. Then tell students to consider the types of markets that these brands are in, such as the soft-drink market. Ask students if most of these markets are highly competitive or not. Have students make a list of markets they consider to be highly competitive and a list of what they consider to be the characteristics of a highly competitive market. Explain to students that they are going to be studying two types of competitive markets—markets with perfect competition and markets with monopolistic competition. Tell students to keep this activity in mind as they read Section 1 of the chapter.

TEACH

Building a Vocabulary

Have students use spiral notebooks to create an Economics Dictionary to be used throughout the chapter. This dictionary might be used as an activity at the start of each new section or as a learning aid for sheltered English students or students having difficulty. List words that students will be expected to know for this section on the chalkboard. Have students use the information provided in the textbook or on the *Researcher CD-ROM* to list, define, and give an example of each term.

Understanding Main Concepts, Comparing and Contrasting

Ask students to name the two types of competitive markets covered in Section 1 *(perfect competition and monopolistic competition)*. Next, have students list the characteristics of each of these types of markets. Discuss each characteristic with students. Then have students compare and contrast the two types of competitive markets. *(Monopolistic competition differs from perfect competition in one key respect—sellers offer different, rather than identical, products.)*

Have students name several products that they use on a regular or semi-regular basis. List at least 10 of these products on the chalkboard. Have students speculate how competitive the market for each of these products is. As students do this activity, have them examine how well each market fulfills each characteristic of perfect or monopolistic competition. If some of the products students name are in markets that are monopolies or oligopolies, explain to students that these products are in noncompetitive markets, which the class will learn about in the next section, Imperfectly Competitive Markets.

Next, ask students if many markets are perfectly competitive. *(No; perfect competition is an ideal market structure that economists use as a model by which to gauge competitiveness in other markets.)* Encourage students to name other markets, besides the agricultural market mentioned in the text, that come close to perfect competition. Have students explain how each of these markets satisfies the characteristics of perfect competition. ★9C, 23A

Applying Ideas

Ask students how sellers in monopolistic competition differentiate between their products and those of their competitors *(through nonprice competition, such as advertising and promoting brand names)*. Then ask students what companies hope to achieve through nonprice competition *(better market share and increased profits)*.

Organize students into groups of three or four and present the following scenario: You are advertising account managers for a small athletic shoe company. The company's product design department has just come up with a new model of athletic shoes. Your job is to prepare a marketing strategy to promote the new shoes and to increase your company's share of the athletic shoe market. Brainstorm ways to differentiate your company's new product from existing products in the market. Select a brand name for the new shoes and create a proposal outlining the marketing strategy that you think the company should follow.

When students are done, have each group share its marketing strategy with the class. Encourage students to provide feedback. Then have the class select the ideas they like best and create a class marketing strategy. ★23C

Synthesizing and Presenting Information

To extend the previous activity have student groups design a logo and create a jingle for their company's athletic shoes. In addition, have groups select the market niche at which they are going to direct their marketing strategy. Then tell each group to prepare a 5-minute presentation of its marketing strategy to present to the company board of directors (the class). Encourage students to use visual aids or multimedia to enhance their presentations. Group members might also want to divide up tasks. When students have completed the activity, have each group pitch its product and marketing strategy to the class.

CLOSE

Review with students the characteristics of perfect and monopolistic competition, and how producers in monopolistic competition differentiate their products. Have students review the list of the characteristics of highly competitive markets that they made at the start of the lesson. Ask students to describe how accurate or inaccurate this list is and why. ★9C

OPTIONS

Gifted Learners

Have interested students research a successful or popular advertising campaign. Students can use the Internet, telephone book, or other available resources to research the origin of the advertising campaign and answer questions such as who developed the campaign and how long it took, how the campaign was market tested, how the campaign has been received, and how the campaign has affected profits for the company being promoted. Have students prepare a presentation of their results. Encourage students to use visual aids or multimedia to enhance their presentations. Following students' presentations, have the class discuss each advertising campaign and then vote on which of the campaigns they like the most.

Refer students who are interested in a career in advertising to the Advertising Account Manager career profile, located in the Careers section on the *Researcher Online*. You might also invite someone in the community who works as an advertising account manager to come speak to the class as a follow-up activity. The speaker might describe the process of creating and market testing advertising campaigns as well as the types of activities an advertising account manager performs on a daily basis.

Interpersonal Learners

Organize students into small groups. Tell each group to select a market or industry that is in monopolistic competition and to research the most common ways that the companies in this market differentiate their products. Have students find out who the largest sellers are in the market, which brand names are the best known, and which companies dominate specific segments of the market. Have each group prepare a presentation that describes product differentiation in their market. ★9C

Visual-Spatial Learners

Tell students to select a product that is in monopolistic competition and then design a World Wide Web page that promotes that product by using nonprice competition to differentiate it from the existing competition. Students' Web pages should provide information about the product as well as exciting visuals to capture viewers' attention. Tell students that their Web pages should provide at least three reasons that consumers should purchase their product instead of a competing product. Before beginning their Web pages, students should research how their product is currently being differentiated from the competition, which products make up the competition, and how the companies that produce those products are using nonprice competition to differentiate them. ★9C

REVIEW

Have students complete the Section 1 Review on page 122. Use the answers in the Annotated Teacher's Edition to assess student mastery of this section.

ASSESS

To assess student mastery of this section, have students complete Daily Quiz 6.1 in *Daily Quizzes with Answer Key*. For additional assessment options, see *Alternative Assessment Handbook* on the *One-Stop Planner CD-ROM*.

ADDITIONAL RESOURCES

Branding: The Marketing Advantage. (videotapes, 7-part series). Films for the Humanities & Sciences.

Economics U$A: Perfect Competition and Inelastic Demand. No. 17. (videotape, 60 min.). The Annenberg/CPB Projects.

Market Structure. (film, cassette). National Council for Economic Education.

LESSON 6.2 — IMPERFECTLY COMPETITIVE MARKETS

TEXTBOOK PAGES 123–29

HOLT PRESENTATION MAKER: Access Illustrated LECTURE NOTES using Microsoft® PowerPoint® on the One-Stop Planner CD-ROM

OBJECTIVES

- Describe the structure of an oligopoly.
- Define a monopoly.
- Identify the types of monopolies that exist.
- Describe the factors that affect price in oligopolies and monopolies.

MOTIVATE

Make a list of the following items on the chalkboard and ask students how much they would be willing to pay for them:

- a can of soda
- a domestic automobile
- a month of cable television service

Then ask students how and why they decided on those prices. Tell students that in this lesson they will be examining noncompetitive markets. Have students read Section 2 of the chapter.

TEACH

Building a Vocabulary

List the important terms for this section on the chalkboard and tell students to add them to their Economics Dictionary. Tell students to use the information provided in the text or on the *Researcher CD-ROM* to list, define, and give an example of each term.

Evaluating Information, Applying a Model

Following up on the Motivate activity, ask students how much money they would be willing to pay for a box of cereal. On a table in the front of the room, display three different brands of the same kind of cereal (for example, the Kellogg's, General Mills, and Post brands of raisin bran.) Ask students if they can name another brand of raisin bran. Then remind them that the existence of a few large sellers is the defining characteristic of an oligopoly.

Next, ask three students to come forward to read aloud the ingredients in each of the boxes of cereal. The ingredients will be nearly identical. Remind students that another condition of an oligopoly is that sellers offer identical or similar products. Tell students that the final condition on which an oligopoly exists is that in general, other sellers cannot enter the market easily. Ask students to list reasons why oligopolistic markets are relatively difficult to enter *(high startup costs, government regulation about entering the market, and consumer loyalty to the established sellers' products)*. Finally, ask students to determine whether the breakfast cereal industry is oligopolistic. Discuss students' answers with them. ★9C

Demonstrating Understanding

Organize students into small groups. Have each group think of as many oligopolistic markets as they can (e.g., the soft-drink market, the cereal market, the soap detergent market, the automobile market, the steel industry, the rough diamond industry). Tell students to write down each example that they think of and explain how that market or industry meets the three criteria of an oligopolistic market. After about 10 minutes, have a representative from each group share the group's list with the class. Encourage feedback and class discussion. ★9C

Applying Ideas, Evaluating Information

Ask students how sellers in oligopolistic markets maintain a strong degree of control over prices *(through nonprice competition and interdependent pricing, and through illegal means such as collusion and cartels)*. Discuss each of these factors with students, including a discussion of price leadership and price wars.

On the chalkboard, write a list of 10 or 15 products that are sold by one company, such as Procter & Gamble or General Mills, or bring the products to class and display them on a table in the front of the room. Ask students to determine which of the products compete on a price basis and which compete on a nonprice basis. Then have students evaluate the impact of advertising and price leadership on the sale of these products. ★9C

Synthesizing Ideas, Solving Problems

Organize the class into small groups. Tell students that they work for an oligopoly. Then have each group simulate a corporate meeting focusing on the conditions that exist in an oligopoly and devising strategies to compete with other companies in the same market or industry. Tell each group to write down the decisions of its meeting. After the groups have completed their meetings, have each group share its strategies with the rest of the class. ★25A

Evaluating and Debating Ideas

Ask students to name and define the other type of noncompetitive market structure that they read about in Section 2 *(a monopoly—there is a single seller; no close substitute goods are available, other sellers cannot enter the market easily)*. Write the names of the four main types of monopolies on the chalkboard: natural, geographic, technological, and government. Organize students into four groups and have each think of and list market examples of their type of monopoly. Then tell each group to discuss this question: Do you think a particular type of monopoly (natural, geographic, technological, or government) benefits the economy, or not? Why or why not? Give each group 5 to 10 minutes to debate the question, and then ask a spokesperson from each group to report on the group's discussion to the entire class. ★9C

Analyzing Ideas

Remind students of the Motivate activity. Ask students to explain why monopolistic companies do not feel free to charge whatever price they want to for their goods and services. *(If sellers charged too much, consumers wouldn't buy their goods or services.)* Refer students back to the answers they provided in the Motivate activity as an example of consumer demand as a force that limits sellers' control over prices. Explain that potential competition and government regulation are the other two forces that help limit monopolistic sellers' control over prices. ★7A, 9C

CLOSE

Have students examine Figure 6.3: Comparing Market Structures (Transparency 23) on page 124. Review with students the structure and characteristics of perfect competition, monopolistic competition, oligopolies, and monopolies. Then, call on students to list and briefly describe the four main types of monopolies, and to identify the factors that affect price in each type of market structure. ★7A, 9C

OPTIONS

Gifted Learners

Organize students into groups. Have each group research the history and current marketing strategies of either a market leader in an oligopolistic market (such as the Coca-Cola Co.) or a company that has a monopoly. Have student groups prepare presentations of their results. Encourage groups to use visual aids or multimedia to enhance their presentations. After groups have finished their presentations, have students discuss the ways in which companies maintain oligopolistic and monopolistic control of their markets. ★9C, 23A

Linguistic Learners

Have students use the Internet, telephone, newspapers, and other available resources to research the local cable television provider(s) in their community. Students should answer questions such as:

▶ How many cable television providers are there in my community? Who are they, and what percentage of the market does each company have?
▶ Is the local cable television market an oligopoly or a monopoly?
▶ What competition does the cable television market in my community face now, and what competition might it face in the future, given our rapidly changing technological society?
▶ Why is it so difficult to penetrate the cable television market?
▶ How do cable companies determine rates?
▶ What specific technologies and services are consumers paying for in their monthly cable bill?
▶ Does the price of cable vary among communities and regions in the United States?

Have students prepare a written report of their findings. Students may want to include their reports in their portfolios. ★9C, 23D

REVIEW

Have students complete the Section 2 Review on page 129. Use the answers in the Annotated Teacher's Edition to assess student mastery of this section.

ASSESS

To assess student mastery of this section, have students complete Daily Quiz 6.2 in *Daily Quizzes with Answer Key*. For additional assessment options, see *Alternative Assessment Handbook* on the *One-Stop Planner CD-ROM*.

ADDITIONAL RESOURCES

Bagdikian, Ben H. *The Media Monopoly*. 2000. Beacon Press.
Frech, H. E., III. *Competition and Monopoly in Medical Care*. 1996. AEI Press.
Geisst, Charles R. *Monopolies in America: Empire Builders and Their Enemies from Jay Gould to Bill Gates*. 2000. Oxford University Press.
Hudgins, Edward L., ed. *Mail @ the Millennium: Will the Postal Service Go Private?* 2000. Cato Institute.
The Diamond Empire. (videotape, 90 min.). PBS Video.
Economics U$A: Monopoly/Oligopolies. Nos. 19 & 20. (videotapes, 30 min.). The Annenberg/CPB Projects.

LESSON 6.3 MARKET REGULATION

TEXTBOOK PAGES 130–34

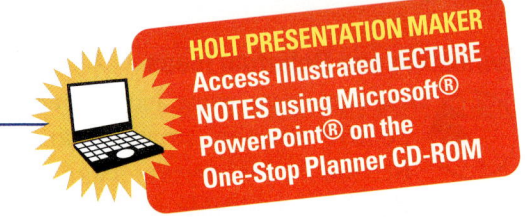

HOLT PRESENTATION MAKER — Access Illustrated LECTURE NOTES using Microsoft® PowerPoint® on the One-Stop Planner CD-ROM

OBJECTIVES

- Describe the relationship between the U.S. government and business before the 1880s.
- Explain the purpose of early antitrust legislation.
- Summarize how the government has enforced antitrust legislation.

MOTIVATE

Review with students the characteristics of a monopoly. *(There is a single seller, no close substitute goods are available, and other sellers cannot enter the market easily.)* Then have each student make a list of the problems he or she would anticipate for the economy, businesses, and individual consumers if the government did not regulate monopolies in any way. Have students discuss their ideas as a class. Then ask students how they think the government should regulate monopolies. List students' suggestions on the chalkboard. Tell students to keep this discussion and their suggestions in mind as they read Section 3 of the chapter. ★9C, 25A

TEACH

Building a Vocabulary

List the important terms for this section on the chalkboard and tell students to add them to their Economics Dictionary. Tell students to use the information provided in the text or on the *Researcher CD-ROM* to list, define, and give an example of each term.

Using Time Lines, Identifying Cause and Effect

Organize students into groups of four or five. Provide large supplies of butcher paper and tell each group to create an illustrated time line of government regulation of business from the Civil War to the present. Students should list all major antitrust legislation, the effects of this legislation, and any other cause-and-effect relationships that they see. In addition, students' time lines might include descriptions of key figures in government and industry and case studies of industries particularly affected by government regulation. Tell students to use color or some other device to separate their time lines into three sections, one representing the relationship between government and business before the 1880s, one representing the period of early antitrust legislation, and one representing more recent antitrust legislation.

Groups may use the textbook, the Internet, newspapers, business journals, and any other available resources to complete their time lines. Have students display their time lines around the classroom when they are finished. Refer students who need additional instruction on the skills used in this activity to the *Global Skillbuilder* Lesson 9: Using Time Lines. ★23A

Mastering Concepts

Follow up the time line activity by having students examine Figure 6.4: U.S. Antitrust Legislation (Transparency 24) on p. 133. Review each law with the class. As you go through the chart, call on students to use their time lines to explain what each law accomplished. Then have students summarize how the U.S. government has enforced antitrust legislation throughout the years. ★23A

CLOSE

Review the material covered in the lesson. Then ask students the following questions and promote class discussion in response to each one: Do you support more or less government regulation of business? Why? What additional regulations are needed, in your opinion? Do you think the government should deregulate more industries, as it has done with the airline industry? Do you agree with the government's decision to let several of the Baby Bells form mergers? Why or why not? ★23D

OPTIONS

Students Having Difficulty, Linguistic Learners

Organize the class into groups of three. Match students having difficulty with students who have mastered the material. Assign one student in each group one of the following readings, located in *From the Source: Readings in Economics and Government:*

- Reading 39: Interstate Commerce Act of 1887
- Reading 40: Sherman Antitrust Act of 1890
- Reading 42: Federal Trade Commission Act of 1914

As students go through the readings, tell them to think about the following questions:
- What is the main purpose, or goal, of the law?
- What problems did this law address?
- Which groups or individuals supported this law, and why?
- Which groups or individuals opposed this law, and why?

When students are through, have each describe his or her reading to the other members of the group. Students should answer each of the above questions when explaining their reading. If a student does not know the answer to a question, encourage the other members of the group to help figure out the answer. When the groups are through, have the class discuss each reading. ★23A

Gifted Learners

Have students research the Federal Trade Commission (FTC) and describe its functions, the types of legal decisions it has made, and the effects of these decisions on the U.S. economy. In addition, have students research an instance of when the FTC has investigated and found proof of the use of unfair methods of competition by a business or industry. Tell students to find out what actions were taken against the company or industry and if it has changed its methods of doing business as a result of the FTC investigation. Have students present their findings in an oral report. A starting point for students' research is the FTC profile located in the Executive Departments section on the *Researcher Online*. ★23A

Linguistic Learners

Have a student read aloud the two paragraphs on page 134 of Section 3, which describe the 1982 breakup of AT&T. Discuss the breakup and then explain to students that in addition to the results mentioned in the text, the breakup of AT&T had many other effects. Have students research the breakup of AT&T, how the telecommunications industry has changed as a result of the breakup, and the effects of the breakup for consumers, other industries, and technology. Have students present their findings in a written report. Students may want to include their reports in their portfolios. ★23A

Interpersonal Learners, Body-Kinesthetic Learners

Organize students into groups. Tell them that they are writers and anchor people for a popular news magazine show on television. The producer of the show has decided to air a 10-minute segment covering antitrust legislation and government regulation of businesses in the United States. Tell groups that their task is to prepare and present the news segment. Explain that they can focus their segment on any aspect of the topic that they want. For example, groups might focus on one individual, industry, law, or event, or they might want to focus on a current antitrust issue, debate, or investigation. Have groups start the assignment by preparing a written proposal explaining the topic they want to cover so that the producer (the teacher) can approve it. Then tell groups to divide up tasks and research the topic. Have each group present its segment to the rest of the class. ★23D, 24D

Interpersonal Learners, Logical-Mathematical Learners

Organize the class into two groups. Have each group research arguments either for or against the following statement: The federal government should not break up large firms in oligopolies. Students should find at least four or five arguments to support their position and at least one specific example to back up each point or argument. Have students select two or three representatives from each group to debate the statement in front of the class. ★23D

REVIEW

Have students complete the Section 3 Review on page 134. Use the answers in the Annotated Teacher's Edition to assess student mastery of this section.

ASSESS

To assess student mastery of this section, have students complete Daily Quiz 6.3 in *Daily Quizzes with Answer Key*. For additional assessment options, see *Alternative Assessment Handbook* on the *One-Stop Planner CD-ROM*.

RETEACH

For students having difficulty with the lessons, have them complete Reteaching Activity 6. This activity is located in *Reteaching Activities with Answer Key*.

ADDITIONAL RESOURCES

Crandall, Robert W., and Harold Furchtgott-Roth. *Cable TV: Regulation or Competition?* 1996. Brookings Institution.

Eisenach, Jeffery A., and Thomas M. Lenard. *Competition, Innovation and the Microsoft Monopoly: Antitrust in the Digital Marketplace.* 1999. Kluwer Academic Press.

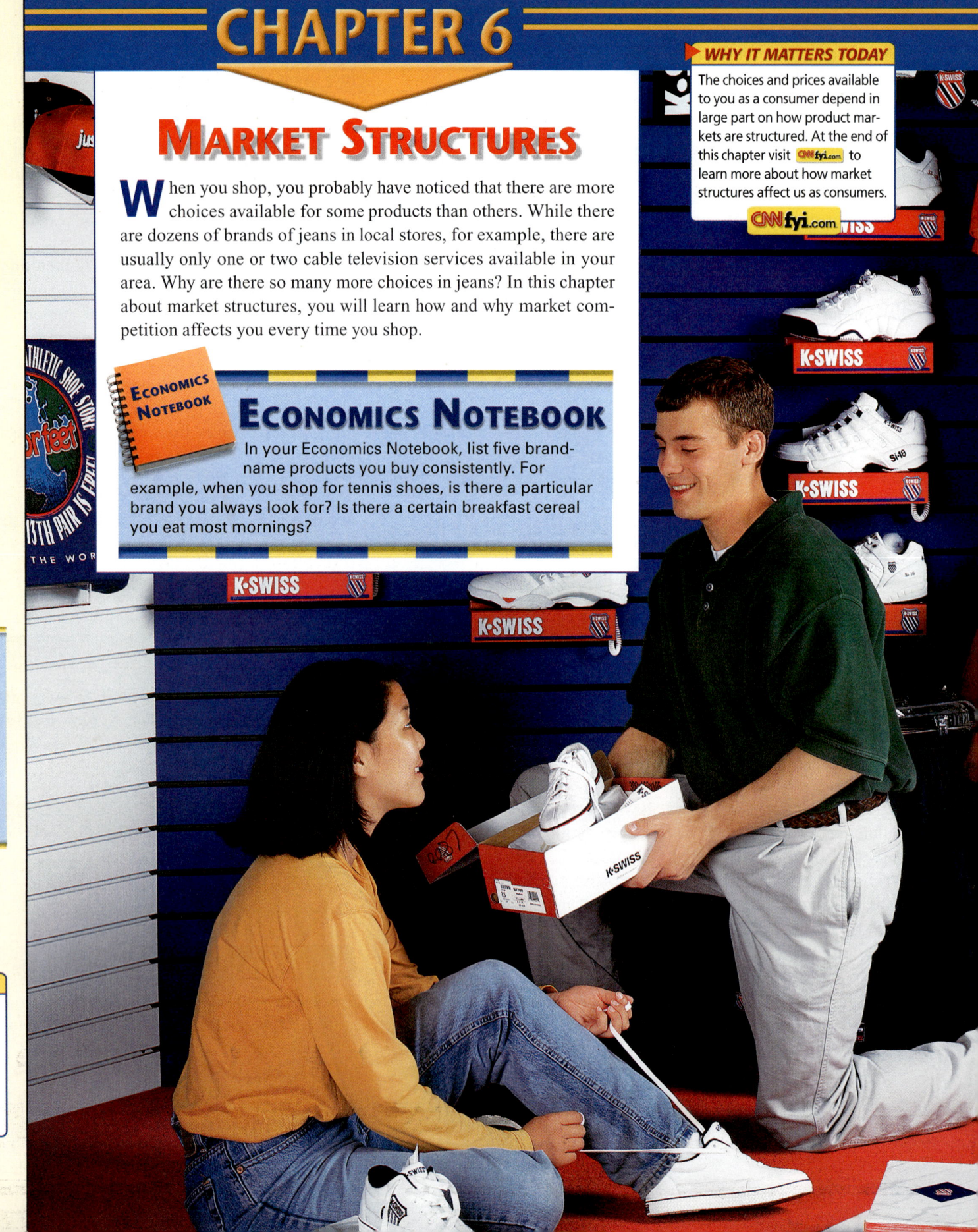

CHAPTER 6

TOPICS INCLUDE

- competitive markets
- perfect competition
- monopolistic competition
- product differentiation
- nonprice competition
- brand loyalty
- noncompetitive markets
- oligopolies
- interdependent pricing
- collusion and cartels
- monopolies
- market regulation
- antitrust policies and legislation

ECONOMICS NOTEBOOK

The Economics Notebook is a journal activity that encourages students to consider basic concepts of economics that relate to their lives. A follow-up notebook activity appears on page 136.

WHY IT MATTERS TODAY

To find additional lesson plans dealing with market structures, visit CNNfyi.com or have students complete the ECONOMICS IN THE NEWS activity on page 135.

CNNfyi.com

CHAPTER 6

MARKET STRUCTURES

When you shop, you probably have noticed that there are more choices available for some products than others. While there are dozens of brands of jeans in local stores, for example, there are usually only one or two cable television services available in your area. Why are there so many more choices in jeans? In this chapter about market structures, you will learn how and why market competition affects you every time you shop.

ECONOMICS NOTEBOOK

In your Economics Notebook, list five brand-name products you buy consistently. For example, when you shop for tennis shoes, is there a particular brand you always look for? Is there a certain breakfast cereal you eat most mornings?

WHY IT MATTERS TODAY

The choices and prices available to you as a consumer depend in large part on how product markets are structured. At the end of this chapter visit CNNfyi.com to learn more about how market structures affect us as consumers.

CNNfyi.com

SECTION 1

HIGHLY COMPETITIVE MARKETS

READ TO DISCOVER

1. What is perfect competition?
2. What is monopolistic competition?
3. How do sellers differentiate their products under monopolistic competition?

ECONOMICS DICTIONARY

perfect competition
buyers
sellers
monopoly
monopolistic competition
differentiate
product differentiation
nonprice competition

As a consumer, you tend to benefit most from competitive markets. These types of markets provide consumers with a range of products that are priced lower, reflect costs more accurately, and are offered by more sellers than in any other kind of market. The jeans market, for example, is highly competitive.

Why do highly competitive markets ensure such a large selection of goods and services? Supply and demand determine what items are produced and at what price they are available. The forces of supply and demand promote competition by encouraging producers to supply consumers with a wide selection of goods and services.

There are two types of highly competitive markets: those with perfect competition and those with monopolistic competition. Each is characterized by certain key conditions.

Perfect Competition

Perfect competition, also called pure competition, is an ideal market structure in which **buyers**, or consumers, and **sellers**, or producers, each compete directly and fully under the laws of supply and demand. This means that no one buyer or seller controls demand, supply, or prices. It also means that nothing prevents competition among both buyers and sellers.

How can you tell if a market is perfectly competitive? In general, perfect competition exists when four conditions are present:

▶ Many buyers and sellers act independently.
▶ Sellers offer identical products.
▶ Buyers are well informed about products.
▶ Sellers can enter or exit the market easily.

Many Buyers and Sellers When there are many buyers and sellers, each one accounts for only a small share of the overall purchases or sales in the market. Therefore, no single buyer or seller in a market has enough power to control

MARKETS & PRICES *Perfect competition enables buyers and sellers to compete under the laws of supply and demand.* **What four conditions indicate perfect competition?** TEKS

SECTION 1

HIGHLY COMPETITIVE MARKETS

Lesson Plans
For teaching strategies, see Lesson 6.1 located at the beginning of this chapter, or the One-Stop Planner Strategy 6.1.

Economics Dictionary
To reinforce the section's vocabulary terms, refer students to the Electronic Glossary on the *Researcher CD-ROM*.

Section Assessment
To assess students' mastery of this section, have them complete Daily Quiz 6.1 in *Daily Quizzes with Answer Key*.

Caption Answer
many buyers and sellers act independently, sellers offer identical products, buyers are well informed about products, sellers can enter or exit the market easily ★9C

Content
2B, 7A, 9C
Social Studies Skills
23A, 23C, 23F, 24A, 24D

MARKET STRUCTURES 117

Cultural Perspectives

Dating is big business. In 2001 a World Wide Web search using the Google search engine found 46,000 sites related to dating services. These sites ranged from small businesses that enable people to set up their own dating home page (complete with a picture), to sites providing matchmaking services, to advice on how to meet one's ideal mate or select the perfect floral arrangement, to help finding an international pen pal.

What Do You Think? Answers

1. Jeremy and Joshua identified a real need—a high-school matchmaking service; identified their market—high-school students; designed surveys and software to obtain and process client information; came up with a successful way to distribute their product through student organizations; offered each organization half of the $1 fee collected per survey as an incentive for the clubs to sponsor the service; and made the wise decision to hire additional companies to help out when demand exceeded capacity. **2B**

2. Answers will vary, but students might suggest that such a business create an Internet site, distribute pamphlets at school dances or at club functions, or advertise in local or school newspapers.

ECONOMICS IN ACTION

Matchmaker, Matchmaker

Have you ever wondered whom to ask to the next school dance? Jeremy Elson and Joshua Adler, founders of Scholastic Matchmakers, bet that you have. While in high school, Jeremy and Joshua started their business with just a computer and an idea—that students might need some help meeting people who shared their interests.

Jeremy and Joshua discovered that the matchmaking market was fairly easy to enter. First, they developed two multiple-choice questionnaires. The first asked basic questions, such as "How would your best friend describe you?" with possible answers such as "outgoing" and "intense." The second questionnaire asked for more personal information, such as what traits and qualities a respondent finds attractive. Jeremy also designed a computer program that analyzed student responses to the surveys.

To distribute the surveys, Jeremy and Joshua contacted business clubs and student councils in a number of high schools. In exchange for sponsoring the surveys, these organizations split with Jeremy and Joshua the $1 fee that students paid to find their "matches." Jeremy said, "There's such a curiosity to know who's out there. Normally talking to girls is so awkward. . . . It's a glimpse into this world you can't see."

By February 14—Valentine's Day—of 1995, Scholastic Matchmakers had received thousands of completed questionnaires from some 200 schools. The volume was completely unexpected—and overwhelming. Jeremy, who had entered Johns Hopkins University since starting Matchmakers, had to choose between focusing on his college studies and concentrating on the business. He said, "I'm embarrassed to say I dropped out for a semester." After he got the business stabilized, however, Jeremy returned to school.

Jeremy and Joshua realized that they needed to adapt their business practices to meet demand. They hired a company to enter the survey responses into a computer. Using the Internet, the responses were transferred to Jeremy's computer, where they were processed using software he had written. Then the results went to another company, which printed out each student's list of "matches" and sent the results to the appropriate high school.

What risks did Jeremy and Joshua face? First, they did not know how many high schools would choose their service or how many students would participate. Additionally, students were not charged until the "match" lists were delivered, and the sponsors at the schools were responsible for collecting fees. Thus, Jeremy and Joshua were not sure that they would be paid everything they were owed. Fortunately for them, the risks paid off.

What Do You Think? TEKS

1. What business practices and decisions helped make Jeremy and Joshua's business successful?
2. What do you think would be the most effective way to publicize a business like Scholastic Matchmakers? Explain your answer.

Scholastic Matchmakers was a business designed to help students meet people who share their interests.

demand, supply, or prices. Instead, levels of production and prices are set by the market forces of supply and demand.

Note that in perfect competition, the many buyers and sellers must act independently. Otherwise, a group of sellers or buyers acting together could influence—or even set—prices. Of course, when there are many sellers and buyers in a market, they are less able to act together to control prices. Having a large number of independent buyers and sellers thus promotes competition.

Identical Products Under perfect competition, sellers offer identical products, so buyers make purchasing decisions by comparing "apples to apples" rather than "apples to oranges." This means that buyers choose one product over another primarily on price, not on unique characteristics. Buyers' decisions thus give sellers accurate information about whether they are charging the best price for their products.

What would happen if buyers chose among nonidentical products? In this case, buyers' purchases would not be based on price alone, as in perfect competition. Each product's unique features would lead to a separate market, with a single firm providing that product to the market. This type of single-firm market is the basis for the market structure known as **monopoly**, in which one seller controls all production of a good or service. Monopolies will be discussed in greater detail in Section 2.

Informed Buyers Under perfect competition, buyers must be knowledgeable about products. Without accurate and readily available product information, buyers cannot compare products effectively. Sellers can compete perfectly only when buyers can make informed decisions.

Easy Market Entry and Exit For sellers to compete perfectly, they must be able to enter a profitable market—or leave an unprofitable one—easily. The freedom to switch from market to market helps ensure that a single seller or small group of sellers cannot dominate a particular market.

The ease of entering or exiting a market depends on start-up costs, the level of technical knowledge needed, and the amount of control held by existing companies in the market. If any of these factors—known as barriers to entry—are high, sellers cannot compete easily and fully.

Perfect Competition As a Model

Of course, no market is perfectly competitive. As noted above, perfect competition is a model of an ideal competitive market structure. This model helps economists analyze markets and determine how competitive they are. (See Figure 6.1.)

Some markets do approach perfect competition, however. One example is the agricultural

COMPETITION AND MARKET STRUCTURE

More Competition
- PERFECT COMPETITION
- MONOPOLISTIC COMPETITION
- OLIGOPOLY
- PURE MONOPOLY

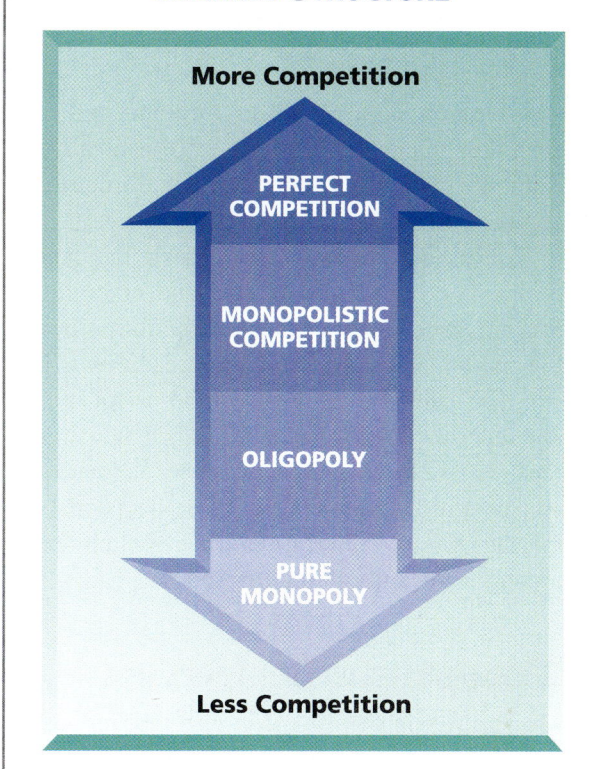

Less Competition

FIGURE 6.1 Market structure is largely determined by the amount of competition among producers. **Which market structure is the least competitive?**

Themes in Economics

THE ROLE OF GOVERNMENT

In today's health-conscious society, many consumers read nutrition labels closely. To improve food labels and ensure their accuracy, the U.S. government passed the Nutrition Labeling and Education Act in 1990. The act requires that all food labels be consistent, list ingredients, and provide specific dietary information.

To make certain that the information provided is accurate, the Food and Drug Administration (FDA) occasionally checks nutrition labels. Standardized nutrition labels and checks on their accuracy promote fair competition in the food industry. ■

Caption Answer
pure monopoly ★9C, 23F

Transparency
An overhead transparency of Figure 6.1 is available in *Transparency Resources*. See Transparency 21: Competition and Market Structure.

markets in the United States. Consider how well agricultural markets meet the four conditions of perfect competition.

First, many buyers and sellers act independently. Thousands of independent farmers and growers compete to sell their products to millions of buyers. No single buyer or seller controls enough of the market to affect the price of corn, peaches, or most other agricultural products.

Second, sellers offer identical products. Agricultural products are uniform: one apple is basically like another apple; one ear of corn is basically like another ear of corn. Buyers make their decisions based solely on the price of the apple or the corn, not on any distinguishing characteristics.

Third, buyers are well informed about the market's products. Labels on apples, for example, tell buyers the variety (McIntosh, Granny Smith, Golden Delicious), the price, the place of origin (Washington State, Michigan, Virginia), and often even how the apples were grown (organically, for example). Buyers can thus use this information to compare the price of identical products.

Fourth, sellers can enter or exit the market easily. The high price of land and other inputs prevent some potential suppliers from entering the market. But farmers who already own land can, for example, easily leave the carrot market and enter the tomato market if they believe tomatoes will become more profitable. Climate and soil conditions may restrict these decisions, but on the whole, U.S. farmers can switch easily among many agricultural markets.

Monopolistic Competition

Monopolistic competition differs from perfect competition in one key respect—sellers offer different, rather than identical, products. Each firm seeks to have monopoly-like power by selling a unique product. Product variation is much more common than having identical products. As a result, monopolistic competition is much more common than perfect competition.

There are, however, similarities between the two systems. First, both buyers and sellers in monopolistic competition compete under the laws of supply and demand, just as they do in perfect competition. In addition, both systems feature many buyers and sellers acting independently, buyers who are well informed about products, and ease of market entry or exit.

Product Differentiation Sellers in monopolistic competition try to **differentiate**, or point out differences, between their products and those of their competitors. By pointing out differences—which can be real or merely seem real to consumers—sellers use **product differentiation** to set their products apart.

Nonprice Competition Sellers differentiate their products through **nonprice competition**. That is, they compete on a basis other than price. Consider the jeans market, for example. Designer jeans that cost $75 and "no-name" jeans that cost $25 are basically the same product. If consumers decided which jeans to buy based solely on price, no one would buy the more expensive designer jeans. In this market, however, manufacturers have succeeded in competing on a nonprice

MARKETS & PRICES *Many sellers use famous celebrities to differentiate their products.* **What is the main goal of product differentiation?**

Caption Answer
Sellers use product differentiation to set their products apart.

Themes in Economics

COMPETITION & MARKET STRUCTURE U.S. companies spent more than $215 billion on advertising in 1999. Although critics assert that advertising makes goods and services more expensive for consumers, it can provide a valuable quality-control service. Consumers often choose goods with well-established brand names because they believe that these products are higher in quality than private-label or generic products. As a result, brand-name producers have a great deal to lose if they do not provide the quality that consumers expect. For example, in 1990 Perrier lost a large amount of its share of the bottled water market when the FDA discovered that benzene, an industrial solvent and carcinogen, had tainted some of Perrier's product. ■

Cultural Perspectives

Coca-Cola's and McDonald's investments in establishing brand loyalty among consumers have paid off. Coca-Cola and McDonald's are two of the world's most valuable brand names, worth an estimated $68.9 and $25.3 billion, respectively.

basis. They compete through advertising and by emphasizing their brand names.

In fact, many manufacturers spend millions of dollars on advertising to persuade buyers to purchase a particular brand of jeans based on style or the brand name instead of price. Many consumers are persuaded by such advertising. They are willing to buy the more expensive jeans because they believe that the designer's brand name makes the jeans more stylish and thus more valuable.

Profits The main goal of product differentiation and nonprice competition is to increase profits. By setting its product apart from the competition and convincing buyers to base their decision on nonprice factors, a seller can raise the price of its product above the competitive level and make more profit. The seller does this by increasing demand for its product, thereby shifting the market price upward.

You can see this type of shift in demand and equilibrium price in Figure 6.2. The demand

CAREERS IN ECONOMICS

Advertising Account Manager

Who creates the attention-getting advertisements that you see on television or in your favorite magazine? One person responsible for bringing those advertisements from the drawing board to the television screen or magazine page is the advertising account manager.

Most ads are the result of a team effort by researchers, designers, and the account manager. While researchers analyze consumer needs and wants, designers develop an ad campaign that presents the product to the public. The account manager is the team captain, overseeing the campaign's development and ensuring that the client is happy with the ads.

Suppose that you are the account manager for Clinique cosmetics. You must determine what distinguishes Clinique products from other companies' cosmetics. Does the company offer makeup in a wider range of colors? Does a famous model or actress use Clinique products? As the account manager, you must persuade consumers to buy cosmetics from Clinique rather than from other companies such as Prescriptives and Max Factor.

Typically, account managers have college degrees in advertising. In addition to knowing how to produce an ad, communicate with the ad team and the client, and understand the market, an account manager must maintain a careful budget. By managing the team, market approach, and budget, an advertising account manager can create a winning campaign that ensures a successful product.

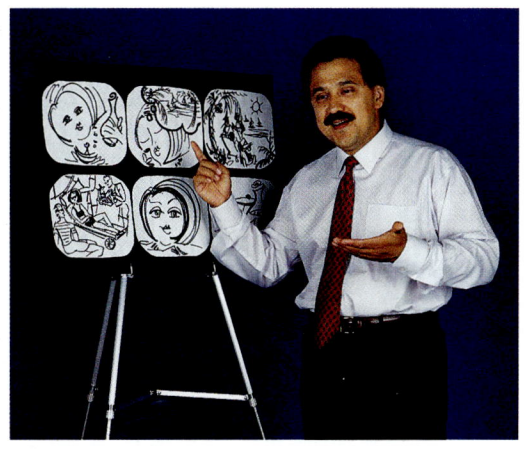

Advertising account managers organize the work of researchers and designers to meet the needs of the client.

Careers in Economics

To help students learn about other careers in economics, refer them to the Careers section on the *Researcher Online*.

---

internet connect

TOPIC: Monopolistic Competition
GO TO: go.hrw.com
KEYWORD: SM EC6

Have students access the Internet through the HRW Go site to conduct research on two retailers that sell the same item to the same market (for example, two stores that sell clothes to teens). Students should select one item (hats, for example) sold by both stores and create an advertisement urging customers to buy that product. Remind students to think about the fact that these stores compete directly with each other. How does each store use product differentiation and non-price competition to increase their profits? ★9C

MARKET STRUCTURES

Transparency
An overhead transparency of Figure 6.2 is available in *Transparency Resources*. See Transparency 22: Shift in Demand and Equilibrium Price.

Caption Answer
Demand at each and every price has increased, resulting in a new equilibrium point. ★7A, 23F

SECTION 1 REVIEW ANSWERS

1. perfect competition (117), buyers (117), sellers (117), monopoly (119), monopolistic competition (120), differentiate (120), product differentiation (120), nonprice competition (120) 9C, 24A

2. branches should read: many buyers and sellers acting independently, sellers offering identical products, well-informed buyers, a market that sellers can easily enter or exit 9C

3a. price 9C, 24D

3b. sellers offer different rather than identical products 9C, 23A

3c. the jeans industry 9C

3d. sellers use product differentiation and nonprice competition 9C

4. Agricultural markets meet all four conditions of perfect competition. Fishing markets are another example of nearly perfectly competitive markets because they also offer identical products. 9C, 23A

SHIFT IN DEMAND AND EQUILIBRIUM PRICE

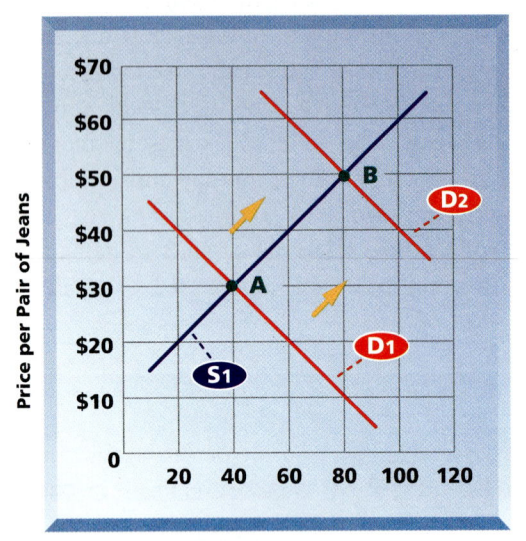

FIGURE 6.2 A demand curve shift results in a new equilibrium price. **What does point B indicate about supply and demand?** ★TEKS

curve D_1 represents the initial demand for Jean Luc brand jeans. The equilibrium price is $30 (point A). After the company launches a successful national advertising campaign, demand for Jean Luc jeans soars. The demand curve shifts to the right (D_2) as consumers are willing and able to buy more jeans at each and every price.

The equilibrium price of Jean Luc jeans shifts upward to $50, from point A on the old demand curve (D_1) to point B on the new demand curve (D_2). Thus, although the product did not change and basically is the same as other jeans on the market, the equilibrium price is different for this brand of jeans.

Generally, by differentiating its product and creating brand-name loyalty, a seller can gain some monopolylike control over price. The seller can use nonprice competition to carve a niche, or small share, for itself in the market—a niche it can monopolize, or dominate, and from which it can profit.

Sellers realize, however, that they are still subject to the law of demand. If the maker of Jean Luc jeans increases its price too much, there will be a surplus of Jean Luc jeans. Many buyers will return to making their decisions based on price and switch to a lower-priced competitor's jeans.

SECTION 1 REVIEW

★TEKS Q: 1, 2, 3a, 3b, 3c, 3d, 4

1. Identify and Explain:
- perfect competition
- buyers
- sellers
- monopoly
- monopolistic competition
- differentiate
- product differentiation
- nonprice competition

2. Analyzing Information: Copy the diagram below. Use it to identify the four conditions that must exist for a market to be perfectly competitive.

Perfect Competition

3. Finding the Main Idea

a. How do buyers choose between products in perfect competition?

b. How does monopolistic competition differ from perfect competition?

c. Give an example of monopolistic competition.

d. How do sellers in monopolistic competition compete with one another?

4. Writing and Critical Thinking

Summarizing: Identify which conditions of perfect competition agricultural markets meet. Now identify at least one other perfectly competitive market. Explain your answer.

Consider:
- the characteristics of perfect competition
- similarities and differences in the agricultural and fishing industries

Homework Practice Online
keyword: SM3 C6

SECTION 2
IMPERFECTLY COMPETITIVE MARKETS

READ TO DISCOVER
1. How is an oligopoly structured?
2. What is a monopoly?
3. What types of monopolies exist?
4. What factors affect price in oligopolies and monopolies?

ECONOMICS DICTIONARY

oligopoly
interdependent pricing
price leadership
price war
collusion
cartel
natural monopolies
economies of scale
geographic monopolies
technological monopolies
patent
copyrights
government monopoly

You now know why you have such a large selection of jeans to choose from when you go shopping. The competitive structure of the jeans market encourages sellers to meet consumer demand but also encourages them to differentiate their jeans.

Not all markets, however, are structured as competitively as the jeans market. The cable television market, for example, typically has been imperfectly competitive, or even noncompetitive. In most areas of the United States, this market has been dominated by just one or two sellers. Fewer sellers generally means fewer products and less choice for consumers like you. An imperfectly competitive structure also usually results in higher prices.

Oligopolies

The most common noncompetitive market in the United States is the **oligopoly**—a market structure in which a few large sellers control most of the production of a good or service. In general, an oligopoly exists when three conditions are present:

- There are only a few large sellers.
- Sellers offer identical or similar products.
- Other sellers cannot enter the market easily.

Few Large Sellers The existence of a few large sellers is the defining characteristic of an oligopoly. No other market structure has this feature. A market is considered an oligopoly when the largest three or four sellers produce most—perhaps 70 percent or more—of the market's total output.

Identical or Similar Products When there are a few large sellers, each one has a large share of the overall sales in the market. Because the sellers have so much at stake, they are less likely to take risks, such as offering new products. If a seller introduced a new product that failed, for example, that seller's share of the market—and its profits—likely would drop significantly. Thus, sellers in an oligopoly tend to offer identical or similar products.

Difficult Market Entry A few sellers can maintain their control only if other sellers cannot easily enter the market. The relative difficulty of entering an oligopolistic market depends on start-up costs, government regulation about entering the market, and consumer loyalty to the established sellers' products. If any of these factors is insignificant enough, other sellers can enter the market, compete with the original few sellers, and end those sellers' oligopoly.

MARKET STRUCTURES 123

COMPARING MARKET STRUCTURES

CHARACTERISTICS	PERFECT COMPETITION	MONOPOLISTIC COMPETITION	OLIGOPOLY	PURE MONOPOLY
NUMBER OF FIRMS IN EACH INDUSTRY	Many	Many	Few (Three or Four)	One
MARKET CONCENTRATION	Low	Low	High	Absolute
TYPE OF PRODUCT	Similar or Identical	Similar or Identical	Similar or Differentiated	Unique (No Substitutes)
AVAILABILITY OF INFORMATION	Much (Product Advertising)	Much (Product Advertising)	Much (Product Advertising)	Some (Product and Institutional Advertising)
ENTRY INTO INDUSTRY	Very Easy	Fairly Easy	Difficult	Prohibitive
CONTROL OVER PRICES	None	Little	Some	Complete
EXAMPLE INDUSTRIES	•Agriculture	•Long-distance telephone service	•Automobiles •Breakfast Cereals	•Electric Power •Cable Television

FIGURE 6.3 Market structure involves several characteristics other than level of competition. **How do oligopolies and pure monopolies differ in terms of the availability of product information?**

Oligopolies at Work

The few sellers in an oligopolistic market have more control over prices than do the many sellers in a monopolistically competitive one. (See Figure 6.3.) This control stems mainly from legal methods of determining prices. Sometimes, however, oligopolies try to control prices through illegal means.

Nonprice Competition Like sellers in monopolistic competition, sellers in an oligopoly control prices somewhat through nonprice competition. That is, oligopolistic sellers attempt to differentiate their products through advertising and by encouraging consumers to develop loyalty to particular brand names.

Nonprice competition can become fierce among sellers in an oligopoly. Consider the market for breakfast cereals. Although a trip to the grocery store might make you think that dozens of cereal makers battle for the highest market share, three companies—Kellogg's, General Mills, and Post—account for about 80 percent of sales. The market is actually an oligopoly in which a few companies differentiate their products by creating numerous brand names.

Transparency

An overhead transparency of Figure 6.3 is available in *Transparency Resources*. See Transparency 23: Comparing Market Structures.

Caption Answer
Product information is more available in oligopolies than in pure monopolies. ★9C

Themes in Economics

COMPETITION & MARKET STRUCTURE The concentration ratio—the percentage of total industry sales made by the four largest firms in an industry—measures the extent to which a few large firms dominate an industry. The ratio varies between zero and 100, with 100 indicating that the four largest firms accounted for all industry sales. An industry is considered an oligopoly if it has a concentration ratio of about 70 or more.

The concentration ratio is only a rough measure of competitiveness, however. An industry may have a low concentration ratio, and still be highly uncompetitive. For example, the newspaper publishing industry has a low concentration ratio. However, most cities have only one or two newspapers, which means that within local markets, newspapers face limited competition. ■

CHAPTER 6

Interdependent Pricing Sellers in an oligopoly also maintain a degree of control over price through **interdependent pricing**, or by being very responsive to—or dependent on—the pricing actions of their competitors. Interdependent pricing is particularly common in oligopolies because sellers are reluctant to risk their market share—causing them to not only offer similar products but also offer them at similar prices.

The most common form of interdependent pricing is **price leadership**, in which one of the largest sellers in the market takes the lead by setting a price for its product. If competitors also institute that price, the market leader has in effect controlled the price of all products.

What happens if the competing companies do not institute the same price as the market leader? In this case the leader has not successfully affected the price of its product. In fact, it may be forced to change its price again to be competitive with the other sellers' prices.

A failed pricing policy may spark a **price war**, in which sellers aggressively undercut each other's prices in an attempt to gain market share. Price wars can initially benefit consumers by lowering prices. Some sellers, however, can be severely hurt by price wars. If this level of competition lasts a long time, a seller may lose so much money that it is forced out of business—something that has happened to some airline carriers in the United States, for example.

When a price war ends, prices tend to rise again as oligopolistic sellers return to price leadership and nonprice competition. If one or more sellers have gone out of business, prices may rise even higher than before the price war because of reduced competition. Thus, in the long run, consumers may not benefit from severe price wars.

Collusion Nonprice competition and price leadership are legal methods of determining prices. On the other hand, **collusion**—when sellers secretly agree to set production levels or prices for their products—is illegal and carries heavy penalties such as fines and even prison sentences for those involved. Collusion tends to raise prices higher than they would be under the

Global Exchange

Driving Prices Up

Whether you're driving to school, going to the mall, or heading out on a vacation, you'll need gasoline to get there.

Have you ever wondered why the price of gas goes up or drops from time to time? Gas is made from refined petroleum. One factor affecting the price of gas is that we have to import much of the petroleum we need. Outside of the United States, most countries with oil to sell belong to a cartel called the Organization of Petroleum Exporting Countries (OPEC), which includes Algeria, Indonesia, Iran, Iraq, Kuwait, Libya, Nigeria, Qatar, Saudi Arabia, the United Arab Emirates, and Venezuela.

A cartel is a group of suppliers of an identical product that acts together to protect the price at which that product sells so that their profit margins do not shrink. All members agree on the price, and no member can drop its price to attract more customers.

How can members protect their price? One way is by controlling supply. For example, OPEC sometimes cuts production to reduce available supply. When supply falls below demand, the price of oil increases.

OPEC is not the only factor affecting the price of gas. National and local conditions and policies also determine how much you pay at the pump. For example, states tax gasoline to pay for such activities as keeping the air clean. Also, periods of high demand may push prices up, as before a holiday weekend.

Themes in Economics

COMPETITION & MARKET STRUCTURE The top two soft-drink sellers, Coca-Cola Co. and PepsiCo Inc., have an oligopoly in the soft-drink market. In 2000 the two companies controlled more than 70 percent of industry sales. Both companies use nonprice competition to differentiate their products—each provides numerous brands of soft drinks—and the "cola wars" have been a mainstay of advertising for many years. ■

Themes in Economics

MARKETS & PRICES Government agencies often investigate claims of price setting. For example, just before Passover in 1997, Florida's attorney general questioned why the price of a 5-pound package of matzo—the unleavened bread eaten during the religious holiday—was more than twice as expensive in Florida as it was in New York City. The attorney general launched an investigation to determine if nine manufacturers and distributors of matzo were colluding to fix prices.

Price differences do not necessarily mean companies are in collusion, however. The differences might simply be a result of the forces of supply and demand at work. During times of increased demand, such as holidays, sellers often raise prices, which is perfectly legal in the U.S. economy. ■

Themes in Economics

COMPETITION & MARKET STRUCTURE In addition to markets with limited numbers of sellers, there are also markets with limited numbers of buyers. A monopsony is a market in which there is only one buyer. For example, in the British coal-mining industry, the National Coal Board is the sole buyer of British coal. In a situation such as this, the buyer has monopolistic control within the market. Monopsonistic firms tend to hire fewer workers and pay lower wages than companies in more competitive markets.

An oligopsony is a market in which there are only a few buyers. For example, in the United States, just a few companies purchase the majority of the nation's tobacco crop. ■

Caption Answer

because they fix prices ★23A

COMPETITION & MARKET STRUCTURE South Africa's De Beers company produces a small portion of the world's diamonds, but through a cartel it controls the sale of rough gems by buying and stockpiling stones. **Why are cartels illegal in the United States?**

---

competitive forces of supply and demand. This interference with competitive trade is viewed as undesirable, but the lure of higher profits may sometimes tempt companies in oligopolistic markets to set prices.

Cartels Collusion is sometimes based on an informal agreement to coordinate production decisions. In other cases, however, sellers form a **cartel**, in which companies openly organize a system of price setting and market sharing.

Cartels are illegal in the United States because they fix prices. Many other countries, however, allow the formation of cartels. Several cartels are international organizations that coordinate the production levels and prices of natural resources such as oil and diamonds. These types of goods lend themselves to being controlled by a cartel because they do not vary much—one country's oil is very much like another's. This means that sellers in the market cannot significantly differentiate their product and thus encounter incentives to coordinate with other sellers.

Cartels often are unstable and short-lived. Members may be tempted to produce more than their agreed-upon market share in order to earn more profits. In response, the other sellers in the cartel may raise their output to protect their market share and profits. As production rises and supply increases, prices fall and competitive pressure increases among the cartel members. A price war can then break out, effectively dissolving the cartel.

Some cartels have maintained power over their markets for generations. For example, an international diamond cartel headed by South Africa's De Beers company has controlled the sale of rough diamonds around the world since the 1920s. Although De Beers directly produces only a fraction of the world's diamonds, it dominates the market, creating scarcity by buying and stockpiling stones from other producers.

Monopolies

Because a monopoly's market structure dictates that a single seller controls all production of a good or service, the conditions found in a monopoly are the opposite of those found in perfect competition. (See Figure 6.3 on page 124.) In general, a monopoly exists when three conditions are present:

- there is a single seller.
- no close substitute goods are available.
- other sellers cannot enter the market easily.

A Single Seller A monopoly is identifiable by the presence of only one seller. No other market structure has this feature. By establishing total control of the production of a good or service, the single seller can monopolize the market. In most regions of the United States, a single cable television company traditionally has controlled the market. Homes and businesses in a community must buy their cable television service from the single cable company because there are no other sellers in their area.

No Close Substitutes A lack of close substitute goods reinforces a single seller's monopoly over the market. As noted in Chapter 3, a substitute good is one that consumers will use to replace the purchase of a similar but higher-priced good.

In the case of a monopolistic cable television market, consumers cannot buy the service from another seller or easily substitute a similar good for it. Some households need cable to have basic television reception, including network broadcasts. Moreover, many viewers who receive network broadcasts without cable do not consider network programming to be a substitute for the hundreds of channels available on cable.

Difficult Market Entry For a single seller to maintain a monopoly, other sellers must not be able to easily enter the market. The difficulty of entering a monopolistic market depends on start-up costs and the level of technical knowledge needed. If either of these factors is low enough, other sellers can enter the market, compete with the original single seller, and end that seller's monopoly. The development of monopolies is made more difficult by government regulation.

The cable television market, for example, is hard to enter. Installing a cable system into homes—and then maintaining it—is an expensive task that requires technological expertise. In addition, government restrictions traditionally have prevented competitors from entering cable markets. Although the government is changing its regulations, most cable markets today remain monopolistic.

Types of Monopolies

How does a single seller establish a monopoly over a market? Certain conditions make it likely, and sometimes even advantageous for consumers, that a monopoly will form in a particular market. There are four main types of monopolies: natural, geographic, technological, and government. Each of these forms under different conditions.

Natural Monopolies In some markets, competition is inconvenient and impractical. These **natural monopolies**, feature a single large seller that produces a good or service most efficiently. Usually this seller can do so because of its **economies of scale**. That is, the seller's large scale, or size, allows it to use its human, capital, and other resources more efficiently and economically than if those resources were divided among several smaller producers.

Traditionally, public and private utilities, like electric companies and cable television services, have been natural monopolies. Because of the immense start-up, equipment, and maintenance

COMPETITION & MARKET STRUCTURE *In a monopoly a single seller controls the total production of a good or service.* **What three conditions indicate the existence of a monopoly?** ⭐TEKS

Across the Curriculum

TECHNOLOGY Cable companies across the nation are now providing Internet access by using cable modems hooked to television cable lines or fiber optic lines, which transmit data much faster than traditional modems hooked to phone lines. Because cable lines have larger bandwidths than phone lines, they are able to transmit data at speeds up to 1,000 times faster than a 28.8 kbs modem, even faster than high-capacity T1 lines. This increased access speed enables people to view full-motion video over the Internet without time delays.

Although the cable TV industry is a natural monopoly, the availability of alternative broadband technologies such as ADSL has prevented the direct transfer of this monopoly to the Internet. However, now some people are concerned that mergers such as that of AOL, the U.S.'s largest Internet service provider, with Time Warner, a major content provider, will give ISPs too much control over what people can access over the Internet, just as cable companies control which channels are available in specific areas. ■

Caption Answer
There is a single seller; no close substitute goods are available; other sellers cannot enter the market easily.
⭐9C, 23E

Caption Answer
They provide public goods and services that cannot always be supplied through the normal workings of the price system because they have low potential for profit. ⭐15A

internet connect
TOPIC: U.S. Monopolies
GO TO: go.hrw.com
KEYWORD: SM3 EC6

Have students access the Internet through the HRW Go site to conduct research on monopolies in the United States. Then have students create a table describing the four main types of monopolies—natural, geographic, technological, and government—using an actual U.S. company for each type of monopoly. In the table, students should describe the three conditions that allow their monopoly to exist and explain why that particular seller's control of prices is limited. ⭐9C

Caption Answer
It will give them competition and may end some of them. ⭐26B

COMPETITION & MARKET STRUCTURE *In the United States, governments maintain monopolies over road construction and maintenance.* **What purpose do government monopolies serve?** ⭐TEKS

costs of utilities, it is often inefficient for more than one seller to provide this type of service in an area.

As a result, governments have given natural monopolies the exclusive right to provide certain goods or services in a specific area. The government closely regulates these monopolies, however, to ensure that they provide quality service at reasonable prices.

Geographic Monopolies Sometimes a monopoly forms because a market's potential profit is so limited by its geographic location that only a single seller decides to enter the market. These markets are **geographic monopolies**. A general store in a remote community, for example, has a geographic monopoly on groceries and many common household items.

The number of geographic monopolies in the United States has declined in recent decades. One reason is that as people have become increasingly mobile, they can travel longer distances to shop. This means that, even in rural areas, more sellers can reach more buyers than ever before. Sellers in remote areas also face competition from mail-order companies, which use telephones, fax machines, and delivery services to compete in markets that were once geographic monopolies. The Internet has also led to increased competition in remote areas as more people use home computers to shop on line.

Technological Monopolies Some monopolies develop when a producer develops new technology that enables the creation of a new product or that changes the way an existing product is made. These types of markets are **technological monopolies**. General Dynamics, for example, developed the technology to build Trident submarines for the U.S. Navy. It is the only company with this technology, giving it a monopoly in the Trident submarine market.

What prevents other sellers from using General Dynamics's technology to produce Trident submarines and compete in the market? Sellers may protect the inventions or technology they develop by applying to the U.S. government for patents. A **patent** grants a company or an individual the exclusive right to produce, use, rent, and sell an invention or discovery for a limited time—20 years in the United States. In effect, a patent gives a seller a 20-year monopoly over its product.

Written works and works of art are protected in much the same way. By granting **copyrights**, the U.S. government gives authors, musicians,

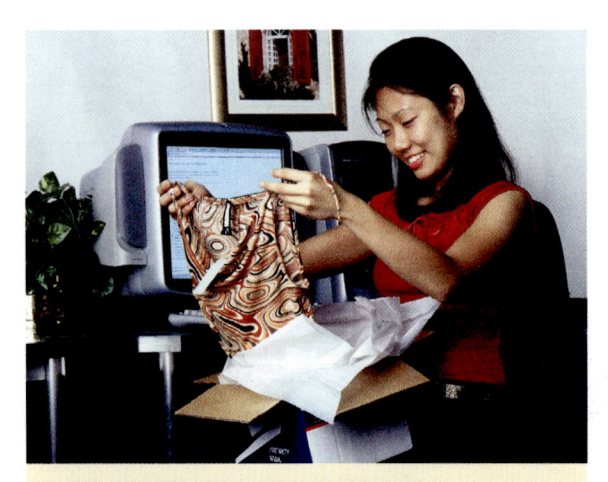

COMPETITION & MARKET STRUCTURE *Geographic monopolies have declined as mail-order shopping has become increasingly widespread.* **How might the Internet affect geographic monopolies?** ⭐TEKS

128 CHAPTER 6

and artists exclusive rights to publish, duplicate, perform, display, and sell their creative works.

Government Monopolies Governments often run monopolies, usually of basic necessities like public utilities. In the United States, cities and towns may monopolize water and sewer services. The federal and state governments have a monopoly over the building and maintenance of roads, bridges, and canals in the United States. Any market in which a government is the sole seller of a product is a **government monopoly**.

Government monopolies provide public goods that cannot always be supplied through the normal workings of the price system. Because these monopolies are providers of goods and services that enhance the general welfare, they usually have public support.

Monopolies at Work

The single seller in a monopolistic market has a great deal of control over prices. Think again about a cable television company. In theory, the company can dictate the price of its cable service. In practice, however, the seller in a monopoly cannot just charge any price it wants. Three forces limit the seller's control over prices: consumer demand, potential competition, and government regulation.

Consumer Demand The first factor influencing the seller's ability to set prices is consumer demand for its product. At some point, the price of a product can become so high that the quantity demanded falls to zero. If the price of cable television, for example, were to reach $300 a month, most consumers would stop subscribing to the cable service.

Potential Competition The second condition limiting the seller's control is potential competition. A monopolistic cable company may make enormous profits from an excessively high service price. At some point, however, these profits are high enough to attract other cable providers in the market, whereas high entry costs had kept competitors out at lower price levels.

Government Regulation The third force affecting sellers in a monopoly is government regulation. To protect consumers from paying unnecessarily high prices, governments monitor and regulate monopolies. This regulation watches over quantity, quality, and prices of products.

SECTION 2 REVIEW

1. Identify and Explain:
- oligopoly
- interdependent pricing
- price leadership
- price war
- collusion
- cartel
- natural monopolies
- economies of scale
- geographic monopolies
- technological monopolies
- patent
- copyrights
- government monopoly

Homework Practice Online
keyword: SM3 C6

2. Identifying Concepts: Copy the diagram below. Use it to identify the factors that affect prices in oligopolies and monopolies.

Factors Affecting Prices → OLIGOPOLY | MONOPOLY ← Factors Affecting Prices

TEKS Q: 1, 2, 3a, 3b, 4

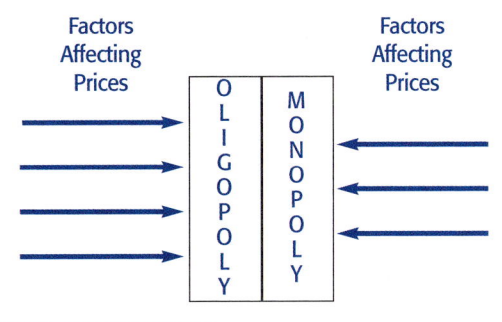

3. Finding the Main Idea
a. Compare the characteristics of oligopolies and monopolies. Give an example of each.
b. What are the four main types of monopolies?

4. Writing and Critical Thinking
Categorizing: Identify two oligopolistic and two monopolistic markets and describe how they exhibit the characteristics of oligopolies and monopolies.
Consider:
- the characteristics of oligopolies and monopolies
- how each example meets the characteristics of a monopoly or oligopoly

MARKET STRUCTURES 129

SECTION 2 REVIEW ANSWERS

1. oligopoly (123), interdependent pricing (125), price leadership (125), price war (125), collusion (125), cartel (126), natural monopolies (127), economies of scale (127), geographic monopolies (128), technological monopolies (128), patent (128), copyrights (128), government monopoly (129) 9C, 24A

2. oligopolies—nonprice competition, interdependent pricing, collusion, cartels; monopolies—consumer demand, potential competition, government regulation 9C, 23A, 24D

3a. oligopolies—a few large sellers offer identical or similar products, market is difficult to enter; monopolies—a single seller offers a product with few or no substitutes, market is difficult to enter; oligopoly—distance phone companies, cereal makers, airlines; monopoly—cable tv, electric company 9C, 23A

3b. natural—one large producer provides a product more efficiently than several smaller producers; geographic—isolated market has limited profit potential, so it attracts only one seller; technological—one producer owns the rights to the technology that created the market; government—product has low profit but enhances the public good 9C

4. Answers should demonstrate understanding of monopolistic and oligopolistic markets. 9C, 23A

SECTION 3
MARKET REGULATION

READ TO DISCOVER
1. What was the relationship between the U.S. government and business before the 1880s?
2. What was the purpose of early antitrust legislation?
3. How has the government enforced antitrust legislation?

ECONOMICS DICTIONARY
trusts
laissez-faire
antitrust legislation
price discrimination

As noted in Section 2, in order to ensure competition and protect consumers, governments often monitor and regulate noncompetitive markets such as monopolies. In the United States, for example, the government has done so for more than 100 years.

Era of Big Business

In the decades after the Civil War ended in 1865, a wave of fierce competition swept through many U.S. markets. This competition affected the oil, steel, coal, sugar, tobacco, meatpacking, and railroad markets. Small companies were forced out of business or were taken over by larger companies. The result was an era of "big business" as huge monopolies called **trusts** dominated the marketplace.

At first the U.S. government did not interfere with the trusts. Most policy-makers at the time firmly believed in a **laissez-faire** economic philosophy. This philosophy states that economic systems prosper when the government does not interfere with the market in any way. (*Laissez-faire* is a French term meaning "let [the people] do [as they will].") Thus, the federal government initially favored leaving the market and the trusts alone.

By the 1880s, however, many people became concerned about the amount of control the trusts held over the marketplace. In response, the federal government passed a number of important laws that were intended to control unfair business practices in the United States.

Early Antitrust Legislation

The first antitrust laws passed were the Interstate Commerce Act (ICA) of 1887 and the Sherman Antitrust Act of 1890. These acts signaled a new era in the relationship between business and government. Called **antitrust legislation**, these acts were designed to monitor and regulate big business, prevent monopolies from forming, and dismantle existing monopolies. Two U.S. presidents who made "trust-busting" a priority of their administrations were Theodore Roosevelt and William Howard Taft.

Interstate Commerce Act The ICA created the Interstate Commerce Commission (ICC) in order to oversee the railroad freight business. Rates for transporting goods by train had soared under the control of trusts. Numerous complaints from farmers and merchants across the country prompted the government to act as it did. The ICC

President Theodore Roosevelt 1901–1909

President William Howard Taft 1909–1913

COMPETITION & MARKET STRUCTURE *The economic power of trusts became a concern during the late 1800s.* **How does this cartoon suggest that trusts—rather than voters—held the majority of political power as well?**

continued to regulate the railroads, along with trucks and other freight carriers, until the commission was abolished in 1995.

Sherman Antitrust Act

The Sherman Antitrust Act was more far-reaching. It banned any agreements and actions "in restraint of trade." This legislation was a milestone in the fight against trusts and set the tone of antitrust legislation for decades.

Unfortunately, the act did not clearly define what actions were or were not in restraint of trade. Because of its vague language, many trusts were able to avoid obeying the law. In fact, most of the lawsuits filed against trusts in the 1890s lost in court.

The Standard Oil Company was the best-known monopoly to be broken up as a result of the Sherman Antitrust Act. In 1870 John D. Rockefeller and his associates formed the Standard Oil Company of Ohio. By 1882 Rockefeller's group controlled almost all the U.S. oil industry through the Standard Oil Trust.

In 1911 the Supreme Court found that unlawful monopoly power existed and ordered the breakup of Standard Oil. Nevertheless, one branch of the company—Standard Oil of New Jersey—remained the largest single industrial corporation in the United States. In 1972 this company changed its name to Exxon, which is one of the largest industrial corporations in the United States and the world today.

Clayton Antitrust Act

To further define the principles in the Sherman Antitrust Act, the U.S. government passed additional antitrust legislation in the early 1900s. This period of time is sometimes called the Progressive Era because of the spirit of reform that swept through many areas of political, economic, and social life in the

---

Cultural Perspectives

Certain industries, such as hair salons and dry cleaners, have traditionally charged women higher prices than men for similar services. In one survey, the Massachusetts Attorney General's Office found that half of Boston dry cleaners charged women three times more than men to dry clean similar articles of clothing. Some states, however, have begun addressing the issue of gender-based pricing discrimination. On January 1, 1996, California became the first state to pass legislation requiring service industries, such as hair salons, to use gender-neutral pricing. As of 1998, California, Massachusetts, the District of Columbia, New York City, and some counties in Virginia had laws requiring gender-neutral pricing.

Caption Answer

The cartoonist used two tactics to suggest that trusts held the political power. The men representing the trusts were drawn much larger than the senators, and the sign above the trust figures reads, "This is a Senate of the monopolists, by the monopolists, and for the monopolists."

Holt Economics Videodisc

The videodisc segment Preserving Competition: Skiing in New England complements the Chapter 6 case study: Is Microsoft a Monopoly? Barcodes for the Spanish version of the video segment are available in the *Holt Economics Videodisc Teacher's Guide.*

PLAY SEGMENT

PAUSE

RESUME PLAY

PLAY OPTION A

PLAY OPTION B

PLAY EPILOGUE

Caption Answer
Sherman Antitrust Act

United States. One such reform was the Clayton Antitrust Act, which the U.S. government passed in 1914.

This act prohibited a number of specific unfair business practices, including price setting and **price discrimination**—the practice of offering different prices to different customers under the same circumstances. Large manufacturers that buy great quantities of resources can pressure suppliers into charging them lower prices. Because this practice gives large sellers an advantage over smaller competitors, it can lead to the formation of monopolies.

Federal Trade Commission Act Another antitrust law passed in 1914 was the Federal Trade Commission Act. This act created the Federal Trade Commission (FTC) to investigate charges of unfair methods of competition and commerce. If the FTC discovers such practices, it can order a company to change its methods of doing business.

The Robinson-Patman Act With the 1936 Robinson-Patman Act, the federal government again strengthened antitrust legislation. This law reinforced the section of the Clayton Antitrust Act dealing with price discrimination.

More recent antitrust laws such as the Celler-Kefauver Act of 1950, the Antitrust Procedures and Penalties Act of 1975, and the Parens Patriae Act of 1976 have strengthened the early antitrust legislation. For a summary of important antitrust legislation, see Figure 6.4.

Antitrust Policy in Recent Decades

The federal government must balance sellers' right to run their businesses with the need for market competition and consumer protection. To help accomplish this goal, the government has enforced the Sherman Antitrust Act and subsequent antitrust legislation.

COMPETITION & MARKET STRUCTURE *John D. Rockefeller was the founder of the Standard Oil Company of Ohio.* **Which piece of antitrust legislation was used to break up the Standard Oil Trust?**

CASE STUDY

An Entertainment Monopoly?

COMPETITION & MARKET STRUCTURE With holdings in a wide variety of entertainment and advertising-related businesses, Clear Channel Communications is one of the biggest players in the entertainment industry. The $34.6 billion company controls 1,170 radio stations and 19 television stations as well as 700,000 billboards in 45 countries worldwide. The firm was one of the most successful of the 1990s, with its stock rising about 9,000% between 1992 and 2000.

In 2000 Clear Channel expanded its media empire by purchasing SFX, the world's largest producer and marketer of live music and theater entertainment. Clear Channel now owns, operates, or has exclusive booking privileges for 135 live entertain-

U.S. Antitrust Legislation

YEAR	LEGISLATION	PURPOSE
1887	Interstate Commerce Act	created the Interstate Commerce Commission (ICC) to oversee railroad rates; currently regulates railroads, motor vehicles, and other freight carriers
1890	Sherman Antitrust Act	prohibits any agreements, contracts, or conspiracies that would restrain interstate trade or cause monopolies to form
1914	Clayton Antitrust Act	clarified and strengthened the Sherman Antitrust Act by prohibiting price discrimination, local price cutting, mergers that reduce competition, and exclusive sales contracts
1914	Federal Trade Commission Act	created the Federal Trade Commission (FTC) to investigate charges of unfair methods of competition and commerce
1936	Robinson-Patman Act	(also called the Antiprice Discrimination Act) protects small retail businesses by prohibiting wholesalers from charging small retailers higher prices than they charged large retailers and by prohibiting large retailers from setting artificially low prices
1950	Celler-Kefauver Act	amended the Clayton Act to prohibit corporate acquisitions when they substantially decrease competition
1975	Antitrust Procedures and Penalties Act	increased penalties for violating antitrust laws
1976	Parens Patriae Act	gives states the right to sue companies on behalf of citizens harmed by the company's antitrust violations; requires large companies to notify the government of planned mergers; strengthened the federal government's power to investigate antitrust violations

FIGURE 6.4 The federal government has passed a number of laws designed to end or prevent monopolies. **How does the Robinson-Patman Act attempt to guarantee fair pricing policies?**

---

ment venues worldwide. The company is involved in 25,000 events with more than 62 million attendees a year.

In 2001 Nobody in Particular Presents, a small, local promoter of music concerts in Denver, Colorado, sued the entertainment giant for violating antitrust laws. It charged that Clear Channel had engaged in "monopolistic, predatory and anticompetitive business practices" by using its strength in the radio market to create a monopoly in the live-music market. Specifically, the suit charged that Clear Channel used its radio stations—the company owns eight in the Denver area alone—to play music by artists promoted by Clear Channel while excluding or limiting air time for artists promoted by other companies. The suit also alleges that Clear Channel used similar tactics to force artists to use the company to promote their performances.

The media giant's expansion into concert promotion first raised concerns when the company sought government approval of its purchase of SFX. Several Senators expressed concern that the company might favor artists it promoted.

Caption Answer
Each company's card can look different and provide slightly different services.

SECTION 3 REVIEW ANSWERS

1. trusts (130), laissez-faire (130), antitrust legislation (130), price discrimination (132) **15A, 24A**

2. see figure 6.4, p. 133 **15B, 24D**

3a. A laissez-faire philosophy gave way to trustbusting regulations. **15A, 15B**

3b. to monitor and regulate big business, prevent monopolies from forming, and dismantle existing monopolies **15A, 15B**

4. The government used the Sherman Antitrust Act to force AT&T to split into several companies. The government did not believe the monopoly benefited the marketplace; consumers did not benefit; new technology made it more efficient for more than one company to provide service. Students can debate as to whether telephone service in the US is better described as an oligopoly or a competitive monopoly: answers will depend on their view as to how much product differentiation there is and whether or not it is easy for a company to get into the market. **9C, 23D**

Another recent example of the power of the Sherman Antitrust Act is the federal government's case against American Telephone and Telegraph (AT&T). In 1982 an antitrust decision broke up AT&T, which was the world's largest corporation and private utility. The government believed that this natural monopoly was no longer beneficial to the marketplace. New technology such as satellites and microwave-based communications had made it possible and more efficient for more than one company to provide telephone service. AT&T—sometimes called "Ma Bell"—was forced to create several independent companies, called "Baby Bells," from its local telephone service operation.

The federal government does not automatically oppose the existence or creation of large corporations, however. In fact, in 1996 the government permitted two of the Baby Bells—Pacific Telesis and SBC Communications—to combine into one company. The new company was by no means a re-creation of the AT&T monopoly, and the government did not believe the merger would pose a threat to competition in the marketplace. The creation of this new company encouraged a similar merger between Bell Atlantic and NYNEX, two other Baby Bells.

COMPETITION & MARKET STRUCTURE *In recent years, a number of companies have offered "pre-paid" phone cards to attract customers.* **How might the sale of these cards assist with product differentiation?**

SECTION 3 REVIEW

⭐ TEKS Q: 1, 2, 3a, 3b, 4

1. Identify and Explain:
- trusts
- laissez-faire
- antitrust legislation
- price discrimination

2. Summarizing: Copy the diagram below. Use it to identify the purpose of each piece of antitrust legislation listed on the left.

Legislation	Purpose
Sherman Antitrust Act	
Clayton Antitrust Act	
Celler-Kefauver Act	
Parens Patriae Act	

Homework Practice Online keyword: SM3 C06S3

3. Finding the Main Idea

a. How did the relationship between government and business change in the late 1800s?

b. Why did the government pass the Sherman Antitrust Act and other antitrust legislation?

4. Writing and Critical Thinking

Analyzing Information: In years past, AT&T had a monopoly on providing telephone service. What was the government's role in breaking up its monopoly? Why do you think the government decided that telephone service should be more competitive? What sort of market structure does today's telecommunications industry have?

Consider:
- the definition of monopoly, perfect competition, oligopoly, and monopolistic competition
- government regulations affecting monopolies
- what factors your family considered when selecting its telephone service provider

Economics IN THE NEWS

Is Microsoft a Monopoly?

In 1975, after realizing that personal computers (PCs) were the wave of the future, a Harvard drop out named **Bill Gates** decided to become an entrepreneur. He started the software company Microsoft with a childhood friend, and together they built one of the world's largest businesses. Microsoft now produces the most commonly used word-processing and Internet software. In 2001 it employed more than 40,000 people in 61 countries and had revenues of $25.3 billion.

In 1994 the U.S. government filed a complaint in federal court against Microsoft, asserting that it used monopolistic practices to promote its operating systems (OS), including Windows. An OS is a piece of software that functions as a computer's "central nervous system," telling the computer how to function and how to respond to commands from software applications, such as computer games.

Microsoft was able to maintain control over a large portion of the OS market by requiring that computer manufacturers who wanted to install their OS on any of their machines pay a fee for all of their PCs—even those that used operating systems developed by companies other than Microsoft. This practice discouraged hardware manufacturers from using other operating systems, contributing to the growth of a monopoly.

While Microsoft eventually agreed to end the practice, it soon landed in hot water again. Among other things, the company was charged with attempting to extend its OS monopoly to the Internet by forcing computer makers who wanted to install Windows to also install Microsoft's Internet Explorer, a piece of software used to browse the Internet. In 1998, after several attempts to negotiate a settlement regarding the practice, the U.S. Department of Justice and a number of states filed suit.

In 1999 the judge in the case held that Microsoft had monopoly power. Later, the court determined that the proper remedy was to split Microsoft into two companies—one for operating systems and one for other types of software.

Microsoft appealed and, in November 2001, settled the federal case. According to the agreement, Microsoft may not prevent other PC makers from working with competing software makers. However, Microsoft will not be split in two.

Microsoft founder Bill Gates built a phenomenally successful computer business that has faced stiff competition from giants like IBM as well as smaller companies like Apple, founded by Steve Jobs, another famous entrepreneur.

What Do You Think?

1. In your opinion, do the above facts suggest that Microsoft is a monopoly?
2. If Microsoft is a monopoly, what remedy would you propose?
3. What contributions has Bill Gates made in his role as entrepreneur?

WHY IT MATTERS TODAY

As of August 2001, the Microsoft case was still under appeal. Use CNNfyi.com or other **current events** sources to find out more about the outcome of the Microsoft case, or other antitrust cases.

Economics in the News Answers

1. Answers will vary, but students should consider the definition of monopoly and the ways in which Microsoft controlled the software market. **23D**

2. Answers will vary, but students should consider remedies historically used to end monopolies as well as the remedies suggested by the courts and the agreement Microsoft later made to resolve the case. **23D**

3. Gates founded Microsoft, which sells the world's most popular word-processing program and Internet browser. **19D**

CHAPTER 6
Review Answers

Writing a Summary
Summaries should focus on the main points of each section. These may be found in the Read to Discover questions at the start of each section. Summaries should also use standard grammar, spelling, sentence structure, and punctuation. **24B, 24D**

Identifying People and Ideas
perfect competition (117), monopoly (119), monopolistic competition (120), product differentiation (120), nonprice competition (120), oligopoly (123), collusion (125), cartel (126), antitrust legislation (130), Bill Gates (135) **9C, 15A, 19D**

CHAPTER 6 Review

(Continued from page 135)

Understanding Main Ideas

1. Under perfect competition, sellers offer identical products. In contrast, under monopolistic competition, they offer different products; perfect—agriculture; monopolistic—clothes. **9C, 23A**
2. oligopolies—a few large sellers offer identical or similar products; monopolies—a single seller offers a product with few or no substitutes **9C, 23A**
3. openly organizes a system of price setting and market sharing; illegal in the U.S. because they fix prices **9C**
4. less choice and higher prices than competitive markets **9C**
5. Many people were concerned about the amount of control the trusts had over the marketplace.

Reviewing Themes

1. to raise prices, thereby increasing profits
2. monopoly **9C**
3. to monitor and regulate big business, to prevent monopolies from forming, and to dismantle existing monopolies **9C**

Thinking Critically

1. Answers should reflect an understanding of the conditions of perfect competition. **9C, 23D**
2. using a celebrity spokesperson; promoting brand names **23A**

Writing a Summary ★TEKS

Using standard grammar, spelling, sentence structure, and punctuation, write a summary of the information in this chapter.

Identifying People and Ideas ★TEKS

Identify the following terms or individuals and explain their significance.

1. perfect competition
2. monopoly
3. monopolistic competition
4. product differentiation
5. nonprice competition
6. oligopoly
7. collusion
8. cartel
9. antitrust legislation
10. Bill Gates

Understanding Main Ideas ★TEKS

SECTION 1 *(pp. 117–22)*

1. How does perfect competition differ from monopolistic competition? Give an example of each.

SECTION 2 *(pp. 123–29)*

2. How are oligopolies different from monopolies?
3. How does a cartel operate? Why are cartels illegal in the United States?
4. How do oligopolies and monopolies affect product choice and price?

SECTION 3 *(pp. 130–34)*

5. What factors encouraged the U.S. government to abandon its laissez-faire economic policies in the 1880s?

Reviewing Themes ★TEKS

1. **Competition & Market Structure** What is the purpose of nonprice competition under monopolistic competition?
2. **Competition & Market Structure** Which market structure gives sellers the greatest control over prices? Explain your answer.
3. **Competition & Market Structure** What is the purpose of antitrust legislation?

Thinking Critically ★TEKS

1. **Evaluating** Select a market in your community, such as movie theaters or shoe stores. How closely do these markets meet the conditions of perfect competition? Explain your answer.
2. **Evaluating** Determine which of the following are examples of non-price competition: using a celebrity spokesperson, issuing discount coupons, holding a storewide sale, promoting product brand names.
3. **Categorizing** Provide one example not listed in the chapter for each of the following: natural monopoly, geographic monopoly, technological monopoly, government monopoly. Explain how each example displays the characteristics of the corresponding monopoly.
4. **Making Predictions** Would you expect monopolies to develop as the result of competition or a lack of competition? Explain your answer, and then compare your response to the way in which monopolies developed after the Civil War.

Writing about Economics ★TEKS

Review the products you listed in your Economics Notebook at the beginning of this chapter. Now that you have studied market structures, can you explain why you are "loyal" to these brand names? What non-price factors persuade you to buy these products? Record your answers in your Notebook.

Building Social Studies Skills

Interpreting the Cartoon

Editorial cartoons have been used for hundreds of years to influence public opinion about a variety of topics. After examining the cartoon, being careful to read all the labels and captions, answer the questions below.

1. What will happen when the consumer can no longer reach the coal bucket?
   a. The monopolists will raise prices again.
   b. The monopolists will stop raising prices.
   c. The consumer will grow six inches taller.
   d. The monopolists will stop selling coal.

2. Using what you know about price setting by monopolies, explain why the artist chose to portray it as an athletic event.

Analyzing Primary Sources

The following is from a series of articles Ida Tarbell wrote denouncing the business practices of John D. Rockefeller's Standard Oil Company at the turn of the century.

"The profits of the present Standard Oil Company are enormous. For five years the dividends have been averaging about $45 million a year. . . .

"[That $45 million] must be invested. . . . It must go to other industries. Naturally, the interests sought will be allied to oil. They will be gas, and we have the Standard Oil crowd steadily acquiring the gas interests of the country. They will be railroads, for on transportation all industries depend. . . . And we have the directors of the Standard Oil Company acting as directors on nearly all of the great railways. . . .

"So long as. . . a company [may] own the exclusive carrier on which a great natural product depends. . . and [may] use this carrier to limit a competitor's supply. . . . and always to make him pay a higher rate than it costs the owner, it is ignorance and folly to talk about constitutional amendments limiting trusts."

3. Which of the following statements best describes Tarbell's point of view?
   a. Tarbell is a disinterested journalist.
   b. Tarbell is an advocate for the trusts.
   c. Tarbell is disturbed by the trusts' stranglehold on key industries.
   d. Tarbell wants to become a trust.

4. What points might John D. Rockefeller have made in a rebuttal to Tarbell's article?

Alternative Assessment

Building Your Portfolio

Write down any advertising slogans you think successfully differentiate a product. Using these slogans, create a puzzle such as a word search or crossword. For example, if the slogan is Nike's "Just Do It.(TM)," you might give the clue, "What brand wants you to just do it?" Exchange puzzles with a classmate. Did the slogans you selected differentiate the products enough for your classmate to identify them?

Internet Activity: go.hrw.com
KEYWORD: SM3 EC6

Access the Internet through the HRW Go site to research gas prices in your community. Use the **HOLT Grapher** to create a graph of prices from the present to one year ago. Use the results of your graph and more research to speculate on the factors driving prices of gas higher or lower.

---

3. Answers should reflect an understanding of each type of monopoly. Examples include: natural monopoly—cable tv; geographic monopoly—local telephone service; technological monopoly—patent medicines; government monopolies—water and sewer services. 9C, 23A

4. Answers will vary but should include supporting evidence. After the Civil War, monopolies grew out of competition as larger companies bought out smaller ones. 23D

Writing about Economics

Answers will vary. Students might say that they like the athlete who advertises the product, that that particular brand has sponsored events they have attended, or that that company supports charities that they like. 24A, 24B, 24D

Building Social Studies Skills

1. b 23E

2. One answer might point out that the monopolists are testing the consumer's ability to pay, just as an athletic event tests an athlete's physical limits. 23A, 23E

3. c 23E

4. Answers will vary but might include the potential for lower costs to the consumer resulting from economies of scale. 23D

UNIT 2

LAB OBJECTIVES

During the lab, students will
- describe the interaction between demand and supply.
- explain the determinants of demand and supply.
- graph demand and supply curves.
- demonstrate product differentiation.

Using the Lab

Before beginning the lab, organize students into groups and distribute copies of the Unit 2 Lab Activity found in *Unit Tests and Unit Lab Activities with Answer Key*. Have students read the assignment on this page and then discuss the assignment as a class. Point out the documents on pages 139–141 that students will use during the lab.

The What Do You Think? questions on pages 140 and 141 will help guide students during the project. In addition, the lab activity sheet includes a step-by-step checklist for students to monitor their progress. ★25B

UNIT 2

ECONOMICS LAB
You Make the Decision

Pricing to a "T"

*I*magine that your school is planning a craft fair for next summer to raise funds to expand the school library. You and many other students have volunteered to help in the fund-raising. In fact, the fair's director has just assigned you and a group of your classmates to paint cotton T-shirts for sale at the fair. Before you decorate the shirts, however, the director needs your group to recommend a selling price that will bring in the most money for the school library project. She also wants your advice on what key points about the T-shirts to highlights in advertising flyers for the fair.

As you know, there are many factors to consider in determining the price of the shirts. To help you make your pricing and advertising decisions, the director has collected materials and information for you to analyze. These include:
- several newspaper articles
- an ad from the local paper
- market research on supply and demand.

Economics Notebook Assignment ★TEKS

1. Write a clear, one-sentence statement of the situation requiring a decision.
2. Review the documents to gather information.
3. Answer the accompanying questions in your Economics Notebook.
4. Work with other group members to develop a recommendation for the fund-raising director. Be sure to identify different options and predict the consequences of each. Support your pricing and advertising decisions with clear arguments based on your document analysis. Discuss how the newspaper articles and other items influenced your decision. The recommendation should be neatly written or typed.
5. Create a sample of the advertising flyer and describe the action you would take to implement your decision.

John F. Kennedy High School
MEMO

To: T-Shirt Fund-Raising Volunteers

From: Ms. Albright, *Ms. Albright*
Fund-Raising Director

I am looking forward to hearing your pricing recommendation for the T-shirts. Please review the following price list of supplies you will need to make the T-shirts. I called several stores to find the best price on these materials, but of course, these prices could change by the time we are ready to make the shirts next summer.

I also have included two newspaper articles and an advertisement that might influence your pricing and advertising decisions. Look these materials over carefully.

Thanks for all your help. I know the fund-raising fair will be a success with you on the team. Good luck!

---

plain white cotton T-shirts
  $5 each if we buy fewer than 100
  $4 each if we buy 100 or more
paints (8 colors) $110
brushes $15
sequins, beads, ribbons $75
glue $10

What Do You Think? Answers

1. If severe, the floods might destroy the cotton crop, reducing supply and causing the price of cotton—and of products made from cotton—to rise. The cost of resources for the school's cotton T-shirt project would then rise.

2. Crazy Clothing's expansion increases competition in the T-shirt market, which will most likely lower the price students can charge.

3. Yes. Students might stress the hand-painted quality and design work of the school's T-shirts. In addition, they might emphasize that the purchase of the school's T-shirts raises funds for the school instead of raising profits for a private retailer.

ECONOMICS LAB *continued*

Discount Clothing Store Opens

Crazy Clothing announced that it will be opening two new stores this month within city limits. The new stores will employ 145 workers. The huge clothing discounter vows to compete fiercely for customers by slashing prices on its entire inventory. The store specializes in casual clothing, shoes, and accessories. Competition among clothing retailers is already tight, and local business owners believe a price war could break out when the new stores open.

Floods Cut Cotton Production

Some of the worst flooding of the decade has left thousands of acres of prime cotton farmland in several southern states under 10 inches of water. Heavy rain continued to batter the region over the weekend, and floodwaters are not expected to subside before Friday. Several states have asked that the flooded counties be declared federal disaster areas. As much as one fifth of the country's cotton crop may be lost. Economic analysts are already predicting that higher cotton prices will ripple throughout the clothing industry within the next month.

crazy clothing
Is Coming to Town!
Attend our Grand Opening Sale!

All items in the store will be discounted **20, 40, even 60%**

- Solid-Color Sweatshirts $19.99!
- Solid-Color T-Shirts $9.99!
- Sport and Other Printed T-Shirts $15.99!
- Shoes, Sandals, and Boots $12.99–$39.99!
- Handbags $14.99–$29.99!

Shop from 8:00 am to 10:00 pm Every Day!

WHAT DO YOU THINK?

1. What impact might the floods have on the price and availability of cotton clothing? How might the prices you have to pay for your resources (plain white cotton T-shirts) change?

2. How might the clothing retailer's expansion and pricing policies affect the price you can charge for your T-shirts?

3. Will you be operating in a competitive market? If so, how can you differentiate your T-shirts from those of the competition?

T-Shirt Painters—

I almost forgot to give you these two tables. The one on the left is a supply schedule for the painted T-shirts. The one on the right is a demand schedule. These schedules are only preliminary, of course. I based them on the price information I collected and on a survey the school did for the fair. We asked parents and other community residents who are likely to attend the fair about what kinds of products they would like to be able to buy at the fund-raiser.

Mr. Albright

Demand Schedule

Price per T-Shirt	Quantity of T-Shirts Demanded
$24	175
$21	225
$18	275
$15	300
$12	325
$9	375
$6	400

Supply Schedule

Price per T-Shirt	Quantity of T-Shirts Supplied
$24	400
$21	375
$18	325
$15	300
$12	275
$9	225
$6	175

WHAT DO YOU THINK?

1. How many T-shirts will your group supply at $12 each? at $24?
2. How many shirts are consumers willing to buy at $6 each? at $21?
3. At what point does the market reach equilibrium?
4. Use the demand and supply schedules to graph demand and supply curves for your painted T-shirts. Label the market's equilibrium point on the graph.
5. How might the equilibrium point change between now and next summer because of nonprice factors such as resource costs?

internet connect

Internet Activity: go.hrw.com
KEYWORD: SM3 ECL2

Have students access the Internet through the HRW Go site to learn more about a career in marketing. Tell students that marketing professionals analyze data like that in the Lab, make pricing decisions, and recommend advertising strategies. Have students create lists of pros and cons of a marketing career and then write a short paragraph explaining if they would ever consider such a career, and why or why not.

ECONOMICS LAB

What Do You Think?
Answers

1. at $12—275; at $24—400 7A
2. at $6—400; at $21—225 7A
3. at $15 and a quantity of 300 7A
4. Demand and supply curves should accurately graph the data in the demand and supply schedules. The equilibrium point should be marked at $15 and 300 T-shirts. 7A, 7B, 23B, 23C, 24D
5. If the price of cotton rises significantly, the supply curve, and in turn the equilibrium point, will then move to the right. 7A, 7B, 23A

UNIT 3

Lesson Options
Suggestions for customizing the material in Unit 3 to fit the specific schedule and curriculum of your classroom are located at the beginning of each chapter.

Main Ideas
Ask each student to read the Main Ideas and briefly answer each question in writing. Later, when you have finished Unit 3, ask students to return to their original answers and revise them using what they learned in the unit.

Economics Lab
The Unit 3 Economics Lab appears on pages 222–25. This lab project is a real-world assignment in which students will work in groups to prepare a business report to persuade a bank to give them a small-business loan to open a Spaegel's Bagels franchise. Support materials for the lab appear in *Unit Tests and Unit Lab Activities with Answer Key.* ★25A

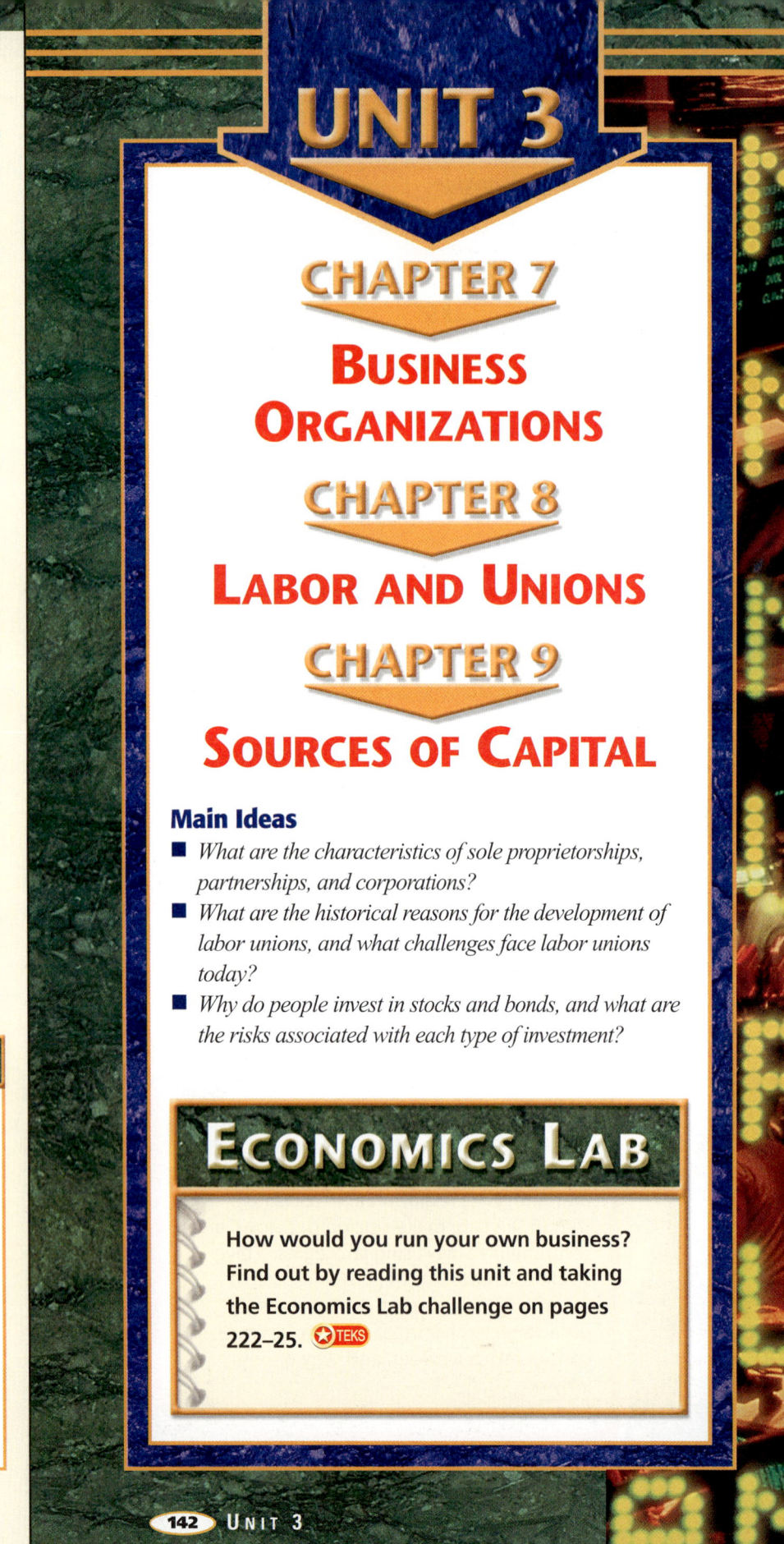

UNIT 3

CHAPTER 7
BUSINESS ORGANIZATIONS

CHAPTER 8
LABOR AND UNIONS

CHAPTER 9
SOURCES OF CAPITAL

Main Ideas
- *What are the characteristics of sole proprietorships, partnerships, and corporations?*
- *What are the historical reasons for the development of labor unions, and what challenges face labor unions today?*
- *Why do people invest in stocks and bonds, and what are the risks associated with each type of investment?*

Economics Lab
How would you run your own business? Find out by reading this unit and taking the Economics Lab challenge on pages 222–25. ★TEKS

Free Enterprise at Work

UNIT 3 OVERVIEW

Unit 3 covers business organizations, labor and unions, and sources of capital. Chapter 7 describes the basic forms of business organization in the United States—sole proprietorships, partnerships, corporations, franchises, cooperatives, and nonprofit organizations. Chapter 8 describes the characteristics of the U.S. labor force, the development and growth of labor unions, major labor legislation, labor negotiations, and labor tactics such as boycotts and strikes. Chapter 9 covers credit and saving, investing, and borrowing.

Teaching with Photographs

This photograph shows an overhead shot of the New York Stock Exchange (NYSE). In 2000 the NYSE listed about 3,000 companies, of which more than 400 were international firms. On average, more than 1 billion shares of stock were traded on the exchange each day, for a combined annual stock value of more than $11 trillion. As a motivating activity for this unit, ask students how the image illustrates the influence of technology on the U.S. economy.

CHAPTER RESOURCE MANAGER

CHAPTER 7 — BUSINESS ORGANIZATIONS

	Objectives	Pacing Guide	Reproducible Resources
SECTION 1 **Sole Proprietorships** (pp. 145–49)	• What are the advantages of establishing a sole proprietorship? • What are the disadvantages of establishing a sole proprietorship?	**Regular** 1.5 days **Block Scheduling** 0.5 day	**ELL** Spanish Study Guide 7.1 **ELL** English Study Guide 7.1 **SM** Mathematics for Economics: Activity 7
SECTION 2 **Partnerships** (pp. 150–52)	• How do general partnerships and limited partnerships differ? • What are the advantages of organizing a partnership? • What are the disadvantages of organizing a partnership?	**Regular** 2 days **Block Scheduling** 1 day	**ELL** Spanish Study Guide 7.2 **ELL** English Study Guide 7.2
SECTION 3 **Corporations** (pp. 153–58)	• How is a corporation formed, and what are the characteristics of a corporation? • How is a corporation organized? • How do stocks and bonds differ? • What are the advantages and disadvantages of organizing a corporation?	**Regular** 1.5 days **Block Scheduling** 1 day	**ELL** Spanish Study Guide 7.3 **ELL** English Study Guide 7.3 **PS** Reading 26: New Nationalism **SM** Consumer Economics: Activity 7
SECTION 4 **Other Forms of Organization** (pp. 159–64)	• How do vertical combinations differ from horizontal and conglomerate combinations? • Why might a business owner decide to open a franchise? • What is the customer's role in a cooperative? • How does a nonprofit organization differ from other types of business organizations?	**Regular** 1.5 days **Block Scheduling** 1 day	**ELL** Spanish Study Guide 7.4 **ELL** English Study Guide 7.4 **E** Challenge and Enrichment: Activity 7 **S** Simulations and Strategies for Teaching Economics: Activity 7

Chapter Resource Key

- **PS** Primary Sources
- **RS** Reading Support
- **E** Enrichment
- **S** Simulations
- **SM** Skills Mastery
- **A** Assessment
- **REV** Review
- **ELL** Reinforcement and English Language Learners
- Transparencies
- CD-ROM
- Video
- Videodisc
- Internet
- Holt Presentation Maker Using Microsoft® PowerPoint®
- TEKS and TAKS

TECHNOLOGY RESOURCES	REINFORCEMENT, REVIEW, AND ASSESSMENT
• One-Stop Planner: Lesson 7.1 • Researcher Online • Homework Practice Online • CNN Presents Economics: Would You Care for a Souvenir with That Burger? • Transparency 25 • Global Skillbuilder CD-ROM	**REV** Section 1 Review, p. 149 **A** Daily Quiz 7.1 ★ TAKS Every Day!
• One-Stop Planner: Lesson 7.2 • Researcher Online • Homework Practice Online • Global Skillbuilder CD-ROM	**REV** Section 2 Review, p. 152 **A** Daily Quiz 7.2 ★ TAKS Every Day!
• One-Stop Planner: Lesson 7.3 • Researcher Online • Homework Practice Online • Transparencies 26 and 27 • Global Skillbuilder CD-ROM	**REV** Section 3 Review, p. 158 **A** Daily Quiz 7.3 ★ TAKS Every Day!
• One-Stop Planner: Lesson 7.4 • Researcher Online • Homework Practice Online • Global Skillbuilder CD-ROM	**REV** Section 4 Review, p. 164 **A** Daily Quiz 7.4 ★ TAKS Every Day!

Chapter Review and Assessment

SM Global Skillbuilder CD-ROM
  HRW Go site
REV Reteaching Activity 7
REV Chapter 7 Review, pp. 166–67
A Chapter 7 Test Generator (on the One-Stop Planner)
A Chapter 7 Test
A Alternative Assessment Handbook

One-Stop Planner CD-ROM

It's easy to plan lessons, select resources, and print out materials for your students when you use the *Texas One-Stop Planner CD-ROM with Test Generator.*

---

internet connect

HRW ONLINE RESOURCES
Go To: go.hrw.com
Then type in a keyword.

TEACHER HOME PAGE
KEYWORD: **SM3 Teacher**

CHAPTER INTERNET ACTIVITIES
KEYWORD: **SM3 EC7**
Choose an activity to:
▶ learn about nonprofit organizations.
▶ research Ben & Jerry's Homemade Ice Cream, Inc.
▶ research Andrew Carnegie.

CHAPTER ENRICHMENT LINKS
KEYWORD: **SM3 CH7**

HOLT RESEARCHER ONLINE
KEYWORD: **Holt Researcher**

ONLINE ASSESSMENT
Homework Practice
KEYWORD: **SM3 HP7**
TAKS Review
KEYWORD: **SM3 T7**
Rubrics
KEYWORD: **SS Rubrics**

CONTENT UPDATES
KEYWORD: **SS Content Updates**

HOLT PRESENTATION MAKER
KEYWORD: **SM3 PPT7**

ONLINE READING SUPPORT
KEYWORD: **SS Strategies**

CURRENT EVENTS
KEYWORD: **S3 Current Events**

LESSON 7.1 SOLE PROPRIETORSHIPS

TEXTBOOK PAGES 145–49

HOLT PRESENTATION MAKER Access Illustrated LECTURE NOTES using Microsoft® PowerPoint® on the One-Stop Planner CD-ROM

OBJECTIVES

- Analyze the advantages of establishing a sole proprietorship. 9B
- Analyze the disadvantages of establishing a sole proprietorship. 9B

MOTIVATE

Option 1: Ask students whether any of them have considered opening their own businesses in the future. Ask for volunteers to describe what types of businesses they hope to open and what challenges they think they might encounter as business owners. Alternatively, organize students into small groups and have them discuss the types of business they might like to start someday and the challenges they think they would face as individual business owners. Tell students to keep this discussion in mind as they read this section, in which they will learn about the advantages and disadvantages of owning a business as a sole proprietor. 9B

Option 2: Find a story in a local newspaper that highlights the successes, struggles, or failures of a sole proprietor or sole proprietors in your community. Share this story with the class. Discuss with the class the advantages and disadvantages of individual business ownership this story illustrates. Write student responses on the chalkboard. Tell students to remember this story as they read this section, in which they will learn about the advantages and disadvantages of owning a business as a sole proprietor. 9B

TEACH

Building a Vocabulary

Have students use spiral notebooks to create an Economics Dictionary to be used throughout the chapter. This dictionary might be used as an activity at the start of each new section or as a learning aid for sheltered English students or students having difficulty. List words that students will be expected to know for this section on the chalkboard. Have students use the information provided in the text or on the *Researcher CD-ROM* to list, define, and give an example of each term.

Evaluating Ideas

Write the term *sole proprietorship* on the chalkboard. Ask for student volunteers to help define this term. *(A sole proprietorship is a business owned and operated by one person.)* Discuss with the class what types of businesses are typically organized as sole proprietorships. Remind the class that because sole proprietorships are owned and operated by a single individual, they give that individual a number of advantages. Write these three advantages on the chalkboard: *ease of start-up, full control,* and *exclusive rights to profits*. Organize the students into groups of three or four. Ask each group to discuss why these three aspects of sole proprietorships are advantages and how such advantages may motivate an individual to become the sole proprietor of a business. 9A, 9B

Evaluating Ideas, Creating Charts and Graphs

Remind the class that sole proprietorships have several disadvantages as well as advantages. On the chalkboard, make a chart to illustrate the disadvantages of sole proprietorships. Across the top of the chart, write the following disadvantages: *unlimited liability, sole responsibility, limited growth potential,* and *lack of longevity*. First, discuss with the class the meanings of the terms *liability* and *longevity*. *(Responsibility for debt is called liability; longevity is the length of a firm's life.)* Next, ask for student volunteers to explain how each of the four aspects of a sole proprietorship written on the chalkboard is a disadvantage, and briefly write these explanations under each disadvantage on the chalkboard. *(For example, under* unlimited liability, *students might suggest that you write, "Sole proprietors are responsible for all business debts.")* 9B

Role-Playing, Judging Information

Tell the students that business people must weigh the advantages and disadvantages of sole proprietorship before choosing to become sole proprietors. Organize students into groups of three or four (you might wish to use the same groups from the first exercise of this lesson). Ask students to imagine that they are giving advice to a fellow businessperson deciding whether to start a sole-proprietorship business. Have each group choose a specific business that its colleague is interested in forming. *(Examples might*

143C

include a restaurant, a small retail clothing store, an auto-repair shop, a law office, a dentist's office, or a flower-and-gift shop.) Ask each group to discuss the particular advantages and disadvantages its friend might encounter if he or she opened a sole proprietorship in a chosen business. Have each group write a short list that summarizes how each advantage and disadvantage might affect its friend and the friend's business. ⭐9B

CLOSE

Discuss with students whether they think the advantages or disadvantages of sole proprietorships are greater. Ask for student volunteers to share with the class any observations they may have from their own experiences—in their families, for example—about a business operated as a sole proprietorship. Next, ask if any student in the class still hopes to become a sole proprietor and how he or she plans to overcome the challenges of sole proprietorships. ⭐9B

OPTIONS

Interpersonal Learners

Discuss with students that many ordinances and regulations apply to the establishment of a business and that the government also places other restrictions on the general use of business property. Have students conduct interviews with local business owners to identify some of the restrictions they face regarding establishing a business and utilizing the property. Ask students to evaluate the purpose for and effectiveness of these restrictions. Do certain types of businesses face more regulations? ⭐2D, 3B

Sheltered English Students

Pair students acquiring English with fluent English speakers. Give each pair seven 5" x 7" blank index cards, or seven pieces of poster board cut into these approximate dimensions. Ask each pair to make two sets of flash cards, one with the advantages and the other with the disadvantages of sole proprietorships written on them. Students should write one advantage or disadvantage on the front of each flash card *(such as "exclusive rights to profits")*, and should write a brief definition on the back of each flash card *(such as "the owner keeps all of the profits from a sole proprietorship")*. Have students quiz each other with the flash cards. ⭐9B

Gifted Learners, Linguistic Learners, Logical-Mathematical Learners

Have students conduct research on the success and failure rates of sole proprietorships for a given year in the recent past. Have students use the *Researcher Online,* the library, in-class resources, and the Internet to conduct their research. You may wish to have students limit their research to a given county or state rather than research national statistics. Have students compile the following information: how many sole proprietorships were opened during that year, how many of these sole proprietorships lasted longer than a year or longer than five years, and how many of these sole proprietorships failed in less than a year or less than five years. Have students display their results in a chart or graph that illustrates the statistics they found, and also include a brief paragraph that explains why they think the business succeeded or failed. You may wish to have students work on this project individually or in pairs.

REVIEW

Have students complete the Section 1 Review on page 149. Use the answers in the Annotated Teacher's Edition to assess student mastery of this section.

ASSESS

To assess student mastery of this section, have students complete Daily Quiz 7.1 in *Daily Quizzes with Answer Key.* For additional assessment options, see *Alternative Assessment Handbook* on the *One-Stop Planner CD-ROM.*

ADDITIONAL RESOURCES

Ash, Mary Kay. *Mary Kay—You Can Have It All: Lifetime Wisdom from America's Foremost Woman Entrepreneur.* 1998. Diane Publishing Company.

Mayo, Todd L. *The Joy of Self-Employment: Entrepreneurship and Education in a Changing World.* 1997. Pinnacle Press.

LESSON 7.2 PARTNERSHIPS

TEXTBOOK PAGES 150–52

OBJECTIVES

- Explain how general partnerships and limited partnerships differ.
- Analyze the advantages of organizing a partnership. ★9B
- Analyze the disadvantages of organizing a partnership. ★9B

MOTIVATE

Option 1: Ask students to discuss the advantages and disadvantages they have found in working with a partner on classroom projects. Next, discuss with students whether any of their parents or adult friends are partners in a local business or work for a business partnership. Ask students: What seem to be the advantages and disadvantages of these types of business partnerships? Tell students that in this section they will learn about the advantages and disadvantages of business partnerships.

Option 2: Have students locate the most recent edition of the *World Almanac* or *Statistical Abstract of the United States* (or another yearly summary of national business statistics) and look up the following: how many business partnerships currently exist in the United States, how many business partnerships were formed in the most recent year listed, and how many business partnerships failed in the most recent year listed. Discuss with students what advantages people might see in founding partnerships, and why partnerships might fail. Tell students to keep this discussion in mind as they read this section, which outlines the advantages and disadvantages of business partnerships.

TEACH

Building a Vocabulary

List the important terms for this section on the chalkboard and tell students to add them to their Economics Dictionary. Tell students to use the information provided in the text or on the *Researcher CD-ROM* to list, define, and find an example of each vocabulary term.

Understanding Main Concepts

Tell students that there are two types of partnerships. On the chalkboard, write *general partnership* and *limited partnership*. Ask for volunteers to recall from their reading what is meant by a general partnership *(partners have equal decision-making authority and unlimited liability should the business fail)*, and what is meant by a limited partnership. *(In limited partnerships, partners join as investors who provide financial capital in return for a share of the profits, they rarely take an active role in business decisions, and they have limited liability should the business fail.)* Write student responses on the chalkboard beside each term. Discuss with the class how these types of partnerships differ. ★9A

Organizing Ideas, Creating Charts and Graphs

Tell the class that like sole proprietorships, both general and limited partnerships have distinct advantages and disadvantages. On the chalkboard, write the advantages of partnerships listed in the textbook: *ease of start-up, specialization, shared decision making,* and *shared business losses*. Organize the students into groups of three or four. Have each group make a flowchart that illustrates the cause-and-effect relationship between each advantage and its benefits to business partners. Have each group fill in its flowchart with information gained from a discussion of the following questions:

- What is meant by ease of start-up, and how does it benefit business partners?
- What is meant by specialization, and how does it benefit business partners?
- What is meant by shared decision making, and how does it benefit business partners?
- What is meant by shared business losses, and how does it benefit business partners?
- How are these advantages similar to and different from the advantages of sole proprietorships? *(Sole proprietorships have the advantages of ease of start-up, full control, and exclusive rights to profits.)*

Ask for volunteers to share their flowcharts. Refer students who need additional instruction on the skills used in this activity to the *Global Skillbuilder CD-ROM* Lesson 12: Creating Graphic Organizers. ★9B, 23F

Role-Playing, Applying Ideas

Next, tell students that partnerships also have disadvantages, although they are not as severe as those for sole proprietorships. Write the following disadvantages on the chalkboard: *unlimited liability, potential for conflict,* and *lack of longevity.* Briefly discuss with the class how each of these aspects is a disadvantage in partnerships. Organize students into pairs. Ask each pair to imagine that they are planning to start a business partnership. Have each pair decide what type of business they plan to start and whether they will organize a general or a limited partnership. Have student pairs develop strategies

143E

for overcoming the possible disadvantages of partnerships while trying to improve on the advantages. Ask each pair to write a few brief paragraphs that explain their partnership and their strategies. ⭐9B, 24D

CLOSE

Ask student volunteers from each pair to share their paragraphs explaining their strategies for overcoming the disadvantages and building on the advantages of partnerships. Next, ask students who said that they hoped to open sole proprietorships if they now think that a partnership might be preferable. ⭐9B

OPTIONS

Interpersonal Learners

Ask the members of a successful local business partnership to visit the class and discuss how they have benefited from the advantages and dealt with the disadvantages of their partnership. Have students prepare questions to ask the business partners in advance. ⭐9B

Students Having Difficulty

Pair students having difficulty with students who have mastered the lesson material. Have each pair arrange the following aspects of partnerships into three categories: characteristics of partnerships, advantages of partnerships, and disadvantages of partnerships.
- specialization
- unlimited liability
- limited partnership
- lack of longevity
- shared business losses
- ease of start-up
- general partnership
- potential for conflict
- shared decision making

Next, ask each pair to write a brief sentence that defines each of the two types of partnerships listed. Also, have pairs write sentences describing how each of the remaining aspects of partnerships on the list may be advantages or disadvantages. *(For example, students may write: "In a limited partnership, partners act as investors who provide financial capital in return for a share of the profits, but they rarely take an active role in business decisions and their liability is limited," or "One disadvantage of partnerships is that disagreements may arise among partners, which can lower employee morale and decrease efficiency.")* ⭐9A, 9B

Gifted Learners, Linguistic Learners

Ask motivated students to research a successful business partnership known in the local community, or one that has gained national attention. Have students use the *Researcher Online,* the library, in-class resources, and the Internet to conduct their research. Ask students to discover how the partnership is organized (as a general or limited partnership), how the partners overcame the disadvantages of partnerships, and how they have made the best of the advantages of partnerships. Have students write summaries of their findings into a report that can be submitted for teacher evaluation or presented to the class. You may want to encourage students to include charts or graphs that help to explain the business partnership.

REVIEW

Have students complete the Section 2 Review on page 152. Use the answers in the Annotated Teacher's Edition to assess student mastery of this section.

ASSESS

To assess student mastery of this section, have students complete Daily Quiz 7.2 in *Daily Quizzes with Answer Key.* For additional assessment options, see *Alternative Assessment Handbook* on the *One-Stop Planner CD-ROM.*

ADDITIONAL RESOURCES

Jaffe, Azriela. *Let's Go into Business Together: Eight Secrets to Successful Business Partnering.* 2001. Career Press.

Minars, David. *Partnerships Step-by-Step.* 1997. Barron's.

LESSON 7.3 CORPORATIONS

TEXTBOOK PAGES 153–58

HOLT PRESENTATION MAKER: Access Illustrated LECTURE NOTES using Microsoft® PowerPoint® on the One-Stop Planner CD-ROM

OBJECTIVES

- Explain how a corporation is formed, and describe the characteristics of a corporation. ★9A
- Describe how a corporation is organized.
- Explain how stocks and bonds differ.
- Analyze the advantages and disadvantages of organizing a corporation. ★9B

MOTIVATE

Find a news story about a well-known corporation and share it with the class. *(Examples include Apple Computer, Nike, Ford Motor Company, Dow Chemical, Coca-Cola, etc.)* Discuss with students how they think this corporation was formed, how it gained its initial funds, and how it became successful. Also, ask students if anyone they know has bought stock in this company. Bring in a stock market page from the newspaper and examine the present value of the corporation's stocks with the class. Tell students that in this section they will learn about what a corporation is, how a corporation is formed, how corporations raise funds, and the disadvantages and advantages of organizing a corporation.

TEACH

Building a Vocabulary

List the important terms for this section on the chalkboard and tell students to add them to their Economics Dictionary. Tell students to use the information provided in the text or on the *Researcher CD-ROM* to list, define, and find an example of each vocabulary term.

Role-Playing, Applying Ideas

Write the term *corporations* on the chalkboard. Ask for student volunteers to recall from their Chapter 7 reading the definition of a corporation. *(Corporations are legally distinct from their owners and are treated as if they were individuals, meaning they can own property, hire workers, make contracts, pay taxes, sue and be sued, and sell products.)* Discuss with the class the types of companies that are typically organized as corporations. *(Industries such as food, steel, and oil, and companies such as insurance, supermarket chains, and auto manufacturers tend to be corporations.)* Tell the class that when companies incorporate, they first need to apply for a license from the state using an application referred to as the articles of incorporation; then, when the state approves this application, the company receives a corporate charter for its new corporation. Organize students into small groups and have them imagine that they are business partners interested in forming a corporation. Ask each group to think of a specific good or service that its corporation hopes to provide and have each group create an articles-of-incorporation application that offers the six pieces of information specified on page 154 of Chapter 7. ★9A

Organizing Ideas

Tell the class that in addition to the corporate officers listed in the articles of incorporation, corporations have formal structures that are not necessarily listed in articles of incorporation. With the help of the class and using the example from Figure 7.4 in the textbook, illustrate on the chalkboard how one of the corporations created by student groups in the last exercise might be organized. Emphasize that the board of directors is the most important decision-making body in any corporation. Other aspects of organization may vary. Ask the class to help define the responsibilities of most corporate boards of directors, and write these duties on the chalkboard as well. *(These duties include determining how the corporation should develop, what policies it will follow, in what directions to expand, when and how to hire or fire corporate officers, and how the corporation will raise funds.)*

Analyzing Ideas

Tell the class that there are two basic ways corporations raise funds: they sell stocks and they issue bonds. On the chalkboard, write the terms *stock, shares, dividends, common stock, preferred stock, corporate bond, principal,* and *interest*. Review the meanings of these terms with the class and write brief definitions next to the terms on the chalkboard. Emphasize that stockholders own part of the company, which means they receive part of the profits and are able to vote on company policies and elect the board of directors. Bondholders, on the other hand, do not own any part of the company and have no voice in company policies or leadership. Organize students into groups of three or four. Give each group a magazine or newspaper, such as *Forbes, Money Magazine, Business Week,* the *Wall Street Journal,* or the business section from a national or local newspaper. Ask each group to find articles about corporate finance and have groups answer the following questions for two or three companies discussed in the periodical:

143G

- If the company is doing well, are stockholders receiving larger dividends than they were previously?
- Does any one individual or a small group of individuals own a very large number of the company's shares?
- Are shares selling rapidly (i.e., at a high volume) for a high price or a low price? Or are shares selling slowly (i.e., at a low volume) for a high price or a low price? How does this reflect the financial well-being of the corporation?
- Is the corporation issuing bonds? If so, how does this reflect the financial well-being of the corporation?

Ask groups to write brief responses to the questions and take notes on other applicable information they discover about stocks and bonds. ★11C

Applying Ideas, Creating Charts and Graphs

Next, discuss with students the advantages and disadvantages of corporations. Organize students into small groups and give each group a piece of poster board. Have the groups plan two tables or charts that illustrate the advantages and disadvantages of corporations for both the stockholders and the corporation. For example, in the left-hand column of the *Advantages* chart, students may want to write the benefits *(such as limited liability, flexibility, separation of owner from management, ease of raising capital, longevity),* and write the terms *stockholders* and *corporation* across the top row. Students should then indicate whether stockholders or the corporation, or both, receives these advantages by using check marks in appropriate boxes on the chart or table. Allow students to devise an alternate system if they wish. Encourage students to write brief explanations of these benefits on their chart or graph. Have students plan the *Disadvantages* chart or table similarly. ★9B, 24D

CLOSE

Review with the class the advantages and disadvantages of corporations for stockholders and corporations. Discuss with the class the following question: Would you rather be an officer or a stockholder in a corporation, a member of a business partnership, or a sole proprietor? ★9B

OPTIONS

Gifted Learners, Linguistic Learners

Have motivated students research the history of a successful corporation. Ask students to prepare a written or oral report that answers the following questions: Who founded the corporation and for what purpose? How well did the corporation do in its first year? Has the corporation relied on stocks or bonds for funding? If it has relied on stocks, how has the value of its stock changed over time? How has the corporation grown? How has growth affected its organization? Have students use the *Researcher Online,* the library, in-class resources, and the Internet.

Students Having Difficulty

Pair students having difficulty with students who have mastered the lesson material. Have pairs discuss the following questions and then write sentences or brief paragraphs to answer them: What is a corporation? What is the purpose of articles of incorporation? What are the responsibilities of a corporation's board of directors? How do stocks and bonds differ? What influence do shareholders have in corporations?

Logical-Mathematical Learners

Tell students that they are going to pretend to buy stocks and then trace how the stocks perform for two weeks. First, give students stock market pages from the business section of the local newspaper or the *Wall Street Journal* and have them choose three corporations. Then have students imagine that they own 100 shares of stock in each company they have chosen. Students should figure out how much money the shares they "own" in each company are presently worth. Students should check their stocks each day and keep a written daily record of the how the value of their stocks changes. After two weeks, have students draw a line graph illustrating each company's stock's performance. Ask them to determine if they made money or lost money on their "investments." Discuss with students the advantages and disadvantages of owning stock in today's market. ★11B, 11C, 23F, 23G

REVIEW

Have students complete the Section 3 Review on page 158. Use the answers in the Annotated Teacher's Edition to assess student mastery of this section.

ASSESS

To assess student mastery of this section, have students complete Daily Quiz 7.3 in *Daily Quizzes with Answer Key.* For additional assessment options, see *Alternative Assessment Handbook* on the *One-Stop Planner CD-ROM.*

ADDITIONAL RESOURCES

Lerner, Josh. *Venture Capital and Private Equity: A Casebook.* 1999. John Wiley & Sons.

National Council on Economic Education. *Financial Fitness for Life: Bringing Home the Gold.* 2001.

LESSON 7.4 OTHER FORMS OF ORGANIZATION
TEXTBOOK PAGES 159–64

HOLT PRESENTATION MAKER
Access Illustrated LECTURE NOTES using Microsoft® PowerPoint® on the One-Stop Planner CD-ROM

OBJECTIVES

▶ Analyze how vertical combinations differ from horizontal and conglomerate combinations.
▶ Explain why a business owner might decide to open a franchise.
▶ Describe the customer's role in a cooperative.
▶ Analyze how a nonprofit organization differs from other types of business organizations.

MOTIVATE

On the chalkboard, write the names of the following businesses and organizations: Supercuts, Dow Chemical, Boy Scouts of America, McDonald's, REI (Recreational Equipment Incorporated), The American Heart Association, and Coca-Cola. Ask students to help determine what type of business they think each of these businesses may be. *(Some may fall into more than one category.)* Guide students to accurately categorize the businesses as corporate combinations, franchises, cooperatives, nonprofit organizations, sole proprietorships, partnerships, or standard corporations. Tell students that in this section they will learn about different types of business organizations.

TEACH

Building a Vocabulary

List the important terms for this section on the chalkboard and tell students to add them to their Economics Dictionary. Tell students to use the information provided in the text or on the *Researcher CD-ROM* to list, define, and find an example of each vocabulary term.

Applying Ideas

Ask students to recall from their reading the two ways that corporations typically grow. *(They grow from within by building new facilities, or they expand by combining legally with another enterprise.)* Discuss what happens in corporate mergers, which are the most common method of joining businesses. *(A merger occurs when one company joins with or absorbs another.)* Remind students that there are three types of corporate mergers: *horizontal combinations, vertical combinations,* and *conglomerates.* Write these three types of mergers on the chalkboard and discuss them. *(A horizontal combination occurs when two or more companies producing the same good or service, or engaging in one phase of production, merge; a vertical combination occurs when two or more companies involved in different production phases of the same good or service merge; and a conglomerate combination occurs when two or more companies producing or marketing unrelated products merge.)*

Tell students that when conglomerate corporations form, some of the companies involved in the merger become subsidiary companies. *(Explain that subsidiaries continue to make products under their own name and frequently keep their own top management.)* Briefly discuss the advantages and disadvantages of each form of merger. Next, organize students into small groups. Give groups pages from the business section of a newspaper or from a financial magazine and ask them to find examples of each type of merger. Have groups determine what type of merger occurred, what aspect(s) of the production process the companies specialize in (if horizontal or vertical combinations), and if the formation of subsidiary companies resulted from the merger.

Analyzing Ideas

Remind the class that another form of business organization they read about in Chapter 7 is the franchise. Discuss the following questions:
▶ What is a franchise? *(an enterprise that, for a fee, uses the original company's name to sell goods and services)*
▶ What kinds of businesses frequently operate as franchises? *(hotels and motels, fast-food restaurants, real-estate agencies)*
▶ Can you give examples of franchises in the local area?
▶ How does a franchisor ensure consistent quality of goods and services among its franchises? *(It often provides training for employees and may pay for national advertising.)*
▶ What benefits does a franchisee have in opening a franchise, as opposed to opening a sole proprietorship? *(Because the franchisor often provides training for employees, pays for national advertising, and offers a well-known name, franchisees can lower costs associated with starting new businesses and may draw a greater number of customers who are familiar with the franchise name and services.)*

Applying Ideas

Ask for student volunteers to help define another form of business organization: the cooperative *(a business owned by its customers).* Organize students into groups of three or four. Ask each group to discuss the role

143I

customers have in cooperatives. *(They own shares in the company and vote on company leadership, but do not own any part of the physical structures, the production equipment, or the land the company occupies.)* Have each group brainstorm a list of businesses that have organized cooperatives in the United States and in their community. If necessary, have students research these questions using the *Researcher Online,* the library, in-class resources, and the Internet.

Comparing and Contrasting

Tell the class that another important form of business organization is the nonprofit organization. Discuss with the class the ways in which nonprofit organizations may be different from or similar to other types of business organizations, such as standard corporations or cooperatives. *(Nonprofit organizations are structured like standard corporations but are not focused on financial gain for their members, which is why they are called nonprofits; they are different from cooperatives because they are not owned by customers, but by stockholders.)* Ask the class to brainstorm all the nonprofit businesses that operate in your local community, and write the names of these businesses and the services they provide on the chalkboard. Next, ask students to name and describe any national or international nonprofit organizations with which they are familiar. Ask if any students have volunteered or worked for a nonprofit organization and what their experiences were. ⭐23A

CLOSE

Discuss with students the following question: Which type of business organization would you be most satisfied working for, and why? Have students consider the advantages and disadvantages of their choices.

OPTIONS

Sheltered English Students

Have students use outside resources to analyze the effect of technology and combinations on productivity. Encourage students to provide historic examples, such as information about Carnegie's vertical combination, and modern examples, such as the use of robotics in development. ⭐19D, 26A

Students Having Difficulty

Pair students having difficulty with students who have mastered the lesson material. Give each pair pages from a newspaper or magazine and have them find advertisements for the following types of business organizations: franchises, cooperatives, and nonprofit businesses. *(They may want to look for fast-food restaurant coupons or ads, co-op membership or sale ads, and American Red Cross, Girl Scouts, or American Cancer Society ads.)* Ask each pair to discuss how each of these businesses is structured, what its purpose is, and what the advantages and disadvantages of each type of business may be for its owners and customers.

Interpersonal Learners

Ask professionals from the community from different types of business organizations to participate in a panel that you organize for the class. You may wish to include franchise operators, nonprofit organization directors, subsidiary corporation officers, and a member from a co-op board of directors. Have students prepare questions for the panel ahead of time, and give a copy of the chapter and lesson plans to each panel participant. Encourage students to ask questions such as: What is the purpose of your business? How is your business organized? What is your role in the business? Are there stockholders in your company? If so, what is their role? What are the advantages and disadvantages of the type of business organization of your business or company? Do you have an ethics policy? Please describe it. ⭐2C

REVIEW

Have students complete the Section 4 Review on page 164. Use the answers in the Annotated Teacher's Edition to assess student mastery of this section.

ASSESS

To assess student mastery of this section, have students complete Daily Quiz 7.4 in *Daily Quizzes with Answer Key.* For additional assessment options, see *Alternative Assessment Handbook* on the *One-Stop Planner CD-ROM.*

RETEACH

For students having difficulty with the lessons, have them complete Reteaching Activity 7. This activity is located in *Reteaching Activities with Answer Key.*

ADDITIONAL RESOURCES

Business Education Index 2000: Index of Business Education Articles and Research Studies Compiled from a Selected List of Periodicals and Yearbooks. 2001. Delta Pi Epsilon.

Hopkins, Bruce. *Starting and Managing a Nonprofit Organization: A Legal Guide.* 2001. John Wiley & Sons.

CHAPTER 7

TOPICS INCLUDE

- sole proprietorships
- liability
- collateral
- general and limited partnerships
- corporations
- articles of incorporation and corporate charters
- common and preferred stocks
- corporate bonds
- principal and interest
- mergers
- corporate combinations
- subsidiaries
- franchises
- cooperatives
- nonprofit organizations

ECONOMICS NOTEBOOK

The Economics Notebook is a journal activity that encourages students to consider basic concepts of economics that relate to their lives. A follow-up notebook activity appears on page 166.

WHY IT MATTERS TODAY

To find additional lesson plans dealing with business organizations, visit CNNfyi.com or have students complete the ECONOMICS IN THE NEWS activity on page 166.

CHAPTER 7

BUSINESS ORGANIZATIONS

Would you like to start your own business? For many people, owning a business provides the opportunity to make their own decisions and to earn a profit. A successful business, however, requires a great deal of work. In addition to deciding what products to provide, a businessperson must determine how that business will be organized.

Free enterprise allows business owners to select the type of organization that suits their needs. Most businesses are organized as sole proprietorships, partnerships, or corporations. This chapter describes the forms of business organization in the United States.

ECONOMICS NOTEBOOK

In your Economics Notebook, list the names of at least 10 businesses in your community. You might include restaurants, clothing-alteration shops, bookstores, shoe-repair shops, law firms, jewelers, department stores, and music stores.

WHY IT MATTERS TODAY

Business ethics is increasingly important in the global economy. Use CNNfyi.com or other **current events** sources to find more examples of companies with a code of ethics.

SECTION 1

SOLE PROPRIETORSHIPS

READ TO DISCOVER
1. What are the advantages of establishing a sole proprietorship?
2. What are the disadvantages of establishing a sole proprietorship?

ECONOMICS DICTIONARY
sole proprietorship
zoning law
liability
collateral
longevity

Suppose that you decide to start a weekend house-cleaning business. You must determine which type of organization will best suit your needs. If you alone will own and control the house-cleaning service, your business may be a **sole proprietorship**. A sole proprietorship is a business owned and controlled by one person. The sole proprietorship is the oldest, simplest, and most common type of business organization.

What kinds of businesses are typically organized as sole proprietorships? The financial resources available to one person often are limited. As a result, sole proprietorships generally tend to be enterprises that require small amounts of financial capital, or money, to start and operate. Many lawyers, plumbers, carpenters, hairstylists, florists, and farmers are sole proprietors. (See Figure 7.1.)

Advantages of Sole Proprietorships

Why might someone choose to organize his or her business as a sole proprietorship? There are a number of advantages to this type of business organization:

- ease of start-up,
- full control, and
- exclusive rights to profits.

Easy Start-Up The chief advantage of sole proprietorships is that they are easy to form. Sole proprietorships require fairly small amounts of financial capital and involve few legal considerations. For example, to start your house-cleaning business, you would not need to file complicated legal documents with your state or federal government.

TYPES OF BUSINESS ORGANIZATIONS, 1997

- Sole proprietorships: 72.6%
- Corporations: 19.9%
- Partnerships: 7.4%

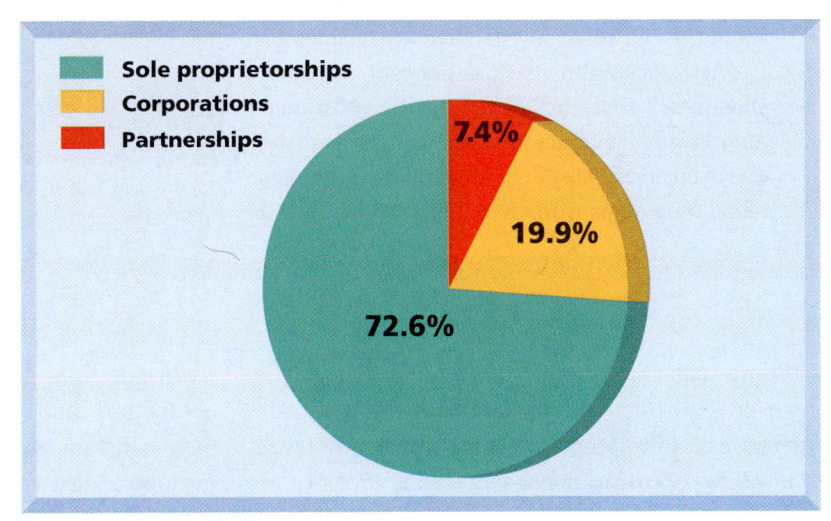

Source: *Statistical Abstract of the United States: 2000*

FIGURE 7.1 Sole proprietorships are the most common type of business organization. **What percentage of businesses are established as sole proprietorships?**

BUSINESS ORGANIZATIONS 145

Careers in Economics

To help students learn about other careers in economics, refer them to the Career section on the *Researcher Online*.

Global Connections

In Cuba, entrepreneurial citizens are giving the country's large, state-owned restaurants a run for their money. *Paladares*—small, privately owned restaurants, often run out of people's homes—have become all the rage. The small restaurants started appearing in 1993, when the Cuban government passed a law allowing for specific types of self-employment. The law did not specifically mention *paladares*, but its loose wording easily allowed for them. Enterprising Cubans everywhere started turning their homes into restaurants or selling food from stands set up next to their houses. The Cuban government, shocked at the response, outlawed *paladares* in late 1993. The spirit of capitalism could not be held back, however. The decision of many owners to operate their restaurants illegally caused the Cuban government to relent and declare *paladares* legal once again. The government has benefited by levying heavy taxes on *paladares,* and owners must pay expensive license fees.

CAREERS IN ECONOMICS

Entrepreneur

If you like the idea of being your own boss, you might consider a career as an entrepreneur. Everyone from a pushcart vendor to a television-station owner can be considered an entrepreneur. Some of these people have graduate degrees in business or finance, while others may have never attended college.

Successful business owners tend to be confident, creative, persistent, hardworking, and flexible. One outstanding example of a successful entrepreneur is Mary Kay Ash (1918-2001). Mary Kay Ash founded the cosmetics company Mary Kay Inc. With a more than 750,000-person sales force working in 37 countries worldwide, Mary Kay had annual sales of more than $1.2 billion in 2000. Mary Kay is one of the most popular brands of cosmetics in the United States.

Mary Kay Ash founded her company after retiring from a 25-year career as a salesperson. Upon retirement, Ash began writing a how-to career book. While writing the book she realized that she should just go ahead and start her own business.

Ash decided to use independent salespersons to sell cosmetics directly to the consumer. After buying a formula for a skin-care cream, she was in business. Starting with an 11-person sales force, the company made $198,000 in its first year. Today the company is the leading direct seller of skin-care products in the United States.

Although becoming an entrepreneur can bring financial rewards, many people simply enjoy being their own boss. With this benefit, however, comes responsibility. Business owners often endure long hours, must oversee every area of operation, and risk failure. You—and other potential entrepreneurs—nevertheless may consider the potential rewards to be well worth the challenges.

Entrepreneur Mary Kay Ash created the cosmetics company Mary Kay Inc.

Some legal and governmental restrictions, however, do affect sole proprietorships. Like all businesses, sole proprietorships must observe zoning laws. **Zoning laws** specify the areas of a city or county where various types of business activities can be pursued. For example, zoning laws in your neighborhood may not permit you to operate your business from your home.

In addition, sole proprietorships may have to obtain city and county licenses before opening their businesses. Some professionals—for example, doctors, child-care providers, and hairstylists—also must be licensed by the state.

Control A second advantage of sole proprietorships is control. While the operation of a larger firm often requires extensive paperwork or group decisions, a sole proprietor can act quickly to correct problems or take advantage of opportunities. If you want to hire more workers so that you can clean more houses, for example, you can expand your staff right away. Similarly, if few people in your neighborhood want to pay for house-cleaning services, you can reduce your staff without the complicated procedures experienced by larger firms.

This control gives sole proprietors a high degree of personal satisfaction. If your house-cleaning business succeeds, you will know that you earned that success through your own efforts—because you alone run the business. A sole proprietorship thus can be rewarding both personally and financially.

Profit Another advantage of sole proprietorships is that the owner keeps all of the profits. In fact, for many people profit is the main reason for starting a business. Will you make a fortune from your house-cleaning business? Perhaps not. In some cases, however, people who started out as small proprietors have made huge fortunes. This possibility of wealth is at the heart of the free-enterprise system.

Disadvantages of Sole Proprietorships

Although sole proprietorships have some appealing advantages, they also have several disadvantages. Sole proprietors face

- unlimited liability,
- sole responsibility,
- limited growth potential, and
- lack of longevity.

Unlimited Liability According to the law, sole proprietors are personally responsible for all business debts. This responsibility for debt is called **liability**. Suppose that you borrow money to publicize your house-cleaning business. If the publicity fails and your company cannot repay the loan, you as a sole proprietor must make the payments—even if that means selling personal

ECONOMIC INSTITUTIONS & INCENTIVES *Sole proprietors have the responsibility of running all aspects of their business.* **What are some other disadvantages of sole proprietorships?** TEKS

ECONOMIC INSTITUTIONS & INCENTIVES *Ninfa Laurenzo established a sole proprietorship.* **What are the advantages of sole proprietorships?** TEKS

Caption Answer
unlimited liability, limited growth potential, lack of longevity 9B

Across the Curriculum

TECHNOLOGY Thanks to the Internet, starting and operating a small business is even easier than it used to be. In the past, if owners of small businesses wanted to promote their products, they had to advertise or print and mail out catalogs, all at high expense. The tremendous growth of the World Wide Web, however, has enabled small-business owners to reach potential customers around the world with a minimal investment of time and money. With a Web page, small-business owners can easily and cheaply display and advertise their products, take customer orders, obtain customer profiles, and track the number of people who visit their sites.

Cybermalls, or virtual shopping malls, have enabled small-business owners to lease space in a group site. As with real shopping malls, cybermalls draw traffic because of the variety of shops available at one location. ■

Caption Answer
ease of start-up, full control, exclusive rights to profits 9B

BUSINESS ORGANIZATIONS 147

Across the Curriculum

GOVERNMENT Another government initiative designed to help small-business owners is the Small Business Institute (SBI), funded by the Small Business Administration. Under this program, owners of small businesses that have been in operation for less than eight years can receive business counseling and technical advice from business students and faculty at participating universities. The program is an all-around success. Owners receive free advice and information, and students gain valuable, real-world experience. ■

What Do You Think?
Answers

1. Answers will vary. Students might mention that businesses must balance the goals of economic growth with the public interest. Students might also mention that businesses have various federal, state, and local reporting requirements. ⭐2A, 3B, 15B

2. Regulations ensure that business owners must adhere to local and federal standards when purchasing, using, and disposing of business property. ⭐3A, 3B, 15A

LINKING ECONOMICS and GOVERNMENT

Government and the Responsibilities of Business Ownership

While running your own business can be a profitable venture, it also involves a great deal of effort. Major responsibilities of business ownership include keeping track of the ordinances and regulations imposed by local, state, and federal governments.

Those responsibilities can often begin even before a business is up and running. For example, a person who buys or starts a dry-cleaning business must obtain various state and local permits and pay other start-up fees.

Dry cleaners, in particular, are bound by many local, state, and federal environmental regulations that pertain to the chemicals used in the dry-cleaning process. Dry cleaners must ensure that they are using chemicals in a manner that does not endanger the health of employees. They must also hire licensed waste-management companies to dispose of the used dry-cleaning solvents, which can be carcinogenic, or cancer causing. Finally, the Environmental Protection Agency (EPA) requires dry cleaners to file a report to prove that they have disposed of chemicals in a safe and legal manner.

In addition to zoning and environmental regulations, businesses must comply with government tax regulations and reporting requirements. Often businesses have to hire lawyers, accountants, and additional personnel to make sure they are in compliance.

Why does government impose so many requirements on business owners? It is the government's role to promote business practices that balance the sometimes-competing goals of economic growth and the public interest. Regulations can help ensure that business owners make responsible choices when starting, running, or selling a business.

It should also be remembered that governments often provide assistance to businesses. Federal, state, and local governments may offer tax breaks or subsidies to help businesses provide goods and services and create jobs to stimulate the economy.

The federal government also has set up programs aimed at reducing the burden imposed by regulations. One program, for instance, gives small businesses a grace period to comply with environmental laws without incurring a fine. Another involves setting up local "stores for business." Business owners can go to the store, which is staffed by federal workers, for free advice on complying with government regulations.

What Do You Think? ⭐TEKS

1. What are the pros and cons of government regulation for business owners?
2. How do various government regulations promote the responsible purchase, use, and disposal of business property?

The U.S. government's store for business offers tax, regulation, and financial advice for small businesses.

property that belongs to you as an individual to satisfy your business debts.

Sole Responsibility A second disadvantage of sole proprietorships is that the owner is responsible for all aspects of running the business. What does this mean for your house-cleaning business, for example? You will have to be a market analyst, advertiser, accountant, and cleaner—at least until you are able to hire others to fill some of these jobs. With so many job requirements, you will need to have skills in many different fields. Even if you hire people to fill these positions, you must check their work if the business is to be successful. These demands on your time and energy may create frustration and reduce your sense of satisfaction and accomplishment.

Limited Growth Potential A third disadvantage of sole proprietorships is limited potential for growth. You probably will start your house-cleaning business by using your savings or borrowing a small amount of money. To guarantee repayment, a bank or other lender often will require you to put up **collateral**—anything of value that a borrower agrees to give up if he or she is not able to repay a loan. Sole proprietors generally have limited collateral, which may include the business itself, supplies and unsold merchandise, and even their homes and other personal possessions.

Like other businesses, sole proprietorships need financial capital to make improvements and to expand their companies. Creditors, however, usually will not lend money that exceeds the value of the borrower's collateral. In other words, if your business and all your personal possessions are already serving as collateral for existing loans, you probably will have trouble finding more credit to expand your business. To increase your credit, you will have to increase your collateral—a difficult task if you cannot expand your business. Thus, because most owners have limited collateral, sole proprietorships often have a limited potential for growth.

Lack of Longevity A final disadvantage of sole proprietorships is lack of longevity. **Longevity** is the length of a firm's life, or the length of time the business operates. Because sole proprietorships depend on the health, commitment, and competence of one person, they often have a shorter life span than other types of business organizations. For example, your house-cleaning service may fail if you become sick or lose interest in the enterprise. Because a sole proprietorship depends on one person, the risk of failure is very great.

SECTION 1 REVIEW

TEKS Q: 1, 2, 3a, 3b, 4

1. Identify and Explain:
sole proprietorship
zoning laws
liability
collateral
longevity

2. Summarizing: Copy the graphic organizer below. Use it to list the challenges faced by a sole proprietor.

Challenges Faced by a Sole Proprietor

Homework Practice Online
keyword: SM3 HP7

3. Finding the Main Idea
a. What are the advantages of organizing a business as a sole proprietorship?
b. What are the main government restrictions on sole proprietorships? Why might government impose such restrictions?

4. Writing and Critical Thinking
Drawing Conclusions: Think about the qualities that a successful entrepreneur must possess. How might Mary Kay Ash have demonstrated those qualities?
Consider the following:
- why she founded her company
- the success of Mary Kay Inc. today

Enhancing the Lesson

For more information on the Small Business Administration (SBA), see the Executive Departments section on the *Researcher Online*.

SECTION 1 REVIEW ANSWERS

1. sole proprietorship (145), zoning laws (146), liability (147), collateral (149), longevity (149) **2D, 3B, 9A, 24A**

2. unlimited liability, sole responsibility, limited growth potential, and lack of longevity **9B, 23A, 24D**

3a. It is easy to form, and the sole proprietor has complete control and the exclusive rights to any profits earned. **9B**

3b. zoning laws and city, county, and state licenses; to protect neighborhoods and the environment and to ensure that service providers are properly qualified **2D, 3B, 9B, 15A**

4. Answers will vary. Students should mention that entrepreneurs tend to be confident, creative, hard-working, persistent, and flexible. Mary Kay Ash demonstrated many of these qualities when she started a new business after retiring from a 25-year career. The growth of her company from a very small one into the largest direct-sales company in the United States at least demonstrates her hard-working nature and her persistence. **19D, 23A**

SECTION 2

PARTNERSHIPS

READ TO DISCOVER

1. How do general partnerships and limited partnerships differ?
2. What are the advantages of organizing a partnership?
3. What are the disadvantages of organizing a partnership?

ECONOMICS DICTIONARY
partnership
general partnership
limited partnership

You know that a sole proprietorship is a business that is owned and controlled by one person. A business that is owned and controlled by two or more people is called a **partnership**. Like sole proprietorships, partnerships are most often found in enterprises that require relatively little financial capital to start and operate.

What kinds of businesses are typically formed as partnerships? In many cases, partnerships are the same types of businesses that are formed as sole proprietorships. Doctors, lawyers, and accountants may form partnerships. Small retail stores, farms, and construction companies also may be organized as partnerships.

Forms of Partnerships

Partnerships take different forms. In a **general partnership**, partners enjoy equal decision-making authority. Each also has unlimited liability. Unlimited liability means that general partners, like sole proprietors, are responsible for paying all of the debts and other financial losses of the business. A general partner's personal property is therefore at risk if the business fails.

A second type of partnership is a **limited partnership**, in which partners join as investors who provide financial capital in exchange for a share of the profits, but rarely take an active role in business decisions. Additionally, their liability is limited, or confined to the amount of money they invest in the business. Unlike sole proprietors or general partners, limited partners cannot lose personal property to creditors if the business fails.

Advantages of Partnerships

Many partnerships begin as sole proprietorships. Business owners often decide to transform their sole proprietorships into partnerships because of the following advantages:

- ease of start-up,
- specialization,
- shared decision making, and
- shared business losses.

Easy Start-Up Like sole proprietorships, partnerships are fairly easy to form. Few government

ECONOMIC INSTITUTIONS & INCENTIVES *Ben Cohen and Jerry Greenfield started their ice cream business as a partnership.* **Why might they have chosen this form of business organization?**

regulations apply to partnerships, and costs tend to be low.

A partnership begins when two or more people agree to operate a business together. To avoid later conflicts, the partners usually develop a written agreement called a partnership contract. This contract outlines the distribution of profits and losses among the partners. It also details each partner's responsibilities and includes conditions for adding or dropping partners and for dissolving the partnership.

Specialization

Another advantage of partnerships is specialization. Specific business duties can be assigned to different partners depending on the partnership contract. Unlike sole proprietors, partners are better able to specialize in those areas of the business in which their skills and talents can best be used.

For example, suppose that Jason Fernandez, Tom Reiner, and Stacey Caserma are partners in a sporting-goods store. Jason is an excellent accountant and money manager, Tom is an experienced salesperson, and Stacey is skilled in sales promotion and maintaining inventory. The three partners are able to pool their skills so that one person does not need to meet all of these job requirements.

Shared Decision Making

A third advantage of partnerships is shared decision making. Partners can minimize mistakes by consulting with each other on business matters. For example, to make wise purchasing decisions, Stacey needs to consult with Tom about which items are selling well and which are selling poorly. Without this information, she might order too many footballs and too few tennis rackets. Similarly, Tom and Jason need to work together to determine prices that customers will be willing to pay but that will bring the store as much profit as possible. This decision-making process allows the partners to compare points of view, rather than relying on one person for ideas.

Shared Business Losses

Just as partners share the process of decision making, they also share any business losses. The sharing of losses may enable a partnership to survive a situation that would cause a sole proprietorship to fail. Furthermore, partnerships usually are better able than sole proprietorships to obtain needed financial capital for business expansion and modernization. Creditors are more likely to extend larger loans to partnerships than to sole proprietorships because the risk is shared among several people. Groups of people typically are better able to repay a debt than is a single owner and are likely to have more collateral. Banks and other lenders thus feel more confident that loans to partnerships will be repaid.

Disadvantages of Partnerships

Some of the problems associated with sole proprietorships are less severe for partnerships.

PARTNERSHIPS BY INDUSTRY, 1997

Industry	Number (in thousands)
Finance, Insurance, and Real Estate	974
Services	311
Wholesale and Retail Trade	173
Agriculture, Forestry, and Fishing	127
Construction	72
Manufacturing	40
Transportation and Public Utilities	31
Mining	28

Source: *Statistical Abstract of the United States: 2000*

FIGURE 7.2 Partnerships offer many advantages, including shared risks. **Which industry contains the largest number of partnerships?**

Caption Answer

finance, insurance, and real estate 23F, 23G

Cultural Perspectives

The small-town general store, where you can buy everything from groceries and clothing to fishing tackle and hardware supplies, is quickly becoming a thing of the past. The increasing spread of superstores, like Wal-Mart and The Home Depot, is putting many general stores out of business. In Vermont, however, general stores remain an important part of small-town life. Local mom-and-pop stores, some of which have been operated by the same families for generations, provide places for people to gather and socialize, and Vermont wants to keep it that way. When Wal-Mart decided to open a store in the small town of Glover, Vermont, the townspeople protested. They successfully lobbied to have the store built in a larger city, to protect Glover's small, locally owned businesses. On a statewide level, the Preservation Trust and the Vermont Country Store mail-order house are doing their part to support mom–and–pop stores by giving selected general stores $3,500 grants.

SECTION 2 REVIEW ANSWERS

1. partnership (150), general partnership (150), limited partnership (150) **9A, 24A**

2. advantages—ease of start-up, specialization, shared decision making, shared business losses; disadvantages—unlimited liability, potential for conflict, lack of longevity **9B, 24D**

3a. General partners have equal decision-making authority and unlimited liability; limited partners have little participation in decisions, and their liability is confined to the amount of money they invested. Answers will vary but should reflect an understanding of the two types of partnerships. **9A**

3b. Answers will vary but should reflect an understanding of the benefits and liabilities of working with partners. See graphic organizer answers. **9B**

4. Answers will vary. A hot dog vendor might take on a partner to have someone with whom to share the workload, decision making, liability, and responsibility. At the same time, the vendor might decide against a partner because he or she does not want to share the profits or have to deal with any personality conflicts or disagreements over how to run the business. **9B, 23A**

However, partnerships do have three distinct disadvantages:

- unlimited liability,
- potential for conflict, and
- lack of longevity.

Unlimited Liability One major disadvantage of general partnerships is unlimited liability. Each general partner has a role in the business, and each is responsible for debts incurred by the business. For example, Jason, Tom, and Stacey all are responsible for repaying their company's loans. If Tom refuses to pay his share, Jason and Stacey still are responsible for the entire payment. Like sole proprietors, partners might have to sacrifice personal property to cover the debts of a failed business. Thus, general partners may lose more than they originally invested in the business.

Potential for Conflict A second disadvantage of partnerships is that disagreements or other conflicts may arise among partners. Partners may have personality conflicts and different management styles. A partner with poor communication skills might fail to relay important information either to the other partners or to employees. Partners who have opposing views may be unable to compromise. These types of conflicts can lower employee morale, delay important business decisions, and decrease overall efficiency. Disagreements also can affect the personal satisfaction that the partners get from the business.

Suppose that Tom thinks that the sporting-goods store should introduce a new line of exercise gear with a celebrity endorsement. Jason, on the other hand, feels that a celebrity endorsement would cost the store more money than would be earned from the new product. If this conflict is not resolved, Tom and Jason could spend too much time arguing and not enough time on their main responsibilities.

Lack of Longevity A final disadvantage of partnerships is that the life of the business is dependent on the willingness and ability of the partners to continue working together. Illness, death, conflict among partners, and other problems can end the partnership.

Following the disagreement about celebrity endorsements, Jason may decide that he can no longer work effectively with Tom. If he withdraws from the partnership, Stacey and Tom will have to find a new partner to assume Jason's responsibilities, divide Jason's former responsibilities between them, or dissolve the partnership and close the business.

SECTION 2 REVIEW

TEKS Q: 1, 2, 3a, 3b, 4

1. Identify and Explain:
partnership
general partnership
limited partnership

2. Contrasting: Copy the chart below. Use it to recount the advantages and challenges involved in forming a partnership.

Advantages of Partnerships	Disadvantages of Partnerships

Homework Practice Online
keyword: SM3 HP7

3. Finding the Main Idea

a. Compare general and limited partnerships. Would you rather be a general partner or a limited partner? Explain your answer.

b. Describe a situation in which you have worked with one or more partners. What were the advantages and disadvantages compared with working alone?

4. Writing and Critical Thinking

Making Predictions: Why might a sole proprietor such as a hot dog vendor decide to take on a new partner? Why might that proprietor decide not to take on a partner?
Consider the following:
- what advantages a partner might offer
- what disadvantages a partner might offer

152 CHAPTER 7

SECTION 3
CORPORATIONS

READ TO DISCOVER

1. How is a corporation formed, and what are the characteristics of a corporation?
2. How is a corporation organized?
3. How do stocks and bonds differ?
4. What are the advantages and disadvantages of organizing a corporation?

ECONOMICS DICTIONARY

corporations
articles of incorporation
corporate charter
board of directors
stock
shares
dividends
common stock
preferred stock
corporate bond
principal
interest

You have learned that sole proprietorships and partnerships are forms of business organization that are owned and controlled by one or a few people. Unlike sole proprietorships and partnerships, **corporations** are legally distinct from their owners and are treated as if they were individuals. This means corporations can own property, hire workers, make contracts, pay taxes, sue and be sued, and make and sell products.

What kinds of companies are organized as corporations? Companies in industries such as food, steel, and oil tend to be organized as corporations. Insurance companies, supermarket chains, and major companies that sell to businesses or consumers also tend to be organized as corporations.

Forming a Corporation

As you have learned, forming a sole proprietorship or a partnership is fairly simple. Forming a corporation, however, is much more complex.

Suppose that Michael Abeyto, Lisa Arnaud, Ben Wallace, and Caroline Jee are partners in a company that develops and sells computer games for a small market in California. The four partners want to expand their business and market their games nationally. Adding a fifth partner would not increase their borrowing power enough to pay for the planned expansion. To put themselves in a better financial position, they decide to transform their partnership into a corporation. Caroline suggests that they consult a lawyer to handle the extensive paperwork and many legal issues.

The first step in forming the new corporation is to apply for a state license known as the

NET INCOME OF BUSINESSES, 1997

- Corporations: 72%
- Sole proprietorships: 14.7%
- Partnerships: 13.2%

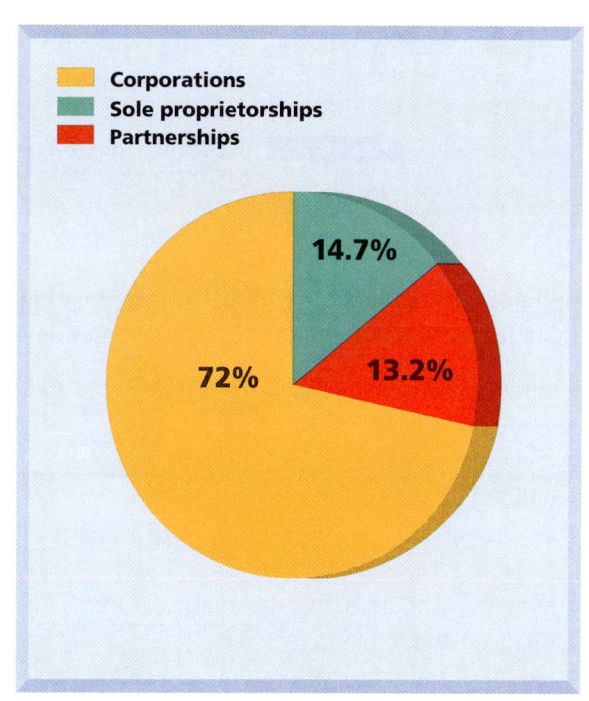

Source: Statistical Abstract of the United States: 2000

FIGURE 7.3 A corporation is considered to be legally distinct from its owners. **What percentage of net income is earned by corporations?**

BUSINESS ORGANIZATIONS 153

Transparency

An overhead transparency of Figure 7.4 is available in *Transparency Resources*. See Transparency 27: Organization and Control in a Typical Corporation.

Caption Answer

owners/shareholders

---

internet connect

TOPIC: Ben & Jerry's Homemade Ice Cream, Inc.
GO TO: go.hrw.com
KEYWORD: SM3 EC7

Have students access the Internet through the HRW Go site to conduct research on the history of Ben & Jerry's, which began as a partnership, became a corporation, and is now owned by Unilever, an Anglo-Dutch conglomerate. Have each student prepare a time line to present important dates and facts about the company. Ask students to discuss regulations that might have applied to establishing the business as a partnership and as a corporation. Conclude by leading a discussion about the characteristics of partnerships and corporations and why the founding partners of Ben & Jerry's Homemade Ice Cream, Inc., might have decided to incorporate their business. ★ 2D, 9B, 12B, 23C

154

ORGANIZATION AND CONTROL IN A TYPICAL CORPORATION

OWNERS/SHAREHOLDERS who elect the
↓
BOARD OF DIRECTORS that selects
↓
CORPORATE OFFICERS who hire
↓
VICE PRESIDENTS
PRODUCTION   OPERATIONS   MARKETING   DISTRIBUTION
↓
DEPARTMENT HEADS
R&D QUALITY CONTROL PERSONNEL FINANCE ADVERTISING SALES WAREHOUSING DELIVERIES
↓
EMPLOYEES

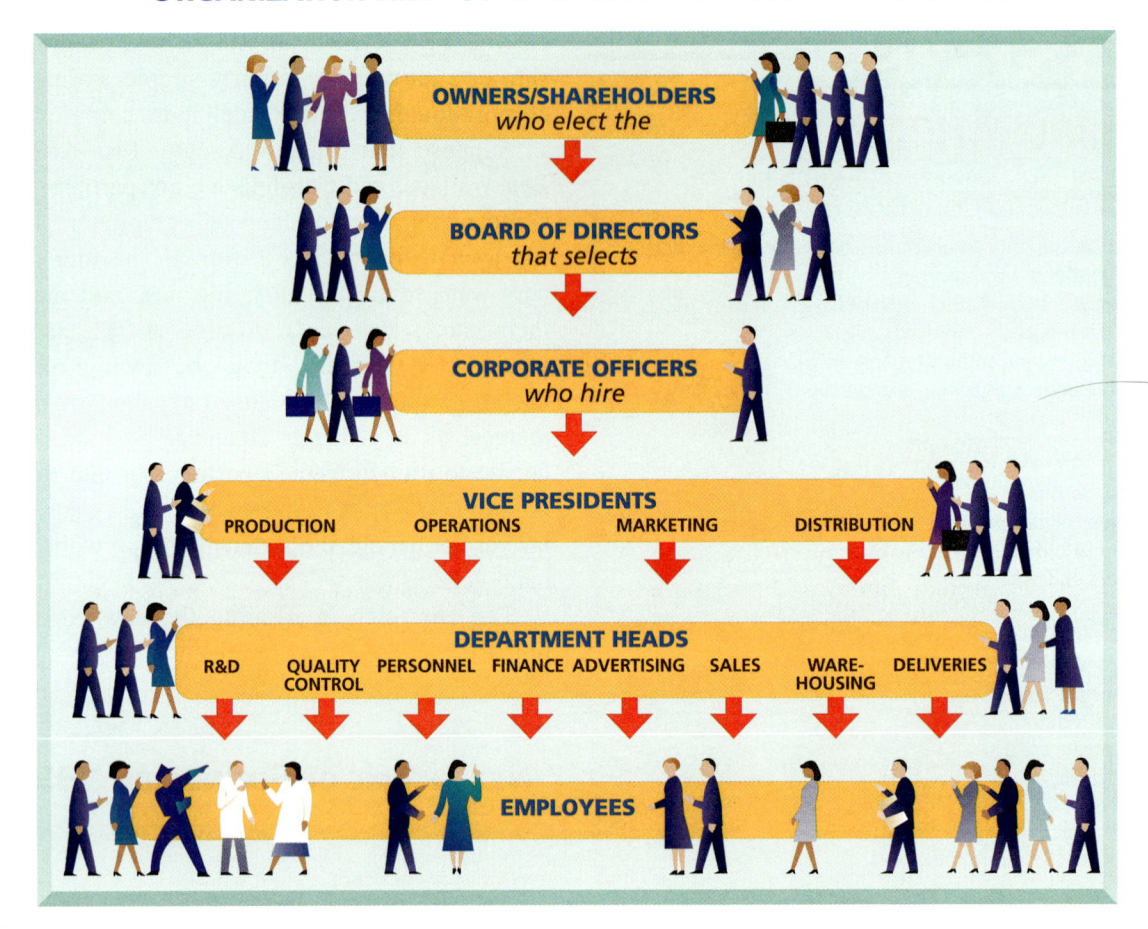

FIGURE 7.4 The board of directors is the most important decision-making body in a corporation. **Who selects the board of directors?**

---

articles of incorporation. This application includes the following six pieces of information:

▸ name and purpose of the proposed corporation,
▸ address of the corporate headquarters,
▸ method of fund-raising the corporation will undertake,
▸ amount of money the corporation expects to raise,
▸ names and addresses of the major corporate officers, and
▸ length of time the corporation is intended to exist—either indefinitely or for a specified period of time.

The articles of incorporation are reviewed by state officials, who—if everything is in order—grant a license, or **corporate charter**, which permits the formation of the new corporation. Michael, Lisa, Ben, and Caroline submit their articles of incorporation and receive the corporate charter for their business, which they have named CompuFun.

Corporate Structure

The corporate charter identifies the corporation's officers—for example, Lisa as president and chief executive officer (CEO), Caroline as vice president of sales, Michael as vice president of product development, and Ben as treasurer. Corporations have other formal structures as well—and generally many more of these structures than

154 CHAPTER 7

do businesses organized as sole proprietorships or partnerships.

Figure 7.4 shows the structure of a typical corporation. The structures of specific corporations may vary somewhat from the diagram because corporations differ in size and in the goods and services they produce. In any corporation, however—including CompuFun—the **board of directors** is made up of people from inside or outside the company. The board is the corporation's key decision-making body.

What kinds of decisions does the board of directors make? The board must determine how the corporation should develop and what policies it will follow. Michael recommends that CompuFun develop a series of educational games to help children study geography, math, and biology. This new product line would require hiring additional product-development specialists and programmers. The board must determine if expansion into educational software is in the company's best interest.

In addition, the board selects new corporate officers as needed. Although the original corporate officers are identified in the articles of incorporation, these individuals may leave the company. The board of directors would then select new officers to ensure that business continues smoothly. Corporate officers typically are experienced, professional managers hired to make day-to-day decisions and to advise the board about production plans. These officers also see that the policies and plans approved by the board are carried out by the corporation's various department heads.

Corporate Finances

The board of directors also is responsible for deciding how the corporation will raise funds. The most common way in which corporations raise funds is by selling stock. **Stock** represents ownership of the firm. This ownership is issued in portions known as **shares**. If you buy 100 shares of stock in a company, you own 100 pieces of that company. If that company has issued 10,000 shares, you own 1 percent of the firm.

Why might you want to own stock? It is an investment—you hope that the company will do well, so that your shares will increase in value and you will receive part of the profits. The profits paid to you as a shareholder are called **dividends**. You receive dividends as a "return," or profit, on your investment.

What other benefits do you enjoy as a shareholder? The answer depends on the type of stock you own. Corporations issue two kinds of stock—common and preferred. **Common stock** provides shareholders with a voice in how the company is run and a share in any potential dividends. **Preferred stock** provides guaranteed dividends—paid before any received by holders of common stock—but does not grant shareholders a voice in running the corporation.

Corporations can have thousands of shareholders and, therefore, thousands of owners. As a result, corporations can raise enormous amounts of money through the sale of stock.

Corporations also raise money by issuing corporate bonds. A **corporate bond** is a certificate issued by a corporation in exchange for money borrowed from an investor. How do stocks and bonds differ? Stock, as you have learned, represents ownership in a corporation. A bond, on the other hand, indicates that the corporation is in debt to the person who holds the bond. The bondholder does not own any part of the company.

As a moneylender, the bondholder is repaid the principal of the loan, plus interest. The **principal** is the actual amount of money that was borrowed. **Interest** is the amount that the borrower—the corporation in this case—must pay for the use of those funds. For example, if you hold a one-year $1,000 bond that pays interest at a rate of 5 percent, you are in fact lending $1,000 for one year. In return, at the end of the year you will receive your $1,000 of principal plus $50 interest ($1,000 × 5% = $50), thereby earning $50 on the loan.

After analyzing the different methods of raising money, the CompuFun board of directors decides to sell common stock. After its first year of sales, CompuFun finds it has made enough profit to issue a dividend of 10 cents per share.

Across the Curriculum

TECHNOLOGY Twenty-four-year-old Mark Andreessen became $58 million richer when Netscape Communications Corporation gave the public its first opportunity to buy stock in August 1995. Andreessen pioneered the user-friendly Web browser called Netscape Navigator™ and had to quickly adjust to corporate culture when his product became a Wall Street blockbuster. Within minutes of going public, Netscape's stock price jumped from $28 to more than $74 per share. The phenomenal rise in Netscape's stock price on its first day of public trading occurred even though the company had yet to turn a profit.

In late 1998 America Online purchased Netscape. Subsequently, Andreessen founded Loudcloud, an Internet consulting company. Loudcloud's initial public offering, which came during a market downturn in March 2001, was received very differently from Netscape's—Loudcloud had to cut its stock price twice to attract buyers. Despite Andreessen's reputation, investors were reluctant to put their money into an unprofitable company. Investors had become leery of technology stocks, particularly Internet stocks, which had lost 75 percent of their value in the preceding six months. ■

Caption Answer
the South ★ 23F, 23G

Themes in Economics

THE ROLE OF GOVERNMENT
The failure of a large corporation can have serious repercussions for the overall economy. For this reason, the government sometimes helps large corporations in financial trouble. The Chrysler Corporation provides an example of one such case.

During the 1970s rising fuel prices hurt sales of Chrysler's luxury cars, which were not fuel efficient and accounted for most of its inventory. By 1979 the company was facing bankruptcy. Chrysler's new chairman, Lee Iacocca, asked the government for a loan to help "bail out" the company. In 1980, after heated debate, Congress voted to give Chrysler guaranteed loans totaling $1.5 billion, if Chrysler agreed to raise another $2 billion itself. Under Iacocca's leadership, the company slashed its workforce, cut wages, and closed plants to save money. At the same time, Chrysler shifted production to more fuel-efficient cars.

The plan worked. By 1981 Chrysler had bounced back. By 1983 it had repaid its government loans, and in 1984 the company enjoyed record profits of more than $2.4 billion.

After its 1998 merger with German automaker Daimler-Benz, Chrysler became a division of DaimlerChrysler Corporation. ■

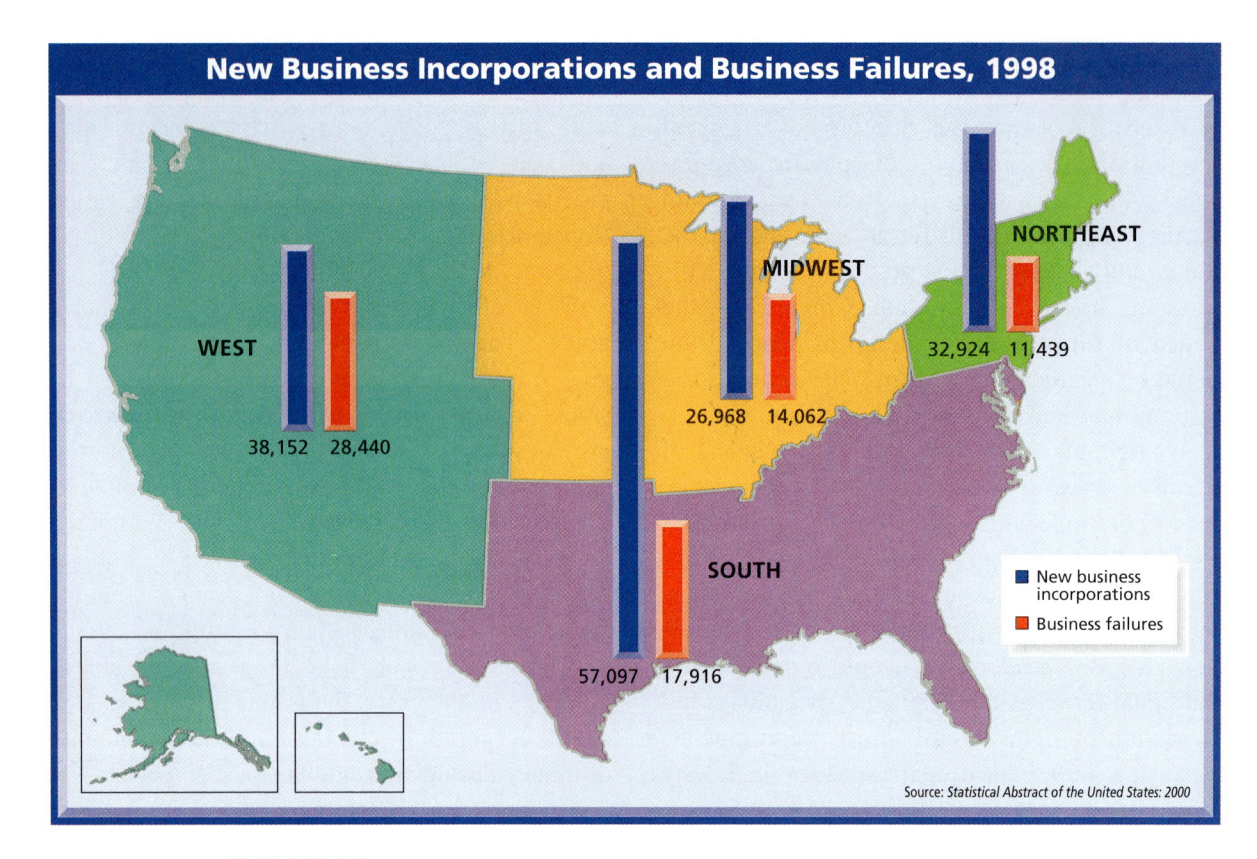

New Business Incorporations and Business Failures, 1998

- WEST: 38,152 / 28,440
- MIDWEST: 26,968 / 14,062
- NORTHEAST: 32,924 / 11,439
- SOUTH: 57,097 / 17,916

■ New business incorporations
■ Business failures

Source: Statistical Abstract of the United States: 2000

FIGURE 7.5 Many new businesses are opened each year. **Which region was home to the largest number of new businesses?** ★TEKS

This means that a person owning 1,000 shares of CompuFun stock receives $100 of the company's profits for the first year (1,000 × $0.10 = $100). Additionally, CompuFun shareholders are able to vote on company policies and elect the board of directors.

Advantages of Corporations

Corporations have two sets of advantages. One group of advantages is enjoyed by the stockholders, and the other is enjoyed by the corporation itself.

Benefits for Stockholders For stockholders, the major advantage is limited liability. If a corporation fails, the loss to its stockholders, for example, is limited to the amount they invested. A shareholder's assets, or private property, cannot be seized to pay corporate debts. If you buy 100 shares of CompuFun stock and the company goes out of business, you will not have to pay the company's remaining debts. You will lose only what you paid for the stock.

The corporate structure also gives stockholders flexibility, allowing them to take back all or part of their investment by selling their shares. You can sell your CompuFun shares at any time, provided that you can find someone who is willing to buy the shares of stock at a price you are willing to accept.

Benefits for Corporations Limited liability also benefits a corporation's founders. The owner of a sole proprietorship who intends to borrow in order to expand the business may decide to incorporate to avoid losing his or her personal possessions. Similarly, partners who incorporate are no longer liable for the loss of anything beyond their own investments.

A second advantage for a corporation is the separation of ownership from management. Because the owners are not involved in daily operations, the corporation can assign specialists to complex management tasks. For example, the CompuFun shareholders do not make day-to-day decisions about company activities. Instead, professional managers, who are skilled at operating a business, make the decisions concerning the production and marketing of the corporation's products. A corporation also can hire additional specialists, such as lawyers and accountants, to advise the professional managers.

A third advantage for a corporation is the relative ease with which capital can be raised. Unlike sole proprietorships and partnerships, which generally rely on collateral to gain credit, corporations can raise money by expanding ownership through the sale of stock. Bonds allow corporations to borrow from individuals as well as from institutions such as banks. A corporation, therefore, has many more potential sources of capital than do sole proprietorships and partnerships.

The final advantage for a corporation is longevity. A corporation often continues to exist after the deaths of its founders and original management. This long life span is possible because the corporation's structure is not dependent on one or a few individuals, as in a sole proprietorship or partnership. A corporation's pool of ownership changes constantly as stock is bought and sold, and as corporate directors, officers, and employees quit, retire, and are hired or fired. Although these changes could force a proprietorship or partnership to close, a corporation would most likely continue to exist. CompuFun, for example, can continue to do business even if Ben is fired, Caroline quits her job to go back to school, or you sell your stock.

Disadvantages of Corporations

Although there are several disadvantages to this form of business organization, most affect the corporation itself rather than individual stockholders. What are these disadvantages?

Corporate Issues First, a corporate charter can be expensive and difficult to obtain. Costs vary from state to state, but attorney fees and filing expenses may total several thousand dollars.

Second, the federal and state governments regulate corporations much more closely than they do sole proprietorships and partnerships. In addition to obtaining a license, a corporation must follow specific government guidelines when selling stock. A corporation also may face stiffer legal regulations, such as having to publicize financial information about its sales and profits.

A third disadvantage for a corporation is the slow process of decision making. In a corporation—particularly a large one—decisions are made only after extensive study of the issues by specialists and discussion and debate among managers. The process can be further slowed if

ECONOMIC INSTITUTIONS & INCENTIVES *Annual meetings offer stockholders the opportunity to vote on company policies.* **What are some of the advantages of forming a corporation?**

Themes in Economics

ECONOMIC INSTITUTIONS & INCENTIVES In general, corporations enjoy greater longevity than sole proprietorships and partnerships. Nevertheless, the average life span for multinational corporations is 40 to 50 years. In Japan and Europe, the typical corporation lasts less than 13 years. Corporations can merge with other firms, break up into smaller companies, or simply fail.

Some corporations have managed to survive for centuries, however. Stora, a Swedish company that produces paper and chemicals, was founded during the 1200s. Sumitomo, a Japanese corporation, is more than 400 years old. In the United States, Du Pont is over 200 years old, and Mutual Assurance Society of Virginia, an insurance company, is also more than 200 years old.

What traits help a company outlive its competitors? One of the most important is being the first company to expand broadly into a new market. ■

Caption Answer

for stockholders—limited liability, flexibility to trade shares; for corporations—limited liability, separation of ownership from management, relative ease of raising financial capital, longevity 9B

disagreements take place between top-level managers and the board of directors over such matters as establishing hiring practices and setting production goals.

Stockholder Issues The main disadvantage for stockholders seems, at first glance, like an advantage. Stockholders can earn a profit without actually working for the company. This may seem very appealing as a way of earning an income without having to work for it. In reality, however, this situation means that stockholders are far removed from the actual running of the business. Although you earn money in the form of dividends from your CompuFun stock, you have no direct participation in developing and selling new products. As a result, you—and other stockholders—are not likely to have the sense of pride, accomplishment, and personal satisfaction often felt by sole proprietors or partners, even though you are an owner of the corporation.

A second, related disadvantage for stockholders is lack of control. Although stockholders technically are able to influence the company, their power generally is limited. Annual shareholder meetings offer owners a chance to vote on company policies. Most stockholders, however, own only a small percentage of a company's shares, making it difficult to influence policy and corporate objectives unless a majority of shares are held by people with similar views. In addition, stockholders cannot affect a corporation's day-to-day activities. For example, if you as a shareholder think that CompuFun should sell a computerized time-management program, you must count on the corporation's officers to decide whether to develop such a product.

Shared Issues For some people, there is an additional disadvantage that applies both to the corporation and to its stockholders. These people point out that corporate profits are taxed twice—once as corporate profits and again as dividends. The income, or profit, of a corporation is taxed because legally—as you learned earlier in this section—the corporation is treated as if it were an individual. Next, these after-tax profits are distributed to shareholders as dividends. The government views dividends as income for the stockholder, so he or she must pay income tax on this money in addition to the taxes paid by the corporation.

SECTION 3 REVIEW

★TEKS Q: 1, 2, 3a, 3b, 3c, 4

1. Identify and Explain:
- corporations
- articles of incorporation
- corporate charter
- board of directors
- stock
- shares
- dividends
- common stock
- preferred stock
- corporate bond
- principal
- interest

2. Compare: Copy the graphic organizer below. Use it to explain the two ways that corporations can raise money from the public.

Sources of Corporate Funds

3. Finding the Main Idea
a. What advantages does incorporation give to the shareholders and to the company?
b. What disadvantages does incorporation give to the shareholders and to the company?
c. What is the economic impact of investing in the stock and bond markets?

4. Writing and Critical Thinking
Drawing Conclusions: How might you consider your school to be a corporation?
Consider the following:
• who makes up the board of directors
• who are the shareholders, and what dividends are paid

Homework Practice Online
keyword: SM3 HP7

SECTION 4
OTHER FORMS OF ORGANIZATION

READ TO DISCOVER

1. How do vertical combinations differ from horizontal and conglomerate combinations?
2. Why might a business owner decide to open a franchise?
3. What is the customer's role in a cooperative?
4. How does a nonprofit organization differ from other types of business organizations?

ECONOMICS DICTIONARY

merger
horizontal combination
vertical combination
conglomerate combination
subsidiaries
franchise
cooperatives
nonprofit organization

Sole proprietorships, partnerships, and corporations are the three most common forms of business organization in the United States. There are, however, other forms business owners may choose, including

- corporate combinations,
- franchises,
- cooperatives, and
- nonprofit organizations.

Like sole proprietorships, partnerships, and corporations, these types of business organizations meet the needs of particular enterprises. As you read this section, consider how each form can benefit a business.

Corporate Combinations

Many of the advantages associated with forming a corporation—longevity, separation of ownership from management, and ease of raising financial capital—are associated with one characteristic: size. As noted in Chapter 6, large size often brings economies of scale. In order to make the most of these advantages, many corporations try to expand. To expand, a corporation either grows from within by building new facilities or legally combines with another enterprise.

The most common method of joining businesses is through mergers. A **merger** occurs when one company joins with or absorbs another. In a merger the absorbed company often loses its identity. Suppose that the computer games company known as CompuFun Corporation is purchased by a company known as CyberAce Corporation. If CompuFun's games are popular, CyberAce will probably continue to produce them, but under the CyberAce name.

Companies may form different types of corporate combinations. The three most common types of combinations are

- horizontal,
- vertical, and
- conglomerate.

Horizontal Combinations A merger between two or more companies producing the same good or service (or the acquisition of one such company by another) is called a **horizontal combination**. A horizontal combination also may involve companies that dominate one phase of production.

As noted in Chapter 6, John D. Rockefeller and his associates organized the Standard Oil Trust—which was later broken up by the federal government—to control the U.S. oil industry. This trust was a horizontal combination in that it included many companies involved in the same industry—oil refining.

Vertical Combinations A merger between two or more companies involved in different production phases of the same good or service is a **vertical combination**. For example, the United

States Steel Corporation, founded in 1901, combined companies that owned ore deposits, iron mines, steel mills, railroads, and shipping lines. All of these companies were involved in different phases of the production and distribution of steel. Today the company, which is now a part of USX Corporation, produces 10 percent of all the steel manufactured in the United States.

Conglomerate Combinations A merger of companies producing unrelated products is known as a **conglomerate combination**. (See Figure 7.6.) Whereas horizontal and vertical combinations have existed since the late 1800s, conglomerate combinations did not become common until the 1960s and 1970s.

One example of a conglomerate is the International Telephone and Telegraph Corporation (ITT). Until the 1950s, ITT manufactured only telecommunications equipment. During the 1960s and 1970s, however, ITT acquired hundreds of companies that became **subsidiaries**, or distinct divisions, of ITT. Although owned by ITT, these subsidiaries continued to manufacture

CONGLOMERATE COMBINATION

THE GILLETTE COMPANY

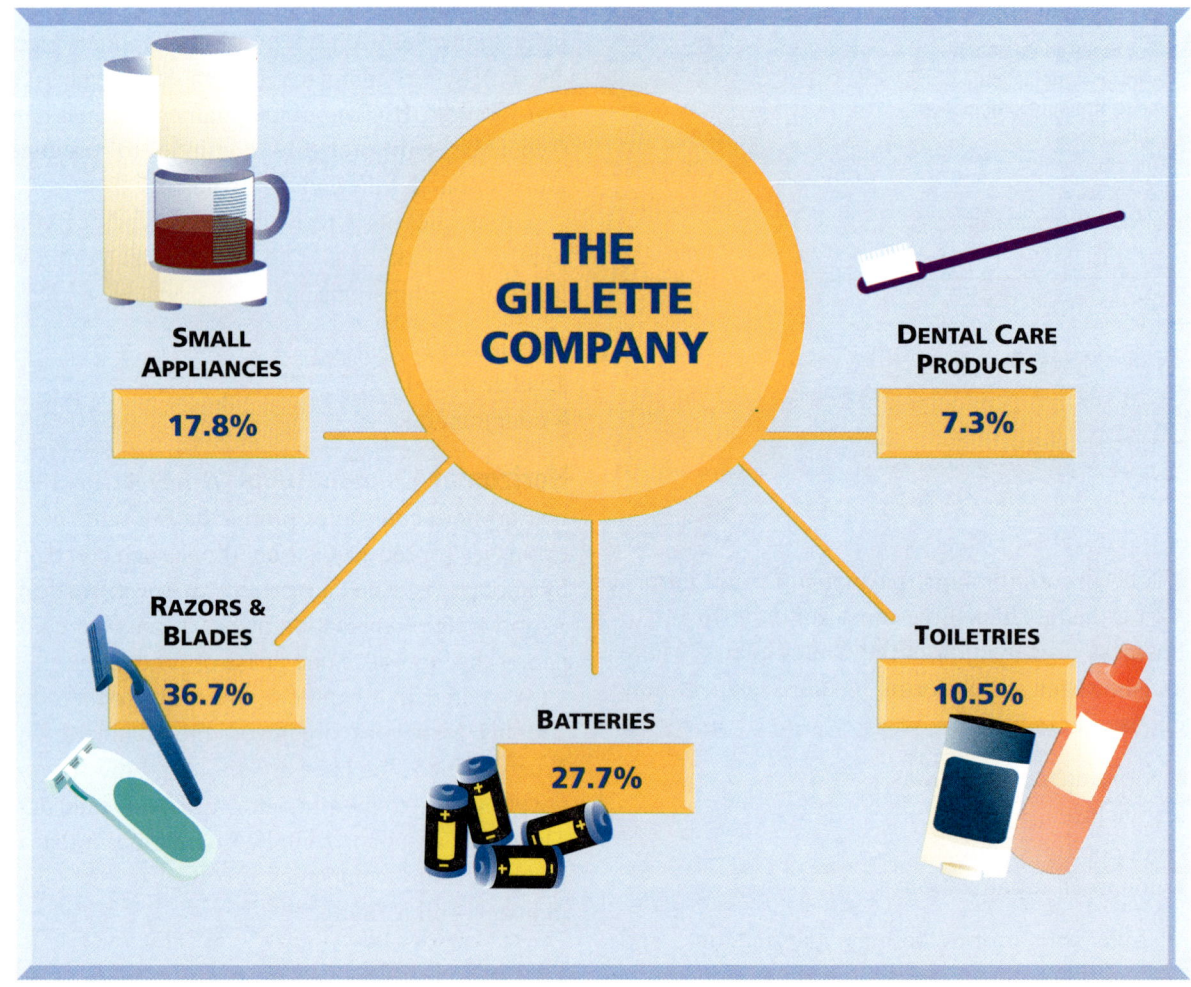

- SMALL APPLIANCES — 17.8%
- DENTAL CARE PRODUCTS — 7.3%
- RAZORS & BLADES — 36.7%
- BATTERIES — 27.7%
- TOILETRIES — 10.5%

Source: *The Gillette Company 2000 Annual Report*

FIGURE 7.6 A conglomerate combination produces two or more unrelated products. What is the Gillette Company's largest product line?

products under their own names—often noting that the companies were subsidiaries of ITT. Today ITT has subsidiaries in such varied enterprises as insurance, financial services, defense technology, and automotive products.

To ensure competent and knowledgeable decision making, combinations often allow subsidiaries to keep their own top management. For example, when General Motors (GM) acquired Hughes Aircraft Company in the mid-1980s, GM permitted Hughes to conduct its own affairs largely without interference.

Advantages of Combinations One major advantage of corporate mergers is efficiency. By centralizing decision making within an industry, a combination usually can increase efficiency through the elimination of overlapping jobs and departments. For example, when CyberAce purchases CompuFun, the new combination may not need two vice presidents of product development and thus may eliminate Michael's job.

A second advantage is the potential for lower costs. Buying an existing business is often less expensive than building new plants and offices, hiring new employees, and acquiring additional financial capital to expand. CyberAce will not need to pay to recruit and relocate new employees because the merger has brought CompuFun's employees into the corporation.

A third advantage is that the increased size of a combination often makes it easier to acquire financial capital. Just as partnerships typically have more collateral than sole proprietorships, corporate combinations typically have a greater ability to raise financial capital than separate corporations. Additionally, larger companies often are believed to be more successful, which encourages shareholder investment. The new financial capital that CyberAce raises can be used to increase the sales force or to modernize production facilities, enabling the combination to compete more effectively in the marketplace.

Disadvantages of Combinations Although combinations can lead to increased efficiency, their practices also can lead to higher rates of

Global Exchange

Andrew Carnegie, Innovator

Andrew Carnegie was one of the most successful and innovative American industrialists. Born in 1835 in Scotland, Carnegie immigrated to the United States with his family at the age of 12.

Carnegie's family settled in a part of what is now Pittsburgh, Pennsylvania. After working as a telegraph operator, Carnegie was hired by a railroad company. He rose quickly through the ranks, and by his 30s Carnegie was a wealthy man with investments in blast furnaces and iron mills as well as railroads.

Carnegie decided to concentrate on the steel business in the 1870s, when he found that British manufacturers were producing steel rails that were superior to the mostly iron rails produced in his plants. The Bessemer process, a new steelmaking process, had been developed in Great Britain, which was then the world's largest steel producer. The process greatly increased the efficiency of steel production, and Carnegie adopted this and other innovative processes. By directing his energy and resources toward the production of steel in the most efficient and technologically advanced manner, he soon dominated the American steel industry.

Carnegie was also creative in the way he organized his businesses. Carnegie organized his holdings by the principle of vertical integration, which involves owning all the businesses related to the manufacture and distribution of a product. By controlling the entire process, from mining to finished products and transportation, Carnegie built a reliable and efficient model for mass-producing industrial goods.

Across the Curriculum

HISTORY When J.P. Morgan bought the Carnegie Steel Company in 1901, he merged it with the Federal Steel Company and eight other companies to create the United States Steel Corporation. Until the late 1990s, the merger remained the largest in U.S. history.

Profiles in Economics

For a biography of John D. Rockefeller, Andrew Carnegie, and other noted people in economics, see the Biographies section on the *Researcher Online*.

Cultural Perspectives

Business-savvy rap group Wu-Tang Clan has created a hip-hop conglomerate. Already successful with their group's recordings, two members have started their own record labels and four others are starting business projects of their own. Group members also own a clothing line, for which they design and sell items ranging from watches to ski jackets. Founded by the RZA (born Robert Diggs), Wu-Tang Clan has gone from selling records from the trunks of their cars to operating a music empire.

Enhancing the Lesson

For a historical perspective on the regulation of business combinations, see Reading 26: New Nationalism, located in *From the Source: Readings in Economics and Government with Answer Key.*

Caption Answer

Answers will vary but should reflect an understanding of the characteristics of franchises.

Global Connections

U.S. franchises that have established overseas operations face potential cultural clashes. In 1996 McDonald's opened its first franchise in India, where the dominant religions—Hinduism and Islam—prohibit followers from eating beef and pork, respectively, and where a large percentage of the population are vegetarians. In keeping with these religious customs, the restaurant is the first McDonald's to not serve beef or pork. Instead, hungry Indians can order a Maharajah Mac—a Big Mac® made with mutton. Also available are veggie burgers and Vegetable McNuggets with McMasala sauce. ■

Caption Answer

to own a share in the business and thereby receive a share of profits or lower prices or rates ★1B, 23A

ECONOMIC INSTITUTIONS & INCENTIVES *Franchises share the original company's name but are individually owned.* **What franchises are you familiar with?**

unemployment. Employees may be reassigned or may lose their jobs. If Michael no longer works as vice president of product development, he may become unemployed or be assigned to new duties—perhaps as vice president of production. Even employees who keep their jobs, however, sometimes suffer low morale from altered job responsibilities or other changes in working conditions. Michael may not enjoy his new job, or employees in product development may not like working for the CyberAce vice president.

Additionally, because mergers may result in reduced competition in the marketplace, they can lead to higher prices for consumers. Since CyberAce games no longer need to compete with CompuFun games—because they all are now produced by CyberAce—prices may increase.

Franchises

Some businesses share a name even though they are separately owned. In this case, one company agrees—for a fee—to let another person or group set up a **franchise**, an enterprise that uses the original company's name to sell goods and services. The parent company—the company owning the name—is called the franchisor. The person or group opening the franchise is called the franchisee.

What kinds of businesses are operated as franchises? Hotel and motel chains including Holiday Inn, restaurants such as Burger King, and real estate agencies such as Century 21 are organized as franchises.

Franchise agreements generally include requirements designed to uphold the reputation of the parent company. For example, the franchisee has to maintain quality standards and must provide a particular good or service.

To ensure consistent quality and service, the franchisor often provides training for employees. It also may pay for national advertising. Because of these advantages, as well as use of the parent company's name, the franchisee can lower the costs associated with starting a business.

For example, suppose that Nalani Ling wants to open a shoe repair store. She can establish a sole proprietorship, but she also has the opportunity to open a franchise of the widely known Zippy Fix Shoe Repair company. Nalani may

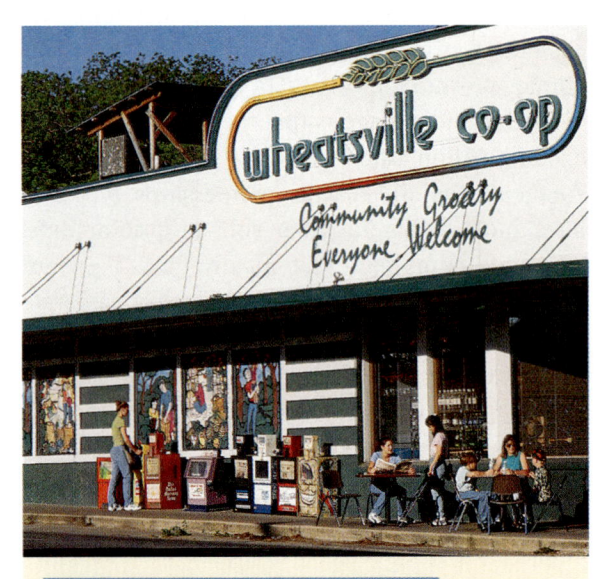

ECONOMIC INSTITUTIONS & INCENTIVES *Cooperatives are owned collectively by their members.* **Why might a consumer join a co-op such as the one pictured here?** ★TEKS

162 CHAPTER 7

decide to become a franchisee because, even though she will have to pay for the use of the Zippy Fix name, she knows that she can count on the franchisor to provide standards of quality, access to tools and materials, and advertising. Additionally, she knows that customers will recognize the Zippy Fix name from the moment she opens the doors of her business, increasing her share of the shoe-repair market. The name Ling Shoe Repair, on the other hand, would be less familiar to the public and would take longer to attract customers. Nalani may determine that a franchise suits her business needs better than a sole proprietorship.

ECONOMIC INSTITUTIONS & INCENTIVES *The Red Cross provided aid in response to the September 11, 2001, attacks.* **How do nonprofit organizations raise money?**

Cooperatives

Some businesses are organized as **cooperatives**, or co-ops—businesses that are owned collectively by their members. For example, residents of an apartment building may join together to buy their building as a housing cooperative, rather than allow it to be purchased by a shopping-mall developer. Suppose that residents of Blue Moon Apartments decide to form a cooperative and buy the building. Some of the residents decide to move, but Janelle Franklin is one of many who agrees to invest money and join the cooperative. Janelle now owns shares in the Blue Moon Apartment Cooperative and has the right to occupy one of the apartments. As an individual, however, she does not own a specific part of the physical structure of the building. Additionally, she and the other co-op members share the building's maintenance costs.

There are many types of cooperatives. Purchasing cooperatives are retail stores that buy large quantities of merchandise at reduced prices and pass these savings on to their members. Marketing cooperatives are commonly established by groups of farmers who hope to secure higher prices for their farm products. Service cooperatives provide members with services such as electrical power, health care, or legal assistance. Credit unions are financial cooperatives that allow members to borrow money at reduced interest rates.

Nonprofit Organizations

One form of business organization does not focus on financial gain for its members. Instead, a **nonprofit organization** works in a businesslike way to provide goods and services while pursuing other goals, such as improving educational standards, providing health care, or maintaining museums and other cultural institutions. Nonprofit organizations include the American Red Cross, the Boy Scouts of America, the Girl Scouts of the U.S.A., and the American Heart Association, as well as some churches, labor unions, and some hospitals.

Nonprofit organizations often are structured like corporations, in part so that they can benefit from unlimited longevity. Revenues for nonprofit organizations generally come from the sale of products, fees for services, and charitable contributions. The income of nonprofit organizations is not taxed by the government.

Across the Curriculum

HISTORY Farming cooperatives have existed in the United States since the 1860s, when the National Grange, a farmers' organization, began forming them. The Grange patterned its cooperatives after those created by the Rochdale Society of Equitable Pioneers. This organization established the first retail cooperative with its store in Rochdale, England, in 1844. The store provided members with quality goods at fair prices. Profits were distributed among members according to the amount each purchased. Membership was open to all, regardless of race, sex, or religious or political affiliation. Each member also had one vote in decision-making matters. ■

Caption Answer
from charitable contributions, the sale of products, and fees for services

BUSINESS ORGANIZATIONS

SECTION 4 REVIEW ANSWERS

1. merger (159), horizontal combination (159), vertical combination (159), conglomerate combination (160), subsidiaries (160), franchise (162), cooperatives (163), nonprofit organization (163) **9A, 24A**

2. all combinations are mergers of two or more companies; horizontal—companies produce the same product or service; vertical—companies in different production phases of the same product or service; conglomerate—companies make unrelated products or services **23A, 24D**

3a. to provide goods and services while pursuing goals other than profit; examples will vary

3b. to own a share in the business and thereby receive a share of profits or lower prices or rates

4. Answers will vary. Students may respond that their school is most like a nonprofit organization because it provides services without financial gain. **23A**

ECONOMIC INSTITUTIONS & INCENTIVES *The Green Bay Packers football team is organized as a nonprofit organization.*

CASE STUDY

The Green Bay Packers, Inc.

ECONOMIC INSTITUTIONS & INCENTIVES Owners of pro sports teams look for many things in a hometown—a large population, a modern stadium, and widespread local television coverage. Because of this, many teams have left familiar cities and fans for greener, richer hometowns. Why, then, have the Packers stayed in Green Bay, Wisconsin, since 1919, when the city is not even among the 100 largest in the United States nor is it one of the biggest television markets?

Most sports teams are organized as sole proprietorships, partnerships, or parts of corporations. The Green Bay Packers, however, are a nonprofit corporation. The original shares of Packer stock were purchased by Green Bay residents. (During a limited-time offering in 1997–98, Packer fans throughout the United States were allowed to purchase Packer stock.) A shareholder can pass his or her original shares on to a relative, but cannot sell the shares to a nonrelative unless the corporation approves. The corporation also limits stock ownership to 200,000 shares per person, and shares cannot be resold, except back to the team. The relatively low price offers an investment in civic pride, not a chance to earn a profit. Any profits earned by the Packer organization are spent on improvements to the stadium and facilities.

Is the choice to make the team a nonprofit organization working? Fans think so. Packer games consistently are sold out, and the waiting list for season tickets contains more than 56,000 names.

SECTION 4 REVIEW

TEKS Q: 1, 2

1. Identify and Explain:
- merger
- horizontal combination
- vertical combination
- conglomerate combination
- subsidiaries
- Andrew Carnegie
- franchise
- cooperatives
- nonprofit organization

2. Comparing: Copy the graphic organizer below. Use it to compare horizontal, vertical, and conglomerate combinations.

Types of Combinations

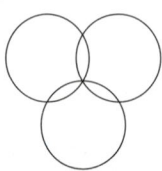

3. Finding the Main Idea

a. What is the purpose of a nonprofit organization? List three nonprofit organizations not mentioned in the text.

b. What are the advantages of membership in a cooperative?

4. Writing and Critical Thinking

Comparing and Contrasting: Is your school more like a franchise, a cooperative, or a nonprofit organization? Explain your answer.

Consider the following:
- characteristics of franchises, cooperatives, and nonprofits
- characteristics your school has in common with these types of businesses

Homework Practice Online
keyword: SM3 HP7

Economics IN THE NEWS

Business Ethics in a Global Economy

Businesses in a free-enterprise economy possess certain legal rights, such as the right to own private property and enter into contracts. They also have legal responsibilities, such as the obligation to comply with government regulations.

A second type of responsibility, ethical conduct, involves adherence to a set of moral values other than legal obligations imposed by government. In recent years there has been growing support for the notion that businesses have an obligation to conduct their operations in an ethical manner. Issues involving business ethics include environmental protection and worker health and safety.

While ethical conduct is its own reward, there are also practical reasons to follow a code of conduct. For one, ethical conduct enhances a business's reputation. Some investors have even begun to base their investment decisions in part on the company's reputation for ethical conduct or its commitment to social good. A second reason is that unethical conduct is also often illegal. For instance polluting the environment is both unethical, based on the idea that one should clean up after oneself, and is in many cases illegal. Finally, having a clear set of ethical guidelines can help standardize business practices. This is especially important in a large corporation that may have employees in a number of different locations worldwide. Moreover, a recent study of 300 large companies found that those with a written ethics policy economically outperformed those without one. In other words, ethics pays.

One company with a written ethics code is the blue-jeans manufacturer Levi Strauss. With its clothing made by over 600 manufacturers in 60 different countries, the ethics code helps ensure that all these separate businesses act in a responsible manner. The company's ethical code imposes a number of requirements on its business partners. For instance, they must follow certain health and safety standards, may not use child or prison labor, and must respect their workers' rights to form labor unions.

Levi Strauss is one of a growing number of businesses, such as the computer company IBM and the telecommunications company Nortel, that have found it makes good business sense to practice corporate citizenship by spelling out their core values in an ethics policy.

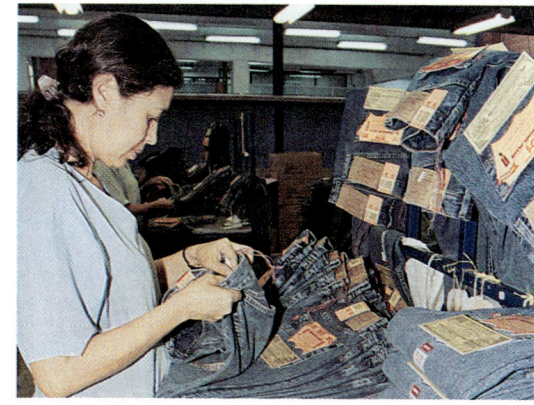

Levi Strauss contracts manufacturers in numerous foreign countries, including Colombia. Levi's ethics policies help to prevent health and safety violations, child labor exploitation, and anti-union policies.

What Do You Think?

1. What are some of the economic benefits that Levi Strauss might gain by having a written code of ethics?
2. How might an ethics code be particularly important in a large global corporation?

WHY IT MATTERS TODAY

The ethics policies of businesses can affect the quality of the goods you receive and the price you pay for them. Use CNNfyi.com or other **current events** sources to find other examples of companies with ethics policies. Record your findings in your journal.

Economics in the News Answers

1. Students might suggest that ethical conduct enhances a business's reputation, that it is legally prudent, and that standardized business practices can ultimately lead to better economic performance. 2C
2. by ensuring workers' rights are respected in both the domestic and overseas operations 2C

CHAPTER 7
Review Answers

Writing a Summary
Summaries should focus on the main points of each section. These may be found in the Read to Discover questions at the start of each section. Summaries should also use standard grammar, spelling, sentence structure, and punctuation. 24B, 24D

Identifying Ideas
sole proprietorship (145), zoning laws (146), general partnership (150), limited partnership (150), corporations (153), board of directors (155), stock (155), corporate bond (155), vertical combination (159) cooperatives (163) 3B, 9A, 15A, 15B, 24A

Understanding Main Ideas
1. It involves little financial capital and involves few legal considerations. 9B

CHAPTER 7 Review

2. partners can specialize and share decision making and business losses **9B**

3. stocks—ownership of a corporation; corporate bonds—loans to a corporation; they sell shares of stock for money and issue bonds in exchange for loans from investors. **11C**

4. It can own property, hire workers, make contracts, pay taxes, sue and be sued, and make and sell products. **9A, 9B**

5. vertical—merger of two or more companies involved in different production phases of the same product; horizontal—merger of two or more companies that produce the same product; by acquiring businesses related to all phases of steel production and distribution **9A, 19D**

6. not focused on financial gain, income not taxed by the government

Reviewing Themes

1. zoning laws and city, county, and state licenses; to protect neighborhoods and the environment and to ensure that businesses are properly qualified **2D, 3B, 15B**

2. by submitting articles of incorporation to, and obtaining a corporate charter from, the state; stockholders—do not receive satisfaction of working in company, lack control, profits taxed twice; corporation—difficult/expensive to obtain charter, complex regulations, slow decision-making process **9B**

3. use of parent company's name, quality standards, tools, materials, national

166

Writing a Summary

Using standard grammar, spelling, sentence structure, and punctuation, write a summary of the information in this chapter.

Identifying Ideas

1. sole proprietorship
2. zoning law
3. general partnership
4. limited partnership
5. corporations
6. board of directors
7. stock
8. corporate bond
9. vertical combination
10. cooperatives

Understanding Main Ideas

SECTION 1 *(pp. 145–49)*

1. Why is a sole proprietorship the easiest type of business to establish?

SECTION 2 *(pp. 150–52)*

2. How does forming a partnership solve many of the problems that are associated with sole proprietorships?

SECTION 3 *(pp. 153–58)*

3. Compare stocks and corporate bonds. How do corporations raise money through stocks and bonds?

4. Legally, how is a corporation treated as an individual?

SECTION 4 *(pp. 159–64)*

5. Explain how vertical combinations differ from horizontal combinations. Describe how Andrew Carnegie created a vertical combination.

6. How do nonprofit organizations differ from other forms of business organization?

Reviewing Themes

1. **Role of Government** Name the main government restrictions on sole proprietorships. Why might government impose such restrictions?

2. **Economic Institutions & Incentives** How is a corporation formed? What are the disadvantages of organizing a business this way?

3. **Economic Institutions & Incentives** What are the advantages of opening a franchise?

Thinking Critically

1. **Evaluating** Suppose you want to start a business selling pizza. Which type of organization do you feel would best suit your business needs? Explain your answer.

2. **Finding the Main Idea** If you purchase stock in a corporation, what is your role as an owner?

3. **Finding the Main Idea** Have you ever participated in—or benefited from—the activities of a nonprofit organization? Explain your answer.

Writing about Economics

Refer to the businesses you listed in your Economics Notebook at the beginning of this chapter. Classify each of these businesses as a sole proprietorship, partnership, corporation, franchise, cooperative, or nonprofit organization.

166 CHAPTER 7

Building Social Studies Skills

Interpreting the Graph

Study the graph, then answer the questions that follow.

SOLE PROPRIETORSHIPS, 1997 BY SIZE OF RECEIPTS

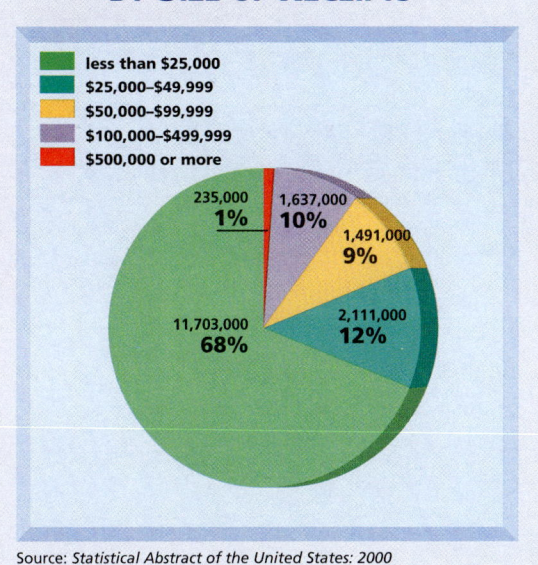

- less than $25,000
- $25,000–$49,999
- $50,000–$99,999
- $100,000–$499,999
- $500,000 or more

235,000 — 1%
1,637,000 — 10%
1,491,000 — 9%
2,111,000 — 12%
11,703,000 — 68%

Source: *Statistical Abstract of the United States: 2000*

1. In 1997 most sole proprietors earned
  a. less than $25,000.
  b. $25,000–$49,000.
  c. $50,000–$99,000.
  d. $500,000 or more.

2. What characteristics of sole proprietorships might contribute to the trend depicted in the pie graph?

Analyzing Primary Sources

Read the following excerpt from Lee Iacocca recalling his early day as president of Chrysler. Then answer the questions.

"It turned out that my worries were justified. I soon stumbled upon my first major revelation: Chrysler didn't really function like a company at all."

What I found at Chrysler were thirty-five vice-presidents, each with his own turf. There was no . . . system of meetings to get people talking to each other . . . Everybody worked independently. I took one look at that system and I almost threw up. That's when I knew I was in really deep trouble. . . ."

3. How might Iacocca's frame of reference have shaped his view of the Chrysler organization?

  a. As the new president of a troubled corporation, it might have been difficult for Iacocca to have a positive view of the organization.

  b. As a person who was immersed in the operation of Chrysler, Iacocca would not have a particular frame of reference.

  c. As a company newcomer, Iacocca was a neutral observer of the events at Chrysler.

  d. As a manager at Chrysler, Iacocca was sympathetic toward other managers.

4. Do you think Iacocca's opinion of Chrysler's organizational structure would have been different had Chrysler been prosperous? Explain.

Alternative Assessment

Building Your Portfolio

As a group, select a good or service that you wish to provide and organize a corporation in order to limit your liability. Assign the roles of president, vice president of product development, vice president of marketing, and treasurer. Prepare a pamphlet that explains your corporate structure, describes the good or service provided by your corporation, and identifies whether your corporation will sell common stock, preferred stock, or corporate bonds. You may wish to include charts or diagrams in your pamphlet.

internet connect

Internet Activity: go.hrw.com
KEYWORD: SM3 EC7

Access the Internet through the HRW Go site to conduct research on different types of nonprofit organizations. Then select one nonprofit organization and write a report to explain the organization's goals, its structure, and how it obtains its funding. Your report should incorporate charts and graphs that illustrate aspects of the organization's finances.

BUSINESS ORGANIZATIONS

---

advertising, training; lower start-up costs; higher initial market share

Thinking Critically

1. Answers will vary but should reflect an understanding of the characteristics of each type of business organization. **9B, 23A**

2. common stock—to provide capital in exchange for dividends and to vote on important company issues; preferred stock—to provide capital in exchange for guaranteed dividends **11C**

3. Answers should reflect an understanding of the characteristics of nonprofits.

Writing about Economics

Students should classify each of these businesses as a sole proprietorship, partnership, corporation, franchise, cooperative, or nonprofit organization and briefly explain why. **9A, 24D**

Building Social Studies Skills

1. a **23F, 23G**

2. Many sole proprietorships begin with very little capital and rely on the labor of a few individuals, thus contributing to the small size of the total receipts. **9A, 23A**

3. a **23E**

4. Students might say that Iacocca's view would have been more favorable if the firm had been doing well, or that he might have objected to the company's practices because they didn't foster teamwork. **23A, 23E**

CHAPTER RESOURCE MANAGER

CHAPTER 8 — LABOR AND UNIONS

	OBJECTIVES	PACING GUIDE	REPRODUCIBLE RESOURCES
SECTION 1 **THE U.S. LABOR FORCE** (pp. 169–76)	▶ What factors affect workers entering the labor force? ▶ How has the U.S. labor force changed over time? ▶ How does the U.S. government affect labor?	**Regular** 1.5 days **Block Scheduling** 1 day	**ELL** Spanish Study Guide 8.1 **ELL** English Study Guide 8.1 **SM** Consumer Economics: Activity 8 **SM** Mathematics for Economics: Activity 8
SECTION 2 **THE GROWTH OF LABOR UNIONS** (pp. 177–83)	▶ What is the history of the labor movement in the United States? ▶ How are labor unions organized? ▶ What are the main challenges facing unions today? ▶ How have government attitudes toward labor unions changed?	**Regular** 2 days **Block Scheduling** 1 day	**ELL** Spanish Study Guide 8.2 **ELL** English Study Guide 8.2
SECTION 3 **UNIONS AND MANAGEMENT** (pp. 184–90)	▶ What major issues are discussed in labor contract negotiations? ▶ How do unions and management reach a contract agreement? ▶ What negotiation tactics do unions and management use?	**Regular** 1.5 days **Block Scheduling** 1 day	**ELL** Spanish Study Guide 8.3 **ELL** English Study Guide 8.3 **PS** Reading 33: César Chávez on Nonviolent Protest **S** Simulations and Strategies for Teaching Economics: Activity 8 **E** Challenge and Enrichment: Activity 8

Chapter Resource Key

- **PS** Primary Sources
- **RS** Reading Support
- **E** Enrichment
- **S** Simulations
- **SM** Skills Mastery
- **A** Assessment
- **REV** Review
- **ELL** Reinforcement and English Language Learners
- Transparencies
- CD-ROM
- Video
- Videodisc
- Internet
- Holt Presentation Maker Using Microsoft® PowerPoint®
- TEKS and TAKS

TECHNOLOGY RESOURCES

- One-Stop Planner: Lesson 8.1
- Researcher Online
- Homework Practice Online
- CNN Presents Economics: Debating the Minimum Wage
- Transparencies 28, 29, and 30
- Global Skillbuilder CD-ROM

- One-Stop Planner: Lesson 8.2
- Researcher Online
- Homework Practice Online
- Transparency 31
- Global Skillbuilder CD-ROM

- One-Stop Planner: Lesson 8.3
- Researcher Online
- Homework Practice Online
- Global Skillbuilder CD-ROM

REINFORCEMENT, REVIEW, AND ASSESSMENT

REV Section 1 Review, p. 176
A Daily Quiz 8.1
★ TAKS Every Day!

REV Section 2 Review, p. 183
A Daily Quiz 8.2
★ TAKS Every Day!

REV Section 3 Review, p. 190
A Daily Quiz 8.3
★ TAKS Every Day!

Chapter Review and Assessment

SM Global Skillbuilder CD-ROM
HRW Go site
REV Reteaching Activity 8
REV Chapter 8 Review, pp. 192–93
A Chapter 8 Test Generator (on the One-Stop Planner)
A Chapter 8 Test
A Alternative Assessment Handbook

One-Stop Planner CD-ROM

It's easy to plan lessons, select resources, and print out materials for your students when you use the **Texas One-Stop Planner CD-ROM with Test Generator.**

internet connect

HRW ONLINE RESOURCES
Go To: go.hrw.com
Then type in a keyword.

TEACHER HOME PAGE
KEYWORD: **SM8 Teacher**

CHAPTER INTERNET ACTIVITIES
KEYWORD: **SM3 EC8**
Choose an activity to:
- research labor reform.
- create an advertisement for Lowell Mills.
- learn about César Chávez and the United Farm Workers.

CHAPTER ENRICHMENT LINKS
KEYWORD: **SM3 CH8**

HOLT RESEARCHER ONLINE
KEYWORD: **Holt Researcher**

ONLINE ASSESSMENT
Homework Practice
KEYWORD: **SM3 HP8**
TAKS Review
KEYWORD: **SM3 T8**
Rubrics
KEYWORD: **SS Rubrics**

CONTENT UPDATES
KEYWORD: **SS Content Updates**

HOLT PRESENTATION MAKER
KEYWORD: **SM3 PPT8**

ONLINE READING SUPPORT
KEYWORD: **SS Strategies**

CURRENT EVENTS
KEYWORD: **S3 Current Events**

TEXAS ONLINE RESOURCES
KEYWORD: **S3 TX**

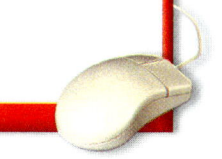

LESSON 8.1 THE U.S. LABOR FORCE

TEXTBOOK PAGES 169–76

HOLT PRESENTATION MAKER Access Illustrated LECTURE NOTES using Microsoft® PowerPoint® on the One-Stop Planner CD-ROM

OBJECTIVES

▶ Describe factors that affect workers entering the labor force.
▶ Explain how the U.S. labor force has changed over time.
▶ Analyze how the U.S. government affects labor.

MOTIVATE

Ask students to share their childhood dreams of careers or jobs. Then ask students: How many of you have held on to that dream and plan to pursue that particular job or career? How many of you have changed your career goals? What career or job do you currently plan to pursue? Why? What factors have led you to this career choice? As students respond, list on the chalkboard the factors that have led them to choose particular jobs or careers. ★23D

TEACH

Building a Vocabulary

Have students use spiral notebooks to create an Economics Dictionary to be used throughout the chapter. This dictionary might be used as an activity at the start of each new section or as a learning aid for sheltered English students or students having difficulty. List words that students will be expected to know for this section on the chalkboard. Have students use the information provided in the text or on the *Researcher CD-ROM* to list, define, and give an example of each term. ★24A, 24B

Classifying Ideas/Information

On the chalkboard, write the factors that affect workers entering the U.S. labor force: *wages, skills, working conditions, location, intrinsic rewards,* and *market trends*. Ask students to compare these factors to the class's responses in the Motivate activity. Did the class consider any of these factors? Discuss each factor, asking the class why each might be important. Next, have students rank the factors in order of importance. Poll the students on each factor to determine its order of importance for the class as a whole. ★23A

Comparing and Contrasting

Review with students some of the ways the U.S. labor force has changed during the past 200 years *(industrialization—primarily during the 1800s—caused the United States to shift from a labor-intensive economy to a capital-intensive economy; increasing numbers of women began to receive wages for work outside the home; and the labor force became better educated)*. You may wish to reproduce the graph below on the chalkboard. Use the graph to illustrate the dramatic transformation of the U.S. labor force since

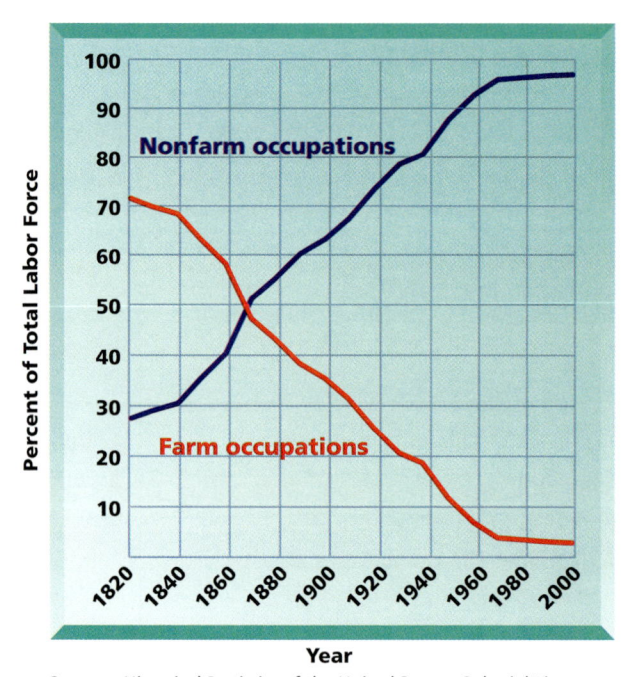

[Graph showing Percent of Total Labor Force vs Year from 1820 to 2000, with Nonfarm occupations rising from about 28 to nearly 100, and Farm occupations falling from about 72 to near 0]

Year

Sources: *Historical Statistics of the United States: Colonial Times to 1970, Part 1; Statistical Abstract of the United States, 1986 and 1996*

1820 and point out the year (~1870) when the nation changed from a primarily agricultural to primarily industrial economy. Then ask the following questions to demonstrate how changes in the labor force have affected students: What kinds of jobs did your grandparents have? What careers do your parents have? Can you detect ways the U.S. labor force has changed over time based on the careers and jobs of those in your own family? ★23A, 23F, 23G

Debating Ideas, Taking a Stand

Review with students the history of affirmative action in the United States. As part of this review, refer

167C

students to *Regents of the University of California* v. *Bakke* found in the Supreme Court Docket section of the *Researcher Online*. Divide students into two groups and assign each group one side of the affirmative action debate. Have each group discuss the issue and make a list of points that support its side of the argument. Then have each group try to predict the arguments from the other side and create counterarguments. Acting as facilitator, start a debate by asking one representative from each side to begin with an opening statement defending his or her group's position on affirmative action. Then continue the exchange with comments from other group members. Finally, ask each side to discuss the college-admissions process in light of affirmative action. ★24D

CLOSE

In a class discussion format, call on students to answer these questions: What factors affect workers entering the U.S. labor force? What is the importance of each of these factors? Which of these are most important to you? In what ways has the U.S. labor force changed over time? What are some ways the U.S. government affects labor? Why do some people oppose affirmative action programs?

OPTIONS

Intrapersonal Learners

Have interested students research career opportunities using the Careers section of the *Researcher Online* as a starting point. Students also should read advertisements for employment in the newspaper. Using the Internet and other available resources, students should write a report that summarizes market trends for careers and jobs that interest them. Encourage students to carefully evaluate their own strengths and weaknesses, skills, and the elements they find desirable in a career. High school counselors may have additional resources available such as job inventories and personality tests designed to guide students in their career choices. ★23A, 24D

Interpersonal Learners, Linguistic Learners

Refer students to the Global Exchange feature Maquiladoras on textbook page 174. Then have students choose several articles of their own clothing (not made in the United States) and attempt to trace their origins. What company produced the clothing? Where was the clothing made? Who are the laborers who produced the clothing? Are they primarily male or female? Under what conditions was the clothing produced? Have interested students research current international labor practices of American companies. Students should record their findings and share them with the class. As an extension, some students may wish to make their opinion on this issue known to legislators. These students should write persuasive letters to appropriate legislators. ★24C, 24D

Gifted Learners

Refer students to the minimum wage table in the Economic Indicators section of the *Researcher Online*. Then have students investigate minimum and/or average wages in other countries, as well as the standard of living and level of economic development in those countries, and compare it to similar information on the United States. Have students display their findings in the form of a chart or graph. ★22A, 23A, 23C

REVIEW

Have students complete the Section 1 Review on page 176. Use the answers in the Annotated Teacher's Edition to assess student mastery of this section.

ASSESS

To assess student mastery of this section, have students complete Daily Quiz 8.1 in *Daily Quizzes with Answer Key*. For additional assessment options, see *Alternative Assessment Handbook* on the *One-Stop Planner CD-ROM*.

ADDITIONAL RESOURCES

Brody, David. *In Labor's Cause: Main Themes on the History of the American Worker*. 1995. Oxford University Press.

Walden, Nancy Elder. *Gender Bias as Related to Women in the Workplace*. 2000. Xilibris Corporation.

LESSON 8.2 THE GROWTH OF LABOR UNIONS

TEXTBOOK PAGES 177–83

HOLT PRESENTATION MAKER
Access Illustrated LECTURE NOTES using Microsoft® PowerPoint® on the One-Stop Planner CD-ROM

OBJECTIVES

▸ Trace the history of the labor movement in the United States. ⭐19B
▸ Describe how labor unions are organized.
▸ Identify the main challenges facing unions today.
▸ Examine how government attitudes toward labor unions have changed.

MOTIVATE

Ask students to describe their ideal working environment. Have the class brainstorm a list of issues that would be important for creating such a workplace and write these issues on the chalkboard. Then ask students what conditions they would be unwilling to tolerate at their workplace (*examples might include unreasonably low wages, hazardous conditions that jeopardize health and safety, and unreasonably long work hours*) and write these on the chalkboard. Ask students who have worked in a job to share their experiences about the positive and negative aspects of their working environment. Then tell students that in this section they will be reading about workers' efforts to ensure safe, fair, and productive working conditions. ⭐23A, 24B

TEACH

Building a Vocabulary

List the important terms for this section on the chalkboard and tell students to add them to their Economics Dictionary. Tell students to use the information provided in the text or on the *Researcher CD-ROM* to list, define, and find an example of each term. ⭐24A

Demonstrating Understanding

Discuss the development of the labor movement in the United States. Call on volunteers to describe working conditions in the late 1800s. Ask students the following questions:
▸ Why did these conditions exist?
▸ What was the effect of industrialization on workers?
▸ What was the effect of industrialization on their working environment and the workplace?
▸ In general, how do these conditions compare with today's workplace? Consider factors such as wages, safety, child labor, and number of working hours per week.
▸ How did workers respond to these conditions?
▸ What were the first major U.S. labor unions? ⭐19B, 23A

Organizing Information

Explain the organization of labor unions by drawing an organizational chart on the chalkboard or on a transparency. On the left-hand side of the chalkboard draw a circle around the term *local unions* and describe the make-up of these unions (*people working for a particular company or in a particular field, such as carpentry*). Directly above *local unions* write the term *national unions* (*explain that national unions are made up of chapters of local unions, and generally have more political and economic power*). Draw a circle around both *national* and *local* to illustrate their relationship (*i.e., local unions are a subset of national unions*). Write the term *AFL–CIO* in the circle and explain that this is one of the most well-known national unions. On the right-hand side of the chalkboard write the term *independent unions* and explain that this term means that these unions are not members of the AFL–CIO. Write the terms *local* and *national* under *independent* and explain that both local and national unions can be independent. Circle all three terms (*local, national,* and *independent*) to illustrate their relationship with each other and their separation from AFL–CIO unions. ⭐23B, 23C, 24C

Analyzing Information, Recognizing Point of View

On the chalkboard, write the three main reasons for the decline of labor unions in the United States today: *employer opposition, changes in employment,* and *negative public opinion.* Divide students into three groups, one for each of the challenges facing unions today. Ask groups to imagine they are leaders in a labor union charged with tackling a particular challenge facing unions. First, tell students to review their group's challenge (as outlined in the textbook). Next, tell groups to brainstorm ways unions could combat opposition. Finally, have students write a formal strategy outlining steps they would take to improve labor unions in the United States. Have a representative from each group share the strategy with the class. ⭐2B, 24D, 25A

167E

Evaluating Information

Using Transparency 31—Major Labor Legislation, discuss changing government attitudes toward labor unions. Review each piece of legislation, asking students questions such as:

- What was the motivation for this law?
- How does this legislation affect workers today?
- Do you personally experience the impact of this law? If so, is the impact positive or negative?

Finally, ask students to identify periods in U.S. history when government has had a positive relationship with labor unions and to give examples of instances when the relationship has been negative. ★15A, 23A

CLOSE

Call on student volunteers to answer these questions: What working conditions led to the development of the labor movement? How are labor unions structured? What are the major challenges facing labor unions today? What periods in U.S. history were marked by a favorable attitude of government toward labor unions? What periods were marked by an unfavorable attitude? ★19B, 23A

OPTIONS

Sheltered English Students, Visual-Spatial Learners

Pair students who are acquiring English with fluent English speakers. Have pairs write a paragraph summarizing the working conditions that led to the rise of the labor movement. Then have pairs create a poster or editorial cartoon that illustrates the working conditions that led to the rise of the labor movement in the 1800s. ★19B, 23A

Interpersonal Learners

Refer students to the *Union Summer* Economics in Action feature on textbook page 181, which profiles young union activists. Ask students to identify other such union activists, using resources including the library and the Internet. Encourage students to interview young people involved in organized labor if possible. Students could ask: Why did you become involved in organized labor? What are your goals as a young union member/organizer? What do you think the goals of organized labor should be in our society? How do those goals relate to the goals historically associated with unions? After students have completed their research, have them present their findings to the class. ★23E, 24D

Gifted Learners, Linguistic Learners

Have students read Upton Sinclair's novel *The Jungle*. Then instruct them to do library and Internet research to supplement their reading of the book. Have students address one of the following topics or one of their own choosing: labor conditions in the early 1900s, the plight of immigrant workers, sanitation in the food industry, or the enactment of pure food laws. Instruct students to prepare brief reports documenting their research and relating it directly to material in *The Jungle*. You might suggest that students present their reports from the point of view of someone from the novel's time period—for example, a legislator, a food industry worker, or a concerned citizen writing a letter to the editor. If several students are working on this project, bring them together to have a group discussion about the book. Ask volunteers to present their reports to the class. ★15A, 23C, 23D, 24B, 24D

REVIEW

Have students complete the Section 2 Review on page 183. Use the answers in the Annotated Teacher's Edition to assess student mastery of this section.

ASSESS

To assess student mastery of this section, have students complete Daily Quiz 8.2 in *Daily Quizzes with Answer Key*. For additional assessment options, see *Alternative Assessment Handbook* on the *One-Stop Planner CD-ROM*.

ADDITIONAL RESOURCES

Craver, Charles. *Can Unions Survive? The Rejuvenation of the American Labor Movement.* 1995. New York University Press.

Green, Max. *Epitaph for American Labor: How Union Leaders Lost Touch with America.* 1996. AEI Press.

LESSON 8.3 UNIONS AND MANAGEMENT

TEXTBOOK PAGES 184–90

HOLT PRESENTATION MAKER
Access Illustrated LECTURE NOTES using Microsoft® PowerPoint® on the One-Stop Planner CD-ROM

OBJECTIVES

- List the major issues that are discussed in labor contract negotiations.
- Explain how unions and management reach a contract agreement.
- Identify the negotiation tactics unions and management use.

MOTIVATE

As students walk into the room, hand them a note card with either an *L* or an *M* written on one side. Then instruct them to sit at the desks on the *L* or *M* side of the room. (You will need to divide the desks and label them accordingly ahead of time). After students are seated, announce that today all students in the class have gone to work for the nation's largest package delivery service. Tell students that their company employs 300,000 workers in the United States, 185,000 of whom are union members represented by the Teamsters union (including drivers, sorters, and package handlers). Tell students that the *L*s are labor union members, and the *M*s are members of management. Finally, tell students that although labor and management have been meeting on a regular basis, they are in conflict over a number of issues in their new contract, and ask them to brainstorm what these issues might be. Record student responses on the chalkboard or on a transparency that can be referred to later. Tell students that they should keep these issues in mind as they read this section. ★23A

TEACH

Building a Vocabulary

List the important terms for this section on the chalkboard and tell students to add them to their Economics Dictionary. Tell students to use the information provided in the text or on the *Researcher CD-ROM* to list, define, and find an example of each term. ★24A

Applying a Model

Review with students the five major issues usually discussed during negotiations between labor and management *(wages and fringe benefits, working conditions and hours, job security, union security,* and *grievance procedures)*. Ask students to look at the list they brainstormed during the Motivate activity and classify those responses according to the five major issues. Next, inform students that in their situation labor and management stand apart on a number of issues. The union members want the company to create more full-time jobs for its part-time workers, eliminate the use of outside contractors, increase wages, and improve pension benefits and job safety. In regards to job safety, the union is concerned that the company has increased weight limits on packages that employees must lift, thereby risking injury. Instruct the labor union group to meet and create a list of points they want to discuss about each of these issues so that they will be ready to articulate their concerns at the bargaining table with management. Instruct the management group to take these concerns into consideration and to be ready to propose a counter offer at the bargaining table. ★2A, 2B, 23A, 23D

Analyzing Ideas

Tell students that now that they are familiar with some of the issues, it is time to negotiate a new contract. Remind students that when negotiating a new contract, union leaders speak for all the members they represent. When representatives of union and management meet, the process is called *collective bargaining*. Ask the two groups to send three representatives each to the bargaining table set up in the middle of the classroom. Notify other students that they may use their note cards to pass notes to their representatives at any point during the talks. Ask union representatives to articulate their issues of concern and have management representatives respond. Periodically, allow each group of representatives to go back and meet with all the other members of the group. Tell the groups their goal is to come to an agreement through the process of collective bargaining. ★23A, 24A

Making Decisions

Tell students that each group will have to make decisions about which issues it will compromise on, and which are non-negotiable. Ask each group to make a list of negotiable and non-negotiable items. Then have representatives come back to the table with these lists and continue to try to come to an agreement. Make sure they understand the other means of reconciliation available to them if the bargaining process breaks down:

167G

mediation and arbitration. If necessary, take on the role of mediator.

If the class cannot come to an agreement on a contract, inform them of their remaining options, including: picketing, boycotting, coordinated campaigning, replacement workers, lockouts, and injunctions. If the class does come to an agreement before any of these methods would be used, explain each tactic and ask the groups what methods they would choose to use and why. ★24A, 25B

CLOSE

Ask students to answer these questions: What were the major issues discussed in your simulation? How do those compare with issues in real labor-management conflicts? What are some ways unions and management reach a contract? What seem to be the most effective tactics used by unions and management? Why? ★23A

OPTIONS

Gifted Learners

Have interested students research a recent or current strike using the newspaper, the Internet, and appropriate journals. Students should answer key questions and present their findings to the class:
- Why did laborers resort to striking?
- Did the federal government intervene? Why or why not?
- How did management respond to the strike?
- What effect did the strike have on the U.S. economy?
- How was the situation finally resolved? ★24D, 25A

Body-Kinesthetic Learners

Have interested students play the role of a labor organizer and write a a speech designed to persuade workers to join their labor union. Using the *Researcher Online*, library, and the Internet, students should research the union they have chosen and read speeches by union organizers such as César Chávez to make their speeches as realistic as possible. Have students "perform" their speeches for the class. ★24B, 24D

Linguistic Learners

Ask students: Can you think of workers in any occupation who should be prohibited by law from striking? *(police officers? teachers? firefighters? doctors?)* Have students write a persuasive essay explaining their point of view, supported by specific evidence for their opinion. Students should research the history of striking workers to support their arguments. ★23D, 24D

REVIEW

Have students complete the Section 3 Review on page 190. Use the answers in the Annotated Teacher's Edition to assess student mastery of this section.

ASSESS

To assess student mastery of this section, have students complete Daily Quiz 8.3 in *Daily Quizzes with Answer Key*. For additional assessment options, see *Alternative Assessment Handbook* on the *One-Stop Planner CD-ROM*.

RETEACH

For students having difficulty with the lessons, have them complete Reteaching Activity 8. This activity is located in *Reteaching Activities with Answer Key*.

ADDITIONAL RESOURCES

Colman, Penny. *Strike: The Bitter Struggle of American Workers from Colonial Times to the Present.* 1995. Millbrook Press.

Gifford, Courtney D. *Directory of U.S. Labor Organizations.* 1997. BNA Books.

Meltzer, Milton. *Bread and Roses: The Struggle of American Labor, 1865–1915.* 1991. Facts on File.

CHAPTER 8

TOPICS INCLUDE

- changes in the labor force over time
- switch from labor-intensive to capital-intensive economy
- women in the labor force
- increasing educational level of the labor force
- antidiscrimination laws
- minimum-wage laws
- history of the labor movement
- history of the AFL–CIO
- union organization
- recent decline in labor-union membership
- major labor legislation
- union strike tactics and management responses

ECONOMICS NOTEBOOK

The Economics Notebook is a journal activity that encourages students to consider basic concepts of economics that relate to their lives. A follow-up notebook activity appears on page 192.

WHY IT MATTERS TODAY

To find additional lesson plans dealing with the importance of organized labor to contemporary workers, visit CNNfyi.com or have students complete the ECONOMICS IN THE NEWS activity on page 191.

CNNfyi.com

CHAPTER 8

LABOR AND UNIONS

What kind of job would you like to have? Perhaps you would like to be an accountant or a television reporter, an artist or a zoologist. When you choose a career, you decide how you will use one of the factors of production—human resources.

The term resources is generally used to describe tools, raw materials, or money. In an economic sense, however, labor is a valuable resource—one that cannot be separated from the people who provide it. In this chapter you will learn about the labor force in the United States and the choices you will face when you enter it.

ECONOMICS NOTEBOOK

In your Economics Notebook, list the kinds of labor you perform during the course of one week. Consider the work you do as a student, as a member of a household, and—if you have an after-school job—as an employee.

WHY IT MATTERS TODAY

Organized unions are important for the protection of the resources provided by labor. At the end of this chapter visit CNNfyi.com to learn more about the importance of organized labor.

168

SECTION 1
THE U.S. LABOR FORCE

READ TO DISCOVER
1. What factors affect workers entering the labor force?
2. How has the U.S. labor force changed over time?
3. How does the U.S. government affect labor?

ECONOMICS DICTIONARY
- labor force
- wage
- intrinsic reward
- derived demand
- industrialization
- capital-intensive
- labor-intensive
- affirmative action
- quota

A re you part of the U.S. labor force? The **labor force** includes all people who are at least 16 years old and are working or actively looking for work. In the United States more than 130 million people—two thirds of all people 16 years of age or older—are members of the civilian labor force. The civilian labor force makes up about 98 percent of all people in the United States who are working or looking for work. The remainder are members of the armed forces or are employed by the military.

How do people decide what kinds of jobs they want in the labor force? For many people, the most important factor in choosing an occupation is the salary or **wage**—the hourly, weekly, monthly, or yearly pay that a worker receives in exchange for his or her labor.

Entering the Labor Force

Suppose that Sally Cromwell is looking for a job. In her search she considers:

- wages
- skills
- working conditions
- location
- intrinsic rewards
- market trends

Wages First, Sally should consider what kinds of jobs are in demand and the supply of different kinds of workers. Why is this information important? Just as supply and demand affect the prices of other resources, they also affect the price of labor, or workers' wages.

LABOR FORCE, 1999

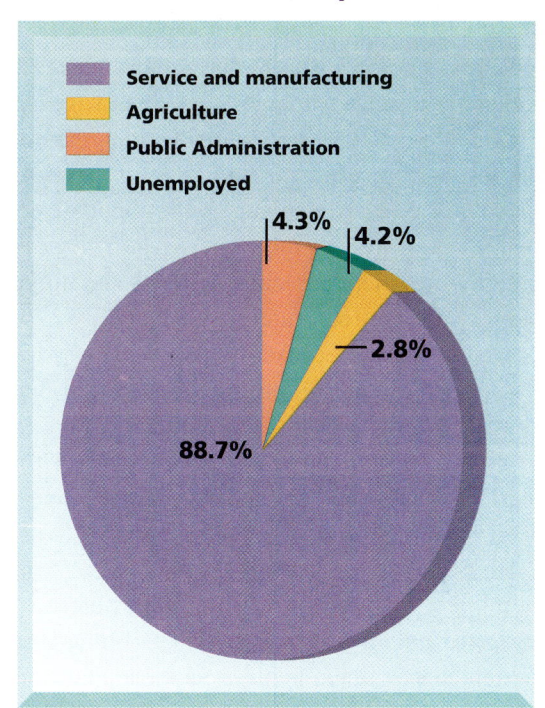

- Service and manufacturing: 88.7%
- Agriculture: 2.8%
- Public Administration: 4.3%
- Unemployed: 4.2%

Source: U.S. Census Bureau, Statistical Abstract of the United States: 2000

FIGURE 8.1 The labor force is made up of U.S. residents who are working or looking for work. **Which employment category provides jobs for the largest percentage of workers?**

LABOR AND UNIONS 169

Sidebar

Transparency
An overhead transparency of Figure 8.2 is available in *Transparency Resources*. See Transparency 28: Equilibrium Wage.

Caption Answer
because the supply of brain surgeons is lower and the demand higher than for waiters ⭐ 23A, 23F, 23G

Cultural Perspectives

Are American laborers overworked? A 1997 nationwide *Money* magazine survey of 500 U.S. workers found that respondents value their free time more than making additional money. When asked if they would prefer time off or extra money for working overtime, 64 percent chose the former. Almost half of those surveyed (49 percent) said they would rather receive a bonus of an extra week off than of an extra week's salary. And when asked what they would do with an extra hour a day away from work, the number one answer respondents gave was "sleep."

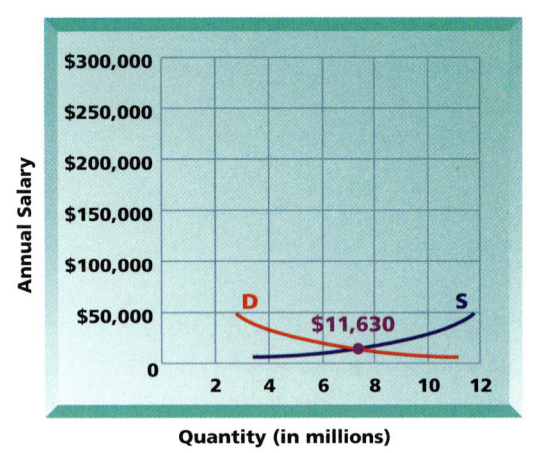

Equilibrium Wage

WAITERS — equilibrium at $11,630

BRAIN SURGEONS — equilibrium at $262,700

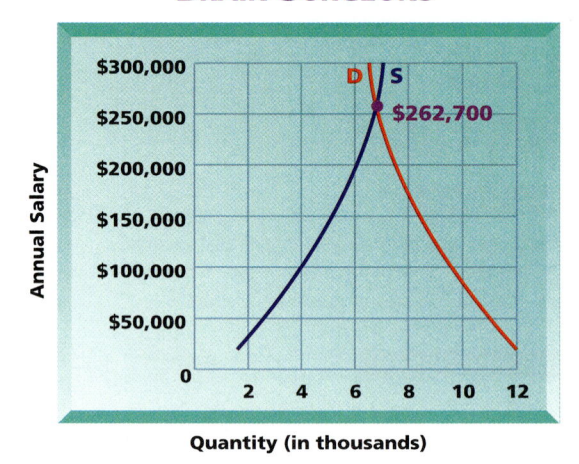

Source: *Statistical Abstract of the United States: 1996*

FIGURE 8.2 The equilibrium wage is established when the quantity of workers supplied and the quantity of workers demanded is the same at a particular salary. **Why is the equilibrium wage for brain surgeons so much higher than that for waiters?** ⭐TEKS

When an occupation has many potential workers but few available jobs, the wage rate tends to be low. For example, imagine that Charles Bernini wants to find a job as an admissions counselor for a university. Many other people are interested in this type of job, however, and although there are many colleges and universities in the United States, each has only a few admissions jobs. Because so many people (a high quantity supplied) are interested in a small number of jobs (a low quantity demanded), there is a surplus of workers and the wages are lower than Charles—and other applicants—might hope to receive.

High wages, on the other hand, occur when the number of workers who are interested in—or are qualified for—an occupation is limited, and the demand for them is high. Suppose that housing construction increases in a city and the current number of workers is insufficient to complete the construction projects. Additional workers cannot appear instantly, so a shortage of workers results. If Joe Wilson, a general contractor for house-building projects, wants to ensure that he will have enough workers to complete his projects on time, he must offer a higher wage than that offered by other contractors.

So how do supply and demand affect what occupation Sally should choose? She is more likely to find a good-paying job in an occupation with a high demand for—and a low supply of—workers. This does not mean, however, that she should base her decision solely on this consideration. Sally should also consider her skills.

Skills Think about your skills as a worker. Education, experience, and abilities all affect your skills and help determine what jobs you are—and are not—eligible to hold. Do you have the skills needed to be a brain surgeon, an airline pilot, or a chef? You probably have yet to develop all the skills needed for these jobs, and employers likely would not hire you for these positions.

Because businesses want to hire only qualified people, skill level can limit the supply of workers (see Figure 8.2). For example, relatively few people attain the skills required to be a professional baseball player or an intensive care nurse. The more skills a particular job requires, the fewer qualified people there are who can

CHAPTER 8

perform the job. As you know, this limited supply of labor means that jobs requiring high skill levels usually offer higher wages. Conversely, the fewer skills a job requires, the greater number of qualified people there are for the position. Because of this large supply of labor, low-skilled occupations usually offer lower wages.

You, Sally, and other workers thus face the same skill-related questions. Do you want to invest a great deal of time, money, and effort in acquiring the skills needed for a high-paying job? Or are there other considerations you might take into account when entering the labor force?

Working Conditions As Sally continues her job search, what might she want to know about conditions in the workplace? In most U.S. workplaces, federal and state laws carefully regulate health and safety concerns such as noise levels and cleanliness. Some high-risk occupations, however, are simply more dangerous to workers. Skyscraper construction, fire fighting, and coal mining are examples of hazardous occupations. To compensate for these dangers and to encourage qualified workers to apply, hazardous occupations sometimes pay higher wages than those jobs with low risks to life and limb.

Location In addition to workplace conditions, Sally should consider the locations of the jobs that interest her. Does she want to move to a new area, or would she rather continue to live where she does now? Sometimes employers offer higher wages to encourage workers to move to a different area. In some cases, jobs in distant or remote locations pay higher wages to help make up for the isolation. For example, engineers and other specialists who are recruited to work in other nations may receive high salaries. Workers performing the same jobs in more desirable locations generally receive lower wages.

Intrinsic Rewards Although Sally certainly wants to earn a good salary, she might seek other types of job satisfaction. **Intrinsic rewards** are nonmonetary reasons for working at a particular job. They include a worker's pride and satisfaction in the quality of work done and the status, prestige, or respect that accompanies a job.

People who value a particular intrinsic reward often are willing to accept lower salaries than they might receive in another job that calls for comparable levels of skill and training. Consider the case of Patrick Sloan, who is graduating from college with a degree in English. He has the skills to go to law school or to earn a teaching certificate. He knows that he may be able to earn a higher salary as a lawyer than as a teacher. Patrick, however, wants to increase people's appreciation for literature. He decides to pursue a teaching career because he believes that the intrinsic rewards of teaching are greater than the possible financial rewards of a legal career.

Market Trends Sally also should investigate trends in the careers that interest her. What industries are expanding or contracting? Industries expand to meet increasing needs and wants of consumers, leading to an increase in the need for workers. In other words, consumers' demand for a particular good creates a demand for the labor—and other resources—needed to produce that good. This process is called **derived demand**, because the demand for workers and other resources is derived, or follows, from the consumers' demand for the good.

Derived demand can cause great changes in employment patterns as producers try to meet the

INCOME DISTRIBUTION *Jobs in remote locations such as Alaska may pay relatively high wages to make up for the isolation.*

Global Connections

In increasing numbers, college graduates are looking abroad to find jobs. This trend coincides with the growing global marketplace. Many American companies now have strong presences overseas. Many college graduates work for American companies abroad. Whereas students in the past most often looked to Western Europe for jobs abroad, graduates now more often accept jobs in the Pacific Rim, Latin America, and Eastern Europe, including the countries of the former Soviet Union. What is drawing graduates abroad? Students cite a lack of high-paying, interesting, and challenging jobs at home and the increased chance of finding a first job that provides high levels of recognition and responsibility. ■

Enhancing the Lesson

For a list of the industries expected to expand and contract the most by 2008, see Figure 11.2: Fastest-Growing Occupations and Fastest Declining Industries, 1998–2008, on page 255.

Caption Answer

Machines for sewing and weaving made it easier to produce large quantities of clothing and other textiles. 23A, 26D

Across the Curriculum

HISTORY In the early 1800s, some New England textile factory owners initially recruited whole families to work in the mills. In addition, they provided each family with housing. As the need for workers increased, however, it became impractical to house entire families. To keep expenses down, textile mill owners in Lowell, Massachusetts, decided to recruit young, single women instead of families. These women became known as Lowell girls. They lived in company-owned boardinghouses, where housekeepers strictly enforced curfews, rules of conduct, and church attendance. Young women, eager to earn money, flocked to the mills. By the early 1850s, some 60,000 women and girls worked in New England textile mills.

ECONOMIC INSTITUTIONS & INCENTIVES *Women began working in New England textile mills in the early 1800s.* **What technological advances in the picture changed the way clothing was manufactured?** TEKS

new needs and wants of consumers. For example, in the early 1900s consumer demand shifted from the horse and carriage to the automobile. As a result, the demand for industrial workers in automobile plants increased, while the demand for skilled carriage makers declined.

Changes in the Labor Force

Now you know what people consider before entering the labor force, but who exactly is looking for jobs? The people who make up the labor force—and the jobs that they hold—are very different today from laborers and jobs in the past. Why is this so?

Capital-Intensive Economy For much of American history, most people in the United States earned their living from agriculture. The introduction of new technologies during the late 1700s and early 1800s, however, encouraged **industrialization**—the process of mechanizing all major forms of production.

Widespread industrialization first occurred in Great Britain in the mid-1700s, during a period that became known as the Industrial Revolution. Soon other nations—including the United States—followed Britain's lead.

Industrialization created new, factory-based jobs, which contributed to an economic shift away from agriculture. This shift led not only to a vast increase in the number and kinds of goods and services available but also to a greater reliance on the capital goods needed in factory production. Industrialization thus caused the U.S. economy to become **capital-intensive**, or dependent on machines to produce goods. In contrast, agricultural economies are **labor-intensive**, producing goods primarily through animal and human power.

How did the shift to an industrialized, capital-intensive economy change the makeup of the U.S. labor force? In the late 1700s about 80 percent of the labor force was employed in farm labor. By 1850, farmworkers made up only 63 percent of the labor force, and by 1900 they made up only 37 percent. Today less than 3 percent of the U.S. labor force works in agriculture. In contrast, almost 90 percent of workers hold service and manufacturing jobs.

Women in the Labor Force Industrialization also increased the number of females who received wages for their labor. Women often worked on family farms without being paid a separate income. In the early 1800s, however, textile factories in New England began to employ women. By 1900, women working for wages outside the home made up about 18 percent of the labor force.

The number of females in the labor force increased again during World War I, when many women took jobs in defense plants to replace men who had entered the military. In fact, during the war some 1.5 million American women worked as automobile mechanics, truck drivers, bricklayers, metalworkers, railroad engineers, and other industrial laborers.

Although many of these women stopped working outside their homes when the war ended, women again entered the labor force in large numbers during World War II. From 1940 to 1944, more than 4 million women held jobs in workplaces such as airplane factories, newspaper offices, and shipyards. The millions of women who joined the labor force in these times of national emergency helped establish a pattern for working outside the home and contributed to a change in public attitudes toward women in the workplace.

The number of women in the labor force continues to increase. Today six out of every ten women in the United States are members of the labor force, compared to three out of every four men. Smaller family size and an increase in affordable day care have enabled many women to pursue careers outside the home. In addition, improved access to educational facilities allows women to gain the same level of training as men, and therefore to compete for jobs traditionally held by men. Legislation protecting equal access to jobs also has opened up employment opportunities for women.

Higher Education Levels As you know, increased education has helped improve employment opportunities for women. These improvements have not been limited to women, however. The U.S. labor force in general has become better educated over the years.

Many states did not have public school systems until the early 1900s, so education in some areas was largely limited to the wealthy. The development of free public schools and the passage of mandatory-attendance laws, however, caused education levels to rise dramatically throughout the 1900s.

For example, in 1960 about 41.1 percent of people over the age of 25 had completed high school. By 1995 this number had nearly doubled, with almost 82 percent completing high school. Similarly, the number of U.S. residents completing at least four years of college increased, from 7.7 percent to 23 percent.

How do workers benefit from greater access to education? A direct relationship exists between a worker's level of education and his or her income. If you stay in school for at least 16 years—earning a college degree—you probably will be able to get a better job and earn a higher salary than workers with less education. How much more could you earn? In 1998 the average salary for a college graduate in the workforce was $45,584 per year, while the average salary for a person with a master's degree was $53,459. In contrast, the average salary for a high school graduate without any further education was $28,166 per year, and the average high school dropout earned only $20,602. (See Figure 8.3.)

Government and Workers

You read earlier that governments passed attendance laws so that more workers would get an education. This is one example of how the government can affect the labor force. In fact, over time the U.S. government has become more

EDUCATION AND SALARY, 1998

HIGHEST EDUCATION LEVEL ATTAINED	AVERAGE YEARLY INCOME
Professional degree	
Doctoral degree	
Master's degree	
Bachelor's degree	
Associate's degree	
Some college, no degree	
High school graduate	
Some high school, no degree	
No high school	

= $10,000

Source: National Center for Educational Statistics

FIGURE 8.3 Higher levels of education generally increase the potential for higher wages. **How does the average yearly income of a person with a professional degree compare to that of a person who did not attend high school?**

Transparency
An overhead transparency of Figure 8.3 is available in *Transparency Resources*. See Transparency 29: Education and Salary, 1998.

Caption Answer
It is more than five times as high. 23E, 23G

internet connect
TOPIC: Lowell Mill Girls
GO TO: go.hrw.com
KEYWORD: SM3 EC8

Have students access the Internet through the HRW Go site to conduct research on the women who worked in the Lowell Mills. Then have students create a job advertisement for the mill owners that attempts to lure women from the farms into the mills. Finally, have students create a second advertisement for a woman who used to work in the mills but now runs a cooperative farm and is trying to draw mill workers to the country. 24D

Across the Curriculum

GOVERNMENT When World War II ended, 9 million service personnel returned home to the United States. Worried that the economy would not be able to absorb these new workers, Congress passed two acts. The Servicemen's Readjustment Act of 1944, more commonly known as the GI Bill, gave veterans loans and financial aid to attend college, start businesses, and buy houses or land. The Employment Act of 1946 committed the federal government to promoting maximum employment and production. To assist lawmakers in this effort, the act also created the Council of Economic Advisers to provide the government with economic information and guidance. These acts were the first of many laws that the federal government has passed to boost employment in the United States. ∎

Global Connections

Maquiladora laborers in Guatemala, with grassroots help from supporters in the United States, persuaded Philips-Van Heusen, a shirt manufacturer, to negotiate a union labor contract in 1997. The event marked the first time that workers at a Guatemalan maquiladora had a labor contract. ∎

Global Exchange

Maquiladoras

Business owners often find that labor is one of their highest costs. To remain competitive in the global market, businesses always are searching for ways to pay less for labor.

For this reason, many U.S. companies have built factories called maquiladoras (mah-kee-lah-DOHR-ahs) on the Mexican side of the 2,000-mile border between the United States and Mexico. These factories save money by employing Mexicans, who typically are paid less than workers in the United States. Maquiladoras began as a result of a 1965 agreement between the United States and Mexico that was designed to generate jobs for Mexicans while allowing U.S. companies access to low-cost labor.

The passage of the North American Free Trade Agreement (NAFTA) among the United States, Mexico, and Canada in 1993 caused a surge in the number of maquiladoras. For a product to qualify for NAFTA's lower tariff rates, a certain percentage of its parts must come from a NAFTA country. Of the three countries involved, Mexico usually has the lowest labor costs, making it a prime location for factories.

Although maquiladoras added close to 200,000 jobs in the border region in 1995 and 1996, not all the effects have been positive. In 1996, for example, the population of the border town Tijuana grew at twice the pace of population growth for Mexico as a whole. A lack of adequate housing has forced many people in Tijuana and other border towns to live in unsafe shelters. In addition, roads and bridges are overburdened, and water and energy supplies are running low.

---

involved in the economy and other issues affecting the labor force. Specifically, since the 1960s the federal government passed several antidiscrimination and minimum-wage laws to protect the rights of individual workers. During the 1900s the government also passed legislation concerning labor unions, which you will learn about in Section 2.

Antidiscrimination Laws During the 1960s Congress passed a series of laws aimed at protecting workers from discrimination in hiring, promotion, and firing. For example, the Equal Pay Act of 1963 requires that employers pay the same wages to male and female workers who perform the same job. The Civil Rights Act of 1964 protects workers from employer discrimination based on race, sex, religion, or national origin. The act also established the Equal Employment Opportunity Commission (EEOC). The main task of the EEOC is to monitor and enforce the act's provisions.

In addition, in 1965 President Lyndon Johnson began pursuing a policy of **affirmative action**, or making up for patterns of discrimination against women, members of minority groups, and others who were traditionally disadvantaged in the workplace. Programs were aimed at eliminating racial and gender bias in the employment practices of firms doing business with the federal government. The Department of Labor soon established a practice of relying on what amounted to **quotas**, or numerical goals, for hiring and promoting women and minorities.

Affirmative action has stirred up controversy between employees and employers. Supporters have argued that affirmative action is the only effective method of ending workplace discrimination. Opponents counter that affirmative action is itself a form of discrimination because it offers special treatment to one group of citizens at the expense of another.

The Supreme Court has acted to make sure that affirmative action does not discriminate against people who are not members of minority groups. In the case *Regents of the University of California* v. *Bakke* (1978), the Court ruled that a

ECONOMIC INSTITUTIONS & INCENTIVES *President Lyndon Johnson signs civil rights legislation.* **What was the name given to Johnson's antidiscrimination policy?**

California medical school could not reserve a certain number of seats for minority students in an incoming class. According to the Court's ruling, that quota violated the Civil Rights Act of 1964 because it made race the sole factor in admissions. The Supreme Court did maintain, however, that race could be one of several factors used to determine admissions.

A shift away from quotas has continued. In *Hopwood* v. *University of Texas* (1996), a federal appeals court ruled that the University of Texas law school could not use race alone as a factor in admissions. Later that year, California voters approved a state constitutional amendment forbidding state agencies—including universities—to consider race or gender in admissions, hiring, promotions, and firing. A federal judge, however, prevented the amendment from going into effect until a federal court could determine whether it violated the U.S. Constitution. In 1997 a federal appeals court ruled that the amendment was constitutional.

CASE STUDY

Equal Pay for Equal Work

INCOME DISTRIBUTION Legally, men and women who perform the same or similar jobs must be paid the same amount of money. But even today, women are often paid less than men. Why?

Historically, men and women have held different jobs. Some occupations—including nursing, secretarial work, and child care—traditionally have been dominated by women. Similarly, men have dominated the fields of law, construction, and engineering. Different jobs pay different wages, and in the past "women's jobs" generally paid less than "men's jobs."

To guarantee women fair wages, some people support the concept of comparable worth, which calls for analyzing the requirements for various jobs in order to set similar wages for jobs requiring similar skill levels. Supporters of comparable worth argue that assigning wages based on job knowledge, problem solving, accountability, and working conditions would remove the traditional wage bias.

Opponents of comparable worth, on the other hand, argue that the laws of supply and demand already are impartial. If women earn less money than men, they say, it is because wages in so-called women's jobs have been driven down by a surplus of available workers. Rating jobs, they argue, thus would interfere with supply and demand and discourage free enterprise.

Minimum-Wage Laws In addition to antidiscrimination laws, the government has passed legislation to ensure that workers are paid a basic level of income. One of the most important pieces of legislation to do this established a national minimum wage, or the lowest hourly wage an employer legally can pay a worker for a job.

The first minimum wage was set at 40 cents per hour by the 1938 Fair Labor Standards Act. This wage applied only to businesses engaged in interstate commerce—trade that crosses state boundaries. Furthermore, the law did not apply to farm laborers, domestic servants, and some other groups.

Over time the Fair Labor Standards Act was extended to a wider range of jobs. For example, the Supreme Court ruled in *Garcia* v. *San Antonio Metropolitan Transit Authority* (1985) that

---

Caption Answer
affirmative action

Across the Curriculum

GOVERNMENT About 45 years before the *Hopwood* case, the University of Texas law school was embroiled in another case involving race and admissions. Herman Sweatt, an African American postal worker from Houston, Texas, applied to the University of Texas law school for the 1946 term. The university rejected his application solely because he was African American, however. In keeping with the Equal Protection Clause of the Fourteenth Amendment, the state of Texas opened a law school for African Americans. Sweatt, however, refused to attend it, claiming that it did not provide education, facilities, staff, or prestige equal to those at the University of Texas law school. In 1950 the U.S. Supreme Court agreed with Sweatt and ordered the University of Texas law school to admit him. Sweatt's victory helped lay the foundation for the 1954 Supreme Court case *Brown* v. *Board of Education*, which ruled that racially segregated educational facilities were unequal. ■

Enhancing the Lesson

For more information on *Regents of the University of California* v. *Bakke* see the Supreme Court Docket on the *Researcher Online*.

LABOR AND UNIONS 175

Transparency

An overhead transparency of Figure 8.4 is available in *Transparency Resources*. See Transparency 30: Minimum Wage, 1950–2000.

Caption Answer
1997 ★ 23F, 23G

SECTION 1 REVIEW ANSWERS

1. labor force (169), wage (169), intrinsic reward (171), derived demand (171), industrialization (172), capital-intensive (172), labor-intensive (172), affirmative action (174), quota (174) **24A**

2. capital-intensive—more goods produced, based on machines, factory production; labor-intensive—based on human labor, agricultural production, fewer goods; common—need workers and consumers **23A, 24C, 26D**

3a. wages, skills, working conditions, location, intrinsic rewards, and market trends **23A**

3b. more capital-intensive, more gender-balanced, better educated **19B**

4. Employers might discriminate in hiring practices, might not check on the safety of new technology, might pay workers as little as possible, and might make them work long hours. **15B, 23A, 26D, 27B**

MINIMUM WAGE, 1950–2000

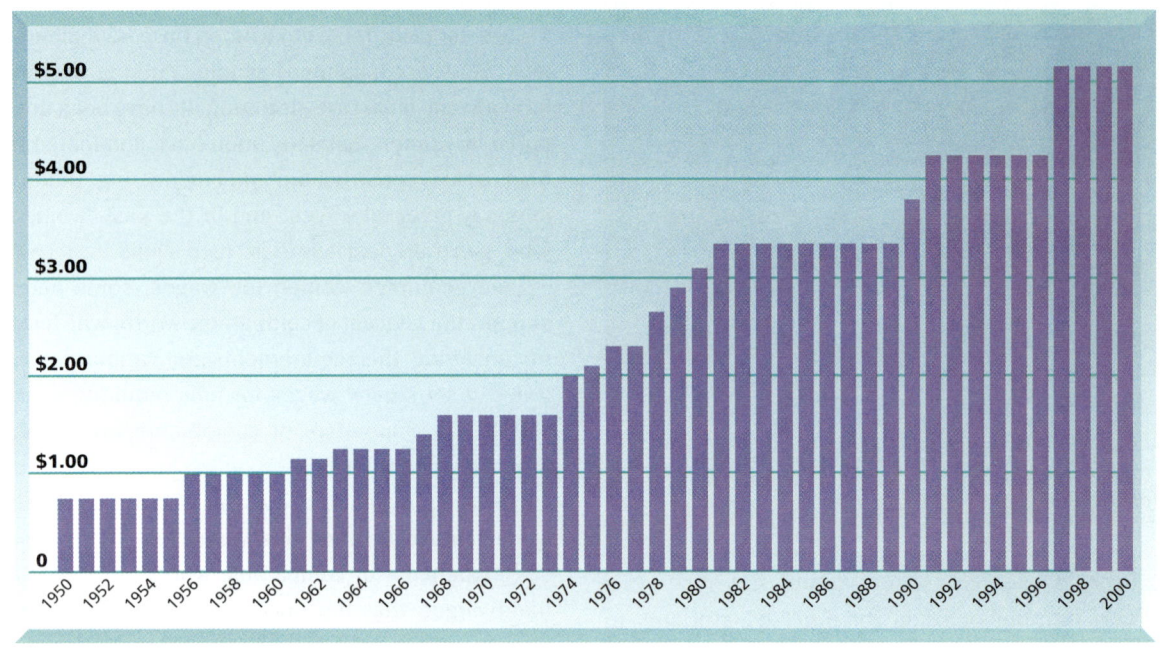

Source: *Statistical Abstract of the United States: 2000*

FIGURE 8.4 The minimum wage is designed to provide workers with a base level of income. **In which year did the minimum wage increase by the greatest amount?** ★TEKS

the federal minimum-wage and overtime regulations should be applied to the millions of people who work for state and local governments. Today more than 80 percent of all employees are covered by the minimum-wage law. (For minimum-wage rate changes since 1950, see Figure 8.4.)

SECTION 1 REVIEW

★TEKS Q: 1, 2, 3b, 4

1. Identify and Explain:
- labor force
- wage
- intrinsic reward
- derived demand
- industrialization
- capital-intensive
- labor-intensive
- affirmative action
- quota

2. Comparing and Contrasting: Copy the Venn diagram below. Use it to compare a capital-intensive economy with a labor-intensive one.

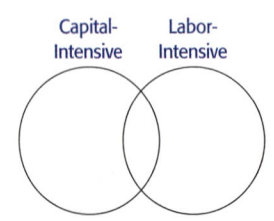

Capital-Intensive / Labor-Intensive

3. Finding the Main Idea
- **a.** What are the six factors that affect a worker's job choice?
- **b.** List three ways in which the composition of the labor force in the United States has changed since the 1700s.

4. Writing and Critical Thinking

Making Predictions: Without the government protections listed in this section, how might worker/employer relations be different today?

Consider:
- the minimum wage and other laws
- changes in technology

Homework Practice Online keyword: SM3 HP8

176 CHAPTER 8

SECTION 2

THE GROWTH OF LABOR UNIONS

READ TO DISCOVER
1. What is the history of the labor movement in the United States?
2. How are labor unions organized?
3. What are the main challenge facing unions today?
4. How have government attitudes toward labor unions changed?

ECONOMICS DICTIONARY
labor union
open shop
closed shop

As you know, in the last several decades the government has acted to protect the rights of workers. For more than two centuries, however, workers in the United States have taken steps to secure their own rights. For example, as early as 1778, printers in New York joined forces to demand higher pay.

Workers also have organized into labor unions. A **labor union** is an organization of workers that negotiates with employers for better wages, improved working conditions, and job security. Labor unions—and the government's attitude toward them and their activities—have a long and varied history in the United States. Today, unions face some of their greatest challenges.

Development of Unions

You have learned how industrialization affected the kinds of jobs available to workers. Industrialization also changed the relationship between employers and their workers. The switch from labor-intensive agriculture to capital-intensive industries meant that employers, or the owners of capital, had increasingly more power than workers, or the owners of labor. This shift in power allowed some industrial business owners to make enormous profits while paying their workers only pennies a day. Owners grew increasingly rich, while workers remained poor and ever more dependent on the low wages they were forced to accept.

Thus, in the mid- and late 1800s, owners had almost complete control over both pay scales and the length of the workday. In 1860, for example, the average workweek for a factory laborer was 60 hours, for which he or she received just over 10 cents an hour. To make ends meet, families often sent their children to work in jobs outside the home. By 1890 nearly 20 percent of children aged 10 to 15 worked for wages.

At that time workplaces frequently were unsafe, noisy, and unsanitary. In 1911 more than 140 people died in a fire at the Triangle Shirtwaist Company in New York City because most of the exits were locked. In his novel *The Jungle*, Upton Sinclair described conditions in meatpacking plants, where people's hands were eaten away by the acid used to help remove the wool from sheep carcasses and where infectious diseases like tuberculosis thrived and spread in the rooms where meat was cooked.

ECONOMIC INSTITUTIONS & INCENTIVES *During the late 1800s workers began to join together in labor unions to protect their rights.* **What are the two major types of unions?**

LABOR AND UNIONS 177

Caption Answer
Congress of Industrial Organizations ⭐19B, 23A

Across the Curriculum

HISTORY The American Federation of Labor (AFL) mainly limited membership to unions of skilled workers. The result was the exclusion of many women, immigrants, and African, Asian, and Hispanic Americans—the groups that made up the majority of unskilled workers. In 1905, however, many of these workers found support in a new union with a different agenda. The Industrial Workers of the World (IWW), a radical labor union that opposed capitalism and cooperation with business owners, encouraged unskilled and semiskilled workers to join. The union actively recruited women, new immigrants, African Americans, and migrant workers.

Wobblies, as the union's members were called, advocated strikes and industrial sabotage to protect workers' rights. The IWW's influence was short-lived, however. Internal squabbling, several unsuccessful strikes, and increasing government resistance to the union all contributed to its eventual decline. By 1920 the IWW had lost most of its influence. Nevertheless, it still maintains headquarters in Chicago, Illinois. ■

ECONOMIC INSTITUTIONS & INCENTIVES *Terence Powderly served as the head of the Knights of Labor from 1879 to 1893.* **Name one major labor organization formed after 1900.** ⭐TEKS

Recognizing that they could bring about change only by acting together, workers formed a number of labor unions. The two major types that developed were craft unions and industrial unions. A craft union is composed of one trade's skilled workers—for example, plumbers, electricians, or carpenters. The International Union of Bricklayers and Allied Craftsmen is a craft union. An industrial union, on the other hand, includes all workers in an industry, whether they are skilled, semiskilled, or unskilled. The United Auto Workers is an industrial union.

Knights of Labor The most successful of the early unions was the Knights of Labor, an industrial union that was open to workers from nearly all trades. A loosely structured organization, the Knights brought together skilled and unskilled workers from a wide variety of crafts and industries. Additionally, the union offered membership to women and African Americans. At the height of its power in 1886, the Knights had nearly 700,000 members.

The Knights of Labor supported setting an eight-hour workday, ending child labor, and replacing capitalism with a system of consumers' and producers' cooperatives. The Knights worked to achieve social and political reform through a combination of marches, demonstrations, and violent protests.

The loose structure of the Knights of Labor and its support of radical political change eventually led to its downfall. In addition, when the Knights attempted to improve the working conditions of unskilled laborers, skilled members refused to support the union's actions. Without the support of skilled workers, the union began to lose power. By 1900 it was no longer a significant force.

American Federation of Labor The modern period of the U.S. labor movement began in 1886, when a loose association of craft unions organized as the American Federation of Labor (AFL). Samuel Gompers, the first AFL president, felt that unions should focus their efforts on gaining higher wages and better working conditions rather than striving for social changes such as the cooperatives supported by the Knights. The AFL mainly included unions of skilled workers, excluding unions of unskilled workers. In 1914 the AFL had more than 2 million members. By 1920 its membership had doubled.

The 1920s, however, were difficult for labor unions. Internal struggles plagued the AFL, and opponents challenged Gompers's leadership. When he died in 1924, the presidency of the union changed hands, but the internal struggles did not disappear. At the same time, a strong antiunion sentiment arose as many unions supported radical platforms and actions. Businesses, with the aid of the government, attacked organized labor. Many business owners set up **open shops**, in which workers did not have to join a union. Unions, of course, preferred **closed shops**, in which workers could be hired only if they first joined a union. (See Figure 8.5.)

Massive unemployment during the Great Depression of the 1930s decreased the AFL's membership. The continuing internal disputes, particularly over the inclusion of unskilled workers, eventually pushed several AFL unions to form a new, separate labor organization.

178 CHAPTER 8

Congress of Industrial Organizations

Although the AFL was made up primarily of craft unions, a few industrial unions did join. To further widen the AFL's membership, John L. Lewis, president of the United Mine Workers (UMW), formed the Committee for Industrial Organizations within the AFL in 1935. One of the committee's main goals was to organize both unskilled and semiskilled workers in several industries and bring them into the American Federation of Labor.

By 1937, AFL leaders—determined to keep the organization focused on craft unions—had expelled Lewis and all of the industrial unions that he had helped organize. A year later, Lewis became president of the newly named Congress of Industrial Organizations (CIO). Under his leadership, millions of unskilled industrial workers—including women as well as African Americans and other minorities—were organized. Large industrial unions that joined the CIO included the United Steel Workers (USW), the United Automobile Workers (UAW), and Lewis's own UMW.

Union Organization

As workers in many industries and regions joined together to claim their rights, labor unions began to structure themselves in certain ways. What are these forms of organization?

Local Unions

Local unions are made up of people who work for a particular company or in a particular area. One local union might be made up of all the workers at the Fantastic Furniture Company. Another might include only saw operators from several lumber companies in the same city.

National Unions

At the next level of organization, local unions from different parts of the country are organized into national unions. Suppose, for example, that the Saw Operators Union of Toledo is one chapter of the Saw Operators Union of America. Although union members are more likely to be active in their local unions, national unions often are better known to the public and hold greater political and economic

States with Right-to-Work Laws

- States with right-to-work laws
- States without right-to-work laws

Sources: Statistical Abstract of the United States: 2000; National Right to Work Legal Defense Foundation: 2001

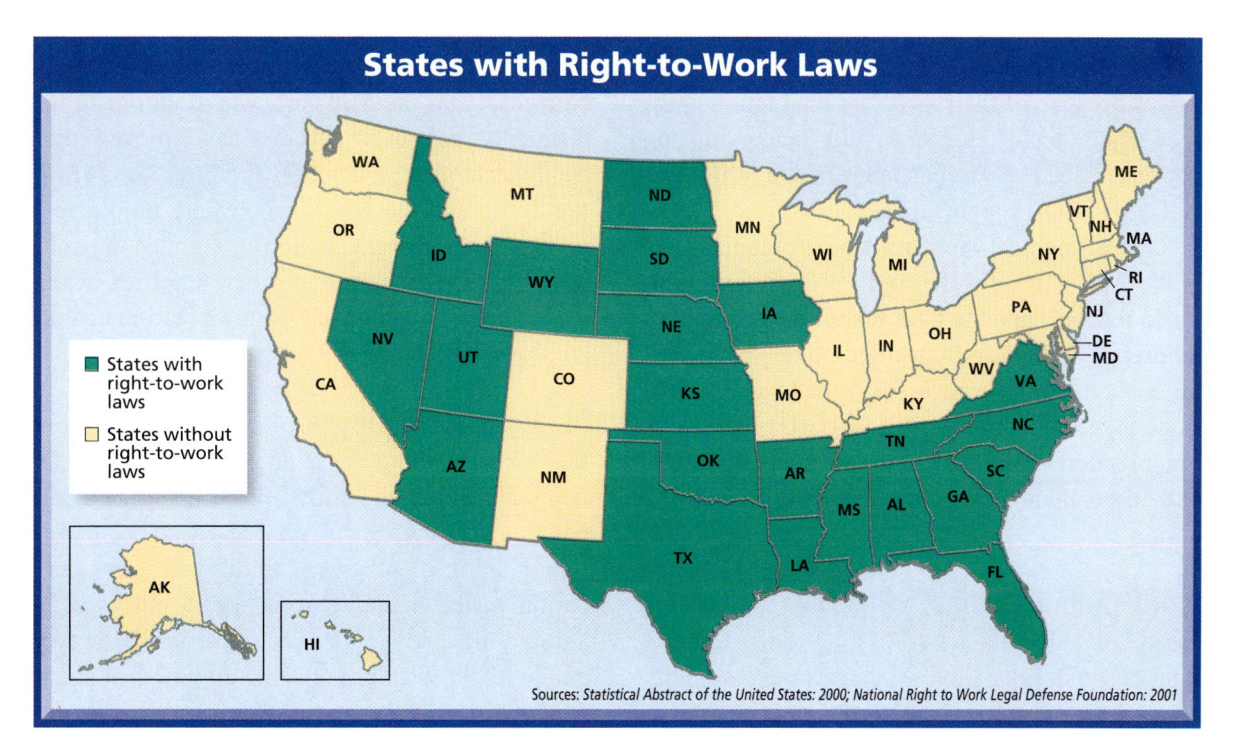

FIGURE 8.5 States establish right-to-work laws, which prohibit shops that are closed to nonunion workers. **Which states have right-to-work laws?**

Profiles in Economics

For biographies of Samuel Gompers, John L. Lewis, and other noted labor leaders, refer students to the Biographies section on the *Researcher Online*.

Cultural Perspectives

Women played an important role in the early labor movement. During the 1830s and early 1840s, New England textile factory owners cut wages, sped up production, and lengthened the workday in an attempt to increase profits. In 1844 Sarah Bagley—a factory worker employed at the textile mills of Francis Lowell—organized the Lowell Female Labor Reform Association to work to improve working conditions. The group's first action was to petition the Massachusetts legislature to limit the workday to 10 hours. Although the legislature turned down the request, the petition did lead to the first investigation of working conditions by a government body in the United States. ■

Caption Answer

Alabama, Arizona, Arkansas, Florida, Georgia, Idaho, Iowa, Kansas, Louisiana, Mississippi, Nebraska, Nevada, North Carolina, North Dakota, Oklahoma, South Carolina, South Dakota, Tennessee, Texas, Utah, Virginia, and Wyoming ★23F

Enhancing the Lesson

For more information on the AFL–CIO see the National Organizations section on the *Researcher Online*.

Caption Answer

employer opposition, changes in employment patterns, and negative public opinion ★19B, 23F, 23G

Themes in Economics

ECONOMIC INSTITUTIONS & INCENTIVES In 1999 some 16.4 million American workers belonged to labor unions. Of these, 9.4 million, or nearly three fifths, worked in the private sector and 7 million held government jobs at the federal, state, and local levels. Within the private sector, the transportation, public utilities, construction, manufacturing, and mining industries had the highest union participation rates. The farming, forestry, and fishing industries had the lowest.

So just who are labor union members? Most are between the ages of 35 and 64, and most work full-time as opposed to part-time. Union members are more likely to be men than women, and to be African American than white or Hispanic. Of these groups, African American men have the highest union participation rate; white women, the lowest. ■

CHANGES IN UNION MEMBERSHIP

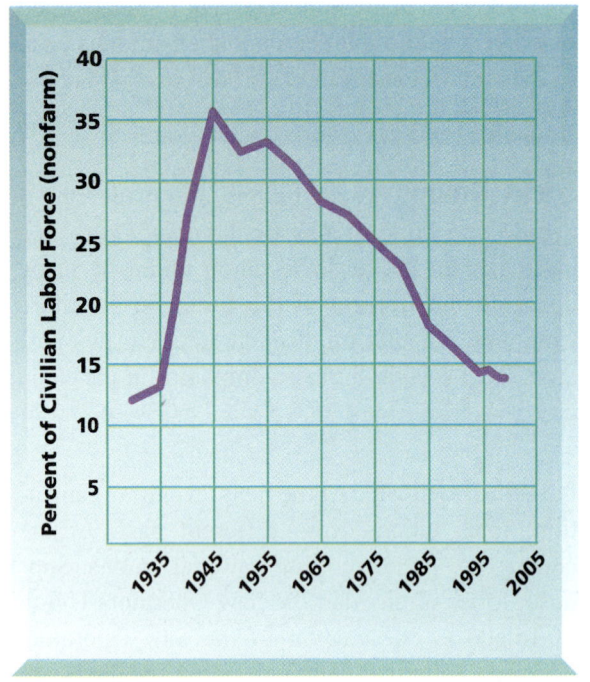

Source: *Statistical Abstract of the United States: 2000*

FIGURE 8.6 Union membership declined sharply after World War II. **What factors contributed to this decline?** ★TEKS

---

power because of their size. National unions provide their local chapters with leadership on national issues, as well as lawyers and other specialized staff to support local causes.

One of the best-known national organizations is the AFL–CIO. By the mid-1950s, union leaders in the AFL and the CIO acknowledged that all laborers—skilled and unskilled alike—had similar economic concerns. In 1955 the two organizations merged, forming the AFL–CIO. Today this organization includes dozens of smaller unions and more than 13 million members across the nation.

Independent Unions Many labor unions are not affiliated with the AFL–CIO. For example, the National Education Association is an independent union with more than 2 million members. Local unions also may be independent of national organizations.

Challenges to Labor Unions

In recent decades the labor movement in the United States has experienced a period of crisis. Union membership has dropped dramatically, as shown in Figure 8.6. The three main reasons for the decline are

▶ employer opposition
▶ changes in employment patterns
▶ negative public opinion

Employer Opposition The managements of many companies have opposed the development of unions because increased wages for workers mean lower profits for owners. Rather than attacking the unions directly, however, in recent years some employers have tried to make unions seem unnecessary by changing company labor policies to recognize the invaluable role of workers. For example, some employers have made workers part of management teams. Others have allowed employee representatives to sit on their boards of directors, thus giving workers a voice in company decision making.

Other companies simply try to avoid dealing with unions. For example, some companies in the Northeast and the Midwest, where unionism traditionally has been strong, have moved their headquarters or production facilities to cities in the South and the Southwest, where unions tend to hold less power. Similarly, some companies have moved production to other countries, where wages are low and a lack of unionization enables employers to cut costs significantly.

Changes in Employment Patterns A second factor contributing to the decline of unions in the United States is the shift from a manufacturing-based economy to a service-based economy. Labor union membership traditionally has been strong in the manufacturing sector, such as the automobile and appliance industries. However, employment in this sector has dropped in recent years, while employment of office and service workers—who generally have low union participation rates—has increased.

Economics in Action

Union Summer

Meet the face of modern organized labor: University of Texas student Gladiola Campos. Although most labor activities in the past were carried out by older white males, many labor activists today are like Gladiola—female members of minority groups in their twenties and thirties.

The American Federation of Labor-Congress of Industrial Organizations (AFL–CIO) is working to energize the labor movement by recruiting young people. Gladiola was one of more than 2,000 volunteers who have participated in the AFL–CIO's Union Summer program between 1996 and 2000. The campaign is modeled after the historic Freedom Summer of 1964, which promoted civil rights and voter registration for African Americans.

Union Summer volunteers have worked in over 40 cities across the United States. For $250 a week and free housing, they have demonstrated against unfair labor practices, registered voters door to door and encouraged local union activism.

As an immigrant and the daughter of an El Paso janitor, Gladiola Campos felt it her duty to fight for immigrants who were not able to attend college as she was. "Around campus, I see so many Mexicans cleaning dorms. We are all immigrants, but I got lucky." She also knows firsthand the power of unions; before her mother's workplace was unionized in 1989, "she had to work two jobs and we couldn't afford health insurance."

Rafael Garcia, Jr., a volunteer from Santa Monica College, was eager to work with the United Farm Workers (UFW). Inspired to join Union Summer by his idol, the late UFW leader and founder César Chávez, Rafael explained his reasons for union activism: "People aren't active. They don't want to get involved in things... A lot of workers don't want to unionize because they are afraid of being fired... I'm hoping to get workers to join unions and not be afraid to stand up for themselves."

Employers' reaction to the enthusiasm of young union activists has been lukewarm. Jeffrey McGuiness—president of the Labor Policy Association in Washington, D.C., which represents the interests of large corporations—says, "College students breezing in and telling people they are better off joining a union—and then breezing back to school again—that's not likely to be very effective." However, many of the student volunteers have worked before or have blue-collar backgrounds.

The AFL-CIO has already seen results from Union Summer. Many of the participants have gone on to careers in union organizing. Moreover, newspapers such as the *Wall Street Journal* have given it credit for the recent resurgence in student activism.

What Do You Think? ★TEKS

1. Why would the AFL–CIO want to recruit union members and organizers with a variety of backgrounds?
2. Why might college students be attracted to a project like Union Summer?

More than 1,000 student volunteers participated in the AFL–CIO's 1996 Union Summer.

What Do You Think? Answers

1. To increase its declining membership, the AFL–CIO needs to reach as many types of people as possible. Recruiting organizers with a wide variety of backgrounds is one way to achieve this goal. Workers may respond better to labor organizers with backgrounds similar to their own. For example, many immigrants may have come to the United States from countries where labor unions had little power or where joining a union meant automatically being fired. Labor organizers who can relate to their experiences may be able to approach these people more easily. In addition, by recruiting people in their twenties, the AFL–CIO is increasing the awareness of the labor movement among the nation's youth and ensuring continued support for decades to come. ★23D

2. Labor unions might have played a strong role in their families; they might want to serve what they see as a worthy cause; and they might want to gain hands-on experience to enhance their resumé.

Sidebar

Transparency

An overhead transparency of Figure 8.7 is available in *Transparency Resources*. See Transparency 31: Major Labor Legislation.

Caption Answer

Most early legislation favored unions and increased their power. Since 1947, however, labor legislation has tended to place limits on unions. ★19B, 23A, 23F

Cultural Perspectives

Labor-union organizers have set their sights on the booming high-tech industry. Although a rapidly growing number of people work for high-tech companies, only 3 percent of these workers are members of unions. Whether high-tech workers are open to labor unions is questionable, however. Traditionally, workers have sought out the solidarity and strength of unions to improve low wages and poor benefits. Most employees working for high-tech companies are generally well paid, however. Aware of these hurdles, union organizers are focusing instead on high-tech workers' long hours and growing job insecurity. As union membership continues to decline, the success of labor unions to expand into new industries may be the deciding factor in the continued influence of the labor movement. ■

MAJOR LABOR LEGISLATION

YEAR	LEGISLATION	PURPOSE
1914	Clayton Antitrust Act	exempts unions from antitrust suits and gives labor the right to strike, picket, and organize a boycott of a firm's products in an effort to settle contract disputes; made it more difficult for businesses to obtain injunctions against unions; not always effective because courts often sided with businesses
1932	Norris–La Guardia Act	guarantees the right of a worker to join a union and engage in normal union activities; outlaws contracts prohibiting employees from joining unions; restricts the issuing of court injunctions during labor disputes
1935	Wagner Act	(also called the National Labor Relations Act) guarantees workers the right to form unions and to bargain collectively; requires management to bargain in good faith and refrain from unfair labor practices; established the National Labor Relations Board
1938	Fair Labor Standards Act	(also called the Wages and Hours Law) established a minimum wage and set a maximum workweek of 44 hours (which was later reduced to 40 hours); guarantees time-and-a-half pay for overtime, and restricts child labor
1947	Taft-Hartley Act	(also called the Labor-Management Relations Act) reversed some earlier union gains by prohibiting closed shops; allows states to enact right-to-work laws, which prohibit closed shops; requires a "cooling-off" period of 60 days prior to strike or termination of a contract and allows federal injunctions to block certain strikes for up to 80 days; outlaws union campaign contributions to national political candidates
1959	Landrum-Griffin Act	(also called the Labor-Management Act) passed in an effort to prevent corrupt union practices; requires union officials to be elected democratically; requires that union funds be recorded with the Department of Labor; set up strict guidelines to be followed in establishing unions and in conducting union activities
1964	Civil Rights Act	title VII established the first federal fair employment practices law, prohibiting employers to discriminate on the basis of race, color, religion, national origin, or sex; established an Equal Opportunity Commission to investigate and rule on complaints

FIGURE 8.7 The federal government has passed a number of laws designed to regulate the workplace. **How do the laws listed here reflect changes in government attitudes toward unions?** ★TEKS

Additionally, growing numbers of women and teenagers have entered the labor force. Although unions do not exclude them, such workers have not been at the center of union organizing efforts and often have not been attracted to union membership. Thus, as employment of women and teenagers has increased, the percentage of employees involved in unions has declined.

Negative Public Opinion The third factor in the decline of unions is the public's generally negative view of them. Many people—including economists—feel that union demands for higher wages and increased benefits have encouraged companies to move their factories outside of the country, thereby decreasing the number of jobs available to workers in the United States. Some also believe that union members' wages are too high considering the skill level needed to perform their jobs.

In addition, the public has at times opposed the actions of union leaders, some of whom have been accused of accepting political favors in exchange for lowering union demands. Others are thought to have used violence and other offensive tactics to maintain their power. These incidents have contributed to a negative public attitude toward unions.

CHAPTER 8

Union Responses

One union response to the drop in membership has been to adopt a more cooperative spirit in their dealings with management. For example, during the 1980s labor and management in some industries agreed to wage and benefit reductions to help their companies remain competitive in the marketplace.

Additionally, labor and management have come together on other national issues. For example, both groups have opposed rapidly rising insurance costs for businesses.

To increase membership, organized labor has addressed new issues that are of concern to workers, such as skill training, career development programs, quality of life in the workplace, and worker involvement in decision making on the job. Other issues, such as the availability of day care facilities, are designed to appeal to parents and other specific groups of workers.

Unions also have attempted to gain members by improving the training they provide to union organizers. Unions also are hiring professional union organizers to explain the benefits of membership to nonunion workers.

Finally, unions have experimented with a number of incentives to make membership more attractive. For example, unions have offered incentives such as life and health insurance plans, retirement accounts, low-interest credit cards, and legal services.

Government and Unions

The government's responses to unions have changed over time. During the 1800s the government generally favored business interests over those of labor unions. For example, in 1894, workers at Chicago's Pullman Palace Car Company factory, which produced sleeping cars for trains, protested wage cuts by refusing to work. Eugene V. Debs, leader of the American Railway Union, then urged union members to refuse to work on any train with a Pullman car. When railroad traffic across the country was disrupted, the railroad companies attached mail cars to Pullman cars. This action caused the government to oppose the protests on the grounds that they were preventing mail delivery. Federal troops were sent to enforce order, and protesters were jailed.

The government's attitude toward unions changed during the first decades of the 1900s, however, when the country entered a period of social and political reform. The U.S. Congress and state legislatures passed laws protecting the rights of workers. Since 1947, though, legislation once again has tended to place limits on the power of unions. (For a description of major labor legislation, see Figure 8.7.)

SECTION 2 REVIEW

TEKS Q: 1, 2, 3a, 4

1. Define and explain:
- labor union
- open shop
- closed shop

2. Identifying Concepts Copy the flowchart below. Use it to trace the development of the labor movement.

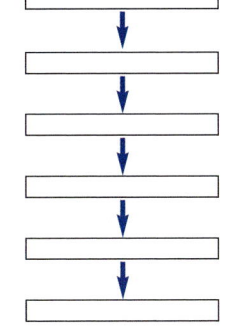

3. Finding the Main Idea
a. What conditions led to the development of labor unions?
b. How do national unions support local unions?

4. Writing and Critical Thinking
Identifying Bias: How has bias in the United States against labor organizers affected the development of the labor movement?
Consider:
- employer opposition
- general public opinion

Homework Practice Online keyword: SM3 HP8

SECTION 3

UNIONS AND MANAGEMENT

Lesson Plans
For teaching strategies, see Lesson 8.3 located at the beginning of this chapter or the One-Stop Planner Strategy 8.3.

Economics Dictionary
To reinforce the section's vocabulary terms, refer students to the Electronic Glossary on the *Researcher CD-ROM*.

Section Assessment
To assess students' mastery of this section, have them complete Daily Quiz 8.3 in *Daily Quizzes with Answer Key*.

Caption Answer
wages and fringe benefits, working conditions, job security, union security, and grievance procedures ★23A

TEKS
Section 3
Content
2A, 2B, 15A
Social Studies Skills
23A, 23D, 24A, 24B, 24C, 24D, 25A, 25B
Chapter Review
Content
7A, 15B, 19B, 26D
Social Studies Skills
23A, 23D, 23E, 23F, 23G, 24A, 24B, 24D

184

SECTION 3

UNIONS AND MANAGEMENT

READ TO DISCOVER
1. What major issues are discussed in labor contract negotiations?
2. How do unions and management reach a contract agreement?
3. What negotiation tactics do unions and management use?

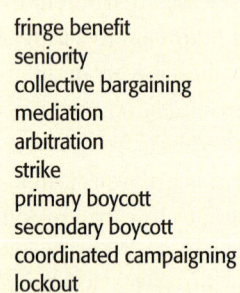

ECONOMICS DICTIONARY
fringe benefit
seniority
collective bargaining
mediation
arbitration
strike
primary boycott
secondary boycott
coordinated campaigning
lockout
injunction

As noted in Section 2, unions are organizations of workers who pool their resources and efforts to secure fair pay, better benefits, safe working conditions, and job security. How can labor unions work to achieve these goals? What tactics do dissatisfied workers sometimes employ? How does management respond to these tactics?

Labor Contract Issues

The labor movement in the United States traditionally has focused on practical issues that affect workers on a daily basis. In negotiations between labor and management, five major issues usually are discussed:

184 CHAPTER 8

◗ wages and fringe benefits
◗ working conditions
◗ job security
◗ union security
◗ grievance procedures.

Suppose that Kara Langley is a leader of the Tour Workers Union in San Francisco. The union includes local tour guides, bus and van drivers, and office workers. For several years Kara worked as a tour guide, so she understands many of the challenges faced by tour workers. The union is currently negotiating a labor contract with a new tour company, and the five issues listed above are under discussion.

Wages and Fringe Benefits The union's first major concern is about wages paid to tour guides, drivers, and office workers. Wages are set by labor contracts and vary according to the type of position held and the number of years a worker has been on the job. Tour guides and drivers probably will be paid different amounts, just as a guide with 10 years of experience will most likely earn more money than a newly hired guide.

ECONOMIC INSTITUTIONS & INCENTIVES *Workers' concerns usually are focused on issues that they confront on a daily basis.* **What are the five major issues that generally are discussed in labor negotiations?**

The labor contract also outlines the policy for paying overtime to tour employees working more than the standard 40-hour work week. In addition, the contract includes a cost-of-living adjustment (COLA). A COLA automatically raises employee wages to match widespread price increases, allowing workers to maintain their purchasing power.

In addition to negotiating for higher wages, Kara—as a union representative—tries to ensure that the tour workers will receive fringe benefits in the labor contracts. **Fringe benefits** are nonwage payments, commonly including paid sick days, holidays, and vacation days; health and life insurance; and savings and retirement plans. Many companies also provide profit sharing as well as employee stock ownership plans (ESOPs). Under profit sharing, a firm distributes a portion of its profits to workers. An ESOP provides workers with stock in the company. By providing higher benefits only if the company does well, profit sharing and ESOPs provide an incentive for employees to work hard.

Working Conditions Kara also tries to secure good working conditions for union employees. In addition to conditions at the tour office, Kara works to improve conditions at the tour locations that workers will visit, such as Fisherman's Wharf, Golden Gate Park, and Lombard Street. Desirable working conditions include a clean and safe workplace, clearly defined work responsibilities, and reasonable working hours. Kara tries to make sure that the labor contract specifies the number of tours a guide is expected to lead each week, the types of vehicles drivers will operate, the ease of contacting and gaining assistance from the tour office, and the maximum number of visitors on each tour.

ECONOMIC INSTITUTIONS & INCENTIVES *Pilots take shifts walking the picket line during a strike over higher pay and other issues.* ***What other labor issues might be important to pilots?***

Job Security As she negotiates the contract, Kara focuses on the need for the new company to provide job security. The legal system provides some job security for workers. For example, the law prohibits an employer from firing an employee because of race, sex, religion, age, or union activity.

Union negotiators typically seek contracts that give greater job security through the seniority system. **Seniority** is the holding of privileges based on the number of years a worker has been employed by a firm. Labor contracts usually protect seniority by requiring that workers with the least seniority be the first to lose their jobs in the event that the company must reduce its workforce. In other words, if the tour company is forced to lay off workers, a tour bus driver who has been working for six months will lose his job before a driver who has held her job for three years.

Union Security As she negotiates the terms of the labor contract, Kara also ensures that workers are free to join the union. In other words, employees of the new tour company will be able to participate in the union without worrying

---

Themes in Economics

ECONOMIC INSTITUTIONS & INCENTIVES American companies are increasingly offering workers more creative and innovative perks. Flexible benefit packages, valet services, on-site banks, fitness centers, and day care facilities are among the services being offered. Anderson Consulting in Chicago, Illinois, provides a full concierge service for employees. Runners perform a variety of services, from picking up dry cleaning and meeting repair workers to shopping for gifts and watering houseplants. Companies hope these benefits will increase workers' morale, productivity, and loyalty and reduce employee turnover.

Caption Answer
fringe benefits, working conditions, union security, and grievance procedures

Enhancing the Lesson
For more information about labor-management relations, see the entries for the National Labor Relations Board and the Federal Labor Relations Authority in the Executive Departments section on the *Researcher Online*.

LABOR AND UNIONS 185

Enhancing the Lesson

For more information about mediation organizations, see the entries for the Federal Mediation and Conciliation Service and the National Mediation Board in the Executive Departments section on the *Researcher Online*.

Caption Answer

National Labor Relations Board ⭐15A, 24A

Profiles in Economics

George W. Taylor was a leader in the field of U.S. labor arbitration and mediation. Born July 10, 1901, in Philadelphia, Pennsylvania, Taylor went on to serve as labor adviser to five U.S. presidents, from Franklin Roosevelt to Lyndon Johnson. In addition, Taylor taught industrial relations at the University of Pennsylvania's Wharton School for more than 40 years.

Known as the Father of American Arbitration, Taylor helped resolve more than 2,000 disputes between labor and management. He believed that both parties in collective bargaining should receive equal consideration and that it is vital to understand a conflict in its entirety before trying to resolve it.

Taylor died in 1972 at 71 years of age. In 1995 he was inducted into the U.S. Labor Hall of Fame.

ECONOMIC INSTITUTIONS & INCENTIVES *Union organizers negotiate for union security.* **What organization enforces workers' right to join a union?**

about whether company owners approve of union activities.

In its broadest sense, union security provides workers with the right to organize and join a union. This right is enforced by the National Labor Relations Board (NLRB).

How does a union become the negotiating body for workers in a company? First, at least 30 percent of a firm's employees must sign a petition informing the NLRB that they want to hold an election to determine whether a majority of employees want to unionize. Second, the NLRB conducts the election using a secret ballot, which allows workers to vote without fear of harassment or intimidation. If the majority of workers favor unionization, the NLRB recognizes the union as the only bargaining representative for the company's employees.

Grievance Procedures

When a work-related dispute arises, either labor or management may seek resolution by following a particular set of steps. For example, suppose that one of the tour guides feels that she is not receiving as many tour assignments as she should. If union representatives agree and feel that management has violated provisions outlined in the labor contract, the union may begin grievance procedures.

Grievances, or formal complaints, usually are resolved by committees made up of representatives of the union and the management. If this procedure does not resolve the problem, a negotiator is brought in by the NLRB. Both sides—union and management—must agree to give the negotiator all applicable information and to abide by the negotiator's decision.

Contract Negotiations

You have learned about the major issues in contract negotiations. How do union representatives and management arrive at an agreement on these issues?

Collective Bargaining

When negotiating a new contract with management, union leaders speak for all the members they represent. During this process, known as **collective bargaining**, union and management representatives meet to discuss their goals and offer solutions and compromises. In most cases, collective bargaining results in a contract settlement. At times, however, other negotiation methods must be used.

Mediation

Sometimes the bargaining process breaks down, and labor and management are unable to make any progress. In this case, they may resort to mediation. In **mediation**, negotiators call in a neutral third party, or mediator, to listen to the arguments of both sides and to suggest ways in which an agreement may be reached.

Who serves as a mediator? Mediation services are offered by private citizens and government agencies alike. In addition, the Taft-Hartley Act of 1947—which gives the government the power to regulate relations between labor and management—established the Federal Mediation and Conciliation Service (FMCS). The FMCS mediates thousands of disputes every year.

Arbitration In some cases, neither collective bargaining nor mediation results in a contract settlement. A third method of reaching an agreement is **arbitration**. Like mediation, arbitration calls for the assistance of a negotiator to arrive at a contract. An arbitrator, like a mediator, is a neutral third party. Unlike in mediation, however, an arbitrator's decision is legally binding.

Union Tactics

What happens when unions and management are unable to reach an agreement through collective

CAREERS IN ECONOMICS

Labor Relations Consultant

As business decisions become increasingly complex, many companies are turning to outside experts for information and ideas. These experts—called consultants—bring their experience and knowledge to many kinds of companies.

Consultants generally have undergraduate and professional degrees in business or law, as well as several years of work experience in a particular field or industry. In addition, many consultants take courses to improve their skills and expand their understanding of business practices and policies.

Consultants are often called in during contract negotiations between labor and management. Suppose, for example, that union representatives want to know if their fringe benefits are comparable to those received by workers in other companies. They may hire a labor relations consultant who can bring knowledge of employment conditions in many regions and industries. Similarly, management may hire a labor relations consultant who can analyze union demands and support management's position during negotiations.

Labor relations consultants have to be intelligent, well informed, persistent, and able to think quickly under pressure. Experience in public speaking and debate, as well as strong research abilities and writing skills, can help a consultant be both persuasive and knowledgeable.

One of the most important skills for a labor relations consultant is the willingness and ability to compromise. Although a consultant may support union positions and have strong views about what actions should be taken, he or she must recognize when to agree to management's terms in order to gain other advantages. You might think of labor relations as a game of checkers. Although your goal is to capture as many pieces—or win as many concessions—as possible, sometimes you may have to lose some of your own pieces—or give up on some issues—to keep moving forward.

Labor relations consultants must be highly skilled in the art of compromise.

Across the Curriculum

GOVERNMENT The federal government rarely intervenes in labor disputes. In recent years it has done so only when it has concluded that a strike might harm the economy or the public good. In 1997, when pilots and management for American Airlines could not reach an agreement, the National Mediation Board stepped in to offer suggestions. The board presented several proposals; however, a majority of pilots voted against them. At this point, having determined that a pilot strike would not be in the public's best interest, President Clinton opted to intervene and sent a presidential emergency board to help the two sides reach an agreement. Because of this action, thousands of travelers were spared flight cancellations or delays.

Careers in Economics

To help students learn about other careers in economics, refer them to the Careers section on the *Researcher Online*.

LABOR AND UNIONS

Across the Curriculum

HISTORY In addition to organizing millions of unskilled industrial workers during the 1930s, the Congress of Industrial Organizations also pioneered a new form of protest—the sit-down strike. In December 1936, General Motors workers sat down in their factories in Flint, Michigan, and refused to leave until management recognized their local union of the United Automobile Workers (UAW). The strike lasted 44 days and involved some 40,000 workers. Other industries were quick to adopt the sit-down strike as well.

In 1939, however, the U.S. Supreme Court declared sit-down strikes illegal, and organized labor ceased to use the tactic. The sit-down strike did not disappear though. During the Civil Rights Movement of the 1960s, protesters used a slightly different form of the sit-down strike—the sit-in—with great success. ■

Caption Answer
picketing, boycotting, and coordinated campaigning
⭐23A

---

bargaining, mediation, or arbitration? In some cases unions may resort to a **strike**, in which they call for union members to stop working until contract demands are met.

Most strikes are called over wage disputes. For example, a salary dispute between professional baseball players and major-league team owners led to a shortened 1994 season and the cancellation of that year's World Series, as well as a delayed start for the 1995 season.

Other strikes have been called because of poor working conditions, lack of benefits, and unfair management practices. In August 1997, for example, the Teamsters Union organized a strike against United Parcel Service (UPS). Demanding more full-time jobs and improved benefits such as pensions, some 185,000 employees participated in the strike. The company's delivery rate dropped from an average of 12 million packages a day to about 120,000. Mediation by the federal government helped to end the 15-day strike, as UPS management agreed to a number of union demands.

Strikes often involve more than the stoppage of work. Three tactics commonly are used in carrying out strikes:

▶ picketing
▶ boycotting
▶ coordinated campaigning.

Picketing Imagine that the assembly line workers at the Merry Marker Crayon Company go on strike. They decide to picket the company, parading in front of the plant while carrying signs that explain their grievances. Why might they decide to adopt this tactic?

The tactic of picketing has three purposes. First, it informs the public that a strike is in progress. Passersby will see the striking workers and read the grievances listed on their signs. Second, picketing may arouse public support. Some

ECONOMIC INSTITUTIONS & INCENTIVES *Teamsters held a 24-hour strike at a hospital in Rhode Island after rejecting a contract proposal.* **What are three common strike tactics?**

CHAPTER 8

members of the public will identify with the problems of the striking workers. Third, picketing discourages nonstrikers from entering the plant. Some workers who did not join the strike may be too intimidated to return to work if they must walk through the group of striking workers. Workers who cross the picket line, called scabs, are often insulted by strikers.

Boycotts If picketing does not help resolve a contract dispute, a union might decide to organize a boycott. A **primary boycott** is an organized effort to stop purchases of a firm's products.

Most primary boycotts are organized on a local level, but some have been successful on a national scale. During the 1960s César Chávez led the National Farm Workers Association in an attempt to improve the wages and working conditions of migrant agricultural laborers. The union expanded and became known as the United Farm Workers (UFW). In 1965 the union organized a primary boycott of grapes. Millions of consumers across the United States supported the union by refusing to buy grapes. This primary boycott lasted for five years, until grape growers in California agreed to a contract with the union.

A **secondary boycott** is a refusal to buy the goods or services of any firm that does business with a company whose employees are on strike. For example, you would be participating in a secondary boycott if you refused to buy lunch or any other goods at the Griffin's Nook Comic and Sandwich Shop because the store carried comic books by White Tiger Press, whose employees are on strike. The Taft-Hartley Act, however, made secondary boycotts illegal if workers are striking in an attempt to make that employer join a boycott of another firm.

Coordinated Campaigning The third tactic that unions may use is called **coordinated campaigning**, which involves the use of picketing as well as boycotts. For example, from 1985 to 1986, a local union of the United Food and Commercial Workers (UFCW) organized a coordinated campaign against George A. Hormel & Company, which makes hot dogs, chili, and many other food products. The UFCW local picketed and boycotted the Hormel company as well as corporations and banks that did business with Hormel. Union members also distributed leaflets to community members and to other unions to try to gain support for the UFCW local's demands.

ECONOMIC INSTITUTIONS & INCENTIVES *César Chávez led the United Farm Workers in an attempt to improve working conditions for migrant laborers.* **What is a boycott?**

Management Responses

Suppose that the dispatchers at the sanitation department go on strike. How will the city government respond? Officials might agree to the demands of the sanitation workers' union. On the other hand, they might oppose the strike. Three common management actions are

- hiring replacement workers
- introducing a lockout
- asking for an injunction.

LABOR AND UNIONS

Caption Answer

hiring replacement workers, introducing a lockout, asking for an injuction ⭐23A

SECTION 3 REVIEW ANSWERS

1. fringe benefit (185), seniority (185), collective bargaining (186), mediation (186), arbitration (187), strike (188), primary boycott (189), secondary boycott (189), coordinated campaigning (189), lockout (190), injunction (190) 24A

2. Both use neutral, third-party negotiators; however, mediators suggest ways to resolve disputes, whereas arbitrators stipulate how disputes will be resolved. 23A, 24D

3a. wages and fringe benefits, working conditions, job security, union security, grievance procedures; descriptions should show an understanding of the issues. 23A

3b. advantages—one-on-one negotiating, experienced negotiator, power of unity; disadvantages—breakdown of communication, not all desires represented, loss of control 23A, 25A

4. unions—striking by picketing, boycotting, or coordinated campaigning; management—hiring replacement workers, introducing a lockout, and asking for an injunction; students might suggest that asking for an injunction is easiest because it involves very few people 23A

Replacement Workers The police department may decide to hire replacement dispatchers so that police officers will be able to respond to reports of crime. Finding qualified workers can be difficult, however, and picketing workers often try to intimidate strikebreakers as they attempt to go to work.

ECONOMIC INSTITUTIONS & INCENTIVES *These workers have been locked out of their jobs.* **What are three common management responses to a strike?**

Lockouts A **lockout** occurs when an employer closes a company's doors to striking workers until negotiators reach a contract agreement that is satisfactory to management. Striking dispatchers who have been locked out by the police department will not be allowed to return to work—even if the strike ends before an agreement is reached. Lockouts can cause problems for employers, however. Employers may lose money if they are unable to hire other workers and production stops.

Injunctions The police department also might ask the government to issue an **injunction**, or court order, to prohibit the dispatchers from striking. There are restrictions on injunctions, but the Taft-Hartley Act permits the issuing of an injunction when a strike threatens the health or safety of the public. A police dispatcher strike might pose just such a threat, as police officers would not be informed of which crimes or disturbances required their attention.

SECTION 3 REVIEW

1. Identify and Explain:
fringe benefit
seniority
collective bargaining
mediation
arbitration
strike
primary boycott
secondary boycott
coordinated campaigning
lockout
injunction

2. Comparing and Contrasting: Copy the chart below. Use it to compare and contrast the concepts of mediation and arbitration.

	Compare	Contrast
Mediation		
Arbitration		

⭐TEKS Q: 1, 2, 3b

3. Finding the Main Idea
a. What major issues generally are discussed in contract negotiations?
b. Explain the advantages and disadvantages of collective bargaining.

4. Writing and Critical Thinking
Evaluating: What options are available to unions and to management when contract negotiations fail to reach a labor agreement? Which of these methods do you think would be easiest to organize?
Consider:
• the number of people involved
• the national scope of the company

Homework Practice Online
keyword: SM3 HP8

CHAPTER 8

Economics IN THE NEWS

Technology and Labor

Technological change can have a powerful effect on the production and distribution of goods. Technological advances often reduce costs by increasing efficiency. For instance, Henry Ford's introduction of the assembly line for manufacturing automobiles reduced assembly time and thus cut production costs dramatically.

Technological changes can have a similar effect on the distribution of goods. One example involves the maritime shipping industry. Ships have been used to transport goods for centuries. Until recently, cargo was shipped in separate boxes and unloaded by hand or with the help of simple technologies such as ropes and pulleys. As a result, the process was labor intensive.

After World War II, however, maritime shippers began to ship their cargo in large containers unloaded with the help of mechanized cranes. The large containers allowed ships to be unloaded quickly and efficiently. Thus, like Henry Ford's assembly line, they reduced production costs, which in turn meant higher profits.

While shippers praised the increases in productivity caused by containerization, dockworkers, known as longshoremen, worried about their jobs. It took 2 minutes to unload a container weighing 20 to 25 tons. Before containerization it took four men five hours to unload the same amount of cargo. After years of dispute between labor unions and shipping companies over the threat containerization posed to jobs, an agreement was reached in 1960. In exchange for agreeing to containerization, under the Mechanization and Modernization Agreement, workers were granted better wages and benefits and guaranteed their work hours.

In recent years, technological change has once again threatened the jobs of dockworkers. This time the threat is new computer technology.

A loaded container ship heads up river in Washington State. Modern-day shipping utilizes containerization, permitting large quantities of goods to be more efficiently transported.

For instance, shippers who use the Port of Los Angeles—the nation's busiest port—have begun to modernize the container trade by using computers to track the flow of cargo.

Both shippers and longshoremen realize that computerization will eliminate some jobs and change existing ones. Both sides, however, hope to reach a mutually beneficial agreement in the spirit of the historic Mechanization and Modernization Agreement.

What Do You Think?

1. What effect might computers have on the way shipped goods are distributed?
2. What tactics might longshoremen use to influence negotiations concerning the introduction of computer technology?

WHY IT MATTERS TODAY

Technological changes can have a variety of effects on labor. Visit CNNfyi.com to find more examples of the relationship between technological and economic change.

LABOR AND UNIONS 191

CHAPTER 8 Review

This shift led to low wages, long days, more child labor, and unsafe working conditions. **19B, 23D**

4. 1800s—favored business interests over labor unions; early 1900s—favored labor unions and passed legislation protecting workers' rights; since 1940s—has favored management and passed legislation limiting labor union power **19B, 23A**

5. wages and fringe benefits, working conditions, job security, union security, and grievance procedures **23A**

6. unions—striking by picketing, boycotting, or coordinated campaigning; management—hiring replacement workers, using lockouts, asking for injunction **23A**

Reviewing Themes

1. offering more profit sharing and retirement opportunities, stock option plans, and better work environments **23A**

2. In the 1800s, unions had to develop on their own and gains were few. After legislation such as the Wagner Act and the Fair Labor Standards Act, government took a stronger role in helping organized labor. With the Taft-Hartley Act, government switched roles again, reducing the power of organized labor in the United States. **19B, 23D**

3. High inflation leads to high prices, which diminish the purchasing power of people making minimum wage. **15B, 23A**

Thinking Critically

1. Answers will vary. Students might suggest that the

Writing a Summary

Using standard grammar, spelling, sentence structure, and punctuation, write a summary of the information in this chapter.

Identifying Ideas

Identify the following terms and explain their significance.

1. labor force
2. wage
3. industrialization
4. capital-intensive
5. labor-intensive
6. labor union
7. fringe benefit
8. collective bargaining
9. mediation
10. arbitration

Understanding Main Ideas

SECTION 1 *(pp. 169–76)*

1. Explain how supply and demand affect the labor force.
2. How has the composition of the U.S. labor force changed since the 1800s?

SECTION 2 *(pp. 177–83)*

3. Why did workers in the 1800s and early 1900s begin to organize unions?
4. Describe how government attitudes toward labor unions have changed over time.

SECTION 3 *(pp. 184–90)*

5. What major issues generally are addressed during labor contract negotiations?
6. What tactics might a labor union use during contract negotiations? What tactics might management use?

Reviewing Themes

1. **Income Distribution** To satisfy union employees during contract negotiations, what kinds of concessions might companies make to distribute profits?
2. **Role of Government** What role did the federal government play in the development of the labor movement?
3. **Inflation and Deflation** Why does high inflation lead Congress to consider raising the federal minimum wage?

Thinking Critically

1. **Comparing and Contrasting** Study the labor force at your school. How does it compare with the national labor force? How is it different?
2. **Sequencing** What steps does a workplace take to become a union workplace?
3. **Summarizing** On what issues do unions and management usually compromise?
4. **Categorizing** Would manufacturing computer chips in a high-tech factory be capital-intensive or labor-intensive work? What about harvesting lettuce?
5. **Finding the Main Idea** How did women's roles in the labor force change during wartime?
6. **Supporting a Point of View** Should the minimum wage in your community be raised? Why or why not? Consider the effect on employers, jobs, and workers.

Writing about Economics

Review the list you wrote in your Economics Notebook of the kinds of labor you perform. How do you decide how to use your own labor? What influences your decisions about where and how to work? Explain your answer in your Notebook.

Building Social Studies Skills

Interpreting the Chart ⭐TEKS

Study the chart showing women's employment in the United States from 1900 to 1999. Then use it to help you answer the questions that follow.

Year	Women in the labor force (in thousands)	Percent of women in the labor force	Women as percent of total labor force
1900	5,319	18.8	18.3
1910	8,076	23.4	21.2
1920	8,550	21.0	20.5
1930	10,752	22.0	22.0
1940	12,887	25.4	24.5
1950	18,389	33.9	29.6
1960	23,240	37.7	33.4
1970	31,543	43.3	38.1
1980	45,487	51.5	42.5
1990	56,829	57.5	45.2
1999	64,855	60.0	46.5

Sources: *Historical Statistics of the United States: Colonial Times to 1970, Part 1: (1900–1960); U.S. Bureau of Labor Statistics*

1. Which best describes how the statistic regarding women as a percentage of the total labor force has changed since 1910?
   a. fallen
   b. risen
   c. risen then fallen
   d. fallen then risen

2. What differences do you notice between the percentage of women in the labor force and the percentage of the labor force made up of women? What is your conclusion?

Analyzing Primary Sources ⭐TEKS

Read the following excerpt from a memorial speech delivered by César Chávez for nineteen farmworkers killed in a bus accident on their way to work. Answer the questions that follow.

"There have been too many accidents in the fields, on trucks, under machines, in buses; so many accidents involving farm workers. People ask if they are deliberate. They are deliberate in the sense that they are a direct result of a farm labor system that treats workers like agricultural implements [tools] and not human beings. . . .

"We are united in sorrow, but also in our anger. This tragedy happened because of the greed of the big growers who do not care about the safety of the workers and who expose them to grave dangers when they transport them in wheeled coffins to the field."

3. Chávez feels that the growers are _____
   a. directly responsible for the bus accident.
   b. finally interested in change because of this tragedy.
   c. indirectly responsible for the bus accident.
   d. finally interested in supporting the workers' families.

4. Which expression from the passage shows a powerful use of propaganda?

Alternative Assessment

Building Your Portfolio ⭐TEKS

Research the symbols, emblems, and logos used by unions to identify products made by union members. Create a board game that challenges players to identify which logo matches which union, and then share the game with your classmates.

internet connect

Internet Activity: go.hrw.com
KEYWORD: SM3 EC8 ⭐TEKS

Access the Internet through the HRW Go site to research muckraking literature from the late 1800s and early 1900s. Then create a time line that shows the publication dates of each piece of literature you find along with the dates of major labor legislation (found in the textbook). Finally, write a short paragraph explaining how muckraking literature fostered public interest in labor reform.

TAKS REVIEW ONLINE
Keyword: SM3 T8

---

labor force at a school has low-end wage earners (maintenance and cafeteria workers), as well as mid-level (teachers) and high-end wage earners (administrators). It has unions, but there is less room for negotiation since school systems are non-profit. **23A**

2. need to have 30 percent of workers sign petition, then have a vote to become local union; if there are enough local unions, they can band together to become a national union **23A**

3. compensation, fringe benefits, working conditions **23A**

4. capital-intensive; labor-intensive **23A**

5. Women replaced the men who went to war. **23A**

6. Answers will vary; students should consider effects on employers, workers, and the number of jobs. **23D**

Writing about Economics

Students should explain their reasons for doing the kind of work they do and the influences that led them to that kind of work. **24D**

Building Social Studies Skills

1. d **23F, 23G**

2. The former is higher than the latter. Students can infer from this that the percentages for men are higher in both cases. **23A, 23F, 23G**

3. c **23E**

4. the expression "wheeled coffins" when used to describe the buses **23E**

LABOR AND UNIONS

CHAPTER RESOURCE MANAGER

CHAPTER 9: SOURCES OF CAPITAL

	OBJECTIVES	PACING GUIDE	REPRODUCIBLE RESOURCES
SECTION 1 **Saving** (pp. 195–99)	▶ What benefits do people gain by saving money? ▶ How do savings accounts differ from time deposits? ▶ How do economists measure savings?	**Regular** 1 day **Block Scheduling** 0.5 day	**ELL** Spanish Study Guide 9.1 **ELL** English Study Guide 9.1 **PS** Reading 46: Depository Institutions Deregulation Act **SM** Mathematics for Economics: Activity 9 **SM** Consumer Economics: Activity 9
SECTION 2 **Investing** (pp. 200–03)	▶ What are the goals and elements of a personal financial plan? ▶ How do financial investment and real investment differ? ▶ How does real investment affect economic growth?	**Regular** 1.5 days **Block Scheduling** 0.5 day	**ELL** Spanish Study Guide 9.2 **ELL** English Study Guide 9.2
SECTION 3 **Stocks, Bonds, and Futures** (pp. 204–13)	▶ Why and how do people invest in stocks? ▶ What factors influence stock prices? ▶ How do corporate and government bonds differ from stocks? ▶ What are the advantages and disadvantages of futures?	**Regular** 2 days **Block Scheduling** 1 day	**ELL** Spanish Study Guide 9.3 **ELL** English Study Guide 9.3 **E** Challenge and Enrichment: Activity 9
SECTION 4 **Borrowing and Credit** (pp. 214–18)	▶ How do lenders make money on loans? ▶ What factors influence a credit rating? ▶ How can credit help the economy?	**Regular** 1.5 days **Block Scheduling** 0.5 day	**ELL** Spanish Study Guide 9.4 **ELL** English Study Guide 9.4 **S** Simulations and Strategies for Teaching Economics: Activity 9

Chapter Resource Key

- **PS** Primary Sources
- **RS** Reading Support
- **E** Enrichment
- **S** Simulations
- **SM** Skills Mastery
- **A** Assessment
- **REV** Review
- **ELL** Reinforcement and English Language Learners
- Transparencies
- CD-ROM
- Video
- Videodisc
- Internet
- Holt Presentation Maker Using Microsoft® PowerPoint®
- TEKS and TAKS

	TECHNOLOGY RESOURCES	REINFORCEMENT, REVIEW, AND ASSESSMENT
	One-Stop Planner: Lesson 9.1 Researcher Online Homework Practice Online CNN Presents Economics: The Fine Art of Investing Transparency 32 Global Skillbuilder CD-ROM	**REV** Section 1 Review, p. 199 **A** Daily Quiz 9.1 ★ TAKS Every Day!
	One-Stop Planner: Lesson 9.2 Researcher Online Homework Practice Online Global Skillbuilder CD-ROM	**REV** Section 2 Review, p. 203 **A** Daily Quiz 9.2 ★ TAKS Every Day!
	One-Stop Planner: Lesson 9.3 Researcher Online Homework Practice Online Transparencies 33, 34, and 35 Global Skillbuilder CD-ROM	**REV** Section 3 Review, p. 213 **A** Daily Quiz 9.3 ★ TAKS Every Day!
	One-Stop Planner: Lesson 9.4 Researcher Online Homework Practice Online Transparencies 36 and 37 Global Skillbuilder CD-ROM	**REV** Section 4 Review, p. 218 **A** Daily Quiz 9.4 ★ TAKS Every Day!

Chapter Review and Assessment

- **SM** Global Skillbuilder CD-ROM
- HRW Go site
- **REV** Reteaching Activity 9
- **REV** Chapter 9 Review, pp. 220–21
- **A** Chapter 9 Test Generator (on the One-Stop Planner)
- **A** Chapter 9 Test
- **A** Alternative Assessment Handbook

One-Stop Planner CD-ROM

It's easy to plan lessons, select resources, and print out materials for your students when you use the **Texas One-Stop Planner CD-ROM with Test Generator**.

---

internet connect

HRW ONLINE RESOURCES
Go to: go.hrw.com
Then type in a keyword.

TEACHER HOME PAGE
KEYWORD: SM3 Teacher

CHAPTER INTERNET ACTIVITIES
KEYWORD: SM3 EC9
Choose an activity to:
▶ learn about financial planners.
▶ create a brochure about the FDIC.
▶ research securities exchanges in the United States.

CHAPTER ENRICHMENT LINKS
KEYWORD: SM3 CH9

HOLT ONLINE RESEARCHER
KEYWORD: Holt Researcher

ONLINE ASSESSMENT
Homework Practice
KEYWORD: SM3 HP9
TAKS Review
KEYWORD: SM3 T9
Rubrics
KEYWORD: SS Rubrics

CONTENT UPDATES
KEYWORD: SS Content Updates

HOLT PRESENTATION MAKER
KEYWORD: SM3 PPT9

ONLINE READING SUPPORT
KEYWORD: SS Strategies

CURRENT EVENTS
KEYWORD: SM3 Current Events

TEXAS ONLINE RESOURCES
KEYWORD: S3 TX

193B

LESSON 9.1 SAVING

TEXTBOOK PAGES 195–99

HOLT PRESENTATION MAKER Access Illustrated LECTURE NOTES using Microsoft® PowerPoint® on the One-Stop Planner CD-ROM

OBJECTIVES

- Describe the benefits people gain by saving money.
- Illustrate how savings accounts differ from time deposits. ★11B
- Explain how economists measure savings.

MOTIVATE

Ask students how many save their money in a bank or other lending institution. Ask for volunteers to share with the class the reasons they are saving money. Write students' reasons on the chalkboard. Next, ask students how they think they benefit from saving money in a bank or other lending institution, rather than in a piggy bank. Write these reasons on the chalkboard as well. Tell students that in this section they will learn more about the benefits of saving money in a lending institution.

TEACH

Building a Vocabulary

Have students use spiral notebooks to create an Economics Dictionary to be used throughout the chapter. This dictionary might be used as an activity at the start of each new section or as a learning aid for sheltered English students or students having difficulty. List words that students will be expected to know for this section on the chalkboard. Have students use the information provided in the text or on the *Researcher CD-ROM* to list, define, and give an example of each term.

Analyzing Ideas

Review with students the five main reasons people save money *(major purchases, large annual or semiannual bills, unexpected expenses, major long-term expenses,* and *to amass wealth).* Tell students that there are two main benefits to saving money. Write these two benefits on the chalkboard: *security* and *interest.* Ask students to discuss the two major ways that lending institutions provide security for a person's savings and write these on the chalkboard under the term *security. (First, money deposited in a bank account cannot be lost; second, financial institutions are usually covered by insurance which protects savers from losing their money if the financial institution closes.)* Discuss with students why and how financial institutions pay interest and why interest rates vary. *(Financial institutions pay interest in exchange for using the saver's money while it is in the bank; interest rates on savings vary according to the financial institution in which the money is deposited; interest rates fluctuate to reflect the general availability of money in the economy.)* Ask students with savings accounts to share with the class what interest rate they are presently receiving.

Creating Charts, Comparing and Contrasting

Next, tell students that there are several ways to save money in a financial institution. Organize students into groups of three or four and give each group a piece of poster board and colored markers. Ask each group to create a chart that illustrates the differences and similarities among various types of savings accounts and time deposit accounts. On one axis of the chart students should list the four types of accounts discussed in Section 1: *regular savings accounts, money market deposit accounts, certificates of deposit,* and *savings bonds.* On the other axis of the chart, students should write in the following categories: *minimum deposit required, minimum balance allowed without a fee, liquidity, interest rate, maturity required (amount of time the saver must leave money in the account),* and *financial risk.* Have student groups define what each of the category terms means, referring to the textbook when necessary. Also, have the groups discuss the differences between these accounts. When students have completed the activity, display their posters around the classroom. Refer students who need additional instruction on the skills in this activity to the *Global Skillbuilder* Lesson 12: Creating Graphic Organizers. ★11B, 23A, 24D

Learning from Visuals, Evaluating Ideas

Tell students that economists measure the savings rate in order to determine the strength of the economy. Ask for student volunteers to explain the savings rate *(The savings rate is the percentage of people's disposable income that is not spent. Disposable income is the amount of money available after taxes are paid.)* Discuss with students the factors that most influence the personal savings rate. *(The personal savings rate is usually higher when wages and employment are high.)* Next, organize students into groups of two or three. Have students examine the cartoon on page 199 of the textbook. Ask student groups to discuss what is being depicted in the cartoon and have them create captions for this cartoon that illustrate the way that personal savings is measured. Ask for student volunteers from each group to share their captions with the class.

CLOSE

Review with students the different types of savings and time deposit accounts and ask the class to discuss the following questions: Which type of savings account might be the best option for a young person with a limited income? Which type of savings account might be best for an older person with a large amount of disposable income?

OPTIONS

Gifted Learners, Logical-Mathematical Learners

Have motivated students research the present interest rates for various types of savings and time deposit accounts and prepare a report summarizing their findings. Ask students to also find the personal savings rate for the last year and determine which type or types of accounts made up the majority of personal savings. In addition or alternatively, students may want to compare recent changes in interest rates and personal savings rates for a period of 5, 10, or 20 years. You may want to have students include charts, graphs, or tables to illustrate the information in their reports. Have students use the *Holt Researcher Online,* the library, in-class resources, and information from business journals or newspapers, such as the *Wall Street Journal, Forbes,* or *Money Magazine* to conduct their research. ★24C, 24D

Students Having Difficulty

Pair students having difficulty with students who have mastered the lesson material. Have students in each pair quiz each other with the following questions:
▶ Why do people save money?
▶ What are the two major ways people benefit from saving money in banks or other lending institutions?
▶ How does a savings account differ from a money market account?
▶ What is a time deposit account? A certificate of deposit?
▶ What is a savings bond, and how does it acquire value?
▶ What is the savings rate, and how do economists use it?

Interpersonal Learners

Ask students to imagine that they have $5,000 they want to save at the highest interest rate possible. Have students visit a local bank and ask for a brief interview to explore the different types of savings accounts offered. As an additional activity, encourage students to open their own savings accounts with a small amount of cash they have saved, or evaluate an account they already have. Students should present the results of the activity to the class in an oral report that focuses on the benefits of different savings plans.

REVIEW

Have students complete the Section 1 Review on page 199. Use the answers in the Annotated Teacher's Edition to assess student mastery of this section.

ASSESS

To assess student mastery of this section, have students complete Daily Quiz 9.1 in *Daily Quizzes with Answer Key*. For additional assessment options, see *Alternative Assessment Handbook* on the *One-Stop Planner CD-ROM*.

ADDITIONAL RESOURCES

Bamford, Janet, et al. *The Consumer Reports Money Book: How to Get It, Save It, and Spend It Wisely*. 2000. Consumer Reports Books.

Bamford, Janet. *Street Wise: A Guide for Teen Investors*. 2000. Bloomberg Press.

LESSON 9.2 INVESTING

TEXTBOOK PAGES 200–03

HOLT PRESENTATION MAKER Access Illustrated LECTURE NOTES using Microsoft® PowerPoint® on the One-Stop Planner CD-ROM

OBJECTIVES

▶ Describe the goals and elements of a personal financial plan.
▶ Analyze how financial investment and real investment differ. ★11B
▶ Describe how real investment affects economic growth. ★4B

MOTIVATE

Find an article in a local or national newspaper that discusses how an individual's or group's investment in the development of a new business is positively influencing the economy. Use the article to begin a discussion of the following question: How do you think the economy might be affected when people invest in the development of new housing, supermarkets, factories, or malls? Ask students to keep this discussion in mind as they read this section.

TEACH

Building a Vocabulary

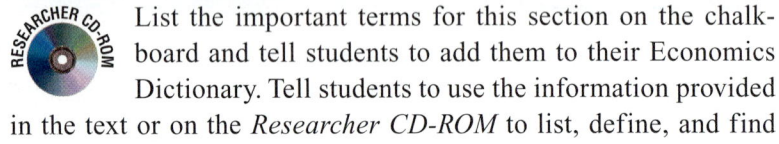

List the important terms for this section on the chalkboard and tell students to add them to their Economics Dictionary. Tell students to use the information provided in the text or on the *Researcher CD-ROM* to list, define, and find an example of each term.

Role-Playing, Analyzing Information

Tell students that one of the best ways to manage money for savings and investment is to develop a personal financial plan. Organize students into pairs. Ask the students in each pair to imagine that they are financial advisers who are helping a single person develop a financial plan. Assign pairs to work with clients with a $30,000, a $45,000, or a $60,000 yearly disposable income. Have each pair design a financial plan that includes a budget with fixed and flexible expenses, a diversified investment plan, a retirement plan, and an estate plan.

Students also should make up actual figures for their clients' budgets and investments that total $30,000, $45,000, or $60,000 a year or less. *(For example, students should make a list of their client's monthly or yearly fixed expenses, such as rent or mortgage, and car, property, and health insurance; they also should make a list of flexible expenses, such as groceries, eating out, clothing, travel, new furniture, and entertainment.)* Then students should determine how much money can be allocated to savings and investments. They should decide how much money they are advising their clients to put towards investments, such as CDs and bonds, as well as towards retirement plans, such as IRAs. Finally, student pairs should write a brief estate plan that indicates who the designated beneficiary is for their client's life insurance and investments. ★23G, 24D

Classifying and Applying Ideas

Remind students that when people are deciding how to invest their money, they usually choose between two basic types of investment. On the chalkboard, write the terms *financial investment* and *real investment*. Ask for student volunteers to help define each of these terms. *(Financial investment is a transfer of property ownership between two individuals, such as stocks, bonds, or real estate; financial investment produces no new goods. Real investments involve the creation of a new capital good, such as the building of a factory, and are made by individuals as well as private companies and the government.)* Next, ask students to give examples of financial investments and real investments being made in the local community. *(For example, if a community member has bought a house with the hope that its value will increase, or if another community member invests in stocks, each is making a financial investment; if another community member is part of a business that invests in the construction of a new grocery store, or a toll road, then that company is making a real investment.)* ★11B

Evaluating Ideas

Tell students that while financial investment can improve the living conditions of individuals, real investment stimulates the economy more actively in four important ways: *capital accumulation, infrastructure, technological change,* and *entrepreneurship (venture capital).* Organize students into groups of three or four. Ask each group to discuss what each of these factors means and how real investment in a free-market economy encourages capital accumulation, technological change, entrepreneurship, and the improvement of a nation's infrastructure. ★4B

193E

CLOSE

Call on student volunteers from the different pairs organized for the first lesson activity to share the personal financial plans they devised for their client. Discuss the following questions:

- How important is a budget to a person's ability to save and invest money?
- Is it possible for a person who takes home $20,000 a year to invest as much as a person who takes home $50,000 a year? How can this be accomplished?
- What factors limit a person's ability to save and invest money? How many of these factors can a person change?

OPTIONS

Gifted Learners

Ask motivated students to explore how real investment in your state or county has promoted economic growth. Students may wish to focus on the building of new stores or on the construction of new factories or businesses important to the local economy, such as lumber or mining, microchip, or textile manufacturing. Encourage students to examine how a lack of real investment may have hurt the local economy. Have students use the *Holt Researcher Online,* the library, in-class resources, and information from business journals or newspapers, such as the *Wall Street Journal, Forbes,* or *Money Magazine*. Students should present their findings in an oral or written report. 24D

Interpersonal Learners

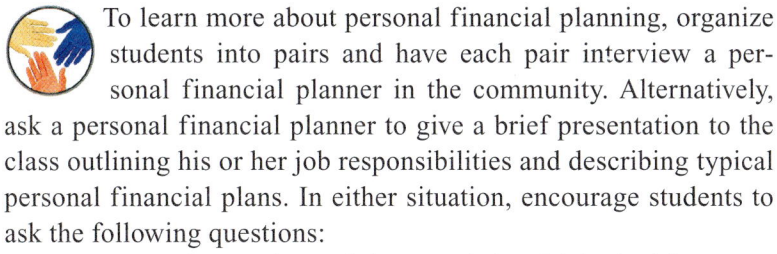

To learn more about personal financial planning, organize students into pairs and have each pair interview a personal financial planner in the community. Alternatively, ask a personal financial planner to give a brief presentation to the class outlining his or her job responsibilities and describing typical personal financial plans. In either situation, encourage students to ask the following questions:

- What issues do people need the most help with in devising a personal financial plan?
- How difficult is it for people to make and stick with a realistic budget that will allow them to save and invest?
- What types of investments and retirement plans are the most popular or common among young wage earners? Among older wage earners?
- Do people with children tend to make personal financial plans that differ greatly from those made by people without children?
- What are the most important things to consider and prioritize when making a personal financial plan?

Sheltered English Students, Visual-Spatial Learners

Pair students acquiring English with fluent English speakers. Have each pair write a brief paragraph that describes the differences between financial investment and real investment. Also, have each pair create a separate flowchart that illustrates how real investment promotes economic growth. Students should show in their flowcharts how real investment leads to capital accumulation, development of national or local infrastructure, technological change, and entrepreneurship. *(For example, students might have a central box with the statement: "real investment," with an arrow leading to a box with the statement: "real investment enables companies to purchase new technology," with an arrow leading to a box with the statement: "new technology increases productivity," with an arrow leading to a box with the statement: "increased productivity leads to increased sales and more new technology.")* You may want to provide students with poster board and colored markers with which to make their charts. Refer students who need additional instruction on the skills used in this activity to the *Global Skillbuilder* Lesson 12: Creating Graphic Organizers.

REVIEW

Have students complete the Section 2 Review on page 203. Use the answers in the Annotated Teacher's Edition to assess student mastery of this section.

ASSESS

To assess student mastery of this section, have students complete Daily Quiz 9.2 in *Daily Quizzes with Answer Key*. For additional assessment options, see *Alternative Assessment Handbook* on the *One-Stop Planner CD-ROM*.

ADDITIONAL RESOURCES

Downes, John, and Jordan Elliot Goodman. *Dictionary of Finance and Investment Terms*. 1998. Barron's.

Tobias, Andrew. *The Only Investment Guide You'll Ever Need*. 1999. Harvest Books.

LESSON 9.3 STOCKS, BONDS, AND FUTURES
TEXTBOOK PAGES 204–13

HOLT PRESENTATION MAKER
Access Illustrated LECTURE NOTES using Microsoft® PowerPoint® on the One-Stop Planner CD-ROM

OBJECTIVES

▸ Explain why and how people invest in stocks. ★11B
▸ Analyze the factors that influence stock prices.
▸ Describe how corporate and government bonds differ from stocks. ★11C
▸ Identify the advantages and disadvantages of investing in futures.

MOTIVATE

Tell students that in this section they will learn about why and how people invest in stocks, what factors influence changes in stock prices, the differences between various types of stocks and bonds, the advantages and disadvantages of investing in a type of commodity exchange called futures, and the economic consequences of buying and selling investments at various prices. ★1B, 11C

Organize students into groups of three or four. Find several articles from local or national newspapers or magazines (such as the *Wall Street Journal, Forbes, Money Magazine,* the *New York Times,* etc.) that discuss an individual's or company's recent success, failure, or concerns with their investments in stocks, bonds, or futures in the current market. Assign an article to each group and tell students to read the article and then discuss the following questions:

▸ What is the main point of this article?
▸ What are the main concerns of the person or company featured in the article regarding their investment, and what kinds of risks are they taking with their investment?
▸ How did the person or company go about making this investment?
▸ How does this type of investment compare with other types of investments?

TEACH

Building a Vocabulary

List the important terms for this section on the chalkboard and tell students to add them to their Economics Dictionary. Tell students to use the information provided in the text or on the *Researcher CD-ROM* to list, define, and find an example of each term.

Analyzing Ideas

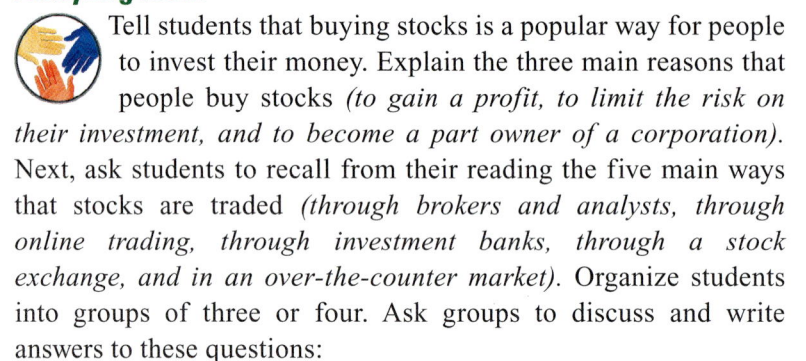

Tell students that buying stocks is a popular way for people to invest their money. Explain the three main reasons that people buy stocks *(to gain a profit, to limit the risk on their investment, and to become a part owner of a corporation).* Next, ask students to recall from their reading the five main ways that stocks are traded *(through brokers and analysts, through online trading, through investment banks, through a stock exchange, and in an over-the-counter market).* Organize students into groups of three or four. Ask groups to discuss and write answers to these questions:

▸ What are two ways that stocks can provide a profit?
▸ What risks are stockholders protected from?
▸ What function do stock brokers and brokerage firms serve?
▸ What is the purpose of the stock exchange?
▸ What is the over-the-counter-market?
▸ What types of economic information are available to investors as a result of technological innovations? ★11B, 11C, 27A

Learning from Visuals

Remind students that because stocks represent partial ownership of a company, the success or failure of a company influences the price of the company's stocks, and therefore the economic consequences to investors. Ask the class what happens to the price of a company's stocks if demand for its stocks is high. *(The price of its stocks rises.)* Next, ask the class what happens if demand for its stocks is low. *(The price of its stocks drops.)*

Organize students into groups of three or four. Give each group the same copy of a recent stock market report found in a local or national newspaper. First, choose any company in the stock report and review with students what each figure and abbreviation represents in that company's stock listing. (Refer to Figure 9.4 on page 208 for assistance.) Next, ask each group to choose one company whose products or services it is familiar with. Tell each group to discuss how corporate finances, investor expectations, and external forces may have influenced the recent rise, fall, or steady value of that company's stocks. Have students discuss how the current status of the market (bull or bear) may have influenced the value of their companies' stocks. ★1B, 11C

193G

Using Charts, Comparing and Contrasting

Remind students that in addition to stocks, investors also can choose to buy bonds. On the chalkboard, draw the outline for a chart to help students understand the differences between corporate bonds, government bonds, and stocks. Along the top of the chart, write the names of the investments: *corporate bonds, government bonds,* and *stocks*. On the left side of the chart, write in a vertical column the factors for comparison: *interest or dividends, tax liability,* and *risk of investment*. Discuss with the class the differences between these types of investments and fill in the chart with information provided by students during the discussion. ★11B, 23A

Applying Ideas, Role-Playing

Remind the class that another type of investment, called futures, includes agricultural products, industrial goods, and precious metals. Organize students into pairs. Give one student in each pair an index card with a commodity written on it *(such as coal, steel, gold, silver, diamonds, soybeans, oats, corn, wheat, hogs, cattle, sheep, etc., giving each pair a different commodity),* a number representing the amount of the commodity *(such as 400 tons of coal, 500 oz. of gold, 25,000 bushels of wheat, 150,000 pounds of cattle, and 75,000 pounds of sheep),* and a price written beneath the name of the commodity *(such as $100 per ton for coal, $200 per oz. for gold, $100 per carat for diamonds, $6 per bushel for oats, $5 per bushel for wheat, and $.40 per pound for cattle).* Cardholders should imagine that they are trying to sell the amount of the commodity they own at the price suggested on their cards. The other student in each pair should imagine that he or she is an investor.

Give the "investor" an index card with an amount of money written on it, which represents how much he or she has to offer for the commodity. Ask the students in each pair to negotiate for a price that is agreeable to both of them. After students have agreed upon a price, have them write this price on each of their cards with the amount of the commodity purchased. Next, tell the students to imagine that six months have passed and the commodities are ready for delivery to the investors. Read the "current" value of the commodities from a list that you have prepared, in which the value of the various commodities has clearly risen or fallen *(for example, $60 per ton for coal, $250 per oz. for gold, $200 per carat for diamonds, $5 per bushel for oats, $.35 per pound for cattle).* Have students determine who lost money and who made money in the exchange.

CLOSE

Using the previous activity as an example, discuss with students the advantages and disadvantages of trading in futures. Call on student volunteers to discuss which type of investment they think usually offers the highest rewards for the least risk: stocks, bonds or futures. ★11B

OPTIONS

Students Having Difficulty

Pair students having difficulty with students who have mastered the lesson material. Have each pair write a sentence or two that describes the following:
- how corporate finances influence demand for a stock
- how investor expectations influence demand for a stock
- what types of external forces influence demand for a stock
- the difference between a bull market and a bear market
- how corporate bonds differ from government bonds
- the meaning of the term *futures* ★7A

Gifted Learners, Linguistic Learners

Ask motivated students to explore one aspect of the stock market crash of 1929. Students may focus on the causes of the crash, the effect of the crash on Wall Street businesspeople, farmers, education, or the regulation of trade in securities. Encourage students to choose a variety of formats in which to present their findings to the class, including collages, poems, songs, short stories, graphs, charts, or a written summary. ★19C, 24D

REVIEW

Have students complete the Section 3 Review on page 213. Use the answers in the Annotated Teacher's Edition to assess student mastery of this section.

ASSESS

To assess student mastery of this section, have students complete Daily Quiz 9.3 in *Daily Quizzes with Answer Key*. For additional assessment options, see *Alternative Assessment Handbook* on the One-Stop Planner CD-ROM.

ADDITIONAL RESOURCES

Common Stocks and Uncommon Profits and Other Writings (Wiley Investment Classics). 1996. John Wiley & Sons.

Galbraith, John Kenneth. *The Great Crash, 1929.* 1997. Houghton Mifflin Co.

LESSON 9.4 BORROWING AND CREDIT

TEXTBOOK PAGES 214–18

HOLT PRESENTATION MAKER Access Illustrated LECTURE NOTES using Microsoft® PowerPoint® on the One-Stop Planner CD-ROM

OBJECTIVES

- Describe how lenders make money on loans.
- Identify the factors that influence a credit rating.
- Explain how credit can help the economy.

MOTIVATE

Cut out a variety of ads from different newspapers or magazines offering goods for sale at different interest rates (ads for cars would be especially useful). Show the ads one at a time to the class and ask students to help determine which ads they think might offer the best deals. Ask students if the ads state whether a buyer must put up collateral in order to finance the goods. Next ask students: If you wanted to buy a car partially on credit, what do you think might be required for you to obtain credit? Tell students that in this section they will learn about the factors that influence a person's ability to gain credit and how credit can help the economy.

TEACH

Building a Vocabulary

List the important terms for this section on the chalkboard and tell students to add them to their Economics Dictionary. Tell students to use the information provided in the text or on the *Researcher CD-ROM* to list, define, and find an example of each term.

Building a Vocabulary, Comparing and Contrasting

On the chalkboard, write the terms *principal* and *interest*. Ask students to explain these terms based on what they have learned from the textbook. *(The principal is the amount borrowed in a loan, while the interest is the amount the borrower pays the lender for the privilege of using the money.)* Next, write *secured loan, unsecured loan, collateral,* and *installments* on the chalkboard. Call on students to help explain these terms. *(A secured loan requires that the borrower offers collateral; an unsecured loan does not require collateral and is thus rare; collateral is something of value, such as a car or a house, offered by the borrower as a guarantee that the loan will be repaid; installments are repayments of loans that have been divided into equal amounts.)* Emphasize that unsecured loans generally require higher interest rates. Discuss with the class the following questions:

- How do lenders make money on loans? *(primarily by charging interest on loans)*
- Which loan would make the most money for the lender, and which loan would save the borrower the most money: a $1,000 loan with a 7 percent interest rate, a $1,000 loan with a 9 percent interest rate, a $1,000 loan with a 12 percent interest rate, or a $1,000 loan with a 16 percent interest rate? *(The loan with a 16 percent interest rate would make the lender the most money, while the loan with the 7 percent interest rate would save the borrower the most money.)* ⭐23G

Analyzing Information

Remind students that consumers do not automatically receive credit, but must first apply and be approved for credit. On the chalkboard, write the term *credit rating* and ask students to explain its meaning. Ask students to recall from their reading of Section 4 the three factors affecting a person's credit rating *(ability to pay, assets,* and *credit history)*. Organize students into groups of three or four. Ask students in each group to make a list of at least six things a person can do to develop a good credit rating based on these factors, and a list of at least six things a person might do to develop a poor credit rating based on these factors *(examples of ways to develop a good credit rating include holding a steady job, paying off all loans and credit debt in a timely fashion, and owning several valuable pieces of property, or assets, such as a house, car, or jewelry; examples of ways to develop a poor credit rating include defaulting on a loan, declaring bankruptcy, failing to hold a steady job, and paying bills late)*. ⭐11A

Evaluating Ideas, Creating Charts

Tell students that while credit helps people buy things they want and need, it also can help to strengthen the economy. Organize students into groups of two or three. Have each group make a flowchart that answers the following questions:

- How does credit stimulate the economy?
- How does credit promote economic stability?

Encourage students to be as specific and creative as possible in constructing their flowcharts. If groups are having difficulty thinking of specific examples to use in making a flowchart, you may

193I

suggest that they use examples such as: a person using credit to buy a $5,000 set of living-room furniture; a person using credit to pay $3,000 of college tuition; a person using $8,000 in credit to put towards a $20,000 boat; a person using credit to buy $20 in gasoline for their car. Refer students to Figure 9.9: Promoting Economic Growth through Saving and Credit *(Transparency 37)* for assistance in making their flowcharts. (An example flowchart addressing the first question might read as follows: a young woman uses $65 borrowed on credit to buy numerous CDs; the music store that sold her the CDs uses the money she spent to help build a second store; the second store can sell more CDs to more people; some of the profit from the CDs goes to the musicians who can use their profits to produce more CDs.) Refer students who need additional instruction on the skills in this activity to the *Global Skill Builder* Lesson 12: Creating Graphic Organizers. ⭐24D

CLOSE

Ask for volunteers to present their flowcharts to the class. Discuss how the economy can be strengthened by the use of credit; then ask the class to discuss how the economy would be affected if everyone in the U.S. stopped using credit. Next, ask students to discuss how and why people can get themselves into trouble by abusing credit, even if credit can be good for the economy.

OPTIONS

Interpersonal Learners

Have students work in pairs or individually for this activity. Ask each pair to research the terms for several major bank credit cards and for credit cards from other sources, such as oil companies (for gasoline) and department stores. Have students compare the finance charges (interest rate on the unpaid balance), the line of credit available, and the yearly fee required for each card. Also, have students investigate eligibility requirements for these different credit cards, including minimum income requirements. Have students present their findings in a brief written or oral report, with graphs or charts that show the differences between what the different cards offer. ⭐23A, 24D

Logical-Mathematical Learners

Ask motivated students: If you could buy anything you wanted, what would it be? Then ask students: How much do you think this item would cost? Tell students to imagine that they are going to finance this dream item by applying for credit. Ask students to call a store or bank that offers credit to find out the present finance charge rate *(monthly and yearly interest rates)*, and any other fees *(for example, a bank might offer a credit card with a 15% yearly interest rate and a $20 yearly fee)*. Have students decide how much they plan to put towards paying off their credit account each month, and how many months it will take for them to pay for their dream item if paying this particular monthly amount *(if they are planning to buy a car that costs $30,000, and they plan to put $300 a month towards their credit plan, then it will take them over eight years to pay off their credit for the car)*. Next, have students calculate how much they would have to pay in total for the item they are buying on credit when the monthly and/or yearly finance charges are added to the total cost of the item *(for the example used here, they would need to calculate 15% yearly interest added to the $30,000 cost of the car, minus the monthly payments made, but adjusting the interest paid to reflect the overall decrease in amount owed on the credit plan)*. Once students have calculated the final cost of the item, ask them to compare the original cost to the cost when credit is used. Discuss with students whether they would still want to buy the item on credit. ⭐23G

REVIEW

Have students complete the Section 4 Review on page 218. Use the answers in the Annotated Teacher's Edition to assess student mastery of this section.

ASSESS

To assess student mastery of this section, have students complete Daily Quiz 9.4 in *Daily Quizzes with Answer Key*. For additional assessment options, see *Alternative Assessment Handbook* on the *One-Stop Planner CD-ROM*.

RETEACH

For students having difficulty with the lessons, have them complete Reteaching Activity 9. This activity is located in *Reteaching Activities with Answer Key*.

ADDITIONAL RESOURCES

McNaughton, Debra. *The Insider's Guide to Credit Power: How to Establish, Maintain, Repair and Protect Your Credit*. 1999. Berkley Publishing Group.

Sullivan, Teresa A., et al. *The Fragile Middle Class: Americans in Debt*. 2000. Yale University Press.

193J

CHAPTER 9

TOPICS INCLUDE

- benefits of saving
- types of savings accounts
- types of time deposits
- investment and risk
- financial planning
- types of investments
- investment and economic growth
- stocks, bonds, and futures
- buying and trading securities
- stock exchanges
- securities regulation
- loans and credit
- credit and economic growth and stability

ECONOMICS NOTEBOOK

The Economics Notebook is a journal activity that encourages students to consider basic concepts of economics that relate to their lives. A follow-up notebook activity appears on page 220.

WHY IT MATTERS TODAY

To find additional lesson plans dealing with information technology and economic information, visit CNNfyi.com or have students complete the ECONOMICS IN THE NEWS activity on page 219.

CNNfyi.com

CHAPTER 9

SOURCES OF CAPITAL

In this chapter you will learn about the choices available to consumers for saving, investing, and borrowing money. Additionally, you will learn how the government regulates these activities.

ECONOMICS NOTEBOOK

Imagine that you have just won $500 in a trivia contest on the radio. Write a brief paragraph in your Economics Notebook explaining what you will do with the money and how you made your choices.

WHY IT MATTERS TODAY

Today information technology changes very quickly. Use CNNfyi.com or other **current events** sources to find more examples of information technology's impact on access to economic information.

CNNfyi.com

SECTION 1

SAVING

READ TO DISCOVER

1. What benefits do people gain by saving money?
2. How do savings accounts differ from time deposits?
3. How do economists measure savings?

ECONOMICS DICTIONARY

disposable income
balance
liquidity
time deposits
maturity
savings rate

In a free-enterprise economy business owners can choose how to organize their companies and workers can make choices about how to use their labor. Similarly, consumers have an important choice to make—how to use the income at their disposal. They may spend this income or save it, consume it or not consume it. Spending is the consumption of **disposable income**—money available after taxes have been paid. Saving is the nonconsumption of disposable income.

Spending and saving are equally important to a strong economy. Spending reflects demand—how much of a product consumers will buy at a particular price. As spending increases, producers expand supply, and as spending decreases, producers reduce supply. But how is saving important?

Why Save Money?

Think about what people can do with money they have saved. In general, people save for five main reasons: for major purchases such as a car, house, or refrigerator; to pay large annual or semiannual bills such as property taxes or automobile insurance; for unexpected expenses such as medical treatment or home repairs; for major long-term expenses such as college tuition or retirement needs; and to amass wealth or leave an inheritance to their children.

No matter what reasons people have for saving money, they experience two benefits: security and interest.

Security Saving money in a bank or other lending institution provides two types of security. First, money in a bank account cannot be lost because of misfortunes in the home, such as fire or theft. Second, most financial institutions are protected by state and federal deposit insurance. These insurance plans protect savers from losing their money if the institution closes.

Interest When you deposit money in a financial institution, you may receive a payment called interest. The financial institution pays interest in exchange for the use of your money while it is deposited. (See Figure 9.1 on page 196.)

Interest rates on savings vary according to the type of account chosen and the financial

ECONOMIC INSTITUTIONS & INCENTIVES *One major expense that many people save for is college.* **What are two benefits of saving?**

SOURCES OF CAPITAL 195

Transparency

An overhead transparency of Figure 9.1 is available in *Transparency Resources*. See Transparency 32: Compound Interest.

Caption Answer

Interest rates vary according to the type of account and financial institution chosen, and the supply of money in the economy. ⭐23F

Themes in Economics

EXCHANGE, MONEY, & INTERDEPENDENCE To determine how much the money you deposit in a savings account will be worth in the future, you need to consider both nominal and real interest rates. For example, suppose that you deposit $100 in a savings account earning 8 percent interest. This rate is the *nominal* interest rate. After one year, your $100 will have grown to $108. Suppose, however, that overall prices increased by 3 percent during the year. As a result, $108 no longer buys the same amount of goods and services as it did a year ago. Thus, the *real* interest rate that you earned on your savings was only 5 percent—that is, the nominal interest rate minus the inflation rate, or the rate at which overall prices increased. ■

COMPOUND INTEREST

Compounded Interest on a Single Investment of $1,000

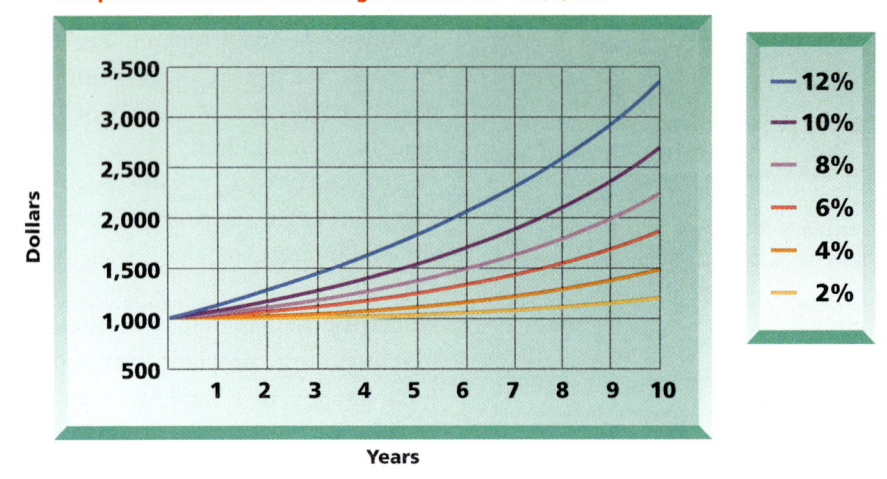

FIGURE 9.1 Financial institutions pay interest in exchange for the use of customers' money. **What causes interest rates to change?** ⭐TEKS

---

institution in which the money is deposited. Interest rates also fluctuate, or change, to reflect the general availability of money in the economy. When the supply of money in the economy is reduced, interest rates generally increase. When more money is available, on the other hand, interest rates are lower.

Financial institutions such as banks also *charge* interest on the loans they make to individuals and businesses. Again, this interest is a payment for the use of the loaned money. Basically, a bank or other financial institution makes a profit in part by charging more interest on loans than it pays on savings deposits.

Savings Accounts

Suppose that Monique Foster decides to open a savings account. She already knows that savings accounts offer very little risk. While her money is deposited in a financial institution such as a bank, her funds—up to $100,000—are insured by the federal government. When Monique arrives at her local bank, she discovers that she can choose from among different types of accounts, including regular savings accounts and money market deposit accounts.

Regular Savings Accounts Regular savings accounts, which are among the most common types of accounts, usually require only a small deposit. Many financial institutions, however, charge a fee if the **balance**—the amount of money in the account—drops below a specified level.

Some depositors open regular savings accounts because they offer liquidity. **Liquidity** means that assets such as an account can be converted into cash with little or no loss in interest payments. Monique could withdraw her savings from this type of account at any time. In exchange for high liquidity, the interest rate on a regular savings account is relatively low compared to the interest paid on other types of savings accounts.

Money Market Deposit Accounts Monique may decide to open a money market deposit account. Like regular savings accounts, money market deposit accounts pay interest and allow relatively easy access to savings. These accounts offer variable interest rates that generally are higher than those of regular savings accounts.

To determine interest rates for money market deposit accounts, financial institutions invest funds from these accounts in interest-bearing securities such as Treasury bills. The financial institution passes on part of the interest to account holders and keeps the rest as profit. Because these interest rates fluctuate, however, account holders may not always receive higher interest rates.

Money market deposit accounts have a fair amount of liquidity. Account holders can make withdrawals without penalty, but they are usually restricted to making a certain number of withdrawals each month. Some financial institutions place other restrictions on these money market accounts as well, such as requiring advance notice of withdrawals.

Time Deposits

Suppose that Monique decides that savings accounts do not offer enough interest. She may open an account known as a time deposit. **Time deposits** require the saver to leave money in the account for a specific amount of time. Savers who want to open time deposits probably will buy certificates of deposit or savings bonds.

Certificates of Deposit Monique may decide to deposit her money for a particular length of time. If she does, she will receive a certificate of deposit (CD) that represents her funds. The length of time that money must be deposited is called the **maturity**. The maturities of CDs range from less than a month to several years.

CDs with longer maturities generally offer higher interest because the higher rates compensate for reduced liquidity. Because people who invest in CDs lose the use of their money for a longer period of time, they receive a higher interest rate. In return, someone who withdraws funds before the maturity date must pay a penalty. CDs usually require a minimum deposit, which may range from $250 to $100,000.

Both the maturity and the interest rate are established when the account is opened, and the interest rate stays constant until the maturity date. Fixed interest rates offer both benefits and

NATIONAL SAVINGS RATES

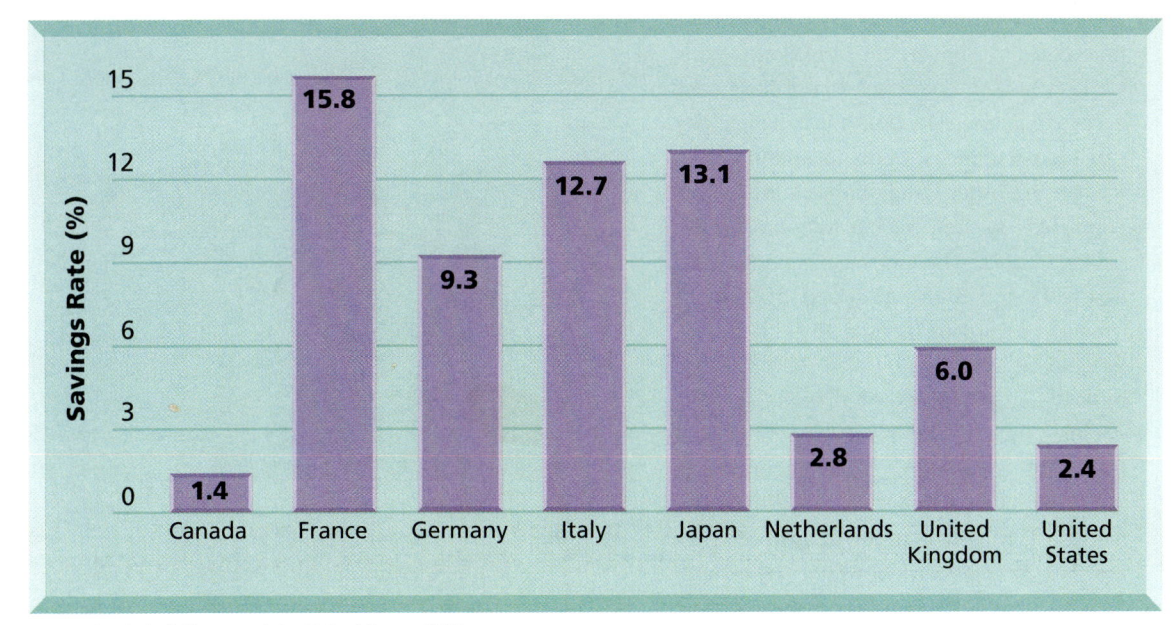

Country	Savings Rate (%)
Canada	1.4
France	15.8
Germany	9.3
Italy	12.7
Japan	13.1
Netherlands	2.8
United Kingdom	6.0
United States	2.4

Source: *Statistical Abstract of the United States: 2000*

FIGURE 9.2 Savings rates vary considerably from country to country. **What are some of the reasons for this variation?**

---

internet connect

TOPIC: The FDIC, Savings Accounts, and Government Regulation
GO TO: go.hrw.com
KEYWORD: SM3 EC9

Have students access the Internet through the HRW Go site to conduct research on the history of the Federal Deposit Insurance Corporation and the federal regulation of savings accounts. Then have students work in pairs to create a list of frequently asked questions (FAQs)—and the answers to them—about the FDIC and the federal regulations governing savings accounts. Tell each pair to create a brochure with FAQs that the FDIC might give banks and/or consumers to explain its history and purpose. ★15A, 15B, 24A

Caption Answer
whether the nation has a government-sponsored savings plan, the availability of products for purchase, the nation's average income, the availability of banks and other savings institutions, the amount of overall consumer debt

Across the Curriculum

GOVERNMENT & HISTORY

During World War I the U.S. government needed money to loan to the Allies and to purchase military supplies and munitions. One way the government raised money was through the sale of U.S. goverment bonds, called Liberty Loans. Film celebrities of the time, such as Charlie Chaplin and Mary Pickford, attended public rallies across the United States to promote the sale of these bonds. The drive was successful. During the course of the war, the U.S. government raised $21 billion through the sale of defense bonds and was able to loan $10 billion to the Allies to help fund the war effort. ■

Caption Answer

It earns interest over time.

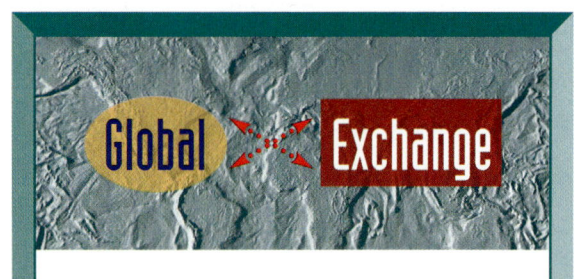

Global Exchange

Savings Around the World

Because many factors influence savings rates, it is not surprising that such rates vary dramatically from country to country. In some countries—Singapore, for example—workers must contribute a portion of their pay to a government-sponsored savings plan, making savings rates relatively high.

The availability of goods for consumers to purchase is another factor that influences savings rates. For example, before the fall of communism, Eastern European countries often suffered from chronic shortages of consumer goods. Without products to purchase, many Eastern Europeans simply saved their money.

Savings rates are naturally lower in countries where incomes are low. In the poorest countries, food purchases might account for as much as 60 to 70 percent of a household's budget. In addition, many workers in poor countries do not have easy access to financial institutions in which they can deposit money they do not spend.

On the other hand, workers in wealthy countries do not necessarily have high savings rates. The personal savings rate in the United States dropped from more than 8 percent of income to less than 1 percent between 1970 and 2000. Economists suggest different reasons for this decline, such as high levels of debt carried by many consumers. Some economists believe, however, that the U.S. savings rate will rise as members of the baby boom generation—people born between 1946 and 1964—get older and put more money away for retirement.

---

drawbacks. If interest rates in general go down after Monique buys a CD, she will still receive the higher, agreed-upon rate. On the other hand, interest rates may go up—but Monique will receive only the CD's relatively lower, established interest rate.

Savings Bonds Monique may decide to limit her risk by purchasing savings bonds, which are issued by the federal government to pay for federal programs. The purchasers assume little risk because the savings bonds are guaranteed by U.S. government funds.

Savers like Monique purchase the bonds for less than face value and redeem them at their face value upon maturity. Savers can purchase a $50 Series EE government savings bond for $25 and redeem it later for $50. If a bondholder chooses to keep the savings bond beyond its

SIGN UP FOR PAYROLL SAVINGS TODAY.

ECONOMIC INSTITUTIONS & INCENTIVES *Savings bonds are issued by the U.S. government.* **How does a bond acquire value?**

maturity date, the bond continues to earn interest until redeemed.

Like corporate bonds, government bonds are a kind of loan. By selling bonds, the government gains money for programs. Similarly, consumers know that they will receive interest while they hold the bond. The increased value of a bond reflects the money borrowed from, plus the interest paid to, the bond buyer. Someone redeeming a $50 bond, for example, gets back the initial $25 plus $25 in interest.

Measuring Savings

Economists measure savings to help determine the health of the economy. The main factor they consider for this process is the savings rate. The **savings rate** is the percentage of people's disposable income—money available after taxes are paid—that is not spent.

One of the most important determinants of the personal savings rate in the United States is income. High-income households tend to save more money than low-income households. As a result, the average rate of personal savings for the nation is likely to be high when wages are high. In contrast, the average rate of personal savings is usually lower when wages are lower—for example, during economic slowdowns and periods of high unemployment. (See Figure 9.2 on page 197.)

ECONOMIC INSTITUTIONS & INCENTIVES *Economists use the savings rate to measure the strength of an economy.* **How is the savings rate determined?**

SECTION 1 REVIEW

Q: 1, 2, 3a

1. **Identify and Explain:**
   - disposable income
   - balance
   - liquidity
   - time deposits
   - maturity
   - savings rate

2. **Comparing:** Copy the chart below. Use it to compare how liquidity and interest rates influence people's choice between savings accounts and time deposits.

Savings Accounts	Time Deposits

3. **Finding the Main Idea**
   a. How do people gain security and profits through savings?
   b. Describe how economists measure savings.

4. **Writing and Critical Thinking**
   Drawing Conclusions: Suppose that you have an after-school job in a music store, and you decide to save $10 from each paycheck. What are the trade-offs?
   Consider the following:
   - the trade-offs involved in choosing to save your money instead of spending it
   - the trade-offs involved in choosing either savings or time deposit accounts

Homework Practice Online keyword: SM3 HP9

Caption Answer
by calculating the percentage of people's disposable income—money available after taxes are paid—that is not spent

SECTION 1 REVIEW ANSWERS

1. disposable income (195), balance (196), liquidity (196), time deposits (197), maturity (197), savings rate (199) **11B, 24A**

2. savings accounts—liquid, but low interest rates; time deposits—higher interest rates, but limited liquidity **11B, 24D**

3a. security—money deposited in financial institutions cannot be lost because of misfortune in the home, and most financial institutions are protected by state and federal deposit insurance; profits—deposits earn interest **11B**

3b. by calculating the savings rate—the percentage of people's disposable income that is not spent

4. Answers will vary, but students should discuss the trade-offs involved in choosing to save their money instead of spending it. In addition, students should discuss the trade-offs involved in choosing either savings or time deposit accounts (liquidity vs. higher interest rates). **23A**

SECTION 2

INVESTING

Lesson Plans
For teaching strategies, see Lesson 9.2 located at the beginning of this chapter or the One-Stop Planner Strategy 9.2.

Economics Dictionary
To reinforce the section's vocabulary terms, refer students to the Electronic Glossary on the *Researcher CD-ROM*.

Section Assessment
To assess students' mastery of this section, have them complete Daily Quiz 9.2 in *Daily Quizzes with Answer Key*.

Caption Answer
flexible

★ TEKS
Content
4B, 11B
Social Studies Skills
23A, 23G, 24A, 24D

SECTION 2

INVESTING

READ TO DISCOVER
1. What are the goals and elements of a personal financial plan?
2. How do financial investment and real investment differ?
3. How does real investment affect economic growth?

ECONOMICS DICTIONARY
investment
budget
fixed expenses
flexible expenses
diversification
real investment
capital accumulation
infrastructure
venture capital

As you decide what to do with your money, saving and spending are not your only options. In the United States, freedom of choice also extends to investment. **Investment** occurs when people exchange their money for something of value with the expectation of earning a profit on it in the future.

Some people who make investments must decrease their current consumption of goods and services because invested money cannot be spent on other goods. These investors make a trade-off, choosing to sacrifice some purchasing power in the present in exchange for the chance of maintaining or increasing their purchasing power in the future.

As you know, keeping your savings in a bank or buying a savings bond involves relatively little risk. On the other hand, most investments—such as stock and corporate bonds—involve greater risk because of the possibility that the firm you invested in will lose money. Governments do not guarantee such investments.

Suppose that Janis Johansen decides to invest some of her money. She knows that as her potential profit increases, her risk is likely to be greater. Why might Janis decide to take the increased risk? She might do so because she feels that the potentially higher returns offered by investments outweigh the greater level of risk.

Financial Planning

As Janis decides how to invest her money, she develops a personal financial plan. A financial plan provides Janis with an organized system of balancing her wants and needs with her ability to pay for them. Such a plan includes a spending and saving plan, an investment plan, a retirement plan, and an estate plan. Janis practices financial planning to ensure that she uses her money wisely and meets her investment goals.

Spending and Saving Plan All financial planning begins with a spending and saving plan, or **budget**. The budget lists fixed expenses and

ECONOMIC INSTITUTIONS & INCENTIVES *Financial planning begins with a spending and savings budget.* **Is eating out a fixed or a flexible expense?**

flexible expenses. **Fixed expenses** are those payments that remain constant from month to month, such as payments for a mortgage and insurance premiums. Your own fixed expenses might include monthly car payments or, in the future, rent. **Flexible expenses** can vary from month to month. Examples include expenditures for pizza and movies. The budget should also include the amounts that a person is willing and able to set aside for saving and investing.

Investment Plan
An investment plan is the way Janis puts her money to work. To devise an investment plan, Janis first must determine her reasons for investing. For example, does she want her investments to provide current income, or does she want them to increase in value over time? Once she answers this question, Janis can decide what kinds of investments to make.

An investment plan often reflects a program of diversification. **Diversification** means that a person chooses a variety of investments—CDs, stocks, bonds, and so on. By diversifying her investments, Janis can balance risk, income, and liquidity. Investment choices will be discussed more fully later in this section.

Retirement Plan
Janis knows that it is time to begin saving for retirement. She must decide how much money to set aside, choosing investments that will grow while she is working.

Janis's retirement plan probably will be influenced by her employer. If she works for a company, it may offer her a pension or other plan such as a 401(k). If she is self-employed, however, she may establish her own program such as an individual retirement account (IRA).

Estate Plan
An estate plan provides for a smooth transfer of a person's property after death. Janis does not yet own a home or have large amounts of savings and investments, but she has designated a beneficiary—or person who will receive payments—for her life insurance. Additionally, her new investments will become part of her estate. Financial experts recommend that people develop estate plans to avoid paying large estate taxes and to guarantee that their inheritance is distributed according to their wishes.

ECONOMIC INSTITUTIONS & INCENTIVES *Saving for retirement is an important part of an individual's financial plan.* **What are three other common components of financial planning?**

Types of Investment
Now you know how to go about creating an overall financial plan. Several investment decisions remain, however, to make the plan complete. For example, what goals do you (the investor) have for your money? Perhaps you hope only that an investment will grow in value during the time you own it. On the other hand, you may hope that your investment increases in value by helping to create new goods. These two types of investment are financial investment and real investment.

Financial Investment
The exchange of property ownership and payment between two individuals or groups is known as a financial investment. Although ownership of the property changes hands, financial investment produces no new goods. People make financial investments when they buy existing stocks, bonds, real estate, or other property. Both individuals and firms make financial investments, in the hope of profiting from them in the future. For example, suppose that two brothers—Johnny and Charlie

---

Themes in Economics

ECONOMIC INSTITUTIONS & INCENTIVES Many companies provide 401(k) retirement plans. With this plan, employees specify a percentage of their salary to contribute to the 401(k), and this amount is automatically deducted from their paychecks each pay period. As a bonus, many companies match from 25 to 100 percent of each employee contribution, up to a certain percentage amount. Companies usually hire a financial institution or brokerage firm to invest employees' 401(k) contributions for them. As an added incentive, money placed in a 401(k) plan is not taxed until it is removed. ■

Caption Answer
spending and saving plan, investment plan, estate plan

Themes in Economics

ECONOMIC SECURITY People should diversify their retirement savings by choosing a variety of investments. For example, planning for retirement by investing only in a company 401(k) plan can backfire. Some companies' 401(k) plans are invested heavily or exclusively in the company's own stock. If a company like this goes under, the value of its 401(k) plan plunges as well. By keeping investments diversified, people can limit their overall losses if any one investment loses money. ■

SOURCES OF CAPITAL

Cultural Perspectives

One popular type of financial investment is to collect items that are expected to increase in value. Some examples are art, jewelry, classic cars, antiques, coins, stamps, comic books, and baseball cards. Many collectibles are sold through famous auction houses, like Sotheby's and Christie's, in London and New York City.

Caption Answer

real investment—using money to create new capital goods; financial investment—exchanging property ownership and payment to make a profit 11B

Across the Curriculum

SCIENCE & TECHNOLOGY In 1998 the U.S. patent office issued more than 163,000 patents to individuals, businesses, and governments. Many of these patents would not have been possible without public and private investments in research and development (R&D). In 1998 R & D expenditures in the United States were almost $227 billion. Of this amount, the federal government contributed 29 percent, industry contributed 66 percent, and universities and nonprofit organizations contributed 2 percent.

ECONOMIC INSTITUTIONS & INCENTIVES *Building construction represents real investment.* ***What is the difference between real and financial investment?*** TEKS

Abela—buy a sizable plot of land as a financial investment. The Abelas have created no new capital goods. They have purchased the property only in the hope that it will increase in value so they can resell it at a profit in the future.

Real Investment When investors use money to create a new capital good, they practice **real investment**. Suppose that Johnny and Charlie Abela decide to form a development company. The new company clears the land and constructs an apartment complex. The Abelas have now created a new capital good—the apartment complex. The money spent on the complex now represents a real investment. Such investments are not only made by individuals, but also by firms and by the government.

Investment and Economic Growth

How does real investment in the public and private sectors promote economic growth? Real investment increases the number of capital goods used by producers. The expansion of the capital goods existing in an economy is called **capital accumulation**. Money spent to *replace* existing capital merely keeps the capital stock at its present level. Capital accumulation, on the other hand, promotes economic growth.

For example, suppose that Brian Flanagan is the owner of a shipping company. If one of his barges sinks in a hurricane and he purchases a replacement barge, he is maintaining his capital stock. If, on the other hand, Brian decides to expand his business and purchases three more barges, he is practicing capital accumulation. In expanding his own business, Brian has provided money to a shipbuilding company, which hires more workers to meet the increased demand for barges. These new jobs provide income to more people, enabling them to purchase consumer goods and further expanding a variety of businesses.

In the public sector, federal, state, and local governments make real investments when they improve the nation's economic **infrastructure**—transportation systems including roads, bridges, harbors, and airports, and public facilities such as schools and universities. The infrastructure is the network that enables producers and consumers to participate in the economy. In the private sector, real investment stimulates technological change and entrepreneurship.

Technological Change How can real investment stimulate technological change? Real investment enables companies to develop or purchase new technology, which increases productivity and economic growth. The development of these new technologies is the result of research and development by major firms or by individual entrepreneurs.

Suppose that Alex Kihara invests in a local business called Print 'n' Copy Store. As a result of this investment, the owners of the copy store are able to afford new software to computerize their billing system. Real investment has improved the technology used by Print 'n' Copy. Additionally, higher sales of the computerized billing program encourages the owners of the

202 CHAPTER 9

software company to develop a new upgraded version of the program.

Entrepreneurship Real investment also can encourage entrepreneurship, which in turn fosters economic growth and the development of new products. Money invested in entrepreneurial enterprises is called **venture capital**, and it encourages economic growth. Venture capital helps entrepreneurs develop an idea into a marketable product, improve production facilities, or finance product distribution.

For example, suppose that Ana Guajardo wants to start a new music magazine. She is able to write the articles, but she needs venture capital to hire a designer to create a "look" for the magazine, pay for photographs and printing, and cover the distribution costs.

Where will Ana acquire this venture capital? She may know friends and local business owners who are willing to invest their money, or she may take out a loan. She might acquire capital from a private venture capital firm that specializes in seeking out and financing promising businesses. In the United States these firms spend billions of dollars annually to support entrepreneurs and their projects.

ECONOMIC INSTITUTIONS & INCENTIVES *Entrepreneurship fosters economic growth and the development of new products.* **How would venture capital encourage economic growth and help a small business such as this one?**

The government also provides funding to entrepreneurs with promising businesses. The Small Business Administration, a federal agency, invests money in smaller-size firms by extending low-interest loans. Some state governments also provide venture capital to small businesses.

SECTION 2 REVIEW

TEKS Q: 1, 2, 3b, 4

1. Identify and Explain:
- investment
- budget
- fixed expenses
- flexible expenses
- diversification
- real investment
- capital accumulation
- infrastructure
- venture capital

2. Sequencing: Copy the flow chart below. Use it to explain how real investment promotes economic growth by putting the steps into sequence.

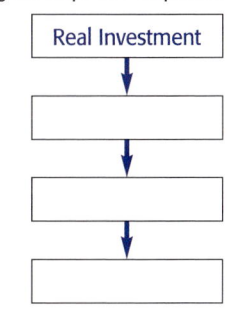

[Flow chart: Real Investment → □ → □ → □]

3. Finding the Main Idea
a. Describe the four elements of a personal financial plan.
b. How do the purposes of financial and real investment differ?

4. Writing and Critical Thinking

Categorizing: Suppose that you have a part-time job after school. At the end of the month, you have $150 left. Design and describe a plan for spending, saving, and investing your money.

Consider the following:
- your financial goals
- the four elements of financial plans

Homework Practice Online
keyword: SM3 HP9

Caption Answer
by helping entrepreneurs and small businesses develop ideas into marketable products, improve production facilities, and finance product distribution

SECTION 2 REVIEW ANSWERS

1. investment (200), budget (200), fixed expenses (201), flexible expenses (201), diversification (201), real investment (202), capital accumulation (202), infrastructure (202), venture capital (203) **11B, 24A**

2. Real investment spurs capital accumulation, thus creating new jobs. The holders of these jobs then purchase more consumer goods and thereby stimulate the expansion of a variety of businesses. **4B, 11B, 23A**

3a. spending and saving plan—a personal budget; investment plan—plan for putting one's money to work; retirement plan—plan for investing and saving for retirement; and estate plan—plan for the transfer of one's property after death

3b. financial investment—to make a profit; real investment—to create new capital goods **4B, 11B**

4. Answers will vary but should reflect an understanding of the four elements of financial plans. **23A, 24D**

SECTION 3

STOCKS, BONDS, AND FUTURES

READ TO DISCOVER

1. Why and how do people invest in stocks?
2. What factors influence stock prices?
3. How do corporate and government bonds differ from stocks?
4. What are the advantages and disadvantages of futures?

ECONOMICS DICTIONARY

capital gain
capital loss
stock split
brokers
investment bank
bull market
bear market
yields
futures
prospectus

Saving and investing require you to make decisions about how to use your money. If you decide to invest your money, further choices arise. For example, do you want to own part of a corporation by becoming a shareholder, or simply lend money by becoming a bondholder? Are you most concerned about low risk or high return? As you read this section, think about the factors that contribute to financial decisions.

Why Buy Stocks?

"Stock Prices Rise." "Experts Predict Market Downturn." You may have seen newspaper headlines like these. Sometimes stocks can seem like an uncertain investment with random price changes. Why, then, do people buy stocks?

There are three main reasons that people choose to invest in stocks. People often hope to

- gain a profit,
- limit the risk on their investment, and
- become a part owner of a corporation.

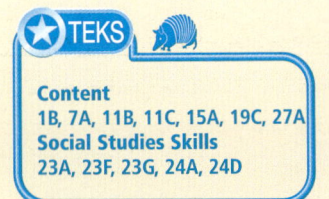

Profit Potential Stocks can provide a profit in two ways. First, many stockholders receive regular dividends on the money invested in stocks. As noted in Chapter 7, dividends are paid to a shareholder in return for an investment. Most corporations pay dividends quarterly, while others pay them annually or semiannually.

Stocks that pay consistent dividends are called income stocks. These stocks provide a steady amount of current income to investors. Stocks that pay few or no dividends but that increase in value are called growth stocks. Investors generally purchase growth stocks in order to increase the value of their assets.

A second way to earn profit on a stock is to sell it at a higher price than the original purchase

ECONOMIC INSTITUTIONS & INCENTIVES *Owning stock in a utility company is a popular form of investment.* **What are the three main reasons that people choose to invest in stocks?**

STOCK SPLITS

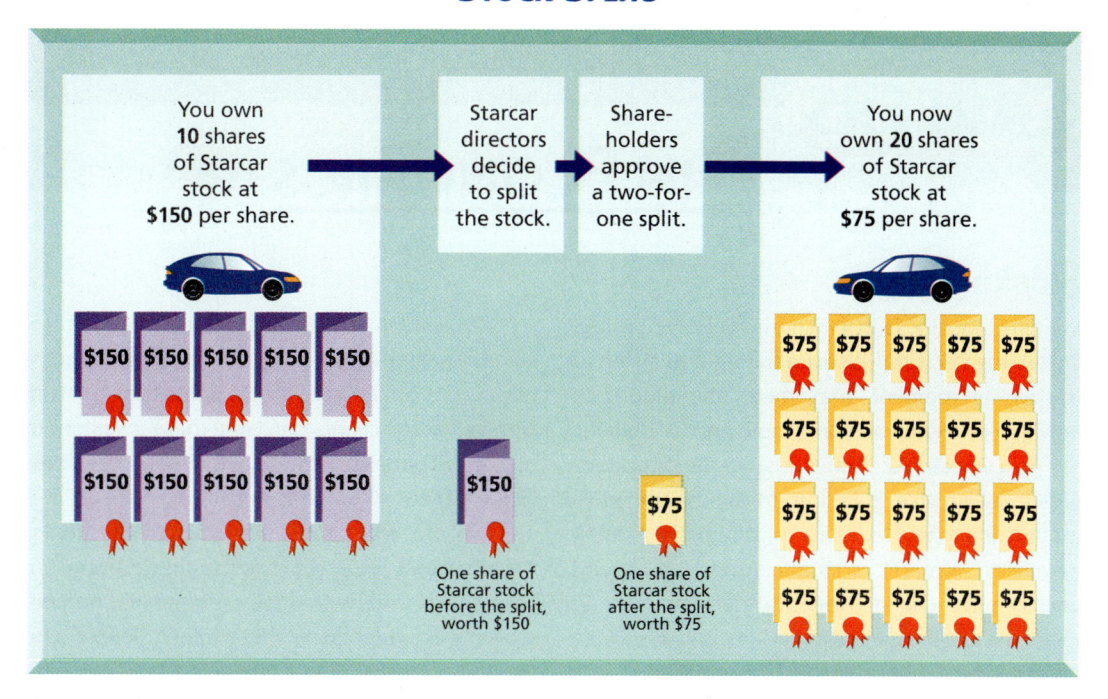

FIGURE 9.3 When the price of stock becomes so high that it discourages potential investors from buying it, the directors of a company may decide to split each share into two. **What usually happens to stock prices after a split?**

You own 10 shares of Starcar stock at $150 per share. → Starcar directors decide to split the stock. → Shareholders approve a two-for-one split. → You now own 20 shares of Starcar stock at $75 per share.

One share of Starcar stock before the split, worth $150. One share of Starcar stock after the split, worth $75.

---

price. The difference between the higher selling price and the lower original purchase price is the investor's **capital gain**. An investor who sells a stock at a price lower than the purchase price, however, incurs a **capital loss**.

Limited Risk Stockholders are protected from some risks. Unlike sole proprietors and partners, stockholders in corporations enjoy limited liability. As noted in Chapter 7, the amount of money a stockholder can lose is limited to the amount he or she invested in the stock.

Ownership People also invest in stocks to become owners in a corporation and to vote on company matters. The number of votes a shareholder has is equal to the number of shares of stock he or she owns.

As owners, shareholders vote to elect the board of directors as well as to decide a variety of other business issues. One such issue involves when to initiate a **stock split**. (See Figure 9.3.) Suppose that the directors of Gadsen Publications determine that the price of Gadsen's stock has become so high that it discourages potential investors from purchasing shares. The directors may decide to "split" each share into two. After the shareholders approve the two-for-one stock split, a shareholder will have two shares of Gadsen stock for every single share held before the split. The price is divided along with the stock, so that stock previously selling for $100 will sell for $50 after the split. Shareholders generally like stock splits because share prices tend to rise afterward.

How Stocks Are Traded

Suppose that Brad Halsey wants to buy stock. Does he call a corporation and place a purchase order? Probably not—very few corporations sell stock directly. Instead, Brad contacts a company

---

Caption Answer
Though stock prices are adjusted to reflect the split, they tend to rise afterward. ★23G

Themes in Economics

COMPETITION & MARKET STRUCTURE During the 1980s large public companies increasingly became victims of "hostile takeovers." In such situations, a company or an individual gains control of a corporation against the wishes of its management by buying a controlling amount of its stock. The buyer obtains large amounts of stock by "making a tender offer," or offering a price higher than the market price.

Hostile takeovers usually occur with companies whose stock has become devalued. Thus, the threat of a takeover can benefit a company by forcing its management to maximize efficiency and profitability so as to keep its stock price high. When takeovers are successful, new management usually increases the company's profitability by selling or closing unprofitable or inefficient parts of the company. As a result, stock prices usually go up following a takeover, which benefits stockholders. On the other hand, takeovers can result in layoffs, wage cuts, and decreased employee morale. ∎

SOURCES OF CAPITAL 205

Careers in Economics

To help students learn about other careers in economics, refer them to the Careers section on the *Holt Researcher Online*.

Themes in Economics

ECONOMIC INSTITUTIONS & INCENTIVES Researching the best stocks and bonds to buy requires a great deal of time and knowledge. As a result, many investors buy shares in a mutual fund. A mutual fund is a professionally managed portfolio of securities. Each share in a mutual fund is actually an investment in multiple stocks and bonds. Administered by investment companies, mutual funds offer two advantages. First, the investment companies employ experts whose sole jobs are to research the market and determine which stocks and bonds are likely to be the most profitable and the best risks. In addition, with a mutual fund, an investor's financial risk is diversified across many different stocks and bonds, limiting the effect of market volatility. ∎

CAREERS IN ECONOMICS

Stockbroker

Imagine a business in which timing is everything. The wrong decision—or even the right decision at the wrong moment—may mean the difference between collecting or losing thousands of dollars.

To a stockbroker, timeliness is vital. Stockbrokers must be able to find up-to-the-minute information and make decisions quickly. Brokers must be able to interpret economic developments and predict price changes on the stock market. To meet these goals, research skills and a college degree in business or finance are essential.

Stockbrokers must be able to find up-to-the-minute information and make wise financial decisions quickly.

Basically, a stockbroker is a salesperson. Instead of selling cars, shoes, or kitchen appliances, however, a broker sells stock. Some brokers work with individual clients, advising these investors to buy or sell particular stocks. Other brokers work in large call centers for brokerage firms.

Brokers often must find their own clients. Because they must be comfortable introducing themselves and their services to people, brokers typically are aggressive, determined people who like to take risks. These characteristics also help brokers make decisions about how their clients' money would best be invested.

Some stockbrokers do not receive hourly wages or a yearly salary. Instead, they are paid commissions—percentages of each sale. These commissions pay stockbrokers for their services, including time, research, and professional advice. To maximize profits brokers work to purchase stock at the lowest possible price and sell it at the highest possible price.

Earning money on commissions can be both risky and rewarding. On the one hand, stockbrokers may not receive steady paychecks. On the other hand, they have the potential to earn much more money from commissions than they might earn from a fixed salary.

---

that specializes in selling stocks. These companies belong to a network of brokerage firms, investment banks, and stock exchanges.

Brokers and Analysts Stockbrokers, often called **brokers**, link buyers and sellers of stock. Brokers work for brokerage firms, which are businesses that specialize in trading stocks and other securities. Brokers and brokerage firms earn a profit by collecting a commission, or fee, on each transaction.

Investment Banks Corporations usually do not issue new stock or trade large blocks of other stocks without help. They usually contact an **investment bank**, which buys and sells large blocks of stock. Investment banks usually buy the stock when offered by a company and then offer that stock to the general public. Like brokers, investment banks collect commissions on transactions.

Stock Exchanges When people speak of the "stock market," they generally are referring to the New York Stock Exchange (NYSE). The NYSE, the largest stock exchange in the United States, began informal operations in 1792 on Wall Street in New York City, providing a place to buy and sell corporate stocks and government bonds.

Before the Civil War, other brokers founded the New York Curb Agency, a name that arose because the brokers actually met on the street. In 1953 the name was officially changed to the American Stock Exchange (AMEX). Besides the NYSE and the AMEX, five regional stock exchanges are located in other U.S. cities. Major world cities such as Tokyo, Hong Kong, London, Frankfurt, and Paris also have stock exchanges on which some U.S. firms are able to trade.

Changes in technology have improved the buying and selling of stocks on the NYSE. For example, the NYSE spent millions of dollars modernizing its equipment from 1980 to 1985. Powerful computers in the exchange and in other locations throughout New York City connect with similar equipment in the nation's major brokerage firms. The computer linkup makes it possible to handle as many as 2,000 stock transactions each second. On December 15, 2000, more than 1.56 billion shares were traded on the NYSE, setting a record for daily trading volume.

The nearly 3,000 companies that now have their shares traded on the NYSE must meet rigorous standards concerning number of shareholders, number of shares, and minimum earnings. Companies on the NYSE also must follow standard accounting practices in calculating their earnings.

Before a brokerage firm's representatives can buy and sell shares on the NYSE, it must purchase a "seat" on the exchange. Prices for the 1,366 seats vary. In April 2001, for example, the auction price of a seat was $2,300,500. The all-time high for a seat was $2,650,000 in August 1999; the low was $2,750 in 1871.

Over-the-Counter Market Stocks that are not listed on the NYSE or other stock exchanges are traded on the over-the-counter (OTC) market. Many smaller corporations that do not meet the standards set by the nation's stock exchanges can still trade their stocks OTC. These stocks are sometimes called OTC stocks.

Investors still need brokers to trade OTC stocks. First, buyers and sellers place buy or sell orders with their brokers. Second, the brokers arrange the purchase or sale by using a market service called the National Association of Securities Dealers Automated Quotations (NASDAQ), which lists thousands of stocks not listed on the stock exchanges. To arrange for the sale or purchase of stocks not listed on NASDAQ, the brokers contact other brokers who might have clients interested in trading the stock directly.

Determinants of Stock Prices

Suppose that you decide to invest in a company's stock. How can you find out the price? If you look in the business section of the local newspaper, you will find a list of stock prices listed in

EXCHANGE, MONEY, & INTERDEPENDENCE *The NYSE began informal operations in 1792 on Wall Street in New York City.* **What other cities in the world have major stock exchanges?**

Across the Curriculum

TECHNOLOGY When companies want to make a public stock offering, they usually turn to an investment bank or a venture capital firm for assistance. These options are often too expensive for smaller or newer firms, however. Now, the Internet provides smaller companies with another option. In February 1996 Spring Street Brewing, a New York brewery, became the first company to offer stock directly to investors over the Internet. The company raised $1.6 million during the first month of going public.

internet connect

TOPIC: Investing, Stock Exchanges
GO TO: go.hrw.com
KEYWORD: SM3 EC9

Have students access the Internet through the HRW Go site to conduct research on one of the major securities exchanges in the United States. Tell students to search for pertinent facts about the history of the exchange, including regulations governing trading on the exchange floor and milestones. Then have each student create a time line to show major events from the exchange's founding through today. 24D

Caption Answer
Tokyo, Hong Kong, London, Frankfurt, and Paris

SOURCES OF CAPITAL

UNDERSTANDING STOCK MARKET REPORTS

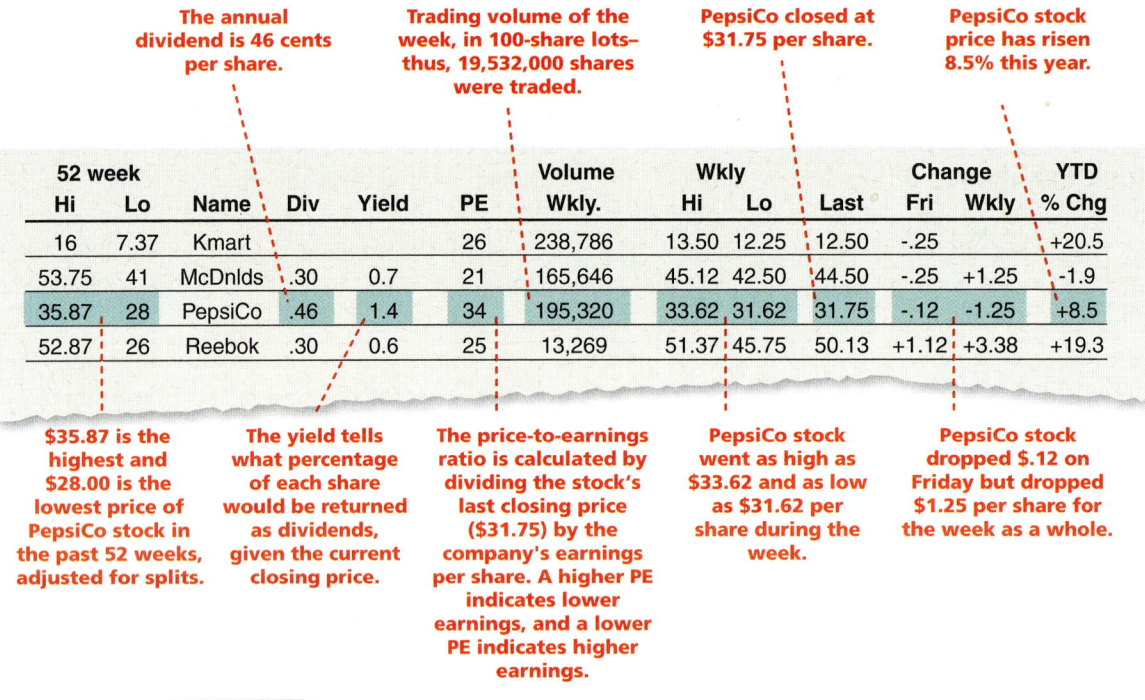

- The annual dividend is 46 cents per share.
- Trading volume of the week, in 100-share lots—thus, 19,532,000 shares were traded.
- PepsiCo closed at $31.75 per share.
- PepsiCo stock price has risen 8.5% this year.

52 week Hi	52 week Lo	Name	Div	Yield	PE	Volume Wkly.	Wkly Hi	Wkly Lo	Last	Change Fri	Change Wkly	YTD % Chg
16	7.37	Kmart			26	238,786	13.50	12.25	12.50	-.25		+20.5
53.75	41	McDnlds	.30	0.7	21	165,646	45.12	42.50	44.50	-.25	+1.25	-1.9
35.87	28	PepsiCo	.46	1.4	34	195,320	33.62	31.62	31.75	-.12	-1.25	+8.5
52.87	26	Reebok	.30	0.6	25	13,269	51.37	45.75	50.13	+1.12	+3.38	+19.3

- $35.87 is the highest and $28.00 is the lowest price of PepsiCo stock in the past 52 weeks, adjusted for splits.
- The yield tells what percentage of each share would be returned as dividends, given the current closing price.
- The price-to-earnings ratio is calculated by dividing the stock's last closing price ($31.75) by the company's earnings per share. A higher PE indicates lower earnings, and a lower PE indicates higher earnings.
- PepsiCo stock went as high as $33.62 and as low as $31.62 per share during the week.
- PepsiCo stock dropped $.12 on Friday but dropped $1.25 per share for the week as a whole.

FIGURE 9.4 Based on this market report, if a person bought 20 shares of Reebok stock at its 52-week low, how much money would he or she make (or lose) if they sold it today? Look for the most current Reebok quote in a newspaper or on the Internet.

---

dollars and cents. (Prior to 2001, stock prices were listed in fractions.) Shares of stock are typically traded in lots, or amounts, of 100. Smaller amounts are referred to as odd lots.

The stockbroker's task is to make a sale by reconciling a "bid" price with an "asked price." For example, a buyer bids $37.37 a share, and the seller asks $38.12. If the stockbroker persuades the buyer to pay 50 cents more for a share and the seller to sell for 25 cents less, a sale is made at $37.87. The process is somewhat different for investors who trade online. Potential buyers and sellers are able to see the bid and ask prices for a stock at a given moment. However, online orders are not routed to an individual stockbroker, but into a much larger pool of orders that are prioritized electronically.

When many buyers compete for a scarce supply of stock, demand pushes up the price. Similarly, when there is a large supply of stock and few buyers, low demand pushes down the price. In this way, demand affects stock prices. The main factors influencing demand for a stock are corporate finances, investor expectations, and external forces.

Corporate Finances A corporation's financial strength usually is measured in terms of profits and losses. A company's quarterly and annual earnings reports are read carefully by investors, market analysts, and brokers. When confident that a corporation produces high-quality products and has good long-term prospects, investors will buy its stock. Such stocks are called "blue chip" stocks and are in high demand during both upswings and downswings of the stock market because of their long-term stability and value.

Investor Expectations As noted in Chapter 3, consumer expectations can influence demand. Similarly, investors' expectations about the future price of a stock can affect the stock's current market price. Investors increase their demand for (buy) a stock when they expect it to increase in value and tend to decrease their demand (sell) when they believe a stock's value will decrease. (See Figure 9.5.)

Investors, market analysts, and brokers form their expectations in part by watching fluctuations in stock indexes, such as the Dow Jones Industrial Average, or the Dow. The Dow records changes in the stock prices of a select group of 30 major industrial companies.

When the Dow steadily rises over a period of time, a **bull market** is said to exist. When the Dow average falls for a period of time, on the other hand, a **bear market** is said to exist. In a bull market, investors expect an increase in profits and thus buy stock. During a bear market, however, investors sell their stock in the expectation of reduced profits.

External Forces Sometimes forces over which neither the stock market nor private firms have any control influence the price of stocks. For example, the price of Johnson & Johnson stock fell in 1982 after someone put poison in a few bottles of Tylenol® capsules in the Chicago area. Johnson & Johnson voluntarily withdrew all Tylenol capsules from store shelves.

Some investors feared that Johnson & Johnson's profits would fall. These investors rushed to sell their Johnson & Johnson shares, contributing to a drop in the stock's price. This drop was temporary, however. After Johnson & Johnson introduced new forms of Tylenol that were more difficult to tamper with, public confidence increased and the stock's price rose again.

Other external forces include government statistics on unemployment, inflation, interest rates, and the number of new houses being built. National and international events such as revolutions, terrorist attacks, and elections also can affect investor confidence. For example, when the New York Stock Exchange resumed following the September 11, 2001, attacks on the World Trade Center, stock prices plunged as investors sold large numbers of shares. In the weeks following the attack, however, major market indices returned to pre-September-11, levels, in part because the Federal Reserve acted quickly to reassure investors.

Why Buy Bonds?

Corporate bonds and government bonds are other forms of investment. Although bond **yields**—or interest on money owed to a bondholder—are frequently lower than stock dividends, they generally offer less risk. Additionally, if a company goes out of business, bondholders must be paid before stockholders.

STOCK MARKET PERFORMANCE

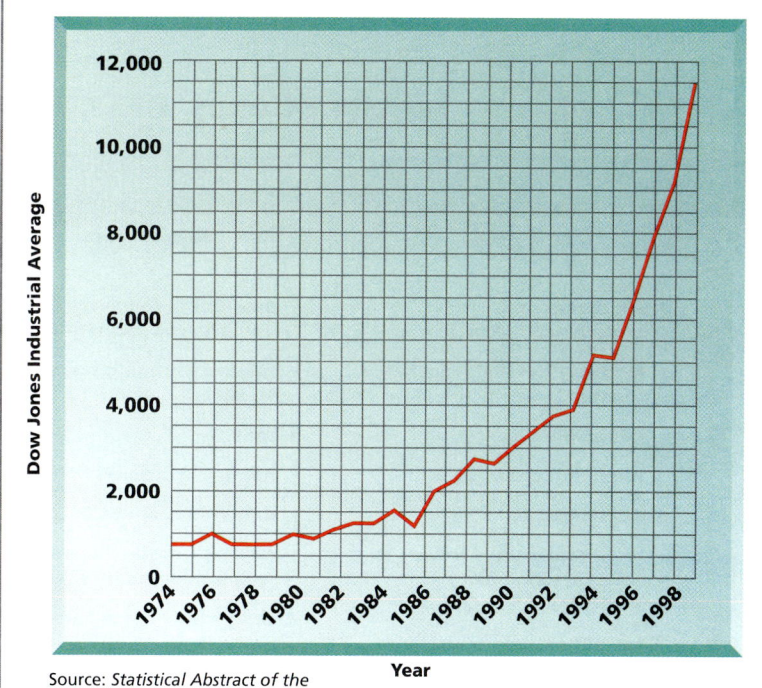

Source: *Statistical Abstract of the United States: 1975, 1980, 1996, 2000*

FIGURE 9.5 Investors buy stock when they expect it to increase in value and sell stock when they expect it to decrease in value. **In the above graph, identify a time period in which a bull market existed and a time period in which a bear market existed.**

Cultural Perspectives

Over the years, investors have used many innovative and downright bizarre approaches to predict stock prices. In one experiment, *Forbes* magazine selected stocks by throwing darts at a dartboard. Ironically, these stocks outperformed the leading mutual funds.

Another method of predicting stock prices revolves around the Super Bowl. Some investors hold that if the team who wins the Super Bowl was a member of the old American Football League (AFL), then stock prices will drop during the coming year. If the team was a member of the old National Football League (NFL), then stock prices will rise. What is the only problem with this method? If the winning team was created after the merger of the AFL and NFL in 1970, then it's back to the dartboard to choose the best stocks for the coming year.

Transparency

An overhead transparency of Figure 9.5 is available in *Transparency Resources*. See Transparency 34: Stock Market Performance.

Caption Answer

bull—1975–76, 1979–80, 1981–83, 1985–88, 1990–94, 1995–99; bear—1976–79, 1980–81, 1994–95

Themes in Economics

MARKETS & PRICES Many factors influence the prices of bonds. Like stock prices, bond prices are closely connected to interest rates. When interest rates rise, the price of previously issued bonds falls, and vice versa.

The risk that the bond issuer will default on payments also affects bond prices—the higher the risk, the lower the price. For example, junk bonds are low-priced, high-risk bonds that often have little solid financial backing. Investors or companies often sell junk bonds to raise money for a new venture or to finance a corporate takeover. ■

Transparency

An overhead transparency of Figure 9.6 is available in *Transparency Resources*. See Transparency 35: Treasury Bonds, Bills, and Notes.

Caption Answer

Treasury bills—3 months to 1 year; Treasury notes —1 to 10 years; Treasury bonds—10 to 30 years ★11B

Corporate Bonds As noted in Chapter 7, corporations sell bonds to raise large sums of money that might be difficult to obtain from a bank. Corporate bonds come in large units, such as $1,000, $5,000, or $10,000 each. The investor purchases a bond at face value—the value listed on the bond when issued—and receives an annual interest payment. On the maturity date, the investor collects the final interest payment and the principal, or the amount of the original bond. Brokerage firms sell the corporate bonds to the public over the counter or on the NYSE and AMEX bond markets.

Government Bonds Corporate bonds are similar to government bonds that, as noted in Section 1, represent debt that the government must repay the investor. The U.S. government—specifically the Treasury Department—issues not only Treasury bonds, but also Treasury bills and notes.

These three investments offer different lengths of maturity and require the same minimum investment of $1,000. They all carry fixed interest rates and are redeemable at stated maturity dates, which vary in length from 90 days to 30 years past the date of purchase. In contrast to corporate bonds, whose interest is taxed as normal income, bonds issued by the federal government pay interest that is exempt from state and local taxes but not from federal income taxes. Backed by the "full faith and credit" of the federal government, these Treasury bonds, bills, and notes are among the safest of all investments. For information about the differences between these three investments, see Figure 9.6.

State, county, and local governments and municipalities such as water districts also issue bonds. For the most part, these bonds have been safe investments since the Great Depression, but they do carry an element of risk. For example, for 18 months beginning in late 1994, people were uncertain whether they would be able to redeem municipal bonds they had purchased from Orange County, California. Orange County was in severe financial difficulty as a result of risky investments by Orange County officials.

TREASURY BONDS, BILLS, AND NOTES

TYPE OF FEDERAL SECURITY		
Treasury Bill	**Treasury Note**	**Treasury Bond**
• short-term U.S. government security	• medium-to-long-term U.S. government security	• long-term U.S. government security
• maturity ranging from three months to one year	• maturity ranging from 1 to 10 years	• maturity ranging from 10 to 30 years
• liquid and safe	• safe	• safe
• minimum order: $1,000	• minimum order: $1,000	• minimum order: $1,000
• denomination: $1,000	• denomination: $1,000	• denomination: $1,000
• yield rate usually lower than on long-term securities	• pays at a stated interest rate semiannually	• pays at a stated interest rate semiannually
• price fluctuation usually lower than for other government securities	• redeemed at face value at maturity	• redeemed at face value at maturity

FIGURE 9.6 Treasury bonds represent debt that the government must repay the investor. **How do the maturity periods differ between these three government investments?** ★TEKS

LINKING ECONOMICS and HISTORY

The Crashes of 1987 and 1929

History often holds important clues to understanding economic events in more modern times. Take, for example, the stock market crashes of 1987 and 1929. On October 19, 1987, the Dow Jones Industrial Average dropped 508 points—a record 22.6 percent. Coming on top of earlier, steep declines in the Dow, the "Black Monday" crash rocked stock markets around the world. Panic set in among some investors and stock traders, adding to fears that the stock slide would batter the U.S. economy and throw people out of work.

To many economists and historians, the crash seemed eerily similar to a stock market crash 58 years earlier. On October 29, 1929—"Black Tuesday"—the Dow fell 12.8 percent. This crash helped trigger a financial panic as stock values continued to plunge for weeks. Banks were forced to close as people rushed to withdraw savings. With access to capital sharply limited, businesses closed, and millions of people lost their jobs.

Prior to the 1929 crash, the U.S. economy appeared to many observers to be very healthy. Stock values were soaring, profits for many companies were high, and consumers were spending—and investing—like never before. Many investors in 1929 and 1987 simply did not see—or refused to see—signs of a coming crash. Reports in 1929, for example, warned that industrial production, certain stock values, and other economic indicators in the United States were falling. Prior to the 1987 crash, some observers warned that the U.S. government was borrowing too much money, thus making capital for private industry more expensive and difficult to obtain.

Certain factors made the effects of the 1929 crash much worse than those in 1987. For example, investors in 1929 often purchased their stocks with credit. An investor would pay cash for only a small portion of the price of the stock and agree to pay off the debt later with profits from the stock after it rose in value. Unfortunately, when brokers began to worry that values might not continue to rise, they began to require purchasers to come up with the money owed, or lose the stock. When prices began to fall, investors who had bought stock with credit could not cover their debts.

In 1987, however, various reforms instituted by the government in response to the 1929 crisis worked to keep a similar financial catastrophe from occurring. One reform restricts the purchase of stocks with credit. Also, the federal government now insures bank deposits. If a bank does not have enough money to cover its deposits during a crisis, a federal agency steps in to pay depositors. In 1987, then, while stock investors indeed lost a great deal of money—at least on paper—U.S. consumers did not have to worry that they would lose money they had deposited in banks.

What Do You Think? TEKS

1. Analyze the impact of the 1929 and 1987 crashes on U.S. history.
2. In a free-enterprise system, people are free to invest. What are the benefits of an investment opportunity? Should the government make stock investments as safe as bank deposits? Explain your answer.

Cultural Perspectives

The classic movie *It's a Wonderful Life* provides an excellent example of how to prevent bank panics. In one scene, George Bailey, the executive secretary of a savings and loan, faces an angry mob of customers demanding their money. It's the early 1930s, and Bailey's bank is out of cash. To save the business, Bailey puts up his own money to calm customers and to persuade them not to pull out their savings. He succeeds and the Bailey Building and Loan survives.

During the 1987 crash, the Federal Reserve acted in much the same way. It persuaded banks not to call in their loans to the brokerages and offered to put extra money into the financial system. As a result, the crash did not create a panic. ■

What Do You Think? Answers

1. 1929—business closures, massive unemployment, runs on banks, stock market reforms, federal insurance of bank deposits; 1987—losses less catastrophic, thanks to reforms instituted after 1929 ★19C

2. Investors can earn a profit if the firm is successful; cannot lose more than they invest; and, through stock ownership become part owners of a firm. Answers will vary but should point out that the high risk of investing in stocks is what enables investors to earn high returns, but too many bad investments can hurt the economy if the market crashes. ★4B, 23D

SECURITY REGULATIONS

YEAR	LEGISLATION	PURPOSE
1890	Sherman Antitrust Act	prohibits business trusts; because its vague language left loopholes it was strengthened in 1914 by the Clayton Antitrust Act
1933	Federal Securities Act	(also called the Truth-in-Securities Act) requires anyone offering securities for public sale to disclose information about them; requires companies to disclose the securities holdings of their officers and directors
1934	Securities Exchange	sought to eliminate dishonest practices in the stock market; created the Securities and Exchange Commission (SEC) to enforce the regulations
1984	Insider Trading Sanctions Act	established triple penalties against violators in addition to requiring the return of any illegally acquired money or property; was extended in 1988 to include corporate supervisors

FIGURE 9.7 During the past 100 years, Congress passed several acts to regulate the securities industry and protect investors. **What is the role of the Securities Exchange Commission?**

Not until June 1996 did the municipal bonds become redeemable.

Why Buy Futures?

Futures are another type of investment. In futures markets such as the Chicago Board of Trade, instead of trading stock, investors trade various types of products called **futures**. Futures include agricultural products such as corn, wheat, soybeans, and oats. They also include industrial goods such as copper and crude oil and precious metals such as gold and silver. Because futures trading carries a high risk, investors must have specialized knowledge about the commodities being bought and sold.

How does futures trading work? When traders sell futures, they accept an investor's money today in exchange for a promise to deliver a commodity to the investor at a later date. The terms of a futures trade are stated in a contract.

For example, suppose that Joanne Kaehler decides to invest in hog futures. She signs a contract in which she agrees to pay a certain amount of money for a later delivery of hogs—perhaps six months after the purchase. Joanne probably does not want to own the hogs, however. She is hoping that the price of hogs will increase within the six-month period so that she can resell the contract and make a profit.

How can the futures market benefit Joanne? If the market price of hogs rises above the price listed on the contract, the hog owner still must honor the contract and deliver the hogs to Joanne at the lower-than-market price that it lists. Joanne then can resell the hog contract at the current market price and make a profit.

The hog owner, on the other hand, hopes that the price will drop within the contract's six-month period. Why? If the market price of hogs drops below the price that Joanne paid in the contract, the hog owner has made a greater profit than is available at the current market price. If the owner had not sold the hogs in advance, he or she would have received the later, lower market price for the hogs.

Both Joanne and the hog owner face tremendous risks. The buyer and the seller essentially are betting that the price of hogs will reach a certain level by a particular time. Depending on whether the price rises or falls, either the seller or the buyer could lose a great deal of money.

Regulation of the Securities Industry

Throughout the 1800s, trade in securities was not monitored by any organizations outside the stock exchanges. As a result, dishonest securities dealers often provided investors with misleading or false information.

During the early 1900s, Congress passed several acts to regulate trading in securities. As noted in Chapter 6, the Clayton Antitrust Act (1914) outlawed many monopolistic practices. The act discouraged the formation of monopolies by forbidding corporations from buying stock in competing companies when doing so could result in monopolistic control over an industry.

The next key piece of legislation came in 1933. The Federal Securities Act, also called the Truth-in-Securities Act, requires all companies to register their securities with the Federal Trade Commission (FTC). Just a year later the Securities Exchange Act established the Securities and Exchange Commission (SEC) to enforce the Federal Securities Act. For a summary of securities regulations, see Figure 9.7.

Companies must meet rigorous standards to sell their stock in a stock exchange. Additionally, companies register their securities by providing a detailed financial statement to the SEC and a prospectus to potential investors. A **prospectus** is a fact sheet containing data on the company's finances. Investors use the prospectus to evaluate securities that are offered for sale. The SEC is empowered to charge heavy fines for violations of these requirements.

The SEC also regulates the procedures for the trading of securities. The SEC licenses all stock exchanges in the United States and regulates the activities of brokers and brokerage houses to guard against fraud and other unethical actions.

SECTION 3 REVIEW

TEKS Q: 1, 2, 3a, 3b, 3c, 4

1. **Identify and Explain:**
   - capital gain
   - capital loss
   - stock split
   - brokers
   - investment bank
   - bull market
   - bear market
   - yields
   - futures
   - prospectus

2. **Categorizing:** Copy the graphic organizer below. Use it to explain the main reasons people choose to purchase stock.

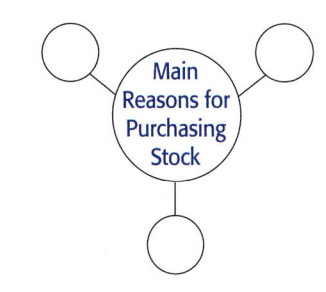

   [Graphic organizer: Main Reasons for Purchasing Stock]

3. **Finding the Main Idea**
   a. What are the benefits of the sale or purchase of bonds?
   b. How do corporate finances, investor expectations, and external forces influence stock prices and possibly pose a risk to investors
   c. How does the futures market offer risks to sellers as well as to investors?

4. **Writing and Critical Thinking**
   Drawing Conclusions: Suppose you own stock in a corporation, and you hear that the stock is about to split. How can you benefit from ownership of this stock?
   Consider the following:
   - the effects of a split on the stock's price
   - what a stock split might signal about a company's prospects

Homework Practice Online keyword: SM3 HP9

SECTION 3 REVIEW ANSWERS

1. capital gain (205), capital loss (205), stock split (205), brokers (206), investment bank (206), bull market (209), bear market (209), yields (209), futures (212), prospectus (213) **24A**

2. to gain a profit, limit the risk on their investment, become a part owner of a corporation **11B, 11C, 24D**

3a. The issuer, or seller, benefits through receipt of capital. The consumer benefits as bonds are a low-risk investment, and government bonds are exempt from federal tax. **11C**

3b. corporate finances—company's profits/losses affect investor confidence; investor expectations—expectations of future stock prices affect investor demand; external forces—the rise or fall of economic indicators, the state of the housing market, national and international events, and unexpected events that affect corporations all affect investor confidence **7A, 11B**

3c. Both sellers and investors speculate that a good's price will reach a certain level by a certain time. Depending on what actually happens, either party can lose money. **11B**

4. After the split the price of the stock will most likely rise, increasing the value of the investment. **11C, 23A**

SOURCES OF CAPITAL

SECTION 4

BORROWING AND CREDIT

READ TO DISCOVER
1. How do lenders make money on loans?
2. What factors influence a credit rating?
3. How can credit help the economy?

ECONOMICS DICTIONARY
installment
credit rating
credit bureau
finance charge
annual percentage rate
usury
bankruptcy

Suppose that you want to buy a car. You know that your friend's parents are selling their car for $5,000. For the past two years you have been saving money from your after-school job and have saved $1,500. If you want to buy the car, you will need to borrow the remaining $3,500 or perhaps pay for the car on credit. Before you do so, however, there are several things you need to know about borrowing and credit.

Borrowing is the transfer of a specified amount of money from a lender to a borrower for a specified length of time. Business owners borrow money to begin or expand their businesses. Governments borrow money to finance their programs and operations.

People also may rely on credit when they do not have enough money for a purchase. Even wealthy consumers may use credit when purchasing expensive items such as houses and cars.

Why do consumers borrow money or rely on credit? Try considering the used-car purchase mentioned earlier. A loan or credit will enable you to use the car now while paying off the loan or credit debt, and you can extend payments for the car over a period of time. Paying a smaller amount every month thus makes large purchases more affordable for many people.

Borrowing Money

As noted in Chapter 7, the amount borrowed in a loan is called the principal. The amount paid by the borrower for the privilege of using the money is called the interest. Both the principal and the interest are included in the loan's repayment.

Most loans require that borrowers put up collateral. Collateral is something of value offered by the borrower as a guarantee that the loan will be repaid. In a mortgage loan the house is the collateral, and in an automobile loan the car is the collateral. If the loan is not repaid according to the terms of the loan agreement, the lender may take possession of the borrower's collateral. That is, the lender can foreclose on the house or repossess the car.

How are loans repaid? In the repayment of most loans, the principal and interest are divided

EXCHANGE, MONEY, & INTERDEPENDENCE *Credit is the purchase of goods and services on the promise to pay later.* **Why do consumers use credit?**

into equal amounts, or **installments**, according to the length of the loan period. The length of repayment is important in determining the monthly payment amount. The longer the loan period, the smaller the amount of money the consumer must pay each month. A longer loan period, however, means that the total interest payment is greater.

Buying on Credit

Unlike borrowing, buying on credit does not involve the direct exchange of money. Instead, businesses allow customers to charge their purchases and to pay for them later. This is done through the use of a charge, or credit, account. Think of a charge account as a type of loan offered by businesses to their clients. Businesses that offer credit include banks, department stores, gasoline companies, and financial service firms such as VISA®, MasterCard®, and American Express®.

Credit Ratings Consumers cannot use credit without first applying for it and being approved. The creditor evaluates information about the purchaser and assigns that person a credit rating. A **credit rating** is an estimation of the probability of repayment. Creditors are particularly concerned about three factors that can influence the likelihood that an applicant will repay credit:

- ability to pay,
- assets, and
- credit history.

Suppose that Julie Solomon is applying for credit. A creditor evaluates the three factors and assigns a credit rating. If Julie's financial status satisfies the creditor, she receives a high credit rating—meaning that she is a good credit risk. Perhaps Julie has no assets, however, or has failed to repay an earlier loan. In that case she may receive a low credit rating. The higher the credit rating a person has, the easier it is for him or her to receive credit.

How do creditors obtain financial information about applicants? Many creditors consult a credit bureau. A **credit bureau**, or credit reporting service, is a business that specializes in collecting financial information about consumers. Consumer information comes from banks and other financial institutions as well as stores and credit card companies. Consumers also may request a copy of their own credit report to guarantee that the information is accurate.

Credit Terms Once a customer is approved for a charge account, he or she can make purchases with a credit card. The consumer is then billed—usually every 28 or 30 days—for the amount of their purchases. These accounts have specified credit limits that indicate the maximum amount the customer can purchase on credit.

A customer who does not pay his or her balance in full will have to pay an additional **finance charge**—the total cost of credit expressed in dollars and cents. This charge includes interest, service charges, and any other miscellaneous fees. Most states allow credit card issuers to set their interest rates as high as 1.5 percent per month, or 18 percent per year. This 18 percent figure is the **annual percentage rate** (APR), or the total cost of credit expressed as a yearly percentage. Some credit card companies

"Sorry, but I hope you'll try us again sometime when you don't need it quite so badly."

ECONOMIC INSTITUTIONS & INCENTIVES *If consumers want credit, they must apply for it.* **What factors do creditors consider?**

Themes in Economics

ECONOMICS INSTITUTIONS & INCENTIVES Credit bureaus have access to a great deal of information about consumers, such as their age, income, activities, and shopping habits. Although credit card companies use the information to determine to whom to extend credit, they have traditionally also compiled it into mailing lists and sold it to other companies—accounting for a lot of junk mail! However, the Gramm-Leach-Bliley Act of 1999 sought to restrict this practice. The legislation, which took effect in July 2000, requires companies to tell consumers what their privacy policies are so that consumers know how their information is used and with whom it is shared. Consumers must also be permitted to "opt out" of having their information shared. An opt-out policy, however, places the burden on the consumer to notify the company that he or she does not want to have his or her personal data given to other companies. ■

Caption Answer

the applicant's ability to pay, assets, and credit history ★11A

SOURCES OF CAPITAL **215**

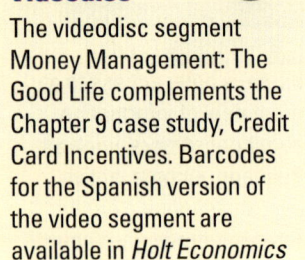

Holt Economics Videodisc

The videodisc segment Money Management: The Good Life complements the Chapter 9 case study, Credit Card Incentives. Barcodes for the Spanish version of the video segment are available in *Holt Economics Videodisc Teacher's Guide*.

PLAY SEGMENT

PAUSE

RESUME PLAY

PLAY OPTION A

PLAY OPTION B

PLAY OPTION C

---

also charge annual fees that must be paid whether or not the card is used.

CASE STUDY

Credit Card Incentives

EXCHANGE, MONEY, & INTERDEPENDENCE Have you ever received an offer from a credit card company? According to the National Consumer Law Center, more than 3 billion credit card offers are mailed to Americans every year. Some companies now even offer credit cards to high school seniors.

The credit card market is highly competitive, so many credit cards offer a variety of incentives to gain consumers' business. Some target specific groups of consumers, such as college students or school alumni. For example, in 2001 the credit card company MBNA offered college students credit cards with no annual fee and an introductory APR of 3.9 percent.

Some other cards offer a rebate. General Motors (GM) issues credit cards that offer rebates on the price of a GM automobile. Other credit cards offer rebates on everything from gas and groceries to compact discs, books, movies, and concert tickets.

Still other cards try to appeal to consumers' interests. Some cards are printed with a picture of the cardholder's college, while others are aimed at animal lovers and vegetarians. Another card donates a percentage of the cardholder's purchases to the environmental group Sierra Club.

Credit card offers are so numerous and provide such a wide range of incentives that consumers need to choose carefully. How much credit is necessary? Which is more important—a low APR or a low annual fee? To use credit wisely, you must examine more than the artwork on the card. Take a critical look at the incentives and costs to determine which card, if any, meets your needs.

Credit Regulation Some critics claim that the interest rates on credit card balances are too high. Banks and credit card companies, however, point to the high number of defaults by credit card users, the lack of collateral for the extended credit, and the high costs of processing credit card loans compared with other types of loans.

To balance the interests of both consumers and creditors, the government limits the amount of interest that can be charged. Charging interest above that limit is illegal and is called **usury**.

The federal government also has passed a number of laws to protect consumers from other kinds of unfair credit practices. Additionally, during the 1960s and 1970s, Congress passed a series of laws to define more clearly the rights and responsibilities of borrowers and lenders. (See Figure 9.8.)

Credit Abuse Increasingly, credit abuse has become a problem for both consumers and businesses. Consumers sometimes take on more credit debt than they can handle. When repayment of loans and credit debts becomes a problem, consumers usually have two courses of action. First, they can seek credit counseling. Counselors advise consumers on ways to pay off present debts through a repayment program and how to avoid recurring credit problems.

Counselors sometimes advise people with severe credit problems to take out a debt consolidation loan to repay several smaller loans and credit balances. Debt consolidation loans carry high interest rates because of the high risk they pose to creditors.

Second, consumers with large debts may be advised to declare bankruptcy. **Bankruptcy** is a legal declaration of inability to pay debts. Those who have abused credit, particularly individuals, usually declare bankruptcy only as a last resort, for it has serious consequences. By law, bankruptcy information remains on a person's credit history for 14 years, making it nearly impossible for the person to borrow money or receive credit.

For businesses, bankruptcy may mean the end of the firm's existence, a reduction in size, or intense regulation by courts and government agencies. Declaring bankruptcy, however, often saves a business by giving it time to rebuild much of its strength.

Credit in the Economy

The use of credit helps people to satisfy many of their personal wants and needs. It also can have a major effect on the economy of the United States by stimulating economic growth and by promoting economic stability—two important goals for the nation.

Stimulating Growth Economic growth is a major goal of the United States. Economic growth occurs when the per capita, or per person, output of goods and services in a nation increases during a specified period of time.

Figure 9.9 on page 218 illustrates how credit—as well as saving and borrowing—helps

FEDERAL REGULATION OF CREDIT

NAME OF LEGISLATION	MAJOR PURPOSE	PROVISIONS
Civil Rights Act, 1968	to outlaw discrimination by lenders in providing home mortgages	• forbids lenders from rejecting a home loan application because of the applicant's race, national origin, religion, or sex
Truth-in-Lending Act, 1968	to ensure that borrowers are fully informed about the costs and conditions of credit	• requires lenders to disclose all costs and finance charges, as well as the annual percentage rate, so that consumers can comparison-shop for credit • sets a $50 maximum that credit card users can be required to pay for charges incurred on a card that is reported lost or stolen and eliminates all liability for purchases made after the loss is reported • establishes a 3-day "cooling off period" during which consumers can cancel most credit contracts except first-home mortgages • requires that credit advertisements include all credit conditions of the agreement
Fair Credit Reporting Act, 1971	to protect consumers against the use of any inaccurate or outdated information gathered by credit bureaus	• entitles consumers to see a summary of their credit reports • allows consumers to insist that disputed information be reinvestigated and corrected and permits consumers to insert in the reports their own versions of the disputed information • requires that most negative credit information be removed from the reports after 7 years, but permits bankruptcy information to remain for 14 years
Equal Credit Opportunity Act, 1974 and 1977	to expand the 1968 Civil Rights Act's protection against discrimination in credit matters	• prohibits discrimination in granting credit because of such personal factors as race, national origin, religion, sex, or marital status • requires that the same credit guidelines be applied to all applicants • requires that applicants be notified within 30 days of a decision on their credit application
Fair Credit Billing Act, 1975	to promote prompt correction of billing errors	• sets up a procedure that allows consumers to challenge billing errors • requires consumers to notify creditors of errors within 60 days of receiving a bill and requires creditors to respond to that notification within 30 days • permits unresolved disputes to be settled in court or through other legal means
Fair Debt Collection Practices Act, 1977	to protect consumers from harassment by professional collection agencies	• prohibits bill collectors from making harassing telephone calls to consumers and their families and friends and from using other methods of intimidation

FIGURE 9.8 The federal government has passed a number of laws to protect consumers from unfair credit practices. **Which law protects consumers against inaccurate credit reports?** TEKS

Global Connections

The number of people filing for bankruptcy is on the rise in the United States. In 1999 more than 1.3 million people filed for bankruptcy, an increase of 71 percent from 1994. The United States is not the only nation where consumers are having a hard time controlling their spending, however. In Japan over 56,000 individuals filed for bankruptcy in 1996, an increase of 30 percent from the year before, a trend expected to continue.

The perception of bankruptcy in Japan differs significantly from that in the United States. Many people in the United States see bankruptcy merely as a way to get a fresh start. In Japan, however, filing for bankruptcy carries a tremendous amount of shame. People who have filed may not be able to find a job or get married. As a result, many Japanese choose to escape debts they cannot repay by going into hiding instead of filing for bankruptcy.

Transparency

An overhead transparency of Figure 9.8 is available in *Transparency Resources*. See Transparency 36: Federal Regulation of Credit.

Caption Answer

Fair Credit Reporting Act, 1971 ★15A, 15B

SOURCES OF CAPITAL **217**

Transparency

An overhead transparency of Figure 9.9 is available in *Transparency Resources*. See Transparency 37: Promoting Economic Growth through Saving and Credit.

Caption Answer

It increases demand and supply, which promotes economic growth. ⭐4B

SECTION 4 REVIEW ANSWERS

1. installments (215), credit rating (215), credit bureau (215), finance charge (215), annual percentage rate (215), usury (216), bankruptcy (216) **24A**

2. It stimulates economic growth and promotes economic stability. **4B, 23A, 24D**

3a. as compensation for lending out their money **11A**

3b. by examining credit applicants' probability of repayment based on their assets, credit history, and ability to pay **11A**

4. It might encourage a consumer to spend beyond his or her ability to repay; some students will say no, because the risk of having a credit card with a limit beyond a person's ability to repay outweighs the benefit. **11A, 23A**

---

promote economic growth. Individuals use the borrowed money and credit to buy consumer goods and services, while businesses buy capital goods such as new equipment and raw materials. Governments provide schools, bridges, and fire and police protection.

As businesses, individuals, and governments spend the borrowed money and use credit, more goods and services are purchased, and demand increases. Businesses then increase their supply of goods to meet consumer demand.

Promoting Stability Credit also affects a nation's economic stability, a companion goal to economic growth. Key indicators of a nation's economic stability are employment and price stability. Credit, when used in moderation, promotes high employment and stable prices.

How does the use of credit accomplish this stability? As consumers use credit to buy goods and services, demand increases. To meet this demand, business owners speed up production and hire more workers, increasing employment. With the supply now sufficient to meet demand, prices reach a level that is acceptable to both producers and consumers. Prices remain stable at this level until supply or demand decreases.

PROMOTING ECONOMIC GROWTH THROUGH SAVING AND CREDIT

[Diagram showing flow:]
- Individuals and businesses save money in financial institutions.
- Financial institutions lend money and extend credit to consumers, businesses, and government.
- Businesses use borrowed money and credit to buy capital goods. / Consumers use borrowed money and credit to buy consumer goods. / Government uses borrowed money and credit to pay for public goods.
- Demand increases.
- Supply increases.

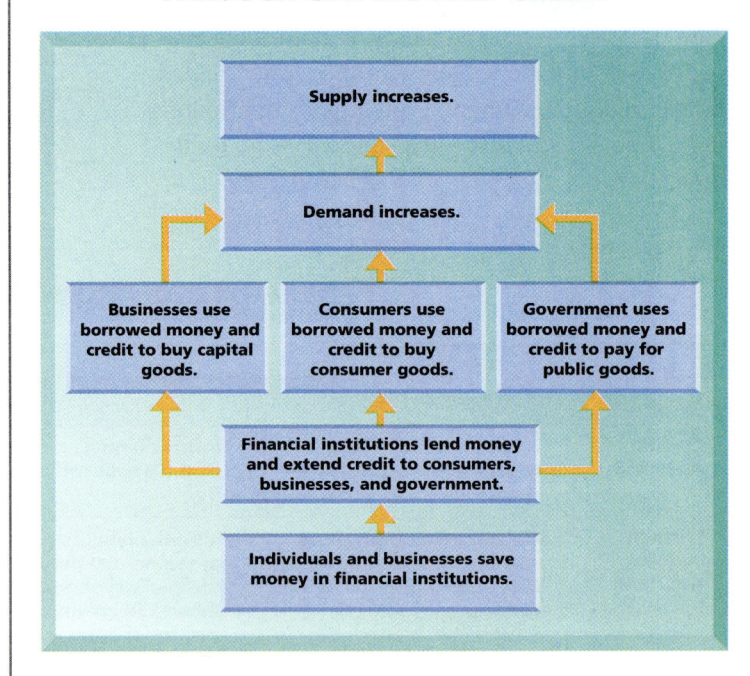

FIGURE 9.9 Economic growth occurs when per capita output of goods and services in a nation increases. **In this diagram, how does the use of credit affect economic growth?** ⭐TEKS

SECTION 4 REVIEW

⭐TEKS Q: 1, 2, 3a, 3b, 4

1. Identify and Explain:
- installment
- credit rating
- credit bureau
- finance charge
- annual percentage rate
- usury
- bankruptcy

2. Drawing Conclusions: Copy the graphic organizer below. Use it to describe the impact of credit on the U.S. economy.

Impact of Credit on U.S. Economy
1.
2.

3. Finding the Main Idea
a. Why do lenders charge interest on loans?
b. How is a credit rating determined?

4. Writing and Critical Thinking
Identifying Cause and Effect: How can having too much credit be harmful to a consumer? Explain your answer.
Consider the following:
- whether it would truly benefit you to have a credit card with a $50,000 credit limit
- the temptation to live beyond your means

Homework Practice Online keyword: SM3 HP9

Economics IN THE NEWS

Information Technology and the Stock Market

On August 23, 2001, the Internet equipment company Cisco Systems unexpectedly announced that its profits appeared to be stabilizing after months of poor performance. The next day the Dow Jones Industrial Average, the major index (measure) of stock prices, responded by rising almost 2 percent. The NASDAQ composite index, the main index for technology shares, responded with even larger gains. Such fluctuations in the stock market make it essential for investors to have real-time access to stock prices and other market information. For years, stock market investors have used the most advanced technology available to obtain timely market information.

For instance, in the early 1900s the most advanced information technology was the stock ticker machine. Based on an invention by Thomas Edison, the machine converted telegraph signals into text, allowing stock prices to be received with only a 15-minute delay. The machine produced a ticker tape, a thin ribbon of symbols and numbers.

Many of today's stock market investors increasingly rely on the Internet to receive stock market information as well as to access the markets. Online trading allows investors to place orders to buy and sell stocks over the Internet, in contrast to the traditional method of placing trades with a stock broker. By 2001, 23 percent of all stock trades were made online.

To capitalize on the Internet's capabilities, several brokerage firms offer trading and other services online. These companies' Web sites provide access to a variety of financial data, such as real-time stock quotes, the latest stock-related newspaper and magazine articles, and investment recommendations from professional financial analysts, that can help their clients make informed

New technology has made real-time stock quotes available through a number of sources, including the Internet, television, and this Nasdaq board in New York City.

decisions. Many brokerage firms also offer wireless stock trading. Wireless trading allows investors to place stock trades using a mobile phone or personal digital assistant.

The Internet also provides investors with access to financial data collected by local, state, and federal governments. For instance, on the U.S. Department of Commerce's Web site, www.statusa.gov, investors can view the latest economic data on everything from e-commerce to national employment figures and foreign investment opportunities.

What Do You Think? TEKS

1. What new types of economic information are available as a result of recent changes in information technology?
2. How might wireless trading technology increase the volume of trading?

WHY IT MATTERS TODAY

Today information technology changes very quickly. Use **CNNfyi.com** or other **current events** sources to find examples of information technology's impact on access to economic information.

CNNfyi.com

Economics in the News Answers

1. stock quotes, news stories, and other market information, as well as government data **27A**

2. by enabling people to trade while they are away from dedicated telephone or computer connections **26A, 26B**

CHAPTER 9
Review Answers

Writing a Summary
Summaries should focus on the main points of each section. These may be found in the Read to Discover questions at the start of each section. Summaries should also use standard grammar, spelling, sentence structure, and punctuation. **11A, 11B, 11C, 24B, 24D**

Identifying Ideas
balance (196), liquidity (196), time deposits (197), savings rate (199), real investment (202), infrastructure (202), brokers (206), yields (209), futures (212), annual percentage rate (215) **24A**

Understanding Main Ideas

1. regular savings accounts, because certificates of deposit charge a penalty for early withdrawal and savings bonds take time to mature **11B**

2. to determine the strength of the economy; income

3. financial investment exchanging property ownership and payments to make

(Continued on page 220)

219

CHAPTER 9 Review

(Continued from page 219)

a profit; real investment—using money to create new capital goods; students' examples will vary **11B**

4. Profits can be earned from dividends and by selling stock at a higher price than the purchase price; capital gain—profit earned from the sale of stock; capital loss—money lost through the sale of stock **11B, 11C**

5. Brokers link buyers and sellers of stock. Market analysts research the strengths and weaknesses of firms to inform brokers.

6. benefits—consumers can have products before paying for them and extend payments over time; liabilities—consumers may take on more debt than they can handle, and those who fail to make payments on time may have to return products and may lose the ability to buy on credit. See Figure 9.8 (p. 217) for descriptions of legislation that protects consumers from unfair credit practices. **1A, 11A, 15B**

Reviewing Themes

1. money available after taxes have been paid; security and interest **1B**

2. money invested in entrepreneurial enterprises; it can help turn an idea into a business venture that produces goods and services and employs people **11B**

3. loss of his or her investment; a stockholder would incur a capital loss **1B, 11C**

Writing a Summary ⊛TEKS

Using standard grammar, spelling, sentence structure, and punctuation, write a summary of the information in this chapter.

Identifying Ideas ⊛TEKS

1. balance
2. liquidity
3. time deposits
4. savings rate
5. real investment
6. infrastructure
7. brokers
8. yields
9. futures
10. annual percentage rate

Understanding Main Ideas ⊛TEKS

SECTION 1 *(pp. 195–99)*

1. Identify which of the following savings plans would provide the greatest possible liquidity: regular savings accounts, certificate of deposits, savings bonds. Explain your answer.

2. Why do economists study savings rates? Name one important determinant of savings rates in the United States.

SECTION 2 *(pp. 200–03)*

3. Explain the difference between financial investment and real investment. Provide an example of each type of investment.

SECTION 3 *(pp. 204–13)*

4. Describe the different ways you can earn profits from stock purchases. Compare a *capital gain* and a *capital loss*.

5. How does a broker's job differ from that of a market analyst?

SECTION 4 *(pp. 214–18)*

6. What are the benefits and liabilities of credit? Describe three pieces of legislation that protect consumers from unfair credit practices.

Reviewing Themes ⊛TEKS

1. Economic Institutions & Incentives What is disposable income? What are the benefits of saving disposable income instead of spending it?

2. Productivity What is venture capital, and how might it promote economic growth?

3. Economic Institutions & Incentives What is the greatest risk a stockholder can incur? Analyze the consequences of buying a stock at a high price and selling it at a low price.

Thinking Critically ⊛TEKS

1. Drawing Conclusions Choose three goods and services that you want to purchase in the future. Explain why either a savings account or time deposit is the most appropriate method of saving for each purchase.

2. Analyzing Information Does construction of a new school represent financial investment or real investment? Explain your answer.

3. Evaluating Suppose that you receive an inheritance of $1,000, with the limitation that it must be invested in stocks and bonds for five years before you can spend it. Decide whether you will purchase stocks, bonds, or a combination of the two. Explain the reasons for your decision.

Writing about Economics ⊛TEKS

Review the financial plan you outlined for your contest winnings in your Economics Notebook at the beginning of the chapter. Now that you have learned about saving, investing, borrowing, and credit, would you make any changes to your plan? Explain your answer in your Notebook.

Building Social Studies Skills

Interpreting the Visual Record

Examine the poster promoting a payroll savings plan for U.S. savings bonds.

SIGN UP FOR PAYROLL SAVINGS TODAY.

1. Why does the poster depict a chalkboard?
   a. To appeal to people's nostalgia for their school days
   b. To appeal to employees in an elementary fashion
   c. To appeal to people's love of artwork
   d. To appeal to those employees who might be saving for their own or their children's education
2. What features of savings bonds might make them an appealing instrument for saving money?

Analyzing Primary Sources

Read the following excerpt from an essay by the American industrialist and philanthropist Andrew Carnegie. Then answer the questions.

"This, then, is held to be the duty of the man of wealth: . . . to consider all surplus revenues, which come to him simply as trust funds, which he is called upon to administer . . . in the manner which, in his judgment, is best calculated to produce the most beneficial results for the community—the man of wealth thus becoming the mere trustee and agent for his poorer brethren, bringing to their service his superior wisdom, experience, and ability to administer, doing for them better than they would be able to do for themselves. . . ."

1. How might Carnegie's frame of reference have shaped his view that the man of wealth had the "superior wisdom, experience, and ability" that would enable him to do better for the poor than they could do for themselves?
   a. As a wealthy person, Carnegie believed in the abilities and superior wisdom of his own class.
   b. While he was poor, Carnegie had been dependent on the wealthy for his own betterment.
   c. Carnegie was being ironic by describing the wealthy in such a way.
   d. Carnegie's views were shaped by his admiration of the poor.
2. What might you infer from the title of Carnegie's essay, *The Gospel of Wealth*?

Alternative Assessment

Building Your Portfolio

As a group, develop a prospectus describing the finances of an imaginary company. Divide tasks among the various "company officers." For example, the vice president of sales might prepare a report on last year's sales. You may want to model your prospectus after a company report found in the library or on the Internet. As a group, design a portfolio that contains charts and graphs illustrating the most important company information.

internet connect

Internet Activity: go.hrw.com
KEYWORD: SM3 EC9

Access the Internet through the HRW Go site to learn about financial planners. Collect data on the training and experience required to become a financial planner, average salaries, what a financial planner does, etc. Then prepare a profile for a fictitious financial planner. Introduce your financial planner to the class.

Thinking Critically

1. Answers will vary but should reflect the benefits and limitations of the different methods of saving. 1B, 11A, 11B, 23A
2. It represents a real investment because the construction produces a new capital good—the school building. 23A
3. Answers will vary but should reflect an understanding of the benefits and limitations of stocks and bonds. 11B, 23A

Writing about Economics

Students' responses will vary but should reflect an understanding of saving, investing, borrowing, and credit. Students should be able to support their answers with concepts they have learned from the chapter. 11A

Building Social Studies Skills

1. d 23E
2. Students should mention that there is minimal risk associated with savings bonds, there is guaranteed interest, and bonds can be purchased at a discount to face value. 11C, 23E
3. a 23E
4. Answers will vary. Students might infer that Carnegie believed that his writings about wealth should be studied and people should use his ideas. 23E

SOURCES OF CAPITAL 221

UNIT 3

LAB OBJECTIVES

During the lab, students will
- explain the benefits of opening a Spaegel's Bagels franchise.
- describe the benefits of working at a Spaegel's Bagels franchise.
- prepare a help-wanted ad for the bagel shop.
- estimate costs, sales, and profits for the bagel shop.
- prepare a financial plan for the bagel shop.
- determine how the shop's profits will be distributed.
- compile the information into a formal business plan for the bagel shop.

Using the Lab

Before beginning the lab, organize students into groups and distribute copies of the Unit 3 Lab Activity found in *Unit Tests and Unit Lab Activities with Answer Key*. Have students read the assignment on this page and then discuss the assignment as a class. Point out the documents on pages 225–227 that students will use during the lab.

The What Do You Think? questions on pages 225–227 will help guide students during the project. In addition, the lab activity sheet includes a step-by-step checklist for students to monitor their progress.

⭐25A

UNIT 3

ECONOMICS LAB
You Solve the problem

Opening a Bagel Franchise

*I*magine that you and the other members of your group want to open a Spaegel's Bagels franchise. You and your partners are convinced that you can offer a wide variety of bagels in a location that is easily accessible to many potential customers. Plus, you want your shop to be part of a well-known, national bagel shop like Spiegel's.

To open your shop, you will need to obtain a small-business loan from a bank. The bank will want to know how you plan to spend the money it loans you, so you should prepare a report outlining your projected costs and profits. The president of Spaegel's has sent you these materials:

- a promotional brochure explaining the benefits her company provides for Spaegel's franchise owners
- a summary of suggested wages and benefits for Spaegel's franchise employees.
- information describing wages and compensation in other service industry businesses.
- an outline of projected costs and sales.

Economics Notebook Assignment ⭐TEKS

1. Write a clear, one-sentence statement of the problem to solve.
2. Review the documents to gather information.
3. In your Economics Notebook, answer the questions that accompany the documents.
4. Review and share your answers with the other members of your group.
5. Prepare a financial plan for your bagel shop. This report should be neatly written or typed, as it will be presented to other potential investors and to the bank you want to provide your business loan. In your plan, consider the various options for how to spend your money, and weigh the advantages and disadvantages of each. Decide upon a workable spending solution you will implement, and evaluate how effective you think the solution will be.
6. Prepare a sample help-wanted advertisement for potential employees.

SPAEGEL'S bagels

Dear Prospective Franchisee:

Thank you for expressing interest in opening a Spaegel's Bagels franchise in your town. Spaegel's Bagels' first shop opened in 1978 in Brooklyn, New York. Today, more than 100 Spaegel's Bagels' shops employ more than 1,200 people in the United States. Our tasty, chewy bagels are loved by customers around the country, and we believe our bagels will be very popular with customers in your town, too.

Spaegel's Bagels offers its franchisees a variety of benefits, including the use of our special bagel recipe and cooking methods. Potential customers from other towns will see our name on your shop and know that they can stop in for a quality bagel.

In addition, opening a Spaegel's Bagels franchise will help keep your costs down. We will pay for national advertising, for example, leaving to your franchise the responsibility only for local advertising.

Spaegel's Bagels also will train your employees in the "Spaegel way" of service, thereby saving you money on training costs. Last, but not least, we will serve as a resource of information and materials you need to make your business a success. For example, all Spaegel's Bagels franchises can purchase supplies, such as flour and spices, at discount rates from one supplier.

If you are interested in opening a Spaegel's Bagels shop, please write us for more information about employee benefits and projected costs and sales for your franchise. Those estimates should help you in developing financial plans for your business and yourselves. I look forward to hearing from you.

Molly Spaegel
President, Spaegel's Bagels

▲ WHAT DO YOU THINK?

1. What are the advantages of opening your bagel shop as a franchise rather than as a sole proprietorship, partnership, or corporation?

2. What might be the disadvantages of opening a national franchise? For example, could problems with a franchise in one town affect other franchises?

3. How could opening a Spaegel's Bagels franchise save on business costs?

What Do You Think?
Answers

1. You can rely on the parent company to pay for national advertising, build brand loyalty, provide discounted supplies, and help train employees. 9B

2. If the brand name develops a bad reputation among consumers, either because of an incident at another franchise or for some other reason, then customers may stop frequenting all Spaegel's Bagels locations.

3. It would reduce overhead costs. Spaegel's Bagels franchise owners do not have to pay for national advertising or employee training and can purchase supplies at discounted rates, as long as they use the company supplier.

ECONOMICS LAB

What Do You Think?
Answers

1. advantages—the minimum wage ensures workers a livable income level, which benefits everyone in society by reducing poverty; disadvantages—the minimum wage may be higher than the "market price" for this job, thereby increasing operating expenses and reducing profits; advantages of paying higher than minimum wage—easier for franchise owners to hire and keep quality employees; disadvantages—increased operating expenses decrease profits

2. Spaegel's Bagels officials believe that providing employees with benefits is important because employees tend to remain with a company longer if they receive good benefits. It is worthwhile for Spaegel's Bagels to try to make employees happy because the more employee turnover they have, the more time and money they will have to spend hiring and training new employees.

3. Answers will vary but students might suggest paid vacation days and company holidays, because many companies do not provide these benefits to employees making low-level wages.

224

Economics Lab *continued*

Spaegel's Bagels

Suggested Wages and Benefits for Spaegel's Bagels Franchise Employees

Starting wage for sales clerks: $5.15/hour
Starting wage for bagel makers: $7.00/hour
Starting wage for shift supervisors: $8.50/hour

Other benefits: job training, potential for advancement, health insurance, two weeks' paid vacation, five company holidays, company retirement plan

Company philosophy:

Spaegel's Bagels values its many hard-working employees. To show our support and appreciation for their hard work, Spaegel's Bagels offers a valuable package of benefits for franchise employees. These benefits include health insurance, vacation and other paid time off, and a company pension plan for longtime employees. These benefits are designed to help our employees support themselves and their families, enjoy their time off, and prepare for their retirement. In return, each Spaegel's Bagels franchise receives the support of a loyal, committed workforce.

Facts to Consider:
- In the U.S. about one fourth of service industry labor costs involve benefits such as health insurance, vacation and sick days, Social Security, and unemployment and workers' compensation insurance.
- The average hourly wage for restaurant employees is $5.59, although the minimum wage for servers is $2.13 because these workers also receive tips.

Source: *Statistical Abstract of the United States: 1996*

◀ WHAT DO YOU THINK?

1. From a business owner's point of view, what are the advantages and disadvantages of the required minimum wage? What would be the advantages and disadvantages of paying workers at a rate higher than the minimum wage?

2. From the fact sheet, you can see that paying for health insurance, vacation days, and other nonwage benefits can be a big part of an employer's costs. Nevertheless, Spaegel's Bagels' officials believe that paying for those benefits is important. Why do you think this is so?

3. What parts of the suggested employee wages and benefits would you emphasize in recruiting new employees for your store? Explain your reasoning.

224 UNIT 3

Spaegel's Bagels

PROJECTED COSTS AND SUGGESTED FINANCING

START-UP COSTS:
Franchise fee to Spaegel's Bagels: $20,000
Other start-up costs (construction, supplies): $50,000

SUGGESTED FINANCING:
$20,000 from partners' savings and other resources
$50,000 business loan

Projected monthly sales: $17,000

PROJECTED MONTHLY COSTS

Item	Cost	Percent of Sales
Rent	$1,700	10
Labor	$5,100	30
Supplies	$1,700	10
Loan repayment ($50,000 at 9.5% for 5 years)	$1,000	06
Total	$9,500	56

Projected monthly profit: $7,500 (before payments to partners)

◀ WHAT DO YOU THINK?

1. How high is the projected start-up cost for the Spaegel's Bagels franchise? According to the tables, what percent of sales will be left as profit (before partners are paid)?

2. What additional costs might your bagel shop face in the future?

3. How much of each month's profits do you think should be saved? How much should be used to pay the partners a monthly salary?

4. What elements would you include in a personal financial plan for managing the money you earn from the bagel shop? Use the information you learned in Chapter 9 to describe how you would save and invest your money.

internet connect

Internet Activity: go.hrw.com
KEYWORD: SM3 ECL3

Access the Internet through the HRW Go site to investigate various franchise opportunities. Choose an actual franchise, then present the pros and cons of buying and operating that franchise. Consider the cost of the franchise, the risk that is associated with the franchise, the type of work you and your employees would be doing, and the potential return you might earn. Present your analysis to the class.

What Do You Think?
Answers

1. $70,000; 44 percent ★23F

2. updating equipment; expanding or renovating the building; payments for beautifying the property, such as landscaping; insurance ★23A

3. Answers will vary but should reflect an understanding of the reasons why franchises need to save and reinvest company profits; answers will vary based on the number of members in each group. However, answers should correspond with the group's other answers in this section.

4. Answers will vary but should reflect an understanding of financial plans and the methods of saving and investing money that are discussed in Chapter 9. ★23A

UNIT 4

Lesson Options

Suggestions for customizing the material in Unit 4 to fit the specific schedule and curriculum of your classroom are located at the beginning of each chapter of the unit.

Main Ideas

Ask each student to read the Main Ideas and briefly answer each question in writing. Later, when you have finished Unit 4, ask students to return to their original answers and revise them using what they learned in the unit.

ECONOMICS LAB

The Unit 4 Economics Lab appears on pages 272–75. This lab project is a real-world assignment in which students will work in groups to examine and synthesize the information in a number of hypothetical economic reports and then use the information to develop recommendations for promoting economic growth in their community, town, or city. Support materials for the lab appear in *Unit Tests and Unit Lab Activities with Answer Key.* ★25B

UNIT 4

CHAPTER 10
ECONOMIC PERFORMANCE

CHAPTER 11
ECONOMIC CHALLENGES

Main Ideas
- What factors do economists look at to measure economic performance?
- What are the requirements of economic growth?
- What factors can lead to inflation?

ECONOMICS LAB

How would you predict the future of the U.S. economy? Find out by reading this unit and taking the Economics Lab Challenge on pages 272–75. ★TEKS

Elements of Macroeconomics

UNIT 4 OVERVIEW

Unit 4 covers the basic macroeconomic concepts of gross domestic product (GDP), economic growth, business cycles, unemployment, inflation and deflation, and poverty and income distribution. Students will learn the phases of the business cycle, the factors that promote economic growth, and how economists measure GDP and calculate the unemployment rate, the inflation rate, and the poverty rate.

Teaching with Photographs

This photograph shows an overhead shot of a busy street in New York City. Tell students that just as photographers zoom out to incorporate more elements into a photo and to show the big picture, economists look at aspects of an entire economy to get an idea of a nation's overall strength and well-being—that is, to see the big economic picture. Explain to students that in this unit they will be studying macroeconomics, the examination of entire economies.

As a motivating activity for this unit, ask students to identify ways in which the elements in this photograph symbolize aspects of the overall economy.

CHAPTER RESOURCE MANAGER

CHAPTER 10 ECONOMIC PERFORMANCE

	OBJECTIVES	PACING GUIDE	REPRODUCIBLE RESOURCES
SECTION 1 **GROSS DOMESTIC PRODUCT** (pp. 229–35)	▸ How do economists calculate gross domestic product? ▸ What are some of the limitations of gross domestic product? ▸ What other statistics do economists use to measure the economy?	**Regular** 1.5 days **Block Scheduling** 1 day	**ELL** Spanish Study Guide 10.1 **ELL** English Study Guide 10.1 **SM** Mathematics for Economics: Activity 10
SECTION 2 **BUSINESS CYCLES** (pp. 236–40)	▸ What are the four phases of the business cycle? ▸ What factors influence the business cycle? ▸ What are the three leading indicators used to determine the current phase of the business cycle and predict where the economy is headed?	**Regular** 1.5 days **Block Scheduling** 1 day	**ELL** Spanish Study Guide 10.2 **ELL** English Study Guide 10.2 **SM** Consumer Economics: Activity 10 **E** Challenge and Enrichment: Activity 10
SECTION 3 **ECONOMIC GROWTH** (pp. 241–46)	▸ Why is economic growth important? ▸ What are the requirements of economic growth? ▸ What is the relationship between economic growth and productivity?	**Regular** 1.5 days **Block Scheduling** 1 day	**ELL** Spanish Study Guide 10.3 **ELL** English Study Guide 10.3 **E** Simulations and Strategies for Teaching Economics: Activity 10

Chapter Resource Key

- **PS** Primary Sources
- **RS** Reading Support
- **E** Enrichment
- **S** Simulations
- **SM** Skills Mastery
- **A** Assessment
- **REV** Review
- **ELL** Reinforcement and English Language Learners
- Transparencies
- CD-ROM
- Video
- Videodisc
- Internet
- Holt Presentation Maker Using Microsoft® PowerPoint®
- TEKS and TAKS

TECHNOLOGY RESOURCES	REINFORCEMENT, REVIEW, AND ASSESSMENT
• One-Stop Planner: Lesson 10.1 • Researcher Online • Homework Practice Online • CNN Presents Economics: The Great Depression: Can It Happen Again? • Transparencies 38, 39, and 40 • Global Skillbuilder CD-ROM	**REV** Section 1 Review, p. 235 **A** Daily Quiz 10.1 ★ TAKS Every Day!
• One-Stop Planner: Lesson 10.2 • Researcher Online • Homework Practice Online • Transparency 41 • Global Skillbuilder CD-ROM	**REV** Section 2 Review, p. 240 **A** Daily Quiz 10.2 ★ TAKS Every Day!
• One-Stop Planner: Lesson 10.3 • Researcher Online • Homework Practice Online • Transparency 42 • Global Skillbuilder CD-ROM	**REV** Section 3 Review, p. 246 **A** Daily Quiz 10.3 ★ TAKS Every Day!

Chapter Review and Assessment

SM Global Skillbuilder CD-ROM
HRW Go site
REV Reteaching Activity 10
REV Chapter 10 Review, pp. 248–49
A Chapter 10 Test Generator (on the One-Stop Planner)
A Chapter 10 Test
A Alternative Assessment Handbook

One-Stop Planner CD-ROM

It's easy to plan lessons, select resources, and print out materials for your students when you use the *Texas One-Stop Planner CD-ROM with Test Generator*.

---

internet connect

HRW ONLINE RESOURCES
Go To: go.hrw.com
Then type in a keyword.

TEACHER HOME PAGE
KEYWORD: SM3 Teacher

CHAPTER INTERNET ACTIVITIES
KEYWORD: SM3 EC10
Choose an activity to:
• create a newspaper about economic factors of the Great Depression.
• write a biography of John Maynard Keynes.
• research OPEC.

CHAPTER ENRICHMENT LINKS
KEYWORD: SM3 CH10

HOLT RESEARCHER ONLINE
KEYWORD: Holt Researcher

ONLINE ASSESSMENT
Homework Practice
KEYWORD: SM3 HP10
TAKS Review
KEYWORD: SM3 T10
Rubrics
KEYWORD: SS Rubrics

CONTENT UPDATES
KEYWORD: SS Content Updates

HOLT PRESENTATION MAKER
KEYWORD: SM3 PPT10

ONLINE READING SUPPORT
KEYWORD: SS Strategies

CURRENT EVENTS
KEYWORD: S3 Current Events

TEXAS ONLINE RESOURCES
KEYWORD: S3 TX

LESSON 10.1 GROSS DOMESTIC PRODUCT

TEXTBOOK PAGES 229–35

HOLT PRESENTATION MAKER Access Illustrated LECTURE NOTES using Microsoft® PowerPoint® on the One-Stop Planner CD-ROM

OBJECTIVES

- Determine how economists calculate gross domestic product.
- Explain some of the limitations of gross domestic product.
- Identify other statistics economists use to measure the economy.

MOTIVATE

Write the term *GDP* on the chalkboard. Ask students if they have heard of this term before and if they know what these letters stand for. If students are unable to give the correct response, explain that GDP stands for *gross domestic product,* and write this term on the chalkboard. Tell students that GDP is the most common measurement that economists use to assess the strength of the economy. Then ask students what they think is meant by *gross domestic product.* Ask them to speculate about the things that might make up the gross domestic product and list these on the board. After students have discussed what might be included in the gross domestic product, write the following definition on the board and ask students to record it in their notes: *GDP = total dollar value of all goods and services produced within a country during one calendar year.* Return to the list on the board and identify which items would be included in GDP. Tell students that in this section they will learn how to calculate GDP, what limitations GDP carries, and about the other ways economists measure economic performance.

TEACH

Building a Vocabulary

Have students use spiral notebooks to create an Economics Dictionary to be used throughout the chapter. This dictionary might be used as an activity at the start of each new section or as a learning aid for sheltered English students or students having difficulty. List words that students will be expected to know for this section on the chalkboard. Have students use the information provided in the text or on the *Researcher CD-ROM* to list, define, and give an example of each term. ★24A

Identifying the Main Idea

Tell students that the first step in exploring the gross domestic product is to understand how economists calculate GDP. Write the following equation on the chalkboard and ask each student to record it in their notes next to the definition they recorded in the Motivate activity: $C + I + G + (X - M) = GDP$. Next, organize students into home groups of four and have them assign themselves letters in the GDP equation. For example, each group will have a C person (an expert on personal consumption expenditures), an I person (an expert on gross private domestic investment), a G person (an expert on government purchases of goods and services), and an X – M person (an expert on net exports of goods and services). Next, have students leave their home groups to meet with others in their expert groups.

When students are in their expert groups, have them read the information in the text about their particular part of the GDP equation. Tell students to discuss their part of the equation and determine the most effective way to teach the others in each of their home groups about the importance of their part of the equation. Challenge expert groups to come up with a clever, interesting way to teach the information to others in their home groups *(for example, students might create cartoons, diagrams, or graphs to illustrate their component).* Next, have students return to their home groups and teach the information about their part of the equation to the others. To review and clarify any questions, ask one student volunteer from each component to explain his or her part of the equation to the entire class. ★24D

Analyzing Ideas/Information

Explain to students that GDP must be calculated in both nominal and real prices. *(nominal GDP, or current GDP, is expressed in current prices of the period being measured; real GDP is adjusted for price changes.)* Ask students to recall from their reading why this is so *(to account for price increases).* Tell students that now that they are familiar with exactly what makes up GDP, you want them to think about what is missing from the equation. Ask students: What are some of the limitations of GDP as a measuring tool? If GDP is measured by market activity, what can you as see as potential limitations to this reporting mechanism? *(Student answers will vary, but should include factors such as accuracy and timeliness of data, nonmarket activities, underground economy, and "goods" and "bads.")* On the chalkboard, create a chart that lists each of these limitations as a heading. As each of these limitations is mentioned (by the students or by the teacher), have students identify an example not already mentioned in the textbook. Record each example under the appropriate heading on the board. You may wish to have students copy this chart into their notes.

227C

Writing about Economics, Comparing and Contrasting

Tell students that economists use measures other than GDP to track the nation's economy. Using Transparency 40 and referring students to Figure 10.3 on page 234, review with students the five most common national income and product accounts: *gross national product, net national product, national income, personal income, and disposable personal income.* For each account, ask students the following questions:

- What does this measurement include?
- How is it different from gross domestic product?
- What are the advantages of using this measurement?

Have each student write a brief explanation of each of these national income and product accounts, explaining how each compares and contrasts with GDP. 24A, 24B

Classifying Ideas/Information, Solving Problems

Ask students to determine gross national product, net national product, national income, personal income, and disposable personal income for a fictitious year. Students should replicate the calculations that they saw in Figure 10.3 using their notes and the following new numbers (in billions of dollars). (Note: these figures are listed in a different order than Figure 10.3 so that students can practice identifying where each component belongs.) Students should present their results in a chart or graph that illustrates the relationships among categories. Refer students having difficulty with the skills in this activity to the *Global Skillbuilder* Lesson 11: Presenting Data Graphically. 23G, 24D

	billions of U.S. $
Gross domestic product	10,063.7
Subsidies	16.1
Fixed capital depreciation	750.2
Goods produced in foreign countries with U.S. capital	302.5
Indirect business taxes, nontax liabilities, and other items	642.5
Goods produced in the U.S. with foreign capital	200.6
Corporate profits, net interest, and social insurance contributions	1852.3
Personal taxes and nontax payments	856.7
Personal interest and dividend income and transfer payments	2134.4

CLOSE

Ask students to recite the formula for GDP without referring to their notes, if possible. Next, have volunteers describe each of the parts of the GDP formula *(personal consumption expenditures, gross private domestic investment, government purchases of goods and services, and net exports of goods and services)*. Call on other volunteers to describe some of the limitations of using the GDP as an economic measure, and finally, have students identify other national income and product accounts that economists use to measure the economy.

OPTIONS

Logical-Mathematical Learners

Using the Internet or economics journals and newspapers, have interested students find the current figures that comprise the different parts of the GDP formula. Have students present their findings in a chart or graph using the formula $C + I + G + (X - M) = GDP$.

Students Having Difficulty

Pair students having difficulty with those who have mastered the material. Ask pairs to review the GDP formula and create a mnemonic device for remembering the formula. Then have pairs share their devices with other pairs.

REVIEW

Have students complete the Section 1 Review on page 235. Use the answers in the Annotated Teacher's Edition to assess student mastery of this section.

ASSESS

To assess student mastery of this section, have students complete Daily Quiz 10.1 in *Daily Quizzes with Answer Key*. For additional assessment options, see *Alternative Assessment Handbook* on the *One-Stop Planner CD-ROM*.

ADDITIONAL RESOURCES

Carrier, David J. *Industrial Restructuring, Financial Instability, and the Dynamics of the Postwar U.S. Economy.* 1997. Garland Publishers.

GDP and the Multiplier Process (video). Films for the Humanities and Social Sciences.

LESSON 10.2 BUSINESS CYCLES

TEXTBOOK PAGES 236–40

> **HOLT PRESENTATION MAKER**
> Access Illustrated LECTURE NOTES using Microsoft® PowerPoint® on the One-Stop Planner CD-ROM

OBJECTIVES

- Examine the four phases of the business cycle.
- Explain the factors that influence the business cycle.
- Identify the three leading indicators used to determine the current phase of the business cycle and predict where the economy is headed.

MOTIVATE

Ask students: When I say the words *Great Depression*, what images come into your mind? *(Answers may include soup lines, unemployment, homelessness, poverty, hunger, etc.)* Then ask students to attempt to define the word *depression* in economic terms. Write the the word *depression* on the chalkboard and list definitions under it as students respond. Tell students that a depression is one part of the business cycle that they will learn about in this section.

TEACH

Building a Vocabulary

List the important terms for this section on the chalkboard and tell students to add them to their Economics Dictionary. Tell students to use the information provided in the text or on the *Researcher CD-ROM* to list, define, and give an example of each vocabulary term. ★24A

Using and Creating Charts and Graphs, Demonstrating Understanding

Divide students into groups of three or four. After reviewing with the entire class the different phases of the business cycle *(expansion or recovery, peak, contraction or recession, and trough)*, have groups list the kinds of events that would be taking place during each of these phases *(employment, unemployment, high prices, low prices, bonuses for employees, layoffs, etc.)*. Have each group prepare an illustrated graph that depicts each phase of the business cycle, related events, and the general mood that would be present among people during each phase. Students should draw cartoons or cut pictures out of magazines to illustrate the different phases in their graphs. Have a representative from each group share its graph with the class. Display graphs in the room. ★24D

Identifying Cause and Effect

Explain to students that the factors that affect supply and demand also cause the fluctuations in the business cycle. Ask student volunteers to identify factors that influence the business cycle *(level of business investment, availability of money and credit, expectations about future economic activity, and other external factors)*. Write each of these factors on the chalkboard and ask students to explain the effect each one has on the business cycle. Underneath each term, write key words or a brief summary that reflects students' responses. Answers should resemble the following: *Business investment: high levels of business investment promote expansion in the business cycle, low levels of investment contribute to contractions; money and credit: total output changes as the availability and affordability of credit rise and fall; public expectations: individuals and businesses tend to increase spending when they believe the economy is strong, and they tend to decrease spending when they fear a recession; external factors: changes in the world's economy or political climate can cause expansions and contractions.* ★23A

Writing About Economics

Ask students to describe the three types of economic indicators that economists use to predict the business cycle: leading indicators *(anticipate the direction in which the economy is headed)*, coincident indicators *(provide information about the current state of the economy)*, and lagging indicators *(predict the duration of economic upturns and downturns)*. Divide students into groups of three or four. Supply each group with a copy of the *Wall Street Journal* or another economics periodical that publishes current economic indicators. Ask students in each group to identify the indicators as either leading, coincident, or lagging. Then ask students to use the indicators to assess the current state of the U.S. economy (its place in the business cycle). From their knowledge of current political and economic events (both national and global), ask students to identify any influencing factors on the business cycle. ★23A

CLOSE

To review students' knowledge of the business cycle ask the following questions:

- What is the business cycle?
- What are the different phases of the business cycle?

227E

- What factors indicate that the business cycle is entering a period of expansion? What factors indicate that it is entering a period of contraction?
- What additional factors may influence the business cycle?
- How do economists predict changes in the business cycle?
- Describe the three types of economic indicators and their purposes.

- What are the different phases of the business cycle?
- What factors cause the business cycle to shift into another phase?
- What are three examples of the factors that influence the business cycle? What are their effects?
- What tools do economists use to predict changes in the business cycle?
- What are the different purposes of the three types of economic indicators?
- Analyze the impact of the business cycle on U.S. history. 19C

OPTIONS

Gifted Learners
Have interested students assume the role of an economist describing the current place of the U.S. economy in the business cycle. Require students to support their hypotheses with evidence such as specific leading, coincident, or lagging indicators, as well as current news stories about consumer and/or macroeconomics, politics, etc. Students may wish to use a variety of formats to share their research: a research paper, a series of charts and graphs, or a multimedia presentation. 23D

Interpersonal Learners
Have interested students interview older family members who experienced the gas lines of the 1970s or who lived through the Great Depression of the 1930s. Before students conduct interviews, have them prepare by researching the economic and political causes of the economic crisis and by writing questions in advance. Students may wish to record or videotape interviews in order to share their research with the entire class.

Sheltered English Students
Pair students acquiring English with fluent English speakers. Ask students to write answers to the following questions:

REVIEW

Have students complete the Section 2 Review on page 240. Use the answers in the Annotated Teacher's Edition to assess student mastery of this section.

ASSESS

To assess student mastery of this section, have students complete Daily Quiz 10.2 in *Daily Quizzes with Answer Key*. For additional assessment options, see *Alternative Assessment Handbook* on the *One-Stop Planner CD-ROM*.

ADDITIONAL RESOURCES

Gordon, Robert J. *The American Business Cycle: Continuity and Change.* 1990. University of Chicago.

Rothbard, Murray N. *America's Great Depression.* 2000. Ludwig von Mises Institute.

Sherman, Howard J. *The Business Cycle: Growth and Crisis under Capitalism.* 1992. Princeton University Press.

Economics U$A: John Maynard Keynes. No. 5. (video). The Annenberg/CPB Projects.

LESSON 10.3 ECONOMIC GROWTH

TEXTBOOK PAGES 241–46

HOLT PRESENTATION MAKER: Access Illustrated LECTURE NOTES using Microsoft® PowerPoint® on the One-Stop Planner CD-ROM

OBJECTIVES

- Explain why economic growth is important.
- Identify the requirements for economic growth.
- Describe the relationship between economic growth and productivity.

MOTIVATE

Ask students if they are familiar with the phrase, "It's the economy, stupid!" Tell them that the phrase was the centerpiece of then-governor Bill Clinton's successful 1992 campaign for the presidency against former president George Bush. Ask students why they think Clinton's campaign focused on an economic theme. Tell students that it has been said that Americans tend to "vote their pocketbook" in presidential election years. Ask them what they think that statement might mean. Ask them why the economy and economic growth is such an important issue in the minds of citizens of the United States. Remind students that one of the six major goals of the U.S. economy is economic growth, and that in this section they will learn more about this goal.

TEACH

Building a Vocabulary

List the important terms for this section on the chalkboard and tell students to add them to their Economics Dictionary. Tell students to use the information provided in the text or on the *Researcher CD-ROM* to list, define, and give an example of each vocabulary term. ★24A

Evaluating Ideas/Information, Writing About Economics

Discuss with students the importance of economic growth to the welfare of the United States. Explain and discuss some of the main reasons economic growth is so important: *to maintain a high standard of living, to compete effectively in global markets, and to provide the resources to deal with domestic problems.* Next, ask students to decide which of these three reasons for economic growth is most critical to the welfare of the United States. Ask for volunteers to give persuasive arguments on behalf of their specific point of view. Finally, have each student write a paragraph in support of the most important reason for U.S. economic growth. Students may wish to include these paragraphs in their notes. ★16B, 23D, 24D

Demonstrating Understanding

Explain to students that because economic growth is so important to the United States, economists devote considerable effort investigating the factors that help stimulate the country's economy. On the chalkboard, write the terms *natural resources, human resources, capital resources,* and *entrepreneurship.* Ask students to provide an example of each factor of production and write their responses on the chalkboard. Next, divide the class into groups of four. Each group member should focus on one factor of production. Tell the groups to determine how increases in each factor of production could increase output. After about 10 minutes of discussion, ask for volunteers to present their group's conclusions to the rest of the class.

Synthesizing Ideas/Information

Write the terms *labor productivity* and *productivity growth* on the chalkboard. Ask volunteers to define the terms, and write the definitions on the chalkboard. *(labor productivity—how much each worker produces in a given period of time; productivity growth—an increase in the output of each worker per hour of work)* Explain to students that economic growth requires an increase in either a nation's inputs—its factors of production—or in the output, or productivity, of these inputs. Explain that certain factors have a great impact on productivity growth. These factors are: *technological advances, capital deepening, educated and skilled labor force, and other external factors.* Divide students into four groups, one group for each of the factors that impacts productivity growth. Ask each group to discuss how their factor affects productivity growth and to brainstorm a list of examples that illustrate this effect. Have a representative from each group present their examples to the class.

CLOSE

Remind students that economic growth is one of the six major goals of the U.S. economy. Point out that economic growth is important for an improved standard of living, global competitiveness, and expanding domestic resources. Ask students the following questions:
- How would you like your standard of living to improve?
- How might you expand your personal resources?

▶ How might you make yourself more competitive, for example, in the job market?

Have students write brief answers to these questions and then compare their responses to the information about the U.S. economy presented in the textbook. Ask students to write a paragraph explaining how their personal economic growth reflects or contrasts with the principles involved in national economic growth.

OPTIONS

Gifted Learners

As noted in the text, although the United States had become the leading economic world power among industrialized nations by the 1990s, the economies of some other nations grew at a faster rate. Have interested students research these other countries using the *Researcher Online,* library sources, and the Internet. Students should address the following questions: What contributes to the growth of these nations? How are these economies growing? Why are they growing at a faster rate than the U.S. economy? What contributes to their increased productivity? How is this productivity measured? Students may share their findings in a written or oral report, a chart or graph, or a multimedia presentation. ★23D, 24D

Students Having Difficulty

Pair students having difficulty with students who have mastered the material. Ask pairs to write brief answers to each of the following questions:
▶ What is the importance of economic growth to the welfare of the United States?
▶ What are three examples of factors of production that stimulate economic growth? How do they work?
▶ Why is labor productivity important to a healthy economy?
▶ Why is productivity growth important to a healthy economy?

Interpersonal Learners

Direct interested students' attention to the *Retraining* case study on textbook pages 245–46. Have interested students research retraining efforts in various companies in order to discover how U.S. industries are facing the challenges of the changing global and U.S. marketplace. As a culmination of their research, encourage students to arrange an interview with a representative of a company that has met these challenges through retraining programs. Students may wish to record or videotape their interviews in order to share information with classmates.

REVIEW

Have students complete the Section 3 Review on page 246. Use the answers in the Annotated Teacher's Edition to assess student mastery of this section.

ASSESS

To assess student mastery of this section, have students complete Daily Quiz 10.3 in *Daily Quizzes with Answer Key.* For additional assessment options, see *Alternative Assessment Handbook* on the *One-Stop Planner CD-ROM.*

RETEACH

For students having difficulty with the lessons, have them complete Reteaching Activity 9. This activity is located in *Reteaching Activities with Answer Key.*

ADDITIONAL RESOURCES

Barro, Robert J. *Determinants of Economic Growth: A Cross-Country Empirical Study.* 1998. MIT Press.

Goudsblom, Johan, et al. *The Course of Human History: Economic Growth, Social Progress, and Civilization.* 1996. M. E. Sharpe.

Peterson, Wallace C., Estenson, Paul S. *Income, Employment, and Economic Growth.* 1997. W. W. Norton & Company.

Economics U$A: Productivity. No. 11. (video). The Annenberg/CPB Projects.

CHAPTER 10

TOPICS INCLUDE

- gross domestic product (GDP)
- output-expenditure model
- real and nominal GDP
- limitations of GDP
- other national income and product accounts
- phases of the business cycle
- influences on the business cycle
- leading, coincident, and lagging indicators
- importance of economic growth
- real GDP per capita
- requirements for economic growth
- ways to measure and increase productivity

ECONOMICS NOTEBOOK

The Economics Notebook is a journal activity that encourages students to consider basic concepts of economics that relate to their lives. A follow-up notebook activity appears on page 248.

WHY IT MATTERS TODAY

To find additional lesson plans dealing with economic performance, visit CNNfyi.com or have students complete the ECONOMICS IN THE NEWS activity on page 247.

CNNfyi.com

CHAPTER 10

ECONOMIC PERFORMANCE

Just as you use weather forecasts to plan daily activities, consumers and producers use economic forecasts to help them make important economic decisions. In this chapter you will learn about the business cycle and the factors that influence it. Additionally, you will learn how economists measure economic performance. These methods form the basis of economic forecasts, which are used to plan future business activities and develop economic policy.

ECONOMICS NOTEBOOK

In your Economics Notebook, write three predictions about your own economic future. Consider your skills, education, job possibilities, and future living conditions.

WHY IT MATTERS TODAY

The performance of the U.S. economy directly impacts almost every aspect of American life. At the end of this chapter, visit CNNfyi.com to learn more about how economic performance affects your life.

CNNfyi.com

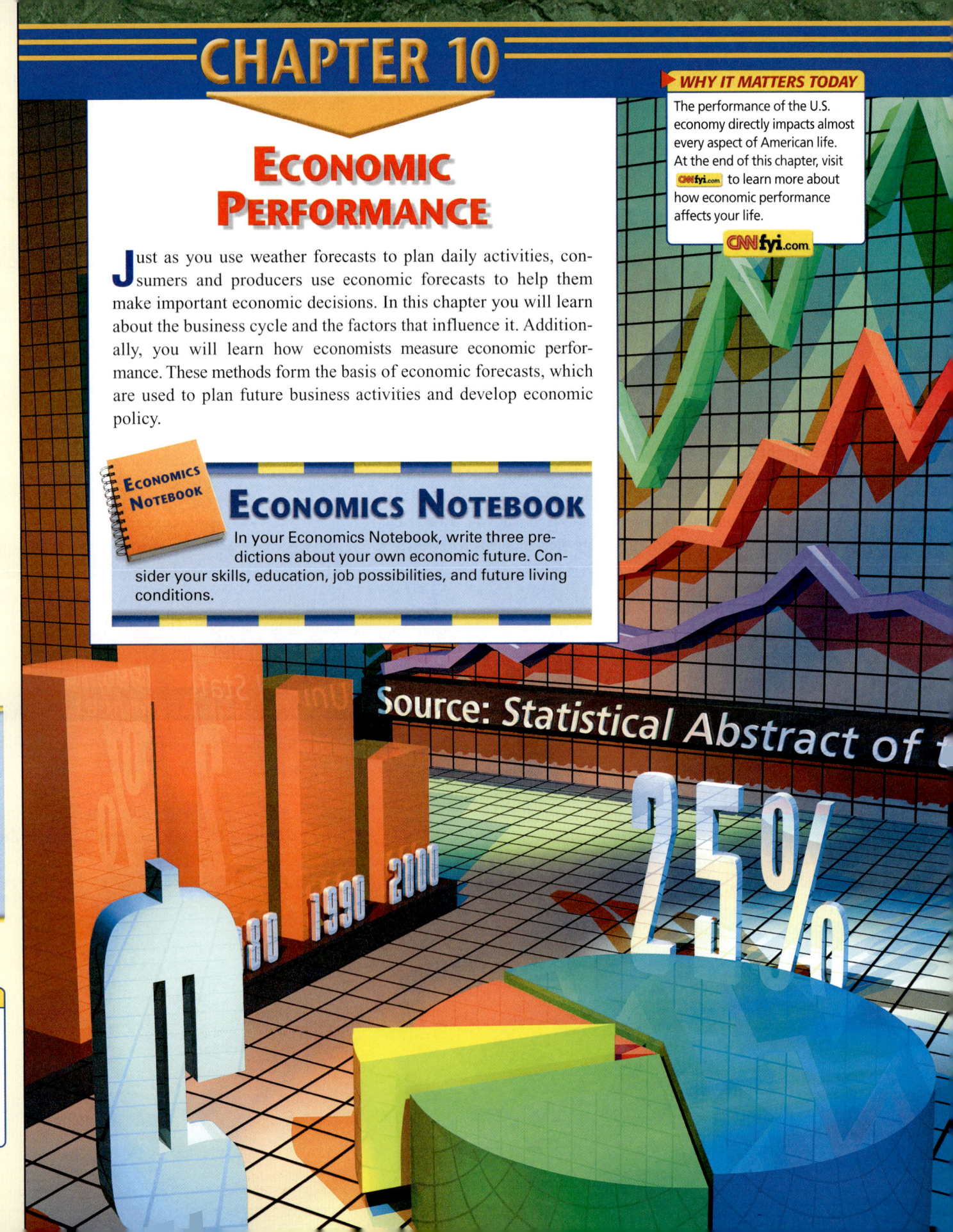

228

SECTION 1
GROSS DOMESTIC PRODUCT

READ TO DISCOVER
1. How do economists calculate gross domestic product?
2. What are some of the limitations of gross domestic product?
3. What other statistics do economists use to measure the economy?

ECONOMICS DICTIONARY
national income accounting
gross domestic product
output-expenditure model
personal consumption expenditure
gross investment
nominal GDP
real GDP
price index
underground economy
gross national product

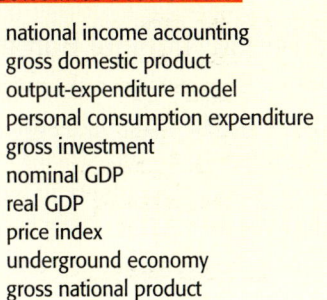

How do economists predict economic performance? Although predicting the future might seem like something done by a fortune teller at a carnival, economists do not rely on crystal balls or tea leaves for their information. Instead, they study the past and current performance of the economy as a whole.

As noted in Chapter 1, the study of entire economies, as opposed to individual actors or markets within an economy, is called macroeconomics. Macroeconomists use measures called national income and product accounts (NIPAs) to track production, income, and consumption in a nation's economy. This tracking process is known as **national income accounting** and provides information about a nation's economic activities.

Measuring Economic Production

Total production, or output, is one measure of an economy's strength. The most widely used NIPA is **gross domestic product** (GDP)—the total dollar value of all final goods and services produced within a country during one calendar year. A closer look at three components of the definition of GDP will help you better understand what it says about a nation's economy.

Final Output To avoid counting products more than once, economists include only the value of final goods and services when calculating GDP. How is a good identified as "final"?

Suppose that a woodcutter cuts down a tree and sells it to a sawmill operator. The sawmill then processes the tree into lumber, which is sold to a furniture manufacturer. The furniture manufacturer in turn uses the lumber to build a dining table, which is purchased by a consumer.

"HOW DO YOU WANT IT — STATISTICAL PROBABILITY, OR THE ANCIENT ART OF CRYSTAL GAZING?"

GROSS DOMESTIC PRODUCT *Economists generally do not use crystal balls to predict the future of the economy.* **What measures do macroeconomists use to predict economic performance?**

ECONOMIC PERFORMANCE 229

Across the Curriculum

HISTORY British economist John Maynard Keynes published his monumental work, *The General Theory of Employment, Interest, and Money*, in 1936, during the midst of the Great Depression. This work revolutionized economic thinking and the role of government in the economy. In his book, Keynes organized the economy into the four sectors that combine to make up GDP—consumer expenditures, investment, government expenditures, and exports and imports. Having analyzed these sectors, Keynes developed the theory that the national economy had no self-correcting mechanism to end a sustained depression. Business investment was not reliable enough to maintain high levels of employment. Thus, government needed to increase spending to offset the decline in business investment and spur economic growth. ■

---

internet connect

TOPIC: Keynes, Economic theory
GO TO: go.hrw.com
KEYWORD: SM3 EC10

Have students access the Internet through the HRW Go site to conduct research on John Maynard Keynes. Each student should write a short biography of Keynes, including information about his family, life, and theories. ★24C

Global Exchange

All Work and No Play . . .

Many companies in the United States hope to increase profits by participating in global markets. One of these firms is Toys "R" Us, America's largest chain of toy stores. As the biggest toy store in the world, Toys "R" Us has opened stores all over the globe, including Japan, Hong Kong, Spain, Germany, and Singapore.

The chain often has had to adjust its way of doing business in order to respond to local conditions. For instance, in Japan Toys "R" Us officials had to undergo a difficult approval process and were required to follow regulations designed to keep smaller stores from going out of business.

The chain also has had to adapt toys for the foreign market. In Hong Kong, for instance, the board game Monopoly® replaces Boardwalk and Park Place with local suburbs Sheko and Repulse Bay.

Even the company name required modification in foreign countries. The backward *R* was unfamiliar to non-English speakers, so many overseas stores added the name by which the store was locally known. Hong Kong toy shoppers therefore can visit Big Toy City, while in Germany the chain is called *Spielwaren das sind wir*.

While Toys "R" Us has had to make adjustments in order to compete in global markets, the company's founder and chairman Charles Lazarus is confident about its success. "Kids are the same all over the world. They all know what Nintendo is; they all know what Ninja Turtles are," he says. Lazarus is hoping that kids the world over will soon add Toys "R" Us to that list.

Of these items, only the dining table is considered the final product. The tree and the lumber are considered intermediate products—goods and services used to make other products. The value of the tree and the lumber are figured into the value of the dining table. To avoid counting these intermediate products twice, GDP includes only the value of the dining table.

Current Year GDP also does not include products such as used cars and secondhand clothing. Because GDP is a gauge of production—not sales—for the current year, sales of secondhand items are not counted. These goods were counted in the year they were produced.

Output Produced Within National Borders
You should note that GDP measures only output produced within a nation's borders, regardless of who produces it. For example, the Coca-Cola Company owns several production plants in Russia. When economists calculate U.S. GDP, however, they do not include these plants' output because the production occurs outside U.S. borders. U.S. GDP does include, however, the output of foreign workers and firms within the United States—for example, the automobiles that are produced at the Japanese-owned Nissan factory in Tennessee.

Output-Expenditure Model

How is GDP determined? Four sectors of the product market combine to make up GDP:

- personal consumption expenditures (C);
- gross investment (I);
- government purchases of goods and services (G); and
- net exports of goods and services, or exports minus imports (X − M).

Figure 10.1 uses these categories to represent the 2000 U.S. GDP. To actually compute GDP, economists add the output produced by these four sectors by using the **output-expenditure model**. This process is represented by the formula $C + I + G + (X - M) = GDP$.

Personal Consumption Expenditures The first element of GDP is **personal consumption expenditures**, or consumer purchases. Personal consumption expenditures include durable goods, nondurable goods, and services. Durable goods are items that have a useful lifetime of more than a year, such as automobiles and computers. Nondurable goods are items that have a short useful lifetime, such as food and cosmetics. Services—such as medical care, entertainment, and public education—are the fastest-growing area of consumer expenditures.

Gross Investment As noted in Chapter 9, real investment is the use of money to produce new capital goods. The results of this real investment—the capital goods produced—are measured as gross investment, which is the second part of GDP. **Gross investment** is the total value of all capital goods produced in a given nation during one year as well as changes in the dollar value of business inventories. Economists divide gross investment into two subcategories: fixed investment and inventory investment.

Fixed investment includes spending on residential structures, nonresidential structures such as office space and factories, and capital goods such as new machinery and office equipment. Inventory investment refers to the increase or decrease in the total dollar amount of the stock of raw materials, intermediate goods, and final goods of domestic businesses during a given period. Note that gross investment does not include the purchase of financial assets—such as stocks, bonds, and land—because these purchases do not result in the production of any new goods or services.

Government Purchases The third component of GDP consists of the total dollar value that federal, state, and local governments spend on goods and services such as highways, public education, and national defense. Government transfer payments—expenditures for which the government receives no goods or services in exchange—are not included when calculating government purchases. Transfer payments include Social Security payments and various types of government aid.

Net Exports The final component of GDP is net exports—total exports minus total imports. As you have learned, GDP measures goods and services produced within a given nation's borders. Thus, GDP includes the value of goods and services produced domestically but sold in other countries (exports) and does not include goods and services produced in other countries but purchased locally (imports).

Some goods and services included in GDP, however, are actually produced in other countries. Likewise, some items produced in the

U.S. GROSS DOMESTIC PRODUCT, 2000

$C + I + G + (X - M) = GDP$

Component	Value (billions of dollars)
C (Personal consumption expenditures)	6,728.4
I (Gross investment)	1,767.5
G (Government purchases)	1,741.0
X−M (Net exports)	−364.0
GDP (Total GDP)	9,872.9

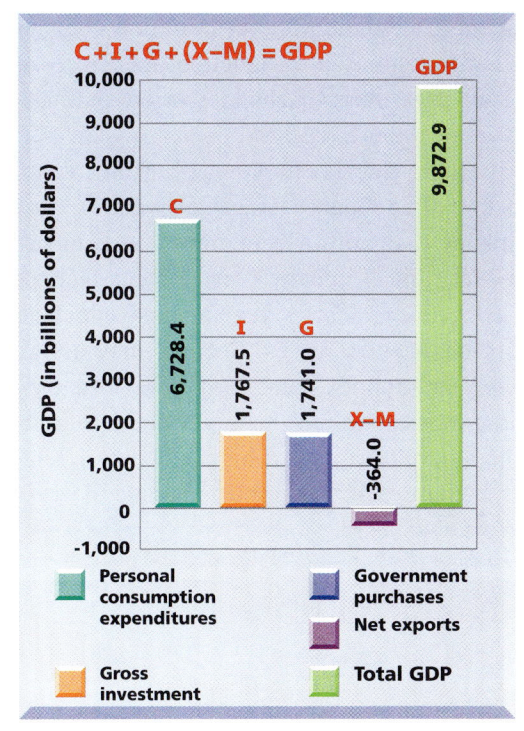

Source: *Bureau of Economic Analysis; Survey of Current Business: August 2001*

FIGURE 10.1 The most common measure of an economy's output, or strength, is gross domestic product. **What four sectors of the product market combine to make up GDP?**

Themes in Economics

THE ROLE OF GOVERNMENT To gather data on consumer purchases, economists do not ask each and every individual to keep records of their daily spending. Instead, the U.S. Bureau of the Census surveys a sample of 5,000 consumers each year. This survey, called the Consumer Expenditure Survey, consists of two parts—consumer interviews and diaries. Every three months, the Census Bureau interviews five of the sample consumers about major purchases they made during that time period. In addition, different consumers in the sample keep diaries of their daily purchases for two weeks throughout the year. Data from these interviews and diaries are combined to determine total U.S. personal consumption expenditures. ■

Transparency

An overhead transparency of Figure 10.1 is available in *Transparency Resources*. See Transparency 38: U.S. Gross Domestic Product, 2000.

Caption Answer

personal consumption expenditures, gross investment, government purchases, net exports

★17C, 23A

ECONOMIC PERFORMANCE 231

Transparency

An overhead transparency of Figure 10.2 is available in *Transparency Resources*. See Transparency 39: Nominal and Real GDP.

Caption Answer

nominal GDP—GDP expressed in the current prices of the period being measured; real GDP—GDP adjusted for price changes ⭐16B, 23A

Themes in Economics

MARKET FAILURES Measuring a nation's underground economy takes a great deal of detective work and a little guesswork. Friedrich Schneider, a professor at Austria's Linz University, studied the underground economies in several countries by examining the amount of unexplained cash circulating in each country. He based his approach on the theory that most underground business is conducted through cash transactions.

Schneider estimated that in 1994 the underground economy made up about 25 percent of Italy's total GDP; more than 20 percent of Spain's and Belgium's GDP; about 15 percent of Canada's, France's, and Germany's GDP; and close to 10 percent of GDP in the United States and Japan. These countries pale in comparison to Russia, however, whose underground economy was approximately the same as its reported 1997 GDP. ■

NOMINAL AND REAL GDP

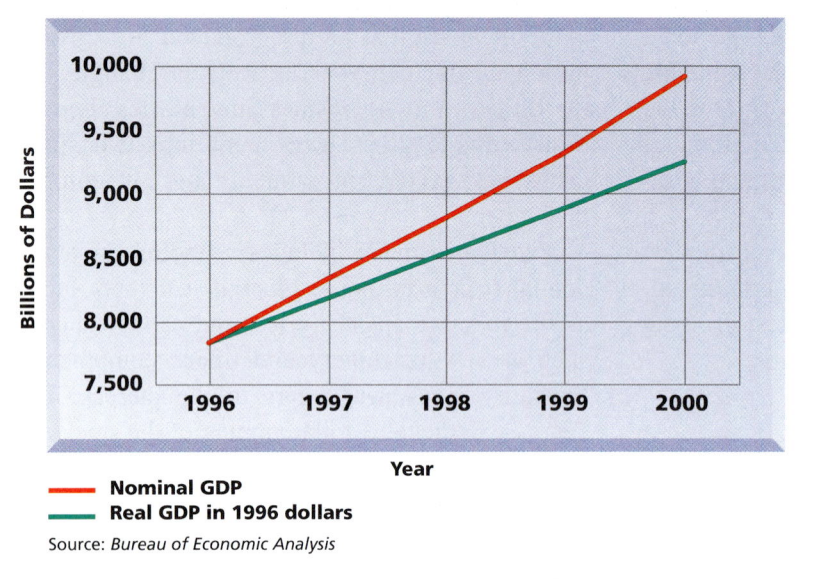

FIGURE 10.2 Nominal GDP grew 26 percent from 1996 to 2000, while real GDP grew only about 18 percent. **What is the difference between real and nominal GDP?** ⭐TEKS

Source: *Bureau of Economic Analysis*

United States are sold in other countries and fail to get included in the other components of GDP. To account for this movement of goods and services in and out of countries, economists subtract total imports from total exports and add the result to the other GDP components to obtain total domestic output.

Adjusting GDP for Price Increases

Suppose that Rosa Quintanilla serves as treasurer for the math club at her high school. In preparation for the club's annual candy sale, Rosa reviews the sales figures for the last two years. Although the club raised almost twice as much money last year as the year before, Rosa notices that the price collected by the club for each candy bar increased from $1.25 to $2.50 from the first year to the next. However, the number of candy bars sold each year was approximately equal. The rise in price had masked the lack of increase in candy-bar sales.

In 1999 U.S. GDP was nearly nine times greater than in 1970, and more than three times what it was in 1980. As in Rosa's case, however, these increases do not necessarily derive from real increases in the output of goods and services. As prices increase, so does GDP. Consequently, economists calculate GDP in both nominal and real prices.

Nominal GDP, or current GDP, is GDP expressed in the current prices of the period being measured. **Real GDP** is GDP adjusted for price changes. Figure 10.2 shows the nominal and real U.S. GDP for 1996 through 2000. A close examination shows that while nominal GDP grew more than 26 percent during that period, real GDP increased by only about 18 percent. Calculating real prices allows economists to determine if production increased or decreased, regardless of changes in the purchasing power of the U.S. dollar.

To measure changes in prices over time, economists use price indexes. A **price index** is a set of statistics that allows economists to compare prices over time. To create a price index, economists first select a base year against which to measure changes in prices. Second, they assign the base year an index number of 100. Third, they calculate index numbers for other years to indicate the amount prices are higher or lower relative to the base year. Economists update the base year every few years.

Limitations of Gross Domestic Product

Although GDP is the most common measure of the state of a nation's economy, it is not an entirely accurate measure of output and economic growth. To properly interpret GDP and other national accounts based on it, one must understand its limitations.

Accuracy and Timeliness of Data When computing GDP, economists use estimates and sampling techniques to determine prices and quantities of goods and services. Gathering the necessary data is a slow and time-consuming process. As a result, initial GDP figures are often inaccurate, and the Commerce Department may have to issue revised figures. Government and business decision makers who use GDP and other NIPAs must either rely on initial figures that may change or they must wait several months for more accurate figures to be calculated. Even then, decision makers must keep in mind that GDP and other NIPAs are only approximations of total output and income.

Nonmarket Activities Suppose that every Saturday, Tim Murphy mows his parents' lawn. Routinely, he also makes his bed, cleans his room, and washes the car—all at no charge. Although these activities are productive, no financial exchange takes place. As a result, Tim's household chores are not included in GDP.

For the most part, GDP measures only market transactions—exchanges of goods and services for money that are recorded in the marketplace. Transactions that do not involve money and are not recorded are nonmarket activities. Barter transactions, housework, and do-it-yourself home repairs are examples of nonmarket activities.

If Tim decides to start charging his parents for the household chores he performs, measured GDP will increase; however, the amount of real output will not have changed. Thus, GDP does not measure all output, and changes in GDP do not necessarily equate to changes in real output.

Underground Economy Suppose that Fran LaSalle spends many of her afternoons working at her auto repair business. She works out of her garage, does not advertise, and accepts only cash for payment. In this way, Fran avoids reporting her income and paying taxes to the Internal Revenue Service.

Fran is taking part in the **underground economy**—illegal activities and unreported legal activities. Although Fran's business is a legally acceptable activity, her failure to report that activity—and any income from it—is illegal.

"Goods" and "Bads" Just as GDP is an imperfect indicator of economic growth in a nation, it is also an imperfect indicator of a nation's overall well-being. The value of many "goods"—things that make for a better society—are not reported in GDP, while the value of many "bads"—things that make society worse—are.

Governments and economists must carefully analyze costs and trade-offs when considering policies designed to stimulate economic growth. Some policies that protect the environment or improve society result in decreased GDP. Nevertheless, the government sometimes decides the trade-off is worthwhile. Automotive emissions standards and regulations that prohibit development in ecologically sensitive areas reduce GDP but improve the nation's well-being.

Some economists have proposed using a new measure of the economy that accounts for the "goods" and "bads," and thus more accurately measures a nation's well-being. Positive dollar values would be assigned to "goods" such as

GROSS DOMESTIC PRODUCT *GDP does not measure all output in an economy—only money transactions that are recorded in the marketplace.* **What other limitations must be considered in the interpretation of GDP?**

Global Connections

Acknowledging that the gross domestic product (GDP) is a poor rating of a nation's well-being, the United Nations Development Program created two indexes by which to rate nations. The Human Development Index considers national income as well as life expectancy and adult-literacy rates. The Gender-Related Development Index considers the same data plus the level of gender inequality. A third index, created by an economist at Cambridge University, considers even more factors, such as political and civil rights and infant survival rates, to rate the well-being of a nation's people.

With these types of indexes, economists hope to indicate not only how a nation's people are doing economically but also aspects of how healthy and educated they are, whether they live long lives, and how much discrimination they face. Several international organizations now use these indexes, in addition to GDP, to compare people's well-being in different countries and to rate various policies.

Caption Answer

Initial GDP figures may be inaccurate; GDP does not include output from the underground economy; GDP does not accurately reflect national economic well-being. 16B, 23A

ECONOMIC PERFORMANCE

Transparency
An overhead transparency of Figure 10.3 is available in *Transparency Resources*. See Transparency 40: National Income and Product Accounts, 1999.

Caption Answer
gross national product, net national product, national income, personal income, and disposable personal income ⭐23F

Themes in Economics
GROSS DOMESTIC PRODUCT
In 1999, U.S. employees' income constituted the largest part of national income, with employees earning about $5.310 trillion, or about 71 percent of national income. Corporate profits accounted for $825 billion, or 11 percent of the total. Proprietors' income accounted for $672 billion, or 9 percent of the total. Net interest accounted for $506 billion, or almost 7 percent of the total. Rental income, the smallest component, accounted for just $148 billion, or 2 percent of total national income. ■

NATIONAL INCOME AND PRODUCT ACCOUNTS, 1999

	in billions
Gross Domestic Product (GDP)	**$9,256.1**
PLUS: The value of goods produced in foreign countries with U.S. capital	+ 302.3
LESS: The value of goods produced in the U.S. with foreign capital	- 322.3
Gross National Product (GNP)	**9,236.2**
LESS: Fixed capital depreciation	- 1,135.8
Net National Product (NNP)	**8,100.4**
PLUS: Subsidies	+ 26.5
LESS: Indirect business taxes, nontax liabilities, and other items	- 716.3
National Income (NI)	**7,496.3**
PLUS: Personal interest and dividend income and transfer payments	+ 2,313.8
LESS: Corporate profits, net interest, and social insurance contributions	- 2,018.4
Personal Income (PI)	**7,791.8**
LESS: Personal taxes and nontax payments	- 1,152.1
Disposable Personal Income (DPI)	**$6,639.7**

Source: *Statistical Abstract of the United States: 2000*

FIGURE 10.3 In addition to GDP, economists use a number of other measures of macroeconomic performance. **What are the five most common national income and product accounts?** ⭐TEKS

---

leisure time and urban renewal. Likewise, negative dollar values would be assigned to "bads" such as pollution and traffic congestion.

Other National Income and Product Accounts

Besides GDP, economists use a number of other national income and product accounts to track and measure a nation's economy. The five most common accounts are

- gross national product,
- net national product,
- national income,
- personal income, and
- disposable personal income.

Figure 10.3 shows the relationship between GDP and the other accounts. Although all five measures are important in macroeconomics, economists most often use the measure of GDP.

Gross National Product
Until December 1991 the U.S. Department of Commerce used a NIPA called **gross national product** (GNP) to measure the U.S. economy. GNP measures the total dollar value of all final output produced with factors of production owned by residents of a country during one year. Consider the Coca-Cola plants from the earlier example. The plants employ mostly local labor. The contribution that these Russian workers make to production would count as part of Russian GNP. If production involves any capital owned by U.S. residents, however, the value of that production would count as part of U.S. GNP.

Although GDP and GNP are similar, GDP more accurately reflects short-term resource use changes in the economy. In addition, the United Nations and most countries use GDP as the primary measure of economic production. For this reason, the Commerce Department switched to GDP—and stopped using GNP—in December 1991. The change has made it easier for U.S. economists and business firms to make international economic comparisons.

Net National Product
As you have learned, GDP includes money invested in capital goods.

234 CHAPTER 10

This investment includes money spent on replacing defective or outdated equipment and machinery. When this depreciation is subtracted from GNP, the result is a nation's net national product. Because net national product does not include investment spent to maintain current equipment, it is a more representative measure than GNP of a nation's actual output of new goods and services during a given year. Nevertheless, even though net national product is a better measure of a nation's output, economists use it less frequently than they use GNP. Net national product usually accounts for about 90 percent of GNP.

National Income To determine the total income paid to the owners of a nation's factors of production, economists use the measure national income. National income refers to the sum of employees' and proprietors' income, real and estimated rental income, corporate profits, and net interest.

To calculate national income, economists subtract subsidies and indirect taxes from net national product. Indirect taxes—as opposed to direct taxes on income—are taxes included in the final price of goods and services.

Personal Income Sometimes economists are interested in the total amount of income earned by people in a given nation. To estimate this measure, economists subtract from national income all income that does not go to people, such as profits that firms retain and reinvest and money that firms spend on corporate income taxes and employees' Social Security. Economists then add to this amount the money that individuals receive from government transfer payments, such as Social Security checks. The result is personal income, the total amount of income paid to individuals living in a given nation.

Disposable Personal Income If you have ever received a paycheck, you are familiar with the difference between your gross pay and your net pay, or the amount of money that you actually take home. Your take-home pay shrinks noticeably once deductions are made for government programs such as Social Security and income tax. Thus, only a portion of personal income is available to consumers.

To estimate a given nation's disposable personal income—the total amount of income available to a nation's people to spend or save—economists subtract personal taxes and nontax payments from personal income. Personal taxes include income, estate, gift, property, and motor vehicle taxes. Nontax payments include fines and passport fees.

SECTION 1 REVIEW

TEKS Q: 1, 2, 3a, 3b, 3c, 4

1. Identify and Explain:
- national income accounting
- gross domestic product
- output-expenditure model
- personal consumption expenditure
- gross investment
- nominal GDP
- real GDP
- price index
- underground economy
- gross national product

2. Analyzing Information: Copy the diagram below. Use it to identify the four sectors of the product market that combine to make up GDP.

3. Finding the Main Idea
a. What are the main components of GDP, and how are they determined?
b. What are the limitations of GDP?
c. How does GDP differ from GNP?

4. Writing and Critical Thinking
Supporting a Point of View: Do you think that economists should place a dollar value on "goods" and "bads" when computing GDP? Explain your answer.
Consider:
- trade-offs between higher GDP and other factors such as the environment, pollution, and traffic
- which "goods" and "bads" are overlooked by GDP

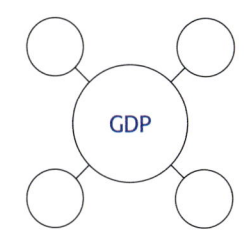

Homework Practice Online keyword: SM3 HP10

SECTION 1 REVIEW ANSWERS

1. national income accounting (229), gross domestic product (229), output-expenditure model (230), personal consumption expenditure (231), gross investment (231), nominal GDP (232), real GDP (232), price index (232), underground economy (233), gross national product (234) 16B, 24A

2. outer circles should be labeled personal consumption expenditures, gross investment, government purchases, net exports 16B, 24C

3a. personal consumption expenditures—total value of final goods and services; gross investment—total value of new capital goods and changes in the dollar value of inventories; government purchases—total dollar value that all levels of government spent on goods and services; net exports—total exports minus total imports 16B, 23A

3b. initial figures are often inaccurate; does not include nonmarket activities or the underground economy; does not accurately measure a nation's well-being 16B, 23A

3c. GNP—final output produced with factors of production owned by the residents of a given country; GDP—final output produced within a nation's borders 16B, 23A

4. Answers will vary but should reflect an understanding of "goods" and "bads," as well as address the trade-offs between these and GDP. 23D

ECONOMIC PERFORMANCE

SECTION 2
BUSINESS CYCLES

READ TO DISCOVER
1. What are the four phases of the business cycle?
2. What factors influence the business cycle?
3. What are the three leading indicators used to determine the current phase of the business cycle and predict where the economy is headed?

ECONOMICS DICTIONARY
business cycle
expansion
peak
contraction
recession
depression
trough
leading indicators
coincident indicators
lagging indicators

Business cycles are fluctuations, or changes, in a market system's economic activity. These fluctuations are measured by increases or decreases in real GDP. While fluctuations are inevitable, the duration of upturns or downturns varies and can last from a few months to several years.

Phases of the Business Cycle

The business cycle is divided into four stages or phases:

- expansion, or recovery,
- peak,
- contraction, or recession, and
- trough.

Figure 10.4 on page 238 illustrates the business cycle and its four phases. The **expansion** phase is a period of economic expansion and growth. For example, between 1940 and 1944 current GNP in the United States increased from $99.7 billion to $210.1 billion, indicating a period of economic expansion. This tremendous growth was mainly because of high levels of military spending during World War II.

Periods of expansion eventually hit a **peak**, or a high point, at which the economy is at its strongest and most prosperous. At a peak, high consumer demand encourages producers to use plant capacity more fully and to hire workers.

When real GDP stops increasing, the business cycle enters a period of business slowdown known as a **contraction**, or a recession. Technically, a **recession** is a decline in real GDP for two or more consecutive quarters—that is, for six months or more. A **depression** is a prolonged and severe recession, such as the Great Depression of the 1930s—the most severe contraction in U.S. economic history.

The final stage in the business cycle is the **trough**, which occurs when demand, production, and employment reach their lowest levels. Following the trough, the economy enters a period of recovery, and the expansion phase begins once again.

Influences on the Business Cycle

The factors that affect supply and demand also cause the fluctuations in the business cycle. Many economists agree that the level of business investment, availability of money and credit, expectations about future economic activity, and external factors affect the business cycle.

Business Investment Businesses invest in capital goods—such as new machinery—to increase their production. High levels of business investment promote expansion in the business cycle, while low levels of investment contribute to contractions.

Economics IN ACTION

How Does Your Garden Grow?

Many students hope to attend college after graduating from high school. However, with the cost of a college education rising, students and their families find paying for college increasingly difficult. A group of high school students in South Central Los Angeles came up with a solution to the problem of financing their college education—they started their own business.

Shortly after the 1992 Los Angeles riots, 39 students at Crenshaw High School—with the help and encouragement of their biology teacher—converted an empty field next to their school into a vegetable garden. They then formed a company, Food from the 'Hood, to sell their produce at local farmers' markets. Soon the students were turning a profit while helping to clean up and beautify their neighborhood.

The business was so successful the students began to think of ways to expand. With the help of several start-up grants and the donated expertise of local investment bankers, financial planners and public relations consultants, the students decided to introduce their own brand of salad dressing—Straight Out 'the Garden. Within months 50,000 bottles of their dressing were sold in stores throughout southern California. Soon the students were promoting their product nationwide at food trade shows. In fact, the business was so successful that Business Week magazine named the students Entrepreneurs of the Year in 1995.

Business decisions are made by vote at weekly meetings held at Food from the 'Hood's company office. Students receive a share of the profits in the form of college tuition grants. After three years of service in the company, a student with good grades can earn as much as $45,000 in scholarship money. As of 2001, more than seventy students have used the money to continue their educations.

Running a company has influenced the future career choices of many of the student-owners. For instance, Ben Osborne's experience designing the label for the dressing encouraged him to study commercial art in college with the goal of working as an art director at an advertising firm. Many other students have decided to pursue college degrees in business after working in the program. Dennis Famond, who earned a football scholarship to the University of California, thinks his experience with the program could provide an alternative career. "I know I can always garden. And my friends and I, we think of opening a restaurant someday."

High school students in South Central Los Angeles formed their own company to finance their college educations.

What Do You Think?

1. What role did the idea of community play in the founding of Food from the 'Hood?
2. The salad-dressing market is extremely competitive. If you were planning an advertising campaign for Straight Out 'the Garden, how might you differentiate the product from its competitors?

Cultural Perspectives

Young entrepreneurs may have great ideas for businesses but limited funds. Youth entrepreneurial organizations at the community level can often help. Many of these organizations have venture capital boards that provide financing to young businesspeople. These boards usually require applicants to submit a formal business plan and a proposal as to how they plan to use the requested funding. In addition, some organizations require that applicants complete an entrepreneurial training program before they can submit a business plan.

What Do You Think? Answers

1. Students located their garden in an empty field that was next to their school. They then sold the produce from their garden at local farmers' markets. The garden improved and beautified the neighborhood, while giving high school students in the community improved chances for earning money for college. ★23A

2. Answers will vary but students might mention that all ingredients are organic or grown in their own garden (if true), and that a portion of the proceeds generated from sales of the salad dressing go to finance students' college educations. ★25B

Business Cycle

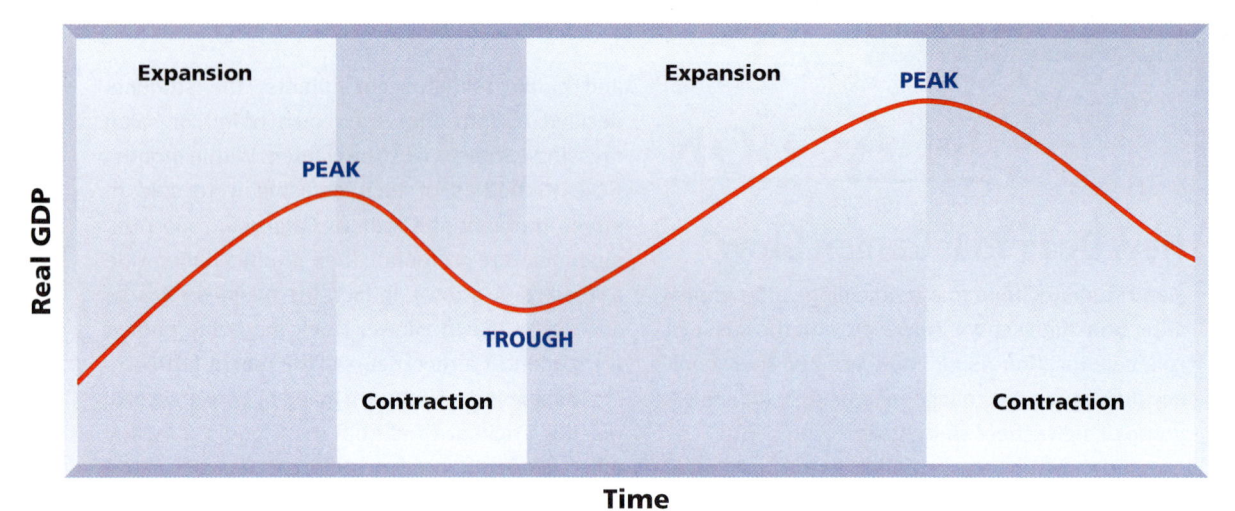

FIGURE 10.4 Increases and decreases in GDP represent fluctuations in the business cycle. **What factors influence the business cycle?**

Business investment is important to expansion for three reasons. First, by purchasing new capital goods, businesses create a demand for these goods. This demand encourages further increases in production. Second, businesses use the new capital to moderate production methods and promote efficiency. Third, increased business investment, particularly in the research and development (R&D) of new capital goods, tends to stimulate technological change and generally results in higher output at lower production costs.

Money and Credit The availability of money and credit also affects the business cycle. The amount of money in circulation depends mainly on government policies. Individuals and businesses generally borrow more money to make purchases when interest rates are low. When interest rates are high, borrowing tends to fall. Thus, total output changes as the availability and affordability of credit rise and fall.

Public Expectations Expectations about future economic conditions can shape current economic behavior as well. For example, if consumers believe that the economy is heading toward a recession, they may decide to limit their spending in order to save money for the hard times ahead. When consumers believe that the economy is strong and the future looks prosperous, however, they tend to increase spending.

Expectations also contribute to fluctuations in the business cycle. The possibility of prosperity encourages business owners to invest in new capital or to hire more workers. Conversely, a negative view of future business prospects causes firms to decrease investment and hiring.

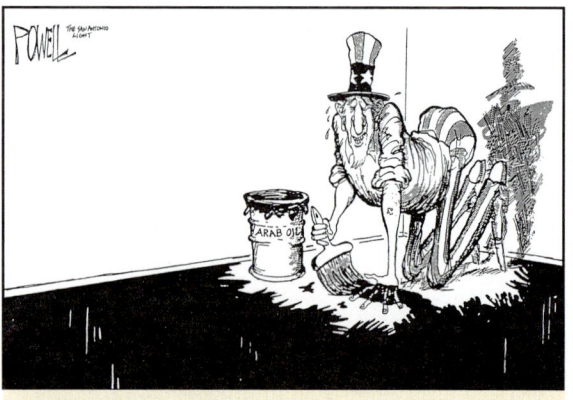

INFLATION & DEFLATION External factors can affect the business cycle in the United States. **What effect did sharp increases in OPEC oil prices have during the 1970s?**

External Factors Changes in the world's economic or political climate also affect the business cycle in the United States. For example, the sharp increase in world oil prices in 1973–74 and again in 1979–80 contributed to recessions in 1974–75 and 1980–82. The Organization of Petroleum Exporting Countries (OPEC) quadrupled oil prices beginning in late 1973, causing severe price shocks throughout the U.S. economy. This external factor kept oil prices high and eventually led to an energy crisis in the United States. Conversely, the dramatic decline in oil prices in the mid-1980s strengthened the expansion phase of the business cycle.

War is another external factor that affects the business cycle. Large government expenditures

CAREERS IN ECONOMICS

Financial Analyst

Suppose you want to invest your hard-earned money in a business. How would you go about determining which one would provide the highest profit—without being too risky? You might start by looking at the stock market quotations in the business section of a newspaper. For more detailed advice you might consult a financial analyst. In many ways, a financial analyst is like a weather forecaster. Instead of predicting the week's weather, he or she predicts the long-range performance of a company or industry.

A financial analyst usually chooses one of three job specializations. First, he or she may analyze the performance of a particular company or industry, focusing on how well it will perform in the future. To do this, analysts review the company's or institution's history, products, markets, operations, and financial stability. Other financial analysts are responsible for evaluating the "health" of the overall economy by studying factors such as the timing of business cycles, interest rates, and the performance of the global economy.

Finally, analysts may manage a large number of investments at one time. This "portfolio" is a group of investments spread over various types of businesses and industries. By distributing investments in this way, financial analysts hope to create the most profit with the least amount of risk. In other words, they try to avoid poor returns by not putting all their clients' eggs (investments) in one basket (business or industry).

Financial analysts usually work for large businesses or investment funds with substantial portfolios. They also usually specialize in a particular type of business such as banking, airlines, or oil and gas. Financial analysis can be a high-paying career. A career in financial analysis requires extensive college training in business and finance, including a familiarity with statistics and the way governments manage the economy.

Financial analysts predict the long-range performance of businesses.

ECONOMIC PERFORMANCE 239

for national defense traditionally have strengthened business activity in the United States. For example, periods of expansion accompanied U.S. involvement in World War I, World War II, and both the Korean and the Vietnam Wars.

Predicting the Business Cycle

Economists try to predict fluctuations in the business cycle. Decision makers in business use these predictions of future economic activity to help plan for plant construction, expansion, or modernization, production goals, and hiring. Similarly, government decision makers rely on economic forecasts when they develop taxation and spending policies.

Economists often rely on three types of economic indicators to determine what phase of the business cycle the economy is currently in and in which direction it is heading. The three types of economic indicators are

- leading indicators,
- coincident indicators, and
- lagging indicators.

All three types are sets of statistics collected by the U.S. Department of Commerce.

Leading Indicators When attempting to predict changes economists often examine **leading indicators**, which anticipate the direction in which the economy is headed. Among the most important leading indicators are changes in the number of building permits issued, the number of orders for new capital and consumer goods, the price of raw materials and stock prices.

Coincident Indicators Some indicators provide information about the current status of the economy. These **coincident indicators** change as the economy moves from one phase of the business cycle to another and tell economists that an upturn or a downturn in the economy has arrived. The most important coincident indicators include personal income, sales volume, and industrial production levels.

Lagging Indicators Not all changes take place instantly. **Lagging indicators** change months after an upturn or a downturn in the economy has begun and help economists predict the duration of economic upturns or downturns. Important lagging indicators include the use of consumer installment credit and the number and size of business incomes.

SECTION 2 REVIEW

1. Identify and Explain:
business cycle
expansion
peak
contraction
recession
depression
trough
leading indicators
coincident indicators
lagging indicators

2. Summarizing: Copy the diagram below. Use it to identify the four factors that influence the business cycle.

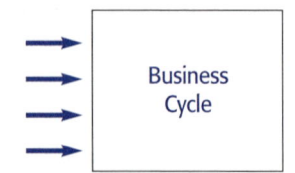

→
→   Business
→   Cycle
→

3. Finding the Main Idea

a. What are three signs that the business cycle is entering a period of expansion?

b. What are three signs the business cycle is entering a period of recession?

c. Contrast leading indicators, coincident indicators, and lagging indicators.

4. Writing and Critical Thinking

Drawing Inferences and Conclusions: How might a prediction by a well-known economist shape future economic activity?

Consider:
- the role of expectation in the economy
- how consumers might respond to a forecast of an imminent recession

TEKS Q: 1, 2, 3c

Homework Practice Online
keyword: SM3 HP10

SECTION 2 REVIEW ANSWERS

1. business cycle (236), expansion (236), peak (236), contraction (236), recession (236), depression (236), trough (236), leading indicators (240), coincident indicators (240), lagging indicators (240) 16B, 24A

2. business investment, money and credit, public expectations, external factors 23A, 24C, 24D

3a. high levels of business investment, low interest rates, increased consumer spending 23A

3b. low levels of business investment, high interest rates, decreased consumer spending 23A

3c. leading indicators—show in which direction the economy is headed; coincident indicators—show the economy's current status; lagging indicators—show a recent fluctuation in the business cycle, help economists predict the duration of the current phase of the business cycle 16B, 23A

4. Answers should address the role of public expectations in shaping economic behavior; e.g., consumers tend to spend less when they feel the economy is heading toward a recession, businesses invest and hire new workers when anticipating economic expansion. 23A

SECTION 3

ECONOMIC GROWTH

READ TO DISCOVER
1. Why is economic growth important?
2. What are the requirements of economic growth?
3. What is the relationship between economic growth and productivity?

ECONOMICS DICTIONARY
real GDP per capita
labor productivity
productivity growth
capital-to-labor ratio
capital deepening

As noted in the previous section, economic activity fluctuates in business cycles. These expansions and contractions usually represent short-term changes in the economy. Economic growth, however, refers to long-term overall improvements in the economy.

For example, consider the Keynes High School basketball team, the Wizards. Throughout the season, they experience both winning and losing streaks. By the end of the season, however, they have won far more games than they have lost, and consider it a winning season. Similarly, even though the economy may fluctuate in short-term ups and downs, as long as the ups are more frequent, the economy will experience growth.

Importance of Economic Growth

As a nation's economy grows, its capacity to produce goods and services increases. Thus, this economic growth is defined as the increase in the output of final goods and services produced within a nation's borders over a specified period of time—that is, an increase in a nation's real GDP over time. To account for population increase, economists usually measure economic growth in terms of *per capita* increase in real GDP. **Real GDP per capita** is an increase in the real dollar value of all final goods and services that are produced *per person* for a specified period of time. (See Figure 10.5 on page 242.)

As noted in Chapter 2, economic growth is one of the six major goals of the U.S. economy. Continued economic growth is important to the welfare of the United States for a number of reasons—to maintain a high standard of living, to compete effectively in global markets, and to provide the resources to deal with domestic problems.

Increasing the Standard of Living Without long-term economic growth, a nation's standard of living declines. The standard of living—the economic well-being of a nation's people—improves when production per person increases

PRODUCTIVITY *The late trade secretary Ronald Brown was in charge of the opening of a U.S. technology office in Beijing, China.* **Why is continuous economic growth important for the United States to remain competitive in the global market?**

ECONOMIC PERFORMANCE 241

Transparency

An overhead transparency of Figure 10.5 is available in *Transparency Resources*. See Transparency 42: Real GDP Per Capita, 1970–1999.

Caption Answer

does not measure quality of life, differentiate between "goods" and "bads," or indicate income distribution ⭐16B, 23A

Global Connections

In 2000, real GDP in the United States increased by 5 percent. This increase was relatively low compared to the growth rate of many developing nations' economies. For example, South Korea's GDP grew by 9 percent, India's grew by 6 percent, and China's grew by 8 percent.

Does this mean that these nations have stronger economies than the United States or that their standards of living are higher? Not necessarily. Many developing nations have much smaller GDPs and real GDPs per capita than the United States, even though their economies are growing at faster rates. For example, although India's GDP is growing faster than U.S. GDP, India's standard of living is much lower than the standard of living in the United States. For example, the United States had one of the highest GDP per capitas in the world in 1999—$32,392. ■

REAL GDP PER CAPITA, 1970–1999

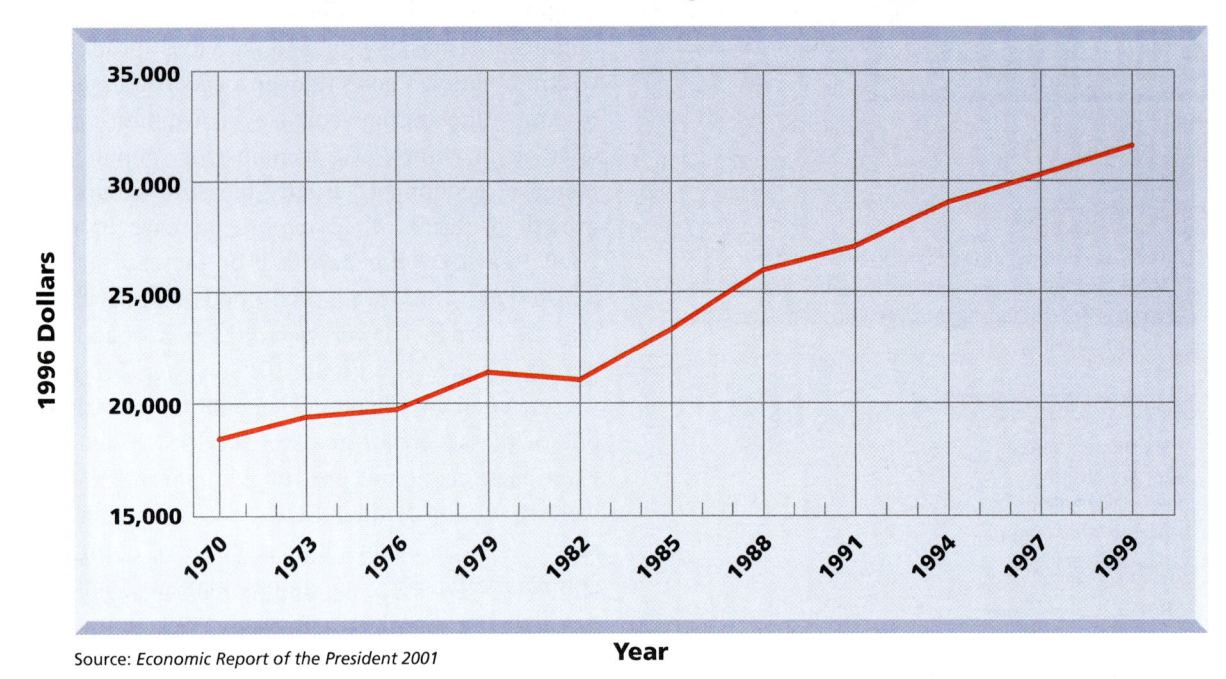

Source: *Economic Report of the President 2001*

FIGURE 10.5 Real GDP per capita provides a good estimate of a nation's standard of living. **Despite this fact, how might this measure be an inaccurate indication of a people's well-being?** ⭐TEKS

---

faster than the total population. Thus, people have more money to spend, an increased supply of goods and services to choose from, and the means to enjoy more leisure time. On the other hand, a decrease in the number of available goods and services results in a decline in the standard of living.

A higher standard of living can benefit society in many ways. People do not have to devote so many hours to work and have more time to spend on family, travel, and entertainment. In addition, people have more time to spend helping their community and can better afford to volunteer their time. More money in the economy also may help lessen domestic problems such as poverty, crime, and lack of health care—all of which are associated with low incomes.

Keep in mind, however, that an increase in a nation's real GDP per capita is not a true measure of that nation's standard of living. As noted in Section 1, real GDP does not measure quality of life or differentiate between "goods" and "bads," and it says nothing about the distribution of income across the population. Obviously, if most material possessions are in the hands of only a few people, then many people are not experiencing a high standard of living. Nevertheless, real GDP per capita does provide a good approximation of a nation's standard of living.

Competing in the Global Market During the twentieth century the United States was the leading economic world power among industrialized nations in terms of GDP. To maintain this position, however, it must continue to experience economic growth. Although the U.S. economy leads the world in overall production levels, the economies of some other nations are growing at a faster rate.

Increasing Domestic Resources Another benefit of economic growth is an expanded tax base. As people's incomes increase, they generally pay more in taxes. Thus, the government can spend more money on national defense, education, fire protection and police services, and

242 CHAPTER 10

other important services such as welfare and job training programs. In addition, the government can devote more money to reducing the federal deficit. Alternatively, the government might lower taxes.

Requirements for Economic Growth

As you can see, economic growth is essential to the strength and prosperity of a nation and its people. Thus, macroeconomists devote a great deal of time to examining ways to stimulate the economy. In order to devise policies that promote growth, economists first examine the factors that contribute to growth.

For a nation to increase its long-term output and income, it must either increase its inputs—its factors of production—or increase the productivity of these inputs. Policies designed to promote economic growth usually seek to increase both available resources and productivity levels, in combination.

Natural Resources The United States possesses a wealth of natural resources. Businesses in the United States, for example, have access to plentiful amounts of timber, coal, natural gas, and minerals. Despite this wealth of natural resources, however, the United States still must import many resources, such as oil and diamonds. As a result, economic growth in the United States is, to a certain extent, dependent on the state of international markets and politics—conditions that can change with little warning. Therefore, it is important that the existing resources be protected, particularly those that cannot be replenished or restocked.

Human Resources When estimating a nation's capacity to produce goods and services, economists examine the amount of labor input that is available. Labor input is the size of the employed labor force multiplied by the length of the average workweek. Although the average workweek has decreased in length significantly since the early 1900s, the size of the labor force has increased. As noted in Chapter 8, this increase has been a result of dramatic population growth and more women and minorities joining the labor force.

Capital Resources Increasing the total stock of capital goods increases total production. The more farmland, machines, factories, and production plants in a nation, the more it is likely to produce and the more its economy will grow. A workforce that has access to plentiful supplies of modern, quality equipment and facilities is generally more productive and more efficient. Just as a high level of investment in capital goods promotes expansion in the business cycle, it also leads to long-term economic growth. The relationship between capital stock and economic growth is examined in further detail later in this section.

Entrepreneurship The willingness of entrepreneurs to take the risks involved in starting new businesses and creating and selling new products is vital to economic growth. These entrepreneurs create new products, new markets, and new jobs, all of which contribute to

PRODUCTIVITY *Natural resources—such as the diamonds used in this industrial saw—are important for economic growth.* **What other factors affect economic growth?**

Themes in Economics

PRODUCTIVITY Another necessity for economic growth is a high level of capital utilization—the percentage of a nation's capital goods being used to produce goods and services. Unused capital goods indicate economic waste and inefficiency. On average, businesses use more of their capital goods during periods of growth, and less during periods of recession. ■

Enhancing the Lesson

For information on GDP and GDP per capita for a number of nations, see the Country Profiles and the Trade Statistics sections on *Researcher Online*.

Caption Answer

human resources, capital resources, entrepreneurship, increased productivity ★23A

ECONOMIC PERFORMANCE **243**

Across the Curriculum

SCIENCE Yearning for a replicator like those on the *Starship Enterprise?* The wait may not be as long as you think. Scientists at the Massachusetts Institute of Technology (MIT) in Cambridge have developed printers that can produce three-dimensional metal, ceramic, or polymer objects based on computer models. The new printers have enabled manufacturers to produce parts that were difficult or impossible to make before. Using special liquids and powders that bind and harden when combined, the printers build objects layer by layer.

One area in which 3-D printers have increased productivity is in the production of metal casts, molds used to create other objects. Normally, it takes several weeks or months to make a metal cast. A 3-D printer, however, can do the job in just a week. ■

Caption Answer
Answers will vary. Students may suggest that the artist believes that even a higher education does not ensure job security. ★ 23A, 23E

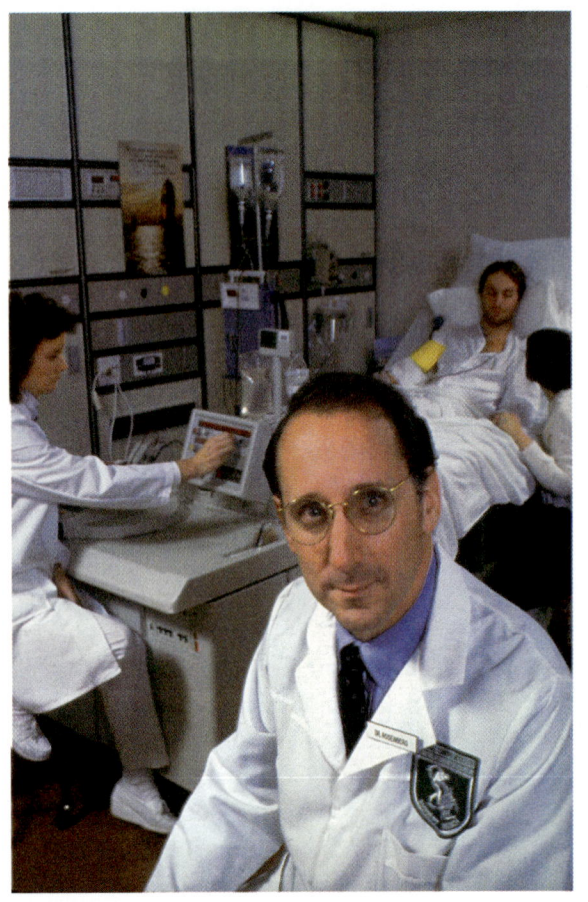

Dr. Steven Rosenberg is a pioneer in cancer research. Advances in technology have given doctors and researchers new tools to diagnose illness and helped them find new treatments for many life-threatening diseases.

---

increased output and demand. Policies that make it easier for entrepreneurs to start new businesses and to compete successfully in the marketplace help a nation's economy grow. At the same time, the new goods and services that entrepreneurs provide give consumers more choices and improve the overall standard of living.

Increasing Productivity

When estimating and determining ways to increase a nation's capacity to produce goods and services, economists often focus on labor productivity. **Labor productivity** is a measure of how much each worker produces in a given period of time, usually one hour. Economists define **productivity growth** as an increase in the output of each worker per hour of work. The factors that have a significant impact on productivity growth are

- level of available technology,
- quantity of capital goods available per worker, and
- education and skill level of the labor force.

Technological Advances
Invention and innovation—new knowledge and new ways of applying this knowledge—are the leading sources of productivity growth. New ideas, methods, and tools increase efficiency and output and often lower costs.

Research and development (R&D) expenditures indicate the percentage of total GDP that a nation devotes to improving its technology.

Capital Deepening
Another measure of productivity is the **capital-to-labor ratio**, or the amount of capital stock available per worker. This ratio is calculated by dividing the total amount of capital stock by the size of the workforce. When the amount of a nation's capital goods increases faster than the size of that nation's workforce, **capital deepening**—an

PRODUCTIVITY *An educated and skilled labor force is critical to a nation's productivity. What is the artist's point of view in this cartoon?* ★ TEKS

244 CHAPTER 10

LABOR PRODUCTIVITY, 1964–1999

Source: Statistical Abstract of the United States: 2000

FIGURE 10.7 Economists use labor productivity to estimate a nation's capacity to produce goods and services. **Did U.S. productivity increase or decrease between 1964 and 1999?**

---

increase in the amount of capital goods available per worker—results.

Workers who have access to more and better capital goods—machines, tools, equipment, and work facilities—usually will produce more in less time. Thus, capital deepening results in increased labor productivity.

Educated and Skilled Labor Force

The third influence on productivity is the education and skill level of the labor force. As trade becomes more global and people become more mobile, workers entering the labor force face greater and stiffer competition for jobs. In addition, as the level of skill required to perform certain jobs increases, employees must continue to learn and to improve their skills to keep their jobs. For U.S. citizens to compete in the workplace, it is vital that the nation and its businesses invest in human resources through better education, improved access to college and vocational programs, and increased numbers of job training programs.

CASE STUDY

Retraining

ECONOMIC INSTITUTIONS & INCENTIVES One business that recognizes the importance of education in the global marketplace is the Will-Burt Company in Orrville, Ohio. During the mid-1980s the machine parts producer found itself losing business to both domestic and foreign manufacturers.

Will-Burt's chairman, Harry Featherstone, realized that his company's main problem was its percentage of machine parts with problems. This high defect rate forced customers to look to competitors for better-quality parts. The defect rate was blamed mostly on undereducated workers. Will-Burt's workers, on average, had a 10th-grade educational level, and most did not have the skills to perform technically complex tasks such as reading blueprints.

Featherstone decided it was time for the company to invest in retraining its workers. The company hired a high school teacher, a university instructor,

---

Themes in Economics

PRODUCTIVITY Like steam power and electricity before it, the computer has revolutionized the workplace. Has it increased productivity, however? Economist Jeremy Greenwood says that it can take businesses 25 to 30 years before they learn to use major technological advances efficiently and effectively. Productivity levels can even drop at first. Greenwood estimates that the computer revolution, which began in the mid-1970s, began to boost overall per-worker output only in the late 1990s. ■

Caption Answer
It increased. 23F, 23G

Across the Curriculum

TECHNOLOGY California researchers estimated that U.S. workers spent an average of 5.1 hours a week in 1995 "futzing" with their computers—that is, playing games, surfing the Internet, sending personal e-mail, chatting on-line, and playing with the look of their screens. Technology has stepped in to fix the problem it created, however. A number of software programs now enable managers to scan workers' computers for unauthorized software and to monitor and restrict employees' use of the Internet. ■

ECONOMIC PERFORMANCE

SECTION 3 REVIEW ANSWERS

1. real GDP per capita (241), labor productivity (244), productivity growth (244), capital-to-labor ratio (244), capital deepening (244) **16B, 24A**

2. technological advances, capital deepening, and a highly skilled and better-educated workforce **23A, 24C, 24D, 26A**

3a. A nation's standard of living increases when its real GDP per capita grows. **23A**

3b. increased inputs or increased productivity of these inputs; real GDP per capita **16B, 23A**

4. Answers will vary, but students might respond that the United States needs to be able to compete to ensure its place as the leading world power, to sustain economic growth, and to maintain a good standard of living for its citizens. **23A, 23D**

---

and a specialist in industrial training to teach classes in everything from basic math and blueprint reading to algebra, geometry, and statistics. Over the next several years the company spent over $200,000 of its own money, as well as several state-funded retraining grants.

The program was an astounding success. The company's defect rate fell dramatically, from 10 percent to less than 3.7 defects per million parts. Moreover, the program led to higher worker morale. For instance, workers took far fewer days off work, and the cost of workers' compensation claims for injuries dropped from $500 per person per year to $3.

Investment in worker retraining can pay off handsomely. Whether through government programs, local community colleges, or the initiative of private companies, retraining plays a crucial role in an increasingly competitive marketplace.

Additional Factors Many factors other than education can affect productivity levels. The attitudes and motivation levels of workers, their dedication to their jobs, and the amount of loyalty they have to their companies directly affect productivity. Highly dedicated workers produce more, as do workers who enjoy their jobs.

A larger percentage of the labor force working in highly productive fields also results in increased productivity. As noted in Chapter 8, industrialization provided many new jobs for U.S. workers. As more people went to work in industry, productivity increased.

Productivity in the United States

Figure 10.7 on page 245 shows labor productivity levels for the United States from 1964 to 1999. U.S. productivity growth has slowed since the mid-1960s. Moreover, in several of the countries that compete with the United States, productivity is increasing at a faster rate.

Economists disagree as to why U.S. labor productivity is increasing at slower rates than in the past. Some of the more commonly cited reasons include decreased saving and investment, decreased investment in research and development, increased government regulation, and the shift to a more service-oriented economy.

Economists also disagree as to the best ways to stimulate economic growth in the United States. As mentioned before, policies designed to promote economic growth usually seek to increase both input and productivity. Different approaches and specific government policies for doing this are discussed in later chapters.

SECTION 3 REVIEW

★TEKS Q: 1, 2, 3b, 4

1. Identify and Explain:
real GDP per capita
labor productivity
productivity growth
capital-to-labor ratio
capital deepening

2. Summarizing: Copy the diagram below. Use it to identify three factors that lead to increased productivity.

[Diagram: three arrows pointing to a box labeled "Increased Productivity"]

3. Finding the Main Idea
  a. Describe the relationship between economic growth and a nation's standard of living.
  b. What changes result in economic growth? How is that growth measured?

4. Writing and Critical Thinking
  Evaluating: Explain why it is important for the United States to be able to compete in the global economy.
  Consider:
  • the relationship between economic growth and standard of living
  • the benefits of economic growth

Homework Practice Online
keyword: SM3 HP10

Economics IN THE NEWS

The Internet and the Global Market Revolution

Until the early 1800s, most Americans lived along the Atlantic seaboard or near a major river because waterways were the only efficient connection to markets. There were few roads, so it took too much time to transport goods more than a short distance by land.

As a result, much of the country's interior (the area west of the Appalachian Mountains) was unable to participate fully in the national economy. This situation began to change when road improvements and the development of steamboats, canals, railroads, and the telegraph opened the west to national commerce.

These innovations in transportation and communication technology had several major economic consequences. Cheaper, faster transportation led to a rapid increase in the volume and pace of trade. This increase in turn stimulated migration, as Americans rushed into the newly opened interior in pursuit of these new economic opportunities. Thus, these innovations had a decisive impact on the early development of the national economy—so much so that many historians believe that this so-called market revolution was the era's defining feature.

Since the market revolution, transportation and communications innovations such as the telephone and the interstate highway system, have continued to drive economic growth. The Internet is the latest communications breakthrough to have a major economic impact, and it has affected a wide variety of business activities. For instance, it has made the distribution of goods more efficient and has given rise to e-commerce, or shopping on line. E-commerce transactions were worth an estimated $7 billion dollars in the first three months of 2001, and their value is forecast to reach more than $41 billion a year by 2002.

The most profound impact of the Internet and e-commerce may be on the global economy, as businesses can expand their potential markets worldwide. Consumers stand to benefit from e-commerce, too, as it affords them a variety of goods at more competitive prices. Whereas canals and railroads triggered a national market revolution, the Internet, with its ability instantly to connect producers and consumers worldwide, may be helping to bring about a global market revolution.

The Internet has revolutionized the global marketplace. Customers can order everything from groceries to CDs to medications online, and businesses can more easily market their goods and services to both domestic and overseas markets.

What Do You Think? TEKS

1. What effect did improvements in transportation and communications technology in the early 1800s have on the economy?
2. How might businesses benefit from the growth of e-commerce? How might consumers benefit?

WHY IT MATTERS TODAY

The recent development of wireless Internet technology will likely produce profound economic changes. Use CNNfyi.com or other **current events** sources to find information about the economic impact of the latest developments in Internet technology.

Economics in the News Answers

1. increased volume and pace of trade 26B
2. expanded markets; variety of goods 4B

CHAPTER 10
Review Answers

Writing a Summary
Summaries should focus on the main points of each section. These may be found in the Read to Discover questions at the start of each section. Summaries should also use standard grammar, spelling, sentence structure, and punctuation. 24B, 24D

Identifying Ideas
gross domestic product (229), nominal GDP (232), real GDP (232), price index (232), gross national product (234), business cycle (236), expansion (236), recession (236), depression (236), leading indicators (240), real GDP per capita (241), labor productivity (244) 16B, 24A

Understanding Main Ideas
1. Nominal GDP is calculated with current prices. Real GDP is adjusted for price changes over time, which gives a clearer picture of the current GDP as compared to past years. 16B, 23A
2. Personal income is the total amount of income individuals in a nation receive.

247

CHAPTER 10 Review

Disposable personal income is personal income minus personal taxes and nontax payments. **23A**

3. expansion—period of growth; peak—point at which economy is strongest and most prosperous; contraction or recession—a period of business slowdown (technically, a recession is a decline in real GDP for two or more consecutive quarters); trough—point at which demand, production, and employment are at their lowest levels **23A**

4. Economic growth requires either more inputs or an increase in the productivity of these inputs. **23A**

5. It accounts for both increases in prices and population. **16B**

Reviewing Themes

1. Involvement in a war typically strengthens the business cycle and leads to expansion because of increased spending on national defense. **23A**

2. The GDP would increase, but quality of life would be unchanged. Answers will vary but should indicate that nonmarket activities and the underground economy exist as part of the economy but are not included in GDP. **16B, 23A**

3. Answers will vary but should suggest that productivity will likely increase because workers will improve their skills and may feel happier and more dedicated to the company. **2B, 23A**

Writing a Summary

Using standard grammar, spelling, sentence structure, and punctuation, write a summary of the information in this chapter.

Identifying People and Ideas

Identify the following terms or individuals and explain their significance.

1. gross domestic product
2. nominal GDP
3. real GDP
4. price index
5. gross national product
6. business cycle
7. expansion
8. recession
9. depression
10. leading indicators
11. real GDP per capita
12. labor productivity

Understanding Main Ideas

SECTION 1 (pp. 229–35)

1. Explain the difference between nominal GDP and real GDP. Why is real GDP a better measure to use when examining changes in GDP over time?
2. Explain the difference between personal income and disposable personal income.

SECTION 2 (pp. 236–40)

3. Identify and explain the four phases of the business cycle.

SECTION 3 (pp. 241–46)

4. How are economic growth and productivity related?
5. Why is real GDP per capita used to measure economic growth?

Reviewing Themes

1. **Inflation and Deflation** How does warfare affect the business cycle?
2. **Gross Domestic Product** What might happen to the GDP if all nonmarket and underground products and services were included? Would this GDP then reflect a higher quality of life? Why or why not?
3. **Productivity** Imagine that the DoRight Company has started an in-house day care and a job skills training program for its employees. What impact might this have on the company's productivity? Explain your answer.

Thinking Critically

1. **Problem Solving** How might you calculate GDP for your school? What products would you include? Which ones would you exclude? Explain your answers.
2. **Problem Solving** What actions might the government take to help the economy when the nation is experiencing a recession?
3. **Comparing and Contrasting** Consider the ways productivity applies to your own life. List five ways that you can improve your productivity at school. Are any of the actions you listed similar to ways in which nations can increase their productivity? Explain your answer.

Writing about Economics

Review the predictions about your economic future that you made in your Notebook at the beginning of this chapter. Are your predictions similar to economic predictions made on the national level? Record your answer in your Notebook.

Building Social Studies Skills

Interpreting the Graph

Use the information in the graph below to help you answer the questions that follow.

LEADING ECONOMIC INDICATORS, 1995–1998

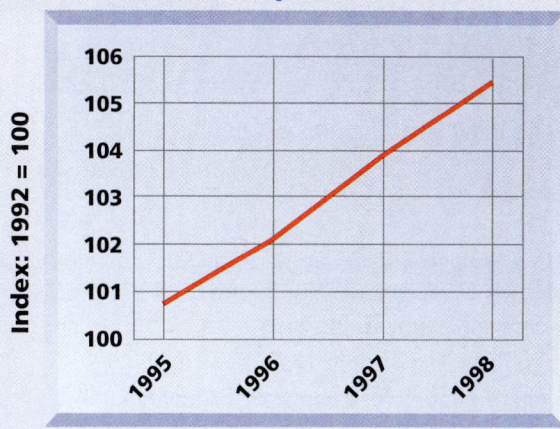

Index: 1992 = 100

Year	Value
1995	~100.5
1996	~102
1997	~104
1998	~105.5

Source: U.S. Census Bureau, *Statistical Abstract of the United States: 2000*

1. In which year did the leading economic indicators peak?
   a. 1995
   b. 1996
   c. 1997
   d. 1998

2. What does the graph indicate about the economy from 1995 to 1998?

Analyzing Primary Sources

Read the following excerpt from Gregg Easterbrook's 1989 article "The Sky Is Always Falling" from *The New Republic*. Then answer the questions that follow.

"Better sit down and brace yourself: there's an economic trend in progress. It's bad, real bad. What trend? Makes no difference.

"Let's take employment. U.S. ECONOMY ADDS 400,000 JOBS IN MONTH: REPORT SPURS FEARS, declaimed the *Washington Post* last February. Some economic naïf [uninformed person] might consider job growth to be good news. To the cognoscenti [especially knowledgeable people], though, it was a frightening omen: high employment might inspire the Federal Reserve to raise interest rates, the *Post* worried. . . . Of course, later when employment expansion slowed somewhat, that was bad too: APRIL JOB GROWTH EASED DECISIVELY, STIRRING CONCERN, the *New York Times* warned. . . .

"[There is a] central truth about economics: almost any economic development is both good *and* bad—good in some ways, bad in others. An expanding economy reduces unemployment, but at some point risks inflation. . . .

3. Which of the following statements best describes the author's point of view?
   a. Economic trends are always bad.
   b. Economic developments always have both a positive and a negative side, but the media favors the negative.
   c. Economic statistics are relentlessly fatuous.
   d. The cognoscenti believe that job losses cause higher interest rates.

4. Easterbrook's piece raises the question: Why does the media so frequently focus on the negative aspects of economic developments?

Alternative Assessment

Building Your Portfolio

Imagine that you are an economist who foresees a recession in the near future. Write an editorial about the recession's impact. Form groups of several editors and discuss your forecasts. Then discuss how the country might address a recession if it is already under way.

Internet Activity: go.hrw.com
KEYWORD: SM3 EC10

Access the Internet through the HRW Go site to research the Great Depression. What economic factors led to the depression? What was life like for people living during the depression? Create a newspaper that details your findings.

Thinking Critically

1. Answers will vary but students should use the output-expenditure model and should display an understanding of the four sectors of the product market that comprise GDP. **16B, 25A**

2. Answers will vary but might include lowering the interest rate to promote borrowing and spending, reducing taxes to encourage spending and investment, or increasing government spending. **15A, 17C, 25A**

3. Answers will vary but should reflect an understanding of the three factors that nations use to increase productivity. **25A**

Writing about Economics

Students should consider how economic predictions are made—the tools that economists use and the factors that they consider.

Building Social Studies Skills

1. d **23F**
2. The economy was growing. **23F**
3. b **23E**
4. Answers will vary, but students might mention that bad news sells papers. **23D, 23E**

ECONOMIC PERFORMANCE

CHAPTER RESOURCE MANAGER

CHAPTER 11 ECONOMIC CHALLENGES

	OBJECTIVES	PACING GUIDE	REPRODUCIBLE RESOURCES
SECTION 1 **UNEMPLOYMENT** (pp. 251–56)	▸ What is the unemployment rate? ▸ What are the four major types of unemployment? ▸ What are the main economic costs of high unemployment?	**Regular** 1.5 days **Block Scheduling** 0.5 day	**ELL** Spanish Study Guide 11.1 **ELL** English Study Guide 11.1 **PS** Reading 60: Principles of Economics
SECTION 2 **INFLATION** (pp. 257–63)	▸ What do economists look at when evaluating price changes over time? ▸ What causes inflation? ▸ What are the two main price indexes that economists use to measure inflation? ▸ How does inflation affect the economy?	**Regular** 2 days **Block Scheduling** 1 day	**ELL** Spanish Study Guide 11.2 **ELL** English Study Guide 11.2 **SM** Mathematics for Economics: Activity 11 **SM** Consumer Economics: Activity 11
SECTION 3 **POVERTY AND INCOME DISTRIBUTION** (pp. 264–68)	▸ How do economists determine the number of poor people in the United States? ▸ How do economists measure the distribution of income? ▸ What policies does the U.S. government use to reduce the income gap and decrease poverty?	**Regular** 1.5 days **Block Scheduling** 0.5 day	**ELL** Spanish Study Guide 11.3 **ELL** English Study Guide 11.3 **E** Challenge and Enrichment: Activity 11 **S** Simulations and Strategies for Teaching Economics: Activity 11

Chapter Resource Key

PS	Primary Sources	**A**	Assessment		Video
RS	Reading Support	**REV**	Review		Videodisc
E	Enrichment	**ELL**	Reinforcement and English Language Learners		Internet
S	Simulations		Transparencies		Holt Presentation Maker Using Microsoft® PowerPoint®
SM	Skills Mastery		CD-ROM		TEKS and TAKS

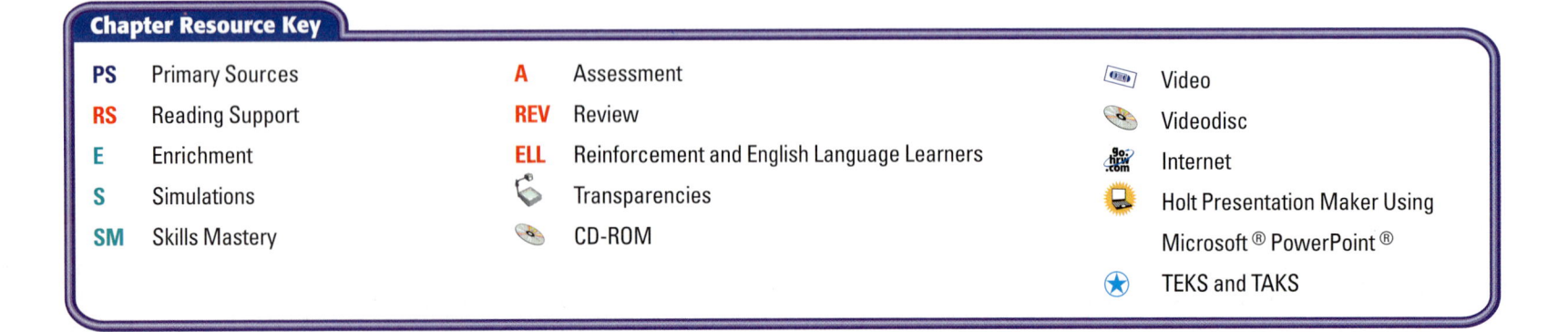

249A

TECHNOLOGY RESOURCES	REINFORCEMENT, REVIEW, AND ASSESSMENT
• One-Stop Planner: Lesson 11.1 • Researcher Online • Homework Practice Online • CNN Presents Economics: Where the Jobs Are • Transparency 43 • Global Skillbuilder CD-ROM	**REV** Section 1 Review, p. 256 **A** Daily Quiz 11.1 ★ TAKS Every Day!
• One-Stop Planner: Lesson 11.2 • Researcher Online • Homework Practice Online • Transparency 44 • Global Skillbuilder CD-ROM	**REV** Section 2 Review, p. 263 **A** Daily Quiz 11.2 ★ TAKS Every Day!
• One-Stop Planner: Lesson 11.3 • Researcher Online • Homework Practice Online • Transparencies 45, 46, and 47 • Global Skillbuilder CD-ROM	**REV** Section 3 Review, p. 268 **A** Daily Quiz 11.3 ★ TAKS Every Day!

Chapter Review and Assessment

SM Global Skillbuilder CD-ROM
  HRW Go site
REV Reteaching Activity 11
REV Chapter 11 Review, pp. 270–71
A Chapter 11 Test Generator (on the One-Stop Planner)
A Chapter 11 Test
A Alternative Assessment Handbook

One-Stop Planner CD-ROM

It's easy to plan lessons, select resources, and print out materials for your students when you use the *Texas One-Stop Planner CD-ROM with Test Generator.*

---

internet connect

HRW ONLINE RESOURCES
Go to: go.hrw.com
Then type in a keyword.

TEACHER HOME PAGE
KEYWORD: SM3 Teacher

CHAPTER INTERNET ACTIVITIES
KEYWORD: SM3 EC11
Choose an activity to:
▸ research the consumer price index (CPI).
▸ write an ad for the Bureau of Labor Statistics.
▸ create a map showing house prices across the country.

CHAPTER ENRICHMENT LINKS
KEYWORD: SM3 CH11

HOLT RESEARCHER ONLINE
KEYWORD: Holt Researcher

ONLINE ASSESSMENT
Homework Practice
KEYWORD: SM3 HP11
TAKS Review
KEYWORD: SM3 T11
Rubrics
KEYWORD: SS Rubrics

CONTENT UPDATES
KEYWORD: SS Content Updates

HOLT PRESENTATION MAKER
KEYWORD: SM3 PPT11

ONLINE READING SUPPORT
KEYWORD: SS Strategies

CURRENT EVENTS
KEYWORD: S3 Current Events

TEXAS ONLINE RESOURCES
KEYWORD: S3 TX

LESSON 11.1 UNEMPLOYMENT

TEXTBOOK PAGES 251–56

HOLT PRESENTATION MAKER
Access Illustrated LECTURE NOTES using Microsoft® PowerPoint® on the One-Stop Planner CD-ROM

OBJECTIVES

▸ Define the unemployment rate. ★16B
▸ Identify the four major types of unemployment.
▸ Discuss the main economic costs of unemployment.

MOTIVATE

Ask students to raise their hands if they have ever been unemployed. Ask volunteers to describe what type of work they were seeking and why it was difficult to be hired for this type of work. Discuss with students the steps that they think young people can take to improve their chances of getting a job. Tell the class that in this section they will learn how economists and policy makers measure unemployment, how these experts define different types of unemployment, and what the consequences of high unemployment can be.

TEACH

Building a Vocabulary

Have students use spiral notebooks to create an Economics Dictionary to be used throughout the chapter. This dictionary might be used as an activity at the start of each new section or as a learning aid for sheltered English students or students having difficulty. List words that students will be expected to know for this section on the chalkboard. Have students use the information provided in the text or on the *Researcher CD-ROM* to list, define, and give an example of each term.

Analyzing Information, Comparing and Contrasting

Tell the class that in order for economists and policy makers to make decisions about how to reduce unemployment, they must first measure the rate of unemployment. Call on students to give a basic definition of the unemployment rate (*the percentage of people in the civilian labor force who are unemployed*). Write this definition on the chalkboard. Remind the class that in order to measure the rate of unemployment, the federal government must classify people as employed or unemployed. Organize students in PP groups of three or four. Have students discuss the following questions, and assign one person in each group to record the group's answers to these questions on a piece of paper:

▸ What are the three major requirements for employed status? (*For employed status, a person must have: 1. worked for pay or profit one or more hours, 2. worked without pay in a family business 15 or more hours, or 3. held a job but did not work as a result of illness, weather, vacations, or labor disputes.*)

▸ What percentage of the population must be employed for the government to claim that there is "full employment"? What is the reason for this? (*About 95 percent of the labor force must be employed; the government uses this figure because economists claim that a small amount of unemployment is natural in a healthy economy.*)

▸ What are the major requirements for unemployed status? (*A person is classified as unemployed if he or she does not meet any of the criteria for being employed, and he or she must have been actively looking for work during the past four weeks.*)

▸ Why is the unemployment rate not completely accurate? (*It does not indicate the differences in intensity with which people look for jobs, and it excludes people from the unemployment rate who most Americans would consider unemployed.*)

▸ Do you think that the people in these categories should be included in the unemployment rate? Explain your answer.

For the last question, encourage students to express a variety of opinions, and instruct the person recording the group's answers to record the different opinions expressed. ★16B, 23A

Evaluating Information, Creating Charts

Explain to the class that economists have divided unemployment into four types based on cause. On the chalkboard, draw the outlines for a chart in which to compare these four types of unemployment (*frictional, structural, seasonal, cyclical*). Write the names of the four types of unemployment in a row along the top of the chart (on the horizontal axis), or in a column on the left side of the chart (on the vertical axis). On the other axis, write *definition*, *examples*, and *effect on economy*. Ask students what defines and differentiates each type of unemployment and write a brief summary for each type in the chart. Finally, discuss with students how each type of unemployment affects the economy (mildly, moderately, or severely), and write this information in the chart. Ask students to copy the chart in their notes as they help you create it.

Identifying Cause and Effect
Remind students that there are many serious economic consequences to high unemployment rates. Organize students into groups of three or four. Ask each group to list the possible consequences of high unemployment rates, particularly long-term high unemployment rates, and have them determine which they think is the most serious. Ask students in each group to refer to the chart that the class created in the last exercise, and have them brainstorm ways that each type of unemployment might be reduced. Ask students to take notes of their discussion to submit for evaluation. ⭐16B

CLOSE

Call on volunteers to share with the class the different ideas their groups discussed for lowering structural unemployment. Discuss with students the following question: How important is education in helping people gain employment after technology causes occupational obsolescence? ⭐26C

OPTIONS

Gifted Learners, Interpersonal Learners
Ask motivated students to make an appointment for an interview with a manager or public relations officer at a local government unemployment office. Encourage them make a list of questions before their visit, or have them ask some of the following:
- What services does this office provide for people who are unemployed?
- Which types of jobs are many people seeking right now, and what kinds are most available now in this region?
- How long does it take the people whom you assist to find jobs?
- Do many people who have part-time jobs already visit your office in hope of finding another part-time job, or a full-time job? How is the growth in the availability of part-time jobs affecting unemployed people?

Ask students to write a paragraph describing what they learned in the interview or how it changed their opinion about unemployment or unemployed people.

Sheltered English Students
Pair students who are acquiring English with fluent English speakers. Have each pair research the unemployment rate for different months in the last 5 or 10 years, and choose 10 different months' estimates for comparison. Ask each pair to make a graphic display of the statistics that they have chosen. Displays may be in the form of bar graphs, pie graphs, line graphs, charts, or a representative model. Have students use the *Researcher Online*, the library, in-class resources, the Internet, and information from business journals or newspapers to conduct their research. ⭐23F

Linguistic Learners
Ask students to write an essay, a newspaper article, or a short research paper that explores the social costs that may result from long-term unemployment. Social costs might include poverty, frustration that leads to violence or crime, or the break-up of families. Have students use the *Researcher Online*, the library, in-class resources, the Internet, and information from magazines or newspapers to conduct their research or get background information for their essay or news story.

REVIEW

Have students complete the Section 1 Review on page 256. Use the answers in the Annotated Teacher's Edition to assess student mastery of this section.

ASSESS

To assess student mastery of this section, have students complete Daily Quiz 11.1 in *Daily Quizzes with Answer Key*. For additional assessment options, see *Alternative Assessment Handbook* on the *One-Stop Planner CD-ROM*.

ADDITIONAL RESOURCES

Rifkin, Jeremy. *The End of Work: The Decline of the Global Labor Force and the Dawn of the Post-Market Era*. 1995. JP Tarcher.

Sucher, Billie, and Alice B. Acheson (eds.). *Between Jobs: Recover, Rethink, and Rebuild*. 1997. Sta Kris.

LESSON 11.2 INFLATION

TEXTBOOK PAGES 257–63

> **HOLT PRESENTATION MAKER**
> Access Illustrated LECTURE NOTES using Microsoft® PowerPoint® on the One-Stop Planner CD-ROM

OBJECTIVES

- Explain how economists evaluate price changes over time.
- Describe what causes inflation.
- Identify the main two price indexes that economists use to measure inflation. ★16B
- Analyze how inflation affects the economy. ★16B

MOTIVATE

Give each student one piece of play money and tell them that each piece of money is worth one dollar. Show them a box of five pencils. Tell them that each student will need one of these pencils to use on their next test, and that at this moment, one pencil will cost one dollar. Ask students who would like to buy a pencil. Tell the class that because so many people want pencils, you have decided to raise the price to two dollars per pencil. However, you can tell the class that half a pencil will cost only one dollar. Ask the class: What happened to the buying power of their money? Is the money worth as much as it was only a minute or two ago? Tell students that essentially, this is often what happens when the national economy experiences sharp inflation. Tell students that in this section they will learn about the causes of inflation, its effects, and how it is measured by economists.

TEACH

Building a Vocabulary

List the vocabulary terms for this section on the chalkboard and tell students to add them to their Economics Dictionary. Tell students to use the information provided in the text or on the *Researcher CD-ROM* to list, define, and find an example of each term.

Applying a Model, Identifying the Main Idea

Explain to students that inflation represents a certain kind of change in prices. In order for economists to know how prices have changed, they need to analyze the price level at different points in time. Discuss with students how supply and demand affect price levels. First, ask students to explain the definition for *aggregate supply,* and write the term and its definition on the chalkboard (*total goods and services produced throughout the economy*). Second, ask students to explain the definition for *aggregate demand,* and write the term and its definition on the chalkboard (*total amount of spending throughout the economy*). To help illustrate the relationship between aggregate supply, aggregate demand, and the price level, draw a simple equation on the chalkboard, such as this:

quantity supplied high = price level high
quantity demanded high = price level low

Call on students to explain what this equation shows. (*When aggregate quantity supplied is high, the price level tends to be high; when aggregate quantity demanded is greater, the price level tends to be low.*) Now discuss with students the following questions:
- What is inflation? (*an increase in the average price level of all goods and services in an economy*)
- Does inflation occur when aggregate demand is high or low? (*inflation usually occurs when aggregate demand increases faster than aggregate supply*).

Demonstrating Understanding

Tell students that economists need to understand the causes of inflation in order to recommend ways to control it. Remind students that there are two general types of inflation, and a third factor that can influence inflation. Ask students to recall from the textbook what these types are, and write them on the chalkboard (*demand-pull inflation, cost-push inflation, price expectations*). Organize students into groups of three or four. Have each group discuss the different causes for each type of inflation. Ask each group to imagine a business scenario that demonstrates each type of inflation in action, and have them write these scenarios into short paragraphs.

Evaluating Information, Applying a Model

Explain to students that in addition to understanding the causes of inflation, economists also need to measure it. Because inflation is a reflection of a high price level, economists have created two indexes to help them measure changes in prices. On the chalkboard, write the names of the two indexes: consumer price index (CPI), and producer price index (PPI). Ask students to explain what

249E

each of these indexes measures. (*The CPI is a measure of the average change over time in the price of a fixed group of community purchased goods and services; the PPI is a measure of the average change over time in the prices of goods and services bought by producers.*) Ask students to describe how the Bureau of Labor Statistics arrives at the amount of goods bought by a typical consumer each month (*by using a representative sampling called the market basket*). Next, display Transparency 44, which shows the inflation rate for 1943–1999 (also represented in Figure 11.4 on textbook page 262). Ask students to assist you in calculating how figures represented in the graph were computed using the example given in the text. ⭐16B

Identifying Cause and Effect, Predicting Outcome

Tell the class that economists are also concerned with the numerous consequences of inflation. Organize students into groups of three or four. Have the members of each group discuss the five effects of inflation presented in the textbook. Keeping these effects in mind, have each group evaluate how a sharp increase in inflation would impact the following people:

- A person who has just withdrawn a considerable amount from a savings account. (*Money will have less value, or buying power, than when it was initially saved.*)
- A doctor on staff at a large hospital. (*Work will be largely unaffected, because demand for medical care services is relatively inelastic, and doctors can increase fees to increase their income.*)
- A retired autoworker on a fixed pension. (*Fixed incomes are susceptible to a loss of purchasing power.*)
- A borrower about to repay a loan. (*The money paid back will have less value than that borrowed.*) ⭐23A

CLOSE

Call on volunteers to explain the possible impacts of inflation on the people and businesses discussed in the last activity. Ask students: What steps can the government take to help curb inflation?

OPTIONS

Interpersonal Learners

Ask students to select a particular retail business in the area and interview the owner to find out how inflation affects his or her business. Suggest that students ask questions not only about prices of products sold but also about the retailer's costs of doing business. Then have students write a few paragraphs describing the impact of inflation on their selected business.

Students Having Difficulty

Pair students who are having difficulty with students who have mastered the lesson material. Have each pair quiz each other using the following questions:

- What is inflation?
- What is the consumer price index? How are consumer prices measured for the CPI?
- What is the producer price index? What data are used for this index?
- What are five effects of inflation?
- Which groups of people are most strongly affected by inflation?

You may want to instruct students to write the answers to these questions on a piece of paper for later reference. ⭐16B

Gifted Learners, Logical-Mathematical Learners

Ask motivated students to lead a class discussion or give a presentation on how the inflation rate is calculated. Ask them to find inflation statistics from recent years to use as a model, and have them go through the mathematical calculations that economists use to figure the rate on the chalkboard. Have students use the *Researcher Online*, the library, in-class resources, the Internet, and information from business journals or newspapers to find statistics from recent years. Remind students to make their presentation or discussion as clear as possible and to keep it within the time constraints of the class. ⭐16B

REVIEW

Have students complete the Section 2 Review on page 263. Use the answers in the Annotated Teacher's Edition to assess student mastery of this section.

ASSESS

To assess student mastery of this section, have students complete Daily Quiz 11.2 in *Daily Quizzes with Answer Key*. For additional assessment options, see *Alternative Assessment Handbook* on the *One-Stop Planner CD-ROM*.

ADDITIONAL RESOURCES

Romer, Christina D., and David Romer (eds.). *Reducing Inflation: Motivation and Strategy.* 1997. University of Chicago Press.

Solow, Robert M. *Inflation, Unemployment, and Monetary Policy.* 1999. MIT Press.

LESSON 11.3 POVERTY AND INCOME DISTRIBUTION

TEXTBOOK PAGES 264–68

HOLT PRESENTATION MAKER
Access Illustrated LECTURE NOTES using Microsoft® PowerPoint® on the One-Stop Planner CD-ROM

OBJECTIVES

- Explain how economists determine the number of poor people in the United States.
- Describe how economists measure the distribution of income.
- Identify the policies that the U.S. government uses to reduce the income gap and decrease poverty.

MOTIVATE

Ask students: How would you define *poverty*? What level of income or opportunities makes a person or family impoverished (poor)? Write students' suggestions on the chalkboard. Also ask students: What do you think causes poverty? Write these suggestions on the board as well. Explain to the class that the federal government clearly defines poverty every year by establishing a poverty level, measured in an exact dollar amount for different kinds of families. Tell students that in this section they will learn about the poverty level, the income gap, and possible solutions to poverty.

TEACH

Building a Vocabulary

List the vocabulary terms for this section on the chalkboard and tell students to add them to their Economics Dictionary. Tell students to use the information provided in the text or on the *Researcher CD-ROM* to list, define, and find an example of each term.

Role Playing, Developing Life Skills, Judging Information

Tell students that the government and economists use a specific mathematical model to determine which individuals, families, or households are living in poverty. Write the term *poverty threshold* on the chalkboard and ask students to describe what this term means (*the lowest income that a family or household of a certain size needs to maintain a basic standard of living*). Ask students to recall from the textbook how the government arrives at the figure that marks this poverty threshold each year, and what role the Department of Agriculture plays in developing information for this calculation. (*The Department of Agriculture designed economical food plans to estimate how much money families of different sizes would spend on food each year; the Social Security Administration (SSA) estimates that the average family of three or more spends one third of its income on food, so they take the figure for yearly food expenditures and multiply it by three to reach the dollar amount for the poverty threshold.*)

Organize students into groups of four. Ask each group to imagine that they are a family of four living on the 2000 poverty threshold rate of $17,603. Tell students that this means their monthly income is approximately $1,467, making their weekly income about $339. Ask each group to make a weekly or monthly budget for a family of four, making sure that their budget does not exceed $17,603 for the year. Give students the following categories to use as the minimal necessities that most families need:

- rent or mortgage
- food
- clothing
- heat/electricity/telephone
- transportation (to/from work)
- child care
- health/car/renter's insurance (if possible)
- medical (dentist, doctor, prescriptions)

Discuss with the class the difficulties they found in making a budget, and what kinds of things they had to leave out. Ask students: Do the family members have any money remaining for movies? for eating at restaurants? for going on vacations? for living in a home with more than one bedroom? for buying a used car? How can they save for retirement? Encourage students to discuss alternative models that the government could use to figure out the poverty threshold (*such as taking a fairly inflexible expense, such as rent/mortgage, and multiplying that by three, or calculating each major cost of living expense individually and then adding them up, rather than using the ×3 method*).

Understanding Graphs

Explain to students that while there are many people living below the poverty level in the United States today, there are also many people who live on much larger incomes. Call on volunteers to help explain how a Lorenz Curve illustrates income inequality. (*It shows the amount that a nation's distribution of income varies from a perfect proportional distribution of income.*) On the chalkboard, draw a

Lorenz Curve similar to the one in the textbook, and point out that the lower the curve dips below the line indicating equality of income, the greater the amount of income inequality.

Discuss with students how the Gini Index is computed. Do some sample equations on the chalkboard if possible. ⭐23F

Solving Problems

Tell students that many economists and politicians think that the income gap between the rich and the poor is growing wider, while others do not believe this is so. Call on volunteers to recall from the textbook what the four main causes of the widening income gap are, and write these on the chalkboard. Organize students into small groups and have them discuss how each of these factors contributes to the income gap. Next, ask each group to discuss at least three possible ways of reducing the income gap.

CLOSE

Call on volunteers from each group to discuss which of the possible solutions they thought offered the most benefits at the least cost. Next, ask students if they are aware of any of these types of solutions operating in the community in which they live. Finally, discuss with students the following question: What things can young people do to help narrow the income gap and ease poverty?

OPTIONS

Gifted Learners, Logical-Mathematical Learners

Ask motivated students to plan and lead a class or panel discussion about the Lorenz Curve—how it is constructed, how cumulative percentages are calculated, and what a "wider" curve means. Be sure that students limit the focus of the discussion and take into account the class time allowed. ⭐23F

Interpersonal Learners

Have students investigate which local government agencies provide assistance for low-income families in the community. Then have students interview an official at one of these agencies to determine the answers to the following questions:
- What assistance programs does the agency oversee?
- Who is eligible for benefits?
- How much is given in benefits?
- Are there any restrictions on those receiving benefits?
- In your opinion, what are the strengths and weaknesses of your assistance programs?

Have students present their findings to the rest of the class.

Students Having Difficulty

Pair students having difficulty with students who have mastered the lesson material. Give each pair a piece of graph paper. Have each pair first look at the Lorenz Curve in the textbook and discuss what the percentages represent that make up the curve. Then ask each pair to draw a Lorenz Curve based on the following hypothetical information:

	2016 Quintile	2035 Quintile
Lowest Fifth	3.5%	2.0%
Second Fifth	8.6%	5.4%
Third Fifth	12.9%	7.5%
Fourth Fifth	23.0%	17.3%
Highest Fifth	52.0%	67.8%

When pairs have completed their graphs, have them discuss the changes in the income gap represented by the Lorenz Curves that they drew. ⭐23F

REVIEW

Have students complete the Section 3 Review on page 268. Use the answers in the Annotated Teacher's Edition to assess student mastery of this section.

ASSESS

To assess student mastery of this section, have students complete Daily Quiz 11.3 in *Daily Quizzes with Answer Key*. For additional assessment options, see *Alternative Assessment Handbook* on the *One-Stop Planner CD-ROM*.

RETEACH

For students having difficulty with the lessons, have them complete Reteaching Activity 11. This activity is located in Reteaching Activities with Answer Key.

ADDITIONAL RESOURCES

Harrington, Michael. *The Other America: Poverty in the United States.* 1997. Scribner.

Wilson, William Julius. *When Work Disappears: The World of the New Urban Poor.* 1997. Vintage Books.

CHAPTER 11

TOPICS INCLUDE

- unemployment rate
- full employment
- types of unemployment
- aggregate supply and aggregate demand
- price levels
- inflation and deflation
- types of inflation
- causes of inflation
- measuring inflation
- consumer price index
- effects of inflation
- poverty thresholds and the poverty rate
- distribution of income
- measuring income inequities
- Lorenz Curve and Gini Index
- reasons for the growing income gap

ECONOMICS NOTEBOOK

The Economics Notebook is a journal activity that encourages students to consider basic concepts of economics that relate to their lives. A follow-up notebook activity appears on page 270.

▶ WHY IT MATTERS TODAY

To find additional lesson plans dealing with the public goods gap, visit CNNfyi.com or have students complete the ECONOMICS IN THE NEWS activity on page 269.

CNNfyi.com

250

CHAPTER 11

ECONOMIC CHALLENGES

To plan for the future, people must anticipate many unknown factors, such as changes in prices, the job market, and technology. The government also encounters these challenges as it tries to meet the nation's economic goals. In this chapter you will learn about three challenges faced by individuals and the U.S. economy as a whole: unemployment, inflation, and poverty and income distribution.

ECONOMICS NOTEBOOK

In your Economics Notebook, list five economic challenges you have faced in the last month, such as a job search or an increase in movie ticket prices. Describe how you responded to each challenge.

▶ WHY IT MATTERS TODAY

Today the U.S. economy faces many challenges. Use CNNfyi.com or other **current events** sources to find examples of some of these challenges.

CNNfyi.com

SECTION 1
UNEMPLOYMENT

READ TO DISCOVER
1. What is the unemployment rate?
2. What are the four major types of unemployment?
3. What are the main economic costs of high unemployment?

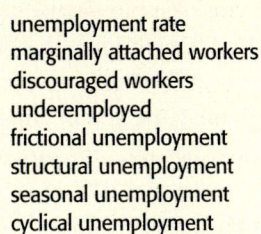

ECONOMICS DICTIONARY
- unemployment rate
- marginally attached workers
- discouraged workers
- underemployed
- frictional unemployment
- structural unemployment
- seasonal unemployment
- cyclical unemployment

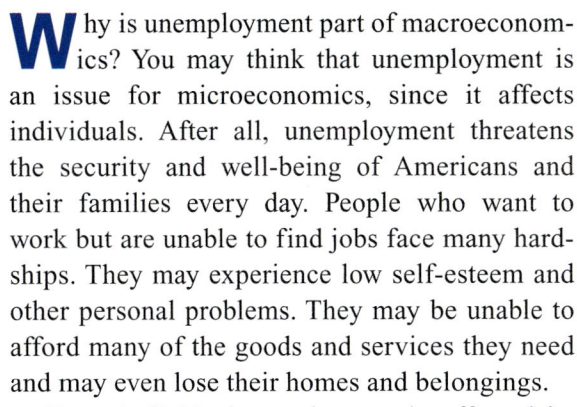

Why is unemployment part of macroeconomics? You may think that unemployment is an issue for microeconomics, since it affects individuals. After all, unemployment threatens the security and well-being of Americans and their families every day. People who want to work but are unable to find jobs face many hardships. They may experience low self-esteem and other personal problems. They may be unable to afford many of the goods and services they need and may even lose their homes and belongings.

True, individuals can be greatly affected by unemployment. At the same time, however, high rates of unemployment also hurt the economy as a whole. The nation loses the goods and services that the unemployed would produce if they were working. Businesses lose sales because the unemployed cannot buy as many products. Moreover, the government must decide how and to what extent to support the unemployed and their dependents.

Measuring Unemployment

Policy makers and economic analysts gauge the health of the U.S. economy by examining the labor force and unemployment: How many workers are unemployed? How long have they been jobless? How does unemployment differ for specific industries and geographic regions?

To answer such questions, the U.S. Bureau of the Census, also known as the Census Bureau, conducts a monthly study called the Current Population Survey. Census Bureau employees interview a sample of about 60,000 households across the country. These data are then analyzed and published by the Bureau of Labor Statistics (BLS) in the U.S. Department of Labor.

Identifying the Employed and Unemployed

The Census Bureau uses specific definitions for the terms *employed* and *unemployed*. Individuals ages 16 and older are classified as employed if during the survey week they

- worked for pay or profit one or more hours,
- worked without pay in a family business 15 or more hours, or
- have jobs but did not work as a result of illness, weather, vacations, or labor disputes.

UNEMPLOYMENT *Economists measure the health of the U.S. economy.* **Which government bureaus study unemployment and full employment?**

SECTION 1
UNEMPLOYMENT

Lesson Plans
For teaching strategies, see Lesson 11.1 located at the beginning of this chapter or the One-Stop Planner Strategy 11.1.

Economics Dictionary
To reinforce the section's vocabulary terms, refer students to the Electronic Glossary on the *Researcher CD-ROM*.

Section Assessment
To assess students' mastery of this section, have them complete Daily Quiz 11.1 in *Daily Quizzes with Answer Key*.

Caption Answer
U.S. Bureau of the Census, Bureau of Labor Statistics ★16B

Content
15B, 16B, 19C, 26C
Social Studies Skills
23A, 23C, 23F, 24A, 24D

ECONOMIC CHALLENGES 251

internet connect

TOPIC: Careers, Bureau of Labor Statistics
GO TO: go.hrw.com
KEYWORD: SM3 EC11

Have students access the Internet through the HRW Go site to conduct research on careers at the Bureau of Labor Statistics. Then have each student write a help-wanted ad for the Bureau. Students' ads should address the types of experience and training that the Bureau seeks in job applicants and the various kinds of work that a Bureau employee could expect to perform. Have each student read his or her ad to the class. ★23C

Themes in Economics

GROSS DOMESTIC PRODUCT

Okun's Law, developed by economist Arthur Okun, states that for every 1 percent rise in the unemployment rate, real gross domestic product drops 3 percent. Thus, if the unemployment rate rises from 5 percent to 7 percent, real GDP drops by 6 percent. The reverse is also true; if the unemployment rate drops, real GDP rises. ∎

The bureau classifies individuals as unemployed if during the survey week they do not meet any of the criteria for employed status. In addition, these people must have been actively looking for work during the past four weeks.

These definitions do not account for every person in the United States. Anyone who is not classified as either employed or unemployed is considered to be "not in the labor force."

Unemployment Rate

The most closely watched and highly publicized labor force statistic is the **unemployment rate**, the percentage of people in the civilian labor force who are unemployed. Unemployment tends to increase during times of recession and decrease during times of expansion.

Problems with the Unemployment Rate

The unemployment rate does not measure all aspects of unemployment. First, it does not indicate the differences in intensity with which people look for jobs. Second, the conditions for being included among the unemployed exclude some individuals who most people would think of as unemployed. Among this group are **marginally attached workers**—people who once held productive jobs but have given up looking for work. In 2000 some 1.1 million people were marginally attached workers. **Discouraged workers**—a subset of marginally attached workers—are people who want a job but have stopped looking for work for job-related reasons.

Suppose, for example, that Ben Greene is a discouraged worker. Ben is 57 years old and worked as a senior programmer for a computer company for 15 years. Two years ago a company merger eliminated his department. He actively searched for employment for over a year, but without success. Now, faced with stiff job competition, Ben has stopped looking. He still wants a job, but sees no point in continuing to look.

A third shortcoming of the unemployment rate is that it does not indicate the number of underemployed workers. Workers who have jobs beneath their skill level or who want full-time work but are only able to find part-time jobs are considered to be **underemployed**. Like unemployment, underemployment represents wasted resources and lost output. For example, a recent college graduate who is unable to find a job in his or her field and takes a job waiting tables is underemployed.

Labor Force Statistics

Figure 11.1 shows the main labor force statistics for the civilian population for 1999. Because unemployment can vary widely among different groups, the Bureau of Labor Statistics (BLS) provides employment and unemployment information for the total population as well as figures that have been broken down by age, sex, race, marital status, industry, and occupation. In addition, the BLS provides unemployment information based on job-seeking methods and reasons for—and duration of—unemployment.

Determining Full Employment

As noted in Chapter 2, full employment is an important part of economic stability. Full employment does not, however, mean that everyone has a job and the unemployment rate is zero. Some unemployment is unavoidable and a natural part of even a healthy economy. As a result, economists generally consider an unemployment rate of about 5 percent—that is, employment of about 95 percent of the labor force—to represent full employment.

In addition, some economists assert that extremely high levels of employment can cause dramatic increases in the average prices of goods and services. These economists state that a "natural rate of unemployment" exists when prices are relatively stable.

Types of Unemployment

To better analyze the factors that contribute to joblessness, economists break unemployment into four categories:

- frictional,
- structural,
- seasonal, and
- cyclical.

CHAPTER 11

Some types of unemployment do not hurt the economy as much as others. In addition, different approaches and policies are needed to deal with the different types of unemployment.

Frictional Unemployment When workers are moving from one job to another, they experience what is known as **frictional unemployment**. This category includes people who have decided to leave one job to look for another, as well as new entrants and re-entrants into the labor force. For example, suppose that Heather Gibson leaves her job as a receptionist to find a job as a data processor. During her job search, Heather is considered frictionally unemployed.

Economists consider frictional unemployment a normal part of a healthy and changing economy. This type of unemployment reflects workers' freedom of choice in the labor market, as they select the jobs that are most satisfying to them. Frictional unemployment often is a signal that new jobs in new industries are becoming available.

Structural Unemployment Unemployment that occurs as a result of changes in technology or in the way the economy is structured is known as **structural unemployment**. Technological advances and shifts in consumers' tastes can result in the change or decline of entire industries. For example, when the television industry began to build TVs that relied on transistors rather than tubes, this technological change reduced the need for television repair specialists. (See Figure 11.2 on page 255 for information on unemployment and current occupations.)

Some industries decline and even disappear as natural resources in a region are used up. Industries in Appalachia, for example, enjoyed high employment and prosperity during the late 1800s and early 1900s because many natural resources such as timber and coal were available there. As

UNEMPLOYMENT BY SEX AND AGE, 1999

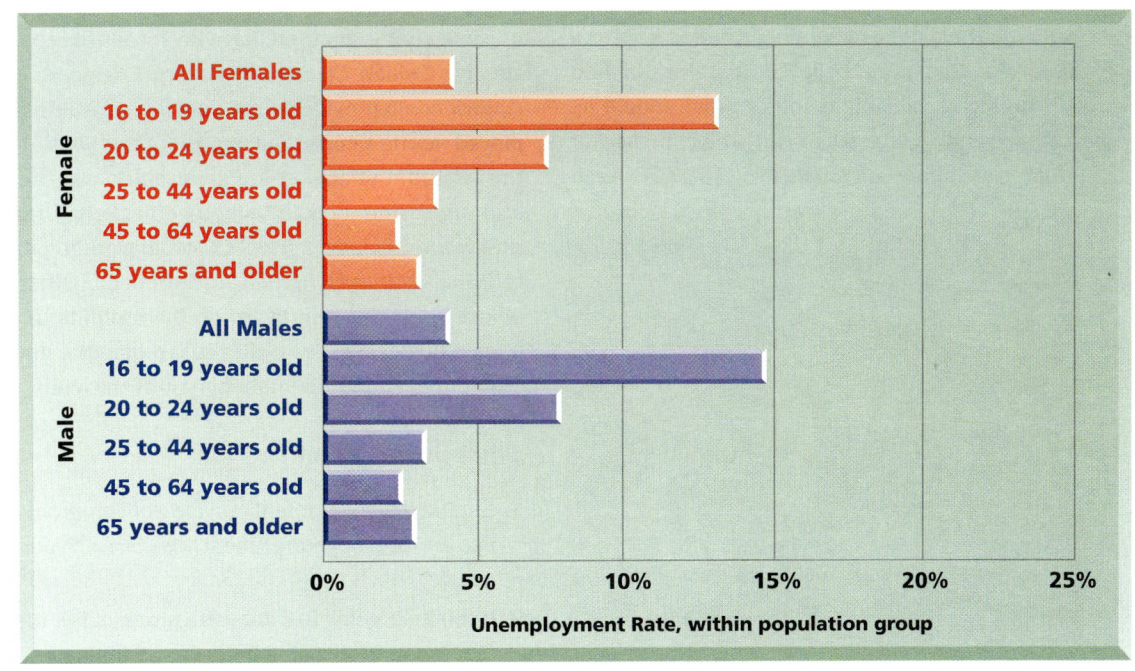

Source: *Statistical Abstract of the United States: 2000*

FIGURE 11.1 The unemployment rate is the percentage of unemployed people in the civilian labor force. **Which population group has the highest unemployment rate?**

Themes in Economics

THE ROLE OF GOVERNMENT
Unemployment insurance, part of the Social Security Act of 1935, provides an income to people who have lost their jobs. The program's goal is not only to aid the involuntarily unemployed but also to help keep up the demand for goods and services in areas with high unemployment in hopes of preventing, or at least not worsening, recessions.

The money for unemployment insurance comes out of federal and state payroll taxes collected from employers. Federal law requires that all states collect a tax from employers of at least 0.8 percent of each employee's first $7,000 of income. The amount collected varies by state and by business. Businesses that have high layoff rates pay more.

In most states, unemployment insurance provides income equal to about one third of the average worker's wages for up to 26 weeks. The average jobless person receives benefits for 13.6 weeks. ■

Transparency
An overhead transparency of Figure 11.1 is available in *Transparency Resources*. See Transparency 43: Unemployment by Sex and Age, 1999.

Caption Answer
males, 16 to 19 years old

ECONOMIC CHALLENGES 253

Themes in Economics

FULL EMPLOYMENT As a group, welfare recipients have high rates of unemployment. Some people think that the government should create jobs for welfare recipients through work programs similar to those of the New Deal. Opponents of the idea, however, criticize "make-work" programs as inefficient, unprofitable, and costly for taxpayers.

An approach seeking the middle ground is workfare, a program to encourage corporate America to hire more welfare recipients for existing jobs. In his 1997 State of the Union Address, President Bill Clinton challenged corporate America to hire 2 million welfare recipients by 2003. The program faces many obstacles, but firms are experimenting with ways to help people make the welfare-to-work transition. ■

What Do You Think? Answers

1. Answers will vary, but students should consider the benefits, costs, and trade-offs of taking different actions. ★15B, 23A

2. Answers will vary, but students should specify the proposed program's goals, which groups the program will help, and how it will be funded. ★23A

LINKING ECONOMICS and GOVERNMENT

Civilian Conservation Corps

The Great Depression of the 1930s was the most serious economic crisis the United States has ever faced. At its worst point in 1933, about one in every four working Americans was unemployed. The unemployment rate among young men was even higher. As many as 250,000 jobless youth had taken to wandering the country in search of employment.

In the first few years of the depression, the federal government did little to lessen the hardships created by severe unemployment. However, with Franklin D. Roosevelt's election to the presidency in 1932, the government began to take action. Within days of taking office in 1933, President Roosevelt set out a recovery plan that became known as the New Deal. One of the plan's first steps was to employ the nation's youth.

To this end, Roosevelt called for the immediate creation of the Civilian Conservation Corps (CCC), a program designed to put young men back to work while helping to maintain the nation's natural resources. Roosevelt believed that forests and farmland were valuable resources that should be managed and protected to ensure their survival for future generations of Americans. The CCC hired young men between the ages of 18 and 25 to work on a variety of conservation-related projects such as combating soil erosion on farmland, replanting overlogged forests, and building dams and other flood control barriers.

The CCC was one of the most successful New Deal programs. From its founding in 1933 until 1942, when it was discontinued because of America's entrance into World War II, the program employed almost 3 million young men, paying them $1 a day, plus room and board.

The program had other economic benefits as well. Farmers benefited from reduced soil erosion, businesspeople received profits from trade with local work camps, and CCC workers sent paychecks to their families. Workers also planted millions of acres of trees, built hundreds of miles of flood control levees, and constructed improvements in the National Park system that are still being enjoyed across the country today.

In recent years there have been calls to recreate the Civilian Conservation Corps. Supporters claim it could provide useful work for many unemployed young people and expose urban youth to the healthful effects of the great outdoors. They also argue that it could bring together urban and rural youth. Finally, a new CCC could work to protect the country's natural environment. Others object to any such program on the grounds that private businesses are better suited than the government to employ the nation's youth efficiently.

The Civilian Conservation Corps, which employed depression-era youth, encouraged hard work, discipline, and cooperation.

What Do You Think? ★TEKS

1. Should the government provide work programs like the CCC for young Americans? Explain your answer.

2. If you were going to establish a program like the CCC today, what would be its focus? Explain your answer.

FASTEST-GROWING OCCUPATIONS AND FASTEST-DECLINING INDUSTRIES, 1998–2008

Fastest-Growing Occupations	Fastest-Declining Industries
Computer engineers	Crude petroleum, natural gas, and gas liquids
Computer support specialists	Apparel
Systems analysts	Coal mining
Database administrators	Footwear (except rubber and plastic)
Desktop publishing specialists	Federal electric utilities
Paralegals and legal assistants	Metal cans and shipping containers
Personal care and home health aides	Watches, clocks, and parts
Medical assistants	Tobacco products
Social and human service assistants	Metal mining
Physician assistants	Luggage, handbags, and leather products

Source: U.S. Census Bureau, Statistical Abstract of the United States: 2000

FIGURE 11.2 Technological innovations can cause entire industries and occupations to disappear. **What might be the economic impact of technological innovations on the industries listed in the right-hand column?**

---

these resources were used up, however, the region developed high structural unemployment.

Seasonal Unemployment The unemployment rate may also fluctuate in a predictable way from season to season as a result of regular occurrences such as holidays, the school year, harvest schedules, and industry production schedules. Economists call these regular fluctuations in jobs **seasonal unemployment**. Agricultural workers are particularly affected by seasonal unemployment. Spring, summer, and fall are busy seasons for many farmers because most crops can be planted, cultivated, and harvested only during warm weather. During the winter months, however, many farmworkers temporarily lose their jobs.

CASE STUDY

Migrant Workers in California

UNEMPLOYMENT For years, California has been an important source of agricultural products. Farming is the state's largest business. In fact, Californians grow over half the nation's fruit and vegetables.

Although this level of productivity might suggest high levels of employment, the nature of the work instead results in significant seasonal unemployment. The instability, low pay, and grueling labor involved in agricultural work, along with the fact that workers frequently have to live in over-crowded labor camps, discourages many U.S. citizens from becoming migrant farm laborers. For more than 100 years, therefore, California growers have relied on the labor of migrant workers—many of whom come from other countries—to harvest their crops.

The state's strawberry industry provides a glimpse of the lives of migrant laborers, as the vast majority of the labor force consists of migrant workers. While strawberries can be highly profitable, they require intensive labor. The berries are planted, tended, and picked by hand, and they have a short harvest period.

When the harvest is at its peak, workers can make as much as $100 a day. These wages—and the prospect of employment—attract many workers. Soon, however, this intense competition causes wages to drop. Additionally, workers often have to live in overcrowded labor camps. Because employment is so short-term, most migrants spend as much as three months each year seasonally unemployed.

ECONOMIC CHALLENGES 255

Caption Answer
seasonal unemployment

SECTION 1 REVIEW ANSWERS

1. unemployment rate (252), marginally attached workers (252), discouraged workers (252), underemployed (252) frictional employment (253) structural unemployment (253), seasonal unemployment (255), cyclical unemployment (256) **16B, 24A**

2. frictional, structural, seasonal, and cyclical; examples will vary. **23A, 24D**

3a. No, it does not indicate the differences in intensity with which people look for jobs, and it does not include marginally attached workers or underemployed workers. **16B**

3b. Economists consider an unemployment rate of about 5 percent to be full employment, because some level of unemployment always exists. Full employment indicates that the economy is healthy. **16B**

4. When the economy slows, producers tend to reduce production and lay off workers. Unemployment rises, leading to less consumer demand, less output, and more layoffs. As the economy enters the recovery phase, producers increase production and hire more workers. Unemployment goes down, and consumer demand goes up. Historical examples will vary. **19C, 24D**

UNEMPLOYMENT *The strawberry industry depends on migrant workers to harvest its crops.* **What type of unemployment affects agricultural laborers?**

Cyclical Unemployment Unemployment resulting from recessions and economic downturns is called **cyclical unemployment**. This type of unemployment harms the economy more than any other type of unemployment. When sales decline, producers tend to reduce output and lay off workers. Increased unemployment further reduces total demand and leads to more layoffs and even higher unemployment. When the economy begins to expand again, total demand for goods and services rises, producers hire more workers to increase output, and the level of unemployment begins to decrease.

Cyclical unemployment has challenged the U.S. economy during the 1900s. In 1933, during the Great Depression, unemployment reached an all-time high of about 25 percent of the labor force, or some 12.8 million workers. Serious recessions in 1974–75, 1980–82, and 1990–91 also were characterized by high levels of cyclical unemployment. Increased unemployment rates may lag slightly behind the development—or even the end—of a recession. For example, in the case of the 1990–91 recession, the unemployment rate did not reach its peak of 7.5 percent until 1992. The complete elimination of cyclical unemployment, on the other hand, indicates that the economy has reached full employment.

Although seasonal fluctuations in unemployment are fairly easy for economists to predict, these changes make it difficult to determine whether unemployment shifts between two periods are the result of changing conditions or normal seasonal changes.

SECTION 1 REVIEW

★ TEKS Q: 1, 2, 3a, 3b, 4

1. Identify and Explain:
- unemployment rate
- marginally attached workers
- discouraged workers
- underemployed
- frictional unemployment
- structural unemployment
- seasonal unemployment
- cyclical unemployment

2. Categorizing: Copy the graphic organizer below. Use it to list the major types of unemployment and give an example of each.

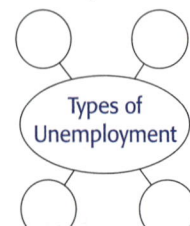

Types of Unemployment

Finding the Main Idea

3. Does the unemployment rate accurately estimate the number of people who are unemployed? Explain your answer.

4. Explain the concept of full employment.

5. Writing and Critical Thinking

Drawing Conclusions: Explain the relationship between recessions in the business cycle and high rates of unemployment. Provide an example to illustrate your explanation.

Consider the following:
- the behavior of consumers and producers in a slowing economy
- the Great Depression or any other historical example of a recession or depression

Homework Practice Online keyword: SM3 HP11

256 CHAPTER 11

SECTION 2

INFLATION

READ TO DISCOVER
1. What do economists look at when evaluating price changes over time?
2. What causes inflation?
3. What are the two main price indexes that economists use to measure inflation?
4. How does inflation affect the U.S. economy?

ECONOMICS DICTIONARY

aggregate supply
aggregate demand
inflation
deflation
demand-pull inflation
cost-push inflation
supply shock
wage-price spiral
consumer price index
market basket
producer price index
inflation rate
hyperinflation

As noted in Chapter 5, when quantity demanded exceeds quantity supplied, prices go up and the purchasing power of a dollar goes down. When quantity supplied is greater than quantity demanded, prices go down and the purchasing power of a dollar goes up. These changes in prices and in the purchasing power of money have many immediate and far-reaching effects for society and can threaten the stability of a nation's economy. To understand the effects of these forces, economists study price changes throughout the economy.

Examining Price Fluctuations

When discussing prices, economists talk about the price level, inflation, and deflation. The price level reflects prices throughout the economy at a particular time. Inflation and deflation refer to changes in the price level over time.

Price Level The price level influences aggregate supply and aggregate demand. **Aggregate supply** is the total amount of goods and services produced throughout the economy. As noted in Chapter 4, the law of supply states that quantity supplied increases as prices rise. Similarly, the aggregate quantity of goods supplied is likely to be higher when the price level is higher.

Aggregate demand is the total amount of spending by individuals and businesses throughout the economy. The law of demand applies to aggregate demand, which means that there is a greater aggregate quantity of products demanded when the price level is lower.

Although the price level reflects a particular point in time, it is used for comparative purposes. For example, economists may compare today's

MARKETS & PRICES *Changes in prices have many effects on society and can threaten the stability of a nation's economy.* **What terms describe changes in price level over time?**

ECONOMIC CHALLENGES 257

Caption Answer
demand-pull inflation and cost-push inflation

Across the Curriculum

History Inflation has existed throughout history. One example is the Great Inflation of the Roman Empire. The ancient Roman currency, the *denarius*, was based on a silver standard. Over time, however, Roman emperors replaced the silver in the coin with other metals. As prices rose, each successive emperor minted more coins with less real value. Inflation resulted.

Some emperors tried to stop rising inflation through legislation, such as making it punishable by death to charge more than certain prices. These attempts did little, however. Inflation continued to rise until the Roman Empire adopted a new currency, the *bezant*, which was based on a gold standard. ■

INFLATION & DEFLATION *Inflation reduces the real purchasing power of the dollar.* **What are the two types of inflation?**

price level with price levels in 1990 or 2000 to see how the economy has changed.

Inflation An increase in the average price level of all products in an economy is called **inflation**. Usually, inflation occurs when aggregate demand increases faster than aggregate supply. When quantity demanded exceeds quantity supplied, consumers must compete for limited products, and prices go up. As prices increase, the amount that a dollar buys decreases. Thus, inflation reduces the real purchasing power of the dollar.

Deflation A decrease in the average price level of all goods and services in an economy is known as **deflation**. Deflation may occur when aggregate demand decreases more rapidly than aggregate supply. In such situations, sellers are forced to lower prices to attract buyers. As prices decrease, the amount a dollar buys increases. Thus, deflation boosts the real purchasing power of the dollar. The most prolonged—and most recent—deflationary period in U.S. history occurred during the Great Depression, when high unemployment coupled with reductions in wages caused aggregate demand and prices to fall.

Causes of Inflation

Economists classify inflation into two general categories based on cause—demand-pull inflation and cost-push inflation. Prices can either be *pulled* up by high demand or *pushed* up by high production costs. In addition, expectations about future prices strongly affect inflation.

Demand-Pull Inflation
When aggregate demand increases faster than the economy's productive capacity, **demand-pull inflation** results. Following the laws of supply and demand, prices increase when quantity demanded exceeds quantity supplied. As demand continues to increase, the prices of goods are *pulled* even higher. Demand-pull inflation can result from an increase in the money supply or an increase in the use of credit.

The Federal Reserve system, commonly known as the "Fed," controls the money supply in the United States. (The Federal Reserve system is discussed in greater detail in Chapters 13 and 14.) When the Fed increases the supply of money and credit, aggregate demand increases as consumers, businesses, and governments purchase more goods. Spending thus outpaces the available supply of goods, and demand-pull inflation results. Economists refer to this situation as "too much money chasing too few goods."

Cost-Push Inflation
When producers raise prices to cover higher resource costs, **cost-push inflation** results. As noted in Chapter 4, resource costs are one of the determinants of supply. Producers must set prices high enough to cover their costs and to earn a profit. Thus, increased production costs *push* producers to raise prices even if demand has not increased.

Supply shocks are one of many sources of cost-push inflation. A **supply shock** is an event that increases the cost of production for all or many firms, resulting in overall higher prices. Crop failures, natural disasters, and political upheavals can cause supply shocks. As noted in Chapter 10, for example, in 1973–74 members of the Organization of Petroleum Exporting Countries (OPEC) quadrupled the price of oil after a war with Israel. Producers in the United States had to raise prices to cover increased energy costs. The result was a ripple of price increases for everything from gasoline and home heating oil to plastics and cosmetics. By 1974 inflation had spiked to 11 percent, up from 6 percent in 1973.

The relationship between wages and prices can also lead to cost-push inflation. Suppose that a worker bargains for a wage increase. These higher wages—when paid to workers throughout

CAREERS IN ECONOMICS

Loan Officer

The use of credit often spurs economic growth. At some point, nearly all companies must borrow money to buy new equipment and finance other improvements that will help their business grow. Families and individuals also borrow money to purchase a new house or car or finance a college education. The high demand for credit means that loans are an important source of income for financial institutions.

To borrow money from a bank, you would need to meet with a loan officer, the person responsible for loan applications. Loan officers determine whether a potential borrower is likely to repay the loan. Once money is lent, the loan officer keeps track of whether the borrower is keeping up with his or her loan payments.

In the 1980s some U.S. banks and savings institutions made unwise lending decisions. When some borrowers stopped making loan payments, the lost revenue threatened the entire banking system. In part to avoid repeating this crisis, the banking industry has since made a concerted effort to raise the training standards for loan officers.

Most banks look for loan officers with training beyond an undergraduate college degree. A loan officer is expected to have business school training in finance and a familiarity with the many federal laws that apply to lending money. He or she is also expected to have excellent writing skills and to possess the ability to communicate clearly.

While becoming a loan officer requires extensive training and preparation, the rewards can be generous. The loan officer is a highly paid employee and has an opportunity to participate in the economic growth of his or her community.

Loan officers evaluate borrowers' needs and their ability to repay loans.

Themes in Economics

INFLATION & DEFLATION

Disinflation occurs when the inflation rate drops. Disinflation is not a drop in prices—which is deflation—but rather a slowing of the rate of inflation. During the mid- to late 1990s, the United States experienced a period of disinflation. This situation occurred despite strong economic growth, low unemployment, and rising wages and profits—all events which many economists argue usually lead to higher inflation.

As some causes for the disinflation, analysts cited increased productivity; the growth of the high-tech industry, where prices tend to drop rapidly as technology improves; and rising global competition, which forces prices of U.S. goods down to compete with foreign goods. Some economists think that as the world changes, the United States may even experience deflation again. ■

Careers in Economics

To help students learn about other careers in economics, refer them to the Careers section on the *Researcher Online*.

Themes in Economics

INFLATION & DEFLATION

Many economists think that the consumer price index (CPI) inaccurately measures inflation. They charge, first, that the CPI's market basket is updated only once a decade or so and, therefore, does not reflect the average consumer's purchasing habits. For example, cellular phones were not included in the market basket in 1997. (Cellular phones were added in 1998.) Second, the CPI does not reflect substitutions that consumers make when products become more expensive—for example, substituting chicken for beef when beef prices rise.

Third, the CPI does not reflect changes in the quality of goods and services over time. For example, an increase in the price of cars may be the result of improvements in quality, not because of a general rise in the level of prices. The main criticism against the CPI, however, is that the Bureau of Labor Statistics' data-collection methodology makes it difficult to compare the prices and quality of products over time and across regions.

As a result of these problems, many economists think that the inflation rate is overstated and thus that policies enacted to control it are inappropriate. ■

---

the economy—encourage producers to raise prices, continuing the cycle. Some economists refer to this cycle as the **wage-price spiral**.

Price Expectations Expectations about future prices can affect inflation. When consumers expect prices to increase, they tend to buy immediately to take advantage of lower prices. As a result, aggregate demand increases and inflation rises. When consumers expect future prices to be lower, they are likely to postpone buying, which decreases aggregate demand and slows inflation.

Similarly, producers adjust prices to match their expectations of future inflation. When producers expect inflation to increase, they raise prices. As prices continue to rise, consumers' and producers' expectations of future inflation grow even more, and prices spiral upward.

Measuring Inflation

When measuring price level fluctuations, economists look at changes in the average price level of goods and services in a nation. They look at the average price level as opposed to specific prices, because in any given period the prices of some goods are rising while the prices of others are falling. While the prices of specific items might be lower than they used to be, if most items are more expensive, then the purchasing power of the dollar in general has decreased.

To measure the price level, economists construct a price index. The two most common price indexes are the consumer price index and the producer price index.

Consumer Price Index When news reports declare that inflation is up or down, they are usually referring to a change in the consumer price index. The **consumer price index** (CPI) is a measure of the average change over time in the price of a fixed group of products.

The Bureau of Labor Statistics (BLS) calculates and reports the CPI each month. First, the bureau selects a base year against which to measure price changes. Currently the CPI is based on the period 1982–84 instead of a single base year.

Second, the bureau selects a representative sample of commonly purchased consumer items, called the **market basket**. This sample includes items that the typical urban consumer might buy, such as food, clothing, shelter, utilities, transportation, entertainment, and health care. Each item in the market basket is weighted based on its importance in consumers' budgets. The bureau then samples the prices of these goods and services in selected areas across the nation. Some prices are reviewed every month; others every other month. Every 8 to 10 years the BLS conducts a survey to identify items that should be included in the market basket.

Economists set the index price for the base year at 100. To calculate the CPI for another year, the BLS determines the price of the market basket for that year, divides the amount by the cost of the market basket in the base year, and multiplies the result by 100. For example, if the market basket cost $4,000 in 1982–84 and $7,000 in a later year, the CPI for the later year would be 175: ($7,000 ÷ $4,000) × 100 = 175. The average price level in the later year is 75 percent higher than it was in 1982–84. In other words, purchasing power has declined, and consumers must spend 175 percent of the cost in 1982–84.

Producer Price Index The **producer price index** (PPI) is a measure of the average change over time in the prices of goods and services bought by producers. PPIs are compiled for selected types of products as well as for production stages or particular industries. Price data are based on some 3,200 products. The current base year for the PPI is 1982 and, like the CPI base year, has a value of 100.

Inflation Rate

Economists use price indexes like the CPI to calculate the **inflation rate**, the monthly or annual percentage change in prices. To use the CPI to calculate the inflation rate from one year to another, economists use the formula: inflation rate = [(CPI Year B − CPI Year A) ÷ CPI Year A] × 100. For example, if the price level, or CPI,

CONSUMER PRICE INDEX, 1943–1999

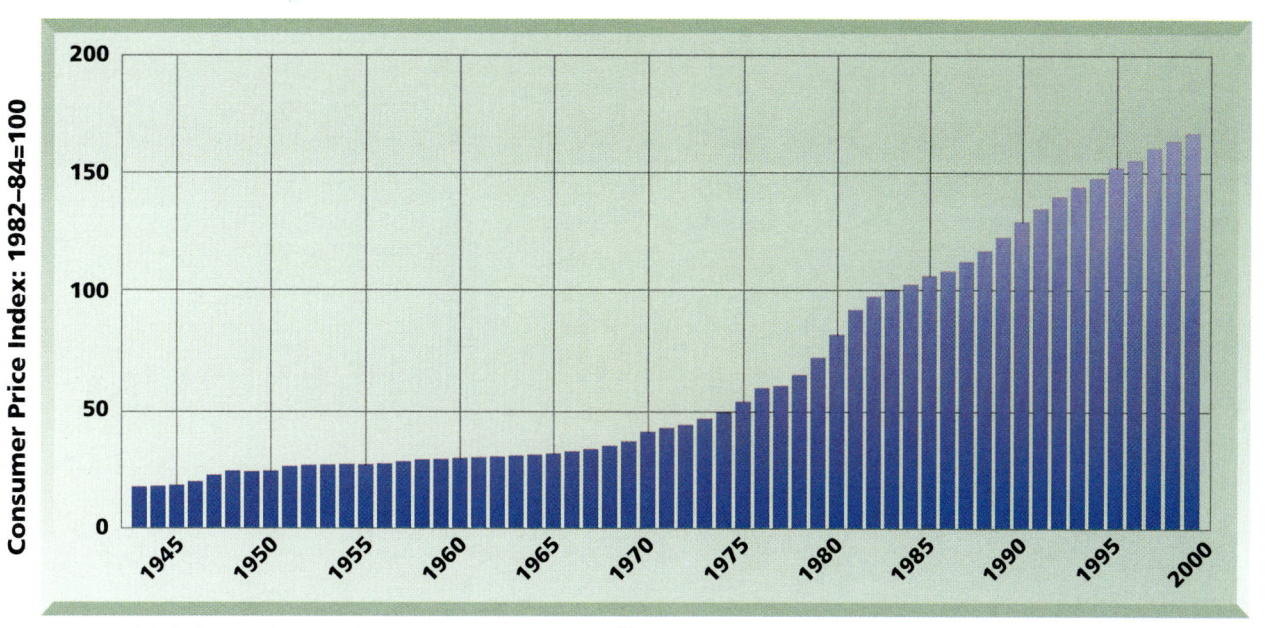

FIGURE 11.3 The consumer price index measures prices for a specific group of products. **What was the consumer price index for 1995?**

Source: *Statistical Abstract of the United States: 2000*

is 140 in Year A and 145 in Year B, the inflation rate is 3.57 percent for that period: [(145 − 140) ÷ 140] × 100 = 3.57 percent. Figure 11.3 shows the CPI for the United States from 1943 to 1999, and Figure 11.4 on page 262 graphs the inflation rate, based on the annual percent change in CPI, for the same period.

Most economists consider inflation rates from 1 to 3 percent to be low to moderate, with inflation rates of less than 1 percent to be negligible. Depending on the severity of the inflation rate, economists may describe it as *creeping* or *galloping*. **Hyperinflation**, the worst degree of inflation, is a situation in which inflation is increasing at a rate of several hundred percent a year. Hyperinflation can result in complete economic collapse. After Germany lost World War I, for example, it was forced to pay heavy reparations to the victorious countries. Germany tried to pay this debt simply by printing more money. By November 15, 1923, it took 4.2 trillion marks (German currency) to equal the value of one U.S. dollar—meaning that the mark was worth so little that even the paper on which it was printed had greater value.

Effects of Inflation

Although inflation benefits some people, it affects most people negatively. Inflation causes changes in

- the purchasing power of the dollar,
- the value of real wages,
- interest rates,
- saving and investing, and
- production costs.

Decreased Purchasing Power You may have heard an older family member or friend talk about how inexpensive things were when they were young. They are discussing one of the effects of inflation—decreased purchasing power. (See Figure 11.5 on page 263.)

Enhancing the Lesson

For information on the consumer price index before 1943, see the Economic Indicators section on the *Researcher Online*.

Caption Answer

Answers should fall between 150.5 and 153. ★23F

Global Connections

The inflation rate in Hungary soared to uncontrollable levels after World War II. By 1948, workers in Hungary were being paid three times a day. Because the Hungarian currency was being devalued at such a rapid rate, the wives of Hungarian workers had to spend much of their time running between their husbands' workplaces and the bank to deposit paychecks before they became worthless.

internet connect

TOPIC: Inflation, Prices
GO TO: go.hrw.com
KEYWORD: SM3 EC11

Have students access the Internet through the HRW Go site to conduct research on the House Price Index. Then have students—individually or in groups—investigate the relative prices of houses in various states. Each student or group should use their findings to create a map showing areas in the country with the most significant increases in house prices over the past decade. Display students' maps around the classroom. ★23C

ECONOMIC CHALLENGES 261

Transparency

An overhead transparency of Figure 11.4 is available in *Transparency Resources*. See Transparency 44: Inflation Rate, 1943–1999.

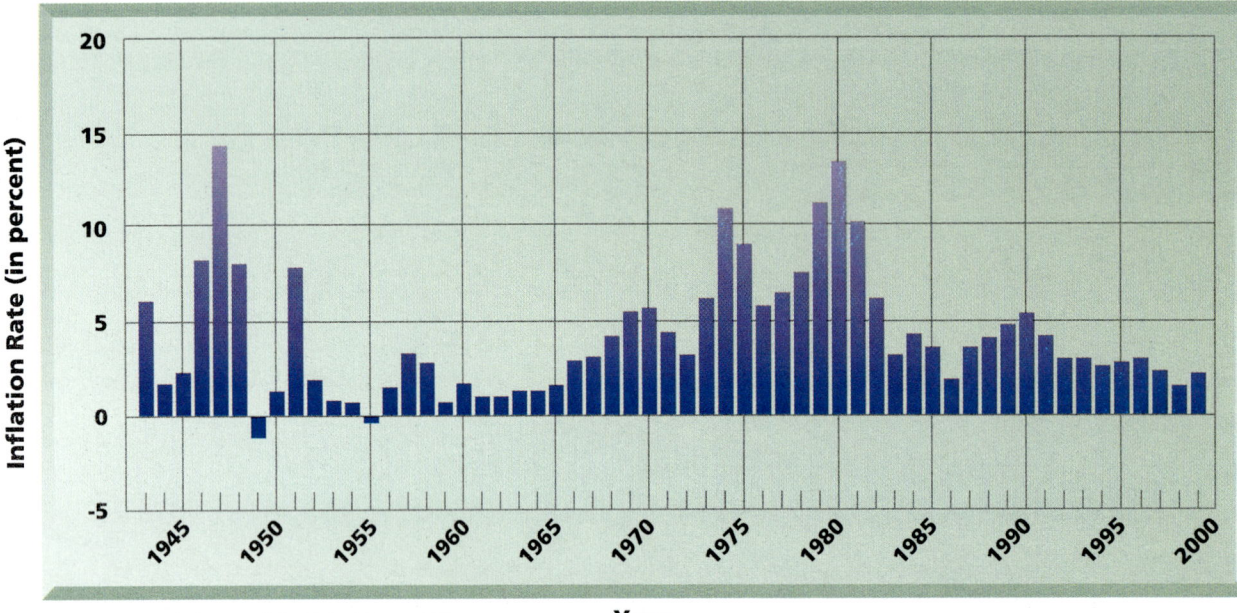

Caption Answer

1949, 1955 ⭐23F

Cultural Perspectives

Inflation measures changes in the overall price level of goods and services over a period of time. In some industries, however, prices increase at a rate faster than the inflation rate. One of these industries, as most parents are painfully aware, is higher education. The cost of college has continued to rise over the years. In 2000–2001, the average cost of tuition, room, and board for one year at a four-year public university was about $8,470 and more than $22,500 at a private university. On average, the cost of college has risen 5 percent per year. However, the inflation rate in 1999 was a low 2.2 percent. The 88 percent increase in financial aid at public universities between 1989–1990 and 1999–2000 only partially offset higher tuitions. ■

INFLATION RATE, 1943–1999

Source: *Statistical Abstract of the United States: 2000*

FIGURE 11.4 The inflation rate is the percentage change in prices during a specific period such as a month or a year. **In which years did the U.S. economy experience a negative inflation rate?** ⭐TEKS

The decreasing value of the dollar particularly hurts people on fixed incomes. As the value of the dollar falls, the purchasing power of people who rely on set pension checks or other fixed income decreases as well. To combat this problem, many labor contracts, government benefits, and retirement plans include cost-of-living adjustments (COLAs). As noted in Chapter 8, COLAs automatically raise wages or payments to account for inflation.

Decreased Value of Real Wages Inflation also reduces the value of workers' real wages when pay increases fail to keep pace with rising prices. For example, suppose that Donald Ming earned $20,000 in 1979 and $47,000 in 2000. In current dollars, Donald's $47,000 salary is more than double what he made in 1979. Once Donald's 2000 income has been adjusted for inflation, however, it becomes clear that his purchasing power has remained about the same. Therefore, his salary increase has just enabled him to keep pace with the cost of living. Overall, wages tend to stay ahead of or at the pace of inflation.

Increased Interest Rates As prices increase, interest rates—the price of borrowing money—tend to increase as well. High interest rates can decrease consumer spending, particularly on goods that are usually purchased on credit or through loans, such as computers, automobiles, and houses. High interest rates can double or even triple consumers' monthly credit card or loan payments.

Decreased Saving and Investing The inflation rate also affects the return that people receive from their savings and investments. For example, suppose that Jody Bailey deposited $2,000 in a savings account yielding 5 percent interest. After a period of five years, during which time the inflation rate averaged 7 percent, she withdrew her savings—which had grown to $2,550. Although Jody has more money than

CHAPTER 11

when she started, she has "lost" money overall because inflation was running at a higher rate than the interest she earned on her savings. As a result, the purchasing power of Jody's savings has declined. High inflation thus tends to discourage saving.

Increased Production Costs

Businesses that issue long-term bonds with interest rates lower than the inflation rate benefit from inflation. For the most part, however, high inflation rates hurt businesses because inflation increases their costs of production. Businesses that can pass these additional costs on to buyers survive. Consumers, however, may refuse to pay the higher prices.

REAL VALUE OF THE DOLLAR, 1982-1999

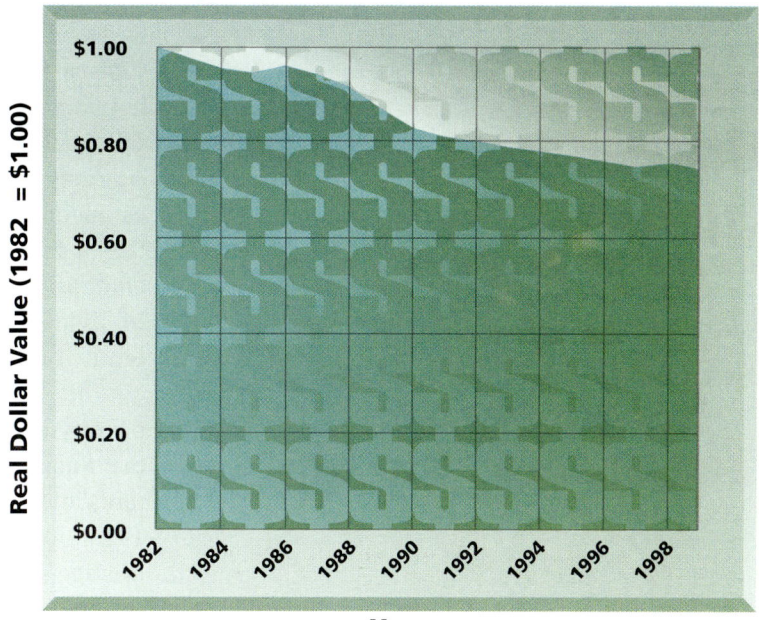

Source: Statistical Abstract of the United States: 2000

FIGURE 11.5 Inflation reduces purchasing power. **How much was a 1982 dollar worth in 1998?**

SECTION 2 REVIEW

TEKS Q: 1, 2, 4

1. Identify and Explain:
aggregate supply
aggregate demand
inflation
deflation
demand-pull inflation
cost-push inflation
supply shock
wage-price spiral
consumer price index
market basket
producer price index
inflation rate
hyperinflation

2. Comparing and Contrasting: Copy the table below. Use it to compare and contrast what economists measure with the two most common price indexes.

Two Most Common Price Indexes

3. Finding the Main Idea

a. How is price level different from inflation and deflation?

b. What are the two major types of inflation?

4. Writing and Critical Thinking

Making Predictions: Imagine that a political revolution in a country containing most of the world's gold mines results in a 15 percent increase in the price of gold in the United States. Predict how the event would affect the rate of inflation.

Consider the following:
- the various types of inflation and their causes
- the prices of items dependent upon gold

Homework Practice Online
keyword: SM3 HP11

ECONOMIC CHALLENGES 263

SECTION 3

POVERTY AND INCOME DISTRIBUTION

READ TO DISCOVER

1. How do economists determine the number of poor people in the United States?
2. How do economists measure the distribution of income?
3. What policies does the U.S. government use to reduce the income gap and decrease poverty?

ECONOMICS DICTIONARY

poverty threshold
poverty rate
Lorenz Curve
Gini Index

The income gap between the richest and the poorest Americans was wider in the 1990s than at any other time since World War II. Moreover, income inequality in the United States had become greater than in any other large industrialized country. How does a growing income gap affect a nation's economy and society? Should the U.S. government take action to reduce this gap? These are the sorts of questions that U.S. policy makers must address as they try to balance economic equity with other goals in an increasingly competitive and global economy.

Poverty in the United States

Another way to examine the economic well-being of a nation is to measure the number of people who are living in poverty. In 1998, for example, 34.5 million people in the United States—12.7 percent of the total population—were living in poverty.

How is poverty defined? According to the Census Bureau, individuals, families, or households are living in poverty if their total incomes fall below designated income levels. The **poverty threshold**, or poverty level, is the lowest income—as determined by the government—that a family or household of a certain size or composition needs to maintain a basic standard of living. In 2000 the poverty threshold for a family of four was $17,603.

The official method of determining the poverty threshold was established in 1963–64 by the Social Security Administration (SSA). The thresholds are based on economical food plans. A 1955 study of food consumption found that the average family of three or more spent approximately one third of its after-tax income on food. Based on this information, the Department of Agriculture designed economical, nutritionally balanced food plans for different family sizes. The SSA then multiplied each plan by three to determine the poverty thresholds. Today poverty thresholds are adjusted annually based on changes in the consumer price index (CPI).

The **poverty rate** is the percentage of individuals or families in the total population, or a

INCOME DISTRIBUTION *Many people in the United States with incomes below the poverty threshold are white and live in rural areas.* **How is the poverty threshold determined?**

subset of the population, that are living in poverty. Figure 11.6 shows the number and percentage of individuals and families living in poverty from 1981 to 1999. Both the number and percentage of Americans living in poverty have dropped in the last several years. In 1999 the poverty rate was 11.8 percent.

Distribution of Income

In his 1890 book *How the Other Half Lives*, journalist Jacob Riis wrote about the widening gap between the rich and the poor. The situation that Riis described was not limited to the late 1800s, an era often called the Gilded Age. Economists refer to this inequality in income among individuals and households as the distribution of income.

Several factors contribute to differences in income. People come from different economic and social backgrounds. They have different skills and talents, grow up in different neighborhoods, attend different schools, and face different economic and social difficulties. Moreover, in a market economy, an individual's income is determined in large part by the market value of the goods and services that person has to offer. People with resources or talents that are in high demand will earn more money than people whose resources and talents are not in such high demand. For example, in the United States a professional basketball player's income will likely dwarf a pro soccer player's income because basketball games draw larger crowds and generate more money than soccer games do.

Measuring Income Inequality When news reports describe the "income gap," they are referring to the amount of income inequality in the nation. If the richest 20 percent of families earn 49 percent of the total income and the poorest 20 percent of families earn only 5 percent of the total income, as in 1995, there is a high level of income inequality.

To measure the amount of inequality in the distribution of income, economists plot a **Lorenz Curve**, which illustrates the amount that a

POVERTY RATE, 1981–1999

Year	Individuals — Number in Poverty (in millions)	Individuals — Percent in Poverty	Families — Number in Poverty (in millions)	Families — Percent in Poverty
1981	31.8	14.0	6.9	11.2
1982	34.4	15.0	7.5	12.2
1983	35.3	15.2	7.6	12.3
1984	33.7	14.4	7.3	11.6
1985	33.1	14.0	7.2	11.4
1986	32.4	13.6	7.0	10.9
1987	32.2	13.4	7.0	10.7
1988	31.7	13.0	6.9	10.4
1989	31.5	12.8	6.8	10.3
1990	33.6	13.5	7.1	10.7
1991	35.7	14.2	7.7	11.5
1992	38.0	14.8	8.1	11.9
1993	39.3	15.1	8.4	12.3
1994	38.1	14.5	8.1	11.6
1995	36.4	13.8	7.5	10.8
1996	36.5	13.7	7.7	11.0
1997	35.6	13.3	7.3	10.3
1998	34.5	12.7	7.2	10.0
1999	32.3	11.8	6.7	9.3

Sources: *Statistical Abstract of the United States: 2000; Economic Report of the President*

FIGURE 11.6 The poverty rate is the percentage of individuals and families in the population that are living in poverty. **In what year was the overall poverty rate highest for families?**

nation's distribution of income varies from a perfectly proportional distribution of income. To create a Lorenz Curve, economists plot the proportion of the total income that various percentages of the population received.

Figure 11.7 on page 266 shows the Lorenz Curve for U.S. household incomes in 1998. Point A equals the percentage of the total income that the lowest population quintile, or the poorest 20 percent of the population, earned. Point B equals the percentage of the total income that the bottom two population quintiles, or the poorest 40 percent of the population, earned. Point C equals the percentage of the total income that the bottom three population quintiles earned, and so on. A perfectly proportional distribution of income—one in which each population quintile earns exactly 20 percent of the nation's total income—results in a 45-degree diagonal line

ECONOMIC CHALLENGES 265

Transparency

Overhead transparencies for Figure 11.7 and Figure 11.8 are available in *Transparency Resources*. See Transparency 46: Lorenz Curve, 1998 and Transparency 47: Gini Index, 1970–1998.

Caption Answer

(top)
15.7 percent ⭐23F, 23G

Cultural Perspectives

One of the most shocking facts about poverty in the United States is who makes up the poor. In 1999 the U.S. economy had strong growth, low unemployment, and low inflation. Nevertheless, during that prosperous time, more than 4.2 million U.S. children under the age of 6—nearly one in five—were living in poverty, more than in any other industrialized nation.

Child poverty is growing faster in suburban areas. Overall, some 39 percent of American children live in or near poverty. Moreover, many poor children live in two-parent families where one of the parents works, challenging the stereotype that these are the children of single "welfare mothers." ■

Caption Answer

(bottom)
1997 ⭐23F

LORENZ CURVE, 1998

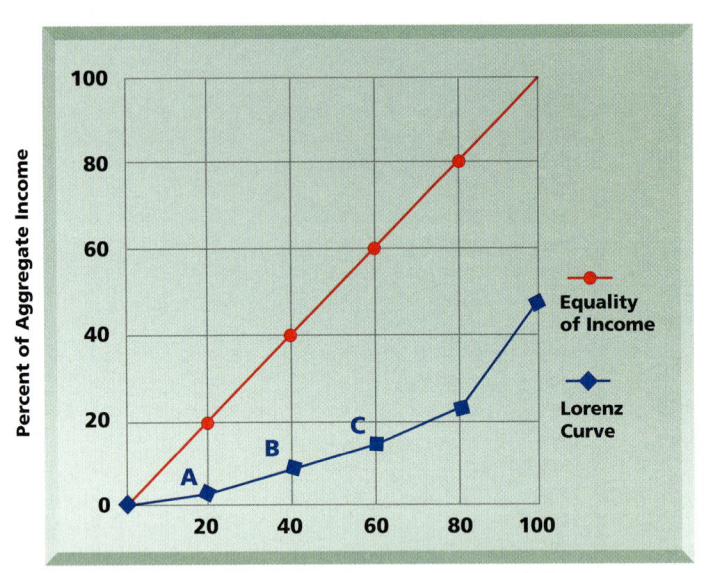

Source: *Statistical Abstract of the United States: 2000*

FIGURE 11.7 The Lorenz Curve illustrates income distribution. **What percentage of income did the lowest 60 percent of households earn in 1998?** ⭐TEKS

extending from the bottom left corner of the graph to the upper right corner. The more an actual Lorenz Curve dips below this 45-degree line of absolute equality, the greater the amount of income inequality.

The data used to plot a Lorenz Curve enable economists to compute the **Gini Index**, another statistical measure of income inequality. The Gini Index ranges from 0.0, where each family or household receives an equal share of the total income, to 1.0, where one family or household receives all of the income. To compute the Gini Index, economists take the area between the 45-degree equality line and the actual Lorenz curve and divide it by the area below the 45-degree line. Figure 11.8 shows the Gini Index from 1970 to 1998.

Limitations of Income Distribution

Measures of income distribution tend to overemphasize income inequality for two main reasons. First, the definition of income for this purpose is very limited. The data that are used to determine the distribution of income are based on families' or households' gross incomes before deductions for such expenses as personal income taxes, Social Security, Medicare, health insurance, and union dues. Income does not include capital gains or the value of noncash benefits that families or households may receive,

GINI INDEX, 1970–1998

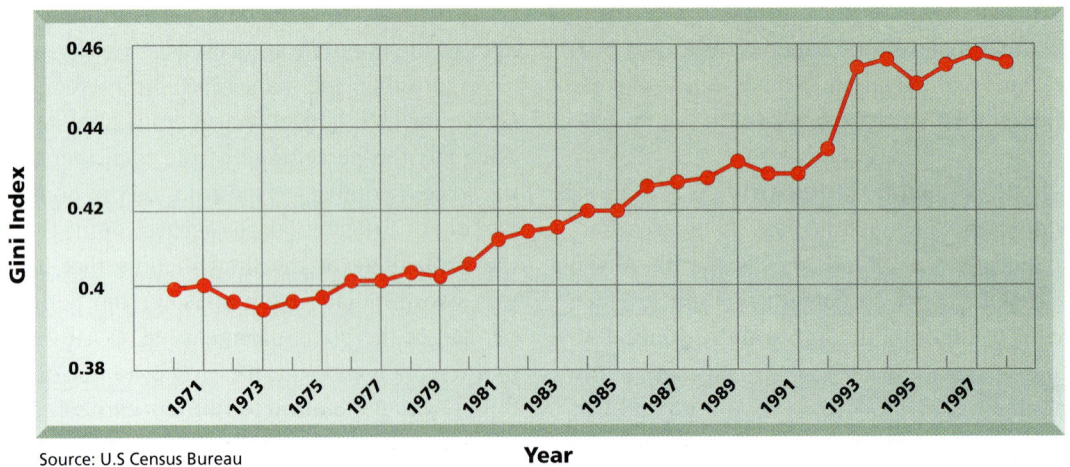

Source: U.S Census Bureau

FIGURE 11.8 The Gini Index indicates whether the income gap is increasing or decreasing. **Based on this graph, in what year did the Gini Index reflect the greatest income gap?** ⭐TEKS

CHAPTER 11

such as food stamps, health benefits, or low-cost housing.

Second, most measures of income distribution do not differentiate among families or households of different sizes, ages, or numbers of wage earners. People tend to earn different amounts of income at different stages in their lives, and families of different sizes and ages need different amounts of income. As a result, families or households in the same income bracket can have very different standards of living.

Growing Income Gap

Are the rich getting richer and the poor getting poorer? This question has become a heated political issue in the United States in recent decades. Some politicians and economists assert that the income gap is not really increasing as much as it may seem, since income estimates are based on pretax figures and do not include noncash benefits. Others argue that even if the gap is increasing, incomes may simply be rising at a faster rate for rich families than for poor.

The growing income gap in the United States stems from a variety of economic and social changes. Economists usually cite the following factors as the main causes of the widening disparity in income:

- changes in households,
- changes in the labor market,
- rapid changes in technology, and
- the growth of a global economy.

Changes in Households
Historically, married couples living with their children have made up a large percentage of the wealthier households in the United States. Well-paid men and women tend to marry each other, thus concentrating wealth in one household and boosting income at the top of the income distribution. Single-parent and single-person households, on the other hand, have tended to have lower incomes. Higher divorce rates, more out-of-wedlock births, and increasing numbers of people who live alone have resulted in more of these households.

Global Exchange

New Horizons

Some Americans respond to economic challenges in the United States by seeking better prospects in other countries. Each year some 250,000 to 300,000 U.S. citizens—about one third the number of people immigrating to the United States—move overseas. Although many are returning to their nation of origin, as many as 100,000 were born in the United States.

Why are these people moving to other countries? Some seek better job opportunities, while others want a more relaxed lifestyle. Still others are in search of a safer place to live, with less social tension.

The growth of a global economy, improved communications networks, and convenient travel opportunities have made living overseas seem very appealing to some people. Dennis Raphael, for example, left Brooklyn, New York, for Toronto, Canada, to attend graduate school in the 1970s. In 1995 he became a Canadian citizen. "Americans are concerned with individualism and the pursuit of happiness. Canadians are concerned with peace, order, and good government," he said.

Others have moved elsewhere for the opportunity to test themselves in a society undergoing dramatic change. For example, Barbara Duvoisin found that her studies of Russian history, economics, and international finance provided her with the ideal qualifications for running the Moscow office of a corporation. "There is no doubt . . . that in Russia you are given more responsibility and more exposure within your organization than anyplace else in the world," she said.

Across the Curriculum

SOCIOLOGY One of the most difficult issues of our time is the persistent socioeconomic separation between blacks and whites in the United States. Although much progress has occurred in recent years and a strong black middle class has emerged, a tremendous amount of racism still exists. This racism makes it difficult for poor blacks in inner cities to get the services and education they need to bridge the gulf.

Recent studies show that job discrimination is still widely practiced, particularly in smaller businesses. Also, more ethnically diverse areas are less likely to receive adequately funded education, roads, trash removal, and even welfare. ■

ECONOMIC CHALLENGES 267

SECTION 3 REVIEW ANSWERS

1. poverty threshold (264), poverty rate (264), Lorenz Curve (265), Gini Index (266) **24A**

2. changes in households, changes in the labor market, rapid changes in technology, growth of a global economy **23A, 24D**

3a. by determining the lowest income that a family or household of a certain size or composition needs to maintain a basic standard of living, based on the cost of economical food plans and the CPI. **16B**

3b. programs that increase access to educational resources and provide training for low-skilled workers; programs that redistribute income; raising the minimum wage; setting wage levels; prohibiting companies from building plants in foreign countries where labor is cheaper **23A**

4. Answers will vary but should reflect an understanding of income distribution within free-enterprise systems. (See page 265.) **15B, 23A**

Changes in the Labor Market Analysts cite changes in the labor market—such as those that have resulted from corporate downsizing—as one cause of the income gap. The heavy corporate downsizing and restructuring of the late 1980s and early 1990s increased unemployment and resulted in many workers settling for lower-paying jobs. The decline in the real value of the minimum wage due to inflation and the increased use of temporary workers, who generally are paid less and receive fewer fringe benefits, have also contributed to lower income levels.

In addition—as noted in Chapter 8—labor union membership has decreased since the 1970s. As the power of labor unions declines, workers lose an important means of negotiating salaries with employers. In countries where labor unions are not as powerful, a greater income gap exists between workers with similar jobs.

Changes in Technology Rapid changes in technology have led to a drop in demand for lower-skilled workers. Additionally, increased automation has lowered income levels for the bottom 20 percent.

The increase in jobs for highly skilled, trained, and educated workers has helped boost incomes for the top 20 percent. Income levels tend to reflect education levels because technological changes make advanced education and computer skills a necessity. The need for education is more important than ever.

Growth of a Global Economy As the economy becomes more global, more U.S. companies are relocating production to other countries where laborers will work for less pay. As a result, the demand for unskilled workers in the United States has decreased, and low-skilled workers in the United States find it harder to find employment. This means that these U.S. workers end up at the bottom of the income distribution.

Narrowing the Income Gap

A variety of policies, some controversial, can narrow the income gap. Programs that increase access to educational resources and provide training for low-skilled workers may help narrow the income gap. The government also can redistribute income by increasing taxes for the wealthy or spending more on programs that provide assistance to low-income groups. Other suggestions for improving income equality include raising the minimum wage, setting wage levels, and prohibiting companies from building plants in foreign countries where labor is cheaper.

SECTION 3 REVIEW

TEKS Q: 1, 2, 3a, 4

1. Identify and Explain:
- poverty threshold
- poverty rate
- Lorenz Curve
- Gini Index

2. Identifying Cause and Effect: Copy the graphic organizer below. Use it to show the factors that have contributed to the income gap in the United States.

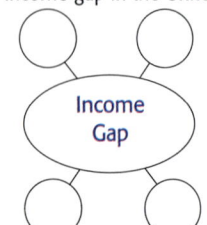

(Graphic organizer with "Income Gap" in center circle)

3. Finding the Main Idea
- **a.** How is the poverty threshold determined?
- **b.** Describe three programs that experts think would decrease the U.S. income gap.

4. Writing and Critical Thinking
Drawing Conclusions: Many economists maintain that a certain level of income inequality is a natural side-effect of a free-enterprise system. Do you agree or disagree? Explain your answer.
Consider the following:
- the market value of goods and services in a free-market economy
- the role of government in the economy

Homework Practice Online keyword: SM3 HP11

Economics IN THE NEWS

The Public Goods Gap

The economic boom of the 1990s was the longest-lasting economic expansion in American history. Because of the boom, many Americans saw significant advances in their personal wealth. For instance, Americans are now twice as likely to own a computer than before the expansion began. At the same time, the U.S. business community also benefited from years of economic expansion.

However, the economic boom of the 1990s was different from earlier periods of economic growth in one key respect. During earlier periods of prosperity, a significant amount of the wealth generated by economic growth was spent on public goods—new highways, universal phone service, and environmental clean up, for example—that benefit all Americans. This time, however, investment in public goods fell to what is likely the lowest level in a century as consumers spent their new wealth on cars and new homes, and private companies rapidly grew.

The public goods gap may have a significant negative impact on the economy. Such public goods as utilities and the network of transportation facilities are vital to the country's economic infrastructure and enable consumers and producers to participate in the economy.

Most experts agree that the public goods gap is a problem. In the words of former Speaker of the U.S. House of Representatives Newt Gingrich—a conservative Republican—"If you ask people what they're looking for, it's clear a lot of the things require collective assets and common action." Nonetheless, there is disagreement over how best to provide public goods, with some supporting free-market solutions and others calling for increased support for government-run projects. However, the problem needs to be addressed by both the public and private sectors. The free market offers the private sector few incentives to provide goods such as public transportation and medicine for diseases that mostly affect poor people. On the other hand, the private sector may be a more efficient provider of phone service and electric power.

So the next time you see a luxury car in a traffic jam or, more seriously, hear of a shortage of life-saving medicines, you may want to consider the degree to which the nation's economic prosperity depends on maintaining its public goods.

An Environmental Protection Agency worker tests car emissions to determine whether or not lead is present. The federal government is responsible for providing a number of public goods, including environmental protection.

What Do You Think?

1. Under what conditions might the public sector be better able to provide public goods than the private sector?
2. How might greater access to medicines and vaccines benefit the economy?

WHY IT MATTERS TODAY

The public goods gap is one of several challenges facing the U.S. economy. Use CNNfyi.com or other **current events** sources to find examples of the impact of public goods spending on economic growth.

Economics in the News Answers

1. in conditions where there is little profit in the provision of public goods 15A, 23A
2. Greater access to medicines might contribute to a healthier workforce and greater economic productivity. 23A

CHAPTER 11
Review Answers

Writing a Summary

Summaries should focus on the main points of each section. These may be found in the Read to Discover questions at the start of each section. Summaries should also use standard grammar, spelling, sentence structure, and punctuation. 16A, 16B, 24B, 24D

Identifying Ideas

unemployment rate (252), structural unemployment (253), aggregate supply (257), aggregate demand (257), inflation (258), deflation (258), consumer price index (260), poverty threshold (264), Lorenz Curve (265), Gini Index (266) 16A, 16B, 24A

Understanding Main Ideas

1. cyclical, because it can weaken the economy overall and deepen a recession 16B
2. Economists have defined an unemployment rate of about 5 percent as full employment, because some level of unemployment always exists.

269

CHAPTER 11 Review

Writing a Summary

Using standard grammar, spelling, sentence structure, and punctuation, write a summary of the information in this chapter.

Identifying Ideas

1. unemployment rate
2. structural unemployment
3. aggregate supply
4. aggregate demand
5. inflation
6. deflation
7. consumer price index
8. poverty threshold
9. Lorenz Curve
10. Gini Index

Understanding Main Ideas

SECTION 1 (pp. 251–56)

1. Which type of unemployment is most damaging to the U.S. economy? Explain your answer.
2. Explain the concept of full employment.

SECTION 2 (pp. 257–63)

3. Identify the following as examples of demand-pull inflation or cost-push inflation: (a) an increase in the price of a popular toy at Christmas when the stores are sold out of the product, (b) an increase in the price of orange juice because of a drought in Florida, (c) an increase in the price of Chunky Chicken products because of a union-negotiated wage increase for production workers.
4. Calculate the consumer price index using the following hypothetical information, and determine the percentage of change in the price level from 1998 to 2000: 1998 market basket ($7,000), 2000 market basket ($10,000).

SECTION 3 (pp. 264–68)

5. What are some of the limitations of income distribution measurements?
6. What is the relationship between the Lorenz Curve and the Gini Index?

Reviewing Themes

1. **Unemployment** How do economists define full employment? What might be the effect of extremely high levels of employment?
2. **Markets & Prices** How does the Bureau of Labor Statistics select the market basket?
3. **Income Distribution** What types of policies can narrow the income gap?

Thinking Critically

1. **Comparing** Explain the relationship between price level, aggregate supply, and aggregate demand.
2. **Finding the Main Idea** Why does unemployment increase during a recession and decrease during an expansion?
3. **Identifying Cause and Effect** Explain how changes in technology have influenced the growth in the income gap.
4. **Categorizing** Give an example of a class of workers that is underemployed and explain why those workers are underemployed.

Writing about Economics

Refer to the list you made in your Economics Notebook at the beginning of this chapter. Does your list include items that might correspond to inflation, unemployment, or poverty? Of these economic challenges, which do you think harms the U.S. economy the most? In your Notebook, provide reasons to support your answer.

(Continued from page 269)

3. (a) demand-pull; (b) cost-push; (c) cost-push
4. CPI = 142.9; inflation rate = 42.9 percent **23G**
5. They overemphasize income inequality because they are based on pre-tax income excluding noncash benefits, and because they do not differentiate among families or households of different sizes or ages or with different numbers of wage earners. **16B**
6. The size of the area between the 45-degree Lorenz equality line and the actual Lorenz Curve, divided by the area below the 45-degree line, equals the Gini Index. **16B**

Reviewing Themes

1. about 5 percent unemployment; dramatic increases in the prices of goods and services **16B**
2. It is a sample of items that the typical urban consumer might buy, such as food, clothing, shelter, utilities, transportation, entertainment, and health care.
3. programs that increase access to educational resources and provide training for low-skilled workers, raising the minimum wage, setting wage levels, and prohibiting companies from building plants in countries where labor is cheaper **15A, 16A**

Thinking Critically

1. Aggregate supply and aggregate demand tend to increase when the price level rises and decrease when the price level drops. **7A, 23A**

Building Social Studies Skills

Interpreting the Visual Record

Examine the cartoon below and answer the questions that follow.

1. What economic challenge might the cartoon be depicting?
   a. The public goods gap
   b. Inflation
   c. Seasonal unemployment
   d. Marginally attached workers
2. Why would the cartoonist show George Washington hanging onto the dollar for dear life?

Analyzing Primary Sources

Read the following excerpt from *The Economics and Politics of Race,* by Thomas Sowell. Then answer the questions.

"Historically, there is little question that non-whites have encountered more economic and social barriers than whites in the United States. . . . Yet what is surprising is the cold fact that there has been little correlation [connection] between the degree of discrimination in history and the economic results of today. It would be hard to claim that Puerto Ricans have encountered as much discrimination as the Japanese—who have about *double* their incomes. . . .

"[T]he translation of subjective prejudice into overt [open] economic discrimination—or of discrimination into poverty—is by no means automatic. . . ."

3. What is Sowell's view regarding poverty and the degree of discrimination against non-white groups—does he believe there is an automatic link?
   a. He does not address the link between income and discrimination against non-whites.
   b. Yes—he claims that Puerto Ricans have historically encountered higher levels of discrimination than Japanese or blacks, and therefore earn lower incomes.
   c. No, because various non-white groups have done as well if not better economically than white groups. He does not think that prejudice automatically translates into economic discrimination.
   d. He states that attempting to link the degree of discrimination with poverty is beside the point.
4. How might Sowell's thesis be evaluated for bias or propaganda?

Alternative Assessment

Building Your Portfolio

Imagine that you are an economist who has just received information about the personal distribution of income for the current year. You learn that the richest fifth of the population earns 68 percent of the total income, while the poorest fifth earns only 7 percent of the total income. With your group, use a problem-solving process to gather data, consider and implement a solution, and evaluate the effectiveness of a solution to the income gap.

internet connect

Internet Activity: go.hrw.com
KEYWORD: SM3 EC11

Access the Internet through the HRW Go site to conduct research on the consumer price index (CPI). Then prepare a 10-question quiz about various aspects of the CPI. Exchange quizzes with another student and then grade each other's quiz. Study any questions you answered incorrectly.

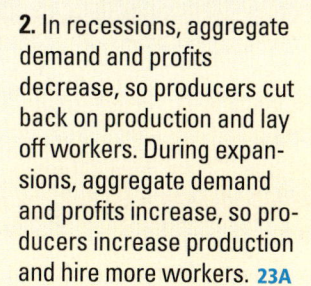

ECONOMIC CHALLENGES 271

UNIT 4

LAB OBJECTIVES

During the lab, students will
- examine, interpret, and synthesize information in economic reports.
- prepare a summary of current economic conditions in their town or city.
- prepare recommendations for promoting economic growth in their town or city.
- assemble their summary and recommendations into a written report.
- present their report to the city council (the class).

Using the Lab

Before beginning the lab, organize students into groups and distribute copies of the Unit 4 Lab Activity found in *Unit Tests and Unit Lab Activities with Answer Key*. Have students read the assignment on this page and then discuss the assignment as a class. Point out the documents on pages 273–275 that students will use during the lab.

The What Do You Think? questions on pages 273–75 will help guide students during the project. In addition, the lab activity sheet includes a step-by-step checklist for students to monitor their progress. ★23B, 25B

UNIT 4
ECONOMICS LAB
You Make the Decision

Macroeconomic Measures

*I*magine that you are a city manager who must develop recommendations for promoting economic growth in your town or city. You will soon have to present your recommendations to the city council. To help you put together the recommendations, Professor Lott O. Pfigurin and a group of her economics graduate students have prepared economic reports about the current condition of the national and local economies.

Professor Pfigurin and her students know that measuring economic performance and creating a plan for economic growth requires information. The data they have provided includes:

- figures on gross domestic product
- last year's index of leading economic indicators
- local unemployment rates
- local market basket information
- factors affecting local economic growth.

Economics Notebook Assignment ★TEKS

1. Write a clear, one-sentence statement of the situation requiring a decision.
2. Review the documents to gather information.
3. Answer the accompanying questions in your Economics Notebook.
4. Prepare your recommendations for the city council. Include specific and general goals for your local economy; you will need to reference the information provided by Professor Pfigurin. Identify various options you could pursue, and predict the consequences of each. Prepare a plan to put your recommendations into action.
5. Create visual guides to help explain your plan. You might, for example, draw line or bar graphs representing key national and local economic data.
6. Present your report to the city council (the rest of the class).

CENTER FOR ECONOMIC RESEARCH

City Manager
Anytown, USA

Dear City Manager:

Thank you for your recent request for assistance from the Center for Economic Research. Several graduate students and I have compiled some information to help you prepare recommendations for developing the local economy. If you need any further assistance after reviewing the data provided here, please feel free to contact me.

I have enclosed figures on gross domestic product, economic indicators, and unemployment and inflation rates. The last figure includes additional information that you should consider about the local economy. I hope this information is helpful in designing your plans for economic growth.

Sincerely,

Prof. Lott O. Pfigurin

FIGURE 1: GROSS DOMESTIC PRODUCT
(in billions of dollars)

GDP four years ago	$8,117.3
GDP three years ago	$7,995.8
GDP two years ago	$7,899.5

Key economic data for last year's GDP:
(in billions of dollars)

Personal consumption expenditures	$5,875.5
Gross private domestic investment	$1,251.9
Government purchases of goods and services	$1,564.7
Exports of goods and services	$1,203.5
Imports of goods and services	$1,339.8

◀ WHAT DO YOU THINK?

1. Using the information in Figure 1 and the formula you studied on page 230, calculate the gross domestic product (GDP) for last year. Compare that number to the GDP figures provided for previous years. Did GDP last year appear to grow faster or slower than GDP in the previous three years?

2. Review the information in Figure 2. Is the index of leading economic indicators rising or declining? What does this trend suggest about economic growth in future months?

3. Review the information about GDP and leading economic indicators on this page. In what phase of the business cycle would you say the economy was at the end of last year?

CENTER FOR ECONOMIC RESEARCH

FIGURE 2: LAST YEAR'S INDEX OF LEADING ECONOMIC INDICATORS

The Conference Board is a business membership and research organization. In an effort to anticipate economic performance in future months, the board examines economic indicators. Information from all of these indicators is then used to create an index of leading economic indicators. In general, a rising index of leading economic indicators shows that future economic growth is expected. A declining index shows the opposite. Figure 2 shows the performance of the index of leading economic indicators over the past 12 months.

What Do You Think? Answers

1. $8,555.8; GDP grew faster last year than it did in the previous three years. ★23F, 23G

2. The index is rising, indicating good potential for economic growth in the coming months. ★23F

3. The economy was in the expansion phase of the business cycle. ★23F

ECONOMICS LAB

What Do You Think? Answers

1. Unemployment was highest three years ago at 7.7 percent. Unemployment has declined since then. ⭐23F, 23G

2. CPI—four years ago: 102.5; three years ago: 106.6; two years ago: 109; last year: 111 inflation rate—four years ago: 2.5 percent; three years ago: 4 percent; two year ago: 2.25 percent; last year: 1.8 percent ⭐23F, 23G

3. moderate, although inflation did rise to 4 percent three years ago ⭐23F, 23G

ECONOMICS LAB continued

CENTER FOR ECONOMIC RESEARCH

In an effort to gauge the strength of the local economy, my graduate students and I estimated the average annual local unemployment rates in recent years. National unemployment figures for the same period are roughly the same.

FIGURE 3: LOCAL UNEMPLOYMENT RATES

- 4 years ago: 6.9%
- 3 years ago: 7.7%
- 2 years ago: 6.4%

◀ WHAT DO YOU THINK?

1. Review the information in Figure 3. When was unemployment highest in the local economy? How much lower was last year's unemployment rate?

2. Using the data in Figure 4, and the formula on page 260, calculate the local consumer price index (CPI) over the last four years. After you have calculated the CPI, use those figures and the formula on page 261 to calculate the rate of inflation over the same period.

3. How would you characterize the local inflation rate over the last four years: non-existent, creeping, moderate, or galloping?

CENTER FOR ECONOMIC RESEARCH

The Center for Economic Research estimated the cost of a list of local market basket items after each of the last several years. These figures can be used to calculate local inflation. In the base year when the market basket was valued at $5,000.

FIGURE 4: LOCAL MARKET BASKET

Four years ago	$5,125
Three years ago	$5,330
Two years ago	$5,450
Last year	$5,550

CENTER FOR ECONOMIC RESEARCH

Factors Affecting Local Economic Growth

Now that you have examined the economic data my students and I have provided, please review the following examination of factors important to growth in the local economy.

- The presence of Central State University in our community is significant in regards to worker-training opportunities. The city government might consider working with the university to develop training programs for local workers.
- Current inflation data is encouraging because it indicates that interest rates for bank loans, which can be used for capital investment, will probably be relatively low in the coming months.
- Natural resources in the local area include significant timberland and natural gas deposits. These resources have not yet been developed.

◀ WHAT DO YOU THINK?

1. How can the presence of Central State University and the training and educational opportunities it provides help local economic growth?

2. In what way does current inflation data indicate that bank loans may be made at relatively low interest rates? How does low inflation help consumers?

3. What advantages are provided by the presence of significant and untapped resources, such as timber and natural gas deposits?

internet connect

Internet Activity: go.hrw.com
KEYWORD: SM3 ECL4

Access the Internet through the HRW Go site to learn more about economic indicators. The Conference Board creates the Index of Leading Economic Indicators, which is designed to signal peaks and troughs in the business cycle. The LEI is derived from ten leading, four coincident, and seven lagging indicators. Explore the Conference Board Web site to identify the indicators. Create a graphic organizer that explains why each indicator is seen as leading, coincident, or lagging.

What Do You Think? Answers

1. An educated and skilled labor force is a strong, positive influence on productivity, which promotes economic growth. ★23A

2. Local inflation is low to moderate, and lower inflation causes interest rates to drop. Lower interest rates indicate that loans for starting and expanding businesses will be less expensive. Low to moderate inflation reduces the costs of consumer borrowing by keeping interest rates low. It also helps people on fixed incomes and encourages saving and investing. ★23A, 23F

3. These significant and untapped resources offer opportunities for economic growth as entrepreneurs and other businesspeople seek to develop and use these resources to produce goods and services. ★23A

ECONOMICS LAB

UNIT 5

Lesson Options
Suggestions for customizing the material in Unit 5 to fit the specific schedule and curriculum of your classroom are located at the beginning of each chapter.

Main Ideas
Ask each student to read the Main Ideas and briefly answer each question in writing. Later, when you have finished with Unit 5, ask students to return to their original answers and revise them using what they learned in the unit.

Economics Lab
The Unit 5 Economics Lab appears on pages 370–73. This project is a real-world assignment in which students imagine that they are members of the organization Citizens for a Good Economy (CGE), which works to promote government policies to strengthen the U.S. economy. Students will work in groups to develop fiscal policy proposals for strengthening the economy and then present these proposals to other CGE members (the class). Support materials for the lab appear in *Unit Tests and Unit Lab Activities with Answer Key*.

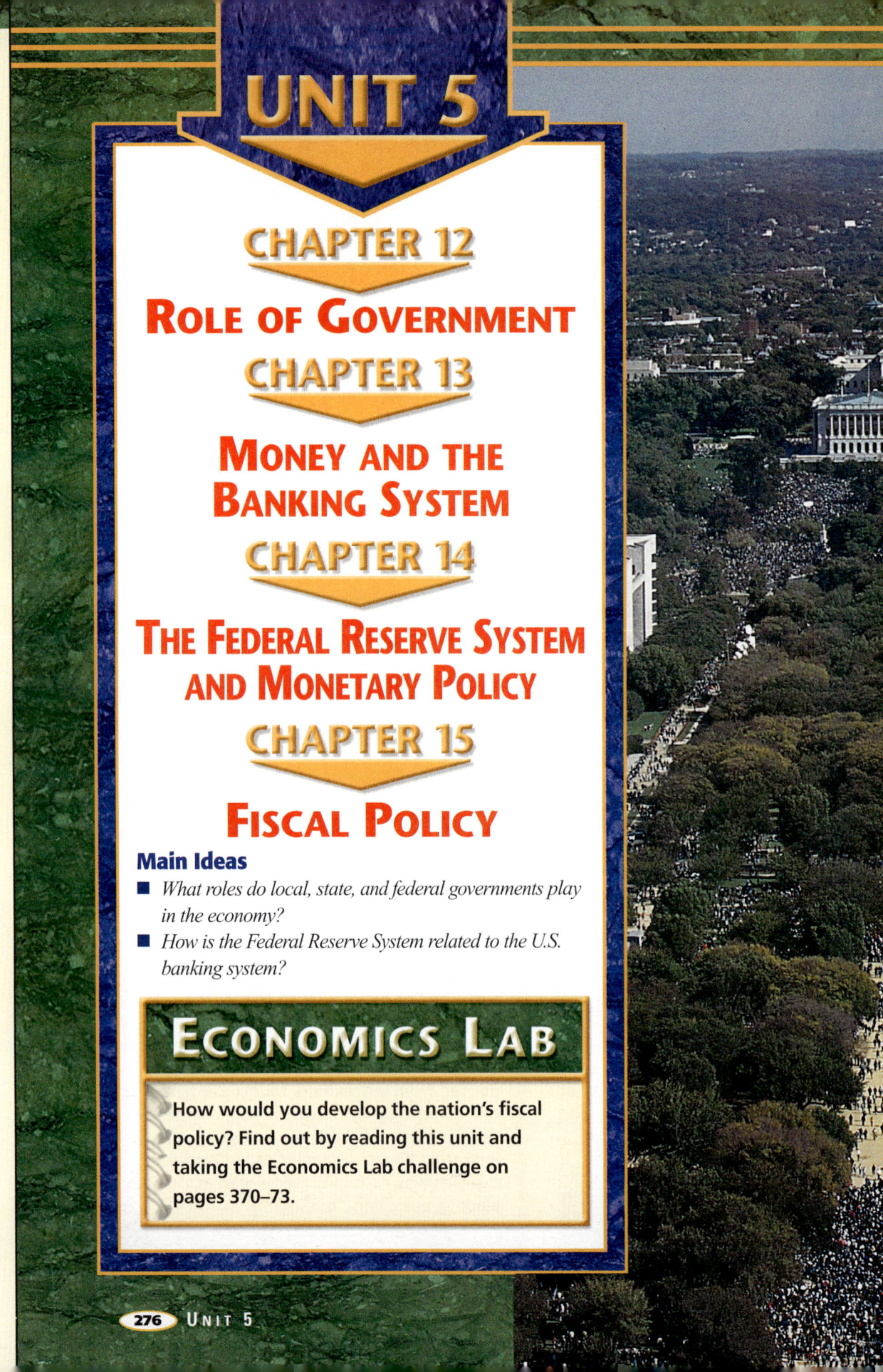

276

UNIT 5

CHAPTER 12
ROLE OF GOVERNMENT

CHAPTER 13
MONEY AND THE BANKING SYSTEM

CHAPTER 14
THE FEDERAL RESERVE SYSTEM AND MONETARY POLICY

CHAPTER 15
FISCAL POLICY

Main Ideas
- What roles do local, state, and federal governments play in the economy?
- How is the Federal Reserve System related to the U.S. banking system?

ECONOMICS LAB
How would you develop the nation's fiscal policy? Find out by reading this unit and taking the Economics Lab challenge on pages 370–73.

276 UNIT 5

Government and the Economy

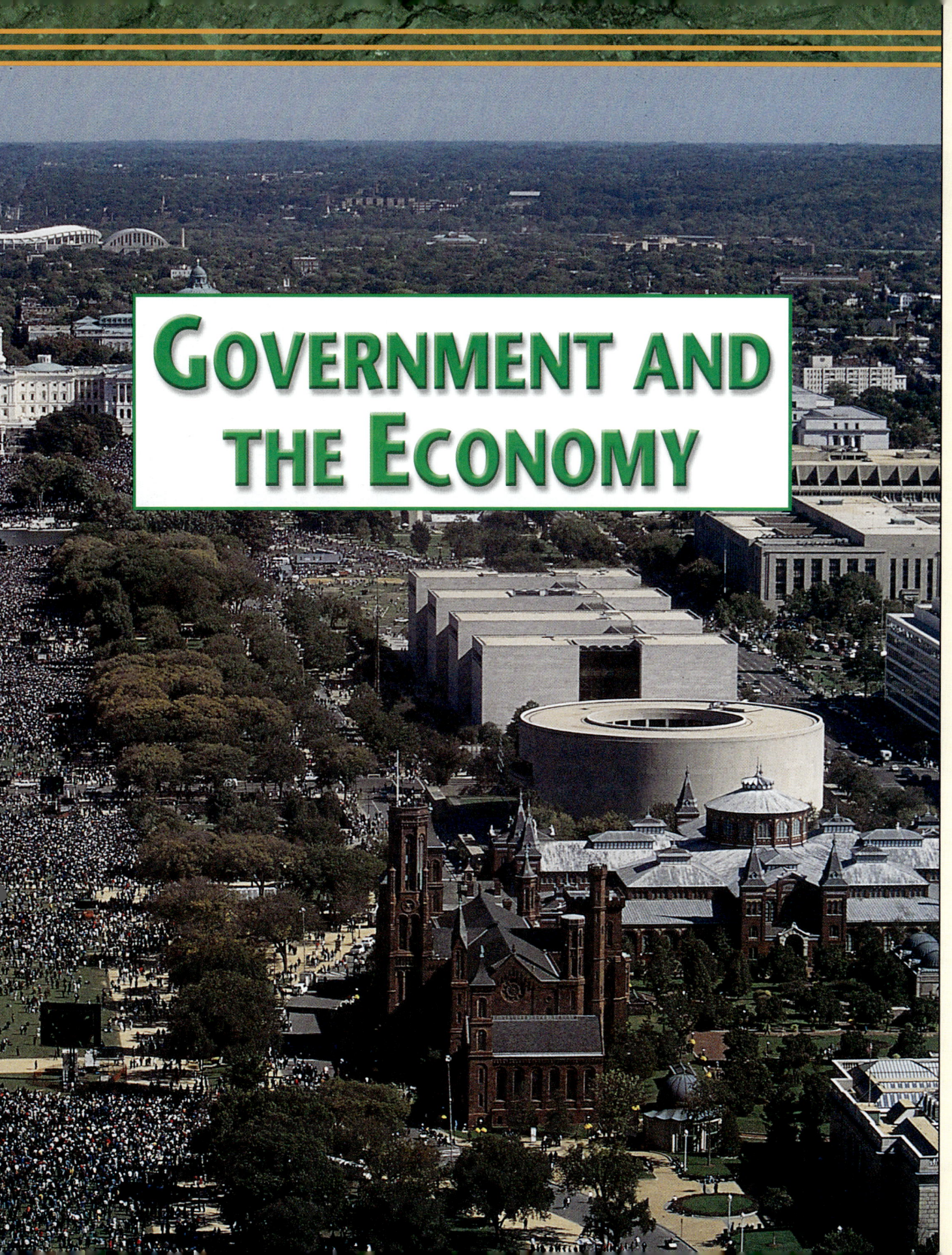

UNIT 5 OVERVIEW

Unit 5 covers the role of the government and financial institutions in the U.S. economy. Students will learn about the government's main economic goals and functions, how the government raises and spends revenue, the development of the U.S. banking system and the Federal Reserve system, and the fundamentals of monetary and fiscal policy. In addition, students will examine the characteristics and functions of money, the methods and goals of supply-side and demand-side economics, the role of the federal budget, and the problems associated with the federal deficit and the national debt.

Teaching with Photographs

This photograph shows the Mall in Washington, D.C. The Capitol Building (center) is located at the east end of the Mall and faces the Washington Monument, which is located at the midpoint of the Mall and is not visible in the photo. Most of the buildings lining the Mall are museums. The Mall is frequently a site of protests, rallies, and demonstrations.

As a motivating activity for this unit, ask students why individuals, groups, and organizations might hold protests and rallies on the Mall. Then ask students to describe some of the ways in which the U.S. government is involved in the economy.

277

CHAPTER RESOURCE MANAGER

CHAPTER 12 — ROLE OF GOVERNMENT

	OBJECTIVES	PACING GUIDE	REPRODUCIBLE RESOURCES
SECTION 1 **GROWTH OF GOVERNMENT** (pp. 279–83)	▸ What factors influence the growth of government? ▸ Why have government expenditures increased over time? ▸ How do federal, state, and local governments spend their money?	**Regular** 1.5 days **Block Scheduling** .5 day	**ELL** Spanish Study Guide 12.1 **ELL** English Study Guide 12.1 **PS** Reading 47: Americans with Disabilities Act of 1990 **E** Challenge and Enrichment: Activity 12 **SM** Mathematics for Economics: Activity 12
SECTION 2 **ECONOMIC GOALS** (pp. 284–90)	▸ Why does the government regulate businesses? ▸ How does the government work to provide public goods? ▸ In what ways does the government promote individuals' well-being? ▸ How does the government work to stabilize the economy?	**Regular** 1.5 days **Block Scheduling** 1 day	**ELL** Spanish Study Guide 12.2 **ELL** English Study Guide 12.2 **S** Simulations and Strategies for Teaching Economics: Activity 12 **SM** Consumer Economics: Activity 12
SECTION 3 **GOVERNMENT AND THE PUBLIC** (pp. 291–96)	▸ How does the government determine the public interest? ▸ What consequences may result from government promotion of the public interest? ▸ How can individuals and interest groups affect government policies?	**Regular** 1.5 days **Block Scheduling** 1 day	**ELL** Spanish Study Guide 12.3 **ELL** English Study Guide 12.3

Chapter Resource Key

- **PS** Primary Sources
- **RS** Reading Support
- **E** Enrichment
- **S** Simulations
- **SM** Skills Mastery
- **A** Assessment
- **REV** Review
- **ELL** Reinforcement and English Language Learners
- Transparencies
- CD-ROM
- Video
- Videodisc
- Internet
- Holt Presentation Maker Using Microsoft® PowerPoint®
- TEKS and TAKS

TECHNOLOGY RESOURCES	REINFORCEMENT, REVIEW, AND ASSESSMENT
One-Stop Planner: Lesson 12.1 Researcher Online Homework Practice Online Transparencies 48 and 49 Global Skillbuilder CD-ROM	REV Section 1 Review, p. 283 A Daily Quiz 12.1 ★ TAKS Every Day!
One-Stop Planner: Lesson 12.2 Researcher Online Homework Practice Online CNN Presents Economics: Deregulating the Cable TV Industry Transparencies 50 and 51 Global Skillbuilder CD-ROM	REV Section 2 Review, p. 290 A Daily Quiz 12.2 ★ TAKS Every Day!
One-Stop Planner: Lesson 12.3 Researcher Online Homework Practice Online Global Skillbuilder CD-ROM	REV Section 3 Review, p. 296 A Daily Quiz 12.3 ★ TAKS Every Day!

Chapter Review and Assessment
- SM Global Skillbuilder CD-ROM
- HRW Go site
- REV Reteaching Activity 12
- REV Chapter 12 Review, pp. 298–99
- A Chapter 12 Test Generator (on the One-Stop Planner)
- A Chapter 12 Test
- A Alternative Assessment Handbook

One-Stop Planner CD-ROM
It's easy to plan lessons, select resources, and print out materials for your students when you use the **Texas One-Stop Planner CD-ROM with Test Generator.**

---

internet connect

HRW ONLINE RESOURCES
Go To: go.hrw.com
Then type in a keyword.

TEACHER HOME PAGE
KEYWORD: SM3 Teacher

CHAPTER INTERNET ACTIVITIES
KEYWORD: SM3 EC12
Choose an activity to:
- research Presidents Ronald Reagan and Bill Clinton.
- explore careers in all levels of government.
- learn about the Social Security Administration.

CHAPTER ENRICHMENT LINKS
KEYWORD: SM3 CH12

HOLT RESEARCHER ONLINE
KEYWORD: Holt Researcher

ONLINE ASSESSMENT
Homework Practice
KEYWORD: SM3 HP12
TAKS Review
KEYWORD: SM3 T12
Rubrics
KEYWORD: SS Rubrics

CONTENT UPDATES
KEYWORD: SS Content Updates

HOLT PRESENTATION MAKER
KEYWORD: SM3 PPT12

ONLINE READING SUPPORT
KEYWORD: SS Strategies

CURRENT EVENTS
KEYWORD: S3 Current Events

TEXAS RESOURCES
KEYWORD: S3 TX

LESSON 12.1 GROWTH OF GOVERNMENT

TEXTBOOK PAGES 279–83

HOLT PRESENTATION MAKER — Access Illustrated LECTURE NOTES using Microsoft® PowerPoint® on the One-Stop Planner CD-ROM

OBJECTIVES

- Describe the factors that influence the growth of government.
- Explain why government expenditures have increased over time.
- Identify how federal, state, and local governments spend their money.

MOTIVATE

Begin the lesson by asking students: How does government affect your lives on a daily basis? (Students may not have many responses to this question because they may not think about the effect of government on their daily lives very often.) To help students answer the question, have them brainstorm a list of daily activities. Then help them link these activities to the government's involvement in their lives *(e.g., students may come to school on a road maintained by their state government)*. Continue the activity until students realize how pervasive government is in the lives of citizens. Tell students to consider the role of government in their lives and in the economy as they read Section 1 of the chapter. ★23A

TEACH

Building a Vocabulary

Have students use spiral notebooks to create an Economics Dictionary to be used throughout the chapter. This dictionary might be used as an activity at the start of each new section or as a learning aid for sheltered English students or students having difficulty. Have students use the information provided in the text or on the *Researcher CD-ROM* to list, define, and give an example of each vocabulary term. ★24A

Understanding Main Concepts, Organizing Information

Have students list and describe the four key factors that have influenced the growth of government in the United States *(population growth, changing public attitudes, a rising standard of living, and national emergencies)*. Then have the class work together to create a graphic organizer that shows how each of these four factors has led to the growth of government at all levels. Students should choose the structure of the graphic organizer and what information to include. Have a volunteer draw the organizer on the chalkboard or on an overhead transparency as the rest of the class creates it. Have students copy the completed graphic organizer into their notes. Refer students who need additional instruction on the skills used in this activity to the *Global Skillbuilder* Lesson 12: Creating Graphic Organizers. ★23A, 23C, 24C, 24D

Acquiring Information, Drawing Conclusions

To extend the previous activity, refer students to the U.S. Population Statistics section on the *Researcher Online*. Organize students into four or five groups. Assign each group one geographic region of the United States and have each group examine the population trends for the states in its region. Then have each group report its findings to the class. After students have made their reports, have the class determine which U.S. regions have experienced the most population growth during recent years and speculate about the reasons for this growth. Then have students discuss how this regional growth has affected the size of local and state governments in these regions. ★23A, 24D

Reading Charts and Graphs, Evaluating Ideas

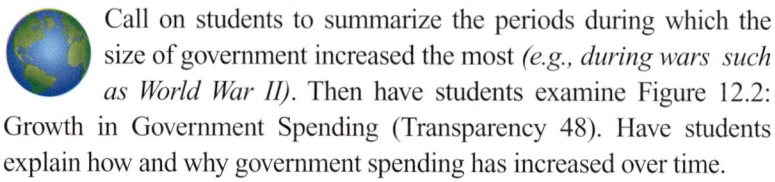

Call on students to summarize the periods during which the size of government increased the most *(e.g., during wars such as World War II)*. Then have students examine Figure 12.2: Growth in Government Spending (Transparency 48). Have students explain how and why government spending has increased over time.

Next, have students examine Figure 12.3: How Federal, State, and Local Dollars Are Spent (Transparency 49). Ask students to name the three largest categories for federal expenditures, state expenditures, and local expenditures. Have students give opinions as to why the government spends the most on these types of services. Ask students whether they agree with how federal, state, and local governments prioritize their spending and to explain their answers.

Then remind students of the Motivate activity and the ways in which government affects their daily lives. Have students discuss which level of government has the greatest effect on their lives now—federal, state, or local—and which level of government they think will have the greatest effect on their lives in five years. Refer students who need additional instruction on the skills used in this activity to the *Global Skillbuilder* Lesson 10: Reading Graphs. ★17B, 23A, 23F, 23G

277C

CLOSE

Have the class discuss the following question: What are some advantages and disadvantages of the growth of government for the citizens of the United States? You might also have students write a short essay in response to this question as a homework assignment. ⭐23D, 25A

OPTIONS

Gifted Learners

Direct students' attention to the Global Exchange feature, Embargoes, on page 280 of the textbook. Have students read the feature and discuss it as a class. Then have interested students use the library, in-class resources, and the Internet to research the ramifications of either the U.S. embargo against Cuba or the United Nations embargo against Iraq. Students should answer questions such as: What are/were the political and/or philosophical reasons for the embargo? What is/was the goal of the embargo? What effect does/did the embargo have on the daily lives of the people in Cuba/Iraq? How have other countries responded to the embargo? Have students present their findings in a written or oral report. Students may want to include their reports in their portfolios.
⭐13C, 14A, 23A, 24D

Gifted Learners

Point out to students that government has increased partially because the size and number of disadvantaged groups have increased. Have students use the *Researcher Online*, the library, in-class resources, and the Internet to research the following questions: Have government expenditures to disadvantaged groups caused these groups to expand? What other factors might have contributed to the expansion of these groups? Have the class discuss each of the questions. ⭐23A

Interpersonal Learners

Organize students into groups of four or five. Tell each group to write and conduct an opinion poll to determine local citizens' expectations regarding government spending in education, medical and health care, defense, welfare, transportation, and special projects such as the space program. Students may want to poll other students in their school as well as members of the community. Have each group report its findings to the class.

As a follow-up activity have students compare how the people in the community think local, state, and federal governments should be spending their money to the way that each level of government is actually spending its money. Then poll the class to see whether students agree more with the community or the government. ⭐15A, 23A, 23C, 23E, 24C, 24D

Interpersonal Learners, Linguistic Learners

Organize the class into small groups. Have each group use the library, in-class resources, and the Internet to research a New Deal reform program that is still in effect today. Each group should be prepared to describe its program to the rest of the class and to answer the following questions: ⭐15A, 23A, 23D

◗ What was the original purpose of the program?
◗ Was the goal of the program accomplished?
◗ What is the role of the program in the U.S. economy today?
◗ How do people feel about the value of this program?
◗ Should it continue into the future?

Logical-Mathematical Learners

Have students use the library, in-class resources, and the Internet to research the local budget decision-making process of their county or city. Who proposes the local budget? Who approves the local budget? What voice do citizens of the community have in the budget process? What is the breakdown of local funds? Tell students to create a chart or graph depicting their findings. Help students turn their chart or graph into a transparency to show the class. Refer students who need additional instruction on the skills used in this activity to the *Global Skill Builder* Lesson 12: Creating Graphic Organizers. ⭐23B

REVIEW

Have students complete the Section 1 Review on page 283. Use the answers in the Annotated Teacher's Edition to assess student mastery of this section.

ASSESS

To assess student mastery of this section, have students complete Daily Quiz 12.1 in *Daily Quizzes with Answer Key*. For additional assessment options, see *Alternative Assessment Handbook* on the *One-Stop Planner CD-ROM*.

ADDITIONAL RESOURCES

America in the Thirties: Creating the Safety Net. (videotape, 30 min.). Films for the Humanities & Sciences.
The Great Depression. (CD-ROM, for Macintosh/Windows). Projected Learning Programs Inc.
The Role of Government in the Economy. (filmstrip). Random House. Educational Enrichment Materials.

LESSON 12.2 ECONOMIC GOALS

TEXTBOOK PAGES 284–90

HOLT PRESENTATION MAKER
Access Illustrated LECTURE NOTES using Microsoft® PowerPoint® on the One-Stop Planner CD-ROM

OBJECTIVES

- Explain and evaluate why government regulations are applied to businesses. ⭐2D
- Describe how the government works to provide public goods.
- Explain how the government promotes individuals' well-being.
- Describe how the government works to stabilize the economy.

MOTIVATE

Write this question on the chalkboard: What do you think the economic goals of the government should be? Have students think about the question on their own and then make a list of responses in their notes. Then discuss students' responses and make a class list. Conclude this activity by telling students that they will learn about the economic goals of government in this lesson. Have students read Section 2 of the chapter. ⭐23A

TEACH

Building a Vocabulary

List the important terms for this section on the chalkboard and tell students to add them to their Economics Dictionary. Tell students to use the information provided in the text or on the *Researcher CD-ROM* to list, define, and give an example of each vocabulary term. ⭐24A

Classifying Information

List the government's four main economic goals—regulating business, providing public goods, promoting citizens' economic well-being, and stabilizing the economy—on the chalkboard and summarize each goal for students. Then review with students the economic goals of the government that the class thought of during the Motivate activity. Have students classify each of their goals under one of the four main goals. ⭐16A, 2D, 23A

Understanding Main Concepts

Next, organize students into five groups. Two of the groups will represent the government's goal of regulating business, and the remaining groups will represent each of the remaining economic goals. Have students review the textbook material that pertains to their group's goal and then create a public-service announcement describing and promoting this governmental role. (The two groups covering the goal of regulating business should divide up the material. For example, one group might cover the information on preventing abuses and protecting consumers, and the other group might cover the information on limiting negative externalities and promoting competition.) Have each group perform its public-service announcement for the class. Students may want to use props or visual aids to enhance their presentations. Students may want to include a description of their presentations in their portfolios. ⭐23D, 24C, 24D

Role-Playing

To extend the previous activity, have each group prepare a short skit illustrating its governmental economic goal in action. Students might illustrate their goal by portraying a government worker interacting with one or more individuals or checking to be sure a new business owner has met all established regulations and ordinances. Have volunteers perform their skits for the class. ⭐16A, 2D, 24D

Conducting Research, Organizing Ideas

Have students examine Figure 12.4: Federal Regulatory Agencies (Transparency 50). Next, organize students into groups of two or three and assign each group one of the agencies listed in the chart. Tell each group to research its agency and to create a chart depicting the history of the agency, how it has developed and changed over time, its current functions and goals, the groups it supports, who currently heads it, how many government employees it employs, and how much government funding it receives. Each group might also examine its agency's site on the World Wide Web to see what sorts of information and services the agency offers online. Students might use the *Researcher Online*, the library, the Internet, or other resources to research their agency. Display groups' charts around the classroom and have each group share its findings with the class. ⭐15A, 23C, 24C, 24D

CLOSE

Review the four main economic goals of government with the class. Then have students discuss which of the four goals of government is most important and why. Then ask students whether they think that the government should be more or less involved in the nation's economy. Encourage class discussion. ⭐16A, 23D, 25B

277E

OPTIONS

Students Having Difficulty, Linguistic Learners

Organize students into groups of three or four. Group students having difficulty with students who have mastered the material. Have each group complete Reading 47: Americans with Disabilities Act of 1990, located in *From the Source: Readings in Economics and Government with Answer Key*. Tell students to go through the reading, discuss it with the other members of their group, and then work together to answer the questions that follow. When students are through, discuss the reading as a class.

Gifted Learners

Have students use the library, the Internet, or other resources to research arguments supporting and opposing privatization. Students might also research privatization efforts in other countries and how those efforts have affected free enterprise. Have students use the information to write a one- or two-page position paper supporting or opposing privatization in the United States. You might want to encourage motivated students to extend the content of their papers by examining the arguments for and against privatization of utility companies in the United States. Students may want to include their papers in their portfolios. ★15B, 23D, 24D

Gifted Learners

Have students use the *Researcher Online*, the library, in-class resources, and the Internet to research the current debate over the welfare system in the United States. Have students use their research to write persuasive letters to the editor of a local newspaper or to their congressperson. Students should present their views on the nation's welfare system and explain the problems they see with the current system. Encourage students to outline their suggestions or solutions for improving the system. Have students exchange papers and evaluate each other's solutions. ★23D, 24D, 25A

Intrapersonal Learners

Have students examine Figure 12.5: Redistributing Income (Transparency 51). Review with students the ways in which the U.S. government redistributes wealth. Next, have the class discuss the following question: Should the U.S. government ensure the same standard of living for all U.S. citizens? Encourage students to provide support for their responses. Then have students write a one-page essay giving their own responses to the question. Students may want to include their essays in their portfolios. ★23A, 23D, 24D

Linguistic Learners

Have students watch an evening news program on television. Tell students to make a note of each news story that illustrates one of the government's roles in the economy as described in Section 2 of the chapter. The next day, have students share the stories they noted with the rest of the class. Encourage students to discuss each story. Ask students to evaluate as a class how each instance of government intervention affected the free-enterprise system. ★15A, 15B, 23A

Visual-Spatial Learners

Have students use posterboard and clippings from newspapers and magazines to create a collage illustrating the four main economic goals of the government. Students might use both images and words in their collage. Have students organize the collage into four sections—one for each goal—and write a descriptive caption to accompany each section. Have students display their collages around the classroom. ★16A, 24C, 24D

Visual-Spatial Learners, Students Having Difficulty

Organize students into groups of two or three. You might want to group students having difficulty with students who have mastered the material. Have students create a chart, such as a Venn diagram, that illustrates the concept of shared responsibility among levels of government. Students should illustrate how federal, state, and local governments share responsibility for promoting the economic goals of regulating business, providing public goods, and promoting citizens' economic well-being. Refer students who need additional instruction on the skills used in this activity to the *Global Skillbuilder* Lesson 12: Creating Graphic Organizers. ★23B

REVIEW

Have students complete the Section 2 Review on page 290. Use the answers in the Annotated Teacher's Edition to assess student mastery of this section.

ASSESS

To assess student mastery of this section, have students complete Daily Quiz 12.2 in *Daily Quizzes with Answer Key*. For additional assessment options, see *Alternative Assessment Handbook* on the *One-Stop Planner CD-ROM*.

ADDITIONAL RESOURCES

Getting Out of Business: Privatization and the Modern State. (videotape, 59 min.). Films for the Humanities & Sciences.

Products on Trial. (videotape, 60 min.). PBS Video.

United States Federal Register. (CD-ROM series). CPI Electronic Publishing.

LESSON 12.3 GOVERNMENT AND THE PUBLIC

TEXTBOOK PAGES 291–96

HOLT PRESENTATION MAKER Access Illustrated LECTURE NOTES using Microsoft® PowerPoint® on the One-Stop Planner CD-ROM

OBJECTIVES

- Explain how the government determines the public interest.
- Identify the consequences that may result from government promotion of the public interest.
- Describe how individuals and interest groups can affect government policies.

MOTIVATE

Ask students the following questions: How does this school identify the public interest of the student body? Can school officials satisfy the student body's public interest as well as the needs and wants of all individual students? What are some of the policies that school officials have passed to promote the public interest of the student body? What actions can students take to influence and change school policies? Are students more effective acting individually or in groups to change school policies? Why might students want to change school policies?

Encourage class discussion. Then tell students that in this lesson they are going to study how the government determines and promotes the public interest, and how individuals and groups can affect government policies. Tell students to keep these issues in mind as they read Section 3 of the chapter. ★23A

TEACH

Building a Vocabulary

List the important terms for this section on the chalkboard and tell students to add them to their Economics Dictionary. Tell students to use the information provided in the text or on the *Researcher CD-ROM* to list, define, and give an example of each vocabulary term. ★24A

Understanding Main Concepts

Ask students how governments identify the public interest. *(The public interest is based on the collective needs of many people.)* Remind students of the questions that they discussed in the Motivate activity. Then ask students whether the U.S. government can satisfy the public interest as well as all individuals' interests, wants, and needs. *(No, public interest outweighs the wishes of the individual.)* Ask students whether they agree with this reasoning. Promote class discussion. ★23A

Applying Ideas, Mastering Concepts

To extend the previous activity, organize students into pairs and tell each pair to create something that illustrates the meaning of the term *public interest*. Some pairs may choose to create a poster. Others may choose to write poems or songs that capture the essence of the public interest. Some students may start by renaming the public interest—perhaps "the common good," "the public good," or "the common interest." Have pairs share their work with the class. ★24A, 24C, 24D

Identifying Cause and Effect, Judging Information

Next, explain to students that there are consequences of policies and regulations related to public-interest programs, and that these consequences can affect all aspects of the free enterprise system, including prices, services, profits, and productivity. Call on volunteers to summarize these consequences.

Then organize students into four groups, one for each aspect of production and consumption listed above. Tell groups to think of examples other than those mentioned in the textbook that illustrate how government policies and regulations related to public-interest programs affect their aspect of production and consumption. Give each group 10 to 15 minutes to think of ideas. Then have each group share its ideas with the rest of the class, and have the class as a whole judge whether the examples are valid. ★15B, 23A

Comparing and Contrasting, Acquiring Information

Review with students some of the actions they listed in the Motivate activity that students can take to influence and change school policy. Then ask students to describe how individuals and interest groups can influence government policies. Have students compare and contrast individuals' and interest groups' methods of influencing government policies. Then ask students: Which is more effective, acting as an individual or as a group? *(Most students will respond that groups can frequently achieve results when individuals acting alone can not)*. Ask students to describe examples of how interest groups can achieve better results than individuals when working to influence or change government policy.

Next, organize students into groups of two or three. Tell each group to research the political agenda and goals of one interest group. Students can use the library, in-class resources, and the Internet to find information on their group. In addition, the National Organizations section on the *Researcher Online* provides information on a variety of U.S. national interest groups. Have groups create a chart or poster that describes an interest group, the date of its creation, current issues and laws it supports or opposes, and its current political agenda and goals. ⭐24C, 24D

Role-Playing, Synthesizing Information

To extend the previous activity, have students take on the role of lobbyists for the interest group that they researched. Tell student lobbyists that a special session of Congress is meeting soon and that all lobbyists will have a chance to address the members and present their goals. Have each group prepare a presentation to teach the members of Congress (the class) about the goals of its interest group and to convince Congress of the importance of passing legislation in keeping with these goals. ⭐23D, 24D

CLOSE

Ask students whether they or any members of their families belong to an interest group. Ask students what sorts of interest groups might be useful for students at their school to form. Have the class choose several interest groups that they would like to form and vote on the one they prefer.

OPTIONS

Gifted Learners
Have students use the library, the Internet, or other resources to research restrictions on lobbyists and interest groups. Students should examine, among other issues, the arguments for and against restricting the actions of lobbyists and the amount of money that interest groups can contribute to candidates. Have students write two to four pages on the topic and conclude by presenting their own opinions on the subject. Students may want to include their papers in their portfolios. ⭐23D, 24D, 25B

Linguistic Learners
Have interested students research the activities of consumer advocate Ralph Nader. Students should research his beginnings as a consumer-rights activist, the groups he has been instrumental in founding, the legislation his groups have initiated, and his overall influence on government policy. Students can use the library, the Internet, or other resources to find information. In addition, the Biographies section on the *Researcher Online* includes a profile of Nader. Have students present the information in a written report. ⭐24D

Interpersonal Learners
Invite a local lobbyist to speak to your class. Ask the speaker to describe what he or she does and the group he or she represents. Encourage students to prepare several questions beforehand to ask the speaker. For example, students might ask what the main obstacles are that lobbyists face, how often politicians keep their word when they promise to support specific legislation, how new scientific discoveries and technological innovations create the need to lobby more than once for similar legislation, and what sorts of information or arguments are most successful when trying to convince others to support one's views. ⭐27B

Interpersonal Learners, Logical-Mathematical Learners
Organize students into groups. Have each group identify a problem in the school or community, research current public policy related to the problem, and devise a plan to solve the problem. The plan should be specific, including a time line for meeting specific goals. In addition, groups should form interest groups to carry out their plans. If time allows, have student interest groups actually work to carry out their plans. Students might use the Internet, local newspapers, bulletin boards, or community-access television stations to inform the community about the problem and to promote their group's goals and plan of action. ⭐25A

REVIEW

Have students complete the Section 3 Review on page 296. Use the answers in the Annotated Teacher's Edition to assess student mastery of this section.

ASSESS

To assess student mastery of this section, have students complete Daily Quiz 12.3 in *Daily Quizzes with Answer Key*. For additional assessment options, see *Alternative Assessment Handbook* on the *One-Stop Planner CD-ROM*.

RETEACH

For students having difficulty with the lessons, have them complete Reteaching Activity 12. This activity is located in *Reteaching Activities with Answer Key*.

ADDITIONAL RESOURCES

Bowen, Charles. *Modem Nation: The Handbook of Grassroots Activism Online*. 1996. Times Books.

Isaac, Katherine, and Ralph Nader. *Ralph Nader's Practicing Democracy 1997: A Guide to Student Action*. 1997. St. Martin's Press.

Seo, Danny. *Generation React: Activism for Beginners*. 1997. Ballantine Books.

CHAPTER 12

Topics Include

- factors influencing the growth of government
- federal, state, and local government spending
- goals of the U.S. government
- government regulation
- role of government in providing public goods
- role of government in redistributing income
- role of government in stabilizing the economy
- role of government in moderating the business cycle
- methods of influencing government

Economics Notebook

The Economics Notebook is a journal activity that encourages students to consider basic concepts of economics that relate to their lives. A follow-up notebook activity appears on page 298.

WHY IT MATTERS TODAY

To find additional lesson plans dealing with the importance of the government to local and national economies, visit CNNfyi.com or have students complete the ECONOMICS IN THE NEWS activity on page 297.

CNNfyi.com

CHAPTER 12

ROLE OF GOVERNMENT

How do you get to school each day? How do you know the number of calories in your favorite snack food? How is the mail delivered in your neighborhood?

The answers to these questions probably involve the government. In the United States the government's involvement in the economy is widespread. As you read this chapter, consider the role of the government in the U.S. economy and how you can have an influence on the government's economic actions.

ECONOMICS NOTEBOOK

In your Economics Notebook, list five ways the government affects your daily activities. Consider how the government affects your education, employment, and consumption of products.

WHY IT MATTERS TODAY

From funding public schools to helping to control inflation, the government's role in the economy today is greater than ever. At the end of this chapter visit CNNfyi.com to learn more about the importance of the government in your life.

CNNfyi.com

SECTION 1
GROWTH OF GOVERNMENT

READ TO DISCOVER
1. What factors influence the growth of government?
2. Why have government expenditures increased over time?
3. How do federal, state, and local governments spend their money?

ECONOMICS DICTIONARY
cabinet
embargo
per capita

What organization employs the greatest number of people in the United States? The answer is the government. Federal, state, and local governments employ about 20.7 million workers.

The U.S. government was not always so large. When the United States was established in 1776, it had little government. Unlike older countries that had many professional officials, the United States was developing new institutions that were small and operated on limited funds. For example, when George Washington took office as president in 1789, he had no official staff beyond the members of the cabinet. To help him carry out his duties, he hired one assistant—his nephew—whom he paid at his own expense. Today the White House staff consists of hundreds of government employees who assist and advise the president.

Factors Encouraging Growth

The growth of government has taken place as the result of four key factors:

- population growth,
- changing public attitudes,
- a rising standard of living, and
- national emergencies.

Population Growth The United States has grown dramatically over time—from 13 states along the Atlantic coast to 50 states that stretch across North America and into the Pacific. As the nation's territory has increased, so has its population. Meeting the many needs of this expanding population has meant increasing the number of government employees. Why? A larger population requires, for example, more educational facilities, increased road construction and repair, more police protection, and larger national defense forces.

How much has the U.S. population increased? When it was founded, the United States was home to fewer than 4 million people. By 2000 the population had grown to more than 276 million,

POPULATION GROWTH

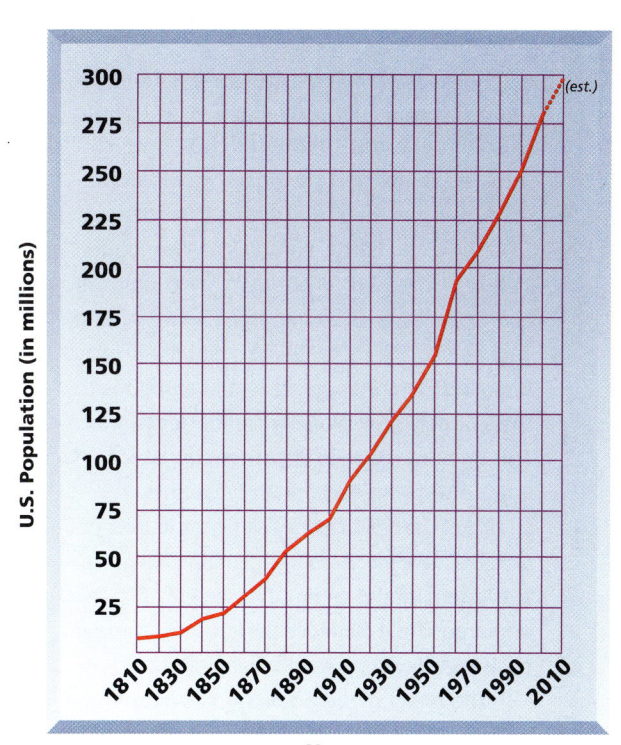

Source: *Statistical Abstract of the United States, 2000*

FIGURE 12.1 The population of the United States has grown dramatically since the nation's founding. **How is population growth related to growth in government?**

ROLE OF GOVERNMENT 279

Caption Answer

People began to recognize—and accept—the need for government intervention in the economy. ⭐23A

Themes in Economics

THE ROLE OF GOVERNMENT

Roosevelt's New Deal created some 59 government agencies. This "alphabet soup" of programs included the Civilian Conservation Corps (CCC), which provided public-works jobs for unemployed young men; the Tennessee Valley Authority (TVA), which funded dam and power station construction in the impoverished Tennessee Valley region; the Federal Deposit Insurance Corporation (FDIC), which insured bank deposits; the Securities and Exchange Commission (SEC), which regulated the securities market; the Public Works Administration (PWA), which provided jobs for the unemployed; and the Social Security Act, which provided unemployment insurance and payments to the retired, disabled, and survivors of employees who died on the job. As a result of the New Deal, the number of federal government employees increased 46 percent from 1932 to 1936. ■

Profiles in Economics

For a biography of Franklin D. Roosevelt and other U.S. presidents, refer students to the *Biographies* section on the *Researcher Online*.

Global Exchange

Embargoes

An **embargo** is an act restricting or prohibiting commerce between countries. Governments sometimes use embargoes to influence the policies and activities of another country.

For example, the United States is trying to topple Fidel Castro's communist regime in Cuba by prohibiting the export of U.S. goods to that country and the import of Cuban products to the United States. Because Cuba previously had depended largely on U.S. trade, this embargo has severely damaged Cuba's economy.

In 2001 President Bush pledged to continue the embargo until the Castro regime "respects the basic human rights of its citizens, frees political prisoners, holds democratic free elections, and allows free speech."

Between 1990 and 2000 the United Nations imposed economic sanctions on eight countries, including Iraq, Somalia, and Yugoslavia. The toughest embargo was imposed in 1990 against Iraq in response to that country's invasion of neighboring Kuwait. This embargo banned the international sale of Iraq's oil—its largest source of revenue.

After the defeat of Iraq's military in the Persian Gulf War, the embargo remained in place. The international community hoped that the embargo would influence the Iraqi government to change its aggressive foreign policy.

The effect of the embargo has been devastating, resulting in famine and disease in Iraq. To lessen these hardships, the United Nations and Iraq agreed to a plan in 1995 that allows Iraq to sell oil in exchange for food and medicine.

ROLE OF GOVERNMENT *Private efforts such as this soup kitchen proved unable to combat the widespread poverty created by the Great Depression.* **How did people's attitudes toward government involvement in the economy change during this period?**

making the United States the third-most-populous nation in the world. (See Figure 12.1.)

Changing Public Attitudes As noted in Chapter 6, laissez-faire economics is based on the belief that the economy does best without government interference. Before the Great Depression of the 1930s, most Americans supported a laissez-faire economic policy. During the depression, however, millions of people lost their jobs and had great difficulty supporting themselves. Homelessness increased dramatically. In cities, people waited in lines for hours to receive a hot meal from "soup kitchens" that sprang up to help the poor.

These relief efforts, however, were not sufficient. Communities and private charities proved unable to ease the hardships of the vast numbers of people hurt by the Great Depression. As a result, many people began to recognize the need for—and accept—government intervention in the economy.

Under President Franklin D. Roosevelt the federal government introduced a number of programs designed to ease the hardships of the Great Depression and to put people back to work. Although these programs—known as the New Deal—did not end the depression, they did contribute to a change in public attitudes about the government's role in the economy. A number of New Deal reform programs remain a central part of the U.S. government today.

Population increases and changing attitudes have led to more assistance for traditionally disadvantaged groups such as minorities and the poor. For example, because the number of people in poverty has risen from more than 25 million in 1971 to more than 32 million in 1999, government assistance programs such as Medicaid and veterans' pensions also have expanded.

Rising Standard of Living

As was the case during the Great Depression, economic hardship can lead to the growth of government. Economic success, however, also can lead to larger government. How does this happen?

Once people earn enough to meet their basic needs, they then look for ways to fulfill their wants—usually through increased spending. In turn, as people spend more and improve their standard of living, they expect goods and services to improve—which frequently means new government programs. As a result, the U.S. government has grown in areas such as education, health care, and consumer protection.

National Emergencies

A national emergency such as a war also can cause the government to increase in size. For example, during World War I the number of civilian employees of the federal government more than doubled, from just fewer than 402,000 workers in 1914 to nearly 855,000 workers in 1918. Similarly, the number of federal employees increased during World War II, from about 1 million in 1940 to almost 4 million in 1945. Government spending increased as well. (See Figure 12.2.)

Although the number of federal employees dropped after both wars, the number never fell to prewar levels—and the government continued many of the programs that were introduced during wartime. Why? Even after the wars ended, people wanted the benefits from these programs to continue. For example, in 1944 Congress passed the GI Bill of Rights, which provided funds for veterans to attend college. Members of the armed forces continued to benefit from this

GROWTH IN GOVERNMENT SPENDING

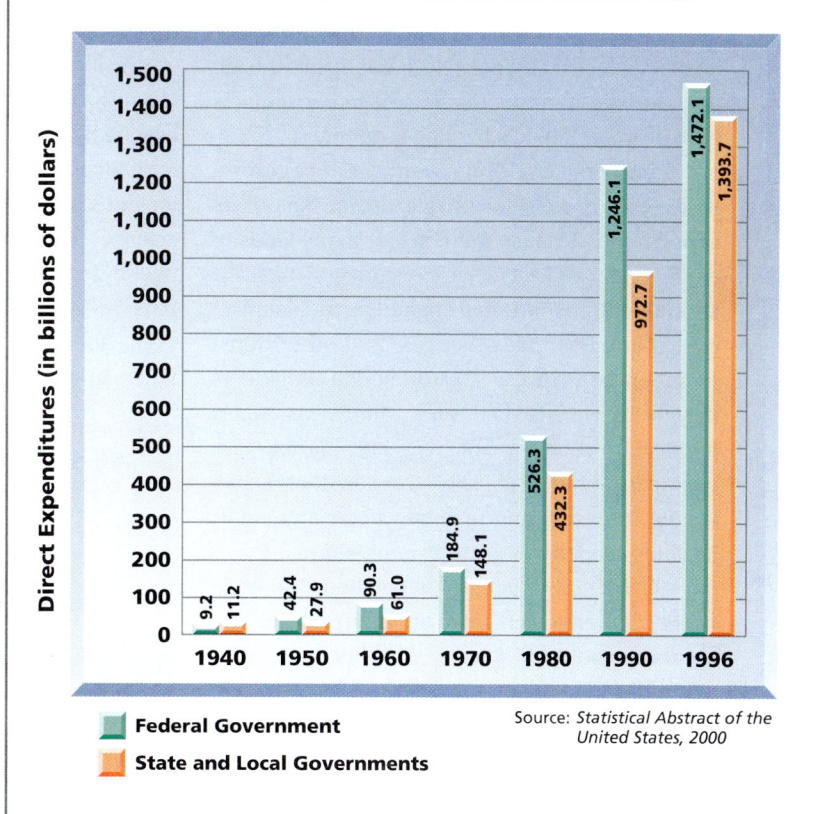

Year	Federal Government	State and Local Governments
1940	9.2	11.2
1950	42.4	27.9
1960	90.3	61.0
1970	184.9	148.1
1980	526.3	432.3
1990	1,246.1	972.7
1996	1,472.1	1,393.7

Direct Expenditures (in billions of dollars)

Source: *Statistical Abstract of the United States, 2000*

FIGURE 12.2 Government spending often increases in times of national emergency such as war. **In what decade did federal government spending more than quadruple?** TEKS

Cultural Perspectives

The Tennessee Valley Authority (TVA), created in 1933, remains one of the most successful of Roosevelt's New Deal programs. The TVA was established to improve the economic conditions of the people living in the Tennessee Valley region, which comprises parts of Tennessee, Kentucky, Virginia, North Carolina, Georgia, Alabama, and Mississippi. During the depression era, frequent flooding, poor farming practices, and overcutting of timber resulted in soil depletion and erosion in the region. In addition, the people suffered from extreme poverty, disease, and illiteracy.

TVA workers built dams and power stations to control flooding and provide electricity for the region, replanted forests, helped farmers improve soil conditions, and worked to combat disease and illiteracy. At the same time, the program created jobs in the area and spurred industry. Today the TVA provides electricity and utility services to the Tennessee Valley.

Transparency

An overhead transparency of Figure 12.2 is available in *Transparency Resources*. See Transparency 48: Growth in Government Spending.

Caption Answer

1940 to 1950 23F, 23G

internet connect

TOPIC: Careers in Government, Pendleton Civil Service Act, Plum Book
GO TO: go.hrw.com
KEYWORD: SM3 EC12

Have students access the Internet through the HRW Go site to conduct research on the Pendleton Civil Service Act, the Plum Book, and Careers in Government. Students should choose a topic that interests them and prepare a poster, speech, or editorial to convey what they've learned. ★24D

Across the Curriculum

GOVERNMENT The *United States Government Policy and Supporting Positions*, known as the plum book, is one of the most highly sought-after government publications. The book, published every four years following the presidential election, lists over 8,000 choice government jobs, all of which are filled through political appointments and pay anywhere from $85,000 to $150,000 a year. Many of the people appointed to these jobs are friends of the president and campaign fund-raisers and organizers. Critics of big government cite many of the jobs listed as examples of government waste. The Plum Book is published in printed form and also on the World Wide Web. ■

---

program—which was later expanded—for decades after World War II had ended.

Growth in Government Spending

Suppose you take up a new hobby, such as competitive skateboarding. You will need to increase your expenditures to buy the required equipment, including a skateboard, pads, and a helmet. Just as your new hobby increases your expenses, new government programs lead to increased government spending. For example, spending by federal, state, and local governments in the United States in 1950 was about $70 billion. Dramatic increases in the number of government programs

CAREERS... IN ECONOMICS

Civil Engineer

Who plans the construction of your city's power plant, sewage system, city hall, stadiums, office buildings, and many other public structures? The answer is a civil engineer. Civil engineers design and oversee the construction of many projects that are important to a healthy economy.

Some civil engineers work for the government. Others work for private businesses or as consultants. Because there are so many kinds of engineering projects, civil engineers typically specialize. Transportation engineers, for instance, design and test roads, bridges, and other transportation structures. Environmental engineers design and construct such things as water purification systems and recycling plants. Civil engineers—of any specialty—are constantly challenged to design and maintain the many public facilities needed by a growing population.

What kinds of people make good civil engineers? Civil engineers must be detail oriented and excellent problem solvers. For instance, they might be asked to determine the best way to construct a canal through rough terrain to link two bodies of water. Or they might have to determine what kinds of materials are best for building a bridge needed to support heavy freight traffic. They must know how much a given material costs, how strong it is, and how it will stand up under various conditions. Civil engineers also must ensure that their constructions are stable and safe.

Civil engineers undergo extensive study and training. A bachelor's degree in engineering is essential, and many civil engineers earn a master's degree or doctorate. Coursework usually includes mathematics, physics, and computer science. To become a state-registered civil engineer or to obtain a state license, a candidate must have a college degree from a school that is officially approved by the Accreditation Board for Engineering and Technology.

Some civil engineers work for the government, designing public facilities such as this airport terminal.

CHAPTER 12

HOW FEDERAL, STATE, AND LOCAL DOLLARS ARE SPENT

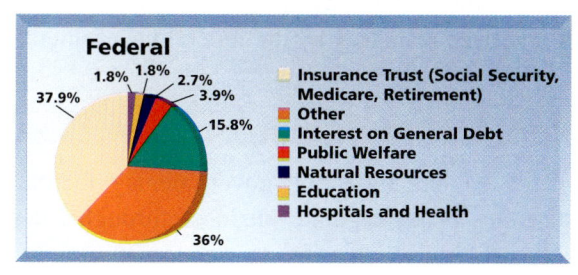

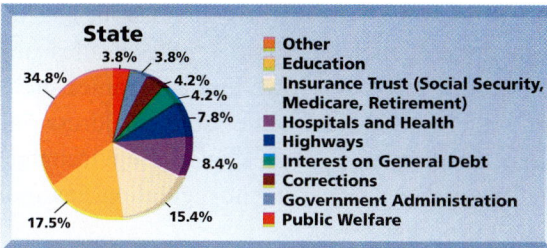

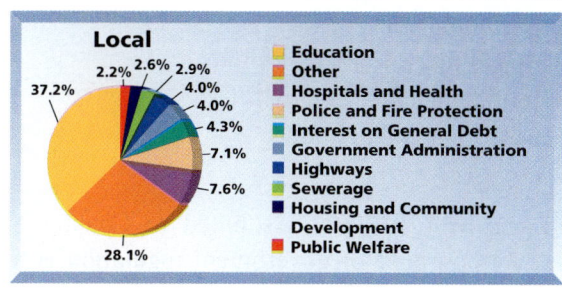

Federal
- 1.8% 1.8% 2.7%
- 3.9%
- 37.9%
- 15.8%
- 36%
  - Insurance Trust (Social Security, Medicare, Retirement)
  - Other
  - Interest on General Debt
  - Public Welfare
  - Natural Resources
  - Education
  - Hospitals and Health

State
- 3.8% 3.8%
- 34.8%
- 4.2%
- 4.2%
- 7.8%
- 8.4%
- 17.5%
- 15.4%
  - Other
  - Education
  - Insurance Trust (Social Security, Medicare, Retirement)
  - Hospitals and Health
  - Highways
  - Interest on General Debt
  - Corrections
  - Government Administration
  - Public Welfare

Local
- 37.2%
- 2.2% 2.6% 2.9%
- 4.0%
- 4.0%
- 4.3%
- 7.1%
- 7.6%
- 28.1%
  - Education
  - Other
  - Hospitals and Health
  - Police and Fire Protection
  - Interest on General Debt
  - Government Administration
  - Highways
  - Sewerage
  - Housing and Community Development
  - Public Welfare

Source: *Statistical Abstract of the United States: 2000*

FIGURE 12.3 Federal, state, and local governments have different spending priorities.

---

meant that by 1996, total government expenditures had risen to more than $3 trillion, or more than $11,760 **per capita,** or per person.

The federal government spends the largest share of this figure—some $1.7 trillion in 1996, for example. About half of federal expenses go toward paying for insurance benefits and interest on debts. Other federal expenses include national defense, education, public hospitals, housing and community development, and law enforcement.

State and local governments also spend large sums of money—an average of more than $3.8 billion a day, or $44,318 a second, in 1996. Spending by state governments, for example, rose from about $15 billion in 1950 to nearly $860 billion in 1996. During the same time, spending by local governments increased from about $17 billion to more than $794 billion.

The largest expenditures in state and local budgets are generally for education, public welfare, and road construction and maintenance, accounting for just less than 45 percent of all state and local spending. The rest goes to public libraries, hospitals and health care, police and fire protection, public buildings, sanitation services, and government administration. (For a breakdown of government spending, see Figure 12.3.)

SECTION 1 REVIEW

1. Define and Explain:
- embargo
- per capita

2. Comparing: Copy the Venn diagram below. Use it to compare how federal, state, and local government dollars are spent.

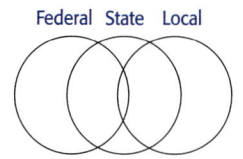

Federal State Local

3. Finding the Main Idea
a. Why has the U.S. government grown in size?
b. Why has U.S. government spending increased over the years?

4. Writing and Critical Thinking
Drawing Inferences: Look at Figure 12.3. The majority of the federal budget goes to "Other" expenses. What might at least three of those expenses be?
Consider:
- responsibilities of the federal government
- federal government departments

Homework Practice Online keyword: SM3 HP12

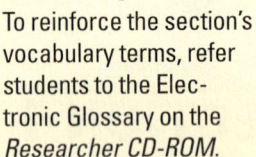

SECTION 2

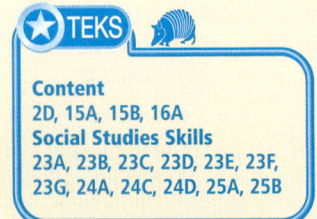

ECONOMIC GOALS

READ TO DISCOVER
1. Why does the government apply regulations to businesses?
2. How does the government work to provide public goods?
3. In what ways does the government promote individuals' well-being?
4. How does the government work to stabilize the economy?

ECONOMICS DICTIONARY
economic stabilization
privatization
transfer payment

Think about what government does for you. Does your community have garbage collection? Do you use a public library? What kind of financial aid is available to students who plan to attend college?

Currently, the federal, state, and local governments provide these services—and many others—to you and other citizens. This has not always been the case, however. Throughout much of U.S. history, popular acceptance of laissez-faire economic practices limited the government's economic role. As government grew, however, it took on an increasing number of functions that affected the economy.

Specifically, federal, state, and local governments began to regulate businesses, provide public goods, promote citizens' economic well-being, and stabilize the economy. Today the governments share the first three of these goals, while economic stabilization is practiced primarily by the federal government.

Regulating Business

In the United States, all governments—federal, state, or local—regulate business through rules and procedures that guide economic activity. (See Figure 12.4 for information about federal regulatory agencies.) Some of these rules and procedures affect the ways that companies interact with individuals, while others address the effect of company policies on the environment and the market. Government regulation has four main purposes:

▶ preventing abuses,
▶ protecting consumers,
▶ limiting negative externalities, and
▶ promoting competition.

Preventing Abuses As noted in Chapter 8, one key purpose of government regulation is to

ROLE OF GOVERNMENT *Most local governments maintain parks for citizens' recreational use.* **What are two other ways that government affects your life?**

284 CHAPTER 12

FEDERAL REGULATORY AGENCIES

Agency	Abbreviation	Year	Description
Interstate Commerce Commission	ICC	1887–1995	regulated rates and other aspects of commercial transportation by railroad, highway, and waterway
Federal Trade Commission	FTC	1914	administers antitrust laws forbidding price-fixing, other deceptive or fraudulent practices, and unfair competition
Food and Drug Administration	FDA	1927	enforces laws to ensure purity, effectiveness, and truthful labeling of food, drugs, and cosmetics; inspects production and shipment of these products
Federal Communications Commission	FCC	1934	licenses and regulates radio and television stations; regulates interstate telephone and telegraph rates and services
Securities and Exchange Commission	SEC	1934	regulates and supervises the sale of listed and unlisted securities and the brokers, dealers, and investment bankers who sell them
National Labor Relations Board	NLRB	1935	administers federal labor-management relations laws; settles labor disputes; prevents unfair labor practices
Federal Aviation Administration	FAA	1958	regulates air commerce; sets standards for pilot training, aircraft maintenance, and air traffic control; controls U.S. airspace
Equal Employment Opportunity Commission	EEOC	1964	investigates and rules on charges of discrimination by employers and labor unions
Environmental Protection Agency	EPA	1970	coordinates federal programs to protect public health and to safeguard and improve the natural environment—air, water, and land
National Highway Traffic Safety Administration	NHTSA	1970	enforces laws to promote motor vehicle safety and to protect drivers, passengers, and pedestrians; sets safety and fuel economy standards for new motor vehicles produced or sold in the U.S.
Occupational Safety and Health Administration	OSHA	1970	investigates accidents at the workplace; enforces regulations to protect employees at work
Consumer Product Safety Commission	CPSC	1972	enforces safety standards for consumer products
Federal Energy Regulatory Commission	FERC	1977	fixes rates for and regulates the interstate transportation and sale of electricity, oil, and natural gas

FIGURE 12.4 Federal agencies regulate a wide range of activities. **What are the four main purposes of regulating businesses?**

prevent business from taking unfair advantage of workers. For example, you may have noticed the initials *EEOC* in job advertisements in newspapers. The government, through the Equal Employment Opportunity Commission (EEOC), makes and enforces regulations that protect workers from discrimination in hiring or promotions based on age, sex, race, religion, or national origin.

The government also sets standards for working conditions. Federal agencies such as the Occupational Safety and Health Administration (OSHA) monitor businesses and punish violators. According to government statistics,

Across the Curriculum

GOVERNMENT The Americans with Disabilities Act, passed in 1990, protects individuals with disabilities from discrimination and guarantees them equal access to public and workplace facilities, as well as equal accommodations. Before the act was three years old, more than 14,000 people had filed claims of violations of the act. Most cited that they had been unfairly dismissed from their jobs or that they did not receive reasonable accommodations. ■

Transparency

An overhead transparency of Figure 12.4 is available in *Transparency Resources.* See Transparency 50: Federal Regulatory Agencies.

Caption Answer

preventing abuses, protecting consumers, limiting negative externalities, and promoting competition ★2D, 15B, 23A

Enhancing the Lesson

For more information about the federal regulatory agencies listed in Figure 12.4, see the Executive Departments and Agencies section on the *Researcher Online.*

Across the Curriculum

LITERATURE In 1906 Upton Sinclair wrote *The Jungle*, an exposé of the unsanitary practices and gruesome working conditions in the Chicago stockyards and meatpacking industry. His vivid descriptions outraged the nation and led to a public outcry for increased regulation. As a result, that same year Congress passed the Meat Inspection Act, requiring meatpackers to date their products and pass factory inspections. In addition, Congress passed the first Food and Drug Act, authorizing the government to ensure the purity and safety of foods and medicines, tasks that are now the responsibility of the Food and Drug Administration. These acts paved the way for the strict food and drug laws of today. ■

Themes in Economics

THE ROLE OF GOVERNMENT
The Food and Drug Administration (FDA), created in 1927, tests, approves, and sets standards for foods, drugs, chemicals, cosmetics, and medical devices. The agency operates under several laws, including the Federal Food, Drug, and Cosmetic Act, the Fair Packaging and Labeling Act, the FDA Modernization Act, and the Public Health Service Act. The FDA can seize or stop the sale of unapproved or harmful products and prosecute individuals and firms. ■

---

enforcement of OSHA regulations contributed to a more than 75% decrease in workplace fatalities in the last three decades. OSHA regulations continue to get stronger.

Protecting Consumers In addition to passing regulations that protect workers, the government also passes laws that protect consumers, savers, borrowers, and investors. For example, the Food and Drug Administration (FDA) and Consumer Product Safety Commission (CPSC) protect people from products such as unsafe foods, medicines, and toys. The Federal Trade Commission (FTC) and the Federal Communications Commission (FCC) ensure that advertising and sales practices are ethical, truthful, and fair.

The federal government also insures citizens' checking and savings deposits and oversees insured banks to make sure that they follow banking laws. (This topic is more fully explained in Chapter 13.) Federal credit laws also protect borrowers. The Securities and Exchange Commission (SEC), meanwhile, protects investors against fraud in the securities trade. It sets procedures for the registration and sale of stocks and the licensing of securities dealers. The SEC has the power to punish any violators.

Many state and local governments have developed regulations that further protect consumers within state and local boundaries.

Limiting Negative Externalities Another way in which governments protect workers, consumers, and society is through regulations that minimize the negative side effects of some economic activities. As noted in Chapter 5, these side effects are called externalities. Examples of negative externalities include pollution, traffic congestion, and soil erosion. The Environmental Protection Agency (EPA), Nuclear Regulatory Commission (NRC), and other government agencies establish and enforce regulations intended to limit these negative externalities.

For example, in 1991 the EPA awarded a $350,000 grant to Robert Smee, director of the Pacific Materials Exchange in Spokane, Washington. Smee's company allowed companies and cities to sell their waste products, such as scrap steel and used Freon™ (a coolant used in refrigerators and air conditioners), to organizations using these products as raw materials. The EPA grant enabled Smee to develop a computerized network linking waste exchanges across the United States.

Promoting Competition Another purpose of government regulation is to promote competition. As noted in Chapter 6, government accomplishes this goal through the creation and enforcement of antitrust legislation. This type of regulation prevents the formation of monopolies and breaks up existing ones. Critics suggest that such regulations negatively affect the U.S. free enterprise system. The Sherman Antitrust Act of 1890 was the first major antitrust legislation in the United States. Later legislation clarified and strengthened this act.

Providing Public Goods

In addition to regulating businesses and the products they make, governments themselves provide

ROLE OF GOVERNMENT *The Environmental Protection Agency inspects toxic waste sites to protect citizens from negative externalities.* **What are three additional purposes for regulating businesses?**

goods. These public goods are goods and services made available to—and consumed by—all citizens.

Why does the government provide public goods? As noted in Chapter 6, the price system fails to assign the cost of public goods among all consumers. The government, however, *can* accomplish this goal. It can charge—or tax—all citizens for the cost of public goods, even if some people do not use the goods directly. For example, the government charges Maryann Ellis for the public school attended by Jaime Montez, even though Maryann does not have children enrolled in the school.

Additionally, the government can ensure that public goods are available to all citizens who need them. For example, an education is available for Jaime whether he decides to attend a public school or a private one. Furthermore, government must make public goods available to all citizens, though citizens can decide for themselves whether to use those goods. Jaime's parents may indeed choose to enroll him in a private school, but the government cannot prohibit him from gaining an education at a public school if he so chooses.

How are public goods provided to citizens? Federal, state, and local governments frequently share the responsibility of funding and distributing public goods. Governments have sometimes decided, however, that private industry is capable of providing certain public goods.

Shared Responsibility

How do governments share the responsibility for providing public goods? Some goods, such as courts, corrections departments, and law enforcement agencies, are found at each level of government. Other goods are the primary responsibility of one level of government with funding from—and the cooperation of—the other levels. Local government, for example, manages public education but receives state and federal funding to help pay the costs. An exception to this system of shared responsibility is national defense, which is provided solely by the federal government.

Privatization

In recent years some governments have turned to the privatization of public goods. **Privatization** refers either to the sale of government property or to the handling of government services by private businesses. Garbage collection, for example, has been privatized in many cities. Even some hospitals formerly run by the government are now operated by private hospital chains.

Why would a government decide to privatize some of its services? Supporters of privatization justify it in three ways. First, they argue that private firms can operate certain industries more efficiently than the government can. A case in point is mail delivery. The U.S. Postal Service faces considerable competition from private carriers.

ROLE OF GOVERNMENT *A New York City police officer assists victims of the September 11, 2001, attack on the World Trade Center.* **How is local law enforcement funded?**

internet connect

TOPIC: U.S. Social Security System
GO TO: go.hrw.com
KEYWORD: SM3 EC12

Have students access the Internet through the HRW Go site to conduct research on the Social Security Administration. Have students choose different topics, such as: How much money does a retired person receive? What problems does Social Security face? How is the Administration organized? Then have students, individually or in groups, prepare short presentations to teach their classmates what they've learned. ★15A, 24D

Caption Answer

by improving people's standard of living and by redistributing income ★16A, 23A

Many businesses opt to use Federal Express or United Parcel Service (UPS), for example, for mail or packages that must be delivered quickly.

Second, supporters of privatization argue that the government should not compete with private business. The Federal Housing Administration (FHA), for example, provides housing loans in direct competition with private lenders.

Third, supporters point out that government could reduce its costs and pay off some of its debt through the sale of public properties and services. Great Britain, for instance, has raised more than $20 billion since 1979 through the sale of certain government-run businesses.

Opponents of privatization argue that public goods are provided by the federal government because private industry was unable or unwilling to provide those goods to all consumers in the first place. Opponents also point to the tremendous resources that government has available to meet the special requirements and circumstances of providing public goods.

ROLE OF GOVERNMENT *The U.S. government works to promote citizens' economic well-being.* **How does it pursue this goal?** ★TEKS

Promoting Economic Well-Being

The third major economic role of government is promoting economic well-being. To fulfill this function, the government works to improve people's standard of living and to redistribute income among citizens.

Improving the Standard of Living

The standard of living for a nation, state, or region reflects how people live and how many goods and services they consume. Consider your community. Where do you and your neighbors buy food? How many people are likely to own consumer goods such as television sets, computers, and stereo systems? What educational opportunities are available, and how many people take advantage of them?

Diet, product consumption, medical care, and education are four areas that affect people's standard of living and for which the government has shown a high degree of concern. Another is medical care. Programs like Medicare and Medicaid provide health insurance to older Americans and to people with low incomes. The government also helps hospitals cover the cost of treating people who do not have insurance.

How do these programs raise people's standard of living? Obviously, people receiving medical care are helped by this policy as their health improves. At the same time, the general public is helped as regular and preventive health care reduce both the need for expensive long-term care and the likelihood of epidemics—diseases that spread quickly through a population.

Redistributing Income

To promote economic well-being, some government programs also are designed to reduce the gap between rich and poor. The government tries to accomplish this through a system of transfer payments. In a **transfer payment**, the government takes money collected from one group of citizens and distributes (transfers) it to another group of citizens.

Transfer payments work by the government establishing specific aid programs that distribute

288 CHAPTER 12

REDISTRIBUTING INCOME

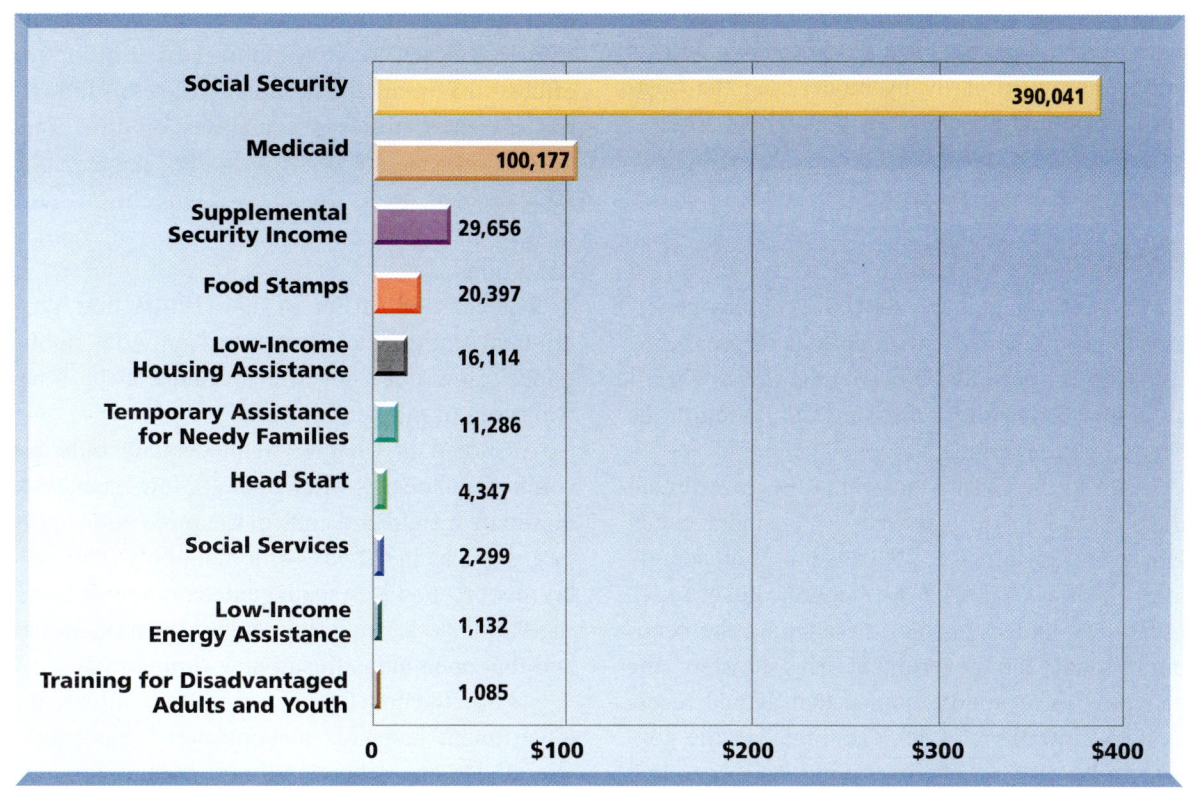

Program	1998 Federal Government Expenditure (in millions)
Social Security	390,041
Medicaid	100,177
Supplemental Security Income	29,656
Food Stamps	20,397
Low-Income Housing Assistance	16,114
Temporary Assistance for Needy Families	11,286
Head Start	4,347
Social Services	2,299
Low-Income Energy Assistance	1,132
Training for Disadvantaged Adults and Youth	1,085

Source: *Statistical Abstract of the United States: 2000*

FIGURE 12.5 The government tries to reduce the gap between rich and poor through transfer payments. **Which three transfer programs account for the greatest government expenditures?**

---

income to anyone who meets certain qualifications. Some of these programs provide incomes for households, while others help pay for medical care, higher education, housing, and job training or retraining.

Some programs are wholly financed and administered by the federal government. The federal government, for example, provides monthly Social Security payments to older people and to people with disabilities. In 1998 the federal government also distributed more than $20 billion worth of food stamps to 21 million low-income Americans. (See Figure 12.5.) Other programs are sponsored by state and local governments. These programs include aid to people who are sick, elderly, and poor—for example, food deliveries and supplemental security income.

Some private businesses and public agencies also receive transfer payments—usually in the form of grants-in-aid—to ensure continued service or production of certain goods. The government, for example, assumes some of the costs of subways, bus lines, commuter trains, and other systems of mass transportation. In this way the government ensures that such services are available and affordable for many people.

Stabilizing the Economy

Although federal, state, and local governments all regulate business, provide public goods, and promote economic well-being, the federal government generally works alone to stabilize the economy. The justification for the government's

ROLE OF GOVERNMENT

SECTION 2 REVIEW ANSWERS

1. privatization (287), transfer payment (288) **16A, 24A**

2. Preventing abuses—EEOC, OSHA; Protecting Consumers—FDA, FTC; Limiting Negative Externalities—EPA, NRC; Promoting Competition—antitrust legislation **2D, 15B, 23A, 23B**

3a. by improving people's standard of living and by redistributing income **15A, 23A**

3b. by moderating the business cycle and by limiting the effects of market failures **16A, 23A**

4. Government regulations tend to limit the U.S. free-enterprise system through rules and ordinances regarding what businesses can and cannot do. This usually means that businesses are in favor of weaker regulations, while individuals—who are protected by government regulation of businesses—are in favor of stronger regulations. **2D, 15A, 15B, 23A, 23E**

---

role in stabilizing the economy comes from the Constitution's mandate to promote the general welfare of the people. The government stabilizes the economy primarily by moderating the business cycle and by responding to market failures.

Moderating the Business Cycle

As noted in Chapter 10, the U.S. economy generally follows a pattern, with periods of prosperity followed by periods of economic slowdown, or recession. This pattern of rising and falling of the economy is called the business cycle.

Prior to the Great Depression the government did not attempt to stabilize the business cycle. However, during the 1930s—and increasingly after World War II—the federal government greatly expanded its role in managing the economy. Today the government tries to steer the economy on a middle course that avoids recession and inflation. To achieve this goal, the government today varies its taxing and spending policies and controls the nation's money supply. These government actions are explained more fully in Chapters 14 and 15.

Responding to Market Failures In addition to moderating the business cycle, the government tries to ensure economic stability by limiting the effects of market failures. Market failures include externalities, the inability or unwillingness of private enterprise to produce some public goods, inadequate business competition, and consumers' inadequate knowledge of market conditions.

You learned earlier in this section how government limits externalities and provides public goods. How does government address the other two types of market failures?

As noted in Chapter 6, inadequate business competition occurs when one or a few businesses dominate a field and control the price and supply of a good, as in the case of a monopoly. The government responds to inadequate competition with regulations that prohibit and dissolve monopolies and that open industries to new competitors.

As for the fourth type of market failure, the government responds to consumers' inadequate knowledge of market conditions by ensuring that information is available to the public. You are already familiar with two agencies that act as "friends of consumers": the CPSC and the SEC.

SECTION 2 REVIEW

★ TEKS Q: 1, 2, 3a, 3b, 4

1. **Define and Explain:**
   privatization
   transfer payment

2. **Summarizing:** Use the web organizer to identify the four main ways government regulates business and give examples of each.

   (web organizer: How Government Regulates Business)

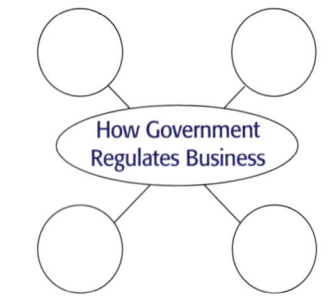

3. **Finding the Main Idea**
   a. Explain how the government works to promote people's economic well-being.
   b. How does government economic policy work to stabilize the economy?

4. **Writing and Critical Thinking**
   Identifying Points of View: Consider the effect government regulations have on the free-enterprise system. Which people or groups favor stronger regulations and which favor weaker regulations?
   Consider:
   • government regulations on businesses
   • government promotion of the common good

Homework Practice Online
keyword: SM3 HP12

SECTION 3

GOVERNMENT AND THE PUBLIC

READ TO DISCOVER
1. How does the government determine the public interest?
2. What consequences may result from government promotion of the public interest?
3. How can individuals and interest groups affect government policies?

ECONOMICS DICTIONARY
interest group
lobbyist

You have learned that the government develops economic policies to promote the public interest. Determining the public interest—and how best to promote it—is a complicated process, however. Government economic policies and regulations affect all aspects of production and consumption. Even well-intentioned economic policies can fail to achieve their goals.

Fortunately, in a free-enterprise system citizens can act to influence government policies. Individuals can support or protest issues through voting and other forms of political activism. People also can work together in groups to express their interests and concerns. This interaction between the government and citizens ensures that careful attention is paid to the public interest.

Identifying the Public Interest

How do governments identify the public interest? The public interest is based on the collective needs of many people. Sometimes these needs can conflict with personal preferences. Although the government acknowledges the importance of individual choice in the U.S. economy, public interest can sometimes outweigh the wishes of an individual or a specific group.

For example, as noted in Chapter 8, the government may forbid a group of workers to strike if their doing so would endanger the health or safety of the public. The government recognizes that workers must be able to voice their concerns about business practices or working conditions, but believes that in some cases the specific concerns of a particular group may conflict with the public interest as a whole.

CASE STUDY

AmeriCorps

ROLE OF GOVERNMENT Sometimes the government's attempts to act in the public interest can become controversial. For example, many people have opposed AmeriCorps, the national service program introduce by President Bill Clinton in 1994.

AmeriCorps is part of a nonprofit organization funded by the federal government. Each of the program's 40,000 AmeriCorps participants receives a salary to cover expenses as well a $4,725 grant to attend college. In return, he or she works full-time for

ROLE OF GOVERNMENT *Believing it would endanger the public interest, President Ronald Reagan outlawed an air traffic controllers' strike in 1981.* **How do governments identify the public interest?**

SECTION 3

GOVERNMENT AND THE PUBLIC

Lesson Plans
For teaching strategies, see Lesson 12.3 located at the beginning of this chapter or the One-Stop Planner Strategy 12.3.

Economics Dictionary
To reinforce the section's vocabulary terms, refer students to the Electronic Glossary on the *Researcher CD-ROM*.

Section Assessment
To assess students' mastery of this section, have them complete Daily Quiz 12.3 in *Daily Quizzes with Answer Key*.

Caption Answer
They weigh the collective needs of the many against the preferences of individuals. ★15A

TEKS

Section 3
Content
1A, 7A, 15A, 15B, 27B
Social Studies Skills
23A, 23B, 23D, 23E, 24A, 24C, 24D, 25A, 25B
Chapter Review
Content
2B, 2D, 7A, 13C, 14A, 15A, 15B, 16A, 18B, 27B
Social Studies Skills
23A, 23D, 23E, 23F, 23G, 24B, 24D

ROLE OF GOVERNMENT 291

Themes in Economics

THE ROLE OF GOVERNMENT

The Office of Management and Budget (OMB), part of the executive branch, reviews budget requests submitted by various government agencies and makes budget recommendations to the president. In addition, the OMB applies cost-benefit analysis to proposed government regulations. That is, the OMB tries to determine whether a regulation's benefits to the public exceed the amount it would cost businesses and others to comply with the regulation.

The supporters of cost-benefit analysis argue that government should be run more like private businesses and that all regulations should be submitted to cost-benefit analysis. Critics argue that it is sometimes hard to put a dollar value on the benefits of a regulation and that one can never put a monetary value on human life. *(Ask students why they might support or oppose applying government regulations to cost-benefit analysis.)* ★15A, 23D

Caption Answer

because the public interest is based on the collective needs of many people, which can sometimes conflict with individuals' needs and wants ★23A

---

a public-service group such as the American Red Cross or Habitat for Humanity.

AmeriCorps members may assist teachers in needy school districts, provide help for disaster victims, or work toward improving health education. In 2001, for example, AmeriCorps volunteers in Amarillo, Texas, tutored 400 educationally at-risk students in reading and other literacy skills.

Nonetheless, the program has its critics. Opponents of AmeriCorps believe that the responsibility to help others lies with the individual and not the federal government. They see government involvement as unnecessary and expensive. Some wonder whether AmeriCorps members are motivated more by the college scholarship than by a sense of compassion or satisfaction in helping others.

AmeriCorps supporters, on the other hand, argue that the program encourages the spirit of community service. These supporters claim that the program directly benefits two groups by increasing the services available to disadvantaged people and by enabling more students to pursue a college education. Finally, they believe the AmeriCorps program teaches the value of public service to young men and women, making them more likely to continue to volunteer as they grow older.

ROLE OF GOVERNMENT *AmeriCorps is a national service program for young Americans. Why is determining the public interest sometimes controversial?*

Effects of Government Regulation

What are the consequences of policies and regulations related to public interest programs such as AmeriCorps? Such government actions affect all aspects of production, distribution, and consumption, including

- prices,
- services,
- profits, and
- productivity.

Prices Government regulation often causes prices to increase. For example, if the government determines that taxi rides are in the public interest, it may try to ensure a minimum supply of taxis by setting a price floor to keep prices from falling below a certain level. Even if a lower price would increase quantity demanded and bring a higher profit, suppliers cannot set prices of their own choosing. Prices thus tend to be higher when a price floor is in effect.

Government regulation also may increase prices indirectly by raising production costs. Suppose that the Petro Plenty Chemical factory pumps its waste products into a nearby river. To protect the public's interest in a clean environment, new government rules require Petro Plenty to limit the amount of waste it produces. These regulations require Petro Plenty to introduce new processing techniques that increase the costs of production. The higher costs are passed on to consumers in the form of higher prices.

Services Different types of government regulation can affect services in different ways. In some cases, regulation can encourage greater levels of service. Suppose that the View Now Cable Television Company wants to offer 32 cable channels to subscribers. Local regulations, however, require the cable company to carry 58 channels. In this case, regulations have increased the cable service available to consumers.

Other forms of regulation can reduce service. For example, if regulations force producers to supply services at a lower price than they otherwise would, producers may reduce service to avoid losing money. Suppose that a city council determines that affordable transportation is in the public interest. The council contracts out bus service on the condition that fares cost no more than 25 cents per passenger. The bus company finds, however, that it cannot make a profit at this price—and reduces bus service to some areas.

Profits Private companies' profits may increase when government regulations result in higher prices and difficult market entry. Generally, however, regulation tends to lower profits. This fact may become most obvious when regulations are lifted.

Consider the airline industry. When the elimination of federal regulations on airline service was concluded in 1984, airlines were able to reorganize their flight patterns. By reducing the number of nonstop flights and requiring many passengers to change planes at central connecting locations, some airlines were able to increase their profits dramatically.

Productivity In some cases, government regulation causes labor productivity to decline. As workers spend more time meeting government regulations instead of producing goods and services, the number of goods and services produced per worker declines.

Suppose that Eric and Laura Pineda own a fishing boat and employ five workers who catch 750 fish per day. Productivity, therefore, can be measured at 150 fish caught per worker per day (750 ÷ 5 = 150).

The government determines that the public interest is best promoted by limiting current fishing to ensure that fish are available both now and in the future. As a result, new government regulations require fishing-boat workers to throw back any fish under a certain length.

How does the regulation affect productivity? Some of the workers' time now must be spent sorting the fish and throwing back those that do not meet the new size requirement. Either the five workers must spend less time fishing in order to sort the fish, or Eric and Laura must hire additional workers to sort the fish. Either choice reduces the average number of fish caught per worker, and therefore results in decreased levels of productivity.

Influencing Government

You have learned how government tries to promote the public interest through regulation. Suppose, however, that people are opposed to these rules. How can individual citizens make their voices heard and try to influence government decisions?

In the United States, government regulations can be changed if the public opposes them. Both individuals working alone and groups of people working together can affect the policies and direction of government.

Courtesy of the Chattanooga Times

ROLE OF GOVERNMENT *Government deregulation of the airline industry was designed to lower the cost of air travel. According to this cartoon, what are the consequences of deregulation?*

Caption Answer
lower prices, but poorer service 15B, 23A, 23E

Themes in Economics

THE ROLE OF GOVERNMENT
President Ronald Reagan, in the 1982 *Economic Report of the President*, endorsed submitting government regulations to a cost-benefit analysis.

"Many Federal rules have yielded benefits to the public.... Regulations, however, can also impose substantial costs on society.... The resources used to comply with regulations are diverted from other activities, with a resultant loss in productivity and economic growth....

"The motive for incorporating benefit-cost analysis into the regulatory decision-making process is to achieve a more efficient allocation of government resources by subjecting the public sector to the same type of efficiency tests used in the private sector. In making an investment decision, for example, business executives compare the costs to be incurred with the expected revenues. The investment is... pursued only if the expected costs are less than the expected revenues....

"The aim of requiring agencies to perform benefit-cost analysis is to... eliminate regulatory actions that, on balance, generate more costs than benefits."

Across the Curriculum

GOVERNMENT Political action committees (PACs) are organizations that raise money for political candidates to encourage them to support their causes. PACs serve as fund-raising machines for interest groups, labor unions, and corporations. The amount of money PACs can raise is not limited, but restrictions limit the amount of money a PAC can give to any one candidate to $5,000. PACs have grown in number and in size since the 1970s and have become a major force in national campaigns. ■

Profiles in Economics

For a biography of Ralph Nader and other noted people in economics, refer students to the Biographies section on the *Researcher Online*.

Enhancing the Lesson

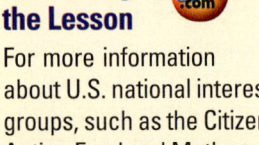

For more information about U.S. national interest groups, such as the Citizen Action Fund and Mothers Against Drunk Driving (MADD), see the National Organizations section on the *Researcher Online*.

Caption Answer

People can vote for public officials who have an economic philosophy similar to their own. ★1A, 23A

Role of Individuals One way that individuals may take action is by voting. By electing public officials with an economic philosophy similar to their own, citizens make their economic opinions heard. For example, the victory of President George W. Bush over opponents Al Gore and Ralph Nader in the 2000 election indicated support for his tax-cut proposal. Elected representatives are particularly sensitive to public opinion because they must satisfy voters if they hope to be re-elected.

To ensure that you are using your vote wisely, you must become informed about the economy and the candidates. Identify the issues that concern you and find out how each candidate plans to address your interests. For example, what are the candidates' stands on taxes, the minimum wage, and job training? By paying attention to the words and actions of each person running for office, you can determine which one would best represent your views.

Another way individuals can influence the government's impact on the economy is through political activism. For example, Ralph Nader, one of the most well-known activists in the United States, has worked for more than 30 years to influence government policy and hold corporations accountable for their practices.

During the late 1950s Nader became concerned about the number of fatal car accidents taking place on the nation's highways. As a result, he began to research the connection between legal standards for safety and the way automobiles were designed. Nader believed that many more people would survive car accidents if their vehicles were made crashworthy—equipped with features such as padded dashboards, seat belts, collapsible steering wheels, and stronger door latches. To publicize the results of his research and to improve government safety regulations, Nader testified before state legislatures in 1965 and published the book *Unsafe at Any Speed*.

Nader soon gained national attention. After getting the media interested in the issue, he persuaded members of Congress to hold hearings on regulations for the auto industry. His actions contributed to passage of the National Traffic and Motor Vehicle Safety Act of 1966. Many of the automobile safety features we take for granted today were developed and required by law as a result of Nader's car-safety crusade.

Role of Interest Groups Individuals also may take action collectively as part of interest groups. An **interest group** is an organization of citizens who work together to achieve their common goals, often by influencing government policy. Interest groups frequently achieve results when individuals acting alone could not.

In the United States, interest groups represent diverse ethnic and minority groups, labor unions, farmers, and businesspeople. Some large interest groups, such as those involved with unions, have considerable influence because they represent the votes of millions of members.

How do interest groups try to influence economic policy? Interest groups may give money to political campaigns and encourage group members to vote for a particular candidate.

In addition to his work as an individual activist, Ralph Nader has also led several interest groups. "Nader's Raiders"—as the groups' members often were called—wrote and published many reports on industrial hazards, pollution, unsafe products, and government neglect of safety laws. These groups' efforts encouraged the

ROLE OF GOVERNMENT *In the United States, the public can change government economic policy.* **How does voting exercise this influence?** ★TEKS

Economics in Action

Young Lobbyist

Suppose that you believe the government should invest more money in protecting the environment. How would you make your views known?

You might try writing letters to your elected representatives, urging them to propose legislation to raise the level of funding for environmental protection. Before the next election, you also could research the various candidates' positions on the issue and then suggest to people of voting age that they vote for the candidate who supports your position. You could join a pressure group that has lobbyists who urge politicians to support the same goal. The most direct way to voice your opinions, however, would be to become a lobbyist yourself.

At age 21 Dan Stafford became director of the Austin, Texas, field office of the grassroots citizen organization United States Public Interest Research Group (U.S. PIRG). His job was to lobby government officials, urging them to support a variety of political and economic initiatives ranging from environmental issues to consumer protection and campaign finance reform.

Dan began working for PIRG as a canvasser, going door to door through neighborhoods asking people to sign petitions, write letters to their representatives, and donate money to advance the group's goals. He quickly assumed the position of field manager, in charge of coordinating canvassing efforts. Within a year he became director of the Austin field office.

Today, Dan works in the Berkeley, California, office. Dan believes PIRG should build "strength through the grassroots and then . . . go and meet with our representatives and do the lobbying." He simply follows through on these goals from a new location.

A significant portion of the issues that PIRG confronts involve economics. In addition to his efforts to strengthen environmental protection, Dan's group has defended consumers' rights to sue makers of dangerous or defective products. The group also has forced the recall or modification of dangerous toys through its annual toy safety study. In addition, PIRG recently published reports documenting how fees have skyrocketed for basic banking services such as automated teller machine (ATM) transactions.

Why would someone want to become a lobbyist? Dan points to the influence of his parents. His father—a minister—and his mother—a nurse—were both politically active. "Watching my parents be active in other people's lives and working to help the community . . . instilled that (drive) in me."

Dan believes that young people who work for pressure groups and become lobbyists "actually put themselves to use and have responsibility. You feel like part of a team. I can't stand up and say I single-handedly did something, but I can say I have been part of a team of people across the country that has been influential in making positive changes."

What Do You Think?

1. Do you believe lobbying is an effective way to make your voice heard? Why or why not?
2. What advantages do you think a young lobbyist brings to the job? What are the possible disadvantages of hiring a young person for this job?

Lobbyists bring a group's concerns to elected representatives to effect change.

Caption Answer

to have someone to express the group's point of view to legislators in hopes of swaying them to support the group's political agenda ⭐23A

SECTION 3
REVIEW ANSWERS

1. interest group (294), lobbyist (296) **24A**

2. prices may rise; service may get better or worse; profits may increase, but will more likely decrease; productivity may decline **15B, 23A, 23B**

3a. Price floor—raises prices and can lead to inflation; Deregulation—decreases prices, but often increases efficiency and profits **7A, 15B, 23A**

3b. Individuals can vote for public officials with an economic philosophy similar to their own. Interest groups can contribute to political campaigns, encourage group members to vote for particular candidates, or pay a lobbyist to express the group's point of view.

4. The government weighs the collective needs of the nation against the preferences of individuals. People's needs can conflict, making it difficult to identify the policies that will best serve the entire nation. **23A, 23E**

---

creation of several government regulatory agencies, including the Environmental Protection Agency, the Occupational Safety and Health Commission, and the Consumer Product Safety Commission. Nader's bid for the presidency in 2000 was unsuccessful, but it focused political attention on important environmental issues.

Most interest groups advance their plans through **lobbyists**—people hired to express a particular point of view to legislators. Lobbyists research issues and provide lawmakers with valuable information about the effect of upcoming legislation. Lobbying groups affect government policies at all levels of government.

How does a lobbyist exert pressure on elected officials? Suppose that Jeff Brenner is a lobbyist for the Small Business Owners League. The league provides grants and low-interest loans to new businesses. Jeff arranges a meeting with Rebecca Lavoie, a candidate for the state legislature, and tells her that the Small Business Owners League will officially support her in the election. Jeff outlines the league's goals and proposes a piece of legislation that will lower the taxes paid by small businesses. Jeff and other members of the league hope that Rebecca will promote the league's goals if she is elected to the legislature. Rebecca, however, may choose not to support the league's goals and its proposed tax policy once she is elected.

ROLE OF GOVERNMENT *Members of an interest group work together to achieve common goals.* **Why might an interest group hire a lobbyist?**

SECTION 3 REVIEW

⭐TEKS Q: 1, 2, 3a, 4

1. Define and Explain:
interest group
lobbyist

2. Cause and Effect:
Copy the chart below. Use it to determine the effects of government regulations on the economy.

Regulation	Result
Prices	
Services	
Profits	
Productivity	

3. Finding the Main Idea

a. What are the effects on the free-enterprise system of such government policies as a price floor and deregulation?

b. Describe how individuals and interest groups can influence government policy.

4. Writing and Critical Thinking

Analyzing Information: What factors must the government weigh in trying to determine the public interest? Why might the public interest be difficult to identify?

Consider:
- the public interest vs. individual wants
- special interest lobbyists

Homework Practice Online
keyword: SM3 HP12

Economics IN THE NEWS

The Economic Impact of September 11, 2001

The economic effects of the terrorist attacks of September 11, 2001, on the United States were felt throughout the economy.

After hijacked airliners struck the World Trade Center in New York's financial district, the federal government responded to address the crisis. The Federal Aviation Administration ordered all U.S. airplanes worldwide and every plane in U.S. air space to land. This move alone had an enormous effect on the economy as travel and many industries were brought to a halt. The federal government took additional steps to ensure the safety of the population, including federalizing the National Guard to patrol airports for added security.

U.S. stock markets remained closed until Monday, September 17, the longest shutdown since the start of World War II. Once the stock markets reopened, it took about three months before stock prices were back to their pre-September-11 levels.

The shocking attacks contributed to a deepening recession as consumers lost confidence. Vacation travel came to a halt, and tourist destinations like Orlando and Disney World saw airplanes arrive almost empty. The tourism industry nationwide began laying off thousands of workers as hotels, theme parks, and convention centers saw attendance drop record amounts.

Not only did Americans stop traveling, they also stopped buying. In the weeks after September 11, retail sales fell sharply. New home sales and home starts dropped. To revive auto sales, car makers offered interest-free financing on new vehicles.

Many states that relied on sales taxes for revenue to provide public goods and services faced the prospect of deficits as tax revenues fell below budgeted levels. School budgets were cut. Many states saw health and welfare agency budgets reduced, even as the need for these services grew as a result of the faltering economy.

In times of crisis, the government's primary role becomes protecting the population, but the government also has the responsibility of stabilizing the economy. The Federal Reserve pumped billions of dollars into bank reserves and made loans so that no banks or brokerages failed. Over the course of 2001, the Fed cut interest rates eleven times in its attempts to stimulate the economy, reducing them to their lowest levels in 40 years in its effort to head off a recession.

President George W. Bush meets New York firefighters and other rescue workers participating in rescue and recovery operations after the September 11 attack on the World Trade Center.

What Do You Think?

1. How did the federal government react quickly to provide for the public good?
2. How can the Federal Reserve affect the economy?

WHY IT MATTERS TODAY

The impact of the September 11 attacks had long-term effects on many aspects of American life. Visit **CNNfyi.com** or other **current events** sources to find out more about the government's response to the crisis and the steps it has taken to ensure the safety and stability of the country.

Economics in the News Answers

1. by ordering air travel to a halt and federalizing the National Guard

2. by pumping money into bank reserves, making loans to banks, and cutting interest rates **18B**

CHAPTER 12
Review Answers

Writing a Summary

Summaries should focus on the main points of each section. These may be found in the Read to Discover questions at the start of each section. Summaries should also use standard grammar, spelling, sentence structure, and punctuation **24B, 24D**

Identifying Ideas

embargo (280), per capita (283), privatization (287) transfer payment (288) interest group (294), lobbyist (296) **13C, 14A**

Understanding Main Ideas

1. population growth, changing public attitudes, a rising standard of living, and national emergencies **23A**

2. preventing abuses, protecting consumers, limiting negative externalities, and promoting competition **2D, 23A**

CHAPTER 12 Review

3. When the price system fails to distribute the cost of public goods among all citizens, the government must do so to ensure that they are available to all who need them. **23A**

4. by improving standard of living and by redistributing income **15A, 16A, 23A**

5. by regulating business, providing public goods, promoting citizens' economic well-being, and stabilizing the economy **16A, 23A**

6. prices may rise; service may get better or worse; profits may increase, but will more likely decrease; productivity may decline **7A, 15B, 23A**

Reviewing Themes

1. promoting economic well-being **16A, 23A**

2. Answers will vary. Students might suggest that the government's role in the economy is likely to expand as the population grows, or that business lobbyists will get stronger and reduce the government's role in the economy. **15A, 23A, 23D**

3. Productivity would likely increase since private businesses are more likely to use cost-benefit analyses. **2B, 23A**

Thinking Critically

1. Government regulations protect consumers' rights; businesses benefit because protected consumers are loyal customers. Businesses may suffer a loss of productivity and profit; consumers lose freedom from government interference. **7A, 15A, 15B, 23A**

298

Writing a Summary

Using standard grammar, spelling, sentence structure, and punctuation, write a summary of the information in this chapter.

Identifying Ideas

Identify the following terms and explain their significance.

1. cabinet
2. embargo
3. per capita
4. economic stabilization
5. privatization
6. epidemic
7. transfer payment
8. deregulation
9. interest group
10. lobbyist

Understanding Main Ideas

SECTION 1 (pp. 279–83)

1. What are the key factors that encourage government expansion?

SECTION 2 (pp. 284–90)

2. What are the main purposes of government regulation of businesses?
3. Why do governments provide public goods?
4. How does the government promote economic well-being?

SECTION 3 (pp. 291–96)

5. How does the government work to promote the public interest?
6. What effects can regulation have on prices, service, profits, and productivity?

Reviewing Themes

1. **Income Distribution** With income transfers, what goal of economic policy is the government fulfilling?

2. **Role of Government** How is the government's role in the economy likely to change in the future?

3. **Productivity** What effect would the privatization of government services have on worker productivity?

Thinking Critically

1. **Comparing and Contrasting** Compare and contrast the advantages and disadvantages of government regulations on the free-enterprise system.

2. **Sequencing** How has the United States moved from a laissez-faire government economic policy to one of complex regulations?

3. **Drawing Inferences** When regulating new technology or scientific discoveries, what factors should the government consider?

4. **Making Predictions** Based on the history of the creation of government regulatory agencies, do you think there will be more or fewer federal agencies created in the future? Give evidence to support your answer.

5. **Generalizations** Many states are experimenting with privatization of government-run social services. If these experiments are successful, what are the states likely to do?

Writing about Economics

Refer to the list you made in your Economics Notebook at the beginning of this chapter. Which of these effects of government might be considered economic? Explain your answer in your Notebook.

298 CHAPTER 12

Building Social Studies Skills

Interpreting the Chart

Study the chart showing people's opinions of the economy in 2001. Then use it to help you answer the questions that follow.

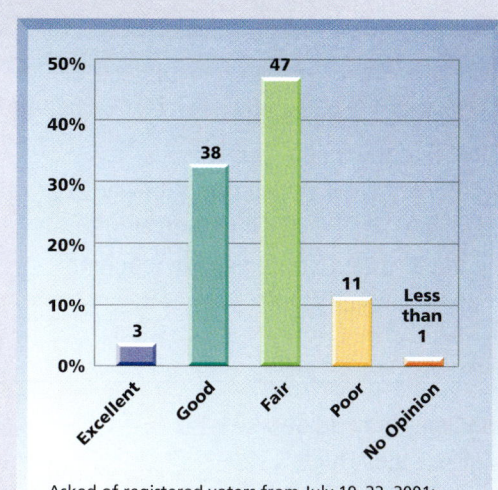

[Bar chart showing:
- Excellent: 3%
- Good: 38%
- Fair: 47%
- Poor: 11%
- No Opinion: Less than 1%

Asked of registered voters from July 19–22, 2001: "How would you rate economic conditions in this country today — excellent, good, only fair, or poor?"]

Source: *The Gallup Poll News Service*

1. What percentage of people probably believed that the government should be doing more to affect the economy?
   a. 1 percent
   b. 11 percent
   c. 58 percent
   d. 99 percent

2. How might the information in this poll have predicted presidential approval?

Analyzing Primary Sources

Read the following excerpt from Franklin D. Roosevelt's first inaugural address. Then answer the questions that follow.

"Our greatest primary task is to put people to work. This is no unsolvable problem if we face it wisely and courageously. It can be accomplished in part by direct recruiting by the government itself, treating the task as we would treat the emergency of a war, but at the same time, through this employment, accomplishing greatly needed projects to stimulate and reorganize the use of our natural resources. . . .

"If I read the temper of our people correctly, we now realize as we have never before, our interdependence on each other; that we cannot merely take, but we must give as well; that if we are to go forward we must move as a trained and loyal army willing to sacrifice for the good of a common discipline. . . ."

3. Roosevelt believed that government should be—
   a. directly involved in the economy
   b. indirectly involved in the economy
   c. involved in the economy only when necessary
   d. not involved in the economy

4. Why did Roosevelt believe people must be "willing to sacrifice for the good of a common discipline"?

Alternative Assessment

Building Your Portfolio

Create a pie chart showing what percentage of your school district's funds comes from federal, state, and local government. Write a caption explaining how these funds are spent. Then include your pie chart in a report regarding the role government plays in the administration of your school. Be sure to include whether or not you agree with the current role of the government. What more could the government be doing for your school?

internet connect

Internet Activity: go.hrw.com
KEYWORD: SM3 EC12

Access the Internet through the HRW Go site to conduct research on Presidents Ronald Reagan and Bill Clinton. Reagan wanted smaller government and fewer government programs, but Clinton started AmeriCorps—a new program. Create a poster comparing these two well-known American presidents and their policies.

---

2. Laissez-faire government began with the country's founding; change began with the Sherman Anti-trust Act; then the most profound changes came as a result of the Great Depression and World War II. 23A

3. Students should suggest that government needs to consider the needs of individuals and businesses, as well as the collective good. 23A, 23D, 27B

4. Answers will vary. Students might suggest that the trend of more regulation will continue. Others might suggest that the state governments will take over regulatory duties. 15A, 15B, 23A

5. Answers will vary. Students should suggest that all states will probably attempt privatization if it is successful. 15B, 23A

Writing about Economics

Students should explain which effects they consider to be economic and provide support from the chapter. 23D, 24B, 24D

Building Social Studies Skills

1. c 23F, 23G

2. Since most people polled felt that the economy was less than "good", blame is usually placed on the president. 23A, 23F, 23G

3. a 2D, 23E

4. The government works for the good of all of its citizens but cannot achieve the common good without the people's help. 15A, 15B, 23E

ROLE OF GOVERNMENT

CHAPTER RESOURCE MANAGER

CHAPTER 13 — MONEY AND THE BANKING SYSTEM

	OBJECTIVES	PACING GUIDE	REPRODUCIBLE RESOURCES
SECTION 1 **MONEY** (pp. 301–07)	▸ What functions does money serve? ▸ What characteristics must an item have to be used as money? ▸ What are the sources of money's value? ▸ What types of money are used in the United States?	**Regular** 1 day **Block Scheduling** 0.5 day	**ELL** Spanish Study Guide 13.1 **ELL** English Study Guide 13.1 **SM** Mathematics for Economics: Activity 13 **E** Challenge and Enrichment: Activity 13 **S** Simulations and Strategies for Teaching Economics: Activity 13
SECTION 2 **HISTORY OF U.S. BANKING** (pp. 308–14)	▸ What were the views of Federalists and Antifederalists about U.S. banking? ▸ How did the development in the 1860s of nationally chartered banks affect the power of state-chartered banks? ▸ How did the government reform and regulate the banking system after World War II?	**Regular** 1.5 days **Block Scheduling** 1 day	**ELL** Spanish Study Guide 13.2 **ELL** English Study Guide 13.2 **PS** Reading 25: Cross of Gold **PS** Reading 41: Federal Reserve Act of 1913
SECTION 3 **U.S. BANKING TODAY** (pp. 315–22)	▸ What are the most common types of U.S. financial institutions? ▸ How has automation affected banking practices? ▸ What were the results of banking deregulation? ▸ What crises did financial institutions face in the late 1980s?	**Regular** 2 days **Block Scheduling** 1 day	**ELL** Spanish Study Guide 13.3 **ELL** English Study Guide 13.3 **PS** Reading 46: Depository Institutions Deregulation and Monetary Control Act of 1980 **SM** Consumer Economics: Activity 13

Chapter Resource Key

- **PS** Primary Sources
- **RS** Reading Support
- **E** Enrichment
- **S** Simulations
- **SM** Skills Mastery
- **A** Assessment
- **REV** Review
- **ELL** Reinforcement and English Language Learners
- Transparencies
- CD-ROM
- Video
- Videodisc
- Internet
- Holt Presentation Maker Using Microsoft® PowerPoint®
- TEKS and TAKS

TECHNOLOGY RESOURCES	REINFORCEMENT, REVIEW, AND ASSESSMENT
• One-Stop Planner: Lesson 13.1 • Researcher Online • Homework Practice Online • CNN Presents Economics: Money Makes the World Go Round • Transparency 52 • Global Skillbuilder CD-ROM	REV Section 1 Review, p. 307 A Daily Quiz 13.1 ★ TAKS Every Day!
• One-Stop Planner: Lesson 13.2 • Researcher Online • Homework Practice Online • Global Skillbuilder CD-ROM	REV Section 2 Review, p. 314 A Daily Quiz 13.2 ★ TAKS Every Day!
• One-Stop Planner: Lesson 13.3 • Researcher Online • Homework Practice Online • Transparency 53 • Global Skillbuilder CD-ROM	REV Section 3 Review, p. 322 A Daily Quiz 13.3 ★ TAKS Every Day!

Chapter Review and Assessment

SM Global Skillbuilder CD-ROM
   HRW Go site
REV Reteaching Activity 13
REV Chapter 13 Review, pp. 324–325
A Chapter 13 Test Generator (on the One-Stop Planner)
A Chapter 13 Test
A Alternative Assessment Handbook

One-Stop Planner CD-ROM

It's easy to plan lessons, select resources, and print out materials for your students when you use the *Texas One-Stop Planner CD-ROM with Test Generator.*

---

internet connect

HRW ONLINE RESOURCES
Go To: go.hrw.com
Then type in a keyword.

TEACHER HOME PAGE
KEYWORD: SM3 Teacher

CHAPTER INTERNET ACTIVITIES
KEYWORD: SM3 EC13
Choose an activity to:
▸ research U.S. currency.
▸ research foreign currency and exchange rates.
▸ learn about historical figures associated with the banking system of the United States.

CHAPTER ENRICHMENT LINKS
KEYWORD: SM3 CH13

HOLT RESEARCHER ONLINE
KEYWORD: Holt Researcher

ONLINE ASSESSMENT
Homework Practice
KEYWORD: SM3 HP13
TAKS Review
KEYWORD: SM3 T13
Rubrics
KEYWORD: SS Rubrics

CONTENT UPDATES
KEYWORD: SS Content Updates

HOLT PRESENTATION MAKER
KEYWORD: SM3 PPT13

ONLINE READING SUPPORT
KEYWORD: SS Strategies

CURRENT EVENTS
KEYWORD: S3 Current Events

TEXAS ONLINE RESOURCES
KEYWORD: S3 TX

LESSON 13.1 MONEY

TEXTBOOK PAGES 301–07

HOLT PRESENTATION MAKER
Access Illustrated LECTURE NOTES using Microsoft® PowerPoint® on the One-Stop Planner CD-ROM

OBJECTIVES

- Explain the functions that money serves.
- Describe the characteristics that an item must have to be used as money.
- Identify the sources of money's value.
- Identify and describe the types of money that are used in the United States.

MOTIVATE

Bring several beads, shells, bags of flour, and large stones to class. Set the items on a table in the front of the room and tell students that the items represent the new forms of U.S. money. (You may want to assign each item a value, such as one bag of flour is equivalent to $1 or $5, etc.) Ask students to discuss why each new form of money might be difficult to use in daily economic transactions. For example, if one bag of flour is equivalent to $5, ask students how they would give or receive change if they wanted to buy or sell something worth only $2. Have students consider the durability, portability, divisibility, stability, and acceptability of using each type of item as money. Then tell students that in this lesson they will learn about the functions, characteristics, and forms of money. Have students read Section 1 of the chapter.

TEACH

Building a Vocabulary

Have students use spiral notebooks to create an Economics Dictionary to be used throughout the chapter. This dictionary might be used as an activity at the start of each new section or as a learning aid for students having difficulty or sheltered English students. List words that students will be expected to know for this section on the chalkboard. Have students use the information provided in the text or on the *Researcher CD-ROM* to list, define, and give an example of each term.

Understanding Main Concepts, Evaluating Information

Ask students to list and describe the three functions that money serves in the United States *(medium of exchange, standard of value, and store of value)*. Have students summarize money's advantages over barter, based on these three functions of money.

Next, ask students how they can determine if a particular item would work well as money. *(Students should list and describe the five characteristics that an item must have to work well as money—durability, portability, divisibility, stability, and acceptability.)* Remind students of the items that they examined in the Motivate activity. Select one of the items, such as a bag of flour, and have students evaluate how well that item fulfills the five characteristics of money. Next, have the class rate how well the item would work as money based on a scale of 1 to 10. Repeat the activity with a variety of objects. Then have students evaluate how well a quarter, a $1 bill, a personal check, and a credit or debit card fulfills the five characteristics of money.

Demonstrating Understanding, Creating Charts

Organize students into groups of three or four. Tell each group to create a chart that consists of five columns and five rows. In the cells in the first column, tell students to list the five characteristics of money. Then tell each group to select four items that vary in size, availability, and perishability that they would like to use as money. Have students list one of these items above each of the four remaining columns. (You might want to draw an example chart on the chalkboard for students to use as a guide.) Tell students to indicate whether each item fulfills each of the five characteristics of money by writing a *yes* or *no* in the appropriate cell. When students have finished their charts, have a representative from each group explain to the class how one of the items listed in that group's chart fulfills or fails to fulfill each of the characteristics of money. Refer students who need additional instruction on the skills used in this activity to the *Global Skillbuilder* Lesson 12: Creating Graphic Organizers. 23F

Comparing and Contrasting

Remind students that even if a society agrees to use an item as money—such as pieces of paper or coins—the item must still have and retain value. Ask students to list and describe the three sources of value for money *(commodity money, representative money, and fiat money)*. Have students compare and contrast each source of value and provide examples of each.

Remind students that for many years the United States used representative money because the government backed paper money with specie, but that this is no longer the case. Ask students from what source U.S. coins and paper bills derive their value today *(from a government fiat)*.

299C

Then ask students what forms of fiat money are used in the United States today *(coins and paper money, checks or demand deposits, and near money)*. List each form of money on the chalkboard. Discuss with students the differences and similarities between these types of money and how each is used. ⭐23A

Evaluating Information

Have students consider how each form of money fulfills the three functions and the five characteristics of money. For example, to help students understand why checks are considered money but savings accounts and certificates of deposit (CDs) are considered near money, have students evaluate whether each fulfills the three functions of money. Explain that because savings accounts and CDs cannot be used directly to buy goods or to pay debts, they do not fulfill the function of medium of exchange. However, because they can be readily converted to cash, they are considered near money.

CLOSE

Have students write a short essay on the role of money in the United States and the benefits of using each of the three different forms of money discussed in the chapter. You might want to have students complete this activity as a homework assignment. Students may want to include their essays in their portfolios. ⭐24D

OPTIONS

Gifted Learners

If you have or can obtain one, bring to class a Susan B. Anthony $1 coin and a Sacagewea $1 coin and have students pass the coins around. Tell students that in 1979 the United States replaced the Eisenhower $1 coin with a new, smaller $1 coin that carried the image of Susan B. Anthony. Explain to students that the new coin did not catch on with the U.S. population, however, and the government ceased minting it in 1981. Have interested students research the reasons why the Susan B. Anthony coin was unpopular. Students should consider each of the functions and characteristics of money in the United States when evaluating why the coin did not catch on. To research the topic, students can use the library, in-class resources, and the Internet. Students also may want to interview bank tellers, coin collectors, and adults in their community to learn their opinions about the Susan B. Anthony coin.

Tell students to use their findings to compare the characteristics of the Susan B. Anthony coin and the new $1 coin. Students should write reports that describe the problems associated with the Susan B. Anthony coin and explain how the design of the new coin may or may not solve those problems. Students may want to include their reports in their portfolios. ⭐24D

Interpersonal Learners, Visual-Spatial Learners

Organize students into groups of three or four. Tell each group to contact a representative at the U.S. Mint or someone at a local bank to learn about the coins and paper money that are currently being issued in the United States. Students should research both commemorative and regular currency. Each group should then prepare a poster or chart that lists and describes the variety of coins and paper money available in the United States today. Refer students who need additional instruction on the skills used in this activity to the *Global Skillbuilder* Lesson 12: Creating Graphic Organizers. ⭐24D

Linguistic Learners

Have students investigate the steps that various countries have taken to prevent or combat the counterfeiting of money. Have students use the *Holt Researcher Online*, the library, in-class resources, the Internet, and information from business journals or newspapers to conduct their research. Students also might want to contact a representative at the Federal Bureau of Investigations to learn about how they investigate counterfeiting and the punishments for those who are caught counterfeiting money. Have students present their findings in a written report. Students may want to include their reports in their portfolios. ⭐24D

REVIEW

Have students complete the Section 1 Review on page 307. Use the answers in the Annotated Teacher's Edition to assess student mastery of this section.

ASSESS

To assess student mastery of this section, have students complete Daily Quiz 13.1 in *Daily Quizzes with Answer Key*. For additional assessment options, see *Alternative Assessment Handbook* on the *One-Stop Planner CD-ROM*.

ADDITIONAL RESOURCES

Bressett, Kenneth, compiler. *Guide Book of United States Currency*. 1999. Golden Books Publishing Co.

Doty, Richard G. *America's Money, America's Story*. 1998. Krause Publications.

Weatherford, Jack. *History of Money: From Sandstone to Cyberspace*. 1998. Three Rivers Press.

United States Currency. (software, IBM/Macintosh). The World of Money Series. Projected Learning Programs Inc.

299D

LESSON 13.2 HISTORY OF U.S. BANKING

TEXTBOOK PAGES 308–14

HOLT PRESENTATION MAKER
Access Illustrated LECTURE NOTES using Microsoft® PowerPoint® on the One-Stop Planner CD-ROM

OBJECTIVES

- Discuss the Federalist and Antifederalist views about U.S. banking.
- Explain how the development in the 1860s of nationally chartered banks affected the power of state-chartered banks.
- Describe how the government reformed and regulated the banking system after World War I.

MOTIVATE

Ask students to imagine the following scenario: The year is 1845. They are merchants living in a small town on the Pennsylvania side of the Pennsylvania–New York border. They trade many types of goods, from copper cookware to plows, to cheese and other farm products. They are interested in trading goods across the border into New York, but Pennsylvania and New York use different currencies with different denominational values. No national currency exists. Besides creating a national currency, what are some ways that merchants might be able to solve their dilemma and successfully trade goods across the state border? Have students discuss the possible benefits and drawbacks that merchants and other people faced during this period when each state, or even each bank, had its own currency. Tell students that in this section, they will learn about the history and development of U.S. banking, including the federal government's decision to create a national currency in the 1860s. Have students read Section 2 of the chapter.

TEACH

Building a Vocabulary

List the vocabulary term for this section on the chalkboard and tell students to add it to their Economics Dictionary. Tell students to use the information provided in the text or on the *Researcher CD-ROM* to list, define, and give an example of this vocabulary term.

Organizing Information

As you go through the lesson, create a time line on the chalkboard or on an overhead transparency of the major events in U.S. banking history. Separate the time line into three main segments, one for each period in the development of banking (1780s to 1860, 1860 to 1913, and 1913 to the present). Have students create a copy of the time line across the top or down the side of the page on which they are taking notes. Refer students who need additional instruction on the skills used in this activity to the *Global Skillbuilder* Lesson 9: Using Time Lines. ★8A, 24D

Comparing and Contrasting, Evaluating Ideas

Remind the class that in the early years of the United States, the nation's leaders knew that a stable form of money and a banking system were necessary, but they did not agree on how to obtain these goals. Explain that the debate over banking reflected a more fundamental debate at the time over the role and power of the federal government versus the state governments. On the chalkboard, write the name of the two groups in opposition over the creation of a national bank—the Federalists and the Antifederalists. Have students list the reasons the Federalists supported and the Antifederalists opposed the creation of a national bank. Write each reason down under the appropriate heading. Have students copy the lists into their notes.

Next, tell students to write down what they think were the advantages and disadvantages of creating a national bank and what would have been the advantages and disadvantages of not creating the bank. After a few minutes, call on students to share some of the items on their lists. Then have the class discuss whether they would have supported or opposed the creation of a national bank in 1791. ★23A

Drawing Conclusions

Review with students the creation of the Second Bank of the United States and President Andrew Jackson's opposition to it. Then ask students to describe the problems that eventually resulted when Jackson vetoed legislation to extend the Second Bank's charter. Tell students that the panic of 1837 led to some reform in banking. Have students describe the nature of this reform *(some states imposed stricter guidelines on state-chartered banks)*. Then ask students why they think government leaders did not establish another national bank at the time, even though the banking system was experiencing a crisis. *(Students might mention the growing sectionalism in the nation and the strong support for states-rights in the South as reasons that leaders opposed a national bank.)* ★23A

Identifying Cause and Effect

Ask students what main development defined the second period in the U.S. history of banking *(the creation of a dual banking system made up of state- and nationally chartered banks)*. Explain to students that after the Civil War, it was necessary to rebuild and strengthen the nation's banking system. On the time line, write the names of the following acts: the National Banking Acts of 1863 and 1864, the Coinage Act of 1873, and the Gold Standard Act of 1900. Have students describe the goals of each act and what each act accomplished. Then call on students to explain how these developments affected state-chartered banks. *(Their power declined as the power of national banking increased.)* ⭐8A

Creating Charts

Ask students what problems still existed in the banking system in the early 1900s. *(The system still did not provide for an efficient method of regulating the amount of money circulating in the economy and it lacked any central organization.)* Ask students what system the government created to try and solve these problems *(the Federal Reserve system)*. Have students describe the successes and failures of the Fed and then name the major event those failures helped create *(the Great Depression)*.

Next, organize students into small groups. Tell each group to create a chart outlining the major reforms and regulations that the government passed between 1930 and the present to improve the banking system. Students should write one or two sentences describing each entry in their charts. When students are finished, have them use their charts to complete the class time line. ⭐8A, 24D

CLOSE

Finish the lesson by having the class give each major segment of the time line a title that summarizes the main aspects of banking during that period. For example, students could title the period in U.S. banking history from 1913 to the present "The Period of Reform and Regulation."

For a homework assignment, you might have students make a larger version of the class time line on a clean piece of paper. Students might enhance their time lines by writing a caption for each segment, illustrating any cause-and-effect relationships, and adding major historical events, such as the Civil War, as points of reference.

OPTIONS

Interpersonal Learners, Linguistic Learners

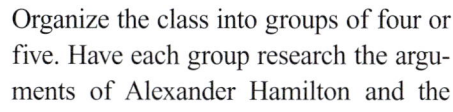

Organize the class into groups of four or five. Have each group research the arguments of Alexander Hamilton and the Federalists for the establishment of a national bank, and the arguments of Thomas Jefferson, James Madison, and the Antifederalists against a national bank. Students might use the library, in-class resources, and the Internet to conduct their research. In addition, the Biographies section of the *Holt Researcher Online* contains profiles of Thomas Jefferson, Alexander Hamilton, and James Madison.

When students are through, organize the class into two groups. Assign one group the role of the Federalists, and the other group the role of the Antifederalists. Tell the two groups to imagine that the year is 1791, and Congress has approved a bill to establish a national bank. President George Washington, however, is unsure that a national bank is constitutional. Before he signs the bill, he would like to hear the opinions of the members of his cabinet (the class). Have the two groups debate the creation of a national bank.

Linguistic Learners

Have students complete Reading 25: "Cross of Gold," located in *From the Source: Readings in Economics and Government with Answer Key*. Discuss the reading and the questions that follow it as a class. Then have each student write a one-page essay responding to William Jennings Bryan's speech. Have students summarize what they think are Bryan's main points, the economic issues or debates that Bryan is addressing, and whether, in students' opinions, Bryan's points are persuasive and convincing. Students may want to include their essays in their portfolios. ⭐24D

REVIEW

Have students complete the Section 2 Review on page 314. Use the answers in the Annotated Teacher's Edition to assess student mastery of this section.

ASSESS

To assess student mastery of this section, have students complete Daily Quiz 13.2 in *Daily Quizzes with Answer Key*. For additional assessment options, see *Alternative Assessment Handbook* on the *One-Stop Planner CD-ROM*.

ADDITIONAL RESOURCES

Chernow, Ron. *The House of Morgan: An American Banking Dynasty and the Rise of Modern Finance.* 1991. Touchstone Books.

Skousen, Mark. *Economics of a Pure Gold Standard.* 1997. Foundation for Economic Education.

Wicker, Elmus. *The Banking Panics of the Great Depression.* (Studies in Monetary and Financial History). 1996. Cambridge University Press.

LESSON 13.3 U.S. BANKING TODAY

TEXTBOOK PAGES 315–22

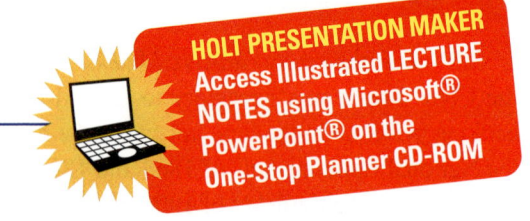

HOLT PRESENTATION MAKER
Access Illustrated LECTURE NOTES using Microsoft® PowerPoint® on the One-Stop Planner CD-ROM

OBJECTIVES

- Identify the most common types of U.S. financial institutions.
- Analyze how automation has affected banking practices.
- Identify and discuss the results of banking deregulation.
- Describe the crises that financial institutions faced in the late 1980s.

MOTIVATE

Examine recent magazines and business journals and find a brief article that discusses the ways in which technology and automation are changing banking. Give copies of the article to each student to read. When students are finished, have them discuss whether they think increased automation of banking is good or bad. Then have students discuss what they think some of the effects of increased automation in banking might be (e.g., more convenience for consumers, but perhaps more structural unemployment for bank tellers). Tell students that in this section they will learn about the state of U.S. banking today as well as recent trends in banking, including automation. Tell students to keep these ideas in mind as they read Section 3 of the chapter. ★8B

TEACH

Building a Vocabulary

List the important terms for this section on the chalkboard and tell students to add them to their Economics Dictionary. Tell students to use the information provided in the text or on the *Researcher CD-ROM* to list, define, and give an example of each vocabulary term.

Classifying Information

Tell students that four major types of financial institutions have emerged as the U.S. banking system has evolved—commercial banks, savings and loan associations, mutual savings banks, and credit unions. On the chalkboard or on an overhead transparency, create a four-column comparative chart. In the left-hand column, list the four types of financial institutions. Above the remaining columns, write the column headings *Main Functions, Customers,* and *Benefits*. Organize the class into groups of three or four. Have each group make a copy of the chart and use the information in Section 3 of the chapter to complete it. When groups are finished, call on group representatives to share their answers. As students supply information, fill in your chart with the correct information. Have students copy the chart into their notes. ★8B, 24D

Evaluating Information, Hypothesizing

Tell students that each of these types of financial institutions has come to rely more and more on automation in recent years. Ask students to recall from the textbook what the four main types of automated banking are *(automated teller machines, automatic clearing house services, point-of-sale terminals, and home banking)*. Keeping students in their same groups, tell each group to write a few sentences describing each type of automation and how it has changed or is changing banking for households and businesses. Then tell each group to make a list of the pros and cons of automated banking. When students are finished, have group representatives share their lists of pros and cons with the class. Encourage student feedback. Then have students discuss what future technological advances they predict for or would like to see occur in banking. ★8B

Analyzing Information, Recognizing Point of View

Tell students that a second recent trend in banking is deregulation. Have students define the term *deregulation*. Write the definition on the chalkboard. Then ask students what the two main results of deregulation have been *(increased competition and an increase in regional, or interstate, banking)*. Have students get into their groups once again. Tell each group to analyze the pros and cons of banking deregulation from the point of view of large banks, small banks, and banking customers. Students might want to create a chart to organize the information. When students are finished, have group representatives share their lists of pros and cons with the class. Encourage student discussion. ★8B

Reading and Writing about Economics

To extend the previous activity, have students complete Reading 46: Depository Institutions Deregulation and Monetary Control Act of 1980, located in *From the Source: Readings in Economics and Government with Answer Key*. When students are finished, have them discuss the reading and the questions that follow it as a class. Then have each student write a short essay describing how this act ended many of the legal differences between commercial banks and other types of financial institutions. ★24D

Solving Problems, Judging Information

Tell students that the third recent trend in banking has been an effort to stabilize financial institutions to deal with increasing numbers of loan defaults and bank failures and to resolve the S&L crisis. Have students return to their groups. Tell each group to draw two columns on a piece of paper and to title one column *Problem* and the other *Solution*. Have groups write brief summaries in the *Problem* column of the three types of problems that financial institutions faced in the 1980s and 1990s. Then tell students to use the *Solution* column to describe how banks and the government worked to solve the three problems. When students have finished, go over their answers with them. Then ask students what else individuals, banks, and the government might do to prevent these types of financial problems from occurring in the future. ⭐15A

CLOSE

Have students consider the advances in electronic banking. Ask them if they think that the United States will operate as a cashless society in the future and, if so, what changes that development might involve. Then have students discuss what the potential benefits and drawbacks of a cashless society might be.

OPTIONS

Gifted Learners

Have interested students research the increasing use of debit cards and smart cards. Students should prepare a written report evaluating the factors that could influence the cards' acceptance and use by consumers in the future. Students should also determine whether debit cards and smart cards have any advantages over the use of checks and credit cards, as well as any disadvantages. Students might use the library, in-class resources, and the Internet to conduct their research. Have students include their reports in their portfolios. ⭐24D

Interpersonal Learners

Have interested students visit a local financial institution and interview one of the institution's officers. Encourage students to focus on trends or recent changes in banking services. Students should make a list of questions before their interview, such as

- How has banking deregulation affected this financial institution?
- What steps has this financial institution taken to discourage loan defaults?
- What changes are occurring in financial institutions, and what new services are being offered?

Have students write a summary of their interview. Students may want to include their summaries in their portfolios. ⭐24D

Visual-Spatial Learners

Have students access the Internet through the HRW Go site to conduct research on the FDIC. Then tell students to design their own Web page that describes the services that the FDIC offers and the importance of these services. Students might also provide links to other Web sites related to banking and banking regulations. Students can find additional information on the FDIC in the Executive Departments section on the *Holt Researcher Online*. ⭐24D

REVIEW

Have students complete the Section 3 Review on page 322. Use the answers in the Annotated Teacher's Edition to assess student mastery of this section.

ASSESS

To assess student mastery of this section, have students complete Daily Quiz 13.3 in *Daily Quizzes with Answer Key*. For additional assessment options, see *Alternative Assessment Handbook* on the *One-Stop Planner CD-ROM*.

RETEACH

For students having difficulty with the lessons, have them complete Reteaching Activity 13. This activity is located in *Reteaching Activities with Answer Key*.

ADDITIONAL RESOURCES

Brandeis, Louis D., Urofsky, Melvin I. (ed.). *Other People's Money and How the Bankers Use It*. (Bedford Series in History and Culture). 1995. Bedford Books.

Cronin, Mary J. (ed.). *Banking and Finance on the Internet*. (Internet Management Series, No. 1). 1997. Van Nostrand Reinhold.

Engler, Henry and James Essinger. *The Future of Banking*. 2000. Financial Times Prentice Hall.

Mayer, Martin. *The Greatest-Ever Bank Robbery: The Collapse of the Savings and Loan Industry*. 1990. Macmillan Press.

Olson, G. N. Banks in Distress: *Lessons from the American Experience of the 1980s*. Kluwer Law International. 2000.

Economics U$A: The Banking System. No. 8. (videotape, 30 min.). The Annenberg/CPB Projects.

Electronic Banking. (software, IBM/Macintosh). The World of Money Series. Projected Learning Programs Inc.

CHAPTER 13

Topics Include
- functions, characteristics, and forms of money
- sources of money's value
- development of the U.S. banking system
- government regulation of banking
- types of financial institutions
- automation of financial transactions
- banking deregulation and its consequences
- financial troubles in banking

Economics Notebook
The Economics Notebook is a journal activity that encourages students to consider basic concepts of economics that relate to their lives. A follow-up notebook activity appears on page 324.

WHY IT MATTERS TODAY
To find additional lesson plans dealing with the Bank Modernization Bill's impact, visit CNNfyi.com or have students complete the ECONOMICS IN THE NEWS activity on page 323.

CNNfyi.com

CHAPTER 13

MONEY AND THE BANKING SYSTEM

Jerry and Ryan are playing basketball. Jerry mentions that he only has chicken feed, and he needs some lettuce.

"What are you talking about?" Ryan asks.

"You know—simoleons," answers Jerry as he sinks his next shot. "Mazuma? Spondulicks?"

"What kind of store sells spondulicks?"

"Why would I go to a store?" Jerry responds. "When I want dough, I go to the bank."

The unfamiliar words Jerry used are slang terms for money. In this chapter you will learn why money is important in economics. Additionally, you will learn about the history of the U.S. banking system.

Economics Notebook
In your Economics Notebook, write a brief paragraph describing what you do with your money in daily life. For example, do you earn money at an after-school job? Do you store money in a checking or savings account?

WHY IT MATTERS TODAY
The full impact of the Bank Modernization Bill is yet to be determined. Use CNNfyi.com or other current events sources to find recent information on the Bank Modernization Bill's impact on consumers and businesses.

CNNfyi.com

SECTION 1

MONEY

READ TO DISCOVER
1. What functions does money serve?
2. What characteristics must an item have to be used as money?
3. What are the sources of money's value?
4. What types of money are used in the United States?

ECONOMICS DICTIONARY
medium of exchange
standard of value
store of value
commodity money
representative money
specie
fiat money
currency
near money

S uppose that you go shopping and decide to buy a jacket. When you pay for the jacket you hand the clerk a live chicken. The clerk refuses to accept the chicken, so you offer him 12 oranges, a walrus tusk, a picture of your cousin, and a coffee mug. The clerk refuses all of these items as well. Finally you open your wallet and offer the clerk several pieces of paper, each bearing a picture of an 18th-century politician named Alexander Hamilton and the number *10* printed in green. Why does the clerk accept these pieces of paper but not the other items? Both the clerk and you recognize the pieces of paper—a form of money—as a guaranteed standard of value in the United States.

What is money, and what gives it value? In this section you will find the answers to these questions as you learn about the functions and characteristics of money, the sources of money's value, and the various forms of money.

Functions of Money

As noted in Chapter 1, it is possible to barter, or exchange goods and services, without using money. In bartering, no medium of exchange is needed. Bartering still occurs in many parts of the world, particularly in traditional economies. Also, in some highly developed economies, individuals barter by performing services for one another. In the United States, for example, a carpenter might exchange his or her services with an electrician or a plumber rather than pay for the services with money.

How does money differ from barter? Money is anything that people commonly accept in exchange for goods and services. Money was developed to overcome the problems associated with bartering, such as those in the example of buying a jacket.

In the United States, money has three basic functions, each of which makes it a more efficient system than barter. Money serves as a medium of exchange, a standard of value, and a

EXCHANGE, MONEY, & INTERDEPENDENCE *Money is anything that people commonly accept in exchange for goods and services.* **What are the three basic functions of money?**

SECTION 1

MONEY

Lesson Plans
For teaching strategies, see Lesson 13.1 located at the beginning of this chapter or the One-Stop Planner Strategy 13.1.

Economics Dictionary
To reinforce the section's vocabulary terms, refer students to the Electronic Glossary on the *Researcher CD-ROM*.

Section Assessment
To assess students' mastery of this section, have them complete Daily Quiz 13.1 in *Daily Quizzes with Answer Key*.

Caption Answer
Money serves as a medium of exchange, a standard of value, and a store of value.

★ TEKS

Content
11A, 15A
Social Studies Skills
23A, 23C, 23F, 23G, 24A, 24C, 24D

MONEY AND THE BANKING SYSTEM 301

Caption Answer

in dollars and cents

Global Connections

The term *dollar* comes from a silver coin that was minted in 1518 in Bohemia (part of what is now the Czech Republic). The coin was circulated widely in Europe, and took on various names. It was known as the *daalder* in Holland, the *daler* in Scandinavia, and the *dollar* in England.

Today, in addition to the United States, other countries that have named their unit of currency *dollar* include Australia, the Bahamas, Barbados, Belize, Bermuda, Brunei, Canada, the Cayman Islands, Dominica, Fiji, Guyana, Jamaica, New Zealand, St. Lucia, St. Vincent, Singapore, the Solomon Islands, Trinidad and Tobago, and Zimbabwe. ■

Caption Answer

The money must be nonperishable and must keep its value over time.

EXCHANGE, MONEY, & INTERDEPENDENCE *Money provides a way to judge the relative values of two products.* **How is the standard of value expressed in the United States?**

store of value. Any item that serves any of these three functions is a type of money.

Medium of Exchange Money primarily is a medium of exchange. A **medium of exchange** is any item that sellers accept as payment for goods and services. As a medium of exchange, money assists in the buying and selling of goods and services, because buyers know that sellers will accept money in payment for products. For example, if you have a part-time job in a restaurant, you will be paid in money rather than in barbecue sauce. You can, of course, use that money to buy barbecue sauce—as well as movie tickets and concert T-shirts—if you so choose.

Standard of Value Another use of money is as a **standard of value**. That is, money provides people with a way to measure the relative value of goods and services by comparing their prices. In this way, people can compare the worth of items such as a television and a bicycle. They also can use prices to judge the relative values of two different models or brands of the same type of item.

In the United States the standard of value is expressed in dollars and cents. Goods and services for sale are marked with a price that shows their value using these forms of measurement. If an audiocassette costs $10 and a pizza costs $5, a consumer knows that the relative value of the cassette is twice that of the pizza.

In addition to allowing consumers to compare prices, money as a standard of value helps clarify opportunity costs. Suppose that Melanie Chu has $10 to spend. She knows that this amount of money allows her to choose either a cassette or two pizzas. If Melanie chooses to buy two pizzas, she gives up the chance to buy the cassette—the opportunity cost of her decision. Consumers like Melanie make more informed choices when they consider both the price and the opportunity cost of their decisions.

Money's function as a standard of value also is important in record keeping. Whether measured in pounds of salt, sacks of rice, bales of cotton, or dollars and cents, businesses need to determine profits and losses. Similarly, governments must be able to figure tax receipts and the cost of expenditures. Money provides a standard system of measurement for these accounting tasks. That is, it allows businesses and the

EXCHANGE, MONEY, & INTERDEPENDENCE *Money's function as a store of value is evidenced by this sunken treasure.* **What two conditions must be met for money to serve as a store of value?**

302 CHAPTER 13

government to calculate their expenses and profits in a recognizable standard of value.

In turn, this system of measurement allows investors to compare two businesses' performance by looking, for example, at how many dollars they made in profit during a specific time period. It would be much more difficult to compare one business's "profit" of 500,000 pounds of salt with another's 300,000 sacks of rice.

Store of Value A third function of money is that it can be saved, or stored for later use. For money to serve as a **store of value**, two conditions must be met. First, the money must be nonperishable. That is, it cannot rot or otherwise deteriorate while being saved. Would steak make a good store of value? Probably not, because the steak would spoil. Second, the money must keep its value over time. In other words, the purchasing power of the money must be fairly constant. Water would be a poor store of value because it evaporates—you would lose purchasing power as quickly as your water supply dried up.

If both of these conditions are met, people can accumulate their wealth for later use. If not, most people would be hesitant about saving money today, for it would be worth little or nothing tomorrow.

Characteristics of Money

Now that you know what money does, how can you determine if a particular item would work well as money? To be used as money, an item must have certain characteristics. The five major characteristics of money are

- durability,
- portability,
- divisibility,
- stability in value, and
- acceptability.

Durability Durability refers to money's ability to be used over and over again. Eggs would be a poor choice for money because they are fragile and perishable. Metals such as gold and silver,

Global Exchange

Promoting Local Trade in a Global Economy

Many Americans are concerned that the global economic system poses a threat to local economies and communities. This concern has been expressed in campaigns throughout the country aimed at halting the spread of large chain stores such as Wal-Mart. Campaign supporters argue that chain stores—which hold a competitive advantage of scale—drive small, locally owned stores out of business. Unlike small businesses that are concentrated in downtown areas, chain stores tend to locate on the outskirts of a town and so help diminish the sense of community in the town.

In 2000, a group of locally owned businesses in Lawrence, Kansas, created the Lawrence Trade Organization (LTO). The group decided to counter the spread of chain stores by creating a local currency called REAL dollars (REAL stands for Realizing Economic Alternatives in Lawrence). The currency features local historical figures such as the African American poet Langston Hughes.

In 2001, eighty-six businesses were accepting the $8,000 of REAL dollars in circulation. Although the dollars are purchased with and backed by U.S. dollars, they can be used only in local businesses. The LTO plans to use the U.S. dollars to make loans to small businesses.

Thus far, some businesses participating in the program have noted that accepting two currencies results in extra work. Others have emphasized that REAL dollars raise awareness of the local economy.

Themes in Economics

MONETARY POLICY The euro remains a controversial issue among the member nations of the European Union. While the member nations want the benefits of increased economic integration, many have been reluctant to give up control of their money supply. Traditionally the ability to issue money has been the prerogative of national governments. In addition, some European countries have a long history of strong government management of their economies. They fear that giving up the power to create money will severely limit their ability to shape economic policy. ■

Themes in Economics

THE ROLE OF GOVERNMENT The U.S. Bureau of Engraving and Printing works hard to produce currency that is extremely durable. A U.S. dollar can be folded forward and backward in the same crease approximately 4,000 times before it will tear. How quickly a bill wears out depends on its denomination. A typical $1 bill is in circulation for 18 months before being replaced, and a $5 bill for about two years. Tens and twenties average three and four years, respectively. The larger denominations, such as $50 and $100 bills, remain in circulation for about nine years. ■

Transparency
An overhead transparency of Figure 13.1 is available in *Transparency Resources.* See Transparency 52: Sources of Money's Value.

Caption Answer
fiat money 11A

internet connect

TOPIC: Foreign Currency, Exchange Rates
GO TO: go.hrw.com
KEYWORD: SM3 EC13

Have students access the Internet through the HRW Go site to research foreign currencies and exchange rates. Each student should choose five countries that he or she would like to visit. (Make sure that only one of the countries has the Euro as its unit of currency.) Then have students determine the value of a U.S. dollar in the currencies of their chosen countries. Ask each student to create a world map showing the currencies in the countries they have researched. 23C, 23G, 24C, 24D

SOURCES OF MONEY'S VALUE

Type of Money	Definition	Examples
Commodity Money	**an item that has value of its own and is used as money**	• **precious metals, gems** • **salt in ancient Rome** • **tobacco, beaver skins, wampum in early colonial America** • **cowrie shells in Ashanti society**
Representative Money	**an item that has value because it can be exchanged for something valuable**	• **bills of credit in Massachusetts Bay Colony**
Fiat Money	**an item that has value because a government decree says it does**	• **U.S. coins and paper money**

FIGURE 13.1 Money can be categorized by its source of value. **Which of the three types of money do you use to acquire goods and services?** TEKS

however, are ideal because they can withstand wear and tear. In fact, many coins minted thousands of years ago are still in existence. Are U.S. dollars durable? Yes, because they can be used many times. Additionally, a damaged dollar bill can be replaced easily.

Portability Money's usefulness may depend on its portability, or ability to be carried from one place to another and transferred from one person to another. As a medium of exchange, money must be convenient for people to use. Large stones, such as those used for money on the island of Yap in the South Pacific, would be difficult to use in a large region because of the problems of moving them. U.S. paper money, on the other hand, is small and lightweight, making it portable.

Divisibility Divisibility refers to money's ability to be divided into smaller units. The U.S. dollar is divisible into any amount between 1 and 100 cents. By combining the various coins and bills, buyers and sellers are able to make transactions of any amount down to the nearest penny.

Divisibility also enhances money's use as a standard of value, because exact price comparisons between products can be made. For example, many grocery stores display shelf labels that list the price of a good and the price per unit, such as an ounce. One 24-ounce bottle of POWERāDE® may cost $1.29, while a 32-ounce bottle may cost $1.59. Each ounce of POWERāDE in the smaller bottle costs about 5.4 cents ($1.29 ÷ 24), while each ounce in the larger bottle costs about 5.0 cents ($1.59 ÷ 32). The divisibility of the dollar into cents enables consumers to compare prices of various products.

Stability in Value As you know, for money to be useful as a store of value, it must be stable in value. Stability in value encourages saving and maintains money's purchasing power. Most people who save money are confident that it will have approximately the same value when they want to buy something with it as it had when they put it into savings. Suppose that you put $50 in a savings account and withdraw it in one year. Although prices probably will have increased somewhat because of inflation, you still will be able to pay for goods and services with the money you have saved.

Acceptability Acceptability means that people are willing to accept money in exchange for their goods and services. People accept money because they know that they, in turn, can spend it for other products. Tourists from the United States to a Pacific island where shells are used as money, for example, would have trouble buying goods with their dollar bills. Shopkeepers would not accept the paper money because it could not be used to buy more merchandise on the island. If the tourists exchanged their dollars for shells, however, they would be able to make purchases with the local money.

Sources of Money's Value

As you have learned, money must have—and retain—value. But how does money acquire this value? Economists have identified three sources of value for money. In fact, money can be identified by its source of value. The three types of money are commodity money, representative money, and fiat money. (See Figure 13.1.)

Commodity Money An item that has a value of its own (as a commodity) and that also is used as money is called **commodity money**. Throughout history, societies have used many commodities as money. Precious metals such as gold and silver—and gems such as rubies, emeralds, and diamonds—often have been used as money. Today salt is a commonplace commodity, but in ancient Rome salt was so rare and desirable that it was used as money.

Rather than being a rare item, commodity money is in some cases the most convenient type of money available. For example, tobacco was used as money in Virginia in the early 1600s. Why? Tobacco was plentiful because tobacco farming was the major source of income for individuals as well as for the colony.

Representative Money An item that has value because it can be exchanged for something else of value is **representative money**. Such items have no intrinsic value. That is, their only value is the value they represent.

The first use of representative money in colonial America occurred in the late 1600s. In 1690 the Massachusetts Bay Colony issued bills of credit to help finance King William's War, which was fought against American Indians. Printed on these bills of credit was the amount of money that colonists had loaned to the Massachusetts government. These bills could be redeemed with the colony's treasurer.

Other colonies soon followed the Massachusetts example and issued bills of credit that could be redeemed for **specie**—gold or silver. The amount of specie held by a government "backs," or defines, the worth of representative money. If a government has large reserves of specie and limits the amount of representative money issued, then the money has a high value. This value decreases, however, if a government has a small reserve of specie and issues more representative money.

During the American Revolution the Continental Congress issued representative money, called Continentals, to finance the war for

EXCHANGE, MONEY, & INTERDEPENDENCE *Precious metals such as gold and silver have been used as money. What are some other commodities that have been used as money?*

Themes in Economics

EXCHANGE, MONEY, & INTERDEPENDENCE Commodity money was the typical form of currency for many societies until recent times. Some of the more intriguing items used as commodity money include elephant hair in Africa, whales' teeth in Fiji, and brick tea in Siberia. In 14th-century Europe, a pound of saffron could buy a horse; a pound of ginger, a sheep. Ancient societies in Egypt and Asia Minor, which had high levels of interaction with outside groups, turned to precious metals to facilitate commerce. Copper, gold, and silver were the most commonly used forms of commodity money in these regions. ∎

Caption Answer
gems, salt, and tobacco

MONEY AND THE BANKING SYSTEM

Across the Curriculum

TECHNOLOGY The Treasury Department takes special precautions to discourage counterfeiting. The engraved plates from which paper money is printed are designed with special curves and lines that make copying difficult. The magnetic ink used in the printing process comes from a secret formula, and the exact composition of the paper is also kept secret. However, computer scanners and color copiers have minimized the skill required to be a counterfeiter. In 1999 counterfeiters produced approximately $180 million in bogus money. Moreover, after a decline in counterfeiting in the mid 1990s, the amount of counterfeit money has been rising since 1997. This rise has been attributed to computer-generated money. The initial investment to produce passable bills comes to a mere $1,000. One company in the early 1990s went so far as to brag about its scanner, claming that "No other scanner can scan a hundred bucks and capture the hidden detail as well as ours." ■

Caption Answer

by gradually replacing the designs for all U.S. paper currency with new designs that incorporate security features that make the bills extremely difficult to forge ★15A

---

independence from Great Britain (1775–1783). Few Continentals were redeemed for specie, however, because the government had little of it. The Continentals lost so much of their value that they became nearly worthless, and colonial merchants often refused to accept them.

Fiat Money Value is attached to **fiat money** because a government fiat, or decree, says that it has value. In the United States, coins and paper money are examples of fiat money.

Like representative money, fiat money has little or no value without this government decree. The materials used to produce U.S. coins are, in fact, worth much less than the face value of the coins. The money has value solely because the government says that the paper money and coins must be accepted for all transactions. Thus, unlike representative money, fiat money cannot be redeemed for specie or other items. Its value ultimately stems from citizens' faith in the U.S. government.

The majority of nations in the world today use a form of fiat money called **currency**—coins and paper bills—for money. The Lydians, an ancient people in Asia Minor, minted the world's first coins about 635 B.C. The Chinese developed the first paper currency, perhaps as early as A.D. 650.

EXCHANGE, MONEY, & INTERDEPENDENCE *Paper currency is printed by the Bureau of Engraving and Printing in Washington, D.C.* ***How does the U.S. government work to prevent counterfeiting?*** ★TEKS

Forms of Money

The United States primarily relies on fiat money. Its money takes the form of coins, paper money, checks, and another type of money known as near money.

Coins and Paper Money
Coins and paper money make up U.S. currency. Coins are made by the U.S. Mint, a bureau of the Department of the Treasury. Paper currency is printed by the Bureau of Engraving and Printing in Washington, D.C. Although the government held gold and silver as partial backing for paper money until 1971, today U.S. currency is not redeemable in specie.

CASE STUDY

Counterfeit Money

EXCHANGE, MONEY, & INTERDEPENDENCE Next time you open your wallet, look at your money. How can you tell whether the bills are genuine or counterfeit?

In the early 1990s, counterfeiting was an increasing problem in the U.S. economy. Forgers illegally copied checks, money orders, and grocery coupons.

What steps has the U.S. government taken to combat the rise in illegally created currency? In 1996 the Treasury Department introduced a new $100 bill—the first major currency redesign since 1929. The design incorporated several security features that make it difficult to forge the new bill. These features include an almost-invisible watermark, or design in the paper, of Benjamin Franklin whose enlarged portrait also appears on the bill; a multicolored shade of ink for the numeral in the lower front right-hand corner; a synthetic security thread embedded in the paper; and microprinting.

New designs were introduced for the $50 bill in 1997, the $20 bill in 1998, and the $5 and $10 dollar bills in 2000. The $1 bill has not yet been redesigned, perhaps because its low value discourages counterfeiting. As criminals take advantage of technological developments, however, the United States and other countries will have to find even more sophisticated ways to stop counterfeiters. Only by stopping the efforts of these forgers can a government maintain control over the amount of its currency in circulation.

Demand Deposits Checking accounts make up the largest segment of the U.S. money supply. Because checks can be paid "on demand," in other words at any time, checking accounts sometimes are referred to as demand deposits.

Checking accounts are fiat money because they stand for the bank's willingness to pay on demand in currency issued by the government. Checks generally are accepted because banks are willing to pay the amount of the check when it is presented for payment. Checking accounts, therefore, are considered money because they are a medium of exchange, a standard of value, and a store of value.

Near Money Many financial assets are similar to money. These assets, such as savings accounts and time deposits, are referred to as **near money**, and they are not always counted as part of the nation's money supply. Although such assets are easily accessible, these accounts cannot be used directly to buy goods or to pay debts. Depositors, for example, cannot pay their bills with a certificate of deposit (CD). Because funds in these accounts can easily be converted into cash, however, they are considered near money.

SECTION 1 REVIEW

Q: 1, 2

1. Identify and Explain:
medium of exchange
standard of value
store of value
commodity money
representative money
specie
fiat money
currency
near money

2. Categorizing: Copy the graphic organizer below. Use it to describe the three basic functions of money that make it more efficient than barter.

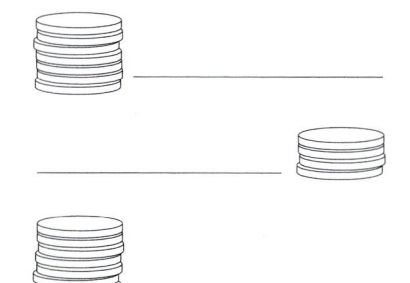

3. Finding the Main Idea
a. Using the five major characteristics of money, explain why popcorn, beads, and oranges would or would not be suitable items to use as money.
b. What are the possible sources of money's value?
c. What forms does money take in the United States?

4. Writing and Critical Thinking
Drawing Conclusions: Suppose that you and the members of your class decide to establish a monetary system for your school's money. What will you use as money (currency)? Explain why you chose that item, why it functions as money, and how it matches the characteristics of money.
Consider the following:
• the source of your new money's value
• the functions of money

Homework Practice Online
keyword: SM3 HP13

SECTION 1
REVIEW ANSWERS

1. medium of exchange (302), standard of value (302), store of value (303), commodity money (305), representative money (305), specie (305), fiat money (306), currency (306), near money (307) **24A**

2. Money serves as a medium of exchange, store of value, and standard of value. **23A, 24D**

3a. Popcorn and oranges are portable, divisible, and may be acceptable but are not durable and may vary in value according to crop success or failure. Beads are durable, portable, and divisible but may not be stable in value over time, reducing acceptability.

3b. commodity—has value of its own; representative—can be exchanged for something else of value; fiat—valuable by government decree

3c. coins, paper money, checks (demand deposits), near money

4. Answers will vary but students' monetary systems should satisfy money's functions as a medium of exchange, a standard of value, and a store of value. Proposed "money" should be durable, portable, divisible, stable in value, and acceptable. **23A**

MONEY AND THE BANKING SYSTEM

SECTION 2

HISTORY OF U.S. BANKING

READ TO DISCOVER
1. What were the views of Federalists and Antifederalists about U.S. banking?
2. How did the development in the 1860s of nationally chartered banks affect the power of state-chartered banks?
3. How did the government reform and regulate the banking system after World War I?

ECONOMICS DICTIONARY
gold standard

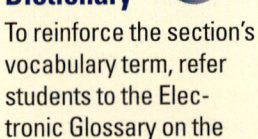

Why might you deposit money in a bank? You probably would do so because you are confident that your money will retain its value and will be available when you want to withdraw it.

Consumers like you have not always been so confident about the security of banks, however. The U.S. banking system has had to earn consumers' confidence as it has developed along with the nation.

Before the American Revolution, the British government discouraged the establishment of banks in the American colonies. Merchants ran unofficial banks by allowing their customers to deposit their money in accounts and take out loans. These banks were only as secure as the individual merchant's business, however. Establishing a stable banking system thus was seen as a key task for the new nation's leaders.

The U.S. monetary and banking systems have gone through three main periods of development. During those periods, banking power has shifted between a centralized, national banking system and independent state and local banks. The result over time has been an increase in stability and public confidence in the nation's money and banking systems.

Before the Civil War

The first period of development, from the 1780s to 1860, was a time of experimentation and debate in U.S. banking. During this period, money and banking were part of a larger political battle over the role of government.

Conflicting Views of Banking The nation's early leaders generally considered themselves to be allied with one of two groups. The Federalists believed that only a powerful central government could keep the United States strong. The Antifederalists opposed a strong central government and favored leaving most power in the hands of state governments. These two groups viewed the young country's monetary problems quite differently. Although the nation's leaders agreed that the United States needed a stable form of money and a stronger banking system, they disagreed about how to reach these goals.

Federalists such as Alexander Hamilton believed that a strong, centralized banking system was necessary to develop U.S. industry and trade. As secretary of the treasury under President George Washington, Hamilton proposed that a national bank have the power to handle the government's funds, to establish and monitor other banks throughout the country, and to issue currency.

Antifederalists such as Thomas Jefferson opposed the creation of a national bank. They feared that the concentration of economic and political power at the national level would weaken the power of individual states. Jefferson supported a decentralized banking system in which the states, rather than the federal government, would establish and regulate the banks within their borders.

First Bank of the United States Hamilton and the Federalists were successful. In 1791 Congress established the First Bank of the United

Alexander Hamilton

Thomas Jefferson

States as a private business. Its 20-year charter, or legal permission to operate, outlined the First Bank's responsibilities, which included the issuing of representative money in the form of banknotes. These banknotes were backed by gold and silver specie. Additionally, the First Bank collected fees and made payments for the federal government.

One year later in 1792 Congress established a national coinage system, and the federal government began to mint gold and silver coins. The government also established the dollar as the official unit of currency.

How successful was the First Bank? It did bring some order to the monetary and banking systems in the United States. It also was successful in regulating banks chartered by the states. For example, the First Bank of the United States required state-chartered banks to hold gold and silver that could be exchanged for currency.

Nonetheless, congressional opponents of the First Bank succeeded in voting down the renewal of its 20-year charter in 1811. As a result, the number of state-chartered banks increased almost threefold, from about 90 in 1811 to nearly 250 in 1816. These state-chartered banks adopted many of the powers associated with the national bank. In the absence of government regulation, these state-chartered banks often issued far more currency than they could back with gold and silver. As a result, many of these banks were unable to redeem paper money, causing a loss of confidence in the banks and their money.

Second Bank of the United States The chaos in the nation's banking system after 1811 caused Congress once again to establish a national bank. Chartered in 1816, the Second Bank of the United States slowly restored confidence in the banking system and in the representative money that state-chartered banks issued.

The Second Bank, however, was not without its critics. Opponents argued that the concentration of wealth in the federal banking system gave too much power to those who controlled it. Other critics argued that the Second Bank restricted economic growth by failing to provide enough credit and currency for the needs of the nation. Still others claimed that it issued too much credit and currency, weakening the U.S. money supply.

Dismantling the Bank The Second Bank came under increasing attack after Andrew Jackson, a vocal critic of the Bank, was elected to the presidency in 1828. In 1832, four years before the official end of the Second Bank's charter, President Jackson vetoed legislation that would have extended it for another 20 years. Jackson's withdrawal of federal government funds in 1833 further blocked the Second Bank's effectiveness for the remaining three years of its life. The fall of the Second Bank set off another rise in the number of state-chartered banks. Between 1830 and 1837 the number of state-chartered banks nearly tripled.

Because state-chartered banks often issued their own currency, bills and coins varied widely from state to state. For example, in 1835 the government of New York prohibited banknotes valued at less than $10. Some banks, on the other hand, issued notes with values as low as 5 cents. Although by 1830 most states required banknotes to carry round-dollar values such as $1 or $5, many people continued to use pieces of dollar bills to represent fractional amounts. In other words, if you visited a store in the 1830s and paid for a 25-cent item with a $1 bill, the clerk might cut the bill into four equal pieces and return three of them to you as change.

In addition to issuing their own banknotes, state-chartered banks issued more credit with

Profiles in Economics

For biographies of Alexander Hamilton, Thomas Jefferson, and other noted people in economics, refer students to the Biographies section on the *Holt Researcher Online*.

Global Connections

Alexander Hamilton modeled the First Bank of the United States after the Bank of England. He believed that the Bank of England was a major factor in Great Britain's rise to political and economic dominance in the 1700s.

Britain's Parliament established the Bank of England in 1694 to supply funds for the nation's wars. Over the next 100 years, the Bank lived up to its expectations by providing the government with the finances it needed to fight seven major wars. In the process, the Bank helped create a stable and universally respected currency. The strength of this currency encouraged greater commerce and contributed to Britain becoming a major economic power. Hamilton hoped the First Bank of the United States would provide similar benefits to the young United States.

MONEY AND THE BANKING SYSTEM

Across the Curriculum

HISTORY The man who most shaped the direction of the Second Bank of the United States was Nicholas Biddle, who became its president in 1822. Biddle supported strong central-banking controls, and during most of his reign the U.S. economy remained relatively stable. Andrew Jackson, hero of the common man, loathed the sophisticated and well-educated Biddle, however, which only increased Jackson's desire to do away with the Second Bank. Although Biddle fought to save the bank, Jackson won. In 1836, the charter for the Second Bank ended, leading to the Panic of 1837. ■

Profiles in Economics

For a biography of Andrew Jackson and others who shaped U.S. economic history, refer students to the Biographies section on the *Holt Researcher Online*.

Caption Answer

The number of state-chartered banks increased. These banks issued more currency and credit and decreased gold and silver reserves. Public confidence in bank notes declined, leading to bank failures and the economic panic of 1837.

---

fewer restrictions. They also kept smaller and smaller reserves of gold and silver to back the growing supply of paper money. By 1837, people found it increasingly difficult to exchange their paper money for gold or silver. Public confidence in the notes issued by state-chartered banks diminished, and many of those banks failed when they were unable to redeem their banknotes in specie.

The resulting economic panic of 1837, however, did not revive public support for another single national bank. Instead, some states coped with the banking crisis by imposing stricter guidelines on state-chartered banks. Most states, for example, adopted the Second Bank's policy requiring state-chartered banks to hold a specie reserve equal to a certain percentage of the notes they issued.

Civil War to World War I

During the second main period of development—between 1860 and 1913—the federal government created a dual banking system made up of state- and nationally chartered banks. The system

EXCHANGE, MONEY, & INTERDEPENDENCE *President Andrew Jackson opposed central banking. What was the effect of the fall of the Second Bank of the United States?*

brought more uniformity and stability to the money supply and U.S. banks. This system also meant that the power of national banking increased, while state-chartered banks became less powerful.

Fragmented Banking

The fall of the Second Bank of the United States in 1836—and the lack of uniformity among the nation's state-chartered banks—created a patchwork banking system during the mid-1800s. By 1861 most of the country's 1,601 state-chartered banks were issuing paper money of questionable value.

The Civil War created even more problems for the nation's monetary system. During the war, Congress issued currency to pay the North's war expenses. Called greenbacks or U.S. notes, the new currency was not backed by specie. Instead, greenbacks were fiat money backed only by the federal government's promise to repay the notes' face value at some future date.

The Confederacy also relied on paper currency during the Civil War. These notes were issued by the Confederate government as well as by individual southern states. This money was worthless by the end of the war, and the banking system in the South was virtually destroyed. In early 1861 nine of the southern states had a combined total of 121 chartered banks. By the end of the war, in 1865, no banks existed in North Carolina, Mississippi, or Florida. Only three banks still operated in Georgia, and South Carolina had only one.

Unifying the Banking System

To rebuild and strengthen the country's banking system, Congress passed the National Banking Acts of 1863 and 1864. These acts gave the federal government the power to charter, or officially establish, banks and to require banks to hold gold and silver reserves. The government's power

310 CHAPTER 13

THE ARAB AND THE CAMEL.
An Arab asked the loaded Camel whether he preferred to go up or down hill. "Pray, Master," said the Camel dryly, "is the straight way across the plain shut up?"—Æsop.

EXCHANGE, MONEY, & INTERDEPENDENCE *Greenbacks were issued by Congress during the Civil War to pay U.S. war expenses. What does the cartoonist suggest about the government's financial policies?*

to charter banks enabled it to establish a system composed of nationally chartered and state-chartered banks.

Additionally, the federal government issued a single national currency through the nationally chartered banks. Unlike the greenbacks issued during the war, this national currency was backed by government bonds. The new currency contributed to the elimination of the many different state bank currencies in use. Most of these state bank currencies were good for local purchases only and relied on the strength and reputation of an individual bank for their value. A national currency provided a nationally acceptable medium of exchange and stabilized the supply of money in the United States.

With the passage of the Coinage Act of 1873, Congress began reducing the country's reliance on silver as specie. The Gold Standard Act of 1900 committed the U.S. government to the **gold standard**—a monetary system in which paper money and coins carry the value of a specified amount of gold. A gold standard allows people to exchange their banknotes for gold and keeps the government from issuing an unlimited number of banknotes.

Suppose that in 1901 you had U.S. banknotes valued at $150. You would know that you could exchange your paper money for $150 in gold. You would probably choose to keep your paper money, however, because it would be much easier to carry. Additionally, the gold standard ensured that the paper money carried an established and recognizable value—so you would feel no need to exchange it for specie.

All of these government decisions increased public confidence in paper currency and in the banking system. The system did not, however, provide for an efficient method of regulating the amount of money circulating in the economy. Also, the system lacked any central organization.

World War I to the Present

The third developmental period in U.S. banking, from 1913 to the present, has been marked by reform and regulation. As noted in Chapter 12, government involvement in the U.S. economy has increased during the 1900s. Specifically, it has focused on regulating the amount of money in the economy in order to stabilize currency values. The banking system has experienced successes as well as failures from this government involvement.

MONEY AND THE BANKING SYSTEM **311**

Caption Answer

so that federal auditors could examine each bank, determine which ones were financially sound, certify them, and let them reopen ★15A

---

internet connect

TOPIC: U.S. Banks
GO TO: go.hrw.com
KEYWORD: SM3 EC13

Have students access the Internet through the HRW Go site to conduct research on historical figures associated with the banking system in the United States. Each student should choose one figure and then create a short biographical sketch of the individual. Have students present their sketches to the class. ★23C, 24D

Profiles in Economics

For a biography of Franklin D. Roosevelt and others who shaped U.S. economic history, refer students to the Biographies section on the *Holt Researcher Online*.

ECONOMIC INSTITUTIONS & INCENTIVES *Thousands of people rushed to withdraw their savings during the Great Depression.* **Why did Franklin D. Roosevelt order a "bank holiday" in 1933?** TEKS

Federal Reserve System In 1913 Congress passed the Federal Reserve Act, establishing the Federal Reserve system—now commonly called the "Fed." The Fed became the nation's central bank, and all nationally chartered banks were required to join the Fed. State-chartered banks, however, were free either to join the Fed or to operate as nonmember banks. In 1996 more than 2,760 commercial banks—including about 15 percent of all state-chartered banks—were members of the Federal Reserve.

In its early years the Fed experienced both success and failure. The chief success was its ability to provide the government with enough credit to finance the U.S. military effort during World War I (1914–18). Its major failures were an inability to control credit during the 1920s and a lack of support for the banking system during the 1930s. In fact, the overextension of credit and the resulting borrower defaults contributed to consumer hardships during the early years of the Great Depression.

New Deal Banking Reforms

The Great Depression was brought on by financial panic that swept the nation. Thousands of people withdrew their savings, causing many banks to fail. In the years 1930–33, nearly 8,000 banks went under, some 4,000 in 1933 alone.

Franklin D. Roosevelt's election to the presidency in 1932 brought lasting changes to the monetary and banking systems. Promising a "New Deal" to the nation's people, Roosevelt sought to restore public confidence in the economy and the nation's banking system.

First, Roosevelt kept the nation's banks closed for four days in March 1933. The president's order for the "bank holiday" allowed banks to reopen only after federal auditors judged them to be financially sound. Most banks were reopened within two weeks. Certification by the auditors helped restore confidence in the reopened banks, and soon people and businesses began to use them again.

Another New Deal reform, the Banking Act of 1933, separated investments from savings in order to protect deposits. Many people felt that bank officials had persuaded them to invest in overvalued stock, destroying their life savings. For example, in 1933 Edgar Brown testified before Congress that he had lost $125,000, in part because he had been pressured to invest in National City Bank stock. After the crash in 1929, the bank had bought the stock back at only two thirds the price Brown had paid.

The Banking Act of 1933 thus prohibited the Fed's member banks from providing investment services such as selling stocks and bonds. The act also established a temporary Federal Deposit Insurance Corporation (FDIC), which insured each savings account up to $5,000. The Banking Act of 1935 made the FDIC permanent and

CHAPTER 13

LINKING ECONOMICS and SCIENCE

Shake, Rattle, and Roll

Earthquakes are one of nature's most powerful and destructive forces. Both engineers and earthquake scientists—known as seismologists—work hard to prevent and lessen the damage caused by earthquakes. Their research allows people to make decisions about how to allocate resources and reduce the chances of economic crisis.

Although earthquakes may strike in several regions of the United States, they are most likely to occur in California. California is particularly subject to earthquakes because of its location on several fault lines, or places where tectonic plates — enormous portions of the earth's crust—meet.

In 1994 the "Northridge quake" caused extensive damage to the city of Los Angeles and much of the rest of densely populated southern California. This quake alone left more than 60 people dead, 5,000 injured, and 25,000 without homes. The region's transportation and communications networks were crippled, and property damage was estimated at more than $20 billion.

The economic impact of the earthquake, however, extended far beyond southern California. The quake closed down highways, railroads, and airports that are critical to nationwide distribution of goods and services. A quake of rarely matched intensity—the "Big One" that seismologists predict has a better than 50-50 chance of occurring during the next 20 years—could pose a serious threat to the national economy.

Seismologists know that earthquakes are caused by tectonic plates grinding against each other. Stress builds up between the plates over time, eventually causing the earth's crust to shift— what we experience as an earthquake. By studying these fault lines, seismologists hope to predict future earthquakes.

While the science of earthquake prediction is far from perfect, it provides important information. For instance, emergency planners use scientists' predictions to locate emergency resources where they will most likely be needed.

Predicting the location and intensity of earthquakes also aids structural engineers, who design devices that can lessen the property damage caused by quakes. One device, for example, cradles a building's foundation on a set of steel rollers, enabling it to move with an earthquake rather than staying rigid and breaking apart.

Recent advances in structural engineering have led many people to call for retrofitting existing buildings and structures—that is, adding quake-resistant structural devices. The California Department of Transportation has worked to retrofit more than 2,000 roads and bridges in the state.

Scientists use antennae connected to a network of satellites called Global Positioning System (GPS) to measure and predict earthquakes.

What Do You Think?

1. Should the federal government discourage people from building near fault lines in order to reduce the potential costs of disaster relief? Explain your answer.
2. Is the cost of retrofitting buildings and transportation structures worthwhile if scientists can make only vague predictions about the location and likelihood of future earthquakes? Explain your answer.

Themes in Economics

THE ROLE OF GOVERNMENT

Floods, another costly type of disaster, occur even more often than earthquakes. In 1968 the government launched the National Flood Insurance Program to help protect home owners and business owners in flood-prone areas. Under this program, the government provides flood insurance to communities that either restrict development in flood-prone areas or follow specific guidelines when building in those areas. Communities that do not take part in this program are ineligible for federal aid in the event of a flood. In addition, federally regulated financial institutions are prohibited from making loans on property in a flood plain unless the land is covered by flood insurance. ■

What Do You Think? Answers

1. Answers will vary but should demonstrate an understanding of the conflicting issues involved—the political freedom to choose where one lives versus the economic costs to society when the government has to provide federal aid to earthquake victims at taxpayer expense. ★15A, 23A

2. Answers will vary but students should weigh the costs of this protection against the potential savings in lives and money should an earthquake hit. ★23A

Caption Answer

banks lend more money directly to consumers ★8A

SECTION 2 REVIEW ANSWERS

1. gold standard (311) **24A**

2. gave federal government power to charter national banks; required banks to hold gold and silver reserves; issued national currency that helped eliminate state-bank currencies **8A, 23A, 24D**

3a. Federalists favored more federal power to regulate state banks, specie, and currency. Antifederalists favored less federal power, with each state controlling its own banks and currency.

3b. The government established the Federal Reserve system and passed the Banking Acts of 1933 and 1935 and the Gold Reserve Act of 1934 to regulate the amount of money in the economy, control credit, restore confidence in the economy, stabilize exchange rates. **8A, 15A**

4. Answers will vary but students should recognize that each government's failure to back its currency by specie and the Civil War's destruction of southern banks created the need for a national banking system to stabilize the money supply and to rebuild and strengthen the nation's banking system. **8A, 15A, 23A**

ECONOMIC INSTITUTIONS & INCENTIVES *During the 1960s and 1970s a number of banks were established to meet the needs of particular groups.* **How has banking changed since the Great Depression?** ★TEKS

expanded its insurance for each account. Today depositors' money is insured up to $100,000 for each account.

The Gold Reserve Act of 1934 eliminated the gold standard in the United States and allowed the government to purchase all gold held by U.S. banks. Further, Federal Reserve notes were no longer to be backed by gold. The act also prohibited the use of gold coins and the redemption of Federal Reserve notes at banks. Gold held in the Treasury was used to set up a fund designed to help stabilize the value of the dollar.

Expanded Banking Services After the Great Depression, banking practices changed dramatically. Banks began to lend money directly to consumers, as well as to corporations and finance companies. Consumer loans made up less than 1 percent of total bank assets in 1945, but by 1995 more than 12.5 percent of bank assets came from consumer loans. Sales and consumer finance companies, on the other hand, saw their percentage of consumer loans drop from about 40 percent of assets in the early 1940s to less than 23 percent by the late 1980s.

Some consumers felt that their needs were not met by most commercial banks. In response, during the 1960s and 1970s a number of banks were established to serve particular groups. These banks, such as Women's Bank in San Diego and Freedom National Bank in Harlem, focused on providing checking and savings accounts, loans, and other financial services to members of specific gender and ethnic groups. Although many of these banks failed, some expanded to offer services to the general population. For example, Women's Bank soon changed its name in an attempt to gain more business, becoming known instead as California Coastal Bank.

SECTION 2 REVIEW

★TEKS Q: 1, 2, 3b, 4

1. Identify and Explain:
gold standard

2. Identifying Cause and Effect: Copy the graphic organizer. Use it to describe three ways in which the development of a national banking system in the 1860s weakened state banks.

Development of a National Banking System

↓

[| |]

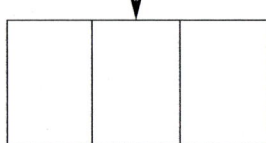

Homework Practice Online
keyword: SM3 HP13

3. Finding the Main Idea
   a. How did conflict over the First and Second Banks of the United States reflect Federalist and Antifederalist views of government?
   b. Explain how and why the government tried to regulate the banking system after World War I.

4. Writing and Critical Thinking
   Drawing Conclusions: How did the turmoil of the Civil War encourage the development of a national banking system?
   Consider the following:
   • the value of currencies during wartime
   • the state of the nation's economy after the war

314 CHAPTER 13

SECTION 3
U.S. BANKING TODAY

READ TO DISCOVER
1. What are the most common types of U.S. financial institutions?
2. How has automation affected banking practices?
3. What were the results of banking deregulation?
4. What crises did financial institutions face in the late 1980s?

ECONOMICS DICTIONARY
commercial banks
savings and loan associations
mutual savings banks
debit card
deregulation
default

As you have learned, the U.S. banking system has changed dramatically over time. Changes such as home banking and debit cards continue to take place all around you. Recently, the three main trends in banking have been automation, deregulation, and stabilization of the banking industry. Before looking at these trends, however, you must be able to identify the players in the field—the financial institutions.

Types of Financial Institutions

Today you have many banking options. Suppose that you decide to open a savings account. You visit each of the several different financial institutions located near your home to find out what services are offered. Soon your mind is whirling with interest rates, regular savings accounts, money market accounts, and certificates of deposit. How do you choose among financial institutions? What do you want to know about these institutions before handing over your hard-earned money?

Three major types of financial institutions have emerged as the U.S. banking system has evolved. Figure 13.2 on page 316 shows some types of financial institutions in the United States today and how many of each type exist, broken down by the value of their assets. For many years these institutions offered different services and different interest rates. Today, however, they are much more similar in their services and functions. The most common types of financial institutions have included

- commercial banks,
- savings and loan associations,
- mutual savings banks, and
- credit unions.

ECONOMIC INSTITUTIONS & INCENTIVES *Commercial banks lend money, accept deposits, and transfer funds.* **What other types of financial institutions are common in the United States?**

MONEY AND THE BANKING SYSTEM 315

Across the Curriculum

HISTORY The first mutual savings bank in the United States was the Philadelphia Savings Fund Society, founded in 1816. Philadelphia's working class residents made up most of the bank's customers. The vast majority were mechanics, tradespeople, laborers, and domestic servants. Ethnically, they included Germans, Jews, Slavs, Italians, Irish, and African Americans. The local business community treated the bank as an experiment designed to teach poor people the values of thrift and honesty. Workers deposited their savings in order to accumulate interest. Accounts were limited to $3,000, and annual deposits to $500 until 1865. Most of the bank's loans were for home mortgages. Historians have used the bank's records to reconstruct the social history of ordinary urban residents of 19th-century America. ■

Transparency
An overhead transparency of Figure 13.2 is available in *Transparency Resources*. See Transparency 53: Financial Institutions, 1999.

Caption Answer
credit unions; FDIC-insured commercial banks ★23F

Commercial Banks The main functions of **commercial banks** today are to lend money, accept deposits, and transfer money among businesses, other banks and financial institutions, and individuals. Loans from commercial banks help businesses expand and make capital improvements. Commercial banks make almost 40 percent of all mortgage loans and almost 50 percent of all other loans.

In the 1800s commercial banks developed as institutions for business and commerce. In the early 1900s, however, commercial banks began to offer services to individuals. Today commercial banks generally offer customers the widest range of services of all financial institutions.

Numbers of Financial Institutions, 1999

Assets	FDIC–Insured Commercial Banks	FDIC–Insured Savings Institutions	Credit Unions
Less than $5.0 million			4,511
$5.0 million–$9.9 million	161	139	683
$10.0 million–$24.9 million			72
$25.0 million–$49.9 million	1,839	198	1,054
$50.0 million–$99.9 million	2,157	327	688
$100.0 million–$499.9 million	2,729	705	698
$500.0 million–$999.9 million	300	124	86
$1.0 billion–$2.9 billion	216	96	32
$3.0 billion or more	178	51	4
TOTALS	**8,580**	**1,640**	**10,628**

Source: *Statistical Abstract of the United States: 2000*

FIGURE 13.2 There are several types of financial institutions in the United States. **Which type was most common in 1999? Which type had the largest number of institutions with more than $500 million in assets?** ★TEKS

Savings and Loan Associations Like commercial banks, **savings and loan associations** (S&Ls) were established to lend money and accept deposits. Sometimes called "thrifts," these savings and loan associations were begun as "home-building societies" in the mid-1800s. Members deposited money into a large general fund and took turns borrowing it—and paying it back—until each member was able to build a house. Individuals and families continue to make up the majority of S&L customers.

Federal regulations and laws allowed S&Ls to expand, enabling them to offer many of the same services available at commercial banks, such as credit cards and insured deposits. Interest rates—both on savings accounts and on loans—vary among savings institutions. Today the nation has about 1,600 FDIC-insured savings institutions, including S&Ls and mutual savings banks.

Mutual Savings Banks In the early 1800s institutions called **mutual savings banks** were set up to serve people who wished to make small deposits that large commercial banks did not want to handle. Like an S & L, business for a mutual savings bank traditionally came from personal savings and home mortgage loans. Interest rates for loans at mutual savings banks often were slightly lower than those at commercial banks.

Credit Unions Employees of large businesses and institutions and members of large labor unions often belong to credit unions. Today approximately 10,600 credit unions are in operation in the United States. When credit union

CAREERS IN ECONOMICS

Bank Teller

Are you interested in learning about how a bank works? Do you have good interpersonal skills as well as strong math ability? If so, you might consider a job as a bank teller.

What does a bank teller do? The word *teller* comes from the Dutch word *tellen*, meaning "to count." Tellers do indeed count money—but they also are responsible for many other transactions between the bank and its customers. These duties include cashing checks, providing account information, accepting loan payments and account deposits, paying withdrawals, and selling bank products. To successfully perform these tasks, a teller must be familiar with the bank's policies and procedures and be able to clearly explain them to customers.

Although accurately handling a wide variety of transactions is a key part of their job, tellers' most important role is to represent the bank to its customers. For many clients, the teller is the only form of personal contact they have with their bank. For this reason, banks expect their tellers to be courteous and helpful. "People friendly" tellers are an important part of a bank's public image.

Banks require that tellers have a high school diploma and the ability to operate various types of bank and office equipment such as personal computers and adding machines. Classes in math, business, and secretarial skills are helpful training for this position. Many employers also look for candidates with experience in retail sales.

Technological innovations, such as electronic funds transfers and automated teller machines, are expected to alter significantly the nature of teller positions in the future. However, as long as there is a need for personal contact between clients and their bank, tellers will continue to play an important role in the nation's banking system.

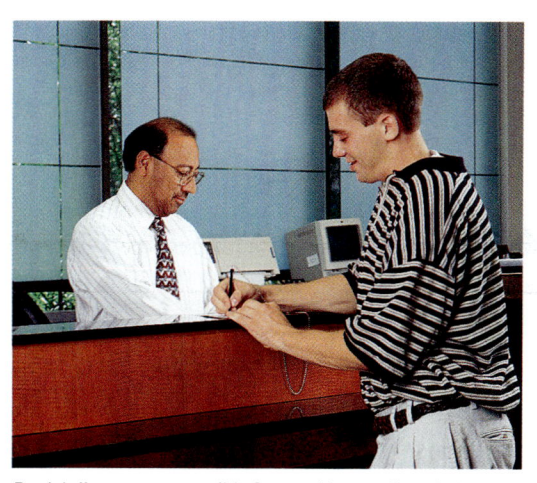

Bank tellers are responsible for most transactions between banks and their customers.

---

members deposit money, they purchase shares that pay interest. Credit unions use this savings pool to supply low-cost loans to their members.

Credit unions usually offer higher interest rates on savings and lower interest rates on loans than do other financial institutions. Personal, automobile, and home improvement loans account for the majority of the loan activity.

Automation

Three main trends have influenced financial institutions in recent years. The first trend is automation, which means reliance on computers to handle transactions. Also called electronic funds transfer (EFT), automated banking increases banks' efficiency by allowing them to execute banking transactions electronically, by

---

Careers in Economics

To help students learn about other careers in economics, refer them to the Careers section on the *Holt Researcher Online*.

Themes in Economics

COMPETITION & MARKET STRUCTURE Credit unions have become quite popular among U.S. employers and employees in recent years. Membership is often offered as an employee benefit. At no cost to their company, employees receive access to low-cost auto loans, special savings clubs, automatic deposit of their paychecks, and numerous other services. Worried about competition and loss of market share, banks obtained a Federal court injunction in 1996 that forbade credit unions from offering membership to customers beyond the employees they were created to serve. This threat to credit unions was removed in August 1998 when Congress approved the Credit Union Membership Access Act. The bill gave credit unions the ability to expand their base of membership again. ■

Enhancing the Lesson

For information about the National Credit Union Administration (NCUA), see the Executive Departments section on the *Holt Researcher Online*.

Across the Curriculum

TECHNOLOGY Although automation is revolutionizing the banking industry, a surprising number of transactions still involve the exchange of cash. In 1998 cash accounted for more than 43 percent of customer transactions, while electronic transfers, debit and ATM cards, and credit cards combined accounted for less than 25 percent of consumer transactions. However, the number and value of non-cash payment methods is growing, and most of the value exchanged in trade flows through electronic means. Between 1994 and 1998, the value of payments by credit and debit cards grew 83 percent, from $764 billion to nearly $1.4 trillion. The number of point-of-sale (POS) machines in grocery stores, gas stations, and other retail stores has also been growing rapidly. However, while electronic payment methods have made inroads, paper remains the most convenient and cost-effective method of exchange for transactions of small value. ■

Caption Answer

Banking at ATMs is more convenient. People usually do not have to wait in long lines and they can use ATMs 24 hours a day.

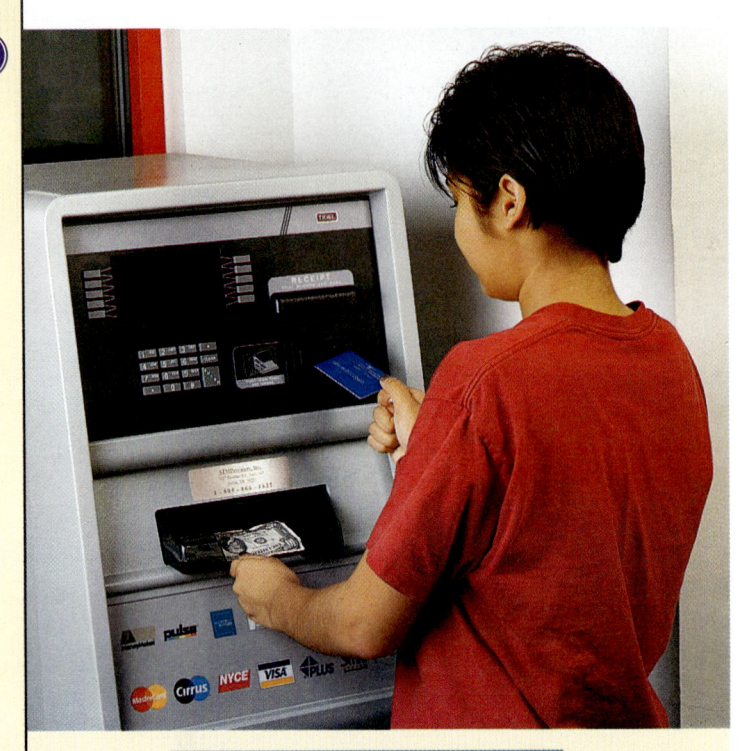

ECONOMIC INSTITUTIONS & INCENTIVES *Many routine banking tasks now are handled by ATMs.* **What are some advantages of using an ATM?**

computer. This process allows transactions to affect accounts immediately. It saves banks money by decreasing the number of workers needed for banking operations. The four main types of automated banking are

- automated teller machines,
- automatic clearing house services,
- point-of-sale terminals, and
- home banking.

Automated Teller Machines Are you among the millions of people who use an automated teller machine (ATM) to deposit or withdraw money from a bank account? If not, you probably know someone who is—in 2000 approximately 230 million ATM cards were in circulation. Those ATM cards, if laid end to end, would stretch across the United States from coast to coast four times.

Many routine banking tasks that had been handled by bank tellers now are handled by ATMs. Bank customers, for example, make deposits or withdrawals from checking and savings accounts at ATMs. They can also make payments on bank loans or transfer money from one account to another automatically.

What are the advantages of using an ATM? You may not have time to stand in line at the bank, or you may need the money after the bank closes. Most ATMs operate 24 hours a day, making them convenient for customers. ATMs are convenient for the bank, too, because fewer tellers are needed. In fact, some banks now charge a fee to customers who rely on tellers for transactions that can be handled by ATMs.

Automatic Clearing House Services Some banks make it possible for you to pay bills without writing checks. Of course, you still have to supply the money, but your bank will transfer funds automatically. Banks do this through automatic clearing house services (ACH), a system that transfers money from a customer's account to those of his or her creditors. Usually, ACH is used to pay regular monthly bills, such as home mortgage payments and rents, insurance premiums, and utility bills. Why might you decide to pay your bills through automatic clearing house services? You would save time as well as money on postage and would have fewer envelopes to seal—and you would know that your payments will arrive in time.

Point-of-Sale Transactions Have you seen someone pay for gasoline or groceries by running a plastic card through an electronic scanner? Customers are able to purchase items in this way at gas stations, grocery stores, and convenience stores that have point-of-sale terminals. A point-of-sale transaction involves the direct transfer of money from a buyer's bank account to a seller's bank account. A buyer pays for goods at the checkout counter by inserting a plastic card, called a **debit card**, into the terminal. Money then is transferred automatically from the buyer's account to the seller's account. By 1999 more than 2.3 million point-of-sale terminals were in use across the United States.

318 CHAPTER 13

How do point-of-sale transactions benefit you? A debit card requires you to use a personal identification number (PIN). Without knowing this PIN, the card is useless, thereby reducing the problems caused by theft. You also can check the amount of money available in your account anytime you want by inserting your card into a point-of-sale terminal.

Some banking experts believe that the use of debit cards soon will replace the use of checks in the U.S. economy. They note that debit cards help merchants by ending the risk of bad checks and eliminating the inconvenience and expense of processing credit card transactions.

The use of debit cards, however, has some drawbacks. For example, debit cards can be used only in stores with the terminals. In addition, consumers are accustomed to the grace period, or lag time, offered by credit cards. When consumers make a credit card purchase, they do not have to pay for the good or service until they are billed for it. This period of credit that allows a purchaser to "buy now and pay later" is the grace period. Consumers lose their grace period with debit cards because a point-of-sale transaction transfers money out of their accounts instantly. Debit cards mean you "buy now and pay now."

Home Banking One of the most dramatic developments in banking involves the Internet. Many banks offer a variety of services to Internet customers. For example, Citizens Bank—headquartered in Indiana—opens accounts over the Internet for customers who are unable to come to one of the bank's branches. Georgia State Bank offers similar services, and Wilber National Bank in New York permits customers to download software for banking transactions and bill payment. In California the Bank of Stockton allows customers to download and reconcile their account statements, transfer funds, and pay bills through the Internet.

Even more popular than Internet banking are telephone and home banking. For example, Bank One offers its customers in Texas the opportunity to check account balances, transfer money, and even apply for loans over the telephone. Electronic home-banking services link personal computers in homes with the bank's computers. Bank records can be accessed by a customer's computer, enabling the transacting of bank business from home. Home banking provides convenience to customers and helps banks by reducing the time and money spent recording transactions.

Deregulation

The second major trend is **deregulation**, or the reduction of government restrictions. Deregulation has resulted in more competition in banking, as well as the rise of interstate, or regional, banking in the United States.

Increased Competition Banking deregulation began in 1980 when Congress passed the Depository Institutions Deregulation and Monetary Control Act. This act eliminated many of the

ECONOMIC INSTITUTIONS & INCENTIVES *Point-of-sale transactions transfer money directly from the buyer's bank account to the seller's bank account.* **How do debit cards provide security?**

Cultural Perspectives

The use of coins is declining as technology eliminates the need to fumble for correct change. Coins are increasingly being replaced by stored value cards, also called smart cards. Some of these cards have a set value, or amount of credit, stored on them. In other cases, the cardholder determines the amount of credit on his or her card. The cards are then used in place of coins in pay phones, vending machines, photocopiers, laundromats, subways, and even parking meters. Each time the card is used, the proper amount of money is automatically debited from the card until the total value stored on the card has been spent.

Global Connections

Europe has been the driving force in the development of a cashless society, followed closely by Asia. Debit cards and stored value cards were common in Europe long before they gained acceptance in the United States. Europeans' reluctance to use credit cards is viewed as an obstacle by companies trying to do Internet commerce in Europe. In 2000, 74 percent of Internet users in North America had made an online purchase with a credit card, compared to 41 percent of Internet users in western Europe.

Caption Answer

They require a personal identification number (PIN).

Themes in Economics

THE ROLE OF GOVERNMENT

The 1994 Riegle-Neal Interstate Banking and Branching Act enables national banks to merge with other banks and establish branches in other states. This act furthered the trend toward regional banking. In the first two years after the law was passed, a record number of bank mergers occurred. About 40 percent of these mergers were the combination of several small banks into one large bank. The growth of regional banking in the United States brings the nation's banking system closer to those of several other industrialized nations, such as Britain, France, and Japan, where a handful of major commercial banks serve consumers. ■

Caption Answer

pros—banking market is more competitive, larger banks can offer a wider variety of services and can benefit from economies of scale; cons—larger banks in distant regions may be unresponsive to customers' needs, smaller banks may not be able to compete against larger banks or may be absorbed by them

---

traditional differences between financial institutions such as commercial banks and S&Ls. In effect, the portions of the act that concern interest rates, checking accounts, and required reserves made banking both more competitive and more uniform in the services offered.

Suppose that you decide to buy a car. Traditionally, you would have arranged a loan from an S&L or a credit union. Deregulation has allowed banks to offer interest rates comparable to those available from other institutions, so you have many more loan offers from which to choose. Similarly, traveler's checks were once issued only at banks. Today, however, vacationers have the convenience of buying traveler's checks at almost any financial institution.

Regional Banking Another major change as a result of deregulation has been the growth of regional banking. Historically, banks and their branches had been limited by law to their home states. In 1985, however, the Supreme Court affirmed that the states—not just the federal government—have a role in regulating regional banking. This ruling allowed banks to merge with other banks and to build branch offices in other states whose state legislatures were agreeable to the expansion.

Would you prefer to do business with a local bank or with one based in a different state? Many banking experts view the trend toward regional banking as beneficial, primarily because larger financial institutions can offer a wider variety of services to consumers. Other experts foresee problems with regional banking—for example, that larger banks from distant regions may be unresponsive to customers' needs. In addition, smaller banks fear that the larger banks' greater size gives them a competitive edge in the market. Small banks also worry that they might be absorbed by larger banks—even when wishing to remain independent.

ECONOMIC INSTITUTIONS & INCENTIVES *Deregulation has encouraged the growth of regional banking and increased the number of bank mergers.* **What are the pros and cons of regional banking?**

CHAPTER 13

BANK FAILURES, 1974–1999

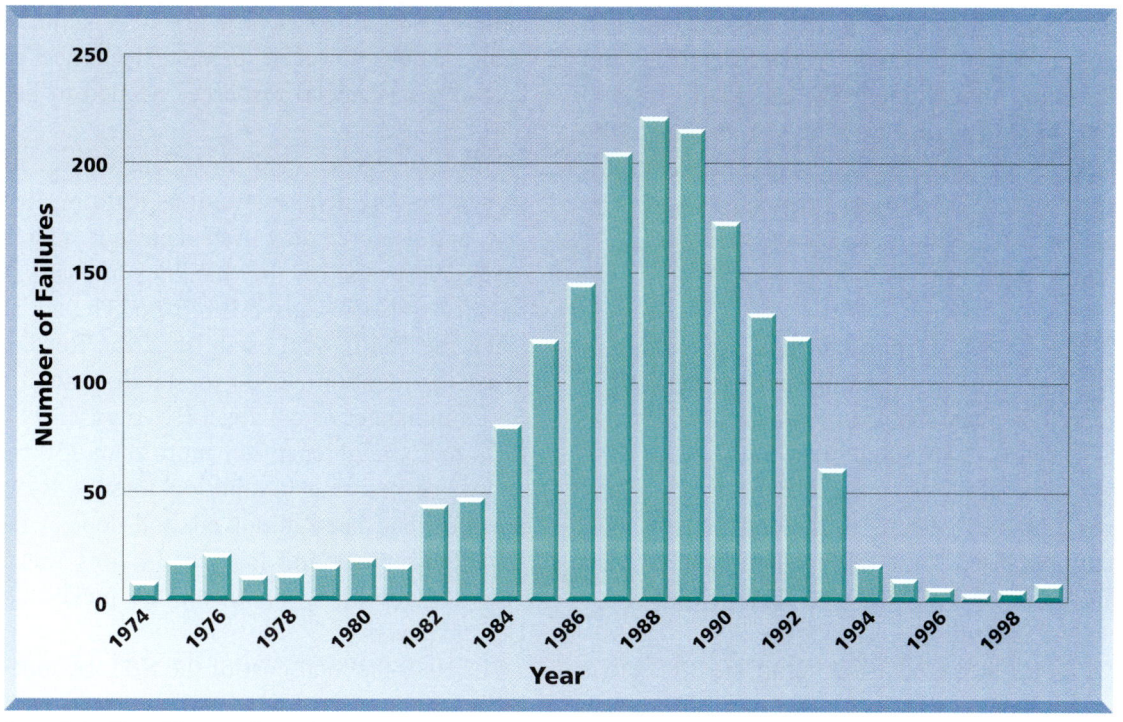

FIGURE 13.3 More banks failed in the 1980s than in any other decade since the Great Depression. **How is bank failure defined?**

Source: Federal Deposit Insurance Corporation

Larger banks generally support the expansion of regional banking to full interstate banking, or nationwide banking. Nationwide banking would allow any bank to open branches and to merge with banks in any state. Supporters argue that national banking would create more competitive markets. Further, they note that "bigness" in the banking industry would allow it to benefit from economies of scale.

Financial Troubles in Banking

The third major banking trend of recent years is the stabilization of financial institutions. The need for increased stability could be seen in three main areas: loan defaults, bank failures, and what became known as the savings and loan crisis.

Loan Defaults During the 1980s many people and businesses relied heavily on borrowed money. In some cases they were unable to repay the funds they had borrowed. This failure to make payments on a loan is called a **default**. Although loan defaults occurred in many parts of the economy, there were a particularly large number of defaults among farmers. The Farm Credit System (FCS), a network of 37 banks that offer loans to farmers nationwide through so-called farm banks, suffered from a wave of loan defaults in the 1980s. Many farmers were unable to make payments on property and equipment that had been purchased with FCS credit. Although the Farm Credit System at that time was the largest farm lender in the United States—with about $61.5 billion in outstanding loans—the organization was on the verge of bankruptcy in 1986.

Bank Failures Loan defaults and other financial worries led to more bank failures in the

---

Caption Answer
A bank fails when it no longer has enough assets on deposit to cover its accounts.

Global Connections

The Cosmo Credit Union, the largest credit union in Tokyo, Japan, failed in August 1995, when customers withdrew some $680 million in one day. The credit union's bad loans at that point equaled 40 percent of its deposits. Cosmo's situation was not unique. When Japanese land prices plummeted in the early 1990s, some $550 billion in assets disappeared from the nation's banking system. This development chilled additional investment and reduced consumer spending, causing a recession. The situation worried U.S. leaders because of Japan's large overseas investments, particularly those in U.S. stocks and bonds. U.S. policy makers feared that Japan's banking problems could lead to a major international economic crisis. The situation illustrates how, in today's global economy, one nation's financial troubles can have worldwide ramifications. ■

MONEY AND THE BANKING SYSTEM

1980s than in any decade since the Great Depression. A bank fails when it no longer has enough assets to cover its accounts. Between 1980 and 1985 the annual number of FDIC–insured banks that failed rose from 11 to more than 100. Added to this total are the numerous near failures and banks in serious financial trouble. The trend in bank failures is shown in Figure 13.3 on page 321.

S&Ls in Crisis Perhaps the most visible sign of instability in U.S. banking during the 1980s involved savings and loan associations. A number of factors contributed to the S&L crisis. First, borrowers failed to make payments on many loans granted by S&Ls in the early 1980s. This situation caused some savings and loan associations to fail and others to be absorbed by larger financial institutions.

Another factor contributing to the S&L crisis was that some S&Ls had only private insurance. About 30 states approved private deposit insurance during the mid-1980s, which allowed state-chartered S&Ls to choose private insurance instead of insurance provided by the Federal Saving and Loan Insurance Corporation (FSLIC). By 1986 nearly 18 percent of the nation's S&Ls had chosen private insurance. In some states, however, private insurance plans lacked the financial resources needed to handle S&L failures.

In response, in 1989 President George Bush signed the Financial Institutions Reform, Recovery, and Enforcement Act. This act addressed several aspects of the banking industry, but focused primarily on S&L reform. The act abolished the FSLIC and established the Resolution Trust Corporation (RTC) to stabilize additional S&Ls in danger of collapse. By August 1994 the RTC had straightened out more than 730 S&Ls and was overseeing 11 additional S&Ls. By 1996 the RTC had been dissolved, and deposit insurance for savings and loan institutions was provided by the FDIC—with the tab picked up by U.S. taxpayers.

In 1999 the total cost of the S&L bailout was estimated at nearly $165 billion, plus interest. One economics reporter pointed out that if the money had not been needed for the bailout, it could conceivably have paid for 57,692 M-1 Abrams tanks—seven times the number used by the U.S. Army.

SECTION 3 REVIEW

TEKS Q: 1, 2, 3b, 3c

1. Identify and Explain:
commercial banks
savings and loan associations
mutual savings banks
debit card
deregulation
default

2. Identifying Cause and Effect: Copy the graphic organizer below. Use it to describe the main types of financial institutions and how these institutions affect households and businesses.

Main Types of Financial Institutions

3. Finding the Main Idea
a. How have automation and the spread of computers made banking more accessible to consumers?
b. How did deregulation affect banks and other financial institutions?
c. How did the U.S. government work to resolve the S & L crisis?

4. Writing and Critical Thinking
Analyzing Information: Suppose that your classroom is a state and that you and your classmates have decided to establish a bank. What services will your bank offer? Will people in other "states" be able to use your bank?
Consider the following:
- the effects of deregulation and the rise of regional banking
- the services offered by different types of financial institutions

Homework Practice Online
keyword: SM3 HP13

Economics IN THE NEWS

Financial Modernization and the Repeal of the Banking Act of 1933

The passage of the Banking Act of 1933, also known as the Glass-Steagall Act, resulted in the prohibition of the Federal Reserve System's member banks from providing both deposit and investment services to their customers. The idea behind the law was to promote financial stability, create public confidence in the banking system, and prevent conflicts of interest. Many economists believed that the conflicts of interest caused by banks pressuring their customers to buy stock contributed to the 1929 stock market crash.

Over the years, however, many critics called for its repeal. Some critics supported repeal on free-enterprise grounds, arguing that the government should avoid involvement in the economy. They also pointed to the fact that banks in many other countries were also providing insurance and investment services. These critics argued that repealing the law would enable American banks to more effectively compete in the global economy. Finally, some argued that the economies of scale that would result from allowing banks to provide insurance and securities services would make the entire financial services industry more efficient.

The Glass-Steagall Act also had its supporters, who feared that allowing banks to re-enter the securities and insurance markets could result in a crisis similar to the stock market crash of 1929, especially if the rest of the economy went into a downturn. Other supporters argued that repealing the law might greatly increase the number of mergers in the banking industry, leading to reduced competition and the formation of monopolies.

In 1999 Congress repealed the Glass-Steagall Act. In its place Congress enacted the Gramm-Leach-Bliley Act (also known as the Bank Modernization Bill), which allows banks to provide banking, insurance, and securities services to their customers. According to Lawrence H. Summers, who was treasury secretary at the time, the Bank Modernization Bill promised to "better enable American companies to compete in the new economy."

According to one estimate, the ability of American banks to provide one-stop financial services to their customers could result in savings of as much as $18 billion a year.

The Bank Modernization Bill enables banks to expand their services to include securities and insurance services.

What Do You Think? TEKS

1. What benefits might the Bank Modernization Bill provide to consumers and businesses?
2. What are some of the possible negative effects of the Bank Modernization Bill on consumers and businesses?

WHY IT MATTERS TODAY

The full impact of the Bank Modernization Bill is yet to be determined. Use CNNfyi.com or other **current events** sources to find recent information on the Bank Modernization Bill's impact on consumers and businesses.

CNNfyi.com

Economics in the News Answers

1. consumers—ability to obtain a variety of financial services through one company; businesses—ability to compete with European and Asian counterparts that offer an array of services **8B, 15B**

2. bank mergers leading to reduced competition and possibly higher prices for consumers; banks pressuring clients to make unwise investments **8B, 15B, 23A**

CHAPTER 13
Review Answers

Writing a Summary

Summaries should focus on the main points of each section. These may be found in the Read to Discover questions at the start of each section. Summaries should also use standard grammar, spelling, sentence structure, and punctuation. **8A, 8B, 24B, 24D**

Identifying Ideas

medium of exchange (302), standard of value (302), store of value (303), specie (305), currency (306), gold standard (311), commercial banks (316), savings and loan associations (316), mutual savings banks (316), default (321) **24A**

Understanding Main Ideas

1. to serve as a medium of exchange, a store of value, and a standard of value

CHAPTER 13 Review

(Continued from page 323)

2. coins, paper money, checks, near money
3. Federalists—Federal control over state banks; Antifederalists—state control over banks
4. In the 1800s, commercial banks served businesses; in the 1900s, they began offering services to individuals; today they offer the widest range of banking services. **8A**
5. Federal Reserve Act created the Fed; Banking Act of 1933 required banks to be sound; Banking Act of 1933 created the FDIC; Gold Reserve Act of 1934 eliminated the gold standard; in 1980s and 1990s federal law deregulated banking, enabled regional banking, and reformed some banking practices and S&Ls **8A, 15A**
6. increased efficiency, lower operating expenses, availability of services, such as ATMs, ACH, point-of-sale transactions, and home banking **8B**
7. passed the Financial Institutions Reform, Recovery, and Enforcement Act, which established the Resolution Trust Corporation (RTC) to reform and stabilize S&Ls **15A**

Reviewing Themes

1. durability, portability, divisibility, stability in value, and acceptability
2. It serves as the central bank of the United States. The Fed was able to provide the government with enough credit to finance World War I; it was unable to control credit during the 1920s and was unable to support the banking system during the 1930s. **8A, 15A**

Writing a Summary

Using standard grammar, spelling, sentence structure, and punctuation, write a summary of the information in this chapter.

Identifying Ideas

1. medium of exchange
2. standard of value
3. store of value
4. specie
5. currency
6. gold standard
7. commercial banks
8. savings and loan associations
9. mutual savings banks
10. default

Understanding Main Ideas

SECTION 1 *(pp. 301–307)*

1. What are the major functions of money?
2. Identify the types of money used in the United States.

SECTION 2 *(pp. 308–314)*

3. Compare the views of Federalists and Antifederalists on banking.

SECTION 3 *(pp. 315–322)*

4. How has the role of commercial banks changed over time?
5. How did the U.S. government work to regulate the banking industry during the 1900s?
6. How has banking changed as a result of automation?
7. How did the U.S. government respond to the S&L crisis of the 1980s?

Reviewing Themes

1. **Exchange, Money, & Interdependence** What are the five major characteristics of money?
2. **Economic Institutions & Incentives** What function does the Fed serve? What were the successes and failures of the Federal Reserve System between 1913 and the early years of the Great Depression?
3. **Economic Institutions & Incentives** What have been the results of banking deregulation?

Thinking Critically

1. **Comparing** Imagine that the U.S. government is considering introducing a one-dollar coin to replace all of the paper dollar bills. What do you believe would be the pros and cons of this move?
2. **Summarizing** What were the long-term consequences of the failures of the First and Second Banks of the United States?
3. **Drawing Conclusions** Where would (or do) you choose to do your banking—a commercial bank, savings and loan association, mutual savings bank, or credit union? Explain your answer.
4. **Drawing Conclusions** Consider the effects of automated banking on households and businesses. Which form of automated banking do you believe is most useful? Explain your answer.

Writing about Economics

Review what you wrote in your Economics Notebook at the beginning of this chapter about your monetary activities. How do recent trends in banking, such as automation and deregulation, affect your activities? Record your answer in your Notebook.

Building Social Studies Skills

Interpreting the Chart

Examine the time line of early U.S. banking history and answer the questions that follow.

EARLY U.S. BANKING HISTORY

- **1791** — The charter of the First Bank of the United States expires.
- **1811** — Congress establishes the First Bank of the United States.
- **1816** — Congress establishes the Second Bank of the United States.
- **1829** — Andrew Jackson becomes President.
- **1836** — The charter of the Second Bank of the United States expires.
- **1860** — About 1,600 banks are operating in the United States.
- **1861–1865** — The Civil War disrupts the nation's monetary system.

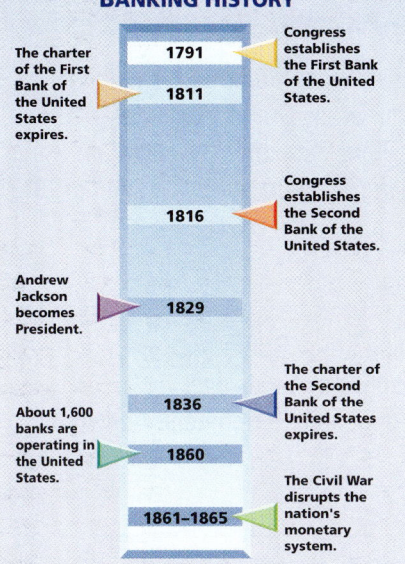

1. When was the U.S. monetary system disrupted?
   a. when the charter of the First Bank expired
   b. when the charter of the Second Bank expired
   c. when the Civil War began
   d. when Andrew Jackson became president
2. Characterize early U.S. banking history—how might early U.S. banking be described?

Analyzing Primary Sources

In 1903 Maggie L. Walker founded the St. Luke Penny Savings Bank and became the first female bank president in the United States. Today Walker's bank thrives as the oldest continuously African American-operated bank in the United States. Read this excerpt from a speech made by Walker in 1901 and answer the questions that follow.

> "What do we need to still further develop and prosper us, numerically and financially? First we need a savings bank. . . .
>
> "We need to start and operate a factory for the making of clothing for women and children, men's underwear and a millinery [women's hat] store. . . .
>
> "What we need is an organ, a newspaper to herald and proclaim [announce] the work. No business. . . . can be pushed successfully without a newspaper. . . .
>
> "We want an executive to run a factory, run a paper, run a bank, that will develop something and give some of the noble women work."

3. Why might Walker have wanted to establish a bank and the other enterprises mentioned?
   a. She wanted to earn a personal fortune from the various enterprises.
   b. She believed that the enterprises would help African Americans and women.
   c. She wanted women executives to hold the top positions at the enterprises.
   d. She wanted to attract publicity for herself.
4. Why did Walker plan to establish a newspaper as well as a bank?

Alternative Assessment

Building Your Portfolio

With your group, develop a banking institution. Compare the services of commercial banks, savings and loans, mutual savings banks, and credit unions. You may want to assign one group member to collect information about each type of institution. Choose which type you will develop, name your institution, and then create an advertisement—designed either for the Yellow Pages or a Web page—that describes the services.

internet connect

Internet Activity: go.hrw.com
KEYWORD: SM3 EC13

Access the Internet through the HRW Go site to research U.S. currency. Individually, or as part of a group, create a poster or a multimedia presentation to teach your classmates about the history and designs of various coins and bills.

---

3. increased competition and the rise of regional banking

Thinking Critically
1. Answers will vary but should reflect an understanding of the forms, characteristics, and functions of money. (See Section 1.)
2. increase in unsound banks, economic instability, currency problems, low public confidence in banks
3. Answers will vary but should reflect an understanding of the functions, services, and benefits of each type of financial institution. **8A, 8B**
4. Answers will vary but should reflect an understanding of the benefits of ATMs, ACH, point-of-sale transactions, and home banking. **8B**

Writing about Economics
Students should mention their use of ATM and debit cards or home banking services. Students might discuss how recent bank mergers have affected their accounts and the level of service provided by their banks. **23A, 24A, 24B**

Building Social Studies Skills
1. c **23A, 23F**
2. Students should mention conflicting views of banking between those who supported and opposed a national bank and fragmentation of the banking system. **23D, 23F**
3. b **23D, 23E**
4. to advertise and promote the bank **23A**

MONEY AND THE BANKING SYSTEM 325

CHAPTER RESOURCE MANAGER

CHAPTER 14: THE FEDERAL RESERVE AND MONETARY POLICY

	OBJECTIVES	PACING GUIDE	REPRODUCIBLE RESOURCES
SECTION 1 **THE FEDERAL RESERVE SYSTEM** (pp. 327–31)	▶ How did the panic of 1907 affect U.S. Banking? ▶ What are the purposes and characteristics of the Federal Reserve System? ▶ How is the Fed organized?	**Regular** 1.5 days **Block Scheduling** 1 day	**ELL** Spanish Study Guide 14.1 **ELL** English Study Guide 14.1 **SM** Consumer Economics: Activity 14 **PS** Reading 41: Federal Reserve Act of 1913
SECTION 2 **THE FEDERAL RESERVE AT WORK** (pp. 332–36)	▶ What services does the Fed provide to banks? ▶ How does the Fed serve the Federal government? ▶ How do economists measure the U.S. money supply?	**Regular** 1.5 days **Block Scheduling** 1 day	**ELL** Spanish Study Guide 14.2 **ELL** English Study Guide 14.2 **E** Challenge and Enrichment: Activity 14
SECTION 3 **MONETARY POLICY STRATEGIES** (pp. 337–44)	▶ Why does the Fed rely on either an easy-money or a tight-money policy? ▶ How does the Fed make monetary policy? ▶ What are the challenges associated with determining monetary policy?	**Regular** 1.5 days **Block Scheduling** 1 day	**ELL** Spanish Study Guide 14.3 **ELL** English Study Guide 14.3 **E** Simulations and Strategies for Teaching Economics: Activity 14 **SM** Mathematics for Economics: Activity 14

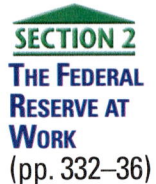

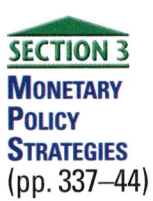

Chapter Resource Key

PS	Primary Sources	**A**	Assessment		Video
RS	Reading Support	**REV**	Review		Videodisc
E	Enrichment	**ELL**	Reinforcement and English Language Learners		Internet
S	Simulations		Transparencies		Holt Presentation Maker Using Microsoft® PowerPoint®
SM	Skills Mastery		CD-ROM		TEKS and TAKS

TECHNOLOGY RESOURCES	REINFORCEMENT, REVIEW, AND ASSESSMENT
One-Stop Planner: Lesson 14.1 Researcher Online Homework Practice Online CNN Presents Economics: The Fed Transparencies 54 and 55 Global Skillbuilder CD-ROM	**REV** Section 1 Review, p. 331 **A** Daily Quiz 14.1 ★ TAKS Every Day!
One-Stop Planner: Lesson 14.2 Researcher Online Homework Practice Online Transparencies 56 and 57 Global Skillbuilder CD-ROM	**REV** Section 2 Review, p. 336 **A** Daily Quiz 14.2 ★ TAKS Every Day!
One-Stop Planner: Lesson 14.3 Researcher Online Homework Practice Online Holt Economics Videodisc: Inflation: The Federal Reserve Responds Transparencies 58 and 59 Global Skillbuilder CD-ROM	**REV** Section 3 Review, p. 344 **A** Daily Quiz 14.3 ★ TAKS Every Day!

Chapter Review and Assessment
SM Global Skillbuilder CD-ROM
HRW Go site
REV Reteaching Activity 14
REV Chapter 14 Review, pp. 346–47
A Chapter 14 Test Generator (on the One-Stop Planner)
A Chapter 14 Test
A Alternative Assessment Handbook

One-Stop Planner CD-ROM
It's easy to plan lessons, select resources, and print out materials for your students when you use the **Texas One-Stop Planner CD-ROM with Test Generator.**

---

internet connect

HRW ONLINE RESOURCES
Go To: go.hrw.com
Then type in a keyword.

TEACHER HOME PAGE
KEYWORD: SM3 Teacher

CHAPTER INTERNET ACTIVITIES
KEYWORD: SM3 EC14
Choose an activity to:
- research the Open Market Committee of the Federal Reserve.
- learn about the Federal Reserve district banks.
- write an editorial on the Government in the Sunshine Act.

CHAPTER ENRICHMENT LINKS
KEYWORD: SM3 CH14

HOLT RESEARCHER ONLINE
KEYWORD: Holt Researcher

ONLINE ASSESSMENT
Homework Practice
KEYWORD: SM3 HP14
TAKS Review
KEYWORD: SM3 T14
Rubrics
KEYWORD: SS Rubrics

CONTENT UPDATES
KEYWORD: SS Content Updates

ONLINE READING SUPPORT
KEYWORD: SS Strategies

HOLT PRESENTATION MAKER
KEYWORD: SM3 PPT14

CURRENT EVENTS
KEYWORD: S3 Current Events

TEXAS ONLINE RESOURCES
KEYWORD: S3 TX

LESSON 14.1 THE FEDERAL RESERVE SYSTEM

TEXTBOOK PAGES 327–31

HOLT PRESENTATION MAKER
Access Illustrated LECTURE NOTES using Microsoft® PowerPoint® on the One-Stop Planner CD-ROM

OBJECTIVES

- Describe how the Panic of 1907 affected U.S. banking.
- Explain the purposes and characteristics of the Federal Reserve system. ★18A, 18B
- Show the organization of the Fed. ★18A

MOTIVATE

Ask students to imagine that they have $100 deposited in a local bank. They hear that many depositors are withdrawing funds and that the bank has made many loans. Ask students if they would still feel that their money was secure in the bank and how many of them would want to withdraw the $100. Have volunteers explain why they would want to withdraw their money. Write their responses on the chalkboard. Explain to students that these sorts of withdrawals—on a much larger scale—were one cause of the Panic of 1907.

On the chalkboard, draw an outline of a pyramid divided into three horizontal sections. Write the words *small, local banks* in the base of the pyramid. In the middle section, write the words *larger city banks*. In the point of the pyramid, write the words *largest commercial banks*. Explain that in the system of pyramided reserves, small, local banks deposited reserves with larger city banks, which in turn deposited reserves with the largest commercial banks in U.S. financial centers such as New York and San Francisco. Ask students what they think would happen if the largest commercial banks loaned out money, and then many smaller local banks tried to withdraw their reserves. Write student responses on the chalkboard and point out that the failure of the system of pyramided reserves was a second cause of the Panic of 1907, which led to the development of a central banking system in the United States. Tell students that in this section they will learn about the development of this system, known as the Federal Reserve system.

TEACH

Building a Vocabulary

Have students use spiral notebooks to create an Economics Dictionary to be used throughout the chapter. This dictionary might be used as an activity at the start of each new section or as a learning aid for sheltered English students or students having difficulty. List words that students will be expected to know for this section on the chalkboard. Have students use the information provided in the text or on the *Researcher CD-ROM* to list, define, and give an example of each term. ★24A

Acquiring Information, Identifying Cause and Effect, Demonstrating Understanding

Review with students the causes of the Panic of 1907 *(runs on banks and the failure of the system of pyramided reserves),* and the effect of these two events *(the creation of a central bank called the Federal Reserve system).* Next, divide students into small groups and instruct each group to create a newscast, set in 1913, announcing the creation of the Federal Reserve system. In addition to having each group report the causes leading up to the creation of the system, also require each group to interview citizens for their reaction to the creation of the Fed. Different groups may interview different kinds of individuals (for example, a farmer, a small-business owner, the president of a major corporation, a commercial bank president). Give each group 10 minutes or so to prepare their newscasts and then have each group perform their newscast for the class. ★18A, 23A, 24D

Evaluating Ideas, Taking a Stand

Organize the class into groups of four or five students. Tell the groups to imagine that they are committees established to develop a central banking system and that they are to discuss a proposed system that has the following three characteristics: lack of a single central bank, ownership and control by the member banks, and optional membership for some banks.

Ask the groups to discuss each of the three characteristics and to determine whether they feel that this proposed system would be successful. When group discussions are concluded, ask volunteers to explain if they would support a system with these characteristics, or how they might alter the characteristics. Suggest that students might want to take notes on the discussions. Have the class vote on whether to adopt the banking system as described. Tell students that the Federal Reserve system—unlike central banks in other countries—has all three of these characteristics. ★23D

Tell students that the lack of a single central bank is very important to the organization of the Fed. Display Transparency 55: Federal Reserve Districts and ask students to identify the district which includes their state. Point out the location of the Federal Reserve Bank for that district.

Synthesizing Information, Creating Charts and Graphs
Ask students if they are familiar with organizational flowcharts. Have them sketch an organizational flowchart of an institution they are familiar with such as the school, the class, or their place of employment. Then tell students that the Fed is also organized in a particular way. After students have reviewed the organization of the Fed as described in the textbook, have them create a flowchart that outlines the organization of the Fed in their Economics Notebooks. Then show students Transparency 54: Organization of the Fed and have students compare their charts with the transparency. Give students time to edit their own charts, if needed. Refer students who need additional instruction on the skills used in this lesson to the *Global Skillbuilder* Lesson 12: Creating Graphic Organizers. ⭐24D

CLOSE

Ask students to name the two causes of the Panic of 1907 and to identify their effect on the U.S. economy. Have students review their notes on the discussions about the organization of the Fed. Ask for volunteers to share and explain their Federal Reserve system organizational flowcharts. ⭐18A

OPTIONS

Students Having Difficulty
Pair students having difficulty with students who have mastered the material. Remind students that the creation of a central banking system was controversial in the United States. Have pairs discuss the newscasts the class groups performed during the first Teach activity. Then ask pairs to write three headlines that convey the causes and effect of the Panic of 1907.

Interpersonal Learners, Linguistic Learners
Have interested students find out more about the qualifications, background, and characteristics of members of the Board of Governors. Chairman Alan Greenspan, for example, studied at the Julliard School of Music and dropped out of school for a year to tour the United States as a musician before beginning his study of economics. Students could access the Internet, write letters to governors, or even call for interviews to gather information for this assignment. Ask volunteers to share their findings with the class.

Visual-Spatial Learners
Encourage interested students to research the locations of the 25 branch offices of Federal Reserve banks around the nation. Ask students to create a map of the 12 Federal Reserve districts that include these branch offices. Students may wish to model their maps after Transparency 55: Federal Reserve Districts (Figure 14.2 on textbook page 330). Remind students to include a map key that distinguishes branch offices from Federal Reserve district banks. ⭐18A

Gifted Learners
Have interested students research the central banking system of a country other than the United States. Students may wish to research the purpose, characteristics, responsibilities, and organization of the system. Then have students create a chart or graph that compares and contrasts that system with the Fed. Students may wish to include their charts in their portfolios, and teachers may wish to display charts in the classroom. ⭐24D

REVIEW

Have students complete the Section 1 Review on page 331. Use the answers in the Annotated Teacher's Edition to assess student mastery of this section.

ASSESS

To assess student mastery of this section, have students complete Daily Quiz 14.1 in *Daily Quizzes with Answer Key*. For additional assessment options, see *Alternative Assessment Handbook* on the *One-Stop Planner CD-ROM*.

ADDITIONAL RESOURCES

Broz, J. Lawrence. *The International Origins of the Federal Reserve System*. 1997. Cornell University Press.

Greider, William. *Secrets of the Temple: How the Federal Reserve Runs the Country*. 1989. Touchstone Books.

America's Central Bank. 1995. Federal Reserve Bank of Boston.

LESSON 14.2 THE FEDERAL RESERVE AT WORK

TEXTBOOK PAGES 332–36

HOLT PRESENTATION MAKER Access Illustrated LECTURE NOTES using Microsoft® PowerPoint® on the One-Stop Planner CD-ROM

OBJECTIVES

- Identify services the Fed provides to banks.
- Describe ways the Fed serves the federal government. ★18B
- Explain how economists measure the U.S. money supply.

MOTIVATE

Ask students to identify services offered by banks, and write responses on the chalkboard. If students have difficulty with this task, refer them to Chapter 13 of the textbook for information. Suggestions may include loans, checking accounts, ATM services, traveler's checks, and safety deposit box rentals. Explain to students that even though the Fed does not provide directly to consumers the kinds of services the students included in their lists, it does provide services indirectly by acting as "the banker's bank" and the "government's bank."

TEACH

Building a Vocabulary
List the vocabulary terms for this section on the chalkboard and tell students to add them to their Economics Dictionary. Tell students to use the information provided in the text or on the *Researcher CD-ROM* to list, define, and find an example of each vocabulary term. ★24A

Hypothesizing, Creating Charts and Graphs
Post two large pieces of paper labeled with the phrases *the banker's bank* and *the government's bank.* Based on their knowledge of the kinds of services provided by commercial banks, ask students to hypothesize the services the Fed provides to member banks through its role as "the banker's bank." As students brainstorm their ideas, record them on the paper labeled "the banker's bank."

Next, review with students the services the Fed provides to banks *(clearing checks and making loans)* by referring them to the appropriate part of the text, and by displaying and explaining Transparency 56: The Fed and Check-Clearing. Ask students to identify reasons the Fed makes loans to banks *(seasonal factors, natural disasters, financial emergencies)*. Have students develop a graphic organizer in their notebooks that displays the services the Fed provides to banks. ★24D

Hypothesizing, Demonstrating Understanding
Now ask students to hypothesize the services the Fed provides to the government through its role as "the government's bank." As students brainstorm their ideas, record them on the chart labeled "the government's bank." Review with students the services the Fed provides to the government *(serves as the government's bank: serves as depository for federal revenues, holds a checking account for the Treasury, records the millions of deposits and withdrawals of federal funds, conducts the purchase and sale of government securities, and advises the legislative and executive branches of government on developing a coordinated economic program; supervises member banks, and regulates the money supply)*. Then have students complete the graphic organizer in their notebooks. Next, divide students into groups of four and ask them to come up with an advertising jingle or rap that illustrates one or more of the services the Fed provides to the government. Have groups perform their work for the class. ★18B, 24D

Understanding Charts and Graphs
Remind students that in its role as the government's bank, one of the duties of the Fed is to regulate the money supply. Explain that before the Fed can regulate the money supply, it must first determine how much money is circulating in the economy. Ask students to brainstorm possible supplies of money the Fed might include in its tabulation of the nation's total circulation. Write their ideas on the chalkboard. Organize students into groups and distribute copies of the *Wall Street Journal.*

Have students find the Federal Reserve Data charts that contain weekly information about the money supply. Direct students to the M1, M2, and M3 columns, and then look in their textbook to find out exactly what is included in each of these measurements of the public money supply. Ask students to compare and contrast the measurements. Then ask students to decide which measurement of the money supply they think is the most accurate and/or useful. ★23A

CLOSE

Ask students to respond to the following two questions in paragraph form in their Economics Notebooks: Why do some people refer to the Fed as "the banker's bank"? Why is the Fed known as "the government's bank"? Ask for volunteers to share their paragraphs with the class. ★18A, 18B

OPTIONS

Students Having Difficulty, Body-Kinesthetic Learners

Display again Transparency 56: The Fed and Check-Clearing. In order to make this process more clear, have the class physically walk through the steps of the process. Organize the students into groups of six. Have each group create signs that read *Local Bank #1, Local Bank #2, Federal Reserve Bank A, Federal Reserve Bank B,* and *Consumer.* Five of the group members should choose signs, and the sixth member will assume the role of the check. Have students position themselves at "stations" that correspond to the stages identified in the transparency. The "check" member will travel among group members just as a real check travels through the check-clearing process. At each stage, the group member at a particular station will explain his or her role in the check-clearing process. When the process is completed, ask each group member to write a brief description of the check-clearing process based on the activity.

Gifted Learners

Refer students to the Global Exchange feature Sharing the Wealth (textbook page 334) that describes some of the functions of the World Bank. Ask students to focus on a particular occasion when the World Bank has extended a loan to a developing country. Students may choose to focus on an instance mentioned in the textbook, or they may choose to research another World Bank funding program. After students have chosen the focus of their research, have them "follow the money trail." Have students start their research by answering these questions: How much money was provided to the country by the World Bank? Why was the money needed? What was the money used for? What projects was the money used to introduce or expand? What economic conditions exist in the country today? Students can report the results of their research in oral or written reports, or by creating a chart or map that illustrates the funding program. ★24D

Logical-Mathematical Learners

Have interested students research the current figures of the M1, M2, and M3, and create a bar graph that shows the major components of the money supply. Students may wish to include their graphs in their portfolios. ★24D

REVIEW

Have students complete the Section 2 Review on page 336. Use the answers in the Annotated Teacher's Edition to assess student mastery of this section.

ASSESS

To assess student mastery of this section, have students complete Daily Quiz 14.2 in *Daily Quizzes with Answer Key.* For additional assessment options, see *Alternative Assessment Handbook* on the *One-Stop Planner CD-ROM.*

ADDITIONAL RESOURCES

Caprio, Gerard, ed. *Preventing Bank Crises: Lessons from Recent Global Bank Failures: Proceedings of a Conference Co-Sponsored by the Federal Reserve Bank of Chicago.* 1998. World Bank.

Khademian, Anne M. *Checking on Banks: Autonomy and Accountability in Three Federal Agencies.* 1996. Brookings Institution Press.

LESSON 14.3 MONETARY POLICY STRATEGIES

TEXTBOOK PAGES 337–44

HOLT PRESENTATION MAKER
Access Illustrated LECTURE NOTES using Microsoft® PowerPoint® on the One-Stop Planner CD-ROM

OBJECTIVES

▶ Explain why the Fed relies on either an easy-money policy or a tight-money policy.
▶ Examine how the Fed makes monetary policy. ★18B
▶ Identify the challenges associated with determining monetary policy.

MOTIVATE

Ask students to imagine that the classroom is a free-enterprise economy like the United States. Tell them that their money supply is 1,000 classbucks. Ask them to consider how their economic activities would be affected by an increase in the money supply to 10,000 classbucks. Write students' responses on the chalkboard. Next, ask students to consider how their activities would be affected if the money supply were suddenly limited to 100 classbucks. Ask students to consider how these changes would affect demand, supply, prices, and employment. Students should also consider the effects on economic actors such as households, businesses, and the government. Point out that the decision to expand or contract the money supply is known as monetary policy, and ask why these changes might be enacted *(to influence the cost and availability of credit)*. Tell students that in this section they will learn about the Fed's use of monetary policy to promote the goals of economic growth and economic stability.

TEACH

Building a Vocabulary

List the vocabulary terms for this section on the chalkboard and tell students to add them to their Economics Dictionary. Tell students to use the information provided in the text or on the *Researcher CD-ROM* to list, define, and find an example of each vocabulary term. ★24A

Comparing and Contrasting, Creating Charts and Graphs

Explain to students that through its monetary policy, the Fed regulates the amount of money and credit available in the economy. Review with students the goals and characteristics of an easy-money policy and a tight-money policy. Have students read the examples in their textbooks of how these policies affect consumers. Instruct students to create a chart in their notebooks that compares and contrasts easy-money policy and tight-money policy. Charts should include a comparison of the policies' goals, how the policies are implemented, and at what point in the business cycle each policy is most useful.

Ask students to imagine that they are thinking of borrowing money from a bank to buy a computer. Would they be more likely to encounter low interest rates during a period when the Fed is enacting an easy-money policy or a tight-money policy *(easy-money policy)*? Have students indicate this information in their charts. ★18B, 24D

Acquiring Information, Analyzing Information, Demonstrating Understanding

Explain to students that there are several ways, formal and informal, that the Fed influences the money supply, the availability of credit, and aggregate demand. These ways include open market operations, the discount rate, the reserve requirement, margin requirements, credit regulation, and moral suasion. Divide students into six groups, each representing one of the ways the Fed makes monetary policy. Tell groups that their task is to explain their assigned tool of monetary policy to the rest of the class. Give each group 15 minutes to think of an innovative way to present their information. After having students refer to the textbook to learn the material, encourage groups to write a poem or song or create a poster or graph that illustrates the information for the class. As each group teaches its concept by presenting it to the class, have the rest of the class take notes on the presentation. ★18B, 24D

Synthesizing Ideas/Information
Review with students the five major challenges facing the Fed: economic forecasts, time lags in developing and carrying out monetary policy, priorities and trade-offs, lack of coordination among government agencies in forming economic policies, and conflicting opinions about monetary policy. After reviewing and explaining the challenges, have students choose one of the challenges and draw a political cartoon that exemplifies this challenge. Display cartoons in the classroom. ★24D

CLOSE

Refer students back to the Motivate activity lists of economic behaviors. In a class discussion format, ask students to make connections between the activities they listed and easy-money and tight-money economic policy. Ask students to summarize the ways the Fed makes monetary policy by referring to the presentations made by each of the groups. Finally, have students share their political cartoons with each other to review the five challenges associated with determining monetary policy. ★18B

OPTIONS

Students Having Difficulty
In order to reinforce the concepts included in the ways the Fed makes monetary policy, have students recall the presentations the six groups made in the second Teach activity. Then have students use the following vocabulary words/phrases in complete sentences: open-market operations, discount rate, prime rate, reserve requirement, margin requirements, credit regulation, and moral suasion. ★24A

Gifted Learners
Have interested students research the history of the interest rate since 1980. Have students create a chart that shows the changing interest rate and depicts the economic and political conditions, factors, and reasons for the changing interest rate. Students may wish to include this research in their portfolios. ★23F

Linguistic Learners
Have students review the five major challenges of carrying out monetary policy. Encourage interested students to scan the newspaper each day during this unit and collect articles that illustrate one or more of the five challenges. Students may also use the Internet to collect these news articles. Have students share synopses of the articles in class. Students may also wish to create an in-class file of news articles related to economics. ★18B

REVIEW

Have students complete the Section 3 Review on page 344. Use the answers in the Annotated Teacher's Edition to assess student mastery of this section.

ASSESS

To assess student mastery of this section, have students complete Daily Quiz 14.3 in *Daily Quizzes with Answer Key*. For additional assessment options, see *Alternative Assessment Handbook* on the *One-Stop Planner CD-ROM*.

RETEACH

For students having difficulty with the lessons, have them complete Reteaching Activity 14. This activity is located in *Reteaching Activities with Answer Key*.

ADDITIONAL RESOURCES

Becker, Stephen K. *Back from the Brink: The Greenspan Years.* 1997. John Wiley & Sons.

Blinder, Alan S. *Central Banking in Theory and Practice (The Lionel Robbins Lectures).* 1999. MIT Press.

Meulendyke, Anne-Marie. *U.S. Monetary Policy and Financial Markets.* 1989. Federal Reserve Bank of New York.

CHAPTER 14

Topics Include

- Panic of 1907
- three main goals of the Federal Reserve system
- characteristics and organization of the Federal Reserve system
- services the Federal Reserve provides to banks
- services the Federal Reserve provides to the government
- components of the money supply
- Federal Reserve's use of monetary policy
- easy-money and tight-money policies
- methods the Federal Reserve uses to institute monetary policy
- limitations of the Federal Reserve's monetary policies

Economics Notebook

The Economics Notebook is a journal activity that encourages students to consider basic concepts of economics that relate to their lives. A follow-up Notebook activity appears on page 346.

▶ WHY IT MATTERS TODAY

To find additional lesson plans dealing with the Federal Reserve and monetary policy, visit CNNfyi.com or have students complete the ECONOMICS IN THE NEWS activity on page 345.

CNNfyi.com

326

CHAPTER 14

THE FEDERAL RESERVE AND MONETARY POLICY

Examine a $1 bill. At the top are the words *Federal Reserve Note*. As discussed in Chapter 13, the Federal Reserve acts as the central bank for the United States. But how exactly does the Federal Reserve system work, and what does it have to do with your money?

In this chapter you will learn about the development and organization of the Federal Reserve system. Additionally, you will learn how the Federal Reserve establishes monetary policy, and what tools are available to the Fed.

ECONOMICS NOTEBOOK

If you had a checking account containing $100, a savings account containing $250, and a CD worth $500, which would you consider to be "readily available"? Explain your answer in your Economics Notebook.

▶ WHY IT MATTERS TODAY

The Federal Reserve sets monetary policy, which is closely tied to economic growth. At the end of this chapter visit CNNfyi.com to learn more about how the Federal Reserve affects your life.

CNNfyi.com

SECTION 1

THE FEDERAL RESERVE SYSTEM

READ TO DISCOVER
1. How did the Panic of 1907 affect U.S. banking?
2. What are the purposes and characteristics of the Federal Reserve system?
3. How is the Fed organized?

ECONOMICS DICTIONARY
pyramided reserves

When first proposed in 1790, the idea of a central bank was controversial, and it remained so throughout much of U.S. history. Although the First and Second Banks of the United States worked to strengthen and stabilize the national economy, many people felt that a central bank placed far too much economic power in the hands of the federal government.

After the demise of the Second Bank of the United States, the government was not able to charter another central bank during the 1800s. Even a series of recessions during the late 1800s failed to revive public support for a central bank. The Panic of 1907, however, which caused the collapse of many banks and endangered the entire monetary system, broke the historic resistance to central banking.

Panic of 1907

The Panic of 1907 had two causes. First, the nation's monetary system at the time had no mechanism for expanding the amount of money in circulation. This meant that business expansion was restricted because consumers and businesses competed for a fixed supply of loanable funds. As individuals and businesses found themselves unable to borrow money, they began to withdraw their savings. During these "runs" on banks, many depositors withdrew funds from an institution at the same time. As a result, financially stable banks went bankrupt in 1907 because they had nowhere to turn for emergency cash, and a widespread financial panic took hold.

Second, the system of pyramided reserves failed. In a system of **pyramided reserves**, virtually all smaller, local banks deposit some of their reserves at larger city banks. These larger city banks, in turn, deposit some of their own cash reserves in the largest commercial banks in a nation's financial centers, such as New York, Chicago, and San Francisco in the United States. These largest banks use part of these deposits to extend loans and hold the rest as reserves.

During periods of prosperity the larger commercial banks receive more deposits and have more funds to loan. At such times a system of pyramided reserves encourages business expansion. During recessions, however, financial panic runs require smaller banks to withdraw their

FINANCIAL INSTITUTIONS & INCENTIVES *During the Panic of 1907, thousands of people rushed to their banks to withdraw the money in their accounts.* **How did these cash withdrawals cause the collapse of many banks?**

THE FEDERAL RESERVE AND MONETARY POLICY 327

Across the Curriculum

PSYCHOLOGY The Panic of 1907 occurred not only as a result of weaknesses in the banking system but also because of anxiety created by rumors. For example, shortly before the start of the panic, some diners in a New York restaurant were discussing problems associated with the Knickerbocker Trust Company, a major New York bank. Waiters overheard the discussion and shared the information with other diners, who in turn told still others. Within two days thousands had panicked and withdrawn their deposits from Knickerbocker Trust. As a result, the bank failed. This bank failure created a domino effect, as people became anxious about the reliability of other banks. The problems that created the Panic of 1907 ultimately led to the formation of the Federal Reserve System in 1913. ■

Enhancing the Lesson

For more information on the Federal Reserve Act, see Reading 41: Federal Reserve Act of 1913 in *From the Source: Readings in Economics and Government with Answer Key.*

Careers in Economics

To help students learn about other careers in economics, refer them to the Careers section on the *Researcher Online.*

---

deposits from the larger banks. As happened in the Panic of 1907, the reserves of the larger banks could not cover the sudden demand for cash because they had loaned out too much of the deposits. Thus, many businesses went bankrupt, and many depositors lost their savings.

To keep these two situations from recurring and causing another panic, in 1908 the newly created National Monetary Commission proposed the re-establishment of a central bank. As noted in Chapter 13, Congress recognized the need and responded to the recommendation by passing the Federal Reserve Act in 1913. The act created a central bank called the Federal Reserve system, more commonly referred to as the "Fed." (See Figure 14.1.)

CAREERS IN ECONOMICS

Accountant

In the complex worlds of banking, business, and personal finance, perhaps one of the most important jobs is that of accountant. You probably have heard accountants referred to by other names: bean counters, for example, or number crunchers. These names imply that accounting is not a glamorous career. Nevertheless, businesses and banks, like the Federal Reserve system, could not function without accountants.

Accountants perform a variety of vital functions. They collect and analyze data and check the accuracy of financial reports. An accountant may determine, for example, how much profit an auto dealership made last month. The dealership's management would then use that information to make decisions about such things as inventory and the size of the sales staff.

In addition, individuals hire accountants to sort through regulations, calculate tax payments, or advise them on investments. In fact, as tax laws have become more complicated, the demand for services provided by accountants has increased significantly. Banks also rely on accountants to keep track of investments, loans, and other financial transactions.

Accountants make up one of the largest professions in business today. By the 1990s more than 1 million people worked as accountants in the United States. What kind of person makes a good accountant? As you might guess, accountants must have strong math skills and an eye for detail. High ethical standards also are essential, for accountants often work with sensitive, confidential information.

Most accountants have a bachelor's degree in accounting, although large accounting firms sometimes require a master's degree. About one third of accountants become certified public accountants, or CPAs, by passing the Uniform CPA Examination of the American Institute of Certified Public Accountants.

Accountants provide financial analysis and advice to businesses, banks, and individuals.

CHAPTER 14

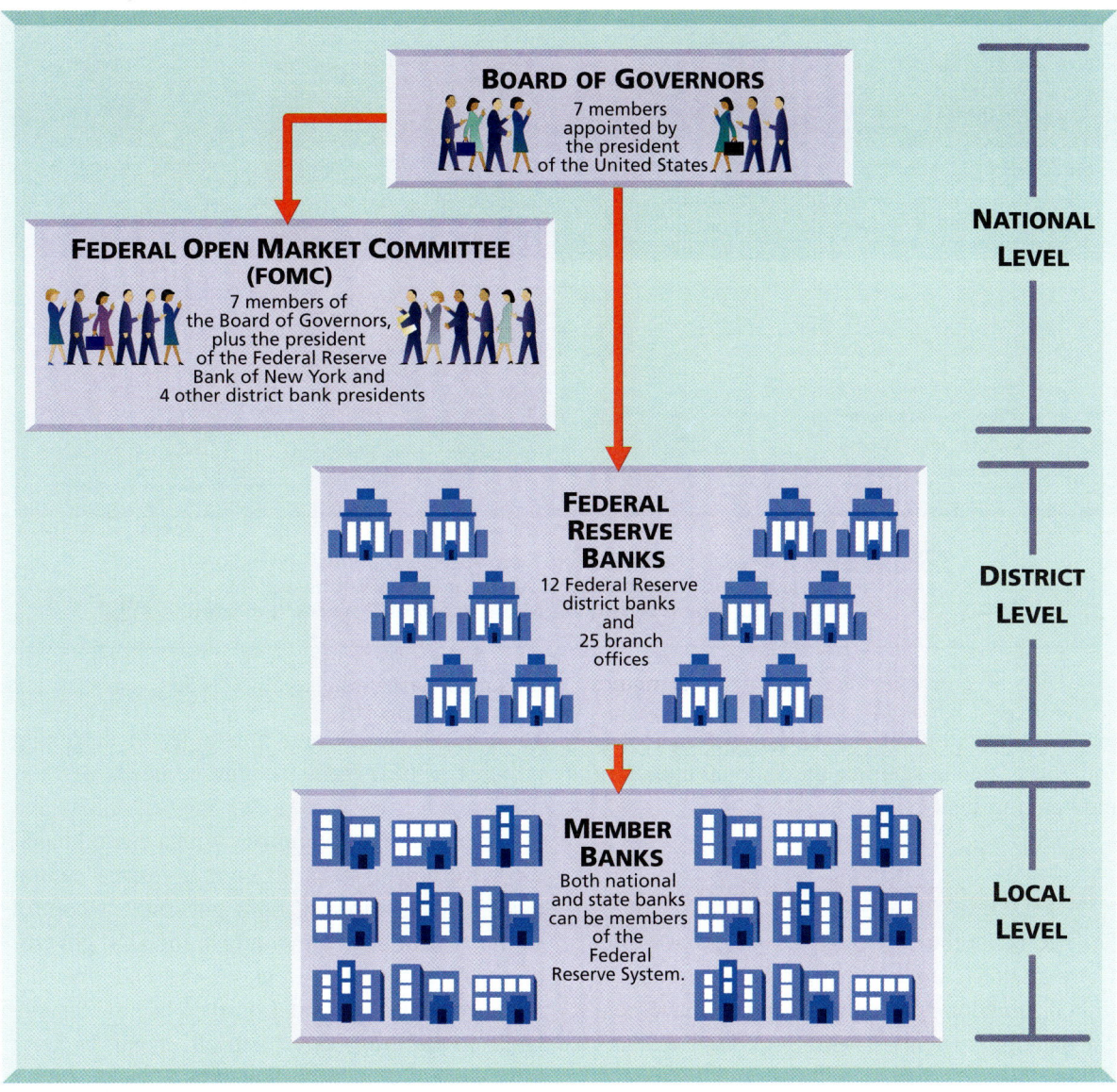

ORGANIZATION OF THE FED

BOARD OF GOVERNORS
7 members appointed by the president of the United States

FEDERAL OPEN MARKET COMMITTEE (FOMC)
7 members of the Board of Governors, plus the president of the Federal Reserve Bank of New York and 4 other district bank presidents

FEDERAL RESERVE BANKS
12 Federal Reserve district banks and 25 branch offices

MEMBER BANKS
Both national and state banks can be members of the Federal Reserve System.

NATIONAL LEVEL • DISTRICT LEVEL • LOCAL LEVEL

Source: Federal Deposit Insurance Corporation

FIGURE 14.1 The Federal Reserve acts as the central bank for the United States but is designed in a way that avoids control of the U.S. economy by a limited group of financiers. **How does the Fed stabilize banking on a national level?**

Role of the Fed

The Fed's stated goals were "to furnish an elastic currency, [and] . . . to establish a more effective supervision of banking in the United States." Today the Fed achieves these goals by serving three main purposes.

First, the Fed supervises member banks. Second, it holds cash reserves. These cash reserves represent funds available for short-term borrowing by commercial banks or by the government. The cash reserves guarantee that money is available in the economy when needed. Third, the Fed

---

Global Connections

The country best known for its banking system is Switzerland, which is one of the world's most important financial centers. Although a reputation for financial secrecy has made Swiss banks attractive to criminals who have money "to hide," most depositors are reputable international investors. Individuals and companies choose to deposit their funds in Swiss banks because of Switzerland's extremely stable economy and its long history and vast experience in the banking industry.

Transparency
An overhead transparency of Figure 14.1 is available in *Transparency Resources*. See Transparency 54: Organization of the Fed.

Caption Answer
by supervising member banks, holding cash reserves, and moving money into or out of circulation ★23A

THE FEDERAL RESERVE AND MONETARY POLICY

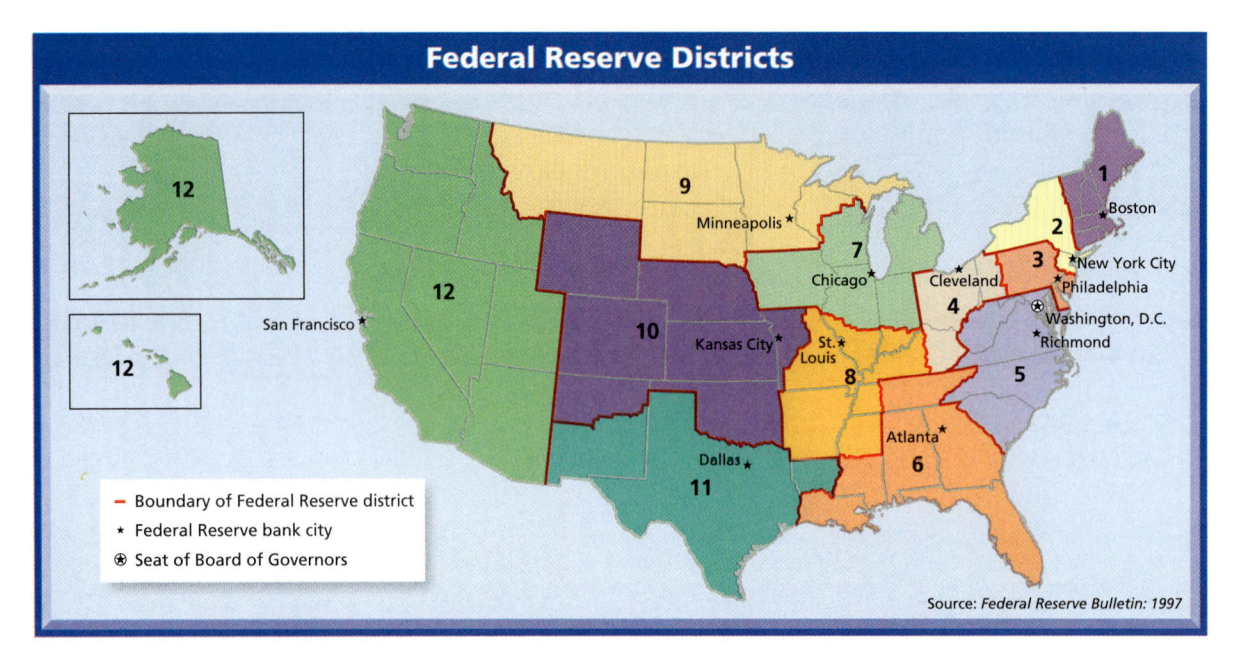

FIGURE 14.2 The Federal Reserve system is organized on national and regional levels, with 12 district banks, the Board of Governors, and the FOMC. **Where is the seat of the Board of Governors located?**

Characteristics of the Fed

The Fed is not the only central bank in the world. Many nations around the world, such as the United Kingdom, Japan, and Canada, have central banking systems. The U.S. Federal Reserve system, however, has several features that distinguish it from central banks in other nations. These features include

- lack of a single central bank,
- ownership and control by the member banks, and
- optional membership in the Fed for some banks.

First, in most countries there is a single central bank. The Federal Reserve system, on the other hand, relies on district banks to carry out the banking policies developed at the national level. These district Federal Reserve banks moves money into or out of circulation. In so doing, it is able to stabilize the national monetary and banking systems.

however, do have some flexibility in designing policies to best meet the unique needs of their districts.

Second, in most countries with a central bank, the government owns all or most of the central bank's stock, allowing tight government control of the central bank. In contrast, the U.S. government does not own stock in the Fed. Instead, member banks own stock in the Federal Reserve banks in their respective districts. In part because this stock is held by member banks rather than by the government, the Fed operates with a high degree of independence from political authorities—although it does ultimately report to Congress.

Third, most nations with a central banking system require all banks within their borders to be members of the central bank. In the United States, all nationally chartered banks are required to join the Fed. For state-chartered banks, however, membership in the Fed is optional. In fact, only about 40 percent of the commercial banks in the United States are members of the Federal Reserve system.

Organization of the Fed

The fact that the Federal Reserve system was designed to oversee banking practices throughout the United States caused many people to be concerned that a single central bank would hold too much power over the nation's economy. To avoid this problem and distribute financial control among different regions, the Fed is organized on two levels: national and district.

National Level The Fed makes its key decisions at the national level. The main decision-making bodies are the Board of Governors and the Federal Open Market Committee (FOMC).

The Board of Governors is the highest policy-making body in the Federal Reserve system. The board supervises the Fed's banking services and issues policies designed to regulate the supply of money in the economy. The president of the United States appoints—and the Senate then confirms—each of the seven members of the Board of Governors.

Each governor is appointed to a 14-year term. These terms are staggered so that one new governor is added to the board every two years. The board's chairperson serves a four-year term. Long terms of office and staggered appointments are designed to free the governors from any political influence by the executive and legislative branches of the federal government, as well as to limit the influence of any one governor.

The seven members of the Board of Governors and the president of the Federal Reserve Bank of New York are permanent members of the FOMC. The remaining four members are district Federal Reserve bank presidents who serve one-year terms on a rotating basis.

District Level The traditional fear of a single bank dominated by a few financiers led to the decision to create 12 separate Federal Reserve banks. Each of these district banks serves a designated geographic region of the United States (see Figure 14.2). In addition, 25 branch offices are located throughout the nation. All commercial banks chartered by the federal government are member banks of the Fed.

The member banks in each Federal Reserve district elect six of the nine directors of their Federal Reserve bank. No more than three of the six directors may be bankers. Other directors often have experience as business owners. The Board of Governors selects the remaining three directors of each bank.

SECTION 1 REVIEW

Q: 1, 2, 3b, 3c, 4

1. Identify and Explain:
pyramided reserves

2. Summarizing: Copy the diagram below. Use it to outline the structure of the Fed at the national, district, and local levels.

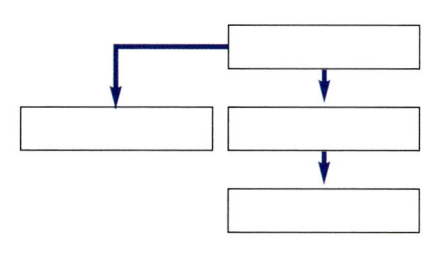

3. Finding the Main Idea
a. List the major causes of the panic of 1907, and explain how the government worked to resolve the panic.
b. Explain the role of the Fed. How does the Fed differ from central banks in other countries?
c. Why is the Federal Reserve System organized on national and district levels?

4. Writing and Critical Thinking
Analyzing Information: How is the Federal Reserve system designed to be largely independent of the federal government? Why would this separation from elected representatives be desirable?
Consider:
- how the Fed differs from most central banks
- how its governors are chosen

Homework Practice Online
keyword: SM3 HP14

SECTION 1 REVIEW ANSWERS

1. pyramided reserves (327) 24A

2. Refer to page 329. 18A, 24C, 24D

3a. The nation's monetary system had no mechanism for expanding the amount of money in circulation and the system of pyramided reserves failed. The government passed the Federal Reserve Act of 1913, which created the Federal Reserve System. 23A

3b. The Fed supervises member banks, holds cash reserves for making loans to commercial banks and the government, and moves money into or out of circulation to stabilize the national monetary and banking systems. The Fed lacks a single central bank, is owned by its members instead of by the government, and requires that only national banks—instead of all banks—become members 18A, 23A

3c. to distribute financial control among regions and prevent a single central bank or a few financiers from holding too much power over the economy 18A, 23A

4. The Fed lacks a single central bank; member banks, rather than the government, own and control the Fed; and members of the Board of Governors serve staggered 14-year terms. It frees the Fed from political influence and enables it to act in the best interests of the economy. 18A, 23A

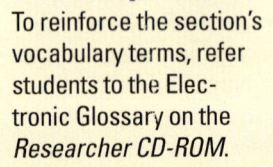

SECTION 2

THE FEDERAL RESERVE AT WORK

READ TO DISCOVER
1. What services does the Fed provide to banks?
2. How does the Fed serve the federal government?
3. How do economists measure the U.S. money supply?

ECONOMICS DICTIONARY
check clearing
money supply

What does the Federal Reserve system do for you? Directly, the Fed does not provide many services to you, for it is not designed to provide services to individuals. Instead, the Fed serves consumers like you *indirectly*—by providing services to commercial banks and to the federal government.

Services to Banks

As you know, one of the Fed's main roles is to supervise and provide services to commercial banks through its 12 Federal Reserve district banks. Although you cannot open a checking or savings account at a Federal Reserve bank, the banking services it provides make transactions at your local commercial bank easier and faster. What Fed activities enable these improvements to commercial banking?

The Fed oversees the flow of money between member banks and its district banks. It does so mainly by clearing checks and by lending reserves to commercial banks.

Clearing Checks Checks are used in millions of financial transactions every day. In fact, Americans write about 30 billion checks every year. The Fed keeps track of these billions of monetary transfers through the service of **check clearing**, which is a method of crediting and debiting banks' reserve accounts—and, in turn, checking accounts.

How does check clearing work? Suppose that you decide to buy a pair of running shoes at Foot Locker. Although the shoes are yours as soon as you write the check, it takes a little longer—and several more steps—to transfer money from your bank account to the store's. Figure 14.3 illustrates check clearing and highlights the Fed's role in the process.

Loans to Banks When you need a loan, you might visit a bank such as Glendale Federal Bank in California or Chevy Chase Bank in Maryland. When a bank or other depository institution needs a loan, it contacts its district Federal Reserve bank. Because their depositors may make large and unexpected withdrawals, banks often need short-term loans to replenish their reserves, or supplies of cash. Federal Reserve banks loan reserves, usually for periods of one day to several weeks.

Most Federal Reserve loans are sought for seasonal factors, natural disasters, and financial emergencies. Seasonal factors are the fairly predictable annual events that deplete reserves in banks. For example, the cash reserves of small rural banks are often reduced during the spring and summer planting and growing seasons when farmers withdraw their cash and apply for loans to pay for farm operations. Similarly, gift purchases during the December holiday season typically involve large withdrawals, and disasters such as floods or hurricanes naturally spur demands for loans. These withdrawals reduce cash reserves in banks. In these cases the Fed often lends money to depository institutions to replenish their reserves. In 1973 the Federal Reserve also established a seasonal credit program to help small banks in particular meet these swings in demand.

In financial emergencies such as a recession, the Fed serves as a "lender of last resort" by making emergency loans to commercial banks. Under special circumstances, a Federal Reserve bank also may extend loans to corporations and individuals who are unable to obtain funding from other financial institutions. To receive a loan from a Federal Reserve bank, financial institutions must meet strict qualifications such as collateral requirements. In deciding whether to make such a loan, the Fed analyzes the effect of the emergency on the national or regional economy. It then makes only those loans considered vital to the economic well-being of the region or

THE FED AND CHECK-CLEARING

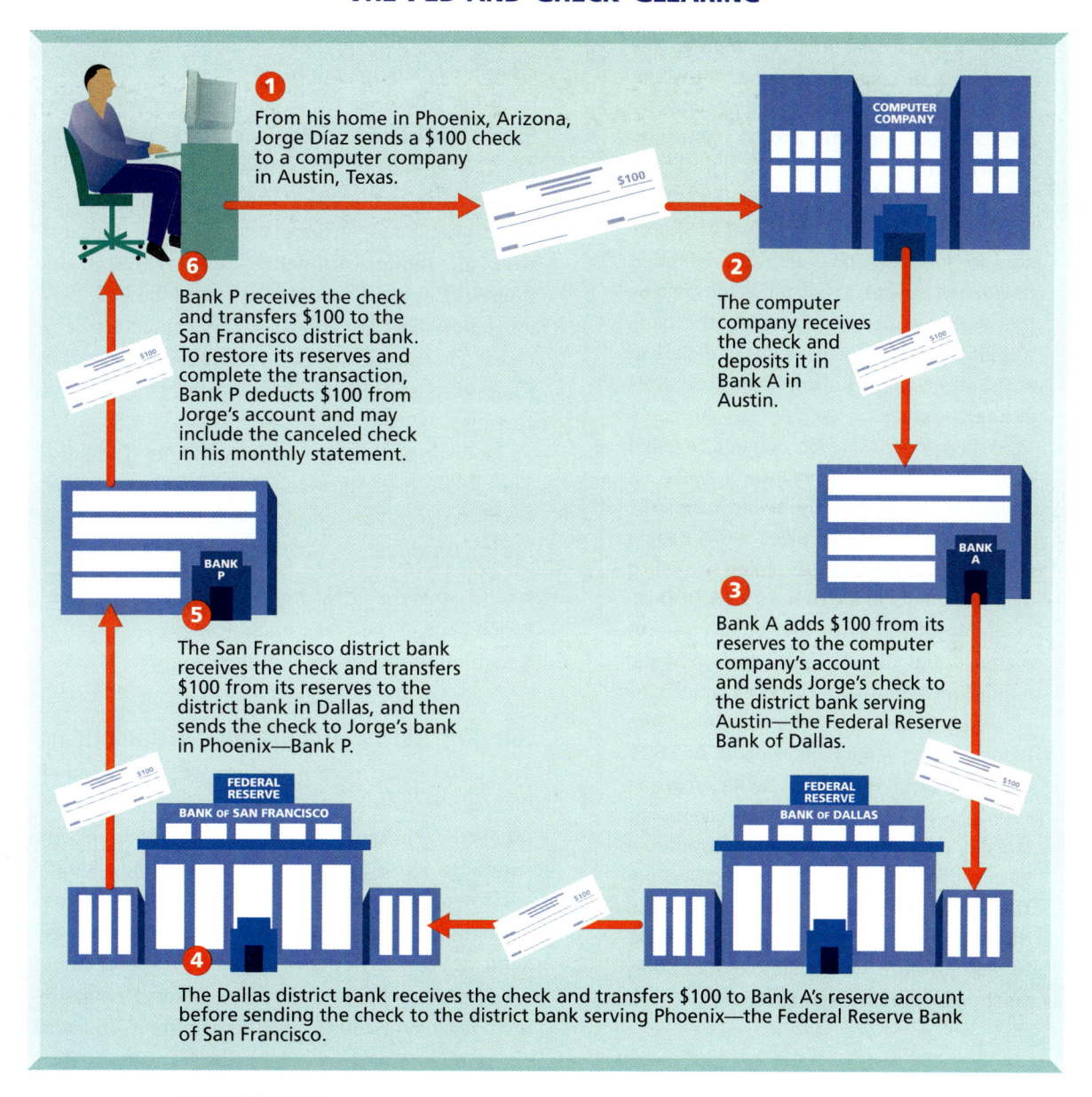

1 From his home in Phoenix, Arizona, Jorge Díaz sends a $100 check to a computer company in Austin, Texas.

2 The computer company receives the check and deposits it in Bank A in Austin.

3 Bank A adds $100 from its reserves to the computer company's account and sends Jorge's check to the district bank serving Austin—the Federal Reserve Bank of Dallas.

4 The Dallas district bank receives the check and transfers $100 to Bank A's reserve account before sending the check to the district bank serving Phoenix—the Federal Reserve Bank of San Francisco.

5 The San Francisco district bank receives the check and transfers $100 from its reserves to the district bank in Dallas, and then sends the check to Jorge's bank in Phoenix—Bank P.

6 Bank P receives the check and transfers $100 to the San Francisco district bank. To restore its reserves and complete the transaction, Bank P deducts $100 from Jorge's account and may include the canceled check in his monthly statement.

FIGURE 14.3 One of the Fed's primary functions is to service commercial banks. **Why must Jorge's check go through both the Dallas and San Francisco district banks?**

Across the Curriculum

TECHNOLOGY Of the billions of dollars exchanged between buyers and sellers, roughly 50 percent is exchanged in the form of checks. The Fed clears all of these checks. The Federal Reserve Bank of Dallas alone processes 4.5 million checks each day. The checks are read by a magnetic scanner at the rate of 100,000 an hour. Today, more and more monetary transactions—such as the direct deposit of paychecks—are being made electronically. To handle these paperless transfers, the Fed developed the automatic clearing house service (ACH). This system enables banks to use computers to electronically transfer funds from a customer's account to another account by way of Federal Reserve district banks. ■

Transparency

An overhead transparency of Figure 14.3 is available in *Transparency Resources*. See Transparency 56: The Fed and Check-Clearing.

Caption Answer

The Fed, through its district banks, tracks monetary transfers by debiting and clearing banks' reserve accounts. Jorge's check is going to a company in Austin (served by the Dallas district bank), and the money is coming from Jorge's account in Phoenix (served by the San Francisco district bank). ⭐23A

THE FEDERAL RESERVE AND MONETARY POLICY 333

Themes in Economics

ECONOMIC INSTITUTIONS & INCENTIVES In addition to providing services to banks and to the government, the Fed compiles information for consumers. For example, it publishes a number of books and pamphlets on such consumer-related topics as using credit cards, understanding mortgages, and filing complaints against banks. The Fed also holds educational workshops and provides free instructional materials to schools. ∎

Global Connections

In addition to the World Bank, other banks assist developing areas around the world. The Inter-American Development Bank was founded in 1959 to promote economic and social development in Latin America and the Caribbean. It now serves some 46 member nations. The African Development Bank aids countries in Africa, and the Asian Development Bank serves countries throughout Asia and the South Pacific. ∎

Enhancing the Lesson

For more information on international aid organizations, see the International Organizations section on the *Researcher Online*.

Global Exchange

Sharing the Wealth

Just as the Federal Reserve System works to stabilize the economy, the World Bank works on an international level to improve the economies of countries around the world. The World Bank has been providing funds for economic development since it was established in 1944.

The World Bank was established to fund Europe's recovery after World War II. Shortly after its founding, however, the institution broadened its work. Using funds provided by the wealthier member countries, the bank has loaned hundreds of billions of dollars to assist the economies of developing countries around the globe.

When Indonesia, for example, needed economic development money in 2001, its government turned to the World Bank. The World Bank agreed to provide $448 million to finance numerous projects, which included grants to the country's 15,000 villages for infrastructure and other improvements, and funds for environmental management and health services projects.

Argentina is one of the many other countries receiving World Bank support. In 2001 the World Bank loaned the South American country $400 million to promote economic stability by improving the administration of government functions such as tax collection. The World Bank also loaned $23.8 million to the African country of Madagascar in 2001 to help privatize several state-owned utility and transportation enterprises.

---

nation. All institutions that borrow often from the Fed become subject to financial review and close supervision by the federal government.

Services to Government

What is your budget? Think about how much money you earn and how much you spend every year. Each year the U.S. government raises and spends more than $1.5 trillion. The Treasury Department and the Fed generally work together to manage this vast sum and the government's complex financial activities.

What role does the Treasury Department play in this task? Think of the Treasury Department as the U.S. government's banker. The secretary of the treasury is the chief financial officer for the government and ensures that the U.S. Treasury pays all the government's bills. Through the Internal Revenue Service (IRS) and the U.S. Customs Service, the Treasury Department collects taxes. Through the U.S. Mint and the Bureau of Engraving and Printing, it produces coins and currency.

How does the Fed work with the Treasury? The Fed's role in managing the government's financial activities consists of providing the following services:

▶ serving as the government's bank
▶ supervising the Fed's member banks
▶ regulating the national money supply

Serving As the Government's Bank If the Treasury Department is the government's banker, then the Fed is the government's bank. That is, the Fed's banking services to government are similar to those that banks provide to individuals.

How does the Federal Reserve act as the government's bank? First, the Fed serves as the depository for federal revenues. Government funds are deposited in Federal Reserve banks by the Treasury. Second, the Fed holds a Treasury checking account on which the Treasury writes checks to cover tax refunds, Social Security payments, and all other government payments. Third, the Fed records the deposits and withdrawals of federal funds and conducts the purchase and sale of government securities such as Treasury bills. Finally, the Fed advises the legislative and executive branches of government on developing a coordinated economic program.

Supervising Member Banks The Fed also functions as the banking system's "watchdog." Each of the 12 Federal Reserve banks has a staff of bank examiners that supervises the financial activities of member banks. These examiners monitor loans and investments and conduct reviews of bank records. All financial depository institutions are required to maintain cash reserves to guarantee that depositors can withdraw their money when needed. The Fed monitors the reserves held by member banks, ensuring that these banks have enough money to meet withdrawal requests. In addition, the Fed regulates bank mergers and the chartering of bank holding companies to ensure that individual commercial banks do not gain too much power over the U.S. economy.

Regulating the Money Supply The Fed's third key function is the regulation of the nation's **money supply**, or the amount of money circulating in the U.S. economy. As noted in Chapter 13, the United States relies on a single form of currency. This money is produced in two forms: Federal Reserve notes—dollars—which are printed by the Treasury Department's Bureau of Engraving and Printing, and coins, which are generated by the U.S. Mint. The 12 Federal Reserve banks distribute this currency.

New currency is put into circulation for two major reasons. One reason is to replace old and worn-out notes, which eventually are destroyed. Banks regularly ship worn-out notes to their district Federal Reserve bank in exchange for new notes. The other reason is to increase the amount of money in circulation by expanding the pool of cash that the Federal Reserve banks can loan.

How does the Fed increase or decrease the U.S money supply? On behalf of the entire system, the Federal Reserve Bank of New York buys and sells U.S. government securities on the open

COMPONENTS OF THE MONEY SUPPLY, 1999

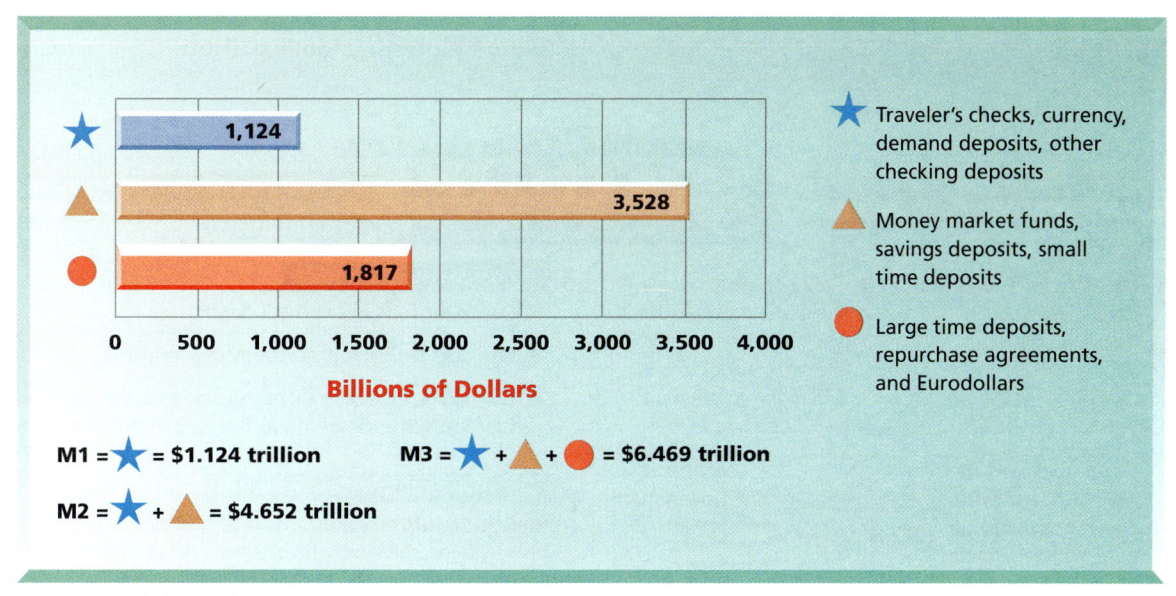

★ 1,124
▲ 3,528
● 1,817

Billions of Dollars (0 – 4,000)

★ Traveler's checks, currency, demand deposits, other checking deposits
▲ Money market funds, savings deposits, small time deposits
● Large time deposits, repurchase agreements, and Eurodollars

M1 = ★ = $1.124 trillion
M2 = ★ + ▲ = $4.652 trillion
M3 = ★ + ▲ + ● = $6.469 trillion

Source: Statistical Abstract of the United States: 2000

FIGURE 14.4 The most common measures of the money supply are M1 and M2. **What additional components are included in M3?**

Themes in Economics

ECONOMIC INSTITUTIONS & INCENTIVES Because monetary policy cannot be effective without a sound banking system, it is important for the Fed to ensure the safety and soundness of all banks. The Federal Reserve is responsible for monitoring all state and national member banks, as well as foreign branches of U.S. banks, and U.S. branches of foreign banks. The Fed uses five criteria to assess the soundness of banks: capital, assets, management, equity, and liquidity. The Fed refers to these criteria with the acronym *CAMEL*. ■

Transparency
An overhead transparency of Figure 14.4 is available in *Transparency Resources*. See Transparency 57: Components of the Money Supply, 1999.

Caption Answer
M3—all large time deposits, repurchase agreements, and Eurodollars. ★23A

Note
The Fed has stopped reporting *L* as a component of the money supply.

SECTION 2 REVIEW ANSWERS

1. check clearing (332), money supply (335) **24A**

2. left side—check clearing and lending reserves; right side—serves as government's bank, supervises member banks, regulates the money supply **18B, 23A, 24C, 24D**

3a. The Fed credits and debits banks' reserve accounts. **23A**

3b. The Fed buys and sells U.S. government securities. **18B, 23A**

3c. M1—all currency in circulation, the value of all travelers' checks, all checking-account deposits, and similar accounts in financial institutions; M2—M1 plus money-market accounts, money-market mutual fund shares, and other easily accessible savings deposits; M3—M2 plus all large time deposits, repurchase agreements, and Eurodollars **23A**

4. Treasury Department deposits government funds in Fed accounts; Treasury writes checks on accounts at the Fed; Fed conducts sales and purchases of all government securities, such as Treasury bills **15A, 18B, 23A**

---

market. Trading in securities allows the Fed both to increase or decrease the money supply and to provide the government with the cash it needs to finance public goods and services. The process by which the Fed trades securities is discussed in greater detail in Section 3.

Money Supply

Before taking action to regulate the money supply, the Fed must determine how much money is circulating in the economy. Economists—those working for the Fed and elsewhere—have determined several ways to measure the nation's money. These measures are called M1, M2, and M3.

M1 The narrowest, as well as the simplest, measure of the money supply is M1. Economists who prefer to use M1 believe that the money supply should consist only of funds that are easily accessible and in actual circulation. Thus, M1 counts all the currency in circulation, the value of all traveler's checks, all checking account deposits, and similar accounts in financial institutions. Checking and checking-type accounts represent nearly 50 percent of the M1 total. (See Figure 14.4 on page 335.) In 1999, M1 totaled more than $1.1 trillion.

M2 A broader measure of the money supply is M2, which totaled more than $4.6 trillion in 1999. Some economists insist that M1 does not include all readily available funds. They consider M2 to be more accurate because in addition to the money counted in M1, M2 includes money market accounts, money market mutual fund shares, and other savings deposits—such as certificates of deposit (CDs) in amounts under $100,000—that allow people easy access to their funds.

M2 also includes money deposited in savings accounts. The development of automated teller machines (ATMs) has allowed savings accounts to serve some of the same purposes as checking accounts. As noted in Chapter 13, ATMs allow depositors instant access to their savings accounts, turning those savings into spendable funds.

M3 Other economists believe that even M2 fails to accurately measure the money supply. They rely on M3, which is a broader measure than M2. M3 includes the money in M2 as well as all large time deposits (such as CDs valued at $100,000 or more), repurchase agreements, and some Eurodollars (U.S. dollars deposited by U.S. residents into U.S.-dollar bank accounts overseas). In 1999 M3 totaled more than $6.4 trillion.

SECTION 2 REVIEW

★TEKS Q: 1, 2, 3b, 4

1. Identify and Explain:
check clearing
money supply

2. Categorizing: Copy the diagram below. Use it to illustrate what services the Fed provides to banks and to the government.

Services to Banks ← Federal Reserve → Services to the Government

3. Finding the Main Idea
a. Explain the Fed's role in check clearing.
b. How does the Fed regulate the money supply?
c. Contrast the three different measurements of the U.S. money supply. Which funds are included in each measurement?

4. Writing and Critical Thinking
Analyzing Information: Analyze how the Fed and the Treasury Department work together to meet the federal government's financial needs.
Consider:
- the services the Fed provides to the government
- the statement, "the Treasury is the government's banker, and the Fed is the government's bank"

Homework Practice Online keyword: SM3 HP14

SECTION 3
MONETARY POLICY STRATEGIES

READ TO DISCOVER
1. Why does the Fed rely on either an easy-money policy or a tight-money policy?
2. How does the Fed make monetary policy?
3. What are the challenges associated with determining monetary policy?

ECONOMICS DICTIONARY
- monetary policy
- easy-money policy
- tight-money policy
- discount rate
- prime rate
- reserve requirement
- margin requirement
- moral suasion

The services provided by the Federal Reserve make the U.S. monetary and banking systems more efficient and sound. The major goal of the Fed, however, is to promote the goals of economic growth and stability. The Fed tries to achieve this goal through the use of monetary policy.

Monetary Policy and Aggregate Demand

Through its monetary policy, the Fed regulates the amount of money and credit available in the economy. **Monetary policy** is the plan to expand or contract the money supply in order to influence the cost and availability of credit. By regulating the money supply and the interest rates charged for credit, the Fed influences aggregate demand. As noted in Chapter 11, aggregate demand is the total demand for all products in the economy. As you also know, demand requires that consumers be willing and able to buy a product. Aggregate demand has the same requirements, but reflects demand for all goods and services in the U.S. economy rather than for a particular product.

The Fed measures both the money supply and aggregate demand in order to develop a monetary policy. Based on the amount of money and the spending habits of people across the United States, the Fed adopts either an easy-money policy or a tight-money policy.

Easy-Money Policy An **easy-money policy** is designed to expand the money supply, increase aggregate demand, create jobs, and thus reduce

MONETARY POLICY *The popularity of computers has made silicon chips such as these a significant part of aggregate demand.* **How does the Fed influence aggregate demand?**

THE FEDERAL RESERVE AND MONETARY POLICY 337

MONETARY POLICY *In 1997 Fed chairman Alan Greenspan was criticized for over-reacting to fears of inflation.* **What monetary policy does the Fed use to rein in inflation?**

unemployment and promote economic growth. The Fed usually adopts an easy-money policy during a recession because the economy needs a financial boost. By charging banks a lower interest rate to borrow money, the Fed makes more money available to those banks. When banks pay less in interest on loans from the Fed, they are able to lower the interest rates they charge their customers.

When banks charge lower interest rates, people and businesses borrow more money. Increased borrowing and spending in turn stimulate economic growth as businesses make more products and hire more workers. Businesses then expand by investing new capital.

Suppose that the Fed charges a lower interest rate to banks, and as a result bank interest rates on car loans drop from 8 percent to 6.5 percent. Samantha Shapiro decides that because interest rates are lower, she can afford to borrow money to buy a car. As other consumers make similar decisions, demand for cars increases. Automobile producers hire more workers and provide more cars. These workers have new income and further stimulate aggregate demand.

Tight-Money Policy In contrast to an easy-money policy, a tight-money policy slows business activity and helps stabilize prices. The Fed may determine that inflation is likely to develop because too much money is circulating and credit is too accessible. To restrict or contract the money supply and thus limit credit, the Fed adopts a tight-money policy. A **tight-money policy** is characterized by higher interest rates and a contraction of the money supply, both of which are designed to reduce aggregate demand.

Suppose that Jack Hendricks wants to buy a new dishwasher. He discovers that interest rates on loans have increased. Jack decides to delay his purchase until interest rates decline. As other consumers also postpone purchases, aggregate demand declines.

CASE STUDY

Alan Greenspan and Tight-Money Policy

MONETARY POLICY Alan Greenspan, chairman of the Federal Reserve's Board of Governors since 1987, is a strong supporter of a tight-money policy. He believes that decreasing the amount of money in circulation and reducing the rate of economic growth will maintain price stability.

For example, in 1995, reports indicated that the U.S. economy was enjoying its highest rate of growth in ten years. Rather than allow this to continue, the Board of Governors—under Greenspan—introduced policies to slow the economy.

Why would the Fed not want the economy to grow even further? Economic growth causes the demand for goods and services to rise, and when demand outpaces supply, prices tend to inflate. To prevent inflation, Greenspan raised the interest rate that the Fed charges banks. Banks were less willing to borrow money, so the money supply was tightened.

The Fed under Greenspan continued its policy of raising interest rates until 2001, when the economy began to slow down. By August 2001, the Fed had lowered the rate seven times in an attempt to revive the sluggish economy, dropping interest rates to what they had been in spring 1994, just before Greenspan began tightening the money supply.

Components of Monetary Policy

How does the Fed put monetary policy to work? There are several ways the Fed can influence the money supply, the availability of credit, and aggregate demand. The key components of the Fed's monetary policy are open-market operations, the discount rate, and the reserve requirement. The Fed also has other formal and informal ways to affect aggregate demand in the economy, including margin requirements, credit regulation, and moral suasion. Figure 14.5 summarizes the Fed's monetary policy tools.

Open-Market Operations The main tool of the Fed is open-market operations, or the buying and selling of government securities. The Federal Open Market Committee (FOMC) makes decisions to buy or sell government securities based on the monetary policy set by the Board of Governors. The Federal Reserve Bank of New York conducts the transactions through private securities dealers, who buy and sell billions of dollars worth of government securities in a single day.

How does the Fed decide whether to buy or to sell government securities? If the Fed wants to contract the money supply, it does so by selling government securities. The cash paid for the securities is ultimately withdrawn from bank reserves, thus shrinking the money supply and decreasing aggregate demand.

When the Fed wants to inject money into the economy, on the other hand, it buys back government securities. The buy-back money paid for these securities ultimately winds up in individuals' and businesses' bank accounts, increasing cash reserves and loan pools. When the government buys securities directly from a bank, the bank's reserves similarly are increased. Either way, the money supply expands. As more money enters circulation, banks make more consumer loans, enabling consumers to purchase more goods and services. To meet this increase in aggregate demand, production rises and the supply of goods and services increases.

Discount Rate A second major component of the Fed's monetary policy is the **discount rate**, the interest rate that the Fed charges member

SUMMARY OF MONETARY POLICY TOOLS

Formal Tool	Fed Action	Effects on Economy	Money Supply
Open-Market Securities	buys government securities	bank reserves increase; aggregate demand and production increase	expands
	sells government securities	bank reserves shrink; aggregate demand decreases	contracts
Discount Rate	lowers discount rate	encourages banks to borrow from the Fed; bank reserves increase	expands
	raises discount rate	discourages banks from borrowing from the Fed; bank reserves decrease	contracts
Reserve Requirement	lowers the reserve requirement percentage	banks hold fewer reserves and extend more loans; interest rates fall; aggregate demand and production increase	expands
	raises the reserve requirement percentage	banks hold more reserves and extend fewer loans; interest rates rise; aggregate demand and production decrease	contracts

FIGURE 14.5 The Fed works to promote economic growth and stability through its monetary policy. **Describe how the Fed can use these tools to enact an easy-money policy.**

Themes in Economics

MONETARY POLICY The Federal Open Market Committee (FOMC) meets regularly to make decisions about expanding or contracting the nation's money supply. One important resource the FOMC relies on to formulate monetary policy is the *Summary of Commentary on Current Economic Conditions*, commonly known as the Beige Book. This book, which is published eight times a year, provides information on current economic conditions across the nation, based on reports from each of the 12 Federal Reserve banks. Each bank examines economic documents and interviews important businesspeople, economists, and market experts in its district to gather information for its report. Researchers then condense each report into a summary to present an overall picture of the current U.S. economy.

Transparency

An overhead transparency of Figure 14.5 is available in *Transparency Resources*. See Transparency 58: Summary of Monetary Policy Tools.

Caption Answer

To enact an easy-money policy, the Fed buys government securities and lowers the discount rate and the reserve requirement percentage.

Themes in Economics

ECONOMIC INSTITUTIONS & INCENTIVES The Federal Reserve assists inner-city development by monitoring banks' compliance with the Community Reinvestment Act (CRA) of 1977. The CRA encourages banks and other depository institutions to provide loans to nearby businesses and individuals in low- and moderate-income neighborhoods. Although the CRA does not force banks to make high-risk loans, it does require them to make fair loan decisions. ■

What Do You Think? Answers

1. Answers will vary, but most students will point out that the businesses need to succeed and grow so that more and greater economic opportunities become available to inner-city neighborhoods. ★23A

2. Answers will vary. Institutions students might identify include banks and other financial institutions, various government agencies, and the local chamber of commerce and other, similar business organizations. ★25A

Economics IN ACTION

Building Businesses in the Inner City

Business decisions can be complicated matters, whether one works with the Federal Reserve or sells hot dogs from a cart on a street corner. In fact, one of the most important resources for business owners is the information they need to make smart decisions about their companies.

The Initiative for a Competitive Inner City (ICIC) was created to meet this need for businesses in inner-city neighborhoods. The national nonprofit organization works to encourage economic development in low-income areas. One ICIC program, for example, matches students in graduate business schools with businesses in inner cities.

Many business owners in inner-city neighborhoods do not have formal business training and are often too busy running their own businesses to plan for the future. "Some places are losing money, but they don't know where the holes are," says program participant Ileana Scheytt. To improve the economic health of these small businesses, students in the ICIC program provide owners with free advice on such things as marketing, borrowing money, and keeping good records.

Scheytt, for example, worked as a consultant to businesses in Harlem while earning a master's degree in business administration (MBA) at Columbia University in the mid-1990s. Harlem, a predominantly African-American neighborhood in New York City, has a rich cultural history. During the 1920s, the neighborhood was one of the most vital African-American communities in the country and was home of the Harlem Renaissance, a literary movement which produced a number of important writers such as the poet Langston Hughes. After World War II, however, overcrowding, racial discrimination, and other factors made Harlem one of this country's poorer neighborhoods.

In recent years, however, Harlem has undergone an economic revival, and students in the ICIC program have made a major contribution. For instance, Columbia's business school students used their knowledge to conduct market surveys, develop business plans, and provide other business services. Among their most important tasks was designing a small-business loan program for the neighborhood's Carver Federal Savings Banks.

One sign of the neighborhood's improved economic fortunes was the opening in 2000 of the $66 million Harlem USA mall. Harlem USA also received support from the ICIC in the form of a study of inner-city shoppers co-authored by the ICIC that encouraged many national retailers to rent space in the mall.

The ICIC has developed consulting programs with a number of business schools across the country and since 1999 has held an annual Inner City Field Study competition that has attracted teams of MBA candidates from schools across the country.

What Do You Think? ★TEKS

1. Why is it important that businesses in inner city neighborhoods get the help they need to be successful and grow?

2. What institutions besides colleges and universities can help businesses in disadvantaged neighborhoods thrive?

Patti Lewis, president of the Alexander Doll Company, received business advice from the Initiative for a Competitive Inner City.

340 CHAPTER 14

banks for the use of its reserves. It adjusts the discount rate to encourage or discourage borrowing. The Fed extends short-term loans to commercial banks to help them maintain sufficient cash reserves. Banks generally attempt to borrow from the Fed only after they have exhausted all other methods of meeting their temporary cash shortfalls.

Lowering the discount rate encourages banks to borrow, increasing the reserves that banks can in turn loan to businesses and individuals. Conversely, increasing the discount rate discourages banks from borrowing from the Fed.

Changes in the discount rate can directly affect the interest rates charged by banks and other financial institutions. Banks and other lenders often pass on the savings from decreases—or costs from increases—in the Fed's discount rate to their customers by lowering or raising their prime rate. The **prime rate**, the interest rate that commercial banks charge on loans to their most reliable business customers, is then used to determine the bank's general interest rate. (See Figure 14.6.) As interest rates fall and consumers and businesses take out more loans, the money supply increases. Why? An interest rate is the "price" of borrowing money. When the Fed lowers the discount rate on loans—charging commercial banks a lower price for borrowed money—banks then can decrease the interest rates they charge individual borrowers.

Reserve Requirement

A third part of the Fed's monetary policy is its reserve requirement. The **reserve requirement** is the money that must be held by banks either in their own vaults or in their accounts at the district Federal Reserve bank. As you have learned, the reserve requirement ensures that banks can meet demand requests.

The reserve requirement is a percentage of each bank's total net transaction accounts. In other words, the Fed determines how much money is in transaction accounts in each bank, and requires the bank to hold a percentage of that total in reserve.

In 1997 the reserve requirement was 3 percent on all such funds on deposit up to $42.8 million and $1,284,000 plus 10 percent on funds over that amount. Banks are not required, however, to hold reserves on time deposits and other accounts that are less liquid than checking accounts.

The Fed can increase or decrease the money supply and influence aggregate demand through its control of the reserve-requirement percentages. When the Fed lowers the percentage, banks

Themes in Economics

MONETARY POLICY Originally, the Federal Reserve was empowered to set reserve requirements for member banks only. Although some state governments also set reserve requirements, generally only commercial banks were affected. The Monetary Control Act of 1980, however, gave the Fed the authority to set reserve requirements for all depository institutions—savings and loans as well as banks—regardless of whether they are members of the Federal Reserve system or not. ■

Enhancing the Lesson

For more information about the discount rate and the prime rate over time, see the Banking and Finance section on the *Researcher Online*.

Transparency

An overhead transparency of Figure 14.6 is available in *Transparency Resources*. See Transparency 59: Discount Rate and Prime Rate.

Caption Answer

The prime rate often rises or falls by about the same amount as the Fed increases or decreases the discount rate. ★23F

DISCOUNT RATE AND PRIME RATE

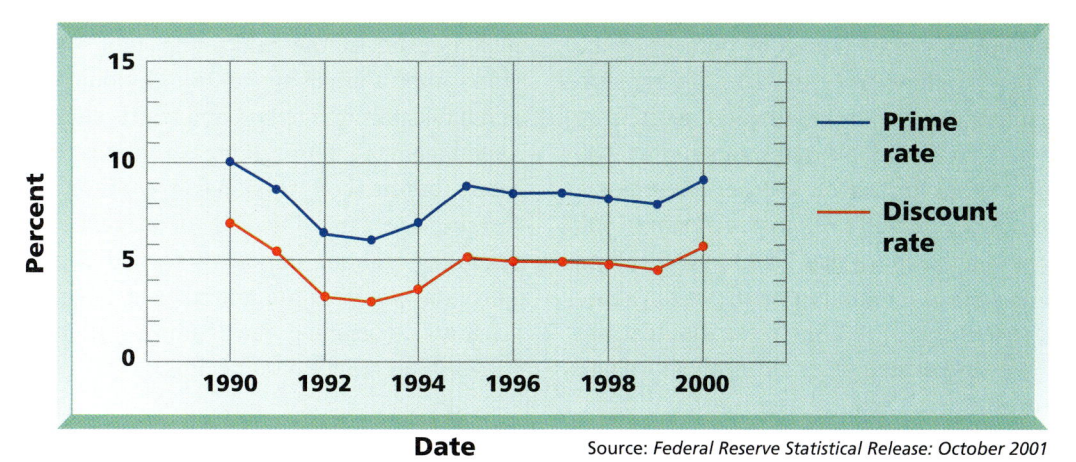

Source: Federal Reserve Statistical Release: October 2001

FIGURE 14.6 Changes in the Fed's discount rate can affect the interest rate charged by banks and other lending institutions. **What does the graph suggest about the relationship between the discount rate and the prime rate?** ★TEKS

Cultural Perspectives

In early 1997 the Federal Reserve used moral suasion to influence lending policies after devastating floods caused severe financial stress in Minnesota, North Dakota, and South Dakota. The Federal Reserve issued a press release outlining steps it had taken to encourage financial institutions to help people affected by the flooding. Among other things, the Fed recommended that banks ease credit terms, refinance existing loans, and extend repayment terms. ■

---

internet connect

TOPIC: Government in the Sunshine Act
GO TO: go.hrw.com
KEYWORD: SM3 EC14

Have students access the Internet through the HRW Go site to conduct research on the Government in the Sunshine Act. Many federal agencies are headed by bodies that make decisions through discussions and voting. To ensure that such decisions not take place in secret, Congress passed the Government in the Sunshine Act in 1976. Research the exemptions that allow the Fed to have closed meetings. Write an editorial in which you oppose or support the existence of closed Fed meetings.
★ 15A, 23D, 24A, 24B, 24D

---

do not need to hold as large a portion of their deposits as reserves. The result is that banks can extend more loans. The combination of more money and easier credit produced by the easy-money policy serves to increase aggregate demand and production in the overall economy.

By raising the percentages of the reserve requirement, on the other hand, the Fed forces banks to hold a larger portion of their deposits as reserves. This enables banks to cut back on their lending, thus contracting the money supply. As the supply of loanable funds shrinks, interest rates rise. As a result, aggregate demand and production slow down. The Fed uses such a tight-money policy to fight inflation.

The percentage requirements change annually according to a formula specified in the Monetary Control Act of 1980. The Fed does not often make frequent or dramatic changes to the reserve requirement, however, because such changes would create uncertainty in the banking system, thus making it more difficult for banks to make long-term loans and investments.

Margin Requirements The Fed also places indirect controls on credit as part of tight-money or easy-money policy. The Securities Exchange Act of 1934 authorizes the Board of Governors to set **margin requirements**, the percentage of cash an investor must have to buy stocks, options, and other investments. If, for example, the margin requirement is set at 60 percent of the stock's value, the investor must put up 60 percent of the investment's purchase price in cash. The remaining 40 percent can be purchased with credit.

Suppose that Elise Donovan wants to buy 100 shares of a stock priced at $10 per share for a total of $1,000. She will need to pay at least $600 in cash, buying no more than $400 of stock with credit. The goal of margin requirements is to prevent the occurrence of wild price fluctuations caused by over-reliance on credit in the purchase of securities.

A high margin requirement discourages investment in the stock market. Low margin requirements, on the other hand, may make stock investing more popular. Since the stock market crash of 1929, the Fed generally has set relatively high margin requirements.

Credit Regulation A second indirect control is the Fed's power to regulate consumer credit in times of national emergency. During World War II and the Korean War, for example, the Fed required high down payments and shorter repayment schedules for consumer loans. These requirements limited the availability of credit, as many people were unable to meet the requirements. As credit became more expensive, fewer people chose to buy consumer goods. The new, lower level of aggregate demand led producers to reduce supply. The government then was able to encourage many suppliers to produce war-related products.

The Fed coordinated its consumer credit policies with its easy- or tight-money policies. Suppose that Evelyn Ogata decides to borrow money so that she can convert her garage into a spare bedroom. Under an easy-money policy, she is able to arrange for a long loan repayment period. If she borrows money while a tight-money policy is in place, however, she may have to make higher payments over a shorter period of time. The Fed's ability to regulate credit was revoked in 1952.

Moral Suasion In addition to its official tools, the Fed can informally restrict aggregate demand in the U.S. economy. **Moral suasion** refers to the unofficial pressures that Federal Reserve policy makers exert on the banking system. Moral suasion can be a direct appeal to individual commercial banks through letters and conferences, public announcements through press releases, and testimony before congressional committees. These techniques enable the Fed to influence banking practices without imposing formal regulations. Through the use of moral suasion, the Fed attempts to channel the lending policies of all banks in the direction it desires.

Policy Limitations

The enormous size of the U.S. economy presents a number of obstacles that the Federal Reserve

MONETARY POLICY *The difficulty of economic forecasting is one of the main challenges to effective monetary policy.* **Why must the Fed make economic forecasts?**

must deal with in order to carry out its duties. The Fed's main challenges are

- economic forecasts
- time lags in developing and carrying out monetary policy
- priorities and trade-offs
- lack of coordination among government agencies in formulating economic policies and
- conflicting opinions about monetary policy.

Economic Forecasting

To develop monetary policy, the Fed first must create an economic forecast, or a prediction of future business activity and consumer spending. Will automobile production increase or decrease? How many laptop computers will be sold? Will consumers buy more gasoline? These economic forecasts provide the assumptions on which the Fed's policies are made. Making these forecasts is a difficult task, however, because the U.S. economy includes millions of economic actors, products, and markets. Incorrect forecasts can lead to inappropriate policies.

Time Lags

Once an economic forecast is developed, time passes before policies go into effect. These time lags are the unavoidable delays that occur before government agencies are able to put their policies into action. Three types of time lags disrupt the effectiveness of the Fed's monetary policy.

First, collecting and studying the tremendous amount of economic data needed for analysis and action by the Federal Reserve can take months. Second, once the data have been studied, time-consuming discussions occur before agreement on an appropriate monetary policy is reached.

Third, additional months may pass before the impact of the monetary policy is felt throughout the economy. Consumers and businesses need time to adjust their buying and selling decisions to tight-money or easy-money policies. Aggregate demand and business activity seldom react instantly to the Fed's actions.

Priorities and Trade-Offs

A third limitation on monetary policy is that it cannot do more than it is designed to do. Monetary policy is designed primarily to fight either inflation or recession. In some cases certain economic policies used to remedy one problem may make another problem worse. For example, an easy-money policy fights the problems of recession but often causes an increase in inflation. Conversely, a tight-money policy is effective in combating inflation, but it tends to decrease business activity and contribute to recession. The Fed must weigh trade-offs and establish priorities for the nation's various economic challenges to develop an effective economic policy.

Lack of Coordination

A fourth limitation on the Fed's actions is that other government agencies sometimes target different economic priorities than those identified by the Fed. This lack of coordination among government agencies can hinder economic stability and often sends mixed signals to the market.

During the early 1980s, for example, some economists believed that the government's

---

Caption Answer
to provide the assumptions on which it can develop monetary policy ⭐23A

Across the Curriculum

GOVERNMENT During the late 1970s and early 1980s the United States experienced what is known as stagflation—a period of both high inflation and high unemployment. Stagflation presented a unique problem for the Federal Reserve. In determining monetary policy, the Fed had to examine various trade-offs. A tight-money policy designed to fight inflation might increase unemployment. An easy-money policy designed to boost the economy and employment might increase inflation. Under the leadership of Paul Volcker, the then chairman of the Board of Governors, the Fed decided to focus on inflation and thus raised the discount rate. The result was a recession that lasted through 1982. Although some criticize Volcker's actions, others credit him with preventing potentially devastating inflation. ■

Caption Answer
Government spending can increase aggregate demand, which would contradict the Fed if it were promoting a tight-money policy. ★23A

SECTION 3 REVIEW ANSWERS

1. monetary policy (337), easy-money policy (337), tight-money policy (338), discount rate, (339), prime rate (341), reserve requirement (341), margin requirement (342), moral suasion (342) 24A

2. open-market operations, discount rate, reserve requirement 18B, 24C, 24D

3a. easy-money policy—to expand the money supply, increase aggregate demand, create jobs and reduce unemployment, and promote economic growth; tight-money policy—to restrict the money supply, reduce aggregate demand, slow business activity, and stabilize prices 17C, 23A

3b. buying and selling government securities, raising or lowering the discount rate, and raising or lowering the reserve requirement 18B, 23A

3c. incorrect economic forecasts, time lags in enacting monetary policy, difficulties in establishing priorities and trade-offs, and lack of coordination among government agencies 23A

4. Answers should reflect an understanding of why the Fed uses moral suasion. 23D, 24A, 24B, 24D

(344)

MONETARY POLICY *Lack of coordination among government agencies can send mixed signals to the market.* **How might government spending on programs such as space exploration contradict the Fed's policies?**

monetary policies and its fiscal policies seemed to contradict one another. The Fed's tight-money policy, targeting inflation as the nation's chief economic problem, sought to restrict the money supply and reduce aggregate demand. At the same time, however, Congress and the president approved massive tax reductions and federal spending hikes. These actions increased demand and total spending in the economy.

Conflicting Opinions A final limitation on monetary policy effectiveness is the disagreement some economists have about the Fed's priorities. For example, monetarists are economists who believe economic growth and stability result from regular, long-term alterations to the money supply. Monetarists argue that the Fed's manipulation of the money supply and aggregate demand damages the economy rather than improves it. Monetarists believe that the Fed should increase the money supply by an established amount each year rather than responding to short-term ups and downs in the economy.

The disagreement over the goals of U.S. monetary policy among policy makers underscores the fact that economics is not an exact science like physics or chemistry. Because of this lack of certainty, the Federal Reserve and other government agencies cannot develop policies that consistently solve all of the complex economic issues in the United States.

SECTION 3 REVIEW

★TEKS Q: 1, 2, 3a, 3b, 4

1. Identify and Explain:
monetary policy
easy-money policy
tight-money policy
discount rate
prime rate
reserve requirement
margin requirement
moral suasion

2. Analyzing Information: Copy the diagram below. Use it to identify the three components of monetary policy.

(Components of Monetary Policy diagram)

3. Finding the Main Idea
a. What are the goals of the Fed's easy-money policy? its tight-money policy?
b. What are the three main tools the Fed uses to implement monetary policy?
c. What obstacles can hinder the Fed's monetary policy?

4. Writing and Critical Thinking
Drawing Conclusions: How has moral suasion influenced your economic activities or other aspects of your daily life? Explain your answer.
Consider:
• what constitutes moral suasion
• why the Fed uses moral suasion

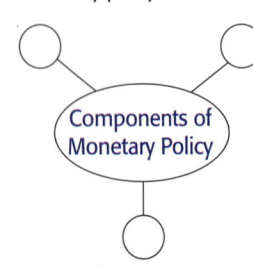

Homework Practice Online
keyword: SM3 HP14

344 CHAPTER 14

Economics IN THE NEWS

Has Alan Greenspan Lost His Magic Touch?

Shortly after Alan Greenspan became chairman of the Fed in 1987, the U.S. economy threatened to go into a tailspin. In just one day in October, the stock market fell over 22 percent. In an effort to keep the declining stock market from infecting the rest of the economy, as it had after the 1929 crash, Greenspan discreetly encouraged banks to continue lending money in spite of poor economic conditions. The strategy worked. Greenspan's actions helped avoid an economic crisis.

During much of the 1990s, Greenspan used the tools of the Federal Reserve wisely. By relying on a tight-money policy, moral suasion, and an understanding that the emerging new economy would allow for higher rates of growth without inflation or unemployment, Greenspan's policies as Federal Reserve Chairman contributed to the longest economic boom in American History.

By 2000, Greenspan's reputation had reached near-heroic status. A biography published in that year hailed the Fed chairman as the "maestro." When Greenspan spoke, the world listened.

Or so it seemed. As early as 1996, Greenspan had warned that investment in the skyrocketing stock market had reached a point of "irrational exuberance." By 2000, profit expectations had far outstripped the actual economic value of the underlying businesses. He again warned that inflated stock prices could lead to a slowdown of the entire economy.

Nonetheless, in 2001, when stock prices began to tumble and the economy began to falter, many blamed Greenspan's interest rate policies. Critics blamed the Fed for not raising interest rates in 1998 and 1999, when it could have helped slow the economy. They also blamed the Fed for raising interest rates too much in 2000 and then

Chairman of the Federal Reserve Alan Greenspan decides U.S. monetary policy. Many people believe that he has even more influence over the U.S. economy than the President.

being too slow to cut interest rates when the economy began to rapidly decline in early 2001.

On the other hand, some economic analysts blamed the 2001 economic slowdown on factors other than the Fed's money policies. Those factors included too much business investment in new equipment and technology, growing consumer debt, falling stock prices, and trade deficits.

Still others questioned the assumption that Greenspan and the Fed have the duty to manage the country's overall economic health. Instead, they argued that Greenspan's main duty is to keep inflation down.

What Do You Think?

1. Cite an example of Alan Greenspan's use of moral suasion.
2. How might time lags have affected the Fed's ability to respond to the economic slowdown of 2001?

WHY IT MATTERS TODAY
Debate over Alan Greenspan's performance will continue. Use CNNfyi.com or other **current events** sources to find the latest information on his performance as Chairman of the Fed.

CNNfyi.com

Economics in the News Answers

1. 1987—urged banks to continue lending in spite of poor economic conditions 23A

2. Answers should reflect understanding of the problem of time lags in setting monetary policy, and might also address the time it takes before the impact of monetary policy is felt in the economy. 23A

CHAPTER 14
Review Answers

Writing a Summary
Summaries should focus on the main points of each section. These may be found in the Read to Discover questions at the start of each section. Summaries should also use standard grammar, spelling, sentence structure, and punctuation. 24A, 24B

Identifying Ideas
pyramided reserves (327), check clearing (332), money supply (335), monetary policy (337), easy-money policy (337), tight-money policy (338), discount rate (339), prime rate (341), reserve requirements (342), moral suasion (342) 24A

Understanding Main Ideas
1. It distributes financial control over two national governing bodies and 12 district banks. 18A

345

CHAPTER 14 Review

Writing a Summary

Using standard grammar, spelling, sentence structure, and punctuation, write a summary of the information in the chapter.

Identifying Ideas

Identify the following terms or individuals and explain their significance.

1. pyramided reserves
2. check clearing
3. money supply
4. monetary policy
5. easy-money policy
6. tight-money policy
7. discount rate
8. prime rate
9. reserve requirements
10. moral suasion

Understanding Main Ideas

SECTION 1 (pp. 327–31)

1. How does the organization of the Federal Reserve System avoid placing too much power in a single bank?

SECTION 2 (pp. 332–36)

2. Why is the Fed considered a "lender of last resort"?

SECTION 3 (pp. 337–44)

3. How does the Fed put monetary policy to work? What are the characteristics of easy-money and tight-money policies?
4. What are the main difficulties the Federal Reserve encounters when developing monetary policy?
5. What tools does the Fed use to implement monetary policy?

Reviewing Themes

1. **Economic Institutions & Incentives** What events led to the development of the Federal Reserve system?
2. **Economic Institutions & Incentives** Do you think the government should control the Fed more directly? Explain your answer.
3. **Monetary Policy** If you were responsible for determining the size of the nation's money supply, which measure would you use and why?
4. **Monetary Policy** Considering the nation's current economic situation, do you believe the Federal Reserve should rely on an easy-money policy or a tight-money policy? Why?

Thinking Critically

1. **Identifying Points of View** Explain how the development of automated banking has led some economists to consider M1 to be too limited a measure of the nation's money supply.
2. **Making Predictions** Why did people in the United States fail to support a central bank for nearly 60 years, despite a civil war and several serious recessions? Do you think another serious national crisis such as a war or depression might change the way the Fed works? Explain your answer.

Writing about Economics

Review what you wrote in your Economics Notebook at the beginning of this chapter. How does your definition of "readily available" compare with the various measurements of money supply? Record your answer in your Notebook.

(Continued from page 345)

2. It makes loans during financial emergencies. **23A**
3. by regulating the money supply and interest rates through open-market operations, discount rates, reserve requirements, margin requirements, and moral suasion; easy-money policy—lowering interest rates, expanding money supply, increasing aggregate demand, creating jobs and reducing unemployment, stimulating economic growth; tight-money policy—increasing interest rates, contraction of the money supply, reduced aggregate demand, slowing economic growth, stabilizing prices **18B, 23A**
4. incorrect economic forecasts, time lags in enacting monetary policy, difficulties in establishing priorities and trade-offs, lack of coordination among government agencies **23A**
5. open market operations, discount rate, and reserve requirement **18B**

Reviewing Themes

1. Panic of 1907, during which runs on banks and the failure of the pyramided reserves caused many banks to collapse; passage of the Federal Reserve Act of 1913 **15A**
2. Answers should address both the need for the Fed to have political independence and the need for coordination among government agencies. **15A, 23D**
3. Answers should address the different measurements of the nation's money supply and how the Fed uses them. **18B, 23D**

Building Social Studies Skills

Interpreting the Chart ⭐TEKS

Growth of the Money Supply, 1989–1999 (in billions)

Year	M1	M2	M3
1989	$ 793	$3,161	$4,091
1990	824	3,281	4,156
1991	896	3,381	4,208
1992	1,024	3,436	4,219
1993	1,130	3,491	4,280
1994	1,150	3,505	4,354
1995	1,127	3,650	4,617
1996	1,081	3,823	4,952
1997	1,074	4,041	5,402
1998	1,097	4,397	5,997
1999	1,124	4,652	6,469

Source: Statistical Abstract of the United States: 2000

1. The table indicates that from 1989 to 1999 the money supply has
   a. increased.
   b. decreased.
   c. remained constant.
   d. disappeared.
2. In which years did one measure of money supply decrease?

Analyzing Primary Sources ⭐TEKS

Read the following excerpts from the Federal Reserve Act of 1913 and its amendments. Then answer the questions.

"The Board of Governors of the Federal Reserve System shall annually make a full report of its operations to the Speaker of the House of Representatives, who shall cause the same to be printed for the entire Congress. . . .

"Federal Reserve notes, to be issued at the discretion of the Board of Governors of the Federal Reserve System for the purpose of making advances to Federal Reserve banks through the Federal Reserve agents as hereinafter set forth and for no other purpose, are authorized. The said notes shall be obligations of the United States and shall be receivable by all national and member banks and Federal Reserve Banks and for all taxes, customs, and other public dues. They shall be redeemed in lawful money on demand at the Treasury Department. . . or at any Federal Reserve Bank. . . ."

1. Which statement best characterizes the writers' purpose in composing this document?
   a. They were attempting to ensure that banks paid taxes and other duties.
   b. They wanted to ensure that the Speaker of the House reported to Congress.
   c. They were attempting to clearly delimit the role and powers of the Fed.
   d. They wanted to make advances on Federal Reserve bank acccounts.
2. How does the Federal Reserve Act define the purpose and use of Federal Reserve Notes?

Alternative Assessment

Building Your Portfolio ⭐TEKS

Individually or in groups, imagine that you are members of the Fed's Board of Governors. Looking at the U.S. economy today, write a proposal for implementing monetary policy in the near future. What are your goals? What tools can you use to implement them?

Internet Activity: go.hrw.com
KEYWORD: SM3 EC14 ⭐TEKS

Access the Internet through the HRW Go site to research the Open Market Committee of the Federal Reserve. Investigate the Beige Book for the previous year or several years. Create an outline of Beige Book topics or a calendar showing upcoming Open Market Committee meetings. Share what you have learned with the class.

---

4. Answers should reflect an understanding of both the current economic situation and when the Fed uses an easy-money or tight-money policy. 23D

Thinking Critically

1. With automated banking, funds in savings accounts are as readily accessible as funds in checking accounts. Thus, many economists think that a measure that does not include savings deposits underestimates the nation's money supply. 23A, 23D
2. Many thought a central bank gave those who ran it too much economic power. Answers should reflect an understanding of the Fed's role during national crises. 23D

Writing about Economics

Students should review and revise their definition of "readily available" in terms of the Fed's three measures of money supply presented in this chapter.

Building Social Studies Skills

1. a 23F
2. M1 decreased between 1994 and 1997. 23F
3. c 23E
4. They are for making advances to Federal Reserve banks, are receivable by all national and member banks, and are used for taxes, customs, and other public dues. 23A

CHAPTER RESOURCE MANAGER

CHAPTER 15 FISCAL POLICY

	OBJECTIVES	PACING GUIDE	REPRODUCIBLE RESOURCES
SECTION 1 **DEFINING FISCAL POLICY** (pp. 349–54)	▸ What role do taxes play in fiscal policy? ▸ What kinds of tax rates do governments set? ▸ Which taxes are the most profitable?	**Regular** 1.5 days **Block Scheduling** 0.5 day	**ELL** Spanish Study Guide 15.1 **ELL** English Study Guide 15.1 **SM** Mathematics for Economics: Activity 15
SECTION 2 **FISCAL POLICY STRATEGIES** (pp. 355–61)	▸ How do supply-side and demand-side theories differ? ▸ What are the chief tools of fiscal policy? ▸ What factors limit the success of fiscal policy?	**Regular** 1.5 days **Block Scheduling** 1 day	**ELL** Spanish Study Guide 15.2 **ELL** English Study Guide 15.2 **E** Challenge and Enrichment: Activity 15
SECTION 3 **FISCAL POLICY AND THE FEDERAL BUDGET** (pp. 362–66)	▸ How is the federal budget developed? ▸ What role does deficit spending play in the U.S. economy? ▸ What methods can the government use to balance the federal budget?	**Regular** 1 day **Block Scheduling** 0.5 day	**ELL** Spanish Study Guide 15.3 **ELL** English Study Guide 15.3 **SM** Consumer Economics: Activity 15 **S** Simulations and Strategies for Teaching Economics: Activity 15

Chapter Resource Key

- **PS** Primary Sources
- **RS** Reading Support
- **E** Enrichment
- **S** Simulations
- **SM** Skills Mastery
- **A** Assessment
- **REV** Review
- **ELL** Reinforcement and English Language Learners
- Transparencies
- CD-ROM
- Video
- Videodisc
- Internet
- Holt Presentation Maker Using Microsoft® PowerPoint®
- TEKS and TAKS

TECHNOLOGY RESOURCES	REINFORCEMENT, REVIEW, AND ASSESSMENT
• One-Stop Planner: Lesson 15.1 • Researcher Online • Homework Practice Online • CNN Presents Economics: Gauging Military Spending • Transparency 60 • Global Skillbuilder CD-ROM	**REV** Section 1 Review, p. 354 **A** Daily Quiz 15.1 ★ TAKS Every Day!
• One-Stop Planner: Lesson 15.2 • Researcher Online • Homework Practice Online • Transparency 61 • Global Skillbuilder CD-ROM	**REV** Section 2 Review, p. 361 **A** Daily Quiz 15.2 ★ TAKS Every Day!
• One-Stop Planner: Lesson 15.3 • Researcher Online • Homework Practice Online • Transparencies 62 and 63 • Global Skillbuilder CD-ROM	**REV** Section 3 Review, p. 366 **A** Daily Quiz 15.3 ★ TAKS Every Day!

Chapter Review and Assessment

SM Global Skillbuilder CD-ROM
HRW Go site
REV Reteaching Activity 15
REV Chapter 15 Review, pp. 368–69
A Chapter 15 Test Generator (on the One-Stop Planner)
A Chapter 15 Test
A Alternative Assessment Handbook

One-Stop Planner CD-ROM

It's easy to plan lessons, select resources, and print out materials for your students when you use the *Texas One-Stop Planner CD-ROM with Test Generator*.

internet connect

HRW ONLINE RESOURCES
Go To: go.hrw.com
Then type in a keyword.

TEACHER HOME PAGE
KEYWORD: SM3 Teacher

CHAPTER INTERNET ACTIVITIES
KEYWORD: SM3 EC15
Choose an activity to:
▸ research the Social Security Administration.
▸ explore the Internal Revenue Service (IRS).
▸ analyze the federal budget.

CHAPTER ENRICHMENT LINKS
KEYWORD: SM3 CH15

HOLT RESEARCHER ONLINE
KEYWORD: Holt Researcher

ONLINE ASSESSMENT
Homework Practice
KEYWORD: SM3 HP15
TAKS Review
KEYWORD: SM3 T15
Rubrics
KEYWORD: SS Rubrics

CONTENT UPDATES
KEYWORD: SS Content Updates

HOLT PRESENTATION MAKER
KEYWORD: SM3 PPT15

ONLINE READING SUPPORT
KEYWORD: SS Strategies

CURRENT EVENTS
KEYWORD: S3 Current Events

TEXAS ONLINE RESOURCES
KEYWORD: S3 TX

LESSON 15.1 DEFINING FISCAL POLICY

TEXTBOOK PAGES 349–54

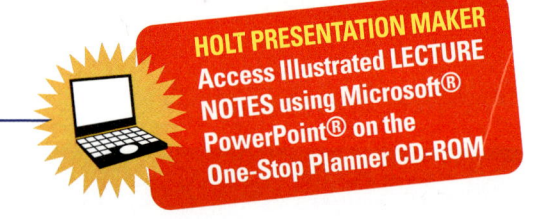

HOLT PRESENTATION MAKER
Access Illustrated LECTURE NOTES using Microsoft® PowerPoint® on the One-Stop Planner CD-ROM

OBJECTIVES

- Explain the role that taxes play in fiscal policy.
- Describe the kinds of tax rates that governments set.
- Identify the most profitable taxes.

MOTIVATE

Direct students to raise their hands if they pay taxes. Ask a student whose hand is not raised if he or she buys clothing, gasoline, food, or magazines, and point out that in almost all states such articles are taxed when they are purchased. Ask another student whose hand was not raised if he or she attends concerts or sporting events, and point out that the cost of the ticket probably includes an entertainment tax. Then ask students to name all the different things that they have bought in the last week or month that they think may have been taxed, and write this list on the chalkboard. Also, have them brainstorm other types of taxes that working adults pay. Tell students that in this section they will learn about different types of taxes and tax rates.

TEACH

Building a Vocabulary

Have students use spiral notebooks to create an Economics Dictionary to be used throughout the chapter. This dictionary might be used as an activity at the start of each new section or as a learning aid for students having difficulty or sheltered English students. List words that students will be expected to know for this section on the chalkboard. Have students use the information provided in the text or on the *Researcher CD-ROM* to list, define, and give an example of each vocabulary term.

Evaluating Ideas

Ask the class to help define the term *fiscal policy*. Write the term on the chalkboard, and beside it write its definition *(taxing, spending, and borrowing policies used to achieve desired levels of economic performance)*. Discuss with the class the main role that taxes play in fiscal policy. *(They provide a primary source of government revenue; they also are used to influence the behavior of individuals.)* Tell the class that the revenues gained from taxes are spent on a variety of government programs. Next, ask the class to name the types of goods that the government might tax to discourage people from consuming them in large amounts *(cigarettes, alcohol, gasoline)*. Discuss with students whether they think these types of taxes are effective in changing people's consumption patterns, and if they affect people with different incomes equally. ★15A

Analyzing Information, Applying a Model

Tell the class that governments can choose among three basic types of taxes and that each tax affects people in different ways. Call on students to help explain what a tax rate is *(the percentage of a person's income that goes toward taxes)*. Write the three basic types of tax rates on the chalkboard *(proportional, progressive, and regressive)*. Ask for student volunteers to help explain how each of the three types of taxes work, and write a summary on the chalkboard beneath each. Then illustrate how each tax works by walking students through the examples for each tax covered in this section. Use the salaries provided in the text to show how the different types of tax rates affect people with higher and lower incomes. Next, organize students into groups of three or four. Have each group work with new scenarios by using the same mathematical calculations as were used for the scenarios in the textbook. You can either have students select their own income amounts, or have them use the following three scenarios in their groups:

- First, have them imagine that they are a family with an income of $130,000 a year. Have them estimate their tax using a proportional tax rate of 8 percent. Then have them estimate their tax using the progressive tax rate formula described in the textbook. Also, to further their understanding of regressive tax rates, have them estimate what percentage of their income they would spend as a family when buying a washing machine that costs $375 and is taxed at a rate of 7.5 percent.
- Next, have them estimate their proportional and progressive taxes on a family income of $54,000 a year. In addition, have them estimate the percentage of their income spent for a $375 washing machine taxed at 7.5 percent tax rate.
- Finally, have them estimate what their proportional and progressive taxes would be if they received a family income of $19,000 per year, and have them estimate the percentage of income required to buy the $375 washing machine taxed at 7.5 percent.

Ask each group to record its calculations on paper and indicate which types of taxes have the heaviest impact on people with lower incomes, and which types of taxes have the heaviest impact on people with higher incomes. ★23G

Comparing and Contrasting, Creating Charts

Now remind students that governments usually rely on five sources of revenue. Ask students to recall from their reading of Section 15.1 what these sources are, and write them on the chalkboard *(individual income taxes, corporate income taxes, Social Security taxes, property taxes, and sales taxes)*. Discuss with the class the constitutional basis for levying taxes and how each of these taxes is usually levied. Next, organize students into groups of three or four. Ask each group to prepare a chart comparing the different tax sources for government revenue. Have each group list on either the horizontal or vertical axis the different taxes, and have them list on the other axis the following: the type of tax (proportional, progressive, or regressive), and the approximate percentage of state or federal revenue that the tax provides. Ask each group to indicate on their charts which type of tax provides the highest revenue for the state or federal governments and which type provides the lowest revenue. You may also wish to have students include a category on relative tax burden (for example, which income bracket bears the greatest burden for this tax and which income bracket bears the lowest), or to present amendments to the Constitution that refer to taxation. ★15A, 17A, 20B

CLOSE

Call on volunteers to present their charts to the rest of the class. Ask students to discuss the following questions:
- Which type of tax rate (proportional, progressive, or regressive) seems the most fair? Which seems the least fair?
- Which type of tax is most commonly used by the federal government for income taxes? Which type is most commonly used by state and local governments? ★17A
- What would happen to local, state, or federal government programs if people were not asked to pay some or all of these taxes?

OPTIONS

Interpersonal Learners

Organize students into groups of four. Ask the groups to each organize a debate in which members discuss whether a proportional or progressive income tax rate should be used in your state. Assign two students to argue for the proportional tax and two to argue for the progressive tax in each group. Then have each group argue for or against levying a new 10 percent sales tax on snack foods in your state. Have students refer to material provided in the textbook or to tax estimates calculated in the second lesson activity.

Students Having Difficulty

Pair students having difficulty with students who have mastered the material. Have each pair make two sets of flash cards: one with different types of tax rates *(proportional, progressive, and regressive)* and the other with the different tax sources *(income tax, sales tax, etc.)*. Have students write one type of tax rate on a card and then on the back summarize how that tax is levied *(for example: proportional taxes take the same percentage of income from individuals at all income levels)*. Pairs should also write each tax source and on the back write whether this tax source is usually used by federal, state, or local governments, and what percentage of revenue this tax source usually provides for each government, if known. Have students in each pair quiz each other about these different tax rates and tax sources by using the flash cards. ★17A

Linguistic Learners

Have students undertake research on the Social Security tax. Topics they might cover include its history (including the impact of President Johnson's removal of Social Security from a separate trust and lumping it in with other national taxes so he could access it for the Vietnam War), its original purpose, changes in collections and payments, and problems with the system. Have students present their findings in an oral report. ★24D

REVIEW

Have students complete the Section 1 Review on page 354. Use the answers in the Annotated Teacher's Edition to assess student mastery of this section.

ASSESS

To assess student mastery of this section, have students complete Daily Quiz 15.1 in *Daily Quizzes with Answer Key*. For additional assessment options, see *Alternative Assessment Handbook* on the *One-Stop Planner CD-ROM*.

ADDITIONAL RESOURCES

Brownlee, W. Elliot. *Federal Taxation in America: A Short History.* 1996. Cambridge University Press.

Graetz, Michael J. *The U.S. Income Tax.* 1999. W. W. Norton & Co.

Hackley, Graham C. *Fiscal Policy: An Introduction.* 1992. Routledge.

LESSON 15.2 FISCAL POLICY STRATEGIES

TEXTBOOK PAGES 355–61

HOLT PRESENTATION MAKER
Access Illustrated LECTURE NOTES using Microsoft® PowerPoint® on the One-Stop Planner CD-ROM

OBJECTIVES

- Explain how supply-side and demand-side theories differ.
- Identify the chief tools of fiscal policy.
- Describe the factors that limit the success of fiscal policy.

MOTIVATE

Find a short article from a newspaper or economic journal that discusses recent fiscal policy proposals or decisions. *(An article about the various proposals debated during a recent presidential election or a session of Congress might be particularly helpful, or perhaps a historical analysis of the Reagan administration economic policies that were based on supply-side economic theories.)* Make copies of the article and distribute them to the class. Discuss with students the main points of the article and ask them what factors they think make it difficult for politicians to enact fiscal policies. Tell the class that in this section they will learn about different economic policy theories, the tools of fiscal policy, and the reasons why it is often difficult for governments to enact fiscal policies.

TEACH

Building a Vocabulary

List the vocabulary terms for this section on the chalkboard and tell students to add them to their Economics Dictionary. Tell students to use the information provided in the text or on the *Researcher CD-ROM* to list, define, and give an example of each vocabulary term.

Evaluating Ideas

On the chalkboard, write the terms *supply-side economics* and *demand-side economics* in two columns. Ask students to recall which economists are known for advocating each of these theories, and write the names of the economists in the appropriate columns. *[French economist Jean-Baptiste Say (18th and 19th centuries) is known for supply-side theories, while John Maynard Keynes (20th century) is known for demand-side theories.]* Ask students to suggest the basic assumptions of each of these two theories, and write these assumptions on the chalkboard in the appropriate columns. Discuss with the class the limitations of these theories and summarize this discussion on the chalkboard in the appropriate columns. Ask the class to discuss which theory they think has been used most by the current administration and whether they think it has been effective. ⭐19A

Creating Charts, Analyzing Ideas

Remind the class that no matter which theory or school of thought guides economists and policy makers in designing fiscal policy, the same basic tools are used. Ask students to recall from their reading what these tools are, and write them on the chalkboard *(taxation, tax incentives, government spending, public transfer payments, and progressive income taxes).* Organize students into groups of three or four. Ask each group to create a chart that compares how each tool is used, what it is used to accomplish, and which level of government tends to use it most (local, state, or federal). You may want to give each group a piece of posterboard and colored pens with which to make their charts. Next, have each group discuss the following questions:

- Which fiscal policy tools do you think the federal and/or state government should use more, and which do you think it should use less?
- Is there an additional purpose for which you think any of these tools might be effectively used? ⭐17C, 23B

Identifying the Main Idea, Applying Ideas

Tell students that governments face several challenges when trying to enact fiscal policy. Ask students to recall from their reading what these challenges are, and write them on the chalkboard *(timing problems, political pressures, unpredictable economic behaviors, and lack of coordination among government policies).* Ask students to suggest how each of these challenges can slow or prevent the application of fiscal policy, and write their suggestions on the chalkboard underneath or beside the corresponding challenge. For the challenge of political pressures, ask students to help explain the differences between restrictive fiscal policy and expansionary fiscal policy and write the definition for each on the chalkboard. Then, to illustrate how each of these challenges might limit the application of fiscal policy in real life, ask students to imagine that a gas shortage is occurring and the federal government has proposed a 25 percent sales tax on gasoline to discourage consumption of so much gas. Ask students to discuss the following questions:

- Why might the application of this proposed tax be delayed?

- What types of political pressures might be exerted to prevent the tax from being enacted?
- How can economists predict the ways in which people might respond to the increased tax?
- Which level of the government (local, state, or federal) will be responsible for monitoring each of the nation's gas stations to ensure that they are including the new tax in the cost of gas that they sell?

CLOSE

Ask students to discuss how the government might make the enactment of fiscal policy smoother. Prompt students with the following questions: Should polls be taken more frequently to determine how citizens might respond to economic changes? Are there ways to protect politicians from being voted out of office if they make unpopular fiscal decisions, or is this an inevitable aspect of a representative, democratic system?

OPTIONS

Gifted Learners, Linguistic Learners

Ask motivated students to conduct a research project on one of the following topics:
- the history of supply-side economic theories
- the history of demand-side economic theories
- the effects of tax incentives on small and large businesses
- different types of public transfer payments and how they work
- the effect of political pressures on a particular fiscal policy

Have students use the *Researcher Online,* the library, in-class resources, and information from business journals or newspapers to conduct their research. Students may wish to include charts or graphs in their finished report, which they should turn in for teacher evaluation. 24D

Sheltered English Students

Pair students acquiring English with fluent English speakers. Have each pair write an outline of the Section 2 material by using a standard outline form. *(For each topic or section listed in the outline, have students write a complete sentence summarizing/defining what that idea means; for example, for supply-side economics, pairs might write, "Supply-side economics focuses on achieving economic stability and growth by increasing or decreasing the supply of goods and services throughout the economy.")* Ask students to make a separate list of unfamiliar words, and have them find and write down the definitions for these words as an extension of this exercise. 24D

Interpersonal Learners

Ask students to interview a local member of Congress, an assistant to a member of Congress, or an economics professor on the topic of fiscal policy strategies. Students may wish to focus their interview on different economic schools of thought—such as supply-side vs. demand-side economics—on the different tools used to enact fiscal policy—such as taxation, tax incentives, or government spending—or on the limitations of fiscal policy. Have students prepare questions before their interview (such as those used in the lesson activities for Section 2) and ask them to turn in a summary of the interview after it has been completed. You might want to suggest some of the following questions:
- Which economic theory do you think is most appropriate for today's economy?
- Which fiscal policy tools do you think are the most important to this state/region?
- Which fiscal policy tools do you think should be changed?

REVIEW

Have students complete the Section 2 Review on page 361. Use the answers in the Annotated Teacher's Edition to assess student mastery of this section.

ASSESS

To assess student mastery of this section, have students complete Daily Quiz 15.2 in *Daily Quizzes with Answer Key*. For additional assessment options, see *Alternative Assessment Handbook* on the *One-Stop Planner CD-ROM*.

ADDITIONAL RESOURCES

Enrique G. Mendoza. *Supply-Side Economics in a Global Economy*. 1995. National Bureau of Economic Research.

Krugman, Paul. *Peddling Prosperity*. 1994. W.W. Norton.

Pugh, Peter and Chris Garratt. *Introducing Keynesian Economics*. 2000. Totem Books.

LESSON 15.3
Fiscal Policy and the Federal Budget

TEXTBOOK PAGES 362–66

HOLT PRESENTATION MAKER Access Illustrated LECTURE NOTES using Microsoft® PowerPoint® on the One-Stop Planner CD-ROM

OBJECTIVES
- Explain how the federal budget is developed.
- Identify what role deficit spending plays in the economy. ★16A
- Describe the methods the government can use to balance the federal budget.

MOTIVATE
Ask students how many of them make a weekly, monthly, or yearly budget. Discuss with students why a budget is necessary for individuals. Next, ask students why they think a budget is considered a necessary and important tool in governmental economic planning, and ask students to analyze the categories of revenues and expenditures in the federal budget. Have students consider the following question: what would happen if different branches of the federal and state governments simply spent whatever amount of money they wanted on the programs that were presented to them first, as U.S. governments did before the mid-1800s? Tell the class that in this section they will learn how the federal government develops a budget, what role deficit spending plays, and how the government can balance the budget. ★17B

TEACH

Building a Vocabulary
List the vocabulary terms for this section on the chalkboard and tell students to add them to their Economics Dictionary. Tell students to use the information provided in the text or on the *Researcher CD-ROM* to list, define, and give an example of each vocabulary term.

Creating Charts
Tell students that producing and passing a federal budget through Congress is a time-consuming process. Organize students into groups of two or three. Have each group prepare a flowchart that illustrates the route that a federal budget travels from inception to final signing by the president. You may want to provide students with pieces of posterboard and colored markers to use in creating their flowcharts. Encourage students to make their flowcharts as clear as possible in showing the possible detours a budget may take before a final version is signed by the president. ★24D

Evaluating Ideas
Tell students that while the federal government creates a new budget every year, it often does not create a balanced budget but instead counts on having a budget deficit. Ask students to define the term *budget deficit*. (*When the government spends more money than it collects, it creates a budget deficit, or shortage.*) Ask the class the following question: What are the four major reasons the government relies on deficit spending? List the four reasons on the chalkboard as students suggest them. (*1. National emergencies such as wars have caused an urgent need for vast spending increases; 2. in providing goods, the federal government may use deficit spending for social programs that many people support, such as national defense or education; 3. the government may use deficit spending to stabilize the economy during recessions; and 4. the government may use deficit spending to promote the economic well-being of its citizens, particularly people who are poor, elderly, or physically challenged.*) Discuss with students whether they think these reasons warrant a regular dependence on budget deficits. Ask students the following questions:
- What would happen if the government decided never to allow a budget deficit again?
- Which government programs might be sacrificed?
- What if a natural disaster such as a hurricane or a flood, caused millions of dollars in damages, and the government refused to help because it did not want to develop a budget deficit?

Also, discuss with students the relationship of the budget deficit to the national debt. Remind students that although many people are presently calling for a balanced budget and an end to deficit spending, many of these same people would probably object to the cancellation of many programs that would have to be sacrificed to achieve a lasting balanced budget.

Debating Ideas, Judging Information
Discuss with students the two main ways that the federal government can develop a balanced budget: it can increase revenues, or it can decrease expenditures (or it can do some of each simultaneously). Ask students to suggest what the primary means for increasing federal revenues is at present (*raising taxes*). Also ask them in what areas the government has tried to decrease expenditures in recent years. (*Military spending, excessive government bureaucracy and waste, and some social programs have been cut.*) Organize students into groups of three or four. Ask each group to discuss the following:

- the costs and benefits of balancing the budget
- the costs and benefits of increasing revenues
- the costs and benefits of decreasing expenditures
- the costs and benefits of passing a constitutional amendment requiring that the government have a balanced budget (and therefore prohibiting deficit spending)

Have each group record on a piece of paper the costs and benefits that they have discussed for each policy and submit these for evaluation. ⭐15A, 17C

CLOSE

Call on volunteers from different groups to share with the class some of the costs and benefits they listed for the different budget policies discussed in the last lesson exercise. Ask students to keep this discussion in mind as they listen to political debates over the federal budget in the near future.

OPTIONS

Gifted Learners
Have motivated students discover who has funded percentages of the national debt. Have each student prepare a pie graph illustrating the comparative percentages. *(Some is funded by state and local governments, some by foreign investors, some by the Federal Reserve system, some by private pension funds, etc.)* You may also want students to write a brief commentary or report on how and why these various groups provide money to cover the debt. ⭐24D

Visual-Spatial Learners
Ask students to clip articles from newspapers and magazines focusing on the federal budget, the federal deficit, and the national debt. Have students use their articles to create a display on a classroom bulletin board.

Linguistic Learners
Have students work individually or in pairs to develop a news magazine story or a live news report that discusses whether the federal deficit is a serious problem. Articles should include topics such as the relationship between the federal deficit and the national debt, the impact of the deficit on the economy (including interest payments), and efforts to reduce the deficit. Students may wish to create graphs or draw pictures illustrating the amount of the current deficit (such as how many times all the dollar bills that make up the deficit could circle the earth if they were strung end to end), or include bar or pie graphs with their articles. Have students present their articles or news story to the class. ⭐23C, 24D

REVIEW

Have students complete the Section 3 Review on page 366. Use the answers in the Annotated Teacher's Edition to assess student mastery of this section.

ASSESS

To assess student mastery of this section, have students complete Daily Quiz 15.3 in *Daily Quizzes with Answer Key*. For additional assessment options, see *Alternative Assessment Handbook* on the *One-Stop Planner CD-ROM*.

RETEACH

For students having difficulty with the lessons, have them complete Reteaching Activity 18. This activity is located in *Reteaching Activities with Answer Key*.

ADDITIONAL RESOURCES

Schick, Allen. *The Federal Budget: Politics, Policy, Process.* 2000. Brookings Institution.

Thompson, Kenneth W. (ed.). *The Budget Deficit and the National Debt.* 1997. University Press of America.

Wetterau, Bruce. *Congressional Quarterly's Desk Reference on the Federal Budget.* 1998. Congressional Quarterly Books.

CHAPTER 15

TOPICS INCLUDE

- proportional, progressive, and regressive taxes
- sources of tax revenue
- supply-side and demand-side economics
- tools and limitations of fiscal policy
- development of the federal budget
- deficit spending
- growth and impact of the national debt
- methods of balancing the federal budget

ECONOMICS NOTEBOOK

The Economics Notebook is a journal activity that encourages students to consider basic concepts of economics that relate to their lives. A follow-up notebook activity appears on page 368.

WHY IT MATTERS TODAY

To find additional lessons plans dealing with the federal and state conflict over economic legislation, visit CNNfyi.com or have students complete the ECONOMICS IN THE NEWS activity on page 367.

CNNfyi.com

CHAPTER 15

FISCAL POLICY

Suppose that you work 15 hours a week in a bookstore, earning $5.50 per hour. At the end of the week, you receive a paycheck, which you expect to be worth $82.50. Instead, you find that your check is for quite a bit less money. On your way home you stop at a music store, where you buy two cassettes for $8 each. Although the cost of the cassettes is $16, the clerk says that you must pay $17.12.

Why do you receive less income and pay more for the cassettes than you expect—and where does that money go? The "missing" money goes to the federal, state, and local governments in the form of taxes. The governments use these taxes for programs and policies that serve a wide variety of purposes. In this chapter you will learn how the governments use taxes and fiscal policy to regulate the economy.

ECONOMICS NOTEBOOK

In your Economics Notebook, list the taxes you have paid during the past month. Have these taxes influenced your spending and saving habits? Write a paragraph explaining your answer.

WHY IT MATTERS TODAY

Sound fiscal policy is essential to the smooth functioning of the economy. Use CNNfyi.com or other current events sources to find examples of the government's taxing, spending, and borrowing policies.

CNNfyi.com

SECTION 1
DEFINING FISCAL POLICY

READ TO DISCOVER
1. What role do taxes play in fiscal policy?
2. What kinds of tax rates do governments set?
3. Which taxes are the most profitable?

ECONOMICS DICTIONARY
fiscal policy
tax rate
excise tax
estate tax
gift tax
customs duty

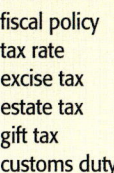

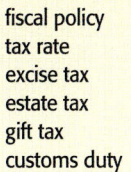

As noted in Chapter 14, the Federal Reserve system uses monetary policy to influence the economy. Another tool the government can use for this is **fiscal policy**—or spending, taxing, and borrowing policies.

The government collects taxes to pay for programs such as road construction, education, and national defense. The government also uses taxes to influence the behavior of individuals. For example, the federal and state governments have placed taxes on products such as tobacco and alcohol in part to discourage people from consuming large quantities of these potentially harmful substances.

Types of Taxes

Taxation is not random. Governments can choose among three basic types of tax rates:

▸ proportional,
▸ progressive, and
▸ regressive.

Whether a tax is proportional, progressive, or regressive depends on the **tax rate**—the percentage of a person's income that goes toward taxes.

Proportional Taxes Some states have proportional taxes, also called "flat rate taxes." A proportional tax takes the same percentage of income from individuals at all income levels.

To understand how this type of tax affects taxpayers, suppose that a state has a 5 percent proportional tax on income. If Nathan Lewis earns $100,000 per year, he pays $5,000 in taxes ($100,000 × 0.05 = $5,000). Stephanie Chisholm earns $10,000 per year and pays the same 5 percent rate, or $500 ($10,000 × 0.05 = $500). Although the tax burden appears to fall equally on all taxpayers, it is probably easier for Nathan to pay the 5 percent tax than it is for Stephanie. Proportional taxes therefore have a greater impact on people with lower incomes.

Progressive Taxes A progressive tax takes a larger percentage of income from a high-income person than from a low-income person. Currently, the main progressive tax in the United States is the federal income tax.

Under current income tax laws, there are different tax rates for people with different levels of income. For example, in 2000 a person with a taxable annual income of $26,250 or less fell into the 15 percent tax bracket, or category. Those individuals who had a taxable income of more than $288,350 were in the highest tax bracket—39.6 percent. These tax brackets cause the burden of the federal income tax to fall more heavily on people with high incomes than on people with low incomes. In addition, income below a certain level is not taxed at all.

Regressive Taxes A regressive tax takes a larger percentage of income from people with low incomes than from people with high incomes. Sales taxes are one kind of regressive tax. A sales tax is levied on the sale of some goods or services.

How is a sales tax regressive? Suppose that Dean Hamilton and April Strong each buy a

FISCAL POLICY **349**

Across the Curriculum

HISTORY A poll tax is a tax that is the same amount for everyone regardless of income levels—in other words, a regressive tax. First imposed by Britain on its American colonies, poll taxes were later used in the U.S. South to keep poor African Americans out of the voting booths. Payment of a poll tax was required for voting, preventing those who could not afford it from exercising their electoral rights. In 1964 Congress passed the Twenty-fourth Amendment to the Constitution, which forbids the use of poll taxes in federal elections. In 1966 the U.S. Supreme Court ruled that poll taxes are unconstitutional in state and local elections as well. ■

---

internet connect

TOPIC: IRS
GO TO: go.hrw.com
KEYWORD: SM3 EC15

Have students access the Internet through the HRW Go site to conduct research on the Internal Revenue Service (IRS). Tell students to investigate the types of information and taxpayer services offered on the IRS Web site. Then have each student create a brochure advising taxpayers of the services that the IRS provides online. ★24C, 24D

Global Exchange

Taxes

Since the 1700s Americans have complained about their taxes. Yet how much do they have to complain about compared with other countries?

The tax burden shouldered by Americans is one of the lowest of the advanced industrial countries. In general, all taxes are lower in the United States than in Europe. For example, in 2000 untaxed gasoline in the United States and Great Britain cost about the same—around $1.15 a gallon. After taxes, however, British drivers paid about $4.40 a gallon while Americans paid around $1.60 a gallon. That same year, a worker in Denmark making about $29,000 a year paid about 34 percent of his or her income in taxes. A worker earning the same salary in the United States would have had a tax burden of about 18 percent.

Why do people in other countries pay higher taxes? European governments use tax revenue to fund medical care, mass transportation systems, generous pension plans and unemployment insurance, college educations, and nursing-home care. Europeans tolerate high taxes because they place a high value on having certain goods and services provided by the government.

In every society, citizens and their governments must make decisions about how to use resources. These decisions necessarily involve trade-offs. Obviously, Europeans' trade-offs for extensive social services take the form of high taxes and result in relatively lower personal income. Likewise, Americans' trade-offs for taking home a higher percentage of their earnings are fewer support services for the general public.

---

paperback book priced at $5.99, with a sales tax of 7 percent. They each will pay $6.41 for the book: $5.99 + ($5.99 × 0.07) = $6.41. The money paid in sales tax, however, is a larger percentage of Dean's $18,000 annual salary than of April's $25,000 salary. With a regressive tax, therefore, the tax burden falls more heavily on people in lower-income groups than on people who earn high incomes.

In 2001, forty-five U.S. states and the District of Columbia had sales taxes, with rates generally ranging from 3 percent to 7 percent. In addition, many cities, such as Chicago, Dallas, Los Angeles, New Orleans, and New York City, have city sales taxes.

Collecting Taxes

Governments rely on a combination of proportional, progressive, and regressive taxes to collect funds. (See Figure 15.1.) The largest sources of tax revenue are

- individual income taxes,
- corporate income taxes,
- Social Security taxes,
- property taxes, and
- sales taxes.

Individual Income Taxes The individual income tax is a progressive—and in some cases proportional—tax on a person's income, including wages or salary, interest, dividends, and tips. Individual income taxes are collected by the federal government and most state governments, as well as some local governments. In 1996 individual income taxes provided about 38 percent of federal revenues, about 14 percent of state revenues, and less than 2 percent of local revenues.

Wage earners pay individual income taxes through a payroll withholding system. Employers deduct tax money from employees' paychecks and forward it to the government. Various government agencies—for example, the federal government's Internal Revenue Service (IRS), a branch of the Treasury Department—collect the taxes.

This "pay-as-you-go" system of tax collection also applies to self-employed workers, who pay regular estimated tax payments—approximations of what is owed—to the government.

Corporate Income Taxes In the United States, governments tax corporate profits. Many corporations pay taxes at reduced rates because they are eligible for tax breaks, such as those designed to promote plant modernization. In 1996, corporate income taxes made up about 10 percent of federal tax revenues, about 3 percent of state tax revenues, and only one third of one percent of local tax revenues.

Social Security Taxes Like individual income taxes, Social Security taxes are withheld from workers' paychecks. Withholding of these taxes was authorized by the Federal Insurance Contributions Act (FICA). They are used to finance two social welfare programs. The first is Old-Age, Survivors, and Disability Insurance (OASDI), or Social Security. The second is Medicare, which provides health care to older Americans, regardless of income.

Social Security taxes are both proportional and regressive. How can this be true? The Social Security tax is proportional because it takes a set percentage of an employee's wages—7.65 percent of incomes up to $76,200 in 2000. Income above that amount is taxed at a lower percentage, making the tax regressive as well as proportional.

For example, suppose that Lily Bell made $30,000 in 2000, Matt Levine made $76,200 that year, and Alicia Fuentes made $90,000. Lily and Matt will have paid the same percentage of their salaries—7.65 percent—in FICA taxes. Alicia will have paid 7.65 percent on the first $76,200 of her salary, and a lower percent on the remaining $13,800. The tax burden therefore fell equally on all people who made $76,200 or less per year, but less heavily on people who made more than $76,200 per year. This means that more of the Social Security tax was paid by people who were less able to afford it.

Social Security taxes are the second-largest source of revenue for the federal government. By 1999 they represented 33.5 percent of the federal government's tax revenue.

Property Taxes State and local governments also rely on property taxes. Most property taxes apply to houses, factory buildings, condominiums, the land on which these structures are built,

FEDERAL TAX RECEIPTS BY SOURCE, 1999

- 48.1% Individual income taxes
- 33.5% Social insurance taxes and contributions
- 10.1% Corporate income taxes
- 3.9% Excise taxes
- 1.9% Miscellaneous
- 1.5% Estate and gift taxes
- 1.0% Customs duties and fees

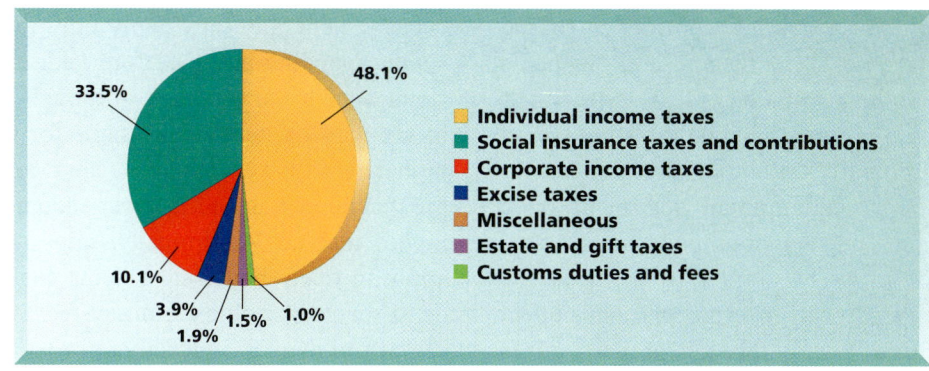

Source: The Budget for Fiscal Year 2001, Historical Tables

FIGURE 15.1 Governments use proportional, progressive, and regressive taxes to enact fiscal policy. **What are the three largest sources of tax revenue for the federal government?**

Themes in Economics

FISCAL POLICY The term *value added* refers to the addition that a company makes to output. For example, if a furniture manufacturer purchases $100 worth of lumber and produces a $300 table, the company has contributed $200 to output, or added $200 to the value of the resources.

Some economists favor a value-added tax (VAT) over a corporate income tax. With the VAT, a company would pay taxes not on its profits but on the amount it adds to the value of the goods and services it produces. Thus, taxes on final goods and services would be levied at various stages of production. ■

Enhancing the Lesson

For information on federal budget net receipts for the years 1940 through 1999, see the Federal Budgets section on the *Researcher Online*.

Transparency

An overhead transparency of Figure 15.1 is available in *Transparency Resources*. See Transparency 60: Federal Tax Receipts by Source, 1999.

Caption Answer

individual income taxes, social insurance taxes and contributions, corporate income taxes 17B, 23F

FISCAL POLICY 351

Caption Answer

because generally they apply only to basic consumer spending and therefore take a larger percentage of lower incomes ★17C

Cultural Perspectives

Religious organizations are exempt from property taxes, but not all taxpayers support this exemption. Property tax exemptions result in the loss of billions of dollars in tax revenues to some states. In some cases, the dollar amount of exemptions exceeds the dollar amount of property tax revenues collected by a state. Supporters of the tax exemptions argue that eliminating them could force small churches to close, thereby limiting religious freedom. Opponents respond that it is unfair that churches and other non-profit organizations do not pay for public goods from which they benefit—for example, police and fire protection. ■

State Sales Tax Rates

WA 6.5%, MT 0%, ND 5%, MN 6.5%, NH 0%, VT 5%, ME 5%, AK 0%, OR 0%, ID 5%, SD 4%, WI 5%, MI 6%, NY 4%, MA 5%, RI 7%, CT 6%, PA 6%, NJ 6%, NV 6.5%, UT 4.75%, WY 4%, NE 5%, IA 5%, IL 6.25%, IN 5%, OH 5%, WV 6%, VA 3.5%, DE 0%, MD 5%, CA 6%, CO 2.9%, KS 4.9%, MO 4.225%, KY 6%, Washington, D.C. 5.75%, NC 4%, HI 4%, AZ 5.6%, NM 5%, OK 4.5%, AR 5.125%, TN 6%, SC 5%, MS 7%, AL 4%, GA 4%, TX 6.25%, LA 4%, FL 6%

Source: Federation of Tax Administrators

FIGURE 15.2 Sales tax rates vary considerably among the 50 states. **Why are sales taxes regressive?** ★TEKS

and undeveloped real estate holdings. Some states also collect taxes on personal property such as household furnishings, boats, and jewelry. Local governments rely on property taxes to finance needs such as education, police and fire protection, and sanitation.

Despite its common use by state and local governments, the property tax often is controversial because it does not take a person's income into account. For example, consider a retired couple living on a fixed income and owning a three-bedroom home on a large lot. Despite their fixed income, the retired couple probably would pay more in property taxes than a wealthier couple living in a condominium apartment on a small lot in the same neighborhood.

Critics of property taxes also point to the unequal results. Local governments that collect large amounts of funds through property taxes can provide quality education, recreation facilities, police and fire protection, and other services. Towns and cities that do not raise much money through property taxes, however, sometimes provide inadequate public goods and services. Although traditionally property taxes make up approximately 1 percent of state revenues, they provide more than a quarter of revenues for local governments.

Sales Taxes A sales tax is a regressive tax assigned to certain goods and services by state and local governments. Sales taxes are regressive because generally they apply only to basic consumer spending and therefore take a larger percentage of lower incomes. Although the *amount* of tax paid on items is the same for people with higher and lower incomes, that amount is a greater percentage of a lower income than of a higher income. Additionally, sales taxes do not apply to many higher-cost items such as houses or to services such as attorney fees. People who can afford these products therefore do not experience the same sales tax burden as people with lower incomes.

Some states that have sales taxes do not tax food, medicine, clothing, and other necessities.

CHAPTER 15

LINKING ECONOMICS and SOCIOLOGY

Everything Old Is New Again

For many Americans, the suburbs represent an ideal life. Home ownership, quiet neighborhoods, and safe streets have become a pull so strong that New York City's suburbs now reach as far west as Pennsylvania—so that work and home may be separated by nearly 100 miles and the entire state of New Jersey.

This urban sprawl is not limited to the East Coast. Michael Fifield, director of Arizona State University's Joint Urban Design Program, has commented that practically the only thing preventing Phoenix from filling all of Arizona is the city of Tucson.

A number of urban planners and property developers have grown dissatisfied with suburbs. They believe that the familiar elements of suburban development—privacy fences, large lawns, and wide streets—serve as barriers between neighbors. These planners, called New Urbanists, argue that people should be able to live in communities that bring neighbors together, in the style of neighborhoods built before World War II.

How do the New Urbanists want to change the way people live? First, they want to build more homes in less space. Today the typical suburb has between one to three houses per acre. New Urbanism, on the other hand, envisions as many as five or six homes per acre. These homes would involve a mix of architectural styles, such as single-family houses, garage apartments, and apartment complexes.

Living closer to the neighbors means smaller lots. Instead of separately owned stretches of grass, New Urbanist communities generally feature small lawns and gardens—with a large open "common" area within walking distance, so that children have space to play.

Additionally, New Urbanism seeks to prevent the need for long-distance drives to shopping malls and huge discount warehouses. Rather, residents in these communities would be encouraged to walk to nearby local businesses.

The ideas generated by the New Urbanism movement have provided a model for several communities. Seaside, Florida, was built in the 1960s and has influenced other developments such as Kentlands, Maryland, and Laguna West, California. Henry Turley, planner of Harbor Town, Tennessee, wanted to offer a wider range of housing prices to make the community "a slice of the world—the more complete and varied the better." As a result, Harbor Town houses range in price from $114,000 all the way to $425,000.

Not all urban planners believe that New Urbanism will work. Instead, many feel that these communities are more like theme parks than neighborhoods. These people also argue that shops such as corner groceries cannot survive without the brisk business that accompanies population densities like those in Manhattan.

What Do You Think?

1. Do you think that smaller yards and shared common areas such as town squares would increase contact with neighbors? Explain your answer.
2. Many U.S. cities have strict zoning codes for suburban development. How might this affect potential New Urbanist communities?

Kentlands, Maryland, is one of a growing number of communities designed to promote interaction among neighbors.

What Do You Think? Answers

1. Answers will vary. Students who think smaller yards and shared common areas would increase contact among neighbors might respond that these factors would encourage residents to feel an increased bond as members of a shared community. The emphasis on community ties would likely lead to more contact among neighbors.

Students who do not think these factors would increase contact might say that people who enjoy meeting their neighbors will do so no matter what, and that those who do not, will not do so no matter what.

2. Strict zoning laws may make it extremely difficult to put into place the changes proposed by New Urbanists. For example, zoning laws that clearly divide residential areas from commercial areas would make it difficult to place shops within walking distance of residents. 15B, 23A

Caption Answer
customs duty, or tariff ⭐17A

SECTION 1
REVIEW ANSWERS

1. fiscal policy (349), tax rate (349), excise tax (354), estate tax (354), gift tax (354), customs duty (354) **24A**

2. individual income taxes (federal and state), Social Security taxes or FICA (federal), property taxes (state and local), and sales taxes (state) **17A, 23A, 24D**

3a. Taxes provide the government with revenue to fund public goods and they are also used to influence the behavior of individuals. **15A, 17A**

3b. Excise taxes are levied on the manufacture, sale, or consumption of certain items; estate taxes apply to items transferred on death to another person; and customs duties are taxes on imported items. **17B**

4. Answers will vary but should reflect an understanding of proportional, progressive, and regressive taxes. **17C, 23A**

FISCAL POLICY *When you bring an item from another country into the United States you may have to pay a tax on that item.* **What is the name of this tax?** ⭐TEKS

Other Taxes and Revenues Excise taxes, estate and gift taxes, and customs duties represented another 6.4 percent of all federal tax revenues in 1999. An **excise tax** is a tax on the manufacture, sale, or consumption of a particular good or service. The federal government places excise taxes on products such as gasoline, tobacco, firearms, alcohol, telephone services, and tires, as well as various forms of gambling. Excise taxes are regressive taxes because they tend to take a larger percentage of income from members of low-income groups than from members of high-income groups.

Estate and gift taxes are taxes on houses, cars, jewelry, and other personal assets when they are transferred from one owner to another under specific circumstances. An **estate tax** is a tax placed on the assets of a person who has died, and is paid out of the estate rather than by an individual. Federal estate taxes were levied only on estates worth more than $675,000 in 2000. A **gift tax** is placed on the transfer of certain gifts of value, such as money or other personal property. The gift-giver pays the tax if his or her gifts to an individual exceed $10,000 annually.

A **customs duty** is a tax on goods that are brought into the United States from other countries. A customs duty is also referred to as a tariff.

These exemptions soften the burden of sales taxes on low- and moderate-income groups. In 1996, sales taxes provided almost 5 percent of federal revenues, 21 percent of state revenues, and 5 percent of local revenues. (See Figure 15.2 on page 352 for state sales tax rates.)

SECTION 1 REVIEW

⭐TEKS Q: 1, 2, 3a, 3b, 4

1. Identify and Explain:
fiscal policy
tax rate
excise tax
estate tax
gift tax
customs duty

2. Categorizing: Copy the chart below. Use it to list the types of taxes that provide federal, state, and local governments with most of their funds.

Types of Taxes		
Federal	**State**	**Local**

3. Finding the Main Idea
a. Explain the importance of taxes to fiscal policy.
b. Explain the differences between excise taxes, estate taxes, and customs duties.

Writing and Critical Thinking
Drawing Conclusions: Compare proportional, progressive, and regressive taxes. Which one seems to be the fairest in the way the tax burden is imposed? Explain your answer.
Consider the following:
- income, property, sales, and excise taxes
- people's income levels

Homework Practice Online
keyword: SM3 HP15

SECTION 2
FISCAL POLICY STRATEGIES

READ TO DISCOVER
1. How do supply-side and demand-side theories differ?
2. What are the chief tools of fiscal policy?
3. What factors limit the success of fiscal policy?

ECONOMICS DICTIONARY
- supply-side economics
- demand-side economics
- tax incentive
- investment tax credit
- restrictive fiscal policy
- expansionary fiscal policy

You know that taxes are an important part of fiscal policy, but how does the government determine that policy? The answer can be found in two schools of economic thought—supply-side economics and demand-side economics.

Supply-Side Economics

What is supply-side economics? **Supply-side economics** focuses on achieving economic stability and growth by increasing the supply of goods and services throughout the economy. Under supply-side economics, the government's role in the economy is limited to providing firms with incentives to increase production. As the supply of goods and services increases, their prices drop. Increased production also requires businesses to hire additional workers, leading to a lower unemployment rate. These workers then spend more money, increasing demand. (See Figure 15.3 on page 356.)

The leading supporter of supply-side thought during its early years was French economist Jean-Baptiste Say (1767–1832). Say is best-known for his statement that supply creates its own demand. According to this theory, producers provide enough goods and services to meet their own needs and produce additional goods and services to exchange for items that meet their wants.

Suppose that Carl Jasper has a computer and a desktop-publishing program. He creates flyers to let people know that he is beginning a desktop-publishing business—in other words, he is advertising the supply of his services. Carl is able to do this because he already has met his own publishing needs. Melissa Hayes sees one of Carl's flyers and decides that she would like him to produce stationery printed with her name and address. Carl's supply, therefore, has created demand for his product.

During the 1980s President Ronald Reagan used many of the ideas of the supply-side economists when formulating his economic policies. Political party conflicts prevented Reagan's supply-side plans from being fully implemented. Instead, tax cuts were accompanied by spending increases.

Elements of Supply-Side Economics

What, according to supply-side economists, is the government's role in the economy? Generally, they believe that the government should adopt a laissez-faire approach. In particular, the government should reduce taxes.

Supply-side economists favor tax cuts to encourage individuals and firms to invest in new businesses and products. They argue that tax cuts increase individuals' disposable incomes and corporations' profits, and that some of this "extra" money will be invested. The increased tax revenues from businesses either begun or expanded with the new investment—along with reduced government spending—will offset the loss in revenue from the tax cuts.

Supply-side economists also view many types of government regulation as obstacles to economic growth. They argue that excessive regulations can increase production costs, delay

FISCAL POLICY

Transparency
An overhead transparency of Figure 15.3 is available in *Transparency Resources*. See Transparency 61: Fiscal Policy Models.

Caption Answer
low unemployment and economic growth ⭐16A

Themes in Economics
MONETARY & FISCAL POLICY

"Reaganomics" was one of the most comprehensive and controversial economic policies in U.S. history. Named after President Ronald Reagan, who served from 1981 to 1989, this economic program entailed four major policy objectives: (1) reduce the growth of government spending, (2) reduce income tax rates, (3) reduce regulation, and (4) reduce inflation by controlling the growth of the money supply. Although nearly everyone agrees that Reagan's was one of the most ambitious economic policies since Roosevelt's New Deal, experts are divided on its outcome. While unemployment and inflation rates declined slightly during the Reagan administration, the national debt increased wildly. ■

FISCAL POLICY MODELS

Supply-Side Model
- Government policies encourage increased aggregate supply.
- Prices drop due to increased quantity supplied. Businesses hire more workers to maintain higher production levels.
- Lower prices and higher incomes and profits encourage individuals and businesses to spend, save, and invest.

Demand-Side Model
- Government policies encourage increased aggregate demand.
- Increased consumer spending encourages businesses to raise production levels and hire more workers to meet higher production goals.
- Lower prices and higher incomes and profits encourage individuals and businesses to spend, save, and invest.

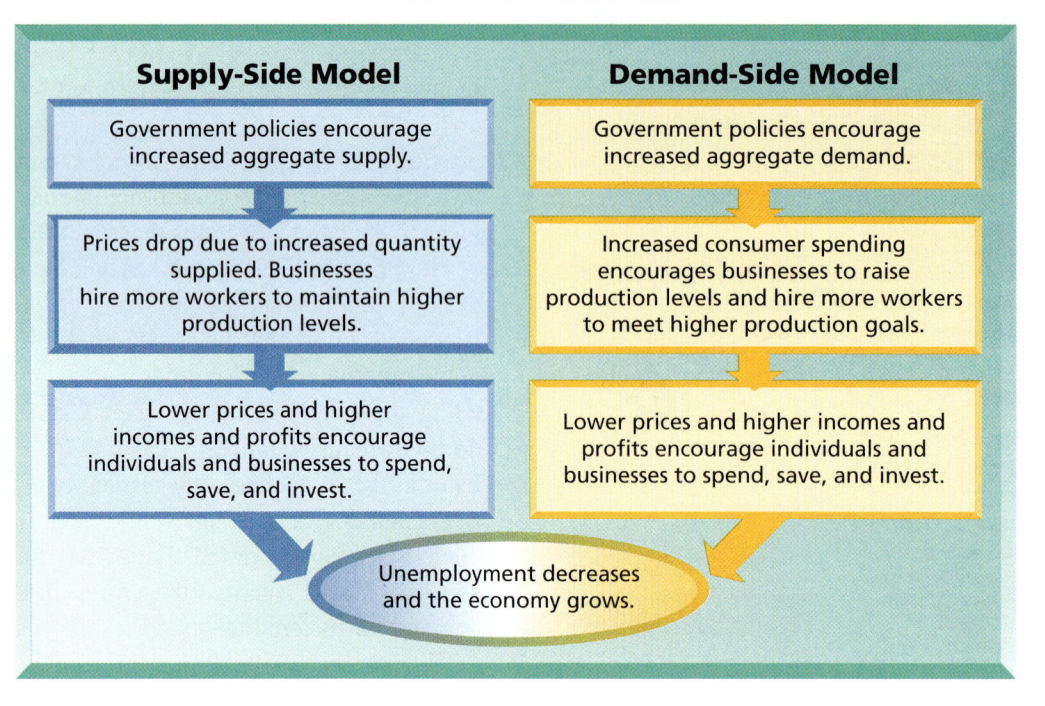

→ Unemployment decreases and the economy grows.

FIGURE 15.3 A government's fiscal policy may be based on either supply-side or demand-side economics. **What goals do these models share?** ⭐TEKS

---

construction on public and private projects, and reduce incentives for businesses to develop new products.

Limitations of Supply-Side Economics
Why do some people disagree with the ideas of the supply-side economists? Critics of the supply-side model question two major assumptions of supply-side theory.

One assumption of all economic philosophies is that economists can predict the economic behaviors of people. Critics point out the limitations of this assumption. For example, in the 1980s supply-side economists assumed that, for the most part, individuals and firms would *invest* the money they gained through tax cuts. Instead, many people chose to *spend* this money, increasing aggregate demand and inflation.

Second, critics of supply-side economics argue that many of the tax cuts are unfair. During the 1980s, for example, the wealthy benefited more from this tax cut legislation than did the poor. These critics also point out that spending cuts made along with the tax cuts fell most heavily on social programs for the poor, the unemployed, and other traditionally disadvantaged groups.

Demand-Side Economics
Instead of concentrating on the importance of supply, demand-side economists emphasize the role of demand. **Demand-side economics** focuses on achieving economic growth through the government's influence on aggregate demand.

The "father" of demand-side economics was British economist John Maynard Keynes [KAYNZ]. In 1936 Keynes published *The General Theory of Employment, Interest, and Money*. With this book, he presented a theory that revolutionized economic thinking.

Economists knew that changes in aggregate demand cause fluctuations in the business cycle.

They recognized that when aggregate demand decreases, businesses produce fewer goods and lay off workers, causing a slowdown in economic growth.

Based on his observations of economic activity during the Great Depression, Keynes reasoned that marketplace forces alone were not enough to increase aggregate demand during economic downturns. Instead, he argued that active government involvement was necessary to achieve full employment and improve sluggish business activity.

Demand-side economics received a boost in the United States when Congress passed the Employment Act of 1946. The act pledged to promote "maximum employment, production, and

CAREERS IN ECONOMICS

Auditor

The mention of an auditor strikes fear into the hearts of many Americans. People often think of auditors solely as Internal Revenue Service (IRS) employees who investigate individuals and businesses to make sure they have complied with the law. In fact, auditors work for private companies as well as the government and their work usually involves routine financial maintenance, rather than pursuing tax evaders.

There are three kinds of auditors. Internal auditors are employed by a company to inspect its financial affairs. Independent auditors work for companies that specialize in auditing. These auditors examine the finances of other companies. Tax auditors are employed by federal and state governments to examine taxpayers' records and assess their tax liabilities.

In general, an auditor's job is to study a business's financial records. They review contracts, business correspondence, and company documents as well as make sure that corporate policies and government regulations are followed. In addition, auditors study ways to improve company operations.

To become an auditor, you must have a bachelor's degree in accounting, although many firms prefer to hire someone with a master's degree in accounting or business administration. Computer and math skills are essential.

The use of computers has increased the need for auditors and changed how they do their job. Computer systems make it easy for companies to gather financial information about their business. Accounting software has eliminated many of the routine mathematical tasks in auditing and made it easier to compile reports. As a result, auditors now spend more time analyzing data, making recommendations on business strategy, and developing better accounting systems.

An auditor reviews a business's financial records to ensure that general accounting practices are followed.

Themes in Economics

UNEMPLOYMENT Keynesian economists typically are more concerned with combating unemployment than with reducing inflation. Demand-side economists think that full employment increases aggregate demand the most and therefore is the best spark for the economy. ■

Profiles in Economics

For biographies of Ronald Reagan, John Maynard Keynes, and other noted people in economics, refer students to the Biographies section on the *Researcher Online*.

Careers in Economics

To help students learn about other careers in economics, refer them to the Careers section on the *Researcher Online*.

FISCAL POLICY

Themes in Economics

THE ROLE OF GOVERNMENT

The U.S. government offers tax incentives to individuals and corporations to encourage certain economic and socially responsible behaviors. For example, during the energy crisis of the late 1970s, the government offered a tax incentive to homeowners who installed solar-powered devices in their homes. In addition, the government has used tax incentives to encourage parents to adopt children and to save for their children's college education and to encourage people to buy and restore historic buildings. ■

Caption Answer

marginal tax rates, tax incentives, government spending, public transfer payments, and progressive income taxes ★17A

---

purchasing power" in the U.S. economy. In effect, the act defined economic growth and stability as goals of the federal government. To meet these goals, the government began to use fiscal policy to fight economic downturns, unemployment, and rising prices.

Tools of Fiscal Policy

Although economists may disagree about the relative importance of supply-side or demand-side theories, they rely on the same methods of enacting fiscal policy. The five chief tools of fiscal policy are

- marginal tax rates,
- tax incentives,
- government spending,
- public transfer payments, and
- progressive income taxes.

Tax Rates Congress often uses taxation to regulate aggregate demand in privately owned businesses. Suppose that businesses in many areas of the country begin to lay off workers. For example, if Leena Al-Nasser loses her job with an advertising agency, she probably will reduce her expenses. As other people make similar choices—either because they have been laid off or because they anticipate losing their jobs—aggregate demand declines and the economy moves toward recession. How might Congress respond to this dilemma?

To help reduce unemployment, Congress decreases taxes. This increases people's disposable incomes and allows firms to retain more of their profits. Additional money encourages more total spending, or higher aggregate demand.

To help limit inflation, Congress raises taxes. Higher taxes decrease an individual's disposable income and a corporation's profits. Higher taxes also slow business activity and reduce the chances of "too much money chasing too few goods."

Tax Incentives The second tool of fiscal policy is tax incentives. A **tax incentive** is a special tax break that government extends to businesses to encourage investment in new capital.

One major tax incentive is the **investment tax credit**, which permits firms to deduct from their corporate income taxes a percentage of the money they spend on new capital. To help reduce unemployment, Congress raises the investment tax credit, encouraging businesses to spend more money on expansion and thereby increasing aggregate demand. To help reduce inflation, Congress decreases the investment tax credit, which restricts business activity and thus lowers aggregate demand.

How do tax incentives work? Suppose that Congress sets the investment tax credit at 40 percent in a given year and that Computer Village, an Internet service provider (ISP), invests $1 million in new capital. Under these conditions, Computer Village is able to deduct $400,000 from its income taxes ($1,000,000 × 0.40 = $400,000). Thus, the real cost of the new capital is only $600,000 because of the $400,000 in tax savings ($1,000,000 − $400,000 = $600,000). On the other hand, if the investment tax credit is

FISCAL POLICY *The Alamodome in San Antonio, Texas, was funded in part by a city tax on public transportation.* **What are the five main fiscal policy tools that governments use?** ★TEKS

10 percent, an investment of $1 million in new capital results in a tax credit of just $100,000 ($1,000,000 × 0.10 = $100,000). As you can see, a lower investment tax credit discourages business investment.

Government Spending
The third tool of fiscal policy is government spending. To help reduce inflation, Congress decreases government spending, resulting in lower aggregate demand and slower business activity.

To help reduce unemployment, on the other hand, Congress increases government spending for goods and services. Higher spending on the nation's infrastructure increases aggregate demand and employment opportunities.

Public Transfer Payments
Some tax dollars are redistributed to nonproductive actors in the economy through public transfer payments. The term *nonproductive* in this context means that no goods or services are created in exchange for these government payments. Today these payments form a "safety net" of social programs for the people of the United States.

One important type of public transfer payment is unemployment compensation. Consider again the case of Leena Al-Nasser. When she loses her job, she becomes eligible for unemployment compensation. As unemployment rises, more people are eligible for this transfer payment, and the government automatically provides these funds to a larger percentage of the population. As the unemployment rate drops, on the other hand, state governments are able to reduce the amount of money they pump into the economy through this transfer payment.

Many federal public transfer payments also tend to keep aggregate demand steady or rising. Social Security payments and veterans' benefits, for example, provide income to elderly and disabled citizens. Likewise, health insurance through Medicare and Medicaid injects billions of dollars into the economy each year.

Progressive Income Taxes
As you know, the personal income tax and corporate income tax both are progressive taxes because higher incomes are taxed at higher rates. During periods of prosperity, the higher incomes of individuals and firms place them in higher tax brackets. When placed in a higher tax bracket, individuals pay a greater percentage of their incomes in taxes. Suppose that Jenna Cooper receives a pay raise and is thus in a higher tax bracket. How do higher taxes affect her wallet? Jenna's disposable income—her income after taxes—does not increase by the same percentage as her total income. By lessening such increases in disposable incomes, higher tax rates lessen the increase in aggregate demand that might be caused by rapidly rising incomes.

During recessions, on the other hand, incomes tend to fall. Many individuals and firms are taxed at lower rates because they earn less and therefore are in lower tax brackets. The lower tax rates lessen the possibility of a disastrous drop in aggregate demand.

Limitations on Fiscal Policy

Although fiscal policy is designed to regulate aggregate demand in the economy, putting policies to work is not always a smooth process. The four most important limitations are

- timing problems,
- political pressures,
- unpredictable economic behaviors, and
- lack of coordination among government policies.

Timing Problems
For fiscal policy to be effective, it must be used—much like a medicine—in proper doses and at the proper time. Timing problems revolve around the challenges of economic forecasting as well as a number of possible delays.

Economic forecasting is an inexact science. Economists rely on a variety of sources to predict future levels of business activity, but interpretations of this data often vary. The uncertainties about future economic problems often lead policy makers to take a "wait and see" position.

Global Connections

By 2025 Japan will have a greater proportion of elderly people than any other nation in the world. This development will put a serious strain on Japan's ability to provide for its elderly. For example, in 1999, about 4 Japanese workers contributed to national pension plans for each person who received an old-age pension. Forecasts suggest, however, that by 2029 that number will have fallen to about 2.

To avoid increasing the size of its national debt, Japanese policy makers will most likely need to either decrease significantly the benefits paid to each pensioner or more than double the amount each worker contributes. Another solution may be to restructure labor practices in Japan and encourage companies to retain workers until they are near or over the current mandatory retirement age. Companies will likely resist, however, because they can pay younger and inexperienced employees lower wages than older employees, which saves money and increases profits.

Enhancing the Lesson

For more information on Social Security and veterans' benefits, see the Executive Departments section on the *Researcher Online*.

Caption Answer

Fiscal policy is established by Congress and the president, all elected representatives of the people. These elected officials can be voted out of office if they make unpopular taxation and spending decisions.

Themes in Economics

FISCAL POLICY Until the early 1990s states could collect sales taxes only from those companies that had a "physical presence" in the state. This restriction meant that companies selling their goods only through mail-order catalogs were legally exempt from charging sales tax.

In 1992, however, the Supreme Court overturned the "physically present" law. Mail-order businesses in the United States earned an estimated $3 billion that year alone. Mail-order companies strongly resisted taxation, not only because they had to start charging their customers more and thus faced losing some sales but also because they had to start paying taxes in some 6,500 jurisdictions in which they do business. ∎

FISCAL POLICY *George W. Bush made a tax-cut proposal a central part of his campaign for the presidency in 2000.* **Who decides fiscal policy, and how can political pressure affect it?**

Significant delays may occur between the time that the government identifies an economic problem and the time that stabilization policies have an impact on the economy. For example, the current process for developing the U.S. budget, which outlines specific taxation and spending policies, takes more than a year to formulate and approve.

Other important delays involve the amount of time that tax or spending policies take to ripple through the economy once they are approved. For example, suppose the government injects $50 billion into the economy by reducing taxes and increasing government expenditures. The full effects of this policy will not be felt for several months or even years because it takes time for this money to be spent and respent in the economy.

Political Pressures Because fiscal policy is established by Congress and the president—the elected representatives of the people—it is more affected by political pressures than is monetary policy. These elected officials, unlike the Fed's Board of Governors, can be voted out of office if they make unpopular taxation and spending decisions. Thus, both political and economic concerns can influence the formulation of fiscal policy in a free-enterprise economy.

Restrictive fiscal policy increases taxes and reduces government spending. As a result, restrictive fiscal policy tends to limit price increases by reducing aggregate demand.

How do people react to restrictive fiscal policy? Consider taxpayers paying higher taxes who will see a reduction in their disposable incomes. Because their expenses do not decrease, they will be less likely to save, invest, or increase the consumption of goods or services. Economists refer to the negative side effects of restrictive fiscal policy as a "fiscal drag" on the economy. In addition, lower government spending often means cutting specific programs. Citizens who benefit from a government program that loses funding and is reduced or even eliminated may decide to vote against the politicians who voted to decrease their benefits.

Expansionary fiscal policy, on the other hand, decreases taxes and increases government spending to stimulate business activity in the economy, thus increasing aggregate demand. Expansionary fiscal policy often is popular because people's disposable incomes rise as their taxes decrease.

Still, political pressures on expansionary fiscal policy do exist. First, some people oppose a larger government role in the economy. Believing that the market—not the government—should ensure long-term growth and stability, these people oppose new government spending. Second, many people have become concerned about the combined effects of lower taxes and higher government expenditures.

Unpredictable Economic Behaviors A third challenge to fiscal policy is the difficulty of predicting how people will respond to the government's economic actions. When developing fiscal policy, government officials rely on models that are based on economic principles and past economic behaviors. Policy makers have no guarantees, however, that people will react to fiscal policies in exactly the same manner as they have in the past.

Lack of Coordination A fourth limitation on fiscal policy is the difficulty of coordinating the efforts of government agencies. At the national level, fiscal policy needs to be coordinated with monetary policy to achieve common goals. For example, if inflation is seen as the most pressing problem, monetary and fiscal policies should work to reduce aggregate demand. The Federal Reserve needs to institute a tight-money policy—reducing the money supply and the availability of credit—while Congress and the president need to agree on a restrictive fiscal policy. If recession and unemployment are the primary concerns, an easy-money policy—increasing the money supply and the availability of credit—and an expansionary fiscal policy are needed. Without this coordination, fiscal policy will be less effective.

In addition, taxation and spending policies on local and state levels must be coordinated with federal stabilization efforts. In many cases, such coordination is not present. For example, local and state governments tend to increase their expenditures for education and other services during periods of prosperity because tax revenues are high and credit is usually easy to obtain. Increased spending by local and state governments during these periods tends to increase aggregate demand and to result in price increases. At the same time, however, the federal government may be following a restrictive fiscal policy to reduce inflation.

FISCAL POLICY *Lack of coordination can lead to conflicting government policies. What type of fiscal policy would a government introduce to combat unemployment and recession?*

SECTION 2 REVIEW

Q: 1, 2, 3a, 3b

1. Identify and Explain
- supply-side economics
- demand-side economics
- tax incentive
- investment tax credit
- restrictive fiscal policy
- expansionary fiscal policy

2. Summarizing: Copy the graphic organizer below. Use it to list the chief tools of fiscal policy.

Chief Tools of Fiscal Policy

3. Finding the Main Idea
a. What type of economic theory did John Maynard Keynes formulate, and why did he favor government involvement in the economy?
b. What are the key limitations on the development of fiscal policy? Analyze the impact of fiscal policy decisions on the economy.

4. Writing and Critical Thinking

Drawing Inferences: Suppose that your school's grading scale changes, and fewer As are awarded each grading period. Does this reflect an explanatory policy or a restrictive policy? Explain your answer.

Consider the following:
- what constitutes expenses and income in this scenario
- whether expenses and income remain the same

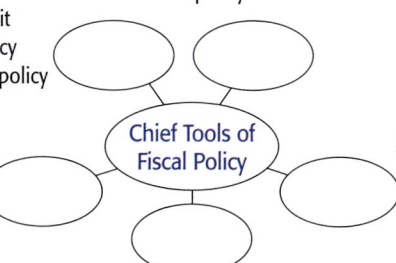

Homework Practice Online
keyword: SM3 HP15

SECTION 3

FISCAL POLICY AND THE FEDERAL BUDGET

READ TO DISCOVER

1. How is the federal budget developed?
2. What role does deficit spending play in the U.S. economy?
3. What methods can the government use to balance the federal budget?

ECONOMICS DICTIONARY

federal budget
fiscal year
budget deficit
budget surplus
deficit spending
national debt
debt ceiling

How do you spend your money? To identify how much you spend on food, clothing, and entertainment, you might keep a record known as a budget. Similarly, businesses and governments also plan how and when to spend funds.

You have learned that for fiscal policy to be effective, it must work with monetary policy. Additionally, fiscal policy must fit the government's spending plan. The **federal budget** is the federal government's plan for the use of government revenues. This budget details government revenues and expenses and predicts any shortfalls. In effect, the federal budget summarizes the ways in which the government uses fiscal policy.

Creating the Federal Budget

Why does the United States have a federal budget? Before the Civil War the United States had no formal process for planning future revenues and expenditures. The various federal departments simply requested funds as needed. After the mid-1800s, however, three developments—wartime spending, increased corruption, and progressive reform—encouraged the creation of an orderly budgeting process.

Wartime Spending Wartime spending caused dramatic increases in the level of government expenditures. For example, federal spending for all programs was just $63 million in 1860, the year before the Civil War began. By 1865, the final year of the war, federal spending had jumped to over $1 billion—more than 16 times the prewar level.

As noted in Chapter 12, the federal government historically has increased in size during a war and remained large after the war. Similarly, federal spending generally remains high after a war. As government officials discovered after the Civil War, this new, higher level of government spending required a more formal system of money management.

Increased Corruption A second factor favoring the creation of an orderly federal budget process was political and financial corruption. During the late 1800s public officials were frequently bribed by individuals seeking government contracts or other favors. People came to believe that a federal budget would reduce financial and political corruption.

Progressive Reform Third, the development of the federal budget was spurred by the general spirit of reform during the Progressive movement of the late 1800s and early 1900s. Progressives like President William Howard Taft worked to make government more accountable to the public and believed that centralized decision making would permit federal resources to be used more efficiently and fairly. These leaders believed that a formal budget would contribute to that goal.

A New Budget Process In response to these factors, in 1921 Congress passed the Budget and

Accounting Act. This legislation created the Bureau of the Budget and empowered the president to formulate an annual federal budget and present it for Congress's approval. In 1971 the Office of Management and Budget (OMB), a part of the executive branch, replaced the Bureau of the Budget and was charged with putting together the president's budget proposal. Further budgetary reforms passed in 1974 established a process for the federal government to follow when creating a budget.

The Budget Process Today How is the federal budget created today? First, the budget is developed by the president, who consults with the OMB, the Council of Economic Advisers, the Department of the Treasury, and other presidential advisers. Although the budget may predict revenues and expenditures for several years, it focuses on the next fiscal year. A **fiscal year** is a 12-month financial period that typically does not duplicate the dates of the calendar year.

After the president has prepared the budget, it is analyzed by Congress. Once the budget has been examined and approved by both houses of Congress, it is returned to the president for signing. By the time the budget is returned to the president, many changes may have been introduced. The president may sign the budget if the changes are acceptable, or otherwise may veto it, requiring the process to continue. (See Figure 15.4 for a breakdown of the 2000 federal budget.)

Federal Budget Deficits

When the government spends more money than it collects, a **budget deficit** occurs. A **budget surplus**, on the other hand, occurs when government revenues exceed government expenditures during the fiscal year. In most years since the 1930s, increases in federal spending were not matched by increases in government revenues. However, the budget showed a surplus in the years 1998–2000, with a $237 billion surplus in 2000.

Economists use the term **deficit spending** to refer to the government policy of spending more

FEDERAL EXPENDITURES, 2000

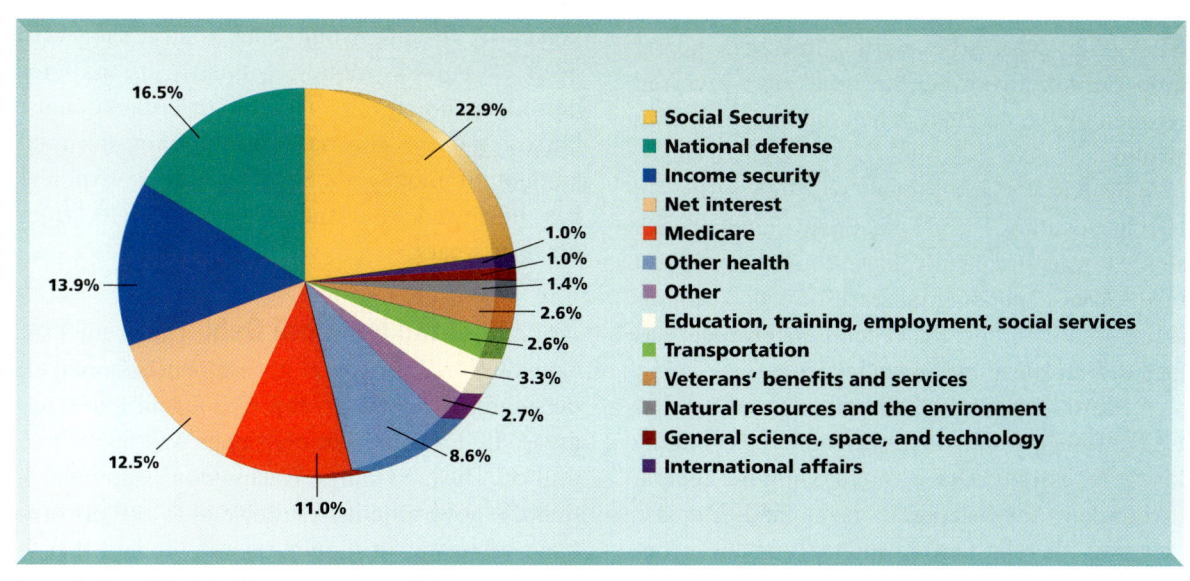

- Social Security — 22.9%
- National defense — 16.5%
- Income security — 13.9%
- Net interest — 12.5%
- Medicare — 11.0%
- Other health — 8.6%
- Other — 2.7%
- Education, training, employment, social services — 3.3%
- Transportation — 2.6%
- Veterans' benefits and services — 2.6%
- Natural resources and the environment — 1.4%
- General science, space, and technology — 1.0%
- International affairs — 1.0%

Source: *Budget of the United States Government: 2000*

FIGURE 15.4 The federal budget is the federal government's plan for spending government revenues. **What are the three largest categories of expenditures in the federal budget?**

FISCAL POLICY

Transparency

An overhead transparency of Figure 15.5 is available in *Transparency Resources*. See Transparency 63: Federal Deficit, 1945–2000.

Caption Answer

to deal with national emergencies, provide public goods, stimulate the economy during recessions, and promote the economic well-being of its citizens ★15A, 16A

Across the Curriculum

HISTORY One might think that politicians may rest easy during times of federal budget surpluses. However, a surplus of more than $100 million in 1889 caused politicians great concern. Although 1889 was a period of significant economic growth, the economy was in danger of shrinking unless the government put more money into circulation. A shortage in the money supply meant tight credit and low wages and prices.

To reduce the surplus, Congress, under President Benjamin Harrison, spent millions improving rivers and harbors, building up the U.S. Navy, and in 1893 awarding $165 million in pensions to Civil War veterans. By that same year, the $100 million surplus had shrunk to $2.5 million. ■

FEDERAL DEFICIT, 1945–2000

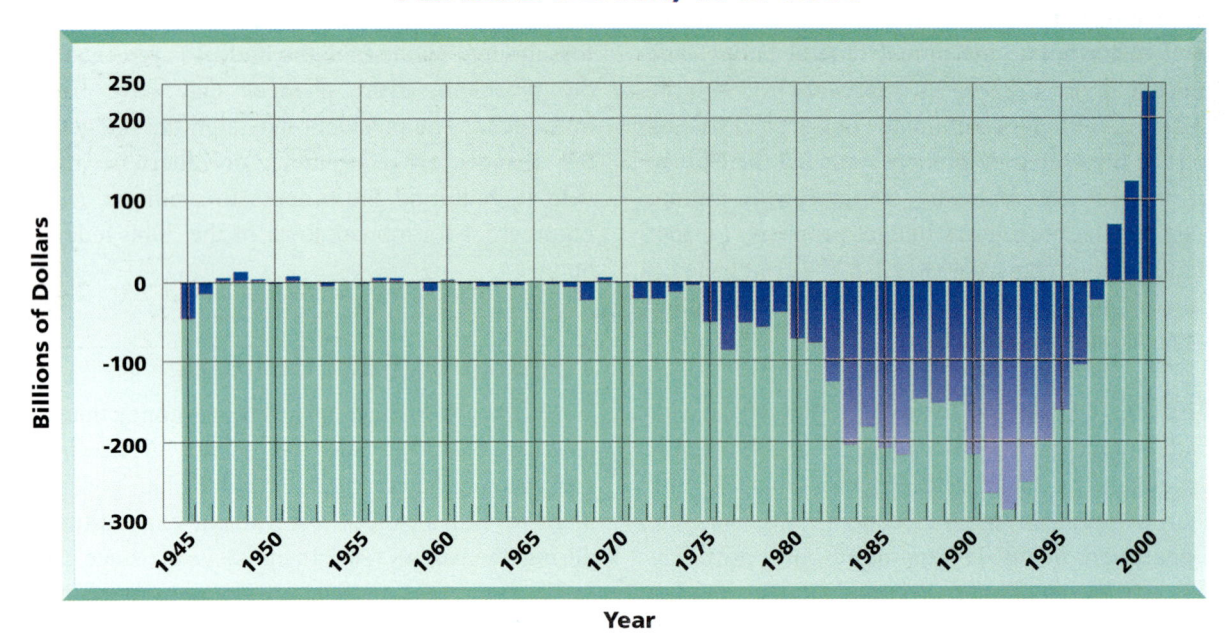

Sources: *World Almanac: 2000*

FIGURE 15.5 The U.S. government has spent more money than it has collected—creating a budget deficit—during most years since 1945. **Why does the government rely on deficit spending?** ★TEKS

money for its programs than it is able to cover with its revenues. Figure 15.5 shows that deficit spending increased dramatically between 1969 and 1992, when the deficit reached nearly $300 billion. However, the trend was reversed between 1998 and 2000, when the budget was in surplus.

Why has the government so often relied on deficit spending? First, national emergencies such as wars frequently have caused an urgent need for vast spending increases. Second, in providing public goods, the federal government has used deficit spending for social programs.

A third reason the federal government has used deficit spending is to stimulate the economy during recessions. During a recession the federal government may decrease taxes and increase spending, thereby putting money into the economy. This process, however, further increases the deficit. The fourth reason for budget deficits has been the federal government's efforts to promote the economic well-being of its citizens.

The National Debt

What happens when you spend more money than you earn? To cover your costs, you probably will need to borrow money. Similarly, to pay for deficit spending, the federal government must borrow money. The **national debt** is the total amount of money that the federal government has borrowed, and includes all deficits from previous years.

Growth of the National Debt
Under the U.S. Constitution, the federal government assumed all outstanding debts of the Confederation Congress. In 1790 the national debt was about $75 million. During George Washington's administration the government first decided to sell government securities, a money-raising method that is still used today.

Since Washington's presidency the national debt has risen and fallen. Sometimes federal budget deficits have increased the size of the national debt, and sometimes budget surpluses have reduced it.

The national debt passed the $1 billion mark for the first time during the Civil War. In 1917, the year the United States entered World War I, the national debt was just under $3 billion. Two years later, the debt had climbed to more than $25 billion. Since World War II the national debt has continued to increase steadily. In 1982 it topped the $1 trillion mark and doubled again within four years. By 2000 the national debt had reached more than $5.6 trillion.

Debt Ceilings Public concern about the size of the national debt has led Congress to approve debt ceilings. A **debt ceiling** legislates a limit on the size of the national debt. The debt ceiling of $11 billion approved during World War I was soon abandoned because of the government's need for additional credit. In 1918 the national debt increased to $12.5 billion, and by 1919 this debt had doubled. The national debt continued to rise, and in 1986 Congress raised the debt ceiling to $2 trillion. By 1997 the debt ceiling had been raised even higher, to $5.95 trillion.

Impact of the National Debt Is the U.S. economy helped or hindered by the national debt? Some economists argue that the benefits achieved from deficit spending—and the resulting rise in the national debt—exceed the costs. They note that government spending on social programs improves the quality of life for many people. Other economists argue that the short-term and long-term economic costs of the debt are severe. For example, in 2000 the federal government paid more than $362 billion in interest on the national debt. These economists argue that annual deficits and the national debt should be reduced so that money used for interest payments could be spent on programs such as national defense, road construction, and education.

Balancing the Federal Budget

The high federal deficits and the rapid rise of the national debt have caused many policy makers to look for ways to balance the federal budget so that expenditures will not exceed revenues. The two ways to balance the budget are to increase revenues and to decrease expenditures. Some policy makers believe that a balanced budget should be required by law.

Increasing Revenues The main tool that the federal government uses to increase revenues is taxation. Many politicians are reluctant to raise taxes because voters rarely want to give more money to the government. In some cases, tax increases may prove unavoidable, however, and Congress passes legislation that changes tax rates and tax brackets. For example, President Bill Clinton signed the 1993 Omnibus Budget Reconciliation Act, which raised individual income tax rates for people in the highest tax bracket. The act also raised taxes on gasoline and provided a number of tax incentives.

Decreasing Expenditures Another way the government can balance the federal budget is by

FISCAL POLICY *Politicians may cut spending to reduce the deficit, but the national debt remains a problem.* **Why is it difficult to elimate the national debt?**

Enhancing the Lesson

For information on the amount of the national debt over time, see the Federal Budgets section on the *Researcher Online*.

Global Connections

Although the leaders of European nations also work to avoid deficit spending, they are much more reluctant than their U.S. counterparts to make cuts in social spending. For example, compared with the United States, France maintains a much wider safety net of social programs, which its citizens are reluctant to give up. In late 1995 French leaders cut back on social spending to reduce the nation's budget deficit. In response, French workers initiated a strike that paralyzed France's transit system for 21 days until the government agreed to restore funding.

Profiles in Economics

For a biography of Bill Clinton and other U.S. presidents, refer students to the Biographies section on the *Researcher Online*.

Caption Answer

because even if the government stops borrowing, the debt grows through interest on it; eliminating the debt would likely mean unpopular tax increases

SECTION 3 REVIEW ANSWERS

1. federal budget (362), fiscal year (363), budget deficit (363), budget surplus (363), deficit spending (363), national debt (364), debt ceiling (365) **24A**

2. After the president, in consultation with advisers, develops the budget, Congress examines it, makes changes, and sends an approved version to the president for signing. The president either signs the budget, if the changes are acceptable, or vetoes it. **23A, 24D**

3a. to deal with national emergencies, provide public goods, stimulate the economy during recessions, and promote the economic well-being of its citizens **15A, 16A**

3b. to reduce high federal deficits and the national debt; by increasing revenues and decreasing expenditures, and, possibly, by a constitutional amendment mandating a balanced budget **20B**

4. The federal deficit is the amount by which annual expenditures exceed annual revenues. The federal debt is the total amount borrowed to finance deficit spending. Some economists believe the cost of interest payments on the deficit deprives government programs of billions of dollars. **16B, 24A**

---

decreasing spending. For example, during the early 1990s a number of U.S. military bases were closed to help reduce spending on national defense. Similarly, of all orders for new aircraft in 1985, about 65 percent were placed by the federal government. By 1993 that number had dropped to 48 percent.

Legislating a Balanced Budget
Despite government actions to increase revenues and decrease expenditures, the remedies did not succeed in bringing federal deficits under control during the 1980s and early 1990s. One proposal, the Balanced Budget and Deficit Reduction Act of 1985—also called the Gramm-Rudman-Hollings Act (GRH)—set up a program to balance the budget within five years. This law required automatic cuts to nearly every government program if the budget deficit exceeded a certain amount.

Although the deficits did decline between 1987 and 1989, the GRH deficit targets proved unachievable. A recession in 1990 and 1991 resulted in increased deficits once again. In response, more lawmakers began to call for an amendment to the U.S. Constitution requiring the government to develop and enact balanced budgets.

CASE STUDY
Balanced Budget Amendment

ROLE OF GOVERNMENT In 1997 Congress seemed likely to approve a constitutional amendment that would force lawmakers to balance the federal budget. Beginning in 2002, Congress would have been able to rely on deficit spending only in times of war or if three fifths of each house gave their permission.

Although the proposal quickly won approval in the House of Representatives, the Senate failed by a single vote to approve the bill. This was not the first time such an amendment had failed. Why do people oppose such amendments?

Opponents of these amendments worry that they would limit the government's ability to maintain many programs or respond to recessions. With a Balanced Budget Amendment in place, the government might be forced to cut spending and raise taxes—even in times of recession. Such actions could make a recession worse. Furthermore, critics argue, a balanced budget amendment would require the government to decrease funding for popular programs. Until Congress can agree on the issues of spending and taxes, it is likely that the debate over this constitutional amendment will continue.

SECTION 2 REVIEW

TEKS Q: 1, 2, 3a, 3b, 4

1. Identify and Explain:
- federal budget
- fiscal year
- budget deficit
- budget surplus
- deficit spending
- national debt
- debt ceiling

2. Comparing: Copy the chart below. Use it to describe the roles played by the president and Congress in developing the budget.

The Budget Process
- President:
- Congress:
- President: or President:

3. Finding the Main Idea
a. Why does the government sometimes rely on deficit spending?
b. Why do many policy makers want to balance the federal budget? How might they do it?

4. Writing and Critical Thinking
Finding the Main Idea: What is the difference between the federal deficit and the federal (national) debt? Why do some economists think that the national debt has severe consequences?
Consider the Following:
- which tally is cumulative
- the costs of spending more than you earn

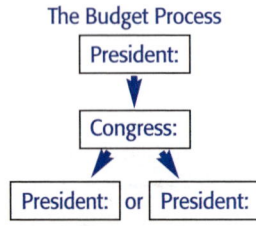

Homework Practice Online
keyword: SM3 HP15

Economics IN THE NEWS

The Commerce Clause and Economic Legislation

In 1824 the Supreme Court handed down the landmark decision *Gibbons* v. *Ogden*. The Court held that the commerce clause, Article 1, Section 8, of the U.S. Constitution, gave Congress the power to regulate interstate commerce, or business activity involving more than one state.

Under the commerce clause, Congress has the power to pass legislation aimed at solving national economic challenges. For example, the commerce clause provided the legal basis for much of the economic legislation passed during and after the New Deal. Some of this legislation pertained to such diverse areas as labor, antidiscrimination, and environmental protection. Until the mid-1990s the Supreme Court consistently held that Congress's power to regulate commerce was broad in scope.

Since 1995, however, the Supreme Court and other federal courts have begun to narrow Congress's lawmaking scope under the commerce clause. Recent laws passed under the commerce clause—such as the Family Medical Leave Act, which provides job protection to workers needing to take time off to care for a newborn baby or sick relative—have been challenged in court on the grounds that Congress has overstepped its authority under the commerce clause. These laws might be affected by the Supreme Court's interpretations of the commerce clause during the 1990s.

Why has the Supreme Court changed its position on the scope of power granted to Congress by the commerce clause? Some observers who oppose the new trend in commerce law cases have accused the Supreme Court of engaging in judicial activism, or ignoring its duty to base its judgments on prior Court decisions.

Supporters of the Court's decisions regarding the commerce clause in the 1990s argue that the Court is merely exercising its power of judicial review. The doctrine of judicial review gives courts the power to review the constitutionality of the legislative and executive branches and to ensure that they do not encroach on powers granted to the states by the Constitution.

The Family Medical Leave Act was a groundbreaking piece of legislation permitting workers to take time off to help a sick family member.

How will Congress's ability to pass economic legislation be affected by recent Supreme Court decisions regarding the commerce clause? For now, it appears that Congress will be more constrained in the ways it can respond to national economic challenges. Whether the states will be able to address such challenges remains to be seen.

What Do You Think?

1. What power does the commerce clause of the U.S. Constitution give to Congress?
2. How might recent changes in the Supreme Court's interpretation of the commerce clause affect legislation such as the Family Medical Leave Act?

WHY IT MATTERS TODAY

Constitutional debate concerning the relative powers of the national and state governments often revolves around the power of Congress to enact economic legislation. Use CNNfyi.com or other **current events** sources to find recent examples of this debate.

CHAPTER 15 Review

(Continued from page 367)

2. by creating a theory of demand-side economics that promotes active government involvement to achieve full employment, improve sluggish business activity, and increase aggregate demand during economic downturns **19A**

3. marginal tax rates, tax incentives, government spending, public transfer payments, progressive income taxes **17A**

4. After the president, in consultation with advisers, develops the budget, Congress examines it, makes changes, and sends an approved version to the president to sign. The president either signs the budget, if the changes are acceptable, or vetoes it.

5. It might increase revenues and/or decrease expenditures. **17C**

Reviewing Themes

1. proportional because they take a set percentage of a worker's wages up to a certain income level; regressive because income above the level is taxed at a lower percentage

2. Answers will vary but should explain that supply-side economics focuses on government's role in increasing the supply of goods and services, and demand-side economics focuses on how government can stimulate aggregate demand. **15A**

3. restrictive policy—increased taxes, reduced government spending leading to reduced aggregate demand and limited price increases; expansionary

Writing a Summary

Using standard grammar, spelling, sentence structure, and punctuation, write a summary of the information in this chapter.

Identifying Ideas

1. fiscal policy
2. excise tax
3. supply-side economics
4. demand-side economics
5. restrictive fiscal policy
6. expansionary fiscal policy
7. federal budget
8. budget deficit
9. budget surplus
10. national debt

Understanding Main Ideas

SECTION 1 *(pp. 349–52)*

1. Explain why federal, state, and local governments collect taxes, and provide an example of each of the following: proportional tax, progressive tax, regressive tax.

SECTION 2 *(pp. 355–61)*

2. How did John Maynard Keynes influence economic thought?

3. What tools do lawmakers use to enact fiscal policy?

SECTION 3 *(pp. 362–66)*

4. Describe the process of developing and approving the federal budget.

5. What actions might the government take to balance the federal budget?

Reviewing Themes

1. Fiscal Policy How are Social Security taxes both proportional and regressive?

2. Fiscal Policy Explain the difference between supply-side and demand-side economics.

3. Fiscal Policy Analyze the impact of fiscal policy decisions on the economy.

4. Fiscal Policy Why does the government sometimes rely on deficit spending?

Thinking Critically

1. Drawing Inferences Why might the excise tax sometimes be referred to as a "sin" tax? (Think about some of the goods and activities that are subject to the excise tax.)

2. Evaluating Why is the property tax controversial? Would you prefer to live in a municipality that levies high property taxes or in a municipality that levies low property taxes? Explain your answer.

3. Summarizing Describe the factors that encouraged Congress to pass the Budget and Accounting Act in 1921. What factors might encourage additional budgetary reforms during the 2000s?

Writing about Economics

Review the taxes you listed in your Economics Notebook at the beginning of this chapter. Now that you have read this chapter, would you change your list in any way? Which governments—federal, state, or local—benefit from the taxes you pay? Have the taxes affected how much you spend and save?

Building Social Studies Skills

Interpreting the Visual Record
Examine the political cartoon below and answer the questions that follow.

1. How is budget deficit reduction portrayed in the cartoon?
   a. as a series of booby traps and hazards
   b. as a series of juvenile pranks
   c. as a cooperative effort between Democrats and Republicans
   d. as an angry elephant
2. Why would the cartoonist depict the deficit-reduction process in such a fashion?

Analyzing Primary Sources
Read the following excerpt from John Maynard Keynes and answer the questions that follow.

"The task of transmuting [changing] human nature must not be confused with the task of managing it. We must recognise that only experience can show how far the common will, embodied in the policy of the State, ought to be directed to increasing and supplementing the inducement [encouragement] to invest; and how far it is safe to stimulate the average propensity [tendency] to consume. . . . It may turn out that the propensity to consume will be so easily strengthened by the effects of a falling rate of interest, that full employment can be reached with a rate of accumulation little greater than at present. . . . for in such matters it is rash to predict how the average man will react to a changed environment."

3. Use the passage and your knowledge of economic history to infer why Keynes might have been particularly interested in the government's ability to stimulate aggregate demand and thereby achieve full employment.
   a. He was committed to state socialism.
   b. He wanted to change the behavior of the average man by putting him to work.
   c. He was interested in lessening the effects of the Great Depression and economic downturns.
   d. He was interested in conducting a social experiment.
4. What is Keynes's point of view regarding the idea that economists can predict economic behavior?

Alternative Assessment

Building Your Portfolio
Work in small groups to develop a "study budget." Consider your "expenditures"—such as time and the cost of supplies—for homework and other projects during a given week. Then consider your "income" in terms of work completed satisfactorily. Do your group's income and expenditures balance? Explain your answer.

internet connect
Internet Activity: go.hrw.com
KEYWORD: SM3 EC15

Access the Internet through the HRW Go site to research Social Security. Some economists predict that the program's funds will run out before today's younger workers retire. Search the Social Security Administration's Web site to see how the agency addresses this issue. Do you believe Social Security benefits will be available for you? Write an editorial to voice your opinion.

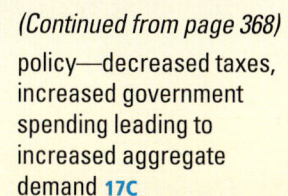

(Continued from page 368)
policy—decreased taxes, increased government spending leading to increased aggregate demand **17C**

4. to deal with national emergencies, provide public goods, stimulate the economy during recessions, and promote the economic well-being of its citizens **17C**

Thinking Critically
1. because the tax is levied on goods and activities such as alcohol, tobacco, and gambling, considered by some to be sinful **17A, 23A**
2. because it does not take into account a person's income, and it results in inequalities in public goods and services; answers will vary. **17A**
3. wartime spending, increased corruption, progressive reform; answers will vary. **23A**

Writing about Economics
Students should revise the list of taxes they have paid, if necessary. Students' paragraphs should mention which governments benefit from the taxes they have paid, and how those taxes might have affected their spending and saving habits.

Building Social Studies Skills
1. a **23E**
2. to show that there are political difficulties involved in implementing deficit-reduction measures
3. c **23A, 23E**
4. He believes it is a rash assumption. **23E**

FISCAL POLICY 369

UNIT 5

LAB OBJECTIVES

During the lab, students will
- examine the functions and limitations of several fiscal policy tools.
- analyze and synthesize information from various sources to develop fiscal policy proposals.
- create a report detailing their fiscal policy proposals.
- prepare arguments to support their fiscal policy proposals.
- devise strategies for winning congressional support for their proposals.
- prepare and give a presentation of their fiscal policy proposals.

Using the Lab

Before beginning the lab, organize students into groups and distribute copies of the Unit 5 Lab Activity found in *Unit Tests and Unit Lab Activities with Answer Key*. Have students read the assignment on this page and then discuss the assignment as a class. Point out the documents on pages 371–73 that students will use during the lab.

The What Do You Think? questions pages 371–73 will help guide students during the project. In addition, the lab activity sheet includes a step-by-step checklist for students to monitor their progress. ★25B

UNIT 5

Economics Lab

You Make the Decision

A Fiscal Fix

*I*magine that you and your classmates have decided to put your recently acquired economic knowledge to work by influencing government policy. Your group has formed a new organization called Citizens for a Good Economy (CGE). The organization's goal is to promote government policies that help strengthen the U.S. economy. In particular, CGE has decided to join the political debate over U.S. fiscal policy.

One of CGE's first tasks will be to decide which fiscal policies to lobby the U.S. government to implement. Each group will prepare fiscal policy recommendations to present to Congress. CGE has hired the consulting firm Bunker, Jefferson, and Stivich, (BJ&S) to provide:

- fact sheets from the campaigns of two key congresspersons
- slides showing recommendations from a leading association of bankers
- a review of recent corporate tax revenues
- the Fed's current monetary policy and available fiscal policy tools.

Economics Notebook Assignment ★TEKS

1. Write a clear, one-sentence statement of the situation requiring a decision.
2. Review the documents to gather information.
3. Answer the accompanying questions in your Economics Notebook.
4. Work with your group to develop fiscal policy recommendations. Support your recommendations by explaining why they would promote a healthy economy. In your recommendations, identify various policy options and discuss their consequences. Your recommendations should also suggest how to implement your decision.
5. Prepare a presentation to the other CGE members (your class). At the direction of your teacher, it may include handouts, posters, or other visual aids.

YOUR VOTE COUNTS

U.S. REPRESENTATIVE JAN LIPSCY

43 years old
fifth-term congresswoman from Michigan
chair, House Budget Committee

SUPPORTS THE FOLLOWING POLICIES:

instituting a flat tax and cutting taxes
cutting government spending
setting strict limits on public transfer payments
eliminating many tax incentives and regulations
balancing the budget
having the Fed set low interest rates

We Need Your Vote!

U.S. SENATOR ABE JENKINS

56 years old
second-term senator from Arizona
chair, Senate Budget Committee

SUPPORTS THE FOLLOWING POLICIES:

★ maintaining a progressive tax with limited or no tax cuts

★ keeping government spending at its current level

★ using public transfer payments to help the needy

★ maintaining tax incentives, particularly those that would promote investment in poor, inner cities

★ balancing the budget, but without deep cuts in social programs

★ having the Fed set low interest rates

▲WHAT DO YOU THINK?▲

1. Which congressperson is more likely to support recommendations that favor supply-side economic policies? Which is more likely to support demand-side policies?

2. The two congresspersons agree that the Fed should encourage low interest rates. Given their differences in other areas, why do you think both congresspersons might support such a policy?

What Do You Think?
Answers
1. supply-side policies—Lipscy; demand-side policies—Jenkins **23A**

2. Lower interest rates would encourage borrowing for both consumption and investment. **17C, 23A**

ECONOMICS LAB

What Do You Think?

Answers

1. It would lower business costs and increase profits that might be used for investment; some students might argue that regulations are needed to promote worker safety, environmental protection, and other goals. **15A, 17E, 23A**

2. Lower corporate taxes and more tax incentives would encourage investment and might bring customers to banks looking to arrange for loans or to deposit money. **23A**

3. Lower spending curbs inflation, thus encouraging the Fed not to raise the discount rate. Lower discount rates mean banks can offer lower interest rates and encourage more business and consumer loans and investment. **23A**

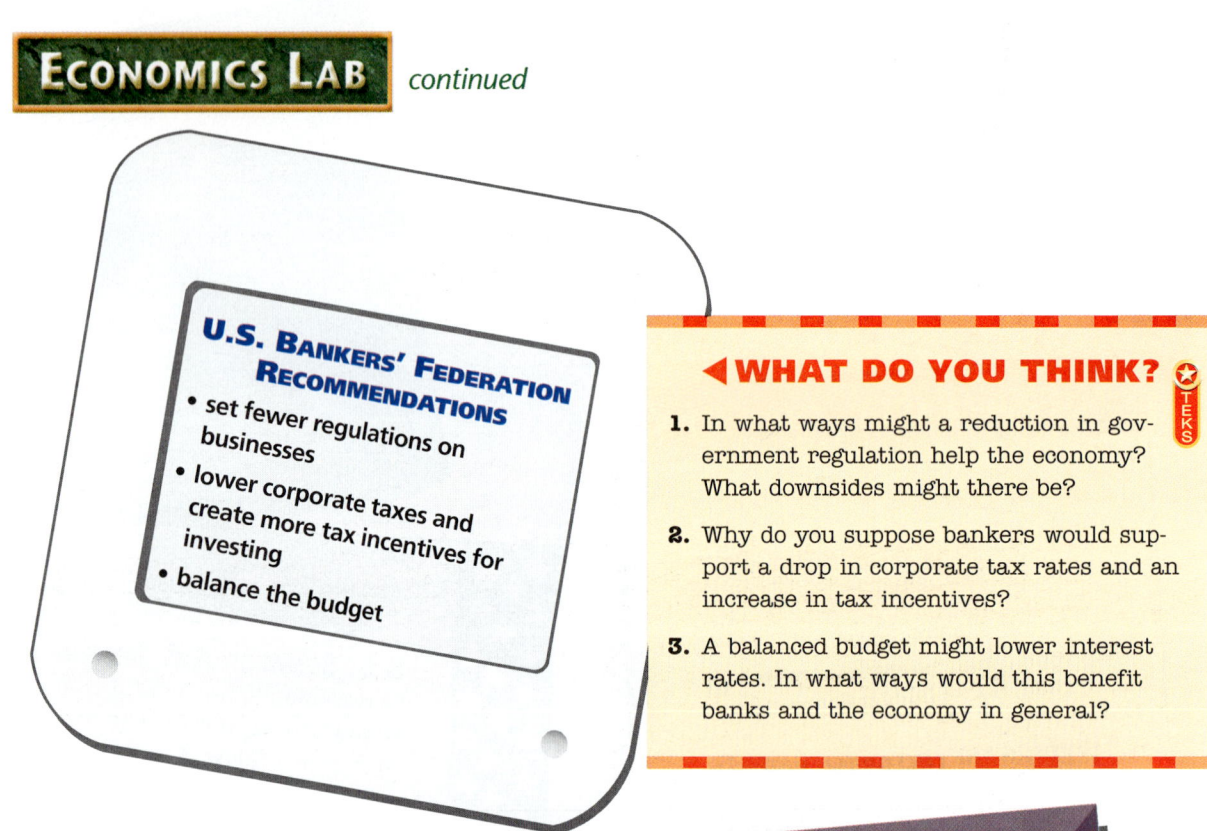

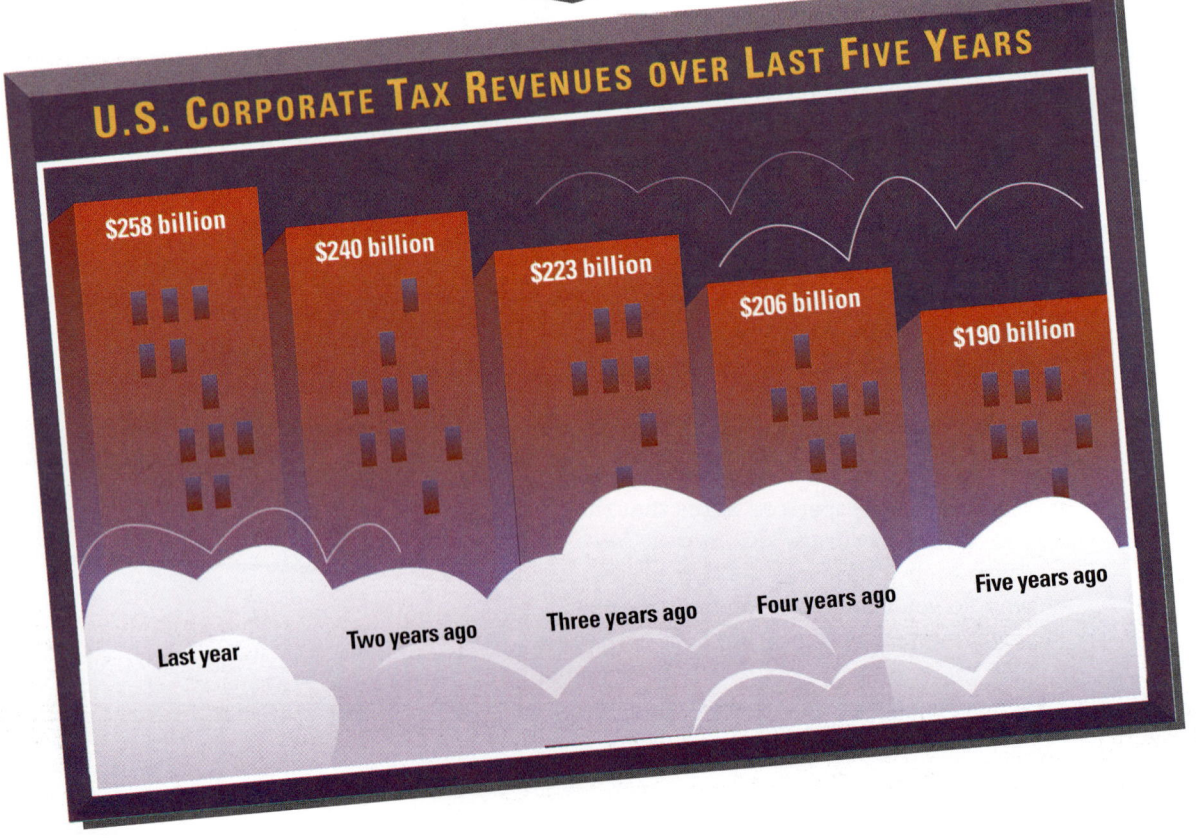

ECONOMICS LAB *continued*

U.S. BANKERS' FEDERATION RECOMMENDATIONS

- set fewer regulations on businesses
- lower corporate taxes and create more tax incentives for investing
- balance the budget

◀ WHAT DO YOU THINK?

1. In what ways might a reduction in government regulation help the economy? What downsides might there be?

2. Why do you suppose bankers would support a drop in corporate tax rates and an increase in tax incentives?

3. A balanced budget might lower interest rates. In what ways would this benefit banks and the economy in general?

U.S. CORPORATE TAX REVENUES OVER LAST FIVE YEARS

- Last year: $258 billion
- Two years ago: $240 billion
- Three years ago: $223 billion
- Four years ago: $206 billion
- Five years ago: $190 billion

CURRENT FED MONETARY POLICY
- slowly raising the discount rate
- increasing the margin requirements
- requiring higher down payments on consumer credit purchases

FISCAL POLICY TOOLS
- taxation
- tax incentives
- government spending
- public transfer payments
- progressive income tax

◀ WHAT DO YOU THINK?

1. What kind of overall monetary policy does the Fed appear to be following? What does that policy indicate about the Fed's thinking concerning the current condition of the economy?

2. What kinds of monetary policies might the Fed adopt to speed economic growth?

3. Recall that Representative Lipscy and Senator Jenkins both favor the setting of lower interest rates. The Fed, however, is increasing the discount rate. What kinds of fiscal policies might Congress adopt to keep interest rates from rising higher than it thinks would be good for the economy?

What Do You Think?
Answers
1. tight-money policy; the economy is growing and demand is high, but inflation is rising. **17C, 23A**

2. lower the discount rate, buy government securities, lower the bank reserve requirement, lower margin requirements, require smaller down payments on consumer credit, practice moral suasion to encourage lending **17C, 18B**

3. reduce government spending, balance the budget **17C, 23A**

internet connect

Internet Activity: go.hrw.com
KEYWORD: SM3 ECL5

Access the Internet through the HRW Go site to investigate current Federal Reserve monetary policy. Look at any recent changes in the discount rate, changes in margin requirements, or other statements from the Fed. Discuss whether the Fed appears to be loosening or tightening the money supply, why you think so, and what affect you would expect this to have on the economy or on you personally in the near future.

ECONOMICS LAB

UNIT 6

Lesson Options
Suggestions for customizing the material in Unit 6 to fit the specific schedule and curriculum of your classroom are located at the beginning of each chapter.

Main Ideas
Ask each student to read the Main Ideas and briefly answer each question in writing. Later, when you have finished with Unit 6, ask students to return to their original answers and revise them using what they learned in the unit.

Economics Lab
The Unit 6 Economics Lab appears on pages 450–53. This lab project is a real-world assignment in which students will take on the role of staff members of the Ministry of Economic Development for the country of Lotsaland, which recently made the transition from command socialism to market capitalism. Students will work in groups to develop and write a speech to encourage foreign businesspeople to invest in their country. Support materials for the lab appear in *Unit Tests and Unit Lab Activities with Answer Key*.

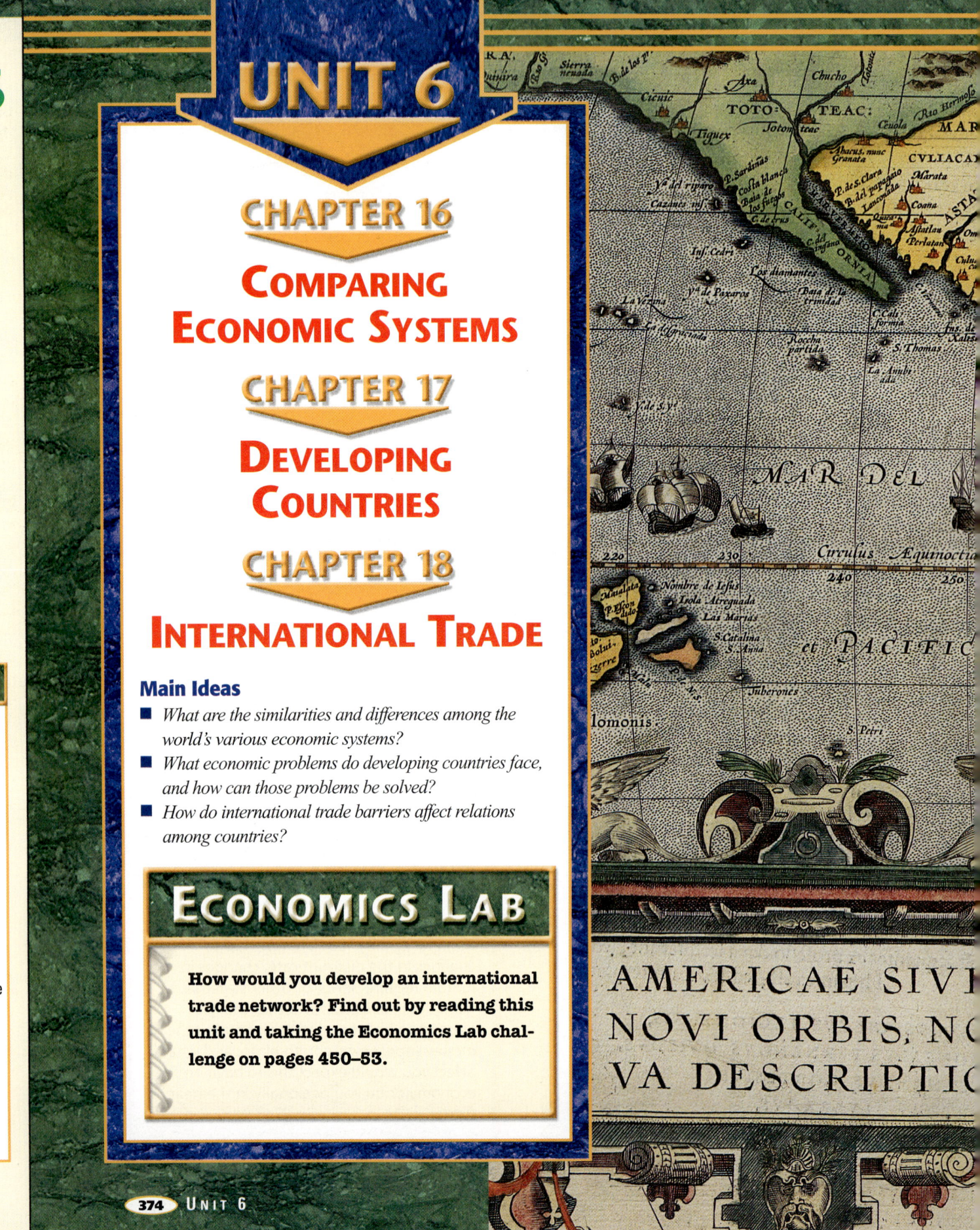

374

UNIT 6

CHAPTER 16
Comparing Economic Systems

CHAPTER 17
Developing Countries

CHAPTER 18
International Trade

Main Ideas
- What are the similarities and differences among the world's various economic systems?
- What economic problems do developing countries face, and how can those problems be solved?
- How do international trade barriers affect relations among countries?

Economics Lab
How would you develop an international trade network? Find out by reading this unit and taking the Economics Lab challenge on pages 450–53.

374 UNIT 6

International Economics

Unit 6 Overview

Unit 6 introduces students to the fundamentals of international economics. Chapter 16 covers the development of capitalism, socialism, and communism and examines some modern forms of these systems. Chapter 17 describes the characteristics of developing nations, the challenges these nations face, and the various sources for financing economic development in these nations. Chapter 18 covers specialization and trade, absolute and comparative advantage, foreign exchange rates, balance of payments and trade, and trade barriers and trade agreements.

Teaching with Photographs

This historic trade map, produced by Dutch mapmaker Abraham Ortelius, illustrates the world view of Europeans in 1587. As a motivating activity for this unit, have students examine a current world map and point out inaccuracies in the map shown here. Next, ask students how a limited knowledge of world geography may have hampered international trade during the 1500s. Then ask students what recent advances have contributed to increased international trade.

CHAPTER RESOURCE MANAGER

CHAPTER 16 COMPARING ECONOMIC SYSTEMS

	OBJECTIVES	PACING GUIDE	REPRODUCIBLE RESOURCES
SECTION 1 **DEVELOPMENT MODELS** (pp. 377–80)	▶ How can ownership of capital be used to identify an economic system? ▶ How do command systems and market systems differ?	**Regular** 1 day **Block Scheduling** .5 day	**ELL** Spanish Study Guide 16.1 **ELL** English Study Guide 16.1 **S** Simulations and Strategies for Teaching Economics: Activity 16
SECTION 2 **CAPITALISM** (pp. 381–85)	▶ What factors contributed to the development of capitalism? ▶ How does the U.S. free-enterprise system compare to capitalist systems in Japan, Germany, France, and South Korea?	**Regular** 1.5 days **Block Scheduling** 1 day	**ELL** Spanish Study Guide 16.2 **ELL** English Study Guide 16.2 **SM** Consumer Economics: Activity 16
SECTION 3 **SOCIALISM** (pp. 386–88)	▶ What conditions led to the development of socialism? ▶ How has high taxation affected Sweden's economy?	**Regular** 1 day **Block Scheduling** .5 day	**ELL** Spanish Study Guide 16.3 **ELL** English Study Guide 16.3 **SM** Mathematics for Economics: Activity 16
SECTION 4 **COMMUNISM** (pp. 389–98)	▶ How did Karl Marx use history to develop the theories of communism? ▶ What economic factors contributed to the fall of the Soviet Union? ▶ How did centralization affect the economy of the People's Republic of China?	**Regular** 2.5 days **Block Scheduling** 1 day	**ELL** Spanish Study Guide 16.4 **ELL** English Study Guide 16.4 **PS** Reading 58: Das Kapital **PS** Reading 59: Communist Manifesto **E** Challenge and Enrichment: Activity 16

Chapter Resource Key

- **PS** Primary Sources
- **RS** Reading Support
- **E** Enrichment
- **S** Simulations
- **SM** Skills Mastery
- **A** Assessment
- **REV** Review
- **ELL** Reinforcement and English Language Learners
- Transparencies
- CD-ROM
- Video
- Videodisc
- Internet
- Holt Presentation Maker Using Microsoft® PowerPoint®
- TEKS and TAKS

TECHNOLOGY RESOURCES	REINFORCEMENT, REVIEW, AND ASSESSMENT
One-Stop Planner: Lesson 16.1 Researcher Online Homework Practice Online Transparencies 64 and 65 Global Skillbuilder CD-ROM	REV Section 1 Review, p. 380 A Daily Quiz 16.1 ★ TAKS Every Day!
One-Stop Planner: Lesson 16.2 Researcher Online Homework Practice Online Global Skillbuilder CD-ROM	REV Section 2 Review, p. 385 A Daily Quiz 16.2 ★ TAKS Every Day!
One-Stop Planner: Lesson 16.3 Researcher Online Homework Practice Online Global Skillbuilder CD-ROM	REV Section 3 Review, p. 388 A Daily Quiz 16.3 ★ TAKS Every Day!
One-Stop Planner: Lesson 16.4 Researcher Online Homework Practice Online Transparency 66 CNN Presents Economics: China's Road to Economic Reform Global Skillbuilder CD-ROM	REV Section 4 Review, p. 398 A Daily Quiz 16.4 ★ TAKS Every Day!

Chapter Review and Assessment
- **SM** Global Skillbuilder CD-ROM
- HRW Go site
- **REV** Reteaching Activity 16
- **REV** Chapter 16 Review, pp. 400–01
- **A** Chapter 16 Test Generator (on the One-Stop Planner)
- **A** Chapter 16 Test
- **A** Alternative Assessment Handbook

One-Stop Planner CD-ROM

It's easy to plan lessons, select resources, and print out materials for your students when you use the *Texas One-Stop Planner CD-ROM with Test Generator*.

---

internet connect

HRW ONLINE RESOURCES
Go To: go.hrw.com
Then type in a keyword.

TEACHER HOME PAGE
KEYWORD: SM3 Teacher

CHAPTER INTERNET ACTIVITIES
KEYWORD: SM3 EC16
Choose an activity to:
▸ research the economy in a region of the world.
▸ research the role of NATO in the modern world.
▸ research the Berlin Wall.

CHAPTER ENRICHMENT LINKS
KEYWORD: SM3 CH16

HOLT RESEARCHER ONLINE
KEYWORD: Holt Researcher

ONLINE ASSESSMENT
Homework Practice
KEYWORD: SM3 HP16
TAKS Review
KEYWORD: SM3 T16
Rubrics
KEYWORD: SS Rubrics

CONTENT UPDATES
KEYWORD: SS Content Updates

HOLT PRESENTATION MAKER
KEYWORD: SM3 PPT16

ONLINE READING SUPPORT
KEYWORD: SS Strategies

CURRENT EVENTS
KEYWORD: S3 Current Events

TEXAS ONLINE RESOURCES
KEYWORD: S3 TX

LESSON 16.1 DEVELOPMENT MODELS

TEXTBOOK PAGES 377–80

HOLT PRESENTATION MAKER
Access Illustrated LECTURE NOTES using Microsoft® PowerPoint® on the One-Stop Planner CD-ROM

OBJECTIVES

- Describe how ownership of capital can be used to identify an economic system.
- Explain how command systems and market systems differ.

MOTIVATE

Ask students what they think of when they hear the word *socialism*. Write students' responses on the chalkboard. Do the same thing for the words *communism* and *capitalism*. Tell students to make copies of each list in their notes. Ask students if the ideas that they have about these three types of economic systems are accurate or if they perhaps are based on opinions they have heard, movies and television programs they have seen, books they have read, and other types of potentially biased information. Tell students that in this lesson they will learn more about these three types of economic systems and the economic systems that exist in the world today. Tell students to try and re-evaluate their preconceived notions of what they think socialist, communist, and capitalist economic systems are like as they study Chapter 16. Have students read Section 1 of the chapter. ★23E, 24A

TEACH

Building a Vocabulary

Have students use spiral notebooks to create an Economics Dictionary to be used throughout the chapter. This dictionary might be used as an activity at the start of each new lesson or as a learning aid for sheltered English students or students having difficulty. List words that students will be expected to know for this section on the chalkboard. Have students use the information provided in the text or on the *Researcher CD-ROM* to list, define, and give an example of each term. ★24A

Reviewing and Mastering Concepts

Review with students the main types of economic systems covered in Chapter 2—traditional, market, and command models, and mixed economic systems such as capitalism, democratic socialism, and authoritarian socialism. Remind students that most nations in the world today have mixed economic systems. Ask students to name some countries with capitalist, democratic socialist, or communist economic systems.
★10A, 23A

Understanding Main Concepts

Have students examine Figure 16.1: Comparing Economic Systems (Transparency 64). Have students use the chart to explain the difference between socialist and capitalist economic systems. *(They differ as to who owns the factors of production; socialist—government owns most capital; capitalist—individuals and businesses own most factors of production.)* Next, ask students to explain the difference between market and command economic systems. *(They differ as to who answers the three main economic questions; market—individuals and businesses generally answer these questions; command—government generally answers these questions.)* Then have students list the four economic systems discussed in Section 1—market capitalism, command capitalism, market socialism (democratic socialism), and command socialism (authoritarian socialism or communism). (Explain to students that Chapter 2 and Chapter 16 use different terms for the last two types of economic systems, in case students are confused.) Have students use Figure 16.1 to describe the main features and characteristics of each economic system. ★10A, 23F, 23G

Comparing and Contrasting

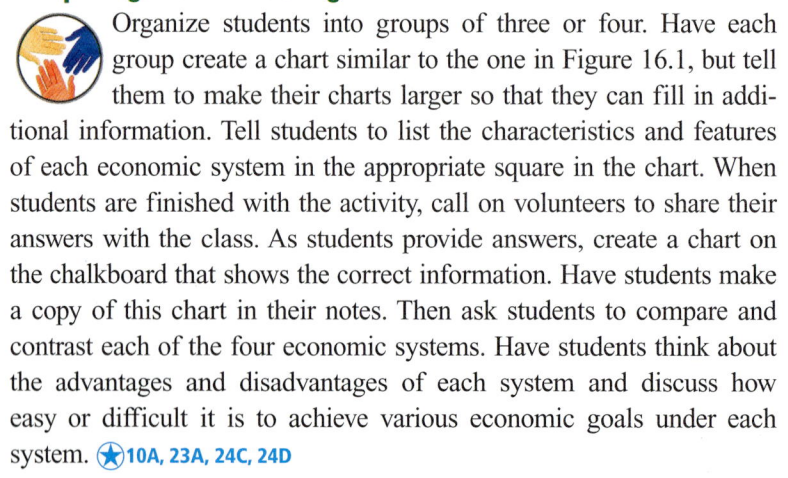

Organize students into groups of three or four. Have each group create a chart similar to the one in Figure 16.1, but tell them to make their charts larger so that they can fill in additional information. Tell students to list the characteristics and features of each economic system in the appropriate square in the chart. When students are finished with the activity, call on volunteers to share their answers with the class. As students provide answers, create a chart on the chalkboard that shows the correct information. Have students make a copy of this chart in their notes. Then ask students to compare and contrast each of the four economic systems. Have students think about the advantages and disadvantages of each system and discuss how easy or difficult it is to achieve various economic goals under each system. ★10A, 23A, 24C, 24D

Acquiring and Organizing Information

To prepare for this activity, bring several recent newspapers and news and business magazines to class. Have students examine Figure 16.2: Independent Nations Formed from the Soviet Union (Transparency 65). Call on one or two students to explain the reasons for the collapse of the Soviet Union in 1991. Then ask students to identify the 15 nations that were formed from the Soviet Union. Ask students what type of economic system most of these nations now have *(a market economic system)*.

Organize students into five groups and assign each group 3 of the 15 nations that emerged after the collapse of the Soviet Union. Tell students to learn as much as they can about their assigned nations in the time allotted. Students might use the Country Profiles section on the *Researcher Online,* the library, in-class resources, the Internet, and newspapers and magazines to find information about their countries. In addition, tell each group to look for recent articles about the political situation or economy in their countries. Students should present the information they gather in three charts, one for each country. In addition, students should write summaries about the current economic situations in their nations based on the articles and information they found. When students are through, have each group brief the rest of the students on its assigned countries. Students may want to include their charts and paragraphs in their portfolios. ★23A, 23F, 23G, 24C, 24D

CLOSE

Ask students which economic system, in their opinion, is the best. Have students explain their answers. Encourage students to consider different points of view and to think about reasons why someone might consider each economic system to be the best. To give students a homework assignment, you might have them complete the following statement: *What I like best about living in a country with a market capitalist economy is* _____. Then have students write a short essay explaining why they chose the answer they did. ★23D, 23E, 24D

OPTIONS

Students Having Difficulty, Sheltered English Students

Organize students into groups of two or three. Match students having difficulty with students who have mastered the material. Have each group create an outline of the information covered in Section 1 of the chapter. Then have students discuss the pros and cons of living in a country with each type of economic system. ★23A

Gifted Learners

Have interested students research the rise and fall of the Berlin Wall. Students should prepare a time line of the events leading up to and following the building of the wall, and the events leading up to and following the destruction of the wall. Have students write a short essay to accompany their time lines. The essay should summarize the events shown in the time line and also describe the impact of the wall's rise and fall on the German economy. Students might use the library, in-class resources, and the Internet to conduct their research. In addition, students might interview adults who remember when the Berlin Wall was built and ask them their reactions when they learned that it had been torn down. Students may want to include their time lines and essays in their portfolios. ★23A, 23E, 24C, 24D

Linguistic Learners

Have students write a paper describing how their school might be run under each type of economic system covered in Section 1. Students should describe briefly how their school is run now, decide which economic system it resembles most, and then describe how things would change if their school were run according to the principles of each of the other three economic systems. Have students end their paper by selecting which of the four economic systems would be best, in their opinion, for school officials to follow. Students may want to include their papers in their portfolios. ★10A, 23A, 23D, 24D

REVIEW

Have students complete the Section 1 Review on page 380. Use the answers in the Annotated Teacher's Edition to assess student mastery of this section.

ASSESS

To assess student mastery of this section, have students complete Daily Quiz 16.1 in *Daily Quizzes with Answer Key.* For additional assessment options, see *Alternative Assessment Handbook* on the *One-Stop Planner CD-ROM.*

ADDITIONAL RESOURCES

Dirlik, Arif. *After the Revolution: Waking to Global Capitalism.* 1994. Wesleyan University Press.

Sachs, Jeffrey. *Poland's Jump to a Market Economy.* (The Lionel Robins Lectures). 1994. MIT Press.

Symynkywicz, Jeffrey B. *1989: The Year the World Changed.* 1995. Dillon Press.

Thurow, Lester C. *The Future of Capitalism: How Today's Economic Forces Shape Tomorrow's World.* 1997. Penguin USA.

Thye Wing Woo et al., eds. *Economics in Transition: Comparing Asia and Eastern Europe.* 1996. MIT Press.

The Berlin Wall. (videotape, 23 min.). Films for the Humanities & Sciences.

Capitalism, Communism, Socialism: An Introduction. (videotape, 28 min.) BFA Educational Media.

LESSON 16.2 CAPITALISM

TEXTBOOK PAGES 381–85

> **HOLT PRESENTATION MAKER**
> Access Illustrated LECTURE NOTES using Microsoft® PowerPoint® on the One-Stop Planner CD-ROM

OBJECTIVES

- Identify and describe the factors that contributed to the development of capitalism.
- Compare the U.S. free-enterprise system to the capitalist economies in Japan, Germany, France, and South Korea. ★10B

MOTIVATE

Ask students if any of them are from or have ever traveled to Japan, Germany, France, or South Korea. Have these students share their knowledge of the economic systems in these countries with the rest of the class. If no students are from or have been to any of these countries, have the class share what they know about each country and its economic system. Then tell students that in this lesson they will learn about the origins of capitalism and the features of the capitalist economic systems in the United States, Japan, Germany, France, and South Korea. Have students read Section 2 of the chapter. ★10A

TEACH

Building a Vocabulary

List the important terms for this section on the chalkboard and tell students to add them to their Economics Dictionary. Tell students to use the information provided in the text or on the *Researcher CD-ROM* to list, define, and give an example of each vocabulary term. ★24A

Understanding Main Concepts, Identifying Cause and Effect

Review with students the origins of capitalism. Discuss manorialism and its decline, the rise of mercantilism, the influence of Adam Smith, and the effect of changing values in U.S. society on the growth of capitalism and free enterprise. As you go through the discussion, have students help you create an outline of the material. Write the outline on the chalkboard or on an overhead transparency and have students make a copy of the outline in their notes. Throughout the lecture, have students point out the various cause-and-effect relationships among events that led to the growth of capitalism. Then review with the class the main features and characteristics of capitalism in the United States today (covered in Chapter 2, Sections 2 and 3). You might want to organize this information into a chart that students copy into their notes as well. ★21B, 23A

Acquiring and Organizing Information

Organize students into groups of four or five. Tell each group to use the information in Section 2 as well as information that they have studied in past chapters to create a chart or other type of graphic organizer comparing and contrasting the free enterprise system in the United States with capitalism in Japan, Germany, France, and South Korea. Tell students that their charts should address the extent of government involvement in economic planning, the amount of government-owned versus privately owned enterprises, the main economic planning organizations, and the current state of each nation's economy. Students also might use the Country Profiles section on the *Researcher Online*, the library, in-class resources, and the Internet to provide additional information on each country, such as geographic size and location, population size, current form of government, main natural resources and industries, type of currency used, and GDP per capita. For students who need additional instruction use the *Global Skillbuilder* Lesson 12: Creating Graphic Organizers. ★10B, 23A, 23C, 24C, 24D

Evaluating and Synthesizing Information

When students are through creating their graphic organizers, go through the information as a class. Discuss the similarities and differences in how each nation practices capitalism and free enterprise. Then draw a horizontal line on the chalkboard. At the left end of the line, write *pure command economy*. At the right end of the line, write *pure market economy*. Briefly review each of these terms with students. Then have students rate where each of the five countries—the United States, Japan, Germany, France, and South Korea—fall along this line, or continuum. Help students understand that not all countries with capitalist economic systems will fall at the same point. Then have students discuss how each of the countries they examined may have moved back and forth along this continuum over the years due to such factors as changing societal values. ★21B, 23A, 24A

CLOSE

Have students discuss which of the five nations they studied in this lesson—the Unites States, Japan, Germany, France, or South Korea—has the best version of capitalism in their opinion. Ask students to provide reasons to support their views. You might also have students write, as a homework assignment, a one-page essay describing which of the capitalist systems they prefer and why. ★23D, 24D

375E

OPTIONS

Students Having Difficulty

Organize students into groups of five. Group students having difficulty with students who have mastered the material. Have a member of each group take on the role of a citizen from one of the five countries studied in the lesson—the United States, Japan, Germany, France, and South Korea. Students should write one to three paragraphs stating where their country is located, describing the form of capitalism in their nation, and explaining the advantages and disadvantages of this form of capitalism. Group members should work together to write the paragraphs. Have one or more groups read their paragraphs to the class. ★10A, 24D, 25A

Gifted Learners

Organize students into groups of four or five. Have each group research the origins of modern capitalism. Students should use the library, the Internet, and other resources to conduct their research. Tell students to create a multimedia presentation that illustrates and describes the growth and development of modern capitalism. Encourage students to enrich their presentations by including images, time lines, charts, maps, three-dimensional objects, and any other appropriate items. Have each group display its presentation in the classroom. Give students time to examine each presentation and then discuss the origins and development of capitalism as a class.
★23A, 23C, 24C, 24D

Interpersonal Learners, Intrapersonal Learners

Have students read the Chapter 16 case study, Capitalism, Singapore Style, on page 385. Discuss with students the strict rule of law in Singapore. Have any students who have traveled to Singapore share their experiences with the class and describe the laws that they noticed while in the country. Then organize students into groups of four to six. Have student groups discuss their views on whether Singapore's social policies have contributed to its strong economic growth. Then tell the groups to discuss whether they think the United States would be a better or worse place to live if it had laws similar to those of Singapore. Monitor discussions to make certain that students stay on topic and that all students can express their views.
★21B

Linguistic Learners

Have students write a report on a capitalist nation not described in Section 2 of the chapter. Students' reports should focus on the extent of government involvement in economic planning, the amount of government-owned versus privately owned enterprises, the main economic planning organizations, and the current state of the nation's economy. In addition, students should compare and contrast capitalism in that nation with the U.S. free-enterprise system. Students can use the *Researcher Online,* the library, in-class resources, and the Internet to conduct their research. Students may want to include their reports in their portfolios. ★10A, 10B, 24D

Logical-Mathematical Learners, Visual-Spatial Learners

Have students work together to create an illustrated and annotated class time line showing the main stages, events, and theories in the development of modern capitalism. Students might use their textbooks, the *Researcher Online,* the library, in-class resources, and the Internet to research the growth of capitalism. Have students include on their time lines images, descriptions of interesting events or anecdotes, and profiles of important people related to the development of capitalism. Students also should organize the time line into major segments to represent the periods of manorialism, mercantilism, and capitalism. Once students finish their time lines, organize a class discussion on what types of societal values can influence a nation's capitalist economy. How can these values lead to change? Refer students who need additional instruction on the skills used in this activity to the *Global Skillbuilder* Lesson 9: Using Time Lines. ★21B, 23A, 23C, 24C

REVIEW

Have students complete the Section 2 Review on page 385. Use the answers in the Annotated Teacher's Edition to assess student mastery of this section.

ASSESS

To assess student mastery of this section, have students complete Daily Quiz 16.2 in *Daily Quizzes with Answer Key.* For additional assessment options, see *Alternative Assessment Handbook* on the *One-Stop Planner CD-ROM.*

ADDITIONAL RESOURCES

Gianaris, Nicholas V. *Modern Capitalism.* 1995. Praeger Publishing.

Tsuru, Shigeto. *Japan's Capitalism: Creative Defeat and Beyond.* 1996. Cambridge University Press.

At the Helm of Korean Business. (videotape, 28 min.). Films for the Humanities & Sciences.

The Culture of Commerce. (videotape, 58 min.). Films for the Humanities & Sciences.

The Japanese Economy: Teaching Strategies. (eight lesson plans). EconomicsAmerica. National Council on Economic Education.

LESSON 16.3 SOCIALISM

TEXTBOOK PAGES 386–88

HOLT PRESENTATION MAKER: Access Illustrated LECTURE NOTES using Microsoft® PowerPoint® on the One-Stop Planner CD-ROM

OBJECTIVES

- Identify and describe the conditions that led to the development of socialism.
- Explain how high taxation has affected Sweden's economy.

MOTIVATE

Review with students the features and goals of socialism. Then tell students that socialist economies, like capitalist economies, fall along a continuum, from pure market socialism to pure command socialism. Draw a horizontal line on the chalkboard or on an overhead transparency. At the left end, write *pure command socialism;* at the right end, write *pure market socialism.* Have students describe each extreme form of socialism. Then tell students to use these models as a basis by which to judge the various socialist systems that they will study in Sections 3 and 4 of Chapter 16. Have students read Section 3 of the chapter. ★24A

TEACH

Understanding Main Concepts, Identifying Cause and Effect

Review with students the origins of socialism. Discuss the influence and contributions of social thinkers such as Robert Owen and Charles Fourier, socialist communities and utopian societies, harsh working and social conditions during the Industrial Revolution, and aspects of capitalism that contributed to the growth of socialism. As you go through the discussion, have students help you create an outline of the material. Write the outline on the chalkboard or on an overhead transparency and have students copy it. Throughout the lecture, have students point out the cause-and-effect relationships that led to the growth of socialism.

Next, review with the class the main features of market socialism. Remind students that market socialism is a model. No nation has a pure market socialist economy, but rather different levels of market socialism. ★10A, 21B, 23A

Organizing Information, Comparing and Contrasting

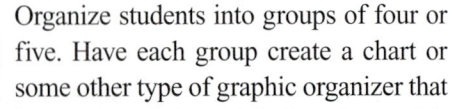

Organize students into groups of four or five. Have each group create a chart or some other type of graphic organizer that describes the main features of the past Swedish model of market socialism and compares and contrasts this model to the pure market socialist model. Groups' charts should address the extent of government involvement in economic planning, the amount of government-owned versus privately owned enterprises, the main economic planning organizations, tax levels and available social programs, and the main advantages and disadvantages of the economic system.

You might also have students use the Country Profiles section on the *Researcher Online,* the library, in-class resources, and the Internet to provide additional information about Sweden, such as geographic size and location, population size, current form of economy and government, main natural resources and industries, type of currency used, and GDP per capita. Refer students who need additional instruction on the skills used in this activity to the *Global Skillbuilder* Lesson 12: Creating Graphic Organizers. ★10A, 23A, 24C, 24D, 25A

Analyzing, Evaluating, and Synthesizing Information

When students are finished creating their graphic organizers, review the information as a class. Discuss the features, advantages, and disadvantages of Sweden's market socialist economy. Then discuss the similarities and differences between Sweden's model of market socialism and the pure market socialist model. Have students rate where Sweden would fall along the continuum from pure market socialism to pure command socialism.

Next, have students explain why Sweden has moved away from market socialism and closer to market capitalism. Help students understand how Sweden's high tax rate and budget deficits hurt its economy and contributed to a severe recession in the early 1990s. Then have students describe how Sweden has since worked to deal with these problems and to reform its economy. ★23A, 25A

CLOSE

Have students discuss the following question: Do you believe market socialism could be a successful economic system? In their responses, students should address the problems that market socialism created for Sweden's economy, possible solutions for dealing with these problems, and the form of market socialism that they think would be the best. For an optional homework assignment, students might write a one- to two-page essay addressing each of these issues. Then, before moving on to the next lesson, have students compare and contrast Sweden's market socialism with the U.S. free-enterprise system again to ensure that students have mastered these fundamental concepts. ★10B, 21B, 23A, 23D, 24D, 25A

375G

OPTIONS

Gifted Learners

Have students research the tax rates in Sweden during its period of market socialism as well as the tax rates in other countries with market socialist economic systems. Tell students to determine how taxes were/are levied and what percentage of incomes were/are paid in taxes in these countries. Have students prepare a chart illustrating their findings. Then have students write an essay relating the level of taxes in these countries to the level of social programs provided. Students should address the following questions in their essays:

- What government programs were/are provided in each country?
- How do these programs compare to the level of social programs provided in the United States?
- How do the level of taxes and social programs affect the overall economy and standard of living in countries with market socialist economic systems?
- Can a market socialist economy work successfully?

Have students use the library, the Internet, and other resources to conduct their research. Students may want to include their charts and essays in their portfolios. ★10B, 23A, 23C, 24C, 24D

Linguistic Learners, Visual-Spatial Learners

Have students use posterboard to create political cartoons that illustrate their opinions of market socialist economic systems. Students might want to have their cartoons specifically address market socialism in Sweden. Tell students to write captions to accompany their cartoons. When students are done, have volunteers share their cartoons with the class. Ask class members to provide feedback and to explain what they think each cartoon is saying. Students may want to include their cartoons in their portfolios. ★24D

Interpersonal Learners

Organize students into groups of four or five. Have each group research the socialist and utopian communities established by Robert Owen, Charles Fourier, and other social thinkers. Students might use the library, the Internet, and other resources to conduct their research. Then have each group create its own imaginary utopian or socialist society. Tell each group to create a poster and a marketing brochure advertising their community. The poster and brochure should describe the community and highlight its "selling points" to explain why people would want to join. Have each group decide if people will use money in their community or have to pay to live in the community, how work and other tasks will be shared in the community, whether the community will do business with other communities and nations or be self-sufficient, and whether the community will be based on certain fundamental values or economic and social principles. Have each group present and describe its community to the class. Then have the class vote on which of the communities they prefer. ★24D, 25B

REVIEW

Have students complete the Section 3 Review on page 388. Use the answers in the Annotated Teacher's Edition to assess student mastery of this section.

ASSESS

To assess student mastery of this section, have students complete Daily Quiz 16.3 in *Daily Quizzes with Answer Key*. For additional assessment options, see *Alternative Assessment Handbook* on the *One-Stop Planner CD-ROM*.

ADDITIONAL RESOURCES

Guarneri, Carl. *The Utopian Alternative: Fourierism in Nineteenth-Century America*. 1991. Cornell University Press.

Hayek, Friedrich A. von. *The Road to Serfdom*. 1994 (1944). University of Chicago Press.

Pitzer, Donald E., ed. *America's Communal Utopias*. 1997. University of North Carolina Press.

Roosevelt, Frank, and David Belkin. *Why Market Socialism?: Voices of Dissent*. 1994. M. E. Sharpe.

Friedrich von Hayek: His Life and Thought. (videotape, 78 min.). Films for the Humanities & Sciences.

Socialism Today. (lesson plans and teaching materials). NewsSource Units. Newsweek Education Department.

Understanding Economics: Free Market vs. Socialist Economy. (filmstrip). Knowledge Unlimited, Inc.

LESSON 16.4 COMMUNISM

TEXTBOOK PAGES 389–98

> **HOLT PRESENTATION MAKER**
> Access Illustrated LECTURE NOTES using Microsoft® PowerPoint® on the One-Stop Planner CD-ROM

OBJECTIVES

- Explain how Karl Marx used history to develop the theories of communism.
- Describe the economic factors that contributed to the fall of the Soviet Union.
- Explain how centralization affected the economy of the People's Republic of China.

MOTIVATE

Have students share what they know about the current economies of Russia and the People's Republic of China. If any students are from or have ever visited either of these countries, have them share their knowledge of these places with the rest of the class as well. Next, remind students of their original ideas about communism that they shared in the Motivate activity of Lesson 1 of this chapter. Tell students that they are going to study two nations that long had command socialist, or communist, economic systems—the Soviet Union and the People's Republic of China. Have students keep in mind their views of what communism is and what they know about the current economies of Russia and China as they read Section 4 of the chapter. ⭐10A

TEACH

Building a Vocabulary

List the important terms for this section on the board and tell students to add them to their Economics Dictionary. Tell students to use the information provided in the text or on the *Researcher CD-ROM* to list, define, and give an example of each term. ⭐24A

Understanding Main Concepts

Review with students Karl Marx's theories about communism. Then have students work together as a class to create a flowchart that shows the steps that Marx believed would lead to communism. Draw the flowchart on the chalkboard or on an overhead transparency, and have students make a copy of the flowchart in their notes. Next, have students point out the problems with Marx's reasoning. Ask students if history has shown Marx's theories to be true. Then have students discuss whether they agree or disagree with Marx's opinion of capitalism and what impact his theory has had on the U.S. free-enterprise system. For students who need additional instruction, use the *Global Skillbuilder* Lesson 12: Creating Graphic Organizers.
⭐19A, 23A, 23B, 23D, 24D, 25A

Reading and Writing About Economics

To extend the previous activity, have students complete Reading 58: *Das Kapital* and Reading 59: *Communist Manifesto*, located in *From the Source: Readings in Economics and Government with Answer Key*. Discuss each reading and the accompanying questions as a class. Then have students write a one- to two-page essay stating why they do or do not agree with Marx's and Engels' views as described in these readings. When students have finished, have a volunteer read his or her essay to the class. Provide feedback and encourage students to provide feedback as well. Students may want to include their essays in their portfolios. ⭐24D

Creating and Using Time Lines, Organizing Information

Review with students the main aspects of Russian communism under Lenin, Russian communism under Stalin, and the changes that have occurred in Russia's economy since Stalin. Then have students examine Figure 16.3: Fall of the Soviet Union (Transparency 66). Go through the events shown in the time line with students. Then tell students to create a similar time line that illustrates the rise of communism in Russia and the Soviet Union. Their time line should begin with Marx's publication of the *Communist Manifesto* in 1848 and end with Mikhail Gorbachev's election as leader of the Soviet Union in 1985, which is where the time line in Figure 16.3 begins. When students have finished, draw a horizontal line on the chalkboard or on an overhead transparency. At the left end, write *pure command socialism;* at the right end, write *pure market socialism*. Have students rate where the Soviet Union would fall along the continuum at various points in history since Lenin took power. Then have students rate where Russia's economic system would fall along the continuum today. Refer students who need additional instruction on the skills used in this activity to the *Global Skillbuilder* Lesson 9: Using Time Lines. ⭐23A, 24C, 24D

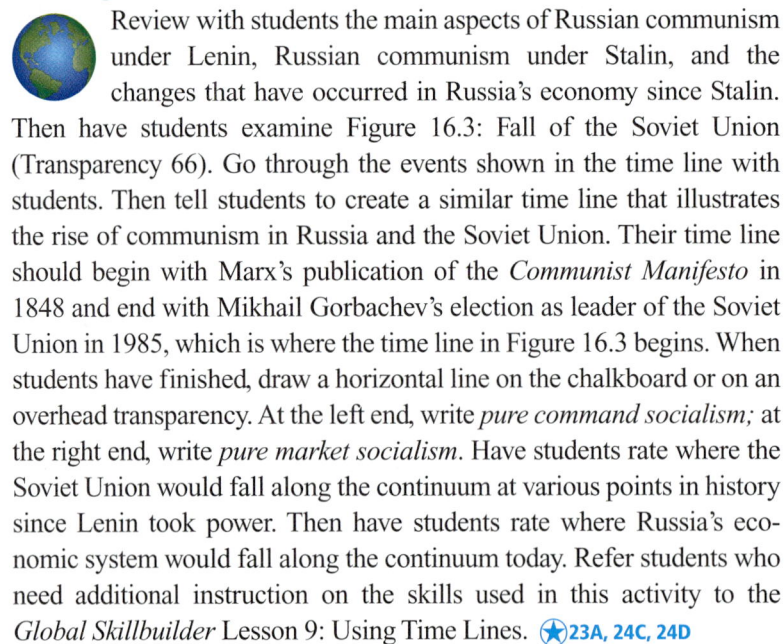

Creating and Using Time Lines, Comparing and Contrasting

Review with students the development of communism in the People's Republic of China. Then have students create a time line similar to the one that they created for the former Soviet Union to illustrate the development of communism in China. The time line should begin in 1949

with Mao Zedong's assuming leadership of China and end in the present. When students have finished their time lines, have the class rate where China's economic system would fall along the continuum from pure command socialism to pure market socialism at different stages since the Chinese communists came to power in 1949. Then have students compare and contrast communism in the Soviet Union with communism in China and with the pure command socialism model.
★23A, 24C, 24D

CLOSE

Have students discuss the advantages and disadvantages of the different stages of communism in the Soviet Union and in China. Then ask students if either system was entirely in keeping with Marx's original theories. Encourage class discussion.

OPTIONS

Gifted Learners
Have interested students research the current economy in Russia or the People's Republic of China. Students might use the library, the Internet, and other resources to conduct their research. Have students report their findings to the class orally. Encourage students to use visual aids such as charts and graphs to enhance their presentation. Then have the class discuss where they think the economies of Russia and China are headed and how they might change. ★23A, 23C, 24C, 24D

Interpersonal Learners, Linguistic Learners
Before class, find three to five recent articles that describe the current economy in Russia or the People's Republic of China. Make several copies of each article. Organize students into groups of four to six. Give each member of each group a copy of one of the articles. Have each student read the article and then discuss it as a group. Then have the group write a summary of the article and their opinion of the information presented. When students have finished, have a representative from each group read that group's summary and opinion to the class. Encourage class feedback and discussion. ★23A, 24D

Interpersonal Learners, Linguistic Learners
Have students research and write a biography of Karl Marx, Vladimir Ilich Lenin, Joseph Stalin, Mao Zedong, or Deng Xiaoping. Students can use the Biographies section on the *Researcher Online,* the library, in-class resources, and the Internet to conduct research for their biographies. When students are finished writing their biographies, have volunteers offer to play the role of the person whose biography they wrote. Try to get a volunteer to represent each of the five men. Have the volunteers hold a round table discussion on the best way to establish and run a communist economy. Each of the other four volunteers should explain the importance of Marx's ideas on their economies, and Marx should explain the importance of his ideas on the U.S. free-enterprise economy. Have students in the audience provide feedback after the round table discussion. Students may want to include their biographies in their portfolios. ★19A, 24D

REVIEW

Have students complete the Section 4 Review on page 398. Use the answers in the Annotated Teacher's Edition to assess student mastery of this section.

ASSESS

To assess student mastery of this section, have students complete Daily Quiz 16.4 in *Daily Quizzes with Answer Key*. For additional assessment options, see *Alternative Assessment Handbook* on the *One-Stop Planner CD-ROM*.

RETEACH

For students having difficulty with the lessons, have them complete Reteaching Activity 16. This activity is located in *Reteaching Activities with Answer Key*.

ADDITIONAL RESOURCES

Evans, Richard. *Deng Xiaoping and the Making of Modern China.* 1997. Penguin USA.

Fischer, Ernst, et al. *How to Read Karl Marx.* 1997. Monthly Review Press.

Kort, Michael G. *China under Communism.* 1995. Millbrook Press.

Marx, Karl, et al. *The Communist Manifesto.* (The World's Classics). 1992 (1848). Oxford University Press.

Skidelsky, Robert. *The Road from Serfdom: The Economic and Political Consequences of the End of Communism.* 1997. Penguin USA.

Volkogonow, Dmitri. *Lenin: A New Biography.* 1994. Free Press.

Whitelaw, Nancy. *Joseph Stalin: From Peasant to Premier.* (People in Focus). 1992. Dillon Press.

The Chinese Revolution. (videotape, 25 min.). Films for the Humanities & Sciences.

Communism. (videotape, 49 min.). Films for the Humanities & Sciences.

Karl Marx and Marxism. (videotape, 52 min.). Films for the Humanities & Sciences.

CHAPTER 16

TOPICS INCLUDE

- capitalist economic systems
- socialist economic systems
- origins of capitalism
- capitalism in various nations today
- origins of socialism
- market socialism
- Swedish socialism
- theories of Karl Marx
- rise of communism
- collapse of the Soviet Union
- Russian economic reform
- communism in the People's Republic of China

Economics Notebook

The Economics Notebook is a journal activity that encourages students to consider basic concepts of economics that relate to their lives. A follow-up notebook activity appears on page 400.

WHY IT MATTERS TODAY

To find additional lesson plans dealing with the impact of different economic systems on the idea of a global economy, visit CNNfyi.com or have students complete the ECONOMICS IN THE NEWS activity on page 399.

CNNfyi.com

CHAPTER 16

Comparing Economic Systems

As noted in Chapter 2, most nations have mixed economic systems. Mixed economic systems combine elements of the pure market model with elements of the pure command model. In this chapter you will learn more about the types of economic systems that exist in the world today. These economic systems include market capitalism, command capitalism, market socialism, and command socialism—also referred to as authoritarian socialism or communism.

Economics Notebook

In your Economics Notebook, list five economic decisions you have made in the past month. How have you answered the questions of what, how, and for whom to produce?

WHY IT MATTERS TODAY

As the idea of a truly global economy becomes more of a reality, the differences in national economic systems become more important. At the end of this chapter, visit CNNfyi.com to learn more about the importance of different economic systems to your life.

CNNfyi.com

376

SECTION 1
DEVELOPMENT MODELS

READ TO DISCOVER
1. How can ownership of capital be used to identify an economic system?
2. How do command systems and market systems differ?

ECONOMICS DICTIONARY
- market system
- command system
- market socialism

Economic systems can be identified in two ways. The first is by ownership of the factors of production capital. An economic system in which most capital is owned by the government is called a socialist economic system. A system in which most capital is privately owned is called a capitalist economic system.

The second way to identify economic systems concerns how decisions about the use of capital and the other factors of production are made. As noted in Chapter 1, all societies must answer three basic economic questions: what to produce, how to produce, and for whom to produce. A system in which these questions primarily are answered by individuals and businesses is called a **market system**. A system in which those decisions are generally made by the government is called a **command system**.

Figure 16.1 shows how these ownership and decision-making characteristics can result in different economic systems. The two columns show public versus private ownership of capital and natural resources. The two rows show public versus private decision-making in the allocation of those resources.

Capitalist Economic Systems

Figure 16.1 describes a market capitalist economy like that of the United States, in which natural, human, capital, and entrepreneurial resources are generally owned or controlled by individuals rather than by the government. Decisions about how these resources are to be used are made primarily by their owners.

The capital and resources used by businesses such as the Walt Disney Company, Apple Computer, or Time Warner Inc. are owned by the shareholders of those firms; the company's management decides how those resources will be used on a day-to-day basis. Most resources in the market capitalist economy of the United States fit the model of private ownership and private decision making.

Not all decisions are made by individuals and businesses; some are made by federal, state, or local governments. For example, the federal government owns the capital that the military uses

COMPARING ECONOMIC SYSTEMS

Ownership of Natural Resources and Capital

Allocation Choices	Private	Government
Private	**Market Capitalism** Examples: United States, Western Europe, Japan	**Market Socialism** Examples: Yugoslavia, China
Government	**Command Capitalism** Examples: many nations in Latin America, Africa, and the Middle East	**Command Socialism** Examples: Soviet Union, Cuba, North Korea

FIGURE 16.1 A nation's economic system is defined by who owns the capital and who decides how capital is used. **Who makes allocation choices in a command capitalist system?**

SECTION 1
DEVELOPMENT MODELS

Lesson Plans
For teaching strategies, see Lesson 16.1 located at the beginning of this chapter or the One-Stop Planner Strategy 16.1.

Economics Dictionary
To reinforce the section's vocabulary terms, refer students to the Electronic Glossary on the *Researcher CD-ROM*.

Section Assessment
To assess students' mastery of this section, have them complete Daily Quiz 16.1 in *Daily Quizzes with Answer Key*.

Enhancing the Lesson
For basic data and information about a number of countries, see the Country Profiles section on the *Researcher Online*.

Transparency
An overhead transparency of Figure 16.1 is available in *Transparency Resources*. See Transparency 64: Comparing Economic Systems.

TEKS
Content
10A, 10B, 21B
Social Studies Skills
23A, 23B, 23D, 23E, 23F, 23G, 24A, 24C, 24D

and determines how those resources will be used. The government also regulates many of the choices that firms make on the use of the capital and other resources they own. For example, the Department of Agriculture may tell farmers participating in a price support program how much of a particular crop to plant. The government also regulates such things as food inspection, maintenance of historic structures, length of the workday, and use of wetlands.

Command capitalism is indicated by a greater degree of government involvement. While individuals continue to play an important role, the government makes a wider variety of economic choices and owns a higher percentage of the factors of production.

CAREERS IN ECONOMICS

Business Geographer

What would be the most profitable location for an ice cream parlor—Alaska or Florida? While the answer may seem obvious, all entrepreneurs must put serious time and effort into finding the best locations for their place of business. One of the best sources of such information comes from the field of geography.

When you think of geography you might think of the names and locations of cities, rivers, mountain ranges, and countries. But geography is more than knowing the location of places on a map. Geography is the study of all the earth's characteristics, be they mountain ranges, human-made places like cities, or the location of populations and natural resources.

Businesspeople seek the services of geographers who specialize in studying the economic aspects of the earth's features. To compete successfully, businesses need to know the most favorable locations for capital investments and market growth. They also must understand the environmental impact of their operations on surrounding areas.

Business geographers, or economic geographers, as they are sometimes called, can provide companies with this information because they study the earth's features as economic resources.

Business geographers analyze the usefulness of natural resources for humans and interpret how the natural and human-made world interrelate. Part of this task is to determine the most profitable location or market for a particular business.

Business geographers have a variety of employment options in manufacturing, retail, and transportation. They typically have undergraduate degrees in geography. Coursework may include various fields of geography—economic, urban, transportation, and population—as well as cartography (mapmaking) and statistics. In addition, classes in marketing, management, and consumer behavior enable business geographers to speak the "language" of business.

Business geographers analyze the earth's features and resources to determine the best locations for businesses.

Socialist Economic Systems

In socialist economies, the society or government owns all or most of the capital and natural resources. Most production is done by state-owned firms. Figure 16.1 shows two versions of socialism: market, also called democratic, and command, also called authoritarian.

Flag of the Soviet Union

The most prominent example of a command socialist economy, which combined state ownership with state decision making, was the Union of Soviet Socialist Republics, known as the Soviet Union. After World War II, the Soviet Union aggressively spread its economic system to nations in Eastern Europe, Central America and the Caribbean, Asia, and Africa.

For decades the Soviet Union represented a political and economic system opposed to the capitalist nations of the West. Economic hardships eventually weakened the Soviet Union, however, and it collapsed in 1991 and dissolved into 15 independent nations. (See Figure 16.2 on page 380.) Most of these nations have rejected socialist economic systems in favor of capitalist economic systems. With the fall of the Soviet Union, former communist nations of Eastern Europe, such as Poland, Romania, and Hungary, also replaced command socialism with market or command forms of capitalism. Today Cuba and North Korea are the only nations that still rely strictly on command socialism as the model for their economic systems.

An alternative to command socialism is market socialism, which emerged in Yugoslavia after World War II. **Market socialism**—or democratic socialism—is identified by government control of major industries, with some decisions made by individuals. Even this form of socialism failed, and Yugoslavia's government and economy collapsed in the 1990s.

Why did these forms of socialism fail? The problem appears to have been fundamentally one of incentives. The "invisible hand" of the market

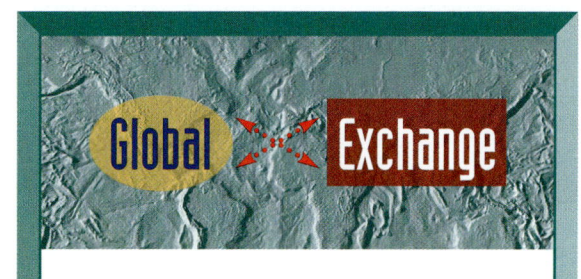

Global Exchange

Marketing Communism

For nearly 30 years the Berlin Wall stood as a symbol of the gulf between capitalism and communism. Built in 1961 to keep East Germans from entering capitalist—and politically democratic—West Berlin, the wall, its concrete guard towers, and barbed wire represented political and economic repression.

Germans on both sides of the wall recognized the power of this historic symbol. When East Germany's communist government collapsed in 1989, East and West Germans worked joyfully together to tear down the wall and reunite the city. The destruction of the Berlin Wall became something of a precelebration for the reunification of all of Germany, which took place a year later. People from all over the country—and around the world—flocked to Berlin to join in the party.

Pieces of the wall were immediately snatched up and sold as souvenirs, turning this symbol of communist rule into a commodity in the global capitalist market. In fact, American entrepreneurs began shipping pieces of the wall to the United States to be sold. One entrepreneur airlifted 20 tons of the rock from Berlin to Chicago.

Meanwhile, price competition among sellers of wall souvenirs became fierce. While the earliest pieces sold for as much as $15, competition quickly brought the price down to $7. In the future, as pieces of the wall become scarce, their value will probably go up. Thanks to the laws of supply and demand, a piece of the wall may one day become a collector's item with significant market value.

Themes in Economics

INTERNATIONAL GROWTH & STABILITY As economic and political reform spread across Eastern Europe and the former Soviet Union during the early 1990s, some countries were more successful making the transition from socialism to capitalism than others. One determinant of success was how quickly a nation instituted economic reform. According to a report by the World Bank, those nations that instituted reforms quickly—despite suffering recessions—experienced smaller drops in national output and were able to recover faster than nations that instituted reforms more slowly. In addition, the better a nation controlled its inflation, the sooner its economy recovered and the faster it grew. ■

Themes in Economics

PRODUCTIVITY Economists John R. Moroney and C. A. K. Lovell compared productivity and efficiency in seven Eastern European command economies and 17 Western European market economies from 1978 to 1980. They found that command economies used resources about 24 percent less efficiently than market economies. For the period, average real GDP per worker in command economies was only $7,775 compared to $12,600 in market economies. ■

Transparency

An overhead transparency of Figure 16.2 is available in *Transparency Resources*. See Transparency 65: Independent Nations Formed from the Soviet Union.

SECTION 1
REVIEW ANSWERS

1. market system (377), command system (377), market socialism (379) **10A, 24A**

2. United States—private ownership of capital; Yugoslavia—government ownership of capital; common—private choices for allocation of resources **10B, 23A, 23B, 24D**

3a. capitalist—most capital is privately owned; socialist—government owns most capital **23A**

3b. The former Soviet Union and Cuba are command systems, while the United States and Japan are market systems. Command—government generally answers the main economic questions of what, how, and for whom to produce; market—private individuals and businesses answer these questions **10A, 23A**

4. capitalist—profit serves as the incentive for private individuals and businesses to use the resources they own wisely; socialist—government has no profit incentive to make wise use of resources; capitalism is more efficient because private individuals have more to gain and to lose, including their social standing, if their businesses are inefficient **21B, 23A**

380

Independent Nations Formed from the Soviet Union

FIGURE 16.2 The Soviet Union was the most prominent example of a command socialist system. In 1991 it dissolved into 15 independent nations.

system was replaced by government orders. These government orders seldom correctly reflected consumer preferences. People who make decisions regarding the use of resources they do not own have no incentive to seek out the most productive use of the resources. In fact the decisions of these socialist economies—both command and market—were usually based on ideology rather than the principal of economic efficiency.

SECTION 1 REVIEW

★ TEKS Q: 1, 2, 3b, 4

1. Define and Explain:
market system
command system
market socialism

2. Compare and Contrast: Copy the Venn diagram below. Use it to compare the market capitalist system of the United States to a market socialist system like that of Yugoslavia in the 1980s.

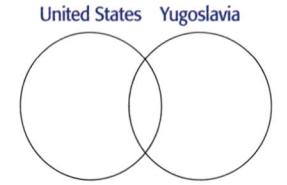

United States   Yugoslavia

3. Finding the Main Idea

a. How do capitalist and socialist economic systems differ?

b. Give two examples of command systems and two examples of market systems and then compare the two systems.

4. Writing and Critical Thinking

Evaluating: What role do incentives play in capitalist and socialist economic systems? Which system is more efficient and why?

Consider:
- ownership of capital
- concept of self-interest

Homework Practice Online
keyword: SM3 HP16

380 CHAPTER 16

SECTION 2
CAPITALISM

READ TO DISCOVER
1. What factors contributed to the development of capitalism?
2. How does the U.S. free-enterprise system compare to the capitalist economies in Japan, Germany, France, and South Korea?

ECONOMICS DICTIONARY
mercantilism
indicative planning
nationalization

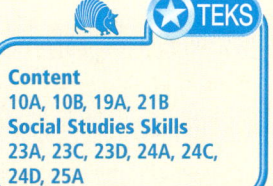

In a capitalist economic system, the ownership of resources is left to individuals and businesses. However, nations differ in their definitions of the role of government in a capitalist system. This difference is often based on their economic history. In command capitalist economies, the government takes an active role in guiding the allocation of resources. Governments may control prices or regulate how resources are to be used. Governments play a more passive role, however, in market capitalism. They influence the allocation of resources through their taxation, spending, and regulatory policies, but leave the bulk of allocation choices to the private sector.

Origins of Capitalism

Capitalism became the dominant economic system in Europe and the United States in the 1800s. This system emerged as part of a series of economic systems over the last several centuries.

Decline of Manorialism During the Middle Ages, Europe's main economic system was manorialism, with land-owning nobles granting peasants the opportunity to work the land in exchange for fixed payments. By the 1100s new agricultural techniques and technological developments led to increased food production, which in turn supported the growing population.

Prosperity and population growth encouraged the expansion of trade—both within Europe and with other regions. As trade increased, people began to invest money in businesses to make a profit.

Over time, the power of landowners began to decline. Just as merchants gained economic power, kings grew stronger politically and were increasingly able to form centralized governments. The rise of these new nations created a need for national currencies and a banking system, two key institutions of capitalism.

Mercantilism Between 1500 and 1800, the governments of major European nations used the

ECONOMIC SYSTEMS *A gold merchant and his wife work together at their banking business in the 1500s. What economic system did European nations use during this period?*

COMPARING ECONOMIC SYSTEMS 381

Themes in Economics

THE ROLE OF GOVERNMENT
In addition to guiding Japan's industrial production and protecting its industries from foreign competition, METI promotes research and development through its National Institute of Advanced Industrial Science and Technology (AIST). AIST oversees 15 national research labs and institutes. These labs perform research in a variety of fields and set industrial standards. AIST's budget is expected to increase as Japan, like many other nations, acknowledges the growing need for research in today's high-tech world. ■

Caption Answer
by imposing tariffs to protect firms from foreign competition, by assisting in joint research efforts, and by encouraging banks to make more credit available to specific industries ★23A

ECONOMIC SYSTEMS *Japanese semiconductor firms captured most of the market during the 1980s.* **How has the Japanese government helped its businesses?**

theory of mercantilism to direct their economies. **Mercantilism** defined a nation's power in terms of its supply of gold and silver. Since these commodities were rare, Europeans generally believed that a nation could grow stronger only by gaining more wealth—and therefore power—than other nations. This accumulation of national wealth took place through a combination of trade and conquest.

Mercantilist power required a steady source of raw materials, encouraging European nations to establish trading posts and colonies around the world. Government leaders then established trade monopolies and introduced trade barriers to maintain control over their supplies of raw materials. Governments thus maintained tight control over national economies.

Adam Smith's Influence By the mid-1700s, many Europeans believed that mercantilism interfered with economic growth. Reform-minded economists urged governments to grant individuals more economic freedom. One of the most influential of the economists opposed to mercantilism was Adam Smith. As noted in Chapter 2, Smith's *Wealth of Nations* argued that economies would prosper without government interference. Smith wrote that the profit motive would make a free economic system efficient, and that competition in the marketplace would eliminate inefficient businesses. Later, this type of economic system became known as a free-enterprise, or capitalist, system.

Capitalism Today

Market capitalism currently functions with varying degrees of government involvement. Governments in every capitalist economy play an active role in assisting the poor and in providing such public goods as law enforcement, education, and environmental protection. Although the amount of governmental control varies from nation to nation, it remains much more limited than in a socialist economy. In the United States, for example, the government intervenes in the economy only on a limited basis. In Japan, South Korea, France, and Germany, on the other hand, the government has had a great deal of influence in how the economy is run.

Capitalism in Japan The Japanese government plays a crucial role in the country's economy. The key players are the Ministry of Economy, Trade, and Industry (METI) and the Ministry of Finance. METI encourages the production of certain goods and discourages the production of others. In the 1970s, for example, when U.S. companies dominated the semiconductor market, METI imposed tariffs to protect Japanese firms from foreign competition and assisted in joint research efforts by Japanese manufacturers. Such tariffs limited the number—and increased the prices—of foreign goods allowed into the country. Goods produced in their own country, therefore, were more affordable for Japanese consumers.

By the mid-1980s, Japanese firms commanded an increasing share of the global market for semiconductors. Although U.S. firms have won back much of the market in recent years,

METI's intervention appears to have helped the Japanese companies.

The Ministry of Finance, which runs the Bank of Japan, Japan's central bank, encourages banks to make more credit available to specific industries. Although the Bank of Japan cannot direct the lending activities of private banks, it can provide guidance to private banks—for example, encouraging them to increase their lending to the desired firms and industries.

Capitalism in Germany Germany emerged from defeat in World War II to a position as an economic superpower. Its economy is the fourth-largest in the world, now behind that of the United States, China, and Japan. Germany has a long tradition of government involvement in the economy and social welfare programs. Many government social welfare programs considered standard by capitalist economies today—such as social insurance—were originally developed in Germany in the 1880s.

Germany's market capitalist economy was created after the Allies divided the defeated nation into four zones following the war. In 1948 the United States, Great Britain, and France economically united their zones, which became known as West Germany, and established a single currency. The Soviet Union's zone became known as East Germany and operated under a command socialist, or communist, economic system.

The Western Allies imposed a command capitalist economic system with extensive price controls. In 1948, when the Allied generals who ruled the occupied nation were away, Ludwig Erhard—the German leader they had appointed—ordered all price controls repealed. Throughout the West German economy, shortages disappeared rapidly. The resulting economic growth continues, although it has slowed since the 1980s.

Like the United States, Germany relies on the types of monetary and fiscal policies noted in

ECONOMIC SYSTEMS *The unification of East Germany and West Germany in 1990 was symbolized by the dismantling of the Berlin Wall.* **What problems have resulted from the reunification of Germany?**

COMPARING ECONOMIC SYSTEMS 383

Across the Curriculum

GOVERNMENT Whether the movement toward increased capitalism and privatization in France will last remains to be seen. In the 1997 French parliamentary elections, the people of France elected a socialist-communist government to power once again. The new socialist prime minister, Lionel Jospin, appointed President Jacques Chirac, promised among other things to create 700,000 more jobs and to stop the privatization of state-owned companies. Faced with a high unemployment rate of 12.5 percent, French citizens were ready for a change. From 1997 to 2000, unemployment in France decreased steadily, and the economy grew by more than 3 percent each year. However, the times are again changing in France. ■

Caption Answer

a system of indicative planning, under which the General Planning Commission creates nonmandatory five-year plans for the economy ★23A

ECONOMIC SYSTEMS *François Mitterrand—president of France from 1981 to 1995—encouraged the nationalization of many French industries.* **What other characteristic defines France's strong central government?**

Chapters 14 and 15. However, German fiscal policy differs from that of the United States in one important respect. In the United States, fiscal policy decisions by state and local governments are largely independent of federal policy. While the federal government may seek to influence state and local spending, it does not regulate their spending and tax choices. Germany, on the other hand, has established two commissions to coordinate the budgets of the federal, state, and local governments in an effort to promote economic stability.

Although Germany has had a history of low inflation and low fiscal deficits, the sudden collapse of East Germany in 1989 and its reunification with West Germany in 1990 created severe economic problems. Low productivity and high unemployment among former East Germans, combined with Germany's generous unemployment benefits, resulted in large deficits. The Bundesbank, Germany's central bank—which is even more independent of elected officials than is the U.S. Federal Reserve system—has helped the nation experience one of the lowest inflation rates in the world over the last two decades.

Privatization of formerly state-owned firms in the former East Germany has moved fairly quickly. Most industrial capacity in the region has been transferred to private ownership. As noted in Chapter 12, privatization is the process in which government-owned firms are transferred to the private sector.

Capitalism in France France has long had a capitalist economy, but it also has a tradition of a strong central government. Perhaps the most striking feature of the French system since World War II was its reliance on a system of **indicative planning**, or providing economic information and setting goals that are not mandatory. Under this system, the General Planning Commission created a series of five-year plans for the French economy. This planning process was not a command system because private firms were not required to base their economic decisions on the growth targets of the plan.

The election of François Mitterrand—a French socialist candidate—as president in 1981 contributed to greater government control over industry through **nationalization**, a policy in which the government purchases and takes over the operation of a private firm. Nationalization efforts in France were concentrated in industries such as iron ore and steel production. The government's ownership share in key industries increased dramatically between 1981 and 1983. At that time the government controlled about one third of the total output of the French economy.

However, in 1993 the French government announced a reversal of the earlier socialist policy through the introduction of privatization. The ownership of 21 state-owned companies, including Renault, was to be shifted to the private sector. This process continued until the 1997 appointment of Lionel Jospin, a more conservative socialist.

Capitalism in South Korea The government-financed Korea Development Institute (KDI),

South Korea's version of METI, is an economic planning agency that brings government planners together with business owners to develop South Korea's economic plans.

Like the Japanese, South Koreans have offered incentives to businesses to direct resource allocation as well as production. For example, in the mid-1970s incentives were provided to the automotive, shipbuilding, steel, and other heavy industries. By the early 1990s South Korean shipbuilders were successful global competitors, and automobiles had become a major export industry.

CASE STUDY

Capitalism, Singapore Style

ROLE OF GOVERNMENT Singapore, a tiny city-state in Southeast Asia, has had one of the fastest growing economies in the world. A former British colony, the country has a total population of only about 4 million. In 1999 the country ranked 53rd in the world in terms of gross domestic product. However, in terms of the amount of gross domestic product produced per person, the tiny country ranked 7th in the world.

Singapore's miracle economy has had its costs, however. Although its economy is capitalist, its government regulates many elements of personal behavior. For instance, the Singapore government imposes fines for failure to flush a public toilet and for chewing gum in public.

According to a former leader of Singapore, Lee Kwan Yew, the country's rapid economic growth is the direct result of its authoritarian principles. "We would not have made economic progress if we had not intervened in very personal matters—who your neighbor is, how you live, the noise you make, how you spit, or what language you use."

However, many economists point to other factors as the more likely reasons for economic growth, such as the country's long history as an international trade center while under British rule.

Nevertheless, some Americans admire Singapore's rigid social policies. For instance, in the mid-1990s an American teenager living in Singapore was convicted of spray-painting graffiti on cars and as punishment was whipped with a bamboo cane. While many Americans viewed the caning as excessively harsh and an affront to humanitarian values, others applauded the Singapore government's tough stand against juvenile delinquency.

An important question, however, is whether or not authoritarianism enhances a capitalist country's economic performance. If it does, is the trade-off between free choice and economic growth worth it?

SECTION 2 REVIEW

TEKS Q: 1, 2, 3b, 4

1. Define and Explain:
- mercantilism
- indicative planning
- nationalization

2. Comparing: Use the chart below to compare the economic systems of Japan, Germany, France, and South Korea to the U.S. free-enterprise system.

	Similar to U.S.	Different from U.S.
Japan		
Germany		
France		
South Korea		

3. Finding the Main Idea
a. What is the economic role of government in Japan, Germany, France, and South Korea?
b. How did privatization change the French economy?

4. Writing and Critical Thinking
Drawing Inferences: What impact did Adam Smith have on the U.S. free-enterprise system?
Consider:
- mercantilism
- government interference

Homework Practice Online keyword: SM3 HP16

SECTION 2 REVIEW ANSWERS

1. mercantilism (382), indicative planning (384), nationalization (384) 24A

2. Japan—similar with private control of capital, different with more government influence in allocation; Germany—similar with little government interference, different coordination of economic regulations; France—similar in increased privatization of industry, different with creation of five-year plans; South Korea—similar with private control of capital; different with high government involvement in allocation 10B, 23A, 23C

3a. The level of governmental control varies among the four nations, but is limited in all four. For the most part, governments work with businesses and industries to plan economic development and to promote economic growth. 23A

3b. The French economy changed from a command economic system to a market economic system. 10A, 23A

4. Adam Smith believed that a country's economy would do better without government interference. He believed the profit motive would increase efficiency and competition. This theory has led directly to the creation of the free-enterprise system in the United States, which is based on the ideas of profit motive, self-interest, and competition. 19A, 23A, 24D

SECTION 3

SOCIALISM

READ TO DISCOVER

1. What conditions led to the development of socialism?
2. How has high taxation affected Sweden's economy?

Socialism is a broad term used to describe several types of noncapitalist economic systems. Whereas capitalism is rooted in the concepts of private property and private decision making about the allocation and use of resources, socialism is an economic system rooted in an entire society's ownership of some or all of the means of production.

Socialists believe that public ownership of industries protects workers from harsh working conditions. Furthermore, socialists believe that central planning is necessary to channel resources into socially desirable areas. One of the goals of central planning is to oversee the distribution of wealth in a nation so that no one is too wealthy or too poor.

Economic socialism does not necessarily indicate the level of political freedom in a country. For example, North Korea and Sweden both have practiced government ownership of some resources and industries. Political freedom, however, is very limited in North Korea but was widespread in socialist Sweden.

Origins of Socialism

In the early 1800s, social thinkers such as Robert Owen and Charles Fourier established a number of socialist communities in which members shared the proceeds of their labor and promoted the good of the community rather than their own interests. These socialist experiments were in part a reaction to harsh working conditions during the Industrial Revolution. Long working

ECONOMIC SYSTEMS *Members of experimental socialist communities such as New Harmony, Indiana, shared the proceeds of their labor.* **How, according to socialist beliefs, does public ownership of industries protect workers?**

hours, low pay, child labor, and hazardous working conditions created workplace conditions that were often unpleasant. Overcrowded tenements, industrial pollution, and the lack of adequate sanitation and medical facilities also contributed to a decline in the workers' quality of life.

Largely in response to these conditions, reformers began to question the capitalist system. Some reformers favored an end to capitalism and the establishment of an economic system that would provide a more equal distribution of wealth. Collectively, these reformers were called socialists. Some socialists called for violent revolutions to topple the capitalists and reorganize ownership of the factors of production. Others supported a peaceful, gradual transition from capitalism to socialism.

Market Socialism

Socialists who believed in peaceful change adapted their economic and political ideals to changes in economic and political conditions during the 1900s. One of these adaptations became known as market, or democratic, socialism. By studying the economic history of Sweden, you can better understand how market socialism has worked.

Socialism in Sweden

Under market socialism, the people retain basic human rights and elect government officials, which gives them some control over economic planning. By electing officials whose economic policies they agree with, the people have a say in their country's economy. Great Britain and France have practiced market socialism in the past. In an effort to reverse their economic declines, both Great Britain and France have privatized many industries that had been nationalized and shifted toward the capitalist system. For many years Sweden's combination of private industry and government-directed services made the country appear to be a model of market socialism. From 1986 to 1991, however, Sweden's system underwent dramatic change.

ECONOMIC SYSTEMS *Sweden's combination of government and private business ownership once made it a model of market socialism.* ***How is Sweden different from a command socialist country?*** TEKS

Industry Ownership Today government ownership of industry stands at approximately 10 percent of the country's industries. Sweden's government has maintained ownership or control of mining and telecommunications, as well as part of the national railway network, broadcasting systems, and hydroelectric facilities. Private firms, such as Electrolux and Volvo, own about 90 percent of industry in Sweden.

Workers' Freedoms During Sweden's socialist period, Swedish workers enjoyed many of the economic freedoms commonly associated with capitalist economies. In some respects, the power of workers was greater in Sweden than in the United States or Japan. For example, Sweden's workforce is the most heavily unionized of the world's industrialized nations. More than 80 percent of Swedish workers belong to unions, compared to about 15 percent of U.S. workers and about 26 percent of Japanese workers. Additionally, Swedish workers routinely have been entitled to representation on the boards of directors of major corporations and shared in corporate decision making.

Caption Answer
The Swedish government does not control all industries and, in most cases, decisions regarding the allocation of resources are made by private citizens. ★10A, 23A

Themes in Economics

ECONOMIC INSTITUTIONS & INCENTIVES Among the benefits enjoyed by Swedish citizens during the socialist period were 12 months of paid leave following the birth of a child, health insurance that paid workers 90 percent of any income lost while ill, and pension plans that paid retired citizens two thirds of their average income earned during their 15 best-paid years.

Opponents of the Swedish model argued that it provided few incentives for employees to work, however. In 1988 Swedish workers called in sick an average of 23.4 days per year. Furthermore, the sizable pensions left workers with little incentive to save. Sweden's experience raises the question of whether capitalism and heavy social spending are compatible. ■

COMPARING ECONOMIC SYSTEMS

Caption Answer
comprehensive health insurance, unemployment insurance, retirement benefits, free education through college, subsidized public housing, child care ⭐23A

SECTION 3 REVIEW ANSWERS

1. government, private businesses, and individuals share economic planning and ownership of industry; workers have many rights and freedoms; people get to elect government officials; a number of social programs are financed through high taxes **10A, 23A**

2a. They set up socialist communities in which people worked for the good of the community and shared the proceeds of their labor. **23A**

2b. More than 80 percent of workers in Sweden's labor force was unionized, compared to about 15 percent of workers in the U.S. labor force. **10B, 23A**

3. advantages—generous social programs, high standard of living; disadvantages—workers demanded higher wages, leading to higher production costs and higher prices of consumer products; tax revenues did not keep pace with rising costs of social programs, led to budget deficits and political unrest **10A, 25A**

ECONOMIC SYSTEMS *The Swedish people have enjoyed one of the highest standards of living in the world. What are some of the social programs the Swedish government has financed?*

Economic Planning Economic planning in the Swedish socialist economy was the responsibility of people who represented both public and private interests. Representatives of the government, labor unions, industry, and agriculture negotiated together to develop annual plans that set production and employment targets.

Taxation Under socialism, taxes in Sweden were among the highest in Europe. The Swedish government used the tax revenues to finance many social programs, including comprehensive health insurance, unemployment insurance, retirement benefits, free education through college, subsidized public housing, and child care. This gave Sweden one of the highest standards of living in the world.

The high taxes that Swedish workers paid were a source of controversy. High taxes forced workers to demand higher wages, which increased the prices of goods produced for domestic and international markets. Moreover, tax revenues did not keep pace with the rising costs of social programs. As a result, the government had to run deficits and borrow heavily to meet its economic and social goals.

In the early 1990s Sweden experienced its worst recession since the Great Depression. Faced with the need to reduce its deficit, the Swedish government launched a program to limit welfare benefits and turn over the production and management of many government services to private firms.

SECTION 3 REVIEW

⭐TEKS Q: 1, 2b, 3

1. Summarizing: Copy the web organizer below and use it to demonstrate the four major characteristics of market socialism.

[Web organizer: Market Socialism]

Homework Practice Online
keyword: SM3 HP16

2. Finding the Main Idea
a. How did social thinkers such as Robert Owen and Charles Fourier contribute to the development of socialism?
b. How does Sweden's labor force differ from that of the United States?

3. Writing and Critical Thinking
Problem Solving: Consider the advantages and disadvantages of market socialism in Sweden and what led to the problems in that country.
Consider:
• taxes and social programs
• increased unionization

SECTION 4

COMMUNISM

READ TO DISCOVER

1. How did Karl Marx use history to develop the theories of communism?
2. What economic factors contributed to the fall of the Soviet Union?
3. How did centralization affect the economy of the People's Republic of China?

ECONOMICS DICTIONARY

bourgeoisie
proletariat
collectivization
perestroika
Great Leap Forward
people's communes
Cultural Revolution
Four Modernizations
household responsibility system
Tiananmen Square Massacre

German philosophers Karl Marx and Friedrich Engels first outlined the theories of communism, or command socialism, in the *Communist Manifesto* (1848) and *Das Kapital* (1867). From these theories, an economic system—and a way of life—was born.

Communism is a type of socialism in which the government owns and controls the means of production. This economic system is closest to the pure command model. The former Soviet Union and the People's Republic of China before the introduction of market-oriented reforms both represent communism.

Theories of Karl Marx

Karl Marx wrote that economic factors determine political and social change. Marx viewed history as a series of class struggles between the oppressors, who owned the means of production, and the oppressed, who supplied the labor.

Rise of the Bourgeoisie Marx's view of the Middle Ages, for example, focused mainly on the decline of manorialism and the rise of mercantilism described in Section 2. Gradually, with the expansion of trade and the growth of cities, a class of merchants arose. As these "middle class" merchants—whom Marx called the **bourgeoisie** (boorzh-wa-ZEE)—became more powerful, they challenged the ruling nobles. Marx noted that the bourgeoisie's triumph over the nobility in this struggle led to the creation of capitalist economic systems in many parts of Europe by the late 1700s.

Rise of the Proletariat Marx did not see the rise of the bourgeoisie as the end of the class struggle. Instead, he saw that during the early

ECONOMIC SYSTEMS *Karl Marx's theories of communism gave rise to the economic system of command socialism.* **What are two prominent examples of communist countries?**

COMPARING ECONOMIC SYSTEMS

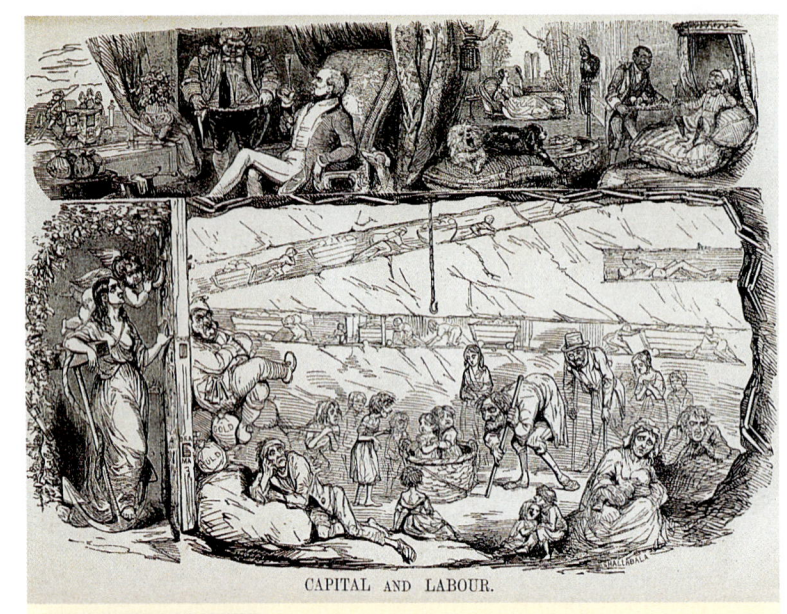

ECONOMIC SYSTEMS *Marx believed that the differences between the bourgeoisie and the proletariat would lead to violent revolution.* **What did Marx believe would happen once capitalism was destroyed?**

Industrial Revolution, the bourgeoisie gained control of the means of production and became the oppressors of the working class. The working class—whom Marx called the **proletariat** (proh-luh-TAYR-ee-uht)—provided the labor needed for the production process in return for very low wages.

Marx saw all of the profits from production going to the bourgeoisie. Their wealth grew while the proletariat continued to work for low wages. In Marx's view, the class struggle would continue to intensify until the proletariat eventually overthrew the bourgeoisie in a violent revolution.

Destruction of Capitalism Marx expected that the working class would organize a government, which he called the "dictatorship of the proletariat," that would oversee the final destruction of capitalism. Marx believed that once capitalism was destroyed, a classless society would develop. Everyone would then be equal and all people would share ownership of the means of production. In his theory, Marx stated that the dictatorship of the proletariat would be temporary. He saw workers in all nations toppling the bourgeoisie and establishing an ideal worldwide society without government.

Simplification of History
Marx believed that the victory of the proletariat was the inevitable conclusion of capitalism. Marx, however, simplified history and ignored political forces by attributing nearly all events to a class struggle. He also incorrectly predicted that capitalism would lead to deteriorating standards of living for the working class. He did not foresee the rising economic status that workers in industrialized nations such as the United States have enjoyed throughout the 1900s.

Finally, the government of the Soviet Union, which practiced communism from 1917 until its breakup in 1991, did not simply wither away after coming to power. Soviet society also was not the classless society that Marx imagined. Instead, the leaders of the Soviet Communist Party enjoyed special privileges and made up the intellectual, political, and social elite of the nation. The majority of the people had—and still have—standards of living below those of capitalist nations.

Rise of Communism

During the early 1900s many revolutionary groups formed in Russia. The Bolsheviks—later called Communists—were one of these opposition groups. Under the leadership of Vladimir Ilich Lenin, in 1917 the Bolsheviks overthrew the existing government in Russia and proclaimed Russia the world's first communist nation.

War Communism The early years of communism were marked by political and economic experimentation. Lenin's first experiment is known as the period of "war communism"

(1917–21). It was a time of civil war and extreme hardship following Russia's defeat in World War I and the overthrow of Czar Nicholas II. Under Lenin's war communism, the state abolished private property, broke up large estates in rural areas, and nationalized and redistributed land. In cities, the communist government took control of factories and allowed the workers to run them. A forced-labor policy relocated scarce labor resources to important industries.

War communism failed because the peasants had no incentive to produce crops when the government confiscated agricultural products to feed the army and urban workers. Furthermore, untrained industrial workers knew little about managing factories. War communism therefore caused agricultural and industrial output to fall dramatically.

New Economic Policy In 1921 Lenin introduced the New Economic Policy (NEP), which restored some private incentives. Peasants were allowed to sell surplus crops on the open market for profit, and small private firms were allowed to open in the cities. Under the NEP, thousands of entrepreneurs revived the economy. Larger enterprises, however, remained in the hands of the government.

Stalin's Rule When Lenin died in 1924, he was succeeded by Joseph Stalin. The new Soviet leader moved toward a more centralized decision-making system. Stalin instituted strict central planning and eliminated private property.

Under Stalin's leadership, a series of Five-Year Plans were established—beginning in 1928—that set long-term economic goals and allocated scarce resources. Under these plans, Stalin and his successors set quotas for increased industrial and agricultural production. Workers who failed to meet quotas were severely punished.

The Soviet government emphasized heavy industries such as steel, concrete, machinery, chemicals, and mining at the expense of many consumer-oriented industries. Shortages of basic necessities such as clothing soon followed.

In agriculture, the government instituted a policy of **collectivization**, under which the state took control of land to form large state-run farms. Many peasants fiercely resisted collectivization, so the government forcibly sent them to work as laborers in factories or in the mines. Exact numbers are not known, but historians estimate that millions of lives were lost in Stalin's centralization of power.

Central Planning A central planning agency called the Gosplan determined the quantities of output that key Soviet firms would produce each year and the prices that would be charged. Other government agencies set output levels for smaller firms. Long-term goals were outlined in the Five-Year Plans, while annual plans set short-term quotas.

Managers of state-owned firms received rewards if they met annual quotas. However, this

ECONOMIC SYSTEMS *Vladimir Ilich Lenin was the first leader of the Soviet Union (1917–24).* **With what economic programs did Lenin experiment?**

Themes in Economics

ECONOMIC SYSTEMS Karl Marx asserted that a socialist revolution could succeed only if it occurred in an advanced and industrialized capitalist society. In pre-industrial societies, such as Russia during the early 1900s, capitalism needed first to fully develop and begin to collapse under its own weight before the proletariat could successfully rise up and destroy it. Lenin disagreed with this view, however, and believed in 1917 that the time was right for socialist revolution in Russia. ■

Across the Curriculum

HISTORY Joseph Stalin ruled the Soviet Union with an iron hand. He was quick to eliminate any dissent or opposition to his policies. Peasants who resisted collectivization were shot or deported to *gulags*, labor camps in Siberia. Political rivals and adversaries received similar treatment. In addition, Stalin had the Red Army and the Communist Party purged of all those he considered to be disloyal. Historians estimate that as many as 20 million to 30 million Russians died as a result of famine, imprisonment, and political persecution under Stalin's leadership. ■

Caption Answer
war communism, New Economic Policy (NEP)
⭐23A

Themes in Economics

SUPPLY & DEMAND Distribution networks were also a problem in the former Soviet Union. Under central planning, factory managers had to follow government directives indicating what to produce and for whom. In addition, managers could not purchase needed resources or refuse unwanted shipments without authorization. As a result, factories often found themselves without the resources they needed, and stuck with items they did not want. Enterprising Soviets known as *tolkachi*, or "fixers," worked behind the scenes to help firms solve these distribution problems. Fixers helped factories find the items they needed and get rid of those they did not. ■

What Do You Think? Answers

1. to enable producers and consumers to find and obtain the goods and services they need and want ⭐11A

2. support for free enterprise—by moving from communism to capitalism, which destroyed the government-controlled distribution network, the Russian government gave many entrepreneurs the opportunity to make money importing goods for resale; challenges to free enterprise—a 50 percent tax on imports into Russia reduces profits ⭐23A

Economics in Action

Brave New World

The collapse of communism in the former Soviet Union has brought many opportunities as well as many challenges for the Russian people. One of the most persistent challenges has been the question of how to distribute economic goods efficiently. Most market capitalist countries rely on the "invisible hand" of the free market to allocate resources in an efficient manner. In the countries formerly governed by the communist Soviet Union, however, distribution was controlled by the government. Thus, when the Soviet command system collapsed, Russia was left without a well-developed distribution network to fill the void.

With virtually no established means of distributing goods, aspiring entrepreneurs had to look for ways to bring products to consumers. Among this group are "shuttle shoppers"—people who travel to other countries to buy goods for resale.

Anchorage, Alaska, is one common stop, where shuttle shoppers visit discount stores such as Costco, Sam's Club, and Kmart. Others frequent bazaars in Turkey. One Russian woman travels from Moscow to Istanbul twice a month, spending at least $10,000 per trip. Profits on Turkish goods—including dolls, clothing, and medical devices—can rise as high as 60 percent.

China is also a center for shuttle shopping. One entrepreneur—the leader of a group of 23 traders—has claimed to sell jogging suits in Moscow for seven times the purchase price in China. Other merchants travel to China in search of consumer electronics and household appliances.

Although the profits can be impressive, these entrepreneurs accept high levels of risk as part of the business. All 23 of the Russian traders traveling to China had been robbed at some point, sometimes repeatedly. Additionally, shuttle shopping involves extensive travel, long hours, and complicated government regulations. For example, Russia imposes a 50 percent tax on imports, which can reduce profits significantly. Documentation requirements may vary as well. Russians entering Turkey can easily obtain multiple entry visas good for five years. On the other hand, when Russia issued new passports for foreign travel, Chinese officials were not aware of the change and turned away travelers carrying the new documents.

Money poses additional problems. Because of the challenges of determining comparative currency values, many traders rely on U.S. dollars for shuttle shopping exchanges.

Shuttle shopping expeditions provide Russian entrepreneurs with the opportunity to import goods that are not available—or are expensive to produce—in their own country. These businesspeople have found a way to earn a profit while participating in Russia's transition from communism to free enterprise.

What Do You Think? ⭐TEKS

1. Why is a distribution network important in an economy?
2. How has the Russian government influenced the development of free enterprise? How have government actions created challenges for free enterprise?

Russian "shuttle shoppers" can make impressive profits, but must accept high levels of risk as part of their business.

system of quotas and rewards created inefficiency in several ways. First, no central planning agency could incorporate consumer preferences and production costs in its decisions concerning how many goods to produce. Decisions about what to produce were made by Communist Party leaders, rather than in response to the market forces of supply and demand. Further, planners could not select prices that would result in equilibrium. As discussed in Chapter 5, prices in a market economy adjust to changes in supply and demand. Given the ever-changing nature of consumer behavior and production costs, it should be no surprise that the central planners could not select equilibrium prices arbitrarily. Soviet planners typically selected prices below equilibrium, causing shortages to develop throughout the economy.

Production Problems Under Stalin, Soviet planners emphasized the production of industrial and military goods at the expense of consumer and agricultural goods. After Stalin died in 1953, central economic plans gradually included more consumer goods. While industrial and military products were still the top priority, many Soviet citizens urged the government to produce more consumer goods and services after the people became aware of higher standards of living.

Agriculture was a major problem area for the Soviet planners. Agricultural productivity was low because of shortages of capital, lack of incentives because of the quota system, and an often harsh climate. About one fifth of the Soviet labor force was employed in agriculture, compared to about 3 percent in the United States. Despite the large agricultural labor force, however, the Soviets had to import large quantities of food each year.

The Soviet Union experienced increasing problems with communism by the 1980s. Because Soviet factory managers had no incentives other than meeting their annual production quotas, they often were reluctant to use new technologies. By the late 1970s Soviet production technologies were outdated compared with those of the United States.

ECONOMIC SYSTEMS *Soviet citizens wait to buy food in a Moscow butcher shop in 1990.* **Why were shortages a chronic problem in the Soviet Union?**

Beginnings of Reform

The republic of Russia dominated the former Union of Soviet Socialist Republics. It contained more than half of the Soviet people and more than three fourths of the nation's land area. Moscow, Russia's capital, was also the capital and center of power for the entire former Soviet Union. In addition to these strengths, Russia was shifting toward market capitalism as a result of reforms that had been introduced during the final years of the Soviet Union. Because of Russia's position within the Soviet Union, any successful shift to market capitalism had to begin there.

Collapse of the Soviet Union During the 1970s and 1980s, some Soviet economists began arguing that the old system could never deliver standards of living comparable to those achieved in market-based economies. The first Soviet leader to introduce the necessary reforms was Mikhail Gorbachev, who became general secretary of the Communist Party—the highest political position in the Soviet Union—in 1985.

Caption Answer
Production decisions were made by central planners instead of by the market forces of supply and demand. Soviet planners typically selected prices below equilibrium, causing shortages throughout the economy. ★10A, 22A, 23A

Global Connections

In 1972 the Soviet Union and the United States entered a period of détente, a relaxing of tensions between the two nations. This period lasted until 1979, when the Soviet Union invaded Afghanistan. During this time, many Russians emigrated to the United States to try their hand at capitalism. Most settled in Chicago, Los Angeles, and New York City. One of the largest Russian communities in the United States, however, is in Brighton Beach, Brooklyn. Known as Little Odessa because of the large number of Russians who moved there from Odessa, a Russian town on the Black Sea, Brighton Beach has been reinvigorated by Russian immigration. The once-sleepy seaside resort now boasts a vibrant city center of shops, markets, and nightclubs, all owned, operated, and frequented by Russian Americans. ■

COMPARING ECONOMIC SYSTEMS

internet connect

TOPIC: NATO, Communism
GO TO: go.hrw.com
KEYWORD: SM3 EC16

Have students access the Internet through the HRW Go site to conduct research on NATO. Have students prepare presentations individually, or in groups, on the evolution of NATO since the breakup of the Soviet Union. What is NATO's role in the modern world now that the Soviet Union no longer exists? How is its membership changing? What sort of activities has NATO conducted recently? Have students present their findings to the class. ★24D

Cultural Perspectives

The economic problems that Russia experienced following its transition to capitalism contributed to the growth of its underground economy. Some analysts estimate that the output of Russia's underground economy in the late 1990s was approximately equal to the nation's official total gross domestic product. ■

Transparency

An overhead transparency of Figure 16.3 is available in *Transparency Resources*. See Transparency 66: Fall of the Soviet Union.

Gorbachev instituted reforms that called for much greater economic independence for state enterprises and increased worker incentives. The policy, called **perestroika**, or "restructuring," was an effort to move the economy toward market socialism. However, Soviet bureaucrats and military leaders in particular wanted none of the reforms pushed by Gorbachev.

To compromise, Gorbachev chose to leave the communist system in place and seek modest reforms that allowed prices for some output to be negotiated between firms that produced the goods and firms that purchased them. Left in place were state ownership of enterprises and the shortages resulting from bad management of the remaining output. In an effort to deal with the shortages of the price-controlled goods, Gorbachev ordered a number of dramatic price increases in 1991.

Gorbachev's price hikes did little to correct the shortages, in part because the state-owned firms had no reason to respond to the higher prices by increasing output. Both managers and workers in these firms were paid salaries set by the government. Thus, there was no means by which either managers or workers could benefit from the higher prices. A firm in a market economy would be expected to increase its quantity supplied in response to a higher price—something that Soviet state-owned firms failed to do.

FALL OF THE SOVIET UNION

1985 — Mikhail Gorbachev becomes leader of the Soviet Union. He calls for restructuring of the economy (perestroika), democratization, and openness (glasnost).

1989–1990 — The collapse of communist regimes in Eastern Europe accelerates the Communist Party's decline in the Soviet Union. Gorbechev refuses to allow the Soviet military to intervene to keep the communist regimes in power.

1990 — The USSR legalizes noncommunist political parties, and Soviet republics begin to restrict the Communist Party's power.

Aug. 18, 1991 — A group calling itself the Extraordinary Commission and led by KGB (secret police) boss Vladimir Kryuchkov holds Gorbachev hostage and attempts a coup, or a government takeover.

Aug. 19, 1991 — Boris Yeltsin, president of the Russian republic, calls for Gorbachev's return. World leaders condemn the coup. Yeltsin gains the support of some soldiers and top military officers.

Aug. 21, 1991 — The coup fails but nevertheless ruins Gorbachev politically. Soviet republics move quickly to gain independence in fear of a successful future coup.

Sept. 1991 — Estonia, Latvia, and Lithuania achieve complete independence.

Dec. 1, 1991 — Ukraine votes for independence.

Dec. 8, 1991 — Russia, Ukraine, and Belorussia declare that the Soviet Union no longer exists and found a loose grouping called the Commonwealth of Independent States (CIS).

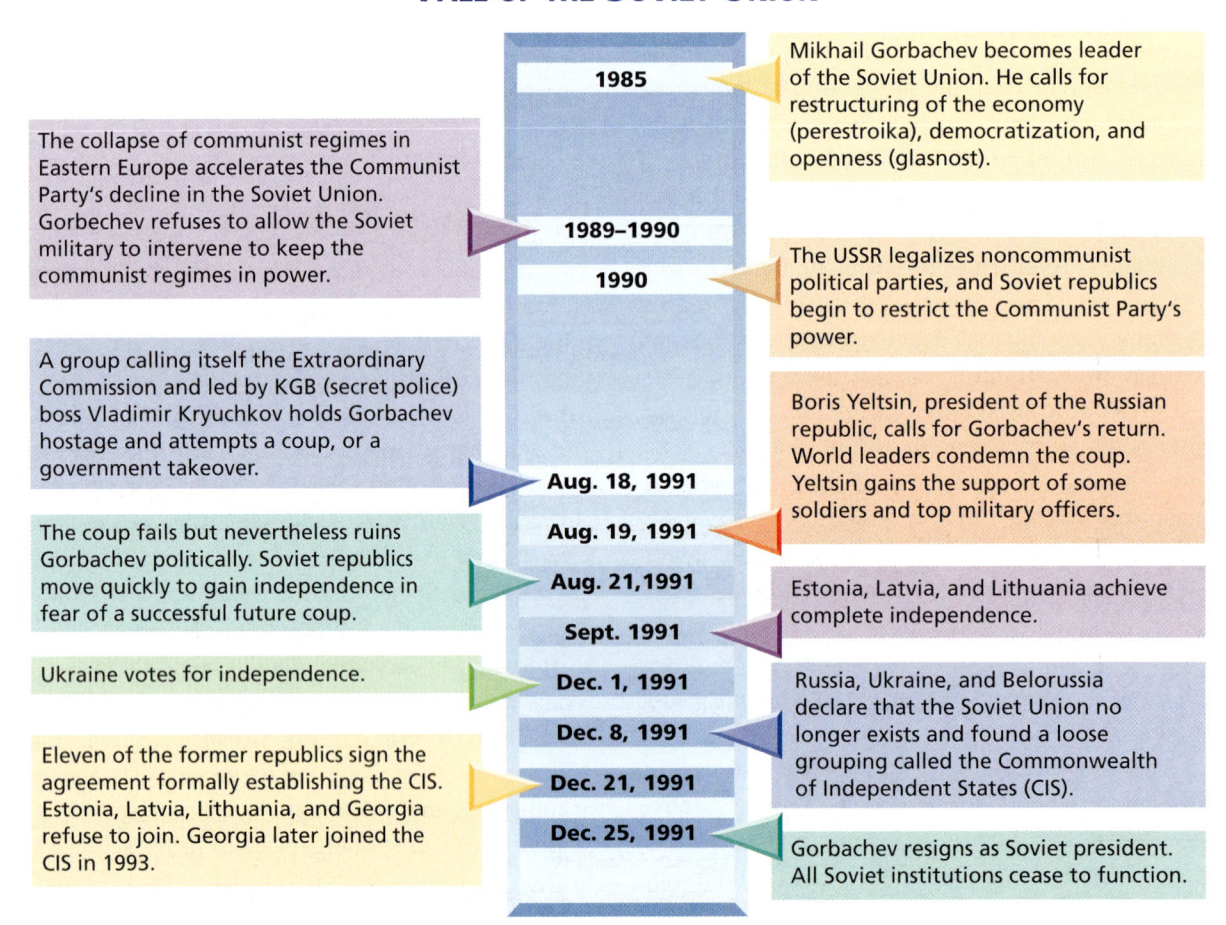

Dec. 21, 1991 — Eleven of the former republics sign the agreement formally establishing the CIS. Estonia, Latvia, Lithuania, and Georgia refuse to join. Georgia later joined the CIS in 1993.

Dec. 25, 1991 — Gorbachev resigns as Soviet president. All Soviet institutions cease to function.

Sources: *Encyclopedia Britannica: 1997* and *Microsoft Encarta*

FIGURE 16.3 Despite Mikhail Gorbachev's attempts at political and economic reform, the Soviet Union collapsed in 1991.

ECONOMIC SYSTEMS *Under Mikhail Gorbachev's leadership, Soviet republics began to break away from the Soviet Union. What new group did many of the former Soviet republics found?*

In the summer of 1991 communist leaders opposed to economic reform tried to overthrow Gorbachev but failed within a few days. Taking advantage of the resulting chaos within the central government, the republics of the Soviet Union declared their independence. For a summary of the events leading to the dissolution of the Soviet Union, see Figure 16.3.

Russian Reform Boris Yeltsin, president of the newly formed Russian Federation, had been a leading supporter of market capitalism even before the Soviet Union collapsed. Once Russia became an independent republic, Yeltsin sought a rapid transition to market capitalism. Yeltsin's efforts were slowed by the remaining former communist officials, however.

Despite these hurdles, Russian economic reformers have accomplished a great deal. Prices and production of most goods have been freed from state controls. Thousands of state-owned firms have been privatized, and Russians now are free to start their own businesses.

To privatize state firms, Russian citizens were issued vouchers that could be used to purchase shares in state enterprises. Under this plan, individuals could use their vouchers to bid for ownership in the firms.

Communism Outside the Soviet Union

The communist nations of the world shared certain characteristics. Each of these nations had a one-party totalitarian political system. The government and the Communist Party controlled the economy.

Since the 1950s communist nations had adapted communism to meet their own needs. Some nations followed a highly centralized command system similar to that in the Soviet Union. Others permitted individuals to make some economic decisions. The most important of these communist nations is the People's Republic of China.

Communism in the People's Republic of China

In recent years, the People's Republic of China has moved toward a more market-responsive communism. This move was a direct result of the failure of overcentralized economic planning, and followed decades of government involvement in the economy.

The Chinese communists came to power in 1949 after a long and bloody civil war. Mao Zedong (MOW zuh-DOOHNG), head of the Chinese Communist Party, assumed leadership of the new government. The economic history of the People's Republic of China can be divided into two periods. In the first period, under strict communism, China launched the Great Leap Forward program and the Cultural Revolution. The second period has been characterized by a more market-responsive communism.

Great Leap Forward In 1953 the Chinese Communists launched the first Five-Year Plan, which stressed industrial development. With the aid of the Soviet Union, China enjoyed some economic successes. Impatient with progress in industry and agriculture, however, Mao pushed

COMPARING ECONOMIC SYSTEMS 395

Caption Answer
Commonwealth of Independent States (CIS) ★23A

Cultural Perspectives

By the end of 1958, China's Great Leap Forward had created some 26,000 people's communes, which housed 98 percent of the rural population. Communes shaped the economic, political, and social structure of Chinese life. Local commune officials issued production and distribution decisions based on party directives. Communist Party policies and propaganda were disseminated through the commune system. In addition, communes provided a number of social services, such as dining facilities, laundry services, public baths, nurseries, schools, health care, police protection, and entertainment. Services were communal to give women more time to work. ■

Caption Answer

dramatic drop in industrial output and low agricultural productivity, leading to economic ruin and mass famine; some 20 to 30 million Chinese died ★22A, 23A

Global Connections

Shortly after the death of Deng Xiaoping in February 1997, Mikhail Gorbachev wrote about whether economic reform is possible without political reform. The following is an excerpt from Gorbachev's editorial, which appeared in the March 3, 1997, issue of *Newsweek*:

"There is much debate about the differences between the way [economic] reforms were conducted under my leadership and in China. Those differences were real and, indeed, inevitable. China and Russia have different histories and traditions, and China's economy was unlike ours in many respects. But it is not quite correct to say that while Deng [Xiaoping] emphasized economic changes, we focused on political reforms. After all, we too started with an attempt at economic reform. But the entrenched and dogmatic *nomenklatura* [bureaucrats] stood in the way of any such attempt and thwarted the economic changes we proposed in 1987."

---

for more rapid industrial and agricultural development in the second Five-Year Plan. This plan began with what was referred to as the **Great Leap Forward**.

The Great Leap Forward established groups of collective farms called **people's communes** in an attempt to increase the agricultural output of China. Under a new system, farmwork was done in small units called production brigades. Government planners determined what, how, and how much communes produced. All output produced was delivered to the government.

In China's industrial sector, the Great Leap Forward stressed the production of steel and other heavy industries. More than a million small backyard furnaces were built to expand steel production, while light industries were neglected.

These policies caused industrial output to fall dramatically, which spelled economic ruin for China. Misuse of resources also led to low agricultural productivity, which contributed to the deaths of 20 to 30 million Chinese in the worst famine in history. In 1960 China's government abandoned the Great Leap Forward.

Cultural Revolution After a brief economic recovery from 1961 to 1965, China's economy was again plunged into chaos. The chaos lasted from 1966 to 1976 during a period called the **Cultural Revolution**.

The Cultural Revolution was a violent movement aimed at safeguarding the communist system. Leaders of the Cultural Revolution denounced party officials, factory managers, scientists, teachers, college professors, and other professionals as "class enemies." Many factories and schools were closed. Millions of people were forcibly relocated to remote rural areas, where they had to perform manual labor and were "reeducated" to become supporters of Mao and his government.

Four Modernizations In 1976 the death of Mao and the end of the Cultural Revolution marked a shift toward more market-responsive policies. A new program of economic development called the **Four Modernizations** targeted modernization in agriculture, industry, science and technology, and defense.

In the late 1970s Deng Xiaoping (DUHNG SHOW-PING) became China's leader. Deng's brand of Chinese socialism combined state planning with market incentives to achieve the Four Modernizations. Under Deng, the most significant agricultural reform was the establishment of the **household responsibility system**, also called the contract responsibility system. This system permits peasants to lease state-owned land and to pay their rent by delivering a portion of their crop to the government. The remainder of the crop can then be sold for profit on the open market. The government encourages individuals to build homes on their plots, raise animals, and acquire tractors and other capital that will lead to improved productivity.

Deng also instituted reforms in the industrial sector. In a new Five-Year Plan, Deng redirected production into light industries that manufactured televisions, refrigerators, radios, and other consumer goods. This focus away from heavy industries established a better balance between the production of consumer goods and capital goods and reinforced incentives for individual productivity.

ECONOMIC SYSTEMS *Production brigade members attend a class at Shuangwang People's Commune.* **What were the economic outcomes of the Great Leap Forward?** ★TEKS

PER CAPITA GDP: CHINA, 1968–2000

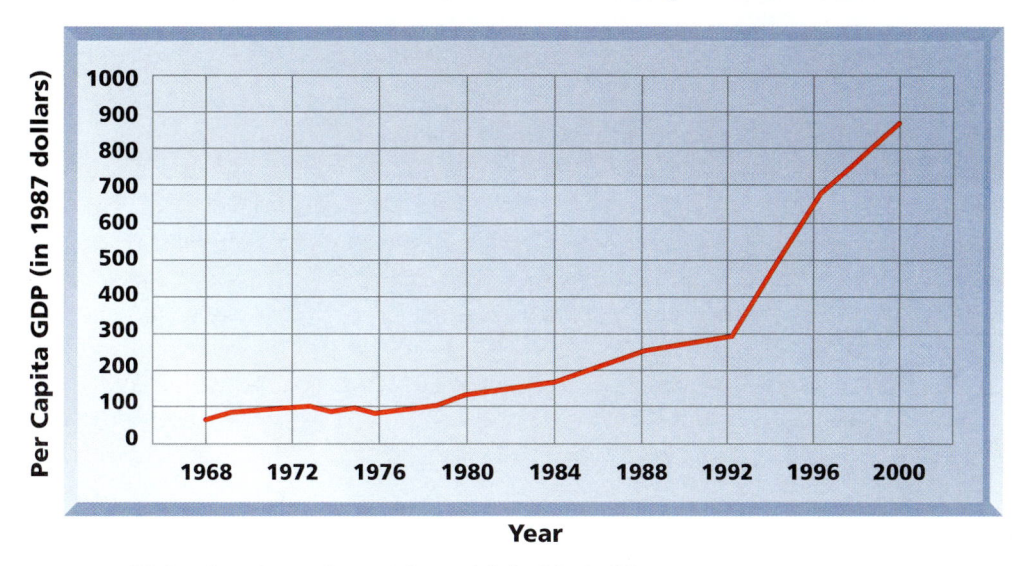

Source: U.S. State Dept. Country Report on Economic Policy & Trade, China

FIGURE 16.4 China's economy has responded favorably to market-oriented reforms begun in the late 1970s. **During which decade did China's per capita GDP increase most dramatically?**

The government also extended to industry the household responsibility system used in agriculture. Under this arrangement, central planners set broad production goals and some quotas, but plant managers are free to hire and fire workers. Further, managers determine what to produce beyond their quotas. Any additional products can be sold for profit. The government levies a progressive income tax on profits, but plant managers can use after-tax profits for reinvestment or workers' pay raises and bonuses.

The government also created free-trade zones in the region around Shanghai and other east-coast ports and joined in ventures with foreign corporations to encourage investment in these zones. The free-trade zones reflected Deng's belief that foreign capital, technology, and management would strengthen the Chinese economy.

China's economy responded favorably to Deng's market-oriented reforms, and agricultural and industrial output rose substantially. Additionally, China now has a greater variety of consumer goods available. Figure 16.4 shows China's growth in per capita output from 1960 to 2000.

Increasingly, economic reforms were accompanied by calls for greater political freedoms. For example, in 1989 a million demonstrators gathered in Beijing's Tiananmen Square. These protesters hoped to gain the freedom to choose their leaders and to improve conditions in universities. Several thousand students went on a hunger strike. Unable to stop the demonstration peacefully, government leaders ordered tanks and armed troops to remove the unarmed protesters by force. Hundreds of protesters were killed and thousands more were injured in the resulting **Tiananmen Square Massacre**, and the political system remained largely unchanged.

The economic reforms of China's Five-Year Plans continued after Deng's death in 1997. Their goals continue to include the reduction of direct government controls.

Challenges for China

In effect, China has a two-tiered economic system, with a central command system and a market system operating at the margin. By leaving the state system in place, the Chinese avoided the disruptions that troubled

---

(Continued from page 396)

In the final analysis, I think one cannot democratize the economy while leaving all the rest as it was before. Even within a one-party system, greater pluralism is necessary.

Economic reform was a great success for Deng's leadership. But the issue of political reform is still there; it has simply been put on hold. Now the Chinese are approaching a stage at which the issue of democratization will become more acute. They will have to conduct political reforms. How are they going to do it? In their own way, I think. We have to hope for the best from this process. All of us have a stake in the stability of the huge world called China."

Caption Answer
the 1990s

Caption Answer

Government tanks and armed troops forcibly removed the protesters, killing hundreds and injuring thousands more. ★23A

SECTION 4 REVIEW ANSWERS

1. bourgeoisie (389), proletariat (390), collectivization (391), perestroika (394), Great Leap Forward (396), people's communes (396), Cultural Revolution (396), Four Modernizations (396), household responsibility system (396), Tiananmen Square Massacre (397) 24A

2. from manorialism to mercantalism to market capitalism to communism to a classless society 19A, 23A, 23B, 24D

3a. did not address consumer demand or production costs; no equilibrium prices; no worker incentives; overemphasis on industrial and military goods; created shortages 10A, 25A

3b. They provided market incentives, which led to the profit motive and increased efficiency. This is similar to the way the profit motive and competition influence the efficiency of the U.S. free-enterprise system. 10B, 23A

4. The communist government under Lenin was modeled partly on Marx's ideals. In the United States, fear of a proletarian revolution, as predicted by Marx, led to many reforms for U.S. labor and strengthened the free-enterprise system. 19A, 23A

398

ECONOMIC SYSTEMS *Student protesters call for political reforms in Beijing's Tiananmen Square in 1989. What was the outcome of this demonstration?*

those countries making the transition to a market economy.

How well has this approach worked? China has one of the fastest-growing economies in the world. Its per capita output increased dramatically. Because of China's huge population, per capita income remains low, but the nation's economy is now the second largest in the world.

SECTION 4 REVIEW

★TEKS Q: 1, 2, 3a, 3b, 4

1. Define and Explain:
bourgeoisie
proletariat
collectivization
perestroika
Great Leap Forward
people's communes
Cultural Revolution
Four Modernizations
household responsibility system
Tiananmen Square Massacre

2. Sequencing: Use the flow chart to describe the progression of an economic system according to the theories of Karl Marx.

Progression of an Economic System

3. Finding the Main Idea

a. What were the drawbacks of central planning in the former Soviet Union?

b. How did the Four Modernizations make the Chinese economy more like the U.S. free-enterprise system?

4. Writing and Critical Thinking

Analyzing Information: Analyze Karl Marx's impact on the former Soviet Union. How did his influence on the Soviets affect the U.S. free-enterprise system?
Consider:
- the Russian Revolution
- U.S. fears of communism

Homework Practice Online
keyword: SM3 HP16

CHAPTER 16

Economics IN THE NEWS

The Cold War and the American Economy

For almost fifty years, from the end of World War II until the collapse of the Soviet Union in 1991, the United States and the Soviet Union engaged in the Cold War. The essence of the Cold War was the notion that the Soviet Union and the United States, the two world superpowers, were involved in a global struggle between the forces of communism, based on the teachings of Karl Marx, and capitalism. While the Cold War did not result in direct military confrontation between the United States and the Soviet Union, it polarized much of the world into separate spheres of influence, helped trigger numerous military conflicts, including the Korean War and the Vietnam War, and brought about an arms race, or buildup of military weapons—especially nuclear weapons—by the two superpowers.

Marx's idea of a violent revolution to overthrow capitalism and replace it with communism had a major impact on many aspects of American society. For instance, this fear of communism and the revolutionary values it represents led to an increased emphasis on values associated with the free-enterprise system, such as individual freedom and limited government. This tendency could be seen in many aspects of American culture such as Hollywood Westerns, where actors like John Wayne often played the part of the rugged individualist.

Another area where the fear of communism had an important impact was the economy. However, economic historians disagree as to the character of its impact. From the end of World War II until the early 1970s, the United States underwent a prolonged period of economic growth. Economic prosperity led to the highest standard of living seen to that point. For instance, home ownership increased greatly and Americans gained wider access to everything from higher education to consumer goods.

This Titan II missile was one component of the military arsenal that the United States built during the Cold War. Although defense spending contributed greatly to the American economy, some people believe that the government's money is better spent on domestic infrastructure and programs.

Some economic historians argue that military spending associated with the Cold War was the major source of this economic growth. Others, however, disagree. They argue that this economic growth was a result of the return to a free market economy after World War II, when much of the American economy had been under the command of the federal government. These historians argue that growth in the consumer economy generated by this return to the free market is what allowed the United States to raise its military spending levels, not the other way around.

Finally, some economic historians argue that military spending may have actually hurt economic growth. They argue that more economic value may have been gained by investing in the production of other goods, such as consumer items.

What Do You Think? ⭐TEKS

1. What does this feature suggest about the impact of Marx's ideology on the American economy?
2. What societal values does the feature suggest are associated with market economies?

▶ **WHY IT MATTERS TODAY**
Economists continue to debate the impact of government spending on economic growth. Visit CNNfyi.com to find additional examples of this debate.

CNNfyi.com

Economics in the News Answers

1. Answers will vary, but students might suggest that the American free-enterprise system and cultural values associated with it were strengthened because of the fear inspired by Marx's ideas. **19A, 23A, 23E**

2. individual freedom and limited government **21B, 23A**

CHAPTER 16
Review Answers

Writing a Summary

Summaries should focus on the main points of each section. These may be found in the Read to Discover questions at the start of each section. Summaries should also use standard grammar, spelling, sentence structure, and punctuation. **24B, 24D**

Identifying Ideas

market system (377), command system (377), mercantilism (382), indicative planning (384), nationalization (384), bourgeoisie (389), proletariat (390), perestroika (394), Great Leap Forward (396), Four Modernizations (396) **10A, 19A**

Understanding Main Ideas

1. a system in which private individuals and businesses make resource allocation choices; the United States **10A, 23A**

2. United States—local and state fiscal policy is largely independent of federal fiscal policy;

(continued on page 400)

399

CHAPTER 16 Review

(continued from page 399)

Germany—commissions coordinate federal, state, and local fiscal policy **10B, 23A**

3. Sweden's emphasis on access to health care and education for all, regardless of income, has led to higher taxes. **21B, 23A**

4. Marx's idea of a proletarian revolution that led to the formation of a communist government influenced the communist governments in the Soviet Union and the People's Republic of China. **19A, 23A**

5. He instituted perestroika to move the economy toward market capitalism. **23A**

6. the initial phase of Mao's second Five-Year Plan; lack of incentives and mismanagement of resources led to low industrial and agricultural output and severe famine. **23A**

Reviewing Themes

1. Who owns the resources and capital? Who makes resource allocation choices? **10A, 23A**

2. The more control a country's government asserts on the economy, the closer that economy is to a command economic system. **10A, 23A**

3. The market economy sets prices based on supply and demand, while the command economy sets prices arbitrarily. **7A, 14A, 23A**

4. When governments make decisions about resource allocation, they take choice from the people and may increase the likelihood of scarcity. **5A, 21B, 23A, 23D**

Writing a Summary ★TEKS

Using standard grammar, spelling, sentence structure, and punctuation, write a summary of the information in this chapter.

Identifying Ideas ★TEKS

Identify the following terms and explain their significance.

1. market system
2. command system
3. mercantilism
4. indicative planning
5. nationalization
6. bourgeoisie
7. proletariat
8. perestroika
9. Great Leap Forward
10. Four Modernizations

Understanding Main Ideas ★TEKS

SECTION 1 *(pp. 377–80)*

1. What are the characteristics of a market system? Give an example of such a system.

SECTION 2 *(pp. 381–85)*

2. How do U.S. and German fiscal policies differ?

SECTION 3 *(pp. 386–88)*

3. How does the value Swedish citizens place on social services influence their economy?

SECTION 4 *(pp. 389–98)*

4. How did Karl Marx's ideas influence the economies in the Soviet Union and the People's Republic of China?

5. How did Mikhail Gorbachev contribute to economic reform in the Soviet Union?

6. What was the Great Leap Forward, and why did it fail?

Reviewing Themes ★TEKS

1. Economic Systems What are the two main questions that all economic systems have to answer?

2. Role of Government How does the government's role in an economy relate to a country's economic system?

3. International Trade Why is it difficult for a country with a market economy to engage in free trade with a country with a command economy?

4. Scarcity and Choice How does the allocation of capital and resources by a government disrupt the economic model of scarcity and choice?

Thinking Critically ★TEKS

1. Comparing What are some of the advantages of living in a capitalist society?

2. Prediction If the communist government in the People's Republic of China were to collapse, what would be the likely economic result?

3. Inference Why did Swedish workers have more power during Sweden's socialist period than workers have in the capitalist nations of the United States and Japan?

4. Summarizing How did Karl Marx's view of communism differ from the point of view held by most U.S. citizens?

Writing about Economics ★TEKS

Refer to the list of decisions you wrote in your Economics Notebook at the beginning of this chapter. How do these decisions—and your answers to the other questions—reflect a market capitalist economy? Record your answer in your Notebook.

Building Social Studies Skills

Interpreting the Chart

Study the chart showing territorial changes in Eastern Europe since World War II. Then use it to help you answer the questions that follow.

Eastern Europe

- Former Soviet republic
- Former East European satellite of Soviet Union
- Member of Commonwealth of Independent States

1. Which of these former Soviet republics is not a member of the Commonwealth of Independent States?
   a. Ukraine
   b. Latvia
   c. Belarus
   d. Russia

2. Was Germany a satellite of the Soviet Union? Explain your answer.

Analyzing Primary Sources

Read the following excerpt from peasant farmer Lou Yumin describing increased responsibility for Chinese agricultural workers. Then answer the questions that follow.

"[U]nder the old policy, good workers and lazy ones were paid the same.... The present system is better. Each family in our village contracts land from the brigade [state].... This year we have been allowed to sell our vegetables independently if we like, and we're all happy about this. In the past I never bothered to plan my work or figure out how to do it better. I just did what our brigade leaders ordered. Now I think about everything—what we should grow, when to apply fertilizer, when to harvest, etc....

"Now, the harder we work, the more money we get. In the first six months of this year we sold 14,000 yuan [about $3,600 in 1986] worth of vegetables to our village's trading center. Deducting our production costs, that gave us a net income of 10,000 yuan, making us one of the best-off families in the village."

3. The new economy Lou Yumin describes is most similar to—
   a. market capitalism
   b. command capitalism
   c. market socialism
   d. command socialism

4. How has the value of self-reliance influenced the economic system in China?

Alternative Assessment

Building Your Portfolio

Design an economic system that combines the advantages of both capitalism and socialism. First list the advantages; then design and present the system to your class. You will want to use graphs and diagrams in your presentation. You may also need to conduct some outside research to find more examples of each type of system.

internet connect

Internet Activity: go.hrw.com
KEYWORD: SM3 EC16

Access the Internet through the HRW Go site to research the current economic situation of various countries. With your assigned group, choose a region of the world. Classify countries in your region as either capitalist, socialist, or communist. As a class, join the regions into a world map of political systems.

Thinking Critically

1. advantages—economic freedom to own property and businesses and to profit from one's work, lower tax rates; disadvantages—fewer social programs, less government control to protect the environment. 10B, 23A, 25A

2. Answers will vary. Students might suggest that China would become a capitalist market economy because of economic reforms it has already introduced. 10B, 21B, 23A

3. Swedish workers were more heavily unionized, had representation on boards of directors of major firms, and shared in corporate decision making. 10B, 23A

4. Marx believed that communism was better for all but the very rich; most U.S. citizens believe they can someday become very rich. 10B, 19A, 23A, 23D

Writing about Economics

Students should explain how their decisions reflect the market capitalist economy of the United States. 10A, 23A, 23D, 24B, 24D

Building Social Studies Skills

1. b 23F, 23G

2. partly; East Germany was a satellite of the Soviet Union. 23A, 23E, 23F, 23G

3. c 10A, 23A

4. When people are self-reliant, they want to improve and work more efficiently. This fact can lead governments to adapt an economic system that allows this kind of self-reliance.

COMPARING ECONOMIC SYSTEMS

CHAPTER RESOURCE MANAGER

CHAPTER 17 DEVELOPING COUNTRIES

	OBJECTIVES	PACING GUIDE	REPRODUCIBLE RESOURCES
SECTION 1 **ECONOMIC DEVELOPMENT** (pp. 403–06)	▸ What characteristics do developing countries have in common? ▸ How can scarcity of resources affect a developing nation?	**Regular** 1.5 days **Block Scheduling** 0.5 day	**ELL** Spanish Study Guide 17.1 **ELL** English Study Guide 17.1 **PS** Reading 71: The Evolution of International Economic Order **SM** Mathematics for Economics: Activity 17
SECTION 2 **CHALLENGES TO GROWTH** (pp. 407–13)	▸ How do many developing countries respond to scarce factors of production? ▸ How can the status of an economic infrastructure help or hinder a developing country? ▸ How can political instability challenge a developing nation?	**Regular** 1.5 days **Block Scheduling** 1 day	**ELL** Spanish Study Guide 17.2 **ELL** English Study Guide 17.2 **PS** Reading 35: Global Environmental Crisis **SM** Consumer Economics: Activity 17
SECTION 3 **PATHS TO ECONOMIC DEVELOPMENT** (pp. 414–22)	▸ What are the characteristics of the socialist and capitalist models of decision making? ▸ What types of aid do governments extend to developing countries? ▸ What are the key public sources of foreign aid?	**Regular** 2 days **Block Scheduling** 1 day	**ELL** Spanish Study Guide 17.3 **ELL** English Study Guide 17.3 **E** Challenge and Enrichment: Activity 17 **S** Simulations and Strategies for Teaching Economics: Activity 17

Chapter Resource Key

PS	Primary Sources	**A**	Assessment		Video
RS	Reading Support	**REV**	Review		Videodisc
E	Enrichment	**ELL**	Reinforcement and English Language Learners		Internet
S	Simulations		Transparencies		Holt Presentation Maker Using Microsoft® PowerPoint®
SM	Skills Mastery		CD-ROM		TEKS and TAKS

TECHNOLOGY RESOURCES	REINFORCEMENT, REVIEW, AND ASSESSMENT
One-Stop Planner: Lesson 17.1 Researcher Online Homework Practice Online CNN Presents Economics: Righting Kenya's Economy Transparency 67 Global Skillbuilder CD-ROM	**REV** Section 1 Review, p. 406 **A** Daily Quiz 17.1 TAKS Every Day!
One-Stop Planner: Lesson 17.2 Researcher Online Homework Practice Online Global Skillbuilder CD-ROM	**REV** Section 2 Review, p. 413 **A** Daily Quiz 17.2 TAKS Every Day!
One-Stop Planner: Lesson 17.3 Researcher Online Homework Practice Online Transparencies 68 and 69 Videodisc: Negotiation: BMW Expands Global Skillbuilder CD-ROM	**REV** Section 3 Review, p. 422 **A** Daily Quiz 17.3 TAKS Every Day!

Chapter Review and Assessment

SM Global Skillbuilder CD-ROM
HRW Go site
REV Reteaching Activity 17
REV Chapter 17 Review, pp. 424–25
A Chapter 17 Test Generator (on the One-Stop Planner)
A Chapter 17 Test
A Alternative Assessment Handbook

One-Stop Planner CD-ROM

It's easy to plan lessons, select resources, and print out materials for your students when you use the *Texas One-Stop Planner CD-ROM with Test Generator.*

internet connect

HRW ONLINE RESOURCES
Go To: go.hrw.com
Then type in a keyword.

TEACHER HOME PAGE
KEYWORD: SM3 Teacher

CHAPTER INTERNET ACTIVITIES
KEYWORD: SM3 EC17
Choose an activity to:
- research the Peace Corps.
- explore immigration to the United States.
- research international foreign aid.

CHAPTER ENRICHMENT LINKS
KEYWORD: SM3 CH17

HOLT RESEARCHER ONLINE
KEYWORD: Holt Researcher

ONLINE ASSESSMENT
Homework Practice
KEYWORD: SM3 HP17
TAKS Review
KEYWORD: SM3 T17
Rubrics
KEYWORD: SS Rubrics

CONTENT UPDATES
KEYWORD: SS Content Updates

HOLT PRESENTATION MAKER
KEYWORD: SM3 PPT17

ONLINE READING SUPPORT
KEYWORD: SS Strategies

CURRENT EVENTS
KEYWORD: S3 Current Events

TEXAS ONLINE RESOURCES
KEYWORD: S3 TX

LESSON 17.1 ECONOMIC DEVELOPMENT

TEXTBOOK PAGES 403–06

> **HOLT PRESENTATION MAKER**
> Access Illustrated LECTURE NOTES using Microsoft® PowerPoint® on the One-Stop Planner CD-ROM

OBJECTIVES

▸ Identify the characteristics that developing nations have in common.
▸ Explain how scarcity of resources can affect a developing nation.
★5B

MOTIVATE

Describe to students the following scenario:

Each student is moving with their family to a beautiful tropical island. There are enough fruits, such as pineapple, and sparkly blue fish to feed all the island's inhabitants indefinitely. A company on the mainland has offered to pay the inhabitants of your island for all the sparkly blue fish that they can catch, which would allow the inhabitants of the island to start an economic development program. This offers the following options: 1) you can catch every sparkly blue fish you can find for the next several years, which would soon exhaust the population of fish; or 2) you can try to manage the island's harvesting of sparkly blue fish so that the population is sustainable and not exhausted; or 3) you can tell the mainland company that you are not interested in selling any sparkly blue fish because the possibility of harvesting the sparkly blue fish to extinction—thereby leaving the inhabitants without a main food source—is too great.

Ask the class to discuss these options. In particular, have students consider: What are the possible risks, or costs, of developing your economy based on a single resource—sparkly blue fish? What are the possible benefits of such a plan? Tell the class to keep this discussion in mind as they read Section 17.1, in which they will learn about developing countries.

TEACH

Building a Vocabulary

Have students use spiral notebooks to create an Economics Dictionary to be used throughout the chapter. This dictionary might be used as an activity at the start of each new section or as a learning aid for English Language Learners students or students having difficulty. List words that students will be expected to know for this section on the chalkboard. Have students use the information provided in the text or on the *Researcher CD-ROM* to list, define, and give an example of each vocabulary term. ★24A

Evaluating Ideas

Remind students that countries around the world are at different stages of economic development. On the chalkboard, write the terms *developed nation* and *developing nation*. Call on students to identify the differences between nations in these two categories and explain what characteristics countries in each of these categories tend to share. *(For developed nations, these shared features include a high level of industrial and technical expertise and a variety of economic institutions, such as banking systems, stock markets, and trade networks; for developing nations, these features include low per capita GNI, limited resources or inefficient use of resources, rapid population growth, and dependency on agricultural production.)* Ask students to explain what GNI is and ask them what information GNI might provide about a nation's economic development. Write students' suggestions on the chalkboard to further motivate discussion. Display Transparency 67—Comparing GNI around the World (represented in Figure 17.1 on textbook page 404). Then ask students: Why might rapid population growth make economic development difficult? Why might the reliance on traditional agricultural economies make economic development difficult? Is industrial development always desirable? Write students' suggestions and comments regarding these issues on the chalkboard as well. ★22A

Using Maps

Explain to students that one of the greatest economic difficulties many nations face is limited resources. Organize students into groups of three or four. Provide each group with a world map that details natural resources and basic landforms. Assign each group a region of the world to examine, or two regions for comparison. Ask student groups to brainstorm on the following questions:

▸ What kind of natural resources might be available in this region?
▸ How do the climate, possible soil type, and elevation affect natural resource availability?
▸ What kinds of development opportunities do the natural resources in this region offer?

Ask each group to take notes or write a short summary of their discussion about the possible resources available in the region(s) assigned to them. Refer students who need additional instruction to the *Global Skillbuilder* Lesson 8: Comparing Maps. ⭐23F

CLOSE

Call on volunteers from each group to discuss the resources in the region of the world that they examined. Next, ask students: How might traditional agricultural or pastoral societies develop their economies, and even industrialize, without sacrificing important aspects of their cultures?

OPTIONS

English Language Learners
Pair students acquiring English with students fluent in English. Have each pair research a developing country that has a one-crop economy. Ask the pair to create a visual display in the form of a flowchart, table, or collage, that demonstrates the limitations and problems of a one-crop economy for the country selected. *(Remind students that "crop" here means any product, agricultural or otherwise; for some countries in the Middle East, oil is their single crop.)* Ask each pair to present their display to the class. Refer students who need additional instruction to the *Global Skillbuilder,* Lesson 12: Creating Graphic Organizers. ⭐24D

Gifted Learners, Linguistic Learners
Tell students that in recent decades, many people have left their native countries to gain an education, enter a profession, and live in the United States and other developed nations. Ask students to explore how the loss of skilled professionals in a nation such as Jamaica or Cuba has affected the economic development of these countries. Ask students to use the *Researcher Online*, the library, in-class resources, the Internet, and information from business journals or newspapers to conduct their research.

Students Having Difficulty, Visual-Spatial Learners
Ask students to research recent population growth rates for at least six different countries. Have students choose three developing countries and three developed countries. Also have them select countries from different regions. Ask students to create a graph *(bar, circular, or other form of their choosing)* that illustrates how population growth rates compare with economic development. *(Usually, developing countries have higher population growth rates, while developed countries tend to have lower population growth rates.)* Have students prepare a caption for their graphs that explains why population growth rates and economic growth are often related. Ask students to use the Country Profiles section on the *Researcher Online,* the library, in-class resources, other Internet resources, and information from business journals or newspapers to conduct their research. Students may wish to include their graphs in their portfolios. ⭐23F

REVIEW

Have students complete the Section Review on page 406. Use the answers in the Annotated Teacher's Edition to assess student mastery of this section.

ASSESS

To assess student mastery of this section, have students complete Daily Quiz 17.1 in *Daily Quizzes with Answer Key*. For additional assessment options, see *Alternative Assessment Handbook* on the *One-Stop Planner CD-ROM*.

ADDITIONAL RESOURCES

Brown, Lester R., et al, eds. *State of the World 2001*. 2001. W. W. Norton & Company.

Sen, Amartya. *Development as Freedom*. 2000. Anchor Books.

Taylor, Lance, ed. *The Rocky Road to Reform: Adjustment, Income Distribution, and Growth in the Developing World*. 1993. MIT Press.

LESSON 17.2 CHALLENGES TO GROWTH

TEXTBOOK PAGES 407–13

HOLT PRESENTATION MAKER Access Illustrated LECTURE NOTES using Microsoft® PowerPoint® on the One-Stop Planner CD-ROM

OBJECTIVES

- Explain the ways in which many developing nations respond to scarce factors of production.
- Describe how the status of an economic infrastructure can help or hinder a developing nation.
- Explain how political instability can challenge a developing nation.

MOTIVATE

Organize students into small groups. Give each group a few pages from the international or economic pages of a recent newspaper. Ask each group to find a story that discusses a developing country and its struggles with economic development. Instruct each group to discuss the following questions:

- What seem to be the obstacles to this country's more successful or more rapid economic development?
- How are people in the country affected by the country's problems with economic development?
- What possible solutions to the country's problems with economic development are suggested in the article?

Tell the class that in this section they will learn how developing nations respond to scarce factors of production, and how weak economic infrastructures and political instability can hurt a country's efforts to develop economically. ★5B, 22A

TEACH

Building a Vocabulary

List the vocabulary terms for this section on the chalkboard and tell students to add them to their Economics Dictionaries. Tell students to use the information provided in the text or on the *Researcher CD-ROM* to list, define, and give an example of each vocabulary term.

Creating Charts

As discussed in the last lesson, the lack or inefficient use of resources can hurt a country's potential for growth. Organize students into groups of three or four. Have each group list the four categories of resources discussed in Section 2 of the textbook *(natural, human, capital, and entrepreneurial)*. Ask each group to discuss how each of these factors can limit economic development. Then ask each group to design a flowchart that illustrates the ways that these limiting factors may be interrelated. Remind students to be sure that their chart identifies the factors' relationship to economic development. Direct students to consider the obstacles faced by developing countries working toward capital formation *(lack of savings and the difficulty of attracting foreign investment; unstable political, economic, and social environments)*. ★24D

Creating Tables, Evaluating Information

Remind students that in addition to scarcity, many developing countries struggle with an inadequate economic infrastructure. Discuss the following question with students: If you were an officer in a corporation thinking of investing in a developing country, would you be more interested in choosing a country that has a solid banking system and a basic national transportation system, such as railroads and paved highways, or one that has a weak banking system and little to no national transportation system? Write the terms *nationalization* and *expropriation* on the chalkboard and ask students to suggest definitions for these. Write these definitions on the chalkboard. Next, organize students into small groups and have them create a table on a piece of notebook paper. Ask each group to use the following factors as labels along the left side of their tables:

- communications networks
- transportation networks
- inadequate educational system
- lack of stable monetary and banking systems
- nationalization or expropriation of private property

Along the top of their tables, ask each group to use these categories as labels:

- How is this factor an obstacle?
- How does this factor challenge development?

Have each group discuss these issues and fill in their tables. Refer students who need additional instruction on the skills used in this lesson to the *Global Skillbuilder*, Lesson 12: Creating Graphic Organizers. ★24D

401E

Analyzing Ideas and Information

When students have finished the last activity, tell them that an additional obstacle to development in many countries is political instability. Discuss the following with students: How might political conflict or instability affect a country's efforts to overcome challenges such as limited natural resources, limited human resources, limited capital resources, lack of entrepreneurs, rapid population growth, reliance on traditional agriculture, and inadequate infrastructure? Write these challenges to development on the chalkboard to use in this discussion. Ask students to identify countries that have struggled with political conflicts and ask them to discuss how economic development may have been affected by these conflicts.

CLOSE

Ask students to imagine that they are businesspeople in one of the countries discussed in the last lesson activity, or entrepreneurs in the United States hoping to start a business in that country. Ask students: As a businessperson, what would you suggest that the government of this country do to ensure future political stability? What suggestions might you make to national leaders regarding ways they might overcome some of the other obstacles faced by their country?

OPTIONS

Linguistic Learners

Have each student select a developing nation. Ask students to write a short report on the most significant obstacles to economic development in their selected nation. Also, have students explore the ways that the government or businesspeople in that country have tried to overcome some of these obstacles. Encourage students to analyze and include in their reports copies of charts or graphs that illustrate the country's GDP, GNI, population growth rate, or natural resources. Students may find useful research information in the Country Profiles section on the *Researcher Online*. ★24D

Students Having Difficulty

Pair students having difficulty with students who have mastered the material. Ask each pair to outline the contents of the chapter, using complete sentences to summarize the section points under each heading. Suggest that students use the following section headings:
I. Scarcity of Resources and Resource Use
   A. Natural Resources
   B. Human Resources
   C. Capital Resources
   D. Entrepreneurship
II. Other Obstacles to Development
   A. Inadequate Infrastructure
      1. Communication and Transportation Networks
      2. Schools
      3. Stable Monetary and Banking Systems
      4. Nationalization and Expropriation
   B. Political Instability ★5B, 24D

Gifted Learners, Linguistic Learners

Ask students to choose a country that has faced political instability in recent years, such as Haiti, Rwanda, or Nicaragua. Have each student explore how the political problems in that country have affected economic development, especially how the political conflict has influenced the availability of basic goods and services for the average citizen. Ask students to write a newspaper article or a short story from the viewpoint of a teenager who lives in an urban area in one of these countries and is concerned about the ways that political conflict has hurt the economy in their country. Encourage students to imagine what goods and services might be missed most during a period of political crisis and economic downturn (although students should first find out what basic goods and services were available to the people of their chosen country before the political conflict affected the economy). Students may wish to include their stories in their portfolio. ★24D

REVIEW

Have students complete the Section 2 Review on page 413. Use the answers in the Annotated Teacher's Edition to assess student mastery of this section.

ASSESS

To assess student mastery of this section, have students complete Daily Quiz 17.2 in *Daily Quizzes with Answer Key*. For additional assessment options, see *Alternative Assessment Handbook* on the *One-Stop Planner CD-ROM*.

ADDITIONAL RESOURCES

Goldman, Marshall I. *Lost Opportunity: What Has Made Economic Reform in Russia So Difficult?* 1996. W. W. Norton & Co.

Hope, Kempe Ronald. *African Political Economy: Contemporary Issues in Development.* 1996. M. E. Sharpe.

Rumer, Boris. *Central Asia in Transition: Dilemmas of Political and Economic Development.* 1996. M. E. Sharpe.

LESSON 17.3 PATHS TO ECONOMIC DEVELOPMENT

TEXTBOOK PAGES 414–22

HOLT PRESENTATION MAKER — Access Illustrated LECTURE NOTES using Microsoft® PowerPoint® on the One-Stop Planner CD-ROM

OBJECTIVES

- Describe the characteristics of the socialist and capitalist models of decision making.
- Describe the types of aid that governments of developed countries extend to developing countries.
- Identify the key public sources of foreign aid.

MOTIVATE

Tell students that in the last few decades, Brazil has constructed a number of large hydroelectric dams that it could not afford to build without outside assistance. Discuss with the class the following questions:
- How might Brazil have chosen countries to ask for economic assistance to build these dams?
- Why would the sources of these funds be willing to extend this type of aid to Brazil for these kinds of projects?

Tell the class that in this section they will learn about the key public sources of foreign aid and the types of economic aid that developed countries extend to developing countries.

TEACH

Building a Vocabulary

List the vocabulary terms for this section on the chalkboard and tell students to add them to their Economics Dictionary. Tell students to use the information provided in the text or on the *Researcher CD-ROM* to list, define, and give an example of each vocabulary term.

Creating Charts, Evaluating Ideas

Tell students that there are two basic economic models being used by countries today in working towards economic development: the socialist model and the capitalist model. Organize students into groups of three or four. Have each group make a chart that compares the advantages and disadvantages of the socialist and capitalist economic models. Have groups write *advantages* and *disadvantages* on the left side of their charts, and have them write *capitalist* and *socialist* along the top of the chart. Ask the students in each group to discuss the possible advantages and disadvantages of each model, including possibilities not listed in the textbook, and then have them write summaries of their discussions in the appropriate boxes in their charts. ⭐24D

Analyzing Ideas

Remind students that regardless of which type of economic model developing countries choose, they need to raise revenue for their economic plans. Tell students that much of this revenue is provided by developed countries. Display Transparency 68—Official Development Assistance from OECD Members (also represented on textbook page 419). Ask students to recall from their reading the different forms of aid offered by developed nations to developing nations and write their suggestions on the chalkboard. Next, ask students to suggest the four main reasons that developed countries offer foreign aid to developing countries. Write these on the chalkboard as well *(for economic, political, military, and humanitarian reasons)*. Discuss these reasons in more detail by asking the class the following questions:
- How does foreign aid encourage international trade? How does increased foreign trade benefit both developed and developing countries?
- What are the political reasons that developed countries offer foreign aid?
- Why might developed nations extend military aid to developing countries?
- Why is foreign aid sometimes controversial in both developed and developing countries?

Classifying Information

Tell students that besides government foreign aid, there are also several international public sources of foreign aid for developing countries. Write three of these on the chalkboard: the World Bank, the International Monetary Fund, and the United Nations. Organize students into groups of three. Give each group 15 index cards. Assign one of the three organizations to each student in each group. Ask each student to write one statement on each card that describes a characteristic or role of their agency and then have them write the name of the agency on the back of the card *(for example: [on one side] The International Development Association (IDA), which has 159 members and makes loans only to the lowest-income developing nations, is part of this organization; [on other side] World Bank).* Have students repeat this process until they cannot think of any more statements to write on their cards. Then have the members of each group shuffle their cards. Students in each group should take turns reading statements to each other and identifying the relevant organization. Encourage students to consult the International Organizations section on the *Researcher Online* for more information.

CLOSE

Discuss with the class the following questions:
- How might the aid given by a multinational corporation to a developing country differ from aid given by the United Nations? What kinds of restrictions might each place on the money put into development projects in the developing country?
- How might aid given by a multinational corporation differ from aid given by the government of a developed country?

Discuss with students the benefits and drawbacks of these different types of aid for developing nations.

OPTIONS

Interpersonal Learners

Organize students into small groups. Ask each group to imagine that they are members of a new government that was just voted into office in a developing country. Tell each group that most of the people in their country are very poor. Ask each group to discuss the possible advantages and disadvantages of the two main models of economic development: socialist and capitalist. Encourage students to explore how socialist and capitalist models might be combined to provide maximum economic development and a better quality of life for as many people as possible. *(For example, socialized medicine in Canada, Britain, and Sweden ensures that no citizen in these countries has to live without basic health care.)* ⭐10A

Linguistic Learners

Have students write an essay supporting or refuting the following statement: *Encouraging economic growth in developing nations can help economic growth in the United States.* Ask students to recall the reasons why developed countries extend aid to developing countries, and to incorporate these into their essays. Call on students from both sides of the issue to read their essays to the class. ⭐24D

English Language Learners, Visual-Spatial Learners

Pair students acquiring English with fluent English speakers. Have students research economic development in a country of their choosing. Ask students to use their findings to construct a time line showing their country's economic growth in the last 20 to 30 years. Encourage students to include in their time lines information about the sources of funding that this country received for development projects. Have students use the *Researcher Online*, the library, in-class resources, other Internet resources, and information from business journals or newspapers to conduct their research. Ask each pair to present their time lines to the class. Refer students who need additional instruction on the skills used in this activity to the *Global Skillbuilder,* Lesson 9: Using Time Lines. ⭐22A, 24D

REVIEW

Have students complete the Section 3 Review on page 422. Use the answers in the Annotated Teacher's Edition to assess student mastery of this section.

ASSESS

To assess student mastery of this section, have students complete Daily Quiz 17.3 in *Daily Quizzes with Answer Key*. For additional assessment options, see *Alternative Assessment Handbook* on the *One-Stop Planner CD-ROM*.

RETEACH

For students having difficulty with the lessons, have them complete the Reteaching Activity 17. This activity is located in *Reteaching Activities with Answer Key*.

ADDITIONAL RESOURCES

Aoki, Masahiko, et al., eds. *The Role of Government in East Asian Economic Development: Comparative Institutional Analysis.* 1998. Clarendon Press.

Van de Walle, Dominique, and Kimberly Nead. *Public Spending and the Poor: Theory and Evidence.* 1995. Johns Hopkins University Press.

Private Capital Flows to Developing Countries: The Road to Financial Integration. 1998. World Bank.

CHAPTER 17

TOPICS INCLUDE

- characteristics of developing nations
- world population growth
- challenges to growth in developing nations
- resource use in developing nations
- entrepreneurship in developing nations
- infrastructure in developing nations
- political instability in developing nations
- socialist and capitalist decision-making models
- sources for financing economic development in developing nations
- multinational corporations
- foreign aid

ECONOMICS NOTEBOOK

The Economics Notebook is a journal activity that encourages students to consider basic concepts of economics that relate to their lives. A follow-up notebook activity appears on page 424.

WHY IT MATTERS TODAY

To find additional lesson plans dealing with the economies of Eastern and Central Europe, visit CNNfyi.com or have students complete the ECONOMICS IN THE NEWS activity on page 423.

CNNfyi.com

CHAPTER 17

DEVELOPING COUNTRIES

Why are some nations more prosperous than others? How can the allocation and use of resources affect economic activity? How do nations work to expand their economies and improve the standard of living for their citizens? The answers to these questions can provide information about why the economies of two countries may operate in very different ways—even if the countries are close geographically.

In this chapter you will learn how nations are classified by economic development. In addition, you will learn why some countries develop more slowly than others, and how national leaders may help speed economic development.

ECONOMICS NOTEBOOK

In your Economics Notebook, define "personal economic development." For example, will you consider yourself "economically developed" when you get your first full-time job or when you buy a car?

WHY IT MATTERS TODAY

Developing nations face many economic challenges. Use CNNfyi.com or other **current events** sources to find examples of some of the challenges specific to developing countries.

CNNfyi.com

SECTION 1

ECONOMIC DEVELOPMENT

READ TO DISCOVER
1. What characteristics do developing nations have in common?
2. How can scarcity of resources affect a developing nation?

ECONOMICS DICTIONARY
- economic development
- developed nations
- developing nations
- arable
- subsistence agriculture

In the world today there are nearly 200 nations, all at different stages of economic development. **Economic development** is a broad term that includes the size and sophistication of a nation's industrial, service, technical, and agricultural sectors.

The industrialized nations of the world, which economists generally classify as **developed nations**, have a high level of industrial and technical expertise, as well as a variety of economic institutions, such as banking systems, stock markets, and trade networks. The World Bank—an international economic organization—has classified some 39 nations as being "high income" or highly developed. The United States, Canada, Japan, most nations in Europe, and several other nations in Asia and the Middle East are among the developed nations. The combined populations of the developed nations make up less than one sixth of the world's population.

Economists classify the remaining nations of the world as developing nations. The majority of the world's population lives in these developing nations. **Developing nations** are characterized by low per capita gross national income (GNI, also called the gross national product or GNP), limited resources or inefficient use of resources, rapid population growth rate, and dependency on agriculture as the main form of production.

Low Per Capita GNI

Per capita GNI, a widely used indicator of the standard of living, is the average dollar value of a nation's annual total output, including overseas investment income, for each person. The per capita GNI is calculated by dividing a nation's total GNI by its total population.

World Bank economists subdivide developing nations according to income level based on per capita GNI. In 2000 the per capita GNI of low-income developing nations was $755 or less. For lower-middle-income countries, per capita GNI ranged between $756 and $2,995. Upper-middle-income countries' per capita GNI ranged from $2,996 to $9,265. In contrast, the developed nations had per capita GNI of more than $9,265. For a comparison of per capita GNI around the world, see Figure 17.1 on pages 404–05.

Limited Resources

Scarcity and the use of resources in developing nations are problems that are caused by both natural and historical forces. Natural forces have affected the distribution of resources through climate and the availability of water resources, mineral deposits, and **arable**—or productive—land. For example, in Libya, Mali, Niger, and other countries that lie across the Sahara in Africa, less than 4 percent of the land is arable, mainly because of the lack of rainfall. On the other hand, in much of tropical Africa, where rainfall is plentiful, the soil is drained of its fertility and is unsuitable for most types of agriculture.

Historical forces that have negatively affected the distribution or use of resources include people's decisions and actions. For example, many developing nations were once European colonies. From the 1500s to the mid-1900s, the European

---

SECTION 1

ECONOMIC DEVELOPMENT

Lesson Plans
For teaching strategies, see Lesson 17.1 located at the beginning of this chapter or the One-Stop Planner Strategy 17.1.

Economics Dictionary
To reinforce the section's vocabulary terms, refer students to the Electronic Glossary on the *Researcher CD-ROM*.

Section Assessment
To assess students' mastery of this section, have them complete Daily Quiz 17.1 in *Daily Quizzes with Answer Key*.

Enhancing the Lesson
For information about a number of countries worldwide, see the Country Profiles section on the *Researcher Online*.

TEKS
Content
5B, 12A, 22A
Social Studies Skills
23A, 23F, 24A, 24D

Cultural Perspectives

Rapid population growth in developing nations has transformed some of their urban areas from small cities into major metropolitan centers in just a few decades. For example, between 1980 and 2000 the population of Bombay, India, increased by about 123 percent; Jakarta, Indonesia's population increased by 83.3 percent; and Cairo, Egypt's by 53.6 percent. In contrast, New York City's population increased by only 6.4 percent.

Although urban growth often helps stimulate economic development, it poses many problems as well. For instance, many rapidly growing cities are located in some of the world's poorest nations, which lack the money and resources to deal with or plan for rapid growth. As a result, many of these cities face severe problems with overcrowding, traffic congestion, pollution, poverty, homelessness, and a lack of adequate housing, sanitation, schools, and hospitals. The challenge for developing nations is to promote economic and social development while alleviating urban problems. ■

Caption Answer

low per capita GNI, limited resources or inefficient use of resources, rapid population growth rate, and a dependency on agricultural production ⭐22A

---

powers used colonies to supply agricultural products and raw materials for Europe's industries. In turn, the European powers made only limited investments in colonial economies, transportation networks, and education systems. Colonialism often slowed economic development in much of Asia, Africa, and Latin America.

Rapid Population Growth

The population growth rate, or the annual percentage of increase in a nation's population, is higher in most developing nations than it is in the developed nations. In 2001 the population growth rate of the many developing nations in Latin America, the Middle East, Africa, and Asia averaged more than 1.5 percent, compared to an average of 0.1 percent in developed countries. The population growth rate of developing nations is therefore more than 10 times higher than the rate of developed nations.

Some experts argue that many statistics downplay population expansion in developed countries. The U.S. population, for example, increased by an average of nearly 3.3 million people each year from 1990 to 2000. About one third of this increase is a result of immigration, but the United States has one of the highest birthrates among developed nations.

Other experts point out that population growth is not the result of higher birthrates. In fact, world birthrates declined from 5.3 children per mother in 1950 to 2.8 children per mother by 2000. Instead, advances in health care, hygiene, and sanitation have enabled people to live longer, so that although fewer people are being born to each mother, more are living to adulthood—and consuming more goods and services.

The world's population in 2001 was more than 6.1 billion and is projected to exceed 7.8 billion in the year 2025. Most of this increase will occur in developing nations. For a comparison of

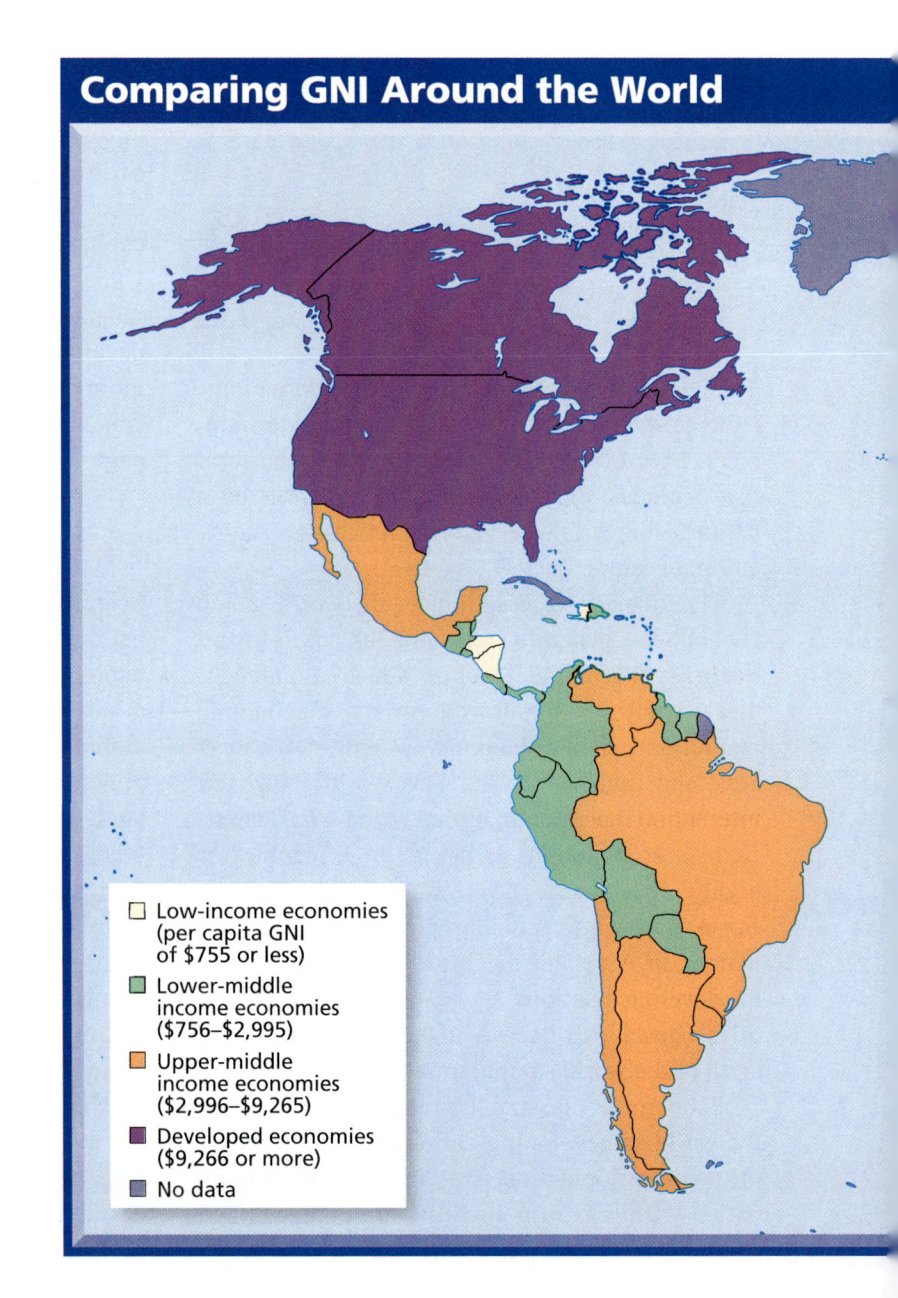

FIGURE 17.1 Developed, or industrialized, nations make up less than one sixth of the world's population. **What characteristics do most developing nations share?** ⭐TEKS

Comparing GNI Around the World

- ☐ Low-income economies (per capita GNI of $755 or less)
- ☐ Lower-middle income economies ($756–$2,995)
- ☐ Upper-middle income economies ($2,996–$9,265)
- ☐ Developed economies ($9,266 or more)
- ☐ No data

selected national population growth rates, see Figure 17.2 on page 406.

Traditional Agricultural Economies

Many people in developing nations still must produce their own food in order to survive. In **subsistence agriculture**, families grow just enough to meet basic needs and do not produce crop surpluses to trade. Most developing nations, however, have been able to produce surpluses of agricultural products to sell in international markets. These surpluses are usually in commercial plantation crops, such as peanuts from Gambia, coffee from Colombia and Brazil, bananas from Honduras, cocoa from Ghana and Côte d'Ivoire, and sugar from Cuba and the Dominican Republic. Generally these cash crops are raised solely for export by the producers, who are usually wealthy landowners.

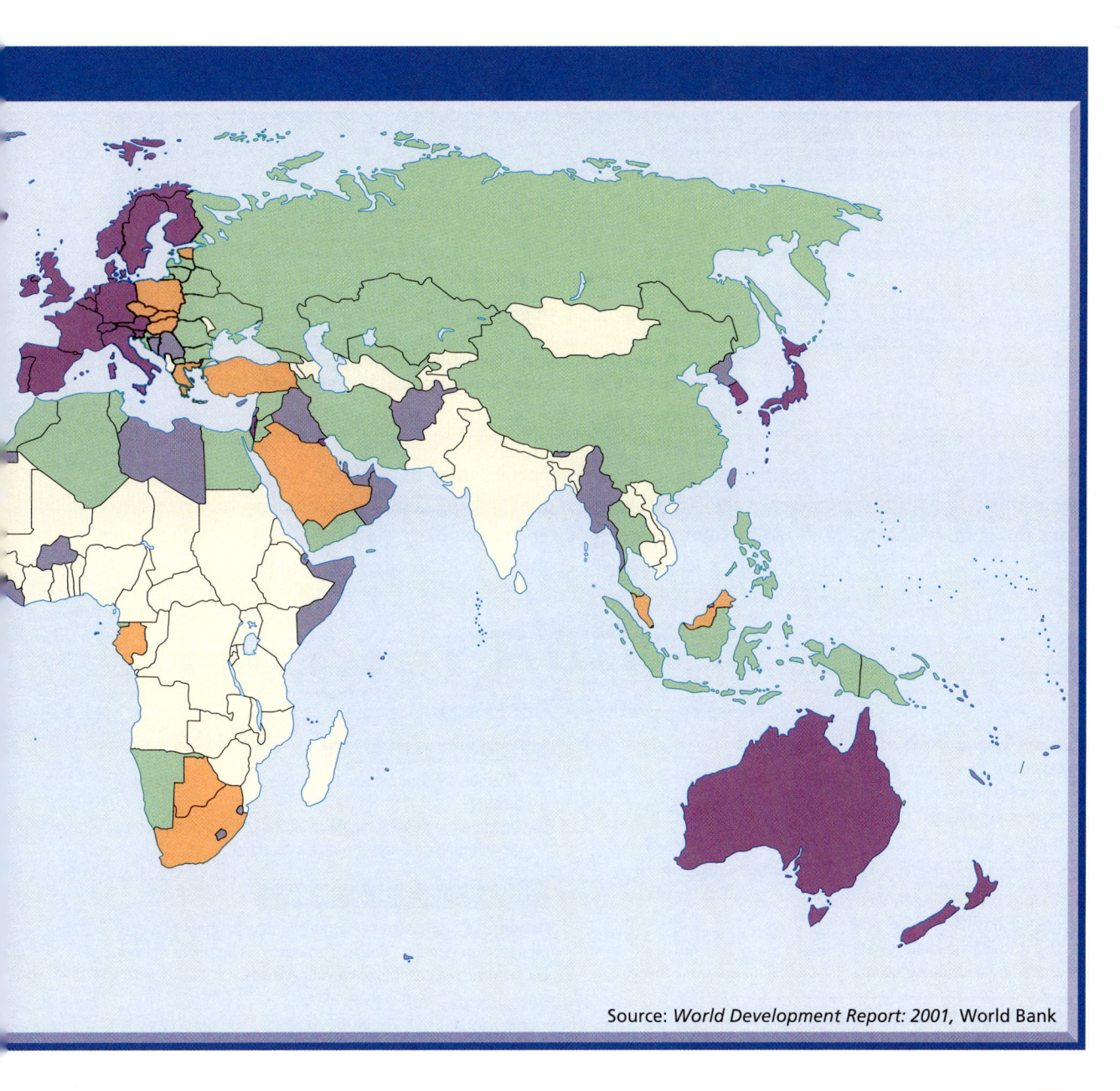

Source: *World Development Report: 2001*, World Bank

Across the Curriculum

GEOGRAPHY In the late 1700s, the economist Adam Smith noted that sea-based trade was less expensive than overland trade, and the same holds true today. Industry and commerce tend to develop sooner and at a faster pace along coastlines and navigable rivers than in areas which have little or no water access. Consequently, landlocked nations and cities tend to experience slower economic growth than those with plenty of accessible ports and navigable rivers. Nations and cities in interior Africa and Asia have experienced slow economic growth in part because of their isolation and lack of accessible water routes. ■

Transparency

An overhead transparency of Figure 17.1 is available in *Transparency Resources*. See Transparency 67: Comparing GNI Around the World.

Enhancing the Lesson

For a discussion on the reasons why some nations develop faster than others, see Reading 71: The Evolution of International Economic Order, located in *From the Source: Readings in Economics and Government with Answer Key*.

Caption Answer
Mexico ⭐23F

SECTION 1 REVIEW ANSWERS

1. economic development (403), developed nations (403), developing nations (403), arable (403), subsistence agriculture (405) 24A

2. low per capita GNI, limited resources or inefficient use of resources, high population growth rate, and dependence on agricultural production 22A, 23A, 24D

3a. tropical or arid climates and limited water resources, mineral deposits, and arable land

3b. Answers will vary. Students might suggest that rapid population growth often leads to greater demands for already scarce resources, higher instances of disease as a result of overcrowding, higher unemployment rates, and lower per capita GNI.

4. Answers will vary. Students might suggest that commercial crops can be exported to other nations for profit, increasing a developing nation's GNI and strengthening its economy. Workers might not benefit as much as producers, who are usually wealthy landowners. 12A, 23A

COMPARING POPULATION GROWTH RATES, 1980–1999

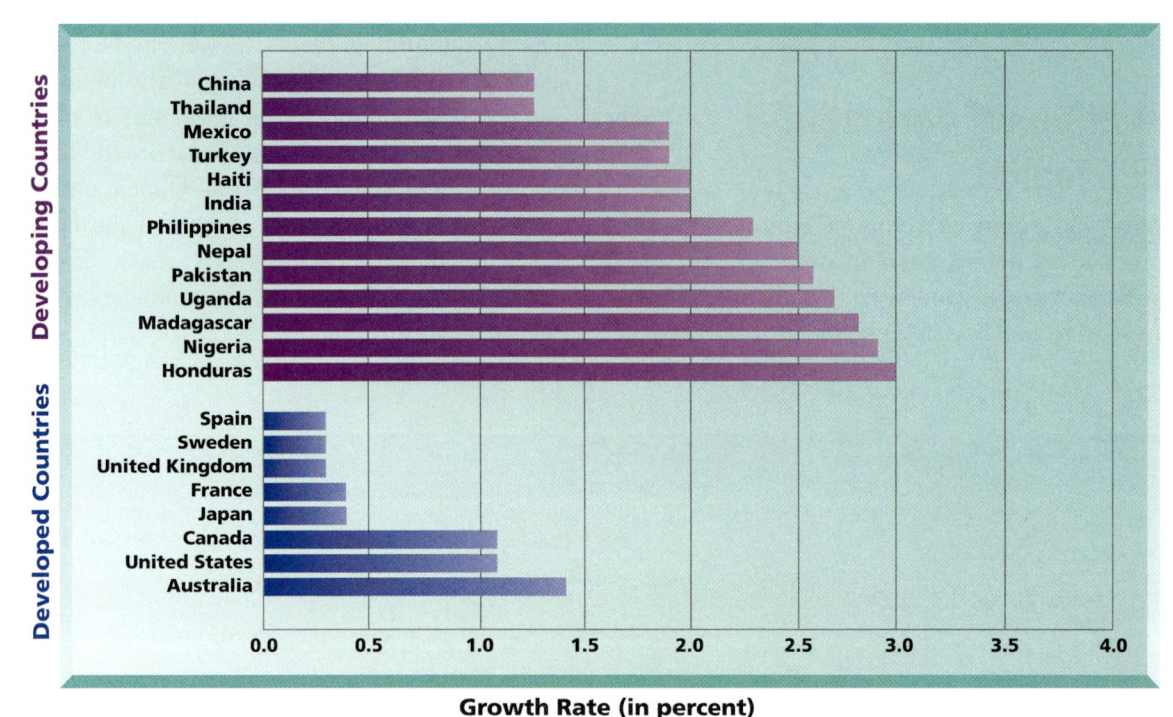

Source: *World Development Indicators: 2001*, World Bank

FIGURE 17.2 Most developing countries experience rapid population growth in comparison to developed countries. **Which neighboring country to the United States has the highest population growth rate?** ⭐TEKS

Subsistence agriculture reinforces a traditional lifestyle because people earn their income from the land, which tends to isolate them from the outside world. Tradition often plays the most important role in shaping religious beliefs, the size of families, and the role of women and children in society—all of which affect the economies of developing nations.

SECTION 1 REVIEW

⭐TEKS Q: 1, 2, 4

1. Identify and Explain:
economic development
developed nations
developing nations
arable
subsistence agriculture

2. Categorizing: Copy the graphic organizer to the right. Use it to list the characteristics shared by developing nations.

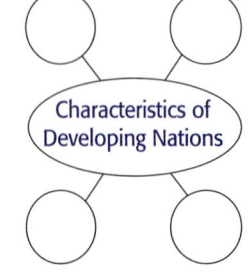

Characteristics of Developing Nations

3. Finding the Main Idea
a. What factors contribute to resource scarcity in developing nations?
b. Describe the possible negative effects of rapid population growth on a developing nation's economy.

4. Writing and Critical Thinking
Drawing Conclusions: How can development of a commercial crop benefit a nation's economy? Who might not benefit from such a crop? Explain your answer.
Consider the following:
• what happens to commercial crops
• resource ownership

Homework Practice Online
keyword: SM3 HP17

SECTION 2
CHALLENGES TO GROWTH

READ TO DISCOVER
1. How do many developing nations respond to scarce factors of production?
2. How can the status of an economic infrastructure help or hinder a developing nation?
3. How can political instability challenge a developing nation?

ECONOMICS DICTIONARY
one-crop economy
capital formation
expropriation

Developing nations face great challenges in pursuing economic growth. Decisions about how to use the factors of production are made more difficult by scarcity. While all societies must respond to scarcity, developing nations generally lack the institutions and systems that would enable them to use resources efficiently, which slows economic growth.

Other obstacles may exist that affect economic development. A limited infrastructure can hinder education, commerce, production, and transportation. Political instability can disrupt trade. Social and cultural traditions may cause some people to resist change. In this section you will learn why many developing nations experience slow economic growth.

Scarcity and Resource Use

To achieve economic growth and development, a nation must be able to increase its total per capita output of goods and services. But to increase the output of goods and services, a developing nation must improve the quantity—and quality—of the available factors of production. This improvement, in turn, relies on the effective use of resources. Scarcity and the inefficient use of natural, human, capital, and entrepreneurial resources can limit the potential for growth in developing nations.

Natural Resources Developing nations tend to specialize in the production of one or a few goods, usually agricultural products or raw materials. Although specialization tends to promote international trade, it can also lead to one-crop economies.

A nation that concentrates on the production of a single item has a **one-crop economy**. When referring to one-crop economies, economists use the term *crop* to include many nonagricultural products, such as minerals. One-crop economies often are unstable because the entire economy depends on the world price for a single product.

SCARCITY & CHOICE *Guatemala specializes in the production of coffee. What are the disadvantages of one-crop economies for developing nations?*

DEVELOPING COUNTRIES 407

Caption Answer
substandard education and job training, inadequate diet, and low level of medical care ★23A

---

internet connect

TOPIC: Human Resources, Immigration
GO TO: go.hrw.com
KEYWORD: SM3 EC17

Have students access the Internet through the HRW Go site to conduct research on immigration to the United States. Then have students create world maps showing the countries from which the greatest number of U.S. immigrants come. ★24C, 24D

Caption Answer
a lack of savings, a lack of private investment, and the rapid deterioration of existing capital

INTERNATIONAL GROWTH & STABILITY *Like most developing nations, India has a large supply of labor. What are some reasons that developing nations often experience low worker productivity?*

Environmental factors also may limit growth in a one-crop economy. Suppose that a country specializing in coffee production experiences a severe winter. If a freeze destroys the crop, producers will not be able to supply coffee to the market. Because the country generates few other products that might provide income, its economy will be weakened.

Human Resources Because of their high population growth rates, most developing nations have enough workers. However, inadequate education, job training, diet, and medical care often result in low worker productivity. In addition, high unemployment and underemployment, each a result of unstable economies, can challenge developing nations.

Most developing nations recognize the importance of investing in human resources. For this reason, many of them are spending more money on primary and secondary education. Shortages of funds, however, tend to limit the number of schools and qualified teachers. As a result, education in some developing nations is available only to people living in urban areas. Many people who attain a higher education take their skills abroad to earn higher wages. This "brain drain" harms the developing countries that have invested in those citizens' educations.

Capital Resources Capital resources and technology are essential to economic growth, but they are in short supply in most developing nations. Capital—when transformed into production plants, machinery, and new equipment—can increase worker productivity. A basic economic goal, therefore, is **capital formation**, the accumulation of the financial resources and capital goods necessary for economic development. Three major obstacles—lack of savings, lack of private investment, and rapid deterioration of existing capital—frequently hinder capital formation in developing nations.

The first obstacle, lack of savings, occurs because people in developing nations find it difficult to put off present consumption. Many people are already living at a subsistence level. After

INTERNATIONAL GROWTH & STABILITY *Capital resources and technology are in short supply in most developing nations. What are some obstacles to capital formation in developing nations?*

408 CHAPTER 17

CAREERS IN ECONOMICS

Urban and Regional Planner

The hope of economic opportunity brings many people to urban areas. In many developing countries, new city-dwellers may instead find crowded living conditions and extreme poverty, because there are not enough jobs in these cities to support rapid population growth.

Urban growth is also common in developed countries. While cities in these nations do experience overcrowding and poverty, decision makers are generally able to avoid the extreme conditions found in developing nations by consulting with experts called urban and regional planners.

Urban and regional planners study the location and extent of housing, hospitals, businesses, transportation networks, and parks and recreational facilities. After evaluating existing conditions, an urban and regional planner then creates a plan for managing a city's growth.

An urban and regional planner generally has an undergraduate or graduate degree in urban planning. Courses in statistics, economics, architecture, and geography may also be helpful. Internships provide students with on-the-job experience, enabling them to apply classroom studies to real-world situations.

An urban and regional planner may have an area of specialization—for example, commercial development in inner cities or the environmental effects of construction. An urban and regional planner might study transportation patterns in a city to determine how people move between homes and workplaces. Should a bus route be discontinued? Should a new highway be built to accommodate increased traffic?

Most urban and regional planners work for government agencies, but some work as consultants with private businesses. If you are interested in helping communities meet the needs of expanding populations, you might consider a career in urban and regional planning.

Urban planners study a city's characteristics to create plans for managing its growth.

---

meeting their basic needs for food, shelter, and clothing, they have no money left to save.

If domestic savings cannot fund capital formation, foreign investment is necessary. Many investors, however, are reluctant to invest in the economies of developing nations for several reasons. First, they fear that business leaders' lack of experience could result in mistakes related to what products to produce or what capital should be used in production. Second, there are few incentives to invest in places where the domestic population cannot support markets by purchasing consumer goods. Third, the economic, political, and social environments of many developing nations are unstable. Outside investors generally try to avoid such situations

Caption Answer
(page 411)
Entrepreneurs suffer from insufficient government financial support in these countries. ⭐22B

What Do You Think?
Answers
1. Opinions will vary. Some students may argue that the label *Third World* has evolved over time to include all developing nations, thus the Third World still exists. Those that disagree may argue that many of the former Second World nations are now developing nations, so referring to all developing nations as the Third World no longer makes sense.

2. Answers will vary. Nonaligned leaders may not agree with either opposing power, they may want to avoid getting involved in any global conflicts, and they may prefer self-sufficiency to political entanglements. The economic effects of nonalignment might include less foreign aid, protection, and military assistance from superpower countries. ⭐22B

LINKING ECONOMICS and HISTORY

How Many Worlds?

You may have heard people refer to "Third World countries." Just where is the "Third World"—and which worlds are "First" and "Second"? Although these terms are not widely used today, historically they reflected international tensions.

When World War II ended in 1945, Europe was divided into capitalist nations allied with the United States and communist nations largely controlled by the Soviet Union. During the postwar years, increased tension led to the struggle known as the Cold War. Each side attempted to extend its military, political, and economic power throughout the world.

In 1955, representatives of 29 African and Asian nations met in Bandung, Indonesia, and formed an association of "nonaligned" nations. In doing so, these countries meant to avoid permanent alliances with either the United States or the Soviet Union. The nonaligned nations—soon joined by Yugoslavia—came to be called the Third World. The United States and its allies thus made up the First World, and the Soviet Union and its Eastern European satellite nations were together referred to as the Second World.

Most Third World countries in Africa and Asia were former colonies. Several European nations had controlled empires that included territories from the Mediterranean to Southeast Asia. Many of these colonies gained their independence after World War II.

Economic development in the colonies had focused largely on the exploitation of natural resources for use in industrialized nations. As a result, newly independent nations often lacked their own economic infrastructure. Because they were less prosperous than industrial countries, they were classified as developing nations. The term *Third World* often was extended to any developing nation, even if it was not part of the nonaligned group introduced at the Bandung Conference.

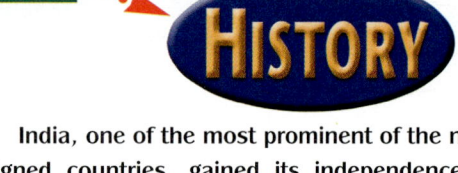

India, one of the most prominent of the nonaligned countries, gained its independence in 1947. Although it has since made some economic progress, its economy is still developing.

India's decision to remain nonaligned was summed up by its first prime minister, Jawaharlal Nehru (juh-WAH-huhr-lal NER-oo), shortly after India became independent. "We do not propose to accept anything that involves in the slightest degree dependence on any other authority," he declared. "Sometimes each country thinks that if you are not completely lined up with it you are its enemy. . . . We have to keep aloof from that and at the same time develop the closest relations with all."

What Do You Think? 🟠TEKS

1. Many economists, political scientists, and historians agree that the Cold War ended with the fall of the Soviet Union in 1991. In light of this, do you think that the "Third World" still exists? Explain your answer.

2. Why might a nation's leaders decide that their country should be nonaligned? What economic challenges might result from this decision?

Financial assistance from the Soviet Union paid for construction of the Aswan High Dam but did not change Egypt's nonaligned status.

INTERNATIONAL GROWTH & STABILITY *Many developing nations spend money on national defense rather than economic development. **How does this choice affect entrepreneurship in developing countries?***

Angola, for example, spent 22 percent of its GDP on national defense in 1999. In contrast, military spending accounted for 1.1 percent of Spain's 1997 GDP. Additionally, a lack of consistent education limits the number of people with training in fields such as mathematics, science, and computer programming, as well as management and finance.

Other Obstacles

In developed nations such as the United States and New Zealand, the economic, political, and social environments have contributed to economic growth. In the developing nations, however, these factors have often created obstacles to economic development.

Inadequate Infrastructure In many developing nations, the economic infrastructure has been inadequate to support economic development. As previously noted, a nation's economic infrastructure is its transportation, communications, banking, education, and other institutions and systems that encourage production and promote trade. Developing nations lack well-developed communications networks and roads, railroads, bridges, harbors, and airports. Inadequate schools and a shortage of teachers restrict the number of literate workers, technicians, scientists, and entrepreneurs who are needed to shape economic progress in developing nations.

In addition, the lack of stable monetary and banking systems in some developing nations discourages savings and investments. For example, during recent decades, extremely high inflation rates in Bolivia and Brazil made their currencies nearly worthless.

Nationalization and expropriation of private property also have discouraged savings and investment. As noted in Chapter 16, nationalization takes place when the government assumes

because of the high risk of losing their investments. Finally, a lack of roads, railroads, ports, and utilities generally discourages investment spending. Shortcomings in the economic infrastructure often make the production and distribution of finished products much more difficult.

Capital goods often deteriorate more rapidly in developing nations than in developed nations. Breakdowns in machinery occur from misuse or because workers are unable to read operation and maintenance manuals. Repairs to factories are delayed because there are not enough trained mechanics. Additionally, spare parts often are available only from manufacturers in other nations, further slowing repairs.

Entrepreneurship The forces that account for the gap in capital formation between developing nations and developed nations also account for a gap in entrepreneurship. The lack of savings and private investment in developing nations discourages entrepreneurship, thus slowing the development of new business.

Entrepreneurs also suffer from insufficient financial support from the government. Many developing nations spend money on national defense rather than on economic development.

Themes in Economics

ECONOMIC INSTITUTIONS & INCENTIVES Many people in developing nations do not have the money and often do not qualify for the bank loans needed to start or expand a business. In response to this problem, a growing number of organizations now provide "microloans" to poor would-be entrepreneurs in developing nations to help people escape poverty.

One such organization is Grameen Bank in Bangladesh. Bank founder, Muhammad Yunus, got the idea for the bank when he met a woman who needed only 20 cents to start her own business. She could not save the money out of the few cents she earned a day, however. Yunus realized that many poor people in Bangladesh were in similar positions. He tried to convince banks to give small loans to some of these people but was told that poor people were credit risks. Yunus disagreed and in 1983 opened his own bank.

Grameen Bank has proven successful. In 2001 it lent out more than $31 million each month, and had branches in more than 40,000 villages. The bank requires small weekly payments with interest, and—disproving the theory that poor people are credit risks—has a loan recovery rate of about 90 percent. The World Bank estimates that as many as one-third of the bank's borrowers have risen out of poverty. ■

DEVELOPING COUNTRIES

Caption Answer
to improve a nation's economy and to promote economic growth

Across the Curriculum

TECHNOLOGY Information technology is helping many developing nations leapfrog out of the past and into the modern age. In 2000 some 2 billion people in developing countries still lacked access to electricity, and about 80 percent of the world's population—about 4.8 billion people—did not have access to telephones. At the same time, satellite linkups, mobile phones, digital pagers, and solar-powered radio-computers were enabling many people in poor and remote areas to connect to the rest of the world, often for the first time. In areas where the existing infrastructure is limited or non-existent, newer technologies are often cheaper, quicker, and easier to set up. ■

Caption Answer
It can inhibit domestic and foreign investments. ⭐23A

INTERNATIONAL GROWTH & STABILITY *In the former Soviet Union, privatization of state farmland has been difficult.* **What is one goal of privatization?**

ownership and control of a business after compensating the former owner. On the other hand, **expropriation** occurs when a nation's government takes control of a firm or industry without compensating the owner. Developing nations have nationalized and expropriated many types of enterprises, such as mines, farms, oil refineries, and factories.

Although many countries have also turned to privatization to improve their economies, this process is not without risk. As noted in Chapter 12, privatization occurs when former public assets such as industry, land, and machinery are sold to individuals or to private businesses. The transition of former communist economies to market economies demonstrates the challenges of privatization. In the former Soviet Union the sale of state-owned farmland and machinery has been difficult. Many factories, for example, were very expensive, making it difficult for individuals or firms to purchase them.

Political Instability The frequent political instability in some developing nations is another disincentive to savings and investments. Both domestic and foreign investors need to be assured that their investments are secure and that there is a reasonable chance for a return. Revolutions, civil wars, and riots generally cause investors to feel that their funds would not be secure, discouraging economic development.

During the 1980s, power struggles in Angola, Nicaragua, El Salvador, Ethiopia, Sri Lanka, Iran, and Iraq disrupted normal business activity. In each of these countries, large sums of money were spent on military goods, and capital investment was destroyed. In 1991 the Persian Gulf War resulted in the destruction of many capital resources in Iraq and Kuwait. To rebuild those countries' economies, new capital goods had to be purchased or developed before consumer goods could be produced.

Social and Cultural Obstacles
In some developing nations, society and culture restrict economic development. A country's traditions,

INTERNATIONAL GROWTH & STABILITY *In 1991 the Persian Gulf War destroyed many capital resources in Iraq and Kuwait.* **In what other ways can political instability affect economic growth?**

412 CHAPTER 17

class structures, and people's wishes for more consumer goods and luxury items may interfere with a nation's economic planning and development.

Strongly rooted customs may lead people to resist changes to traditional production methods. Nations that have primarily agricultural economies generally remain more bound by tradition than nations that are more industrialized and urbanized. In recent decades, however, education, the spread of technology, and increased contact with the developed world have weakened some of the resistance to economic change.

As they begin to experience economic growth, some people in developing nations may expect a rapid increase in the number of goods and services they will be able to consume. These expectations in part come from exposure to the prosperity of developed nations, as shown through the mass media. However, supply is not always able to meet increased demand.

Finally, traditional class structures in some developing nations may limit opportunities for individuals. Fewer opportunities to climb the social and economic ladder may reduce incentives to become better educated. Moreover, the ruling elite often opposes change because the present social system guarantees them a privileged position.

INTERNATIONAL GROWTH & STABILITY *These Japanese workers are performing traditional group exercises.* **How can society and culture influence economic development?**

SECTION 2 REVIEW

1. Identify and Explain:
- one-crop economy
- capital formation
- expropriation

2. Identifying Cause and Effect: Copy the graphic organizer. Use it to explain how scarce factors of production can affect developing nations.

Scarce Factors of Production

3. Finding the Main Idea
a. How do nationalization and expropriation affect economic infrastructures?
b. What are the potential effects of political instability on a nation's economy?

4. Writing and Critical Thinking

Making Generalizations and Predictions: How can privatization pose challenges to a developing nation?

Consider the following:
- the state of capital and capital goods in a developing nation
- the financial situation of people in developing countries

Homework Practice Online
keyword: SM3 HP17

DEVELOPING COUNTRIES 413

SECTION 3

PATHS TO ECONOMIC DEVELOPMENT

READ TO DISCOVER

1. What are the characteristics of the socialist and capitalist models of decision making?
2. What types of aid do governments of developed countries extend to developing countries?
3. What are the key public sources of foreign aid?

ECONOMICS DICTIONARY

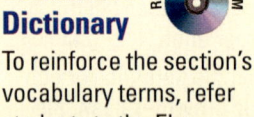

land reform
multinational corporation

Not all developing nations have the same type of economic system. Decision makers in each nation set their own goals for development and thus follow varied paths to economic growth.

Decision-Making Models

Leaders of some developing nations follow the socialist model of decision making, while leaders in other nations follow the capitalist model. The choice of which decision-making model to use is not always made solely with economic growth and development in mind.

Socialist Model Decision making in the socialist model, which is associated with communist governments, is centralized in the hands of national leaders. Although many former command socialist economies are making a transition to a market system, there are still a few developing nations—such as Cuba, North Korea, and Vietnam—using the socialist model of decision making.

The biggest advantage of central planning is the government's ability to direct resources and production toward specific economic goals. This allows the government to change direction quickly. For example, if a government that has traditionally focused on producing military equipment decides that more consumer goods are necessary, it does not need to wait for the forces of supply and demand to take effect. The major disadvantages of central planning are inefficiency, bureaucratic resistance to change, and possible corruption of the bureaucracy that develops and carries out the central plan.

Capitalist Model In a capitalist market economy the decision-making process is decentralized. The government does not control economic decisions; instead, individuals and businesses make most of the decisions through markets. The economic progress of the United States, Japan, and nations in Western Europe has demonstrated

INTERNATIONAL GROWTH & STABILITY *Fidel Castro is the leader of a developing nation—Cuba—that follows the socialist model of decision making.* **What are the key characteristics of this command model of centralized planning?**

CHAPTER 17

that high levels of economic development are possible through decentralized decision making. Therefore, the economies of many developing nations now follow the capitalist model of economic decision making. Some of the most successful nations in East Asia—such as Singapore, Taiwan, and South Korea—have relied on the capitalist model during their development.

One major advantage of the capitalist model of decision making is the opportunity that individuals have to make economic decisions. In a free-enterprise system, individuals are encouraged to become entrepreneurs. Free enterprise also allows businesses to invest however they choose in new capital and technology. Both owners and workers produce because it is in their self-interest to do so.

Decentralized decision making places few direct controls on how resources are used and which goods are produced. This situation presents a problem for the government if it wants to direct more investment into capital goods to encourage growth. Businesses may prefer to produce more consumer goods to meet demand. Government influence in the capitalist model is instead exercised through taxation, subsidies, and regulations. As well, the U.S. government exerts influence in its role as the world's largest consumer, a borrower, and the country's largest employer.

Planning for Economic Development

Whether a developing nation prefers the capitalist or socialist model of decision making, it must create a development plan—an outline of how the nation's resources should be used to meet its economic goals. In socialist economies, central planners in the government are responsible for the development plan. In capitalist economies, where the mix of public and private decision making varies from country to country, private businesses and elected representatives in government each plan for the development and control of resources.

Global Exchange

Changing of the Guard

At midnight on June 30, 1997, the former British colony of Hong Kong—for nearly 100 years a symbol of free-market economics—became part of the communist People's Republic of China. This dramatic change is sure to have far-reaching effects on both Hong Kong and China.

In 1898 the British government leased Hong Kong from China for a period of 99 years. Hong Kong's strategic location on the Kowloon Peninsula and island of Hong Kong contributed to the development of one of the strongest economies in Asia, with one of the busiest ports in the world.

Across the bay created by the Pearl River delta lies the former Portuguese colony of Macao (muh-KOW). Even smaller than Hong Kong, the colony has a population of nearly 500,000 people. For several centuries Macao was a very important port in Asia. Today, however, Macao's main industry is tourism.

China regained control of Macao in 1999. The return of these two territories has caused concern among people in capitalist nations. Both colonies allowed much greater freedom than China offers its own citizens. The Chinese government, on the other hand, sees the return as a time for national pride.

According to a U.S. government report released in 2000, Hong Kong and Macao have thus far been able to sustain their economic success and individual freedoms under Chinese rule. Some analysts, meanwhile, wonder if Hong Kong and Macao's traditions of economic and political freedom will have an impact on China.

Themes in Economics

ECONOMIC FREEDOM In 2001 the Cato Institute, a libertarian think tank, ranked 123 world economies based on economic freedom. Hong Kong, under Chinese rule since 1997, received the top score as having the freest economy. The study considered issues such as tax rates and government regulation to determine the degree of an economy's freedom. The United States was ranked fifth after Hong Kong, Singapore, New Zealand, and the United Kingdom. ■

Themes in Economics

ECONOMIC SYSTEMS When India gained its independence from Britain in 1947, it adopted a socialist system based on self-reliance. Foreign imports were highly restricted, and central planners directed the economy. India's economy, however, grew at a slower pace than that of most other Asian countries. As a result, in 1991, India decided to change course. The nation slowly opened its economy to foreign goods, cut protective tariffs, encouraged direct foreign investment into India, and promoted competition. The results were favorable. Between 1994 and 1997, India's economy grew an average of 7 percent annually. ■

Across the Curriculum

SCIENCE & TECHNOLOGY

Science and technology are helping developing nations expand their production possibilities in a number of ways. To help improve diets in developing countries, scientists are designing foods with increased amounts of nutrients, such as crops rich in zinc. Scientists hope nutrient-rich foods will prevent malnourishment in areas where food supplies are limited.

To help people in developing nations who do not have access to safe drinking water, scientists have invented a device that uses ultraviolet light to quickly and cheaply purify water. This device could save many lives. According to the State of World Index in 2000, about 1.3 billion people—some 20 percent of the world's population—do not have access to safe drinking water. Approximately 25,000 people per day die from drinking contaminated water.

In addition, to help people improve farming techniques and to protect the environment, researchers are working with farmers in developing nations to teach them how to garden more organically and rely on pesticides less. ■

Caption Answer

5 units of capital goods
★5B, 23F

Trade-Offs The problem of scarcity prevents any nation from satisfying all of its economic needs and wants. Therefore, a developing nation must make trade-offs. For example, a developing nation may need a new irrigation system for one region of the country and a new road network for another region. Lacking the resources to meet both needs, the government makes a choice. If the irrigation system receives funding, the road network is the trade-off. As noted in Chapter 1, the next-best or alternative use of resources is the first choice's opportunity cost, so in this case the road network becomes the opportunity cost of building the irrigation system.

Production Possibilities To recognize the realities of trade-offs and opportunity costs, note the production possibilities curve shown in Figure 17.3. The graph shows one major type of production choice faced by all developing nations—whether to produce more capital goods or more consumer goods.

PRODUCTION POSSIBILITIES CURVE FOR DEVELOPING NATIONS

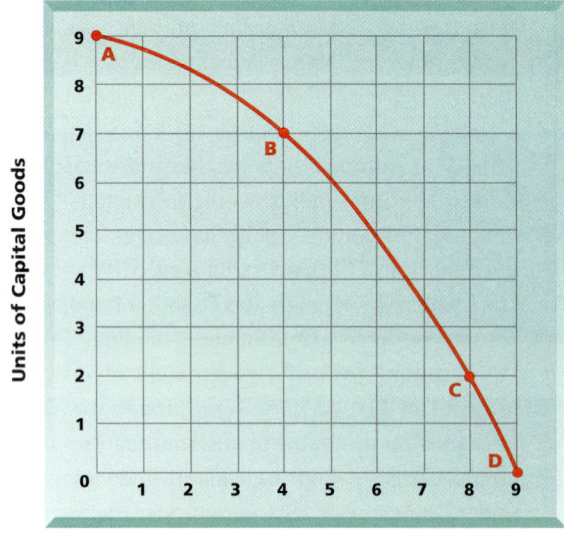

FIGURE 17.3 Production decisions involve opportunity costs and trade-offs. **What is the opportunity cost of producing eight units (point C) as opposed to four units (point B) of consumer goods?**
★TEKS

The horizontal axis shows units of consumer goods, and the vertical axis shows units of capital goods. At point A, nine units of capital goods and zero units of consumer goods are produced, meaning all resources are channeled into the production of capital goods. At point D, nine units of consumer goods and zero units of capital goods are produced, because all resources are devoted to the production of consumer goods.

Decision makers realize that all production decisions have an opportunity cost. For example, suppose a country's development plan focuses largely on the production of capital goods. At point B, seven units of capital goods and four units of consumer goods are produced. Compared to point A, two units of capital goods are given up to gain four units of consumer goods. The opportunity cost of these four units of consumer goods is two units of capital goods.

This curve is a simplified model of the trade-offs and opportunity costs involved in making production decisions. The model assumes that nations can devote all of their resources to just two types of goods—consumer or capital goods. In reality, there are other production choices—such as whether to spend money on military or nonmilitary goods and whether to invest more heavily in agricultural or in industrial capital. The graph also reflects the assumption of a constant level of resources. As a nation's resources or technology increases, the production possibilities curve shifts to the right. The shape of the curve also shows that there are increasing opportunity costs as specialization intensifies.

Expanding Production Possibilities

Developing nations can expand their production possibilities by increasing the quantity or by improving the quality of their factors of production or by improving their production technology. The successes of the "green revolution" illustrate how production possibilities can be expanded.

The green revolution is the use of pest-resistant and high-yielding hybrid seeds, as well as the application of modern technology—advanced machinery, fertilizers, irrigation systems, and pesticides—to agriculture. Since the 1960s the green revolution has expanded agricultural production in many developing nations.

Increasing the amount of land under cultivation and the number of laborers working the land also expands agricultural production. In many developing nations, most of the arable land traditionally has been owned by a small number of wealthy people. **Land reform** is the redistribution of agricultural land from a few major landowners to a larger number of the people who work the land. However, in some command economies the opposite has occurred: small plots have been combined into larger fields to make more efficient use of technology.

Financing Economic Development

To pay for economic development, developing nations rely on both domestic and international funds. Individuals' and corporate savings generally are the most important source of domestic funds. Foreign funds come from businesses and nonprofit organizations, foreign governments, as well as international development organizations.

Domestic Savings

In some developing nations, domestic savings are the major source of funding for economic development. Developing nations have undertaken infrastructure projects such as roads, railroads, dams, and schools without foreign funding, even though many people in developing nations exist at subsistence level. For example, Paraguay and Brazil have worked together to construct a hydroelectric plant. South Africa is undergoing a domestically funded reconstruction program to reduce unemployment and inequities in health care, education, and other social services. Domestic funds also helped pay for construction of Gabon's Transgabonese Railway, which links the coast with the nation's interior.

INTERNATIONAL GROWTH & STABILITY *Bolivian farmers attend an educational workshop held at an experimental farm.* ***How can improved farming techniques expand production possibilities?***

In most developing nations, domestic savings alone are insufficient to finance economic development. Therefore, many developing nations seek international capital.

International Private Capital

Several major sources of private capital are available to developing nations. Although nonprofit organizations may provide funding to developing countries, the primary sources of capital are banks—which extend loans to businesses and to governments in developing nations, and earn a profit by collecting interest payments on these loans—and businesses known as multinational corporations (MNCs).

A **multinational corporation** is a firm that owns production facilities in two or more countries and that usually markets its products worldwide. These companies generally sell a wide range of products. For example, Unilever, a Dutch-British MNC, has about 300 subsidiaries that operate in some 88 countries. In the United States alone, Unilever sells products including Lipton Tea®, Country Crock® margarine, Ben & Jerry's® ice cream, and Lever 2000® soap, as well as perfumes by designers such as Calvin Klein and Karl Lagerfeld. (See Figure 17.4 on page 418.)

Multinational corporations invest money and technology in developing nations and earn

---

Caption Answer
They help increase the quantity and quality of the crops a nation produces. 26A

Themes in Economics

OPPORTUNITY COST & TRADE-OFFS In China, memories of the terrible famine during the Great Leap Forward remain strong. As China's huge population grows—experts predict it will reach 1.5 billion by 2017—many Chinese worry about future food availability as well. Some government officials realize that to continue to feed the people of China, the nation must either increase its agricultural productivity or its imports of food.

Chinese leaders hope to avoid the latter option. They worry that if China becomes dependent on global food supplies, another famine could occur if supplies became inadequate or unavailable. In addition, dependence on food imports makes China vulnerable to foreign control through trade embargoes.

Instead, Chinese leaders want to make China self-sufficient in food production. Toward this end, they have increased research in improving soil and crop yields. Some in China disagree with this approach, however. They assert that China would benefit more by importing grain and using its own fields to grow cash crops for export. ■

DEVELOPING COUNTRIES

profits in local and international markets. The construction of new plants and the use of advanced machinery funded by MNCs in turn add to the host nation's capital goods.

Political and economic instability, however, often discourage banks and MNCs from extending credit to or investing in developing nations. Banks are careful about loaning money to nations that are already heavily in debt, while MNCs must be cautious to avoid losing capital investments in nations experiencing political turmoil. Nevertheless, banks and MNCs continue to make loans to developing nations.

CASE STUDY

Global Links

INTERNATIONAL GROWTH AND STABILITY Multinational corporations are formed in part to increase competitiveness in the global economy. MNCs work to reduce environmental, political, or cultural risks so that they can increase profits and expand their share of their markets.

In the search for higher profits and greater market share, many MNCs attempt to reduce costs. By locating production plants in developing countries, for example, MNCs typically are able to lower labor costs.

Critics of these practices argue that while multinational corporations may rely on inexpensive labor in developing countries, they take profits out of those countries. According to a report prepared by the National Interfaith Committee for Worker Justice, for example, workers in a Guess? blue jeans manufacturing plant that recently relocated to Mexico earn about 50 cents per hour. Opponents also argue that MNCs use up natural resources, interfere with local businesses, and take job opportunities away from skilled, semi-skilled, and unskilled workers in developed countries.

The supporters of multinational corporations counter these arguments by asserting that MNCs are likely to pay taxes in every country in which they do business, thereby contributing to local economies. Additionally, supporters argue, equating U.S. wages with wages in developing countries is complicated and inaccurate. While an international minimum wage is believed by some people to be necessary, others argue that it would be unfair to require an individual corporation such as Guess to pay U.S. wages in developing countries. In addition, they assert, MNCs provide jobs for people in developing countries, provide training for employees around the world, and increase the capital resources of developing nations by constructing new plants and introducing new resources technology.

International Government Sources of Capital

The governments of many developed countries have special programs to help developing nations. The money, products, and services that are extended through these programs are collectively called foreign aid. Each year the governments of developed nations supply billions of dollars through economic assistance, military

MULTINATIONAL CORPORATION: UNILEVER'S 2000 PROFITS

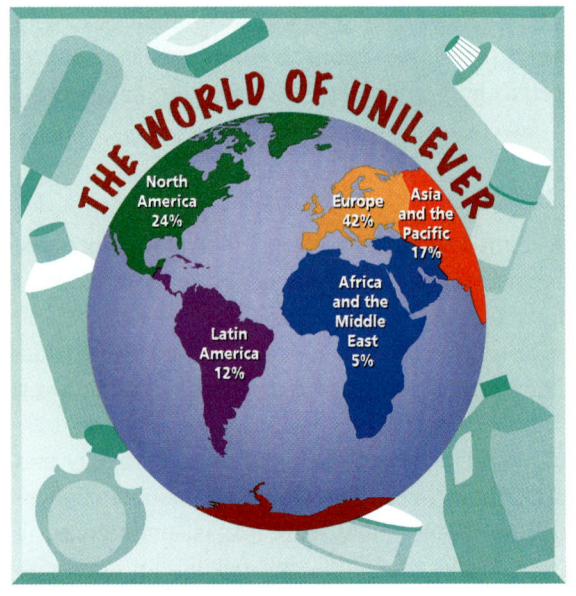

THE WORLD OF UNILEVER
- North America 24%
- Europe 42%
- Asia and the Pacific 17%
- Latin America 12%
- Africa and the Middle East 5%

Source: *Unilever Annual Review 2000*

FIGURE 17.4 Multinational companies invest money and technology in developing nations. **What is another major source of private capital for developing nations?**

OFFICIAL DEVELOPMENT ASSISTANCE FROM OECD MEMBERS, 1999

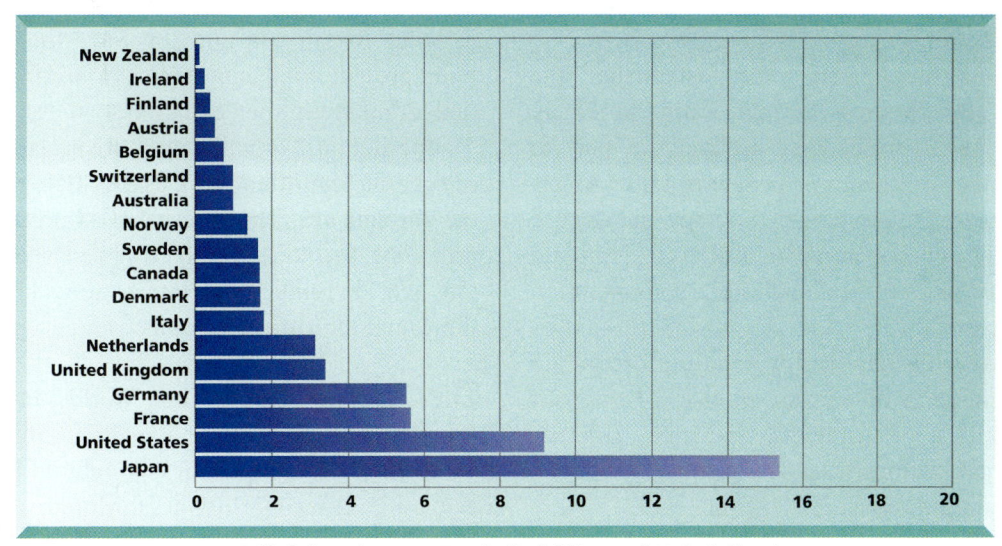

New Zealand	
Ireland	
Finland	
Austria	
Belgium	
Switzerland	
Australia	
Norway	
Sweden	
Canada	
Denmark	
Italy	
Netherlands	
United Kingdom	
Germany	
France	
United States	
Japan	

Official Assistance Totals (in billions of U.S. dollars)

Source: *World Development Indicators: 2001,* World Bank

FIGURE 17.5 The Organization for Economic Cooperation and Development extends aid to developing countries. **What are some of the reasons for extending foreign aid?**

assistance, and emergency assistance to developing nations.

Financial and technical aid, loans, and cash grants that contribute directly to economic development are all types of economic assistance. Supplying the services of specialists such as engineers, scientists, teachers, and physicians is also considered economic assistance.

Military assistance to developing nations takes the form of loans, cash payments, technical expertise, and equipment for military purposes. A developed country is most likely to extend military assistance to its allies, thus making military assistance an important part of the developed nation's foreign policy.

Finally, governments extend emergency aid—food, medical supplies, clothing, and other goods that sustain life—in times of crisis. A major portion of U.S. aid to developing countries is provided in the form of social infrastructure development, such as health care and education. Figure 17.5 shows how much money various governments extend to developing countries around the world.

Reasons for Extending Foreign Aid The United States remains one of the largest sources of foreign aid in the world, even though this aid is a small percentage of the federal budget. Like other developed nations, the United States extends foreign aid for economic, political, military, and humanitarian reasons.

Foreign aid encourages international trade. The economic and social improvements made possible through foreign aid increase the distribution of money throughout the world economy. Foreign aid also can reduce political strife that often disrupts international trade. In addition, foreign aid commonly benefits the supplier because the assisted countries tend to spend money on exports from their donors.

Developed nations sometimes grant foreign aid for political reasons because the aid promotes the donor nation's foreign policy. After World War II, for example, the United States channeled more than $13 billion in military and economic aid to like-minded European nations to stop the spread of communism. By funding economic and physical rebuilding, the Truman Doctrine and the

---

Transparency
An overhead transparency of Figure 17.5 is available in *Transparency Resources*. See Transparency 68: Official Development Assistance from OECD Members, 1999.

Caption Answer
economic, political, military, and humanitarian

Global Connections
Many U.S. citizens think that the United States earmarks a much larger percentage of its federal budget for foreign aid than it actually does. In 1999 U.S. foreign aid equaled less than 0.1 percent of GNI. Moreover, foreign aid as a percentage of GNI was less in the United States than in any other industrialized nation. Those nations with the highest foreign aid as a percentage of GNI were Denmark, Norway, the Netherlands, Sweden, Luxembourg, France, Japan, and Switzerland.

Themes in Economics
INTERNATIONAL GROWTH & STABILITY In 1999 OECD members contributed more than $56 billion in foreign aid, more than 90 percent of total foreign aid worldwide. In recent years, however, several OECD nations, including the United States, have scaled back on foreign aid.

DEVELOPING COUNTRIES

internet connect

TOPIC: Foreign Aid
GO TO: go.hrw.com
KEYWORD: SM3 EC17

Have students access the Internet through the HRW Go site to conduct research on international foreign aid. Then organize the class into pairs, and have each pair choose a development project currently supported by an organization such as the World Bank. Each pair should compile a list of the potential rewards and drawbacks of the project they have chosen. Conclude by having volunteers lead a discussion about the projects that they have analyzed. ★24D

Careers in Economics

To help students learn more about working as a Peace Corps volunteer, refer them to the Careers section on the *Researcher Online*.

Enhancing the Lesson

For more information about the IMF and the UN, see the International Organizations section on the *Researcher Online*.

Caption Answer

the World Bank, the International Monetary Fund, and the United Nations ★23A

Marshall Plan improved postwar conditions while helping support democracy and capitalism in allied nations.

In 1961 the United States established the Alliance for Progress to aid Latin American nations. The Alliance was designed in part to improve the well-being of people in Latin America and in part to promote democracy and oppose the spread of communism. Often foreign aid leads to further political and military cooperation among nations.

A final major motive for granting foreign aid is the reduction of human suffering. Nonprofit organizations, governments, and many international organizations have a humanitarian motive for providing foreign aid.

Effectiveness of Foreign Aid Foreign aid has improved the standard of living and quality of life for millions of people in developing nations. Still, experts question whether people in those nations are receiving the maximum benefit from foreign aid.

Some experts, for example, believe that closer supervision by developed nations can improve the effectiveness of aid programs. Such supervision is often strongly opposed by the people and governments of developing nations, who view it as interference with their economic freedom. Nevertheless, governments and international development organizations are now attaching specific conditions to some loans and other forms of assistance to direct the use of economic resources. See Figure 17.6 for information about the debt owed by developing nations.

International Public Sources of Capital

Agencies such as the U.S. Peace Corps—whose goal is to teach skills that increase workers' productivity—provide agriculture experts, engineers, teachers, and other specialists to developing nations. In 2000 the Peace Corps had about 7,300 volunteers working in 75 countries around the world.

Many nonprofit organizations also provide aid to developing nations. For example, the International Red Cross and the Save the Children Fund provide food and medical assistance to victims of disasters such as famines.

International organizations are a major source of funding and often serve as a vehicle to distribute foreign aid. The international organizations providing the most significant levels of aid are the World Bank, the International Monetary Fund, and the United Nations.

The World Bank The World Bank was founded at the Bretton Woods Conference in 1944. Its initial purpose was to rebuild European economies after World War II. More recently, the organization has focused on economic progress in developing nations. The World Bank Group consists of the International Bank for Reconstruction and Development (IBRD), the International Development Association (IDA), and the International Finance Corporation (IFC). In 1988 the Multilateral Investment Guarantee Agency was added to the World Bank Group. Since its founding the World Bank has lent more than $330 billion to developing countries.

The IBRD is the largest part of the World Bank and is owned by the governments of 180

INTERNATIONAL GROWTH & STABILITY *The Peace Corps sends teachers, engineers, and other specialists to developing nations.* **What international organizations provide the most aid to developing countries?**

EXTERNAL DEBT OF DEVELOPING NATIONS, 1999

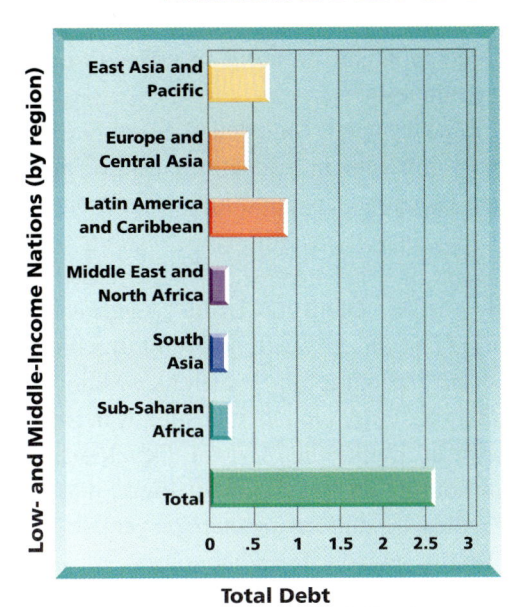

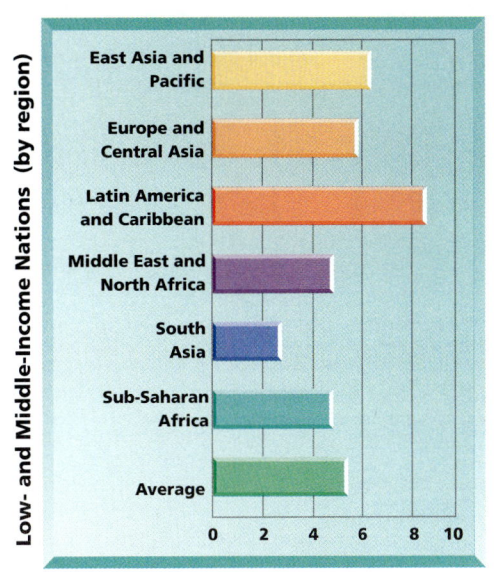

Total Debt (in trillions of U.S. dollars) — by region (Low- and Middle-Income Nations): East Asia and Pacific, Europe and Central Asia, Latin America and Caribbean, Middle East and North Africa, South Asia, Sub-Saharan Africa, Total.

External Debt Service as Percentage of GNI — by region (Low- and Middle-Income Nations): East Asia and Pacific, Europe and Central Asia, Latin America and Caribbean, Middle East and North Africa, South Asia, Sub-Saharan Africa, Average.

Source: *World Development Report: 2001*, World Bank

FIGURE 17.6 Developing nations use public and private loans to improve their economies. **Which region has the greatest external debt service as a percentage of its GNI?**

---

countries. Over the years IBRD loans have been directed at particular types of development. During the 1950s and 1960s, for example, the IBRD granted loans mainly for such internal improvements as roads, railways, and port facilities. During the 1970s the IBRD stressed loans for agricultural development. Since the 1980s loans have focused on economic reorganization rather than building projects.

The International Development Association has 162 members and makes loans only to the lowest-income developing nations. To be eligible for IDA loans, a nation's annual per capita GNI must be in the category of low-income countries.

The 175-member International Finance Corporation encourages private investment in developing nations. To achieve this goal, the IFC works closely with domestic businesses and foreign firms. IFC negotiations and advice help clear the way for direct investment by multinational corporations.

The newest member of the World Bank—the 154-member Multilateral Investment Guarantee Agency—encourages foreign investment and ensures investors protection from noncommercial risk such as war or nationalization.

International Monetary Fund The International Monetary Fund (IMF) also was founded at the 1944 Bretton Woods Conference. The IMF has made hundreds of short-term loans. For a nation to receive an IMF loan, it must introduce certain economic policies or structural reforms.

In 2000 and 2001 the IMF pledged more than $21 billion to Argentina. The aid package is designed to help Argentina pay down its external debt and restore economic growth. In exchange for the funds, Argentina's leaders agreed to increase taxes, cut spending—including wages and pensions of government workers—and introduce other financial reforms.

United Nations The United Nations (UN), established as the world's leading international peacekeeping organization in 1945, also is concerned with economic development. Most of its members are developing nations.

DEVELOPING COUNTRIES 421

Caption Answer
FAO, WHO, and UNIDO 23A

SECTION 3 REVIEW ANSWERS

1. land reform (417), multinational corporation (417) 24A

2. socialist: government can direct, and quickly redirect, resources and production toward specific economic goals, inefficiency, bureaucratic resistance to change, corruption; capitalist: freedom to make economic decisions, difficult to redirect resources and production toward economic goals 10A, 23A, 24D

3a. to promote international trade, provide economic and social improvements, reduce political strife, promote foreign policy, and reduce human suffering

3b. The curve should be downward sloping, with military goods on one axis and nonmilitary on the other, similar to the graph on page 416. 23B

4. Yes. Explanations should reflect the information provided in Section 3. 19A, 23A

INTERNATIONAL GROWTH & STABILITY *The UN promotes economic development through the United Nations Development Program which works closely with other agencies.* **Name three of these agencies.**

The UN promotes economic development through the programs of its specialized agencies. The United Nations Development Program (UNDP) coordinates its efforts with those of agencies such as the Food and Agriculture Organization (FAO), the World Health Organization (WHO), and the United Nations Industrial Development Organization (UNIDO). During the 1990s, for example, the UNDP worked with officials in El Salvador to help former civil war participants become farmers. This program provided tools and training in efficient agricultural techniques.

The UN has financed thousands of development projects in education, health, agriculture, and industry. UN funding comes from its member nations.

Regional Organizations Various regional organizations also extend credit to nations within certain geographic locations. Major regional organizations, such as the Inter-American Development Bank, the African Development Bank, and the Asian Development Bank, make loans to developing nations in their respective regions in order to improve local economies.

For example, in 2000 the African Development Bank provided some $659 million for infrastructure development in southern Africa. The program included such project categories as agriculture and rural development, communications, water supply and sanitation, transport, education, and power supply. These projects were designed to provide greater access to markets in the region.

SECTION 3 REVIEW

TEKS Q: 1, 2, 3b, 4

1. Identify and Explain:
land reform
multinational corporation

2. Comparing: Copy the chart below. Use it to list the characteristics of the capitalist and socialist decision-making models.

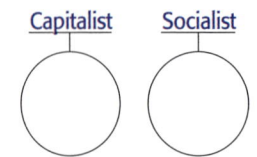

Capitalist   Socialist

3. Finding the Main Idea

a. Why do developed nations extend economic, military, and emergency assistance to other countries?

b. When nations make production choices, they make trade-offs. Draw a production possibilities curve that illustrates the trade-off between military and nonmilitary spending.

4. Writing and Critical Thinking

Finding the Main Idea: When governments, international organizations, and businesses provide foreign aid, do their actions support Adam Smith's theory that pursuing individual self-interest can benefit an entire society? Explain.

Consider the following:
• the reasons for providing foreign aid
• the global economy

Homework Practice Online
keyword: SM3 HP17

Economics IN THE NEWS

Eastern Europe in the post-Communist Era

Since the fall of communism in the Soviet bloc, the formerly communist countries of eastern and central Europe have struggled with the transition from command to free-market economies. In the years immediately following the transition to capitalism, the region went into a steep economic decline. Only recently have the region's most successful economies begun to reach the levels of economic output they had at the end of the communist era.

Russia's economy, which initially went into a steep dive, had achieved three consecutive years of stability by 2001. Nonetheless, the country's gross national product in the year 2000 was still 45 percent below its level under communist rule. More troubling is Russia's reliance on three classes of primary products—oil, gas, and metals—for 75 percent of its export income. This reliance on primary products could subject the Russian economy to the fluctuations of world-market prices. Unless Russia diversifies its export base, it will be difficult for the country to achieve sustained economic growth.

Unlike Russia, Hungary and Poland have achieved a measure of economic success. In 1999 Hungary's gross domestic product rose by 4 percent for the year and was predicted to continue rising at a comparable rate. Over 85 percent of the country's economy is privatized, and foreign investment levels had reached $21 billion by 1999. In fact the country has begun to push for membership in the European Union.

Poland also has been achieving economic growth, with a 4.1 percent rise in GNP in 2000. The country has even begun to establish an Internet economy, with Polish companies bidding for contracts over the Internet to U.S. manufacturers. However, Poland and Hungary have yet to catch up with the standards of living of neighboring western European countries.

Eastern Europe has experienced an economic boom since the fall of the Soviet Union. Economies that were once state-controlled have become more competitive and now attract overseas investors like Daewoo, a Korean car manufacturer that now has assembly operations in Poland.

The economic stagnation of much of the former Soviet bloc has surprised some economists, who expected the region's adoption of market reforms to lead to more rapid growth. Some observers believe that a cause of eastern Europe's slower-than-expected economic turnaround may lie in the failure of many countries to overhaul their legal systems. Although these countries were quick to privatize their economies and adopt other market reforms, old Soviet era economic regulations often remained in place. Scholars have argued that economic growth in a capitalist economy relies on strong legal protections of property rights.

What Do You Think?

1. Name one reason why much of eastern Europe has experienced slow economic growth.
2. What key economic reform have the region's countries implemented?

WHY IT MATTERS TODAY

Eastern Europe continues its efforts to raise its standard of living. Use **CNNfyi.com** or other **current events** sources to find the latest information on economic conditions in Eastern Europe.

CNNfyi.com

Economics in the News Answers

1. failure to implement necessary legal reforms
2. privatization

CHAPTER 17
Review Answers

Writing a Summary

Summaries should focus on the main points of each section. These may be found in the Read to Discover questions at the start of each section. Summaries should use standard grammar, spelling, sentence structure, and punctuation. **24B, 24D**

Identifying Ideas

economic development (403), developed nations (403), developing nations (403), arable (403), subsistence agriculture (405), one-crop economy (407), capital formation (408), expropriation (412), land reform (417), multinational corporation (417) **24A**

Understanding Main Ideas

1. developing—per capita GNI less than or equal to $9,265; developed—per capita GNI over $9,265
2. lack of saving, lack of private investment, rapid deterioration of existing capital
3. can limit potential for economic growth, development **5B**
4. through taxation, subsidies, and regulations **10A**

(continued on page 424)

CHAPTER 17 Review

Writing a Summary
Using standard grammar, spelling, sentence structure, and punctuation, write a summary of the information in this chapter.

Identifying Ideas
1. economic development
2. developed nations
3. developing nations
4. arable
5. subsistence agriculture
6. one-crop economy
7. capital formation
8. expropriation
9. land reform
10. multinational corporation

Understanding Main Ideas

SECTION 1 (pp. 403–06)
1. How is per capita GNI used to classify developing nations?

SECTION 2 (pp. 407–13)
2. What are developing nations' three major obstacles to capital formation?
3. Why is scarcity a problem for developing nations?

SECTION 3 (pp. 414–22)
4. How can leaders influence economic growth and development in a nation that uses the capitalist decision-making model?
5. Provide an example of each of the following: economic assistance, military assistance, and emergency assistance.

Reviewing Themes
1. **Role of Government** What are some reasons that a country might extend foreign aid?
2. **Scarcity & Choice** How can the world market affect an economy that relies on one crop for its export income?
3. **International Growth & Stability** What is a "green revolution"? How might it help a country strengthen its economy?
4. **Scarcity & Choice** How can an inadequate infrastructure affect a country's growth?

Thinking Critically
1. **Contrasting** Explain the difference between developed and developing nations. Select one of the latter and explain how it exemplifies the common characteristics of a developing country.
2. **Evaluating** How might social and cultural issues affect economic progress in developing countries?
3. **Identifying Cause & Effect** How can developing countries expand their production possibilities? What effect does this expansion have on the country's production possibilities curve?
4. **Identifying Cause & Effect** What are some obstacles to capital formation in developing countries?

Writing about Economics
Review the paragraph that you wrote in your Economics Notebook at the beginning of this chapter. How does your definition treat capital formation, economic infrastructure, and other elements of national economic development? Record your answer in your Notebook.

Sidebar

5. economic—financial and technical aid, loans, grants, supplying services of specialists; military—loans, cash, technical expertise and equipment; emergency—food, medical supplies, clothing

Reviewing Themes
1. economic, political, military, and humanitarian **23A**
2. Fluctuations in world-market prices of the crop can lead to decreased income for the country. **12A**
3. use of pest-resistant and high-yielding hybrid seeds, application of modern technology to agriculture; by expanding production possibilities in agriculture **26A**
4. by contributing to low worker productivity, hindering the country's ability to trade, and discouraging savings and investment

Thinking Critically
1. developed—high level of industrial and technical expertise, variety of economic institutions, high per capita GNI, low population growth rate; developing—limited resources or inefficient use of resources, dependency on agriculture, low per capita GNI, rapid population growth rate; examples will vary. **22A, 23A**
2. may cause people to resist changes to traditional production methods and may lead to rising expectations regarding standard of living that cannot be met; may limit opportunities **22B, 23A**
3. by increasing the quantity or improving the quality

(Continued on page 425)

424

424 CHAPTER 17

Building Social Studies Skills

Interpreting the Chart 🟊TEKS

Examine the chart below and answer the questions that follow.

Country	Pop.	GDP (2000 $)	Per Capita GDP
Belize	256,062	790 mil.	$3,200
Costa Rica	3,773,057	25 bil.	$6,700
El Salvador	6,237,662	24 bil.	$4,000
Guatemala	12,974,361	46.2 bil.	$3,700
Honduras	6,406,052	17 bil.	$2,700
Nicaragua	4,918,393	13.1 bil.	$2,700
Panama	2,845,647	16.6 bil.	$6,000

Source: CIA World Factbook 2001

1. Why might it be useful to compare the GDPs of all the countries shown in the chart?
   a. to show readers that the smallest country has the largest GDP of all the countries shown in the chart
   b. to help readers understand why all of the countries shown on the map have dictatorships
   c. because the countries for which GDP information is shown are in the same geographic region
   d. because all the countries shown are wealthy
2. Explain why per capita GDP is higher in Costa Rica than in Guatemala, even though Guatemala has a higher overall GDP.

Analyzing Primary Sources 🟊TEKS

Read the excerpt below from British economist Sir Arthur Lewis and answer the questions that follow.

"From the standpoint of economic development, one may distinguish between types of education which increase productive capacity and types which do not. Teaching an African cook to read may increase his enjoyment of life, but will not necessarily make him a better cook. Education of the former kind I have called 'investment education', while the latter kind is called consumption education'. From the standpoint of economic development, investment education has a high priority, but consumption education is on a par with [equal to] other forms of consumption."

3. Which statement best describes Lewis's point of view about educating people in poor countries?
   a. Poor countries must set priorities in funding education, with "investment education" taking priority.
   b. Poor countries must set priorities in funding education, with "consumption education" taking priority.
   c. Poor countries should fund education for all their citizens.
   d. Poor countries cannot increase their productive capacity by funding education.
4. How might Lewis characterize music education for the general population in poor countries?

Alternative Assessment

Building Your Portfolio 🟊TEKS

Imagine that you and your group are owners of a multinational corporation that is interested in opening a business in a developing country. Have members of your group conduct research on developing countries around the world. Select the economy that seems best suited for your business, and write a proposal for marketing your product. Some group member should develop an outline and text for the proposal while others create illustrations.

Internet Activity: go.hrw.com
KEYWORD: SM3 EC17 🟊TEKS

Access the Internet through the HRW Go site to conduct research on the history and goals of the Peace Corps. Then imagine that you are a Peace Corps applicant. Write a letter to a Peace Corps recruiter to explain why you would like to join the Peace Corps, your qualifications, and the type of work you would like do if you were accepted by the organization.

---

of their factors of production, or by improving their production technology; the curve shifts to the right 5B, 23F

4. a lack of savings, a lack of private investment, and the rapid deterioration of existing capital 23A

Writing about Economics

Students should review and revise their definition of "personal economic development" in terms of capital formation, economic infrastructure, and other elements of national economic development presented in the chapter.

Building Social Studies Skills

1. c 23F
2. Guatemala's population is much larger. 23F
3. a 23E
4. as consumption education 23E

CHAPTER RESOURCE MANAGER

CHAPTER 18 INTERNATIONAL TRADE

	OBJECTIVES	PACING GUIDE	REPRODUCIBLE RESOURCES
SECTION 1 **Specialization and Interdependence** (pp. 427–30)	▸ How does specialization encourage trade? ▸ How can absolute advantages influence economic choices? ▸ How can comparative advantages affect a nation's economy?	**Regular** 1.5 days **Block Scheduling** 1 day	**ELL** Spanish Study Guide 18.1 **ELL** English Study Guide 18.1
SECTION 2 **Foreign Exchange and Currencies** (pp. 431–38)	▸ Why are foreign exchange rates necessary? ▸ How does a nation determine its balance of payments? ▸ What is the significance of the balance of trade?	**Regular** 1.5 days **Block Scheduling** 1 day	**ELL** Spanish Study Guide 18.2 **ELL** English Study Guide 18.2 **SM** Mathematics for Economics: Activity 18
SECTION 3 **Cooperation and Trade Barriers** (pp. 439–46)	▸ Why do nations impose trade barriers? ▸ What are the key arguments made in favor of free trade? ▸ What types of agreements indicate that nations are following a policy of cooperation?	**Regular** 1.5 days **Block Scheduling** 1 day	**ELL** Spanish Study Guide 18.3 **ELL** English Study Guide 18.3 **PS** Reading 13: Open-Door Policy in China **S** Simulations and Strategies for Teaching Economics: Activity 18 **E** Challenge and Enrichment: Activity 18 **SM** Consumer Economics: Activity 18

Chapter Resource Key

- **PS** Primary Sources
- **RS** Reading Support
- **E** Enrichment
- **S** Simulations
- **SM** Skills Mastery

- **A** Assessment
- **REV** Review
- **ELL** Reinforcement and English Language Learners
- Transparencies
- CD-ROM

- Video
- Videodisc
- Internet
- Holt Presentation Maker Using Microsoft® PowerPoint®
- TEKS and TAKS

TECHNOLOGY RESOURCES	REINFORCEMENT, REVIEW, AND ASSESSMENT
• One-Stop Planner: Lesson 18.1 • Researcher Online • Homework Practice Online • CNN Presents Economics: Launching the Euro • Global Skillbuilder CD-ROM	REV Section 1 Review, p. 430 A Daily Quiz 18.1 ★ TAKS Every Day!
• One-Stop Planner: Lesson 18.2 • Researcher Online • Homework Practice Online • Transparencies 70–73 • Global Skillbuilder CD-ROM	REV Section 2 Review, p. 438 A Daily Quiz 18.2 ★ TAKS Every Day!
• One-Stop Planner: Lesson 18.3 • Researcher Online • Homework Practice Online • Transparencies 74 and 75 • Global Skillbuilder CD-ROM	REV Section 3 Review, p. 446 A Daily Quiz 18.3 ★ TAKS Every Day!

Chapter Review and Assessment

SM Global Skillbuilder CD-ROM
• HRW Go site
REV Reteaching Activity 18
REV Chapter 18 Review, pp. 448–49
A Chapter 18 Test Generator (on the One-Stop Planner)
A Chapter 18 Test
A Alternative Assessment Handbook

One-Stop Planner CD–ROM

It's easy to plan lessons, select resources, and print out materials for your students when you use the *Texas One-Stop Planner CD-ROM with Test Generator.*

---

internet connect

HRW ONLINE RESOURCES
Go To: go.hrw.com
Then type in a keyword.

TEACHER HOME PAGE
KEYWORD: SM3 Teacher

CHAPTER INTERNET ACTIVITIES
KEYWORD: SM3 EC18
▸ research NAFTA and the WTO.
▸ learn about foreign exchange.
▸ research the IMF.

CHAPTER ENRICHMENT LINKS
KEYWORD: SM3 CH18

HOLT RESEARCHER ONLINE
KEYWORD: Holt Researcher

ONLINE ASSESSMENT
Homework Practice
KEYWORD: SM3 HP18
TAKS Review
KEYWORD: SM3 T18
Rubrics
KEYWORD: SS Rubrics

CONTENT UPDATES
KEYWORD: SS Content Updates

HOLT PRESENTATION MAKER
KEYWORD: SM3 PPT18

ONLINE READING SUPPORT
KEYWORD: SS Strategies

CURRENT EVENTS
KEYWORD: S3 Current Events

TEXAS ONLINE RESOURCES
KEYWORD: S3 TX

LESSON 18.1 SPECIALIZATION AND INTERDEPENDENCE

TEXTBOOK PAGES 427–30

HOLT PRESENTATION MAKER Access Illustrated LECTURE NOTES using Microsoft® PowerPoint® on the One-Stop Planner CD-ROM

OBJECTIVES

- Explain how specialization encourages trade.
- Explain how absolute advantages can influence economic choices.
- Explain how comparative advantages can affect a nation's economy.

MOTIVATE

The day before you plan to start the lesson, point out to students that many items that they use everyday are produced in other countries. Tell students to make a list of at least 10 products they use during one day, to note where each is made, and to bring the list to class to discuss it. In addition, have students read Section 1 of the chapter.

Place the following two headings on the chalkboard or on an overhead transparency: *U.S.–Made Products* and *Foreign-Made Products*. As students read off the items on their lists, write each item in the appropriate column. Point out that many items have components made in the United States as well as some that are made elsewhere and imported. For example, plastics and some cosmetics are petroleum-based products, and the United States imports a majority of its petroleum. Ask students how a complete absence of imported products would affect their lives. As students respond, help them realize the importance of international trade to the overall U.S. standard of living.

TEACH

Building a Vocabulary

Have students use spiral notebooks to create an Economics Dictionary to be used throughout the chapter. This dictionary might be used as an activity at the start of each new section or as a learning aid for sheltered English students or students having difficulty. List words that students will be expected to know for this section on the chalkboard. Have students use the information provided in the text or on the *Researcher CD-ROM* to list, define, and give an example of each term.

Understanding Main Concepts

Review with students the concepts of specialization and economic interdependence that they learned about in Chapter 1. Ask students whether they think that a nation today can be self-sufficient. *(Most students will respond no.)* Next, ask students to explain how the distribution of the factors of production throughout the world encourages nations to specialize and trade. *(The factors of production are not distributed equally throughout the world, so nations are motivated to trade to improve their citizens' standard of living.)* Then ask students to explain how specialization and international trade benefit nations. *(Without international trade, a nation's people can consume only the goods and services that nation produces. With international trade, a nation can specialize in those goods and services it produces the most efficiently and then trade them for whatever products the nation does not produce efficiently or cannot produce at all.)* ★12A

Hypothesizing, Writing About Economics

Ask students to define the concept of absolute advantage. *(A nation has an absolute advantage at producing a good or service when it can do so more cheaply and more efficiently than the nations with which it trades.)* Next, ask students what absolute advantage they and the other students taking economics in their school probably have over their schoolmates who are not taking economics *(a knowledge of economics)*. Next, have students name some of the products in which they think the United States probably has an absolute advantage. Students should use their knowledge of the geography and climate of the United States, the resources it has in abundance, its leading industries, and the skills of its labor force to formulate their answers. Then tell students to write one or two paragraphs explaining how absolute advantages can influence a nation's economic choices. ★13A

Analyzing Information

Tell students to imagine that they are skilled at a number of tasks, such as gardening, building, sewing, and computer programming. Then ask students whether they would grow all their food, make all their furniture, sew all their clothes, and do all their programming themselves, or whether they instead might specialize in just one of these tasks, such as programming, and then use the money they earn to buy food, furniture, and clothes from others who have specialized in producing those items. *(Most students will respond that they would specialize in one task.)* Then ask students how they would choose which task to specialize in. *(Most students will respond that they would choose the task that they do best, that they enjoy doing the most, and that pays the most money.)*

Then explain to students that nations also specialize in those products that they make the most efficiently and that are the most profitable. Ask students to name the economic concept that describes how nations choose which products to specialize in and the name of the economist who introduced this theory *(comparative advantage; David Ricardo)*. Call on a student to define comparative advantage *(the ability of a nation to produce a certain good or service more cheaply and more efficiently than any other good or service that it produces)*. ★13A

Mastering Concepts, Using Graphs and Models

To illustrate the example provided in Section 1 of the chapter, draw two production possibilities curves on the chalkboard, one for Costa Rica and one for Panama. On each graph, label the vertical axis *coffee (millions of lbs.)*, and the horizontal axis *bananas (millions of lbs.)*. On the vertical axis, make five tick marks and label them, from bottom to top, *5, 10, 15, 20,* and *25*. On the horizontal axis, make five tick marks and label them, from left to right, *1, 2, 3, 4,* and *5*. On the graph for Costa Rica, draw a straight line from the 25 on the vertical axis to the 5 on the horizontal axis. On the graph for Panama, draw a straight line from the midpoint between the 10 and 15 on the vertical axis to the 4 on the horizontal axis.

Review with students the use of production possibilities curves as models (covered in Chapter 1, Section 4). Then have students determine the opportunity cost for each country of producing only coffee *(Costa Rica—one pound of bananas for every five pounds of coffee; Panama—one pound of bananas for every three pounds of coffee)*. Next, have students determine the opportunity cost of producing only bananas *(Costa Rica—five pounds of coffee for every pound of bananas; Panama—three pounds of coffee for every pound of bananas)*. Explain that Costa Rica has the lower opportunity cost for producing coffee, so it has the comparative advantage in that product. Panama has the lower opportunity cost for producing bananas, so it has the comparative advantage there.

Next, have students explain how if Costa Rica specializes in the production of coffee and Panama in the production of bananas, and both countries trade at a rate of four pounds of coffee to one pound of bananas, both countries' production possibilities frontiers would expand. Have volunteers come up to the chalkboard and draw a new line on each graph representing the new trade ratio of 4:1 *(Costa Rica—a line from 25 on the vertical axis to 6.25 on the horizontal axis; Panama—a line from 16 on the vertical axis to 4 on the horizontal axis)*. Refer students who need additional instruction on the skills used in this activity to the *Global Skillbuilder* Lesson 10: Reading Graphs and Lesson 11: Presenting Data Graphically. ★23F

CLOSE

Have students discuss how absolute advantage, comparative advantage, specialization, and international trade can affect and benefit a nation's economy and standard of living. ★13B, 23A

OPTIONS

Interpersonal Learners

Organize students into groups of four. Write the following scenario on the chalkboard: The United States can produce 20 million units of wheat or 10 million units of textiles with all of its resources. Great Britain can produce 12 million units of wheat or 12 million units of textiles with all of its resources. Have each group determine where each nation's comparative advantage lies, determine a trade ratio that would be advantageous for both nations, and draw production possibilities curves for each nation that show the production possibilities before and after trade. Students may want to use the Graphing Tool on the *Researcher Online* to create their graphs. Review the activity when groups are finished. ★23B

Linguistic Learners

Have students research and write a biography of economist David Ricardo. Students should describe Ricardo's main influences and his most important contributions to economics. Students can use the library, the Internet, and other resources to conduct their research. Students may want to include their biographies in their portfolios. ★24B, 24D

REVIEW

Have students complete the Section 1 Review on page 430. Use the answers in the Annotated Teacher's Edition to assess student mastery of this section.

ASSESS

To assess student mastery of this section, have students complete Daily Quiz 18.1 in *Daily Quizzes with Answer Key*. For additional assessment options, see *Alternative Assessment Handbook* on the *One-Stop Planner CD-ROM*.

ADDITIONAL RESOURCES

Ricardo, David. *Principles of Political Economy and Taxation.* 1817 Great Minds Series. 1996. Prometheus Books.

Free Trade. (videotape, 28 min.) Films for the Humanities and Sciences.

Inside the Global Economy. (13 one-hour videotape programs; topics include trade, fixed versus floating exchange rates, and protectionism versus free trade). The Annenberg/CPB Projects.

The Production Possibilities Frontier. (videotape, 60 min.). Macroeconomics Series. Projected Learning Programs Inc.

LESSON 18.2 — FOREIGN EXCHANGE AND CURRENCIES

TEXTBOOK PAGES 431–38

HOLT PRESENTATION MAKER — Access Illustrated LECTURE NOTES using Microsoft® PowerPoint® on the One-Stop Planner CD-ROM

OBJECTIVES

- Explain why foreign exchange rates are necessary.
- Describe how a nation determines its balance of payments.
- Explain the significance of the balance of trade.

MOTIVATE

Ask students to name some different types of foreign currency, such as British pounds, Japanese yen, or the euro. Then tell students that nations, like tourists, must be able to exchange their currency for the currencies of other nations to participate in foreign trade. Ask students to speculate about how nations determine exchange rates for their currency. For example, how does Japan determine how many U.S. dollars one yen is worth? Have students write down their ideas in their notes. Then tell students that in this section they will learn how nations set foreign exchange rates and determine their balance of payments.

TEACH

Building a Vocabulary

List the important terms for this section on the chalkboard and tell students to add them to their Economics Dictionary. Tell students to use the information provided in the text or on the *Researcher CD-ROM* to list, define, and give an example of each vocabulary term.

Understanding Main Concepts

Review with students why foreign exchange rates are necessary. *(To participate in international trade, nations must have a way of determining the values of their currencies in relation to one another.)* Then ask students in what two ways foreign exchange rates are expressed in the United States *(in the U.S. dollar value for each unit of foreign currency; in the number of units of another nation's currency that equals one dollar).*

Acquiring Information, Demonstrating Understanding

Give each student a copy of a list of current currency exchange rates (these are usually provided in the business sections of newspapers) or have students look up a site on the Internet that provides this information. The OANDA 164 Currency Converter site on the World Wide Web provides current and historical exchange rates for 164 currencies (http://www.oanda.com/cgi-bin/ncc). Have students work together to find the current exchange rates for a number of countries, such as Germany, Japan, France, Italy, Russia, Canada, and Mexico. Students should express exchange rates by using both methods employed in the United States. ★13D

Comparing and Contrasting

Next, explain to students that nations have used two different systems since World War II for setting foreign exchange rates—the adjustable-peg system and the floating exchange rates system. Have students define the adjustable-peg system of setting foreign exchange rates and explain the problems that existed with this system. Then have them define the method of floating exchange rates, compare and contrast this method to the adjustable-peg system, and explain how floating exchange rates solved the problems of the adjustable-peg system. Make certain that students understand each system of setting exchange rates and the economic concepts of devaluation and appreciation. ★23A

Analyzing and Evaluating Information

Organize students into groups of three or four. Tell each group to list the pros and cons of having a strong U.S. dollar and of having a weak U.S. dollar. Students should also indicate how various groups, such as exporters and consumers, are affected in each case. When groups are finished, have them share their answers with the class. Discuss students' answers and make a list on the chalkboard of the correct information. ★13D, 23A

Organizing Information

Have students explain how each nation determines the amount of the payments and receipts being transferred annually between its residents, businesses, and governments and other nations' residents, businesses, and governments *(by determining its balance of payments).* Have students help you create a chart that illustrates the balance of payments that form the current account and those that form the capital account. Explain that a nation's total expenditures in other nations rarely balances exactly with its total receipts from other nations.

Using Charts, Hypothesizing

Then tell students that the balance of trade has historically been the most important factor in determining a nation's overall balance of payments. Ask students how a nation determines its balance of trade *(by calculating the difference between its imported and exported products).* Then ask students to define a trade surplus and a trade deficit *(surplus—exports more than it imports; deficit—imports more than it exports).*

Have students examine Figure 18.4: U.S. Trade Balance, 1970–1999 (Transparency 72). Ask students to identify the two years since 1970 in which the United States had the largest trade deficits *(1998 and 1999).* Have students explain the factors that have contributed to the ongoing U.S. trade deficits. Next, have students use a *Statistical Abstract of the United States* or the Internet to find out whether the United States had a trade surplus or a trade deficit in the most recent year for which data is available. Ask students what factors may have contributed to this surplus or deficit. Encourage class discussion. ⭐13C

Conducting Research

Have students examine Figure 18.2: U.S. International Trade (in billions of U.S. dollars), 1997 (Transparency 70). Discuss the information in the chart. Then organize students into groups of four or five. Assign each group one of the nations with which the United States trades to research in depth. Students might use the *Researcher Online,* the library, in-class resources, and the Internet to conduct their research. Have each group prepare a presentation addressing the following questions:
- What products does the United States import from this country?
- What products does the United States export to this country?
- What social, political, cultural, and economic factors influence trade between the United States and this country?

Have each group deliver its presentation to the class. Then have students discuss the various international trade problems that the United States faces with different nations. ⭐13C, 24D

CLOSE

Review with students the material covered in the lesson. Then call on students to summarize the role of foreign exchange markets and the significance of a nation's balance of payments and balance of trade.
⭐13D, 23A

OPTIONS

Gifted Learners

Have interested students research the balance of trade in another nation, such as Canada, Japan, or Mexico. Students should create maps and charts similar to those in Figures 18.2, 18.3, 18.4, and 18.5 to illustrate the nation's main trading partners, its balance of trade over time, the main products that the nation imports and exports, and its inward and outward foreign direct investment. Students might use the *Researcher Online,* the library, in-class resources, and the Internet to conduct their research. Have each student organize the information into an international trade report such as might be prepared by a government agency concerned with international trade. Students may want to include their reports in their portfolios. ⭐23F, 24D

Interpersonal Learners

Organize students into groups of four or five. Tell each group that it is preparing a whirlwind tour of Europe, Asia, or Africa. Have groups select three countries that they would like to visit in their region, find out the currency and the current exchange rate for each country, and then find out the current price of one item that they would like to buy in each country and determine how much that item will cost in U.S. dollars. Students might use the *Researcher Online,* the library, the Internet, business sections from current newspapers, travel agencies, and other sources to obtain information. Tell the groups to present their information in a travel itinerary. Have each group share its itinerary with the class. ⭐24D

REVIEW

Have students complete the Section 2 Review on page 438. Use the answers in the Annotated Teacher's Edition to assess student mastery of this section.

ASSESS

To assess student mastery of this section, have students complete Daily Quiz 18.2 in *Daily Quizzes with Answer Key.* For additional assessment options, see *Alternative Assessment Handbook* on the *One-Stop Planner CD-ROM.*

ADDITIONAL RESOURCES

Preeg, Ernest H. *The Trade Deficit, the Dollar, and the U.S. National Interest.* 2000. Hudson Institute.

Rangan, S., and R. Z. Lawrence. *A Prism on Globalization: Corporate Responses to the Dollar.* 1999. Brookings Institution Press.

Economics U$A: Exchange Rates. No. 28. (videotape, 30 min.). The Annenberg/CPB Projects.

LESSON 18.3 COOPERATION AND TRADE BARRIERS

TEXTBOOK PAGES 439–46

HOLT PRESENTATION MAKER Access Illustrated LECTURE NOTES using Microsoft® PowerPoint® on the One-Stop Planner CD-ROM

OBJECTIVES

- Explain why nations impose trade barriers.
- Describe the key arguments made in favor of free trade.
- Describe the types of agreements that indicate that nations are following a policy of cooperation.

MOTIVATE

Ask students to think of some ways that the United States might deal with a high trade deficit, increased foreign competition in specific industries, or a nation that is acting in some way of which the United States disapproves. Guide students' responses to consider different types of barriers against trade, such as tariffs, import quotas, and trade embargoes. Then have students read Section 3 of the chapter.

TEACH

Building a Vocabulary

List the important terms for this section on the chalkboard and tell students to add them to their Economics Dictionary. Tell students to use the information provided in the text or on the *Researcher CD-ROM* to list, define, and give an example of each vocabulary term.

Understanding Main Concepts, Identifying Cause and Effect

Review with students the trade barriers discussed in Section 3 of the chapter—tariffs, import quotas, voluntary trade restrictions, embargoes, and other types of trade barriers. Have students define and describe each type of trade barrier. Then ask students how each type of trade barrier affects the price, supply, and demand of imported products. You might use a supply and demand curve to indicate the equilibrium price for a particular product to help students visualize the effects of different types of trade barriers. ★14A

Recognizing Point of View, Synthesizing Information

Have students discuss the reasons the United States and other nations impose different types of trade barriers and explain what they hope to achieve from them. Review with students the terms *free trade* and *protectionism*. Then have students summarize the key arguments used by protectionists in favor of trade barriers and by supporters of free trade against trade barriers. Make a chart of these arguments on the chalkboard or on an overhead transparency and have students copy the chart into their notes.

Organize students into seven groups. Have each group take the point of view of a particular group in the economy. Each group should represent one of the following: labor unions, consumers, exporters, importers, owners of multinational corporations, owners of successful domestic businesses, and owners of domestic businesses in an industry facing stiff competition from foreign firms. Instruct each group to determine its point of view toward trade barriers. The groups should examine how trade barriers affect them and then formulate arguments in favor of or against different types of protectionist legislation. Tell each group to write a summary of its arguments supporting or opposing trade barriers. Have a representative from each group read the group's summary to the class. Encourage students to provide feedback. ★14A, 23D, 24D

Debating Ideas, Demonstrating Understanding

To extend the previous activity, have each group select one representative to serve on a panel that will debate trade barriers, protectionism, and free trade. Have students, in their roles, debate these issues. You might also want to present panel members with one or more particular issues to debate, such as the passage of a specific tariff, import quota, voluntary trade restriction, or embargo. When students are finished with the activity, discuss the debate as a class. ★14A, 23D

Analyzing Information, Drawing Conclusions

Explain to students that a government's trade policy rarely is completely protectionist or completely based on free trade, but is usually a combination of the two. Have students describe some of the factors that influence U.S. trade policies. *(Students might mention a variety of international and domestic factors related to the U.S. economy and politics.)* Then ask students what other methods nations use besides trade barriers to improve and regulate international trade *(trade cooperation, such as reciprocal trade agreements, regional trade organizations, and international trade agreements)*. Have students describe and provide some examples of each of these types of trade cooperation. Then write the words *Advantages* and *Disadvantages* on the chalkboard or on an overhead transparency. Have students discuss what they think might be some of the advantages and disadvantages of each type of trade cooperation, and list each under the appropriate heading. ★14B

Conducting Research, Organizing Information

To extend the previous activity, organize students into groups of four or five. Have each group research a trade agreement or a regional trade organization and prepare a fact sheet on it. Students might use the *Researcher Online*, the library, in-class resources, and the Internet to conduct their research. Have groups read their fact sheets to the class. ★23A

CLOSE

Have students summarize the advantages and disadvantages of trade barriers and trade cooperation. Then ask students to discuss whether they support free trade or protectionism. For an optional homework assignment, students might write a one- to two-page essay stating why they support free trade or protectionism. ★23A, 23D, 24D

OPTIONS

Gifted Learners

Have interested students research the effects of the North American Free Trade Agreement (NAFTA) on international trade and the U.S. economy. Students might use the *Researcher Online*, the library, newspapers and business magazines, the Internet, and other sources to conduct their research. Have students present their findings in a written report. Students may want to include their reports in their portfolios. ★14B, 23A, 24D

Interpersonal Learners

Invite a representative of a U.S. firm that is involved in international trade to visit the class to discuss his or her experience in international markets. If possible, find out beforehand what the speaker will be discussing and have students prepare some relevant questions to ask following the discussion. Have each student write a summary of the speaker's presentation and what he or she learned from it. ★23A

Linguistic Learners

Have students complete Reading 13: Open-Door Policy in China, located in *From the Source: Readings in Economics and Government with Answer Key*. Discuss the reading and its accompanying questions as a class. Then have students write an essay stating what they think the implications of this policy were for the United States and China. When students have finished, have a volunteer read his or her essay to the class. Provide feedback and encourage students to provide feedback as well. Students may want to include their essays in their portfolios. ★23A, 24D

Logical-Mathematical Learners, Visual-Spatial Learners

Organize students into groups of four or five. Assign each group a period of U.S. history. Tell each group to construct a time line showing major U.S. trade legislation passed during that period. Students should also include major events and conflicts as points of reference. Have groups display their time lines around the classroom. Refer students who need additional instruction on the skills used in this activity to the *Global Skillbuilder* Lesson 9: Using Time Lines. ★23A, 24C

Visual-Spatial Learners

Have students draw a political cartoon or comic strip in favor of either protectionism or free trade. Encourage students to examine several newspapers and business magazines to find a current issue on which to base their cartoon. Display students' cartoons around the class. Students may want to include their cartoons in their portfolios. ★24D

REVIEW

Have students complete the Section 3 Review on page 446. Use the answers in the Annotated Teacher's Edition to assess student mastery of this section.

ASSESS

To assess student mastery of this section, have students complete Daily Quiz 18.3 in *Daily Quizzes with Answer Key*. For additional assessment options, see *Alternative Assessment Handbook* on the *One-Stop Planner CD-ROM*.

RETEACH

For students having difficulty with the lessons, have them complete Reteaching Activity 18. This activity is located in *Reteaching Activities with Answer Key*.

ADDITIONAL RESOURCES

Irwin, Douglas A. *Against the Tide: An Intellectual History of Free Trade*. 1997. Princeton University Press.

MacArthur, John R., Jr. *The Selling of "Free Trade": NAFTA, Washington, and the Subversion of American Democracy*. 2000. Hill and Wang.

Roberts, Russel D. *The Choice: A Fable of Free Trade and Protectionism*. 2000. Prentice Hall.

Economics USA: International Trade. No. 27. (videotape, 30 min.). The Annenberg/CPB Projects.

CHAPTER 18

TOPICS INCLUDE

- specialization and trade
- absolute and comparative advantage
- foreign exchange rates
- adjustable-peg system
- currency devaluation and appreciation
- floating exchange rates
- foreign exchange markets
- balance of payments and trade
- trade surpluses and trade deficits
- foreign direct investment
- trade barriers
- free trade versus protectionism
- trade agreements and organizations
- multinational corporations and joint ventures

ECONOMICS NOTEBOOK

The Economics Notebook is a journal activity that encourages students to consider basic concepts of economics that relate to their lives. A follow-up notebook activity appears on page 448.

WHY IT MATTERS TODAY

To find additional lesson plans dealing with international trade, visit CNNfyi.com or have students complete the ECONOMICS IN THE NEWS activity on page 447.
CNNfyi.com

CHAPTER 18

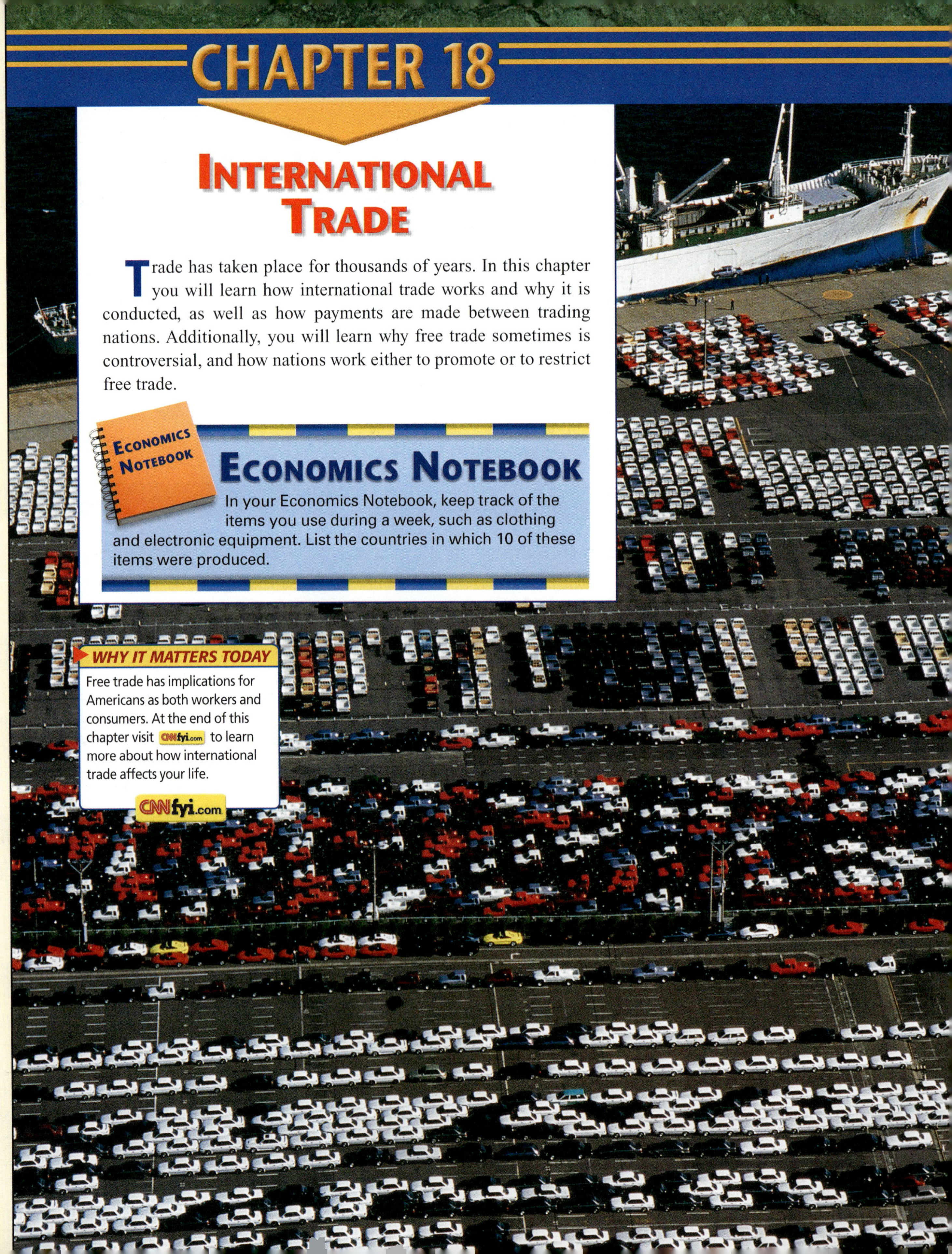

INTERNATIONAL TRADE

Trade has taken place for thousands of years. In this chapter you will learn how international trade works and why it is conducted, as well as how payments are made between trading nations. Additionally, you will learn why free trade sometimes is controversial, and how nations work either to promote or to restrict free trade.

ECONOMICS NOTEBOOK

In your Economics Notebook, keep track of the items you use during a week, such as clothing and electronic equipment. List the countries in which 10 of these items were produced.

WHY IT MATTERS TODAY

Free trade has implications for Americans as both workers and consumers. At the end of this chapter visit CNNfyi.com to learn more about how international trade affects your life.

426

SECTION 1

SPECIALIZATION AND INTERDEPENDENCE

READ TO DISCOVER
1. How does specialization encourage trade?
2. How can absolute advantages influence economic choices?
3. How can comparative advantages affect a nation's economy?

ECONOMICS DICTIONARY
absolute advantage
comparative advantage

Why do nations participate in international trade? International trade is characterized by two features. First, it is selective. Nations choose which resources and products they will trade. Second, it creates wealth. Nations pursue trade in order to increase their wealth in terms of goods, services, or resources.

Specialization and Trade

Specialization and economic interdependence serve as the basis for international trade. As noted in Chapter 1, specialization occurs when producers provide a limited number of goods or services. Such specialization may occur because of a nation's particular resources. For example, much of the world's coffee comes from nations in Central and South America, while countries such as Switzerland—which do not have a climate appropriate for coffee production—must import all their coffee.

Without international trade, a nation can consume only the goods and services it produces. The development of international trade enables a nation to specialize in the production of goods and services that can be traded for other products. Specialization offers a nation the opportunity to become efficient in the production of a few goods and services and to trade them for whatever goods and services that nation cannot supply to its people.

CASE STUDY

The European Union

INTERNATIONAL GROWTH & STABILITY In the early 1990s many Europeans feared that the elimination of trade barriers among European nations would lead to a single European economy and society. Instead of creating a group of distinct nations each with its own language and customs, these people argued, free trade would blur populations—and eventually cultures.

So far, these fears have not materialized. Economists have instead noted increasing specialization based on traditional centers of production. For example, before the European Union (EU) was established, Carrara, Italy, was a marble-carving center for centuries, even long after its quarries were depleted. After the EU was formed, Carrara's carving industry was not challenged by new marble-carving centers. In fact, Carrara remains among the leading marble-carving centers in Europe despite the fact that lowered trade barriers also allow marble to be imported to Naples, Marseilles, or any other location in Europe.

Similarly, moviemakers in Spain have tried to establish a film animation industry in the city of Seville. Film animators continue to flock to London's Soho district, however, where artists and filmmakers have centered their activity for years.

This continued specialization encourages interdependence among European nations. Limited natural, human, capital, and entrepreneurial resources force cities and nations to make choices that result in specialization and interdependence. Simplified trade requirements have not led, for example, to pork production centers all over Europe, but have eased the process of shipping hams and bacon from Denmark to other countries.

SECTION 1

SPECIALIZATION AND INTERDEPENDENCE

Lesson Plans
For teaching strategies, see Lesson 18.1 located at the beginning of this chapter or the One-Stop Planner Strategy 18.1.

Economics Dictionary
To reinforce the section's vocabulary terms, refer students to the Electronic Glossary on the *Researcher CD-ROM*.

Section Assessment
To assess students' mastery of this section, have them complete Daily Quiz 18.1 in *Daily Quizzes with Answer Key*.

★ TEKS

Content
12A, 13A, 13B
Social Studies Skills
23A, 23B, 23F, 24A, 24B, 24D

Caption Answer

by determining where its greatest absolute advantage occurs ★13A

Themes in Economics

INTERNATIONAL TRADE Some people fear that the growing availability of cheap foreign labor means fewer jobs, lower wages, and a lower standard of living for U.S. workers in the future. Comparative advantage helps explain the fallacy of this reasoning. Many developing countries with lower wages and plentiful labor also have lower productivity and fewer highly skilled and educated workers. These nations tend to have a comparative advantage in low-skilled, labor-intensive industries. Highly industrialized nations tend to have a comparative advantage in knowledge-intensive, high-tech industries. Although some low-skilled, manufacturing jobs in the United States are being lost to cheap foreign labor, new knowledge-intensive, high-tech jobs are replacing these jobs.

Even as productivity and skills improve in developing nations, the costs, quality, and availability of the factors of production will continue to vary by nation, and within nations, by industry. Consequently, nations will continue to specialize and trade, and to see overall improvements in their standards of living as a result. ■

428

Absolute and Comparative Advantage

The factors of production—natural, human, capital, and entrepreneurial resources—are not distributed equally throughout the world. This uneven resource distribution encourages nations to trade in order to improve their citizens' standard of living. For example, Japan has very limited oil reserves. To acquire oil, it must produce other goods and services that can be traded. How a nation decides what to produce is determined by two related economic concepts originally described by the nineteenth-century British political economist David Ricardo—absolute advantage and comparative advantage.

Absolute Advantage A nation has an **absolute advantage** in producing a certain good when it can do so with greater efficiency than can its partner in trade. For example, if Costa Rica and Panama both produce coffee, cocoa, and lumber, and Costa Rica can produce each at a lower cost, then it would be correct to say that Costa Rica holds an absolute advantage over Panama for these items. Similarly, if an attorney can type 120 words per minute while her secretary, who is not an attorney and has no training in the law, can type only 100 words per minute, then it would be correct to say that the attorney has an absolute advantage in both practicing law and typing.

Comparative Advantage The existence of an absolute advantage does not mean that the nation with the absolute advantage will produce everything while the other nation will produce no goods and services at all. The particular items each produces will be determined by identifying its comparative advantage. The **comparative advantage** may be found by determining where the greatest absolute advantage occurs for each nation.

Consider again the attorney and her secretary. While the attorney is absolutely more productive in both practicing law and in typing, the greatest advantage is in practicing law. The secretary may

INTERNATIONAL TRADE *A nation decides what to produce—bananas, for instance—by determining its absolute and its comparative advantages.* **How is a nation's comparative advantage determined?** ⊙TEKS

not know anything about practicing law, but may be quite skilled at typing. Therefore, the attorney has the comparative advantage in practicing law. On this basis the attorney would be wise to practice law and let her secretary handle the typing. Comparative advantage thus determines how individuals specialize.

In the same manner, comparative advantage influences specialization on a national level. The key to comparative advantage is the concept of trade-offs. As noted in Chapter 1, trade-offs are the items sacrificed, or not selected, when production choices are made. Suppose that if Costa Rica devoted all its resources to producing coffee it could produce 25 million pounds per year, and if it devoted all its resources to growing bananas it could produce 5 million pounds per year. In terms of resources, Costa Rica thus would be producing five pounds of coffee for every pound of bananas. The pound of bananas would be the trade-off for the five pounds of coffee. Costa Rica's exchange ratio between coffee and bananas would be 5:1.

428 CHAPTER 18

CAREERS IN ECONOMICS

Customs Inspector

Each year nearly a half billion people and billions of dollars of products enter the United States through any one of the country's 300 air, sea, and land ports of entry. The U.S. Customs Service oversees this enormous flow of people and products. Some 19,000 Customs Service employees enforce travel and immigration laws and ensure that incoming products meet the many laws and regulations of the United States.

The customs inspector is the frontline worker in this critical operation. Inspectors are stationed at each national port of entry, where they individually process and inspect each person and shipment of products entering the country. They often work with other government agencies such as the Immigration and Naturalization Service, the Drug Enforcement Administration, and the Department of Agriculture.

To qualify for a position as a customs inspector, applicants must be citizens of the United States and must pass a physical examination, a background check, and a drug test. Inspectors also must have work experience that involves interacting with people and learning and applying a large collection of detailed facts.

In addition, customs inspectors undergo extensive training. Employees begin with 11 weeks of formal law-enforcement instruction, including written and physical tests, practical exercises, and firearms classes. This formal training is then supplemented by continual on-the-job training.

The customs inspector's job is not an easy one. Inspectors are expected to work long, irregular hours, often at remote border locations around the country. Their work, however, plays a crucial role in maintaining the economic health of the United States.

Customs inspectors ensure that products entering the United States comply with U.S. laws and regulations.

Careers in Economics

To help students learn about other careers in economics, refer them to the Careers section on the *Researcher Online*.

Themes in Economics

COMPETITION & MARKET STRUCTURE A nation's comparative advantages can shift over time. By improving and increasing its factors of production, a nation can gain a comparative advantage in an industry in which it previously did not have one. Increased globalization and advances in information technology (IT) are greatly speeding up this process. Japan, for example, took several decades to become a leading carmaker, yet it became a leading manufacturer of memory chips in only about 10 years.

Suppose also that if Panama devoted all of its resources to coffee production, it could produce 12 million pounds per year. If Panama devoted all of its resources to banana production, on the other hand, it could produce 4 million pounds per year. In terms of resources, Panama would be producing three pounds of coffee for every pound of bananas. The pound of bananas would be the trade-off for the three pounds of coffee, making Panama's exchange ratio between coffee and bananas 3:1.

Clearly, Costa Rica would be more productive in both coffee and bananas. However, the country would be comparatively—or relatively—more productive in producing coffee. On that basis, it would benefit both nations to specialize, with

INTERNATIONAL TRADE

Caption Answer
They can become efficient in the production of a few goods and services and then trade for any other goods and services they need. ⭐23A

SECTION 1 REVIEW ANSWERS

1. absolute advantage (428), comparative advantage (428) 13A, 24A

2. Thailand—4:1, rice; Malaysia—2.5:1, rubber 13B, 24D

3a. It results in specialization. Nations specialize in those goods and services that they produce the most efficiently, and then trade them for those that they either do not produce well or cannot produce at all. 12A

3b. By concentrating on making those goods and services that a country produces most efficiently, and trading with other nations for other products, a nation can expand its production possibilities and, thus, benefit from specialization and international trade. 13B, 23A

4. Answers will vary but should reflect an understanding of specialization, comparative advantage, and trade. 13B, 23A

ABSOLUTE AND COMPARATIVE ADVANTAGE

Domestic Pretrade Product Ratios

Costa Rica 5:1

Panama 3:1

Costa Rica–Panama

Trade Ratio 4:1

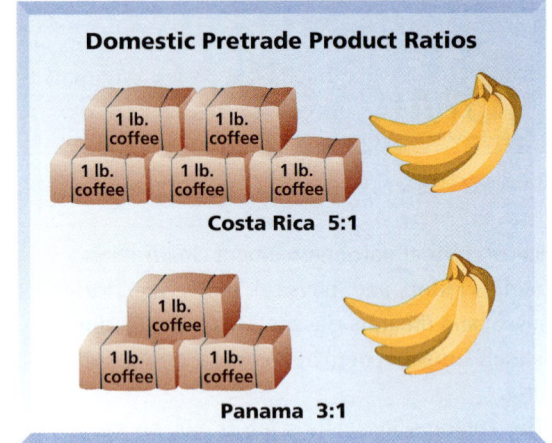

FIGURE 18.1 Pretrade product ratios describe original production possibilities, while trade ratios reflect comparative advantage. **How do countries benefit from specialization?**

Costa Rica producing coffee and Panama producing bananas. The exact trade ratio will determine just how much each country would benefit by trade, but so long as the trade ratio was between 5:1 and 3:1, both nations would benefit from specialization.

Suppose that the trade ratio was determined to be 4:1. If Costa Rica specialized in coffee, with international trade it would only have to give up—or trade off—four pounds of coffee for one pound of bananas. Without trade it would have to give up five pounds of coffee for a single pound of bananas (see Figure 18.1). Costa Rica therefore would benefit from international trade and specialization.

If Panama specialized in bananas at the 4:1 trade ratio, for every pound of bananas it traded it would receive four pounds of coffee. Without trade it would have to give up—or trade off—a pound of bananas for only three pounds of coffee. Thus, Panama, too, would benefit from trade and specialization. The original domestic pretrade production ratios of 5:1 and 3:1 describe each nation's original production possibilities, while the new production ratio of 4:1 describes the situation once the concept of comparative advantage is applied.

SECTION 1 REVIEW

⭐TEKS Q: 1, 2, 3a, 3b, 4

1. Identify and Explain:
absolute advantage
comparative advantage

2. Problem Solving: Copy the chart below. Use it to determine the exchange ratio for each product and in which product each country has a comparative advantage.

Product/Country	Rice	Rubber	Exchange Ratio	Comparative Advantage
Thailand	8,000 tons	2,000 tons		
Malaysia	10,000 tons	4,000 tons		

Homework Practice Online
keyword: SM3 HP18

3. Finding the Main Idea

a. How does the unequal distribution of economic factors of production relate to trade?

b. Why might policymakers choose to pursue a comparative advantage rather than an absolute advantage?

4. Writing and Critical Thinking

Drawing Conclusions: How does specialization affect your choices as an individual? Describe a recent specialization-based exchange of products or resources in which you have participated.

Consider the following:
- areas in which you have a comparative advantage
- areas in which you lack a comparative advantage

430 CHAPTER 18

SECTION 2

FOREIGN EXCHANGE AND CURRENCIES

READ TO DISCOVER
1. Why are foreign exchange rates necessary?
2. How does a nation determine its balance of payments?
3. What is the significance of the balance of trade?

ECONOMICS DICTIONARY
foreign exchange market
foreign exchange rate
adjustable-peg system
devaluation
appreciation
floating exchange rates
balance of payments
balance of trade
trade surplus
trade deficit

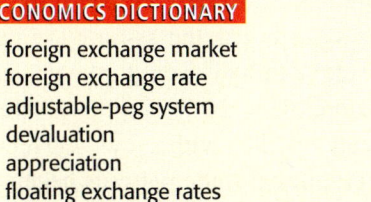

As of 2001 there were 192 nations in the world, each with its own government and national currency. National currencies such as dollars, pesos, and rupees generally are accepted in payment for goods and services within a nation's borders. To participate in international trade, however, nations must have a way of determining the values of their currencies in relation to one another.

Markets exist for the buying and selling of national currencies, just as they do for stocks, bonds, and other commodities. These currency markets are known as **foreign exchange markets**.

Foreign Exchange Rates

When a business in one country imports items, it makes payment in the exporting nation's currency. When a business in another country exports items, it also needs to receive payment in its own currency. Foreign exchange markets are designed to resolve these situations. Through the foreign exchange markets, currencies are converted into other currencies. Once the value of one currency is determined in relation to another, a **foreign exchange rate** for the two has been established.

In the United States, foreign exchange rates are expressed in two ways. The first is the number of units of another nation's currency that equals one dollar. In September 2001, for example, one U.S. dollar equaled 117.6 Japanese yen, and 1.091 Euros. The second is the U.S. dollar value for each unit of foreign currency. At that

EXCHANGE, MONEY, & INTERDEPENDENCE *Currencies are converted into other currencies through foreign-exchange markets.* **How are foreign exchange rates expressed in the United States?**

INTERNATIONAL TRADE 431

Themes in Economics

EXCHANGE, MONEY, & INTERDEPENDENCE When a nation's general price level increases, international demand for its currency tends to decline. As a result, inflation tends to cause a nation's currency to depreciate. Inflation's effect on exchange rates is explained by the theory of purchasing power parity (PPP). This theory states that floating exchange rates will adjust to account for changes in countries' relative price levels.

For example, suppose that the Japan–United States exchange rate is 200 yen to $1, and the U.S. price level doubles compared to that in Japan. PPP theory states that the U.S. dollar would begin to depreciate against the yen until it reached the point at which U.S. products cost the same in Japan as they did before the price increase. In the example, the U.S. dollar would depreciate 50 percent, to 100 yen to $1.

PPP theory does not always hold true, however. Many factors besides inflation affect exchange rates, such as trade barriers. PPP theory is most useful as a predictor of exchange rates when a nation has severe inflation relative to other nations. ∎

Caption Answer
The adjustable-peg system could not keep up with these rapid currency changes. ⭐ 23A, 23E

---

time, the Japanese yen was worth $0.0085, and the Euro was worth $0.9166.

Since World War II, nations have used one of two foreign exchange rate systems: the adjustable-peg system and the floating, or flexible, system. In an **adjustable-peg system**, the currency of one nation was initially pegged, or established, in relation to U.S. dollars, which had a fixed price in gold. The relationship was not fixed permanently, however. As economic situations changed, nations could change the exchange rate of their currency with currencies of other nations. This new rate would remain intact until one country chose to change the relationship between its currency and that of other nations. The adjustable-peg exchange rate system was used from 1944 to 1971.

Bretton Woods Conference
Adjustable-peg exchange rates were introduced at the Bretton Woods Conference in 1944. At that conference, 44 allied nations agreed that each nation should define its currency in terms of U.S. dollars, with an ounce of gold worth $35. Once set, these rates established base rates with all other currencies. Further, with this exchange rate system, each nation agreed to keep its currency stable in relation to other countries' currencies.

The Bretton Woods Conference established the International Monetary Fund (IMF) to make the system work. This organization, based in Washington, D.C., promotes international monetary cooperation, currency stabilization, and international trade. In 2001, 183 countries were members of the IMF.

Eliminating the Adjustable-Peg System
At the heart of this system was the assumption that international trade patterns would remain unchanged. For more than 20 years this system worked relatively well, with few currency changes. As international trade patterns began to change rapidly during the 1960s and 1970s, however, countries found it increasingly difficult to maintain established exchange rates under the adjustable-peg system.

When one nation's currency decreases in value relative to other currencies, **devaluation**, or depreciation, has occurred. When a nation's currency is devalued, its products become cheaper to other nations; at the same time, other nations' products become more expensive to buyers in the nation that has devalued its currency.

On the other hand, when a nation's currency increases in value compared to other currencies, **appreciation** has occurred. Following this appreciation, that nation's products will become

"Sorry, your uncle left nothing of value, only U.S. dollars."

BALANCE OF PAYMENTS When this cartoon was drawn in 1978, the value of the U.S. dollar was decreasing relative to foreign currencies. **How did currency devaluation and appreciation contribute to the elimination of the adjustable-peg system?** ⭐TEKS

432 CHAPTER 18

more expensive for people who purchase them in other countries. Additionally, other countries' products will become relatively less expensive in the nation with the appreciating currency. Because of the constant changes in international trade patterns, nations were unable to rely on the adjustable-peg system, and in 1971 a new system, based on floating exchange rates, was established.

Floating Exchange Rates

With **floating exchange rates**, the value of a currency is determined by the laws of demand and supply. As a result, currency values can change from one minute to the next.

These constant changes in the exchange value of a nation's currency can have both positive and negative effects. For example, during the mid-1980s the demand for U.S. dollars was high. Foreign investors wanted to buy dollars to invest in U.S. businesses and securities, and the U.S. dollar was viewed as one of the world's most secure currencies because of the strength of the U.S. government and a low U.S. inflation rate. In addition, many people around the world relied on dollars as a medium of exchange and investment. As a result of these factors, the U.S. dollar appreciated in value.

This appreciation led to what economists call a "strong" dollar, which has more purchasing power relative to other currencies. The strong dollar had a negative effect on U.S. exporters, who sold products to other nations, while having a positive effect on U.S. consumers buying foreign goods. In other words, foreign-made goods became less expensive in U.S. markets, and goods made in the United States became more expensive in foreign markets.

To understand how a strong dollar affects exports and imports, consider the following example. Suppose that two British pounds equal a single U.S. dollar. At that exchange rate an item priced at $100 would sell in Britain for £200. However, if the exchange rate changes as a result of the dollar's appreciation so that three pounds equal a dollar, it would take £300—instead of £200—to buy the U.S. item. Clearly, this change in the exchange rate would reduce the quantity of U.S. goods demanded in Britain.

The quantity of British goods demanded in the United States would increase, as those goods would decrease in price when the exchange rate changed. A British manufacturer who initially priced his or her products to be sold in the United States at the equivalent of £200 each would have required Americans to pay $100 for that item; however, after the change in relative currency values to three pounds per dollar, Americans could buy the same item for $66.66 each. This price decrease would lead to an increase in the quantity of British goods demanded in the United States.

The previous examples assumed that the forces of demand and supply acted without government involvement. In reality, however, governments do intervene from time to time in foreign exchange markets to keep the value of their own or other nations' currencies from rising or falling too much. Governments do this by buying or selling their currencies on the foreign exchange market.

INTERNATIONAL TRADE *A strong U.S. dollar works to reduce the price of foreign-made goods such as this Mexican rug.* **How does a strong dollar affect goods made in the United States?**

Caption Answer
It makes them more expensive as compared to U.S. imports and also makes them more expensive in foreign markets. ★13D, 23A

Global Connections

Many speculators buy and sell currencies for profit and rely on economic indicators to predict the direction in which exchange rates are moving. Purchasing power parity (PPP) is one such indicator. According to PPP theory, the exchange rate between two currencies moves over time toward the "correct" rate—that is, the rate at which a market basket of identical products costs relatively the same in each country.

The Economist magazine has been using a simplified and lighthearted version of PPP, called the Big Mac index, since the mid-1980s. This index examines the price of a Big Mac® hamburger worldwide to determine whether current exchange rates are correct. For example, in 1997 the average price of a Big Mac in the United States was $2.42, and its average price in Japan was 294 yen. Based on PPP theory, the exchange rate should have been $1 to 121 yen (294 divided by $2.42 equals 121). The actual rate, however, was $1 to 126 yen. Thus, according to the Big Mac index, the yen was undervalued against the dollar and likely to appreciate in the future. ■

What Do You Think? Answers

1. The businesses could learn more about what products consumers in those countries want, what businesses they must compete against, and how best to market their products in other cultures. ★23A

2. advantages—students graduate with real-life business experience, a strong background in business in their region, and the ability to apply business knowledge to a variety of topics; disadvantages—students not interested in future careers in business might want to study and explore nonbusiness-related subjects in more depth or in ways not related to international business with Pacific Rim countries; extra-curricular activities in theater, music, and sports may not receive as much attention; students who graduate may not be as well-rounded as students who attend more traditional high schools. ★25A

3. Answers will vary but should accurately reflect an awareness of the local economic community and of the types of businesses that are lacking or that would do well there. ★25A

ECONOMICS IN ACTION

An Education for the Global Economy

Pacific Rim countries—those bordering the Pacific Ocean—make up one of the fastest-growing trade regions in the world. Mt. Edgecumbe High School in Sitka, Alaska, has developed a unique program to help its students prepare themselves to participate in the Pacific Rim market.

Mt. Edgecumbe High School has a heavier course load than other Alaska high schools and requires several classes not typically taken by American high school students. For example, students must take at least one year of Chinese or Japanese language and a year-long course on Pacific Rim cultures.

Traditional classes also focus on developing future entrepreneurs. For example, math classes involve calculating exchange rates, art classes include lessons in brochure design, and computer classes teach students to analyze business profits and expenses using spreadsheets.

To put these educational skills into practice, the school has also established a number of pilot business projects. For instance, from 1985 to 1991, students ran Edgecumbe Enterprises, a business they founded to export smoked salmon to the Pacific Rim market. Salmon are plentiful in Alaskan waters, and the Asian market often pays high prices for the popular fish.

The company began as a salmon-processing plant, founded with a grant from the U.S. Department of Health and Human Services that paid for the necessary equipment and the development of package and label designs. Money from the grant also allowed students to make trips to Japan and China to meet with businesspeople and to learn about local business practices and culture. For example, students studied Japan's stringent quality-assurance techniques. They then applied their new-found knowledge, incorporating the methods they learned into their own business. This increased efficiency and helped ensure the high product quality needed to compete in the international market. The hands-on experience also enabled students to negotiate Japan's trade barriers and regulations.

By 1991, however, changes in the Pacific Rim market for smoked salmon had made it unprofitable to continue the business, and the student entrepreneurs closed Edgecumbe Enterprises. Meanwhile, Mt. Edgecumbe High School's business research and design class began the search for its next business opportunity.

What Do You Think? ★TEKS

1. How might studying different cultures help businesses involved in international trade?
2. Briefly discuss the advantages and disadvantages of designing a curriculum around a specific subject like international trade.
3. Considering the characteristics of your own school and local economy, how might your high school curriculum be changed to involve students in real business?

Students at Mt. Edgecumbe High School in Sitka, Alaska, developed a business to sell salmon in Asia.

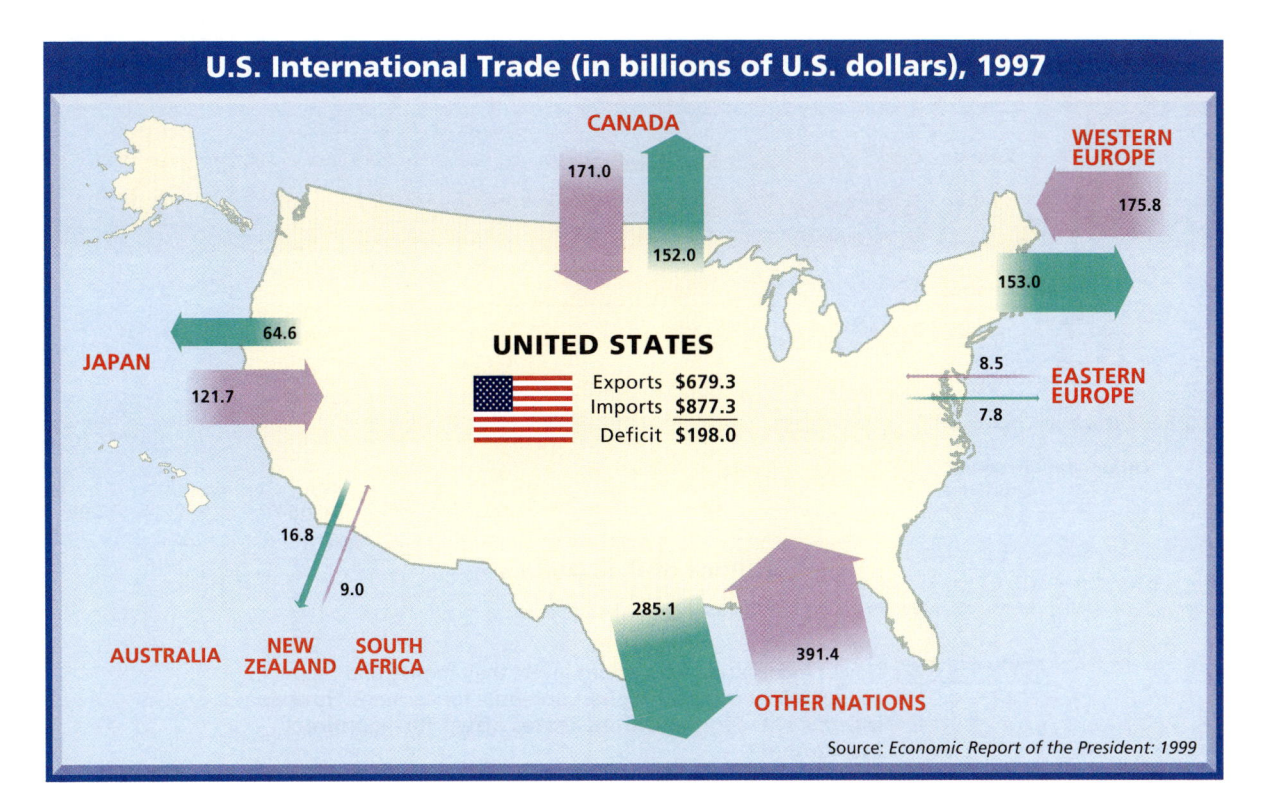

U.S. International Trade (in billions of U.S. dollars), 1997

CANADA: 171.0 / 152.0
WESTERN EUROPE: 175.8 / 153.0
JAPAN: 64.6 / 121.7
EASTERN EUROPE: 8.5 / 7.8
AUSTRALIA, NEW ZEALAND, SOUTH AFRICA: 16.8 / 9.0
OTHER NATIONS: 285.1 / 391.4

UNITED STATES
Exports $679.3
Imports $877.3
Deficit $198.0

Source: *Economic Report of the President: 1999*

FIGURE 18.2 Like individuals, nations buy goods on credit, financing the purchase with funds from sales to other nations. **To what single country does the U.S. export the largest dollar value of goods?**

Foreign Exchange Markets

The economies of the world are linked by foreign exchange markets. Traditionally, the most important function of a foreign exchange market has been to convert one currency into an equivalent amount of a second currency. This currency conversion is needed for three types of international transactions: trade, tourism and travel, and investing. Each of these types of international transactions requires a record of payment and exchange.

Balance of Payments and Trade

Understanding a nation's economic health is much like understanding that of an individual. Individuals earn income by supplying labor and other productive services in the market, and in turn they spend their income buying goods and services in the market. If they earn more than they spend, they have savings. On the other hand, if they spend more than they earn, they accumulate debt. This debt may be financed by various types of borrowing, such as the use of credit cards or loans. However, there are limits to the amount of debt that individuals can accumulate. These limits usually depend on consumers' ability to repay the debt. (Credit is discussed more fully in Chapter 9.)

Nations conduct business in much the same way. For example, the United States buys more than it sells to other nations during certain years and sells more to other nations than it buys in other years. The nations that buy more than they sell must finance those purchases either by borrowing from or selling assets to other nations, or by allowing other nations to hold their currency (see Figure 18.2).

Themes in Economics

BALANCE OF PAYMENTS
Based on the combined values of U.S. imports and exports, the 10 countries with which the United States did the most trade in 1999 were—in order from most to least—Canada, Mexico, Japan, China, Germany, the United Kingdom, Taiwan, South Korea, France, and Singapore. During the same period, the United States carried its largest trade deficit with Japan, and its largest trade surplus with the Netherlands.

Transparency
An overhead transparency of Figure 18.2 is available in *Transparency Resources*. See Transparency 70: U.S. International Trade (in billions of U.S. dollars), 1997.

Caption Answer
Canada

internet connect
TOPIC: International Trade
GO TO: go.hrw.com
KEYWORD: SM3 EC18

Have students access the Internet through the HRW Go site to conduct research on the Commercial Service of the U.S. Commerce Department. Then have each student prepare a 10-question quiz about the Commercial Service and how it promotes international trade. Have students trade quizzes with a partner and then score one another. Be sure students understand any questions they answered incorrectly.

INTERNATIONAL TRADE

Transparency

An overhead transparency of Figure 18.3 is available in *Transparency Resources.* See Transparency 71: Foreign Direct Investment in the United States, 1998.

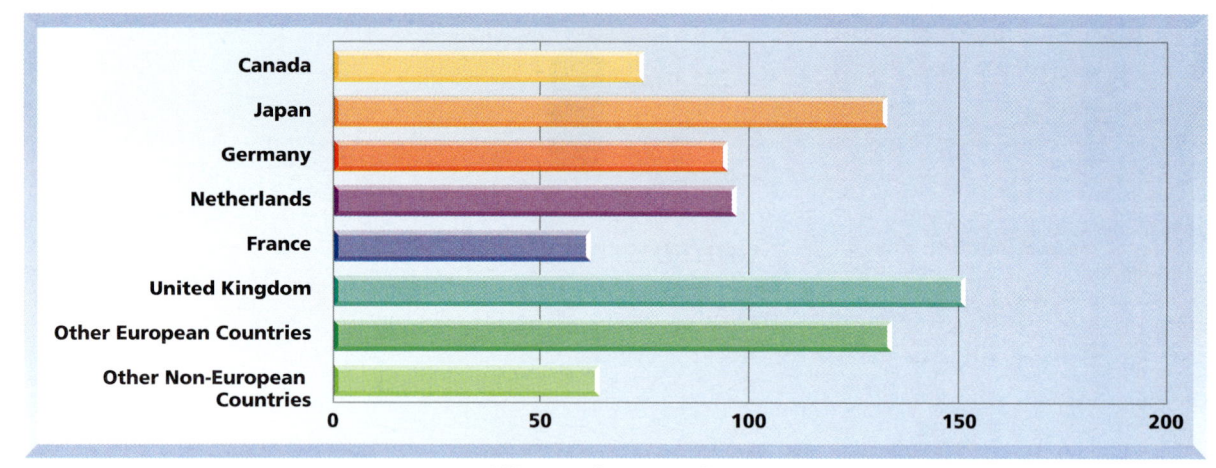

Caption Answer

U.S. interest rates that are higher relative to other nations encourage more foreign direct investment in the United States. ★23A

Global Connections

During the 1980s, Japanese foreign direct investment in the United States increased rapidly, spurred on by a strong yen and Japan's robust economic growth. Japanese investors bought such notable U.S. assets as Rockefeller Center, Columbia Pictures, and Pebble Beach golf course in California. Increased Japanese investment in the United States alarmed many Americans, who feared Japan would buy control of the United States.

As with many economic trends, however, this one did not last. In the early 1990s, Japan's economy collapsed, and U.S. real-estate prices plummeted. Both countries entered recessions. Japanese investments, most made when U.S. real-estate prices were at their peak, fell greatly in value. Many Japanese investors became overextended and had to either sell at a loss or file for bankruptcy. ■

FOREIGN DIRECT INVESTMENT IN THE UNITED STATES, 1998

[Bar chart showing foreign direct investment in billions of U.S. dollars by country: Canada, Japan, Germany, Netherlands, France, United Kingdom, Other European Countries, Other Non-European Countries. Scale 0 to 200.]

Billions of U.S. Dollars

Source: U.S. Census Bureau, *Statistical Abstract of the United States: 2000*

FIGURE 18.3 Governments and corporations invest their money and capital in countries that offer the highest potential for earnings. **How do interest rates in the United States affect foreign direct investment?**

Balance of Payments A nation's **balance of payments** is an annual accounting record of all the payments and receipts occurring between its residents, businesses, and governments and the residents, businesses, and governments of other nations. The U.S. balance of payments provides information about finances and investment between the United States and all its trading partners.

The balance of payments is divided into the current account and the capital account. The current account shows the dollar value of goods and services that U.S. citizens and companies bought from and sold to other countries, the income that Americans and U.S. multinational corporations earned in other countries, and the income that foreign individuals and companies earned in the United States.

The capital-account portion of the balance of payments keeps track of the flow of money or capital between nations. Like individuals, governments and corporations make their investments in places that offer the highest rate of return accompanied by safety and other factors.

For example, relatively higher interest rates in the United States are usually accompanied by an increase of foreign capital flowing to the United States. If interest rates are relatively low in the United States, then foreign capital likely will be invested in other nations.

The international flow of money for investment purposes is nothing new. As of 1998, other nations had more than $811 billion directly invested in the United States (see Figure 18.3). In 1998 Great Britain, the largest foreign investor in the United States, owned more than $150 billion of U.S. assets, including such well-known companies as Burger King and Pillsbury. Japan was the second-largest owner of U.S. assets, including such well-known U.S. businesses as Firestone Tire & Rubber and Columbia Pictures.

When both the current and capital accounts are totaled, rarely will the total expenditures in other nations be balanced exactly with the receipts from other nations. Generally a nation will run a current-account deficit and a capital-account surplus, or a current-account surplus and a capital-account deficit.

CHAPTER 18

Balance of Trade The difference between a nation's imported and exported products is known as its **balance of trade**. This merchandise balance of trade has historically been the most important factor in determining the nation's overall balance of payments.

When the United States exports more than it imports, it has a **trade surplus**. The last year the United States had a trade surplus in goods and services was 1975. When the United States imports more than it exports—as is generally the case—it has a **trade deficit** (see Figure 18.4).

U.S. Trade Deficit Trade deficits have been characteristic of the U.S. economy for many years. When the Organization of Petroleum Exporting Countries (OPEC) dramatically raised the price of oil in the 1970s, the United States had to increase its oil expenditures. That additional spending represented a sharp rise in the dollar value of imports into the United States and resulted in a trade deficit for the United States.

The U.S. trade deficit persisted because of a lag in productivity in the United States compared to other nations such as Japan, Singapore, and South Korea. As productivity increased in these nations, their goods became more competitive in global markets and relatively less expensive in the United States.

This problem was aggravated by the rise in the value of the dollar against other currencies. As this occurred it became even more expensive for people in other nations to buy U.S. goods. As Americans purchased more imported goods such as cars and electronics, and as U.S. exports grew far more slowly, the trade deficit widened. Furthermore, it became less expensive for Americans to buy foreign-made goods. (For a breakdown of U.S. imports and exports, see Figure 18.5 on page 438.)

In the 1990s, however, U.S. productivity began to rise with the increasing use of high technology. As a result, in the mid-1990s, the United States began to be more competitive in the arena of international trade and the domestic economy saw a boom that lasted into 2000.

U.S. BALANCE OF TRADE (GOODS AND SERVICES), 1970–1999

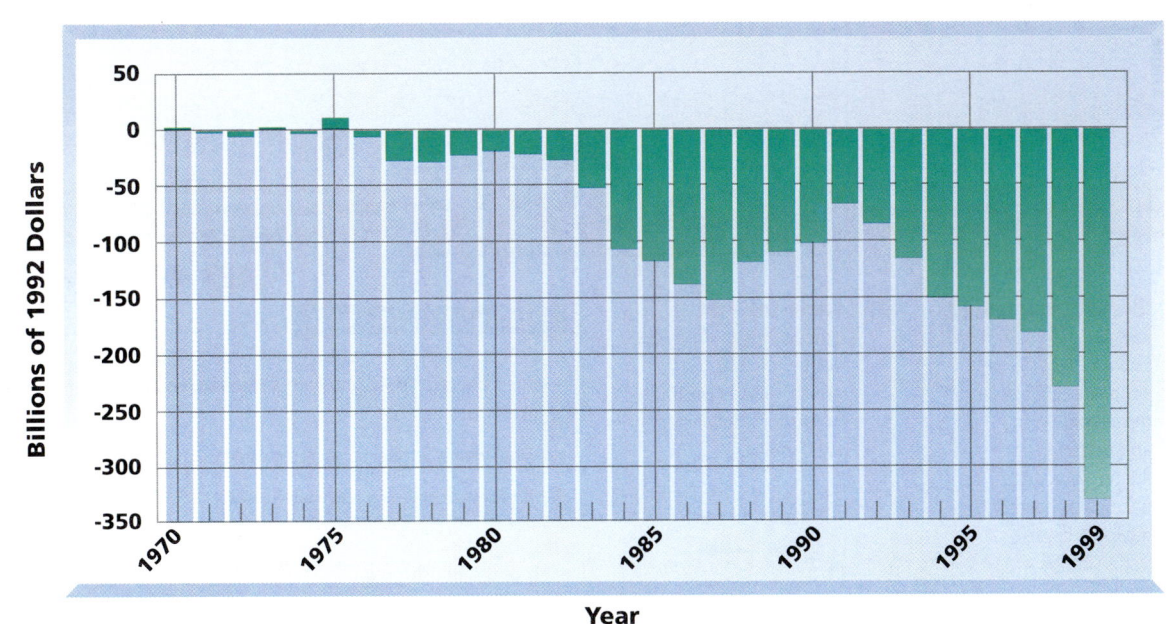

Source: U.S. Census Bureau, Statistical Abstract of the United States: 2000

FIGURE 18.4 The balance of trade historically has been the most important factor in determining the nation's overall balance of payments. **What factors contribute to trade deficits in the United States?**

Themes in Economics

Transparency
An overhead transparency of Figure 18.4 is available in *Transparency Resources*. See Transparency 72: U.S. Balance of Trade, 1970–1999.

Caption Answer
increased productivity and competitiveness of some other nations, which makes their products relatively less expensive in the United States, and a strong dollar relative to other nations ★13C, 23A

Transparency
(p. 438)
An overhead transparency of Figure 18.5 is available in *Transparency Resources*. See Transparency 73: U.S. Imports and Exports, 1999–2000.

Caption Answer

Exports of capital goods are double imports of consumer goods. If foreign goods' prices decline, the U.S. will likely import more. If U.S. goods' prices decline, the U.S. will likely export more. ★13C, 23A, 23F

SECTION 2 REVIEW ANSWERS

1. foreign exchange market (431), foreign exchange rate (431), adjustable-peg system (432), devaluation (432), appreciation (432), floating exchange rate (433), balance of payments (436), balance of trade (437), trade surplus (437), trade deficit (437) **24A**

2. "strong" dollar—increased imports, reduced exports; "weak" dollar—reduced imports, increased exports **13D, 24D**

3a. adjustable peg—pegged to U.S. dollars; floating—set by supply and demand, can change often; nations trade currencies to buy imports **13D, 23A**

3b. rising oil prices; lagging U.S. productivity versus nations such as Japan, Korea, and Singapore; relative strength of U.S. dollar

4. Answers should reflect an understanding of how the relative strength of currencies relates to trade. **13D, 23A**

438

U.S. IMPORTS AND EXPORTS, 1999-2000

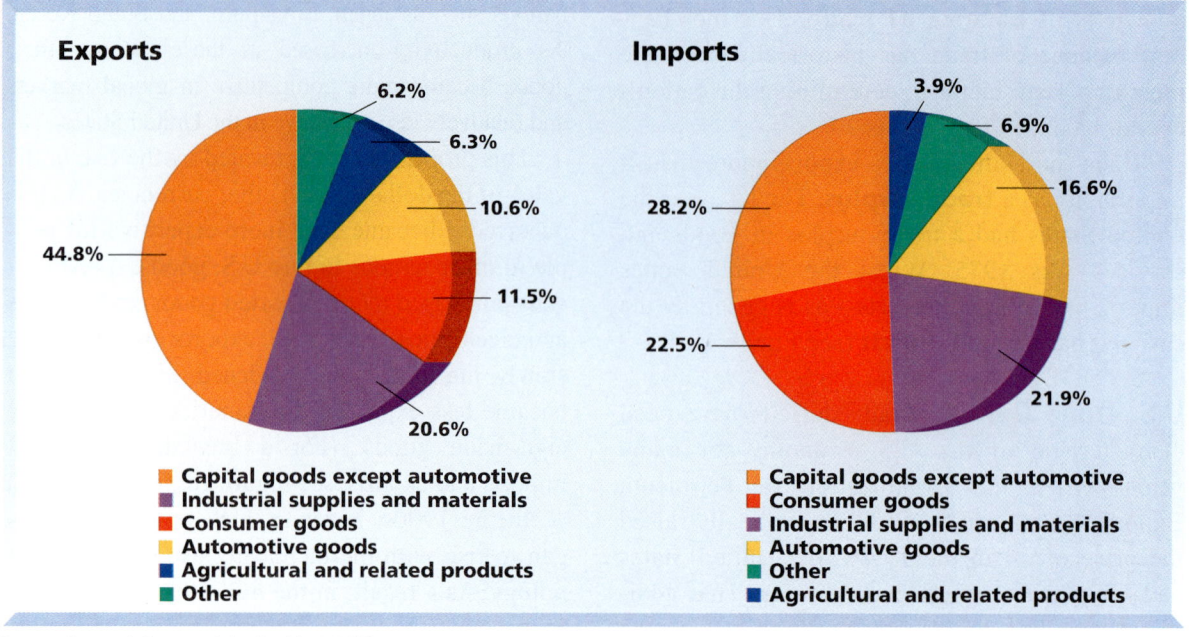

Exports
- 44.8% Capital goods except automotive
- 20.6% Industrial supplies and materials
- 11.5% Consumer goods
- 10.6% Automotive goods
- 6.3% Agricultural and related products
- 6.2% Other

Imports
- 28.2% Capital goods except automotive
- 22.5% Consumer goods
- 21.9% Industrial supplies and materials
- 16.6% Automotive goods
- 6.9% Other
- 3.9% Agricultural and related products

Source: *Economic Report of the President: 2001*

FIGURE 18.5 The kinds of goods imported and exported by the United States affect its balance of trade. **How does the export of capital goods compare to the import of consumer goods? How might prices affect the balance of trade?** ★TEKS

SECTION 2 REVIEW

★TEKS Q: 1, 2, 3a, 4

1. Identify and Explain:
foreign exchange market
foreign exchange rate
adjustable-peg system
devaluation
appreciation
floating exchange rate
balance of payments
balance of trade
trade surplus
trade deficit

2. Comparing and Contrasting: Copy the chart below. Use it to diagram the effects on trade of a "strong" dollar and a "weak" dollar.

Strong Dollar →
Weak Dollar →

3. Finding the Main Idea

a. Contrast adjustable-peg exchange rates with floating exchange rates, and explain why exchange rates are an important factor in international trade.

b. What were the original causes of the U.S. trade deficit?

4. Writing and Critical Thinking

Identifying Cause and Effect: If the value of a currency such as the British pound increases, what is the effect on trade between Britain and the United States? Explain your answer with an example not described in the book.

Consider the following:
- the effects of a strong currency and of a weak currency
- the balance of trade

Homework Practice Online
keyword: SM3 HP18

SECTION 3

COOPERATION AND TRADE BARRIERS

READ TO DISCOVER

1. Why do nations impose trade barriers?
2. What are the key arguments made in favor of free trade?
3. What types of agreements indicate that nations are following a policy of cooperation?

ECONOMICS DICTIONARY

trade barrier
revenue tariff
protective tariff
import quota
voluntary trade restriction
embargo
free trade
protectionism

International trade allows people and nations to specialize in the production of goods and services. Economically, international trade is a positive force promoting efficiency and growth. Because of a variety of factors, however, nations often restrict the free exchange of goods across national borders.

Trade Barriers

Government actions that are designed to protect domestic industries and jobs from foreign competition are called **trade barriers**. The major types of trade barriers are tariffs, import quotas and voluntary restrictions, and embargoes.

Tariffs Any tax on imports is a tariff. Tariffs are either **revenue tariffs**, which raise money for government, or **protective tariffs**, which restrict the number of foreign goods sold in a country. Until the early 1900s, revenue tariffs—or customs duties—were a major source of income for the U.S. government. After the U.S. government adopted the income tax in 1913, revenue from tariffs was considerably less important to government finances.

A protective tariff is designed to favor domestic industries over foreign competitors. By increasing the prices of imported goods, protective tariffs tend to reduce the quantity of foreign goods demanded.

Suppose that a Japanese firm sells a motorcycle for $5,000 and that a comparable U.S.-made motorcycle costs $7,000. The $2,000 price difference would cause many buyers in the United States to purchase the Japanese model. If the U.S. government places a 50 percent protective tariff on Japanese motorcycles, the imported motorcycle's price will jump substantially, to

INTERNATIONAL TRADE *Nations often restrict the free exchange of goods across national borders.* **What are three types of trade barriers?**

INTERNATIONAL TRADE **439**

Caption Answer

Protective tariffs tend to reduce the quantity of foreign products demanded by increasing the prices of imported products. ⭐14A, 23A

Themes in Economics

THE ROLE OF GOVERNMENT

Following World War II, the U.S. steel industry was booming. By the early 1980s, however, it had lost large amounts of market share to foreign steel companies. Burdened with inefficient and outdated technology, high wages, and low productivity, U.S. steel companies could not compete. In an effort to help, the U.S. government placed a voluntary trade restriction on steel imports.

The restriction helped U.S. steel companies earn higher profits, which they reinvested to modernize their plants and to increase efficiency. By 1992, when the voluntary trade restriction expired, U.S. steelmakers had doubled their productivity rates and were a match for foreign competitors. However, supporters of free trade note that many other factors, such as the drop in the U.S. dollar in 1985, may have helped the U.S. steel industry far more than the voluntary trade restriction. ■

AVERAGE TARIFF RATES IN THE UNITED STATES, 1825–1995

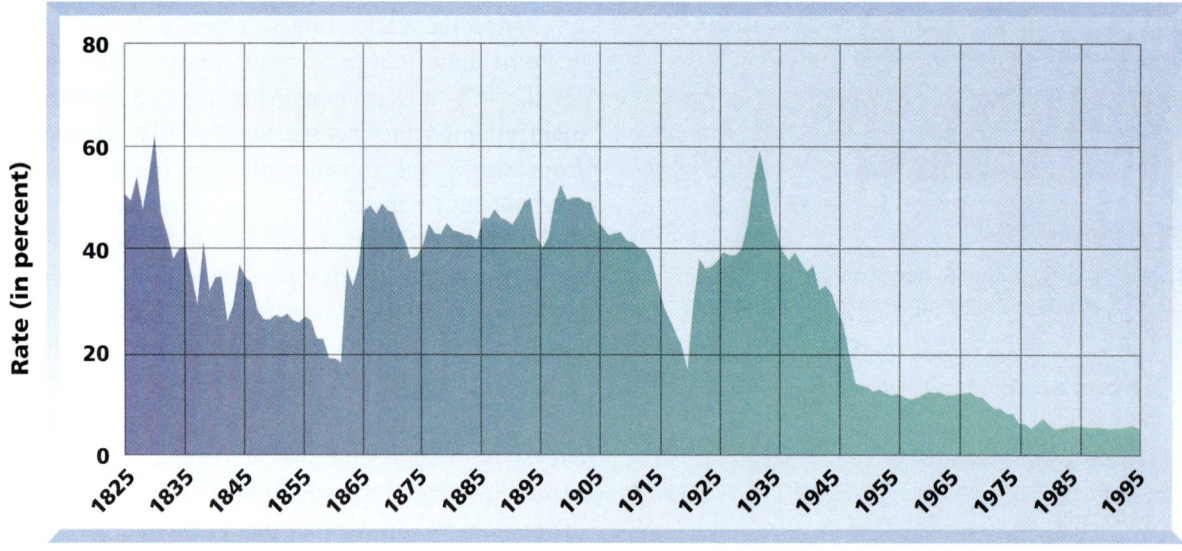

Sources: *Historical Statistics of the United States: Colonial Times to 1970; Statistical Abstract of the United States: 1986, 1996*

FIGURE 18.6 Revenue tariffs were a major source of income for the U.S. government prior to 1913. Since the adoption of the income tax, however, most U.S. tariffs have been protective rather than revenue generating. **How do protective tariffs work to safeguard U.S. companies from foreign competition?** ⭐TEKS

$7,500 [(0.5 × $5,000 = $2,500) + $5,000 = $7,500]. The protective tariff increases the price of the Japanese motorcycle, thus making it more expensive than the American motorcycle. This price difference would encourage many consumers in the United States to buy the American model.

The United States has used protective tariffs for much of its history. The McKinley Tariff Act of 1890 set such high tariffs that many foreign competitors were totally excluded from American markets. The Smoot-Hawley Tariff of 1930, which was enacted at the onset of the Great Depression, decreased imports by almost 60 percent and had a negative effect on all international trade.

Since World War II the United States has reduced its use of protective tariffs (see Figure 18.6). Exceptions to this policy continued into the 1990s, however, and included heavy tariffs on Japanese motorcycles and trucks.

Import Quotas and Voluntary Restrictions

Governments also can use import quotas and voluntary trade restrictions to decrease imports. Both of these forms of regulation are intended to help domestic businesses sell their products by limiting the quantity of a specific product that can be imported into a country. An **import quota**, which sets a fixed amount of an item that can be imported, is a law. A **voluntary trade restriction** is a binding agreement between the U.S. and another nation that does not require congressional action and legislation.

Import quotas and voluntary trade restrictions occasionally are directed at specific goods from specific nations. In 1981, for example, the U.S. government responded to domestic automakers' requests for industry protection from Japanese competition. In that year, Japan agreed to limit the number of cars exported to the United States to about 1.7 million cars each year. In 1985 this voluntary trade restriction agreement was

CHAPTER 18

changed to allow 2.3 million Japanese cars to be imported into the United States annually. Today such voluntary trade restrictions no longer exist on the importation of Japanese cars.

Embargoes A law that cuts off imports from, and exports to, specific countries is called an **embargo**. Historically, embargoes have been enacted for political—rather than economic—reasons. The Embargo Act of 1807, for example, was a politically motivated embargo designed to stop France and Great Britain from raiding ships belonging to American merchants.

More recent embargoes also have been used for political purposes. A 1985 embargo against South Africa sought to pressure that government to end apartheid, a racist system dismantled in the early 1990s. In 1990 Iraq invaded tiny, oil-rich Kuwait. An embargo cut supplies to Iraq during the ensuing Gulf War and remained in place to pressure Iraq's leader, Saddam Hussein, into permitting U.N. weapons inspectors to ensure that Iraq had taken apart its programs to create weapons of mass destruction.

Other Trade Barriers Other trade barriers include licensing requirements and extensive paperwork, which can interrupt the free flow of goods between countries. Some nations require firms to obtain a special license before they can import goods. By restricting the number of licenses, these nations ensure that fewer foreign goods are imported.

In some nations, paperwork delays also interfere with trade. In Japan, for example, imports are subject to extensive testing and inspection, and time-consuming and expensive paperwork must be completed. Many exporters choose not to sell their products in Japan for this reason.

In 1959 Fidel Castro established a communist government in Cuba, expropriating American-owned property. The United States opposed Castro and banned direct trade between the countries. With the passage of the Helms-Burton Act in June 1996, however, companies—even those from nations other than the United States—that do business in Cuba may encounter barriers to trade with the United States. Specifically, the Helms-Burton Act provides various punishments for any companies or their employees who are caught using properties in Cuba that were expropriated from American firms and organizations.

Free Trade versus Protectionism

Free trade is international trade that is not subject to government regulation. Supporters of free trade believe that exports and imports should flow freely between nations. Not everyone supports free trade, however. Some people believe in **protectionism**—the use of protective tariffs between nations to favor domestic industries. The arguments used by both protectionists and supporters of free trade are based on

- infant industries,
- job protection,
- standard of living,
- specialization,
- national security, and
- fairness.

INTERNATIONAL TRADE *Countries often use trade embargoes to apply political pressure.* **Why did the United States enact a trade embargo against South Africa in 1985?**

Across the Curriculum

HISTORY On January 1, 1959, Fidel Castro overthrew Fulgencio Batista and took control of Cuba. With the support and backing of the Soviet Union, Castro then set up a communist government. As part of this process, he expropriated more than $1 billion in U.S. assets in Cuba. U.S. president Dwight Eisenhower, in response to this action and to Cuba's growing alignment with the Soviet Union, cut all diplomatic ties with Cuba in 1961. In addition, he placed a trade embargo on Cuba. The United States eased these trade restrictions slightly in 1999.

Enhancing the Lesson

For information on early U.S. international trade policies, see Reading 13: Open-Door Policy in China, located in *From the Source: Readings in Economics and Government with Answer Key*.

Caption Answer

to pressure the South African government into ending apartheid 14A, 23A

Across the Curriculum

HISTORY & GOVERNMENT

Alexander Hamilton was one of the first vocal protectionists in the United States. In his *Report on Manufactures,* which he wrote in 1791, Hamilton argued that the United States should encourage the development of manufacturing to complement its already developed agricultural base. Hamilton proposed that the U.S. government actively support the growth of "infant" manufacturing industries through the use of trade barriers and subsidies. He suggested the government impose tariffs on foreign products that competed with U.S. goods, use trade restrictions to prevent the export of raw materials that are vital to U.S. manufacturing, establish embargoes to prevent U.S. industrial secrets from leaving the country, and provide subsidies for manufacturing companies. Hamilton's ideas received a lukewarm reception from Congress, however, and few were carried out. ■

Profiles in Economics

For a biography of Alexander Hamilton and other noted people in economics, refer students to the Biographies section on the *Researcher Online.*

Global Exchange

E-Commerce and the Global Economy

In recent years the Internet has facilitated the rapid growth of electronic commerce, or e-commerce. One unique aspect of e-commerce is that it enables entrepreneurs and consumers to easily conduct business across national boundaries. In 1997, the United States government issued "A Framework for Global Electronic Commerce," which set out its vision for the global marketplace created by the Internet.

The document contains a set of principles and policies related to international e-commerce. For instance, it calls on the private sector to take the lead in further developing the Internet and supports business self-regulation when appropriate. It also calls on governments to avoid undue restraints on e-commerce. Where government regulation is necessary, such as to protect consumers, the report calls on governments to create a simple, predictable legal environment.

The report also discusses several areas in which international agreements might facilitate e-commerce. For instance, financial issues, such as customs and taxation; legal issues, such as the protection of intellectual property and privacy; and market access issues, such as infrastructure and technical standards, could all benefit from global cooperation.

A survey of 27 countries in 2000 found that 10 percent of Internet users shopped on line. With a little help from governments and private industry, the Internet promises to remain a major source of global trade.

Infant Industries First, protectionists argue that a nation's "infant" industries should be protected from foreign competition until they are able to establish themselves. By restricting imports by the competitors of these new industries, the government allows the "infants" to build up a strong domestic market. Today, many developing nations use this strategy to help kick-start their economies.

Those on the side of free trade believe that the decreased competition resulting from trade barriers encourages poor resource use, because the protected businesses have less incentive to be efficient. Free-trade supporters also claim that these temporary protective measures are likely to be extended indefinitely because of the political pressures that businesses exert on government. Once protected, always protected, they argue.

Job Protection A second argument in favor of protectionism is based on the claim that reducing foreign competition allows more businesses to compete in the domestic market and provides more jobs for domestic workers. Free-trade supporters, on the other hand, claim that trade restrictions actually reduce the employment of U.S. workers. They note that trade barriers put up by the United States historically have caused other nations to respond by erecting barriers to U.S. trade. These barriers hurt U.S. businesses in the world market and ultimately reduce the number of American jobs.

Standard of Living Protectionists point out that trade barriers help maintain the high wages and standard of living available in the United States. The trade barriers between nations are needed, they say, because other nations' cheap labor gives them an unfair advantage in world markets.

People who support free trade believe that the high wages and high standard of living in the United States can be maintained without trade barriers. They claim that U.S. businesses can afford to pay high wages and still produce competitively priced products because of U.S. workers' skills and efficiency levels.

INTERNATIONAL TRADE *Protectionists opposed the signing of a free-trade agreement among the United States, Mexico, and Canada in 1993.* **What arguments support the creation of trade barriers?**

Specialization

People who favor protectionism argue that free trade encourages businesses to overspecialize. They further claim that overspecialization can cause a nation's economy to be hurt by changes in world demand. These protectionists urge nations to encourage businesses to produce a wide variety of products while protecting businesses that lack an absolute or comparative advantage.

Those who support free trade believe that it benefits the world economy and that competition guarantees the best product at the best price. They recognize that an economy based on a single product is not as strong as a highly diversified economy, like that of the United States.

National Security and Fairness

Both protectionists and free-trade supporters agree that some industries must be protected from foreign competition and failure because they are vital to a nation's national security. In the United States, protected industries include steel and other heavy industries, advanced technology businesses, and energy-based industries. This kind of protectionism makes the United States less dependent on foreign firms during times of national emergency. While acknowledging that vital industries must be protected, people who support free trade claim that non-essential industries abuse this argument with false claims.

On the issue of fairness, protectionists argue that few, if any, nations allow truly free trade. Protectionists feel that U.S. barriers should match those of other nations. Free-trade supporters agree that some nations violate the notion of fair trade, but they prefer to dismantle trade barriers.

Rarely is a government's trade policy completely protectionist or completely based on free trade. Instead, most nations' policies reflect a variety of international and domestic factors that can stem from economic or political factors, or both. The government may protect some industries while allowing free trade in others. In the United States, government officials closely watch the nation's trade situation so they can react to policy changes in other nations.

International Cooperation

To reap the economic and political benefits of global trade, many nations have engaged in international cooperation. Some examples of trade cooperation among nations are reciprocal trade agreements, regional trade organizations, and international trade agreements.

Reciprocal Trade Agreements

With the election of President Franklin Roosevelt in 1932, the United States began an ambitious plan to restore slumping international trade. The Reciprocal Trade Agreements Act of 1934 identified protective tariffs as the leading obstacles to trade and sought to reduce them in two ways. First, it gave the president the power to reduce tariffs by as much as 50 percent, provided that other

---

Caption Answer

arguments related to infant industries, job protection, standard of living, specialization, national security, and fairness ★ 14A, 23A

Themes in Economics

MARKETS & PRICES Dumping refers to the practice of selling an export at a price below either its domestic price or its total production costs. Firms dump products for a number of reasons. For example, firms can get rid of excess stock by selling it cheaply—that is, dumping it—in foreign markets. The most often cited reason for dumping, however, is to undercut competitors in foreign markets, usually to gain dominant market share. Once a company has eliminated its competitors and gained control of the market, it raises its prices.

Many governments have antidumping laws to protect domestic industries from unfair foreign competition. Usually these laws penalize firms caught dumping products by imposing a duty on the products. Opponents of antidumping laws argue that they keep domestic prices above market equilibriums, hurting consumers and companies that buy the protected products. In addition, there are a number of "fair" reasons that companies may sell exports below cost, such as the launching of a new product. ■

Transparency

An overhead transparency of Figure 18.7 is available in *Transparency Resources.* See Transparency 74: European Union.

Caption Answer

Austria, Finland, and Sweden

---

internet connect

TOPIC: NAFTA, WTO, International Cooperation, Trade
GO TO: go.hrw.com
KEYWORD: SM3 EC18

Have students access the Internet through the HRW Go site to conduct research on U.S. trade agreements with other countries. Individually, or in groups, have students select either the WTO or NAFTA and create a chart that summarizes its major benefits or costs. Have students present their charts to the class and explain what they've learned. ★14B, 23B, 24C

---

nations made similar compromises regarding trade regulations.

Second, it allowed Congress to grant most-favored-nation (MFN) status to U.S. trading partners. Any partner awarded this status pays the same, preferred tariffs as those paid by all such partners. Thus, if the United States lowers the wheat tariff from 20 percent to 10 percent for one MFN, the tariff reduction automatically applies to all other MFNs.

Congress has the final authority to grant and to revoke MFN status. Before the Korean War in the early 1950s, for example, the former Soviet Union enjoyed most-favored-nation status. This privilege was revoked during the Korean War, however, as tensions increased between the two nations. Controversy has also arisen with other U.S. trading partners, including China.

Regional Trade Organizations Many nations have formed regional trade organizations or alliances to reduce or eliminate trade barriers among member nations. Such benefits, however, usually are limited to the member nations and may have negative consequences on nations that are not a part of the alliance.

Examples of existing regional trade organizations include the European Union (EU)—which includes Austria, Belgium, Denmark, Finland, France, Germany, Greece, Italy, Ireland, Luxembourg, the Netherlands, Portugal, Spain, Sweden, and the United Kingdom—and the Caribbean Community and Common Market (CARICOM)—which includes Antigua and Barbuda, the Bahamas, Barbados, Belize, Grenada, Guyana, Jamaica, and several smaller nations. Other organizations are the Central American Common Market, which includes Costa Rica, El Salvador, Guatemala, Honduras, and Nicaragua; the Association of Southeast Asian Nations (ASEAN), including Brunei Darussalam, Indonesia, Malaysia, the Philippines, Singapore,

---

European Union

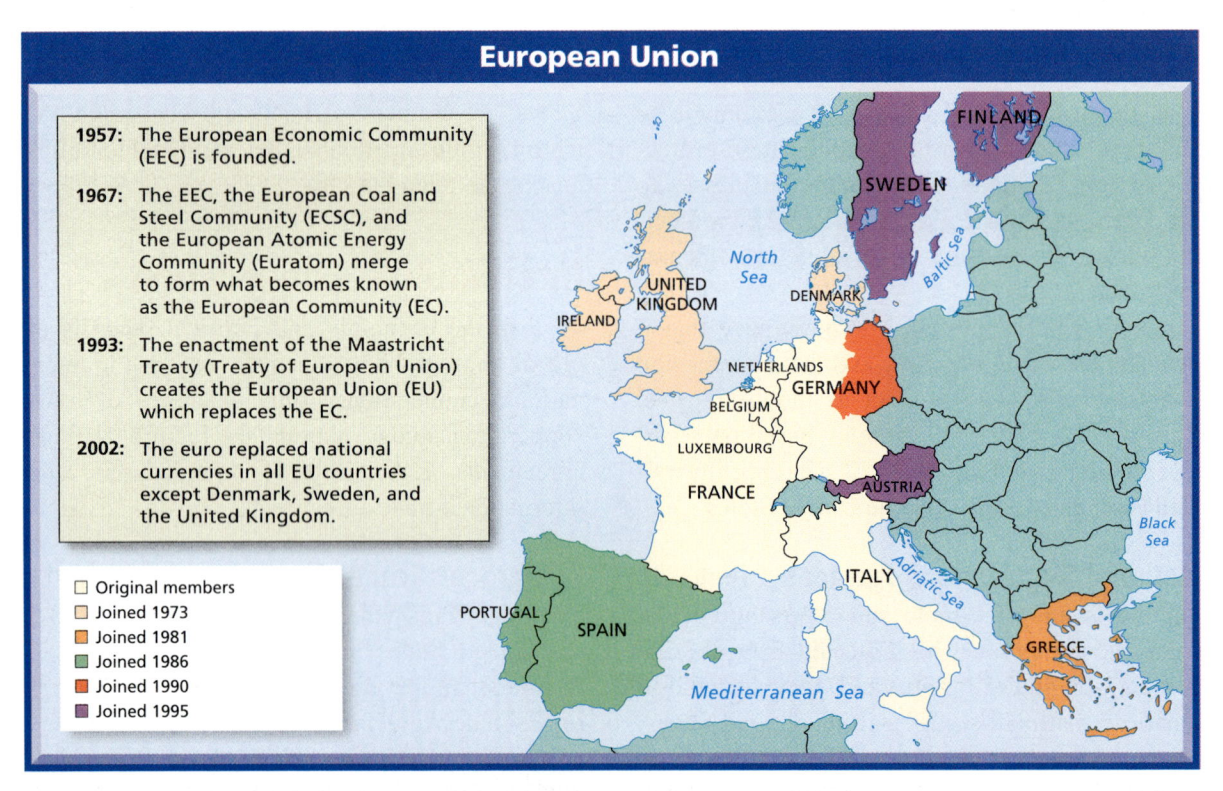

- **1957:** The European Economic Community (EEC) is founded.
- **1967:** The EEC, the European Coal and Steel Community (ECSC), and the European Atomic Energy Community (Euratom) merge to form what becomes known as the European Community (EC).
- **1993:** The enactment of the Maastricht Treaty (Treaty of European Union) creates the European Union (EU) which replaces the EC.
- **2002:** The euro replaced national currencies in all EU countries except Denmark, Sweden, and the United Kingdom.

☐ Original members
☐ Joined 1973
☐ Joined 1981
☐ Joined 1986
☐ Joined 1990
☐ Joined 1995

FIGURE 18.7 The European Union is one of the oldest regional trade alliances in the world. **Which countries are the most recent members of this organization?**

CHAPTER 18

North American Free Trade Agreement (highlights)

- established a free-trade zone across the United States, Canada, and Mexico
- provided for the gradual elimination of tariffs on goods traded among NAFTA countries
- required NAFTA countries to improve access to their agricultural markets
- reaffirmed the right of each member to set and enforce its own level of protection of human, animal, and plant life and health through measures that are scientifically based, necessary, and fair
- required each member country to treat other members' investors and their investments as favorably as it treats its own; set up arbitration rules to settle investment disputes
- affirmed a member's right to establish a monopoly, but required them to minimize impairment of free trade
- established rules to govern temporary entrance by citizens of one NAFTA country into other NAFTA countries for business purposes; identified categories of travelers eligible for temporary access to other countries
- required members to protect and enforce intellectual property rights of the other countries — for example copyrights, trademarks, patents, and trade secrets — and to prevent enforcement measures from hindering legitimate trade
- provided for countries to join or withdraw from NAFTA

Source: Organization of American States

FIGURE 18.8 The economic and political benefits of international trade encourage nations to reduce trade barriers. **What three countries participate in NAFTA?**

Thailand, and Vietnam; and the Southern Common Market (MERCOSUR), which includes Argentina, Bolivia, Brazil, Chile, Paraguay, and Uruguay.

International Trade Agreements

The most significant international trade agreement of the post–World War II period was the General Agreement on Tariffs and Trade (GATT), a multinational trade agreement. Twenty-three noncommunist nations signed this agreement in 1947.

GATT members met periodically in conferences known as rounds to discuss issues in international trade. Two of the best-known rounds of GATT talks were the Kennedy Round, which concluded in 1967, and the Tokyo Round, which was completed in 1979. Each round of talks resulted in substantial tariff reductions and opened additional talks on related issues.

In the 1980s growing concern about nontariff barriers such as quotas, voluntary restrictions, export subsidies, and licensing requirements also were included in GATT negotiations. The GATT talks in Geneva, Switzerland (1982), and the Uruguay Round (1986–1993), reaffirmed nations' support for free trade despite increasing pressures from protectionists.

In 1995 GATT was superseded by the World Trade Organization (WTO). Membership in the WTO now includes more than 140 nations that have pledged work to reduce tariffs and eliminate quotas.

NAFTA Another significant development in international trade was the negotiation of the North American Free Trade Agreement (NAFTA). Signed by the United States, Mexico, and Canada in 1992, this agreement was designed to reduce—and eventually eliminate—tariffs on all goods and services coming into and out of these countries. (For more information on NAFTA, see Figure 18.8.)

Multinational Corporations

In recent years, more global companies have built plants in the countries with which they do business. The decision to build in a foreign nation can benefit both the multinational corporation (MNC) and the host nation. The corporation is able to avoid some shipping fees, protective tariffs, and quotas. The host nation benefits from additional employment opportunities and higher revenues

---

Global Connections

As of 1996, the World Trade Organization (WTO) listed 76 regional trade organizations worldwide. Of these, more than half were created during the 1990s, indicating a strong global move toward freer trade.

Enhancing the Lesson

For more information on regional trade organizations and the World Trade Organization (WTO), see the International Organizations section on the *Researcher Online*.

Transparency

An overhead transparency of Figure 18.8 is available in *Transparency Resources*. See Transparency 75: North American Free Trade Agreement (highlights).

Caption Answer

Canada, Mexico, and the United States

Caption Answer
They can avoid some shipping fees, protective tariffs, and quotas. ⭐14A, 23A

SECTION 3 REVIEW ANSWERS

1. trade barrier (439), revenue tariff (439), protective tariff (439), import quota (440), voluntary trade restriction (440), embargo (441), free trade (441), protectionism (441) **24A**

2. revenue tariffs, protective tariffs, import quotas, voluntary trade restrictions, embargos, licensing requirements **24C, 24D**

3a. benefits—can protect infant industries, maintain a nation's standard of living, prevent overspecialization, protect important industries from foreign competition and failure, protect national security, and promote fairness; opportunity costs—can decrease competition, encourage inefficiency, reduce employment, result in higher-priced and poorer-quality products, and lead to abuses by some industries **14A**

3b. increases competition, leading to better-quality goods at a better price; promotes economic growth **14A**

4. It has increased trade among nations in regional trade organizations, reduced obstacles to trade, and promoted more multinational corporations and joint ventures. **14B, 23A**

INTERNATIONAL TRADE *Recently, many multinational corporations (MNCs) have built plants in the countries in which they do business.* **What are the incentives for MNCs to set up production facilities in the countries in which their products are sold?** ⭐TEKS

from taxes on the corporation's income, profits, and properties.

During the 1980s and 1990s a number of foreign firms located plants in the United States. Nissan, for example, began building cars and trucks in Tennessee, and Honda began making motorcycles and cars in Ohio.

Some companies choose to organize joint ventures. Under joint-ownership arrangements, two companies from different nations can agree to build and operate a production plant. The profits are shared by both companies, usually according to a written agreement.

Joint ventures begun during the 1980s and 1990s include the General Motors and Toyota joint venture to produce cars at a new plant in California, Boeing Corporation's teaming with the Japanese Aircraft Corporation to develop more advanced aircraft, and the agreement between RCA and Japan's Sharp Corporation to build satellites together in the United States. These recent changes in international trade have created new trade issues, such as whether goods produced by joint ventures in the United States should be considered "American made."

Another concern is that MNCs and joint ventures will outproduce and thereby hurt domestic producers in nations in which they build plants. To address this, nations throughout the world have instituted performance standards for multinationals that build plants in their countries. These standards require the corporation to export a certain percentage of its output. The hope is that such requirements will protect domestic industries.

SECTION 3 REVIEW

⭐TEKS Q: 1, 2, 3a, 3b, 4

1. Identify and Explain:
   trade barrier
   revenue tariff
   protective tariff
   import quota
   voluntary trade restriction
   embargo
   free trade
   protectionism

2. Categorizing: Copy the chart below. Use it to identify six kinds of trade barriers.

(Trade Barriers)

3. Finding the Main Idea
   a. How might a nation hope to benefit from trade barriers? What are the opportunity costs of trade barriers?
   b. What are the arguments in favor of free trade?

4. Writing and Critical Thinking
   Evaluating: Explain how economic cooperation among nations has led to increased international trade.
   Consider the following:
   • the benefits of membership in international free-trade organizations
   • the costs of membership in such organizations

Homework Practice Online
keyword: SM3 HP4

446 CHAPTER 18

Economics IN THE NEWS

The NAFTA Debate

The North American Free Trade Agreement (NAFTA) went into effect in 1994. Since then, there has been significant controversy over the agreement's effects.

Nonetheless, advocates and opponents of free trade agree on one thing—NAFTA has increased trade among its members. For instance, Mexico and Canada have increased their exports to the United States. In the 1990s Mexico saw its exports grow by an annual average of 16 percent, while Canada saw a 10-percent annual rise. U.S. exports to its NAFTA partners also grew. By 2000, 23 percent of the United States' exports went to Canada while 14 percent went to Mexico.

In addition, during the 1990s global exports from the NAFTA economies grew at an annual rate of 7 percent, which was similar to that of Asia, but far ahead of the rates for Europe (4 percent) and Latin America (5 percent, excluding Mexico). In 2000 the NAFTA economies were responsible for 20 percent of global exports.

NAFTA has also had other positive effects on business. American businesses, for instance, have been able to take advantage of lower labor costs in Mexico. As a result, Mexico has seen growth in its manufacturing sector.

Opponents of NAFTA point to the problems associated with the agreement. They note a pattern of stagnant wages, increased job insecurity, and rising inequality. In the United States, for instance, NAFTA has resulted in the loss of an estimated 766,000 jobs. In Mexico, opponents of the agreement point out that while manufacturing has risen, wages have declined by 21 percent. They also mention that most growth in manufacturing has occurred along the United States–Mexico border and thus has not provided much benefit to the rest of the country. In Canada, NAFTA's critics note that per capita income has declined and the country's wealth has been redistributed toward the richest 20 percent of Canadians.

Opponents of NAFTA also criticize its investor-protection provisions. NAFTA allows foreign investors to sue their host countries for damages when governmental actions interfere with their profits. NAFTA does not allow labor and environmental activists the same right to sue foreign businesses that harm workers or the environment.

Debate over the costs and benefits of NAFTA has influenced debate over the proposed Free Trade of Area of the Americas (FTAA), which would extend NAFTA to the rest of the Americas by 2005.

A truck crosses from Mexico into the United States. Cross-border trade among Canada, Mexico, and the United States has increased since NAFTA took effect, but the debate over NAFTA's benefits to the average American worker still rages on.

What Do You Think?

1. What are some of the benefits and costs of NAFTA?
2. In your opinion, which groups stand to benefit the most from NAFTA—businesses, consumers, or labor?

WHY IT MATTERS TODAY

Free trade, including the extension of the FTAA, remains a hotly contested issue. Use CNNfyi.com or other **current events** sources to find more examples of this debate.

Economics in the News Answers

1. benefits—increased trade among members, lower labor costs for U.S. businesses, growth in Mexican manufacturing sector, increased exports of Canadian natural resources; costs—stagnant or declining wages, decreased job security, rising inequality, declining per capita income, redistribution of wealth toward the rich, and investors' being able to sue, while labor and environmental interests cannot **14B**

2. Answers should reflect an understanding of the costs and benefits of NAFTA. **14B**

CHAPTER 18
Review Answers

Writing a Summary

Summaries should focus on the main points of each section. These may be found in the Read to Discover questions at the start of each section. Summaries should also use standard grammar, spelling, sentence structure, and punctuation. **24B, 24D**

Identifying Ideas

absolute advantage (428), comparative advantage (428), floating exchange rate (433), balance of payments (436), trade deficit (437), trade barrier (439), protective tariff (439), import quota (440), free trade (441), protectionism (441) **24A**

CHAPTER 18 Review

(Continued from page 447)

Understanding Main Ideas

1. A nation can focus on efficiently producing a few products and trade them for other things it needs, thus expanding its production possibilities.
2. absolute—products a nation produces more cheaply and efficiently than its trading partners; comparative—products in which a nation has the greatest absolute advantage **13A**
3. exports are cheaper; imports are more expensive **13D**
4. tariffs—increase price of imports; import quotas and voluntary trade restrictions—limit import volumes; embargoes—cut off imports to and exports from a country **14A**
5. by enabling businesses to market and sell products to consumers outside their local area. **26D**

Reviewing Themes

1. Nation A has an absolute advantage in both; Nation A should specialize in coconuts, Nation B in pineapples, and the two nations should trade. **13B**
2. absolute advantage—knowledge of economics; comparative advantages—knowledge of economics with science and mathematics nations, knowledge of economics and mathematics with government nation **13A, 23A**

Writing a Summary ★TEKS

Using standard grammar, spelling, sentence structure, and punctuation, write a summary of the information in the chapter.

Identifying Ideas ★TEKS

Identify the following terms or individuals and explain their significance.

1. absolute advantage
2. comparative advantage
3. floating exchange rate
4. balance of payments
5. trade deficit
6. trade barrier
7. protective tariff
8. import quota
9. free trade
10. protectionism

Understanding Main Ideas ★TEKS

SECTION 1 *(pp. 427–30)*

1. Why might a nation practice specialization?
2. Explain the difference between absolute advantage and comparative advantage.

SECTION 2 *(pp. 431–38)*

3. What effect does currency depreciation have on a nation's exports and imports?

SECTION 3 *(pp. 439–46)*

4. What are the three principal types of trade barriers? Explain how each works to restrict international trade.
5. How has the advent of e-commerce affected the marketing and sale of goods?

Reviewing Themes ★TEKS

1. **International Trade** If Nation A devoted all its resources to one product, it could produce 30 million pounds of coconuts or 5 million pounds of pineapples each year. Likewise, Nation B could produce 16 million pounds of coconuts or 4 million pounds of pineapples. Which nation has the absolute advantage in coconuts? Pineapples? What would you suggest each nation produce or trade?

2. **International Trade** Imagine that your economics classroom is a nation and that you and your classmates have the opportunity to engage in a trade of tutoring services with a "mathematics" nation, a "science" nation, and a "government" nation. What are your absolute advantages? Comparative advantages?

Thinking Critically ★TEKS

1. **Supporting a Point of View** Which policy do you think best serves the economic interests of the United States—free trade or protectionism? Explain your answer.

2. **Evaluating** Suppose Japanese car imports are selling better than domestic cars in the United States. Should the United States implement trade barriers to increase domestic car sales? Explain your answer.

3. **Evaluating** Explain how a nation's balance of payments provides information about its trading relationship with other nations. Consider the nation's current account and capital account in your answer.

Writing about Economics ★TEKS

Review the list that you created in your Economics Notebook at the beginning of this chapter. What does this list suggest about international trade? Explain your answer in your Notebook.

448 CHAPTER 18

Building Social Studies Skills

Interpreting the Cartoon

"Sorry, your uncle left nothing of value, only U.S. dollars."

1. What is the cartoonist saying about U.S. dollars?
   a. Their value has skyrocketed.
   b. They are a memorial to the past.
   c. They are worthless.
   d. They are of equal value with the British pound.

2. Based on what you know about exchange rates, what do you think might have happened to U.S. imports and exports at the time this cartoon was written?
   a. They both would have grown.
   b. They both would have declined.
   c. Imports would have risen while exports declined.
   d. Exports would have risen while imports declined.

Analyzing Primary Sources

Laura Tyson is an economic expert on international trade who served as President Clinton's National Economic Advisor. Read this excerpt from her 1993 book and answer the questions that follow.

"During the last half century, America defined its priorities in geopolitical terms. . . . We have succeeded beyond our wildest dreams, emerging as the world's only military superpower. But we are no longer the world's only economic superpower. Indeed, in the full flush of geopolitical triumph, we are teetering over the abyss of economic decline.

"The signs are everywhere: anemic [feeble] productivity growth, falling real wages, a woefully inadequate educational system, and declining shares of world markets for many high-technology products. After more than a decade of faltering American economic performance . . . our economic competitiveness . . . is in slow but perceptible decline."

3. Which of the following statements best describes the author's point of view?
   a. In spite of its geopolitical ascendance, the United States is in an economic decline.
   b. The economy, like our geopolitical power, is triumphant.
   c. America has consistently made its economy a priority.
   d. America should increase its defense spending.

4. Compare and contrast the current condition of the U.S. economy with its condition at the time Tyson was writing her book.

Alternative Assessment

Building Your Portfolio

Suppose in her last letter to you, your French pen pal asked you to buy her some popular music CDs that she cannot get in France. Determine the price in U.S. dollars of five CDs, and research the current exchange rate of Euros to dollars. Write your pen pal a letter explaining how you found the exchange rate, what the exchange rate is, how much each CD costs in U.S. dollars, and how much she would need to send you in Euros for you to be able to make the purchases.

Internet Activity: go.hrw.com
KEYWORD: SM3 EC18

Access the Internet through the HRW Go site to conduct research on the International Monetary Fund (IMF). Find out which countries belong to the IMF, who runs the IMF, and how the IMF works to keep currency stabilized. Write a brief paragraph summarizing your findings.

INTERNATIONAL TRADE 449

Thinking Critically

1. Answers should reflect an understanding of the pros and cons of free trade and protectionism. 14A

2. Answers should reflect an understanding of the pros and cons of using trade barriers to help U.S. companies compete with imports. 14A

3. indicates the nation's finances and investments with other nations; current account shows dollar value of imports and exports, income citizens and firms earn in other countries, and income foreign citizens and firms earn in the nation; capital account shows flow of capital between the nation and other nations 23A

Writing about Economics

Answers will vary but should reflect an understanding of the importance of foreign trade and the concept of comparative advantage. 12B, 13B, 13C, 14A

Building Social Studies Skills

1. c 23E
2. d 13D, 23E
3. a 23E
4. Answers should reflect an understanding of the weakened state of the U.S. economy at the time Tyson was writing, as well as of the current state of the U.S. economy. 23D, 23E

449

UNIT 6

LAB OBJECTIVES

During the lab, students will
- take on the role of staff members of the Ministry of Economic Development for the country of Lotsaland.
- review and analyze information and documents pertaining to the country of Lotsaland.
- prepare a list of reasons why foreign business people should invest in Lotsaland.
- prepare a written or typed speech to encourage foreign business people to invest in Lotsaland.

Using the Lab

Before beginning the lab, organize students into groups and distribute copies of the Unit 6 Lab Activity found in *Unit Tests and Unit Lab Activities with Answer Key*. Have students read the assignment on this page and then discuss it as a class. Point out the documents on pages 451–53 that students will use during the lab.

The What Do You Think? questions on pages 451–53 will help guide students during the project. In addition, the lab activity sheet includes a step-by-step checklist for students to monitor their progress.
★25A

UNIT 6

ECONOMICS LAB

You Solve the problem

Developing an Economy

Imagine that you and other members of the Ministry of Economic Development for the country of Lotsaland. The nation operated under a command socialist economy for more than 50 years. Recently, however, the government—of which you are part—has been moving the country, rather unsuccessfully, toward market capitalism.

As staff members for the Ministry of Economic Development, your group's job is to encourage foreign investment in your country as the economy continues to revert into a market system. Your group has collected the following documents and other information:
- A map and statistical data sheet for the Republic of Lotsaland
- Fact sheet from the Ministry of Economic Development
- A copy of the Regional Association of Free Trade (RAFT) proposal

This information should be used to help you develop a speech encouraging foreign business owners—bankers and the heads of multinational corporations—to invest in your country.

Economics Notebook Assignment ★TEKS

1. Write a clear, one-sentence statement of the problem to solve.
2. Review the documents to gather information.
3. Answer the accompanying questions in your Economics Notebook.
4. Prepare the speech for the Minister of Economic Development to give at the conference of foreign business owners. The speech should point out the reasons why foreign businesspeople should invest in your country. Also remember that your country's goal is to continue to revert into a market system. In your speech, be sure to list and consider the different options for investment and weigh the advantages and disadvantages of each. Your speech should also indicate what solution you recommend, how the solution will be implemented, and how effective you think the solution will be.

What Do You Think?
Answers

1. An advantage, because a highly literate populace is more likely to be educated. Educated and skilled workers improve a nation's productivity levels and its ability to innovate and to adapt—all of which help promote economic growth and development. **23A**

2. iron ore, aluminum, oil, cattle, pigs, sheep; in the mountainous, eastern part of the country **23F**

3. Yes. This infrastructure will enable companies and individuals to easily transport resources and products among the nation's cities. **23A, 23F**

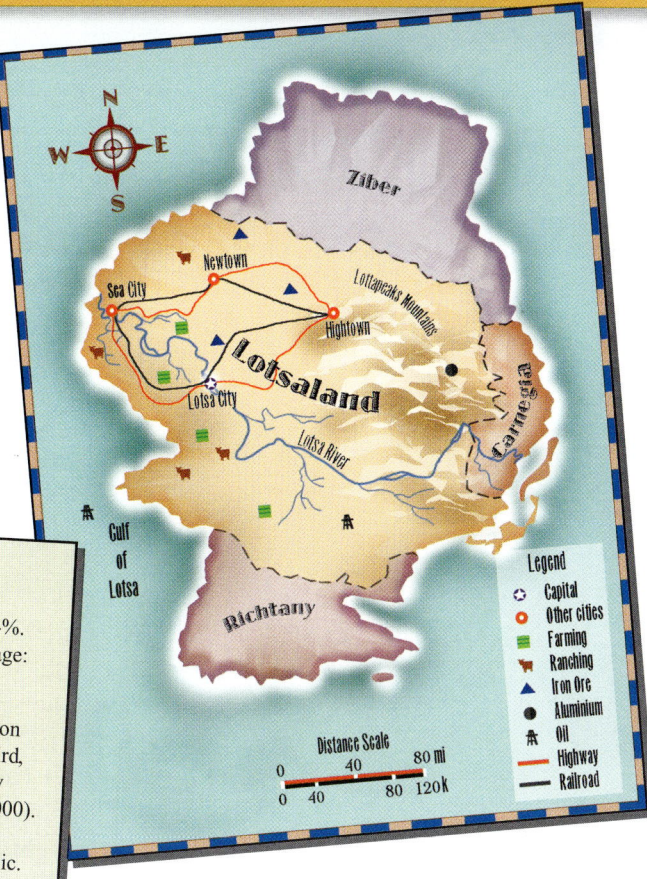

REPUBLIC OF LOTSALAND

People: **Population**: 11,136,777. **Age distribution**: <18: 24%; 65+: 14%. **Pop. Density**: 352.55 per sq. mi. (136 per sq. km). **Urban**: 77%. **Language**: Lotsalandian.

Geography: **Area**: 31,589 sq. mi. (81,815.5 sq. km). **Neighbors**: Ziber on N, Carnegia on E, Richtany on S. **Topography**: mountainous eastern third, flat or low hills elsewhere. **Capital**: Lotsa City. **Major cities**: Lotsa City (1.6 million), Sea City (600,000), Newtown (500,000), Hightown (420,000).

Government: **Form**: Communist state in transition to democratic republic. **Defense spending**: 4.1% of GDP. **Military size**: 200,000.

Economy: **Industries**: Machinery, mining, steel, motor vehicles, oil. **Chief crops**: wheat, corn, potatoes. **Minerals**: iron ore, aluminum, oil. **Livestock**: cattle, pigs, sheep. **Labor force**: 42% industrial, 18% agricultural, 40% service.

Finance: **Monetary unit**: lottabux. **Gross domestic product** (in U.S. dollars): $83.3 billion. **Per capita GDP**: $7,480. **Imports**: $14.2 billion; trading partners: Carnegia 51%, Richtany 30%, Ziber 14%, Other 5%. **Exports**: $22.5 billion; trading partners: Carnegia 54%, Richtany 24%, Ziber 17%, Other 5%. **National budget**: $17.7 billion. **International gold reserves**: 2.1 million oz. **Consumer price change (inflation) over last year**: 10.2%.

Transport: **Railroads**: 5,799 mi. (9,330.6 km). **Motor vehicles**: 1.6 million passenger autos, 420,000 commercial vehicles. **Air transport**: 2 international airports.

Communications: **Television sets**: 1 per 4.1 people. **Radios**: 1 per 2.6 people. **Telephones**: 1 per 4.7 people. **Daily newspaper circulation**: 389 per 1,000 people.

Health: **Life expectancy**: 70, male; 73, female. **Births** (per 1,000 people): 11. **Deaths** (per 1,000 people): 10. **Hospital beds**: 1 per 98 people. **Physicians**: 1 per 344 people. **Literacy rate**: 98%.

–254–

▲ WHAT DO YOU THINK?

1. Would you expect Lotsaland's literacy rate to be an advantage or a disadvantage for its future economic development? Why?

2. What kinds of resources are available for economic development? Where are Lotsaland's aluminum deposits located?

3. Are Lotsaland's cities connected by modern highways and rail lines? How should this affect economic development?

ECONOMICS LAB

What Do You Think?
Answers

1. more business decisions being made by individuals and businesses; steadily increasing rate of economic growth, increasing economic prosperity, loans from the World Bank and IMF for development, decreasing military spending, comparative advantage in steel **23A**

2. Less military spending frees up resources for use in producing more consumer and capital goods. Students' production possibilities curves should be similar to the model in Figure 17.3 on page 416. **5B, 23B**

3. 5:1; any trade ratio from 4:1 to 1:1 **23G**

ECONOMICS LAB continued

REPUBLIC OF LOTSALAND
MINISTRY OF ECONOMIC DEVELOPMENT

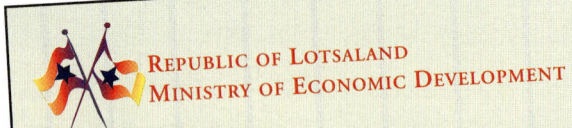

Fact Sheet

- Seven years ago the government of the Republic of Lotsaland began to enact various reforms aimed at moving the country toward market capitalism. These reforms include transferring economic decision making from government officials to individuals and businesses.

- As a result of these economic reforms, the rate of economic growth in Lotsaland has been steadily increasing for six years. This economic growth rate has led to increased prosperity among Lotsalandians. This prosperity, however, has not been felt by all of Lotsaland's citizens.

- The World Bank and the International Monetary Fund have provided billions of dollars in loans to help economic development in Lotsaland. In return for these loans, the government has agreed to allow individuals and businesses to make more economic decisions.

- The government has set a goal of cutting military spending from 4.1 percent of GDP to less than 2 percent within five years. This spending cut will allow more resources to be used to produce nonmilitary goods.

- Because iron ore is plentiful, Lotsaland has a comparative advantage over other countries in the production of steel. On the other hand, the country's aluminum deposits are located in the Lottapeaks Mountains, making mining difficult. As a result, Lotsaland can produce 20 tons of steel for every 4 tons of aluminum products.

WHAT DO YOU THINK?

1. What points on this fact sheet are most likely to encourage foreign investment in Lotsaland?

2. What are some possible outcomes of using fewer resources to produce military goods? Explain your answer by sketching a model of a production possibilities curve.

3. What is the exchange ratio between steel and aluminum products? What ratio would make importing aluminum products more efficient than making them domestically?

**Republic of Lotsaland
Ministry of Economic Development**

A Proposal for the Regional Association of Free Trade (RAFT)

In recent years the Republic of Lotsaland has seen great economic growth as a result of its market reforms. To promote even greater economic growth, the Republic of Lotsaland proposes the creation of a Regional Association of Free Trade (RAFT) that would include itself and neighboring countries seeking improved economies through market reforms.

RAFT would pursue the following goals:
- the gradual elimination of import tariffs and import quotas—or the quantity of goods each country permits to be imported—among member countries,
- the development of a large market in which goods from member countries can be produced and sold freely,
- and cooperation among member countries to promote friendly political and economic relations.

The Republic of Lotsaland proposes that the RAFT agreement—under terms that pursue the above goals—be completely implemented within three years. In addition, Lotsaland invites the following countries to become founding members of RAFT: Richtany, Ziber, and Carnegia.

RAFT does not wish to disrupt free trade among its member countries and non-RAFT members. Therefore, each member country will be permitted to pursue its own trade policies with nonmember countries.

◀ WHAT DO YOU THINK?

1. Why might Lotsaland's membership in the Regional Association of Free Trade appeal to foreign investors?
2. How would a free-trade association help each member country market what it produces most efficiently?
3. Why do you suppose that Lotsaland's government does not want the RAFT agreement to interfere with trade among member and nonmember countries?

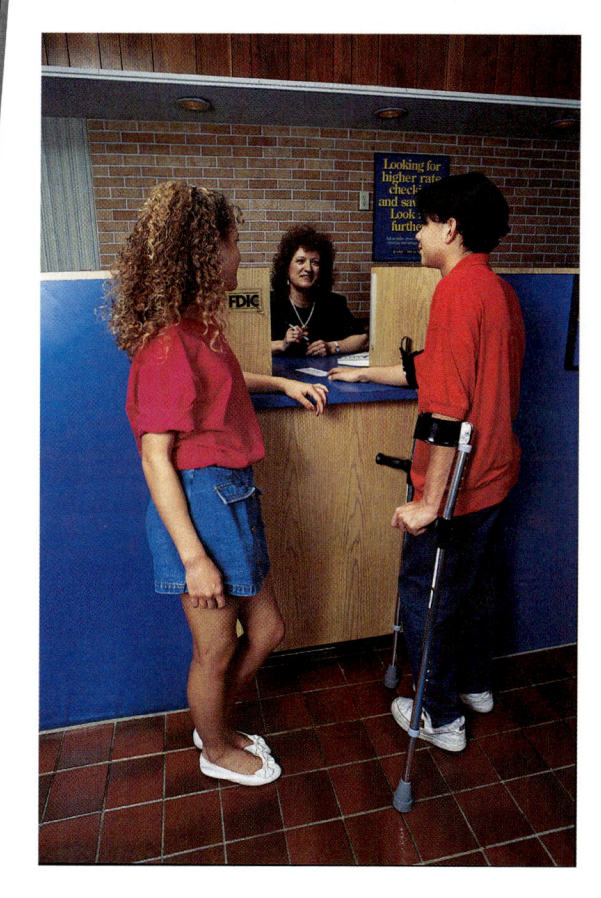

internet connect

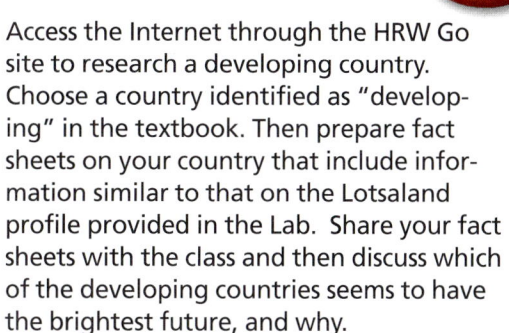

Internet Activity: go.hrw.com
KEYWORD: SM3 ECL6

Access the Internet through the HRW Go site to research a developing country. Choose a country identified as "developing" in the textbook. Then prepare fact sheets on your country that include information similar to that on the Lotsaland profile provided in the Lab. Share your fact sheets with the class and then discuss which of the developing countries seems to have the brightest future, and why.

What Do You Think?
Answers

1. RAFT would reduce tariffs and enlarge the market for goods produced in Lotsaland, increasing the likelihood of higher monetary returns for foreign investors. In addition, RAFT would decrease the likelihood of political conflict or war between Lotsaland and a neighboring country, which would make the nation a safer investment. **14B, 23A**

2. By removing tariffs and import quotas, RAFT would help each member nation better identify the products for which it has a comparative advantage. Lotsaland has a comparative advantage in steel production. **14B, 23A**

3. Lotsaland's government leaders want to ensure that the RAFT agreement does not disrupt existing trade or prevent future trade between Lotsaland and non-RAFT nations. **14B, 23A**

ECONOMICS LAB

HOLT Economics

REFERENCE SECTION

Consumer Handbook	R2
World Economic Statistics	R26
Glossary	R38
Glosario	R51
Index	R67
Acknowledgments	R90
Photo Credits	R91

Reference Section R1

CONSUMER HANDBOOK

1 BUDGETING

Economics is a study of choices—the choices people make in order to satisfy their needs and wants. Such choices are necessary because people's needs and wants often are greater than the economic resources available to satisfy them. For consumers, preparing a personal budget is essential to making wise economic choices.

A budget is a money plan. It identifies the amount of money a consumer can expect to earn and spend during a given period of time. Preparing a personal budget is not a difficult task, but it does take time and careful thought.

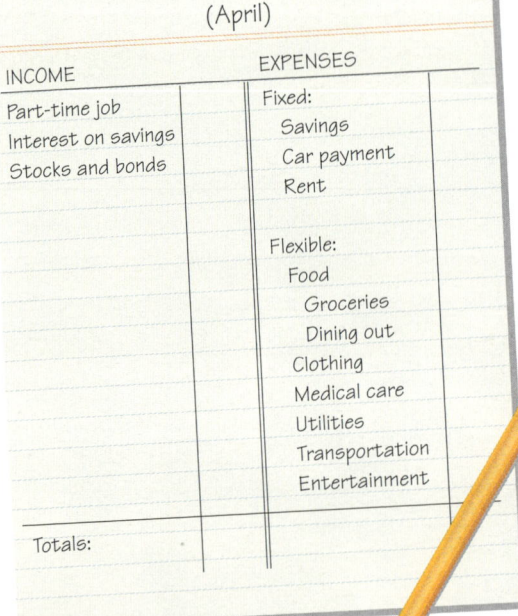

Assessing Your Budget Needs

Before preparing a budget, you should assess your budget needs. You can start by studying your income and expenses for a given period of time, such as one month.

In general, consumers plan their personal budgets on a monthly basis because the payments for many expenses—such as housing, electricity, and telephone service—are due each month. Additionally, many people save a portion of their income on a monthly basis. To assess your budget needs, keep detailed records of the money you earn and the money you spend during a one-month period. You may wish to save copies of your bills as well as cash register and credit card receipts to help you.

At the end of the month, record your findings. You may wish to use a computer software program to assess and organize your budget, or you can prepare a handwritten budget on a sheet of paper. If your budget is handwritten, divide the paper into two columns. Label the first column "Income" and the second column "Expenses." Then list your income and expenses for the month under the proper column. (Note that savings should be entered under the "Expenses" column.) You will begin to see a pattern of earning, spending, and saving money. This pattern reflects your budget needs and can be used as the basis for your personal budget.

Household Budget (April)

INCOME	EXPENSES
Part-time job	Fixed:
Interest on savings	Savings
Stocks and bonds	Car payment
	Rent
	Flexible:
	Food
	Groceries
	Dining out
	Clothing
	Medical care
	Utilities
	Transportation
	Entertainment
Totals:	

Estimating Your Income

Once you have assessed your budget needs, you will be equipped to prepare your personal budget. First, write the name of the month that the budget is for at the top of a sheet of paper. Then divide the paper into "Income" and "Expenses" columns, as you did when assessing your budget needs.

In the Income column, record your estimated income for the month. Be sure to include whatever money you expect to earn from part-time jobs, as well as any money you expect to receive from interest on savings or other investments.

Estimating Your Expenses

In the Expenses column, identify the costs that you anticipate for the month. It is important to include as many details as possible. List all the expenses that you think you will have, including those for personal items and other small purchases.

When listing expenses, it often is helpful to divide them into two categories—fixed expenses and flexible expenses. Fixed expenses are the same from month to month. Rent and car payments, for example, are fixed expenses. Flexible expenses, on the other hand, change from month to month. They include food, clothing, medical care, and medicines.

Your expenses may not be very high if you live with a parent or guardian. When you live independently, however, you probably will find that your highest monthly expenses will fall into the same general categories as those of other consumers. These categories include housing, food, clothing, and transportation.

Housing Expenses Housing costs are high, whether you rent an apartment or own a house or condominium. For most people, their largest monthly expense is housing—whether rent or a mortgage payment. When preparing a budget for housing expenses, however, it also is important to list the costs of utilities. Utilities are essential services such as electricity, gas, water, telephone service, and trash removal. Additional housing expenses include home repairs, property insurance, property taxes, furniture, decorating, maintenance equipment, and cleaning supplies.

Food Expenses Grocery bills usually make up the largest portion of food expenses. Meals and snacks purchased away from home also should be listed under food expenses. If you typically eat dinner in a restaurant twice a month, for example, the money used to pay for these meals should be reflected in your food budget.

Clothing Expenses Clothing costs involve more than the price of new clothes and shoes. Laundry and dry-cleaning bills, shoe repairs, and mending supplies also should be listed under your clothing expenses.

Transportation Expenses Transportation costs may range from bus and subway fares to the expenses of automobile ownership—monthly car payments, gasoline and oil, repairs, insurance, car washes, and accessories.

Other Expenses Most consumers' budgets include expense categories other than housing, food, clothing, and transportation. These categories vary among consumers, depending on their needs, and might include health care, life insurance, education, and entertainment. In addition, some consumers include a category for miscellaneous expenses that are difficult to predict.

Savings One other category should be listed under monthly expenses in every consumer's budget. This category is savings. The main goal of a

CONSUMER HANDBOOK R3

Practicing Consumer Skills
Answers

1. The payments for many expenses, such as rent, electricity, and telephone service are due each month. Additionally, many people are in the practice of saving a portion of their income on a monthly basis. **23A**

2. Answers should include housing, food, clothing, transportation, and savings. **23A**

3. Revision is necessary because people's incomes and expenses change over time. Income often changes significantly with a new job or promotion. Likewise, expenses change as people's circumstances change. **1B, 23A**

---

money plan is to help consumers make wise economic decisions. An important part of being a wise consumer is saving money.

Saving money is important because inflation and unforeseen expenses sometimes can ruin even the most carefully planned budget. Many items in your budget, such as medical bills and home and auto repairs, tend to increase in cost over time. In addition, expenses for unexpected developments—such as flood damage or an automobile accident—cannot be anticipated. For these reasons, it is useful to set money aside each month in an emergency fund for use on those occasions when an unplanned expense occurs.

Saving money is important for other reasons too. You might want to save for certain items that you cannot afford to buy right away, but saving money to satisfy short-term goals is not the only reason for saving. For example, many people save for major expenses such as college tuition. It also is important to save—or invest—for the future in order to assure a comfortable standard of living in later years. Known as unearned income, the interest and dividends from savings and investments also can supplement your earned income.

Revising Your Budget

For a budget that accurately predicts your needs, wants, and priorities, periodic revisions are needed. Revision is necessary because your income and expenses will change over time. Income often changes significantly with a new job or promotion. Likewise, expenses will change as your personal circumstances change.

One useful way of assessing the need for budget revision is to make an annual budget. After you have kept a budget for a number of months, prepare a budget listing all expected income and expenses for one year. An annual budget will help you get an overall picture of your financial situation and decide whether you are allocating enough funds for savings and spending as you planned.

Practicing Consumer Skills TEKS

1. Why are personal budgets traditionally based on one-month periods?
2. What general expense categories should be included in your personal budget?
3. Why is it important to revise your budget from time to time?

② COMPARISON SHOPPING

Buying and selling goods in a free market is the cornerstone of the U.S. free-enterprise system. It also is the means by which consumers satisfy their needs and wants. To satisfy the greatest number of needs and wants in spite of limitations on the amount of resources available, today's consumers must learn to be smart shoppers.

Preparing to Shop

Smart shoppers plan ahead. Before setting out for the grocery store or heading to the mall, there are several things you can do that will help prepare you to shop as efficiently and affordably as possible.

Defining Your Needs and Wants
One of the most important parts of being a smart shopper is defining the particular need or want that you wish to satisfy by purchasing a product. Suppose that you are in the market for a computer. You may need the computer only to perform simple word processing tasks. Such a computer is quite different from one that has the power and capacity to run CD-ROM programs and allow you to access the Internet. By defining your needs and wants and setting priorities ahead of time, you will be better able to make a wise buying decision.

Setting a Spending Limit Many of the buying decisions that you make depend on the amount of money that you have available to spend. To make the best decisions on how to use limited income, you may want to determine a spending limit before going shopping. This assessment will better prepare you to buy a product that will not only satisfy your needs and wants but also fit your budget.

Doing Your Homework Before making a major purchase, you may wish to consult one or more consumer publications. Magazines such as *Consumer Reports* provide useful information on a variety of products, including automobiles, electronic equipment, and appliances. A trip to the library can provide you with information about the features and product histories of items you wish to buy.

Deciding Where to Shop Choosing the best location to make your purchases is part of being a smart shopper. One way to decide where to shop is to pay attention to advertisements that appear in newspapers or are broadcast on the radio and television. If you know that a product is on sale at a certain store, you may wish to start your shopping trip there. It also may be a good idea to consider shopping at a discount store. Discount stores buy products in large quantities and can thus sell them at reduced prices. Before making a decision about where to shop, however, you may wish to phone several stores to make sure that the item you are looking for is in stock—and to check on its price.

Deciding When to Shop The time or season when you shop also can affect your buying decisions. Car dealers, for example, often put new cars on sale in the spring or summer to help clear their showrooms for next year's models, which are delivered in the fall. Being aware of such sale patterns can help you save money.

Other, more personal, factors also should be considered in decisions about when to shop. You may want to avoid going shopping when you are tired, because tired shoppers tend to buy products on impulse so that they can get home faster. Similarly, if you go grocery shopping when you are hungry, you may buy more than you planned.

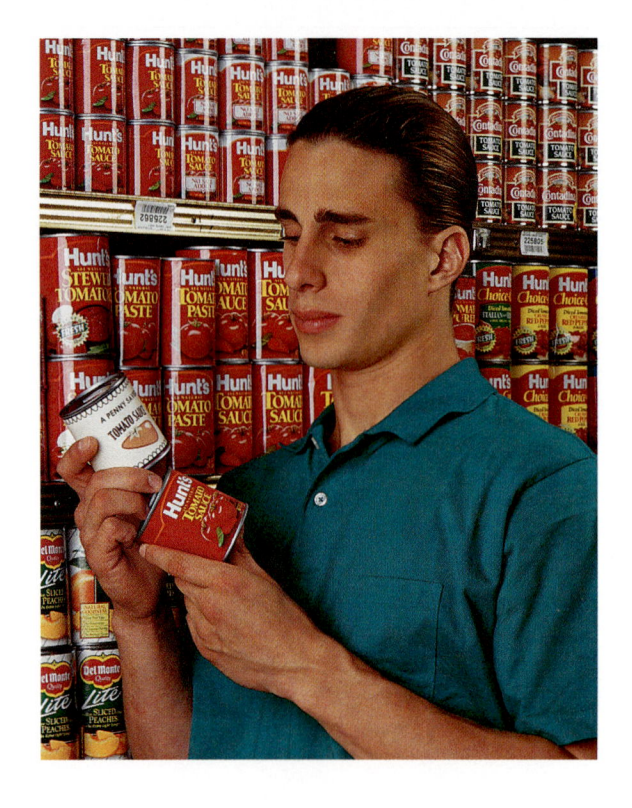

How to Shop Wisely

Making wise buying decisions requires more than advance planning. Once at the store, you must pay careful attention to the products you select.

Reading Food Labels
When shopping for food, it is particularly important that you read labels carefully. One of the first things you should notice is the brand of the product. You probably are familiar with many name brands of foods. The same foods, however, often are available in house brands or generic brands. These products generally have simple package designs and do not carry the advertising costs associated with name brands.

Compare the ingredients that are found in generic and in name-brand products. Some house and generic brands contain the exact same ingredients as the more expensive name brands—but at a lower price—and therefore are the better buys.

Food labels also should be read for information about a product's contents. Federal law requires manufacturers to list the ingredients found in their products, as well as the number of calories and percentage of fat. Additionally, information about vitamins and nutrients is included. These labels can be particularly helpful to people who have allergies or who are on restricted diets. Consumers also should look for the date after which perishable items should not be purchased.

Reading Product Descriptions
Before making a purchase, it also is a good idea to read an item's product description. Most product descriptions contain information about the care of a product. Clothing items, for example, contain information about whether—and how—they should be washed or dry cleaned. Some product descriptions also contain information about a product's proper use and warnings about its misuse. An electrical product such as a space heater, for example, may contain information about how to use the product most efficiently by taking advantage of various settings. It also may contain warnings about placing the heater away from flammable objects.

When reading product descriptions, also be sure to note whether the product must be assembled or if it requires batteries. These factors may affect your buying decision.

Comparing Product Features
Using all of the information available, carefully compare the various features of the product you are considering for purchase. Before purchasing an item, be certain that it will perform all of the tasks you expect of it. You may want to ask the sales clerk to clarify exactly what the product can—and cannot—do. Ask about the product's warranties or guarantees. If practical, ask for a trial use.

Quality Considerations
High-quality items have features that make them more attractive to consumers. Such items may last longer, look nicer, and perform better. Consumers usually are willing to pay more for high-quality products and services.

Quality, however, is often difficult to measure. Certain brand-name products, for example, penetrate the market by appealing to consumer tastes and preferences. Such products become popular to own, but it is important to remember that popularity is not the same as quality. Before buying any product, check the label and product description as

Consumer Handbook

well as the overall appearance to get a better, more accurate idea of the product's quality. Again, you also may want to research the product in consumer magazines.

Quantity and Price Considerations

If you use large quantities of an item that can be stored easily and is nonperishable, you often can save money by buying the item in a larger size—one that contains more units. You can tell if you are getting the most for your money by checking the unit prices marked on the product or on the store shelf. A unit price is the price of a product by unit, weight, or volume. The unit price of a certain brand of canned fruit, for example, may be 44 cents an ounce. The unit price of the same brand of fruit in a larger can may be 42 cents an ounce. By checking the unit prices, you can tell that the larger can is the better buy.

Practicing Consumer Skills ⭐TEKS

1. Why is it important to define specific needs and wants before going shopping?
2. What information can be obtained by reading food labels and product descriptions?
3. What is the unit price of a product?

3 UNDERSTANDING WARRANTIES

As a smart shopper, you should be sure that the products you buy are durable and in excellent condition. Manufacturers generally are required by law to provide a warranty, or written guarantee, of the condition of their products. A warranty specifies the manufacturer's obligations to the consumer; contains information about the quality and attributes of the product, including its expected lifespan; and explains the manufacturer's plan to assure product performance.

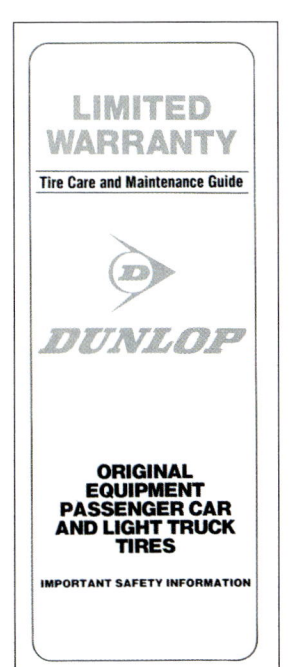

Warranties and the Law

Warranties are subject to both federal and state laws. In many states, warranties are governed by the Uniform Commercial Code, which monitors trade rules and regulations. The Magnuson-Moss Warranty Act, passed by Congress in 1975, states that the seller of a product must explain the terms of the warranty at the time of purchase. The Magnuson-Moss Warranty Act also requires that a manufacturer must specify if and how the warranty is limited.

What Warranties Cover

Most warranties cover the materials from which a product is made, as well as the quality of work used in making it. Should defects be found in the materials or the quality, the product normally will be repaired or replaced.

Be aware, however, that warranty coverage may not include all parts of a product. Specific limitations—also called exemptions—of the warranty often are written in small print. An automobile warranty, for example, may exclude problems stemming from rust. A microwave oven warranty may cover the oven's internal working parts but may exempt its case or its mechanical parts. Be sure to read the entire warranty carefully before you make a major purchase.

Most warranties do not cover repairs that might be necessary because of normal wear, misuse, abuse, negligence, or accidents. In such cases, the warranty may be void.

Most warranties are valid only for a specific time period. After this period expires, the warranty no longer applies. Normally, the longer the warranty period, the better the quality of the product. The warranty period usually starts at the time of purchase. In the case of certain appliances,

---

Practicing Consumer Skills Answers

1. By defining needs and wants and setting priorities ahead of time, people are better able to make wise buying decisions. **1A, 5A, 23A**

2. food labels—ingredients, number of calories and percentage of fat, information about vitamins and nutrients; product descriptions—information about the care of a product, information about a product's proper use and warnings about its misuse, whether the product must be assembled or if it requires batteries **23A**

3. A unit price is the price of a product by unit, weight, or volume. **23A**

CONSUMER HANDBOOK R7

Practicing Consumer Skills
Answers

1. A written guarantee that specifies the manufacturer's obligations to the consumer; provides information about the quality and attributes of the product, including its expected lifespan; and explains the manufacturer's plan to assure product performance. **23A**

2. Most warranties cover the materials from which a product is made, as well as the quality of work used to make it. Warranty coverage may not include all parts of a product, however. **23A**

3. The steps a consumer should take depend on the requirements of the specific warranty. In most cases, consumers can return the product to either the manufacturer or the place of purchase for repair, replacement, or a refund. **23A**

---

however, such as those that must be installed in the home, the warranty may start on the first day of actual use.

When a Product Is Defective

If you find that a product covered by a warranty is defective, you have certain rights. The extent of these rights depends on the manufacturer and the terms of the warranty.

Some warranties require that you return the product to the manufacturer for repair or replacement. Others require that you return the item to the place of purchase. Some warranties cover repairs on the defective merchandise, while others will replace it. Still others offer to refund the purchase price.

Generally, warranties require that you present a proof of purchase before any corrective action can be taken. Because of this requirement, it is a good idea to check the warranty when you first purchase a product to see what will be required if it is found to be defective. Label and save any packaging, receipts, or other items required by the manufacturer's or store's warranty.

Practicing Consumer Skills

1. What is a warranty?
2. What do warranties generally cover?
3. What steps can a consumer take when a product covered by a warranty is found to be defective?

4 CONSUMER CREDIT

As a consumer, one of the most valuable assets you have is credit. Using credit enables you to make purchases now and—with a finance charge—pay for them over time. Most consumers use credit to buy houses, automobiles, appliances, and other large purchases.

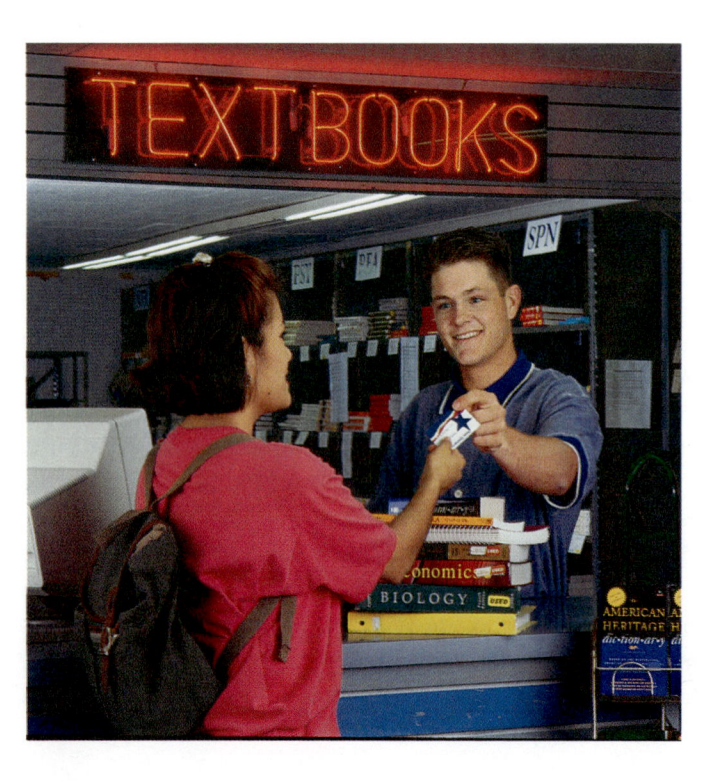

How Credit Is Extended

Credit can be extended to you by a financial institution or by a vendor selling a product. Financial institutions extend credit by issuing loans such as mortgages, short-term notes, and bank cards such as Visa® and Mastercard®. Many vendors such as department stores and oil companies extend credit by issuing credit cards. To apply for most types of credit, you must fill out an application listing such information as your place of employment, income, and outstanding debts. If your application is approved, the institution will assign you a credit limit, indicating the maximum amount you may spend using credit.

Advantages of Credit

One of the most important advantages of credit is its convenience. It allows you to buy what you need when you need it. Suppose, for example, that you need to buy a new refrigerator but do not have enough cash. If you have the ability to pay over time, the use of credit may be a practical and convenient choice.

Disadvantages of Credit

Although credit has many advantages, it also has disadvantages that a smart shopper should consider. The most obvious disadvantage is that credit usually is not free. For this reason, it is very important that consumers understand the terms of any credit arrangement that they make. The 1968 Truth in Lending Act requires that consumers be informed in writing of the finance charge, total transaction cost, and annual percentage rate associated with credit. Even with such requirements, the real cost of using credit can be deceptive. The combination of high interest rates and long term payments can cause the actual cost of credit to increase significantly.

Consumer Credit Ratings

When you first apply for credit, most financial institutions or vendors assign you a credit rating based upon the information that you provide on your credit application. This credit rating is an estimation of the probability that you will repay your debts based on your income and monthly expenditures. Even after you are assigned a good credit rating and your credit is approved, businesses continue to rate your credit behavior as you make purchases on credit. If you misuse your credit or are late making payments. lenders report this information to credit bureaus, which keep records of consumer credit ratings. If you fail to make payment on a loan, for example, the lender will report that information to a credit bureau. If you default on several loans, you will have a very poor credit rating and will find it difficult, if not impossible, to obtain credit in the future.

Practicing Consumer Skills ⭐TEKS

1. How is credit extended?
2. What are the advantages and the disadvantages of credit?
3. Why is it important for you to maintain a good credit rating?

5 CHECKING ACCOUNTS

Today one of the easiest and most common ways to pay bills and transfer money to other individuals or businesses is through the use of a personal checking account.

Opening a Checking Account

If you have money to deposit, you can open a checking account at most banks, credit unions, or savings institutions. These depository institutions offer various kinds of checking accounts. In most cases, the right account for you depends on the amount of money that you plan to keep in the account.

The traditional checking account has no minimum or monthly balance requirements. For most of these accounts, however, the customer must pay monthly service charges and check-printing fees. Typically, money deposited in the account does not earn interest.

An alternative to the traditional checking account is the NOW (negotiable order of withdrawal) account. The NOW account is an interest-bearing savings and checking account. The customer can write checks on the amount that is deposited and collect interest on the amount remaining. However, the customer usually must keep a minimum monthly balance in the account to receive the interest and free-checking privileges.

Practicing Consumer Skills Answers

1. Credit can be extended by financial institutions or by vendors selling a product. Financial institutions extend credit by issuing loans and bank cards. Many vendors extend credit by issuing charge cards or credit cards. **11A, 23A**

2. advantages—very convenient, allows people to buy what they need when they need it; disadvantages—credit is not free, when interest rates are high and payments are extended over a long period of time, the actual cost of credit increases significantly **23A**

3. It will be difficult, if not impossible, to obtain credit in the future. **23A**

CONSUMER HANDBOOK **R9**

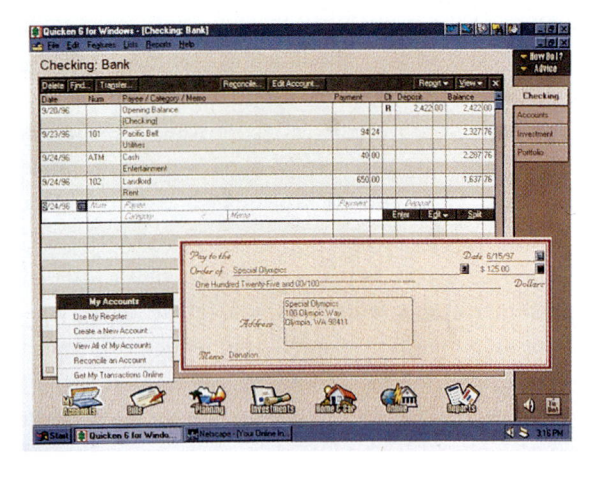

This minimum can nevertheless be quite high. For example, the minimum balance on a special account called a super-NOW account is $2,500.

Writing and Cashing Checks

A signed check represents money. For this reason, it is important that you follow special procedures both in writing and cashing checks.

Writing Checks
Most checks are printed with the account owner's name, address, and telephone number appearing in the upper left corner and the check number in the upper right corner. Checks are numbered consecutively to help people and banks keep track of which ones have been written.

Near the check number is a place for you to write the date. Across the center of the check are the words "Pay to the Order of" and a blank space. In this space, write the name of the person or business to whom you are writing the check. This person or business is known as the payee. To the right of the payee's name is a place to write the amount of the check in numerals. The amount also must be spelled out in words on the next line.

In the lower left corner of the check is a line labeled "Memo." Use this line to record any information that might be helpful to you about the check, such as what was purchased with the check.

In the lower right corner of the check is a space for you to sign your name. Without your signature, the check cannot be cashed. Across the bottom of the check you will see the name of the bank or institution with which you have the account. You also will see a series of numbers. The first series is the bank's identification number. The second series is your checking account number.

Cashing Checks
When someone gives you a personal check, it must be endorsed before it can be cashed. To endorse the check, simply sign your name in the proper space on the back as it appears on the front.

To receive the amount of the check in cash, you must go to a bank in person. There the teller may ask you to write your account number on the check before giving you the cash.

To deposit the check in your checking account, you must fill out a deposit slip. Deposit slips usually are provided to you with your checks. Your name, address, telephone number, and checking-account number are printed on the front of the deposit slip, just as they appear on your checks. The deposit slip also includes spaces in which you must write the date and add up the total amount of the deposit. If you are depositing several checks, these should be listed separately, sometimes on the reverse side of the slip. If you are receiving some of the money you deposit back in cash, you should indicate the amount as "less cash" and sign the deposit slip on the line provided.

You may deposit checks through the mail, at an automated teller machine (ATM), or in person at your bank. If you are sending an endorsed check through the mail or using the ATM machine to make a deposit, however, it is best to write your account number and the words "For Deposit Only" beneath your signature. Taking this precaution could prevent someone else from cashing your check.

Recording Your Transactions

Each time that you write or deposit a check, it is important that you keep a record of the transaction. Some institutions offer checks with carbon copies, and most also provide you with a record book, or register, for this purpose. In the record book, you should note the check number, date, payee, and amount of each transaction. You also should keep track of your current balance: after writing a check, its amount should be deducted from your balance, and after making a deposit, its amount should be added to your balance.

Balancing Your Checking Account

To help you verify the amount of money you have in your checking account, your banking institution will send you an account statement each month. This statement typically includes your balance at the beginning of the month, a list of the transactions made during the month, and your balance at the end of the month. It also includes an explanation of any special charges made against your account during the month, such as service charges or check-printing fees, as well as any monthly interest added to your balance.

Along with the monthly statements, many banks also return the checks that you wrote and that were cashed by the payees. These checks are known as canceled checks. In addition, for occasions when you do not receive receipts when depositing funds into your account, some banks also include your deposit slips with your statement.

When you receive your monthly bank statement, it is important to reconcile, or make sure that the balance you have recorded agrees with the bank's version of your balance. The easiest way to balance your checking account is to follow the directions on the back of the bank's statement. If you find an inconsistency, go back through your record book to verify that you have entered the amounts of all checks correctly. Also, make certain that you have noted which checks have not been cashed. Any time that you cannot reconcile an inconsistency between your records and the bank statement, you should call the bank for assistance.

Practicing Consumer Skills

1. What various kinds of checking accounts are available?
2. What information must be filled in when you write a check?
3. How do you endorse a check?

6 CONDUCTING A JOB SEARCH

When you are looking for a job, the classified section of the newspaper will be invaluable. Also known as the want ads, the classified section contains ads for jobs in businesses in the local area. It may also contain selected ads from businesses across the country.

When searching for the best possible job available, it is helpful to consult more than one newspaper, particularly if you live in a large metropolitan area. In addition to studying the want ads from your city's leading newspapers, you might also study newspapers from nearby suburbs and towns. If you are willing to relocate, it also would be a good idea to consult newspapers from other cities. Most large newsstands or bookstores stock a selection of out-of-town newspapers. Many public libraries also carry a good selection of out-of-town papers. In addition, you can access the classifieds in out-of-town newspapers on the Internet. The Sunday paper usually has the largest help-wanted section.

The Want Ads

Locate the want ads, then refer to the jobs that interest you by checking under the headings that

---

Practicing Consumer Skills
Answers

1. traditional checking accounts, negotiable order of withdrawal (NOW) accounts **23A**

2. the date; the name of the person or business to whom the check is being written; the check amount in numerals and spelled out in words, the signature of the person writing the check; and, in the memo space, any other information that might be helpful **23A**

3. A person endorses a check by signing his or her name on the back of the check as it appears on the front of the check. **23A**

Practicing Consumer Skills
Answers

1. Want ads usually list jobs in alphabetical order by job classification. **23A**

2. A person should read several sections of the want ads when beginning a job search because many jobs can be listed under more than one category. **23A**

3. The Internet provides access to databases, alumni directories, professional organizations and on-line classified ads. **23A**

---

list specific job classifications. Want ads usually are listed in alphabetical order by job classification. Such job classifications might include accounting, administration, bookkeeping, clerical, computer programming, data processing, education, engineering, financial, insurance, marketing, medical, printing, professional, sales, secretarial, and word processing. Concentrate on the listings in which you are most interested and for which you are qualified, but do not limit your search to one particular heading. You should apply for all the jobs that appeal to you, even if you think you may not be fully qualified.

You may find that a job you are looking for is listed under more than one category. Openings for a cook, for example, may be listed under bakers, chefs, and restaurants. By reading through other categories, you also may be able to uncover interesting job openings in related fields. It is helpful to read the want ads thoroughly the first few weeks of a job search to become familiar with the categories that pertain to your qualifications and interests.

The Internet

The Internet is an excellent tool for searching employment opportunities. The Internet provides access to extensive databases, such as college alumni directories and professional organizations, that can provide information that is helpful for networking and contacting potential employers. Many companies have websites that advertise current job openings and some allow you to submit an application over the Internet. In addition, people who are looking for a job can post their resumes on their own home page.

Practicing Consumer Skills

1. How are jobs listed in the classified section of the newspaper?
2. Why should you read several different sections of the want ads when beginning a job search?
3. List three ways that the Internet can be used to find employment information.

7 YOUR RIGHTS AS AN EMPLOYEE

Before you start any new job, you will want to discuss your job description—a written summary of the duties you will actually be responsible for and expected to perform—and the company's benefits with your employer. Ask your employer to explain the responsibilities of the position and the hours you will be expected to work. Your salary is based on the responsibilities of your job, as are employer-provided benefits such as sick leave, vacation pay, and health insurance.

This discussion normally is part of your job interview and provides you with an opportunity to ask questions and understand the terms and conditions of your employment. Be sure to clarify any unclear issues at this time. Most often, you will begin a new job with this type of verbal agreement. Sometimes, employers also will ask you to sign a written contract outlining your duties, responsibilities, and salary. Other conditions of your employment and company procedures will be clarified for you during your first few weeks of work.

Further Clarification of Benefits

Soon after you start your job, you will learn the day-to-day schedule it requires. For example, you may or may not have breaks. You may be enrolled in health insurance, life insurance, dental insurance, and pension programs. Most companies will give you a policy manual outlining your benefits and responsibilities. In addition to clarifying your benefits, it also is important that new employees fully understand the deductions that will be taken from their paychecks on a regular basis.

Payroll Deductions

Employers make payroll deductions for federal and state income taxes, Social Security taxes, insurance plans, and in some cases, pension plans and other optional programs. Your earnings before these deductions are called your gross pay. Your earnings after these deductions are called your net pay.

Federal Income Tax Forms When you begin a new job, you will be asked to fill out a federal income tax form, or W-4. On the form, you need to indicate the number of dependents you want to claim and whether you are married or single. The amount withheld from your gross pay for federal income taxes will be based on the information you provide on the W-4.

Social Security Congress passed the Social Security Act in 1935 to provide workers with disability and accident insurance, unemployment compensation, and old-age retirement benefits. Although not all categories of workers are covered by Social Security, most are. If you are covered under Social Security, Federal Insurance Contributions Act (FICA) payments also will be deducted from your gross pay.

U.S. Labor Laws

Historically, your rights as a worker have been defined and preserved by the interaction of employers, employees, labor unions, and the government. Some of these rights as a worker include a guaranteed minimum wage; the right to freedom from employment discrimination because of age, sex, race, or national origin; and the right to work in a safe environment.

National Labor Relations Act In addition to the Social Security Act, one of the earliest worker-oriented laws passed was the 1935 National Labor Relations Act, or Wagner Act. This law guaranteed employees the right to belong to a union and to engage in collective bargaining. Many states also have passed right-to-work laws, which outlaw closed shops in which workers must join a union to get or keep their jobs.

Fair Labor Standards Act The 1938 Fair Labor Standards Act grants workers the right to a minimum wage. Not all employers are obligated to pay this minimum wage, but most companies with a relatively large number of employees are required to by the law. The Fair Labor Standards Act also sets the standard workweek at 40 hours and grants employees who are paid on an hourly basis the right to overtime pay.

Civil Rights Act The Civil Rights Act was signed into law by President Lyndon Johnson in 1964. This law protects a person's freedom to vote, use public facilities, and seek employment. Title VII of this act broadens the scope of employee rights by preventing employers from discriminating

Practicing Consumer Skills
Answers

1. Before starting any new job, an employee should discuss the job description and the company's benefits with his or her employer. **23A**

2. federal and state income taxes, Social Security taxes, insurance plans, and in some cases, pension plans and other optional programs **17A, 23A**

3. the right to belong to a labor union and to engage in collective bargaining; the right to a minimum wage; the right to freedom from employment discrimination because of age, sex, color, or national origin; and the right to work in a safe environment **19B, 23A**

---

against individuals on the basis of race, color, religion, sex, or national origin. Under this law, employees cannot be discriminated against in hiring, pay, employment privileges and opportunities, or union membership. Employers cannot advertise in a discriminatory manner, and employment agencies may not fail to recommend a person for a job for prejudicial reasons.

Equal Employment Opportunity Commission

The Equal Employment Opportunity Commission (EEOC) administers Title VII of the Civil Rights Act. The commission encourages employers and employment agencies to settle discriminatory charges voluntarily. The commission also can help an injured party file a discrimination suit.

Employment Rights for Minorities and Women

In the 1970s the federal government began to pass laws to further assure employment rights for minorities and women. As part of this effort, the government adopted a program called affirmative action. Affirmative action seeks to make up for past discrimination by requiring that certain employers set hiring and fair employment goals for minorities and women.

In recent years, federal courts and the Supreme Court have acted to make sure that affirmative action does not discriminate against people who are *not* members of minority groups. As a result, employers have begun to shift away from using numerical goals, or quotas, for hiring and promoting women and minorities.

Safety Measures
Employees also have the right to work in a safe environment. Federal safety measures are enacted to help eliminate hazards in the workplace. Many of these laws concern the use of protective clothing and glasses, standards for safe equipment, and other matters that affect workers' safety. The Occupational Safety and Health Administration (OSHA), a division of the U.S. Department of Labor, administers these laws and promotes safe and healthful working conditions in all industries.

Practicing Consumer Skills

1. What should you discuss with your employer before starting a new job?
2. What deductions will be made in your paycheck?
3. List four of your rights as a worker in the United States.

---

8 CONTRACT OBLIGATIONS

A contract is an agreement between two or more parties that is enforceable by law and is used to regulate terms of trade. Both verbal and written agreements are considered to be contracts. A verbal agreement, however, is binding only if it involves a relatively small sum of money over a short period of time and does not involve a real estate purchase.

As a consumer, you probably will enter into a variety of contracts. Some of the more common types of contracts are those involving an installment purchase, the buying and selling of real estate, a personal loan, the purchase of stocks or bonds, the use of a credit card, the purchase of an automobile, a rental agreement, agreements for such services as appliance maintenance and lawn care, and all types of insurance policies.

Contract Criteria

An agreement qualifies as a contract when it meets four basic criteria. First, an offer and a promise to accept the offer must be made. A credit card company may offer you a $2,000 credit line for a $25 annual fee but it would not be a valid contract unless you accepted the offer, paid the $25, and used the card.

Second, all parties must be competent, or legally qualified, to enter into a contract. Contracts that are signed by minors, people who are mentally

R14 CONSUMER HANDBOOK

Before You Sign a Contract

Before signing a contract, first read it thoroughly. You may think the document's legal terminology is confusing, or it may be less complicated than you thought. If you find any part of the contract unclear, you can contact a lawyer who will explain the contract's terms.

Second, be sure you agree with the terms of the contract. Identify what the agreement will require of you. Also identify the obligations of the other parties involved in the agreement.

Third, make certain you understand your options for terminating or changing the contract. Unless a contract specifies a trial period, it may be difficult to change it once it has been signed. In some cases, the terms of a contract can change when other conditions change. A real estate contract, for example, may specify that the interest rate on a loan will fluctuate with changes in the market. Be sure that you understand any circumstances under which the agreement could be changed.

Fourth, be sure you know what will happen if you break your promise. Most contractual obligations still stand even if you are unable to pay your debts. In that case, you could lose the title to your house or car, for example. Some contracts also state that if you die during the life of the contract, your heirs are obligated to repay the debt.

impaired, or people under influence of alcohol or drugs are not legal or binding. Third, the terms of the agreement must be legal. For example, you cannot legally collect money on a promise to deliver a stolen automobile. Fourth, an element of "bargain for exchange" must be present. This means that both parties must agree to fulfill certain promises. These can involve money, goods, an action, and or restraint from action. If one person agrees to deliver something and gets nothing in return, there is no contract.

Practicing Consumer Skills TEKS

1. What criteria must contracts meet?
2. What should you consider before signing a contract?

9 PAYING TAXES

Taxes have a tremendous impact on many aspects of the lives of U.S. consumers. Government at the state, local, and federal levels collects many different kinds of taxes, including sales taxes, property taxes, excise taxes, and income taxes. Money from these taxes pays for a variety of public goods and services. These taxes also pay for many federal programs.

Government and Taxes

The power of the U.S. government to collect taxes dates back to 1788—the year that the Constitution was ratified. The Constitution originally specified that taxes collected by the government had to be divided fully among the states according to population. Responding to an 1894 federal law imposing an income tax, the Supreme Court ruled the tax

---

Practicing Consumer Skills Answers

1. Contracts must be an offer and a promise to accept that offer; all parties to the agreement must be competent, or legally qualified to enter into a contract; the terms of the agreement must be lawful; and an element of "bargain for exchange" must be present. **1A, 23A**

2. Before signing a contract, individuals should read the contract thoroughly, be sure they agree with the terms, understand what the agreement will require of them and what the obligations of the other parties will be, make certain they understand their options for terminating or changing the contract, and make certain that they know what will happen if they default on their promise **1A, 23A**

CONSUMER HANDBOOK R15

FEDERAL TAX RECEIPTS BY SOURCE, 1999

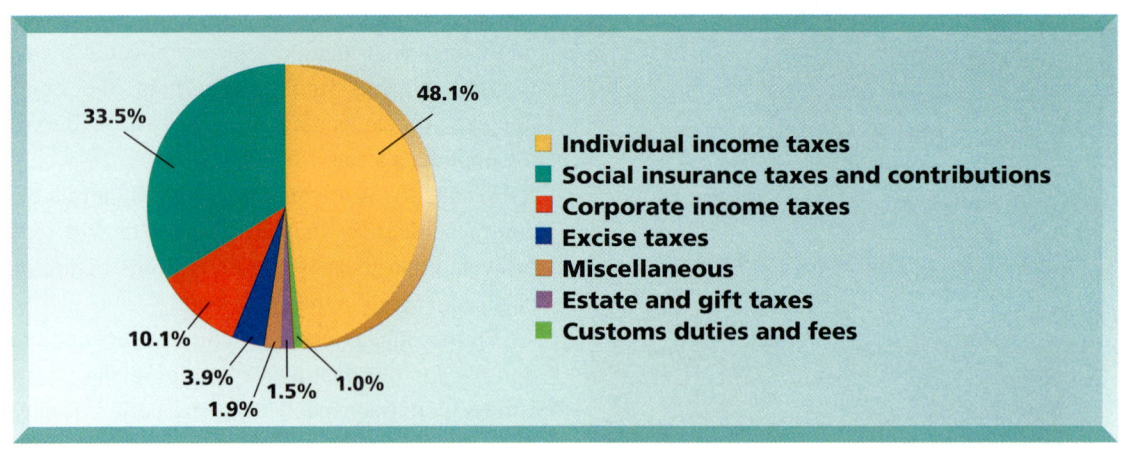

- 48.1% Individual income taxes
- 33.5% Social insurance taxes and contributions
- 10.1% Corporate income taxes
- 3.9% Excise taxes
- 1.9% Miscellaneous
- 1.5% Estate and gift taxes
- 1.0% Customs duties and fees

Source: *The Budget for Fiscal Year 2001, Historical Tables*

---

unconstitutional because it did not meet this requirement.

The increasing costs of government in the growing nation, however, led many to support an income tax. This support eventually resulted in the adoption of the Sixteenth Amendment in 1913. This amendment gave Congress the power to "lay and collect taxes on incomes, from whatever source derived without apportionment among the several States."

Tax Reform Act of 1986

The Sixteenth Amendment provides the basis of the income tax as we know it today. However, many issues concerning taxes have changed in the years following 1913. The primary tax issue of the 1980s was tax reform. Many supporters of reform cited inequities in the tax system, numerous tax loopholes, and overly complicated tax regulations.

The Tax Reform Act of 1986, which resulted from this movement, is the most significant overhaul of the income tax system since 1913. The law restructured the tax code to make it more fair. Among other changes, the new tax law greatly reduced the number of tax brackets. It also changed the tax status of certain tax shelters, real estate investments, and deductions on consumer debts, thereby simplifying the tax code.

IRAs and Other Tax Shelters The Tax Reform Act of 1986 also made significant changes in the status of individual retirement accounts (IRAs) and other tax shelters. A tax shelter is a special investment plan in which the amount invested is not taxed until it is withdrawn from the plan. The IRA, which has been a particularly popular tax shelter, is an account into which people will be able to contribute up to $4,000 of income per year by 2005. Individuals do not pay taxes on this money or on the interest or dividends it earns until the money is withdrawn, usually upon retirement.

Employees who do not have other pension or retirement programs provided by their employer may contribute to an IRA and deduct their contributions from their taxable income. 1997 legislation allowed people who had other pension programs at work to qualify for these IRA investment opportunities only if they had incomes of less than $25,000 for single people or combined incomes of less than $40,000 for married people filing a joint income tax return. Starting with 1998 returns, however, these levels began to goup. For those who qualify, their tax deduction is proportionately reduced as taxable income increases.

At these higher income levels, contributions to IRA accounts are no longer tax-deductible. People who do not qualify under these guidelines are still able to set aside money in IRAs. They also can defer taxes on this money until their retirement. However, they are cannot deduct their contributions from their income taxes.

The Roth IRA, first available in 1998, offers a new method of saving. Single people with an income up to $110,000 and married couples with a combined income of $160,000 will be allowed to contribute up to $4,000 per year to the Roth IRA by 2005. While the contributions are not tax-deductible, the interest on the account is tax-deferred, which means that the IRA–holder does not pay taxes on the interest their savings earns. Furthermore, the proceeds can be withdrawn tax-free after five years if they are withdrawn to pay for a first-time home mortgage or when the IRA–holder reaches the age of 59 1/2. Another popular tax shelter and retirement plan is the 401(k) program, or the Deferred Income Plan. This plan is one in which an employee and his or her employer make deposits into the employee's retirement program. Taxes are deferred on the money in the account until the employee's retirement. The upper limit on employer contributions is 25% of compensation per year.

Real Estate Investments A significant tax break for most people is the fact that home owners are able to deduct mortgage interest—for no more than two home's—from their taxes.

Practicing Consumer Skills
1. Why was the Sixteenth Amendment passed?
2. What problems in the tax codes led to tax reform in the 1980s?
3. How does an IRA function as a tax shelter?

10 HOME MORTGAGES

A loan is a transfer of funds that carries with it the legal obligation of repayment. A mortgage is a type of loan. Consumers typically apply to banks or other lenders for mortgages in order to finance purchases of property. In general, mortgages are associated with the purchase of a home.

Real Estate Agreements
Most consumers in the housing market use a real estate agent to help them find a house to buy. Using a realtor has several advantages. For example, a real estate agent help buyers determine how much money they can afford to spend on housing. Then the agent will help find an affordable house that will meet the buyers' needs.

When deciding to purchase a certain house, most buyers will make a bid on the house to the seller. If the seller agrees to the price, both parties sign a real estate agreement. The price of the house and any special conditions of the sale will be specified in writing in the agreement. Once the agreement is signed, there is a "contract pending" on the house. During this time, the seller of the house may not sell it to anyone else while the buyer awaits mortgage approval.

Practicing Consumer Skills Answers

1. The U.S. Constitution originally specified that taxes collected by the U.S. government had to be apportioned uniformly among the states according to population. However, the federal government needed to raise money to cover the increasing costs of government in the growing United States. To handle this problem, the Sixteenth Amendment was passed. **20A, 23A**

2. inequities in the tax system, numerous tax loopholes, overly complicated tax regulations **23A**

3. Employees do not pay tax on the money they put into an IRA or on the interest this money earns until they withdraw the money from their accounts upon retirement. **23A**

Practicing Consumer Skills

Answers

1. A mortgage is a type of loan used to finance purchases of property. **23A**

2. The price of the house or property and any special conditions of the sale are specified in writing in a real estate agreement. **23A**

3. The lending institution will verify the borrower's income, employment history, current salary, and credit rating. **23A**

Lending Institutions

Any bank, savings institution, or other lender may grant a mortgage loan. Wise consumers should shop around for the lowest interest rate before deciding on a lending institution.

When visiting possible lending institutions, prospective buyers should gather information about the various types of mortgages available. The most common mortgage is the conventional, or fixed-rate, mortgage. This type of loan is made for a stated period of time, such as 30 years, at an established rate of interest. The borrower makes a fixed monthly installment payment that includes repayment of both principal and interest.

Today several alternatives to the conventional mortgage exist. One of the most popular is the adjustable rate mortgage—a loan in which flexible interest rates are built into the mortgage. If interest rates drop, the borrower pays less toward interest and more toward principal in his or her fixed installment payments. Interest on mortgages is almost always tax-deductible.

After a consumer decides to apply for a certain kind of mortgage, the lending institution must determine whether to qualify, or approve credit for, the buyer. This process may take several weeks or even months. During this time, the lending institution will verify the borrower's income, employment history, current salary, and credit rating. The lending institution then notifies the borrower to tell them if the mortgage has been denied or approved.

Closing

Soon after a loan has been approved, the buyer, seller, real estate agent, representatives of the lending institution, and other people involved in the purchase of the house meet to sign the legal papers necessary to close the original agreement. This meeting is referred to as the closing. The closing usually is the last step in what can be a long process of buying a house.

Practicing Consumer Skills

1. What is a mortgage?
2. What is specified in a real estate agreement?
3. What does a lending institution verify before approving a loan?

11 INSURANCE

Careful financial planning should include plans for the unexpected. As a consumer, you need to know about the various types of insurance that can protect you and your family in times of crisis.

Kinds of Insurance

Today many kinds of insurance are available to meet a variety of needs. Among the most important types of insurance are automobile, homeowner's or renter's, medical and disability, and life.

Automobile Insurance Two basic types of automobile insurance—collision and liability—are available. Collision insurance pays for damages to your car if you are involved in an accident. Most collision policies include a deductible, or specified amount of the repair cost that you must pay before the insurance will pick up the cost. Liability insurance pays for the medical expenses of those injured in an accident and for damages to others' property.

R18 CONSUMER HANDBOOK

Homeowner's and Renter's Insurance Like automobile insurance, two kinds of homeowner's or renter's insurance—property and liability—are available. Property insurance will pay for the replacement or repair of a dwelling or other structure on your property, as well as its contents. If you are renting an apartment and do not own the structure, it still is a good idea to buy insurance for the contents of your apartment. Liability insurance pays for the medical expenses of persons who may be injured on your property.

Medical and Disability Insurance Traditionally, medical insurance was available only as part of a major medical insurance plan, which pays for medical expenses billed by the doctors and hospitals of your choice. Not all medical services are covered, however, and some that are include deductibles.

Today two popular new forms of medical insurance—health maintenance organizations (HMOs) and preferred provider organizations (PPOs)—are available. HMOs pay for all or part of medical expenses billed by their doctors and hospitals. Often, these plans cover medical expenses such as yearly examinations and well-baby care to prevent future medical problems. PPOs extend benefits to cover treatment by providers outside of the PPO's network.

Disability insurance provides income assistance to those who become disabled from accident, injury, or illness and can no longer work. This insurance can be either short-term—covering temporary inability to work—or long-term—covering permanent inability to work.

Life Insurance Life insurance pays benefits to the families of policy holders who die. The two kinds of life insurance available are term insurance and whole life insurance. Term insurance expires after a specified period of time. Individuals who have young children or large mortgages may choose to invest in term insurance because it is relatively inexpensive and will provide a surviving spouse with money to raise children and pay off a mortgage or other large debts. Whole life insurance covers you throughout your life and offers dividends that generally are used to pay for more insurance after the policy has been in effect a certain number of years. In most cases, whole life insurance is more expensive than term insurance.

How to Buy Insurance
Various kinds of insurance—particularly medical, disability, and life—usually are offered as part of an employer's benefits package. When you buy other kinds of insurance individually, be sure that the insurance company from which you buy is an established company with a reputation for paying claims readily and in full. If you need more than one kind of insurance, shop around to find the company that can offer you the best insurance package.

Practicing Consumer Skills
1. What are the major kinds of insurance?
2. Analyze the factors involved in the process of acquiring insurance.

12 BUYING A NEW CAR

Buying a car can be complicated. To simplify the process and get the most for your money, consider basic factors in advance, such as the style of the car you want and the amount you can afford to spend.

Size and Style
When you consider the style of the car you want, you will be defining how you plan to use your car and the models that you will consider. A large, comfortable car may be most appropriate for people who do a lot of traveling. Smaller cars usually get better gas mileage and are very practical for driving the short distances. If you use your car to transport several people, like younger siblings or your friends, you will find that some models suit your needs better than others. You can choose from a variety of models including sedans, minivans, hatchbacks, and pickup trucks.

Practicing Consumer Skills
Answers
1. automobile insurance, homeowner's or renter's insurance, medical insurance, disability insurance, life insurance **23A**
2. Consumers should consider what needs to be insured, how much insurance they can afford, how much they want their deductible to be, and whether they can get insurance as part of their employee benefits package, or if they will have to buy it independently. **11A**

CONSUMER HANDBOOK R19

Style typically is a matter of personal preference. Most models will be available in a variety of colors. The basic lines and design of the cars also will vary. In some cases, you may be able to save money if you are flexible about color and detailing because dealers often will accept a lower price for models that they have in stock.

What You Can Afford to Spend

When deciding what you can afford to spend on a car, you must consider the total cost of the car—that is, the base price of the car plus options, initial fees, and maintenance costs.

Options All vehicles are manufactured with standard equipment. The list price of the car is the base price without options. Options are added features that are not necessary for the operation of the car. You will have many options to choose from, but you should know that each increases the price of the car. Among the options available on many cars are air-conditioning, radios, stereo systems, CD players, leather interiors, rear window defoggers, chrome styling, automatic window controls, whitewall tires, antilock brakes, and more.

After you have identified the base price of the car, consider the options you want, one at a time. It may be a good idea to rank the options in order of priority, listing those most important to you first. Then list the prices of the options. This may help you identify those options that meet your needs and that you can afford, as well as those that you are willing to give up. When budgeting for options, also keep in mind that you will need to consider the costs of initial fees and the continuing costs of owning a car.

Initial Fees and Continuing Costs Initial fees are one-time charges for items such as sales tax, title, and original license plates. These costs usually are not included in the base price of the car.

The amount for sales tax may be more than you expect. Sales taxes are a percentage of a products' cost. Depending on the price of the car, the sales tax on an automobile can add up to thousands of dollars.

In addition to initial fees, the continuing costs of owning a car must be considered when thinking about your budget. These include insurance premiums, repair and maintenance costs, license plate renewal fees, and the price of gasoline. Information for most models of domestic and foreign cars may be found in publications such as *Consumer Reports*, generally available at your local library or newsstand.

Once you have compared the prices of car models and options, compare the prices offered at different car dealers before making your final selection. You may

From the sales of domestic compact models, the automakers had reason to believe that Americans would not continue to purchase smaller cars when the price of gasoline went down. As a result, many U.S. manufacturers failed to invest in the styling, safety features, and special options that might have made compact cars more desirable to the American buyer. This trend provided increased opportunities for foreign automobile competition in U.S. markets. The strength of the U.S. dollar in foreign-exchange markets also meant that imported cars were relatively less expensive for consumers in the United States. than they otherwise might have been. Some of the manufacturers that established a significant hold in the U.S. automobile market as a result were Toyota, Honda, Mitsubishi, and Nissan.

Domestic automakers began to take foreign competition more seriously in the 1980s. A new effort was made to produce stylish cars with downsized engines, advanced safety features, better gas mileage, and unique high-tech features. In addition, some Japanese car manufacturers began to build their cars in production facilities in the United States, such as the Honda plant in Ohio.

Whether you decide to purchase a domestic car or a foreign car, you have a wide range of choices as a consumer. Keep in mind that your overall goal is to buy a car that suits your needs as well your budget.

find that certain dealers can make a better offer for the basic car that you want than others can. It is a good idea to shop around, talk to salespeople, and compare your choices until you are satisfied that you are buying the car you want at the best possible price.

Foreign Cars

In the 1960s the most popular imported car was the German-made Volkswagen. It was relatively affordable, easy to repair, and because of its good gas mileage, it was less expensive to operate than many domestic cars.

In the years that followed, many other foreign cars began to compete with Volkswagen in the U.S. car market. Over time, foreign cars became more and more popular in the United States. Many consumers came to believe that the smaller, more economical foreign cars had significant advantages over larger American-made cars.

When gasoline prices skyrocketed in the 1970s—further increasing demand for fuel-efficient foreign cars—U.S. manufacturers began an effort to downsize domestic cars. Almost every major U.S. auto company produced what they called a "compact" model to compete with imported vehicles.

Most domestic car manufacturers, however, believed that high gasoline prices would be temporary.

Practicing Consumer Skills ⭐TEKS

1. What should consumers keep in mind when deciding on the size and style of a car?
2. What costs does the total price of a car include?
3. What impact has foreign competition had on American car manufacturers?

Practicing Consumer Skills Answers

1. Consumers should consider how they plan to use their new car, the number of people who will usually be riding in the car, how comfortable the car is, whether they will do much traveling in the car, and what sort of gas mileage the car gets. **1A, 23A**

2. The total price of a car includes the base price of the car as well as the cost of any options and initial fees. **23A**

3. In the 1970s, foreign competition caused U.S. car manufacturers to produce more economical, compact models of cars. In the 1980s, foreign competition caused U.S. car makers to produce more stylish cars with downsized engines, better safety features, better gas mileage, and unique high-tech features. **4B, 23A**

CONSUMER HANDBOOK R21

13 INVESTING IN STOCKS

Stocks are popular investments because they offer the potential to earn profits with fairly limited risk. Stocks represent partial ownership of a corporation. This ownership is issued in portions called shares. Stocks can provide a profit either through dividends or when resold at a higher price.

Types of Stock

Shares of stock are divided into two types—common and preferred. The type of stock issued by a corporation depends on the legal organization of the corporation and the decisions made within the corporation as the market changes.

Common Stock Owners of common stock receive dividends at a variable rate. When the corporation's profits are high, dividends usually are high; when the corporation's profits fall, dividends also fall. If a corporation is operating at a loss, it does not pay any dividends on common stock.

Preferred Stock Owners of preferred stock receive dividends at a fixed rate, regardless of the level of the corporation's profits. In addition, owners of preferred stock receive their dividends before the owners of common stock do.

Advantages and Disadvantages of Stock Investments

Consumers buy stock as either long-term or short-term investments. As a long-term investment, stocks can

- help protect against inflation,
- serve as a means of increasing financial capital, and
- provide future income.

People who buy and sell stock for short-term gain are called speculators. The object of speculation is to buy low and sell high in order to make a "quick profit." Such investing is extremely risky because prices in the stock market are highly unstable in the short term. While investors hope to sell at a higher price and thus earn a profit, at times they may be forced to sell at the same or a low price and thereby lose money.

R22 CONSUMER HANDBOOK

UNDERSTANDING STOCK MARKET REPORTS

The annual dividend is 46 cents per share.

Trading volume of the week, in 100-share lots– thus, 19,532,000 shares were traded.

PepsiCo closed at $31.75 per share.

PepsiCo stock price has risen 8.5% this year.

52 week Hi	Lo	Name	Div	Yield	PE	Volume Wkly.	Wkly Hi	Lo	Last	Change Fri	Wkly	YTD % Chg
16	7.37	Kmart			26	238,786	13.50	12.25	12.50	-.25		+20.5
53.75	41	McDnlds	.30	0.7	21	165,646	45.12	42.50	44.50	-.25	+1.25	-1.9
35.87	28	PepsiCo	.46	1.4	34	195,320	33.62	31.62	31.75	-.12	-1.25	+8.5
52.87	26	Reebok	.30	0.6	25	13,269	51.37	45.75	50.12	+1.12	+3.37	+19.3

$35.87 is the highest and $28.00 is the lowest price of PepsiCo stock in the past 52 weeks, adjusted for splits.

The yield tells what percentage of each share would be returned as dividends, given the current closing price.

The price-to-earnings (PE) ratio is calculated by dividing the stock's last closing price ($31.75) by the company's earnings per share. A higher PE indicates lower earnings, and a lower PE indicates higher earnings.

PepsiCo stock went as high as $33.62 and as low as $31.62 per share during the week.

PepsiCo stock dropped $.12 per share on Friday but dropped $1.25 for the week as a whole.

Influences on Stock Prices

Almost any economic or political event can affect stock prices in the short term. An increase in the unemployment rate or the election of an unpopular foreign leader can cause stock prices to plummet. Or, the passage of a law in Congress to reduce taxes or the announcement of falling interest rates can cause stock prices to rise.

Stock prices also are influenced by news about specific corporations. The announcement that a corporation exceeded its quarterly profit for example, can cause the price of its stock to rise. Likewise, rumors of problems in a corporation, can cause its stock price to fall.

Purchasing Stock

Consumers thinking about purchasing stock should follow these guidelines:

- look for stock in a growth industry, as opposed to industries in which growth has peaked.
- look for corporations with higher-than-average growth rates.
- read business periodicals and newspapers to identify corporations with good overall performances.
- avoid corporations with large debts.
- look for corporations with consistent dividend increases.

Investing in Stocks

The goal of a stock market investment is to achieve a high rate of return, either as the result of short-term speculation or over the long term. Investments in high-growth stocks represent investments over the long term.

Long-term Investment and Economic Change
High-growth stocks are stocks in corporations that have high rates of growth over time, despite changes in the overall economy. The growth rates of such corporations are higher than the growth rates of other corporations, or of the economy as a whole.

When the economy is expanding and businesses are making profits, many stocks can be categorized

CONSUMER HANDBOOK R23

Practicing Consumer Skills

Answers

1. Common stock pays dividends at a variable rate based on the corporation's profits. Preferred stock pays dividends at a fixed rate, regardless of the corporation's profits, and dividends are paid to preferred stockholders before owners of common stock are paid. **11C, 23A**

2. because prices in the stock market are highly volatile in the short term **1A, 11C, 23A**

3. Recessions or contractions in the economy can cause many stocks to lose their growth status. **11C, 23A**

4. It is difficult to know whether a company or stock that has had high growth in the past will continue to grow, or to identify which companies and stocks that have not been growing will grow rapidly in the future. **11C, 23A**

5. a company with significant present earnings, a high rate of retained earnings and reinvestment relative to the firm's size, products with good market potential, strong managerial leadership, relatively low wage requirements, freedom from government interference, and the ability to adapt to and possibly benefit from technological change or a restructuring of the economy **11C, 23A**

---

as growth stocks. When the economy is contracting, or going through a recession, many stocks lose their growth status. High-growth stocks typically maintain their growth even during other economic downturns.

By definition, growth stocks pay no or few dividends at first. Instead, they grow in value over time. Making money in business almost always requires investing money over the long term. Growing businesses typically invest in capital such as facilities and equipment, new marketing and distribution strategies, research and development, and product or service improvement. For this reason, expanding companies normally do not make significant dividend payouts early on. A person investing in a high-growth stock should do so patiently in hopes of increased long-term value.

Buying High-Growth Stocks Finding the right high-growth stock is the most difficult task involved in making this type of investment. It is not difficult to identify stocks and companies that have performed well in the past. Knowing whether growth will continue into the future or if some presently low-growth stock or new stock will "take off" is much more difficult.

Selecting a high-growth company means choosing a company with good earnings. Earnings must be great enough to create profits to reinvest in expansion. In fact, some experts believe the single most important factor in selecting a high-growth stock is choosing one with a high rate of retained earnings and reinvestment.

Other criteria for selecting a high-growth stock should be the market potential for a company's product or service and the possibilities a company has to benefit from technological change or a restructuring of the economy. You might also consider whether the company has strong managerial leadership and relatively low wage requirements.

No matter how carefully an investor chooses investments, the possibility of losing money always exists. Although companies' annual reports and financial periodicals such as *Money* or *Inc.* help inform consumers, high-growth stocks can be risky. When investing in such stocks, an individual should be in a financial position to sustain a loss.

Practicing Consumer Skills

1. What is the difference between common stock and preferred stock?
2. Why is short-term stock investment especially risky?
3. How can a long-term investment be affected by changes in the economy?
4. Why is it difficult to identify high-growth stocks?
5. What are the criteria for selecting a high-growth stock?

14 MUTUAL FUNDS

One of the most popular investment choices for consumers today is mutual funds. A mutual fund is a fund in which investors' money is pooled to purchase a variety of securities.

As investments, mutual funds have a number of advantages. One of the most important is that, mutual funds are managed by professional financial experts who know market trends, thus freeing investors from the time and effort required to purchase securities on their own. Such management also helps limit the risks of investment. In addition, mutual funds enable investors to buy a variety of securities with a minimal amount of money.

CONSUMER HANDBOOK

STOCK MARKET PERFORMANCE

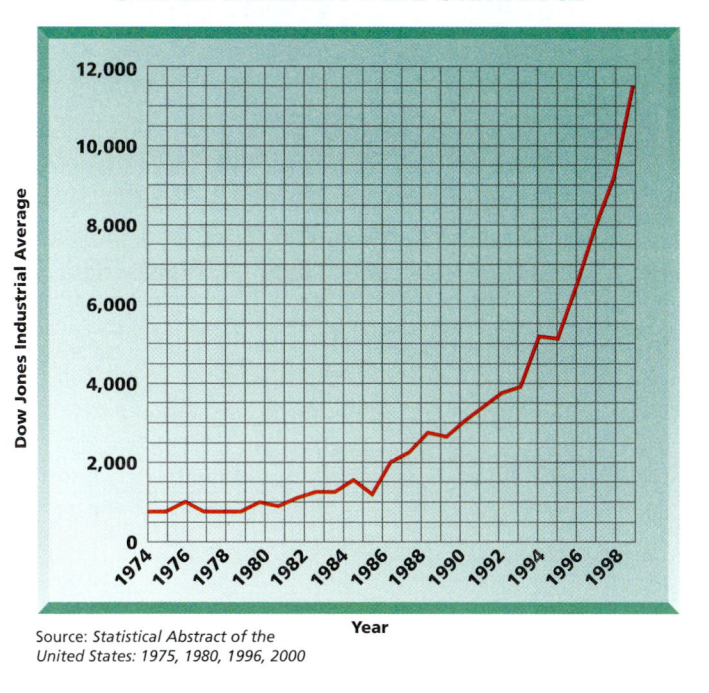

Source: Statistical Abstract of the United States: 1975, 1980, 1996, 2000

Because the funds allow investors to pool their capital, an individual investor can own a few shares each of many stocks.

Kinds of Mutual Funds

Stock, money, and bond securities are three types of securities available through a mutual fund.

Stock Market Mutual Funds
Buying stocks in a mutual fund provides several advantages. Buying a variety of stock minimizes the risk of loss by spreading the investment out over several possible outcomes—a process known as diversification. For their stock investments, many consumers prefer to pool their money with a number of other people, invest in a number of stocks, and hire a professional to manage their investments.

Money Market Mutual Funds
Money markets are markets in which investors lend money on a short-term basis to banks, businesses, and governments. Money market certificates generally pay the current interest rate, called a yield. A money market mutual fund is a mutual fund investing in a variety of short-term money market instruments. The typical interest rate for such funds often is generally higher than regular savings, but lower than stocks. In addition, because they are for the short term, money market mutual funds enable investors to switch to other investments as market conditions change.

Bond Market Mutual Funds
The bond market is the market in which investors buy, sell, and trade government and corporate bonds. Investors thus lend money to governments and corporations for relatively long periods of time and at fixed rates of interest. Investors generally invest in the bond market when interest rates are high or before an expected drop in rates because a bond's yield is guaranteed. Bond market mutual funds, or bond funds, are funds in which investments are made in a variety of bonds and therefore are similar to other mutual funds.

How to Invest in Mutual Funds

Investors can buy a mutual fund from a stock broker, an insurance salesperson, or on their own. Some mutual funds require consumers to pay a sales commission. By law, this commission cannot be more than 8.5 percent. Other funds, called "no-load" funds, do not charge sales commissions. However, all mutual fund accounts charge consumers a management fee averaging 1.0–1.5 percent.

Investors who want to invest in a mutual fund on their own may subscribe to a mutual fund advisory service or study the publications of such services in the library. Charges for advisory service publications range from $20 to $120 per year.

Practicing Consumer Skills

1. What are the advantages of investing in a mutual fund?
2. What is diversification?
3. Describe three types of mutual fund investments.

Practicing Consumer Skills Answers

1. Mutual funds are managed by professional financial experts who know market trends. As a result, mutual funds free investors from the time and effort required to purchase securities on their own, limit the risk of the investment, and enable investors to buy a variety of securities with a minimal amount of money because they can pool their capital. **11B, 23A**

2. Diversification is the process of buying several kinds of stock to minimize the risk of loss by spreading the investment out over several possible outcomes. **23A, 24A**

3. stock market mutual fund—mutual fund investing in a variety of stocks; money market mutual fund—mutual fund investing in a variety of short-term money market instruments, which generally yield high interest rates; bond market mutual fund—mutual fund investing in a variety of long-term bonds, which yield fixed interest rates **23A**

WORLD ECONOMIC STATISTICS

BANKING AND FINANCE

Prime Rate, 1929–2000

Year	Lowest Rate	Highest Rate	Year	Lowest Rate	Highest Rate
1929	5.50	6.00	1965	4.50	5.00
1930	3.50	6.00	1966	5.00	6.00
1931	2.75	5.00	1967	5.50	6.00
1932	3.25	4.00	1968	6.00	6.75
1933	1.50	4.00	1969	6.75	8.50
1934	1.50	1.50	1970	6.75	8.50
1935	1.50	1.50	1971	5.25	6.75
1936	1.50	1.50	1972	4.75	6.00
1937	1.50	1.50	1973	6.00	10.00
1938	1.50	1.50	1974	8.75	12.00
1939	1.50	1.50	1975	7.00	10.50
1940	1.50	1.50	1976	6.25	7.25
1941	1.50	1.50	1977	6.25	7.75
1942	1.50	1.50	1978	7.75	11.75
1943	1.50	1.50	1979	11.50	15.75
1944	1.50	1.50	1980	11.00	21.50
1945	1.50	1.50	1981	15.75	21.50
1946	1.50	1.50	1982	11.50	17.00
1947	1.50	1.75	1983	10.50	11.50
1948	2.00	2.00	1984	10.75	13.00
1949	2.00	2.00	1985	9.50	10.75
1950	2.00	2.25	1986	7.50	9.50
1951	2.50	3.00	1987	7.50	9.25
1952	3.00	3.00	1988	8.50	10.50
1953	3.00	3.25	1989	10.50	11.50
1954	3.00	3.25	1990	10.00	10.50
1955	3.00	3.50	1991	6.50	10.00
1956	3.50	4.00	1992	6.00	6.50
1957	4.00	4.50	1993	6.00	6.00
1958	3.50	4.50	1994	6.00	8.50
1959	4.00	5.00	1995	8.50	9.00
1960	4.50	5.00	1996	8.50	8.25
1961	4.50	4.50	1997	8.25	8.50
1962	4.50	4.50	1998	7.75	8.50
1963	4.50	4.50	1999	7.75	8.50
1964	4.50	4.50	2000	8.50	9.50

Sources: U.S. Congress, *Economic Indicators*; Federal Reserve Bank

Discount Rate, 1914–2000

Year	Lowest Rate	Highest Rate	Year	Lowest Rate	Highest Rate
1914	5.00	6.00	1958	1.75	3.00
1915	4.00	5.00	1959	2.50	4.00
1916	3.00	4.00	1960	3.00	4.00
1917	3.00	3.50	1961	3.00	3.00
1918	3.50	4.00	1962	3.00	3.00
1919	4.00	4.75	1963	3.00	3.50
1920	4.75	7.00	1964	3.50	4.00
1921	4.50	7.00	1965	4.00	4.50
1922	4.00	4.50	1966	4.50	4.50
1923	4.00	4.50	1967	4.00	4.50
1924	3.00	4.50	1968	4.50	5.50
1925	3.00	3.50	1969	5.50	6.00
1926	3.50	4.00	1970	5.50	6.00
1927	3.50	4.00	1971	4.50	5.50
1928	3.50	5.00	1972	4.50	4.50
1929	4.50	6.00	1973	4.50	7.50
1930	2.00	4.50	1974	7.50	8.00
1931	1.50	3.50	1975	6.00	7.75
1932	2.50	3.50	1976	5.25	6.00
1933	2.00	3.50	1977	5.25	6.00
1934	1.50	2.00	1978	6.00	9.50
1935	1.50	1.50	1979	9.50	12.00
1936	1.50	1.50	1980	10.00	13.00
1937	1.00	1.50	1981	12.00	14.00
1938	1.00	1.00	1982	8.50	12.00
1939	1.00	1.00	1983	8.50	8.50
1940	1.00	1.00	1984	8.00	9.00
1941	1.00	1.00	1985	7.50	8.00
1942	0.50	1.00	1986	5.50	7.50
1943	0.50	1.00	1987	5.50	6.00
1944	0.50	1.00	1988	6.00	6.50
1945	0.50	1.00	1989	6.50	7.00
1946	0.50	1.00	1990	6.50	7.00
1947	1.00	1.00	1991	3.50	6.50
1948	1.00	1.50	1992	3.00	3.50
1949	1.50	1.50	1993	3.00	3.00
1950	1.50	1.75	1994	3.00	4.75
1951	1.75	1.75	1995	4.75	5.25
1952	1.75	1.75	1996	5.00	5.25
1953	1.75	2.00	1997	5.00	5.00
1954	1.50	2.00	1998	4.50	5.00
1955	1.50	2.50	1999	4.50	5.00
1956	2.50	3.00	2000	5.00	6.00
1957	3.00	3.50			

Sources: U.S. Congress, *Economic Indicators;* Federal Reserve Bank

Compound Savings of an Annuity

Years Saved	1%	2%	3%	4%	5%	6%	7%	8%	9%	10%
1	1.000	1.000	1.000	1.000	1.000	1.000	1.000	1.000	1.000	1.000
2	2.010	2.020	2.030	2.040	2.050	2.060	2.070	2.080	2.090	2.100
3	3.030	3.060	3.091	3.122	3.153	3.184	3.215	3.246	3.278	3.310
4	4.060	4.122	4.184	4.246	4.310	4.375	4.440	4.506	4.573	4.641
5	5.101	5.204	5.309	5.416	5.526	5.637	5.751	5.867	5.985	6.105
6	6.152	6.308	6.468	6.633	6.802	6.975	7.153	7.336	7.523	7.716
7	7.214	7.434	7.662	7.898	8.142	8.394	8.654	8.923	9.200	9.487
8	8.286	8.583	8.892	9.214	9.549	9.897	10.260	10.637	11.028	11.436
9	9.369	9.755	10.159	10.583	11.027	11.491	11.978	12.488	13.021	13.579
10	10.462	10.950	11.464	12.006	12.578	13.181	13.816	14.487	15.193	15.937
11	11.567	12.169	12.808	13.486	14.207	14.972	15.784	16.645	17.560	18.531
12	12.683	13.412	14.192	15.026	15.917	16.870	17.888	18.977	20.141	21.384
13	13.809	14.680	15.618	16.627	17.713	18.882	20.141	21.495	22.953	24.523
14	14.947	15.974	17.086	18.292	19.599	21.015	22.550	24.215	26.019	27.975
15	16.097	17.293	18.599	20.024	21.579	23.276	25.129	27.152	29.361	31.772
20	22.019	24.297	26.870	29.778	33.066	36.786	40.995	45.762	51.160	57.275
25	28.243	32.030	36.459	41.646	47.727	54.865	63.249	73.106	84.701	98.347
30	34.785	40.588	47.575	56.085	66.439	79.058	94.461	113.280	136.310	164.490
40	48.886	60.402	75.401	95.026	120.800	154.760	199.640	259.060	337.890	442.590
50	64.463	84.579	112.800	152.670	209.350	290.340	406.530	573.770	815.080	1,163.900

Example: If you invested $1,000 yearly in a retirement plan paying 7 percent a year compounded annually, at the end of the thirtieth year you would have saved $94,461 ($1,000 × 94.461).

ECONOMIC INDICATORS
Consumer Price Index for All Urban Consumers, Annual Average of Change, 1914–2000

1982–84 = 100

Year	% Changed
1914	1.0
1915	1.0
1916	7.9
1917	17.4
1918	18.0
1919	14.6
1920	15.6
1921	-10.5
1922	-6.1
1923	1.8
1924	0
1925	2.3
1926	1.1
1927	-1.7
1928	-1.7
1929	0.0
1930	-2.3
1931	-9.0
1932	-9.9
1933	-5.1
1934	3.1
1935	2.2
1936	1.5
1937	3.6
1938	-2.1
1939	-1.4
1940	0.7
1941	5.0
1942	10.9
1943	6.1
1944	1.7
1945	2.3
1946	8.3
1947	14.4
1948	8.1
1949	-1.2
1950	1.3
1951	7.9
1952	1.9
1953	0.8
1954	0.7
1955	-0.4
1956	1.5
1957	3.3
1958	2.8
1959	0.7
1960	1.7
1961	1.0
1962	1.0
1963	1.3
1964	1.3
1965	1.6
1966	2.9
1967	3.1
1968	4.2
1969	5.5
1970	5.7
1971	4.4
1972	3.2
1973	6.2
1974	11.0
1975	9.1
1976	5.8
1977	6.5
1978	7.6
1979	11.3
1980	13.5
1981	10.3
1982	6.2
1983	3.2
1984	4.3
1985	3.6
1986	1.9
1987	3.6
1988	4.1
1989	4.8
1990	5.4
1991	4.2
1992	3.0
1993	3.0
1994	2.6
1995	2.8
1996	3.0
1997	2.3
1998	1.6
1999	2.2
2000	3.4

Source: U.S. Bureau of Labor Statistics

Average Annual Incomes for Selected Occupations

Year	Average for All Workers	Coal Miners	Farm Workers	Federal Employees	Gas and Electric Workers	Health-Care Providers	Public School Teachers	Salespeople
1900	490	547	247	1,033	620	256	548	508
1910	630	805	336	1,108	622	338	677	630
1920	1,489	2,130	810	1,648	1,432	752	1,817	1,270
1930	1,494	909	444	1,492	1,603	933	1,717	1,569
1940	1,392	1,235	463	1,125	1,795	927	1,906	1,382
1950	3,255	3,245	1,454	3,220	3,571	2,067	3,778	3,034
1960	5,260	5,367	1,848	4,721	6,150	3,414	6,241	5,756
1970	7,747	9,790	3,787	8,040	10,028	6,593	10,110	NR
1980	15,757	24,555	7,434	17,217	21,701	14,728	25,372	18,822
1990	15,641	28,460	NA	NA	26,875	21,653	26,875	18,236

Source: U.S. Bureau of Labor Statistics

NR = Income not reported

NA = Information not available. The Bureau of Labor Statistics did not compile this data in 1990.

Prices of Selected Consumer Products
New York City

Year	Beef Roast (per pound)	Butter (per pound)	Chicken (per pound)	Eggs (per dozen)	Rice (per pound)
1900	$0.18	$0.27	$0.13	$0.23	$0.07
1905	0.14	0.28	0.17	0.32	0.09
1910	0.19	0.39	0.19	0.36	NR
1915	0.22	0.36	0.22	0.39	0.09
1920	0.41	0.71	0.44	0.78	0.17
1925	0.39	0.55	0.39	0.63	0.11
1930	0.41	0.46	0.37	0.52	0.09
1935	0.34	0.37	0.32	0.44	0.09
1941*	0.41	0.42	0.34	0.45	0.09
1945	0.33	0.51	0.47	0.60	0.14
1950	0.75	0.74	0.44	0.67	0.17
1955	0.70	0.72	0.45	0.70	0.20
1960	0.76	0.74	0.43	0.63	0.19
1965	0.85	0.75	0.42	0.57	0.20
1970	1.02	0.88	0.46	0.67	0.22
1975	1.78	1.06	0.68	0.85	0.50
1980	3.65	1.99	0.77	0.91	0.52
1986*	4.17	NR	0.88	0.92	NR
1990	4.54	1.92	0.86	1.00	0.49
1995	4.81	1.73	0.94	1.16	0.55

Source: U.S. Bureau of Labor Statistics

*Prices for 1940 and 1985 were not recorded.

NR = Prices not recorded

Unemployment in the United States, 1911–2000

Year	Number of Unemployed People (in thousands)	Unemployment Rate (in percent)	Year	Number of Unemployed People (in thousands)	Unemployment Rate (in percent)
1911	2,518	6.7	1956	2,750	4.1
1912	1,759	4.6	1957	2,859	4.3
1913	1,671	4.3	1958	4,602	6.8
1914	3,120	7.9	1959	3,740	5.5
1915	3,377	8.5	1960	3,852	5.5
1916	2,043	5.1	1961	4,714	6.7
1917	1,848	4.6	1962	3,911	5.5
1918	536	1.4	1963	4,070	5.7
1919	546	1.4	1964	3,786	5.2
1920	2,132	5.2	1965	3,366	4.5
1921	4,918	11.7	1966	2,875	3.8
1922	2,859	6.7	1967	2,975	3.8
1923	1,049	2.4	1968	2,817	3.6
1924	2,190	5.0	1969	2,832	3.5
1925	1,453	3.2	1970	4,093	4.9
1926	801	1.8	1971	5,016	5.9
1927	1,519	3.3	1972	4,882	5.6
1928	1,982	4.2	1973	4,365	4.9
1929	1,550	3.2	1974	5,156	5.6
1930	4,340	8.7	1975	7,929	8.5
1931	8,020	15.9	1976	7,406	7.7
1932	12,060	23.6	1977	6,991	7.1
1933	12,830	24.9	1978	6,202	6.1
1934	11,340	21.7	1979	6,137	5.8
1935	10,610	20.1	1980	7,637	7.1
1936	9,030	16.9	1981	8,273	7.6
1937	7,700	14.3	1982	10,678	9.7
1938	10,390	19.0	1983	10,717	9.6
1939	9,480	17.2	1984	8,539	7.5
1940	8,120	14.6	1985	8,312	7.2
1941	5,560	9.9	1986	8,237	7.0
1942	2,660	4.7	1987	7,425	6.2
1943	1,070	1.9	1988	6,701	5.5
1944	670	1.2	1989	6,528	5.3
1945	1,040	1.9	1990	7,047	5.6
1946	2,270	3.9	1991	8,628	6.8
1947	2,311	3.9	1992	9,613	7.5
1948	2,276	3.8	1993	8,940	6.9
1949	3,637	5.9	1994	7,996	6.1
1950	3,288	5.3	1995	7,404	5.6
1951	2,055	3.3	1996	7,236	5.4
1952	1,883	3.0	1997	6,739	4.9
1953	1,834	2.9	1998	6,210	4.5
1954	3,532	5.5	1999	5,880	4.2
1955	2,852	4.4	2000	5,655	4.0

Note: From 1911 until 1947, figures are for workers aged 14 and older. After 1947, figures are for workers aged 16 and older.
Source: U.S. Bureau of Labor Statistics

FEDERAL BUDGET

Summary of Federal Government Finances, 1789–2000

Year	Total Revenue	Total Expenditures (in mill. of dollars)	Surplus or Deficit (-)	Year	Total Revenue	Total Expenditures (in mill. of dollars)	Surplus or Deficit (-)
1789–91	4	4	*	1833	34	23	11
1792	4	5	-1	1834	22	19	3
1793	5	4	*	1835	35	18	18
1794	5	7	-2	1836	51	31	20
1795	6	8	-1	1837	25	37	-12
1796	8	6	3	1838	26	34	-8
1797	9	6	3	1839	31	27	5
1798	8	8	*	1840	19	24	-5
1799	8	10	-2	1841	17	27	-10
1800	11	11	*	1842	20	25	-5
1801	13	9	4	1843	8	12	-4
1802	15	8	7	1844	29	22	7
1803	11	8	3	1845	30	23	7
1804	12	9	3	1846	30	28	2
1805	14	11	3	1847	26	57	-31
1806	16	10	6	1848	36	45	-10
1807	16	8	8	1849	31	45	-14
1808	17	10	7	1850	44	40	4
1809	8	10	-3	1851	53	48	5
1810	9	8	1	1852	50	44	6
1811	14	8	6	1853	62	48	13
1812	10	20	-10	1854	74	58	16
1813	14	32	-17	1855	65	60	6
1814	11	35	-24	1856	74	70	4
1815	16	33	-17	1857	69	68	1
1816	48	31	17	1858	47	74	-28
1817	33	22	11	1859	53	69	-16
1818	22	20	2	1860	56	63	-7
1819	25	21	3	1861	42	67	-25
1820	18	18	*	1862	52	475	-423
1821	15	16	-1	1863	113	715	-602
1822	20	15	5	1864	265	865	-601
1823	21	15	6	1865	334	1,298	-964
1824	19	20	-1	1866	558	521	37
1825	22	16	6	1867	491	358	133
1826	25	17	8	1868	406	377	28
1827	23	16	7	1869	371	323	48
1828	25	16	8	1870	411	310	102
1829	25	15	10	1871	383	292	91
1830	25	15	10	1872	374	278	97
1831	29	15	13	1873	334	290	43
1832	32	17	15	1874	305	303	2

*$500,000 or less

Year	Total Revenue	Total Expenditures (in mill. of dollars)	Surplus or Deficit (-)	Year	Total Revenue	Total Expenditures (in mill. of dollars)	Surplus or Deficit (-)
1875	288	275	13	1922	4,026	3,289	736
1876	294	265	29	1923	3,853	3,140	713
1877	281	241	40	1924	3,871	2,908	963
1878	258	237	21	1925	3,641	2,924	717
1879	274	267	7	1926	3,795	2,930	865
1880	334	268	66	1927	4,013	2,857	1,155
1881	361	261	100	1928	3,900	2,961	939
1882	404	258	146	1929	3,862	3,127	734
1883	398	265	133	1930	4,058	3,320	738
1884	349	244	104	1931	3,116	3,577	-462
1885	324	260	63	1932	1,924	4,659	-2,735
1886	336	242	94	1933	1,997	4,598	-2,602
1887	371	268	103	1934	3,015	6,645	-3,630
1888	379	268	111	1935	3,706	6,497	-2,791
1889	387	299	88	1936	3,997	8,422	-4,425
1890	403	318	85	1937	4,956	7,733	-2,777
1891	393	366	27	1938	5,588	6,765	-1,177
1892	355	345	10	1939	4,979	8,841	-3,862
1893	386	383	2	1940	6,548	9,468	-2,920
1894	306	368	-61	1941	8,712	13,653	-4,941
1895	325	356	-31	1942	14,634	35,137	-20,503
1896	338	352	-14	1943	24,001	78,555	-54,554
1897	348	366	-18	1944	43,747	91,304	-47,557
1898	405	443	-38	1945	45,159	92,712	-47,553
1899	516	605	-89	1946	39,296	55,232	-15,936
1900	567	521	46	1947	38,514	34,496	4,018
1901	588	525	63	1948	41,560	29,764	11,796
1902	562	485	77	1949	39,415	38,835	580
1903	562	517	45	1950	39,443	42,562	-3,119
1904	541	584	-43	1951	51,616	45,514	6,102
1905	544	567	-23	1952	66,167	67,686	-1,519
1906	595	570	25	1953	69,608	76,101	-6,493
1907	666	579	87	1954	69,701	70,855	-1,154
1908	602	659	-57	1955	65,451	68,444	-2,993
1909	604	694	-89	1956	74,587	70,640	3,947
1910	676	694	-18	1957	79,990	76,578	3,412
1911	702	691	11	1958	79,636	82,405	-2,769
1912	693	690	3	1959	79,249	92,098	-12,849
1913	714	715	*	1960	92,492	92,191	301
1914	725	726	*	1961	94,388	97,723	-3,335
1915	683	746	-63	1962	99,676	106,821	-7,146
1916	761	713	48	1963	106,560	111,316	-4,756
1917	1,101	1,954	-853	1964	112,613	118,528	-5,915
1918	3,645	12,677	-9,032	1965	116,817	118,228	-1,411
1919	5,130	18,493	-13,363	1966	130,835	134,532	-3,698
1920	6,649	6,358	291	1967	148,822	157,464	-8,643
1921	5,571	5,062	509				

Continued on next page

Summary of Federal Government Finances, 1789–2000

Continued from page R33

Year	Total Revenue	Total Expenditures (in mill. of dollars)	Surplus or Deficit (-)	Year	Total Revenue	Total Expenditures (in mill. of dollars)	Surplus or Deficit (-)
1968	152,973	178,134	-25,161	1987	854,396	1,004,164	-149,769
1969	186,882	183,640	3,242	1988	909,303	1,064,489	-155,187
1970	192,807	195,649	-2,842	1989	991,190	1,143,671	-152,481
1971	187,139	210,172	-23,033	1990	1,031,969	1,253,198	-221,229
1972	207,309	230,681	-23,373	1991	1,055,041	1,324,400	-269,361
1973	230,799	245,707	-14,908	1992	1,091,279	1,381,684	-290,404
1974	263,224	269,359	-6,135	1993	1,154,401	1,409,512	-255,110
1975	279,090	332,332	-53,242	1994	1,258,627	1,461,902	-203,275
1976	298,060	371,792	-73,732	1995	1,351,830	1,515,837	-164,007
1977	355,559	409,218	-53,659	1996	1,453,062	1,560,572	-107,510
1978	399,561	458,746	-59,186	1997	1,579,292	1,601,282	-21,990
1979	463,302	504,032	-40,729	1998	1,721,798	1,652,611	69,187
1980	517,112	590,947	-73,835	1999	1,827,454	1,703,040	124,414
1981	599,272	678,249	-78,976	2000 est.	1,956,252	1,789,562	166,690
1982	617,766	745,755	-127,989				
1983	600,562	808,380	-207,818				
1984	666,499	851,888	-185,388				
1985	734,165	946,499	-212,334				
1986	769,260	990,505	-221,245				

Note: Due to rounding, the surplus or deficit may not equal exactly the difference between revenues and expenditures.

Sources: U.S. Bureau of the Census, Executive Office of the President of the United States

Public Debt of the Federal Government, 1803–2000

Year	Total Public Debt (in millions)	Year	Total Public Debt (in millions)	Year	Total Public Debt (in millions)
1803	$86.4	1822	$90.9	1841	$13.6
1804	82.3	1823	90.3	1842	20.2
1805	75.7	1824	83.8	1843	32.7
1806	69.2	1825	81.1	1844	23.5
1807	65.2	1826	74.0	1845	15.9
1808	57.0	1827	67.5	1846	15.6
1809	53.2	1828	58.4	1847	38.8
1810	48.0	1829	48.6	1848	47.0
1811	45.2	1830	39.1	1849	63.1
1812	56.0	1831	24.3	1850	63.5
1813	81.5	1832	7.0	1851	68.3
1814	99.8	1833	4.8	1852	66.2
1815	127.3	1834	*	1853	59.8
1816	123.5	1835	*	1854	42.2
1817	103.5	1836	0.3	1855	35.6
1818	95.5	1837	3.3	1856	32.0
1819	91.0	1838	10.4	1857	28.7
1820	90.0	1839	3.6	1858	44.9
1821	93.5	1840	5.3	1859	58.5

Year	Total Public Debt (in millions)	Year	Total Public Debt (in millions)	Year	Total Public Debt (in millions)
1860	$64.8	1908	$1,177.7	1956	$272,750.8
1861	90.6	1909	1,148.3	1957	270,527.2
1862	524.2	1910	1,146.9	1958	276,343.2
1863	1,119.8	1911	1,154.0	1959	284,705.9
1864	1,815.8	1912	1,193.8	1960	286,330.8
1865	2,677.9	1913	1,193.0	1961	288,970.9
1866	2,755.8	1914	1,188.2	1962	298,200.8
1867	2,650.2	1915	1,191.3	1963	305,859.6
1868	2,583.4	1916	1,225.1	1964	311,712.9
1869	2,545.1	1917	2,975.6	1965	317,273.9
1870	2,436.5	1918	12,455.2	1966	319,907.1
1871	2,322.1	1919	25,484.5	1967	326,220.9
1872	2,210.0	1920	24,299.3	1968	347,578.4
1873	2,151.2	1921	23,977.5	1969	353,720.3
1874	2,159.9	1922	22,963.4	1970	370,918.7
1875	2,156.3	1923	22,349.7	1971	408,176.0
1876	2,130.8	1924	21,250.8	1972	435,936
1877	2,107.8	1925	20,516.2	1973	466,291
1878	2,159.4	1926	19,643.2	1974	483,893
1879	2,298.9	1927	18,511.9	1975	541,925
1880	2,090.9	1928	17,604.3	1976	628,970
1881	2,019.3	1929	16,931.1	1977	706,398
1882	1,856.9	1930	16,185.3	1978	776,602
1883	1,722.0	1931	16,801.3	1979	829,471
1884	1,625.3	1932	19,487.0	1980	909,050
1885	1,578.6	1933	22,538.7	1981	994,845
1886	1,555.7	1934	27,053.1	1982	1,137,345
1887	1,465.5	1935	28,700.9	1983	1,371,710
1888	1,384.6	1936	33,778.5	1984	1,564,657
1889	1,249.5	1937	36,424.6	1985	1,817,521
1890	1,122.4	1938	37,164.7	1986	2,120,629
1891	1,005.8	1939	40,439.5	1987	2,346,125
1892	968.2	1940	42,967.5	1988	2,601,307
1893	961.4	1941	48,961.4	1989	2,868,039
1894	1,016.8	1942	72,422.4	1990	3,206,564
1895	1,096.9	1943	136,696.1	1991	3,598,485
1896	1,222.7	1944	201,003.4	1992	4,002,123
1897	1,226.8	1945	258,682.2	1993	4,351,403
1898	1,232.7	1946	269,422.1	1994	4,643,691
1899	1,436.7	1947	258,286.4	1995	4,921,005
1900	1,263.4	1948	252,292.2	1996	5,181,921
1901	1,221.6	1949	252,770.4	1997	5,369,694
1902	1,178.0	1950	257,357.4	1998	5,478,711
1903	1,159.4	1951	255,222.0	1999	5,606,087
1904	1,136.3	1952	259,105.2	2000 est.	5,686,338
1905	1,132.4	1953	266,071.1		
1906	1,142.5	1954	271,259.6		
1907	$1,147.2	1955	274,374.2		

*less than 0.1

Sources: U.S. Bureau of the Census; Executive Office of the President of the United States

UNITED STATES POPULATION

Population of the United States, 1790–2000

Year	Population (in thousands)
1790	3,929
1800	5,308
1810	7,240
1820	9,638
1830	12,866
1840	17,069
1850	23,192
1860	31,443
1870	39,818
1880	50,156
1890	62,948
1900	75,995
1910	91,972
1920	105,711
1930	122,775
1940	131,669
1950	151,326
1960	179,323
1970	203,302
1980	226,542
1990	248,718
2000	281,422

Source: U.S. Bureau of the Census

Note: Data for years before 1950 do not include the populations of Alaska and Hawaii.

Population of the United States by Race and Ethnicity, 1900–2000

(in thousands)

Year	White	African American	Hispanic/ Latino	Total (Other)	American Indian, Inuit, Aleut	Asian, Pacific Islander
1900	66,809	8,834	NA	351	NA	NA
1910	81,732	9,828	NA	413	NA	NA
1920	94,821	10,463	NA	427	NA	NA
1930	110,287	11,891	NA	597	NA	NA
1940	118,215	12,866	NA	589	NA	NA
1950	134,942	15,042	NA	713	NA	NA
1960	158,832	18,872	NA	1,620	NA	NA
1970	178,098	22,581	NA	2,557	NA	NA
1980	194,713	26,683	14,609	5,150	1,420	3,729
1990	208,710	30,486	22,354	9,523	2,065	7,458
2000	211,461	34,658	35,306	13,118	2,476	10,642

NA=This information is not available because it was not reported in the official census.

Source: U.S. Bureau of the Census

Population of the United States by Gender, 1850–2000

(in thousands)

Year	Male	Female
1850	11,838	11,354
1900	38,816	37,178
1910	47,332	44,640
1920	53,900	51,810
1930	62,137	60,638
1940	66,062	65,608
1950	75,187	76,139
1960	88,331	90,992
1970	98,926	104,309
1980	110,053	116,493
1990	121,284	127,507
2000	138,054	143,368

Note: Before 1870, population figures reported by gender are incomplete. Before 1950, figures exclude Alaska and Hawaii.
Source: U.S. Bureau of the Census

Immigrants to the United States by Region, 1901–1998

Year	Africa	Asia	Australia and Pacific Islands	Europe	North America	South America	Total
1901–10	7,368	196,501	13,024	8,136,016	336,416	25,472	8,795,386
1911–20	8,443	192,559	13,427	4,375,564	1,084,613	59,058	5,735,811
1921–30	6,286	97,400	8,726	2,477,853	1,458,701	58,015	4,107,209
1931–40	1,750	15,872	2,417	348,289	146,348	12,089	528,431
1941–50	7,367	36,471	14,551	621,704	282,032	72,772	1,035,039
1951–60	14,092	150,681	12,976	1,328,293	800,852	196,090	2,515,479
1961–70	28,954	421,464	25,122	1,129,670	1,337,460	378,914	3,321,677
1971–80	91,500	1,633,800	37,300*	801,300	1,645,000	284,400	4,493,300
1981–90	192,300	2,817,400	41,900*	705,600	3,125,000	455,900	7,338,100
1991–94	117,700	1,366,100	21,000*	599,800	2,168,600	236,600	4,509,800
1995–98	183,796	1,902,792	18,283	486,430	1,132,550	205,706	3,095,216

*Figure includes Australia, New Zealand, and countries listed as "unknown."
Source: U.S. Bureau of the Census, U.S. Immigration and Naturalization Service

GLOSSARY

Glossary
This glossary contains terms you need to understand as you study economics. After each term there is a brief definition or explanation of the term as it is used in *Holt Economics*. The page number refers to the page on which the term is introduced in the textbook.

Phonetic Respelling and Pronunciation Guide
Many of the key terms in this textbook have been respelled to help you pronounce them. The letter combinations used in the respellings throughout the narrative are explained in the following phonetic respelling and pronunciation guide. The guide is adapted from *Webster's Tenth New Collegiate Dictionary, Webster's New Geographical Dictionary,* and *Webster's New Biographical Dictionary.*

MARK	AS IN	RESPELLING	EXAMPLE
a	alphabet	a	*AL-fuh-bet
ā	Asia	ay	AY-zhuh
ä	cart, top	ah	KAHRT, TAHP
e	let, ten	e	LET, TEN
ē	even, leaf	ee	EE-vuhn, LEEF
i	it, tip, British	i	IT, TIP, BRIT-ish
ī	site, buy, Ohio	y	SYT, BY, oh-HY-oh
	iris	eye	EYE-ris
k	card	k	KAHRD
ō	over, rainbow	oh	oh-vuhr, RAYN-boh
ù	book, wood	ooh	BOOHK, WOOHD
ȯ	all, orchid	aw	AWL, AWR-kid
ȯi	foil, coin	oy	FOYL, KOYN
aù	out	ow	OWT
ə	cup, butter	uh	KUHP, BUHT-uhr
ü	rule, food	oo	ROOL, FOOD
yü	few	yoo	FYOO
zh	vision	zh	VIZH-uhn

*A syllable printed in small capital letters receives heavier emphasis than the other syllable(s) in a word.

A

absolute advantage the ability of a nation, region, or company to produce a certain good or service more efficiently and cheaply than any other nation, region, or company. 428

adjustable-peg system a system in which the exchange rates between currencies are fixed at specific values instead of reflecting changing economic conditions. 432

affirmative action a program, supported by law, requiring U.S. employers, labor unions, and other institutions to eliminate discrimination against women and minorities by increasing hiring, promotion, training, and other opportunities for members of these groups. 174

aggregate demand the total amount of goods, investments, and services that consumers want to buy during a specific period of time. 257

aggregate supply the total supply of all goods and services available in an economy. 257

allocate to distribute scarce resources—such as money, land, equipment, or labor—in order to satisfy the greatest number of needs and wants. 8

annual percentage rate the total cost of credit expressed as a yearly percentage. 215

antitrust legislation federal and state laws that regulate big business and labor unions to prevent or dismantle monopolies. 130

appreciation 1) an increase in the buying power of money 2) an increase in the value of a possession, such as a share of stock, a work or art, or real estate 3) an increase in the value of a nation's money relative to that of another nation. 432

arable fit for or used for growing crops. 403

arbitration a process for settling a dispute in which a mutually agreed-upon third party listens to each side and makes a settlement decision. 187

articles of incorporation an application to form a new corporation. 154

authoritarian socialism an economic system in which the government owns or controls nearly all factors of production; also known as communism. 27

B

balance 1) the amount on the credit side of an account 2) the difference between the debits and credits in a series of transactions. 196

balance of payments the accounting record of what a nation owes to and is owed by foreign countries and international institutions. 436

balance of trade the difference between the value of a nation's exports and that of its imports. 437

bankruptcy a legal process in which an individual or business whose debts exceed the value of their assets is forgiven those debts in excess of their assets. 216

barter the direct exchange of goods and services without the use of money. 15

bear market a financial market in which in the price of stocks, bonds, or other traded commodities is generally on the decline and in which investors believe that prices will continue to fall. 209

black market buying and selling of goods in violation of the law, typically at a higher price than has been officially established. 112

board of directors a panel elected by the stockholders of a corporation to establish its policies and overall direction. 155

bourgeoisie 1) the middle class, particularly as distinct from the upper class and the poor 2) the people who own the means of production in a capitalist nation. 389

broker a person who carries out investors' orders to buy and sell stocks and bonds. 206

budget a plan listing the expenses and income of an individual or organization. 200

budget deficit the amount that an organization's spending exceeds the revenue it takes in over a designated period. 363

budget surplus the amount that an organization's income exceeds its spending over a designated period. 363

bull market a financial market in which the price of stocks, bonds, or other traded commodities is generally on the rise and in which investors believe that prices will continue to rise. 209

business cycle a recurring pattern in economic activity that is characterized by alternating periods of expansion and contraction. 236

buyer someone who purchases or consumes a good or service. 117

C

call center central location to which a business's customer inquiries are routed. 19

capital accumulation the expansion of an economy's amount of capital goods. 202

capital deepening the increasing of capital resources at a faster rate than the increasing of the labor force, causing a rise in the capital-to-labor ratio. 244

capital formation the accumulation of financial and capital goods that promote increased production and economic development. 408

capital gain the profit earned through the sale of a capital asset. 205

capital good a building, structure, machine or tool that is used to produce goods or services. 5

capital improvements steps taken to increase the quality and efficiency of business resources. 316

capital loss a loss that results when a capital asset, such as a home, equipment, or investments, is sold for less than it cost. 205

capital resource an item that is used in the production of other goods and services. 5

capital-intensive a condition describing a company, industry, or national economy that depends on machines or capital assets to produce goods. 172

capitalism a market-based economic system in which individuals own and control the factors of production. 28

capital-to-labor ratio The amount of capital resources available per worker. 244

cartel group of producers or sellers of a certain good or service who unite to control prices, output, and market share. **126**

check-clearing the daily process of debiting and crediting banks' reserve accounts and checking accounts. **332**

closed shop a business that hires only labor union members. **178**

coincident indicators a set of economic factors that move up or down with the overall economy, measuring current economic activity. **240**

collateral property pledged by a borrower as security for a loan—for example, real estate, automobiles, or equipment. **149**

collective bargaining the process by which labor union leaders, speaking for the members they represent, and management representatives meet to negotiate labor contracts. **186**

collectivization the Soviet Union's policy of taking privately owned land to form large state-run farms. **391**

collusion an effort by producers or sellers of a particular product to secretly set production levels or prices. **125**

command economy an economy in which a central government authority makes all basic economic decisions and controls the factors of production. **25**

command system an economic system in which basic economic decisions are made by the government. **377**

commerce clause section of the Constitution giving Congress the right to regulate business between the United States and other nations, and among the states. **367**

commercial bank a financial institution whose chief purpose is to accept savings and checking deposits, make loans to businesses and individuals, and tranfer money among businesses, other banks, financial institutions, and individuals. **316**

commodity money a money system that is based on an item (a commodity) that has value to a society. **305**

common stock a share of ownership in a corporation; grants dividends and a voice in corporate management to the shareholder. **155**

communism economic system in which the government owns or controls nearly all factors of production; also known as authoritarian socialism. **27**

comparative advantage the ability of a nation, region, or company to produce a certain good or service more cheaply than any other country. **428**

competition in business, a state of rivalry among sellers of the same or similar products, in which each seller tries to gain a larger share of a market and to increase profits. **32**

complementary good a good that is commonly used with another good and for which demand increases (or decreases) when the demand for the related good increases (or decreases). **62**

conglomerate combination a corporation made up of several companies involved in different industries and markets. **160**

consolidation the combining of companies within a single industry. **69**

consumer one who buys goods or services for personal use rather than for resale or use in production or manufacturing. **3**

consumer good a finished product that is consumed by an individual. **7**

consumer price index (CPI) a measure of changes in the prices of market basket items, specific goods and services commonly purchased by a typical family. **260**

containerization putting products into large, standardized containers for shipping. **191**

contract a legally binding agreement, either oral or written, between individuals, such as to buy and sell goods and services. **30**

contraction a period in the business cycle during which business activity slows down and overall economic indicators decline. **236**

cooperative a business that is owned collectively by those who use its goods or services. **163**

coordinated campaigning a strategy in a labor dispute in which workers or a labor union use a variety of tactics, such as picketing, primary boycotts, and secondary boycotts, to force an employer to give in to their demands. **189**

copyright a government-granted right to exclusively duplicate, perform, display, publish, and sell copies of a literary, musical, or artistic work for a specified period of time. **128**

corporate bond a document representing a loan made by an investor to a corporation. **155**

corporate charter a document that a government issues to grant certain rights and impose certain restrictions on a bank or corporation. **154**

corporation a business in which a group of owners, called stockholders, share in the profits and losses. **153**

cost of production the total cost of materials, labor, and other inputs required in the manufacture of a product. **74**

cost-push inflation a general rise in prices that results from a rise in the costs of production. **258**

credit a form of exchange that allows consumers to use items with a promise of repayment over a specified time. **16**

credit bureau a company that collects and reports to its clients information about a person's financial condition and past record in meeting his or her financial obligations. **215**

credit rating an evaluation of a person's or a company's financial condition and reliability, especially concerning its record of meeting financial obligations. **215**

Cultural Revolution a violent movement in China from 1966 to 1976 that sought to preserve the communist system. **396**

currency the paper money and coins that are in circulation in a nation and that make up its money supply. **306**

customs duty a tax on goods brought into the United States. **354**

cyclical unemployment unemployment that is caused by downturns in the business cycle. **256**

D

debit card a plastic card used to make withdrawals at an automatic teller machine or a place of business. **318**

debt ceiling the maximum limit of debt that a local, state, or national government allows for itself by law. **365**

default the failure to make payments on a loan. **321**

deficit spending a government policy of spending more money on its programs than it is able cover with expected revenue. **363**

deflation a general decrease in the prices of all goods and services. **258**

demand the amount of a good or service that consumers are willing and able to buy at various prices during a given period. **5**

demand curve a graphic representation of a demand schedule, showing the relationship between the price of an item and the quantity demanded during a given period, with all other things being equal. **54**

demand schedule a table that shows the level of demand for a particular item at various prices. **54**

demand-pull inflation a general rise in prices that occurs when overall demand for goods increases faster than the output of goods. **258**

demand-side economics an economic theory developed by John Maynard Keynes proposing that government should stimulate the economy through measures that influence the overall demand for goods and services. **356**

democratic socialism an economic system in which some means of producing and distributing goods are owned or controlled by an elected government. **28**

depreciation 1) a decrease in the value of a capital good because of its age, use, or deterioration. Machinery in a factory, for example, declines in value over time and therefore suffers depreciation. **91** 2) a decline in the value of one nation's currency relative to that of another nation. **432**

depression a prolonged and severe recession. **236**

deregulation a lifting or lessening of government control or restrictions on a company, industry, or profession. **319**

derived demand the increased demand for resources, such as labor, that results from consumer demand for a particular product. **171**

determinant of demand a nonprice factor that influences the amount of demand for a good or service. **56**

determinant of supply a nonprice factor that influences the available supply of a good or a service. **79**

devaluation a reduction in the value of a nation's currency. **432**

developed nation a nation with a high level of industrial development and technical expertise, as well as various established economic institutions such as banks and stock markets. **403**

developing nation a nation with little industry and that has a low standard of living in comparison with developed nations. **403**

differentiate to point out something that distinguishes an item from similar items; to make distinctions among similar things. **120**

diminishing marginal utility the natural decreases in the utility of a good or service as more units of it are consumed. **53**

discount rate the interest rate charged by the Federal Reserve for loans to member banks. **339**

discouraged worker an unemployed worker who is not seeking employment because of job-related reasons. **252**

disposable income money that remains after taxes have been paid. **195**

diversification 1) the practice of spreading savings among several types of investments, such as gold, real estate, time deposits, or a variety of different stocks and bonds 2) the practice of reducing business risk by expanding the variety of goods or services offered or the geographic areas served. 201

dividend a stockholder's portion of a corporation's profit. 155

division of labor the division of a complex procedure into small tasks, enabling workers to increase output through specialzation. 10

E

easy-money policy government methods, such as reduced interest rates, to expand the economy's money supply. 337

e-commerce the electronic trading of goods. 247

economic development the degree to which a nation has developed its industrial, service, technical, and agricultural sectors. 403

economics the study of how society chooses to use scarce resources to satisfy its unlimited wants and needs. 3

economies of scale a condition in which, because of the level of resources needed, the cost of producing each unit of a product declines as the total number of units produced increases. 127

economist someone who studies economic theory and applies it to the real world. 3

efficiency the production of goods and services using the smallest amount of resources for the greatest amount of output. 63

elastic demand the situation that exists when quantity demanded changes greatly in response to a change in price. 63

elastic supply the situation that exists when quantity supplied changes greatly in response to a change in price. 77

elasticity of demand the degree to which changes in the price of a good or a service affect quantity demanded. 163

elasticity of supply the degree to which changes in the price of a good or a service affect quantity supplied. 76

embargo a government order that forbids importing or exporting goods with a specified nation. 441

entrepreneur someone who undertakes and develops a new business enterprise or develops a new product, risking failure or loss for the possibility of financial gain. 7

entrepreneurship the organizational abilities and risk taking involved in starting a new business or introducing a new product to consumers. 7

estate tax a tax levied on the assets, or property, of a person who has died. 354

ethics code set of moral rules, usually written, by which a company conducts business. 165

exchange the process by which producers and consumers agree to provide one type of item in return for another. 15

excise tax a tax placed by the federal government and some state governments on the manufacture, sale, or consumption of certain goods, often those considered to be luxury items or socially undesirable products. 354

expansion a period of the business cycle during which economic activity is increasing toward a peak. 236

expansionary fiscal policy a government policy designed to stimulate economic activity by reducing taxes and increasing spending. 360

expropriation the seizure of private property by a government, either with no payment or only partial payment to its owners. 412

externality an effect that an economic activity has on people and businesses that are neither producers nor consumers of the good or service being produced. An externality may be either positive (beneficial) or negative (harmful). 101

F

factor of production a resource used to produce goods and services. 4

federal budget the estimate of the revenues and expenses of the federal government for a fiscal year. 362

fiat money money that is not backed by gold, silver, or other items of value but that has worth because a government requires that it be accepted as a medium of exchange. 306

finance charge the total cost of credit. 215

fiscal policy the overall government program that establishes levels of taxing, borrowing, and spending that promote the desired economic goals for the nation. 349

fiscal year any 12-month period for financial reporting that ends on a date other than December 31. A typical fiscal year may begin on July 1 and run through June 30 of the following calendar year. 363

fixed cost a cost of doing business that remains constant as production increases or decreases. **91**

fixed expense an expense that does not vary from month to month or with a change in the level of a person's activity or, for a business, in the level of output. **201**

flexible expense an expense that may change from month to month according to an individual's or business's level of activity or output. **201**

floating exchange rate a foreign exchange rate that continuously varies according to supply and demand. **433**

foreign exchange market a market in which the currencies of different nations are bought and sold. **431**

foreign exchange rate the rate at which one nation's currency can be exchanged for another's. **431**

Four Modernizations a program for economic development in China that was announced in 1964. The Four Modernizations focused on improving agriculture, industry, science and technology, and defense. **396**

franchise a business that pays another established business to use the latter's name and product line. **162**

free enterprise system in which private business operates with minimal government involvement. **29**

free trade trade among nations that is not restrained by protective tariffs or other governmental restrictions. **441**

frictional unemployment temporary unemployment caused by factors that are not related to the business cycle. **253**

fringe benefit a nonwage payment that employers make to employees in addition to basic wages. **185**

full employment the lowest possible level of unemployment in an economy. **38**

future a commodity that is bought in order to sell at an agreed-upon price and at an agreed-upon time in anticipation of profits. **212**

G

general partnership a partnership in which all members have equal authority and share equally in the business's profits and losses. **150**

geographic monopoly a market whose geographic area is so limited that a single seller can control an item's manufacture, sale, distribution, or price. **128**

gift tax a tax by the federal government and some state governments on large transfers of property that are made without something of value being given in return. **354**

Gini Index a mathematical measure of income inequality in an economy. **266**

gold standard a system in which the value of a nation's money is defined by how many units of its currency are redeemable for a specified amount of gold. **311**

good an object or material that can be purchased to satisfy human wants or needs. **4**

government monopoly a market in which a government is the sole producer or seller of a product. **129**

Great Leap Forward an unsuccessful economic development plan for the People's Republic of China that was introduced by communist leaders in 1958. **396**

gross domestic product (GDP) the total value of all final goods and services produced within a country in a given year. **229**

gross investment the total value of private spending in the economy for capital assets—such as new equipment, machinery, and buildings—over a specific period of time, plus total changes in business inventories. **231**

gross national product (GNP) the total value of all final goods and services produced with factors of production owned by citizens of a given country. Unlike the gross domestic product (GDP), the GNP includes the income of the overseas divisions of U.S. companies. **234**

H

horizontal combination a corporation made up of various businesses that produce the same or similar goods and services. **159**

household responsibility system a government program in rural China enabling farmers to lease state-owned land in exchange for a portion of their crop. **396**

human resource any human activity—mental or physical—used in the production process. **5**

hyperinflation an increase in prices that is so rapid and severe that it disrupts normal economic conditions. **261**

I

import quota a law limiting the amount of a foreign-produced good that may be imported into a nation during a specified period of time. **440**

incentive something that encourages an action or effort. Expectation of rewards and fear of losses are both incentives. **27**

income **1)** money payments that households receive from business firms and the government in exchange for resources **2)** funds that a business takes in for supplying goods or services. **34**

income effect the effect that a change in an item's price has on consumers' ability to purchase goods. **52**

indicative planning the development of non-mandatory economic goals by a government in order to coordinate private and public sector investment and production plans. **384**

industrialization the process of mechanizing all major forms of production. **172**

inelastic demand the situation that exists when quantity demanded changes only slightly or not at all in response to a change in price. **64**

inelastic supply the situation that exists when quantity supplied changes only slightly or not at all in response to a change in price. **77**

inflation an increase in overall prices that results from rising wages, an increased money supply, and increased spending relative to the supply of products. **258**

inflation rate the rate at which the overall price level of goods and services in an economy is changing. **260**

infrastructure the basic facilities and services that an economy needs in order to function. **202**

injunction a court order in a labor dispute that forbids specified acts by specified individuals or groups. **190**

installment a repeated partial payment made to a financial institution or other credit-extending organization to repay a loan or to pay for goods or services that have been purchased. **215**

interdependence the relationship of mutual reliance and influence among people, businesses, industries, regions, and nations. **18**

interdependent pricing the setting of prices in a manner responsive to—or dependent on—one's competitors. **125**

interest **1)** the financial return gained by investing or lending capital **2)** the money that a borrower pays to a bank or other lender in return for a loan **3)** the return on a debt security investment, such as a bond **4)** a share in the ownership of property—for example, a 25 percent interest in a business. **155**

interest group a group whose members hold common political beliefs and work to influence government officials, policies, and practices. **294**

intrinsic reward nonmonetary compensation that has no financial worth but is desirable because of the recipient's personal values. **171**

investment **1)** the purchase of something of value with the expectation that over time it will increase in value and produce a profit **2)** in economic theory, the purchase of capital goods. **200**

investment bank a firm that buys large blocks of stocks and bonds issued by companies and then resells those securities to investors at a profit. **206**

investment tax credit a tax incentive that allows businesses to deduct from their taxes part of their investment in new equipment. **358**

L

labor force all persons in a nation who are at least 16 years old and either working or actively looking for work. **169**

labor productivity a measure of how much each worker produces in a given period of time. **177**

labor union an organization of workers that negotiates with employers for better wages, improved working conditions, and job security. **177**

labor-intensive a term to describe an economy that has a large proportion of labor input relative to capital investment. **172**

lagging indicators a set of economic factors that help economists predict the duration of economic upturns or downturns. **240**

laissez-faire economic philosophy that opposes government intervention in the market. **130**

land ordinance a public order regulating land use. **30**

land reform redistribution, or changes in land ownership, carried out or enforced by the government. **417**

law of demand the principle that, all other factors being equal, consumers will purchase (demand) more of a good at lower prices and less of a good at higher prices. **52**

law of diminishing returns the principle that as more of one input (such as labor) is added to a fixed supply of other resources (such as capital), productivity will increase up to a point, after which the marginal product will diminish. **87**

law of supply the principle that producers will supply more of a product or service at higher prices but less of a product or service at lower prices. **73**

leading indicators a set of economic factors that anticipate the expansions and contractions of the business cycle from one month up to two years before similar changes in overall economic activity occur. **240**

liability 1) a debt obligation 2) a person or business's legally enforceable responsibility for unpaid expenses. **147**

limited partnership a form of partnership in which some members, called limited partners, invest money but take no part in management. **150**

liquidity the ease with which an individual or a business can convert assets into cash without suffering a substantial monetary loss. **196**

lobbyist an individual who is paid to influence legislators and government administrators to act in ways that are favorable to the lobbyist's employer. **296**

lockout a shutdown of a business by an employer, or other refusal to let striking employees come to work, in protest of worker or labor union demands. **190**

longevity the duration of a firm's life. **149**

Lorenz curve a graph showing how equally income is distributed in an economy. **265**

M

macroeconomics the study of an entire economy or one of its principal sectors. **3**

margin requirement the percentage of the price an investor must pay in cash to purchase a stock, convertible bond, or other security. **342**

marginal cost the cost of producing one additional unit of output. **92**

marginal product the additional output obtained by employing one more unit of input. **87**

marginally attached worker a worker who once held a productive job but is now unemployed and no longer looking for work. **252**

market the free exchange of goods and services; also called the market place. **25**

market basket a representative sample of about 400 goods and services that the U.S. Department of Labor has identified as common purchases of a typical consumer. **260**

market economy an economy in which the government has little say in what, how, and for whom goods are produced and in which the factors of production are owned by individuals. **25**

market equilibrium the point at which the quantity supplied and quantity demanded for a product are equal at the same price. **103**

market failure a flaw in a price system that occurs when some costs have not been accounted for and therefore are not properly distributed. **101**

market revolution major change in the way goods are bought and sold. **247**

market socialism a type of socialism in which the means of production are owned or controlled by the government, but individuals and businesses make some economic decisions. **379**

market system an economic system in which the three basic economic questions are answered by individuals and businesses. **377**

maturity the length of time that money must be deposited in a time deposit. **197**

mediation a process for settling disputes in which a neutral third party listens to each side, asks questions and clarifies issues, and proposes a solution. **186**

medium of exchange anything that a seller will accept as payment for a good or service. **302**

mercantilism an economic theory that defined a nation's power in terms of specie; used to direct most European economies between 1500 and 1800. **382**

merger the joining of two or more businesses under a single ownership. **159**

microeconomics the study of a single factor of an economy—such as individuals, households, businesses, and industries—rather than an economy as a whole. **3**

minimum wage the lowest hourly wage rate that an employer legally can pay a worker, as established by federal law. **109**

mixed economy an economy that combines elements of the traditional, market, and command economic models. **27**

monetary policy a government's plan for regulating a nation's money supply and the availability of credit in order to accomplish certain economic goals. **337**

money any item, typically currency, that is commonly accepted in exchange for goods, services, or the settling of debts. **15**

money supply the total amount of money circulating at any given time in a nation's economy. **335**

monopolistic competition a market in which many producers offer a similar—but not identical—good or service. **120**

monopoly a market in which a single seller exercises exclusive or nearly exclusive control over a particular good or service. **119**

moral suasion unofficial pressure that the Federal Reserve uses to persuade member banks to behave in a certain way. **342**

multinational corporation (MNC) a business that is based in one nation but operates divisions or subsidiaries in other nations. **417**

mutual savings bank a bank that is owned by its depositors, who share in its profits. **316**

N

national debt the total amount of money that a nation owes its creditors. **364**

national income accounting the process used for tracking production, income, and consumption in a nation's economy. **229**

nationalization the government takeover of specific companies or of a major segment of a nation's private industry, such as manufacturing, agriculture, or transportation. **384**

natural monopoly a market in which competition is inconvenient and impractical, and thus efficiency is best achieved by a single seller. **127**

natural resource in economics, any material provided by nature that can be used to produce goods or provide services. **4**

near money an asset that can easily be converted into cash when needed. **307**

nominal GDP the value of a nation's gross domestic product (GDP) at the current prices of the period being measured. **232**

nonprice competition any attempt by a seller to attract customers from its competitors other than by lowering its prices. **120**

nonprofit organization an organization that generates revenue from product sales or donations but does not distribute the profits to any owner or trustee. **163**

O

oligopoly a market in which a few large sellers control most of the production of a good or service. **123**

one-crop economy an economy that is dominated by the production of a single item. **407**

open shop a business where membership in a labor union is not a condition of employment. **178**

opportunity cost the value lost by rejecting one use of resources in favor of another. In other words, an action's opportunity cost is the value of the next-best alternative action that is not taken. **11**

output-expenditure model a method of computing the gross domestic product (GDP) by adding the total value of consumer and government spending on goods and services, total private investment, and the total value of exports, and then subtracting the total value of imports. **230**

overhead the sum of a business's fixed costs except for wages and the material costs. **91**

P

partnership a business owned and controlled by two or more people who share in its profits and are responsible for its losses. **150**

patent a government document granting an inventor the right to produce, use, or sell an invention exclusively for a limited period of time. **128**

peak 1) the point of the business cycle during which employment, production, and wages are at their highest. A peak is also called a turning point. 2) the high point of any phase of economic activity. **236**

people's communes large collective farms established in China beginning in 1958. **396**

per capita amount for each person. **279**

perfect competition an ideal market condition that includes a large number of sellers of identical goods and services and in which no one seller controls supply or prices. **117**

personal consumption expenditure total spending by consumers for durable goods, nondurable goods, and services during a specified period of time. **231**

poverty rate the percentage of individuals or families in the total population who are living below the poverty threshold and are thus considered by the government to be poor. **264**

poverty threshold the level of income that the government considers necessary to sustain a family at a minimum standard of living. **264**

preferred stock a share of ownership in a corporation. **155**

price ceiling a government regulation that sets a maximum price for a particular good. **108**

price discrimination the setting of different prices for different buyers under the same circumstances. **132**

price floor a government regulation that sets a minimum price for a particular good. **109**

price index a set of statistics that allows economists to compare prices over time. **232**

price leadership a situation in which one major seller in an industry sets a price and other sellers follow in order to remain competitive. **125**

price stability the condition that exists when overall price levels remain relatively constant over a period of time. **38**

price war a series of price reductions that may become so drastic that each seller involved suffers considerable losses. **125**

primary boycott an organized effort to stop purchases of a firm's products. It is a tactic to express disapproval or to force the other party to take some desired action. Primary boycotts are often part of labor disputes. **189**

prime rate the interest rate for loans that banks charge to their most reliable customers. **341**

principal 1) an amount of money that is borrowed, as in a loan. Principal is distinct from interest and profit 2) the face amount of a bond. **155**

private property property that is owned by individuals and businesses, rather than the government. **29**

privatization the act of returning property or functions previously owned or performed by government to the private sector. **287**

producer a person, group, or business that makes goods or provides services to satisfy consumers' needs and wants. **3**

producer price index (PPI) a measure of the changes in prices of about 3,200 items bought by producers. **260**

product differentiation an attempt by a seller in monopolistic competition to convince buyers that its product is different from and superior to the nearly identical products of competitors. **120**

product market the market in which producers offer—and consumers purchase—final goods and services. **34**

production possibilities curve a graphic representation showing all of the possible combinations of two goods or services that can be produced in a stated period, assuming that the amount of available resources and technology will not change during the period, and that all of the natural, human, and capital resources involved are being used in the most efficient manner possible. **12**

productivity the level of output that results from a given level of input. **9**

productivity growth an increase in output per worker per hour worked. **244**

profit the difference between the revenue received from the sale of a good or service and the costs of providing that good or service. **74**

profit motive the desire to make money. **73**

proletariat the working class, whose members the radical political theorist Karl Marx believed were oppressed by the bourgeoisie and would eventually overthrow the bourgeoisie in a violent revolution. **390**

prospectus a fact sheet that provides detailed financial information about the company issuing the data. **213**

protectionism the use of trade barriers to protect a nation's industries against foreign competition. **441**

protective tariff a tax or customs duty that a nation's government places on certain imports to restrict their sale. **439**

public good any good or service that is consumed by all members of a group, regardless of who has helped pay for it. **102**

public goods gap the difference between the amount of private wealth generated and the amount spent on public goods. **250**

purchasing power the amount of income that people have available to spend on goods and services. **52**

pyramided reserves a system in which smaller banks deposit some of their reserves into larger banks and the larger banks deposit some of their reserves into the largest banks. **327**

Q

quantity demanded the amount of a good or service that consumers are willing and able to purchase at a particular price. **51**

quantity supplied the amount of a good or service that producers are willing and able to sell at a particular price. **73**

quota 1) the minimum number of new hires to be made through an affirmative action program. 2) a maximum or minimum limit to be achieved in dollars or units of something. **174**

R

rationing a system by which a government or other institution decides how to distribute a good or service; rationing is usually the result of limited supply. **110**

real GDP the value of a nation's gross domestic product (GDP) after it has been adjusted for inflation. **232**

real GDP per capita the dollar value—adjusted for inflation—of all final goods and services produced per person in an economy in a given year. **241**

real investment an investment that creates a new capital good. **202**

recession a substantial and general decline in overall business activity over a significant period of time. **236**

regulation a rule that a government establishes and enforces to protect the public or provide equal access to specific goods and services. **82**

representative money a money system in which an item has value because it can be exchanged for something else that is valuable. **305**

reserve requirement money the Fed requires a bank to hold either in its own vaults or in a district Federal Reserve bank. **341**

resource anything used to produce goods or services. **4**

resource market the market in which households exchange resources with businesses and the government. **34**

restrictive fiscal policy a government policy designed to reduce economic activity in times of overexpansion by increasing taxes and/or reducing government spending. **360**

revenue tariff a tax or customs duty that a nation's government places on imports in order to raise money. **439**

S

savings and loan association a financial institution that lends money and in which depositors maintain savings and checking accounts. **316**

savings rate the percentage of disposable income that is not consumed by purchasing goods and services. **199**

scarcity the fundamental condition of economics that results from the combination of limited resources and unlimited wants. **8**

seasonal unemployment unemployment that results from seasonal variations in the economy. **255**

secondary boycott a refusal to buy the goods or services of any firm that does business with a company whose employees are on strike. **189**

self-interest the impulse that encourages people to fulfill their needs and wants. **26**

self-sufficiency the ability to fullfill all of one's needs without assistance. **17**

seller the producer of a good or service. **117**

seniority a ranking of employees based on the number of years a worker has been employed by a firm. **185**

service any action or activity that is performed for a fee. **4**

share 1) the smallest unit of ownership in a corporation, usually expressed as one share of stock 2) the portion of an owner's interest in a business. **155**

shortage a situation in which the quantity demanded of a good or resource exceeds the quantity supplied. **105**

sole proprietorship a business that is owned and managed by one person. **145**

specialization the focus of a worker on only one or a few aspects of production in order to improve efficiency. **10**

specie money in the form of coins. Historically, specie was valued for the metal it was made from, typically gold or silver. **305**

standard of living people's economic well-being as determined by the quantity of goods and services they consume in a given time period. **39**

standard of value a measure of the relative value of various goods or services. **302**

stock 1) a share of ownership in a corporation 2) the inventory of items held for sale by a manufacturer or other seller of goods. **155**

stock quote the price of a particular stock at a given time. **219**

stock split an action by a corporation to divide its stock into a larger number of shares. **205**

stock ticker a machine that converted telegraph signals into text to report stock prices. **219**

store of value a characteristic of a medium of exchange that allows it, and thus value or wealth, to be stored. **303**

strike a work stoppage by employees or labor union members acting together to bring pressure on their employer to give in to their demands on some job-related dispute. **188**

structural unemployment unemployment that is caused by changes in technology, government policies, long-term consumer demand for certain products, population trends, and other factors unrelated to the business cycle. **253**

subsidiary a business that another company either owns or in which it has a controlling interest. **160**

subsidy a payment made by a government to individuals, businesses, or an industry to encourage certain activities that are considered essential or desirable. **82**

subsistence agriculture a type of farming in which there are only enough crops and livestock raised to meet a family's basic needs, with no excess left over to sell or trade. **405**

substitute good a product that purchasers use in place of another product, particularly if the price of the other product rises. **60**

substitution effect consumers' tendency to substitute a lower-priced good for a similar, higher-priced one. **52**

supply the amount of a good or service that producers are willing to sell at various possible prices during a given period. **73**

supply curve a graphic representation of a supply schedule, showing the relationship between the price of an item and the quantity supplied during a given time period, with all other things being equal. **75**

supply schedule a table that lists each quantity of a product that producers are willing to supply at various prices. **75**

supply shock an economic disturbance caused by events outside a nation's economy; increases costs of production for one or more industries and often leads to inflation. **258**

supply-side economics the economic theory that focuses on achieving economic stability and growth by increasing the supply of goods and services throughout the economy. **355**

surplus a situation in which the quantity supplied of an item at a given price exceeds the quantity demanded. **105**

T

tax a required payment to a local, state, or national government, usually made on some regular basis. **81**

tax incentive a provision in a tax law intended to stimulate economic activity by encouraging businesses to invest in new capital. **358**

tax rate the percentage at which income, property, or purchases are taxed. **349**

technological monopoly a market that is dominated by a single producer because of new technology it has developed. **128**

technology scientific and technical techniques used to produce existing products more efficiently or of higher quality. **7**

Tiananmen Square Massacre a 1989 incident in which Chinese demonstrators seeking greater political freedoms were brutally attacked by China's armed forces. **397**

tight-money policy government methods, such as increased interest rates, designed to reduce the economy's money supply. **338**

time deposit a deposit—usually a certificate of deposit or a savings bond—in a bank or other financial institution that earns interest and that must remain on deposit for a specified period of time. **197**

total cost the sum of the fixed and variable costs involved in the production of a good or service. **91**

total product all the goods and services produced by a business during a given period of time with a given amount of input. **86**

total revenue a business's total income; sometimes called total receipts. **66**

trade barrier any limitation on the flow of goods between nations. **439**

trade deficit a condition in international trade in which the value of a nation's imports from another country exceeds the value of its exports to that particular country. **437**

trade surplus a condition in international trade in which the value of a nation's exports to another country exceeds the value of its imports from that particular country. **437**

trade-off the sacrifice of one good in order to purchase or produce another. **11**

traditional economy an economy in which production is based on customs and tradition. **24**

transfer payment a payment made by a government to someone who does not produce a good or service in return. **288**

trough the lowest point of a business cycle, in which demand, production, and employment reach their lowest levels. **236**

trust a group of companies that combine to eliminate competition in an industry and thereby gain a monopoly. **130**

U

underemployed working at a job for which one is overqualified, or working in a part-time job when full-time employment is desired. **252**

underground economy illegal economic activities or unreported legal activities that are not accounted for in national economic measures. **233**

unemployment rate the percentage of people in the civilian workforce who are unemployed. **252**

usury the act of charging borrowers a higher rate of interest than is allowed by law. **216**

utility the usefulness of a good or service that contributes to its value. **17**

V

value the worth of a good or service for the purposes of exchange, expressed as the amount of money that a consumer is willing to pay for a good or service. **17**

variable cost a cost of doing business that changes directly with a change in the level of output, typically rising and dropping as production increases and decreases. **91**

venture capital individual or corporate funds that are invested in entrepreneurial enterprises to encourage economic growth. **203**

vertical combination a corporation made up of various businesses involved in different stages of the production process of the same good or service. **159**

vertical integration owning all of the businesses related to the manufacture and distribution of a product. **161**

voluntary exchange the unconditional and mutually beneficial transfer of products between producer and consumer. **321**

voluntary trade restriction an agreement—not requiring congressional legislation—between two or more nations to limit or control trade by restricting shipments of certain products to a particular country. **440**

W

wage the payment that a worker receives for his or her labor. **169**

wage-price spiral a cycle that develops when increased wages raise production costs, which then lead to higher prices for goods or services, encouraging workers to demand still higher wages. **260**

Y

yield 1) the annual income earned on a stock, bond, or other investment security. It is usually expressed as a percentage of its market price 2) the total income earned on a loan 3) the total interest income paid on a bond if the bond is held by the purchaser until its maturity. **209**

Z

zoning law a law governing what types of structures and businesses are allowed in a particular area. **146**

GLOSARIO

Este glosario contiene términos que necesitas comprender al aprender economía. Después de cada término se presenta una breve definición o explicación dentro del contexto de *Holt Economics*. El número corresponde a la página del libro de texto en donde se encuentra el término.

A

absolute advantage/ventaja absoluta capacidad que tiene un país, región o compañía para producir cierto producto o brindar cierto servicio de manera más eficiente y más barata que cualquier otro país, región o compañía. **428**

adjustable-peg system/sistema de estabilización regulable sistema en el que los tipos de cambio entre una moneda y otra se fijan con base en valores específicos en vez de que reflejen las condiciones económicas cambiantes. **432**

affirmative action/acción afirmativa programa sustentado en la ley que obliga a los patrones, sindicatos y demás instituciones estadounidenses a eliminar la discriminación contra mujeres y minorías mediante el aumento de contrataciones, promociones, capacitación y demás oportunidades para los miembros de estos grupos. **174**

aggregate demand/demanda agregada cantidad total de productos, inversiones y servicios que los consumidores desean comprar dentro de un lapso de tiempo específico. **257**

aggregate supply/oferta agregada oferta total de productos y servicios disponibles en una economía. **257**

allocate/asignar distribuir recursos insuficientes –como dinero, tierras, equipo o trabajo– de modo que se satisfaga el mayor número de necesidades. **8**

annual percentage rate/tasa anual de porcentaje costo total del crédito expresado como un porcentaje anual. **215**

antitrust legislation/legislación antimonopólica leyes federales y estatales que regulan las grandes empresas y los sindicatos para evitar o desmantelar los monopolios. **130**

appreciation/apreciación 1) aumento en el poder de compra del dinero 2) aumento en el valor de una posesión, como las acciones, una obra artística, un producto o un bien raíz 3) aumento en el valor del dinero de un país en relación con el de otro país. **432**

arable/cultivable que está listo o se usa para producir cosechas. **403**

arbitration/arbitraje proceso de resolución de una disputa en el que una tercera parte, por mutuo acuerdo, escucha a cada lado y toma una decisión resolutiva. **187**

articles of incorporation/artículos de incorporación solicitud para conformar una corporación nueva. **154**

authoritarian socialism/socialismo autoritario sistema económico en donde el gobierno posee y controla casi todos los factores de producción; también es conocido como comunismo. **27**

B

balance/saldo 1) monto del crédito en una cuenta 2) diferencia entre el debe y el haber en una serie de transacciones. **196**

balance of payments/balanza de pagos registro contable de lo que un país debe a países extranjeros y de lo que los países extranjeros le deben. **436**

balance of trade/balanza de comercio diferencia entre el valor de las exportaciones de un país y el de sus importaciones. **437**

bankruptcy/bancarrota proceso legal en el que se condonan las deudas a una persona o una empresa cuyas deudas exceden el valor de sus activos. **216**

barter/trueque intercambio directo de bienes y servicios sin el uso de dinero. **15**

GLOSARIO **R51**

bear market/mercado a la baja mercado financiero en que el precio de las mercancías, los depósitos y otros productos comerciales están a la baja y los inversionistas creen que los precios seguirán bajando. **209**

black market/mercado negro compra y venta de bienes fuera de la ley, por lo general a un precio más alto que los establecidos oficialmente. **112**

board of directors/junta directiva grupo de personas electo por los accionistas de una corporación para establecer sus políticas y su orientación en general. **115**

bourgeoisie/burguesía 1) clase media, la clase particularmente distinta de la clase alta y la clase baja 2) los que poseen los medios de producción en un país capitalista. **389**

broker/corredor de bolsa persona que, por instrucciones de los inversionistas, realiza la compra y la venta acciones y bonos. **206**

budget/presupuesto lista del plan de ingresos y egresos de una persona o una organización. **200**

budget deficit/déficit del presupuesto cantidad por la que los gastos exceden los ingresos de una organización en un periodo determinado. **363**

budget surplus/excedente de presupuesto cantidad por la que los ingresos exceden los gastos de una organización en un periodo determinado. **363**

bull market/mercado al alza mercado financiero en el que los precios, las acciones, los bonos y otros productos comerciales están al alza y muchos inversionistas creen que los precios seguirán así. **209**

business cycle/ciclo de negocios patrón que se repite en las actividades económicas y que se caracteriza por periodos alternativos de expansión y contracción. **236**

buyer/comprador persona que compra o consume un producto o un servicio. **117**

C

capital accumulation/acumulación de capital crecimiento de la cantidad de los bienes de capital en una economía. **202**

capital deepening/aceleración del capital incremento de los recursos del capital a un ritmo más rápido que el incremento de la fuerza de trabajo, lo que ocasiona un aumento en la relación capital-fuerza de trabajo. **244**

capital formation/formación de capital acumulación de bienes financieros y de capital que favorece el desarrollo económico y el incremento de la producción. **408**

capital gain/beneficio de inversiones beneficio que se obtiene por la venta de un activo fijo. **205**

capital good/bien de capital edificio, instalación, máquina o herramienta que se emplean para producir bienes y servicios. **5**

capital loss/pérdida de capital pérdida ocasionada cuando un activo fijo, como una casa, equipo o inversión, se vende a menos de su costo. **205**

capital resource/recurso de capital artículo que se emplea en la producción de otros bienes y servicios. **5**

capital-intensive/concentración de capital término que describe a una compañía, industria o economía nacional cuando depende de máquinas o activos fijos para producir bienes. **172**

capitalism/capitalismo sistema económico basado en el mercado, en el cual los individuos son dueños de los medios de producción y los controlan. **28**

capital-to-labor ratio/ relación capital-fuerza de trabajo cantidad de recursos de capital disponibles para cada trabajador. **244**

cartel/cartel grupo de productores o de vendedores de un determinado producto o servicio que se unen para controlar su precio y su producción y compartir el mercado. **126**

check-clearing/registro de saldos proceso diario de registro de débito y crédito de las cuentas de la reserva bancaria y de las cuentas de depósito. **332**

close shop/taller agremiado negocio que contrata sólo a los miembros de un gremio. **178**

coincident indicators/indicadores coincidentes grupo de factores económicos que suben o bajan junto con la economía en general, midiendo la actividad económica. **240**

collateral/garantía propiedad que un prestatario da en prenda a cambio de un préstamo; por ejemplo, bienes raíces, automóviles o equipo. **149**

collective bargaining/contrato colectivo proceso por el que los líderes de un sindicato hablan a favor de los miembros que representan y se entrevistan con los representantes de la dirección para negociar los contratos laborales. **186**

collectivization/colectivización política de la Unión Soviética de apropiarse de extensiones de tierra para formar grandes granjas administradas por el Estado. **391**

collusion/colusión esfuerzo que hacen los productores o vendedores para establecer los niveles de producción o los precios de un producto. **125**

command economy/economía autoritaria economía en que la autoridad de un gobierno central toma las decisiones económicas importantes y controla los factores de producción. **25**

command system/sistema económico autoritario sistema económico en que el gobierno toma las decisiones económicas importantes. **377**

commercial bank/banco comercial institución financiera cuyo propósito principal es captar ahorros y registrar depósitos, hacer préstamos a negocios e individuos y transferir dinero entre negocios, otros bancos, instituciones financieras e individuos. **316**

commodity money/dinero en especie sistema de moneda basado en un artículo (producto o mercancía) que tiene un valor en una sociedad. **305**

common stock/acciones comunes participación de la propiedad de una corporación; concesión de dividendos y derecho a opinión para los accionistas en el manejo de la corporación. **155**

communism/comunismo sistema económico en el cual el gobierno es dueño de casi todos los medios de producción y los controla; también se conoce como socialismo autoritario. **27**

comparative advantage/ventaja comparativa capacidad de una nación, región o compañía de producir cierto producto o servicio de manera más económica que cualquier otro país. **428**

competition/competencia en los negocios, situación de rivalidad entre los vendedores de productos iguales o semejantes, en la cual cada vendedor trata de ganar una mayor porción del mercado y aumentar sus ganancias. **32**

complementary good/producto complementario producto que comúnmente se usa con otro producto y su demanda aumenta (o disminuye) cuando la demanda del producto relacionado aumenta (o disminuye). **62**

conglomerate combination/conglomerado empresarial corporación que se compone de varias empresas que participan en diferentes industrias y mercados. **160**

consumer/consumidor persona que adquiere bienes o servicios para su uso personal más que para venderlos o usarlos en la producción o la manufactura. **3**

consumer good/producto de consumo producto terminado que los individuos consumen. **7**

consumer price index (CPI)/índice de precios al consumidor (IPC) medida de los cambios que ocurren en los precios de productos de la canasta básica y de bienes y servicios específicos que comúnmente adquiere una familia típica. **260**

contract/contrato acuerdo legal, ya sea de palabra o por escrito, entre personas, por ejemplo, para comprar y vender bienes y servicios. **30**

contraction/contracción periodo del ciclo económico durante el cual disminuye la actividad de las empresas y bajan los indicadores económicos globales. **236**

cooperative/cooperativa negocio que es propiedad colectiva de quienes usan sus productos y servicios. **163**

coordinated compaigning/campaña coordinada en un conflicto laboral, estrategia en que los trabajadores de un sindicato usan una variedad de tácticas, tales como piquetes de huelga y boicots primarios y secundarios para obligar a quienes los contratan a cumplir sus demandas. **189**

copyright/registro de propiedad derecho de exclusividad garantizado por el gobierno al reproducir, tocar, escenificar, publicar y vender copias de obras literarias, musicales o artísticas durante un periodo de tiempo determinado. **128**

corporate bond/bono corporativo documento que representa un préstamo que un inversionista hace a una corporación. **155**

corporate charter/carta corporativa documento que emite el gobierno para otorgar ciertos derechos e imponer ciertas obligaciones a un banco o una corporación. **154**

corporation/corporación negocio en que un grupo de propietarios, llamados accionistas, comparten las ganancias y las pérdidas. **153**

cost of production/costo de producción costo total de los materiales, el trabajo y otros insumos o factores de producción que se requieren en la fabricación de un producto. **74**

cost-push inflation/inflación por costos de producción elevación general de los precios como resultado de una elevación de los costos de producción. **258**

credit/crédito forma de intercambio que permite a los consumidores usar artículos con su promesa de pago en un tiempo determinado. **16**

credit bureau/buró de crédito compañía que recoge y proporciona a sus clientes información acerca de la situación financiera de una persona y les reporta acerca del cumplimiento de sus compromisos económicos. **215**

credit rating/capacidad de pago evaluación de la condición financiera y formalidad de una persona o compañía, especialmente en cuanto al cumplimiento de sus obligaciones económicas. **215**

Cultural Revolution/Revolución Cultural movimiento armado ocurrido en China de 1966 a 1976, que buscaba mantener el régimen comunista. **396**

currency/moneda papel moneda y monedas que circulan en un país y que constituyen su provisión de dinero. **306**

customs duty/derechos arancelarios impuesto que grava mercancías traídas a Estados Unidos. **354**

cyclical unemployment/desempleo cíclico desempleo originado por bajas en el ciclo de las empresas. **256**

D

debit card/tarjeta de débito tarjeta de plástico que sirve para hacer retiros de una máquina de cajero automático o de un centro de comercio. **318**

debt ceiling/límite de adeudo límite máximo de adeudo que está permitido por ley en una localidad, estado o nación. **365**

default/incumplimiento omisión en los pagos de un préstamo. **321**

deficit spending/déficit por gastos política gubernamental en la que se gasta más dinero del que es capaz de cubrir según sus expectativas de ingresos. **363**

deflation/deflación descenso general de los precios de los bienes y servicios. **258**

demand/demanda cantidad de un producto o servicio que los consumidores pueden y están dispuestos a comprar a varios precios durante un periodo determinado. **5**

demand curve/curva de demanda representación gráfica de un inventario de demanda en el que se muestra la relación entre el precio de un artículo y la cantidad demandada durante cierto periodo, junto con todas las otras cosas. **54**

demand schedule/inventario de demanda tabla que muestra la demanda de un artículo a varios precios. **54**

demand pull-inflation/inflación por aumento de demanda alza general de los precios que ocurre cuando la demanda general de los bienes aumenta más rápido que su producción. **258**

demand-side economics/economía de demanda teoría económica desarrollada por John Maynard Keynes en la que propone que el gobierno debe estimular la economía por medio de medidas que influyan en la demanda general de bienes y servicios. **356**

democratic socialism/socialismo democrático sistema económico en el que algunos medios de producción y distribución de bienes son propiedad de un gobierno electo o están bajo su control. **28**

depreciation/depreciación 1) baja del valor de un bien de capital a causa de su edad, uso o

deterioro. La maquinaria de una fábrica, por ejemplo, baja de valor con el tiempo y tiene una depreciación. **91 2)** baja de valor de la moneda de una nación en relación con la de otra nación. **432**

depression/depresión recesión severa y prolongada. **236**

deregulation/desregulación aumento o disminución del control de un gobierno o restricciones a una compañía, industria o profesión. **319**

derived demand/demanda indirecta aumento en la demanda de recursos, tales como el trabajo, a consecuencia de la demanda de los consumidores por un producto en particular. **171**

determinant of demand/determinante de demanda factor diferente del precio que influye en la cantidad de demanda de un bien o servicio. **56**

determinant of supply/determinante de oferta factor diferente del precio que influye en la oferta disponible de un bien o servicio. **79**

devaluation/devaluación reducción del valor de la moneda de un país. **432**

developed nation/país desarrollado país con un alto nivel de desarrollo industrial y experiencia técnica, así como con varias instituciones económicas establecidas, como bancos y mercados de valores. **403**

developing nation/país en desarrollo país con pequeña industria y bajos estándares de vida en comparación con los países desarrollados. **403**

differentiate/distinguir señalar algo que distingue a un artículo en particular de otro parecido; hacer distinciones entre cosas similares. **120**

diminishing marginal utility/utilidad marginal decreciente descenso natural de la utilidad de un bien o un servicio a medida que se consumen más unidades. **53**

discount rate/tasa de descuento tasa de interés que aplica la Reserva Federal para los préstamos de los bancos asociados. **339**

discouraged worker/trabajador desalentado trabajador desempleado que no busca empleo a causa de sus relaciones de trabajo. **252**

disposable income/ingreso disponible dinero que queda después de pagar los impuestos. **195**

diversification/diversificación 1) práctica de distribuir los ahorros entre varios tipos de inversiones, como oro, bienes raíces, depósitos a plazos y una variedad de acciones y bonos **2)** práctica de reducir el riesgo de negocios extendiendo la variedad de productos y servicios o el área geográfica. **201**

dividend/dividendo parte de las ganancias de una corporación que le corresponden a un accionista. **155**

division of labor/división del trabajo división de un procedimiento complejo en tareas sencillas que permite a los trabajadores aumentar la producción mediante la especialización. **10**

E

easy-money policy/política de dinero fácil prácticas de un gobierno, como la reducción de las tasas de interés, para aumentar la oferta de dinero en la economía. **337**

economic development/desarrollo económico grado en el que un país ha desarrollado sus sectores industrial, de servicios, técnico y agrícola. **403**

economics/economía estudio de la forma en que las sociedades usan recursos escasos para satisfacer sus interminables deseos y necesidades. **3**

economies of scale/ economía de escala condición en la que, a causa del nivel de recursos necesarios, el costo de producción de cada unidad de un producto disminuye a medida que aumenta el número de unidades producidas. **127**

economist/economista persona que estudia teoría económica y la aplica en el mundo real. **3**

efficiency/eficiencia producción de bienes y servicios con la mínima cantidad de recursos para lograr la máxima cantidad de productos. **63**

elastic demand/demanda flexible situación que ocurre cuando la cantidad demandada cambia considerablemente a causa de un cambio en el precio. **63**

elastic supply/oferta flexible situación que ocurre cuando la cantidad de la oferta cambia considerablemente a causa de un cambio en el precio. **77**

elasticity of demand/elasticidad de la demanda grado en que los cambios en el precio de un producto o servicio afectan a la cantidad de la demanda. **163**

elasticity of supply/elasticidad de la oferta grado en que los cambios en el precio de un producto o servicio afectan la cantidad de la oferta. **76**

embargo/embargo orden de gobierno que prohíbe la importación y la exportación de productos con un país específico. **441**

entrepreneur/empresario persona que emprende y desarrolla un nuevo negocio o un nuevo producto, con riesgo de fallar y perder, a cambio de la posibilidad de obtener beneficio económico. **7**

entrepreneurship/calidad de empresario capacidad de organización y de afrontar riesgos que se toman al emprender un negocio o introducir un nuevo producto para los consumidores. **7**

estate tax/impuesto sucesorio impuesto que recauda los activos y propiedades de una persona que ha muerto. **354**

exchange/intercambio proceso por el que los productores y los consumidores acuerdan dar un tipo de artículo a cambio de otro. **15**

excise tax/impuesto al consumo impuesto que imponen el gobierno federal y algunos estados a la manufactura, venta y consumo de ciertos productos que se consideran de lujo o socialmente indeseables. **354**

expansion/expansión periodo del ciclo de negocios en que la actividad económica está llegando a su máximo nivel. **236**

expansionary fiscal policy/política fiscal de expansión política de gobierno diseñada para estimular la actividad económica mediante la reducción de impuestos y el aumento del gasto. **360**

expropriation/expropiación incautación o embargo de una propiedad privada por parte del gobierno, ya sea sin pago o mediante un pago parcial a los propietarios. **412**

externality/exterioridad efecto que una actividad económica tiene en las personas o negocios que no son productores ni consumidores de los bienes y servicios. Una exterioridad puede ser positiva (benéfica) o negativa (dañina). **101**

F

factor of production/factor de producción recurso empleado en la producción de bienes y servicios. **4**

federal budget/presupuesto federal estimación de gastos y ganancias del gobierno federal en un año fiscal. **362**

fiat money/dinero fiduciario dinero que no está respaldado en oro, plata o en algún otro artículo valioso, pero que tiene su valor porque el gobierno exige que se lo acepte como un medio de intercambio. **306**

finance charge/costo del financiamiento el costo total de un crédito. **215**

fiscal policy/política fiscal programa de gobierno integral que establece las tasas de impuestos, el endeudamiento y los gastos necesarios para promover las metas económicas establecidas para un país. **349**

fiscal year/año fiscal cualquier periodo de 12 meses de reportes financieros que termina en cualquier otra fecha que no sea el 31 de diciembre. El año fiscal clásico puede empezar el 1 de julio y terminar el 30 de junio del año calendárico siguiente. **363**

fixed cost/costo fijo costo que se mantiene constante tanto si la producción de un negocio aumenta o disminuye. **91**

fixed expense/gasto fijo gasto que no varía de mes a mes o que no cambia con el grado de actividad de la persona o, en un negocio, con el grado de producción. **201**

flexible expense/gasto flexible gasto que puede variar de un mes a otro de acuerdo con el grado de actividad o de producción individual o de una empresa. **201**

floating exchange rate/ tasa de cambio de flotación tasa de cambio de una moneda extranjera que varía continuamente de acuerdo con la oferta y la demanda. **433**

foreign exchange market/mercado de divisas mercado en el que las monedas o divisas de diversas naciones se compran y se venden. **431**

foreign exchange rate/tasa de cambio de moneda extranjera tasa en que la moneda de un país puede ser cambiada en otro país. **431**

Four Modernizations/las Cuatro Modernizaciones programa económico desarrollado en China dado a conocer en 1964. Las Cuatro Modernizaciones se enfocaban en el mejoramiento de la agricultura, la industria, la ciencia y la tecnología, y la defensa. **396**

franchise/franquicia negocio que paga a otra empresa ya establecida por usar su nombre y su línea de productos. **162**

free enterprise/libre empresa sistema en el cual funcionan negocios privados con una mínima participación del estado. **29**

free trade/libre comercio comercio entre las naciones que no está regulado por aranceles proteccionistas u otras restricciones gubernamentales. **441**

frictional unemployment/desempleo de fricción falta temporal de trabajo ocasionada por factores que no están relacionados con el ciclo de las empresas. **253**

fringe benefit/beneficio adicional pagos no salariales que los empleadores dan a sus empleados junto con su salario base. **185**

full employment/empleo completo grado mínimo de desempleo posible que puede haber en una economía. **38**

future/mercancía para el futuro mercancía que se compra con el fin de venderla en un precio acordado dentro de un tiempo también acordado como anticipo a las ganancias. **212**

G

general partnership/sociedad colectiva asociación en la que todos los miembros tienen la misma autoridad y comparten igualmente las pérdidas y las ganancias del negocio. **150**

geographic monopoly/monopolio geográfico mercado cuya área geográfica está tan delimitada que un solo vendedor controla la producción de un artículo, su venta, distribución y precio. **128**

gift tax/impuesto a las donaciones impuesto del gobierno federal o de algunos gobiernos estatales para que se realicen grandes transferencias de propiedad sin obtener a cambio algo de valor. **354**

Gini Index/índice Gini medida matemática de la desigualdad de ingresos en una economía. **266**

gold standard/patrón oro sistema en el que el valor del dinero de una nación está determinado por el número de unidades de su moneda que son redimibles o están respaldadas por una cantidad específica de oro. **311**

good/producto objeto o material que puede ser adquirido para satisfacer deseos o necesidades humanas. **4**

government monopoly/monopolio del gobierno mercado en el que el gobierno es el único productor y vendedor de un producto. **129**

Great Leap Forward/Gran Paso hacia Adelante plan de desarrollo económico de la República de China que fue establecido por los líderes comunistas en 1958. **396**

gross domestic product (GDP)/producto interno bruto (PIB) valor total de todos los bienes terminados y servicios producidos en un país en un año determinado. **229**

gross investment/inversión en bienes valor total del gasto privado en la economía de los activos del capital, como equipo nuevo, maquinaria, instalaciones y edificios, dentro de un periodo de tiempo específico, más los cambios totales en los inventarios de la empresa. **231**

gross national product (GNP)/producto nacional bruto (PNB) valor total de todos los bienes terminados y de los servicios producidos con los factores de producción, propiedad de los ciudadanos de una determinada nación. A diferencia del producto interno bruto (PIB), el PNB incluye los ingresos de las divisiones extranjeras de las compañías estadounidenses. **234**

H

horizontal combination/combinación horizontal empresa o corporación conformada por varios negocios que producen bienes y servicios iguales o semejantes. **159**

household responsabilty system/sistema de responsabilidad común programa de gobierno en la China rural que permitía a los agricultores alquilar la tierra propiedad del estado, a cambio de una parte de sus cosechas. **396**

human resource/recurso humano cualquier actividad humana —física o intelectual— que se emplea en los procesos productivos. **5**

hyperinflation/hiperinflación incremento tan acelerado y severo en los precios que trastorna las condiciones económicas normales. **261**

I

---

import quota/cuota de importación ley que limita la importación de un bien producido en el extranjero a una determinada cantidad durante un periodo de tiempo específico. **440**

incentive/incentivo medida que estimula una acción o esfuerzo. Esperar recompensas y temer a las pérdidas son incentivos. **27**

income/ingreso 1) pago en dinero que un empleado recibe de las empresas o del gobierno a cambio de recursos 2) capital que percibe un negocio por proporcionar bienes y servicios. **34**

income effect/efecto en los ingresos efecto que se produce en la capacidad de compra de los consumidores cuando cambia el precio de un artículo. **52**

indicative planning/planeación indicativa desarrollo de metas económicas no obligatorias de un gobierno para coordinar las inversiones y los planes de producción de los sectores público y privado. **384**

industrialization/industrialización proceso de industrialización de las principales formas de producción. **172**

inelastic demand/demanda no flexible situación que ocurre cuando la cantidad demandada cambia muy poco o nada al cambiar el precio. **64**

inelastic supply/oferta no flexible situación que ocurre cuando la cantidad de la oferta cambia muy poco o nada al cambiar el precio. **77**

inflation/inflación aumento de los precios en general como resultado de un alza en los salarios, un aumento en la oferta de dinero y un aumento en los gastos relacionados con la oferta de productos. **258**

inflation rate/tasa de inflación medida en la que todos los precios de los productos y servicios de una economía están cambiando. **260**

infrastructure/infraestructura recursos y servicios básicos que una economía necesita para funcionar. **202**

injunction/prescripción orden judicial, en un conflicto laboral, que prohíbe leyes específicas para individuos y grupos específicos. **190**

installment/pago a plazos pago parcial a una institución financiera u otra institución de crédito para pagar un préstamo, o productos o servicios que se han comprado. **215**

interdependence/interdependencia relación de mutuo acuerdo e influencia entre personas, negocios, industrias, regiones o naciones. **18**

interdependent pricing/precios interdependientes establecimiento de precios en respuesta —o en relación con— los precios de los competidores. **125**

interest/interés 1) rendimiento que se obtiene al invertir o prestar capital 2) dinero que se paga al banco o a cualquier prestamista a cambio de un préstamo 3) rendimiento por un adeudo de un título de inversión, como un bono 4) participación por tener una propiedad, por ejemplo, 25 por ciento de interés en un negocio. **155**

interest group/grupo de presión grupo cuyos miembros tienen tendencias políticas comunes y trabajan para influir en funciones, políticas y prácticas de gobierno. **294**

intrinsic reward/compensación intrínseca compensación que no tiene valor financiero, pero que es deseable por el valor personal de quien lo recibe. **171**

investment/inversión 1) compra de algo de valor con la expectativa de que con el tiempo su valor aumente y rinda beneficios 2) en teoría económica, compra de bienes de capital. **200**

investment bank/banco de inversión compañía que adquiere grandes cantidades de acciones y valores que emiten empresas y vende estos títulos a inversionistas por una utilidad. **206**

investment tax credit/crédito fiscal de inversión incentivo de impuesto que permite a los negocios deducir parte de los impuestos por adquirir nuevo equipo. **358**

L
---

labor force/fuerza de trabajo personas de un país que tienen al menos 16 años y están trabajando o en busca de trabajo. **169**

labor productivity/productividad del trabajo medida de la cantidad de trabajo que produce cada trabajador en un tiempo determinado. **177**

labor union/sindicato organización de trabajadores que negocian con los empleadores para obtener salarios más altos, mejores condiciones laborales y seguridad en el trabajo. **177**

labor-intensive/dependiente del trabajo término que describe una economía que requiere una gran cantidad de trabajo en relación con la inversión de capital. **172**

lagging indicators/indicadores de cobertura grupo de factores económicos que ayudan a los economistas a predecir la duración de las alzas y las bajas. **240**

laissez-faire/laissez-faire (dejar hacer) filosofía económica que se opone a la intervención del gobierno en el mercado. **130**

land reform/reforma agraria redistribución o cambio de propiedad de la tierra realizado o impuesto por el gobierno. **417**

law of demand/ley de la demanda principio de que, si todo lo demás permanece igual, los consumidores comprarán (demandarán) mayor cantidad de un producto a precio bajo, y menor cantidad de un producto a precio alto. **52**

law of diminishing returns/ ley de rendimientos decrecientes principio de que, cuando más de una variable (como el trabajo) se agrega a la oferta fija de otros recursos (como capital), la productividad aumentará hasta un punto después del cual el producto marginal disminuirá. **87**

law of supply/ley de la oferta principio según el cual los productores ofrecerán mayor cantidad de un producto o servicio a precio alto, pero menor cantidad de un producto o servicio a precio bajo. **73**

leading indicators/indicadores principales grupo de factores económicos que anticipan la expansión y la contracción del ciclo de negocios en un plazo desde un mes hasta dos años antes de que ocurran cambios similares en la actividad económica en general. **240**

liability/responsabilidad 1) obligación por una deuda **2)** persona o negocio a quienes se pueden responsabilizar legalmente por gastos no pagados. **147**

limited partnership/asociación limitada forma de asociación en la que algunos miembros, llamados socios limitados, invierten dinero pero no tienen parte en la administración. **150**

liquidity/liquidez facilidad con que un individuo o un negocio pueden convertir activos fijos en dinero en efectivo sin sufrir una pérdida sustancial de dinero. **196**

lobbyist/activista individuo bajo la influencia de legisladores y administradores del gobierno que actúa de manera favorable a los empleados activistas. **296**

lockout/cierre patronal terminación de un negocio por parte de un empresario, u otro tipo de negativa, para que los empleados en huelga vuelvan a trabajar, en protesta por las demandas de los trabajadores o de un sindicato. **190**

longetivity/longevidad tiempo de vida de un negocio. **149**

Lorenz curve/curva de Lorenz gráfica que muestra el grado de igualdad con que se reparten los ingresos de un negocio. **265**

M
---

macroeconomics/macroeconomía estudio de una economía completa o de uno de sus sectores principales. **3**

margin requirement/requerimiento de margen porcentaje del precio que un inversionista debe pagar en efectivo para comprar una acción, un bono convertible u otro título. **342**

marginal cost/costo marginal costo de producción de una unidad adicional de un producto. **92**

marginal product/producto marginal producto adicional que se obtiene al emplear una o más unidades de inversión. **87**

marginally attached worker/trabajador marginal trabajador que tuvo un trabajo productivo, pero que ahora está desempleado y no busca trabajo. **252**

market/mercado libre intercambio de bienes y servicios, también llamado plaza de mercado. **25**

market basket/canasta básica muestra representativa de aproximadamente 400 productos y servicios que el Departamento de Trabajo de Estados Unidos ha identificado como la compra común de un consumidor. **260**

market economy/economía de mercado economía en la que el gobierno tiene poca participación en qué, cómo y por quiénes se producen los bienes de consumo, y qué sectores de la producción están en poder de individuos. **25**

market equilibrium/equilibrio de mercado punto en que las cantidades de demanda y oferta de un producto son iguales y tienen el mismo precio. **103**

market failure/error de mercado falla en el sistema de precios que ocurre cuando algunos costos no se han contabilizado y por lo tanto no están distribuidos de manera apropiada. **101**

market socialism/socialismo de mercado tipo de socialismo en el que los medios de producción son de propiedad o están controlados por el gobierno, pero los individuos y las empresas toman algunas decisiones económicas. **379**

market system/sistema de mercado sistema económico en el que las tres economías básicas están respaldadas por individuos y empresas. **377**

maturity/vencimiento tiempo en que debe depositarse el dinero en un depósito a plazos. **197**

mediation/mediación proceso de conciliación en que una tercera parte neutral escucha a cada bando, hace preguntas, pone en claro los asuntos y propone una solución. **186**

medium of exchange/medio de cambio cualquier cosa que un vendedor acepte como pago por un producto o servicio. **302**

mercantilism/mercantilismo teoría económica que indica el poder de un país en términos de especie; se usó para administrar la mayoría de las economías europeas entre los años 1500 y 1800. **382**

merger/fusión unión de dos o más empresas en una sola propiedad. **159**

microeconomics/microeconomía estudio de un solo factor de una economía, como individuos, familias, empresas e industrias, y no de una economía entera. **3**

minimun wage/salario mínimo cantidad más baja por hora que un empresario puede pagar a un trabajador, como lo establece la ley federal. **109**

mixed economy/economía mixta economía que combina elementos de la tradición, el mercado y la dirección de modelos económicos. **27**

monetary policy/política monetaria plan de gobierno para regular la oferta monetaria de un país y la disponibilidad de crédito para cumplir con ciertas metas económicas. **337**

money/dinero cualquier artículo, por lo general moneda, que se acepta para intercambiar productos, servicios y el pago de adeudos. **15**

money supply/oferta de dinero cantidad total del dinero en circulación de la economía de un país en un tiempo determinado. **335**

monopolistic competition/competencia monopólica mercado en el que varios productores ofrecen un producto o un servicio parecido pero no idéntico. **120**

monopoly/monopolio mercado en el que un solo vendedor ejerce exclusiva o casi exclusivamente el control sobre un bien o servicio determinado. **119**

moral suasion/persuación moral presión no oficial que la Reserva Federal usa para persuadir a los bancos asociados para que se orienten de una manera determinada. **342**

multinational corporation (MNC)/compañía multinacional (CMN) negocio que tiene su base en un país, pero tiene divisiones subsidiarias en otros países. **417**

mutual savings bank/banco de ahorro compartido banco que es propiedad de sus depositantes, quienes comparten sus beneficios. **316**

N

national debt/deuda nacional cantidad total de dinero que debe un país a sus acreedores. **364**

national income accounting/cuenta de renta nacional proceso que se usa para vigilar la producción, los ingresos y el consumo de la economía de un país. **229**

nationalization/nacionalización expropiación que un gobierno hace de determinadas empresas o de gran parte de la industria privada de un país, como de manufactura, agricultura o transporte. **384**

natural monopoly/monopolio natural mercado en que la competencia no es práctica ni conveniente, y es más eficiente con un solo vendedor. **127**

natural resource/recurso natural en economía, cualquier material de la naturaleza que pueda usarse para producir bienes o proveer servicios. **4**

near money/dinero seguro activo que fácilmente puede cambiarse por dinero en efectivo cuando se necesite. **307**

nominal GDP/PIB nominal valor del producto interno bruto (PIB) de un país en los precios vigentes del periodo que se evalúa. **232**

nonprice competition/competencia no basada en el precio cualquier intento de un vendedor por atraer clientes de sus competidores sin bajar los precios. **120**

nonprofit organization/organización no lucrativa organización que genera ingresos de la venta de productos o donaciones, pero no distribuye las ganancias a ningún propietario o fideicomiso. **163**

O

oligopoly/oligopolio mercado en el que pocos vendedores grandes controlan la mayoría de los bienes de producción o servicio. **123**

one-crop economy/economía de un solo cultivo economía en la que prevalece la producción de un solo artículo. **407**

open shop/taller libre negocio en el que no es obligatorio ser miembro de un sindicato para obtener empleo. **178**

oportunity cost/costo de oportunidad valor que se pierde al rechazar el uso de recursos en favor de otro. En otras palabras, la acción de un costo de oportunidad es el valor de la acción de la mejor alternativa siguiente que no fue tomada. **11**

output-expenditure model/modelo de egresos método por computadora del producto interno bruto (PIB) por el que se suma el total del consumo, el gasto del gobierno en bienes y servicios, el total de la inversión privada y el total de las exportaciones, y después se resta el total de las importaciones. **230**

overhead/gasto general total de los costos fijos de un negocio, excepto de los salarios y el costo de material. **91**

P

partnership/sociedad propiedad y control de un negocio por parte de dos o más personas que comparten ganancias y son responsables de sus pérdidas. **150**

patent/patente documento de gobierno que da a un inventor el derecho exclusivo de producir, usar o vender un invento por un tiempo determinado. **128**

peak/máximo nivel 1) punto de un ciclo de negocios en que el empleo, la producción y los salarios están en su punto máximo. También se llama punto de retorno. 2) punto más alto de cualquier fase de la actividad económica. **236**

people's communes/granjas colectivas granjas muy grandes establecidas en China a principios de 1958. **396**

perfect competition/competencia perfecta condiciones de mercado ideales que incluyen un gran número de vendedores de productos y servicios idénticos y en los que ningún vendedor controla la oferta y los precios. **117**

personal consumption expenditure /gasto de consumo personal gasto total que realizan los consumidores en productos duraderos, no duraderos y servicios durante un periodo específico. **231**

poverty rate/índice de pobreza porcentaje de individuos y familias del total de la población que viven en los límites de la pobreza y son considerados así por el gobierno. **264**

poverty threshold/límite de pobreza nivel de ingreso que el gobierno considera necesario para el sostenimiento de una familia en el mínimo estándar de vida. **264**

preferred stock/acciones preferenciales participación del propietario de una corporación. **155**

price ceiling/precio tope regulación gubernamental que establece un precio máximo para un producto en particular. **108**

price discrimination/discriminación de precios establecimiento de precios diferentes para diferentes compradores en las mismas circunstancias. **132**

price floor/precio base regulación gubernamental que establece un precio mínimo para un producto en particular. **109**

price index/índice de precios grupo de estadísticas que permite a los economistas comparar los precios en el tiempo. **232**

price leadership/precio inicial situación en la que un vendedor importante de una industria establece un precio y otros vendedores lo siguen para poder competir. **125**

price stability/estabilidad de precios condición que ocurre cuando todos los precios se mantienen relativamente constantes en un tiempo determinado. **38**

price war/guerra de precios serie de reducciones de precios, en ocasiones tan drásticas que los vendedores sufren pérdidas considerables. **125**

primary boycott/boicot primario esfuerzo organizado para detener la compra de los productos de una compañía. Esta táctica se usa para mostrar desaprobación u obligar a un grupo a realizar una acción determinada. Los boicots primarios suelen ser parte de las disputas laborales. **189**

prime rate/interés primario tasa de interés que los bancos aplican a los préstamos otorgados a sus clientes. **341**

principal/capital principal 1) dinero solicitado en préstamo. El capital principal no es lo mismo que el interés y las ganancias. 2) respaldo de un bono. **155**

private property/propiedad privada propiedad de individuos y comercios independientes del gobierno. **29**

privatization/privatización otorgamiento de propiedades o funciones anteriormente controladas por el gobierno a instituciones del sector privado. **287**

producer/productor persona, grupo o negocio que elabora bienes o proporciona servicios para satisfacer las necesidades de los consumidores. **3**

producer price index (PPI)/índice de precios del productor (IPP) medida de los cambios en los precios de aproximadamente 3,200 productos de consumo. **260**

product differentiation/diferenciación de productor intento de un vendedor en un mercado de monopolio para convencer a los compradores de que su producto es diferente y superior que otros artículos similares de la competencia. **120**

product market/mercado de productos mercado en el que los productores ofrecen bienes y servicios finales a los consumidores. **34**

production possibilities curve/curva de posibilidades de producción representación gráfica que muestra todas las combinaciones posibles de producción de dos bienes o servicios elaborados en un periodo específico, suponiendo que los recursos disponibles y la tecnología no cambien en ese lapso y que los recursos naturales, humanos y de capital se aprovechan de la mejor manera posible. **12**

productivity/productividad efectividad de los resultados obtenidos a partir del inicio de un proceso. **9**

productivity growth/crecimiento de productividad aumento en la producción por trabajador y por hora de trabajo. 244

profit/ganancias diferencia entre los ingresos recibidos con la venta de un bien o servicio y el costo original del mismo. 74

proletariat/proletariado clase trabajadora cuyos integrantes, según la teoría del analista político Karl Marx, eran oprimidos de tal manera por la burguesía que con el paso del tiempo derrocarían a ese grupo social mediante una revolución violenta. 390

prospectus/prospecto hoja de datos con información financiera detallada sobre una compañía en particular. 213

protectionism/proteccionismo uso de barreras comerciales para proteger las industrias de una nación de la competencia extranjera. 441

protective tariff/tarifa de protección impuesto aplicado por el gobierno de un país a ciertas importaciones con la finalidad de restringir su venta. 439

public good/bien público producto o servicio que consumen todos los integrantes de un grupo, sin importar quiénes lo hayan adquirido. 102

purchasing power/poder adquisitivo cantidad de ingreso disponible para adquirir bienes y servicios. 52

pyramided reserves/pirámide de reservas sistema en el que pequeños bancos depositan parte de sus reservas en bancos mayores, quienes a su vez depositan parte de sus reservas en bancos más importantes. 327

Q

quantity demanded/cantidad de la demanda cantidad de bienes o servicios que los consumidores adquieren por un precio determinado. 51

quantity supplied/cantidad de la oferta cantidad de bienes o servicios que los productores ofrecen a un precio determinado. 73

quota/cuota 1) cantidad mínima de nuevas contrataciones en un programa de acciones afirmativas. 2) límite máximo o mínimo que debe alcanzarse en un proceso, por lo general establecido en dólares o unidades. 174

R

rationing/racionamiento sistema aplicado por un gobierno o institución para distribuir ciertos bienes o servicios. El racionamiento es el resultado de una escasez de tales bienes o servicios. 110

real GDP/PIB real valor del producto interno bruto (PIB) de un país después de hacer los ajustes de inflación. 232

real GDP per capita/PIB real per cápita valor en dólares (después de los ajustes de inflación) de los bienes y servicios producidos por cada persona en un año específico. 241

real investment/inversión real inversión que crea nuevos bienes de capital. 202

recession/recesión disminución considerable de las actividades comerciales en un periodo significativo. 236

regulation/regulación reglamentos establecidos por un gobierno para proteger y ofrecer igual acceso a ciertos bienes y servicios. 82

representative money/dinero representativo sistema monetario en el que un artículo adquiere cierto valor porque puede ofrecerse en intercambio por otro artículo de valor. 305

reserve requirement/solicitud de reserva dinero que deben almacenar los bancos por orden de la Reserva Federal, ya sea en sus propias arcas o en un banco de distrito de la Reserva. 341

resource/recurso elemento usado en la producción de bienes y servicios. 4

resource market/mercado de recursos mercado en el que se intercambian acciones entre comercios y con el gobierno. 34

restrictive fiscal policy/política fiscal restrictiva política aplicada por el gobierno para reducir la actividad económica en tiempos de expansión excesiva mediante el cobro de mayores impuestos y/o la reducción del gasto público. 360

revenue tariff/impuesto sobre ingresos impuesto aplicado por el gobierno de una nación a las importaciones con fines de recaudación. **439**

S

savings and loan association/asociación de ahorros y préstamos institución financiera que presta dinero y guarda los depósitos de sus clientes en cuentas de ahorros. **316**

savings rate/índice de ahorros porcentaje de ingresos disponibles que no son usados para adquirir bienes y servicios. **199**

scarcity/escasez condición de la economía que resulta de la combinación de una existencia limitada de recursos y una demanda ilimitada de los mismos. **8**

seasonal unemployment/desempleo de temporada desempleo que resulta de las variaciones temporales de la economía. **255**

secondary boycott/boicot secundario rechazo a la compra de bienes o servicios de una compañía que tiene relaciones comerciales con otra compañía cuyos empleados están en huelga. **189**

self-interest/interés propio impulso que motiva a las personas a satisfacer sus necesidades. **26**

self-sufficiency/autosuficiencia capacidad de satisfacer las necesidades propias sin ayuda. **17**

seller/vendedor productor de un bien o servicio. **117**

seniority/antigüedad clasificación de empleados según el tiempo que han prestado sus servicios a una empresa. **185**

service/servicio acción o actividad realizada a cambio de un pago. **4**

share/acción 1) unidad más pequeña de propiedad en una corporación, por lo general expresada con alguna forma de participación 2) porción de un negocio que posee una persona. **155**

shortage/insuficiencia situación generada cuando la demanda de un bien o servicio en una comunidad es mayor que la producción del mismo. **105**

sole propioetorship/propietario único negocio que una sola persona posee y administra. **145**

specialization/especialización enfoque de un trabajador en aquellos aspectos de la producción que mejoran su eficacia. **10**

specie/especie dinero acuñado en forma de monedas. Históricamente, el valor de la especie se basaba en el metal con el que se fabricaba, principalmente oro y plata. **305**

standard of living/estándar de vida bienestar económico de la población que se determina por la cantidad de bienes y servicios que consumen en un periodo determinado. **39**

standard of value/estándar de valor cálculo del valor relativo de los bienes y servicios. **302**

stock/acción 1) parte que se posee de una empresa 2) inventario de elementos puestos a la venta por un fabricante o distribuidor. **155**

stock split/división de acciones división del total de acciones de una empresa. **205**

store of value/almacén de valores característica de un medio de intercambio que permite almacenar un valor determinado. **303**

strike/huelga paro de labores de empleados o integrantes de un sindicato con la finalidad de presionar a su jefe y obtener las demandas que plantean en su disputa laboral. **188**

structural unemployment/desempleo estructural desempleo ocasionado por cambios en la tecnología, políticas del gobierno, demanda de ciertos productos a largo plazo, tendencias de la población y otros factores relacionados con los ciclos comerciales. **253**

subsidiary/subsidiario comercio que otra compañía posee o en el que ésta controla ciertos intereses. **160**

subsidy/subsidio pago realizado por el gobierno a individuos, comercios o industrias para fomentar las actividades consideradas como recomendables en una sociedad. **82**

subsistence agriculture/agricultura de subsistencia tipo de agricultura en la que una familia cultiva lo necesario para satisfacer sus necesidades básicas sin producir excedentes para la venta. **405**

substitute good/producto de reemplazo producto que los consumidores usan en lugar de otro, especialmente cuando el precio del primero se eleva demasiado. **60**

substitution effect/efecto de sustitución tendencia del consumidor a sustituir bienes de precio bajo por otros más costosos. **52**

supply/oferta cantidad de bienes o servicios que los productores venden a diferentes precios en un periodo determinado. **73**

supply curve/curva de oferta representación gráfica de un calendario de suministros que muestra la relación entre el precio de un producto y la cantidad de piezas ofrecidas en un periodo determinado donde todos los elementos sean equivalentes. **75**

supply schedule/inventario de oferta lista con la cantidad de artículos que un productor ofrece a diferentes precios. **75**

supply shock/impacto en la oferta problema económico ocasionado por sucesos ajenos a la economía de una nación que aumentan el costo de producción de una o más industrias y producen inflación. **258**

supply-side economics/economía basada en la oferta teoría económica que se enfoca en la obtención de estabilidad económica y el crecimiento mediante el aumento de la oferta de bienes y servicios en general. **355**

surplus/excedente situación que se presenta cuando la oferta de un producto de precio específico excede la demanda del mismo. **105**

T

tax/impuesto pago requerido en forma regular por el gobierno local, estatal o federal. **81**

tax incentive/incentivo de impuesto provisión de la ley de impuestos creada para estimular la actividad económica al fomentar la inversión de nuevos capitales. **358**

tax rate/tasa de impuesto porcentaje de pago aplicado a ingresos, propiedades y compras. **349**

technological monopoly/monopolio tecnológico mercado que domina un solo productor gracias a la tecnología que aplica. **128**

technology/tecnología técnicas científicas y tecnológicas para aumentar la eficacia y la calidad de la producción. **7**

Tiananmen Square Massacre/matanza de la Plaza Tiananmen incidente ocurrido en 1989 cuando un grupo de personas que se manifestaba en busca de mayores libertades políticas fue brutalmente atacado por las fuerzas armadas chinas. **397**

tight-money policy/política de austeridad métodos usados por el gobierno (como el aumento en las tasas de interés) para reducir el flujo de circulante. **338**

time deposit/depósito a plazo fijo depósito (por lo general en forma de certificados o bonos de ahorro) que genera intereses si se guarda en un banco durante un periodo específico. **197**

total cost/costo total suma de los costos fijos y variables en la producción de un bien o servicio. **91**

total product/producción total conjunto total de bienes y servicios que produce un negocio en un periodo determinado con una cantidad fija de recursos. **86**

total revenue/ingreso total suma de los ingresos de un comercio, en ocasiones llamados recibos totales. **66**

trade barrier/barrera comercial interrupción del flujo de los bienes intercambiados entre naciones. **439**

trade deficit/déficit comercial condición del comercio internacional en que el valor de las importaciones provenientes de un país supera el valor de las exportaciones a ese país. **437**

trade surplus/excedente comercial condición del comercio internacional que se genera cuando el valor de las exportaciones a un país específico supera el valor de las importaciones provenientes de ese país. **437**

trade-off/comercio de elección sacrificio de la compra de un producto para comprar o producir otro. **11**

traditional economy/economía tradicional tipo de economía cuya producción se basa en las costumbres y tradiciones. **24**

transfer payment/pago de transferencia pago que hace el gobierno sin recibir un bien o servicio a cambio. **288**

trough/fin de ciclo punto más bajo de un ciclo comercial en el que la demanda, la producción y la generación de empleos llega a su mínimo nivel. **236**

trust/consorcio grupo de compañías que unen esfuerzos para eliminar la competencia en una industria y crear un monopolio. **130**

U

underemployment/subempleo trabajo realizado por una persona que tiene destrezas mucho mayores que las que requiere su oficio. Aceptación de un empleo de medio tiempo cuando se busca uno de tiempo completo. **252**

underground economy/economía subterránea actividades económicas ilegales no registradas que no generan beneficios económicos a una nación. **233**

unemployment rate/tasa de desempleo porcentaje de personas desempleadas dentro de la fuerza laboral. **252**

usury/usura cobro de intereses mayores a los permitidos por la ley. **216**

utility/utilidad aprovechamiento de un bien o servicio que contribuye al valor del mismo. **17**

V

value/valor costo de un bien o servicio con propósitos de intercambio comercial, expresado como la cantidad de dinero que un consumidor está dispuesto a pagar por el mismo. **17**

variable cost/costo variable costo de operación de un negocio que cambia de acuerdo con los recursos disponibles para su producción, lo cual genera alzas y bajas de producción. **91**

venture capital/capital de riesgo fondos individuales o de una compañía que son invertidos en actividades empresariales para fomentar el desarrollo económico. **203**

vertical combination/combinación vertical corporación formada por la unión de varias empresas relacionadas con diversas etapas del proceso de producción de un tipo de producto o servicio. **159**

voluntary trade restriction/restricción voluntaria de comercio acuerdo (que no requiere aprobación de la legislatura) entre dos o más países para limitar o controlar el comercio con un país específico mediante la restricción del envío de ciertos productos a dicho país. **440**

W

wage/salario pago que recibe un empleado por su trabajo. **169**

wage-price spiral/espiral de salario y precio ciclo producido cuando el aumento de los salarios genera un aumento en los costos de producción, lo cual a su vez produce un aumento en el precio de los bienes y servicios y, como consecuencia final, la demanda de mayores salarios. **260**

Y

yield/tasa de rendimiento 1) ingreso anual obtenido por el manejo de acciones, bonos y otras formas de inversión. Por lo general se expresa como un porcentaje del mercado relacionado 2) ganancias obtenidas sobre un préstamo 3) interés total pagado por la emisión de un bono cuando el titular del mismo lo conserva hasta su madurez. **209**

Z

zoning law/ley de zonificación ley que regula el tipo de estructuras comerciales y empresas que pueden establecerse en una zon específica. **146**

INDEX

A

absolute advantage, 428, *c430*
accountant, as career, 328
ACH. *See* automatic clearing house services (ACH)
acid rain, 81
adjustable-peg system, 432–433
advertising account manager, as career, 121
Advanced Micro Devices (AMD), 93
affirmative action, 174–175
AFL. *See* American Federation of Labor (AFL)
AFL–CIO. *See* American Federation of Labor–Congress of Industrial Organizations (AFL–CIO)
affirmative action, 174–175
Africa, 303
African Development Bank, 422
aggregate demand: definition of, 257; demand-side economics and, 356–358; Federal Reserve system and, 337–339, 341–342; price levels and, 257–258; restrictive fiscal policy and, 360
aggregate supply: definition of, 257; price levels and, 257–258
agricultural economies, 404–407
agricultural workers, 172, 255
airlines: deregulation and, 293; price wars and, 125
Alaska, 392, 434
Alliance for Progress, 420
allocate, 8
allocation of resources, 8–9
Altair 8000®, 99
AMD. *See* Advanced Micro Devices
AMERCOSUR. *See* Southern Common Market (AMERCOSUR)
American Federation of Labor (AFL), 178
American Federation of Labor–Congress of Industrial Organizations (AFL–CIO), 180, 181
American Railway Union, 183
American Red Cross, 291
American Revolution, 305–306
American Stock Exchange (AMEX), 207
American Telephone and Telegraph (AT&T), 134
AmeriCorps, 291–292
AMEX. *See* American Stock Exchange (AMEX)
Angola, 411, 412
annual percentage rate (APR), 215
Antifederalists, 308
Antitrust and Procedures and Penalties Act of 1974, 132
antitrust legislation, 130–133; free enterprise and, 286; interpretation of, 135
Apple Computer, 99
appreciation, 432–433
APR. *See* annual percentage rate (APR)
arable land, 403
arbitration, 187
articles of incorporation, 154
ASEAN. *See* Association of Southeast Asian Nations (ASEAN)
Ash, Mary Kay, 146
Asian Development Bank, 422
Association of Southeast Asian Nations (ASEAN), 445
AT&T. *See* American Telephone and Telegraph (AT&T)
ATMs. *See* automated teller machines (ATMs)
auditor: as career, 357
Australia, 403
authoritarian socialism, 379; definition of, 27; as mixed economy, 27–28, 41
automated teller machines (ATMs), 318, 336
automatic clearing house services (ACH), 318
automation: in banking, 317–319; in industry, 7

B

Bahamas, 445
balance, 196
balance of payments, 435–436
balance of trade, 436–437, *g438*
Balanced Budget Amendment, 366
Balanced Budget and Deficit Reduction Act of 1985, 366
Bangladesh, 411, 420
bank failures, 321, *g321*, 322
Bank of Japan, 383
bank teller: as career, 315

banking: automated teller machines (ATMs), 318, 336; automatic clearing house services (ACH), 318; automation of, 170, 318–319; bank failures, 321, *g321,* 322; Banking Act of 1933, 312, 323; Banking Act of 1935, 312; **Bank Modernization Bill,** 300, 323; banking reforms of the New Deal, 311, 312; certificates of deposit, 197–198; commercial banks, 315–316, *c316;* competition in, 320; credit unions, 315, *c316,* 317–318; debit cards and, 319; deregulation of, 319–321; discount rate, 339–341, *g341;* electronic funds transfer (EFT), 318; farm banks, 321; Federal Deposit Insurance Corporation (FDIC), 312; Federal Reserve system and, 312, 332–334; Federal Saving and Loan Insurance Corporation (FSLIC), 322; Financial Institutions Reform, Recovery, and Enforcement Act, 322; financial troubles in, 321–322; home banking, 319; Internet and, 319; legislation concerning, 311–312, 314, 320, 322; loan defaults and, 321; money market deposit accounts, 196–197; moral suasion and, 342; mutual savings banks, 315, 316–317; National Banking Act of 1863, 311; National Banking Act of 1864, 311; national currency and, 311; point-of-sale transactions and, 318–319; regional banking, 320–321; reserve requirement, 341–342; Resolution Trust Corporation (RTC), 322; savings accounts, 196–197; savings and loan associations (S&Ls), 315, 316, 321, 322; types of financial institutions, 315–318. *See also* banking history

Banking Act of 1933, 312, 323

Banking Act of 1935, 312

banking history: Antifederalists and, 308; before Civil War, 308–310; Civil War to World War I, 310–311; Coinage Act of 1873 and, 311; Confederacy and, 311; confidence in banks, 308–314; conflicting views of, 308; dual banking system, 310; Federalists and, 308; fiat money and, 311; First Bank of the United States, 308–309, 327; fragmented banking, 310–311; Gold Standard Act of 1900, 311; gold standard and, 311, 314; legislation and, 311–312, 314; National Banking Act of 1863, 311; nationally chartered banks, 311; New Deal and, 311–312, 314; panic of 1837 and, 310; Second Bank of the United States, 309–310, 327; state-chartered banks, 210, 308, 309; unifying the banking system, 311; World War I to the present, 311–312, 314

bankruptcy, 216

banks. *See* banking

Barbados, 445

Barbuda, 445

barter, 15, 301

bear market, 209

Belize, 445

Bell Atlantic, 134

Berlin Wall, 379, *p383*

Bessemer process, 161

black markets, 112

Black Monday, 211

Black Tuesday, 211

BLS. *See* Bureau of Labor Statistics (BLS)

board of directors, 155

Board of Governors of the Federal Reserve system, *c329,* 331, 338, 339, 360

Bolivia, 412, *p417*

bolsheviks, 390

bonds: corporate bonds, 155, 199; government bonds, 210; municipal bonds, 210, 212; reasons for purchasing, 209–210, 212; Treasury bills, 210, *c210,* 212; Treasury bonds, 210, *c210;* Treasury notes, 210, *c210;* yields on, 209

borrowing: credit, 215–216; definition of, 214; interest rates and, 238; loans, 214–215

bourgeoisie, 389

boycotts, 189

Brazil, 412, 417, 445

Bretton Woods Conference, 420, 421, 432

Britain. *See* Great Britain; United Kingdom

brokers, 206–207

Brown* v. *Board of Education, 175

Brunei, 445

budget, 200; fixed expenses and, 201. *See also* federal budget

Budget and Accounting Act of 1921, 363

budget deficit, 363

budget surplus, 363

bull market, 209

Bundesbank, 384

Bureau of Engraving and Printing, 301, 304, 334, 335

Bureau of Labor Statistics (BLS), 251, 260

Bureau of the Budget, 363

Bureau of the Census, 251, 264

Burger King, 436

Bush, George, 322

Bush, George W., 280, 294

business cycles, *g238;* business investment and, 236, 238; coincident indicators of, 240; contraction phase of, 236; credit and, 238; definition of, 236; depression and, 236; expansion phase of, 236; external factors and, 239–240; influences on, 236, 238–240; lagging indicators of, 240; leading indicators of, 240; money and, 238; peak phase of, 236; phases of, 236; political climate and, 239; prediction of, 240; price shocks and, 239; public expectations and, 238–239; recession and, 236; trough phase of, 236; war and, 239–240; world economics and, 239

business ethics, 144, 165

business geography, as career, 378

business investment, 238

business organizations: cooperatives, 163; combinations, 159–162; corporations, *g145,* 153–158; franchises, 162–163; nonprofit organizations, 163–164; partnerships, *g145,* 150–152; sole proprietorships, 145–149, *g145;* types of, *g145*

buyer: as career, 76

buyers: competition and, 117, 119; informed buyers and perfect competition, 119; informed decisions of, 119. *See also* consumers

C

call center, 19, 206

Canada, 81, 174, 403, 436, 437, 446

capital: accumulation of, 202; capital formation, 408–409, 411; saving as, 195–199. *See also* headings beginning with capital

capital accumulation, 202

capital deepening, 244–245

capital formation, 408

capital gain, 205

capital goods, 231; capital deepening, 244–245; as capital resource, 7; definition of, 5, 7; economic expansion and, 238; as factor of production, 5

capital improvements, 316

capital-intensive economies, 172

capital loss, 205

capital resources: definition of, 5; developing nations and, 408–409, 411; economic growth, 243; as factor of production, 7

capital-to-labor ratio, 244

capitalism: Cold War effect on, 399; definition of, 28; examples of, 28; as mixed economy, 28. *See also* capitalist economic system

capitalist economic system: command capitalism, 378; decision-making model of, 414–415; definition of, 377; in France, 384; in Germany, 383–384; government involvement in, 377, 382; in Japan, 382–383; market capitalism, 382–385, 414–415; origins of, 381–382; in Singapore, 385; in South Korea, 385

Caribbean Community and Common Market (CARICOM), 445

CARICOM. *See* Caribbean Community and Common Market (CARICOM)

Carnegie, Andrew, 161, 221

cartel, 126

cash reserves, 329

Castro, Fidel, 280, *p414*

CCC. *See* Civilian Conservation Corps (CCC)

Celler–Kefauver Act of 1950, 132

Census Bureau. *See* Bureau of the Census

central planners, 25

certificates of deposit: maturity of, 197; money supply and, 336; as near money, 307; as savings, 197–198

Chávez, César, 181, 189, *p189,* 193

check-clearing, 332

checks: 307, 318, 319, 332; check-clearing by Federal Reserve system, 332, *c333*

Chicago Board of Trade, 213

China: challenges for, 397–398; "class enemies" in, 396; as command system, 389; communism and, 395–398; Cultural Revolution, 396; currency and, 304; Five-Year Plans and, 396–397; Four Modernizations, 396–397; free-trade zones in, 397; Great Leap Forward, 395–396; Hong Kong and, 415; household responsibility system in, 396–397; international trade and, 434; Mao Zedong and, 395; as most-favored-nation, 444; people's communes in, 395–396; per capita gross domestic product and, *g397;* production brigades in, 396; Tiananmen Square Massacre, 397, *p398;* trade with Russia, 392

choice: price system and, 98; reasons for increase, 247; scarcity and, 8–10

Chrysler Corporation, 167

Cisco Systems, 219

CIO. *See* Congress of Industrial Organizations (CIO)

circular flow model, 34–35, *c34*

civil engineer: as career, 282

Civil Rights Act of 1964, 174, 175, *c182*

Civil Rights Act of 1968, *c217*

Civil War, 310–311, 365

Civilian Conservation Corps (CCC), 254

Clayton Antitrust Act, 131–132, 213

Clear Channel Communications, 132–133

Clinton, Bill, 291, 294, 365, 455

closed shops, 178

CNN.com, 37

Coinage Act of 1873, 311

coincident indicators, 240

coins, 306

COLA. *See* cost-of-living adjustment (COLA)

Cold War, 410

collateral, 149, 214

collectivization, 391

collective bargaining, 186

collusion, 125–126

colonization, 403–404

command capitalism: government involvement and, 378; in West Germany, 383

command economies: central planners in, 25; characteristics of, 25; definition of, 23, 25; economic questions and, 26; Egypt (Old Kingdom) as example of, 25; land reform and, 417; Zhou Dynasty as example of, 25

command socialism, 379, *p387*

command system, 377, 389, *p414*, 423

commerce clause, 367

commercial banks, 315–316, *c316*

commercials, 61

commodity money, *c302, c304,* 305

common stock, 155

communism: bourgeoisie and, 389; central planning and, 391–393; China and, 395–398; class struggle and, 390; Cold War effect on, 399; collectivization and, 391; Five-Year Plans and, 391; historically, 389–398; Industrial Revolution and, 389–390; Karl Marx and, 389–390; New Economic Policy (NEP) and, 391; production problems and, 393; proletariat and, 389–390; rise of, 390–393; Stalin's rule and, 391; war communism, 390–391. *See also* authoritarian socialism

Communist Manifesto, 389

Community College Times, 71

comparable worth: quotas and, 174; wages and, 175

comparative advantage, 428–430, *c430*

competition: creating choice, 98; definition of, 32; effect on prices, 113; free-enterprise system and, 32; market structure and, 119; monopolies and, 120–122, 129; perfect competition, 117, 119–120; supply curve and, 83

complementary goods, 62

computers: in banking, 317–319; in industry, 7; and the Internet, 84, 442; and prices, 99

concentration ratio, 124

Confederacy, 311

conglomerate combinations, 160

Congress of Industrial Organizations (CIO), 179

consolidation, 69

consumer demand. *See* demand

consumer expectations, demand and, 62

consumer goods, definition of, 7

consumer price index 1940–1996, *g261*

consumer price index (CPI), 260–261, 264

Consumer Product Safety Commission (CPSC), *c285,* 286, 296

consumer purchases, 231

consumers: definition of, 3; as economic actors, 33; economic choices of, 32; expectations and demand, 62; tastes and preferences of, 57. *See also* headings beginning with consumer

containerization, 191

Continental Congress, 304

continentals, 305–306

contraction phase, 236, *g238*

contracts: definition of, 30; free-enterprise system and, 29–30; as legally binding, 30

cooperatives: credit unions as, 163; definition of, 163; housing cooperatives, 163; marketing cooperatives, 163; purchasing cooperatives, 163; service cooperatives, 163

coordinated campaign, 189

copyrights, 128–129

corporate bonds, 155, 199

corporate charter, 154, 157

corporate combinations: advantages of, 161; as business organizations, 159–162; competition and, 162; conglomerate combinations, 160–161; costs and, 161; disadvantages of, 161–162; efficiency of, 161; financial capital acquisition and, 161; horizontal combinations, 159; mergers as, 159; subsidiaries of, 160–161; unemployment and, 161–162; vertical combinations, 159

corporate income taxes, 350, 351

corporations: advantages of, 156–157; articles of incorporation, 154; board of directors, 155; as business organizations, 153–158; common stock in, 155; control of, 158; corporate bonds, 155; corporate charter, 154; corporate finances, 155–156; decision-making and, 157–158; definition of, 153; disadvantages of, 157–158; dividends on stock, 155–156; formation of, 153–154, 157; government regulation of, 157–158; limited liability of, 156–157; longevity of, 157; new incorporations and business failures, *m156;* officers of, 155; organization and control, *c154;* preferred stock in, 155; stock in, 155–156; stockholder participation in, 158; structure of, 154–155; subsidiaries of, 160–161; taxes and, 158

cost-of-living adjustment (COLA), 185, 262

cost of production, 74, 93

cost-push inflation, 258–260

Costa Rica, 6, 428–430, 445

costs: corporate combinations and, 161; fixed costs, 91; marginal costs, 92; of production, 74; of rationing, 111–112; resource costs affecting production, 80–81; taxes as, 81; total costs, 91–92; variable costs, 91. *See also* opportunity costs, production costs

costs of production, 74, 93

Council of California Growers, 193

Council of Economic Advisers, 363

counterfeit money, 306

CPSC. *See* Consumer Product Safety Commission (CPSC)

craft unions, 178

credit: abuse of, 216–218; annual percentage rates, 215; business cycles and, 238; buying on, 215–218; charge accounts, 215; credit bureau, 215; credit cards, 215–216, 218; credit ratings, 215; definition of, 16, 215; economy and, 217–218; Federal Reserve regulation of, 312, 342; finance charges, 215; as form of exchange, 16; regulation of, 216; terms of, 215–216; usury and, 216

credit bureau, 215

credit cards, 215–216, 218; incentives and, 216

credit ratings, 215

credit regulation, 342

credit unions, 315, *c316*, 317–318

Cuba, 111, 146, 280, 379, 414; as example of authoritarian socialism, 28; trade barriers and, 441

Cultural Revolution, 396

currency. *See* money

Current Population Survey, 251

customs duty, 354

customs inspector: as career, 429

Customs Service. *See* U.S. Customs Service

cyclical unemployment, 252, 256

D

Das Kapital, 389

De Beers, 126

debit cards, 319

Debs, Eugene V., 183

debt. *See* national debt

debt ceiling, 365

decision-making: corporations and, 157–158; free-enterprise system and, 32; in partnerships, 151; production decisions, 86–87, 89–92; self-interest and, 32; in sole proprietorships, 146–147. *See also* economic decisions

decision-making grid, *c11*

decision-making models, developing nations and, 414–415

default, 321

deficit spending, 363

deflation, 258

Dell Computer Corporation, 7, 93, 104

Dell, Michael, 7

demand, 50–68; changes in, 56–62, 62, 93, 113; commercials and, 61; complementary goods and, 62; consumer expectations and, 62; consumer preferences and, 50, 57, 69; definition of, 51; determinants of, 56–60, 62, 73, 93, 113; elasticity of, 63–68; equilibrium price and, 106, *g122;* floating exchange rates and, 433; foreign exchange rates and, 433; government policy decisions and, 58; income and, 59–60; labor force and, 169–172; law of, 52–54; market size and, 57–59; monopolies' effect on, 125, 129; nature of, 51–55; price of related goods and, 60; shifts in, 56–57, *g57;* substitute goods and, 60. *See also* supply, headings beginning with demand

demand curve, *g55, g57;* definition of, 54; quantity demanded and, 56

demand deposits, 307

demand-pull inflation, 258

demand schedules, 54, *c54, c55, g103*

demand-side economics: aggregate demand and, 356–358; definition of, 356; depression and, 357; Employment Act of 1946 and, 357–358; government's role in, 356–357; Keynes and, 356–357; model of, *c356*

democratic socialism: definition of, 28; examples of, 28; as mixed economy, 28

Deng, Xiaoping, 396–397

Denmark, 282, 427

Department of Agriculture, 429

Department of Commerce, 219, 233

Department of Health and Human Services, 434

Department of Labor, 175, 251

Department of the Treasury, 306, 334, 350, 363

Depository Institutions Deregulation and Monetary Control Act, 320

depreciation, 91

depressions, 236

deregulation, 113, 293, 319–321

derived demand, 171–172

determinants of demand, 56–60

determinants of supply, 79

devaluation, 432

developed nations: Asian Development Bank and, 422; definition of, 403; foreign aid and, 417–420; International Monetary Fund (IMF) and, 420–422. *See also* specific countries

developing nations: African Development Bank and, 422; agricultural economies in, 404–405; arable land and, 403; capital formation and, 408–409, 411; capital resources and, 408–409, 411; capitalist model of decision-making, 414–415; central planning and, 414; colonization and, 403–404; cultural obstacles to growth in, 412–413; decision-making models, 414–415; definition of, 403; domestic savings and, 417; education and, 408; emergency assistance for, 419; entrepreneurship, 411; expropriation and, 412; financing economic development, 417; Food and Agriculture Organization (FAO) and, 422; foreign aid and, 419–422; foreign investment in, 409; growth challenges, 407–413; human resources and, 408; infrastructure and, 411–412; Inter-American Development Bank and, 422; International Bank for Reconstruction and Development (IBRD) and, 420; International Development Association (IDA), 420; International Finance Corporation (IFC), 420–422; International Monetary Fund (IMF) and, 421–422; international public sources of capital, 420–422; International Red Cross and, 420; land reform and, 417; military assistance to, 419; Multilateral Investment Guarantee Agency and, 421; multinational corporations (MNC) and, 417–418; nationalization and, 412; natural resources and, 403–404, 407–408; nonprofit organizations and, 417–418; one-crop economies in, 407–408; Peace Corps and, 420; political instability and, 412, 418; population growth and, 404–405; private capital and, 417–418; privatization and, 412; production possibilities and, 416–417; Save the Children Fund and, 420; scarcity and, 416; socialist model of decision-making and, 414; subsistence agriculture in, 404–405; as Third World countries, 410; trade-offs and, 416; United Nations Development Program (UNDP) and, 422; United Nations Industrial Development Organization (UNIDO) and, 422; World Bank and, 420–421; World Health Organization (WHO) and, 422. *See also* economic development, specific countries

differentiate, 120

diminishing marginal utility: definition of, 53; law of demand and, 53–54

direct retailing, 71

discount rate, 339, *c339*, 341, *g341*

discouraged workers, 252

disposable income, 195, 235

diversification, 201

dividends, 155, 204

division of labor, 10

domestic resources, 242–243

Dow Jones Industrial Average, 209, *g209*, 219

Drug Enforcement Administration, 429

durable goods, 231

---

earthquakes, 313

Easterbrook, Gregg, 249

easy-money policy, 337–338

e-commerce, 247, 297, 442

economic activity: incentives as regulator, 27; self-interest as regulator, 25–26

economic actors, free-enterprise system and, 33–34

economic decisions, 2, 3–4, 119

economic development: African Development Bank and, 422; arable land and, 403; Asian Development Bank and, 422; capital formation and, 408–409, 411; capital resources and, 408–409, 411; colonization and, 403–404; cultural obstacles to, 412–413; definition of, 403; domestic savings and, 417; economic instability and, 418; education and, 408; entrepreneurship and, 411; expropriation and, 412; financing economic development, 417; Food and Agriculture Organization (FAO), 422; foreign aid and, 417–420; human resources and, 408; infrastructure and, 411–412; Inter-American Development Bank and, 422; International Bank for Reconstruction and Development (IBRD) and, 420; International Development Association (IDA), 420; International Finance Corporation (IFC), 420–421; International Monetary Fund (IMF) and, 421–422; international public sources of capital for, 420–422; International Red Cross and, 420; land reform and, 417; Multilateral Investment Guarantee Agency and, 421; multinational corporations (MNC) and, 417–418; nationalization and, 412; natural resources and, 403–404, 407–408; nonprofit organizations and, 417–418; opportunity costs and, 416; paths to, 414–422; Peace Corps and, 420; per capita gross domestic product, 403; planning for, 415–416; political instability and, 412; population growth and, 404–405; private capital and, 417–418; privatization and, 412; production possibilities and, 416–417; Save the Children Fund and, 420; standard of living and, 403; agriculture, 404–405; trade-offs and, 416; United Nations

Development Program (UNDP) and, 422; United Nations Industrial Development Organization (UNIDO) and, 422; World Bank and, 334, 420–421; World Health Organization (WHO) and, 422. *See also* developing nations

economic efficiency, 38

economic equity, 38

economic flows, 34–35

economic forecasting, 359–360; business cycles and, 240; Federal Reserve system and, 343

economic freedom, as goal of U. S. economy, 36

economic goals: and trade-offs, 39–40; of United States, 36

economic growth, 241–246; business cycles and, 236; capital deepening and, 244–245; capital resources and, 243; capital-to-labor ratio, 244; costs and trade-offs, 233; credit affecting, 217–218, *c218;* definition of, 241; domestic resources and, 242–243; entrepreneurship and, 243–244; expanded tax base and, 242–243; expansion and, 236; global markets and, 242; as goal of U.S. economy, 39, human resources and, 243; importance of, 41, 241–243; income distribution and, 242; labor force retraining and, 245; labor productivity and, 244; military spending and, 399; natural resources and, 243; and public interest, 148; productivity and, 244–246; real gross domestic product (GDP) per capita and, 241; requirements for, 243–244; research and development and, 244; savings affecting, *c218;* standard of living and, 241–242; technological advances and, 244

economic indicators, 240

economic interdependence. *See* interdependence

economic production: economic growth and, 241; gross domestic product (GDP) and, 229–235; gross national product (GNP) and, 234; measurement of, 229–232; output-expenditure model, 230–232; underground economies and, 233

economic questions: basic three, 23; command economies and, 26; identification of, 8–9; smarket economies and, 26; traditional economies and, 26

economic resources: classification of, 4–5, 7, 19

economic rivalry. *See* competition

economic sanctions. *See* embargo

economic security: definition of, 38; as goal of U. S. economy, 38

economic stability: credit promoting, 218; definition of, 38; employment and, 38; as goal of U. S. economy, 38–39; in market economies, 33

economic systems, 22–40, *c26;* capitalist economic systems, 377–378; command economies, 25, *c26;* comparison of, 376–398; global economy and, 376; identifying, 377; market economies, 23, 25–26, *c26;* Mbuti as example of, 24–25; mixed economies, 27–28; socialist economic systems, 377, 378–380; traditional economies, 23–25, *c26;* types of, 23–28, *c26, c377*

economics: definition of, 3. *See also* economies; economist; headings beginning with economic

Economics and Politics of Race, 271

economies of scale, 127, 323

economist, 3; as career, 5

ecosystem, 12

ecotourism, 6

Eddie Bauer, 111

Edgecumbe Enterprises, 434

education: in developing nations, 408; and labor force, 173; market economies and, 33; productivity and, 246; salary and, 173, *c173*

EEOC. *See* Equal Employment Opportunity Commission (EEOC)

efficiency: definition of, 10; price system and, 98, 100

EFT. *See* electronic funds transfer (EFT)

Egypt (Middle Kingdom): as example of command economies, 25

El Salvador, 412, 420, 422, 445

elastic demand, *g64;* definition of, 63; markets and, 65–66; measuring, 66; properties of goods having, 63–64; total revenue and, 67

elastic supply, 76–78, *g77*

elasticity of demand, 63–68; definition of, 63; measurement of, 66–68; measuring, 66–68

elasticity of supply, 76–78

electronic funds transfer (EFT), 318

Electronic Numerical Integrator and Computer (ENIAC), 99

Embargo Act of 1807, 441

embargoes, 280, 441

employee stock ownership plans (ESOP), 185

employees. *See* labor force

employment, 251, 252; international, 267

Employment Act of 1946, 357–358

ENIAC. *See* Electronic Numerical Integrator and Computer (ENIAC)

entrepreneur: as career, 146; definition of, 7; example of, 88; young entrepreneurs, 118, 237

entrepreneurship: definition of, 7; developing nations and, 411; economic growth and, 243–244; as factor of production, 7; real investment and, 203; venture capital and, 203

environment: government regulations and, 81; opportunity costs and trade-offs, 12

Environmental Protection Agency (EPA), 148, *c285,* 286, 296

Equal Credit Opportunity Act, *c217*

Equal Employment Opportunity Commission (EEOC), 174, 285, *c285*

Equal Pay Act of 1963, 174

equal pay for equal work, 175

equilibrium: demand and, 106–107, *g122;* equilibrium point, 103; market equilibrium, 103–104; prices and, 103–107; shifts in, 106–107; shortages and, 105; supply and, 106–107; surplus and, 104–105. *See also* market equilibrium

equilibrium point, 103

equilibrium wage, *g170*

Erhard, Ludwig, 383

ESOP. *See* employee stock ownership plans (ESOP)

estate plan, 201

estate tax, 354

ethics code, 165

Ethiopia, 412

EU. *See* European Union (EU)

euro, 303, 431–432

European Union (EU), 427, *m444*

exchange: definition of, 15; forms of, 15–16; global exchange, 16; interdependence and, 17–18; value and, 17. *See also* barter, credit, money

exchange rates. *See* foreign exchange rates

exchange ratio, 428–430

excise tax, 354

expansion phase, 236, *g238*

expansionary fiscal policy, 360

expenses: fixed expenses, 201; flexible expenses, 201

exports: definition of, 231; net exports, 231–232

expropriation, 412

externalities, 101, 286, 290

F

---

factors of production, 2, 4–5, 7, 19; command economies and, 25; definition of, 4; market economies and, 25; mixed economies and, 27–28

Fair Credit Billing Act, *c217*

Fair Credit Reporting Act, *c217*

Fair Debt Collection Practices Act, *c217*

Fair Labor Standards Act, 176

Family Medical Leave Act, 367

FAO. *See* Food and Agriculture Organization (FAO)

farm banks, 321

Farm Credit System (FCS), 321

FCC. *See* Federal Communications Commission (FCC)

FCS. *See* Farm Credit System (FCS)

FDA. *See* Food and Drug Administration (FDA)

FDIC. *See* Federal Deposit Insurance Corporation (FDIC)

Federal Aviation Administration, *c285*

federal budget: balanced budget amendment, 366; balancing the federal budget, 365–366; Budget and Accounting Act of 1921 and, 363; budget deficits, 363–364; budget surplus, 363; corruption historically, 362; creation of, 362–363; debt ceilings and, 365; decreasing expenditures and, 365–366; deficit spending and, 363–364; definition of, 362; federal budget 1996, *g363;* federal deficit, *g364;* fiscal year and, 363; increasing revenues, 365; legislating a balanced budget, 366; national debt and, 364–365; Omnibus Budget Reconciliation Act of 1993 and, 365; preparation of, 363; Progressive Movement and, 362; taxation and, 365; wartime spending and, 362

Federal Communications Commission (FCC), *c285,* 286

federal deficit, *g364;* economic growth and, 243

Federal Deposit Insurance Corporation (FDIC), 312, 320

Federal Energy Regulatory Commission, *c285*

Federal Housing Administration (FHA), 287–288

Federal Insurance Contributions Act (FICA), 351

Federal Mediation and Conciliation Service (FMCS), 187

Federal Open Market Committee (FOMC), *c329,* 331, 339

Federal Reserve Act of 1913, 311, 328, 347

Federal Reserve Bank of New York, 336, 339

Federal Reserve system, 278–296; aggregate demand and, 337–339, 341–342; bank supervision, 334, 335; cash reserves and, 329; characteristics of, 330; check clearing, 332, *c333;* credit regulation and, 312, 342; discount rate, 339–341, *c339, g341;* district level, 331; districts of, 330, *c330;* economic forecasting of, 343; establishment of, 311–312; fiscal policy and, 361; government services and, 334–336; as government's bank, 334–335; inflation and, 258, 338, 342, 345; interagency coordination and, 343–344; loans to banks, 332–334; margin requirements and, 342; monetarists and, 344; monetary policy and, 337–345; monetary policy tools, *c339,* 345; money supply regulator, 334, 335–336; moral suasion and, 342, 345; national level, 331; open-market operations, 339, c339; organization of, c329, 331; policy limitations, 342–344; prime rate and, 341, g341; priorities of, 343–344; reserve requirement, 341–342; role of, 323, 329–330; services to banks, 332–334; time lags and, 343; trade-offs, 343

federal revenue, 352, 354. *See also* taxation; taxes

Federal Saving and Loan Insurance Corporation (FSLIC), 322

Federal Securities Act, *c212,* 213

federal tax receipts by source, *g351*

Federal Trade Commission Act, 132

Federal Trade Commission (FTC), 132, 213, *c285,* 286

Federalists, 308

FHA. *See* Federal Housing Administration (FHA)

fiat money, *c304,* 305, 306, 311

FICA. *See* Federal Insurance Contributions Act (FICA)

final product: example of, 229–231

finance charges, 216

financial analyst: as career, 239

Financial Institution Reform, Recovery, and Enforcement Act, 322

financial institutions: automated teller machines (ATM) and, 318; automatic clearing house services (ACH), 318; automation and, 318–319; bank failures, 321, *g321,* 322; commercial banks, 315–316, *c316;* competition among, 320; credit unions, 315, *c316,* 317–318; debit cards and, 319; deregulation and, 319–321; electronic funds transfer (EFT) and, 318; Federal Deposit Insurance Corporation (FDIC), 312; Federal Saving and Loan Insurance Corporation (FSLIC), 322; Financial Institutions Reform, Recovery, and Enforcement Act, 322; home banking and, 319; loan defaults and, 321; mutual savings banks, 315; point-of-sale transactions and, 318–319; regional banking, 320–321; savings and loan associations (S&Ls), 315, 316, 321, 322; types of, 315–318

financial planning: budget, 200–201; diversification, 201; estate plan, 201; flexible expenses and, 201; investment plan, 201; for investments, 200–201; retirement plan, 201; spending and saving plan, 201

First Bank of the United States, 307, 327

fiscal policy, 348–366; Balanced Budget and Deficit Reduction Act of 1985 and, 366; collecting taxes, 350–354, 354; coordination of government agencies and, 361; customs duty, 354; deficit spending and, 363–364; definition of, 349; demand-side economics and, *c356,* 356–358; forecasting and, 359–360; estate tax, 354; excise tax, 354; expansionary fiscal policy, 360; federal budget and, 362–363; Federal Reserve system and, 361; federal tax receipts by source, *g351;* gift tax, 354; government spending, 359; Gramm-Rudman-Hollings Act (GRH) and, 366; income taxes and, 359; Internal Revenue Service and, 350; investment tax credit, 358; limitations on, 359; Medicaid and, 359; Medicare and, 351, 359; national debt and, 364–365; nonproductive actors and, 359; Old-Age, Survivors, and Disability Insurance (OASDI) and, 351; political pressures and, 360; progressive taxes and, 349, 350–351, 359; proportional taxes and, 349, 351; public transfer payments and, 359; regressive taxes and, 349–350, 351, 354; restrictive fiscal policy, 360; sales tax rates by state, *m352;* strategies of, 355–361; supply-side economics, 355–356, *c356;* tariffs and, 354; tax incentives and, 358–359; tax rates and, 349–350; taxation and, 358; timing problems and, 359–360; tools of, 358–359

fiscal year, 363

Five-Year Plans, 391, 396–397

fixed costs, 91

fixed expenses, 201

fixed investment, 231

flat rate taxes, 349

flexible expenses, 201

floating exchange rates, 433

FMCS. *See* Federal Mediation and Conciliation Service (FMCS)

Food and Agriculture Organization (FAO), 422

Food and Drug Administration (FDA), 119, *c285,* 286

Food From the 'Hood, 237

Ford, Henry, 83

foreign aid: as economic assistance, 419; effectiveness of, 420; as emergency assistance, 419; as military assistance, 419; purposes of, 419–420; as source of capital, 418–420

foreign exchange and currencies: adjustable-peg system, 432–433; appreciation and, 432–433; balance of payments, 435–436; and trade, 436–437; Bretton Woods Conference and, 432; devaluation and, 432; floating exchange rates, 433; exchange markets, 431; foreign exchange rates, 431–433; "strong" dollar, 433; trade surplus and, 437; U.S. trade deficit, 437

foreign exchange markets, 431, 433

foreign exchange rates: adjustable-peg system and, 432; definition of, 431; demand and, 433; floating exchange rates, 433; "strong" dollar and, 433; supply and, 433

foreign investment in United States, *g436*

foreign labor, 428

Four Modernizations, 396–397

Fourier, Charles, 386

France: capitalism in, 384; European Union (EU) and, 445

franchises: definition of, 162; terms of, 162–163; types of, 162

free-enterprise system: antitrust legislation and, 286; comparisons and, 381; business rights in, 165; competition and, 32; contracts and, 29–30; decision-making in, 32; definition of, 29; economic actors and, 33–34; rights of individuals within, 29–33, 399; role of U.S. government in, 33, 323, 399; self-interest and, 32–33; United States as example of, 29–35

free market economy, 399, 415, 423

free trade: definition of, 441; fairness and, 443; implications of, 426; infant industries and, 442; job protection and, 442; national security and, 443; NAFTA and, 447; specialization and, 443; standard of living and, 442–443

Free Trade of Area of the Americas, 447

free-trade zones, 397

freedom of choice, 33–34

frictional unemployment, 252, 253

fringe benefits, 184–185

FTAA. *See* Free Trade of Area of the Americas

FTC. *See* Federal Trade Commission (FTC)

full employment, 252; definition of, 38; as goal of economic stability, 38; government involvement in, 38, *p251*

futures, 212–213; reasons for investing in, 212–213; trading futures, 212–213

Garcia, Rafael Jr., 181

Garcia v. San Antonio Metropolitan Transit Authority, 176

Gates, Bill, 135

GATT. *See* General Agreement on Tariffs and Trade (GATT)

GDP. *See* gross domestic product (GDP)

General Agreement on Tariffs and Trade (GATT), 445

General Motors (GM), 161, 446

general partnerships, 150

General Planning Commission, 384

General Theory of Employment, Interest, and Money, 356, 369

generic products: demand and, 53

geographer: as career, 378

geographic monopoly, 128, 136

Germany: capitalism in, 383–384; East Germany and, 384; European Union (EU) and, 445; fiscal policies of, 384; hyperinflation and, 261; research and development expenditures, *g244*; value of German mark, 302

GI Bill of Rights, 281–282

gift tax, 354

Gillette Company, *c160*

Gingrich, Newt, 269

Gini Index, 265–266, *g266*

Glass-Steagall Act. *See* Banking Act of 1933

global economy, 144, 247, 268, 303, 376

global markets, 230, 242; revolution in, 247

global warming, 409

GM. *See* General Motors (GM)

GNI. *See* gross national income

GNP. *See* gross national product

Gold Reserve Act of 1934, 312, 313–314

gold standard, 311, 312

Gold Standard Act of 1900, 311

Gompers, Samuel, 178

goods: capital goods, 5, 7; consumer goods, 7; definition of, 4; elastic demand of, 63; public goods, 286–288; related goods effect on supply curve, 84

Gorbachev, Mikhail, 393–394

Gore, Albert, 294

Gospel of Wealth, 221

government: business cycle and, 289–290; capitalist economic systems and, 377–378; competition in business and, 286; consumer protection, 286; deregulation, 293, 319–321; as economic actors, 33; economic goals of, 284–290; economic well-being and, 288–290; embargoes and, 280; as employer, 279; federal regulatory agencies, *c285*; government programs, 282–283, 350; government spending, *g281*, 282–283, *g283*, 350; growth of, 279–283; health care programs, 288; interest groups and, 294–296; intergovernmental responsibilities, 287; labor force and, 173–176; labor unions and, 183; laissez-faire economics, 280; lobbyists and, 295–296; emergencies and, 281; negative externalities and, 286; New Deal programs, 281; policy decision affect on demand, 58; population growth and, 279, *g279*; private property and, 22; privatization and, 287–288; public attitudes and, 280–281; public goods, 286–288; public influence on, 293–296; public interest and, 291–296;

redistribution of income, 288–289, *g289;* as regulator, 82, 129, 130–134, 146, 157–158, *c212,* 216, *c217,* 284–286, 292–293; role in market economies, 33; services of, 292–293; standard of living and, 279, 281, 288; transfer payments, 231, 235, 288. *See also* headings beginning with government

government monopoly, 129

government purchases, 231

government regulation: of corporations, 157–158, 297; credit and, 216, *c217;* federal regulating agencies, *c285;* of information, 297; of markets, 130–134; of monopolies, 129; of prices, 96; primary purposes of, 284–286; of private property, 40–41; of production costs, 82; of public utilities, 113; security regulations, *c212;* of small businesses, 148; of sole proprietorship, 145–146; supply and, 82

government securities: types of, 210, *c210*

government spending: at different levels of government, 283, *g283;* gross domestic product (GDP) and, 231; growth in, *g281,* 282–283; transfer payments and, 231

government transfer payments, 231

grace period, 319

Gramm-Leach-Bliley Act, 323

Gramm-Rudman-Hollings Act (GRH), 366

Great Britain, *g244,* 288, 300, 301, 303, 308, 318, 350, 383, 415, 427, 436. *See also* United Kingdom

Great Depression, 211, 254, 290, 312, 314, 357; American Federation of Labor and, 178; deflation during, 258; homelessness during, 280; New Deal programs and, 254, 281, 311–312, 314; unemployment during, 254–256

Great Leap Forward, 395–396

Greece, 445

Green Bay Packers, 164

green cards, 39

"green revolution," 416–417

greenbacks, 311

Greenspan, Alan, 338, *p338,* 345

Grenada, 445

GRH. *See* Gramm-Rudman-Hollings Act (GRH)

grievance procedures, 186

gross domestic product (GDP), 229–235, *g231;* accuracy and timeliness of data, 233; adjustment for price increases, 232; business cycles and, 236, 238; computing, 230–232; current output and, 230; definition of, 229; final output and, 229–230; four sectors of, 230–232; global markets and, 242; "goods" and "bads" and, 233–234; government purchases, 231; gross investment, 231; limitations of, 232–234; national income product accounts, *c234;* national well-being and, 233–234; net exports, 231–232; nominal and real gross domestic product (GDP), *g232;* nominal gross domestic product, 232; non-market activities and, 233; output included, 229–230; output produced within national borders, 230; output-expenditure model, 230–232; per capita, 241; per capita worldwide comparison of, *m404–405;* personal consumption expenditures, 231; price index and, 232; real gross domestic product, 232, 236, *g238,* 241; research and development expenditures, *g244;* underground economies and, 233. *See also* gross national product (GNP) and gross national income (GNI)

gross investments, 231

gross national income (GNI), 423

gross national product (GNP), 234, *c234,* 423

Guatemala, 445

Guyana, 445

H

Hamilton, Alexander, 308, *p309*

Helms-Burton Act of 1996, 441

Holland. *See* Netherlands

home banking, 319

Honduras, 445

Hong Kong, 415, 437

Hopwood **v.** *Univerity of Texas* **(1996),** 175

horizontal combinations, 159

household responsibility system, 396–397

housing cooperatives, 163

human resources: definition of, 5; developing nations and, 408; economic growth and, 243; as factor of production, 5

hyperinflation, 261

I

Iacocca, Lee, 167

IBM. *See* International Business Machines (IBM)

IBRD. *See* International Bank for Reconstruction and Development (IBRD)

ICA. *See* Interstate Commerce Act (ICA)

ICC. *See* Interstate Commerce Commission (ICC)

ICIC. *See* Initiative for a Competitive Inner City (ICIC)

IDA. *See* International Development Association (IDA)

identical products: purchasing decisions and, 119

IFC. *See* International Finance Corporation (IFC)

IMF. *See* International Monetary Fund (IMF)

immigration, 39

Immigration and Naturalization Service, 429

import quotas, 440–441

imports, 231

incentives: definition of, 27; price system and, 98

income: definition of, 34; demand and, 59–60; equal pay for equal work, 175; government redistribution of income, *g289;* net income of businesses, *g153;* redistribution of income by the government, 288–289

income distribution: Gini Index, 265–266, *g266;* limitations of, 266–267; Lorenz Curve, 265–266, *g266;* measuring income inequality, 265–267; poverty and, 264–268; poverty threshold and, 264

income effect, 52

income gap: causes of, 267–268; definition of, 264, 265; global economies and, 268; government redistribution of income, 288–289; labor market and, 268; narrowing of, 268; technology affecting, 268

income inequality: causes of, 267–268; government redistribution of income, 288–289; measurement of, 265–267. *See also* income gap

income taxes: corporate income taxes, 351; income taxes, 350–351

indicative planning, 384

individual choice, free enterprise and, 30–32

individual income taxes, 350–351

Indonesia, 410, 418, 445

Industrial Revolution, 386–387, 389–390

industrial unions, 178

industrialization, 172

inelastic demand, 64–65, *g65;* definition of, 64; properties of, 64–65; total revenue and, 67–68

inelastic supply: definition of, 77; gold as example of, 78; properties of, 77

infant industries, 442

inflation: causes of, 258–260; consumer price index, 260; cost-of-living adjustments (COLA) for, 262; cost-push inflation, 258–260; creeping inflation rate, 261; definition of, 258; demand-pull inflation, 258; effects of, 261–263; Federal Reserve system and, 258; galloping inflation rate, 261; government spending and, 278, 359; hyperinflation, 261; inflation rate, 260–261; rate 1940–1996, *g262;* interest rates and, 261, 262–263; market basket, 260; measuring inflation, 260; monetary policy and, 258; pensions and, 262; price expectations and, 260; price fluctuations and, 257–258; producer price index (PPI), 260; production costs and, 258–259; purchasing power and, 258, 261–262; real wages and, 261–262; return on investments and, 261, 262–263; saving and, 262–266; supply shock and, 258–259; taxation and, 358; tight-money policy and, 338; value of dollar and, *g263;* wage-price spiral and, 260

inflation rate, 1940–1996, *g262*

informed buyers, 119

infrastructure, 202, 269, 411–412, 417

Initiative for a Competitive Inner City (ICIC), 340

injunctions, 190

Inquiry into the Nature and Causes of the Wealth of Nations, 25–26, 382

Insider Trading Sanctions Act, *c212*

installments, 215

Intel, 93

Inter-American Development Bank, 422

interdependence: concept of, 17–18; definition of, 18; specialization and, 427–430

interdependent pricing: oligopoly and, 125

interest: on corporate bonds, 155; on loans, 214–215; on savings, 195–196, *g196*

interest groups, 294–296, 296

interest rates: inflation and, 262

intermediate product, 230

Internal Revenue Service (IRS), 334, 350

International Bank for Reconstruction and Development (IBRD), 420–421

International Business Machines (IBM), 7, 99, 104, 165

International Development Association (IDA), 420–421

International Finance Corporation (IFC), 420–421

international joint venture, 161, 446

International Monetary Fund (IMF), 420–422, 432

International Red Cross, 420

International Telephone and Telegraph Corporation (ITT), 160–161

international trade, 426–446; absolute advantage and, 428, *c430;* adjustable-peg system and, 432–433; balance of payments and, 435–436; balance of trade, 436–437; Bretton Woods Conference and, 432; comparative advantage and, 428–430, *c430;* currency appreciation and, 432–433; currency devaluation and, 432; economic interdependence and, 427; embargoes and, 441; fairness and, 443; floating exchange rates and, 433; foreign currencies and, 431–438; foreign exchange, and,

431–438; foreign exchange markets and, 434–436; exchange rates, 431–433; free trade, 441–442; import quotas and, 440–441; infant industries and, 442; international cooperation and, 443–446; International Monetary Fund (IMF) and, 432; international trade agreements, 445–446; job protection and, 442; licensing requirements and, 441; multinational corporations (MNC) and, 446; national security and, 443; protectionism and, 441–442; reciprocal trade agreements and, 444; specialization and, 427, 443; standard of living and, 442–443; "strong" dollar and, 433; tariffs and, 439–440; trade barriers, 439–441; trade surplus and, 437; U.S. trade deficit of the United States, 437; voluntary trade restrictions and, 440–441

Internet service providers (ISPs), 84

Internet trade, 442

Interstate Commerce Act (ICA), 130

Interstate Commerce Commission (ICC), 130, *c285*

intrinsic rewards, 171

inventory investment, 231

investments: capital accumulation and, 202; definition of, 200; diversification in, 201; economic growth and, 202–203; entrepreneurship and, 203; estate plan, 201; financial investment, 201–202; financial planning for, 200–201; fixed investments, 231; gross investments, 231; inflation and, 261–266; inventory investment, 231; investment plan, 201; nation's economic infrastructure and, 202; real investments, 202, 231; retirement plan, 201; risks of, 200; spending and saving plan, 200–201; technological change and, 202–203; venture capital and, 203

investment bank, 206

investment tax credit, 358

Iran, 412

Iraq, 280, 412

Ireland, 445

IRS. *See* Internal Revenue Service (IRS)

ISP. *See* Internet service providers

Italy, 427, 445; research and development expenditures, *g244*

ITT. *See* International Telephone and Telegraph Corporation (ITT)

J

Jackson, Andrew, 308

Jamaica, 445

Japan, 428; Bank of Japan, 383; capitalism in, 382–383, 414–415; competition in global markets, 230; as developed nation, 403; global markets and, 230; international trade and, 434; investment in United States, 436; Ministry of Finance role in, 382–383; Ministry of International Trade and Industry (MITI), 382–383, 385; multinational corporations (MNC) and, 446; research and development expenditures, *g244*; tariffs in, 382–383; tourism and, 111; deficit of, 437; trade restrictions and, 230; trade with United States and, *c435*; voluntary trade restrictions and, 440–441

Jefferson, Thomas, 308, *p309*

job protection, 442

job security, 185. *See also* labor force, labor unions, unemployment

Johnson & Johnson, 209

Johnson administration: affirmative action and, 174

joint ventures, 446

Jospin, Lionel, 384

Jungle, 177

K

Keynes, John Maynard, 356, 357, 369

King William's War, 305

Knights of Labor, 178

Korea, 384–385

Korea Development Institute (KDI), 385

Korean War, 240, 444

Kuwait, 280, 412

L

labor force: affirmative action and, 175; agriculture and, 172; antidiscrimination laws and, 174–175; capital-intensive economies and, 172; changes in, 172–174; collective bargaining and, 186; contract negotiations and, 186–189; definition of, 169; derived demand for, 171–172; education and, 172–173, 245; employment and, 251, 252; entering the labor force, 169–172; factories in 1800s, 177; global competition, 245; government and, 173–176; income gap and, 267, 268; industrial unions, 178; industrialization and, 172; intrinsic rewards and, 171; labor-intensive economies and, 172; market trends and, 171–172; mediation with, 186–187; productivity and, 244–246, *g245*; quotas and, 175; retraining programs, 245–246; skills and, 170–171, 245; statistics, *g169*, 252; unemployment and, 251–256; women in, 172–173; work location and, 171; working conditions and, 171

labor movement, 177–179

Labor Policy Association, 177–179

labor productivity: definition of, 244, *g245*

labor relations consultant: as career, 187

labor unions: African Americans and, 178; American Federal of Labor (AFL), 178–179; arbitration by, 187; boycotts by, 189; business ethics and, 165; challenges to, 180–182; closed shops, 178; Congress of Industrial Organizations (CIO), 179–180; contract issues, 184–186; coordinated campaigning, 189; cost-of-living adjustments (COLA) and, 185; craft unions, 178; declining membership of, 183; definition of, 177; development of, 177–179; employee stock ownership plans (ESOPs) and, 185; employer opposition to, 180; employment patterns affecting, 180–182; fringe benefits and, 184–185; government and, 183; grievance procedures, 186; of, 177–183; unions, 178; job security and, 185; Knights of Labor, 178; local unions, 179; major labor legislation, *c182*; management and, 183, 184–190; membership demographics, 180; membership statistics, *g180*; National Labor Relations Board (NLRB) and, 186; national unions, 179–180; negotiating body, 186; open shops, 178; picketing by, 188–189; opinion of, 182; right-to-work laws, *m179*; seniority and, 185; strikes, 188, 189; union security, 185–186; union tactics, 187–189; wages and, 184–185; women and, 178; for worker protection, 168; working conditions and, 185

labor intensive, 172

labor-intensive economies, 172

lagging indicators, 240

laissez-faire, 280, 355; definition of, 130. *See also* capitalism

land ordinance, 30

land reform, 417

language of prices, 97

law of demand, 52–54, 257

law of diminishing returns, 87

law of supply, 73–75, 257

Lawrence Trade Organization (LTO), 303

leading indicators, 240

Lee Kwan Yew, 385

legislation: antidiscrimination legislation, 174; antitrust legislation, 130–133; banking legislation, *c217,* 311–312, 314, 320, 322, 342; federal budget and, 363; Federal Reserve system and, 311–312, 328, 347; health and safety, 294; health and safety legislation, 119; international trade regulations, 440, 444; major labor legislation, 176, *c182,* 357–358; minimum-wage laws, 175–176; security regulations, *c212,* 213; tariff laws, 440

Lenin, Vladimir Ilich, 390–391, *p391*

Levi Strauss, Inc. 165

Lewis, John L., 179

Lewis, Sir Arthur, 425

liability, 147

Libya, 403

limited partnerships, 150

liquidity, 196

loan defaults, 321

loan officer: as career, 259

loans: banks as lenders, 314; collateral on, 214; Federal Reserve loans to banks, 332–334; installments on, 215; interest on, 214–215; loan officer, 259; principal on, 214

lobbyists, 296

lockouts, 190

longevity, 149

Lorenz Curve, 265–266, *g266. See also* income gap, income inequality

LTO, *See* Lawrence Trade Organization

Luxemburg, 445

Lydians, 306

Macao, 415

macroeconomics: definition of, 3, 229

Malaysia, 445

Mali, 403

management: labor unions and, 184–190; of prices, 108–112; stockholders' participation in, 158

manorialism, 381, 389

Mao Zedong, 395

maquiladoras, 19, 174

margin requirements, 342

marginal costs, 92

marginal product, 87

marginal returns: diminishing marginal returns, 89; increasing marginal returns, 89; negative marginal returns, 89–90

marginally attached workers, 252

market, 25

market basket, 260

market capitalism, 382, 383, 393. *See also* capitalist economic system

market economies, 23; definition of, 25; economic questions and, 26; economic stability in, 33; Germany as, 25; Japan as, 25; national defense in, 33; public education and, 33; redistribution of wealth in, 33; role of government in, 33; United States as, 25, 33

market entry: monopoly and, 127; oligopoly and, 123–124; perfect competition and, 119; sellers and, 119

market equilibrium: definition of, 103; example of, *g103;* price system and, 103–104

market failures, 101

market researcher: as career, 58

market revolution, 247

market size: demand and, 57–59; factors affecting, 57–59

market socialism, 378, 379–380, 387–388. *See also* socialism, socialist economic systems

market structures: comparison of types, *g124;* perfect competition and, 119

market system, 377

marketing cooperatives, 163

markets: definition of, 25; elasticity of demand and, 65–66; highly competitive markets, 117, 119–122; imperfectly competitive markets, 123–129; product market, 34; profit and, 74–75; regulation of, 130–134; resource market, 34–35. *See also* other headings beginning with market

Marshall, Alfred, 21

Marshall Plan, 420

Marx, Karl, 389–390, 399

Mary Kay Inc., 146

Massachusetts Bay Colony, *c304,* 305

maturity: definition of, 197; of bonds, 210; of time deposits, 197

Mbuti, as traditional economy, 24–25

McGuiness, Jeffrey, 181

McKinley Tariff Act of 1890, 440

measuring unemployment, 251–255

Mechanization and Modernization Agreement, 191

mediation, 186–187

Medicaid, 281, 359

Medicare, 351, 359

medium of exchange, 301, 302

mercantilism, 381–382, 389

merger, 159

Mexico, 115, 174, 445–446

MFN. *See* most-favored-nation (MFN)

microeconomics, 3

Microsoft, 135

Mighty Morphin Power Rangers®, 105

migrant workers, 255

minimum wage: historically, *g176;* definition of, 109; legislation and, 175–176; as price floor, 109

Ministry of Economy, Trade, and Industry (METI), 382–383, 385

METI. *See* Ministry of Economy, Trade, and Industry (METI)

Mitterand, Francois, 384, *p384*

mixed economies: authoritarian socialism as, 27–28; capitalism as, 28; categories of, 27; characteristics of, 27–28; definition of, 27; democratic socialism as, 28

MNC. *See* multinational corporations (MNC)

Monetary Control Act of 1980, 342

monetary policy: aggregate demand and, 337–339, 341–342; components of, 339, 341–342; credit regulation and, 342; definition of, 337; discount rate and, 339, *c339,* 341; easy-money policy, 337–338; Federal Reserve system and, 337–344; inflation and, 258, 338; margin requirements and, 342; monetarists and, 344; moral suasion and, 342; open-market operations and, 339, *c339;* policy limitations, 342–344; reserve requirement and, 339, *c339,* 341–342; tight-money policy, 338; tools of, *c339*

money, 300–307; acceptability of, 304–305; bartering and, 301; business cycles and, 238; characteristics of, 303–305; coins, 306; commodity money, *c304,* 305; counterfeit money, 306; currency as, 306; definition of, 15; demand deposits as, 307; divisibility of, 303, 304; durability of, 303–304; fiat money, *c304,* 305, 306, 311; as form of exchange, 15–16; forms of, 306–307; functions of, 16, 301–303; greenbacks as, 311; history of currency, 308–314; as medium of exchange, 301, 302; national currency, 311; near money, 307; paper money, 304, 306; portability of, 302, 303, 304; purpose of, 299; representative money, *c304,* 305–306; sources of money's value, *c304,* 305–306; specie and, 305; stability in value of, 303, 304; as standard of value, 299, 301, 302; store of value and, 302, 303; U. S. banknotes as, 309

money market deposit accounts, 197

money supply: aggregate demand and, 337; components of, *g335;* definition of, 335; easy-money policy, 337–338; Federal Reserve system as regulator, 334, 335–336; growth of, *c347;* inflation and, 338; L, *g335,* 336; M1, *g335,* 336; M2, *g335,* 336; M3, *g335,* 336; monetary policy and, 337–344; tight-money policy and, 338

monopolies: and anti-trust legislation, 130–133; Clear Channel Communications as, 132–133; competition and, 129; concentration ratio and, 124; conditions of, 126; consumer demand and, 129; definition of, 119; effect of, 129; geographic monopolies, 128; government monopolies, 129; government regulation of, 129; market entry and, 127; Microsoft as, 135; natural monopolies, 127–128; technological monopolies, 128–129; types of, 127–129

monopolistic competition: definition of, 120; nonprice competition and, 120–121; perfect competition compared with, 120; product differentiation and, 120; profits and, 121–122

moral suasion, 342

most-favored-nation (MFN) status, 444

MS–DOS, 133

Multilateral Investment Guarantee Agency, 421

multinational corporations (MNC): definition of, 417; developing nations and, 418; joint ventures and, 446; performance standards for, 446

mutual savings banks, 315, 316–317

N

Nader, Ralph, 294–295, 296

Nader's Raiders, 296

NAFTA. *See* North American Free Trade Agreement

NASDAQ. *See* National Association of Securities Dealers Automated Quotations (NASDAQ)

National Association of Securities Dealers Automated Quotations (NASDAQ), 207, 219

National Banking Act of 1863, 311

National Banking Act of 1864, 311

National Consumer Law Center, 216

national currency, 311, 431

national debt: debt ceilings and, 365; definition of, 364; growth of, 364–365; impact of, 365; war and, 365

National Farm Workers Association, 189

National Highway Traffic Safety Administration, c285

national income, c234, 235

national income accounting, 229

national income and product accounts, 229, c234

National Labor Relations Board (NLRB), 186, c285

National Monetary Commission, 328

national security, 443

National Traffic and Motor Vehicle Safety Act of 1966, 294

nationalization, 384, 412

nationally chartered banks, 308–310, 311, 312

natural disasters: loans for, 332

natural monopoly, 127–128

natural resources: definition of, 4; developing nations and, 403–404, 407–408; economic growth and, 243; as factor of production, 4–5

near money, 307

needs, classification of, 4

Nehru, Jawaharlal, 410

net exports, 231–232

net national product, 234–235, c234

Netherlands, 445

New Deal, 254, 281, 311–312, 314

New Urbanism, 353

New York Curb Agency, 207

New York Stock Exchange (NYSE), 207

Nicaragua, 412, 445

Nicholas II, Czar, 390

Niger, 403

Nike, 418

Nissan, 446

NLRB. *See* National Labor Relations Board (NLRB)

Nobody in Particular Presents, 132–133

nominal gross domestic product, 232

nondurable goods, 231

nonmarket activities, 233

nonprice competition: definition of, 120; monopolistic competition and, 120–121

nonproductive actors, 359

nonprofit organizations: definition of, 163; economic development and, 417–418; Green Bay Packers as, 164; structure of, 163

Nortel, 165

North American Free Trade Agreement (NAFTA), 174, 445–447

North Korea, 386, 414

NRC. *See* Nuclear Regulatory Commission (NRC)

Nuclear Regulatory Commission (NRC), 286

Nutrition Labeling and Education Act of 1990, 119

NYNEX, 134

NYSE. *See* New York Stock Exchange (NYSE)

O

OASDI. *See* Old–Age, Survivors, and Disability Insurance (OASDI)

Occupational Safety and Health Administration (OSHA), 285–286, *c285,* 296

occupations: fastest-declining, 1994–2005, *c255;* fastest-growing, 1994–2005, *c255*

Office of Management and Budget (OMB), 363

Old-Age, Survivors, and Disability Insurance (OASDI), 351

oligopoly: cartels in, 126; collusion in, 125–126; definition of, 123; identical products and, 123; interdependent pricing and, 125; market entry, 123–124; nonprice competition and, 124; price leadership and, 125; price war and, 125; sellers in, 123; three conditions for, 123

OMB. *See* Office of Management and Budget (OMB)

Omnibus Budget Reconciliation Act of 1993, 365

one-crop economies, 407–408

Only One Earth, 95

OPEC. *See* Organization of Petroleum Exporting Countries (OPEC)

open-market securities, *c339*

open shops, 178

Operation Desert Storm, 280

opportunity costs, 11–14, 32; definition of, 11; economic development and, 399, 416; effect on production, 13; trade-offs and, 11–12

Organization for Economic Development (OECD), *g419*

Organization of Petroleum Exporting Countries (OPEC), 125, 239, 259, 437

OSHA. *See* Occupational Safety and Health Administration (OSHA)

output-expenditure model: 230–232; definition of, 230; government purchases, 230, 231; gross investment, 230, 231; investments, 231; net exports, 230, 231–232; personal consumption on expenditures, 230

overhead, 91

Owen, Robert, 386

Pacific Telesis, 134

Panama, 428–430

Panic of 1837, 308, 310

Panic of 1907, 327–328

paper money, 304, 306

Paraguay, 417, 445

Parens Patriae Act of 1976, 132

partnerships: advantages of, 150–151; business losses and, 151; as business organizations, 150–152; conflict potential in, 152; decision-making in, 151; definition of, 150; disadvantages of, 151–152; general partnerships, 150; limited partnerships, 150; longevity of, 152; specialization in, 151; start up of, 150–151; unlimited liability in, 152

patents, 128

Peace Corps, 420

peak phase, 236, *g238*

pensions, 262

people's communes, 395–396

per capita, 279, 283

per capita gross domestic product, 403

per capita income, 447

perestroika, 393

perfect competition: conditions for, 117, 120; definition of, 117; identical products and, 119; informed buyers and, 119; market entry and, 119; structure and, 119; as model, 119–120

Persian Gulf War, 412, *p412*

personal consumption expenditures, 231

personal identification number (PIN), 319

personal income, *c234,* 235

Philippines, 445

picketing, 188–189

Pillsbury, 436

PIN. *See* personal identification number (PIN)

point-of-sale transactions, 318–319

population: comparison worldwide, *g406;* developing nations and, 404–405; government growth and, 279–280; U.S. population growth, *g279*

Portugal, 445

poverty: definition of, 264; income distribution and, 264–268; poverty rate, 264–265, *c265;* poverty threshold, 264; in the United States, 264–265, 281

poverty rate, 1977–1995, *c265*

poverty rate, 264–265

poverty threshold, 264, 265

Powered, Inc., 84

PPI. *See* producer price index (PPI)

preferred stock, 155

price ceiling, *g109;* definition of, 108; control as example of, 108–109

price discrimination, 132

price floor: definition of, 109; minimum wage as example of, 109

price index, 232

price leadership, 125

price shocks, 239

price shortages, *g109*

price stability: definition of, 38; as goal of economic stability, 38

price system: benefits of, 97–98, 100–101; choice generated by, 98; efficiency of, 98, 100; externalities and, 101; flexibility in, 100–101; incentives of, 98; information gained from, 97–98; instability of, 102; language of prices, 97; limitations of, 101–102; market failures, 101; public goods and, 101–102. *See also* prices

price wars, 125

prices, 96–112; aggregate demand and, 257–258; aggregate supply and, 257–258; consequences of setting prices, 109–110; determination of, 103–107; equilibrium and, 103–107; government effect on, 292; language of, 97; management of, 108–112; price levels, 257–258; price war, 125; rationing and, 110–112; setting of, 108–110; shortages and, 105; stock prices, 207–209; surpluses and, 104–105; system of, 97–102. *See also* headings beginning with price and prices

prices of related goods: demand and, 60, 62; supply and, 84

prices of resources, 80–81

primary boycott, 189

prime rate, 341

principal: on corporate bonds, 155; on loans, 214

priorities: changing priorities, 40; conflicting priorities, 40; scarcity and, 39–40; solutions for conflict in, 40; trade-offs and, 39–40

private property, 29–30, 156; government regulation of, 22, 40–41

privatization, definition of, 287; 384, 412, 423

producer expectations, 84–85

producer price index (PPI), 260–261

producers: definition of, 3; as economic actors, 33

product differentiation: definition of, 120; goal of, 121–122; monopolistic competition and, 120; oligopolies and, 123

product market: definition of, 34; and circular flow model, *c35*

production: decision-making and, 86–87, 89–92; factors affecting, 9–10; as cost of, 81–82

production costs: definition of, 74, 90; depreciation and, 91; fixed costs, 91; government regulations and, 82; inflation and, 258–259, 261, 263; marginal costs, 92; overhead, 91; resources as, 80–81; return on investment and, 263; subsidies and, 82; supply shocks and, 258–259; taxes as, 81–82; technology and, 82–83; total costs, 91–92; variable costs, 91

production curve, *g87*

production possibilities, 12–13, 416–417; current production possibilities, 13–14; future production possibilities, 14

production possibilities curve, *g13, g14;* definition of, 12–13; for developing nations, *g41;* shifts in, 14

production schedule: example of, *g87*

productivity: capital deepening and, 244–245; capital-to-labor ratio and, 244; definition of, 9; division of labor and, 10; economic growth and, 244–246; education and, 246; efficiency and, 10; government effect on, 293; increasing productivity, 244–246; labor force and, 244–246; labor productivity, 244, *g245;* mechanization and, 10; and production decisions, 86; productivity growth, 244; retraining programs and, 245–246; specialization and, 10; technological advances and, 244; United States and, *g245,* 246; worker loyalty and, 246

productivity growth, 244

profit margin. *See* profit

profit motive, 73, 74

profits: definition of, 74; government effect on, 293; markets and, 74–75; monopolistic competition and, 121–122; product differentiation and, 121–122; sole proprietorships and, 147

progressive income taxes, 359

Progressive Movement, 362

progressive taxes, 349, 350–351, 359

proletariat, 389–390

property taxes, 351–352

proportional taxes, 349, 351

prospectus, 213

protectionism: definition of, 441; fairness and, 443; infant industries and, 442; job protection and, 442; national security and, 443; protective tariffs, 439; specialization and, 443; standard of living and, 442–443

protective tariffs, 439

public goods: definition of, 101–102; economic boom and, 269; price system and, 101–102

public goods gap, 250, 269

public interest: economic growth and, 148; identifying the public interest, 291–292

public transfer payments, 359

Pullman Palace Car Company, 183

purchasing cooperatives, 163

purchasing power, 258, 262, *g263;* definition of, 52; income effect and, 52; inflation and, 258

pyramided reserves, 327

Q

quantity demanded: definition of, 51; income effect and, 52

quantity supplied, 73

quotas, 174–175

R

rationing: black markets and, 112; causes of, 110–111, 113; consequences of, 111–112; cost of, 111–112; definition of, 110; unfairness of, 111

RCA, 446

Reagan, Ronald, 355, 441

real estate agent: as career, 31

real gross domestic product (GDP), 232, 236, *g238*, 241

real gross domestic product (GDP) per capita, 241, *g242*

real investments, 202, 231

real value of the dollar, *g263*

real wages, 262

recession, 236, 238

reciprocal trade agreements, 443

Reciprocal Trade Agreements Act of 1934, 443

Regents of the University of California v. Bakke **(1978)**, 175

regional banking, 320–321

regressive taxes, 349–350, 351, 354

regulations, 82

related goods: demand and, 60, 62; supply and, 84; types of, 60, 62

relative poverty, 265

relative worth, 17

rent control, 108–109

representative money, 303–304, *c304*, 305–306

research & development expenditures 1992, *g244*

reserve requirement, 339, *c339*, 341–342

Resolution Trust Corporation (RTC), 322

resource market: circular flow model and, *c35*; definition of, 34

resources: allocation of, 8–9; capital, 5, 7; definition of, 4; effect on production costs, 80; human resources, 5; natural resources, 4–5; price system and, 100; profit motive and, 74. *See also* human resources; natural resources

restrictive fiscal policy, 360

retirement plan, 201

retraining programs, 245–246

revenue tariffs, 439

Ricardo, David, 428

right-to-work laws, *m179*

Rivlin, Alice, 5

Robinson-Patman Act, 132

Rockefeller, John D., 132

Roosevelt, Franklin Delano, 254, 281, 311–312, 443

Roosevelt, Theodore, 130

RTC. *See* Resolution Trust Corporation (RTC)

Russia: communism and, 390–391, 393–395; perestroika and, 393; reform in, 395; "shuttle shoppers" in, 392. *See also* Soviet Union

Russian Federation, 395

S

S&Ls. *See* savings and loan associations (S&Ls)

salary: education and, 173, *c173*

sales manager: as career, 104

sales taxes, 352, *m352*, 354

Save the Children Fund, 420

savings: as capital, 195–199; certificates of deposit and, 197–198; inflation and, 261, 262–263; interest on, 195–196, *g196*; measuring savings, 199; national savings rates, *g197*; reasons for, 195–196; savings accounts, 196–197; savings bonds, 198–199; savings rate, 199; security of, 195; time deposits, 197–199

savings accounts: balance on, 196; liquidity of, 196; money market deposit accounts, 196–197; regular savings accounts, 196

savings and loan associations (S&Ls), 315, 316, 321, 322

savings bonds, 198–199

savings rate, *g197*, 198; definition of, 199

Say, Jean-Baptiste, 355

scarcity, *c9*; choice and, 8–10, 38; definition of, 8; developing nations and, 407; economic development and, 416; effect on economics, 23; priorities and, 39–40

Sears, 104

seasonal unemployment, 252–256

SEC. *See* Securities and Exchange Commission (SEC)

Second Bank of the United States, 309–310, 327

secondary boycott, 189

Securities and Exchange Commission (SEC), 213, *c285,* 286

Securities Exchange Act (1934), *c212,* 213, 342

seismologists, 313

self-employed workers: taxes and, 351

self-interest: definition of, 26; as economic regulator, 25–26; free-enterprise system and, 32–33

self-sufficiency, 17

sellers: competition and, 117, 119, 123; definition of, 117; market entry of, 119; single seller as monopoly, 126–127

seniority, 185

services: definition of, 4; government effect on, 292–293

setting prices: government involvement in, 108–109

SFX, 132–133

share: definition of, 155. *See also* stocks

Sharp Corporation, 446

Sherman Antitrust Act, 130–131, 133, *c212,* 286

shortages: definition of, 105. equilibrium and, 105; price ceilings and, 109, 110

"shuttle shoppers", 392

Sinclair, Upton, 177

Singapore, 385, 415, 437, 445

single seller: monopoly, 126–127

skills, 170–171

small business, 148

Small Business Administration, 148, 203

Smith, Adam, 25–26, *p26,* 32–33, 43, 382

Smoot-Hawley Tariff of 1930, 440

Social Security, 231

Social Security Administration (SSA), 264

Social Security taxes, 351

socialism: decision-making model, 414; definition of, 386; economic planning and, 387–388, 414; Industrial Revolution and, 386–387; industry ownership and, 387; market socialism, 379–380, 387–388; origins of, 386–387; in Sweden, 386, 387–388; taxation and, 388; workers' freedoms and, 387. *See also* socialist economic systems

socialist economic systems: authoritarian socialism, 379; command socialism, 379; definition of, 377; market socialism, 379–380, 387–388

sole proprietorships: advantages of, 145–147; as business organizations, 145–149; by size of receipts, *c167;* control of, 146–147; definition of, 145; disadvantages of, 147–149; growth potential of, 149; liability for, 147; longevity of, 149; profit and, 147; responsibility for, 149; restrictions on, 146; start up of, 145–146; types of, 145; unlimited liability of, 147, 149; zoning laws affecting, 146

Sony Playstation 2, 105–106

South Africa, 126, 417, 441

South Korea, 385, 415, 437

Southern Common Market (AMERCOSUR), 445

Soviet Union: agricultural production and, 393; central planning and, 391, 393; as command socialist system, 379, 389; East Germany and, 383; economic reform in, 393–395; fall of, *c394;* Gosplan and, 391; Lenin and, 390–391; as most-favored-nation, 444; nations formed from, *m380;* production problems in, 393; Stalin and, 391, 393. *See also* Russia

Sowell, Thomas, 271

Spain, 411, 427, 445

specialization: definition of, 10; economic interdependence and, 427–430; in partnerships, 151; trade and, 427, 443

specie, 305, 311

Sri Lanka, 412

SSA. *See* Social Security Administration (SSA)

St. Luke Penny Savings Bank, 325

stability. *See* economic stability

stability in value, 302

Stalin, Joseph, 391, 393

standard of living: definition of, 39; developing nations and, 442–443; in Eastern Europe, 402, 423; growth and, 241–242; government growth and, 279, 281; gross domestic product and, 403

standard of value, 301, 302

Standard Oil Company, 137

Standard Oil Company of Ohio, 132

Standard Oil of New Jersey, 131

Standard Oil Trust, 131

state-chartered banks, 209, 308, 310

stock markets: American Stock Exchange (AMEX), 207; bear market, 209; bull market, 209; crashes, 211; Mexican stock market, 209; National Association of Securities Dealers Automated Quotations (NASDAQ), 207; New York Stock Exchange (NYSE), 207; over-the-counter market, 207; regulation of, *c212*

stockbrokers, 206–207; as career, 206

stockholders: benefits for, 156; capitalist economic systems and, 377; control of corporation, 158; and corporate taxes, 158; limited liability of, 205; participation in corporation management, 158, 205

stocks: bear market, 209; blue chip stocks, 208; brokers of, 206–207; bull market, 209; capital gains and, 205; capital losses and, 205; common stock, 155; corporate finances and, 209; corporate stock, 155; definition of, 155; dividends on, 155–156, 204; Dow Jones Industrial Average, 209, *g209;* employee stock ownership plans (ESOPs), 185; external forces and, 209; growth stocks, 204; income stocks, 204; investment banks and, 206–207; investor expectations and, 209; of, 213; limited risk of, 205; over-the-counter market, 207; ownership of, 205–206; preferred stock, 155; price determinants of, 207–209; profit potential of, 204–205; prospectus for, 195, 213; reasons for investing in, 204–206; stock exchanges, 207; stock quotes, 219; stock splits, 205, *c205;* stock ticker, 219; trading of, 206–208

store of value, 302, 303

strikes: boycotts and, 189; coordinated campaigning and, 189; definition of, 188; injunctions against, 190; and lockouts, 190; management responses to, 189–190; picketing and, 188–189; primary boycotts and, 189; reasons for, 188; replacement workers for, 189–190; secondary boycotts and, 189; Taft-Hartley Act applied to, 189, 190

"strong" dollar, 433

structural unemployment, 252, 253, 255

subsidiaries, 160–161

subsidies, 82, 148

subsistence agriculture, 404–405

substitute goods: definition of, 60; monopoly and, 127

substitution effect: definition of, 52; law of demand and, 52–53

suburbs, 353

Superstation TBS, 147

supply, 72–93; changes in, 79–85, 93, 113; competition and, 83; decrease in, *c90*, 93, 113, 125; definition of, 73; determinants of, 79–80, 113; elasticity of, 76–78; equilibrium and, 103, 106–107; foreign exchange rates and, 433; government regulations and, 82; labor force and, 169–171; law of, 73–75; nature of, 73–78; subsidies and, 82; supply-side economics and, 355–356; taxes and, 81–82. *See also* demand; and headings beginning with supply

supply curve: competition and, 83; definition of, 75; examples of, *g74, g80;* price of resources affecting, 80; producer expectations and, 84–85; technology and, 82–83

supply schedule, *g74,* 75, *g103*

supply shifts, 74–75, 79–80

supply shock, 258

supply-side economics: definition of, 355; elements of, 355–356; government's role in, 355; laissez-faire approach, 355; limitations of, 356; model of, *c356;* taxes and, 355

surplus: definition of, 105; equilibrium and, 104–105; price floors and, 110

Sweden: socialism in, 386, 387–388; trade and, 445

Switzerland, 445

T

Taft, William Howard, 130, 362

Taft-Hartley Act of 1947, 186–187, 189, 190

Taiwan, 415

tariffs, 354, 439, *g440*

tax incentives, 358–359

tax rates: definition of, 349; state sales tax rates, *m352*

taxation: federal budget and, 365; fiscal policy and, 358; inflation and, 358; socialism and, 388; unemployment and, 358. *See also* taxes

taxes: collecting taxes, 350–354; corporate income taxes, 158, 351; customs duty, 354; definition of, 81; direct taxes, 235; economic growth and, 242–243; estate tax, 354; excise tax, 354; expansionary fiscal policy and, 360; Federal Insurance Contributions Act (FICA) and, 351; federal tax receipts by source, *g351;* gift tax, 354; indirect taxes, 235; individual income taxes, 350–351; internationally, 350; investment tax credit, 358; Medicare and, 351; Old-Age, Survivors, and Disability Insurance (OASDI) and, 351; progressive income taxes and, 359; progressive taxes, 349, 350–351; property taxes, 351–352; proportional taxes, 349, 351; regressive taxes, 349–350, 351, 354; sales taxes, 352, *m352,* 354; self-employed workers and, 351; for small businesses, 148; Social Security and, 351; supply and, 81–82; supply-side economics and, 355; tax incentives, 358–359; tax rates, 349; types of, 349–350. *See also* taxation

Teamsters Union, 188

technological monopoly: definition of, 128; examples of, 128

technology: definition of, 7; developing nations and, 408; economic development and, 408; economic growth and, 244; income gap and, 267, 268; investments and, 202–203; new markets and, 59; new products and, 59; production costs and, 82–83; productivity and, 244; supply curve and, 82–83; unemployment and, 253

Teen Ink, 37

telemarketing, 88

Thailand, 421–422, 445

"Third World countries," 410

thrifts, 316

Tiananmen Square Massacre, 397

Tickle Me Elmo, 105

tight-money policy, 338

time deposits: certificates of deposit, 197–198; savings bonds as, 198–199

total cost, 91

total product, 86

total revenue: definition of, 66; elastic demand and, 67; inelastic demand and, 67–68; maximizing total receipts, 68; as measurement of elasticity, 66–68

Toyota, 446

Toys "R" Us, 230

trade: Internet and, 442; specialization and, 427. *See also* international trade, headings beginning trade

trade barriers: definition of, 439; import quotas and, 440–441; licensing requirements as, 441; and, 439–440; trade restrictions and, 440–441

trade deficit, 437

trade-offs: comparative advantage and, 428–430; definition of, 11; economic goals and, 39–40; Federal Reserve system and, 343; international trade and, 428–430; opportunity costs and, 11–12; priorities and, 39–40

trade ratio, 428–430

trade surplus, 437

traditional economies: characteristics of, 24–25; definition of, 24; economic questions and, 26, Mbuti as, 24–25

transfer payments, 231, 235, 288

Treasury bills, 210, *c210*

Treasury bonds, 210, *c210*

Treasury Department. *See* Department of the Treasury

Treasury notes, 210, *c210*

Triangle Shirtwaist Company, 177

trough phase, 236, *g238*

Truman Doctrine, 420

trusts: anti-trust legislation, 130–133; definition of, 130

Truth-in-Lending Act, *c217*

Truth-in-Securities Act, 213

Tyson, Laura, 455

UAW. *See* United Autoworker (UAW)

UFCW. *See* United Food and Commercial Workers (UFCW)

UFW. *See* United Farm Workers (UFW)

UMW. *See* United Mine Workers (UMW)

underemployed, 252

underground economies, 232, 233

UNDP. *See* United Nations Development Program (UNDP)

unemployment, 251–256; age and, *g253;* decline of industries and, 253; definition, 251–252; demand-side economics and, *c356,* 357–358; discouraged workers, 252; frictional unemployment, 252, 253; full employment and, 252; government spending and, 359; marginally attached workers, 252; measuring unemployment, 251–252; migrant workers and, 255; public transfer payments and, 359; sex and, *g253;* supply-side economics and, 355, *c356;* taxation and, 358; technological change and, 253; types of, 252–253, 255, 256; underemployed workers, 252; unemployment compensation, 359

unemployment rate, 252, 255, 256

Unilever, 417, *m418*

Union of Soviet Socialist Republics. *See* Soviet Union

Union Summer, 181

unions. *See* labor unions

United Auto Workers (UAW), 418

United Autoworker (UAW), 179

United Farm Workers (UFW), 181, 189

United Food and Commercial Workers (UFCW), 189

United Kingdom, 318, 330, *g436,* 437, 445. *See also* Great Britain

United Mine Workers (UMW), 179

United Nations, 280, 420, 422

United Nations Development Program (UNDP), 422

United Nations Industrial Development Organization (UNIDO), 422

United Parcel Service (UPS), 188

United States: economic features of, 29–35; economic goals of, 36–39, 284–290; features of U. S. economy, 29–35; foreign investment in, *g436;* as free-enterprise system, 29–35; imports and exports, *g438;* income distribution in, 265–268; income gap and, 267; inflation rate 1940–1996, *g262;* international trade, *m435;* natural resources of, 243; poverty in, 264–265; productivity and, *g245,* 246; research and development expenditures, *g244;* trade deficit of, 437; unemployment in 1995, *g253*. *See also* government

United States Airline Deregulation Act of 1978, 133

U.S. banknotes, 311

U.S. Customs Service, 334

U.S. Mint, 306, 334, 335
U.S. PIRG. *See* United States Public Interest Research Group (U.S. PIRG)
United States Public Interest Research Group (U.S. PIRG), 295
United Steel Workers (USW), 179
University of Texas, 175, 181
unlimited liability: in partnerships, 152; in sole proprietorships, 147, 149
Unsafe at Any Speed, 294
UPS. *See* United Parcel Service (UPS)
urban and regional planner: as career, 409
Uruguay, 445
USA Today, 37
usury, 216
USW. *See* United Steel Workers (USW)
utility, 17, 53

V

value, 16–17
variable costs, 91
venture capital, 203
vertical combinations, 159–160
vertical integration, 161
Vietnam, 240, 414, 445
Vietnam War, 240
voluntary exchange, 29, 32
voluntary trade restrictions, 440–441
voting, 294
VOX, 37

W

wage-price spiral, 260
wages: affect of supply and demand on, 169–170; comparable worth and, 175; definition of, 169; equilibrium wage, g170; in foreign countries, 418; labor unions and, 184–185; minimum wage 1950–1997, g176; women and, 175

wage-price spiral, 260
Walker, Maggie L., 325
Wall Street Journal, 181
Wal-Mart, 303
wants: classification of, 4; scarcity and, 8, 23
war: business cycles and, 240
war communism, 390–391
Washington, George, 307, 364
welfare programs, g289
West Germany, 383
WHO. *See* World Health Organization (WHO)
Windows, 133
wobblies, 178
women: antidiscrimination laws and, 174–175; in labor force, 172–173; wages and, 175
workers. *See* labor force
working conditions: labor force and, 171; labor unions and, 185
World Bank, 334, 403, 420–421
World Bank Group, 420–421
World Health Organization (WHO), 422
World Trade Organization (WTO), 445
World War I, 240, 261, 311, 365; growth of government and, 281–282
World War II, 240, 365
World Wide Web, 442
WTO. *See* World Trade Organization (WTO)

Y

yield, 209
Yeltsin, Boris, 395
Yugoslavia, 379, 410
Yumin, Lou, 401

Z

Zhou Dynasty, 25
zoning laws, 30, 41, 146, 148

ACKNOWLEDGMENTS

For permission to reprint copyrighted material, grateful acknowledgment is made to the following sources:

The Economist Newspaper Limited: From "The China Syndrome" from "The World Economy Survey" section from *The Economist,* vol. 340, no. 7985, September 28, 1996. Copyright © 1996 by The Economist Newspaper Limited.

Harcourt Brace & Company: From "Capitalism and Equality" and "Conclusion" from "Created Equal" from *Free to Choose: A Personal Statement* by Milton Friedman and Rose D. Friedman. Copyright © 1980 by Milton Friedman and Rose D. Friedman.

The Gorbachev Foundation: From "Our different paths" by Mikhail Gorbachev from *Newsweek,* vol. 129, no. 9, March 3, 1997. Copyright © 1997 by The Gorbachev Foundation.

For permission to reprint copyrighted material, grateful acknowledgment is made to the following sources:

American Association of Community Colleges: From "Summertime Blues" by Bill Reinhard from *Community College Times,* June 29, 1993. Copyright © 1993 by American Association of Community Colleges.

American Management Association, New York: From quotes by Bill Cunningham from "Upstarts Stand Tall" by Patti Watts from *Management Review,* vol. 78, no. 1, January 1989. Copyright © 1989 by American Management Association. All rights reserved.

Bantam Books, a division of Bantam Doubleday Dell Publishing Group, Inc.: From *Iacocca: An Autobiography* by Lee Iacocca with William Novak. Copyright © 1984 by Lee Iacocca.

César E. Chávez Foundation, P.O. Box 62, La Paz, Keene, CA 93531; Tel. (805) 822-5571, Ext. 230; Fax (805) 822-6103: From a speech by César E. Chávez given on January 19, 1974. Copyright © 1974 by the César E. Chávez Foundation.

China Today: From "Vegetables for City People" (retitled "Lou Yumin's Account of a New System") by Lou Yumin from *China Reconstructs,* vol. XXXV, no. 1, January 1986, pp. 11–12 (North American Edition). Copyright © 1986 by China Today.

Don Curlee: From a letter by Don Curlee to the *Los Angeles Times,* January 1974. Copyright © 1974 by Don Curlee.

Gregg Easterbrook: From "The Sky Is Always Falling" by Gregg Easterbrook from *The New Republic,* vol. 201, no. 8, August 21, 1989. Copyright © 1989 by Gregg Easterbrook.

Jeremy Elson: From quotes by Jeremy Elson from "College Entrepreneurs Help High Schoolers Make a Match" by Peter Behr from *The Washington Post,* vol. 119, February 12, 1996. Copyright © 1996 by Jeremy Elson.

Harcourt Brace & Company: From *The General Theory of Employment, Interest, and Money* by John Maynard Keynes. Copyright 1936 and renewed © 1964 by Harcourt Brace & Company.

Institute for International Economics: From "America's High-Technology Trade Challenge: The Perspective of a Cautious Activist" from *Who's Bashing Whom?: Trade Conflict in High-Technology Industries* by Laura D'Andrea Tyson. Copyright © 1993 by the Institute for International Economics. All rights reserved.

Los Angeles Times Syndicate: From "Youthful Drive: AFL-CIO Hopes Union Summer Will Inspire New Generation" by Stuart Silverstein and Robert A. Rosenblatt from the *Los Angeles Times,* vol. 115, May 2, 1996. Copyright © 1996 by Los Angeles Times Syndicate.

William Morrow & Company, Inc.: From "Economic Differences" from *The Economics and Politics of Race* by Thomas Sowell. Copyright © 1983 by Thomas Sowell, Inc.

The New York Times Company: From "As Piracy Grows in Mexico, U.S. Companies Shout Foul" (retitled "Fighting a Formidable Force") by Julia Preston from *The New York Times,* April 28, 1996. Copyright © 1996 by The New York Times Company.

New York University Press: From *Selected Economic Writings of W. Arthur Lewis,* edited by Mark Gersovitz. Copyright © 1983 by New York University.

W. W. Norton & Company, Inc.: From "The Balance of Resources" from *Only One Earth: The Care and Maintenance of a Small Planet* by Barbara Ward and René Dubos. Copyright © 1972 by Report on the Environment, Inc.

Janet Prindle: From "Adam Smith, Social Investor" by Janet Prindle and Farha-Joyce Haboucha from *The Christian Science Monitor,* December 10, 1996. Copyright © 1996 by Janet Prindle.

21st Century, Box 30, Newton, MA 02161: Quote by John and Stephanie Meyer, quote by David Anable, quote by an anonymous teenager about American art, and quote by an anonymous teenager about problems associated with television as printed in *The Christian Science Monitor,* May 13, 1996. Copyright © 1996 by 21st Century.

SOURCES CITED:

Quotes by Jennifer Hill and Roya Rastegar from "Teens on the Scene: Cub Reporters Cover the Olympics" by Kristine Anderson from *The Christian Science Monitor,* July 30, 1996. Published by The Christian Science Publishing Society.

Quotes by Barbara Duvoisin and Dennis Raphael from "Many Seek American Dream—Outside America" by Warren Richey et al., from *The Christian Science Monitor,* March 19, 1997. Published by The Christian Science Publishing Society.

PHOTO CREDITS

Abbreviations used: (t) top, (c) center, (b) bottom, (l) left, (r) right.

All money borders: HRW photo; 19, 41, 69, 93, 113, 135, 165, 191, 219, 247, 269, 323, 345, 367, 399, 423, 447 (bkgd), Antonio M. Rosario/Picture Quest;

FRONT COVER, Main image: Artbase Inc.; Background: Artbase Inc.; Inset: ©Comstock Images; **TITLE PAGE**: Main Image: CORBIS/Micheal Yamashita; Background: Artbase Inc.; Inset: ©Comstock Images

TABLE OF CONTENTS, ii(t), HRW photo by Peter Van Steen; (c), HRW photo by Peter Van Steen; (b), HRW photo by Peter Van Steen; iv Chris Sorensen; v(b), HRW photo by Peter Van Steen; (t), HRW Photo: Shoes- Victoria Smith; Bike- C Squared Studios/Photodisc/Picturequest;Pizza - Photo Disc; vi (b), (t), HRW photo by Peter Van; vii(b), (t), HRW photo by Peter Van Steen; viii HRW photo by Peter Van Steen; ix(b), (t), HRW photo by Peter Van Steen x(b), CORBIS/AFP Photo/Timothy Clary; x R. Crandall/The Image Works; xi HRW photo by Peter Van Steen; xii David Ball/The Stock Market; xiii(b), (t), HRW photo by Peter

Van Steen; xiv Courtesy Union Summer, AFL-CIO; xv(b), CORBIS/Roger Ressmeyer (t), HRW photo by Peter Van Steen

TX CHAPTER: TX0 Peter Van Steen/HRW; TX5 The Granger Collection, New York; TX7 Franklin D. Roosevelt Library; TX9 CORBIS/Museum of Flight; TX10(t), NASA; TX10(b), CORBIS/Stock Market/Chris Sorensen; TX13 Peter Van Steen/HRW/ Location: Umlauf Sculpture Gardens, Austin, Texas/Work in foreground: Elementals by Mary K. Morse/Work in background by Charles Umlauf

SKILLS HANDBOOK, S2 Courtesy of Union Summer, AFL-CIO; S3 Jay Mallin; S4(br), Digital imagery® copyright 2003 PhotoDisc, Inc.; S5(c), Sam Dudgeon/HRW; S6 HRW Photo; S7(b), Courtesy of the Ford Archives, Henry Ford Museum, Dearborn, S8(t), Digital imagery® copyright 2003 PhotoDisc, Inc. S10(l), Sam Dudgeon/HRW Photo; S11(br), Sam Dudgeon/HRW Photo; S12 Sam Dudgeon/HRW; S16 HRW/Sam Dudgeon; S18 Reprinted with permission, "Star Tribune", Minneapolis.; S19(t), HRW/Sam Dudgeon; S21 HRW photo by Peter Van Steen; S23 Courtesy of the "Chattanooga Times"

UNIT 1, 0-1 HRW photo by Peter Van Steen; **Chapter 1**, 2 HRW photo by Peter Van Steen; 4(b), David Young-Wolff/Tony Stone Images; 4(t), HRW Photo; Shoes- Victoria Smith; Bike- C Squared Studios/Photodisc/Picturequest; Pizza - Photo Disc; 5 AP/Wide World Photos/Gino Domenico; 6 Gary Braasch/ Woodfin Camp & Associates; Michigan; 8 HRW photo by Peter Van Steen; 10 Sergio Dorantes/Sygma; 12 Boudrea and Turnbull/Index Stock Imagery/Picture Quest; 15 Novosti/R.I.A./Gamma-Liaison; 16 HRW photo by Sam Dudgeon; 17 J.L. Atlan/Sygma; 18 Chris Sorensen; 19 CORBIS; **Chapter 2**, 22 HRW photo by Peter Van Steen; 23 N. Rowan/The Image Works; 24 Nick Robinson/Panos Pictures; 25 Giraudon/Art Resource, NY; 26 Bettman/CORBIS; 27(t), Rolando Pujol/Woodfin Camp & Associates; 27(c), Najlan Feanny/SABA Press Photos, Inc.; 27(b), Poincet/Sygma; 29 Leland Bobbie/Getty Images/Stone; 30(t), BABY BLUES reprinted with special permission of King Features Syndicate, Inc.; 30(b), Don Mason/The Stock Market; 31 S. Gazin/The Image Works; 32 HRW photo by Peter Van Steen; 33 Laurence Parent; 35 HRW photo by Peter Van Steen; 36 By permission of Johnny Hart and Creators Syndicate, Inc.; 37 Peter Van Steen/HRW; 38(t), R Lord/The Image Works; 38(b), ©Julie Marcotte/Getty Images/Stone; 40 HRW photo by Peter Van Steen; 41 AP/Wide World Photos/Stephen J. Carrera; **Lab 1**, 44 HRW Photo Research Library/ Michelle Bridwell; 45 NASA; 47 HRW Photo Research Library/Michelle Bridwell;

UNIT 2, 48-49 HRW photo by Peter Van Steen; **Chapter 3**, 50 HRW photo by Peter Van Steen; 51 HRW photo by Peter Van Steen; 53 HRW photo by Peter Van Steen; 56 HRW photo by Peter Van Steen; 58 HRW photo by Peter Van Steen; 59(t), Sam Dudgeon/HRW/Courtesy Sketchers Footwear; 59(b), Art and Chip Sansom/NEA, Inc./1993; 60 Sam Dudgeon/HRW; Bkgd: Richard Pasley/Stock Boston Inc./Picture Quest; 61 Spencer Grant/Gamma Liaison; 62 HRW photo by Peter Van Steen; 63 Peter Van Steen/HRW; 64 HRW photo by Peter Van Steen; 65 HRW photo by Peter Van Steen; 68 HRW photo by Peter Van Steen; 69 CORBIS/Reuters NewMedia Inc.; **Chapter 4**, 72 HRW photo by Peter Van Steen; 73 HRW photo by Peter Van Steen; 75 EEK & MEEK reprinted by permission of Newspaper Enterprise Association, Inc.; 76 HRW photo by Peter Van Steen; 77 Peter Van Steen/HRW; 79 BLONDIE reprinted with special permission of King Features Syndicate, Inc.; 81 Brian Atkinson/Tony Stone Images; 82 Courtesy of the Ford Archives, Henry Ford Museum, Dearborn, Michigan; 83 HRW photo by Peter Van Steen; 84 CORBIS; 85 HRW photo by Peter Van Steen; 88 HRW photo by Michael Lyon; 89 HRW photo by Peter Van Steen; 91 CORBIS/Kevin Flemming; 92 HRW photo by Sam Dudgeon; 93 Index Stock Imagery/Rick Raymond/Picture Quest; **Chapter 5**, 96 HRW photo by Peter Van Steen; 98 CALVIN & HOBBES copyright 1989 Watterson. Reprinted with permission of Universal Press Syndicate. All rights reserved.; 99 Bettman/CORBIS; 100(t), HRW photo by Peter Van Steen; 100(b), Chuck Pefley/Tony Stone Images; 101 HRW photo by Peter Van Steen; 102 HRW photo by Peter Van Steen; 104 Joseph Pobereskin/Tony Stone Images; 105 HRW photo by Peter Van Steen; 107 HRW photo by Sam Dudgeon; 108 Bernard Boutrit/Woodfin Camp & Associates; 109 HRW photo by Peter Van Steen; 110 Jim Anderson/Woodfin Camp & Associates; 112 Paul Meridteh/Getty Images/Stone; 113 AP/Wide World Photos/Justin Sullivan, Stringer; **Chapter 6**, 116 HRW photo by Peter Van Steen; 117 HRW photo by Peter Van Steen; 118 HRW photo by Peter Van Steen; 120 AP/Wide World Photos/ Amy E. Conn; 121 HRW photo by Peter Van Steen; 126 Gerald Cubitt; 127 © Tribune Media Services, Inc. All rights reserved. Reprinted with permission.; 128(t), Baron Wolman/Tony Stone Images; 128(b), Peter Van Steen/HRW; 130(r), Bureau of Engraving and Printing; 130(l), Bureau of Engraving and Printing; 131(tc), Culver Pictures; 132 Archive Photos; 134 HRW photo by Sam Dudgeon; 135 CORBIS/Peter Turnley; **Lab 2**, 137 HRW photo by Sam Dudgeon; 138 Sam Dudgeon/HRW; 139 Randal Alhadeff/HRW; 140 Christine Galinda/HRW; 141 Peter Van Steen/HRW

UNIT 3, 142-143 Seth Resnick/Gamma Liaison/Getty, **Chapter 7**, 144 HRW photo by Peter Van Steen; 146 AP/Wide World Photos/Tommy Hultgren; 147(b), Courtesy of Ninfa's; 147(t), HRW photo by Peter Van Steen; 148 ©Houston Chronicle; 150 AP/Wide World Photos/Toby Talbot; 157 CORBIS/AFP PHOTO/PATRICK KOVARIK; 162(t), HRW photo by Peter Van Steen; 162(b), HRW photo by Peter Van Steen; 163 CORBIS; 164 Todd Rosenberg/Allsport; 165 AP/Wide World Photos; **Chapter 8**, 168 HRW photo by Peter Van Steen; 171 Geoffrey Orth/Alaska Stock Images; 172 Print Collection, Miriam and Ira D. Wallach Division of Art, Print and Photographs, The New York Public Library, Astor, Lenox and Tilden Foundations; 175 Archive Photos; 177 Culver Pictures; 178 Culver Pictures; 181 Courtesy of Union Summer, AFL-CIO; 184 HRW photo by Peter Van Steen; 185 AP/Wide World Photos/David Kohl, Stringer; 186 AP/Wide World Photos/Ron Edmonds; 187 AP/Wide World Photo; 188 AP/Wide World Photos/Victoria Arocho; 189 UPI/Corbis-Bettmann; 190 David H. Wells/The Image Works; 191 AP/Wide World Photos/Roger Werth/The Daily News; **Chapter 9**, 194 Peter Van Steen/HRW; 195 Tom and Deann McCarthy/Corbis Stock Market; 198 U.S. Treasury Department, drawn by Dawn Larson, a 6th grade student from Ute, Iowa. Her poster was awarded first place in the 1996 U.S. Savings Bonds National Student Poster Contest; 199 TOLES copyright 1991 The Buffalo News. Reprinted with permission of Universal Press Syndicate. All rights reserved.; 200 HRW photo by Peter Van Steen; 201 Michael Keller/The Stock Market; 202 ©Vince Streano/Getty Images/Stone; 203 HRW photo by Peter Van Steen; 204 Bryan F. Peterson/The Stock Market; 206 HRW photo by Peter Van Steen; 207 Joan Menschenfreund/The Stock Market; 211 Bettmann Archives; 214 HRW photo by Peter Van Steen; 215 Drawing by Mirachi; © 1975 The New Yorker Magazine, Inc.; 219 Jean Miele/Corbis Stock Market; **Lab 3**, 222 HRW Photo Research Library/Victoria Smith; 223 HRW photo by Sam Dudgeon; 224 HRW photo by Sam Dudgeon; 225 HRW Photo Research Library

UNIT 4, 226-227 R. Berenholtz/The Stock Market; **Chapter 10**, 229 © 1999 by Sidney Harris; 233 HRW photo by Peter Van Steen; 237 HRW photo by Sam Dudgeon; 238 Copyright, 1974. Raleigh News & Observer. Distributed by Los Angeles Times Syndicate. Reprinted with permission.; 239 HRW photo by Peter Van Steen; 241 Forrest Anderson/Gamma Liaison/Getty Images; 243 HRW photo by Peter Van Steen; 244 Reprinted by permission of Josh Beutel from the "New Brunswick Telegraph Journal"; 244(t), Dennis Brack/Black Star Publishing/Picture Quest; 247 Ed Bock/Corbis Stock Market; **Chapter 11**, 250 Mark Houston/Adventure Photos; 251 HRW photo by Peter Van Steen; 254 Culver Pictures; 256 ©Bruce Forster/Getty Images/Stone; 257 CORBIS/ AFP PHOTO/Scott OLSON; 258 ROB ROGERS reprinted by permission of United Features Syndicate, Inc.; 259 HRW photo by Peter Van Steen; 264 Paul Fusco/Magnum Photos Inc.; 269 CORBIS/Ted Spiegel; **Lab 4**, 272 Sam Dudgeon/HRW; 273 HRW Photo Research Library; 275 HRW Photo Research Library/John Langford

UNIT 5, 276-277 A. Tannenbaum/Sygma; **Chapter 12**, 278 HRW photo by Peter Van Steen; 280 Brown Brothers; 282 HRW photo by Peter Van Steen; 284 ©David Young Wolff/Getty Images/Stone; 286 Jeffrey D.

Smith/Woodfin Camp & Associates; 288 HRW photo by Peter Van Steen; 291 ©Paul Chesley/Getty Images/Stone; 292 HRW photo by Peter Van Steen; 293 Courtesy of the "Chattanoga Times"; 294 HRW photo by Peter Van Steen; 295 AP/Wide World Photos/Leslie E. Kossoff; 296 AP/Wide World Photo; 297 The Image Works; 297 CORBIS; **Chapter 13,** 300 HRW photo by Peter Van Steen; 301 HRW photo by Peter Van Steen; 302(tl), HRW photo by Peter Van Steen; 302(br), Mark Greenberg/Gamma-Liaison; 305 Superstock; 306 R. Crandall/The Image Works; 307 HRW photo by Sam Dudgeon; 309(l), National Portrait Gallery, Smithsonian Institution/Art Resource, NY; 309(r), National Portrait Gallery, Smithsonian Institution; gift of the Regents of the Smithsonian Institution, the Thomas Jefferson Memorial Foundation/Art Resource, NY; 310 Courtesy, American Antiquarian Society; 311 Culver Pictures; 312 Brown Brothers; 313 HRW photo by Peter Van Steen; 314 John Van Hasselt/Sygma; 315 HRW photo by Peter Van Steen; 317 HRW photo by Peter Van Steen; 318 HRW photo by Peter Van Steen; 319 HRW photo by Peter Van Steen; 320 ETTA HULME reprinted by permission of Newspaper Enterprise Association, Inc.; 323 Keith Brofsky/PhotoDisc/Getty Images; **Chapter 14,** 326 Comstock, Inc.; 327 HRW photo by Sam Dudgeon; 328 HRW photo by Peter Van Steen; 337 John Madere/The Stock Market; 338 Courtesy of the "Chattanooga Times"; 340 AP/Wide World Photo; 343 © 1999 by Sidney Harris; 344 NASA; 345 AP/Wide World Photos; **Chapter 15,** 348 Wally McNamee/Sygma; 353 Merrick Advertising; 354 HRW photo by Peter Van Steen; 357 HRW photo by Peter Van Steen; 358 HRW photo by Peter Van Steen; 360 CORBIS/AFP PHOTO/Timothy Clary; 361 MORIN reprinted with special permission of King Features Syndicate, Inc.; 365 Reprinted with permission, "Star Tribune", Minneapolis/Steve Sack; 367 CORBIS/Philip James Corwin; 369 Reprinted with permission, "Star Tribune", Minneapolis; **Lab 5,** 370(b) and 370(t), HRW Photo Research Library/LBJ Library; 371(l), HRW photo by Sam Dudgeon; 371(r), HRW photo by Sam Dudgeon; 373 Sam Dudgeon/HRW

UNIT 6, 374-375 Courtesy, Special Collections Division, The University of Texas at Arlington Libraries, Arlington, Texas.; **Chapter 16,** 376 ©Mike McQueen/Getty Images/Stone; 378 HRW photo by Peter Van Steen; 381 AKG London; 382 Karen Kasmauski/Woodfin Camp & Associates, Inc.; 383 Anthony Suau/Gamma-Liaison/Getty Images; 384 Gilles Bouquillon/Gamma-Liaison/Getty Images; 386 Bettman/CORBIS; 387 Lars Sward/Pica Pressfoto; 388 Blaine Harrington III; 389 AKG London; 390 HRW photo by Sam Dudgeon; 391 AKG London; 392 Dennis Cox/ChinaStock; 393 Filip Horvat/SABA Press Photos, Inc.; 395 Courtesy of Glenn McCoy, "Belleville News-Democrat"; 396 New China Pictures/Eastfoto/Sovfoto; 398 Charlesworth/SABA Press Photos, Inc.; 399 John Cancalosi/ Stock Boston/PictureQuest; **Chapter 17,** 402 Arabella Cecil/ Panos Pictures; 407 B. Zaunders/The Stock Market; 408(t), Robert Frerck/Woodfin Camp & Associates, Inc.; 408 Reprinted by permission from the "Earth Summit Times"; 409 HRW photo by Peter Van Steen; 410 T. Pierce/SABA; 411 W. Campbell/ Sygma; 412(b), A. Tannenbaum/Sygma; 412(t), Patrick Morrow; 413 Diego Goldberg/Sygma; 414 Goitia/SABA Press Photos, Inc.; 417 Rhodri Jones/Panos Pictures; 420 Courtesy of Peace Corps; 422 Frank Fournier/Contact/The Stock Market; 423 Piotr Malecki/Liaison/Getty Images; **Chapter 18,** 426 David Ball/The Stock Market; 428 John F. Mason/The Stock Market; 429 HRW photo by Peter Van Steen; 431 Frederick Charles/Gamma-Liaison/Getty Images; 432 ©San Francisco Chronicle. Reprinted with permission.; 433 Everton/The Image Works; 434; 439 Paul Howell/Gamma-Liaison/Getty Images; 441 Tony Savino/The Image Works; 443 Courtesy of Mike Smith, "Las Vegas Sun"; 446 HRW photo by Peter Van Steen; 447 David McNew/Getty Images; **Lab 6,** 450 HRW Photo Research Library; 453 Steve Ferry/HRW

REFERENCE SECTION, 454-455 Seth Resnick/Gamma Liaison/Getty Images; **Consumer Handbook,** 457 HRW photo by Peter Van Steen; 458 HRW photo by Peter Van Steen; 459 HRW photo by Peter Van Steen; 460 HRW photo by Peter Van Steen; 461 courtesy of Dunlop Tires; 462 HRW photo by Peter Van Steen; 464 Courtesy of Intuit; 465 R. Lord/The Image Works; 466 Vince Streano/Getty Images/Stone; 467 Archive Photos/Getty Images; 468 Peter Van Steen/HRW; 471 S. Gazin/The Image Works; 472 AP/Wide World Photo; 474 HRW photo by Peter Van Steen; 475 HRW photo by Peter Van Steen; 476 Joan Menschenfreund/The Stock Market; 478 HRW photo by Peter Van Steen

ART CREDITS

TABLE OF CONTENTS, Page: xvii, Leslie Kell; xx, Leslie Kell; xxiv, Leslie Kell; xxv (t), Leslie Kell; xxv (b), GeoSystems Global Corp.; xxvi, Rose Zgodzinski/Three in a Box; xxvii, GeoSystems Global Corp.

SKILLS HANDBOOK, Page: xxix, Rose Zgodzinski/Three in a Box; xxxi, Kenneth Batelman; xxxiii, Leslie Kell; xxxviii, Leslie Kell; xl, Leslie Kell; xli (t), Rose Zgodzinski/Three in a Box; xli (b), Leslie Kell; xlii, Leslie Kell; xliii, GeoSystems Global Corp.; xliv, GeoSystems Global Corp.

UNIT ONE, Page: 1C, Leslie Kell; 1G, Kenneth Batelman; 9, Rose Zgodzinski/Three in a Box; 11, Kenneth Batelman; 13, Leslie Kell; 14, Leslie Kell; 21D, Kenneth Batelman; 21F, Kenneth Batelman; 26, Kenneth Batelman; 34, Rose Zgodzinski/Three in a Box.

UNIT TWO, Page: 49F, Leslie Kell; 54, Leslie Kell; 55, Leslie Kell; 57, Leslie Kell; 64, Leslie Kell; 65, Leslie Kell; 67, Leslie Kell; 71, Leslie Kell; 74, Leslie Kell; 77, Leslie Kell; 78, Leslie Kell; 80, Leslie Kell; 87, Leslie Kell; 90, Kenneth Batelman; 95E, Leslie Kell; 95, Kenneth Batelman; 103, Leslie Kell; 105, Leslie Kell; 106, Leslie Kell; 109, Leslie Kell; 110, Leslie Kell; 115, Leslie Kell; 119, Rose Zgodzinski/Three in a Box; 122, Leslie Kell; 124, Kenneth Batelman; 133, Kenneth Batelman.

UNIT THREE, Page: 145, Rose Zgodzinski/Three in a Box; 151, Rose Zgodzinski/Three in a Box; 153, Rose Zgodzinski/Three in a Box; 154, Rose Zgodzinski/Three in a Box; 156, GeoSystems Global Corp.; 160, Rose Zgodzinski/Three in a Box; 167, Rose Zgodzinski/Three in a Box; 169, Rose Zgodzinski/Three in a Box; 170, Leslie Kell; 173, Kenneth Batelman; 176, Rose Zgodzinski/Three in a Box; 179, GeoSystems Global Corp.; 180, Rose Zgodzinski/Three in a Box; 182, Kenneth Batelman; 193, Kenneth Batelman; 196, Leslie Kell; 197, Rose Zgodzinski/Three in a Box; 205, Rose Zgodzinski/ Three in a Box; 208, Leslie Kell; 209, Leslie Kell; 210, Kenneth Batelman; 212, Kenneth Batelman; 217, Kenneth Batelman; 218, Rose Zgodzinski/Three in a Box; 221, Leslie Kell.

UNIT FOUR, Page: 227D, Leslie Kell; 231, Leslie Kell; 232, Leslie Kell; 234, Leslie Kell; 238, Leslie Kell; 242, Leslie Kell; 244, Leslie Kell; 245, Leslie Kell; 248, Leslie Kell; 249H, Leslie Kell; 253, Leslie Kell; 255, Leslie Kell; 261, Leslie Kell; 262, Leslie Kell; 263, Leslie Kell; 265, Kenneth Batelman; 266, Leslie Kell.

UNIT FIVE, Page: 279, Leslie Kell; 281, Leslie Kell; 283, Leslie Kell; 285, Kenneth Batelman; 289, Leslie Kell; 299, Leslie Kell; 304, Kenneth Batelman; 316, Kenneth Batelman; 321, Leslie Kell; 325, Leslie Kell; 329, Rose Zgodzinski/Three in a Box; 330, GeoSystems Global Corp.; 333, Rose Zgodzinski/Three in a Box; 335, Leslie Kell; 339, Kenneth Batelman; 341, Leslie Kell; 347, Kenneth Batelman; 351, Leslie Kell; 352, GeoSystems Global Corp.; 356, Leslie Kell; 363, Leslie Kell; 364, Leslie Kell.

UNIT SIX, Page: 377, Kenneth Batelman; 380, GeoSystems Global Corp.; 394, Leslie Kell; 397, Leslie Kell; 401, GeoSystems Global Corp.; 404–405, GeoSystems Global Corp.; 406, Leslie Kell; 416, Leslie Kell; 418, Leslie Kell; 419, Leslie Kell; 421, Leslie Kell; 425 (tl), GeoSystems Global Corp.; 425 (cl), Kenneth Batelman; 430, Leslie Kell; 435, GeoSystems Global Corp.; 436, Leslie Kell; 437, Leslie Kell; 438, Leslie Kell; 440, Leslie Kell; 444, GeoSystems Global Corp.; 445, Kenneth Batelman.

CONSUMER HANDBOOK, Page: 456, Leslie Kell; 463, Leslie Kell; 470, Leslie Kell; 477, Leslie Kell; 479, Leslie Kell.

ATLAS, Page: 480–487, GeoSystems Global Corp.